SECOND EDITION

HUMAN
ARRANGEMENTS

An Introduction to Sociology

1. (A.82.7-234) Marionette, Italy?, late 19th–early 20th c.
2. (393) "Dancer" Puppet, Burma, 20th c.
3. (367) Doll, Central Europe, early 20th c.
4. (3040 GF) Cloth Topsy-Turvy Doll, U.S., early 20th c.
5. (420) Plains Indian Woman, Plains area, U.S., early 20th c.
6. (417) Plains Indian Woman, Plains area, U.S., early 20th c.
7. (A.80.36-284) Cut-out Cloth Doll, possibly Art Fabric Mills, N.Y., early 20th c.
8. (A.68.32-26) Cloth Doll Group, China, ca. 1945
9. (A.65.64-4) "Dury" Sillies, Noginsk, U.S.S.R., late 19th c.
10. (434) Eskimo Doll, Alaska/Canada, 20th c.
11. (2467) Maid of Honor, part of Norwegian wedding procession, Hardanger, Norway, ca. 1920
12. (A.81.1-491) "Punch" Hand Puppet, England?, ca. 1925

Cover: All dolls courtesy of the Museum of International Folk Art, a unit of the Museum of New Mexico, Santa Fe, and its Girard Foundation Collection.

ISBN: 0-15-539769-9

Library of Congress Catalog Card Number: 88-80642
Printed in the United States of America

Preface

TO STUDENTS

Like many others, I spent much of my undergraduate career trying to discover what I wanted to do with my life. Although I changed majors several times, I always knew that whatever field I entered would have to appeal to several important sides of me. It would have to be challenging and interesting; it would have to stimulate and increase my ability to understand how things work, to see the ways in which things that appear unconnected are in fact connected and affect one another. Perhaps most important, it would have to touch my desire to understand not only my own life, but the lives of other people in relation to one another. As a sociologist, I have been able to do all of these things, not simply to make a living, but to live with far more awareness and understanding than I would have otherwise had.

As a writer, I hope you will enjoy what you read, that the care with which I have tried to shape ideas and experience will come across clearly and draw you in as an active reader; and I hope that the examples and analyses of social life will give you reason to stop and reflect on your own life and the circumstances in which you live it.

As a teacher, I hope you will *use* this book as well as read and enjoy it, that you will learn from it and thereby acquire some of the ability to use sociology that has made it such a satisfying part of my life and the lives of other sociologists. This textbook is intended to be worked with, studied, pondered, and, at times, struggled with. It will challenge you to look at the world from what will probably be a very new perspective; to turn the world upside down at times if for no other reason than to get a clearer understanding of what right side up is all about.

Several features of the book were designed to make it more useful to you. Each chapter begins with a detailed table of contents and ends with a summary of major points, a list of key terms, and recommended readings. I suggest you begin each chapter by studying the table of contents and the summary in order to gain an overall sense of what the chapter is about and how it is put together. Each of the key terms is followed by a page number indicating where the term was first introduced and discussed. Together, the table of contents, summary, and list of terms provide an outline for organizing study and review. Also note that at the end of each chapter there is a "Looking Elsewhere" boxed insert that alerts you to related discussions in other chapters of *Human Arrangements*, Second Edition. As you will learn, social life is so inherently complex that it is impossible to discuss one area without touching on others. Using these cross-references will help you to get a clearer grasp of the interconnectedness of different areas of sociological analysis.

You may find several sections at the end of the book useful. The glossary is very extensive and, like the lists of key terms, refers you to the page where each term was first introduced and discussed. The glossary will be particularly helpful when, in later chapters, you encounter key terms first introduced early in the book. Use the glossary to refresh your understanding and, if necessary, use the page reference to go back for a fuller explanation. The reference list also contains page references to where each book or article is mentioned. This is especially useful if you are trying to locate something written by a frequently cited author. If a term paper is part of the requirements for your course, be sure to read Appendix A.

One final note. I wrote this book for you, and I would like to hear from you, especially if you have suggestions for making this book more useful. Please feel free to write to me at 40 Whiting Lane, West Hartford, CT 06119. I will be pleased to respond.

TO INSTRUCTORS

At the first meeting of an undergraduate sociology course, I once asked students to take a few moments to write a short paragraph describing sociology as a discipline. For the most part, these students had completed nothing more than an introductory course, and I wanted to get some idea of what I had to work with. None could produce a short, workable definition of the field. I suspect that too many students leave introductory sociology courses with a great many facts and terms but an unnecessarily fuzzy understanding of what it means to observe and explain the social world in a sociological way. What these students lack is a clear sense that no matter what we look at—from informal interactions among strangers to relationships between large organizations, from the structure of a family to the structure of a world economy—a clear framework exists for defining what makes a problem sociological.

In writing *Human Arrangements*, Second Edition, I had two principal goals: to present sociology so that it makes sense on several different levels, and to do so in a way that is both interesting and challenging on the one hand and accessible to students with a wide range of abilities on the other.

The book is based on a definition of sociology that focuses on three conceptual areas: culture, social structure, and population/ecology. Within this conceptual framework there are, of course, many theoretical frameworks—from major perspectives such as conflict, functional, and symbolic interaction to specific theories such as political process theory in the study of social movements, exchange theory in the study of social interaction, or labeling theory in the study of deviance. Students, then, know from the outset that in order to understand any phenomenon sociologically they must begin by paying attention to its cultural, structural, and population/ecological aspects.

I have organized the book to reinforce this approach to making sense of sociology. It is divided into six parts, the first of which introduces the field in terms of the major concepts that define the kinds of questions we ask as well as in terms of the research

methods we use to look for answers. Part Two describes in detail the three major concepts that I have used to define the discipline, providing a clear framework that forms the basis for everything that follows.

The remaining parts then apply the sociological perspective in a systematic way to increasingly larger levels of analysis. Part Three, for example, moves from relatively small-scale and simple processes to the more complex and large-scale; Parts Four and Five focus on social inequality and social institutions; and Part Six ends with detailed discussions of collective behavior and social change. Thus, the book moves from basic conceptual and theoretical views of the sociological perspective to increasingly large-scale and complex areas in which to apply it clearly and systematically.

Most instructors will probably want to begin with Part One; but I have tried to write chapters to maximize your flexibility. Chapter 2 ("Research Methods"), for example, can be assigned at any time, since it relies on no previously introduced sociological concepts; and most of the remaining chapters can be assigned in any order that fits the needs of your class.

It is in the internal organization of chapters that the priority of making sense of sociology is, I hope, most apparent. I have organized chapters around the central concepts of culture, structure, and population/ecology as well as important theoretical approaches to specific areas so that students can develop a sense of sociology as a coherent framework of concepts and theories that can be applied to any aspect of social life.

Human Arrangements, Second Edition, incorporates a number of features designed to make it both more rewarding and easier to use for teachers and students. "Puzzles" are boxed inserts that pose questions intended to stimulate the reader's curiosity and encourage active participation. Throughout the book, figures and tables abound, both to illustrate and to amplify important points. Each chapter ends with a summary, recommended readings, key terms with page references, and a "Looking Elsewhere" box.

The glossary is exceptionally complete and includes page references to the major discussions of each entry. The reference list is not only unusually thorough, varied, and up-to-date, but also serves as an author index. This gives students not just a string of page numbers after each author's name, but specific page references for each book or article.

A *Study Guide, Test Book* (available both in print and on floppy disk), and an *Instructor's Manual* are available. All of the ancillaries have been either written or revised by me.

Throughout the writing of *Human Arrangements,* Second Edition, I have worked from a conviction that in teaching introductory sociology, instructors should not have to choose between being understood by their students on the one hand and exposing students to the richness of sociology on the other. I have tried to write a book that does the essential work of giving students sociological literacy as well as a sense of sociological ideas and analysis—for this is the heart of sociology. This is, then, more than anything, a book about how to observe and think about the world. To do that, of course, students need to know something about how to label what they observe; but our field is far more than a set of descriptive terms. In short, my goal has been to give instructors and their students the best of both worlds—a clear textbook that is relatively easy to teach and learn from and an engaging, challenging, lively, and interesting exploration of the field.

WHAT'S NEW IN THE SECOND EDITION

Human Arrangements, Second Edition, is thoroughly up to date. With the benefit of hindsight given to textbook authors, I have carefully reedited the entire book to make it still tighter and clearer without sacrificing any of the richness of detail and engaging examples that so many instructors appreciated in the first edition.

I have substantially rewritten Chapter 1 to provide a clearer introduction to the major theoretical perspectives. I have also added major treatments of health, science, medicine, and technology. Chapter 5 (Population) now has a full discussion of health, morbidity, and epidemiology, including the origins of the AIDS pandemic. Science, medicine, and technology are the focus of a new chapter (17) which includes some material on technology from Chapter 5.

I deleted the "Voices" boxes to make way for a unique addition that, I believe, will have more value for both students and instructors. "One Step Further" boxed inserts use clearly presented data to expand on points raised in the text. Many draw on the General Social Surveys and all use nothing more sophisticated

than percentages and, in some cases, colorful graphics. I think you will find these to be an unintimidating and engaging way to take students a bit closer to the serious data sociologists use. The Second Edition has more figures and tables than before, each still carefully integrated with the text and fully explained.

Another unique addition is the "Looking Elsewhere" box at the end of each chapter, which functions as a focused cross-reference to related discussions in other chapters. After studying deviance in Chapter 10, for example, students can look at related discussions, such as deviance in science (Chapter 17) or deviance as a source of religious change (Chapter 20). My purpose is to enhance the usefulness of the book and to underscore the inherent interrelatedness of the enormous range of phenomena sociologists study.

It would be helpful to me to hear your impressions of this edition, especially if you have suggestions for making this a more useful text for you and your students. Please feel free to write to me at the address given at the end of the "To Students" section of the preface.

SPECIAL ACKNOWLEDGMENTS

The complex process of seeing a book from conception through the finished product involves a great deal of work, but it is a labor of the most satisfying sort when an author is fortunate enough to work with the kind of editors, designers, and artists I have had the privilege to know through this project.

It is my pleasure to extend my deep appreciation to HBJ's advisory editor, Robert K. Merton, who continues to lend his unsurpassed depth of knowledge, his critical sense, his timely wit, and his enduring support; to Marcus Boggs for his continuing support for my work; to Martha Berlin who edited the manuscript with sensitivity and skill, knowing that most difficult of distinctions between what to change and what to leave alone; to Jane Carey with whom I have both enjoyed and learned much from the give and take that contributed to her elegant and beautiful design; to Susan Holtz who, with her exceptional photographer's eye, is responsible for finding almost 300 pictures, each of which I think goes far beyond mere decoration to provoke both thought and feeling; to production editor Carol Maxwell for expertly guiding the manuscript into print; and to Lesley Lenox, production manager, who supervised the many and complex phases of typesetting and printing involved in this large, full-color book.

I also want to express my appreciation to others, members of the HBJ staff and outside consultants whose skills went into this book. They include Ann Smith, Alice Harmon, Cheryl Mayville, and Paulette Russo.

Many of my colleagues have helped by sharing critical insights as reviewers for both the First and Second Editions (their names appear in the separate Acknowledgments list). I appreciate their many suggestions that have gone into this work. I also want to thank Joel Levine for making available his PC software (LINTAB) that enabled me to analyze General Social Survey data.

Every book flows from the life of its author, and as my life is connected to many others, so this book is connected to them. What intelligence, insight, wit, and heart readers may find here have benefitted in no small part from the extraordinary people who have, by various routes, found their way into my life: Alice, Valdemar, Geraldine, Annalee, Emily, and Paul Johnson; Stuart Alpert, Naomi Bressette, George Zepko, Charles Levenstein, Leonard Wallace Robinson, Grace Bochain, Brent Harold, Susan Weegar, Ellen Allen, Andrew Mason, Dorothy Mason, Thomas Disher, and, above all, Nora Jamieson, editor and critic, partner in life, and deepest friend, whose wisdom, heart, and courage enrich my life and work beyond measure.

And finally, as the Second Edition goes to press, I feel my abiding appreciation to my friend and former editor, Peter Dougherty, without whom there most likely would never have been a First Edition.

Allan G. Johnson

Acknowledgments

John W. Bardo, Southwest Texas State University

Julie Brown, University of North Carolina, Greensboro

Diane M. Bush, Colorado State University

Craig Calhoun, University of North Carolina, Chapel Hill

Henry Camp, Kansas State University

J. Stephen Cleghorn, Emory University

Albin J. Cofone, Suffolk Community College

Henry Comby, Tulsa Junior College

Nick Costa, Greater Hartford Community College

John Crowley, Manchester Community College

Clark A. Davis, California State University, Chico

Carolyn Ellis, University of South Florida

Charles F. Emmons, Gettysburg College

Robert Freymeyer, Presbyterian College

T. Neal Garland, University of Akron

Avrama Gingold, Intermarket Research, Inc. and The Academic Factor

Vaughn Grisham, University of Mississippi

Gerard Grzyb, University of Wisconsin, Oshkosh

B. G. Gunter, University of South Florida

Patricia Gwartney-Gibbs, University of Oregon

Harry Hale, Jr., Northeast Louisiana University

Kelley Hancock, Portland State University

Allen C. Haney, University of Houston

Charles Henderson, Memphis State University

Donald W. Hinrichs, Gettysburg College

Walter Hirsch, Purdue University

Eric O. Hoiberg, Iowa State University

Joan Huber, Ohio State University

Sidney J. Kaplan, University of Toledo

Will C. Kennedy, San Diego State University

Sally B. Kilgore, Emory University

Thomas Koenig, Northeastern University

Joel Lapin, Cantonsville Community College

Charles Levenstein, University of Lowell

George Lowe, Texas Tech University

Gary Madsen, Utah State University

John Markoff, University of Pittsburgh

Stephen L. Markson, University of Hartford

Anselyn Marshall, San Antonio College

Joseph A. McFalls, Temple University

Robert McLaren, Portland Community College

Scott G. McNall, University of Kansas

Bernard N. Meltzer, Central Michigan University

Eleanor M. Miller, University of Wisconsin, Milwaukee

Harvey Molotch, University of California, Santa Barbara

Charles Nam, Florida State University

Pamela Oliver, University of Wisconsin, Madison

Anne K. Peters, California State University, Dominguez Hills

Donald R. Ploch, University of Tennessee, Knoxville

Jeffrey P. Rosenfeld, Nassau Community College

Martin Scheffer, Boise State University

Eugen Schoenfeld, Georgia State University

Arnold R. Silverman, Nassau Community College

Randall Stokes, University of Massachusetts

Ann Sundgren, Tacoma Community College

Joseph B. Tamney, Ball State University

Edgar Webster, Oklahoma State University

Ronald T. Wohlstein, Eastern Illinois University

Charlotte Wolf, Memphis State University

Thomas J. Yacovone, Los Angeles Valley College

John Zipp, University of Wisconsin, Milwaukee

Contents

TWO
The Sociological Framework

5 Population and Ecology   103

THREE
Social Organization

FOUR
Social Stratification

11 Social Stratification: Who Gets What, and Why?   279

12 Race and Ethnicity   311

13 Gender   341

FIVE
Social Institutions

SIX
Social Change

SECOND EDITION

HUMAN ARRANGEMENTS

An Introduction to Sociology

ONE

What Sociology Is All About

WE ARE SURROUNDED BY all kinds of arrangements. Wherever you happen to be sitting right now, look around you and you will find that everything can be looked at in terms of its relation to other things. The room you are sitting in differs from other rooms, not only by what is in it, but by how things are arranged (try moving about with your eyes closed and you will see what I mean). This book is at its simplest a collection of electrons, atoms, and molecules that are arranged in such a way as to produce paper, ink, and color. The most important arrangement in this book, however, consists of words arranged into sentences, and the most important thing about them is that you understand them and they are thus the link in the arrangement between you the reader and me the author.

Sociologists, physicists, biologists, psychologists, economists, historians, literary scholars—all are interested in arrangements, whether it be the meter and rhyme in a poem, the structure of an atom, or what goes on among human beings. This book is about sociology, the study of the arrangements through which people know, share, and affect one another's lives.

Sociologists focus on three basic types of arrangements: the arrangement of words and ideas (culture) that we use to make sense of one another and our surroundings; the arrangement of social relationships (social structure) such as those that link authors and readers, parents and children, lovers, enemies, rich and poor, powerful and weak, or spectators and performers at a spontaneous break dance exhibition on a New York sidewalk; and the arrangement of people in physical space (ecology), from how the placement of furniture can affect who emerges as a group's leader to the differences between life in large, populous cities and life in small, rural villages.

Part One introduces you to sociology both as a perspective from which we look at the world and ask questions about it and as a set of scientific methods with which we try to answer those questions and see the world more clearly.

1 A First Look at Sociology

This is not an easy world to live in, much less to understand. There probably has never been a time in human history with such widespread day-to-day awareness of the crises and problems that arise from social life. From the news to films to life in our neighborhoods there is no escaping at least some sense that the world is huge and interconnected and a place of much trouble. In the U.S. alone, 1987 saw the Iran-*contra* scandal, homelessness of unprecedented proportions, a full-fledged AIDS epidemic, a stock market crash, the increasing poisoning of ground, air, and water with garbage and toxic wastes, candidates dropping out of the presidential race because of various forms of misconduct, moral scandals involving religious leaders, and new reports showing little progress toward racial or gender equality in spite of decades of social activism. To these we have to add problems that involve us beyond our borders, from the nuclear arms race to the international trade in drugs and weapons, political crises in the Philippines, apartheid in South Africa, terrorism in the Middle East, and civil war in Latin America.

In the face of all this, it is understandable that many people do not even try to make sense of it. It is a world that was already here when we were born into it; a world we did not make, and, which we often think, we cannot change. The world is enormously complex and seems to change as fast as we can grasp a piece of it. For all our collective awareness of the events and problems of our times, we really do not know what to do with it, except, perhaps, to attribute the problems in some vague way to "society" or the flawed personalities of people in general or our leaders in particular. In the end, it often seems easier if we do not read the newspapers, if we turn off the news, and go about our personal lives.

Our personal lives, though, are no less complicated. In the midst of all the world's problems we wrestle with what we tend to think of as personal troubles—of how we appear to other people, of being accepted, liked, and loved; of having our sexuality without giving up our safety; of figuring out who we are and reconciling that with who we want to be; of getting along with (and without) our parents; of earning a living, of deciding whether to marry, to have children, or to divorce.

What we tend to miss is the fact that our personal lives are not truly personal. We are not alone in our troubles, which is precisely the point of this book: everything *is* connected to everything else, and we are inevitably a part of that. We all participate in a social environment that presents us with both the troubles we must struggle with and the resources that are available to us. Each of us has characteristics of gender, race, age, religion, ethnicity, and social class in a society in which these matter a great deal in what happens to us. Our emotional needs are strongly influenced by the social relationships we participate in. The conditions under which we can earn a living depend on the fact that we live in an industrial capitalist society. The food we eat, the water we drink, the clothes we wear, the books we read, the toxic chemicals that make their way into our bodies—all depend on the social environment we live in. Virtually every aspect of our lives connects us to a larger world that most of us barely begin to understand.

A result of this is the frustration felt by Walter Lee, a major character in Lorraine Hansberry's powerful play *A Raisin in the Sun*, the story of a black American family struggling to escape an urban ghetto. "I didn't make this world. It was give to me this way!" he screams in a bitter and helpless rage after years of

Puzzles: The Search for Answers

How has the condition of black people in the United States changed during the 20-odd years since Lorraine Hansberry published *A Raisin in the Sun* and the Civil Rights Act was signed into law by President Lyndon Johnson?

While reading this book you will encounter a number of questions and puzzles much like this one. The answers to them, I think, will not at first be obvious to you. Some may surprise you. *A Raisin in the Sun* depicts a black family's affirmation of pride in itself, in its past, in its future. It is a moving story, filled with feeling, a story that turns on social conflict and ends in personal triumph. There are many similar stories about the black experience—the brutality they as a people have endured, their struggle to overcome the conditions imposed on them and to live with dignity. As you think about a question or puzzle such as the one above and try to answer it, you draw upon your store of personal experience, of things heard and seen, which informs you and leads you to a kind of understanding. You have the makings of a common sense.

Sociology, however, challenges our ordinary and limited personal experience by questioning our ready answers even when those answers express our most humane feelings. It upsets our common sense and proposes something better. Consider the answer to our question about the progress of blacks.

In the 20 years since passage of the Civil Rights Act, in the 30 years since the Supreme Court ordered desegregation of public schools, in the almost 40 years since Jackie Robinson became the first black to play major league baseball, there has been little significant improvement in the relative position of black people as a whole in American society (including no black major league baseball managers). The apparent gains—increased numbers of middle-class blacks, the election of black officials, and higher salaries paid to black profes-

sional athletes—have had little effect on the vast majority of blacks. They remain less well paid for their labor, less well housed, fed, and educated than their fellow citizens. Indeed, many blacks feel farther than ever from full participation in society despite the years of struggle for recognition and despite the hopes that flared when the Civil Rights Act became law. Some explanations for this distressing and perhaps surprising answer to our question will be proposed later, in Chapter 12.

It is in puzzles similar to this one that sociology proceeds as a way of looking at the world in search of answers. Each question flows from a general wonder about why societies are as they are. Each is a matter of concern that sociologists want to understand, and I put them to you as examples of what it means to observe and think about the world from a sociological perspective rather than rely only on the common sense that arises from personal experience.

This book is an invitation to you to acquire the skills that will enable you to dig deeper in search of understanding about the social world we inhabit. If you acquire those skills, then I will have succeeded in what I set out to do.

trying unsuccessfully to find a place for himself in a world dominated by whites.

None of us made this world, but as participants in it, we do affect it. The social world is not frozen; it is a process of continual making and remaking in which we all take part; and it is up to us to choose whether to participate in that process with as much awareness and understanding of it as we can achieve. At the very least it makes life more interesting and full of meaning, for by appreciating the complexity of the world and our connections to it, we also appreciate the richness of our own lives. At the most, this kind of commitment has the potential to help change the world itself, including the terms by which we live.

The purpose of this book is quite simple to state: to offer you the sociological framework as a set of tools for making sense of the social world and understanding your own life by seeing more clearly its connection with the lives of others in a shared social environment.

A SOCIOLOGICAL VIEW OF FAMILIAR WORLDS

We all live out our lives in relation to social and physical environments, and **sociology** *is the systematic study of social and physical environments and their effects on our experience and behavior as individuals.* Sociology is about us—the "us" that preceded you and me and the "us" of which we are now a part.

Sociology helps us see the human arrangements of shared ideas and relationships that connect our otherwise separate lives, just as astronomy helps us see constellations where before we saw only a sea of individual stars. The stars were there all the time, but to see Orion's Belt or the Big Dipper, we have to look for patterns; and to see the constellations of social relationships that characterize life, we have to pay attention to the patterns that exist among individuals.

This chapter has two goals: (1) through a series of examples, to introduce some of the major concepts

 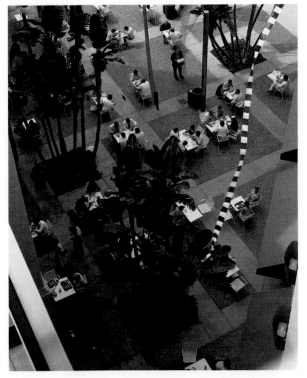

Just as there are patterns among stars, so too are there patterns in relationships among people. In the photo of people on a patio, few tables have an odd number of people. How would you explain this simple pattern? What does it say about life in our society?

that organize sociological thinking; (2) to sketch the history of sociological thought—to show that this way of looking at the world is, itself, one way in which humans respond to the world by trying to make sense of it.

Social Expectations: How Do We Know Who People Really Are?

Perhaps it was just this morning that you entered your first class of the new term, most likely a large room with rows of chairs which may have been bolted to the floor, forcing you to face the front of the room. As students talked among themselves, a person—perhaps it was a woman—entered the room, walked to the front, and stood behind the lectern. Everyone in the room stopped talking soon after she arrived—except for her.

When she wanted to talk, she just talked; when others wanted to talk, they raised a hand and waited for her permission. Students asked questions; she made statements. She did not write down what you said, but you wrote down what she said. This scene repeats itself so often in college classrooms that it may never have occurred to you how remarkable it is.

What is remarkable is that no one ever asks those people behind lecterns if they are who we think they are. Without any personal knowledge of the professor in the scene just described, students pay attention to her and enter into relationships in which she has power over them and controls rewards they value highly. Students do "know" something about her, however, knowledge they substitute for details of her personal identity.

They know that according to the catalogue the course was supposed to meet in that room at that time, that every student was expected to read the catalogue and be guided by it. They went to the room at the designated time and found other people there. Some asked, "Is this Intro Soc.?," were told "yes," and believed what they heard.

The woman entered the room and took the position at the front. Anyone could have stood there, but only she did. This is important, for if anyone had challenged her for that spot, your "knowledge" of who she was would have been shaken. No one challenged her, however, because someone was *expected* to occupy that position, someone who looked as though she was supposed to be there.

You expected her to be older than you, to dress in a certain way, to speak English, and behave appropriately. So long as people's appearance and behavior fit our expectations, we treat them accordingly even though their "real" selves may not be what they appear to be (Goffman, 1959). The acceptance of a teacher's authority in a classroom does not depend only on the personalities of individuals but also on expectations that students and teachers share about one another as students and teachers, not as unique individuals.

One point of this is that we repeatedly enter into relationships with people without any direct personal knowledge of who they are. We take our clothes off in front of people we believe to be physicians and may even allow them to perform surgery on us. We allow dentists to drill our teeth and airline pilots and bus drivers to take our lives in their hands. Even when we drive a car or walk across an intersection, we depend on automobile drivers to behave in predictable ways. Rarely, if ever, do we ask doctors for their credentials or demand assurance that a pilot really knows how to fly a plane.

What we know of one another consists primarily of expectations about people's positions in social relationships (professor, doctor, bus driver) and about ourselves in relation to them (student, patient, passenger). The power of those expectations comes in part from the fact that we share them with one another and in part from our general lack of awareness of them as objective characteristics of our social environment. Rarely are we conscious of the complex social relationships that tie us to one another, and, as a result, we often try to understand who we and others are solely by focusing on characteristics such as personality.

Social Relationships: Mothers

Our positions in social relationships affect not only how we perceive one another, but how we behave. While most of us experience our mothers as unique individuals, from a sociological perspective "mother" is a social position that profoundly affects how those unique individuals behave.

We enter the world knowing not a single soul. Our knowledge of others is largely sensory, consisting of smells and tastes, touch and sound. We soon learn something very useful, however: the magic of words through which things and people can be named. "Mother" is, when we first learn it, a particular

We think of a "mother" as a woman who values the needs of her husband and children more than her own, who loves and accepts her children without conditions, and who never has a cruel or unkind thought about them. However poorly it may fit the reality of actual mothers, it is a powerful image.

woman's proper name. The word "mother" tells us who that woman is, and so we tend to think that this is who she is to everyone.

Enter confusion: other people do not call mother "mother." Also confusing is the fact that many women are called "mother"; and every mother has a mother, so is both "mother" and "daughter." What is hard for small children to understand is that the word "mother" is not like "tree" or "rock," for "mother" describes a *position* in a particular *social relationship* with another person. It need not be the woman who bore the child; it can be any woman who occupies the social position "mother" in relation to someone who occupies the social position "son" or "daughter."

Most of us do not have shared ideas about any particular mother, but we do share ideas about

mothers in general, about what they are like, their behavior, what is important in their lives, and how they are supposed to feel in relation to their children. To the extent that a mother shares these ideas, they influence what she thinks, feels, and does. To understand a woman's behavior as a mother, we cannot pay attention only to her mental life, the ebb and flow of her emotions. "Mother" represents more than biological fact: it represents a complex set of ideas that she and others use to decide who she is, what her children and she may expect of one another, how she should choose between conflicting alternatives. While she may act and feel contrary to those ideas, she does not have the power to remove them from her social environment.

In a social sense, "who we are" depends on the positions we occupy in relation to other people and the shared ideas attached to us as a result. To ignore the social component of our selves is like trying to explain why apples fall from trees by examining only the characteristics of apples without taking into account their relationship to the earth's gravitational pull. This attention to the relationship between individuals and their environments is at the core of sociology.

Perspectives:
How Did J. J. Riordan Come to Die?

In trying to understand life, sociologists pay attention not only to relationships between individuals, but also to the larger *social environments* in which those relationships exist. More than anything else, it is this focus that distinguishes sociology as a point of view, as we will see in the case of James J. Riordan.

According to the *New York Times*, Riordan, 47, left his spacious apartment on New York City's West Side early on a drizzly Friday morning in October. He went to confession, then to work, but he did not stay very long. Shortly before noon he returned home. At 5:30 that afternoon, his sister and brother-in-law found him seated in an overstuffed red plush chair in his bedroom at the rear of the house. His jacket and vest hung neatly on a wooden valet; his right hand dangled over the arm of the chair, and directly beneath it, on the floor, was a revolver from which one shot had been fired. He had a bullet wound in his right temple and was dead. How do we figure out how he came to die?

"Figuring things out" is not simple, because there are many ways to do it. We look at things from different points of view, or *perspectives*. Therefore, we can ask different questions about the same thing and arrive at different explanations. Perspectives influence what we look at and what we make of what we see. It is fairly simple to explain Riordan's death from the perspectives of physics and biology, the points of view coroners use to determine causes of death. These perspectives raise questions about hands holding guns and fingers pulling triggers, about exploding gun powder, the mass and velocity of bullets fired, and bullets' effect on a brain and the life of its owner.

A physical explanation also demands that we determine who pulled the trigger. The gun Riordan was shot with came from a desk drawer in his office; his fingerprints were the only ones found on it; it lay on the floor right where it would have fallen had he shot himself. In the absence of other evidence, we conclude that he committed suicide. From these points of view, then, we know *how* J. J. Riordan came to die.

While these disciplines explain who killed him and how, other points of view produce new questions. Riordan was a human being who had a mind, experienced emotion, sensed the world outside him and responded to it. The psychological perspective raises questions about human choice and the emotional and mental processes that influence what is chosen. The explanations of biology and physics cannot solve the psychological puzzle: *why* did J. J. Riordan come to die?

Riordan's friends told the *New York Times* that he had been emotionally exhausted for weeks prior to his suicide; his doctors feared that he would collapse physically and emotionally. All agreed he was severely depressed. These are classic danger signals of a possible suicide: prolonged exhaustion, feelings of hopelessness and despair, an inability to cope (Lester, 1983). But such an explanation is not a full solution to the psychological puzzle, for other questions remain: Why do such states lead some to kill themselves but do not have this effect on others?

Even a complete biological, physical, and psychological explanation of the suicide falls short, for it looks at Riordan's behavior only in terms of his individual processes and characteristics. What is missing is attention to the fact that he made his choice within a social environment. To understand his death from a sociological point of view, we must understand that environment and his position in it.

J. J. Riordan was feeling depressed because he had recently lost a great deal of money. He shot himself on November 10, 1929, just twelve days after the initial crash of the New York Stock Market, which spun the United States and the world into a decade of severe economic depression. His speculation in that market led to his downfall. But why was his downfall so important to him that he would take his own life?

Riordan's social environment was one in which people valued money and accorded prestige and power to those who had a great amount. He was the president of a large bank, which gave him access to a lot of money to speculate with; it also gave him a great deal of responsibility for the well-being of others. He was a white man in an environment that gave power to white men and expected them to use it successfully. In this environment, Riordan's financial success and ability to exercise power was a major source of standing and security.

The sociological perspective suggests that Riordan was hit particularly hard by the stock market crash because of his social positions in relation to that event: a middle-aged, white, male banker who not only lost material wealth (as did many others) but suffered from intense guilt and a humiliating loss of social prestige, as well.

If Riordan's social positions influenced him to kill himself, then we should find similar effects on people who occupied similar social positions. These effects appear as *patterns* of behavior that differ from one position to another, and we can see the effects of the environment by locating Riordan in patterns of behavior. To do this, we look at the suicide *rate* for people like Riordan to see if they were more strongly affected by the crash than people in different social positions.

If we look at the suicide rate for white males in the U.S., we find that for white men 15 to 34 years old, the rate changed very little between 1929 and 1932 when the stock market reached its lowest ebb. For older white men 45 to 64, who had the greatest investment in the economy, the suicide rate jumped by almost 50 percent. For white women, on the other hand, a great many of whom shared the economic gains and losses of men, there was no such pattern corresponding to the stock market crash. (For comparison, the suicide rate for black males rose only among those 55 to 64 years old.) (National Office of Vital Statistics, 1956.)

While suicide rates tell us only about groups and nothing about the individual, J. J. Riordan, they do tell us about the behavior of people who occupied social positions similar to his and, as such, they give us clues about the pressures exerted on such people and the resulting patterns of response to them. (For more on this, see One Step Further 1-1, pp. 12–13.) It is important to note, however, that, while we will not go into it further here, the sociological work is not done until we can also explain why so many people in Riordan's position did *not* choose to commit suicide. A sociological explanation would also have to account for the absence of a large increase in suicides after the stock market crash of 1987.

Clearly, Riordan was not just an isolated organism that thought, felt, and acted. Although wealthy and powerful, he was part of something much larger than he was, something he neither created nor controlled. He participated in a system of social relationships and shared ideas, through which he constructed his world and made his choices. Had he lived in any other social environment, his circumstances would have been quite different. There have been and still are groups in which the ideas of private property, money, banks, and speculation do not exist, in which prestige does not depend on owning more than others, and whose material existence is so marginal that there is nothing to accumulate in the first place.

When we pay attention to patterns of behavior among people according to their positions in social relationships, we gain insights that other perspectives overlook. As valuable as it is to identify psychological aspects of suicide, we also need an appreciation of the social circumstances affecting the emotional and mental processes through which people make choices. James Riordan's solitary act of suicide tells us things about him; but it also mirrors his social environment.

The crash of the stock market and the Great Depression that followed did not just "happen." They represented the breakdown of an economic system, a way in which humans organized the production and distribution of goods and services. They resulted from a history of events, themselves shaped by the ongoing collective process of social life in the U.S.

The nature of that social life did not just happen, either. The ability to accumulate wealth represents centuries of social development through which it became possible to produce more than people needed for immediate consumption. The development of money and banks, as well as the ideas of private property, credit and the future (about which people might speculate) represents ways in which humans organized

social relationships. Riordan's solitary act is connected to a collective process unfolding through history, and it is by locating him in that process that we come to a fuller understanding of his individual circumstances, experience, and behavior.

Each of the preceding examples shows in its own way that who we are and what we do is affected by our positions in social relationships and in large social environments. This is never more apparent than when we meet someone for the first time.

Puzzles: A Self-Survey

Who do you think you are?

Before reading any further, write down ten words or phrases that, for you, answer the question, "Who am I?" Then, as you read the following section, look again at your answers and think about what this says about "who you are."

Social Identities: Who Do You Think You Are?

Suppose that you live by yourself in an apartment; to make ends meet, you decide to advertise for a roommate. In response to your ad, someone writes to you: "Most people think I'm intelligent and have a good sense of humor. I'm neat, keep regular hours, don't play music too loudly, pay my bills on time. I enjoy most sports, a good book, lively conversation and meeting new people."

Would this be enough information for you? Would you like to know if this person is male or female, homosexual or heterosexual, 16 years old or 55 years old with two grandchildren? Would it matter to you if this person is an illegal alien, a child of the president of the United States, is unemployed, or works as a police officer, a journalist, a farm worker, a computer programmer, a taxi driver, or a restaurant cook? Would you like to know if this person is black, Hispanic, white, or Asian, is fabulously wealthy or desperately poor, went to a posh prep school in Boston or a run-down high school on the south side of Chicago, grew up on a farm or in the Bronx or on an Indian reservation? Does it matter if your roommate is Catholic, Protestant, Jewish, or Muslim, or grew up in a tribe of cannibals on New Guinea?

ONE STEP FURTHER 1-1:
Age, Gender, and the Risks of Suicide

This is the first of the One Step Further boxes that you will find throughout *Human Arrangements*. Each takes a point made in the text and explores it in more detail with the data that sociologists use to test ideas about social life. If you feel uncomfortable with charts, graphs, and tables, just take your time and read along with the explanation that accompanies each box. There is nothing here that requires any statistical sophistication.

The graph in Figure B-1-1 shows how suicide rates changed between the years 1925 and 1939, a period that included the stock market crash. The years are marked off along the horizontal axis, and the suicide rates are marked off along the vertical axis. There are seven lines, each one showing the experiences of categories of white people who differ by gender or age. Each line is marked with a description at the right and a Roman numeral at the left. The top line (VII) shows suicide rates for 65–74 year-old white men; the bottom line (I) shows suicide rates for 25–34 year-old white women. Stop for a moment and make sure you see everything described above in the graph.

Beginning at the bottom (line I), you can see that suicide rates for younger white women changed barely at all from 1925 to 1939—the line is almost straight across. The same is true for white women 55–64 (line II). In addition, notice that the lines for older and younger women are quite close to each other, showing that older women are not much more likely to kill themselves than are younger women.

The situation for white men, however, is dramatically different. First notice that for each year, with each older age group, there is a large jump in the suicide rate, which you can see from the fact that the lines for older age groups are located quite a ways above the lines for younger age groups. In 1932 the suicide rate for white men was 23 per 100,000 for those 25–34, 36 for those 35–44, 62 for those 45–54,.86 for those 55–64, and 92 for those 65–74 (see the small circles on each line). This is a pattern that still holds in the U.S. Why should older men be so much more likely to kill themselves? Is it because they have a more difficult time adjusting to the inevitable disappointments that occur as we age? What do you think?

Now notice how the shape of the lines changes as we move from younger men to older men. The suicide rate for the youngest men (line III) increased only slightly by 1932, but as we move upward to each older age group, the jump is more and more pronounced. For the oldest men (line VII), the rate jumped from 63 per 100,000 in 1925 to 92 in 1932 and then fell back down to its previous level over the next three or four years. Notice also how different the line for 55–64-year-old men (line VI) is from the line for 55–64-year-old women (line II).

Stop for a moment and make sure you see these patterns.

Differences in gender and age go along with sharply different tendencies to commit suicide. Why these patterns exist is still an unsolved puzzle, but they raise intriguing questions about age and gender as social characteristics that affect our behavior.

Figure B-1-1 Rate of Suicides for White Males and Females by Age Group, 1925 to 1939, in the U.S.

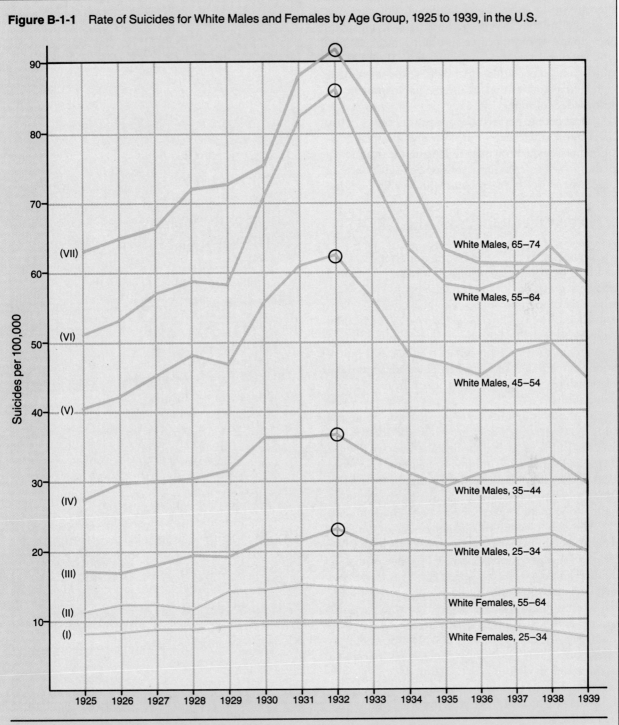

Source: National Office of Vital Statistics, 1956.

Most likely, most or all of these things would interest you to some degree, although none tells us about the individual you are thinking of living with. They do tell us about people's positions in social environments, and this gives us clues about their beliefs, values, and expectations in relation to others. It is such characteristics that we use in shaping our initial "knowledge" of others.

Most people never know our private selves. They know our *social* selves—our positions in social environments—and know us through the ideas attached to those "selves." Similarly, our social selves are an important source of ideas about who *we* think we are.

WHAT SOCIOLOGY IS ALL ABOUT

The preceding examples stress the importance of our positions in social relationships; but most people find it hard to grasp the idea that relationships exist independently of the individuals who participate in them (Durkheim, 1895). The relationship between children and parents is defined by shared ideas about children and parents, their behavior, goals, feelings, and expectations in relation to one another. Those ideas, and the relationships they define, exist apart from you and your parents.

Without individuals acting in those relationships, however, they would not exist, and there is the crux of it: all of us participate in something we did not create, and yet through our involvement we give those relationships life; we stamp them with our own interpretations and thereby participate in changing or maintaining them as parts of our social environment.

The examples in this chapter center on vital aspects of social life that are at the core of sociology. We use shared ideas to make sense of the world, one another, and ourselves; we spend our lives in webs of social relationships with other people, relationships that affect not only how we behave, but who we think we are; and social life is itself affected by physical conditions, including the ways in which societies produce goods. These key aspects of social life correspond to three major concepts that define sociology as a perspective: culture, social structure, and population and ecology. The next three sections briefly introduce each of them.

Culture

Culture consists of two basic products that arise from the collective activity and the experience of human

Cultural beliefs are used to construct basic ideas about reality, especially aspects we cannot observe, such as what happens after death. Bosch's 16th century vision of hell is a cultural attempt to grasp the unknown.

beings. The first is **nonmaterial culture**, which includes language, art, music, and four major types of shared ideas: beliefs, norms, values, and attitudes. The second is **material culture**, objects that humans make and which become part of our physical environment.

Beliefs are statements about what is real and are thus the most fundamental of all cultural ideas. Some examples of such statements are: "The world is round, not flat, and it revolves around the sun." "It is possible to win a nuclear war." "All people are created equal." "People succeed because they work hard." "AIDS can be transmitted through sexual contact."

Norms are rules about people's behavior according to their positions in social relationships. Some examples: Students are supposed to do what teachers tell them to. Teachers are not supposed to abuse students or sell high grades. We may not physically attack one another, steal other people's things, or shout people down because we dislike what they say. Parents may not abuse their children.

In addition to beliefs and norms, we share **values**, which are ideas about what is important and unimportant, good and bad, desirable and undesirable. Some examples are: Honesty and fairness are important (we do not want teachers to grade arbitrarily or tell students there are two papers in the course when in fact there are four). People should do whatever their government tells them to. People should always question authority. Wealth, power, and prestige are desirable.

As a fourth component of nonmaterial culture, **attitudes** are evaluations that predispose us to feel behave positively or negatively toward people, objects, or situations (Allport, 1935; Hill, 1981). Many people have a negative attitude toward people on welfare, based on the value that they should be working and the belief that they could if they wanted to. Attitudes are a key part of culture because they reflect the importance of emotions in social life. Prejudice is difficult to eradicate because it is more than a matter of false beliefs about a particular group. It is also deeply

As a cultural attitude, racial prejudice often includes deep feelings of contempt, hostility, and fear. In this Pulitzer Prize winning picture, whites, who have just recited the pledge of allegiance, attack a black businessman as he walks near a rally against a court-ordered busing plan to integrate schools. The incident took place during the bicentennial year in Boston, a city considered by many to be the "cradle of liberty."

rooted in emotions of hostility, fear, and loyalty to one's own group. Feelings are much harder to change than beliefs, and we often resist changing our beliefs because it will force us to change our feelings as well.

While ideas constitute the major part of cultural products, humans have also developed *material* products: objects that both extend our abilities and limit our choices. Computers, automobiles, telephones, forks, plows, pianos, highways, and cities are all examples of material culture. They affect everything from how we eat and communicate to how we plan our communities and conduct our relationships with one another.

Social Structure

Cultural ideas are organized into social relationships among people who occupy different positions (such as mother and child). On the *micro*—or small-scale—level of social life, **social structure** is the arrangement of people in relation to one another and the patterns of expectation attached to each position in social relationships.

When you and I identify ourselves as children in relation to our mothers and fathers, we define an important part of the social structure of interaction in our families. Parents and children share certain socially prescribed expectations of one another. Each social structure, then, is an arrangement that gives participants a predictable pattern of expectations.

In addition to social relationships among individuals, the concept of **social structure** has two additional meanings on the *macro*—or large-scale—level. First, groups and organizations interact with one another just as individuals do, and they too have patterns of shared expectations. Universities have structured relationships with government agencies through which universities receive financial support.

Second, the concept of social structure also refers to the ways in which people are *distributed* among various social positions as well as how major rewards of social life—in particular, wealth, power, and prestige—are distributed among members of a group or society. The medical profession in the United States is structured so that women rarely occupy the prestigious social position "surgeon" and, as a result, are denied the high income and prestige and influence that accompany that specialty.

The concept of social structure describes how we are arranged in relation to one another, from personal interactions to society as a whole. As a concept, it is extremely useful, because it draws our attention to the predictable, organized patterns of expectation that characterize social life. Together, the concepts of culture and social structure describe social environments. When we describe something as "social," we are saying that it concerns one or both of these aspects of a social environment.

As important as social environments are, we cannot overlook the fact that they exist in *physical* environments that include both the physical world and the biological facts of life on this planet. This brings us to the third major concept in the sociological perspective—population and ecology.

Population and Ecology

Whereas culture and structure describe the social environment, population and ecology focus on human beings as organisms who live in relation to physical environments. In sociology, a **population** is any collection of people who share a physical environment. A population can be as small as a single person living on a desert island or as large as the population of the world, which numbered in excess of 5 billion people in 1988.

Ecology focuses on the characteristics of physical environments and the relation of populations to them. The characteristics of physical environments include the availability of resources such as fertile land, water, and fuel; access to transportation routes such as rivers; and isolation by mountains, deserts, or other barriers. The relation of populations to physical environments includes such factors as how large populations are, how rapidly they grow or shrink, and how they are distributed in physical space. This relation also includes **technology**, a population's ability to make use of natural resources. Plows, electric generators, printing presses, crop irrigation systems, and computers all represent ways in which human beings make use of the physical environment. Population and ecology are important parts of the sociological perspective because the physical conditions of human life have important effects on how social environments develop.

The development of large industrial societies depends on more than culture and social structure, for it also results from rapid population growth, the concentration of workers in large cities, and the successful application of technology to problems of production. In turn, the ability to produce more than people need

Population and ecology are concepts that focus on differences such as those between rural Japanese who cultivate rice largely by hand and urban Japanese who live in crowded cities dominated by the mass production of modern industry. Just as they relate to their physical environments in radically different ways, so too do they relate to one another in different ways—from the structure of family life to politics, religion, education, and social inequality.

to survive allows some people to accumulate wealth and power at the expense of others. The social structures that gave J. J. Riordan the power to speculate with other people's money were made possible by an industrialized society with a large, urban population and vast natural resources.

While the concepts of culture and social structure define the social environment, population and ecology focus on humanity as a species of life, whose numbers shrink and swell, distribute themselves geographically, and learn to use their physical environments.

Society

A **society** is a population with several important characteristics of particular interest in sociology. A society shares a geographical territory, a common culture, and way of life. It is held together by a shared identity, and

is relatively independent and self-sufficient. Because societies combine all the basic elements of culture, social structure, population, and ecology, sociology has a great deal to say about how they are put together and how they operate—as you will see in the chapters to come.

Societies differ greatly from one another. They may differ in how homogeneous or varied their cultures are. Iceland, for example, is culturally homogeneous, with most of its people tracing their cultural heritage back hundreds of years to common roots in Norway. In contrast, the republics that comprise the Soviet Union include scores of languages, and racial and cultural groups that are often at odds with the white, Russian speaking central government. In some ways, the U.S. is similar, for, although we have English as a common language, our population includes many ethnic and racial groups that often go to great lengths to preserve their language, values, and distinctive clothing, food, and customs. As we will see, this heterogeneity is a source of rich cultural diversity and of prejudice, discrimination, and social conflict.

Societies also differ in their independence and self-sufficiency, especially in a world in which international trade and politics are as important as they are now. Japan is an independent nation free from political control of other countries. By comparison, Tibet has a distinct cultural identity, way of life, and territory, but is under the military and political control of China. In other cases, dependence takes more subtle forms. Countries such as South Korea, El Salvador, and the Philippines have been so dependent on military and economic aid from the United States, that the U.S. has been able to exert considerable pressure on the internal affairs of these countries. Similar relations, although in a more extreme form, exist between the Soviet Union and most socialist societies in Eastern Europe.

Societies can be very large (the territory of the Soviet Union is more than twice that of the U.S., and the people of China make up a fifth of the entire world population) or very small (Iceland's population amounts to barely 200,000 people). They vary enormously in their complexity, from modern industrial societies in which many aspects of life are affected by huge bureaucracies to simple societies with no schools, government, military, corporations, banks, or churches.

The most important difference among societies centers on their ability to obtain material needs—how they arrange themselves to produce goods, to grow food, and meet other physical needs. At one extreme, hunter-gatherers grow none of their own food and have few possessions, while at the other extreme, industrial societies grow all of their own food and place a high value on accumulating possessions. Many important aspects of life in a society are affected by these productive arrangements, including the existence of inequality, social oppression, and the variety of religious beliefs.

The Personal and the Social

A crucial element of sociological thinking is the distinction between individuals and their environments. A behavior or experience may be common to many individuals and yet not be social; or be rare and yet profoundly social.

Everyone inevitably experiences death, but death remains a personal activity; by itself, the universality of this experience does not make it social. How people respond to us when they know we are dying, however, as well as how we respond to them and to our own condition are *social*, because they are affected by cultural ideas about death; also, our age at death and the cause of our death are strongly affected by our social positions.

I sit alone in my office writing a book about the social world—a rare activity in any society, but nonetheless a highly social one. To explain this activity only in terms of my motivation and ability ignores the social and material world within which I act. This book is socially possible because humans invented paper, ink, and printing presses, and developed language and the idea that writing books is socially valuable, allowing me to do it in exchange for a share of what other people produce—food, shelter, clothing. I am also writing this book because humans developed a particular way of thinking about social life (sociology) just as they developed ways of thinking about physical life (biology), matter and energy (physics), mental and emotional processes (psychology), the unknown (religion), beauty (art), and other cultures (anthropology).

If I belonged to one of many other societies around the world, I would not be writing this book, because in those environments there would be no paper, presses, or audience of college students trying to understand the social world in a systematic way. So, what I do at this moment cannot be explained solely by my motives and thoughts; I must also understand my position in the social environment within which I act as a human being, a context I did not create.

Sociology provides us with a window on the world and a mirror of our participation in it. To use it, however, is difficult, for we actively participate in the very thing we are trying to understand; the intellectual tools, themselves, are part of culture. In addition, sociology often challenges us to raise uncomfortable questions about the connection between ourselves and social problems.

We could look at J. J. Riordan's suicide as a personal solution to a personal problem. When, however, we see that people like him (middle-aged, white men) were far more likely to kill themselves than were those who differed in age, race, and gender, we can no longer regard his behavior as purely personal. The patterns reflected in suicide rates for people in different social positions indicate that something is going on in the variety of environments in which people find themselves, something that makes people in some positions more likely than others to kill themselves (Durkheim, 1895). Like all behavior, suicide is a personal and a social act (Mills, 1959).

As we begin to understand the social causes of individual troubles, we must acknowledge that as participants in social life we are connected in some way to them. Racism, sexism, and ageism are not problems for only those individuals who happen to have a particular skin color, sex, or age. We are understandably reluctant to connect ourselves with other people's troubles, and we resist giving up comfortable beliefs in order to see the world in a new way. As Berger (1963) wrote, a social environment

> provides us with warm, reasonably comfortable caves, in which we can huddle with our fellows, beating on the drums that drown out the howling hyenas of the surrounding darkness. "Ecstasy" is the act of stepping outside the caves, alone, to face the night. (p. 150)

To "step outside" is to adopt a kind of consciousness that Mills called "the sociological imagination."

THEORETICAL PERSPECTIVES ON SOCIAL LIFE

Culture, social structure, population, and ecology form a conceptual framework for sociology by defining its subject matter, for it is impossible to look at something sociologically without including one or more of these concepts. These, however, are just the groundwork of the sociological perspective. The major reason for paying attention to them is to understand how social life works and affects us. To do this, we have to go beyond concepts, such as culture and social structure, and construct explanations in the form of theories.

A **theory** is a set of interrelated ideas that attempt to explain how things work. As we will see in Chapter 12 one theory argues that when groups compete with each other for resources, such as jobs, they tend to develop prejudiced ideas about each other, and this is one source of racism. Another theory argues that when one group dominates and exploits another, it tends to develop prejudiced ideas about the subordinate group in order to justify inequality. Together, the two theories suggest that racism against blacks in the

A fundamental challenge of sociology is to understand the connection between individuals and their social environments, to explain social life and participate in it at the same time. Our relationship to society is complex, reciprocal, and difficult to unravel, much like M. C. Escher's famous drawing of two hands drawing each other.

Drawing Hands, M. C. Escher, National Gallery of Art, Washington, Rosenwald Collection.

U.S. results partly from competition between blacks and whites, and partly from the need of whites to justify their dominance and privilege.

Where do such theories come from? As with any science, the origins for sociological theory are complex and rooted in our abilities to observe the world, to share ideas with one another, and to think creatively. In doing this, most sociologists use one or more general frameworks—called **theoretical perspectives**—that define basic points of view on the cultural, structural, and ecological aspects of social life. Unlike theories, theoretical perspectives do not explain anything; rather, they define points of view from which we look at whatever it is we are trying to understand.

In trying to explain suicide we saw that disciplines such as biology, physics, psychology, and sociology offer different points of view on the same thing and therefore generate different questions about it. This is also true *within* disciplines: just as sociology and biology offer different perspectives on life, within sociology there are also several major points of view that draw attention to and emphasize different social aspects of the same phenomenon. While all sociologists would consider culture and social structure in trying to explain suicide, the theories they arrive at will depend on their theoretical perspective. The theories of racial prejudice mentioned above are closely connected to the conflict perspective which, as you will see shortly, emphasizes the causes and consequences of tension, struggle, and inequality in social life.

Before the development of science the dominant perspective used to explain the social and physical world was based heavily on the idea of "natural order" dictated by God and nature. In contrast, science represented a radical shift towards reason, logic, and observation and away from religious faith. Rather than accepting things as they are, the idea that the social and physical worlds can be understood, controlled, and improved became increasingly influential.

The world from which sociology emerged was in many ways similar to our own, a world full of rapid, often frightening social change. The French Revolution toppled the monarchy in 1789, and, after Napoleon's unsuccessful attempt to conquer Europe, fifty years of social instability and rapid economic and political change followed. The Industrial Revolution brought unprecedented productivity along with congested cities, high unemployment, increased poverty, and miserable living conditions. In the face of what many saw as anarchy that might destroy their societies, some responded by clinging to old ways of thinking, while others, finding these to be inadequate, looked for new frameworks, new assumptions, and new points of view. The French philosopher Auguste Comte (1798–1857) developed the idea that societies can be understood in terms of scientific laws that govern their development. It was Comte who first used the term "sociology" to refer to what he promoted as the scientific study of social life.

Since Comte, sociology has developed three major theoretical perspectives—functional, conflict, and interactionist—from which most theory flows. Each offers a different point of view on social life by emphasizing different aspects of it.

Understanding Social Systems: Two Perspectives

A **social system** is any set of social relationships that operates as a whole, and a major concern of sociology is to understand how they are formed, how they work and change, and how they affect people's lives. Social systems can be as large as a society or the entire world of interrelated societies (such as the world economy discussed in Chapters 11 and 18); or they can be as small as a married couple or two friends. Social systems are what organize life, from relationships between bus drivers and their passengers, physicians and their patients, and college roommates, to the complexities of the U.S. Congress, the Toyota corporation, and the United States. What they all have in common is that they are sets of relationships that can be thought of as a unit.

Perhaps the most important aspect of social systems is that they are more than the sum of their parts (see Durkheim, 1895). A human body is more than a collection of cells and organs; it is the particular *arrangement* of cells and organs in relation to one another that distinguishes humans from other species. In the same way, a group or society is more than a collection of specific people; it is a particular arrangement of individuals in relation to one another. If you were asked to define a "volleyball team," it would not be enough to simply list the names of the people on a particular team. Instead, you would have to describe the relationships and expectations that bind people together in particular ways that distinguish a volleyball team from a group of office workers (both of which might include the same individuals).

Two of the three major theoretical perspectives focus on how social systems work and how they affect the people who participate in them. These are the functional and conflict perspectives.

The Functional Perspective   The **functional perspective** focuses on how social systems operate (or "function"), the process through which they maintain themselves, and adapt. An aspect of a social system that contributes to this process is called **functional**, and an aspect that interferes with it is called **dysfunctional** (Merton, 1968). In school academic competition is functional insofar as it promotes hard work and high achievement, both of which are certainly integral parts of schools as social systems. Competition, however, can also be dysfunctional when, say, it encourages students to earn high grades by interfering with the work of other students.

In the U.S. legal system, people accused of crimes are protected by rights that make it difficult to convict and punish people unjustly, such as the rights to legal representation and a trial by jury. These norms help to protect citizens from abuse and are functional for a system that exists, in part, to promote justice. However, they also have the effect of making it easier for guilty people to go free, as when murderers are released because arresting officers fail to inform them of their legal rights or seize vital evidence without a search warrant. These norms, then, have dysfunctional consequences. The complexity of social systems makes it probable that their different aspects will have both functional and dysfunctional consequences.

When the functional or dysfunctional consequences of something are intended, they are called **manifest**, and when they are unintended, they are called **latent** (Merton, 1968). The norms that protect those accused of crimes have the manifest consequence of protecting citizens from abuse; but they also have the latent consequence of interfering with the effective prosecution of those who commit crimes. In constructing the protections found in our legal system, no one intended to make it easier for criminals to go free, and yet, however unintended it may be, this is nonetheless a real consequence that interferes with the effective operation of the criminal justice system.

It is important to remember that functional consequences are not necessarily ethically "good," and dysfunctional consequences are not necessarily "bad." The Soviet Union is a social system whose stability depends heavily on a massive secret police (the "KGB") that regularly spies on, harasses, and mistreats Soviet citizens. Although the KGB is functional for the short-run stability of the Soviet political system, this in no way implies that the KGB is "good" in the moral sense of the word. Civil rights activists in the U.S. brought about a great deal of public unrest, conflict, and, in some cases, violence in the 1960s, but, while this may have been dysfunctional for the stability of society in the short run, there can be no doubt that in the long run it has had the positive effect of promoting social change towards a less racist society. A functional analysis enables us to see how a society maintains itself in its present form and how it adapts to pressures for change. Whether we judge the consequences of living in a particular social system to be ethically good or bad is of course an important question; but it is, nonetheless, a separate issue from determining whether something is functional or dysfunctional in a social system.

The origins of the functional perspective are traced to the great French sociologist Emile Durkheim (1858–1917) who wanted to understand what holds societies together. Durkheim was particularly interested in discovering latent functions and dysfunctions, those unanticipated, often surprising consequences of social life. While most early criminologists viewed crime as an abnormal phenomenon caused by defects in people's personalities, Durkheim tried to identify ways in which the existence of crime might actually contribute to the maintenance of social systems. Although crime certainly can be dysfunctional for preserving social order, the functional perspective raises the question of whether there are ways in which crime actually contributes to social systems.

When someone commits a particularly horrible crime, such as murdering a child, community members often feel closer to one another as they share their collective outrage. Since bringing people "closer together" strengthens the ties that hold social systems together, crime has the latent functional consequence of contributing to social cohesion. Crime can also be functional by bringing about needed social change, since it is often only through criminal acts such as civil disobedience that unjust laws are successfully challenged and changed.

It should not be suggested that a functional analysis of crime implies that people commit crime in order to benefit society or that we should promote crime as a way to increase social cohesion. It should be suggested, however, that when a society defines a behavior as "criminal," it contributes to social cohesion by distinguishing between those who obey the law and those who do not. It is a distinction that encourages "law-abiding" citizens to feel closer to one another *simply because they abide by common laws* in contrast to those who do not. This is especially true of laws defined as criminal acts that have no victims (such as homosexual behavior) but which violate shared community standards (see Chapter 10). In spite of its negative effects, then, the existence of crime has some surprising functional consequences.

The Conflict Perspective   Like the functional perspective, the **conflict perspective** focuses on how social systems operate, but with a strong emphasis on a particular consequence of social life.

The conflict perspective emphasizes that however well or badly social systems function, more often than not they involve some degree of inequality and conflict over scarce rewards such as power, wealth, and prestige. Because social systems tend to benefit some groups more than others, they are often held together, to some degree, by coercion and force. Parents dominate children, and in traditional marriages husbands dominate wives. As in most societies, a small percentage of the people in the U.S. own most of the wealth and have far more political power than the average citizen. Whites are more powerful and wealthy than nonwhites and men are more powerful and wealthy than women. Those who own factories and other means of production are more wealthy and powerful than those who work for them.

The conflict perspective looks at questions of how inequality and conflict arise in social systems, from relationships between husbands and wives to those between blacks and whites and between rich and poor nations. What are the consequences of inequality for the quality of people's lives, for their material well-being and health, for their satisfaction and happiness? How does inequality affect the justice that people receive in courts or the education children receive in schools? How do those on top maintain their privileged position and how do those on the bottom improve theirs?

The conflict perspective is most closely associated with the influential work of Karl Marx (1818–1883), a German who, like Durkheim, felt compelled to understand a world that not only was changing rapidly but also was raising serious threats to social justice and the quality of life. After the defeat of

Napoleon, Germans anticipated a new era of freedom, but soon found themselves in a police state that was worse than life under Napoleon. Political meetings were banned, universities were tightly controlled, and there was no representative government, trial by jury, or right of free speech. Like other Germans, Marx's expectations of liberty were frustrated by the power of an elite to oppress and exploit the masses of people.

Because his ideas made him unpopular with German authorities, Marx lived in exile in England. There he saw workers struggling to make a living in a rapidly industrializing country in which the means of production were increasingly concentrated in the hands of a small elite. Marx developed the view that how societies develop depends on how they are arranged to produce the goods that people need in order to live,

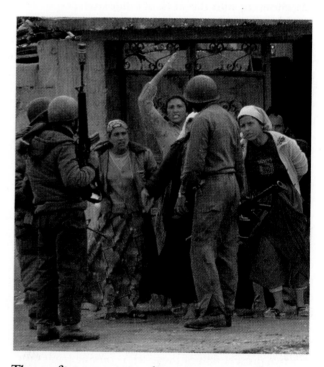

The conflict perspective draws attention to the causes and consequences of divisions between and within societies, especially those that center on social inequality. The struggle between Arabs and Israelis in the Middle East is a complex conflict that involves ethnic, economic, political, and religious differences which, in 1987 and 1988, erupted in violence between Israeli authorities and protecting Palestinians in the Israeli occupied West Bank territory. In this picture, an Arab woman is trying to stop an Israeli soldier from searching her house in Gaza.

and that these arrangements often produce tensions and divisions within and between societies.

In capitalist societies the means of production—machines and factories—can be privately owned. Marx argued that this simple aspect of production—the private ownership of capital—has consequences for virtually all aspects of social life, from religion to politics to the family. It creates class divisions between those who own and control the means of production and those who do not. Those who do not own or control capital must sell their time for wages, and employers increase their profits by paying their workers as little as they can. This arrangement, Marx believed, inevitably creates conflict between social classes, a continuing conflict that may lead to dramatic social change (see Marx and Engels, 1846, 1848). If Marx were alive today he would see that modern industrial nations that control most of the world's wealth are in a position to exploit and dominate poorer nations of the Third World, an arrangement that inevitably produces international conflict.

The conflict perspective is not limited to Marx's analysis of social class, although this is certainly the most influential and widely used example. In general, the conflict perspective emphasizes the social forces that create tension and division within or between societies, the aspects of social life that involve struggle between groups whose interests compete and clash with one another, and which often includes the dominance and exploitation of some groups by others (see Mills, 1956; Dahrendorf, 1959; Collins, 1975). The conflict perspective covers a wide range of social life, but in each instance, it focuses on the ways in which a particular social arrangement reflects and affects competing interests and struggles between people who occupy different positions in social systems.

Together, the functional and conflict perspectives give us powerful vantage points from which to observe and understand the richness and complexity of life in social systems, from the smallest family to the most complex society.

Understanding Behavior: The Interactionist Perspective

While emphasizing the importance of groups and social systems, the functional and conflict perspectives pay relatively less attention to the aspects of social life that we are most aware of—the experience and behavior of individual people. As it has developed since the early work of German sociologist Georg Simmel (1858–1919) the **interactionist perspective** emphasizes the complex social causes and consequences of the ways in which we act in relation to one another, from how we try to control what other people think of us to what motivates us to do what we do.

The key to understanding behavior from an interactionist perspective is the ability to attach meaning to everything that we experience and do. As the great German sociologist Max Weber (1864–1920) argued, we can understand what we do only in terms of the meaning that we attach to experience and behavior, and culture is our primary source of meaning. We cannot understand people's motivations (and, therefore, their appearance and behavior) without knowing what they believe, what they value, and what they think other people expect them to do, and all of these will vary from one social situation to another. In our example of the first day of a college class, students figured out who the "teacher" was by attaching meaning to everything, from what she wore to what she said and did. Since the meaning they attached to her depended on the situation they were in, from an interactionist perspective, the first step toward understanding behavior is to identify the social situation in which it occurs, for the behavior of individuals is always part of a social process of interaction.

In many situations, we are unaware of the unspoken rules and meanings that affect our perceptions and expectations of one another. **Ethnomethodology** is the study of such underlying rules and expectations, which we often discover only when someone violates them (Garfinkel, 1967; Heritage, 1984). When you step into an elevator you might not be aware of the expectation that elevator passengers face front; but you soon would be if you stood facing the rear for a few moments and noticed the reactions of other people. Social life is full of subtle, unconscious understandings and expectations.

Symbolic Interaction and Life as Theater

Within each social situation we participate in a complex process of presenting ourselves to others, interpreting their behavior, and adjusting our own behavior to what we think is going on (see Stryker, 1981). The **symbolic interaction** perspective is a part of the interactionist perspective that focuses on a simple fact with complex implications: we interact with other people by using symbols, especially in the form of language.

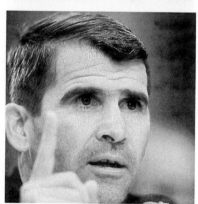

A symbolic interactionist sitting in on the Iran-contra hearings in 1987 would have paid careful attention to the ways in which witnesses, such as Lt. Colonel Oliver North, used language, dress, and gestures to create and sustain a favorable impression. Notice his facial expressions, how he uses his hands, and his wearing of his marine uniform. What impression do these pictures convey?

In some ways, social life is like a game (Mead, 1934); but unlike a game, it has rules and understandings that to some degree are subject to negotiation and interpretation, and symbols play an important part in that process. A "date" is a situation that tends to follow general patterns, but people can present themselves and behave in many ways, each of which can have more than one interpretation. Behaviors, such as a man opening a door for a woman or insisting on driving the car or paying the check, can be interpreted as politeness and a show of respect or as a statement that men are strong and women are weak. When someone acts friendly on a date, does this mean he or she is interested in having sexual relations? Gutek (1985) shows that the answer often depends on whether the person acting friendly is a woman or a man, for men are far more likely than women to interpret friendly gestures as sexual (see also Abbey, 1987). Similarly, when women say "no" to sexual activity, it is more likely to be interpreted by men as "maybe" or even "yes" than when men say "no" to women. The symbolic interaction perspective makes us aware of these small details of social life through which we, as individuals, move through the world, using symbols to present ourselves to others and affect what people think, feel, and do.

Erving Goffman's **dramaturgical perspective** adds an interesting dimension to the interactionist perspective by looking at social life as theater (Goffman, 1959, 1981). As Shakespeare wrote in *As You Like It*,

> All the world's a stage
> And all the men and women merely players;
> They have their exits and their entrances;
> And one man in his time plays many parts.
> (Act II, Scene vii)

As actors and actresses, we present images of ourselves to audiences and construct images of others by watching their "performances." To Goffman, we are always acting, trying to create favorable impressions from one "stage" to the next. We may be confident and aggressive while playing a sport, but meek when a police officer hands us a traffic ticket; wild and crazy at a party, but serious and calm in church. None of this is "faking"; there is no "real self" deceiving the world. From Goffman's point of view, this is just the way it is. *We are who we present ourselves to be.* The "masks" do not hide us; they are part of us.

Goffman's perspective makes the important contribution that although social situations carry certain expectations, we are always in a position to manipulate, circumvent, and resist them. The dramaturgical perspective makes us aware of how creative we often are as social actors, bringing to each role our own particular "touch," creating and maintaining the impressions we want, and affecting other people's perceptions, feelings, thoughts, and behavior.

Towards an Integrated Sociological Perspective

Together, the functional, conflict, and interactionist perspectives emphasize the key elements of social life, from the consequences produced by social systems to the mechanics of social interaction. Although sociologists often prefer one perspective over the others, it is possible—even desirable—to use them all as a single, integrated perspective in order to have an awareness of the different aspects of social life that they emphasize.

Consider the social system known as a "school" (see Chapter 16). Schools barely existed in most societies as recently as a hundred years ago, and yet they now are enormously important in industrial societies. How do we explore and understand this kind of system? What kinds of questions do the different theoretical perspectives suggest?

The functional perspective emphasizes the operation of schools as social systems whose different aspects contribute to and interfere with their functioning and affect their place in society. How is the learning process affected by violence in schools or by the sometimes harsh disciplinary measures used to control it? What are the effects of having schools that are run by teachers and parents rather than by professional administrators? How is learning affected by giving students more or less control over what they study? How does the racial or social class composition of student bodies affect how much and how well students learn? What part do schools play in the operation of society itself, from providing skilled workers and scientists to indoctrinating young people with political ideology and keeping them out of the work

force in order to lessen competition with adults for jobs?

The conflict perspective shifts the emphasis to the part schools play in social conflict. How do the interests of students, teachers, parents, administrators, and politicians differ, and how do such differences generate conflict over how schools are operated? How do schools resolve conflicts between the desires of parents to control what their children are exposed to and the social value of exposing children to a wide range of ideas? Issues such as sex and AIDS education, the teaching of evolutionary and Biblical accounts of creation, censorship of school books deemed offensive by parents, and the treatment of minorities in history and social studies texts all raise questions about a social system whose position in society inevitably places it at the center of competing and conflicting interests and values.

Since schools play a major role in child development, including giving young people a sense of what they are most suited for, we also must raise questions about the effect of schools on social inequality. How does schooling affect the distribution of power, wealth, and prestige in society? Are blacks more likely than whites to be poor in part because they attend schools with fewer resources? Are black and lower-class high school students given as much encouragement to go to college as whites and middle-class students? How do schools promote inequality between men and women? In what ways do teachers treat female and male students differently, and how does this affect gender inequality? Do teachers discourage female students from pursuing studies in science and math? Or, do college professors give female students as much encouragement to attend graduate school as they do male students?

While the functional and conflict perspectives emphasize how social systems operate and the consequences they tend to produce, the interactionist perspective emphasizes the mechanics of social life among individuals through which such effects usually occur. How are classroom interactions affected if students sit in a circle rather than in rows of chairs, or if teachers sit among students rather than standing at the front of the room? How do students and teachers perceive what goes on in classrooms; how do they use language to convey their feelings, expectations, and sense of who they are; and how does all of this affect what goes on among them? How do teachers use and maintain their power over students, and how do students protect themselves while still giving teachers what they expect? How do the effects of race, class, age, and gender differences appear in classrooms through language and behavior?

Although each set of questions is more closely associated with one perspective than the other two, they are all closely related. Interaction between teachers and students is more than a simple, isolated issue of social interaction. It is also the major way in which social conflict occurs within schools and affects how schools operate as social systems. In this sense, there is no question asked from one theoretical perspective that does not have implications for the other two. The differences among the three are differences of emphasis on the aspects that make up the social reality in which we live. To learn to use all three, and to move easily among them, are among the major goals that this introduction to sociology will help you achieve.

The conceptual and theoretical tools of sociology determine the kinds of questions that we ask about social life; but how do we find the answers? For one approach, we turn to Chapter 2.

SUMMARY

1. Sociology is the study of social environments and their effects on individuals. Social environments consist of material and nonmaterial cultural products and social structures that exist independently of the individuals who participate in them. To describe something as social is to say that it is related to the collective experience of people as they interact with one another. However unique we are as individuals, who we are and what we think, feel, do, and experience are social insofar as they arise from shared ideas and our social positions.

2. What we know about one another consists largely of ideas we share about the social positions that we and other people occupy. As individuals we respond to environments in many ways; but sociology focuses on patterns of behavior that are more likely in some social environments or positions than in others. Thus, all personal choices in some way reflect the limitations of social life.

3. Culture consists of nonmaterial and material products. Nonmaterial culture includes language, art, music, and four types of shared ideas: beliefs, norms, values, and attitudes.

4. Social structure is the arrangement of people and the patterns of expectation attached to their positions in social relationships. Social structure also refers to relationships between groups, the distribution of people among social positions, and the distribution of rewards such as wealth, power, and prestige.

5. Individuals, groups, and societies are affected by physical environments, the number of people and their distribution in relation to one another and physical surroundings. A population is a collection of people who share a given territory, and a society is a population that identifies with a common culture. Ecology focuses on the relationships between populations and physical environments.

6. Sociologists use theoretical frameworks to define perspectives from which they then develop theories that explain different aspects of social life. Early sociologists tried to make sense of the chaotic social conditions of nineteenth-century Europe. Comte developed the idea of sociology as a science dedicated to discovering laws which he believed determined how societies develop and which can be understood and used to affect social change.

7. The functional perspective focuses on how social systems work as units and how different aspects of social life affect them.

8. The conflict perspective also deals with how social systems work, but in terms of how the operation of social systems benefits some groups more than others, creating and maintaining various social inequalities.

9. The interactionist perspective focuses on the mechanics of everyday life, especially in terms of the meaning we give to how people appear and what they do. The interactionist perspective includes concerns about symbolic interaction (how we use symbol systems such as language to affect one another), ethnomethodology (the

discovery of underlying rules and understandings of social life), and dramaturgy (the view of life as theater).

10. Although sociologists often have a favorite theoretical perspective, it is important to learn to use them all in approaching any aspect of social life.

KEY TERMS

conflict perspective   22
culture   14

    material culture   15
    nonmaterial culture   15

        attitudes   15
        beliefs   15
        norms   15
        values   15

ecology   16
functional perspective   21

    latent function or dysfunction   21
    manifest function or dysfunction   21

interactionist perspective   23

    dramaturgical perspective   24
    ethnomethodology   23
    symbolic interaction   24

population   16
social structure   16
social system   20
society   17
sociology   7
technology   16
theoretical perspective   20
theory   19

Looking Elsewhere

Although Chapter 1 is an introductory chapter whose themes form the basic structure of the book, having studied it you might want to look at related discussions in *Human Arrangements*, several of which expand on examples used here, such as

- interaction in college classrooms (Chapter 7, p. 174; Chapter 16, pp. 441–43)

- suicide as deviance (Chapter 10, p. 247)

- gender roles and health (Chapter 13, pp. 362–65)

- and see also the political implications of the conflict and functional frameworks (Chapter 17, pp. 463–64)

RECOMMENDED READINGS

BERGER, P. (1963). *Invitation to sociology.* New York: Doubleday (available in paperback). An elegant, personal, and sometimes passionate introduction to the sociological perspective and the dilemmas posed by living as an individual in the social world.

COSER, L. A. (1977). *Masters of sociological thought: Ideas in historical and social context.* New York: Harcourt Brace Jovanovich. A readable, interesting text that takes a detailed look at the historical development of sociology, with an emphasis on the ideas, lives, and times of the sociologists who made it happen, from Comte through the major figures of the 1960s and 1970s.

GOFFMAN, E. (1959). *The presentation of self in everyday life.* Garden City, NY: Doubleday/Anchor. A fascinating classic that introduces the analysis of social interaction from Goffman's dramaturgical point of view.

MILLS, C. W. (1959). *The sociological imagination.* New York: Oxford University Press. This brief paperback is a passionate view of sociology as both a point of view and as a profession. Pay particular attention to Chapter 1 ("The Promise"), which ranks as the classic statement about the relationship between the "personal" and the "social" and to Chapter 8 ("The Uses of History"), in which Mills urges an attention to history as a vital part of sociological thinking.

Asking Sociological Questions

What Do You Want to Know?

    Variables

    Measurement, Meaning, and Validity

How to Find Out: Designing Research

    Populations

    Surveys

    Experiments

    Participant Observation

    Using What Is Already There: Secondary Analysis

Interpretation:
Using Information to Answer Questions

    Some Useful Statistics

    Causal Relationships between Variables

Some Difficulties in Sociological Research

    Complexity and Objectivity

    Ethics, Research, and People's Lives

2 Research Methods

Chapter 1 introduced major concepts that lie at the heart of most sociological questions. This chapter takes a detailed look at how sociologists use scientific research methods to answer such questions.

We begin by looking at the scientific method itself and its importance in sociology; then we follow the research process from deciding what you want to know to designing research, interpreting results, and wrestling with some of the difficulties of studying human beings and their social world.

ASKING SOCIOLOGICAL QUESTIONS

Among full-time, year-round workers, why did men earn almost two-thirds more money in 1985 than women? In the simplest sense, we can answer this or any question by sitting back and thinking about it; but, how can we know whether or not such personal explanations are correct? If you ask enough people, you will get a variety of answers to the above question, ranging from the effects of genes and hormones to cultural prejudice. How do we decide where the truth lies?

As we will see in this chapter, one response to this problem is the **scientific method**, which establishes objective standards for gathering and interpreting evidence. Unlike personal explanations, scientific results rest on *observable, unambiguous facts that lead everyone to the same conclusion.* Scientists try to rise above subjective perceptions and judgments by confining themselves to questions about observable facts. Did God intend that men should be more powerful than women? Science can do nothing with this kind of question, because there are no observable facts that provide an answer.

Other questions, however, can be answered scientifically because relevant facts can be observed: Are women discriminated against in the workplace? Are women as capable as men? Do men have advantages in the labor market? How would economic equality between men and women affect other aspects of social life?

Durkheim's study of suicide (1897) was one of the first sociological attempts to use the scientific method. If suicide is a purely individual act unaffected by social environments, then the *rate* of suicide (the relative number of people who kill themselves each year) should be the same for every group regardless of culture and social structure. Yet when Durkheim examined death records, he found that Protestants were more likely to kill themselves than were Catholics and that Jews had the lowest suicide rate of all. Single people were more likely to commit suicide than married people and soldiers had higher rates than civilians. Durkheim reasoned that such differences reflect forces beyond individual personalities and troubles, forces that affect choices according to positions in social relationships.

Durkheim considered purely cultural factors— shared ideas about suicide—that might explain differences in suicide rates, but logic and evidence led him to discard that explanation. There is no reason to believe that married people disapprove of suicide more than single people do, and while Catholicism views suicide more seriously than does Judaism (regarding it as a mortal sin), Catholics have higher rates of suicide than Jews.

Durkheim turned to social structure for an explanation of the relationships that connect people to one another. In particular, he was interested in the degree of *social cohesion* found among people in different social categories. Protestants stress independence and individualism, while Catholics and Jews stress active involvement with other members of their religious communities. In a similar way, married people tend to have stronger ties than single people. This is reflected in Durkheim's theory to explain patterns of suicide

Although science can answer many questions, there are many it cannot. The story of Adam and Eve—shown in Michelangelo's portrayal on the ceiling of the Sistine Chapel in Rome—is regarded by tens of millions of Christians as a sacred and true account of the origins of the human race, an account that they would never judge on the basis of scientific standards of evidence and truth.

that distinguished one social category from another: When social bonds are weak, people are more likely to kill themselves.

Durkheim also noticed, however, that suicide rates tend to be relatively high in groups with very high levels of cohesion. Professional soldiers are more likely than draftees to take fatal risks in battle, and some widows in India once committed suicide at the funerals of their husbands because it was expected of them. In both cases, people were more likely to commit suicide because they valued the group and its culture more than their individual lives. Consequently, Durkheim's theory of suicide predicted that suicide rates will be relatively high when social cohesion is either very low or very high.

This first attempt to apply scientific methods to sociological questions was understandably flawed. Durkheim used official records that were often distorted to conceal suicides, and while his theory fit the facts, other explanations might fit them as well. Nevertheless, his attempt to find connections between people's behavior and the observable characteristics of their social environments established a model of sociological research that continues to be one of Durkheim's most important contributions. (For a more

recent test of Durkheim's ideas about suicide, see Breault, 1986.)

Sociological research centers on three basic tasks. First, in order to identify the effects of social structure, culture, population, and ecology, we must be able to *describe* them. What beliefs prevail in a society? How are families, schools, governments, and economies structured? How are rewards such as power, wealth, and prestige distributed?

Second, how do we *explain* what we describe—such as variations in people's behavior? How do we explain the recent rise in teenage suicides? How is social inequality maintained, and what are the consequences for those involved? How do we explain why societies differ and why they change?

Third, how can we make *predictions* about the future? Will our cultural emphasis on individuality and mobility weaken our bonds with our families and communities, and will this cause a rise in suicide rates? How many children will be born in the next five years? Will there be enough jobs for them when they become adults?

The remaining chapters in this book are filled with the results of sociological research. To prepare you for them, this chapter focuses on the research

In 1987, four New Jersey teenagers committed suicide by locking themselves in a garage and sitting in a car with the engine running. As the facial expressions on these teenage mourners show, making sense of why someone close to us might commit suicide is a haunting and difficult thing. For sociology, the problem is less personal but no less compelling: why would rates of suicide for young people increase in a society? What social forces are at work, and what can be done to change them?

process that produces such results. Any research project involves four basic phases:

1. Deciding what you want to know.
2. Deciding how you are going to find out.
3. Gathering information.
4. Interpreting your results.

Understanding how research is done will enable you not only to ask critical questions about scientific results, it will also help you do your own research when you write term papers (see Appendix A). In addition, many of the research skills described below are used in a variety of occupations.

WHAT DO YOU WANT TO KNOW?

If you have ever gotten bogged down trying to write a term paper, it was probably because you did not have a clear idea of just what it was you wanted to know. For undergraduates and research scientists alike, deciding what we want to know is the first and often the most difficult part of any research project.

Are we interested in learning about such behavior as lying or telling the truth, stealing, marrying and divorcing, having children or remaining childless, voting or not voting, cheating on college exams or telling on someone who does? Do we want to know about people's beliefs, values, and attitudes and how these ideas are reflected in their behavior? Or are we interested in a society's distribution of wealth, power, and prestige, its vulnerability to revolution? In short, what aspects of individuals, groups, or societies do we want to understand?

Our interest in trying to understand the income gap between men and women might well lead us to study women's liberation. Before we can begin, we have to define "women's liberation" and what, in particular, we want to know about it. "Women's liberation" can have many meanings. It can mean "equalizing rewards such as wealth, power, and prestige," "changing the structure of family life so that fathers are equally responsible for child care," or "changing cultural ideas that define women as inferior." It can also refer to the women's movement—how it began and how different segments of it try to achieve different goals.

Suppose we focus on "removing inequalities." Because that problem has many different aspects, we have to narrow it down and ask questions that can be answered by observing measurable phenomena. To show how the research process works, let us ask the following question: Do most people in the U.S. favor equality for women? Favoring or opposing women's equality are values, and before we can do a study, we have to decide how we are going to *measure* them.

Variables

Favoring women's equality is a characteristic that varies from one person to another; it is called a **variable**. Variables can be events, behaviors, or any measurable characteristic of individuals, groups, or societies. Group size, unemployment rates, believing in God, personal income, criminal behavior, and educational attainment are all variables. Having been born and eventually dying, on the other hand, are *constants*. *When* we are born and how and at what age we die, however, are variables.

Just as we must use a thermometer to measure heat, we now need some way to observe and sort people according to their level of support for equality. One simple possibility is to ask people if they favor the Equal Rights Amendment, which states: "Equality of rights under the law shall not be denied or abridged by the United States or by any State on account of sex."

We could then interpret "yes" answers as favoring equality and "noes" as opposition. This kind of procedure is a **measurement instrument**, because it clearly classifies people according to some characteristic.

Measurement, Meaning, and Validity

A measurement instrument is **valid** if it measures only what we intend it to measure. In 1982 a national sample was asked, "Do you strongly favor, somewhat favor, somewhat oppose, or strongly oppose the Equal Rights Amendment?" The result: 39 percent expressed opposition (Davis and Smith, 1984). Does this mean that 39 percent of U.S. adults oppose women's equality? Is opposition to the ERA a valid measure of opposition to equality?

Opposition to the ERA reflects a general value about women's rights, while equality for women involves a variety of specific goals that have direct and immediate implications for people's lives. It is possible for people to oppose the ERA generally and actually support equality for women in terms of specific issues. (Before reading on, you might want to take a look at the box, "How to Read a Table".)

For example, Table 2-1 summarizes responses to a series of specific questions about men and women, *among respondents who expressed opposition to the ERA in 1982*. Among ERA opponents, 64 percent disagree that women should stay home and leave running the country to men; 67 percent disagree that married women whose husbands can support them should not have jobs themselves; and almost three-quarters say they would vote for a qualified female presidential candidate. A majority disagree with the idea that men are better suited emotionally for politics than women, and almost 40 percent believe married women should have the right to legal abortions if they are too poor to afford additional children.

While opposition to the ERA may be a valid measure of opposition to the ERA, this evidence sug-

---

Table 2-1

Values about Men and Women among Adults Who Oppose the ERA, 1982

VALUE STATEMENT	AGREE	DISAGREE	TOTAL (N)
1. Women should take care of running their homes and leave running the country up to men.	36%	64%	100% (453)
2. A married woman should not earn money in business or industry if she has a husband capable of supporting her.	33%	67%	100% (453)
3. If your party nominated a woman for president, would you vote for her if she were qualified for the job?	73%	27%	100% (453)
4. Most men are better suited emotionally for politics than are most women.	47%	53%	100% (453)
5. It should be possible for a pregnant woman to obtain a legal abortion if the family has a very low income and they cannot afford any more children.	38%	62%	100% (453)

Source: Computed from raw 1982 General Social Survey data.

How to Read a Table

Most research results begin as a set of observations of the characteristics of anything from people to entire societies. Researchers face the problem of organizing and summarizing masses of information in order to answer questions. As a reader, your problem is to understand what researchers present to you. We start with information, such as people's answers to the question, "Are you in favor of the Equal Rights Amendment?" A total of 453 adults answered "no" in a 1982 national study.

Any arrangement of numbers in columns and rows (such as Table 2-1) is called a *table*, and there are several things we can learn from this one. It shows how opponents of the ERA answered some other questions about men and women. Here is how to go about reading it:

1. Read the title, for it tells you what the table is about. Look at the column and row headings to be sure what each number means. Are the numbers percentages or are they frequencies or averages? The first column contains a list of questions the respondents were asked, and the second and third columns give the percentages who answered "Agree" and "Disagree." The last column includes the total (100%) showing that everyone has been included and the number of people—453—who answered each question sometimes represented by the letter "N").

A good way to make sure you know what the numbers represent is to use one in a sentence. For example, 36 is the first number in the "Agree" column: Thirty-six percent of the people who oppose the ERA agree that "It is more important for a wife to help her husband's career than to have one of her own."

2. Next, look to see if there are any footnotes. These often provide important information, including when the information was gathered and by whom as well as the meaning of key words ("adult" might be defined in terms of age).

3. Now you are ready to learn something from the table. This is a relatively simple table because it gives only the percentage breakdown for each variable without comparing the responses of different kinds of people (such as people of different ages); and yet it has some interesting findings. In spite of the fact that everyone in the table expressed opposition to the ERA, substantial percentages nonetheless take quite different positions on more specific questions about men's and women's roles. As the text points out, this table raises questions about the meaning of opposition to the ERA, since many of those who say they oppose the ERA seem to support equality in some more specific areas of social life.

gests that it is an invalid measure of opposition to specific aspects of social life that must be changed in order to bring about equality. In a similar way, people may oppose specific aspects of women's liberation and yet support the ERA as a general idea.

Consequently, "opposition to equality" is too complex to be measured with one instrument. Similarly, when we hear a statement such as "A majority of adults favor equality for women," we have to ask a critical question: What does "favoring women's equality" *mean*? In other words, did the researcher use a valid instrument to measure this concept?

Reliability Measurement instruments must not only be valid; they must be **reliable**: they must produce the same results no matter who uses them. In

addition, if the characteristic they measure remains constant, then the results must remain constant as well.

One way to measure the incidence of crime is to count up the number of crimes reported to police each year. The problem with this is that most crimes are never reported to police (Chapter 10). The incidence of crime might go down from one year to the next, but the *measure* of crime might show an increase if people become more willing to report crimes to police.

Official crime statistics are *unreliable* because they may indicate change even when what they try to measure does not. Their lack of reliability also makes them invalid because they reflect two things at once: the incidence of crime *and* the willingness of people to report it. Whether the official rates go up, down, or remain the same, we cannot be sure about what is happening.

Measurement Problems   Measurement poses difficult problems for social scientists (Schuman and Presser, 1981). Much of what we try to measure is difficult to observe directly. We cannot measure attitudes in the same way that we can measure the weight of an object. We must rely on what people tell us or what they reveal through their actions, and even the latter requires interpretation.

This problem occurs in all sciences. Astronomers rely on what little they can observe in order to construct theories about what they cannot observe—such as the origin of the universe. Atomic physicists developed nuclear reactors long before they could actually see atoms with electron microscopes, and even now the image they see is not the atom itself, but its shadow.

While in some ways the need for interpretation may be seen as a liability in social research, Max Weber

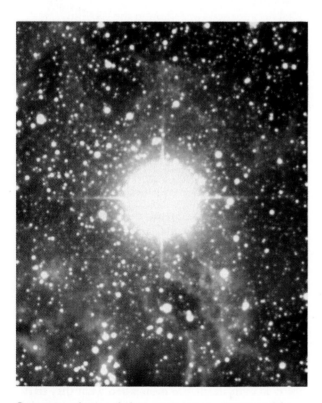

Scientists observed this supernova in 1987, and from it derived theories about what they will never be able to observe—the origins of the universe.

(1949) pointed out that when we study human beings, subjective interpretation of behavior is essential. A falling object has no motives or desires that affect its rate of fall. People are far more complicated, however, and we cannot understand the effects of social environments on our behavior simply by observing people as if they were objects. Research in the social sciences requires a delicate balance of objectivity and subjectivity: we must put ourselves in another's place while at the same time standing apart and trying to observe with objectivity.

An additional problem is that while the characteristics of objects tend to remain the same over time, people are far less constant. Social research relies heavily on how people present themselves, and information about them can easily be distorted. People sometimes lie about themselves in order to make a good impression, or answer questions they do not understand rather than appear to be ignorant. There is evidence that highly educated people tend to give what they believe are "socially acceptable responses" when they report their views and behavior (Crowne and Marlowe, 1980).

Sociological research is also difficult because the act of gathering information about people is itself a social process. When people know they are being observed, their behavior is affected by the social situation and the characteristics of the observer. Most of the interviewers who asked the question about support for the ERA were women, and it is reasonable to assume that people are less willing to express opposition to the ERA to a woman than they are to a man.

Other studies find similar effects by race (see Schuman and Converse, 1971; Summers and Hammond, 1966). Blacks are more likely to express warmth and closeness towards whites when they are interviewed by whites rather than by blacks (Anderson et al., 1987). Such effects can seriously distort research findings. Between 1976 and 1984, national studies found a declining percentage of blacks who said they felt close to other blacks. As Anderson et al. (1987) discovered, however, this was due not to a shift in feelings among blacks but to changes in the racial composition of interviewer staffs of national surveys. As the percentage of blacks who were interviewed by whites increased, the reported feelings of closeness to other blacks went down. Social scientists cannot completely separate themselves from the people they study and take measurements in carefully controlled surroundings.

HOW TO FIND OUT: DESIGNING RESEARCH

Once we decide what we want to know and how we are going to measure it, we next have to decide how we are actually going to *use* our measurement instruments.

Sociologists use a variety of research methods, because all approaches have shortcomings. Some, such as in-depth interviews, allow us to examine social interaction in great detail, but restrict us to small numbers of people who may represent no one but themselves. Other methods, such as surveys, allow us to study large representative samples of a population, but limit us to more superficial kinds of information. While all methods have their advantages and disadvantages, together they produce results that are detailed and broadly representative.

Populations

In scientific research, a **population** is any precisely defined set of people, groups, or societies (notice that this definition differs slightly from that used in the study of population and ecology in Chapters 1 and 5). Once we decide what we want to know, we define the population, which may be as small as a group of two people or as large as the entire human race. "Currently married people in Ohio," "Japanese corporations," and "countries that use the death penalty" can all be defined as populations.

If we want to find the percentage of U.S. adults who support women's equality, we have to decide *whose* support or opposition we want to measure. "U.S. adults" is not a precisely defined population for scientific research, because it does not clearly indicate who is included. What age groups are considered "adult," and will we include citizens who currently live outside the United States? Will we include people living in Alaska and Hawaii? Will we include people who live in the United States but are not citizens— illegal aliens and college exchange students? One solution to the problem is to define our hypothetical population as "U.S. citizens over 18 years old living in the continental United States at the time of the study."

Censuses versus Samples With small populations, it is possible to conduct a **census** by gathering information about all of its members. With large populations, however, the expense and time involved make it difficult if not impossible to observe each

member. The U.S. Census Bureau does this every ten years at a cost of tens of millions of dollars (see Mitroff, Mason, and Barabba, 1983) and, as you will see throughout this book, it provides a rich source of information about social life.

If we want to know if members of a small labor union support women's equality, we could ask all of them; but if we want to pose this question to our population of all adult U.S. citizens (more than 170 million people), we face an enormous task out of all proportion to what we stand to gain from it. (You only need stop a moment and try to imagine the number of different studies we might want to do on the U.S. population and then realize that each would cost tens of millions of dollars.) In such cases, practical necessity forces researchers to select a subgroup—called a **sample**—and use it to represent the population.

The necessary use of samples raises important questions about all scientific research: Are some samples better than others? How do we tell? Can a sample

"How would you like me to answer that question? As a member of my ethnic group, educational class, income group, or religious category?"

Drawing by D. Fradon © 1969, The New Yorker Magazine, Inc.

accurately represent a large population? How, for example, can the Gallup Poll use 1,500 people to accurately describe the beliefs, values, and attitudes of tens of millions?

Good Samples and Bad Samples   Any set of people, groups, organizations, or societies selected from a population constitutes a sample, and there is virtually no way to be certain that a sample accurately represents the population it came from. How, then, can we use samples with confidence?

The answer to this question lies in the way samples are selected. Suppose there are 10,000 students in your college and you want to find out how strongly they support women's equality. You stand at the library door during the evening and question students as they enter. After you question 200 students, you stop. Do their answers accurately represent the student body?

While your sample *may* represent the student population, you have no reason to believe this, because you failed to consider the students who never use the library at night (or who never go there at all); and their views may differ from those of students who spend their evenings in the library. This haphazard sample is likely to be *biased* because you did not actually select the sample; rather, students selected themselves.

What if you used a different procedure, putting each of the 10,000 students' names into a big bowl and then picking 200 names? You would have good reason to feel confident in this sample *because every member of the population had an equal chance to be included.* Samples selected in this way are called **random samples**. Many sampling methods use the principle of randomness (Kalton, 1984). To save time, you might select at random one of the first 50 names on the list of 10,000 students and use that as a starting point to select every 50th name on the list (a **systematic sample**). Or if you wanted to gather information on all U.S. college students, you might first select a sample of colleges and then randomly select students in each one (a **multistage sample**). What all of these procedures have in common is that each member of the population has a known chance of being selected, and this is a crucial characteristic that distinguishes good samples from bad ones.

You might be saying to yourself at this point, "I still don't see how they can use a sample to describe millions of people. So what if it's random?" The answer involves some mathematical reasoning that we will not go into here; but if you are curious, take a look at Appendix B.

Surveys

In most **surveys**, information is gathered either in **interviews**, in which respondents interact with someone who asks questions, or in **questionnaires** which respondents fill out in private. In the simplest sense, we use surveys to find out "what's going on out there" by asking people to tell us (see Alreck and Settle, 1985; Schuman and Presser, 1981).

Surveys are useful because they allow researchers to gather large amounts of information. Surveys can be used to describe prevailing cultural values, beliefs, and attitudes as in Table 2-1. They also allow us to describe broad aspects of social structure—the number of people who are unemployed, the extent and distribution of poverty, or how income, prestige, power, jobs, and education are distributed in a population.

When surveys focus on specific problems, they often go beyond mere description and shed light on the social processes through which social structure and culture affect individuals' lives. Work in skilled blue-collar trades requires a period of apprenticeship. While in 1970 there were 280,000 men apprenticed in 350 skilled trades and crafts, there were only 12,000 women. Is discrimination involved?

In a survey of employers in a Wisconsin town, researchers discovered that most employers said they would not admit women to training programs because they would have to work under harsh physical conditions (Hammel, 1974). The researchers also found, however, that women *were* hired to do unskilled work in the same harsh conditions endured by higher-paid, male workers. Survey results, combined with other observations, produced evidence of discrimination in hiring.

Another survey sheds light on the process of discrimination in medicine, the highest-paid profession in the U.S. A sample of male physicians was asked to rank different medical specialties in terms of prestige, and their replies placed surgery at the top and pediatrics and psychiatry at the bottom (Quadagno, 1976). Women physicians are overwhelmingly concentrated in low-paying, low-prestige specialties such as pediatrics (Epstein, 1970; Association of American Medical Colleges, 1987). How does this happen? When Quadagno asked a sample of female physicians to explain their choice of specialty, two reasons were always given: male surgeons treated them with hostility, and they received far more encouragement from superiors to pursue "feminine" specialties.

> Their awareness of negative attitudes toward them in certain areas combined with positive reinforcement in others led them to avoid situations where conflict might occur. Rather than confront possible rejection, women selected specialties in which they felt comfortable and welcome. (p. 450)

Case Studies   While most surveys attempt to represent entire populations, sociologists often begin by studying samples that may not represent the population they are interested in. These are called **case studies**, and they allow researchers to explore and clarify problems and perfect measurement instruments before mounting an expensive survey. W. F. Whyte (1981) was interested in the intimate details of life in an urban slum; Helen and Robert Lynd (1929) spent years studying social relationships in a small U.S. city; and Erving Goffman (1961a) observed life in a mental institution for many months.

In each of these studies, detailed descriptions of social life required enormous amounts of time and would have been impossible if researchers had focused on large samples of slum neighborhoods, small cities, or asylums. Instead, they used case studies to focus on a single instance that was carefully chosen to make it as representative as possible. In effect, they based their conclusions on samples that contained only one "case."

While a study of a mental hospital cannot be used to describe mental hospitals in general, it can provide insights that can then be tested with more representative samples. In addition, case studies can provide a depth of understanding that is impossible in surveys. While a case study rarely describes a population, the accumulated findings of many case studies often can. If Goffman's observations of a single hospital are added to other studies, the regular patterns that emerge can tell us much about how people behave in those environments.

In-depth Interviews   Like surveys, **in-depth interviews** gather information by asking questions and recording answers. Unlike most surveys, in-depth interviews can last for many hours during which respondents and interviewers can develop a rapport that enables them to explore issues whose subtlety and personal nature are beyond the scope of most surveys.

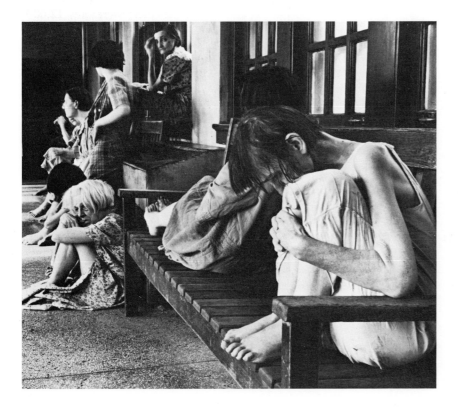

It is difficult to understand what life is like in institutions such as mental hospitals without witnessing the experiences of patients and staff members first-hand.

However, as we will see shortly, the closer observers get to their subjects and, often, the more they come to care about them, the more difficult it becomes to make observations with the objectivity required by science.

Researchers are able to explore the reasons that underlie people's behavior and to record intimate details of their lives.

Rubin (1976) studied life in working-class marriages by interviewing each husband and wife in 50 couples. Some of the interviews lasted as long as ten hours and required repeated visits. Wives and husbands talked about their marriages, their early hopes and dreams, how their families and relationships grew and changed over the years, their disappointments when the reality of married life collided with their dreams, and how they adapted within the limitations and financial hardships of working-class life. Rubin's result is a set of richly textured portraits that reveal, among other things, how husbands and wives often experience their relationship with each other in strikingly different ways.

In-depth studies like Rubin's are limited in several ways. We cannot know if the families in her sample represent anyone other than themselves; and the closeness of her relationship with them carries the danger that her results are distorted because respondents may tell her what they think she wants to hear. In spite of these limitations, in-depth interviews can yield a wealth of detail about social relationships and human experience. They remind us that sociological research concerns the lives of people who are trying to come to terms not only with themselves, but with the cultural, structural, and ecological conditions of their lives.

Limitations of Survey Research   Surveys do have limitations. First, they rely on what people report on questionnaires or to interviewers, and people may either misperceive the question or, for a variety of reasons, give inaccurate reports. If we ask someone, "Why do you oppose the ERA?" the answer may have little to do with actual causes. Some surveys directly observe behavior; but most measure what people *say* about their behavior. The problem is not that verbal behavior is less "real" than other behavior, for we are quite capable of deceiving others through our actions (Merton, 1940). Rather, surveys limit us to a relatively narrow range of behavior (what people say), which may or may not correspond to their actions.

Surveys are also limited in time. A survey is like a still photograph, whereas social life is a continuing process. While surveys measure the results of social processes (gender differences in occupation and income, for example), they are not very effective for discovering how those results come about. One solution is a **longitudinal survey**, in which a sample of people is interviewed at regular intervals and tracked over time to record changes in their social positions,

How will the violent atmosphere of Belfast, Northern Ireland affect the children who grow up there compared with children who grow up away from violence in their streets? How will Protestant and Catholic children learn to see each other and themselves? How will they handle conflict in their personal lives? How will they solve problems in their communities? Questions like these can be answered only with longitudinal surveys taken over long periods of time.

behavior, beliefs, values, and attitudes. The problem with longitudinal surveys is that keeping track of several thousand people over a period of many years is difficult and expensive.

A more practical approach is to use a series of surveys that gather information from *different* samples selected from the *same* population. To find out if support for women's equality changes as people age, we could interview a national sample of 20-year-olds in 1985 and then interview a sample of 30-year-olds in 1995. In both cases, the samples represent the same population: people who were born in 1965.

Because single surveys are "still photographs," however, their results cannot be used to test conclusively ideas about cause and effect, and this is their most serious limitation (see, however, Blalock, 1964, 1985). A scientist cannot answer the question "Does heat make balloons expand?" simply by gathering a sample of balloons and measuring their temperatures and their volumes. Why not? Because other factors—such as the initial size of the balloons—may account for some of the observed differences.

The only way to answer this question is to take a group of balloons of the same size, heat them to different temperatures, and then record differences in volume. In other words, every factor other than heat must be controlled by holding it constant, and then the suspected *cause* (heat) must be manipulated to see how it (and it alone) produces an *effect* (increased volume). This is the experimental method, and it requires time and controlled conditions, both of which are beyond the capability of single surveys.

Experiments

An interest in finding out why men earn much more money than women might lead us to explore the ways in which women are discriminated against. Do people tend to assume that women are less capable than men and evaluate men more favorably than women even when their performances are of equal quality? Assuming they are even aware of it, people would be reluctant to admit such a bias in survey interviews, and even if they did admit it, we could not use a survey to see if women are actually discriminated against simply because they are women.

To see if gender, by itself, affects people's evaluations of ability and performance, we have to *hold constant all other factors that might affect evaluations*— that is, we must use an **experiment**. In experiments,

groups are exposed to conditions that are exactly alike in all ways but one. If people's behavior differs from one group to another, then those differences must be due to the different conditions they were exposed to, since the groups are alike in all other ways.

Etaugh and Kasley (1981) used the experimental method when they randomly selected samples of male and female college undergraduates at a Midwestern university. Each was given a packet of written materials (including a sample newspaper article) which supposedly represented a job application submitted by someone who had recently been hired to write for a local newspaper. Each application was identical except that the applicant was identified as female in one half of the cases and as male in the other half. The experimental subjects were asked to fill out forms in which they assigned letter grades (ranging from "A" for superior to "F" for inferior) in eight areas, including the applicant's overall competence, status in the field, future job success, and the quality of the article itself.

For all eight areas, applicants identified as male consistently received higher evaluations than did those identified as female. Male applicants were seen as more competent professionally, as having a higher chance for success in their profession, and as having a higher professional status. The articles themselves were rated higher in every respect when subjects thought the author was male.

Because the students were randomly assigned to male and female applicants, students were, as subjects, similar in all important respects. They read and evaluated the same articles in the same social situation; thus, any pattern of differences in their evaluations can be due to only one factor—their perception of the author's gender. Experiments allow researchers to control all factors that might account for different responses and to manipulate the one factor they are interested in. In this way, they are able to demonstrate cause-and-effect relationships between variables.

Limitations of Experiments   Like all scientific methods, experiments have limitations. When people know they are participating in an experiment their behavior may be affected in ways that distort the results. Experimental subjects who know that their behavior is observed, are aware that what they do matters. The experimental setting itself may exert an uncontrolled influence on subjects' behavior.

One early study of factory workers suggested that people's behavior in experiments is affected simply because they get more attention than they are accustomed to. Mayo and his colleagues studied workers at the Hawthorne plant of the Western Electric Company to discover how working conditions affect productivity (Roethlisberger and Dickson, 1939). They varied such factors as the amount of lighting and the frequency and duration of coffee breaks and found, to their surprise, that no matter what they did, productivity increased.

They eventually concluded that merely by participating in the experiment, workers received more attention than they were used to, and their feelings of being "special" resulted in higher productivity. Distortions caused by experimental situations came to be known as the "Hawthorne effect" and are a serious problem for experimenters.

Had the researchers been aware of this effect, they might have used a **control group** of workers who were told they were experimental subjects but were *not* exposed to different working conditions. Mayo might then have found that their productivity increased just as the other workers' had.

While the Hawthorne effect made researchers more aware of experimental conditions as sources of error, subsequent studies consistently failed to duplicate Mayo's findings in a variety of settings (Parsons, 1982). This illustrates an important principle in all scientific research: we run a considerable risk of error if we accept the findings of a single study as conclusive proof of any proposition. Science depends on **replication**—repeating studies in different settings to see if the initial findings hold up.

The "Real World" as Laboratory   The experimental method is also limited by the artificial nature of laboratory research settings. The students in Etaugh and Kasley's study knew that their evaluations would not affect the job applicants ("It's just an experiment") and it is impossible to estimate how such settings affect people. If these same students were personnel managers whose decisions affected people's lives, would they still discriminate against women? Laboratory experiments cannot answer such questions, and for this reason researchers often conduct **field experiments** outside the laboratory.

Fidell (1970) sent fake applications for faculty positions to 238 university psychology departments. The résumés that accompanied the applications were the same in each case, but half of the applicants were identified as males ("Patricks") and the other half as females ("Patricias"). The heads of departments were asked to give a "current appraisal of the applicant's chances of getting a full-time position." The results showed that Patricks were judged to be suitable for more appointments and at higher levels than were Patricias, even though their experience and qualifications were identical; and only Patricks were considered to be qualified for full professorships.

Field experiments allow us to control and manipulate key variables in "real world" settings; to do this we must focus on a narrow problem involving only a few variables. This illustrates an important trade-off among research methods: those that allow a large scope (surveys) make it difficult to test ideas under carefully controlled conditions; however, those that permit such controls (experiments) restrict us to simple problems, when in fact behavior is caused by many related factors. When the findings produced by different methods are combined, it is possible to piece together richer, more complex explanations.

Participant Observation

While surveys ask people to describe their social situations, behavior, and experience, and experiments allow researchers to observe behavior in controlled laboratory conditions, with **participant observation** we can directly observe behavior outside of laboratories (R. M. Emerson, 1981). Many sociologists use this technique to gain insights into social behavior. W. F. Whyte (1981) lived for several years in a lower-class neighborhood of Boston and observed urban gangs by participating in their activities. The trust that developed between researcher and subjects allowed Whyte to observe the lives of these gang members in ways that would otherwise be impossible.

Goffman (1961a) observed life in a mental hospital and identified ways in which depersonalization and humiliation aggravate mental problems. Festinger, Riecken, and Schachter (1956) joined a religious cult whose members believed the world would soon be destroyed and that only they would be saved by aliens from outer space. The researchers were able to observe firsthand when cult members reacted to the failure of their prophecy.

Kanter (1977a, 1977b) observed employees in a corporation. Among her findings, three stand out. First, most women were employed as secretaries, and one of their most important responsibilities was attending to such personal needs of their male superiors as listening to personal problems, picking up laundry, and arranging social appointments. Promotions, however, depend on task performance, not attention to personal needs. Many women in corporations are confined to tasks whose successful performance effectively bars them from advancement.

Second, while women numerically dominate secretarial jobs, among managers and executives they are numerical *tokens*—a few among a vast crowd of men. This, Kanter observed, affects behavior. Women tend to feel highly visible and often try to "hide" by blending in—wearing man-tailored suits. Their heightened visibility also makes them self-conscious, and they tend to overachieve because they know that everything they do is closely watched and evaluated as an indicator of "what women can do."

Third, Kanter found that women often perform activities that have little to do with their jobs. They may play "mother" (comforting men) or "seductress," treated as a sex object by men who try to monopolize their attention. They may also play the "pet" who is cute and presents herself as a self-effacing, unthreatening "girl." Kanter found that women are often unaware of such behavior, and her ability to observe life in corporations allowed her to see the unwitting responses of men and women to their social environment.

Limitations of Participant Observation   Participant observation allows us to explore aspects of behavior that individuals are often unaware of, to witness daily life as it occurs. While this method has clear advantages over surveys, it also has limitations. One of the most serious drawbacks is that it requires enormous amounts of time—sometimes as long as several years. More serious is that since researchers participate in the social situations they study, there is always the danger that their presence will affect people's behavior and that the observers may identify so closely with their subjects that their own objectivity is impaired. They may develop positive and negative feelings toward their subjects that lead them to unconsciously select and interpret observations in biased ways.

In the 1920s, anthropologist Margaret Mead lived for several years on the island of Samoa. Her classic book, *Coming of Age in Samoa* (1928/1953), described Samoans as a graceful and gentle people among whom adolescence was a trouble-free time of life. Mead's book was particularly important because it was written at a time of great concern about the "adolescent crises" so common in U.S. society; her discovery of a society in which such crises did not occur supported the view that culture is more important than biology in determining behavior.

In 1983 another anthropologist, Derek Freeman, attacked Mead's study. He argued that Mead went to Samoa looking for evidence of the importance of culture, and her observations and interpretations were determined by what she wanted to see. A storm of controversy followed, and while Mead's research did have its methodological flaws, it appears that her interpretation of Samoan society in the 1920s was nonetheless basically accurate (see Holmes, 1986).

As Marcus (1983) wrote in his comments on this controversy, the outcome is not the most important lesson we can draw from it. More important is the fact that two observers can arrive at "radically different interpretations from fieldwork in the same culture" (Marcus, p. 22). Like all case studies, the results of participant observation must be interpreted in comparison with the findings of other observers. This is an important principle in all scientific research.

Using What Is Already There: Secondary Analysis

Surveys, case studies, experiments, participant observation, and in-depth interviews are methods used to gather fresh evidence that sheds light on sociological problems; but a great deal of information already exists in historical documents, government statistics, and published studies. When researchers apply information gathered by someone else to their own questions, they are using **secondary analysis** (Hyman, 1972). When Durkheim studied suicide he found a new use for information that already existed—death certificates. Using information that has already been gathered is what secondary analysis is all about.

One of the richest sources of sociological information is the U.S. Census, conducted every ten years by the Census Bureau, which at that time gathers detailed information about every citizen. Additional information is gathered several times a year through the Current Population Survey. Other government agencies gather a wealth of information on births, deaths, marriages, and divorces as part of the vital statistics system.

In addition, organizations such as corporations, military units, universities, public school systems, hospitals, and police departments regularly gather information about their activities. When we add to this the thousands of social science research projects conducted over the last half century, we have a rich store of information that can be applied to a variety of research questions never anticipated by those who originally gathered the information.

Sometimes revealing information can be found in the most unlikely places. If you look in the Yellow Pages of your telephone directory under the heading "Physicians" you will find that doctors are listed by their specialties. First names will give you a clue to the gender of each doctor, and by counting patiently you will soon see how women doctors are distributed among different specialties—relatively few in surgery, but many in pediatrics.

Because data gathering is expensive and time-consuming, sociologists are increasingly using secondary analysis. In her study of a corporation, Kanter (1977a) examined forms used to evaluate employee performance. The forms existed for the purpose of making personnel decisions, but Kanter found a new use for them as she looked to see which aspects of men's and women's performances led to high ratings.

Kanter found that secretaries were evaluated according to two main characteristics: "initiative and enthusiasm" and "ability to anticipate and take care of their bosses' personal needs." Secretaries were rewarded on the basis of personal relationships with superiors, while men were rewarded more on the basis of professional skills and performance.

Content Analysis   The methods discussed thus far focus primarily on what people do and what they say. **Content analysis** is an additional method that examines not *what* people communicate, but *how* they communicate it, and this often reveals messages that are conveyed when people write or talk (Riley and Stoll, 1968). Content analysis is widely used to investigate how the mass media transmit cultural ideas and images that reinforce the subordinate position of women in society. How is it done?

Suppose you want to find out if school textbooks portray males and females in different ways. You could do this by assembling a collection of textbooks and perhaps counting the number of characters used in stories or examples and determining what percentage of them are male. Content analyses of school texts find that most characters—whether they are human, animal, or fantasy—are male, and almost all important

people are presented as male. Working women are rarely portrayed, and when they are, their jobs tend to be low in prestige and pay—secretaries, nurses, and elementary school teachers (St. Peter, 1979; Women on Words and Images, 1975a).

Content analyses of television shows reveal similar biases. Whether the shows are aimed at children or adults, the vast majority of leading characters are male, and successful working women are rarely portrayed (Sternglanz and Serbin, 1974; Cantor and Pingree, 1983). In commercials, women are often portrayed as bewildered consumers whose most important concern is clean laundry, and the "voice of authority" is male (Women on Words and Images, 1975b).

While books, television shows, commercials, and movies serve a variety of intended purposes for their creators (education, entertainment, selling products), their contents reveal important aspects of the culture in which they are created, and such messages affect our ideas of who we are and should be as men and women.

Historical Research   Historical documents are an additional valuable source of information for secondary analysis, for they shed light on the ways in which societies develop and change. What light does history shed on the current standing of women in society?

Historical research methods, by definition, focus on what has already occurred. We cannot, therefore, scientifically observe or experimentally manipulate history. We can learn a great deal, however, from records that reflect the social environments in which people once lived. Perhaps the most important lessons to be learned from historical research are that societies are always changing, and that the social arrangements we live in today developed over long periods of time. This may be the only world we have ever known, but it is not the only world that has ever been known or that ever will be.

Baxandall, Gordon, and Reverby (1976) wanted to understand how capitalism and the Industrial Revolution affected working-class women in the U.S. between the early seventeenth century and 1975. How did they do it? Their biggest problem was that most working-class women had neither the time nor the ability to leave written records of their experiences, and even when they did, they often did not consider their lives to be important enough to write about.

Time Table of the Holyoke Mills,

To take effect on and after Jan. 3d, 1853.

The standard being that of the Western Rail Road, which is the Meridian time at Cambridge.

MORNING BELLS.

First Bell ring 4.40, A.M. Second Bell ring is at 5, A.M.

YARD GATES

Will be opened at ringing of Morning Bells, of Meal Bells, and of Evening Bells, and kept open ten minutes.

WORK COMMENCES

At ten minutes after last Morning Bell, and ten minutes after Bell which "rings in" from Meals.

BREAKFAST BELLS.

October 1st, to March 31st, inclusive, ring out at 7, A.M.; ring in at 7.30, A.M.
April 1st, to Sept. 30th, inclusive, ring out at 6.30, A.M.; ring in at 7, A.M.

DINNER BELLS.

Ring out at 12.30, P.M.; ring in at 1, P.M.

EVENING BELLS.

Ring out at 6.30,* P.M.

*Excepting on Saturdays when the Sun sets previous to 6.30. At such times, ring out at sunset.

In all cases, the first stroke of the Bell is considered as marking the time.

Historical documents, such as this 1853 factory worker time table, tell much about the social conditions in which people lived. Notice at what time people were expected to come to work, how little time was allowed to arrive and to eat, how long the work day and the work week were, and how precisely regimented the day was. No mention is made of breaks from work other than for meals. In what ways do you think work has changed, and in what ways are conditions similar?

Although we may believe that men are "naturally" stronger than women, historical research shows that women have often taken on an equal or heavier burden of physical labor. This Japanese woman works in the fields alongside men and makes a contribution that is valued as much.

By systematically scouring libraries and archives for documents, the researchers found union records, diaries, short stories, poems, songs, letters, advertisements, social-worker reports, factory rules and regulations, petitions, newspaper and magazine articles, government reports, and statistical studies.

They found that colonial families met most of their needs through their own labor. While men and women performed different tasks in general, women still played a full role in economic production—weaving fabric, making soap and candles, and trading in the marketplace. It was not uncommon for women to be blacksmiths, tailors, printers, and shopkeepers; and widows often assumed full managerial control of family businesses.

The Industrial Revolution and the rise of capitalism physically separated the family from economic activity, and people no longer worked in the same place they lived. Life was divided into the private sphere of unpaid housework and the public sphere of paid employment. Because most work done at home was unpaid, it gradually lost its cultural value, and the self-esteem of women suffered as a result.

Although many women worked outside the home, they were restricted to low-paying jobs, and census takers routinely ignored wives' earnings when they recorded family income. Because paid work was socially defined as a "secondary" role for women, they were expected to be temporary workers who could be paid little and laid off when it suited their employers' interests. Women played an important part in the labor movement's long struggle for better working conditions, and many rebelled against the domination of their husbands.

The most serious limitation of historical studies is that we cannot use them to demonstrate the cause-and-effect relationships between variables. We cannot manipulate history in order to see what would have happened without an Industrial Revolution and without capitalism.

Cross-cultural studies, which compare different societies, are a partial solution to this problem. By comparing Samoa with the United States, Mead (1928/1953) showed that "adolescent crisis" is not an inevitable part of growing up. Studies of the American Hopi Indians show that families are headed by women, not men, and "women's work"—such as making pottery and baskets—is valued just as highly as men's (Leavitt, 1971). Such studies are important because they provide clues to the mystery of why societies develop in so many ways.

The preceding sections show how the complexity of social life requires sociologists to draw upon a wide range of research designs as they gather data. What happens, however, after the data are gathered? How are thousands of bits of information used to answer the questions we ask?

INTERPRETATION: USING INFORMATION TO ANSWER QUESTIONS

Of all research tasks, the interpretation of data is the most fascinating, for it is here that we must exercise a detective's skills in order to discover the clues and patterns that solve puzzles such as the income gap between men and women. At this stage, statistics are particularly useful.

Some Useful Statistics

Variables that have a small number of categories (such as the "Agree" and "Disagree" in Table 2-1) are easily summarized with percentages, allowing us to compare different groups. Variables such as income, however, present a more difficult problem, for there are thousands of different numbers that represent people's earnings.

In 1985 the Census Bureau interviewed almost 60,000 adults and recorded annual incomes for full-time, year-round workers (U.S. Census Bureau, 1987a). How can we use this massive set of facts to describe and compare the incomes of women and men? The most efficient solution would allow us to describe each category with a single number.

We could simplify the information by sorting people into a small set of income categories (Table 2-2). We could then compare women and men by

Table 2-2

Annual Income of Year-Round, Full-Time Workers by Gender (United States, 1985)

INCOME	WOMEN (%)	MEN (%)
Less than $5,000	3	3
$5,000 to $9,999	16	7
$10,000 to $14,999	27	13
$15,000 to $19,999	22	15
$20,000 to $29,999	23	27
$30,000 to $49,999	8	26
$50,000 to $74,999	1	6
$75,000 or more	*	3
TOTAL	100	100

Source: U.S. Census Bureau, 1987a.

seeing which categories they are most likely to be in. Women are more clustered in the lower income brackets than are men. For men, the *most frequent* income category (the **mode**) is between $20,000 and $29,999, while the mode for women is $10,000 to $14,999. Although these descriptions show that men are better off than women, they are crude, for they do not allow us to gauge how *much* better off men are.

A second approach to this problem is to add up all the money earned by men in 1985 and divide the total by the number of men, giving us the average earnings *per man*. This statistic is what most people think of as an "average" and is called the **mean**. When we calculate means, we find that men earned an average of $28,800—59 percent more than the average of $18,100 earned by full-time women workers in 1985.

As a description of groups, however, the mean has its disadvantages, for a few people who make a great deal of money "pump up" the mean and inflate the group's income. For example, suppose we have five people with the following incomes:

Vincent	$9,000
Joe	$10,000
Teresa	$10,500
Barbara	$11,000
John	$1,000,000
TOTAL	$1,040,500

If we want to summarize the incomes of the people in this group with a single number, would the mean give an accurate picture? Four of the five people have incomes between $9,000 and $11,000, and yet the mean income for the group is $208,100 (or $1,040,500/5). Certainly the mean is not a good indicator of the income of the people in this group. Clearly, whenever a few members of a group have extreme characteristics, the mean is not an effective way to describe the group. The mean does accurately tell us that men *as a group* earned 59 percent more than women did in 1985, but it may give a distorted picture of how *most* men compared with *most* women.

This brings us to a third important statistic—the **median**—which is simply the middle number in any group of numbers that is ranked from high to low or from low to high. In the group above, Teresa's income, $10,500, is the median. In 1985 the median income for full-time women workers was $16,200, while the median for men was $25,000 (U.S. Census Bureau, 1987a). This indicates that half of all women made more than $16,200 and half made less. Because the median is unaffected by extremely large or small incomes, it is a better summary description.

All these measures describe groups imperfectly, but they are useful because they allow us to summarize thousands of observations of individuals and use them to compare different groups. We can use means to see that while in 1955 full-time working women made 64¢ for every dollar earned by men, in 1985 women had actually fallen behind still further and earned only 63¢ for every dollar earned by men (U.S. Census Bureau, 1983b, 1987a).

Note that such statements do not tell us anything about individual men and women. While there are certainly some women who earn more money than most men and some men who earn less than most women, the focus of sociological research is not on individuals per se. Rather, it is on the characteristics of social environments in which individuals live.

Causal Relationships between Variables

If men and women were equally likely to fall in each income bracket, we would say that the variables "gender" and "income" are *independent* of each other. As we saw in the previous section, however, if you are a woman, you tend to have a lower income than if you are a man, and in this sense, the variable "income" *depends on* the variable "gender."

There is, in other words, a relationship between gender and income. In this relationship, gender is an **independent variable**, because we consider it to affect income. Because income depends to some degree on a person's gender, it is a **dependent variable**. Note that for one variable to affect another, it must occur before the dependent variable. In other words, it would be silly to suggest that income determines whether a person is male or female.

How do we explain the relationship between gender and income? That is the function of a **hypothesis**, a statement that predicts a relationship between variables. The first step is to think of other variables—such as educational attainment and occupation—that we know affect people's income, and these generate several possible hypotheses.

Our first hypothesis is that women work at poorer-paying jobs. In the first column in Table 2-3 we find that only 35 percent of working women are in white-collar or blue-collar jobs that pay more than $20,000 a year. Fifty-two percent are in white-collar jobs (such as secretaries) or blue-collar jobs (such as assembly-line workers) that pay less than $20,000 a year, and an additional 13 percent are in farm, service, and private household jobs that pay less than $12,000 a year. By comparison, the second column of Table 2-3

Table 2-3

Occupation by Gender (United States, 1985)

OCCUPATION[1]	WOMEN (%)	MEN (%)
Upper white-collar ($20,000 or more)	32	32
Upper blue-collar ($20,000 or more)	3	21
Lower white-collar (Less than $20,000)	43	18
Lower blue-collar (Less than $20,000)	9	19
Farm and service (Less than $12,000)	13	10
TOTAL	100	100

[1]Ranked by average income for full-time wage and salary workers. Excludes self-employed.

Source: U.S. Census Bureau, 1986a.

Table 2-4

Mean Hourly Earnings of Wage and Salary Workers by Occupation and Gender (United States, 1986)

OCCUPATION	MEAN EARNINGS		FOR EACH DOLLAR MEN EARN, WOMEN EARN:
	WOMEN	MEN	
Executive & managerial	$ 9.89	$16.12	61¢
Professional specialty	$10.47	$15.78	66¢
Accountants	$ 7.31	$10.15	72¢
Computer specialists	$ 8.72	$10.63	73¢
Nurses	$ 7.76	$ 8.52	91¢
Social workers	$ 6.39	$ 8.75	73¢
High school teachers	$ 6.99	$ 8.13	81¢
Lawyers	$10.78	$12.11	63¢
Journalists	$ 7.14	$ 9.39	76¢
Public officials and administrators	$ 7.67	$10.09	72¢
Sales representatives	$ 7.16	$ 9.94	72¢
Office clerks	$ 5.11	$ 6.46	79¢
Waiters/waitresses	$ 3.01	$ 4.63	65¢
Service workers	$ 4.91	$ 8.09	61¢
Farm and forestry	$ 3.26	$ 4.98	65¢
Office supervisors	$ 6.53	$10.20	64¢
Janitors and cleaners	$ 3.44	$ 5.73	60¢

Source: U.S. Census Bureau, 1986a, 1987c.

shows that 53 percent of all male workers are in white-collar and upper blue-collar occupations that pay more than $20,000 a year. The data support the first hypothesis.

Although part of the relationship between gender and income is due to the concentration of women in poorly paid jobs, we have to consider a second hypothesis: Women are paid less than men even when they work at the same job. To test this hypothesis, we compare the average incomes of men and women who have similar jobs, trying to see if men still earn more money. By looking at men and women who have the same kind of job, we are, in a sense, holding occupation "constant"; and when we do this, we are using occupation as a **control variable**.

The result is in Table 2-4, which shows the median incomes of men and women according to their occupations. As we saw before, women in general earn 63¢ for every dollar earned by men. For some occupations, however, the gap is smaller: female high school teachers earn 81¢ for each dollar earned by men. Thus,

some of the difference in earnings is due to different occupations; but notice that in almost *no* occupation do women earn as much as men, and in most jobs, women earn far less (see also Treiman and Hartmann, 1981). (Notice how each new explanation generates more questions: why is the gender gap in income smaller among computer specialists than among lawyers?)

By testing our first two hypotheses we found that women have poorer-paying jobs and are paid less for doing the same work. Why are they concentrated at the low end of the job market and paid less for the same work? These questions lead to our third hypothesis, which focuses on education: Women hold poorer-paying jobs and are paid less for the same work because they have lower average levels of education.

To test the third hypothesis, we control for the variable "education," *by comparing the jobs of men and women who are alike on that characteristic.* Do men and women with similar education hold similar jobs? Table 2-5 provides an answer (this is a multicolumn

Table 2-5

Occupation by Education and Gender (United States, 1985)

YEARS OF SCHOOLING COMPLETED

| | College Grads | | High School Grads | | 0 to 11 Years | |
| | Women | Men | Women | Men | Women | Men |
OCCUPATION	(%)	(%)	(%)	(%)	(%)	(%)
Upper white-collar	69	65	12	11	5	5
Upper blue-collar	1	5	3	30	6	28
Lower white-collar	26	23	54	19	21	8
Lower blue-collar	1	3	11	26	26	37
Farm and service	3	4	20	14	42	22
TOTAL	100	100	100	100	100	100

Source: U.S. Census Bureau, 1986a.

table, so go through it slowly, one column at a time). The first two columns describe the occupations of men and women who have at least a college degree, and show quite similar distributions.

When we look at the occupations of less-educated workers, strong gender differences emerge. Among workers with high school diplomas (the second pair of columns), men are more likely to have upper blue-collar jobs, and women are heavily concentrated in lower white-collar and service occupations. Among the least-educated workers (the last two columns), only 11 percent of women have upper white-collar or upper blue-collar jobs compared with 33 percent of comparably educated men. (Pause for a few minutes and verify these statements by examining the table carefully.)

Table 2-5 suggests that education benefits men more than women in the job market (see also Spenner, Otto, and Call, 1982); but how does education affect income? Do women and men with the same education have the same income? As Table 2-6 (p. 48) shows, controlling for education does not explain the relationship between gender and income, for at each level of education, the median income for men is much higher than that for women. In fact, women with college degrees averaged $2,500 less than men who never went beyond high school ($21,400 versus $23,900), and women high school graduates make

$3,100 less on the average than men who never went beyond elementary school ($15,500 versus $18,600).

This analysis reveals some aspects of the relationship between income and gender. Women earn less than men because they hold poorer-paying jobs regardless of their education, and even when they have similar jobs, they are paid less. While a complete explanation involves other variables (such as job experience), these findings strongly suggest that women are discriminated against on the basis of gender, both in getting jobs and being rewarded for their work (see Bergmann, 1986; Duncan et al., 1984).

This analysis describes a series of patterns—occupation, gender, education, and income—and examines the *relationships* among them. In this way, we can see how social characteristics, such as being male or female, are related to others, such as occupation, education, and income, that have important effects on people's lives. This kind of analysis lies at the heart of sociological research, for it illuminates the complex effects of social environments on human life.

Spurious Relationships between Variables

It should be emphasized that the existence of a statistical relationship between two variables does not necessarily mean that one variable causes changes in the other. Suppose we gather information on fires and

Table 2-6

Median Income by Years of Education and Gender for Year-Round, Full-Time Workers (United States, 1985)

YEARS OF SCHOOL COMPLETED	MEDIAN INCOME		FOR EACH DOLLAR MEN EARN, WOMEN EARN:
	WOMEN	MEN	
Elementary			
0 to 7 Years	$ 9,700	$14,800	66¢
8 Years	$11,400	$18,600	61¢
High School			
1 to 3 Years	$11,800	$18,900	62¢
4 Years	$15,500	$23,900	65¢
College			
1 to 3 Years	$18,000	$27,000	67¢
4 Years	$21,400	$32,800	65¢
5 Years or more	$25,900	$39,300	66¢

Source: U.S. Census Bureau, 1987a.

keep track of two variables: (1) the number of fire-fighters at each fire and (2) the amount of damage caused by each fire. We find this relationship between these variables: the more firefighters at the scene, the more damage. Is the secret to lowering fire losses, then, to reduce the number of firefighters?

Most of us would hesitate to accept such a conclusion. Why? We have to ask a basic question: Why should this relationship exist? In this case, the answer is that both variables are caused by a *third* variable, the seriousness of the fire. Big fires bring more firefighters to the scene *and* cause more damage. If we ignore this third variable, it *appears* that firefighters cause more damage when in fact they do not. The statistical relationship between the number of firefighters present and the extent of fire damage is **spurious**, *for it has nothing to do with cause and effect.*

Whenever we find a relationship between variables, we have to ask ourselves if it might be spurious. Otherwise, we might waste time trying to figure out how firefighters cause damage or urging firefighters to stay away from fires. In this example, logic leads us to conclude that the relationship is spurious, but in many cases, relationships may appear to be causal when they are actually spurious, as in the following example.

In the 1960s the U.S. Department of Health, Education, and Welfare conducted a survey of more than 7,000 adults in which each of them received a detailed physical examination. It was found that 40 percent of those widowed and divorced had high blood pressure compared with only 15 percent of married people and 10 percent of single people (Table 2-7).

Table 2-7

Blood Pressure by Marital Status (United States, 1959–62)

MARITAL STATUS	BLOOD PRESSURE		
	High	*Normal*	*Total*
Single	10%	90%	100%
Married	15%	85%	100%
Widowed or divorced	40%	60%	100%

Source: Derived by the author from unpublished data provided by the National Center for Health Statistics.

There is some evidence that aggressive and violent children and adolescents have watched more violence on television than normally behaved children. Does this mean that watching excessive violence is a cause of the violent behavior? If the relationship is spurious, what other factors might account for it?

It is tempting to accept such findings at face value, because it "makes sense" that widowhood and divorce are high-stress social positions and that, in many ways, marriage is more difficult than single life. Scientists, however, test common-sense explanations, and so we must consider the possibility that this finding is spurious. Is there a causal relationship between marital status and blood pressure?

To answer this question, we have to rephrase it: Is there a factor that causes high blood pressure *and* distinguishes widowed and divorced people from others? An obvious candidate is age, for as people grow older their blood pressure usually increases and they are more likely to be widowed or divorced.

We test the possibility that widowed and divorced people have higher blood pressure not because of their marital status, but because they are generally older than single and married people. We control for age by asking, "Does marital status make a difference among people of the same age?" We find that widowed and divorced people are no more likely to have high blood pressure than single and married people *of the same age*. By controlling for age, the relationship between marital status and blood pressure becomes spurious.

Spuriousness occurs whenever two variables are related to a variable that is causally related to one or both of them. In the firefighter example, both variables were caused by a third variable (seriousness of the fire). In the blood-pressure example, both marital status and blood pressure are related to age, which *does* have a causal effect on the dependent variable, blood pressure.

The possibility of spuriousness is often overlooked when the relationships appear to be reasonable. Scientists rely on cultural beliefs to decide what "makes sense" and what does not. What sets scientists apart, however, is their skepticism, their reluctance to accept "reasonable" findings at face value, and their use of previous research findings to decide what makes sense. The only way to find out if what appears to be true is in fact true is to gather and analyze objective evidence.

Correlation   Percentages, medians, means, and modes enable us to describe groups in terms of single variables, but we also need to describe relationships between variables.

A *perfect statistical* **correlation** is one in which two variables overlap completely. In parts *a* and *b* of Figure 2-1, if we know someone's education, we also

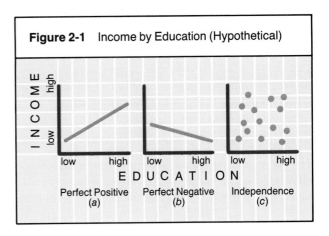

Figure 2-1   Income by Education (Hypothetical)

INCOME (low to high) / EDUCATION (low to high)

Perfect Positive (*a*)   Perfect Negative (*b*)   Independence (*c*)

know his or her income. In *a*, the correlation is *positive*, because the higher education is, the higher income is. In *b*, the correlation is *negative* because the higher education is, the *lower* income is. In *c*, the variables are *independent* of each other, because the chances of having high or low income are the same regardless of education: education does not make a difference.

Most relationships between variables are neither perfect nor independent; rather, they are somewhere in between. In Table 2-7, marital status makes a difference in the likelihood of having high blood pressure, but knowing people's marital status does not allow us to know their blood pressure with complete certainty. While widowed and divorced people are more likely than others to have high blood pressure, 60 percent of them have normal blood pressure.

We need a way to measure the *strength* of relationships between variables. In addition to saying, "marital status makes a difference," we also want to express how much of a difference it makes.

To do this, we use a **measure of association**, which is a number from -1.0 to $+1.0$. The association has a value of zero when the variables are independent, a value of -1.0 when the relationship is perfect and negative, and a value of $+1.0$ when it is perfect and positive. Note that the "$+$" or "$-$" sign of a relationship describes the pattern of association between two variables, telling us what *kind* of effect the independent variable has on the dependent. The number measures the strength of the relationship, telling us how *much* of an effect it has. While "$+.60$" and "$-.60$" describe different patterns, they are of equal strength.

SOME DIFFICULTIES IN SOCIOLOGICAL RESEARCH

The study of people and the characteristics of their social environments poses a number of scientific and ethical problems for sociological researchers.

Complexity and Objectivity

The forces that influence human behavior and cause changes in social environments are enormously complex. The position of women in society cannot be described or explained by a few variables; rather, it flows from many aspects of culture and social structure that are related to each other in complex ways.

In addition, as sociologists study social environments they cannot be immune from the effects of those environments on their own activity as scientists. Survey researchers may ask loaded questions ("You aren't a racist, are you?"); the biases of participant observers may influence what they notice as well as how they interpret their observations; and experimental conditions may themselves produce their own effects. In comparison with most other scientific disciplines, the demands of objectivity are particularly difficult for sociologists to meet. It is for this reason that sociologists so carefully scrutinize their own measures and methods in order to be aware of any possible sources of distorting bias.

As Max Weber argued, however, the complete objectivity of the physical scientist is not only difficult for social researchers to achieve, it is also undesirable. Unlike rocks, beams of light, and barnyard animals, humans behave according to complex perceptions and interpretations, and all of these are influenced by social environments. To understand how the Grand Canyon was formed, we do not have to imagine what it would be like to *be* the Grand Canyon; but we cannot understand people in the same way.

Ethics, Research, and People's Lives

Another difficulty in sociological research involves ethical questions (Reynolds, 1979, 1982). While the experimental manipulation of objects is culturally acceptable, scientists must take far greater care with people. Researchers may not explore the effects of child abuse on emotional development by systematically abusing a sample of children and comparing them with a control group of unabused children. In many cases, however, the ethical issues are less clear-cut.

Humphreys (1970) wanted to learn more about men who have homosexual encounters with strangers in public rest rooms. To gather information, he served as a "lookout," and as an observer he was able to gather detailed data about these interactions. To gather further information, he kept a record of automobile license plates, which he used to locate the subjects a year later. He then presented himself as a survey researcher gathering information having nothing to do

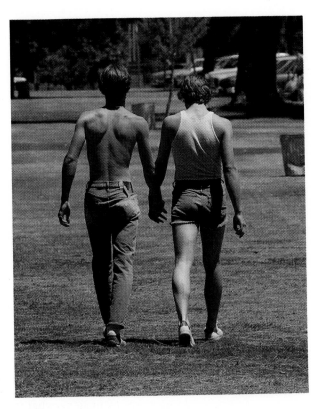

Relatively little research has been done on homosexuals in the United States, in part, because as a minority they are reluctant to be identified and, in part, because of ethical issues. To what degree do social scientists have the right to invade people's privacy in order to do research, even if their findings might bring about positive social change?

with homosexuality, and he found, among other things, that most of these men were married.

In spite of the fact that his study dispelled many myths about homosexual behavior, Humphreys was criticized on ethical grounds because he lied about his identity and, although he safeguarded subjects' identities, he risked exposing them and their actions. He later agreed that he had improperly invaded the privacy of his subjects and unnecessarily endangered them (Humphreys, 1975). For all scientists, but for social scientists in particular, his methods raise a troubling question: Do the research ends justify the research means?

Ethical questions involve not only research methods, but the possible *uses* of research findings. Scientists are bound by professional norms that re-

quire careful interpretation of findings ("the differences are small and apply only to men and women in general"); but parents, teachers, potential employers, and government policymakers are not. There is a danger that scientific findings will be used sloppily or indiscriminately to reinforce damaging cultural stereotypes and the social inequalities they support.

In the 1960s the U.S. Army provided funds for the study of the social conditions likely to cause or prevent revolutions in Latin American countries. From a scientific point of view, Project Camelot (as it was known) was simply one more set of questions to be answered, but from the Latin American perspective, it involved information that would enable the U.S. government to interfere in the domestic affairs of their countries (Horowitz, 1965).

When news of Project Camelot reached Chile, a public furor erupted, the program was canceled, and the researchers confronted ethical issues they had previously ignored. To a scientist, one bit of knowledge is no better or worse than any other, subject only to rigid standards for determining truth. Outside the scientific community, however, knowledge often represents power that can be used destructively as well as constructively.

In spite of the difficulties inherent in their research, most sociologists are committed to the scientific method. By limiting themselves to objective aspects of reality that can be observed and measured, sociologists necessarily limit the kinds of questions they can investigate. For this reason, few would suggest that scientific research alone is sufficient to solve the many puzzles of social life; but by systematically observing social environments and their effects, sociologists obtain the information needed to test a wide range of ideas that contribute to our overall understanding of the human condition.

SUMMARY

1. The scientific method involves careful and exacting procedures for gathering and interpreting objective evidence that helps sociologists accomplish the three major tasks of research: description, explanation, and prediction.

2. Research begins with the problem of deciding what it is that we want to know, which variables are involved, and how best to measure them in a

valid and reliable way. Measurement is particularly difficult in sociology because much of what
is measured is invisible, changes over time, and
depends on how people present themselves.

3. The complexity of social life calls for many
    methods for gathering and interpreting infor-
    mation, and each has its own strengths and
    weaknesses. Research design begins with the
    definition of the population to be studied and the
    decision to study all its members (a census), a
    representative sample, or carefully selected cases.

4. Interview and questionnaire surveys allow re-
    searchers to gather large amounts of information,
    but are limited by time and their dependence on
    the accuracy of people's reports about themselves.
    In-depth interviews yield greater detail, but must
    compromise by focusing on a smaller number of
    people who are less likely to represent a popula-
    tion scientifically.

5. Laboratory and field experiments allow us to dis-
    cover cause-and-effect relationships by carefully
    controlling the conditions in which variables are
    measured. Participant observation allows us to
    observe directly the behavior of subjects, but our
    involvement makes it more difficult to be
    objective.

6. Content analysis and historical research are types
    of secondary analysis in which existing informa-
    tion is applied to new research problems. Cross-
    cultural comparisons of different societies help
    researchers discover how social environments
    change.

7. Regardless of methods, sociologists often use sta-
    tistics to summarize and condense huge amounts
    of detailed information and to discover and ex-
    plain relationships between variables.

8. Sociological research is difficult in several ways.
    We must pay attention not only to the biases that
    threaten any scientist's objectivity, but also to the
    risks that research may pose for the people we
    study. Ethical issues are enormously important in
    sociology, both in relation to the process of gath-
    ering information and to the ways in which that
    information is eventually used.

KEY TERMS

case study   37
census   35
cross-cultural study   44
experiment   39
    control group   40
    field experiment   40

hypothesis   45
    control variable   46
    dependent variable   45
    independent variable   45
        measure of association   50
    spurious relationship   48
longitudinal survey   38
measurement instrument   32
    reliability   33
    validity   32
    variable   32

participant observation   40
population   35
replication   40
sample   35
    multistage sample   36
    random sample   36
    systematic sample   36
scientific method   29
secondary analysis   41
    content analysis   42
    historical research   42
statistics   44
    correlation   49
    mean   44
    median   45
    mode   44
survey   36
    in-depth interview   37
    interview   36
    questionnaire   36

Looking Elsewhere

Having studied Chapter 2, you might want to look at related discussions in *Human Arrangements*, which include

- science and the scientific method (Chapter 17, pp. 461–70)
- gender inequality (Chapter 13)

RECOMMENDED READINGS

COLE, S. (1976). *The sociological method* (2nd ed.). Chicago: Rand McNally (paperback). A clearly written, lively introduction to the logic of sociological research and the many uses of statistical techniques. Full of interesting examples.

GLAZER, M. (1972). *The research adventure.* New York: Random House. A series of accounts of sociological research projects, the practical problems the researchers encountered, and how they solved them.

HUNT, M. (1986). *Profiles of social research: The scientific study of human interactions.* New York: Russell Sage. A wonderfully clear and engaging look at different ways of designing sociological research. Hunt truly manages to convey what it is like to do research.

KATZER, J., COOK, K., and CROUCH, W. (1978). *Evaluating information: A guide for users of social science research.* Reading, MA: Addison-Wesley (paperback). A book for consumers of research reports. It is lively and clearly written and focuses on basic problems that confront anyone trying to make sense of scientific research and trying to decide which findings to accept and which to reject.

REYNOLDS, P.D. (1982). *Ethics and social science research.* Englewood Cliffs, NJ: Prentice-Hall. A recent examination of the ethical problems encountered by social researchers and some of the ways of dealing with them.

ROSSI, A. C. (1982). *Feminists in politics: A panel analysis of the first national women's conference.* New York: Academic Press. A fascinating account of the process of designing and carrying out a large survey.

WHYTE, W. F. (1981). *Street corner society* (3rd ed.). Chicago: University of Chicago Press. In what has become a sociological classic, pay particular attention to the Appendix, "On the Evolution of Street Corner Society." It is a rare and profound look into the problems and promises of participant observation research.

TWO

The Sociological Framework

IF WE WANT TO understand why people behave as they do, we must look at the social and physical contexts in which they experience and interpret themselves and others. These contexts include the culture that people share, the relationships that bind them together, and physical factors such as population and ecological arrangements.

The following three chapters take a detailed look at these three major areas that define sociology as a perspective. In Chapter 3 we outline different kinds of cultural products and see some of the ways in which they affect our lives. Chapter 4 describes the ways in which our participation in social relationships affects not only what we do but who we think we are; and Chapter 5 shows how population and ecology affect the cultural and structural characteristics of social environments.

Symbols, Language, and Meaning

    Language

    The Uses of Language

Cultural Ideas

    Beliefs: The Real and the Unreal

    Values: Shoulds and Shouldn'ts

    Norms: Dos and Don'ts

    Attitudes: Evaluation and Feeling

**Material Culture:
Things from Ideas and Ideas from Things**

3 Culture

As we saw in Chapter 1, **culture** consists of two kinds of products—the symbols and ideas that members of a society share as a framework for interpreting the world and the objects that people create and incorporate into their environments. In this chapter we take a detailed look at language and the ideas that make up most of nonmaterial culture. We close with a brief look at material culture and its connection with cultural ideas.

Because the essence of culture consists of ideas, its existence depends on the human ability to use symbols in order to attach meaning to experience and perceptions and thereby think about the world (Geertz, 1973). Therefore, it is with symbols that we begin this chapter.

SYMBOLS, LANGUAGE, AND MEANING

Take a moment to look at Figure 3-1. What is it? On a piece of paper make a list of all the answers you can think of. Do not read any further until you have at least four items on your list.

What is Figure 3-1 a picture of? "A bunch of dots?" "Two lines of dots, one shorter than the other, joined at a right angle two-thirds of the way up the longer line?" "*X*- and *y*-axes used to plot data?" "Two roads intersecting?" "A 'cross'?" While the first two answers are a mere physical description of Figure 3-1, the remaining three answers go beyond what the lines look like to say what they *are*. They transform the lines into *symbols* by attaching *meaning* to them; and it is meaning that is at the heart of nonmaterial culture.

A **symbol** is anything that represents more than itself. In many cultures a "cross"—whether made of two sticks or lines on a piece of paper—is more than what our eyes see: people pay great attention to it, carry it around their necks, and hang it in their homes. Members of the Ku Klux Klan gather around large ones and watch them burn in the night. In many places, however, and during many periods of history, people would see nothing more than a pair of sticks held together or two lines joined at right angles.

The four kinds of symbols include, first, symbolic *objects*—flags represent nations and money represents labor and goods; second, symbolic *characteristics* of objects—in our culture purple "stands for" royalty, black for mourning, yellow for cowardice, white for purity. *Gestures* are the third type of symbol. **Gestures** are actions that have meaning: smiles and winks, a raised right hand in oath taking, a shrug of the shoulders, a frustrated snap of the fingers—all of these actions have meaning in a particular cultural context (Malandro and Barker, 1983; Patterson, 1983). The fourth type of symbol is the vast range of *spoken and written words* that make up *language*, which is so important that it deserves a separate discussion. Language is the most important set of symbols in any culture, for it embodies the symbolic building blocks used to construct ideas.

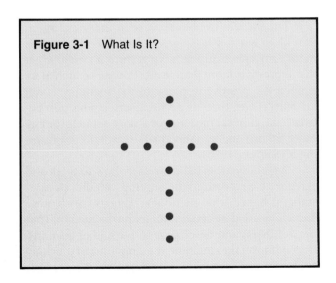

Figure 3-1 What Is It?

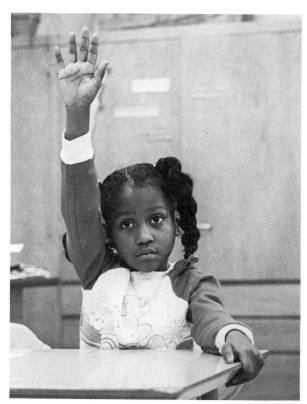

Gestures are physical actions that have meaning, and, as in spoken language, the meaning of a gesture often depends on the social context. In this series of pictures, notice how the gesture of a raised hand has a very different meaning in each case.

In a culture, then, objects, the characteristics of objects, actions, and words are more than our senses perceive them to be; they are what a culture signifies them to be. They *are* what they *mean*. Suppose you walk down a city street on a summer day and come upon an auction in the front yard of an old house. You spy an empty seat in the shade and, being hot and tired, you sit down to watch. On the auction block is a large ornate desk, and the bidding is high. "Two thousand dollars," the auctioneer barks. "Do I hear twenty-one hundred? Going once. Going twice . . ." Suddenly, your nose itches and you scratch it with your index finger. Just as suddenly, the auctioneer points a finger at you and shouts, "Twenty-one hundred! Going once! Going twice! Sold!" You have just bought yourself a $2,100 desk.

Strictly speaking, you only scratched your nose, and you did so just to relieve an itch. You had no intention of bidding for a desk. How do you get out of it? "I didn't *mean* anything by it," you say. "I just scratched my nose." Had you been sitting across from the auctioneer on a subway and scratched your nose in just the same way, the outcome would have been very different.

You got into trouble because in the social situation of an auction it is agreed that a nose scratch is more than a physical act; it is a gesture, a symbolic act that represents more than itself: "A nose scratch at an auction is a positive response to the auctioneer's call for bids." Thus, there is no necessary connection between the cultural meaning of a nose scratch (or any other action) and an individual's reason for performing it (Sahlins, 1976).

Symbol systems tell their users how to mark and categorize perceptions depending on the circumstances; hence, the auctioneer categorizes a nose scratch as a bid at certain points in the auction (but not at others) and never does so outside of auctions. Depending on the situation, the simple act of touching your nose can have many meanings: when con artists are about to "sting" a victim, a finger on the side of the nose means "all is ready"; or a thumb drawn across the nose can signify contempt. A single action can be transformed into many different meaningful gestures, depending on the cultural context.

This example illustrates a vital aspect of symbols: *we respond to them just as we respond to what they represent.* While the word "fire" represents something that can hurt us, the word itself cannot; yet the word "fire" can make us run just as readily as the sight or heat of fire itself. Without the word, we can experience fire only with our senses, by seeing its color, hearing its crackle, feeling its heat. With the word, on the other hand, fire exists as an *idea* even when there is no fire: it exists in our minds, and when we share the symbol with other people, it exists among us. We can think about it, teach each other about it and its uses. We can attach the idea of "fire" to things that have no concrete relation to it, as "the fiery anger in her eyes." Symbols, themselves, then, are *real* to us; and as W. I.

Thomas (1931) pointed out, what we define as real has real consequences.

Symbols are created, which means we can create symbols to which we respond just as we do to physical objects and forces. There is nothing inherent in any symbol that gives it power over us; its power lies in what it signifies to those who share its meaning. If children learn the meaning of "danger" by touching a hot stove and hearing the word from an adult, the word "danger" can be used to keep them away from all kinds of things that may not be dangerous at all. Similarly, the symbol "immoral" can be attached to virtually any behavior. This explains why the meaning of a behavior is often more important to us than its objective characteristics or consequences.

Culture provides a framework of ideas that we use to interpret what we perceive, and people's appearance and behavior are fully understandable only if we pay attention to their cultural context. If we feed our guests roast chicken and after the meal tell them they just consumed the flesh of a dog, their reaction depends only in part on what they actually ate or think they ate. To predict their response, we must know the system of meaning they use to interpret what they did—some Southeast Asians might thank us for the delicacy, while most Europeans would look disgusted.

Language

There would be no culture without **language**, the collection of symbols (words) and rules for their use with which we think and communicate with one another. Without culture, humans would be hard-pressed to survive. We are not born knowing what kinds of berries to eat and which are poisonous, or how to catch and eat a wild animal, but we do have the ability to use symbols. Because "edible" and "inedible" are important distinctions for us, we have symbols for them; we can categorize objects and, most important, we can teach those categories to one another.

Every language has two elements: a collection of words and a set of rules—syntax and grammar—that governs the arrangement of words to express thoughts. Some words—such as "telephone"—have fixed meanings, while many depend on their relation to other words. The phrase "he threw up" means one thing followed by "his lunch," but quite another in the poem, "A Visit From St. Nicholas," in which the father "ran to the window and threw up the sash."

The symbols and their meanings contained in a language represent the distinctions that its users tend to make as they perceive and mark their world. To the Eskimo, a detailed understanding of different kinds of snow is vital for survival. Eskimo languages typically include as many as 20 different words for "snow"— snow that is good for making igloo blocks, hard and crusty snow, dry snow drifted by the wind, and so on—while English has only one (Hoebel, 1966). Argentine cowboys ("gauchos") have over 200 separate words that describe the color of horses (Curtis, 1968). English, on the other hand, has an enormous number of words used in making precise scientific measurements. A nanosecond (one billionth of a second) is a unit of time that exists only in computer operations and is otherwise beyond human experience (see Rifkin, 1987).

The second element of language—syntax and grammar—tells us how to arrange words in order to express ourselves. Different arrangements of the same words convey very different meanings, as in "The

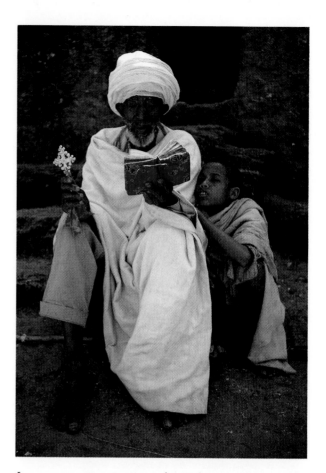

Language exists as a part of social environments only when it is shared. As this elderly teacher in Ethiopia passes on his language to his student, with it follows the gateway to a common culture and way of life.

whale swallowed Jonah" or "Jonah swallowed the whale," or convey nothing at all, as in "Whale Jonah the swallowed."

The Marx Brothers were famous for manipulating language as a source of humor. In the film *The Coconuts* (1929), Groucho owns a hotel, and his bellboys want to be paid. "Oh," Groucho says, "you want your *money*?" "Yes," they reply. "So, you want *my* money," Groucho says, as he changes the meaning by changing the pronoun. "Is that fair? Do I want *your* money? No, my friends, no. Money will never make you happy. And happy will never make you money."

Meaning also depends on the cultural context. The subtlety of such variations is painfully obvious to those who learn a language as adults and thereby often know only literal meanings. A foreign dinner guest who hears "Oh, you *must* try some of this stew" may interpret the statement as an order, not as friendly encouragement. The social relationship between the speaker and the hearer can also be important in determining meanings: "I love you" spoken by a child to a parent has a different meaning than when spoken between two unrelated adults.

The complexity of language reflects the complexity of culture as a system for representing and interpreting the world. As Farb (1975) pointed out, even the simplest statements are impressively complex.

> Children who unravel a simple statement like "The chair broke" must do more than decode a grammatical utterance. They must first master the subtle category of things that *break*, like *chairs* and also *machines* and *windowpanes*. Then they must distinguish the category of things that *break* from things that *tear*, like *paper* and *bedsheets*, or things that *smash*, like *vases* and *cars*. They must next interpret the influence on the chair of the verb *broke* out of all the possibilities that verb implies, such as that the breaking of a chair is conceptually different from breaking the bank at Monte Carlo or from waves breaking on a beach. To achieve all this, children unconsciously unravel the sentence into parts that can be analyzed, and then put the elements together again in a meaningful fashion. (pp. 262–263)

Meaning depends on the symbols used, their arrangement in relation to one another, and the social situation in which they are used.

The language of words is not the only type of language found in cultures (see Figure 3-2). Mathematics is a language used to represent the quantitative aspects of reality: it is a set of symbols (such as "2," "3," "+," "×," "=") with specific rules that define their relationships to each other ("2 + 3 = 5" or "2 × 3 = 6"). Musical notation is also a language, symbols on paper representing sounds.

Language develops from the interactions of group life, and those who share a culture use its language to represent reality (Berger and Luckman, 1967). The fact that the words "wizard," "bachelor," and "Indian brave" have more positive connotations than "witch," "spinster," and "Indian squaw" reflects long-standing patterns of discrimination against women in life as it is lived. To grow up with these categories of meaning affects the way people think about women and men, and thus, as patterns of living foster certain views of reality, those views in turn help to sustain and reproduce those same patterns of social life.

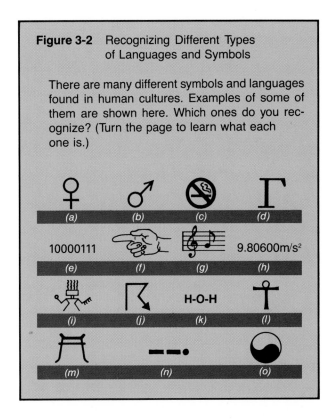

Figure 3-2 Recognizing Different Types of Languages and Symbols

There are many different symbols and languages found in human cultures. Examples of some of them are shown here. Which ones do you recognize? (Turn the page to learn what each one is.)

The limitations of language are clearest when we look at their ambiguities and internal contradictions. Many slang expressions do not mean what they literally say: "it blew my mind," "a heavy idea," "I'll catch you later," "he spilled his guts," "she picked his brain," and "he shot his mouth off" all illustrate the flexibility with which language can be used to describe reality.

The Uses of Language

As a major part of culture, language is more than a system of communication, for sharing a common language fulfills four basic social functions (Farb, 1975). First, our language allows us to assume that those who share it with us (our **speech community**) know what we mean when we talk or write. It is precisely our expectation that strangers will understand us when we speak that makes a language social; a "personal" language is not a language at all, for its meanings are not shared. Because there is practically no one who speaks Latin in an existing social environment, it is described as a "dead" language.

Second, the common language of a speech community allows its members to distinguish themselves from outsiders, helping to maintain group boundaries

Figure 3-2   Identifying the Examples of
(Answers)   Different Types of Languages and
             Symbols

 a. Female, Venus, Friday
 b. Male, Mars, Tuesday
 c. International symbol for No Smoking
 d. Letter "g" in Russian alphabet
 e. Letter "g" in EBCDIC (Extended Binary
     Coded Decimal Exchange Code)
 f. Letter "g" in American Manual Alphabet
     sign language
 g. Musical notation for eighth note G on G clef
     (treble clef)
 h. In physics, the value of acceleration due to
     gravity (at 45° latitude and sea level)
     denoted by the symbol g
 i. Symbol for Animiki, the North American
     Indian god of storm and thunder
 j. Meteorological symbol for thunderstorm
 k. In organic chemistry, the structural formula
     for water
 l. Ankh, ancient Egyptian symbol of enduring life
 m. Torii, emblem of Shinto
 n. Letter "g" in Morse Code
 o. Yin-yang symbol, used by Taoists to
     indicate the universal law of existence: the
     harmonious balance of opposites

own set of slang terms for students who study a lot or who party a lot, for hard courses and easy ones—terms that have different meanings (or none at all) for those outside the college speech community. Ethnic and racial groups have derogatory terms that label the members of other groups; there are more than a thousand such terms in English alone (Allen, 1983).

If immigrants do not learn their new society's language, they must restrict themselves to small pockets that contain their speech community. When the children of immigrants learn the new language while their parents cling to the old, the result is often distance between family members who participate in different speech communities and, in many respects, different cultures.

When Africans were brought to the U.S. as slaves, they were forbidden to speak their native languages and were given new names. Wars have been fought over which language would dominate in a culture (see McRae, 1984, 1986). The struggle between French and English Canadians in Quebec is reflected in the French Canadians' insistence that French have the same importance as English, that bank tellers be able to speak French (Giniger, 1981). In similar ways, there has been great controversy in the United States about the idea of adopting English as our "official" language. Although mainstream social life is certainly carried on in English, some fear that to include other languages—most notably Spanish—in schools and public affairs undermines the sense of social solidarity and national identity that rest on sharing a common language.

The third social function of language is that it often serves as a substitute for physical contact: we "keep in touch" by telephone, letter, and small talk that often appears to be meaningless. When we meet someone and ask, "How are you?" we rarely expect more than a short reply such as "fine" or "OK." Many people look upon such exchanges as phony or trivial, but they allow us to briefly "touch" one another. It is as if we say, "I see you; do you see me?" and thereby make contact, reaffirming our existence in the eyes of others (the importance of which is painfully evident when people ignore us). We also use language as a symbolic substitute for physical violence and yell at each other just as some birds angrily spread their tail feathers or elk toss their antlers.

Fourth, some utterances, known as **performative language**, constitute meaningful actions simply by being spoken (Robinson, 1972). To say "I promise"

and solidarity (see Edwards, 1984; Stevens and Swicegood, 1987). In Shaw's play *Pygmalion* (and later on Broadway as the musical *My Fair Lady*), Eliza Doolittle's cockney accent immediately identifies her social class to Professor Higgins. When blacks in the U.S. leave urban ghettos to attend college, they often find on their return that subtle changes in their use of language alienate them from friends who now see them as outsiders to their speech community.

Children in school create special languages (such as pig Latin) or use little-known languages such as American Sign Language as a part of forming exclusive groups. Prison inmates have their own vocabularies to distinguish them from guards and outsiders (Sykes, 1958). Many occupations use special vocabularies (jargon) to distinguish themselves from others (see Table 3-1). Each generation of college students has its

Table 3-1

Reviving Traditional U.S. Navy Terminology

In November 1984, as part of his campaign to increase the pride and professionalism of Navy personnel, Navy Sec. John F. Lehman, Jr., ordered adherence to traditional language (examples appear below, right). He contended that use of this historic vernacular helps Navy men and women appreciate that they are part of a unique institution with its own heritage and military style.

"CIVILIAN" TERM	TRADITIONAL TERM
Enlisted Dining Facility	Mess Decks or Galleys
Dining Room (for officers)	Mess or Ward Room
Stairs	Ladder
Hall or corridor	Passageway
Floor	Deck
Wall	Bulwark
Ceiling	Overhead
Upstairs	Topside
Downstairs	Below
Replacement when your watch duty is done	Relief
The state of suffering late relief	Gapped
Double shift	Double (or dual) hatted
Shift change	Turnover
Advance pay	Deadhorse
Putting things away downstairs	Strike it below
Ice cream, soda, or soda fountain items	Geedunk (slang)
Argumentative person	Sea lawyer
Older man who teaches a recruit	Sea daddy
To be forgotten or go over the side	Go by the board
Trash can	GI can
Portable radio for distress signals	Gibson girl

Source: Navy Public Affairs Office and the Naval Institute Press's Naval Terms Dictionary.

is to make a promise, just as "I do" seals a marriage. When a friend looks you in the eyes and says "I love you" for the first time, it is often more than an expression of feeling. It is an invitation to enter into a relationship with particular expectations; that it is an offer is painfully clear if you fail to reciprocate with "I love you, too." If you do reciprocate, you, too, may have done more than express feelings. The general terms of your new relationship are established simply by uttering such phrases, and they can be undone only with other performative utterances such as, "I don't love you any more."

Perhaps the most marvelous aspect of language, aside from its sheer complexity and seemingly endless variations, is that we are able to participate in it with little or no conscious effort. It is so familiar to us, so close to our everyday lives, that we are likely to think of it as an inherent part of each human being.

Language, however, does not arise from the isolated psychological experience of individuals, even though each of us possesses the biological and psychological characteristics that make language possible. The creation of a single word is complete only when two or more people share its meaning. While a single mind can create a sound, until it is shared it is only a noise, not a word. The development of separate languages—English, French, Swahili, Chinese, Hebrew, Arabic, or the thousands of others—does not rest on differences in physiology or psychology, but on the endless variations produced by social interactions extending across many generations.

As a collection of symbols and rules, language is the basis of all beliefs, values, norms, and attitudes. The following sections describe in detail each of these components of nonmaterial culture.

CULTURAL IDEAS

Beliefs: The Real and the Unreal

Beliefs are symbolic statements about what is real, such as "The earth is round," "There is a God," "There are 100 centimeters in a meter," and "The way to get ahead in the world is to obey the rules and work hard." All of these are beliefs because they try to describe some aspect of reality.

Not all statements about what is real are *cultural* beliefs. An individual cannot create or change cultural beliefs by waking up one morning and saying, "The earth is a cube." A belief is cultural only if the ultimate authority for its validity lies outside of individuals—in our assumptions that others share in the particular belief. When the astronomer Copernicus observed the heavens and concluded that the earth was not the center of the universe, his sole authority rested in his own observations, and his belief—at least initially—was strictly a personal one. Copernicus and, later, Galileo were persecuted not because their beliefs were objectively incorrect, but because they contradicted those of the surrounding culture and struck at the heart of an entire system of religious beliefs about the relationship between God and humanity.

Beliefs furnish us with the "obvious" facts of our existence: it is "obvious" to anyone reading this book that the earth is round. But it was equally obvious to some living in fifteenth-century Europe that the earth was flat and anyone sailing far enough from land would surely fall off the edge. No thing, then, in itself, is either obvious or obscure. What we call "obvious" is that which we do not question, and whether or not we question it is often more a matter of culture than

---

Table 3-2

Some Aspects of Culture Found in All Known Societies

Beliefs about death	Inheritance rules
Bodily adornment	Interpretation of dreams
Calendar	Joking
Cleanliness training	Language
Cooking	Law
Cosmology	Magic
Courtship	Medicine
Dance	Mourning
Decorative art	Numerals
Divination	Personal names
Education	Population policy
Ethics	Property rights
Etiquette	Puberty customs
Faith healing	Religious ritual
Feasting	Sexual restrictions
Fire making	Soul concepts
Folklore	Sports
Games	Superstition
Gift giving	Surgery
Hair styles	Toolmaking
Hospitality	Trade
Hygiene	Weaning
Incest taboos	Weather control

Source: Murdock, 1943.

Puzzles: What Is a Person?

Is this a person? Why or why not? Are you aware of people who would answer these questions differently? What is the basis of the difference? How does this question differ from "Is the earth round?"

On both sides of the abortion controversy, sincere people argue about not when life literally begins, but at what point a fetus becomes a person in a social sense, subject to the protections of its community. As you can see in the section on beliefs, such arguments persist because they have less to do with objective scientific fact than with the beliefs that make up a basic part of culture.

objective reality. Just as beliefs provide us with categories for sorting perceptions and experiences, so they limit our awareness to those things that have a place in our cultural framework.

Cultural Relativism, Subcultures, and Ethnocentrism   Some aspects of culture—such as dancing, games, and language—are found in every known society and are thus referred to as **cultural universals** (see Table 3-2). In general, cultural symbols and ideas vary enormously among societies: What is regarded as truth in one may be unrecognized or regarded as nonsense in others. Ideas that exist in one culture may not exist in others or, if they do, they may be considered less important. This phenomenon is called **cultural relativism**. The belief that the deliberate killing of a child is murder does not exist in all cultures, for in some—such as Brazil's Tenetehara tribe—the killing of infants is a culturally legitimate practice. Most westerners experience kissing as a very pleasurable activity, but when the Thonga of Africa first encountered

the practice among visiting Europeans, they were horrified by what they regarded as "eating each other's saliva and dirt" (Hyde, 1979, p. 18).

Ideas also vary within cultures. A **subculture** is a distinctive set of cultural ideas that sets a group of people apart from the culture of its surrounding community or society. While U.S. culture generally defines marijuana as a dangerous substance, many knowingly share the belief that it is harmless, and such beliefs support and encourage its use among those who share in that subculture. This is especially true in the criminal subculture of smugglers and dealers who live the "fast lane" life of the drug trade (Adler, 1985).

Because cultural ideas define reality for us, we often judge the ideas of other cultures as incorrect, if not inferior—an attitude called **ethnocentrism** (Sumner, 1906). Most societies have, at one time or another, regarded outsiders as "barbarians" whose cultures were "uncivilized" or "stupid" simply because they were different. "How could they live that way?" we may ask. The essence of ethnocentrism is that we

In some cultures, as in France, dogs are cherished as pets who, when they die, are accorded the kind of treatment usually reserved for humans. In others, such as China, dogs are valued in quite a different way. How do these pictures make you feel, and how do you explain your feelings?

ONE STEP FURTHER 3-1:
Is Premarital Sex Wrong?

Only a minority (36 percent) of U.S. adults hold the value that premarital sex is always or almost always wrong (Davis and Smith, 1987), but like most values in complex societies, the positions people take on this issue depend strongly on their social characteristics. The figures in Table B-3-1 show differences by education, region of the country, family income, age, race, gender, and ethnicity in the percentage of adults saying that premarital sex is always or almost always wrong. If you have not yet studied Chapter 2, you might want to look at "How to Read a Table" on p. 000 before going on.

Notice how strongly some social characteristics affect the tendency to disapprove of premarital sex:

The more education people have, the less likely they are to disapprove.

Those living in New England are far less likely to disapprove than those from other regions, the south in particular.

The higher the family income is, the less likely adults are to disapprove.

The elderly are almost three times more likely to disapprove than younger people (62% vs. 23%).

Protestants disapprove more than Catholics (43% vs. 31%) and "others" (which include Jews and those with no religious preference) are a distant third (16%).

Whites and nonwhites are equally likely to disapprove.

Women are far more likely than men to disapprove (42% vs. 29%).

Those with British, Irish, or Asian ethnic backgrounds are most likely to disapprove, followed by those with African, European, or Latin American backgrounds who are equally likely to disapprove.

There has been a steady decline in strong disapproval of premarital sex, from 46% in 1972 to only 36% in 1986.

It is important, as you study these figures, to begin to acquire an appreciation for the idea of *variation*, that elements of culture such as beliefs and values change over time and differ from one social grouping to another, something which is a source of diversity and conflict.

---

rarely realize that people in other cultures might ask the same question of us.

In our own culture many of us believe that romantic love is essential for marriage, and if ours is the only culture we have ever known, we might believe that this reflects human nature rather than the beliefs and values of our own culture. If we study history, we find that in Western cultures the idea of romantic love is quite recent, dating back only to the fourteenth century, and in our own time there are many cultures, such as China's, in which the importance of romantic love in marriage is considerably less than in our own.

Ethnocentrism distorts our perceptions by encouraging us to think of the world only from our own point of view. People of European ancestry like to think that explorers, such as Columbus, "discovered" the "Dark Continent" of Africa and the "New World" of

North and South America. This would come as a great surprise to the peoples of many cultures who lived and thrived throughout those areas for centuries before any European set sail. To these peoples, what were mysteries to the Europeans were simply part of their everyday environment. It is only through the narrow eye of ethnocentrism that we in the U.S. can believe that before whites set foot in North America it was an "undiscovered" place (see Braudel, 1981).

Values: Shoulds and Shouldn'ts

Whereas beliefs define what is real, cultural **values** define goals by ranking forms of behavior and social arrangements in terms of their relative desirability (see One Step Further 3-1). "Honesty is better than dishonesty," "Competition is better than cooperation," and

Table B-3-1

Percent Who Say Premarital Sex Is Always or Almost Always Wrong by Selected Social Characteristics, United States, 1986

SOCIAL CHARACTERISTICS	PERCENT WHO DISAPPROVE OF PREMARITAL SEX	SOCIAL CHARACTERISTICS	PERCENT WHO DISAPPROVE OF PREMARITAL SEX
Education		*Religion*	
Less than high school graduate	48	Protestant	43
High school graduate	38	Catholic	31
Some college	29	Other	16
College degree or more	19		
		Race	
Region		White	36
New England	23	Nonwhite	38
Midwest	38		
South	45	*Gender*	
West	35	Female	42
		Male	29
Income			
Less than $14,000	41	*Ethnic Background*	
$14,000 to $34,000	36	Africa	32
$35,000 or more	28	United Kingdom/Ireland	40
		Europe	34
Age		Latin America	32
18–39	23	Asia	42
40–59	37		
60 and older	62		

Source: Computed from raw 1986 General Social Survey data.

"People should not engage in premarital sex" are all statements about what *should* be rather than about what *is*. Notice that in everyday speech people often use the word "belief" to refer to what is in fact a value. "I believe people *should* be honest" is a cultural value statement, since it describes what *ought* to be, not what is. "I believe that most people *are* basically honest," however, is a belief since it refers to what is rather than to what should be.

We are born preferring some states of being over others. Infants prefer warmth to extreme cold or heat, satiation to hunger or thirst, comfort to pain, and contact to isolation. There are no ideas involved in such preferences, for infants have no symbols with which to construct ideas.

Values, on the other hand, are abstract ideas about goals. Many readers of this book attend college, even if it involves considerable hardship, because they share the value that education, as an end in itself, is inherently desirable. It is "good" to be educated, and more education is better than less. Many also share the value that being able to use our brains well is more desirable than being able to use our hands well, and that high-prestige, high-paying jobs are more desirable than lower-prestige, lower-paying ones. The cultural desirability of education is reflected in individual choices, but as an idea it exists independently of individuals, just as do cultural beliefs.

Also, like beliefs, values are quite different from personal tastes and preferences. If you say, "I like mayonnaise," no one can say "you shouldn't like it," for it expresses a preference whose sole authority is you as an individual. A value judgment, on the other hand, rests on sources of authority outside the individual.

"You should not eat mayonnaise because the cholesterol in it is bad for your health" is a judgment that rests on the value we place on good health and long life (and the belief that cholesterol contributes to heart disease).

If you reply, "I don't care if I get heart disease," the response will likely be one of shock (except in a subculture that values eating whatever you like more than health), and the shocked person will know that others share that negative judgment. As a value, health is not more important than self-indulgence because you say it is; its relative "goodness" is part of a culture that ranks some ends higher than others.

Because we share them with others in our culture, such ideas influence our choices. They not only predispose us to strive in competition, to be honest and loyal, but they may also be used to manipulate our decisions. The advertising industry regularly uses established values to sell merchandise. The interior of a car may be described as "sexy"; spark plugs may be displayed next to a picture of a beautiful woman. In both cases, the masculine values placed on attracting, possessing, or having power over a woman are paired with the idea of buying something that has no inherent connection to them. If men accept the pairing, they are more likely to buy the product, not because they value it but because they value the goals the advertisement associates with it (Slater, 1970).

While we may pursue what we want, values powerfully influence what it is we want in the first place. As the German philosopher Schopenhauer put it, "We want what we will, but we don't will what we want" (in Harris, 1979, p. 60). We may *think* that we "freely choose" to compete with others rather than cooperate, but we are largely unaware that in a different culture we would place different values on such behavior and make very different choices. The Zuni Indians of the U.S. Southwest value cooperation more than competition:

> Personal authority is perhaps the most vigorously disparaged trait in Zuni. A man who thirsts for power or knowledge, who wishes to be as they scornfully phrase it, "a leader of his people," receives nothing but censure and will very likely be persecuted for sorcery. . . . The ideal man in Zuni is a person of dignity and affability who has never tried to lead, and who has never called forth comment from his neighbors. . . . Even in contests of skill like their foot races, if a man wins habitually he is debarred from running. They are interested in a game that a number can play with even chances, and an outstanding runner spoils the game: they will have none of him. (Benedict, 1934, p. 95)

When Values Conflict   We often hold values that, in a particular situation, produce conflict. Suppose you see a friend cheating on an exam. On the one hand, you value truth and honesty, for these are among the most fundamental values in a university. On the other hand, you value loyalty to friends. No matter what you choose to do—to tell on your friend or not—you will violate a value.

Values produce conflict because they make up a loose "grammar" of thought about the importance of different alternatives, and because we occupy many social positions, each with its own values. The values of "respect for the law" and "loyalty to one's friends" are *general* guidelines that do not tell us what to do in specific situations.

By presenting them with a series of dilemmas, Kohlberg (1963) studied how children choose among conflicting values. In one, a man's wife is desperately ill and can be saved only with a new drug invented by a local pharmacist. The pharmacist demands an exorbitant price, far beyond the man's ability to pay. The husband later breaks into the pharmacy and steals the drug. Was he wrong? The answer depends on which value we consider to be more important.

To Kohlberg, we learn moral rules in the same way we learn grammatical rules that allow us to construct and interpret sentences we have never encountered before. We learn only general rules—such as "It's wrong to steal" and "Put family first"—which we then apply to specific situations. Just as no one ever "taught" you the meaning of the preceding sentence, no one teaches us what to do if someone in our family needs a medicine that we cannot afford to buy. To solve moral dilemmas, then, we participate in a system of values, interpreting and choosing in search of what

---

Puzzles: Is Honesty Always the Best Policy?

How do you know when to lie and when to tell the truth? Have you ever been in a situation in which you were expected to lie and would be punished if you told the truth?

As you will see in the section on norms, both lying and telling the truth are forms of social behavior and whether or not we are expected to do one or the other depends very much on the social situation.

Roger Brown (1965) called "some reasonable consistency among judgment, feeling, and action" (p. 414).

Norms: Dos and Don'ts

Values provide us with general guidelines for behavior; norms are specific rules. A **norm** defines punishments or rewards for various forms of behavior according to people's positions in social relationships. While all actions have objective consequences, norms specify *social* consequences for the person performing the action.

If I kill a man, he dies; if I smack my lips at the dinner table, a noise results. The death and the noise are objective consequences. If I kill a man identified as "the enemy" in a war, however, his death is not the only consequence, for I might be rewarded with a medal. If I kill a man because I do not like the color of his eyes or disagree with his politics, on the other hand, I will be punished. If I smack my lips over dinner in the United States, people may show disapproval by frowning, but if I smack them in India, people are more likely to smile at me. If I am caught stealing a traveler's suitcase in the United States, I might be sent to jail; in the Sudan in 1984, however, the penalty for one unfortunate thief was to have his right hand cut off in a public ceremony.

In each case, the link between the act and the consequences for the actor is artificial; it is not inherent in the act itself. The statements "If you kill an enemy, you will get a medal" and "If you kill a man because you don't like him you will be punished" are norms that link specific acts to social responses that we can expect from other people who share our culture. The responses are called **sanctions**, and they take the form of rewards (such as medals) or punishments (such as imprisonment). When we are punished for violating a norm (or rewarded for conforming to one), it is not because of what we did, it is because of the *rule*; if the rule changes, the same behavior no longer brings with it the same sanctions (Durkheim, 1924).

The basic types of norms are *folkways* and *mores* (pronounced "morayz"), each of which can take the form of a *law*.

Folkways   In a classic work, William Graham Sumner (1906) defined a society's **folkways** as the set of manners and customary acts that characterize everyday life in a society. As a set of norms, folkways regulate behavior whose consequences are relatively trivial and in which the resulting sanctions tend to be correspondingly mild.

Folkways include customs that govern how people greet each other when they meet. Soviet Premier Mikhail Gorbachev would never greet Ronald Reagan as he would one of his own countrymen, and both men would feel quite out of place if they had to bow in a traditional Japanese greeting.

We are not supposed to stare at people or stand too close when talking with them. We are expected to face front in elevators, replace caps on toothpaste tubes, return library books on time, and not refer to our parents by their first name.

Folkways are a particularly fluid form of norm, subject to rapid change, inconsistent application, and enormous variation among the world's cultures. It was not very long ago that men were expected to open doors for women, but now expectations have changed considerably, and the simple act of passing through a doorway can be an occasion for substantial negotiation and uncertainty (Walum, 1974).

The application of folkways, as with all norms, depends on the situation (see Edgerton, 1985). Staring at a stranger on a bus violates a folkway, but we are expected to stare at performers in a theater. To be seen by others is vital to us, but folkways regulate this simple act.

Folkways also vary enormously from one culture to another. In Latin cultures people are expected to stand very close to each other when talking, so close that North Americans and Europeans feel very uncomfortable (Hall, 1969). Compared with the British upper class, Americans are far more likely to assume familiarity by calling people by their first name. The Japanese remove their shoes whenever they enter a house and Icelanders consider it impolite to leave a party before three or four o'clock in the morning.

A society's folkways describe the "fine texture" of everyday life, the manners and customs that its members take for granted as "the way we do things." Only when we encounter the folkways of different cultures do we become aware of ours as peculiar rather than as the "natural" way of going about life.

Mores and Morality   Whereas folkways regulate the trivial aspects of social interaction, a society's mores focus on more serious expectations about behavior. **Mores** are norms that reflect deeply held cultural ideals about how people should behave (Sumner, 1906). While folkways distinguish between relatively unimportant categories—polite and impolite, clean and neat, sophisticated and vulgar—mores make more important distinctions, such as those between "good" and "bad," "virtuous" and "sinful," "laudable" and "repugnant." A society's mores define standards of behavior that are more serious than those defined by folkways, and punishment for their violation tends to be both more certain and more severe.

Puzzles: Making Moral Decisions

Before reading on, imagine that you are a pediatrician and one of your newborn infant patients suffers from a serious condition that will most likely leave it both paralyzed and severely brain damaged. The parents insist that you take no extreme measures to keep the baby alive. One of your colleagues vehemently disagrees, arguing that it is your duty as a doctor to do everything you can to keep every patient alive. What would you do? How would you go about making your decision?

As you read on, think about moral decisions and how we make them.

There is a story about two children, the first of whom has two apples, one large and the other small. The first offers to share them. When the second child takes the large apple, the first protests, "Hey, why'd you take the big one?"

"Which one would you have taken?" asks the second child.

"The small one."

"Then you got what you wanted, didn't you?"

The first child is outraged because the second ignored an important moral principle: When one person offers something to another, the recipient is expected to reciprocate—to return the favor—by not taking full advantage of the choice. There is actually an exchange going on in this interaction—an apple in exchange for restraint and moderation—and the second child's failure to reciprocate violates important cultural ideas about "fairness" and "reciprocity" (Gouldner, 1960; see also Fisher, Nadler, and DePaulo, 1983).

Mores focus on what most of us think of as morality, and several social characteristics distinguish moral acts from immoral ones. First, moral acts never have the actor's self-interest as their only goal. This is what distinguishes Robin Hood's acts of stealing from similar acts by someone who steals for personal gain. This does not imply that an act is immoral if done purely for personal reasons: to run into a burning house to save people's lives is a moral act, but to stay outside out of concern for our own lives usually will be

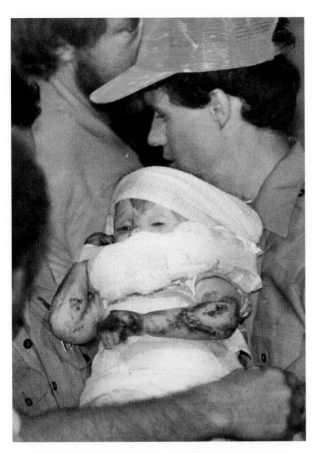

In Midland, Texas, rescuers worked feverishly for 58 hours—some at the risk of their lives—to rescue Jessica McClure, a small child who had fallen down a well. Several months later, two different groups of rescuers organized to compete for financially lucrative contracts for movie rights to their stories. From a social point of view, how does this development affect the moral standing of their heroism?

excused. A moral act thus differs from other acts in that it is performed in the interests of other people.

The second social characteristic of moral acts is that they have a quality of command. We do them because we are supposed to, out of a sense of duty and obligation, not simply to another individual, but to the values embodied in the act (the value of honesty or of a human life). We refrain from some acts simply because they are forbidden in our culture. If a cashier in a store gives us too much change and we knowingly take it, we do not simply hurt the cashier or the company; we violate one of the terms of our participation in social

life. If we return the money, we affirm our place in society and feel the pleasure of belonging.

Third, moral acts have an element of social desirability. They are "good," just as immoral acts are "bad," and we feel genuine pleasure simply from doing "the right thing" (and pain from doing "the wrong thing"), whether or not we tell other people and bask in the glow of their approval.

Finally, ideas about morality are sacred. Because they reflect the deepest collective feelings about who we are and should be, we attach strong feelings to them. While specific laws may allow some people to do things forbidden to others, the idea that "no one is above the law" is a moral one that applies to us all, even, as Richard Nixon discovered, someone who is the president of the United States.

As with folkways, the application of mores often depends on the situation. While dishonesty violates general cultural mores, there are situations in which it is permitted or expected. As Bok (1979) pointed out, mores permit us to lie in order to save a life or mislead an enemy during wartime. Scientists may deceive and lie to subjects about the aims of their research, parents lie to their children about everything from the existence of Santa Claus to the details of sexual behavior, and physicians may lie by understating the true condition of terminally ill patients.

There is also considerable cross-cultural variation in the definition of moral behavior. Cannibal tribes in Oceania do not consider it immoral to eat human flesh, and the Nayar of India do not define adultery as immoral. Eating pork violates the mores of Orthodox Jews, but in other cultures the consumption of pork is part of an annual celebration of great importance (Harris, 1974). In addition, while the mores of all known cultures prohibit murder, there is considerable variation in its definition. In Western cultures, killing for personal revenge is defined and punished as murder, but in some other cultures killing to avenge the murder of a relative is expected (see also One Step Further 3-2, pp. 72—73).

Mores extend beyond the rightness or wrongness of certain acts to the most profound ideas of what life in a society is supposed to be about. Mores have been used throughout history to justify everything from self-sacrifice and charity to outrageous cruelty. The murder of over 6 million Jews during the Holocaust was seen by the Nazis as "the final solution" to the "Jewish problem" that, they believed, stood between them and the realization of the "supremacy of the

ONE STEP FURTHER 3-2:
Homosexuality: Norms and Values

Over many years of national surveys, an over-whelming majority (75%) of the adult U.S. population has held the value that homosexual behavior is always wrong. As the percentages in Table B-3-2 show, however, there is considerable variation in the strength of this value.

Even more interesting, however, is the fact that although there is overwhelming support for *values* against homosexual behavior, in many states—par-ticularly in New England, the Midwest, and the Far West—there are no laws forbidding homosexual behavior, in spite of the 1987 Supreme Court decision upholding the constitutional right of states to enact such laws. As you can see from Figure B-3-2, even when a value is strongly supported, there often are great differences in the kinds of norms that are used to support and enforce it.

Figure B-3-2   Sodomy Laws in the United States

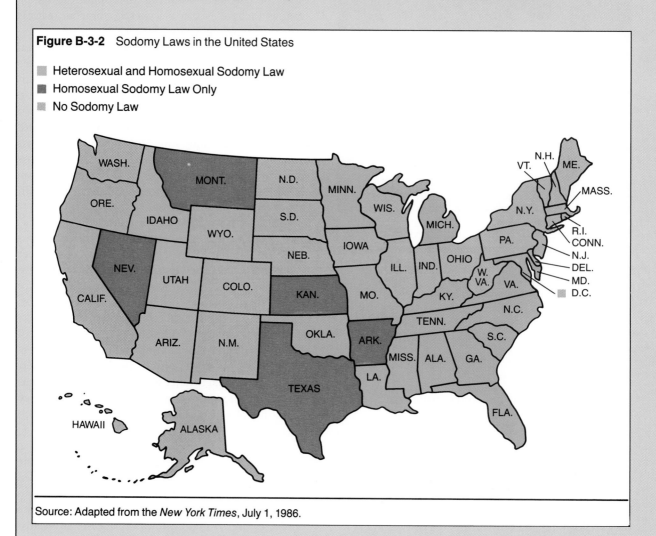

Source: Adapted from the *New York Times*, July 1, 1986.

Table B-3-2

Percent Who Say Homosexual Behavior Is Always Wrong, by Selected Social Characteristics, United States, 1984.

SOCIAL CHARACTERISTICS	PERCENT WHO STRONGLY DISAPPROVE OF HOMOSEXUAL BEHAVIOR
Education	
Less than high school graduate	87
High school graduate	79
Some college or more	58
Income	
Less than $7,000	75
$7,000 to $14,999	70
$15,000 to $24,999	67
$25,000 or more	60
Age	
Less than 30	66
30–39	61
40–49	77
50–64	84
65 and older	86
Religion	
Protestant	80
Catholic	68
Other	49
None	41
Race	
White	71
Nonwhite	86
Gender	
Female	74
Male	72

Source: Computed from raw 1984 General Social Survey data.

Aryan race." To many Nazis, the execution of millions of men, women, and children was part of a crusade for racial "purity," full of moral self-righteousness; while, to those who did not share their vision, the Holocaust was a crime of unimaginable immorality and horror (see Dawidowicz, 1975).

Laws   As norms, both folkways and mores involve sanctions which can be either informal or formal. **Informal sanctions** are not clearly defined and anyone has the right to impose them. If we belch loudly in the company of others, anyone has the right to impose a variety of sanctions ranging from the slightest frown to an angry outburst.

Formal sanctions, on the other hand, are clearly defined and people in specialized social positions have the power and responsibility to impose them. If I steal your radio, it is not up to you to enforce the sanctions attached to the norm prohibiting theft. The sanctions as well as the procedures for deciding if and how to apply them are clearly specified; and specific people are authorized to apprehend me, determine my guilt or innocence, and impose punishment. Norms with formal sanctions are called **laws**.

Criminal law links specific acts with punishments (expulsion from school for cheating; imprisonment for stealing; fines for reckless driving). To violate such a law is not simply an act against an individual, for it represents an act against society itself. When someone commits murder, we may feel outrage regardless of our relationship to the victim, and it is the state that prosecutes the case, not the victim's friends and family.

Civil law regulates social relationships and, when possible, undoes the negative effects of a particular act. Civil law regulates relationships among producers, buyers, and sellers (commercial law); the functioning of courts and their officers (procedural law); the relationship between citizens and their government (constitutional law); and the relationships among family members (family law), determining, for example, which parent gets custody of children in case of divorce. In addition, if you slip on a skateboard on my front porch and break your leg, the state will not prosecute me under criminal law; but you might sue me in order to pay for your hospital bills and compensate you for the effects of my negligence.

One of the most basic cultural ideas in civil law is that of the *contract*, which is an agreement between two parties to exchange one thing for another: I will give you $5,000 if you will paint my house. The idea of a contract clearly illustrates the fact that norms exist apart from individuals, for the power behind the agreement extends beyond the people who are directly involved. If I refuse to pay you when you fulfill your part of the bargain, society itself supports your claim—*not* out of concern for you as an individual, but to preserve the culturally valued idea of a contract. Society is an "interested party" in all contracts made between individuals (Durkheim, 1893/1933).

Formal and informal sanctions are used to enforce both folkways and mores. While mores usually involve formal sanctions (as in the case of murder), in some cases (such as lying to a friend) the sanctions are informal. Spitting on a sidewalk violates a folkway, but the sanctions are formal (it is against the law); but if we spit on the floor at a party, the sanctions are informal (the host cannot have us arrested). Note, however, that while specific laws may or may not have a moral content (overparking is not immoral, but murder is), the *idea* of "the law" is a profoundly moral one.

Attitudes: Evaluation and Feeling

Unlike beliefs, values, and norms, cultural attitudes focus on emotions. As we saw in Chapter 1, **attitudes** are positive or negative evaluations of objects, people, or situations that predispose us to feel and behave toward them in positive or negative ways (Allport, 1935; Hill, 1981). Although they involve beliefs and values, what sets attitudes apart are the feelings that flow from these beliefs and values, feelings such as hatred, reverence, awe, disgust, affection, contempt, and pity. This means that the key to identifying a cultural attitude is to see the emotions that it involves.

We have the ability to experience and display many emotions, but to understand their ebb and flow, we must go beyond the psychology of individual motives to the cultures that produce patterns of belief, feeling, and behavior. The shared love of a country—patriotism—is an attitude that encompasses beliefs ("our country is the best there is") and emotions (pride, excitement, love) and makes us more likely to behave aggressively toward anyone who threatens our positive national image.

In many respects, popular U.S. sports such as hockey and football show many of the characteristics of warfare, complete with injuries and hatred of the "enemy." From a cultural point of view, hockey players (and their fans) are not violent because of an aggressive "human nature"; rather, they are aggressive because they play hockey and share in its subcultural attitudes.

Guilt, pride, shame, sympathy, love, and gratitude are attitudes that exist only in a social context (Clark, 1987; Gordon, 1981; Kemper, 1987). Without culture, there is no occasion for such emotions, for they rest on beliefs and values used to interpret and judge behavior. Fear exists as a primary emotion in many animal species, but only in a cultural context do we find the concept of "cowardice" and the shame that goes with it.

All attitudes are based on beliefs, but people may share an attitude without sharing a particular belief, just as they may share a belief without sharing a related attitude. The attitude of racial hatred is often justified by a variety of beliefs such as a belief in the genetic inferiority of a hated group. Others, however, might feel just as strongly but justify their attitude with a different belief—such as "they're cruel and dirty."

Cultural ideas influence what we believe, value, feel, and do. Just as gravity pulls our bodies toward the center of the earth, cultural ideas "pull" us toward centers of meaning, value, and expectation. We resist—even defy—gravity in many ways; in the simplest act of standing up an individual resists gravity's pull. We also resist, and sometimes defy, the constraining force of culture as when we play with language or violate norms.

Consequently, culture does not determine who we are, what we feel and think, or what we do. Nor do we act in a vacuum, free of the limitations imposed by social environments. The character of our lives and our relationships with one another are, rather, the result of an *interaction* between ourselves and our environments.

MATERIAL CULTURE: THINGS FROM IDEAS AND IDEAS FROM THINGS

The creation of material objects lies at the core of human existence, and the development of material culture takes place only through a web of social relationships. We produce objects not only to satisfy our needs for them, but also because "free, conscious activity" and "productive life" are important aspects of what makes us human (Marx, in Schaff, 1970, p. 125).

Thus, through the course of history, people have developed an astonishing variety of objects that affect our lives. The invention of the plow and wheel, around 6,000 years ago, revolutionized the ability of humans to travel, produce food, and conduct trade. The development of printing, first by the Chinese in the fifth century A.D. and then with Gutenberg's invention of movable type in the fifteenth century, stimulated a rapid spread of literacy and new ideas.

The Industrial Revolution began in the middle of the eighteenth century with the invention of machines such as textile looms and the use of new sources of power, such as steam. The application of the steam engine to transportation in the mid-1800s vastly expanded the markets for goods and hence stimulated their production. The last hundred years have seen the rapid development of mass production, the automobile, light and durable plastics, and revolutions in communications and computer technology.

Such objects are cultural in that they arise from the human ability to think in symbolic terms, to share the resulting knowledge, and to build on previous inventions in the creation of others. They also reflect cultural values and beliefs. The rapid development of industrial technology reflects not only possessions as a value, but, in capitalist societies, the value of profit, which is increased by mechanization and more efficient production.

The development of material culture is often a collective response to the pressures of population and ecology. Growing populations require new methods for satisfying subsistence needs. Those methods, in turn, often create the need for further innovation. When coal was first used as a source of power in the United States it was easy to obtain: in Pennsylvania, it lay on the surface of the earth. As we consumed it in greater and greater quantities, it became necessary to go underground, and this required more sophisticated machines to drill and haul the coal.

Material culture is also social in its influence on our thought, behavior, and experience. The automobile did more than allow increased mobility; it also contributed to the growth of cities and "rush hours" with all their tensions. It became a place for young people to be alone, beyond the watchful eyes of parents; and, for many, it provided an instrument for aggression, self-expression, and displays of wealth and individuality.

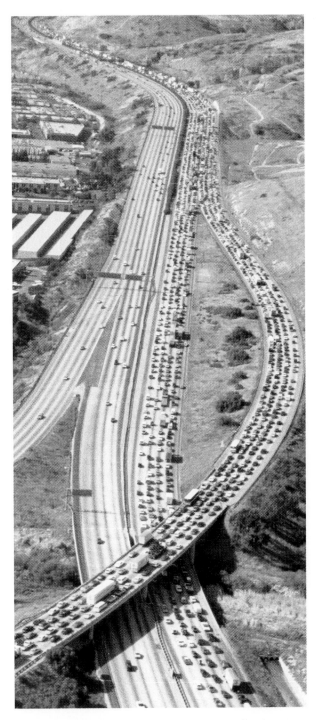

Few examples of material culture have had such dramatic and far-reaching effects as the automobile. From air pollution, patterns of urban development, and massive traffic jams to getting a driver's license as a major sign of growing up, cars are embedded in the American way of life.

The relationship between material and non-material culture is both complex and reciprocal. The explosive growth in electronics and computer technology, for example, raises new threats to rights of privacy. Since 1983 there has been growing alarm over the relative ease with which the operators of home computers can gain access to records stored in computers in hospitals, universities, banks, military research laboratories, and other institutions. When this was first discovered in 1983, there were no laws that defined it as a crime, because the spread of computer technology had been so rapid that such crimes had not come up as a serious possibility. As new laws are passed in order to protect the security of computers and the right to privacy, new technology must be invented to secure computers against unauthorized access.

An even more important aspect of material culture is that objects, once created, become independent parts of their creators' culture. Computers do only what programmers and operators tell them to do, and yet we often blame computers for everything from errors on telephone bills to the junk mail we would rather not receive. With the blame often goes the belief that computers somehow have the power to control our lives, power beyond what their human creators and operators choose to do with them. As machines and other products of material culture assume greater and greater importance in our lives, we may "begin to feel ourselves as things that are parts of the surrounding world of things" (Schaff, 1970, p. 106).

The concepts of material and nonmaterial culture are tools that make up a major part of the sociological perspective. Social environments, however, are more than a vast collection of ideas and objects swirling about us like a thick soup. They are organized into social relationships that produce patterns of expectation and behavior. These patterns represent the second major sociological concept, social structure, the subject of Chapter 4.

SUMMARY

1. Although culture consists of both material and nonmaterial products, the essence of culture is nonmaterial and is made up of abstract beliefs, values, attitudes, and norms. These, in turn, are expressed through symbols: objects, characteristics of objects, gestures, or words that represent more than themselves. Language is a collection of symbols and rules for their use shared by those who make up a speech community.

2. Language serves several social functions. It allows people to express experience, to store records of it, and to assume that others know what they mean when they write or talk; it allows members of a speech community to distinguish between themselves and outsiders; and it often substitutes for physical contact. In addition, performative language is a meaningful action that alters people's positions in social relationships.

3. Cultural relativism refers to the fact that the importance of a particular cultural product varies from one social environment to another. Ethnocentrism describes the tendency of people to regard other cultures or subcultures as inferior to their own. The concepts of cultural relativism and ethnocentrism can also apply within a society in relation to subcultures, which set a group apart from a surrounding community or society.

4. Beliefs are statements about reality, and are cultural only if their authority lies outside of individuals in the shared assumption that other people support them. Values rank behavior and social arrangements in terms of relative desirability. Values often conflict because they are loose guidelines for making choices and because we occupy positions in many different relationships, each governed by its own set of values.

5. Norms are rules that prescribe sanctions—punishments or rewards—for behavior according to people's positions in social relationships. Sanctions may be either informal—loosely defined with no specific people authorized to impose them—or formal—clearly defined with specific people empowered to deliver them.

6. There are three kinds of norms. Folkways are norms (such as table manners) that regulate relatively trivial behaviors in everyday social interactions. Mores, however, reflect deeply held ideas about how people should behave. Norms with formal sanctions are called laws. Criminal law links specific acts with punishments, while civil law regulates social relationships (such as marriage and divorce), deals with contracts, and undoes the effects of an action (as when someone sues someone else to pay for damaged property).

7. Attitudes are predispositions to feel positive or negative emotions toward people and to behave toward them in positive or negative ways. Attitudes also include the feelings people have toward themselves, such as guilt, pride, or shame.

8. Material culture consists of objects people make as they interact with each other and the physical world. The relationship between material and nonmaterial culture is complex and reciprocal. Ideas often lead to the creation of objects, but objects can become so important a part of the environment that they affect the cultural ideas that regulate social interaction.

KEY TERMS

cultural relativism   65
cultural universals   65
culture   57

    attitude   74
    belief   63
    gesture   57
    language   60

        performative language   62
        speech community   61

    norm   69

        civil law   73
        criminal law   73
        folkways   69
        formal sanction   73
        informal sanction   73
        law   73
        mores   70
        sanction   69

    symbol   57
    value   66

ethnocentrism   65
subculture   65

Looking Elsewhere

Although you will be reading about culture throughout *Human Arrangements*, having studied this chapter you may want to look at some discussions with a particularly strong cultural focus, which include

- the importance of language in socialization (Chapter 6, pp. 138–41)
- language and gender roles (Chapter 13, pp. 343–45)
- the controversy over English as the official language of the U.S. (Chapter 12, p. 316)
- technology and material culture (Chapter 5, pp. 123–24; Chapter 17, pp. 470–75)

RECOMMENDED READINGS

BENEDICT, R. (1960). *Patterns of culture.* New York: New American Library (paperback). A classic analysis of cultural relativism with a special emphasis on native American tribes. (Original work published 1934.)

HARRIS, M. (1985). *Good to eat: Riddles of food and culture.* New York: Simon and Schuster. Anthropologist Marvin Harris offers a rich and fascinating look at the cultural basis of what people like (and don't like) to eat.

SLATER, P. (1976). *The pursuit of loneliness* (rev. ed.). Boston: Beacon Press (paperback). A passionate and articulate analysis in which a sociologist shows how cultural values can promote social isolation and loneliness.

ZBOROWSKI, M. (1953). Cultural components in responses to pain. *Journal of Social Issues, 8,* 16–31. A fascinating exploration into ethnic differences in the ways people experience and respond to pain in a hospital setting.

4 Social Structure

Social structure is the second major concept that defines the sociological perspective. It describes the ways in which cultural ideas are organized in patterns of expectation, producing the countless relationships we participate in during our lives, the limits they impose on our choices, and the conflicts that inevitably result; and it describes the place of each relationship in a complex web of patterns that give predictable form to social life.

This chapter looks closely at this key concept and the different characteristics of social relationships that affect how we behave in relation to one another.

THE CONCEPT OF SOCIAL STRUCTURE

One night an insurance agent named George feels ill and goes to the hospital emergency room. A doctor named Mary takes his case, and they talk in a small room. They have never met before, yet they share some expectations: he will call her "doctor," not "Mary"; he will answer her questions as accurately as he can; he will follow her advice; and he will pay for her services. They also share the expectations that she knows what she is doing, that she will confine herself to questions that are relevant to his illness, and that she will keep his answers in strict confidence. While both are capable of a vast array of acts, they limit themselves to a very narrow range: they do not go to sleep or read aloud from the Bible; she does not undress (although he might), and he does not try to sell her an insurance policy.

George and Mary would behave differently relaxing at home with their families, eating dinner in a restaurant, or meeting in the office of his insurance agency. Moreover, if the physician were Harry and the patient were Susan, the expectations would be the same. In a different culture, however—such as one

in which witch doctors heal the sick—the patterns would be very different. Among the Mojave Indians in the American Southwest the "medicine man" was known more for his power to kill than his power to heal, and the Mojave believed that those who were killed by the medicine man's sorcery were under his power in the afterlife. The Mojave medicine man often had more to gain by the death of patients than by their survival (Benedict, 1934).

The behavior of physicians and patients is limited by a set of shared expectations about what is and is not supposed to take place. These expectations form a pattern that we recognize, and the pattern imposes limits on both participants regardless of who they are as individuals.

The Three Aspects of Social Structure

The concept of social structure rests on the idea that "a whole is more than the sum of its parts." A human face is not simply a collection of parts—of two eyes, a nose and mouth, cheeks, lips, chin and forehead. What makes it recognizable as a human face is the *arrangement* of those parts in relation to one another. Similarly, the behavior of physicians and patients cannot be understood solely in terms of their individual characteristics. It is their arrangement in relation to each other, and their orientations to that arrangement that produce the unique interactions of doctor and patient (Merton, 1968). The first aspect of **social structure** is *the arrangement of individuals in social relationships with patterned expectations.*

The second aspect describes *patterned expectations among groups.* The delivery of medical services is not simply organized around interactions between doctors and patients. Complex organizations such as hospitals, insurance companies, and government agencies also have social relationships with one another: insurance companies interact with hospitals in setting fees and paying claims; governments make rules that regulate insurance companies and hospitals and grant physicians the right to practice medicine.

The third aspect of social structure is *the distribution of people among various social positions* (there are many more patients than physicians) *as well as the distribution of various kinds of rewards, the most sociologically important of which are wealth, power, and prestige* (most of the wealth in the U.S. is held by a small fraction of the population). The fact that there are relatively few skilled brain surgeons means that brain surgeons are always in demand; as a result, they can charge very high fees for their work.

In each of its three aspects, the concept of social structure refers to the arrangement of people and groups in relation to one another, and these arrangements exist independently of the people who participate in them. Individuals do not have the power to decide arbitrarily what those expectations will be. A doctor in the U.S. does not have the right to suddenly decide to start behaving like a Mojave medicine man.

Expectations that define social relationships are also reciprocal, and vary from one social relationship to another. Both physician and patient orient their actions in relation to their expectations of the other. A person cannot perform as a physician without a pa-

tient, nor can one be a patient without a physician. If George confides a secret about his health to Mary while he is her patient in the hospital, she may not tell the world about it; but if he meets her in a bar and tells the same secret, she is not bound by the physician–patient relationship to keep it confidential. In addition, while George is legally bound to pay for Mary's advice in the hospital, anything she tells him in a bar is free of charge.

Social Statuses and Status Sets

The positions that we occupy in social relationships are called **social statuses** (not to be confused with the common use of "status" to refer to prestige), and they are the building blocks of social structures (Linton, 1936). To say "He is a doctor's patient" describes one of George's social statuses. The definition of a baseball team centers on a set of statuses—outfielder, pitcher, catcher, shortstop, and so on—that makes up its structure.

A social status exists only in relation to other statuses: the status "college student" has no meaning except in relation to other positions such as "college teacher" or "college administrator." Not all characteristics are statuses. Being left- or right-handed is not a

The Marx brothers make us laugh because they turn the world upside down by violating expectations of how people are supposed to perform their roles. In this scene from "A Night at the Opera," people have crowded into a ship's stateroom to perform a task or take care of a problem created by the person who entered before.

As this picture of John Kennedy as both president and father illustrates, all of us occupy different statuses that make up our status sets.

Puzzles: What Is Your Racial Status?

If you got a copy of your birth certificate and found that it described your race as something other than you consider it to be, would it bother you? Why? How would you feel about showing the certificate to other people? Are there some people you would not want to see it? Why? (See the opening pages of Chapter 12.)

position in a social relationship, for it does not carry with it patterned expectations. Being blind, deaf, or mentally handicapped, however, can be a social status if the condition affects people's expectations.

The most enduring statuses are **ascribed** (or assigned) to us at birth. These include age, race, ethnicity, and gender. Others are **achieved** (or acquired), such as educational attainment and occupation. Unlike achieved statuses, it is very difficult if not impossible to change an ascribed status. (It is true that some people undergo sex-change surgery, and we all change our age status—but only in one direction.) We can, however, control with greater success how others *perceive* our ascribed statuses. People often alter various aspects of their appearance—with hair styles, clothing, cosmetics, and even plastic surgery—to affect others' perception of their age.

The third type of status is **temporary**, and this can be either *situational* or *transitional*. A **situational status** is a position that we occupy only while we are in a particular situation. When we walk into a store, we enter the status of "customer," and when we walk out, we leave that status and enter others such as "pedestrian" or "bus passenger." Some states of being are also temporary statuses: when a person believes another to be asleep or sick their expectations of each

other are different from those they might have when both are awake or well (Parsons, 1951).

A **transitional status** is one that is socially structured to be occupied for a limited time as a bridge between statuses (Coser, 1966). The status "engaged to be married" is a transition from "single person" to "spouse," just as "probation" is a status designed to link "nonemployee" with "permanent employee."

Since statuses are *positions* in social relationships, they exist independently of the individuals who occupy them. Even though no one in a given year might occupy the status of "presidential candidate" the social position still exists. This distinction is crucial, for it draws our attention to the limitations of a particular position over and above the personal characteristics of whoever occupies it. A psychologist, for example, might be interested in President *Reagan*; but a sociologist would be interested in *President* Reagan.

We all occupy a wide variety of social statuses. The most socially important status we occupy is called a **master status** because it affects almost every aspect of our lives. In racially segregated South Africa race is a master status. In countries such as the United States, occupation is usually treated as a master status.

If you made a list of all the statuses you occupy, the result would be your **status set** (Merton, 1968). Figure 4-1 (p. 82) shows a portion of the status set for Mary, the doctor in our opening example.

Roles and Role Sets

The importance of social structure for understanding behavior lies in the patterned expectations of those who occupy social statuses. Attached to each status is a **role**, a set of beliefs, values, attitudes, and norms that define expectations shared by status occupants in their relationships with the occupants of other statuses (Linton, 1936; see also Heiss, 1981). Mary and George

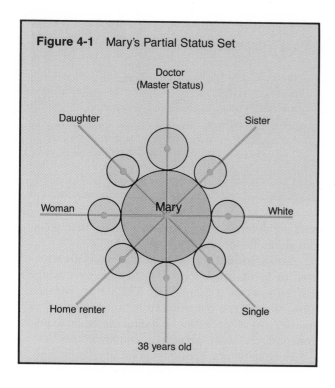

Figure 4-1 Mary's Partial Status Set

Doctor (Master Status)

Daughter

Sister

Woman

Mary

White

Home renter

Single

38 years old

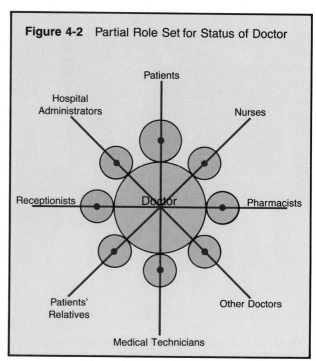

Figure 4-2 Partial Role Set for Status of Doctor

Patients

Hospital Administrators

Nurses

Receptionists

Doctor

Pharmacists

Patients' Relatives

Other Doctors

Medical Technicians

play the roles of doctor and patient in relation to each other.

Roles are collections of ideas about the thoughts, feelings, and behavior of status occupants, and **role performance** is behavior that results from our orientation to those ideas. Infants who cry because they are hungry are not performing a role, because they are not orienting themselves to a set of cultural expectations attached to the statuses of infant and parent. Doctors and patients, however, are limited by cultural ideas such as the value placed on health and the belief that doctors know more about medicine than do patients.

Notice, however, that when doctors interact with one another, the expectations change, even though they still occupy the status of "doctor." They are more likely to treat one another as equals, less likely to tell one another what to do. Why does the role change?

The answer is that the content of a particular role depends on the other statuses involved in the relationship. When Mary performs the role of doctor in relation to George the patient, George is Mary's **role partner**, and Mary is George's role partner. A status occupant may have relationships with several different role partners, and each relationship involves different expectations.

Doctors have role relationships with patients, patients' relatives, nurses, hospital administrators, recep-

tionists, and other doctors. In other words, "doctor," by virtue of being a doctor, has a *set* of roles (called a **role set**) with the occupants of other statuses (Merton, 1968). Figure 4-2 shows the role set for Mary's master status "doctor."

Defining Situations (and Ourselves)

Our status and role sets strongly influence who other people think we are and who *we* think we are. If a stranger asks us to describe ourselves, we are unlikely to talk about our personalities, because personalities do not locate us in social space. Most people want to know our age, gender, occupation, marital status, educational attainment, income, sexual orientation, race, and ethnic background, because such characteristics help locate us in relation to patterns of cultural values, beliefs, norms, and attitudes. If people believe we are married or fabulously wealthy, they perceive and treat us differently than they do if they believe we are single or desperately poor.

When we identify our statuses and those of the people we interact with, we are **defining the situation**, and until we do this, we feel uncomfortable precisely because we do not know "where we are" socially. It is for this reason that people exert so much pressure on us to reveal our social statuses, and take it very seriously when we misrepresent ourselves. If we become romantically involved with someone whom we later discover is married, we are more than disappointed: we feel deceived and embarrassed because we oriented our behavior and feelings to a situation that did not in fact exist.

The structure of social life—which we take for granted most of the time—is complex. We all occupy many different statuses (making up our status set), and for each status, we play a variety of roles (a role set). In addition, we are often influenced by several roles at one time. To see the inherent complexity of our status and role sets helps us appreciate the inevitability of conflict, ambivalence, and ambiguity as we try to satisfy conflicting expectations.

Status Strain and Role Strain

Because we occupy many statuses, each with its own role set, we frequently experience **status strain**—the difficulty in satisfying role requirements for different statuses (Merton, 1968).

In 1986, 59 percent of working women in the U.S. were married, and 37 percent lived with children under the age of 18 (U.S. Census Bureau, 1986a). As a college professor, a woman is expected to devote her days to her work, while as a mother she is expected to care for her children—to stay home with them when they are sick and respond to emergencies at school. As a wife, she is expected to keep house and be supportive of her husband's career. The three statuses—professor, mother, and wife—carry with them roles whose expectations can often produce strain within the status set (see One Step Further 4-1, p. 84).

Not all status strain is so clear-cut, for we are often unaware of statuses that produce conflict. People's expectations of police officers differ according to the officer's gender. When officers are on duty, "police officer" is their **manifest status** because that is the status that defines their role set. Like everyone else, however, police officers occupy other statuses—such as male, female, father, mother, husband, wife—that make up their status sets. When these statuses are socially defined as irrelevant in a situation, they are called **latent statuses**. They are important because although they are defined as irrelevant, they often affect performance in a manifest status.

As a latent status, gender often influences people's expectations. Women police officers may be

People often treat us according to our latent statuses. Jane Fonda is a political activist and an actress testifying before the U.S. Senate on the plight of American farmers. She was an antiwar activist during the Vietnam War, and after traveling to North Vietnam was accused of betraying her country. In 1988, while in New England to make a movie, many people treated her as an actress, but others saw her as a controversial political figure and protested her plans.

barred from hazardous duty (and denied an avenue toward promotion). In some occupations, a latent status is considered to be important enough to be incorporated into the manifest status, creating such statuses as "policewoman," "chairwoman," and "congresswoman."

Strain also occurs within a role set, for when we occupy a status, we must orient ourselves to a variety of role partners. The professor's students expect her to pay attention to them, to give them her time and energy; at the same time, other professors expect her to conduct research, serve on committees, and write books and articles. This kind of conflict, occurring within the role set attached to a single status, is called **role strain**.

Responses to Strain   There are many ways of lowering status and role strain (Merton, 1968). We are often more committed to one role than to another and act accordingly. In the case of the role strain previously mentioned, the professor may choose to comply with the expectations that carry the more severe

ONE STEP FURTHER 4-1:
Status Strain and Changes in Women's Status Sets

As status sets become more complicated, the potential for status strain increases. For women this has been particularly true as they become more likely to combine marriage, motherhood, and paid employment. In Figure B-4-1, the top line shows changes in the percentage of U.S. women who combine two of these statuses—married and working—since 1890. In 1890 only 2.5% of all women were both working and married. By 1986, however, the percentage was twelve times as large—30%—indicating that close to one out of every three women had

to deal with the conflicting demands of marriage and work.

Just as dramatic are more recent increases in the percentage of women combining all three statuses (bottom line). Since 1948, the percentage who are married working mothers has almost tripled from 5.7% to 16.3%. Although the line shows that the rate of increase in this status strain "Triple-Threat" slowed somewhat during the 1970s it is accelerating again in the 1980s as more and more women try to combine work and family life.

Figure B-4-1

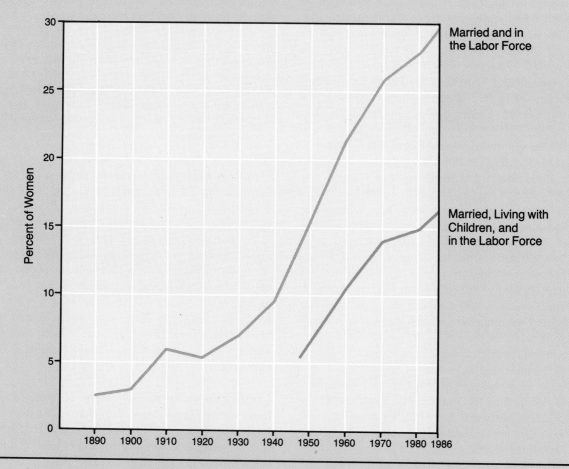

Source: Computed from U.S. Census Bureau, 1975a, 1986a.

punishment if violated (losing a job is more serious than making students angry).

We can also minimize strain by choosing statuses whose roles do not conflict with one another, as students do when they enroll in easy courses to balance their demanding ones. What can we do, however, when we cannot avoid conflicting roles?

One tactic is to make our behavior in one of the roles less visible so that we can violate its expectations in greater safety. National politicians, who must satisfy several conflicting constituencies, may express different opinions before different audiences, hoping that one will not hear about the message delivered to the other. For this to work, the actors must *insulate* their behavior from certain audiences.

Another approach is to **segregate** statuses and roles so that specific individuals are not role partners for more than one of our roles (Goffman, 1961b). Surgeons do not perform operations on their own children—in other words, those who are role partners in family relationships are never role partners in surgical relationships. In this way, surgeons avoid the strain of making life-and-death decisions about the people closest to them.

The most drastic response to strain is to abandon a status or role relationship altogether. Quitting a job, divorcing a spouse, dropping a course, and leaving school are frequent responses to conflicting role demands.

There are other sources of strain in role behavior in addition to status and role conflict. To perform a role, we must know what the expectations are and have the ability and motivation to meet them. Few experiences are as anxiety-producing as entering a status and not knowing what is expected of us. First-time parents are rarely prepared for the demands of child care and often spend a great deal of time and energy worrying about whether or not they are doing what they should. First-year medical residents, fresh from school, face similar anxieties as they begin to apply academic knowledge to living human beings.

Even when we meet the requirements for role performance, we may find the performance itself to be unbearably disagreeable. In combat zones, army doctors are exposed to a steady stream of mutilated bodies day after day, and often use humor or other irrelevant talk to distract themselves from what they are doing (as beautifully portrayed in the television show M*A*S*H). Occupational jargon often serves a similar purpose—referring to the death of a patient as a "negative patient outcome" rather than simply, and more

*Doctors, like those portrayed in M*A*S*H, who act in an unprofessional manner, may do so to protect their ability to be effective physicians during the horrors of war.*

directly, as a death. These are examples of **role distance**—the disassociation from a role—which helps people endure the strain inherent in the performance of difficult roles (Goffman, 1961b; Snow and Anderson, 1987).

Throughout our lives, we move from one role relationship to another, trying to achieve some sense of harmony and continuity among the roles we are expected to play. In a sense, our lives consist of this delicate juggling of expectations and choices, and how we go about it is a major concern of sociological analysis.

Groups and Nongroups

The simplest social relationship is a pair of people—a **dyad**—who interact as the occupants of two statuses such as father and daughter. As important as individuals are in our lives, we also pay an enormous amount of attention to collections of people—families, athletic teams, universities, and governments.

Families and athletic teams are **groups**, which sociologists define as two or more people who interact in patterned ways and are identified as members by themselves (Homans, 1950). A **subgroup** is simply a group within a larger group. Members of a basketball team share a subculture whose most important ideas include expectations that govern the game (who does what in each situation), values such as those placed on winning, and attitudes such as affection toward the team and hostility toward opponents. The team, in turn, may include subgroups such as first-stringers and second-stringers, veterans and rookies. We could not fully describe a group simply by listing the names of its members, for all groups are identified by their cultural and structural characteristics.

Not all collections of people are groups. **Social categories** are sets of people with one or more social statuses in common. Examples include adolescents, college students, lawyers, native Americans, and divorced people. As occupants of similar statuses, they tend to orient themselves to similar cultural ideas; but they usually do not identify themselves as a unit, nor do they interact with one another in regular, patterned ways, as do the members of a group.

An **aggregate** is simply a collection of people who happen to be in the same place at the same time. They share the same situational status. A crowd of pedestrians, the audience at a rock concert, passengers on a bus, and the collection of automobile occupants driving on any highway are all examples of aggregates.

The distinction between groups, social categories, and aggregates is often unclear. "Groupness" is a matter of degree, depending on how much members interact with one another, how strong their sense of "we-ness" is, and how strongly group norms affect its members' behavior.

Groups are basic units of sociological analysis. We perform most of our roles in them, and they are important sources of both social control and conflict. In addition, the social characteristics of groups can affect not only individuals, but entire societies. The relationships in a family affect not only the happiness and welfare of the individual members, but the ability of societies to teach children how to participate in social life.

As we have seen, then, the concept of social structure includes three major aspects: (1) patterns of expectation for participants in social relationships, (2) patterns of expectation in relationships among groups, and (3) the distribution of people among social statuses and the distribution of social rewards among people. At the heart of social structures are social relationships, which may extend from the simplest pair of interacting statuses to social categories, aggregates, or the largest, most complex group.

CHARACTERISTICS OF SOCIAL STRUCTURES

While cultural ideas are the threads of social life, social structure is the fabric, the weaving together of ideas into a vast and fascinating tapestry of relationships. Whether we are looking at a corporation or two people meeting on a street, we can describe social relationships in terms of nine basic structural characteristics that all have one thing in common: they describe the conditions and circumstances under which relationships are acted out. We will look at each of these characteristics.

Boundaries: Insiders and Outsiders

The **boundaries** of a social relationship specify who may occupy statuses within it. All groups have boundaries, for by merely saying "We are a group," members distinguish themselves from nonmembers.

The boundaries of relationships differ in their **clarity**—how easily we can tell who occupies which statuses—and their **openness**—how easily people can occupy or leave statuses. Table 4-1 shows how these two characteristics interact in describing social situations.

The Clarity of Boundaries   The clarity of structural boundaries refers to how easy it is for people to identify others and their statuses—and plays an important part in social life. Military combat units must be able to tell the difference between "friend" and "foe" at every moment, and maintain clarity by wearing uniforms and using passwords. One of the most serious violations of the "rules of war" is to impersonate enemy soldiers.

During the Battle of the Bulge in World War II, some German soldiers dressed in U.S. uniforms, carefully copied speech patterns, and even memorized facts about U.S. cities and baseball teams. As the clarity of group boundaries broke down, U.S. soldiers did not know whom they could trust, and the result was confusion and fear (Goolrich and Tanner, 1980).

Some groups deliberately draw vague boundaries in order to avoid offending potential members. Political parties use positions on issues to define their boundaries. The candidates of these parties may try to be "all things to all people" by never taking a clear position on controversial issues. The vagueness of

Table 4-1

The structural boundaries of social situations differ in their degree of openness and clarity and can best be described in terms of the combination of these two characteristics.

	OPEN BOUNDARY	CLOSED BOUNDARY
CLEAR BOUNDARY	A sidewalk	The wall separating East and West Berlin Football team during a game
UNCLEAR BOUNDARY	Mobs during riots	The population of U.S. citizens College student Terrorist group

their boundaries can allow people with very different political opinions to vote for them.

Thus, the boundaries of social relationships are not fixed walls that never change; and they often depend on the social situation. In relation to civilians, soldiers define the boundary of their group as "military vs. civilian"; but in relation to one another, they draw different lines, separating officers from enlisted men and women, "short-timers" from career soldiers, or military academy graduates from reserve officers (Kaplan, 1955).

The Openness of Boundaries   The clarity of boundaries is related to their degree of *openness*. While almost anyone can enter the status of "pedestrian" at any time, only a relative few can enroll in prestigious universities.

Closed boundaries lie at the heart of discrimination based on such characteristics as race, ethnicity, religion, gender, and age. Many whites exclude nonwhites from neighborhoods and workplaces in the name of supporting group values. Racism, therefore, is a matter both of culture *and* social structure. The forced integration of workplaces and schools is an attempt to open previously closed boundaries, in the hope that by altering the structure of race relations, the increased interaction that results will remove negative beliefs and attitudes.

Some groups close their boundaries to preserve their *idea* of themselves as a group. The "high society" of wealthy families strictly limits entry into their social circles. An elite position is an essential part of their social identity, and if "high society" is easily entered, it is, by definition, no longer an "elite" group.

"Coming out" parties, in which daughters of prominent families are "presented" to high society, have long been used to maintain the exclusiveness of upper-middle- and upper-class membership.

Structuring Time

Within the boundaries that regulate our entry into statuses, a number of structural characteristics affect social relationships (Zerubavel, 1981). One is the way we **structure time**. In his novel *The Magic Mountain* (1924), Thomas Mann wrote:

> Time has no divisions to mark its passage, there is never a thunder-storm or blare of trumpets to announce the beginning of a new month or year. Even when a new century begins, it is only we mortals who ring bells and fire off pistols.

The way we think of and therefore experience time is affected by culture. The 7-day week is a unit of time that is a human creation, for unlike days, months, and years, it does not correspond to any natural cycles such as the seasons or the phases of the moon (see Zerubavel, 1985). Yet, no unit of time so profoundly affects our lives, from terrible Monday mornings to "Thank God it's Friday" and the relief of weekends. Depending on the culture, the week has included as many as twenty days and as few as five. For ten years after the French Revolution in 1792, the French experimented with a 10-day week (and also divided days into 10 hours of 100 minutes, each of which was broken down into 100 seconds).

We "don't have time," we "make" time, "lose" time, and "waste" it as if it were an object. We eat not when we are hungry but when it is "time" for it. We go to bed at "bedtime" and whether or not we are tired may be irrelevant.

In the U.S., we are famous as sticklers for precise schedules; consequently, we often feel "pressed" for time, while Latin Americans are comparatively loose about time, not considering being half an hour late for an appointment to be worthy of comment. We routinely orient ourselves to the "future," while many

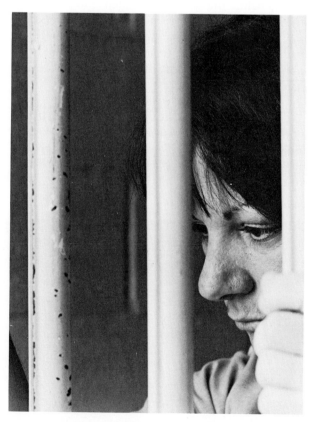

Time is a crucial element in the structuring of social life, whether it is the time that workers sell in return for wages or the time that is "served" by prison inmates.

Arabs view anyone who tries to see into the future as slightly crazy (Hall, 1959, 1969).

As a structural aspect of relationships, time has important effects on social life (Sorokin and Merton, 1937; Lauer, 1981). We tend to make weaker commitments to relationships we expect to last a short time. We may feel we can afford to be rude to a waitress we will never see again; and it is often difficult to arouse the interest of students in the long-term futures of their universities. In prisons, however, the most dangerous inmates are those with life sentences, for without hope of parole, they feel they have nothing to lose: there is no more time in the outside world to take away from them.

Like most aspects of social environments, time structures are something we are unaware of until they are disrupted. When students go on long vacations, they often find themselves feeling lost without a schedule to adhere to, and the unemployed, accustomed to years of knowing what they will do in relation to a clock, often feel that one day drifts into the next. Our social sense of time is thus a vital aspect of the predictable structuring of our lives.

Role Structures: Who's Who

In social relationships, people take on different roles that, together, form a **role structure**. There are many different kinds of roles, but two types are particularly important in most groups—**task roles** and **expressive roles** (Bales, 1950). The first is oriented toward group tasks, ranging from assigning work in an office to being a "critic" who observes and comments on the group but rarely participates in other ways. Expressive roles maintain group harmony, soothing frustrated and angry members, breaking tension with humor, or being a "scapegoat" who takes the blame for group failures (Hare, 1962, 1968).

Role structures describe divisions of labor in relationships. In his study of prisons, Sykes (1958) identified a number of roles that organize life among prisoners. "Rats," for example, betray other prisoners by giving information to prison officials; "gorillas" use force to take what they want from other prisoners; and "merchants" take advantage of prisoners' misery by selling scarce goods.

Prisoners identified as "wolves" aggressively seek homosexual contacts; "punks" submit to the aggression of "wolves" without showing any signs of femininity; and "fags" submit and openly assume a passive role that corresponds to cultural ideas of femininity. "Ball busters" openly challenge the authority of guards, and a "real man" is one who serves his time with quiet dignity, neither dominating nor submitting to other prisoners.

Role structures differ not only in content, but in complexity—the number of statuses recognized in social situations. When two people play tennis, the structure of the game is simple not only in the number of people involved, but in the number of statuses as well. Each occupies the status of "player," and one occupies the status of "server" while the other is "receiver."

When four people play doubles, however, there are more people and more statuses. In addition to those above, we now have the status of "partner," which significantly increases the complexity of the game's structure. The pattern of expectations becomes far more complex as partners orient themselves to each other as well as to their opponents.

While large groups or crowds are usually more complex than smaller ones, this is not always so. A college lecture may include hundreds of people, but since all except one of them occupy the same status ("student"), it has a simple structure. A baseball team, however, has nine different positions and a complex structure whose rules define each status' relationships with all the others. Successful players are not simply those with the strongest arms or the sharpest eyes. They are the ones who can quickly and accurately "read" a situation in relation to the structure of the game and their position in it (a good outfielder does not stand there trying to figure out who to throw the ball to).

We can also use the concept of role structure to describe entire societies. Societies that existed some 10,000 years ago fed themselves by hunting small game and gathering food; they therefore tended to be very small. Their division of labor was simple and few people were specialists capable of performing only one particular job (Lenski, 1975).

In the 1980s, by contrast, there are cities with over 20 million people and production depends on complex relationships among growers, makers, and marketers. The division of labor is complex and specialized: skills that were shared broadly within smaller, simpler communities are now possessed by a relative few. One ironic result of this specialization is that we are more vulnerable as individuals.

> Specialization . . . involves doing many things badly or not at all in order to do other things well. . . . We live in the most powerful societies in the world, but as individuals we are babes in arms compared to members of the most primitive societies, all of whom, unlike us, are generally capable of maintaining their own independent existence. We are utterly dependent on others in a way that they are not. (Barnes, 1985, p. 25)

Structures of Affection: Mapping Friendship

While role structures connect people in webs of shared expectations that vary in content and complexity, participants in social relationships also vary in how much they like one another, and this difference affects the way they play their roles. If you watch a group of people discussing a problem, you may notice that some members tend to "stick together," supporting one another's views and whispering quietly to one another. Sociologists have long noted the importance of these structures of affection—subgroups based on friendship—which can profoundly affect group performance. How can we identify the existence of such groups within groups?

In 1943 J. L. Moreno developed a method called **sociometry** to identify subgroups. Asking members of test groups how much they liked or disliked each other, he "mapped" their answers in a diagram or **sociogram** that revealed the existence of subgroups based on affection. If we repeat his technique, using

six students working together on a group project, what might the sociometric structure look like, and why is it important? The sociograms in Figure 4-3 show two possibilities. In this figure, a single arrow represents one member's affection for another, while an arrow pointing in both directions represents mutual liking between two members.

In (a), all the members like one another, so they will tend to be highly committed to the group and will try to avoid disagreement with one another in order to maintain unity and consensus.

In (b), the group has two subgroups, so there will be a greater possibility for conflict to split the members (which member do you think is most likely to smooth relations between the subgroups?). Opinions will be more varied since members run lower risks of feeling excluded; expressions of frustration and anger are more likely, and decisions may be harder to reach. Sociograms are useful for understanding why groups operate in different ways, for they reveal that members frequently value subgroups more than the group.

In addition to their different structures of roles and affection, relationships also differ in their distribution of power among the occupants of different statuses.

Power and Prestige Structures

Social **power** may be defined as *the potential to have an effect on ourselves, others, or our environment in spite of opposition* (see also Weber, 1925; Wrong, 1980). This can take the form of controlling other people or socially valued resources such as land and factories, but

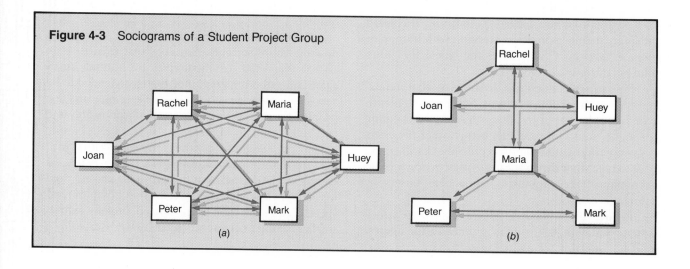

Figure 4-3   Sociograms of a Student Project Group

(a)

(b)

Presidents have authority only as long as they occupy the office of president. In January 1981, Ronald Reagan took the oath of office and the departing president, Jimmy Carter, was instantly transformed from perhaps the most powerful man in the world to someone with no more authority than any other private citizen.

it can also consist of freedom from control by others. The ability to express unpopular opinions is as much an example of social power as the ability to control what others say. Sociology focuses on how power is distributed among status occupants and how this affects interactions among them.

In social relationships, power structures vary in the evenness of the power distribution and whether power is distributed according to norms. When power is distributed evenly, the power structure is **democratic** (or egalitarian), and as power is increasingly concentrated in the hands of a few people, the structure becomes more **authoritarian**. Most relationships fall between these two extremes, with some people having more power than others but none having complete control.

Power assigned according to norms is called **authority**, and a group that distributes power in this way has a **leadership structure**. Corporations, military units, and governments all have leadership structures based on authority. It is important to note that power and leadership are not always the same, for leadership represents authority that is supported by group norms and accepted by members. Power, on the other hand, may result from a person's expertise, persuasiveness, control over valued resources, or physical ability to coerce others. Airplane hijackers who threaten to blow up an airplane unless their demands are met,

have a great deal of power but no authority. While "having power" is sometimes a personal characteristic, "being a leader" is always a social status under group control. For this reason, leadership tends to be more stable over time than personal power, and leadership structures are one of the most enduring characteristics of groups (see Zelditch and Walker, 1984; Ridgeway and Berger, 1986).

Some groups have a **pluralistic structure** in which authority is divided among specialists. Families in which spouses divide task and expressive roles are typical of groups that rely on pluralistic leadership (Bales and Slater, 1955). Groups that exist to accomplish specific goals, however, such as a jury, usually have a single leader who controls the group (Bales, 1954).

Many groups have two power structures: a leadership structure defined by norms, and informal structures reflecting the ability of individuals and subgroups to control the group. An army combat platoon's leadership structure is defined by regulations that assign a lieutenant as the leader; but his sergeants are often more experienced and command greater loyalty and trust from combat soldiers. A lieutenant may allow sergeants to overrule his decisions, giving them greater power than the leadership structure calls for. In extreme cases, when lieutenants refuse to share authority with more competent subordinates, enlisted

Table 4-2

As these examples show, power and prestige often go together, but not always.

	RELATIVELY HIGH PRESTIGE	RELATIVELY LOW PRESTIGE
RELATIVELY HIGH POWER	President of the United States Army general	Blackmailer Airplane hijacker Unpopular dictator
RELATIVELY LOW POWER	College professor Minister Honorary degree recipient Nobel Prize winner	Someone on welfare Assembly-line worker A child

men have murdered their leader rather than suffer from his mistakes in combat. Even when lieutenants do share power, of course, they remain responsible for the actions of their men in combat, so the relationship between lieutenants and sergeants is delicate, and requires them to use the informal power structure in order to survive without threatening the formal leadership structure.

Just as power is distributed among status occupants, so are rewards such as wealth and **prestige** (Chapter 11). Because power and prestige have similar bases, they generally go together (Markovsky, Smith, and Berger, 1984). Jury members who have more highly respected occupations tend not only to exercise more power but to receive higher levels of respect—to be given more opportunities to talk and to have their opinions taken more seriously (Strodtbeck, James, and Hawkins, 1957).

Nonetheless, people can be respected highly without having correspondingly high power (Table 4-2). This is true of former U.S. presidents and members of the British royal family. The Queen of England, although certainly the most respected person in all of Britain, is expected to make no open attempts to influence the official policies of her government. In 1986 there was an uproar over rumors that the queen was preparing to openly disagree with her government's refusal to support sanctions against South Africa. Many Britains were shocked that she would even consider expressing her views in public.

The concept of social structure describes how roles, affection, power, and prestige are distributed in social relationships. These structural aspects of social life create **communication structures** that determine how frequently and extensively the occupants of different statuses interact with one another.

Communication Structures

When four roommates sit down to decide how to arrange furniture, an important characteristic of their interaction is that each person is able to talk with all the others. The pattern resembles a circle in which each person is connected to everyone else. But when they meet with a dean to resolve a dispute among them, the pattern changes: comments are directed mostly to the dean, who acts like the hub of a wheel, holding the four "spokes" together and coordinating their interaction. In armies, the patterns—called a "chain of command"—are dramatically different: generals talk only with high-level officers, and enlisted personnel rarely interact with anyone other than comrades or immediate superiors. Such patterns of communication affect the performance of groups and the lives of their members (Bavelas, 1950).

In an experiment, Leavitt (1951) gave five-man groups a simple problem to solve: each man had a card with a list of symbols, only some of which were on every card. The task was to find out which symbols were held in common by all members of the group. The men sat around a table, separated from each other by partitions, and communicated by passing written notes through slots in the partitions. By using different arrangements of partitions, Leavitt created four different structures of communication (Figure 4-4).

Leavitt found that the "wheel" structure produced correct answers more quickly than any other, whereas the "circle" was the least efficient. People who

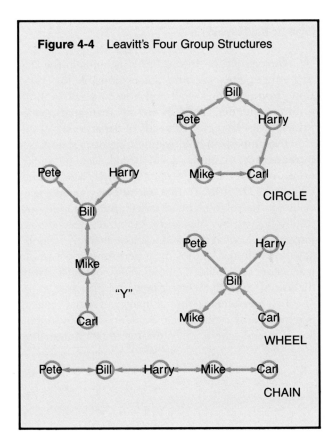

Figure 4-4   Leavitt's Four Group Structures

occupied central positions (Bill in the "Y" and the "wheel," and Mike in the "chain") tended to emerge as leaders and enjoyed the task the most. He also found that the most efficient groups were the least enjoyed by their members.

Other researchers (Shaw, 1954) repeated the experiment using different kinds of tasks and found that for complex problems with more than one solution the group efficiency ranks were reversed, with the circle reaching a consensus faster than the others and the wheel finishing last.

Students find that lectures (wheels) are boring but efficient ways to pass on a lot of information, whereas discussion groups (circles) are more enjoyable but often frustratingly inefficient ("We never get anywhere"). Complex issues are difficult to discuss in wheel structures, while brainstorming to solve a mathematical problem is fast and efficient. Hence the saying, "A camel is a horse put together by a committee."

Authoritarian governments are structured as "wheels," enabling them to make decisions more efficiently than more democratic "circles" such as the U.S. Congress, whose decisions depend on consensus

and whose members are pressured by lobbyists. The slow pace of legislation in the U.S. is due to more than the personalities of legislators: the structure itself is inefficient.

Primary and Secondary Relationships

Primary relationships are the kind we find among friends and within families. Such relationships, in which the welfare of individuals is more important than the achievement of goals, are valued for their own sake. They endure even when circumstances change and involve many aspects of people's lives. Primary ties are based on affection and involve frequent face-to-face interaction (Cooley, 1909). We do not expect to gain from such relationships: we would not say, "She's my friend because she tunes my car and lends me money." It would be more accurate to say, "She tunes my car and lends me money because we're friends."

Secondary relationships focus on specific goals that are valued more highly than the welfare of individuals. They involve only the parts of members' lives that are related to achieving those goals, are based on rational considerations of self-interest rather than feelings of affection, and are relatively short-lived. Interaction is limited to specific times and places and is often impersonal. This is the kind of relationship found most often in complex societies such as our own—buyers with sellers, teachers with students, bosses with employees, judges with lawyers, nurses with patients.

The concepts of primary and secondary relations represent what Max Weber called **ideal types**; "ideal," that is, not in the sense of being desirable, but as purely theoretical. Thus, most relationships contain both primary and secondary characteristics—police officers work together not only to achieve specific, limited goals (such as earning a living and enforcing the law) but, often, because they like one another.

Expectations in both primary and secondary relationships are defined by norms, but sociologists make an important distinction between informal and formal relationships.

Formal and Informal Relationships

Informal relationships—those among friends—are based on loosely defined, flexible norms that are always open to negotiation. **Formal relationships**, on the other hand, are regulated by clearly stated norms that rigidly prescribe the roles associated with each status. Such relationships are found in secondary groups—most business offices—whose goals require careful control and coordination of people's behavior. Especially when organizations are large and complex, groups cannot depend on members to negotiate the terms of their relationships as they go along (Simmel, 1950).

Suppose you and 30 people form a group to improve conditions in your neighborhood. At first, the group is informal. Without clearly stated expectations, you frequently interrupt one another and have little sense of direction. Sooner or later, someone says, "We've got to get organized," which means "We've got to create a structure that everyone can refer to in order to know what to do next." To do this, you first list your goals and then deal with several important questions.

Who will do what? How will you make decisions? How often will you meet and who will be eligible to belong? Will you have officers and, if so, with what authority? How will you collect, spend, and keep track of funds? As these kinds of decisions are made, the group creates a formal structure beyond the personal control of any of its members. In its most complex form, it is a *bureaucracy*.

Bureaucracy   In the 1800s, schools in the U.S. had only one teacher who was responsible for everything from deciding what and how to teach to disciplining students. There were no principals, vice-principals, secretaries, or heads of departments.

By comparison, the twentieth-century school is a **bureaucracy**, a complex set of formal, secondary relationships governed by explicitly stated, rigid norms (Weber, 1922a, 1922b). In a bureaucracy, people specialize in narrowly defined tasks, and their roles are rigidly defined by rules and regulations. Teachers no longer decide what they will teach or, in many schools, *how* they will teach. Jobs once performed by a single teacher are now divided among many specialists, from the lowest clerk to the most powerful principal.

In a bureaucracy, the occupancy of social statuses is regulated by rigid norms. Students are required by law to attend school and cannot graduate unless they

The simple structure of an 1887 Texas public school house (above) had little need for the bureaucratic organization of today's universities (right). These days, registering for classes involves so many forms and procedures that the paperwork often seems more important than the needs of students or teachers.

fulfill specific academic requirements. Teachers must be certified by the state in order to work, and the conditions under which they are promoted or fired are clearly spelled out.

Power is distributed in a hierarchy from the principal at the top to students at the bottom. Written records are kept on every aspect of school life, from test scores to school budgets and teacher performance; and specialists—administrators—do nothing but manage the complex relationships and ensure that everything works as it is supposed to.

One of the most important characteristics of bureaucracies is that decisions are supposed to be based on rational considerations of the best interests of the group, rather than on the personal feelings and welfare of individuals. Schools in the U.S. commonly promote students to the next higher grade whether or not they have mastered basic skills in reading, writing, and mathematics (National Commission on Excellence in Education, 1983). This is clearly not in the individual student's best interests, but from the school's point of view, it promotes efficiency by ridding the school of students who do not learn easily.

While bureaucracies are relatively efficient producers and distributors of goods and services, their higher efficiency comes at a price (see Chapter 8). People tend to feel lost and invisible, participating in something so complex that they easily are kept from understanding how it works. College students often feel as though they are known more by numbers than by names; workers are easily laid off by people they have never met—and then replaced by other workers who are equally unknown as individuals with names and faces. The productive work of the office and the assembly line is split into increasingly specialized tasks performed in efficient, yet impersonal settings. Walk through the offices of any large corporation, and you will see endless rows of desks that, save for a small picture or a flower, look exactly the same.

Bureaucratic norms require people to respond to others as "cases"—not as people with individual needs, desires, and circumstances—and this both solves and creates problems. On the one hand, formal relationships allow us to disclaim personal responsibility for the consequences of our behavior, so long as we adhere strictly to the rules. This, however, requires us to distance ourselves from other people in a way that may make us feel more like machines than human beings.

Consider the example of Clare, who applies for unemployment compensation and is told by the claims processor, Charles, that due to a technicality, she does not qualify for benefits. "If it were up to me," he says, "I'd give you the benefits, but the rule is clear.

I haven't got a choice. It's nothing personal; I'm just doing my job."

Clare tries to make eye contact with Charles, to arouse feelings of sympathy and make it a personal matter between the two of them. Charles, however, sticks to the rules, acting not as a feeling individual but as a status occupant who has no personal control over his clearly and rigidly defined role. Clare wants Charles to treat her as an individual with feelings, to relate to her on a personal level that calls upon his human capacity for empathy and compassion. Charles, on the other hand, uses his status and its role

As an institution, the Supreme Court is a social arrangement designed to interpret and define our fundamental rights under the Constitution. The Court has the power to bring about social change, as did the Court led by Chief Justice Earl Warren (center), which handed down the historic 1954 decision ordering an end to racially segregated schools. It also has the power to prevent change, which has made it a focal point for controversial issues such as abortion, civil rights, and criminal justice.

requirements as a shield against personal involvement, yet he cannot help feeling some responsibility.

The preceding sections describe characteristics of social structures that influence everyday interactions, from the simple building blocks of status and role to groups and their boundaries; the structures of roles, power, prestige, friendship, and communication; and the types of relationships that tie people together—primary and secondary, formal and informal. These patterns, however, are themselves embedded in other patterns that describe social environments on a larger scale.

STRUCTURES WITHIN STRUCTURES

The example that begins this chapter illustrates the fact that most cultures distinguish between "healers" and "patients" and regulate their interactions through social roles. This role relationship, however, exists in a larger structural context that includes *the relative numbers of people who occupy particular social statuses.*

Small societies might have only one healer, whose monopoly on a vital status brings with it great power (you could not afford to be on the wrong side of the tribal healer). In more developed countries, however, there are thousands of doctors; if you dislike one, you can always find another. The power associated with the status "doctor" depends in part on how many doctors are competing with one another. It also depends on the number of patients relative to the number of doctors: the fewer patients there are, the more eager doctors will be to please. The number of status occupants is an important element of large-scale (macro) social structures that affects relationships among individuals in the small-scale (micro) structures of everyday life.

The distribution of people by age is also important (see Table 4-3). In 1850 only 2 percent of the people in the U.S. were 65 or older, whereas 35 percent were in the more economically productive age-group of 20 to 64. There were roughly 17 workers to support each elderly citizen in 1850. By 1985, however, the percentage who were 65 or older had increased by six times to 12 percent, but the percentage of those 20 to 64 years old had increased only to 57 percent. In 1985, then, there were fewer than *five* workers to support each elderly person.

There have been dramatic changes at the lower end of the age scale as well: the percentage under the age of 15 dropped from 42 percent in 1850 to 25 percent in 1940 and, with the post–World War II baby boom, jumped to 31 percent in 1960. By 1985 it had declined to only 22 percent of the population.

The effects of such changes have been clear in recent years. The Social Security system is in serious long-term trouble because an ever larger number of people are depending on the labor of an ever smaller number of workers. The elderly, worried over their

Table 4-3

Distribution of the U.S. Population by Age and the Number of People 20–64 Years Old for Each Person 65 or Older (1850 to 1985)

YEAR	LESS THAN 15	20–64	65 AND OVER	RATIO OF THOSE 20–64 TO THOSE 65 OR OVER
1850	42%	35%	2%	17:1
1900	34%	50%	4%	12:1
1940	25%	59%	7%	8:1
1960	31%	52%	9%	6:1
1985	22%	57%	12%	5:1

Sources: For 1850, 1900, 1940, and 1960: U.S. Census Bureau, 1975a. For 1985: U.S. Census Bureau, 1986a.

declining security, have organized politically (see Chapter 14). In addition, the baby boom that followed World War II resulted in the construction of thousands of public schools and an enormous increase in the demand for teachers; and the subsequent decline in the school-age population closed hundreds of schools (some of which, ironically, are now used as social centers for the elderly) and produced massive unemployment among teachers.

Such long-term structural shifts illustrate the ever changing, fluid nature of social environments. They also illustrate that although social structures are the major source of cohesion in social life, they can produce disruptive change and conflict as well.

Institutions and Societies: Enduring Social Structures

As we have seen, the characteristics of social structures strongly influence the way we experience our lives and the bonds we feel with our work and other people. As we will see in the chapters that compose Part Five, in some cases a social relationship is so important to a group or society that it is preserved as an enduring pattern of expectations—in other words, the relationship becomes an *institution*. An **institution** can be defined as an enduring set of ideas and relationships organized to accomplish important goals. When a social arrangement has a relatively permanent place in a group or society, it has been "institutionalized."

All societies rely on the institution of the family to produce, socialize, protect, and care for new members, and in many societies, schools provide additional training. Economic institutions produce and distribute goods and services; science provides a systematic method for increasing our understanding of the material world; political institutions distribute and apply collective power; and religious institutions help people grapple with important questions about morality, the unknown, and the meaning of life.

It is important to point out that, unlike families or schools, institutions do not always correspond to groups. Our political institutions include not only groups such as "the Senate budget committee," but also ways of doing things that have an enduring place in our political system. No one has the right to prevent voters from casting their ballots, or to observe voters to see whom they are voting for. These procedures clearly define social relationships in political activities, and are as much a part of "political institutions" as the White House staff, the House of Representatives, the Cabinet, or a town council.

Institutions are designed to accomplish goals that societies define as important and continuing; each existed long before our births and will persist long after we die. While their cultural and structural characteristics change and vary from one society to another, institutions themselves exist as long as the needs they meet persist. The family exists in all known societies while schools are peculiar to those societies that require (and can afford) prolonged training for their members.

Just as individuals make a variety of choices within the general limitations of social environments, however, individual families vary from the general institutional guidelines laid down by society. As each of us participates in family life, we do so in relation to "models" that indicate how family relationships should be structured and what goals families should pursue. Institutions are social "blueprints" that describe how to accomplish important goals.

The importance of institutions lies in their relative permanence. Whereas friends can change their expectations of one another and bureaucrats can alter their rigid rules at the stroke of a pen, an institution is far more difficult to change, for it represents deeply imbedded ideas about how goals ought to be achieved. Bureaucrats might explain a particular rule as "most efficient"; but, if we are asked why U.S. families usually consist of a mother, father, and their children, we would tend to reply, "Because that's what a family *is*."

The permanence of institutions places them at the heart of what makes one society different from another. Macro-structural blueprints define the broad course of political, economic, religious, and family life, and in doing so they affect virtually every aspect of human existence, from the most intimate to the most public. It is impossible to understand social relationships today without also understanding the historical transformations that have taken place in major social institutions—the dominance of world capitalism and the emergence of socialism and communism in response to it (Chapter 18); the decline of organized religion and the growing power of the state (Chapters 19 and 20); the bureaucratization of so many aspects of social life, from business to schools to the making of war (Chapters 8 and 16); the enormous influence of science and technology as ways of making sense of and manipulating ourselves and our environments (Chapters 5, 17, and 22); and the transformation of the family in response to a rapidly changing world (Chapter 15).

In order to understand even our intimate lives as individuals, we must place ourselves in the larger context of the major institutional structures that define and dominate our society (see Tilly, 1985).

SUMMARY

1. The concept of social structure draws attention to the recurring patterns of relationships through which people live their lives and perform roles as occupants of social statuses. Whether referring to expectations between lovers, relationships among groups, or the distribution of income, power, and prestige in a society, social structure describes patterns that are more than a sum of their parts and that exist independently of us as individuals even though we participate in them.

2. Statuses and their associated roles are at the heart of any social structure. Status sets include statuses that are ascribed, achieved, or temporary (situational or transitional), and for each status, we are expected to perform a variety of roles (the role set) in relation to different role partners. In each case we must define the situation in order to know which role we are expected to perform.

3. Statuses and roles often subject us to role strain when we have difficulty satisfying the demands associated with a role, and status strain when the roles associated with two or more statuses have expectations that conflict with one another. The roles we are expected to perform in a situation are manifest, whereas those that are defined as socially irrelevant are latent, and conflict often occurs between manifest and latent statuses. A master status is the most important status in a status set.

4. There are a variety of ways to reduce status and role strain. We may insulate our role behavior from those whose expectations we fail to live up to, or make sure that we do not perform differ-

ent roles in relation to the same person. When role performance is unpleasant, we may use role distance to avoid being aware of what we are doing.

5. The simplest unit of sociological analysis is a dyad, a pair of people who interact as the occupants of two statuses. Sociologists, however, also pay attention to larger units: groups, whose members share a common culture, interact with one another, and identify themselves as members; social categories, whose members may have no more in common than a status (such as race or occupation); and aggregates, which are a collection of people who happen to occupy the same temporary status at the same time, such as an audience.

6. The patterns that make up social structures have many characteristics that affect what goes on within them. Boundaries differ in clarity and openness. Time structures affect both how long relationships last and how we feel and behave in them.

7. Role structures differ in their content and their complexity. Large groups are usually but not always more complex than small ones, and in complex structures it is particularly important for everyone involved to have a clear idea of what is supposed to happen.

8. Sociometry uses sociograms to map the ties of affection among members of a group. These ties are often the basis for subgroups, which may be sources of conflict within a group.

9. Groups distribute a number of important rewards and resources. The most sociologically important of these are power, prestige, and wealth. Unlike personal power, which is based on individual characteristics, authority is power assigned according to norms, and results in a leadership structure. Authority is evenly distributed in democratic structures; it is shared among specialists in pluralistic structures; and it is concentrated in the hands of a few people in authoritarian structures.

10. Communication structures determine who interacts with whom and have important effects on the behavior and experience of group members and the effectiveness of groups themselves.

11. There are several kinds of social relationships. Primary relationships, such as friendships, are valued for their own sake and involve many aspects of our lives. Secondary relationships, such as those between clerks and customers, focus on particular goals and tend to be more impersonal. Informal relationships are regulated by loosely defined norms, while the norms in formal relationships are clearly defined. In their most complex form, formal relationships constitute a bureaucracy.

12. Institutions are enduring social arrangements organized to accomplish important goals. They include arrangements such as the family as well as those that focus on education, economics, politics, and religion.

13. Relationships among individuals (found in micro structures) exist within larger macro structures. A primary element of macro structures is the relative numbers of people who occupy particular statuses. The distribution of people by age or occupation, for example, is an important aspect of macro structures.

KEY TERMS

Looking Elsewhere

Although the concept of social structure is fundamental to every chapter in the rest of the text, some of the examples in this chapter are also discussed elsewhere, such as

• gender and status/role conflict (Chapter 13, pp. 349–50)

• relationships between doctors and patients (Chapter 17, pp. 477–78)

RECOMMENDED READINGS

BIDDLE, B. J., and THOMAS, E. J. (Eds.). (1979). *Role theory: Concepts and research*. New York: Wiley. A rich collection of articles dealing with many aspects of social structure including statuses, roles, and conflict.

BLAU, P. M. (Ed.). (1975). *Approaches to the study of social structure*. New York: Free Press. A demanding but highly informative set of articles on various aspects of social structure, written by leading sociologists.

COSER, L. A. (Ed.). (1975). *The idea of social structure: Papers in honor of Robert K. Merton*. New York: Harcourt Brace Jovanovich. A collection of essays that explore the concept of social structure, from the complexity of roles and the uses of power to the present status of functional theory in sociology.

GOFFMAN, E. (1961). *Encounters*. Indianapolis, IN: Bobbs-Merrill. A pair of essays, the second of which focuses on role distance as a means of resolving role conflict, especially in high-stress situations such as hospital operating rooms.

LAUER, R. H. (1981). *Temporal man: The meaning and uses of social time*. New York: Praeger. A look at an aspect of social structure that we rarely think of as social at all.

MERTON, R. K. (1968). *Social theory and social structure* (revised and enlarged edition). New York: Free Press. Perhaps the classic statement on the importance of social structure as a concept in sociology.

ZURCHER, L. A. (1983). *Social roles: Conformity, conflict, and creativity*. Beverly Hills, CA: Sage Publications. An entertaining book at the creative ways in which we perform roles while trying to maintain some sense of personal autonomy.

POET

Population and Demography

    Births

    Mortality, Morbidity, and Health

    Epidemiology and AIDS

    The Rate of Natural Increase

    The Demographic Transition and the Economics of Childbearing

    Migration: Gains and Losses

    Age Structures

    Population Size and Distribution

Physical Environments

    Land, Water, and Air

    Varieties of Life

Organization: Ecosystems and Niches

Technology

    Preindustrial Societies

    Industrial Societies

Too Many People?

5 Population and Ecology

In 1839 Fanny Calderon de la Barca traveled to Mexico City, and as her coach came within view of the Valley of Mexico, she remembered lines from Robert Southey's long romantic tribute to the city:

> Thou art beautiful.
> Queen of the valley! Thou art beautiful!
> Thy walls, like silver, sparkle in the sun.

Later that night, she wrote to a friend:

> At length we arrived at the heights on which we look down upon the superb Valley of Mexico, celebrated in all parts of the world, with its framework of magnificent mountains, its snow-capped volcanoes, great lakes, and fertile plains. (Both quotations in Fisher and Fisher, 1966, p. 87)

Robert Southey and Fanny Calderon would hardly recognize Mexico City now. It is rapidly becoming not only the largest but the poorest city in the world. In 1988, more than 20 million people were living in Mexico City, and by the year 2000 an estimated 31 million—more than the number found in many *nations*—will be living there. Half of its adults have no jobs, there is not enough water to drink, and most residents live in slums. Rush-hour traffic lasts from 6 A.M. to 10 P.M.; and the air is so polluted with dust, smoke from industry and burning garbage, and automobile exhaust that rarely can one see the beautiful mountains that surround the city.

> Old Mexicans still remember spending afternoons in nearby fields and rivers within view of Popocatepetl, the snow-capped volcano. Many of today's school-children must play in dusty streets or open sewers, and they learn about Popocatepetl from books. (Riding, 1983, p. 12)

What happened to transform the "Queen of the Valley" into a congested, polluted center of poverty that one Mexico City doctor described as a "blueprint for hell"?

To answer this question about Mexico City— and similar questions about other cities around the world—we have to understand population and ecology, which focus on how societies adapt to physical environments and how these adaptations affect social life. This chapter describes four key concepts that define this perspective and illustrates some of the ways in which population and ecology help to explain how societies change and why so many are in a state of crisis in the late twentieth century.

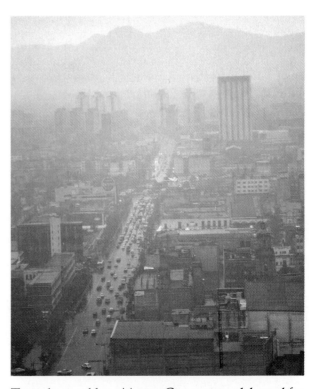

To understand how Mexico City, a city celebrated for its beauty, was transformed into a polluted "blueprint for hell," we have to pay attention to the physical and social factors represented by POET.

POET

The easiest way to remember the concepts that define the population/ecological perspective is to use the acronym POET, which stands for *population, organization, environment, and technology* (Duncan, 1961; Duncan and Schnore, 1959).

In this chapter we will define a **population** as the people who share a geographic territory, and a society as a population whose members share a cultural identity and way of life, and who interact in patterned ways. **Demography** is the study of the size, growth, composition, and distribution of human populations: why birth and death rates rise and fall, why populations are distributed over the land in particular ways, and why people migrate from one place to another. The inhabitants of Mexico City are a population, and we cannot understand their problems without understanding how so many people came to live in one place. A major part of this involves understanding the society of which Mexico City is a part.

Ecology is the study of how *populations*—and societies, in particular—adapt to physical *environments*: climate, the shape of the land, and the availability of natural resources (see Hawley, 1986; Micklin and Choldin, 1984). This adaptation is accomplished in two ways. First, populations *organize* themselves in different ways. Hunter-gatherer societies have relatively simple divisions of labor based on gender and age and do not grow their own food. Industrial societies have complex divisions of labor and produce goods on a massive scale. Second, societies adapt by using technology—the accumulated knowledge of how to use physical environments. The wheel, the horse-drawn plow, computers, automobiles, electricity, telephones, and nuclear energy are all part of cultural adaptations to physical environments.

The four concepts summed up in POET are useful for understanding the large populations of cities, countries, and the world. They also help us understand the tiny populations of families, school classes, and work groups, all of which affect our lives.

POPULATION AND DEMOGRAPHY

Why have conditions in Mexico City deteriorated so much since Fanny Calderon's visit in 1839? From a population perspective, the problems of Mexico, Mexico City, and much of the world are caused by the size,

rate of growth, age characteristics, and physical distribution of populations. The following sections deal with the central questions of demography: what causes rates of birth, death, and migration to rise and fall?

Births

To survive, every society must reproduce its members, but the *rate* of reproduction varies enormously. In the late 1980s the birth rate in Mexico (31 births per 1,000 people) was twice that in the U.S. (Population Reference Bureau, 1987). On a larger scale, birth rates in Africa are roughly three times as high as those in North America and Europe, and rates in Latin America and Asia are about twice as high (Table 5-1). Birth rates also vary within societies. In the U.S., people with high education, occupation, and income tend to have fewer children than those who occupy lower positions. Whites generally have fewer children than nonwhites, and birth rates tend to be higher in rural

Table 5-1

Crude Birth Rates in Major World Regions, Mid 1980s

Crude birth rates range from their highest levels in Africa to their lowest levels in Europe. What is perhaps most troublesome is that most of the world's population lives in those areas that not only have the highest birth rates but also have the most impoverished conditions. Those countries that can least afford rapid population growth are precisely those with the highest birth rates. How would you explain this?

REGION	CRUDE BIRTH RATE[1]
Europe	13
North America	15
Soviet Union	19
Oceania	20
Asia	28
Latin America	30
Africa	44
World	28

[1]Births per 1,000 people.

Source: Population Reference Bureau, 1987.

areas than in cities (U.S. Census Bureau, 1979, 1986a). From a sociological perspective, such variations occur because like any other behavior, having babies is affected by the ideas and relationships that make up social environments (Davis and Blake, 1956; Tilly, 1978b).

Birth rates are much higher in Mexico than in the U.S. for a variety of reasons that include differences in culture and social structure. Mexican women are expected to marry and marry young (see Merrick, 1986). If women marry young and quickly remarry after the death of a husband, they are more likely to become pregnant than if they remain single or marry at older ages.

Mexican parents prefer male children, in part because the family line is traced through men (see Williamson, 1976). This value encourages higher birth rates, for in order to be sure of having a son, parents whose first children are girls must keep trying (Freedman, Freedman, and Whelpton, 1960). Like people in many less developed countries, Mexicans also value large families, in part because societies that rely heavily on manual labor use children to help produce goods. In addition, when parents become too old to work, they often rely on their children for support, an arrangement that encourages having many children (Vos, 1984). In industrial societies, however, children can perform few productive tasks and are more likely to be economic liabilities. As we will see, industrialization has brought with it lower birth rates in many countries, including our own.

Mexicans have more children not only because they want more, but also because their children have a smaller chance of surviving. The **infant mortality rate** is the number of infants under the age of 1 who die each year for every 1,000 births. The infant mortality rate in Mexico is five times that in the U.S. (Population Reference Bureau, 1987). If Mexican parents want to have four children and expect some to die during childhood, they may compensate by having five or six.

Birth rates are also affected by social policies that encourage or discourage childbearing. During this century, Germany, Japan, France, Brazil, Argentina, Rumania, and the Soviet Union have used rewards ranging from medals to cash payments to encourage parents to have large families. Norms have also been used to restrict or prohibit the use of contraceptives in many of these countries—as well as among Catholics in many societies, whose norms forbid the use of contraceptives. As U.S. Catholics have increasingly violated those norms, their birth rates have become similar to those of non-Catholics (Westoff and Bumpass, 1973).

The governments of China and India have deliberately promoted low birth rates for over a decade.

In countries such as France, birth rates have fallen so much that there are public campaigns urging people to have babies. An example is this poster which reads, "Life is not just sex; France needs babies." China, however, has the opposite problem, and has gone to great lengths to promote one-child families as a cultural ideal.

India uses massive advertising campaigns and financial incentives to encourage couples to limit their families to two children—but such programs have had little measurable effect on birth rates. In 1984, China introduced laws limiting each family to one child (Chen, 1985; Croll et al., 1985). Women who became pregnant with their second child were expected to have abortions, and couples who already had more than one child were expected to undergo sterilization. In spite of considerable control, however, the Chinese government's policy quickly lost its grip on the country's more than one billion people. As in most less developed societies, children have economic value in China, particularly in rural farm areas where birth rates tend to be relatively high. By 1986, the birth rate had actually risen (*New York Times*, March 21, 1987, p. A1) and officials were uncertain of what to do next to stem China's population growth.

While pressures to marry and have children are weaker in the U.S. than they are in countries such as Mexico, they do exist (Blake, 1972). Griffith (1973) asked a national sample of adults 18 to 39 years old to imagine how they would feel and how people would treat them if they never had children. Most believed that family and friends would urge them to have children, and almost half said they would feel out of place among other married people and would be accused of selfishness. Most also believed that having only one child was undesirable (see Polit and Falbo, 1987), that friends and parents would urge them to have more, and that it would probably be bad for the child. More recent evidence suggests a decline in the judgment that voluntary childlessness is selfish. Huber and Spitze (1983) found that only a quarter of a national sample of adults made such a judgment about a hypothetical couple that chose not to have children.

An important aspect of social structure is the number of people who occupy different statuses, and birth rates are strongly affected by the relative number of women in a population who are of childbearing age. Imagine two populations, A and B, each with 1,000 females (see Table 5-2). In A, 50 percent (500) of the females are of childbearing age, compared with only 10 percent (100) in B. Even if women in both populations have an average of three children apiece, population A will produce five times as many children as will population B (1,500 children in A vs. 300 in B).

During the late 1940s and early 1950s, there was an enormous increase in the U.S. birth rate known as the "baby boom." As these children became adults, the number of young women increased greatly, and although they generally had smaller families than their predecessors, birth rates rose.

Mortality, Morbidity, and Health

In addition to the birth rate, population size also depends on how high or low death rates are. The

---

Table 5-2

The Effect of Age Structure on the Birth Rate

Both populations have the same number of people and the same number of females, and in both populations each woman of childbearing age has the same number of children; but population A has five times as many children because it has five times as many females of childbearing age.

	CHILDREN BORN IF EACH WOMAN OF CHILDBEARING AGE HAS 3 CHILDREN
POPULATION A: 2,000 PEOPLE	
1,000 females	
500 of childbearing age	$3 \times 500 = 1,500$ children
500 too young or too old	$0 \times 500 = 0$
POPULATION B: 2,000 PEOPLE	
1,000 females	
100 of childbearing age	$3 \times 100 = 300$ children
900 too young or too old	$0 \times 900 = 0$

crude death rate is the number of deaths in a given year for every 1,000 people in a population. A common way of expressing the rate of death in a population is the concept of **life expectancy**, which is the average number of years people of a given age can expect to live if current death rates remain unchanged throughout their lifetime. **Morbidity** refers to disease and illness in a population, which is important in demography because it is the major cause of mortality (Kammeyer and Ginn, 1986).

Like birth rates, death rates, life expectancy, and morbidity vary enormously among and within societies (Table 5-3); and once again, social factors help explain why. Causes of death are frequently divided into five categories: infectious, parasitic, and respiratory diseases; circulatory diseases (such as heart disease and strokes); cancer; violent causes (suicide, homicide, and accidents); and other causes (such as starvation, diabetes, and birth injury). These distinctions are sociologically important, because different causes are related to characteristics of physical and social environments.

Infectious diseases such as tuberculosis and diphtheria are more common among poorly nourished people who live in unsanitary conditions. Prior to the discovery of vaccines and of the importance of sanitation and nutrition, infectious disease accounted for the major portion of deaths in most societies. The incidence of infectious disease depends heavily on material living conditions; it accounts for more than 20 percent of all deaths in developing countries such as Colombia but only 6 percent of all deaths in the U.S. (World Health Organization, 1978).

Cancer and circulatory disease are the most frequent causes of death in industrial societies, causing almost three-quarters of all deaths in the U.S. but only a third of those in Colombia (World Health Organization, 1978). In part this difference occurs because wealthy countries have already conquered infectious diseases, and—since people are mortal—they must die from *something*. However, the difference is also due to factors associated with industrialization such as exposure to cancer-causing agents. Coal miners suffer from black-lung disease, and workers in cotton mills often develop brown-lung disease from continually breathing cotton dust. Other workers are exposed to dangerous pesticides and cancer-causing substances such as asbestos. Cultural factors also contribute to differences among industrialized countries. Heart disease is more common in the U.S. than in Japan in part

Table 5-3

Crude Death Rates and Infant Mortality Rates for Selected Countries, Mid 1980s

Looking down each column, there is enormous variation around the world in health and mortality, especially in the first year of life. Notice, however, that differences in infant mortality rates are much more dramatic (ranging from a low of 6 to a high of almost 200) than differences in crude death rates. As you will see, this has more to do with differences in age structure than with differences in health.

COUNTRY	CRUDE DEATH RATE[1]	INFANT MORTALITY RATE[2]
Japan	6	6
Mexico	7	50
China	8	61
Brazil	8	63
United States	9	10
France	10	8
Soviet Union	11	26
United Kingdom	12	9
West Germany	12	10
Czechoslovakia	12	14
India	12	101
Iran	13	113
Bangladesh	17	140
Afghanistan	22	182
World	10	81

[1] Deaths each year per 1,000 people.
[2] Deaths of infants less than one year old for every 1,000 births in a population.

Source: Population Reference Bureau, 1987.

because of differences in diet (Americans consume far more red meat), personal habits such as cigarette smoking, and levels of stress.

If you look at crude death rates for different countries, you may be surprised to find that the crude death rate is *lower* in relatively poor countries than it is in the U.S. Before concluding that people are healthier in impoverished Mexico than they are in affluent countries, you need to understand what it is about crude death rates that makes them "crude."

Specifically, the population of Mexico has a very high proportion of children. If you walk through a Mexican community on a Sunday afternoon, almost *half* (42 percent) of all the people you see will be under the age of 15. In the U.S., only 22 percent of the population is under 15, and the percentage of elderly people is increasing rapidly (Population Reference Bureau, 1987). How does this affect crude death rates? Children are less likely to die than people at any other age, and a population with a large percentage of children will, as a result, experience relatively few deaths. Although health conditions are certainly worse in Mexico than they are in the United States, the large percentage of children in Mexico—and the correspondingly low percentage of elderly people—pushes the crude death rate down below that of the U.S.

Levels of morbidity and mortality vary not only between societies, but within them, as well. Females generally have lower death rates than males in industrial societies, although in many underdeveloped societies it is males who fare better. This is largely because the resources needed for survival are scarce in underdeveloped societies and the higher value placed on being male is often a matter of life and death among the poorest societies.

Social inequality in the U.S. plays an important part in creating differences in morbidity and mortality. Death rates are higher among blacks than whites, and higher among lower and working classes than among the middle and upper classes (see Kammeyer and Ginn, 1986). In comparison with those with an income of $15,000 or more, poorer people are almost twice as likely to be hospitalized, and when they are disabled by disease or injury, the average length of the disability is three times as long. Poorer people are three times more likely to have heart disease, anemia, and arthritis, and almost four times more likely to suffer from diabetes (U.S. Census Bureau, 1980b, 1983c). In comparison with white infants, black infants are almost twice as likely to die during their first year, and overall life expectancy among blacks is four years shorter than among whites (National Center for Health Statistics, 1988). As Table 5-4 shows, whites and people with a higher income, education, and occupational prestige are more likely to say that they are in excellent health and much less likely to say they are in only fair or poor health than are those lower in the stratification system.

Explanations of such differences draw on many factors, including limited access to medical care (see

Table 5-4

Percent Who Say They Are in Excellent Health, and Percent Who Say They Are in Fair or Poor Health, by Race, Family Income, Education, and Occupational Prestige, United States, 1984

Looking down the first column, you see that higher income, education, occupational prestige, and being white go along with a greater tendency to report being in excellent health. The second column shows how the likelihood of being in poor health has the opposite pattern.

CHARACTERISTICS	EXCELLENT HEALTH	FAIR OR POOR HEALTH
Income		
Less than $6,999	16%	41%
$7,000–$14,999	25%	27%
$15,000–$24,999	33%	21%
$25,000–$34,999	34%	9%
$35,000–$49,999	40%	11%
$50,000 or more	44%	9%
Education		
Less than high school graduate	17%	42%
High school graduate	28%	17%
Some college or more	41%	13%
Occupational Prestige		
Low	24%	31%
Medium	28%	26%
High	36%	15%
Race		
Black	24%	30%
White	31%	21%

Source: Computed from raw 1984 GENSOC survey data.

Chapter 17), poor diet, unsanitary living conditions, and dangerous occupations. Average black workers are in occupations that are between 37 and 52 percent more likely to produce serious illness or accidents (J. Robinson, 1984). As the cost of medical care has risen dramatically, health has become a commodity to be bought and sold in markets limited to those who can afford it. This is especially true in the U.S., which is the only industrial society without a national system of health insurance guaranteeing basic medical care for all.

Epidemiology and AIDS

Epidemiology is the study of where diseases come from, how they are distributed geographically and socially, and how they are transmitted from one place or person to another. Epidemiology is of particular interest to those who work in fields related to public health, but because of the effects that health has on mortality and social life, it is also important to demographers and, increasingly, to sociologists.

Epidemiologists distinguish between diseases that are normally found in a population (an **endemic** disease such as measles or the common cold) and those that are not (an **epidemic** disease such as the Hong Kong flu) but which, from time to time, spread rapidly through a population and then die out. Of the two, epidemic diseases are the most serious because when they are introduced to populations that have not built up resistance to them, they can have devastating effects. When European explorers and conquerors first came to the Americas, they brought with them diseases, such as smallpox, which, although endemic to Europe, were, to the native Indian populations, epidemics that almost wiped out local populations. For their part, the Indians, among whom syphilis was an endemic disease unknown in Europe, passed this disease on to the Europeans who carried it back home.

A **pandemic** disease is an epidemic that spreads across several different populations, even to include the entire world. In the 1980s the newest and certainly most important pandemic disease is AIDS—Acquired Immune Deficiency Syndrome—whose discovery represents a classic case of epidemiological research (see Altman, 1986; Nichols, 1986; Shilts, 1987). First detected by U.S. physicians in 1981, the AIDS virus can destroy the body's immune system, leaving people vulnerable to death from a variety of diseases, especially rare cancers and pneumonia. Infection does not automatically result in an active case of the disease, but it is believed that most who are infected will eventually develop symptoms.

The vital questions of where AIDS came from and how it spreads were answered by studying the social characteristics and behaviors of those who were infected. Most victims share one or more of three characteristics—sexually active bisexual or homosexual men, drug users who share needles, and hemophiliacs who must undergo frequent blood transfusions. Others included the children of AIDS victims and those who received blood transfusions. From these patterns, researchers discovered that AIDS is transmitted through bodily fluids—most notably of which are blood and semen.

Epidemiologists now agree that AIDS originated in central Africa, perhaps through human contact with

A visible sign of the social impact of the AIDS pandemic has been the unprecedented willingness—and need—of schools, the media, and health officials to discuss publicly and graphically the usage of condoms, and the relative safety of different sexual practices.

green monkeys who are known to be infected with a related virus. The virus was probably spread to the Western Hemisphere by Haitians who had worked in Zaire, and to Europe by travelers from Africa. AIDS spread rapidly, expanding to more than 49,000 cases in the U.S. by the end of 1987 and upwards of 150,000 worldwide, just six years after it was discovered. The World Health Organization (1987) estimates that there will be as many as 300,000 cases by the end of 1988, mostly in the U.S., Western Europe, Uganda, and Tanzania. Since it is possible to be infected with the AIDS virus without actually developing the disease, these estimates are only a fraction of some 1 million Americans and 5 to 10 million people worldwide who are believed to be already infected. Although in the U.S. few AIDS victims are women or heterosexuals who do not use drugs, this does not mean that heterosexuality per se provides some protection from the disease. In central Africa most AIDS victims are heterosexual men and women.

AIDS powerfully illustrates the importance of social factors in patterns of disease in a population. The rapid spread of AIDS depended on the movement of infected people over great distances—something quite difficult to accomplish only a few centuries ago and which makes pandemics an inevitable and increasingly common occurrence. Transmission was also facilitated by the existence of a large drug subculture using such modern technology as syringes, and by widespread tolerance for sexual promiscuity, especially among homosexuals in large cities.

Of even greater sociological significance are the dramatic effects that the AIDS epidemic has had on social life. Many AIDS victims have been excluded from schools, workplaces, and housing, and discrimination against homosexuals has intensified in housing, employment, and medical care. The minority status of gays was also apparent in the slowness with which government and health officials responded to the early signs of the epidemic (see Shilts, 1987). The gay communities of major cities such as New York and San Francisco have been devastated as the death toll has mounted. Sexual promiscuity among both homosexuals and heterosexuals has been greatly curbed as a result of the fear of AIDS. The practice of dentistry and medicine has changed dramatically as health care providers have tried to insulate themselves from their patients: rubber gloves, gowns, and masks have become commonplace in settings in which they were

rarely seen before. Some doctors, nurses, dentists, and dental hygienists have refused to treat AIDS patients, prompting the American Medical Association to declare to its members in 1987 that this was unacceptable behavior for a health care professional. Health officials project staggering costs for caring for hundreds of thousands of AIDS patients.

The AIDS pandemic has also raised issues about threats to the civil rights of patients posed by efforts to stop the spread of the disease. The right to privacy has become a key issue as government and health officials have wrestled with the idea of identifying those infected with the virus in order to slow its spread. There is considerable controversy over whether massive screening programs would be of any use, and even greater concern that attempts to identify those carrying the AIDS virus could lead to segregation and massive discrimination. In the hysteria that often accompanies epidemics and pandemics, however, it is difficult to weigh such issues objectively and, as a result, those who already suffer the most are the most likely to suffer the additional damaging effects of a frightened population trying to protect itself.

The Rate of Natural Increase

The rate of population growth is determined primarily by the **rate of natural increase**, which is simply the birth rate minus the death rate. In 1985 the U.S. population increased at a rate of 0.8 percent: the birth rate was 15 births per 1,000 people (1.5 percent) and the death rate was 7 deaths per 1,000 people (0.7 percent). The difference between the two is 0.8 percent (Population Reference Bureau, 1987).

An easy way to see the consequence of a given rate of natural increase is to divide it into 70. The result—88 for the United States—is roughly the number of years it will take for the population to double in size if its current rate of natural increase continues. Rates of natural increase vary widely among the world's societies (Table 5-5).

As Table 5-5 shows, the lowest rate of natural increase in the world today is found in West Germany, where the deaths actually outnumber the births. Britain's rate of natural increase is only 0.1 percent, and at this rate, its population will take 700 years to double. The population of Mexico, on the other hand, is growing at a rate of 2.4 percent per year. Its birth rate in 1985 was 31 per 1,000 and its death rate was only 7 per

Table 5-5

Population Statistics for Selected Countries, Mid 1980s

Crude birth and death rates vary greatly among societies, as does the rate of natural increase. Notice that the rate of increase depends on *both* birth and death rates, which means that high birth rates result in rapid population growth only when death rates are relatively low. India has a higher birth rate than Brazil, but the same rate of natural increase. Japan has a lower birth rate than France, but a *higher* rate of natural increase.

COUNTRY	CRUDE BIRTH RATE	CRUDE DEATH RATE	RATE OF NATURAL INCREASE	YEARS TO DOUBLE[1]
West Germany	10	12	−0.2%	—
United Kingdom	13	12	0.1%	700
Czechoslovakia	15	12	0.3%	233
France	14	10	0.4%	175
United States	15	7	0.8%	88
Japan	12	6	0.6%	117
Soviet Union	19	11	0.8%	88
China	21	8	1.3%	54
India	33	12	2.1%	33
Afghanistan	48	22	2.6%	27
Brazil	29	8	2.1%	33
Mexico	31	7	2.4%	29
Bangladesh	44	17	2.7%	26
Iran	45	13	3.2%	22
World	28	10	1.8%	39

[1]The number of years it would take for the population to double in size if its current rate of growth continues.

Source: Population Reference Bureau, 1987.

1,000, which produces a rate of natural increase of 2.4 percent (3.1 percent minus 0.7 percent). At this rate of natural increase, the population of Mexico will double every 29 years.

The rate of population growth in Mexico and most nonindustrial countries is high because birth rates are far higher than death rates. In the U.S. and Europe growth rates are low because both birth and death rates are roughly equal. The rate of natural increase is already negative in West Germany, and Westoff (1978a) estimates that negative population growth rates are likely to occur in Australia, Great Britain, Luxembourg, Belgium, Sweden, Norway, Denmark, Greece, Italy, and Switzerland by 1990; in the Netherlands and France by 2000; and in the United States by 2020 (see also Westoff, 1983). In most of Europe, from Italy to Norway, there is concern that a declining population will bring a decline in national prosperity and power (Teitelbaum and Winter, 1985). In 1984, Rumania launched a national program to encourage larger families by limiting the availability of contraceptives, banning abortion, and giving financial incentives (van de Kaa, 1987).

Why would fertility decline far enough to cause a negative rate of growth? There are several answers. The percentage of people who have never married continues to rise; so does the cost of raising children—estimated to be from $60,000 to $120,000 per child when the cost of college education is included (Espenshade, 1980, 1984; Hall, 1981). As women become more heavily involved in occupations, the indirect cost of raising children—measured by the income women forgo when they leave work to care for children—also increases (Easterlin, 1978). The dependency of elderly parents on their adult children is lessening as the financial security of the elderly increases (Becker, 1981). In short, "the costs of childbearing are increasing while the rewards are decreasing" (Huber and Spitze, 1983, p. 38; see also van de Kaa, 1987).

The Demographic Transition and the Economics of Childbearing

As we have seen, the sharp differences in growth rates of nonindustrialized and industrialized societies reflect, in part, changing historical circumstances. One attempt to describe these long-term shifts is the theory of the **demographic transition**, which describes a three-stage pattern of population growth that has occurred in most societies that are now industrialized (see Figure 5-1). In the first stage of the transition both birth and death rates are high, and the rate of natural increase is therefore low. In early societies, when food was plentiful, death rates dropped for a while and populations increased; and when food was scarce or epidemics struck, death rates jumped and populations leveled off or shrank.

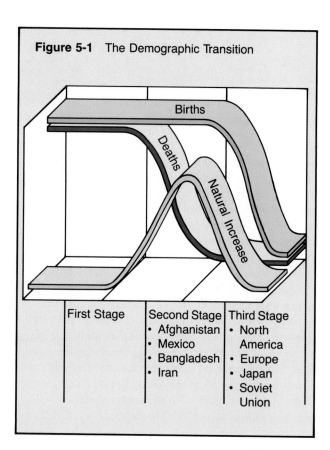

Figure 5-1   The Demographic Transition

Births

Deaths

Natural Increase

First Stage	Second Stage	Third Stage
	• Afghanistan	• North
	• Mexico	America
	• Bangladesh	• Europe
	• Iran	• Japan
		• Soviet
		Union

Although available information is at best sketchy, most demographers agree that the world population was quite stable until around 7000 B.C. when people first started to grow their own food (Weinstein, 1976) (Figure 5-2). Although higher food production probably lowered death rates by improving nutrition, the rate of natural increase was probably very low. Over the next 9,000 years—roughly up to the mid-1600s—growth rates around the world were low and uneven—going up in some years and down in others. Infectious diseases kept death rates high in most years. During the fourteenth century the Black Plague killed more than one-third of the entire population of Europe (Thompson, 1942; Tuchman, 1978).

From the seventeenth century on, however, growth rates shot up dramatically in most of the world and especially in Europe. Although the population of the world took roughly 1,600 years to double (to A.D. 1600), it took only 200 years (from 1600 to 1800) to double again. Improved sanitation and inexpensive cures for infectious diseases resulted in a redoubling of the world population by 1930, and by 1980—only 50 years later—the population of the world had doubled yet again. In 1985 the population of the world was growing at a rate of 1.8 percent, which may seem like a small figure until it is applied to a base of 5 billion people, producing 90 million additional people every year (Population Reference Bureau, 1987). (Question: At this rate, in how many years will the population of the world double to 10 billion?)

Declining death rates in the eighteenth century triggered the second stage of the demographic transition, during which birth rates stayed high while death rates fell, producing higher rates of natural increase. As nutrition and sanitation improved in industrializing Europe, death rates continued to fall and the population of Europe doubled between 1800 and 1850. During this period, however, Europe (and, a bit later, the U.S.) entered the third stage of the demographic transition as birth rates also fell and approached the level of death rates, producing very low rates of natural increase.

The populations of most nonindustrial societies such as Mexico continue to grow rapidly, for although death rates have fallen sharply through the use of medical technology borrowed from industrial countries, birth rates are still high (see One Step Further 5-1, pp. 114–15). These countries appear, in short, to be taking a long time to get through the second stage of the demographic transition. Why?

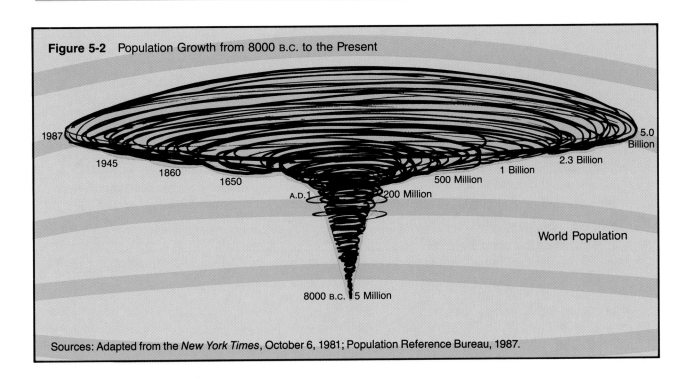

Figure 5-2 Population Growth from 8000 B.C. to the Present

1987
1945
1860
1650
A.D.1
8000 B.C. 5 Million
200 Million
500 Million
1 Billion
2.3 Billion
5.0 Billion
World Population

Sources: Adapted from the *New York Times*, October 6, 1981; Population Reference Bureau, 1987.

You might think that if high birth rates make life so hard, people would have fewer children. Historical evidence suggests, however, that it is the prosperity brought by industrialization that causes families to control their fertility. Birth rates in Europe and the U.S. did not begin to fall until the Industrial Revolution took hold at the beginning of the nineteenth century. Japan experienced a similar decline when it industrialized in the twentieth century (Davis, 1963).

Industrialization not only raises hopes for prosperity, but also converts children from an asset to a liability. Parents who want to exploit expanding opportunities simply have an easier time if they have small families. The desire for upward mobility raises parents' aspirations for their children, and if they have small families, they maximize the resources they can devote to each child's development (see Harris and Ross, 1987; Rindfuss, Bumpass, and St. John, 1980).

At the heart of the ecological problems of most less developed nations are rates of natural increase that add people faster than jobs and goods can be produced. Natural increase is the most important component of population growth, but migration also plays an important part in the growth of many societies and in the distribution of people within them.

The populations of Mexico City and cities in other less developed societies are exploding only in part because fertility is high.

Migration: Gains and Losses

Migration is the movement of people either within or between countries. **Immigrants** are people who enter a population, and **emigrants** are those who leave a population (someone who moves from Mexico to the U.S. emigrates *from* Mexico and immigrates *to* the U.S.). The causes of migration can be divided into "push" factors—poverty or oppression—that drive people away from an area and "pull" factors—the promise of higher income or greater freedom—that attract them to a new area (see Bouvier and Gardner, 1986).

For centuries people migrated to escape poor conditions. Hundreds of thousands of Irish immigrated to the U.S. after the potato famine of 1846. The westward expansion that took place in the U.S. in the nineteenth century resulted as much from crowded living conditions and limited opportunities in East Coast cities as from the lure of exploiting new territories (Limerick, 1987). When the farmers of the Midwest were ruined by years of drought during the Great Depression of the 1930s, hundreds of thousands

ONE STEP FURTHER 5-1:
Sweden, Mexico, and the Demographic Transition

Figure B-5-1 shows how Sweden reached the third stage of the demographic transition in the early 1900s, while Mexico remains, as of today, in the second stage. In the first figure (for Sweden), notice how death rates began to fall in the early 1800s, widening the gap with birth rates (and, therefore, the rate of natural increase). In the later years of the 1800s, the birth

Figure B-5-1   The Demographic Transition in Sweden Compared with the Incomplete Transition in Mexico

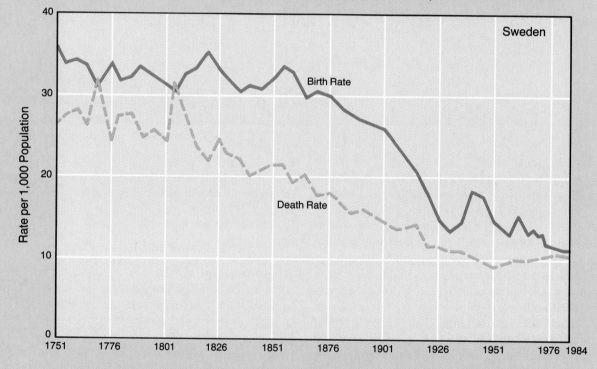

packed up all they could carry and migrated to what they thought would be better conditions in California (a desperate story powerfully portrayed in John Steinbeck's novel *The Grapes of Wrath*, published in 1939).

Since the 1930s, migration has involved millions of people moving within a short time and under intense pressure. Tens of millions of European civilians were uprooted by World War II and Nazi persecution, and in 1948 thousands of Palestinians fled from the territory that is now Israel (Bouvier, Shryock, and Hen-

derson, 1977). Across the world, roughly 50 million people left their homelands between 1946 and 1955 alone (Cook, 1957), and in the 1970s political and economic upheavals created tens of millions of refugees in Southeast Asia.

In the late 1980s many countries, including Mexico and Haiti, still look upon the U.S. as a place for people who cannot be supported by their economies at home. Illegal immigration of Mexicans into the U.S. is so massive that no one really knows just how many rate fell, too, eventually catching up to the death rate in the 1970s. The second figure shows how Mexico's death rate fell sharply in the early 1900s, but the birth rate remains high in spite of declines since 1970. The combination of the two results in a high rate of natural increase.

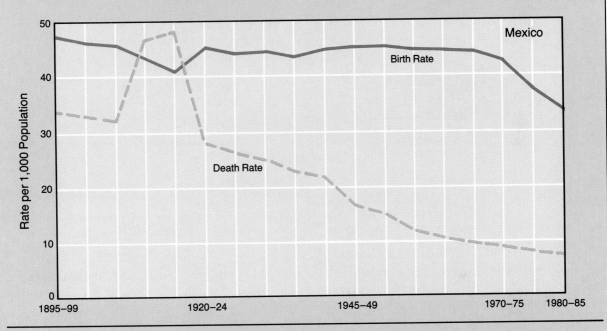

Sources: Adapted from Merrick, 1986, Figure 2. Sweden: Statistics Sweden, *1986 Statistical Yearbook* (Stockholm: 1985); Mexico: 1895–1970: Francisco Alba-Hernandez, *The Population of Mexico* (Mexico: Center of Economic and Demographic Studies, El Colegio de Mexico, 1976); 1970–1985: United Nations, Population Division, *Demographic Indicators by Countries as Assessed in 1984*, New York, December 1985, computer printout.

cross the 1,900-mile border each year (see Massey, 1981a; Massey et al., 1987). The figure could be as high as 2 million (Immigration and Naturalization Service, 1986).

Migration is a major cause of population growth especially in low fertility countries such as the U.S. (Bouvier and Gardner, 1986). Between 1840 and 1930, roughly 52 million people emigrated from Europe, mostly to the U.S. (Davis, 1974). From 1651 to the abolition of slavery in the nineteenth century, between 9 and 11 million Africans were forcibly brought to the United States (Curtin, 1969). These migrations rapidly expanded the populations of receiving countries and substantially redistributed a sizable portion of the world's people. By 1930 one-third of the world's whites lived outside of Europe, and one-fifth of all blacks lived outside of Africa (Davis, 1974).

Migration is the primary cause of the growth of cities. Although birth rates are generally lower in cities than in rural areas, urban populations have increased

These women, on a ship arriving in the United States around 1910, were among the millions of immigrants who sought a better life by leaving their homelands in the late nineteenth and early twentieth centuries.

while rural ones have declined. The populations of many cities such as Mexico City, however, are exploding under the pressures of migration from rural areas. An estimated 1,900 Mexicans migrate from rural areas to the city each *day* in the hope of finding jobs that will improve their standard of living (Fox, 1981). Like many less developed countries, Mexico is trying to industrialize rapidly, and is therefore investing far more in industry than in agriculture. Mexico City acts like a magnet that pulls thousands of poor, unskilled rural workers who are motivated by the false hope that life in the city will be better (see Bradshaw, 1987; London, 1987). The flood of migrants, however, only makes life in the city worse.

As in Mexico, migration affects the distribution of people within the U.S. Between 1980 and 1985, 40 percent of the population moved to a new house, and 45 percent of these moves were across county lines (U.S. Census Bureau, 1986a). During the nineteenth century, migration flows were from east to west and south to north; but since 1970, the northerly flow has reversed as northerners leave home in search of jobs,

and the South and West are the only regions gaining population through migration (U.S. Census Bureau, 1987e).

Patterns of migration often have important social consequences. As people move from the North and East to the West and South the "receiver" areas gain political power in Congress, because representation is based on population. Migration also causes problems for receiver areas, however. Massive migration of unemployed workers severely strains states whose job markets, schools, public services, and natural resources (water) cannot keep up with a rapidly expanding population (Weller and Bouvier, 1981).

Migration is also a major source of change in the social composition of populations (Bouvier and Gardner, 1986) (Figure 5-3). The Detroit area now has the largest concentration of Arab-speaking people outside of the Middle East, and, according to at least one estimate, Spanish-speaking people will constitute a majority of California's population by the year 2000 (*New York Times*, June 30, 1986). These changes have prompted strong opposition to immigration and

Figure 5-3   Legal Immigrants to the U.S., by Region of Origin, 1820–1985

Change in the flow of immigrants from different parts of the world has an enormous potential to affect the ethnic composition of the United States. In 1820–60, virtually all immigrants were from Europe; but by 1961–70, less than half were from Europe, and by the early 1980s, almost half were from Asia and more than a third were from Latin America.

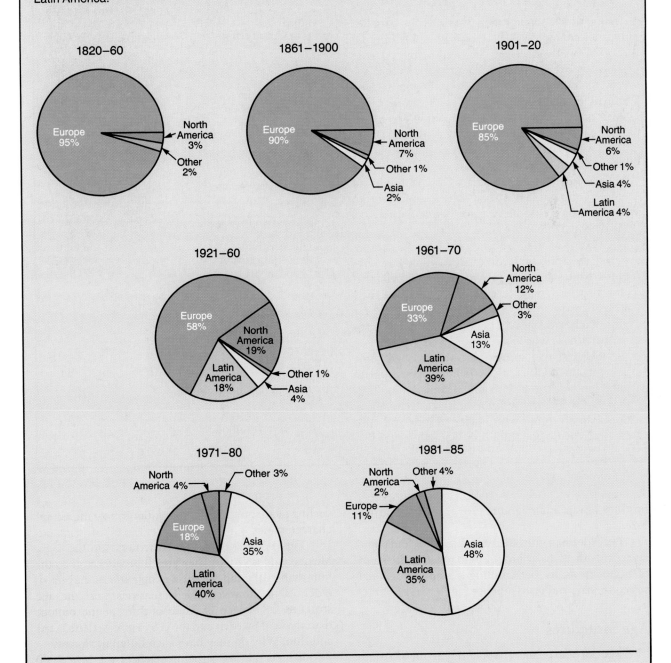

Source: Bouvier and Gardner, 1986, Figure 2.

ONE STEP FURTHER 5-2:
"Send Me Your Poor and Huddled Masses"?

Although the U.S. has long prided itself on being a nation of immigrants, it has also had long periods during which immigration was sharply curtailed and newcomers were greeted with something far short of open arms. Today, there are many countries that have larger foreign-born populations than the U.S., including France, Canada, and Australia, and annual immigration into the U.S. constitutes a very small portion of our annual population growth.

Still, the perception of many is that the U.S. is being inundated by a flood of legal and illegal immigrants. As of mid-1986, just under half of the adult population favored decreasing the number of immigrants, but, as with all values, opposition to immigration has some revealing social patterns, as the data in Table B-5-2 show.

Groups with the most recent immigrant experience are least in favor of decreasing immigration—whites are most in favor, followed by blacks and Hispanics in that order. Those who trace their U.S. ancestry to pre-Revolutionary days are far more likely to be in favor of decreasing immigration than are those who arrived more recently.

The last two sets of percentages shed some light on the social reasons behind opposition to immigration. Those with less income and education tend to be more in favor of decreased immigration than are those with higher income and education. Why do you think this would be true?

Table B-5-2

SOCIAL CHARACTERISTICS	PERCENT WHO BELIEVE IMMIGRATION LEVEL SHOULD BE DECREASED
Race	
White	52
Black	39
Hispanic	31
Ancestry	
First arrived before 1776	50
Born abroad or from family arriving after 1941	29
Income	
Under $12,500	55
$12,500 to $24,999	53
$25,000 to $34,999	51
$35,000 or more	42
Education	
Less than high school graduate	55
High school graduate	51
Some college	49
College graduate	35

Source: *New York Times*/CBS News Poll, *New York Times*, July 1, 1986, p. A21.

hostility towards immigrants (see One Step Further 5-2).

Birth, death, natural increase, migration, and population growth are basic processes that define the study of populations by determining a population's *age structure, size,* and *distribution.*

Age Structures

The **age structure** of a population is the distribution of people according to age. Age structures are usually represented by "pyramids," which give a re-vealing picture of one of a population's most important characteristics.

Figure 5-4 shows age structures for the U.S., Mexico, and Sweden. They are all broader at the bottom than at the top, because people die as they grow older. Here, however, the similarities end: the age structure of Mexico is much broader at the bottom than those of Sweden and the U.S., and Sweden's is tall and thin. Why do they have such different shapes?

In general, age structures reflect the history of births, deaths, and migration in a population; but of these factors, birth rates are by far the most important

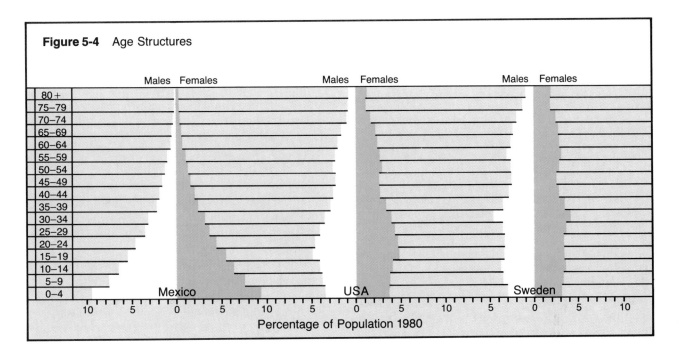

Figure 5-4   Age Structures

(Coale, 1964). Mexico has a history of high birth rates, whereas birth rates in Sweden have remained low. This is why Mexico has such a large proportion of children and Sweden has a large proportion of elderly people. The U.S. age structure, on the other hand, has a bulge that primarily reflects changing birth rates. Prior to World War II, U.S. birth rates had declined steadily for over a century, so that each new generation was smaller than the one that preceded it. Between 1945 and the early 1960s, the United States experienced a "baby boom"; then a drop in birth rates resulted in a "baby bust" in the 1970s. The "bulge" contains maturing "boom babies" and the relatively narrow base contains the "bust babies" born in the 1970s (Harter, 1977).

Age structures have important effects on both societies and individuals. An "old" population such as Sweden's must devote a relatively large share of its resources to the elderly, whereas Mexico is burdened with a disproportionately large number of children who produce less than they consume. A large proportion of children in a population poses difficult problems for economic development, particularly in poor societies that are trying to industrialize.

Pakistan can put little toward industrialization because the huge numbers of dependent children require a great deal just to survive (Easterlin, 1967; Heer, 1966). Rather than investing in higher stand-ards of living, such countries must use much of what they produce simply to maintain their already poor living conditions; and in order to industrialize, they must go into debt by borrowing money from wealthier countries.

Unlike "old" countries such as Sweden and "young" ones such as Mexico, the U.S. is aging and must make a difficult transition between meeting the needs of a young population (building more schools for the "boom babies") and meeting those of an aging one (providing medical care and retirement benefits).

Birth Cohorts   Age is an important social status in all societies, but our experiences and opportunities at different ages depend strongly on the period in history in which we reach each age and the relative numbers of people who are younger or older than we are. A **birth cohort** consists of all people who are born at roughly the same time, and the cohort we belong to has important effects on our lives (Ryder, 1965; Riley, 1987).

If you had been born in the 1930s your cohort would have been smaller than those born before 1930, because the economic hardship of the depression discouraged childbearing. As a member of the depression cohort, you would have enjoyed a relatively rich supply of jobs and educational opportunities, because *the relatively large cohorts that preceded you created more opportunities than your cohort required.* For this reason, Harter (1977) called the 1930s cohort the "Good Times Cohort":

> By virtue of their smaller number, the thirties cohort, upon encountering each important life cycle event, have experienced relative abundance. . . . In all their important life cycle events, the 1930s cohort has "had it made." . . . Insofar as the number of high school classrooms, glee clubs, athletic teams . . . had not diminished, then the 1950 fifteen-year-old had a greater chance than did the 1940 fifteen-year-old of being in a smaller class, of being a class officer . . . and when the 1930s cohort was 21–30, they required fewer new jobs and housing units than did their predecessors ten years earlier. (pp. 3–4)

As a member of a baby boom cohort, however, you would encounter enormous competition in the job market for the relatively few jobs created by the smaller cohorts that preceded yours. If you were born after the late 1960s (a baby-bust baby) your relatively small cohort will have the greater opportunities enjoyed by those that preceded the baby boom (assuming, of course, that other factors do not change for the worse).

Population Size and Distribution

Along with age structure, population *size* and *distribution* are important both for societies and individuals. In comparison with large, densely settled societies, small, sparsely settled ones, such as the Kung Bushmen of Africa, require fewer resources, find it easier to move to more supportive environments, tend to have less complex divisions of labor, and tend to be less urban (Marshall, 1965).

By comparison, the populations of industrial societies are in the tens and hundreds of millions. Such large populations are a continuing source of diversity and innovation because they allow individuals to specialize in specific tasks. Large societies are vulnerable, however, for they demand enormous natural resources and cannot simply move in order to meet their needs.

While large, densely settled populations have greater potential for innovative technology and complex divisions of labor (Bosrup, 1981), their sheer size need not have this result. Many of the poorest countries of the world—Bangladesh, China, India, and El Salvador—have among the largest and most densely settled populations. If the United States were as densely settled as Bangladesh, its population would exceed the current population of the entire world by 39 percent (Population Reference Bureau, 1987).

In part, the poverty of many large, dense populations is due to high birth rates that result in relatively large numbers of children who produce less than they consume. A full explanation, however, involves the characteristics of physical environments and the ways in which human populations organize themselves and use natural resources.

PHYSICAL ENVIRONMENTS

The social characteristics of a society often reflect the problems of adapting to a physical environment— from the isolation imposed by mountains to the splitting of an urban neighborhood by a new highway. For this reason sociologists have paid increasing attention to the relationship between social and physical environments, which include nonliving elements such as land, water, and air as well as other species of life.

Land, Water, and Air

Mountains, deserts, oceans, and seas are barriers to easy movement from one place to another; as a result, they isolate and protect societies from one another. Rivers and seas also allow people to travel and trade over distances that would be difficult if not impossible to cover over land; and landlocked societies without access to major rivers rarely prosper. It is no accident that most of the world's great cities—New York, Los Angeles, Chicago, Rio de Janeiro, London, Paris, Rome, Moscow, Bombay, Calcutta, Shanghai, and Tokyo—lie on seacoasts or major rivers.

The physical characteristics of land profoundly affect the way communities develop. Los Angeles lies in what was once a desert, and the long valley extending from the sea to San Bernardino encouraged the development of a sprawling city with relatively low-rising buildings. The vastness of Los Angeles also makes it difficult to use bus and subway transportation efficiently, and so the city developed as a place in which cars are a necessity. The air pollution generated by cars, in turn, is held and concentrated by the hills that line the valley and intensified by sunlight. The famous smog of Los Angeles results from both geography and the development of the city.

Varieties of Life

Each species of life lives in relation to other species, and ecology focuses on the place of human beings in such relationships (Hawley, 1968, 1986; Park and Bur-

Much of the prosperity enjoyed by the United States results from the richness of its farmland—an ecological condition quite unlike that found in famine-stricken African countries, including Ethiopia, Chad, and Sudan, where, despite international relief efforts, hungry people have been driven to scavenging grains of cattle feed. The suffering, starvation, and death of tens of thousands have been caused, in part, by deforestation, extensive monoculture (cultivation of a single kind of crop, usually for export rather than to sustain those who grow it), and widespread droughts making agriculture all but impossible and creating new deserts.

gess, 1921). To survive, each form of life continually exchanges one thing for another. We take oxygen from the air and give back carbon dioxide (whereas plants do just the opposite); we take coal and oil from the ground and give back heat and pollution as we burn them; cows transform grass into milk, which we then transform into teeth, bones, muscle, fat, heat (energy), and wastes (which bacteria thrive on).

Forms of life often benefit from one another's behavior. As bees gather nectar, they unwittingly pollinate flowers and allow them to reproduce; as worms dig tunnels, they loosen the soil and allow it to absorb air and water more easily, making it more supportive of plants and, in turn, of humans and others who eat the plants.

Just as living things benefit one another, so can they harm one another—and themselves. People cut down forests in order to build homes, make paper, and keep warm; but, although this benefits us in the short run, it destroys forests that thousands of animals depend on for their survival; in the long run, it also deprives us of vital oxygen that green plants add to the air.

ORGANIZATION: ECOSYSTEMS AND NICHES

An **ecosystem** consists of all forms of life that live in relation to one another and a shared physical environment (the word "ecology" refers to the study of such systems). The limits of a particular ecosystem depend on how we define a "shared physical environment"; a vacant lot in a city, a small pond, or the world might all be defined as ecosystems, so long as what goes on in one part of that environment affects life in other parts.

Within ecosystems, species of life survive through relationships with other species and the physical environment, and their positions in such relationships are called **niches**. While a status refers to a position in a social environment, a niche refers to the position of an entire population in its physical environment. Wheat draws nutrients and water from the soil and carbon dioxide from the air. As it grows it gives off oxygen, and when it dies it decomposes, providing food for bacteria and fertilizer to be used by other plants. Much of the carbon dioxide it needs to survive comes from animals (such as ourselves) who extract oxygen from the air and exhale carbon dioxide. What is "waste" to plant life—oxygen—is vital to animals, and what is "waste" to animals—carbon dioxide—is vital to plants.

Human niches in ecosystems are unique because they are extremely complex and can be altered deliberately. Human beings do not dominate the earth because they are bigger, faster, or stronger than other creatures. It is through culture and social structure that we organize our activities and vastly extend our otherwise modest biological endowment (Harris, 1979). Whereas most species must adapt through slow biological evolution, we can quickly adapt to an extraordinary range of environmental conditions.

We have an enormous ability to alter the physical environment itself: we can pollute the waters and clean them, plant trees and cut them down, and build roads and buildings on land that would otherwise sprout vegetation (which would in turn produce oxygen). We can plow the land in such a way that rains wash away the topsoil, ruining it for further cultivation, or we can carefully terrace the land and protect it from erosion.

Most species occupy narrowly defined niches, but the relationship of societies to ecosystems is far more complex. Tiny fish eat plants and microorganisms, then are eaten by bigger fish, which in turn

Puzzles: Why Are Cows Sacred in India but Raised for Slaughter in the U.S.?

A simple answer is that the Hindu religion of India forbids the eating of beef, but this sidesteps the question of why this ever became a part of the Hindu religion. Anthropologist Marvin Harris argues that the holy status enjoyed by cattle in India came about in response to ecological and population conditions. India's recurring droughts and resulting crop failures made it tempting for farmers to use their cattle for food. Farmers who did this, however, faced starvation when the rains returned because they had eaten the only animal that could pull their plows. While eating cows may have made sense in the short run, it was ecologically disastrous in the long run. Making the cow sacred was a way to ensure that even in the most severe crisis, the precious work animals would be preserved. This is one of many examples of the ways in which ecology and population affect human culture in unexpected ways (Harris, 1977).

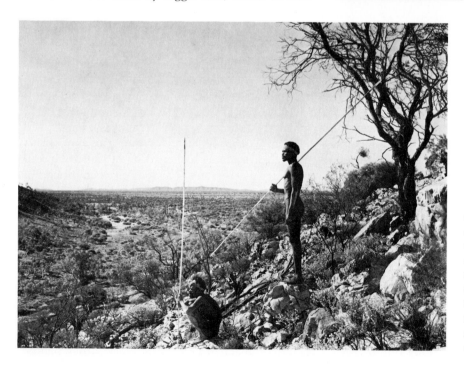

Compared with industrial societies, these Australian aborigines occupy a simple ecological niche. What they take from their environment in the way of food and natural resources is relatively limited, as is what they return to it. For the most part, they leave the ecosystem undisturbed.

provide food for still larger fish. Humans, however, eat all manner of plants and animals and have the ability to exterminate almost any animal species; we mine the earth and send a vast range of radio waves and chemicals into the air. Whereas most species have biological predispositions to slow their consumption before the food supply becomes too scarce, humans have no such inborn checks.

A major point of all this is that societies can deliberately alter and create ecological conditions within which people and other forms of life must survive. The populations that make up societies grow, shrink, distribute themselves over physical environments, and survive by organizing their relationships with one another and the natural environment and its many species of life.

TECHNOLOGY

For humans, a major element of our organization for survival is technology. The number of people who can survive in a physical environment depends on natural resources and the ability to use them, and when a growing population has too few resources, the range of adaptations is limited. The simplest responses are to move the society to a more supportive physical environment or to intensify the use of existing technologies—by increasing kills of wild game, farming more land, or drilling for more oil. These adaptations have limited value, however, for the emigration of an entire society is impractical, and any technology ultimately reaches the limits of its usefulness.

In such circumstances, a society has only four options: to develop new social arrangements and technologies that increase production, to shrink its population through migration, to control reproduction and death, or to wait for nature to take its toll. Throughout history, societies have relied on the first option—developing new technologies—in order to support larger populations. The results have produced four major types of societies—hunter-gatherer, horticultural, agrarian, and industrial.

Preindustrial Societies

In the earliest societies—existing between roughly 35,000 and 7000 B.C.—people survived by gathering vegetation and by hunting animals. They lived in small, autonomous communities, and they searched for food continually, with everyone kept busy at this task (Murdock, 1967). Their division of labor was simple (there were few if any full-time specialists), and wealth, power, and prestige were distributed fairly equally. Because they did not produce their own food, they had to move whenever they exhausted the supply.

Their technology was primitive, but appropriate to their way of life. They domesticated sheep and dogs, developed basketry and fishing, and invented spears, bows and arrows, lamps, combs, spoons, shovels, fish traps, hooks, and nets (Clark and Piggott, 1965); they had no knowledge of how to fabricate metals, however, and the human body was their only source of energy for work.

Horticultural Societies   Around 7000 B.C., people in Asia Minor discovered how to cultivate plants, and for the first time in history human beings produced some of their own food. They planted crops with hoes and digging sticks, and after the harvest they burned the stubble (which eventually provided fertilizer) and started again. Although the technology of these horticultural societies was crude and they often exhausted the soil's fertility, these simple innovations were enormously important, for as food supplies grew, so did populations.

Because people could produce more than they needed for themselves, others could specialize in work that was not necessary for survival, such as pottery and weaving (Childe, 1953, 1964). Plant cultivation provided a more stable food supply, and settlements were more permanent. With a greater variety of goods, people accumulated possessions and built larger dwellings. Although these early communities were still

---

Puzzles: Which Came First, the King or the Plow?

If it were not for the invention of the plow, there might never have been kings, queens, emperors, or popes. Why?

The answer is that without the plow societies might never have had the ability to produce a surplus, and as you will see in Chapter 11, without a surplus societies rarely develop social inequalities of wealth and power.

relatively autonomous, trade began, which made it possible to support larger populations since they could acquire goods they did not produce themselves.

Advanced horticultural societies were more permanent, more complex, and larger than their predecessors, averaging just under 300 people. For the first time, they were linked to multicommunity societies with average populations of more than 5,000. Work was more specialized: whereas metal and leather working, boat and house building, pottery making, and weaving were specialties in only 2 percent of the early horticultural societies, they were specialties in almost 30 percent of advanced horticultural societies (Murdock, 1967).

Agrarian Societies   What historians refer to as "the dawn of civilization" began around 3000 B.C. Although this period saw the development of the wheel, alphabetic writing, numbers, and the calendar, the most important innovation was the plow (Childe, 1964). The plow helped solve the problems of weeds and the exhaustion of the soil's fertility by digging deeply as it turned over the soil. For the first time, plants could be cultivated in large fields rather than in small gardens, and animal and wind power—useless in a technology dependent on sticks and hoes—were harnessed.

The agrarian age coincided with the development of the first real cities, some with populations exceed-

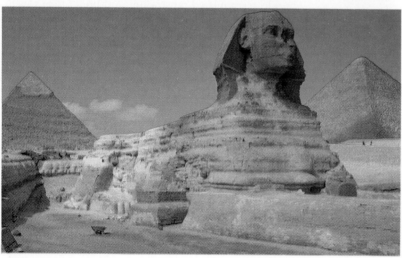

The development of agriculture, through the invention of the plow, in ancient societies, such as Egypt, made it possible to produce a surplus. This, in turn, supported emerging elite classes and their followers. Even with slavery, the millions of workers who built astonishing monuments—the Great Sphinx and Pyramids— would never have been available without ecological conditions that enabled part of the population to produce enough goods to meet the needs of themselves as well as others.

ing 100,000 (Davis, 1955). Cities came into being because technology enabled a relatively small portion of a population to produce the entire food supply, allowing people to live in densely settled communities that did not produce their own food. Permanent settlements were now the rule, and larger crops produced greater surpluses, which in turn supported still more complex divisions of labor.

Industrial Societies

The Industrial Revolution began in England between 1760 and 1830 with the development of more efficient machinery for making textiles (Mathais, 1983). With a "flying shuttle," one worker could weave as much as two could without one, and the resulting demand for yarn prompted the invention of "spinning jennies," which could spin not one but 120 threads at once. This led to such a large supply of yarn that the weavers could not keep up; so England, lacking a large network of rivers and streams to provide water power, had to find a new source of energy.

The idea of using steam to generate power was not new. Hero of Alexandria—a Greek scientist—invented the steam turbine in the first century A.D. Like Leonardo da Vinci's helicopter, however, it was an idea whose time came only after centuries of social development had produced societies such as England (in which someone like James Watt could invent a workable steam engine to provide power for enormous looms). By the early 1800s England depended more on manufacturing than on agriculture, and was, therefore, the world's first industrial society. Iron and coal production grew rapidly, and machines capable of manufacturing interchangeable, precisely tooled metal parts were developed, paving the way for greater, more efficient production.

Most societies continue to rely on technology to cope with the demands of population growth. In the 1980s, scientists are using discoveries in genetics to create new varieties of food plants that are resistant to disease and produce higher yields (Steinhart, 1981), and the Chinese are attempting to increase their supplies of energy by converting human wastes into flammable methane gas on a massive scale (Wren, 1981).

In comparison with biological evolution, cultural technology allows societies to alter their relationship with physical environments at lightning speed. The daily expenditure of energy in large industrial soci-

eties is estimated to be 50 *million* times greater than that in the hunter-gatherer societies of only 10,000 years ago (Harris, 1979). (10,000 years may seem like a long time, but it shrinks in the context of some 2 million years of human history.) World population is estimated to be 880 times greater now than it was at the dawn of horticultural societies around 8000 B.C. The current population constitutes 9 percent of all the people who ever lived (Westing, 1981), and its density has increased from roughly one person per square mile in 8000 B.C. to more than 65 (Harris, 1979).

While technological innovation often improves the ability to survive, it sometimes has unanticipated consequences that create serious problems. Chemical pesticides have dramatically improved usable crop yields by protecting them against insects; but a negative consequence is the chronic introduction of dangerous substances into food supplies—such as the discovery of ethylenedibromide (also known as EDB) in grains and fruits in 1983 and 1984 (see Chapter 17).

TOO MANY PEOPLE?

Historically, population size has been limited by high death rates from infectious disease, but inexpensive medical technology has sharply lowered death rates without also lowering birth rates. Less developed countries such as Mexico are growing at an unprecedented rate, and their young, rapidly expanding populations severely strain their resources. Rapid increases in the size of populations and projections into the future have generated widespread concern about overpopulation (see Johnson and Lee, 1986).

World population has grown dramatically since 1750, from just under a billion to more than 8 billion projected for the year 2025. Of these people, 82 percent will live in less developed countries. Figure 5-5 (p. 126) shows the changing excess of births over deaths (natural increase) in more developed and less developed countries between 1925 and 2025. As the pair of blue "walls" show, the number of births will remain stable in more developed countries while the death rate will rise slightly as the population age structure gets older. The difference between the height of the two "walls" (the amount of natural increase) is small. For less developed countries the number of deaths each year is much higher (the rose-colored "wall") than in more developed countries, but the

Figure 5-5 Population Growth, Births and Deaths in More Developed and Less Developed Countries, 1925–2025

Source: United Nations Fund for Population Activities, *Population Images*, 2ed., 1987.

number of births is so huge that by the year 2000 there will be 60 million more births than deaths each year.

Many social scientists argue that rapid population growth—particularly in underdeveloped societies—makes economic progress all but impossible and continued widespread poverty, poor health, and starvation inevitable (United Nations, 1987). High-fertility societies tend to have young populations, and if economies cannot expand fast enough to employ them, they are likely to be a source of social unrest and political instability (Davis, 1976). In addition, larger populations use up natural resources at faster rates and strain the physical environment's ability to absorb growing amounts of waste and pollution (Worldwatch Institute, 1987).

In 1798 an English clergyman named Thomas Malthus published the first serious discussion of the problem of population size and growth. He used simple reasoning to arrive at a dramatic conclusion: populations grow exponentially (doubling and redoubling as in 2, 4, 8, 16, 32), whereas food supplies grow arithmetically (as in 1, 2, 3, 4) as new land is cultivated. Malthus argued that unless birth rates are controlled, the size of a population will inevitably be controlled through higher death rates caused by starvation, disease, or war.

Although it is obvious that there are upper limits on the number of people who can survive on a planet with finite space and resources, determining how many people constitute "too many" is complicated. Survival and the quality of life depend on ecological factors such as the size and distribution of populations, the characteristics of physical environments, and technology. Bosrup (1981) argues that the development of new technology, in turn, has depended historically on the pressures of expanding populations: rather than face starvation, expanding populations *had* to come up with innovative ways to produce food and other necessities.

Survival also depends, however, on how societies organize production and distribute what they produce. Until recently, Mexico had a rapidly expanding economy, but little of its prosperity has been shared with its large peasant population (Gonzalez Casanova, 1980). From a functional point of view, a population is too large when its social and ecological arrangements are unable to support its members. The functional answer, then, is either to alter those arrangements in order to increase production or to slow—if not reverse—the rate of population growth.

As we saw earlier, many societies with rapidly growing populations have tried to lower birth rates by promoting the use of contraceptives, but historical evidence suggests that people generally do not lower their fertility in order to improve their standard of living. From this perspective, the connection between population size and poverty is reciprocal: countries are poor because their populations are too large, and their populations are too large because they are poor. All of this suggests that an important answer to the problem of overpopulation is to change social and ecological conditions in ways that will both increase production and raise standards of living—and thereby motivate individuals to have fewer children (see Merrick, 1986).

From a conflict perspective, however, those who control societies are unlikely to choose this solution. As we will see in Chapter 11, conflict theorists argue that the poverty found in rapidly growing societies is due both to overpopulation and to social relationships through which an elite exploits workers and hoards wealth (see Hernandez, 1985; Mamdani, 1981). Marx (1867) argued that capitalist societies in particular depend on a "surplus" population to provide a supply of "readily exploitable manpower" (pp. 596–97).

This does not mean that population size and growth do not by themselves help perpetuate poverty. It does suggest, however, that slowing the growth of populations by controlling births may not by itself do much to improve living conditions. It also suggests that the causes and consequences of and the "cures" for problems of overpopulation depend not only on ecological factors such as technology, but on the organization of social life as well.

SUMMARY

1. Each species survives through a complex set of relationships with other species and with its physical surroundings. Ecology is the study of such relationships, and focuses on four basic concepts: population, organization, environment, and technology (POET). Demography is the study of the size, growth, composition, and distribution of populations.

2. The crude birth rate is the number of children born each year for every 1,000 members of a population, and birth rates vary among and within societies. The number of births depends on culture and social structure as well as on the proportion of women of childbearing age.

3. The crude death rate is the number of people who die in a given year for every 1,000 people. The infant mortality rate is the number of children under the age of 1 who die each year for every 1,000 births. Death rates differ among societies primarily because of differences in culture (medical knowledge) and material conditions (sanitation and nutrition). They vary within societies because of differences in the quality of living conditions and access to medical care and knowledge.

4. The epidemiological study of morbidity is of interest to demographers and sociologists because endemic, epidemic, and pandemic diseases affect not only death rates, but the quality of social life as well. As the example of AIDS shows, disease is social both in its causes and in its consequences.

5. The rate of natural increase is the birth rate minus the death rate. The theory of demographic transition is a three-stage pattern of population growth that has occurred in industrialized societies. In the first stage the growth rate is low because the birth and death rates are high. In the second stage the death rate falls while the birth rate remains high, producing a high rate of natural increase. In the third stage the birth rate falls and levels off close to the death rate, producing a low rate of natural increase.

6. Migration is the movement of people within societies or between them. People who leave an area are called emigrants, and those who enter are called immigrants. Migration is primarily responsible for the growth of cities, often contributes to population growth, and has important social consequences for both receiving and sending areas.

7. The age structure of a population is the relative number of people of each age. Prolonged high birth rates tend to produce a young population, whereas low birth rates produce an old one. Young populations have a relatively high proportion of children who consume more than they produce, whereas old populations must devote a relatively large share of what they produce to the support of the elderly. A birth cohort consists of people born in the same year, and a cohort's experiences and opportunities depend on when in history they reach each age as well as the relative numbers of people who are older and younger.

8. In comparison with small, sparse populations, large, dense ones require more natural resources, find it harder to move to more supportive physical environments, tend to have more complex divisions of labor, and tend to be more urban.

9. The survival of a species depends on its relationships with its physical surroundings and other living things. An ecosystem consists of all forms of life that live in relation to one another and a physical environment. A niche is the position a species occupies in an ecosystem. Human niches are unique because they are very complex and can be altered with relative ease.

10. Technology is the major way in which humans adapt to physical conditions. Hunter-gatherer societies relied on wild game and vegetation to meet subsistence needs; and in horticultural societies people cultivated small gardens with digging sticks and hoes. In agrarian societies the use of plows allowed people to cultivate large fields and produce a surplus of food. The Industrial Revolution introduced new sources of energy such as steam and electricity, machinery that multiplied the amount of labor one worker could accomplish, and centralized production in factories.

11. Although technology often has beneficial results, it can also have unanticipated latent consequences that create serious problems such as pollution.

12. Survival and the quality of human life depend on population size and distribution, the characteristics of natural environments, technology, how societies organize production, and how they distribute what is produced. Malthus was one of the first to pay serious attention to the limited ability of physical environments to support large human populations. Although the resources of the earth are certainly finite, overpopulation is a complex problem.

KEY TERMS

age structure   118
birth cohort   119
crude birth rate   111
crude death rate   107
demographic transition theory   112
demography   104
ecology   104

    ecosystem   121
    niche   121

endemic disease   109
epidemic disease   109
epidemiology   109
infant mortality rate   105

Looking Elsewhere

Having studied Chapter 5, you might want to look at related discussions in *Human Arrangements*, which include

- additional major discussion of technology (Chapter 17, pp. 470–75)
- age structure, birth cohorts, and social inequality (Chapter 14, pp. 384, 388–89, 392–94)
- age structure and unemployment (Chapter 18, pp. 505–506)
- cohorts as a source of social change (Chapter 22, pp. 603–604)
- fertility, mortality, and family life (Chapter 15, pp. 415–17)
- the effects of greater longevity on family life (Chapter 17, pp. 481–82)
- the effect of technology on family life (Chapter 15, pp. 417–19)
- technology, production, and the development of capitalism (Chapter 18, pp. 485–92)
- automation and work (Chapter 18, pp. 494–95)
- postindustrial society (Chapter 18, pp. 501–502)
- technology and varieties of religious belief (Chapter 20, pp. 556–57)
- inequality, health, and health care (Chapter 17, pp. 478–81)
- how ecosystems change (Chapter 22, p. 602)
- technology as a source of social change (Chapter 22, pp. 604–607)
- the importance of geography for political power (Chapter 19, pp. 533–34)
- race, ethnicity, and hostility toward immigrants (Chapter 12, pp. 316, 328–30)

RECOMMENDED READINGS

Bogue, D. J. (1985). *The population of the United States: Historical trends and future projections*. New York: Free Press. A useful reference on population dynamics in the U.S., including trends in population growth and composition, with a special emphasis on change since 1960.

Coale, A. J. (1964). How a population ages or grows younger. In R. Freedman (Ed.), *Population: The vital revolution*. New York: Doubleday/Anchor (paperback). A readable and classic analysis of how birth and death rates affect the age structure of populations.

Ehrlich, P. R., et al. (1977). *Ecoscience: Population, resources, environment*. San Francisco: Freeman. An excellent introduction to the ecological perspective.

Ford, T. R., and DeJong, G.F. (Eds.). (1970). *Social demography*. Englewood Cliffs, NJ: Prentice-Hall. Although published some years ago, this collection of articles gives a very useful look at the social aspects of birth, death, migration, and population composition, size, and distribution.

Harris, M. (1974). *Cows, pigs, wars, and witches*. (1977). *Cannibals and kings*. Both New York: Random House. Harris is now famous for his entertaining and provocative uses of the ecological perspective in search of the origins of a marvelous collection of cultural practices.

Jones, L. Y. (1980). *Great expectations: America and the baby boom generations*. New York: Coward, McCann, and Geoghegan. An interesting look at cohort effects, with an emphasis on the Baby Boom and post-Baby Boom generations.

Lenski, G. E., and Lenski, J. (1987). *Human societies* (5th ed.). New York: McGraw-Hill. An excellent description and analysis of the historical development of technology and its effects on human societies.

Papademetriou, D. G., and Miller, M. J. (Eds.). (1984). *The unavoidable issue: U.S. immigration policy in the 1980s*. Philadelphia: Institute for the Study of Human Issues. A thorough, readable, multidisciplinary introduction to the complex issues and debates surrounding immigration to the United States.

Weeks, J. P. (1986). *Population: An introduction to concepts and issues*. Belmont, CA: Wadsworth. A clear introduction to the science of demography.

Weinstein, J. A. (1976). *Demographic transition and social change*. Morristown, NJ: General Learning Press (paperback). A brief and clear description of demographic transition theory with a critical look at its usefulness when applied to nonindustrial and industrializing societies.

THREE

Social Organization

HAVING READ PARTS ONE and Two you should now have a solid introduction to the major concepts that define sociology as a perspective. In Part Three we begin a task that will occupy us throughout the remainder of the book: to use these concepts to focus attention on the world in a new way. Along the way we will introduce you to still more concepts that apply to particular areas of social life.

We begin Part Three with Chapter 6, a look at what is perhaps the most important of all social processes, socialization, through which each generation learns the fundamentals of its culture and how to perform the roles that go along with the many statuses we occupy. Chapter 7 is the first of a series of three chapters that look at social life as it operates on three distinct levels: the level of the individual, the group, and the community. We close Part Three with an in-depth examination of deviance and conformity, problems that exist at all levels of social life.

As you work your way through these chapters, keep in mind that the framework we are using rests on the basic concepts of culture, social structure, and population/ecology, as well as other key ideas introduced in Part One. If you feel uncertain when you encounter them again (or encounter some that you do not remember seeing before) be sure to use the glossary at the end of the book.

Our need to feel that we belong to the social world around us is so strong that we will identify with and imitate behavior long before we are able to understand it. These children are standing on the roof of a white supremacist organization in Boston—the National Socialist White People's Party (NSWPP). By the time they have developed the cognitive ability to appreciate the complexity of politics, race, or ideas such as justice and equality, their racial attitudes, values, and beliefs may already be formed.

Most studies conclude that we choose models who are "attractive"; and, during early childhood, attractiveness appears to be mostly a matter of power. We imitate those who appear to control events and other people: young girls and boys tend to imitate the parent who dominates the family, regardless of that parent's gender (Hetherington, 1967).

Neither the behavioral nor the social learning perspectives includes people's thoughts and feelings in explanations of behavior; and neither can explain behavior that appears when there is no model present. The bomber pilot had no "disobedient" model to imitate. He made a difficult moral decision, weighing what others expected of him against his own moral values about duty and the sanctity of life.

If 3-year-old children were confronted with a moral dilemma, however, they would have little idea of what to do, for moral values mean little if anything to them. At that age, moreover, they are incapable of learning how to make such judgments, regardless of the availability of models or the influence of punishments or rewards.

How is it, then, that adults can make complex judgments and children cannot, regardless of learning opportunities? One answer comes from the **cognitive development perspective**, which focuses on the growth of our mental abilities to make complex judgments about ourselves as well as our environments.

Learning to Think

A 1-year-old boy sits on the floor next to his mother, who holds out a toy. As he reaches for it, she slowly hides it behind her back, letting him see exactly where she puts it. He wants the toy, but shows no sign that he knows where it is. Even though he saw where she hid it, he acts as though it no longer exists.

A 5-year-old girl sits in front of two sets of ten coins spread out on a table. If asked, "Which group has more coins?" she will reply, "They're the same." If we

It is important to emphasize that socialization is not a uniform experience for everyone. Although a culture may contain ideas about what everyone should become—honest, for example—it also includes ideas that make distinctions among people who occupy different statuses. When Bem and Bem (1976) asked adults to predict what a newborn boy would be doing as an adult, it was difficult for the respondents to answer the question, because they could imagine many possibilities for him. When asked the same question about a girl, on the other hand, the respondents tended to predict with ease and confidence that she would be a wife and mother and that these would be her most important roles in life.

Variations also occur because in most societies children are exposed only to portions of the surrounding culture. In a small Vermont town, children might never encounter a black or Asian person, and might have little sense of what racism is. The children of professional parents are unlikely to consider coal min-

ing as an occupation, whereas the sons of coal miners may imagine nothing else. Because our statuses are points of view from which we perceive society, they influence our exposure to cultural ideas as well as to the structures of life.

It is inaccurate to think of complex societies as having a single, universal culture. Although some cultural ideas apply to everyone—laws and a common language—many exist only in subcultures. Russian is the official language of the Soviet Union, but that country includes many different peoples speaking scores of languages that reflect sharp cultural differences. Similarly, walking through Chinatown in San Francisco, a Mexican neighborhood in San Antonio, New York City's Harlem, or the Italian section of Boston makes it clear that although all are located in the U.S., they represent subcultures that foster striking differences in social life.

Whatever culture or subculture we are exposed to, one aspect of socialization is universal: children learn

In large complex societies, socialization cannot be a uniform experience. Among the Amish in Lancaster County, Pennsylvania, children are raised to reject most of what people take for granted in the surrounding society—from politics, science, and electricity to colorful clothing, rock music, cars, alcohol, and movies.

that their bodies and experiences do not belong solely to themselves, that there is an expanding world of "others" who express active interest in what they feel, think, and do. Awareness of other people is perhaps the most fundamental element of socialization, for it underlies the discovery of ourselves and others as participants in social life.

Socialization and Social Structure

At the heart of socialization is the growing awareness that the social world involves more than our own experiences, desires, and needs. Infants are totally absorbed in themselves and their needs experienced through their senses, through hunger and thirst, pain and comfort, cold and warmth, loneliness and contact; but society is more than individuals who act, feel, and think. The core of social life is a complex set of relationships among individual selves, and before children can participate fully they must acquire an awareness of themselves in relation to others.

Id, Ego, and Superego   To the founder of psychoanalysis, Sigmund Freud, the self consisted of three parts (1923/1960). He believed that we are born with desires and impulses—to be sexual and aggressive, and to seek pleasure—and these he called the **id**. After the first few months of life the *ego* begins to develop. According to Freud, the **ego** is the rational part of ourselves that develops as we learn to curb our pursuit of pleasure and instant satisfaction. At about age 6, the *superego*—or conscience—develops in response to feelings of fear of parental power. In Freud's scheme, the **superego** is the source of moral standards and feelings of guilt and shame.

To get a clearer idea of what Freud was trying to describe, consider a teenage boy who steals a cassette tape from a department store because he is unwilling to wait until he can earn the money to buy it. His id is the source of his desire to have the cassette without having to wait; and his superego is the source of the knowledge that what he is doing is wrong—that the theft violates ideas about what kind of person he should be in the eyes of his parents and adult society. His ego is his "manager," who not only figures out how to steal the cassette and get away with it, but also how to soothe the conflict between his id and superego. One way to do this is to say to himself, "It's a big store; they won't miss one cassette." In this way, his ego tries to satisfy the demands of both his id and his superego.

To Freud (1913, 1930), the process of socialization was one of conflict between the desires of infants and the demands of society. But the sociologist George Herbert Mead (1934) focused on a very different aspect of socialization—the process through which we use *symbols* to discover both other people and ourselves and thereby learn to participate in the social world.

"I," "Me," "Others," and "Mind"   As an illustration of Mead's point of view consider anger, which as an emotion is invisible to others. We may feel enraged, and yet present ourselves to other people as contented and calm. We may even hide the truth of our anger from ourselves. When we make an angry face, shake our fist, and say, "Damn it, I'm mad!" we are using gestures and language to communicate otherwise invisible feelings.

Children fear adult anger and may learn to avoid provoking it, but cats and dogs are fully capable of the same kind of learning. It is when children learn to *label* another's feelings, expectations, and actions that they take a crucial step toward full participation in social life. How is this so, and why is it important?

Angry words represent feelings; behind the angry words are selves who think, feel, and act both in relation to themselves and to others. Without symbols, however, infants cannot know that people have points of view; that they think, feel, and make decisions. This is of enormous importance, for "being unaware of other points of view, they are necessarily unaware of their own—as a point of view. It simply is the way things are" (Brown, 1965, p. 220).

When infants are punished for knocking over flower pots, they learn to use the word "angry" to label a person's response. The label marks an important transition because they can apply it to their own feelings as well. Now when someone says, "I'm angry," children know how the speaker feels. Something familiar to them is going on behind the words, in another person. To understand such statements, children must look at their own behavior from another person's point of view. In this way, *they discover themselves through their discovery of others.*

Mead (1934) developed the sociological concept of *mind* to describe this ability to "put ourselves in another's place." **Mind** is the ability to use symbols in order to be aware of other people's feelings, thoughts, and expectations, and we develop mind by using language. Children begin their lives without this aware-

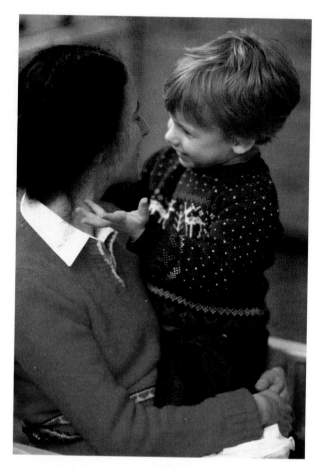

Gestures and language enable us to reveal ourselves and discover others. The intensity and joy on this child's face reflect the importance of this interaction not only to socialization and social life, but to the lives of the participants.

ness, for without symbols they experience the world directly through their senses: things are what they appear to be, not what they mean. Mead identified this "self"—this direct experience of ourselves and others—as "**I**." "I" is that part of us that feels hunger, satiation, pain, frustration, joy, ecstasy, and desire.

As children acquire language, they learn that they live in a social world in which people share ideas about themselves, the world, and their relationships with one another. In this way, Mead believed, children learn to look upon themselves as others look upon them, to view themselves and their behavior from other people's points of view. This transition can be seen in small children when they respond to themselves just as their parents respond to them. When children learn

"no," for example, they often apply it to themselves: it is not uncommon to hear them say "no" to themselves as they are about to do something they should not, or to scold themselves after the fact ("bad boy"). Who are these "selves" who scold and say "no" to themselves?

To Mead, the voice in children that says, "Knock that thing over and see what happens," is the "I"; but the interior voice that says "no" is enormously important to their social development, because it shows that *they have a point of view on their own behavior.* Language enables us to "talk to ourselves," to conduct internal conversations in which one part of us looks at "I," interpreting its desires, needs, feelings, and behavior in terms of cultural ideas. Mead identified this second voice in such "conversations" as the "**me**."

Although we are all born with an "I," our "me" arises *only* from social interaction, for the "me" is that part of ourselves that views ourselves and our behavior just as if we were another person. Without language, Mead asserts, the "me" cannot develop, for it is the medium through which we share our different points of view with one another.

Mead uses the example of a game to demonstrate his concepts of "I," "me," and "mind." When several infants play in the same room, they pay very little attention to one another. They may struggle over possession of a toy, but they do not orient themselves to one another's expectations, for without symbols and ideas they can have no expectations. They are "parallel playing"—alongside one another but not *with* one another.

The first step away from parallel play comes when children use language to pay attention to the expectations of particular people, such as a parent. When a little girl's "I" is tempted to grab every toy in the room, her "me" may say, "I'd better share them with my brother, because if I don't, mommy will get angry." In this case, she is orienting herself to the expectations of what psychiatrist Harry Stack Sullivan called a **significant other**—a particular person whose expectations we pay attention to. She is not yet playing a role, because she has no awareness that she occupies the status of "playmate" and that sharing toys is an expectation of playmates in her culture.

To learn a game such as baseball, she must orient herself not to the expectations of significant others, but to an abstract set of rules that describe the relationships among the players, telling them who does what in each situation. If she fields a hit while George is playing first base and the bases are empty, she does

In these pictures the children differ in their shared focus of activity and in their taking of roles in relation to one another. In which situation are the children being affected by a generalized other? How can you tell?

not base her decision to throw the ball to him on her personal knowledge of what he wants her to do. She throws it to him because that is what a fielder does in that situation regardless of who is playing each position. The person playing first base may be a stranger to her, yet she still knows when to throw the ball to first and when not to.

In a game, players orient themselves less to the expectations of significant others than to what they believe are the expectations shared by players in general. They orient themselves to what Mead (1934) called the **generalized other**, which is our perception of the social environment itself, including role expectations.

The generalized other is important because it is our only source of knowledge about a social situation in which we have no specific knowledge of the people who are involved. When we travel in a bus, buy something in a store, or go to the movies, we have no personal knowledge of what other individuals in the crowd expect of us. Instead, we rely on social knowledge of what people *in general* expect of one another in such situations; and our perception of these expectations *is* the generalized other.

When children learn to orient themselves to the generalized other in a game, they take a crucial step toward fully social behavior, for in order to know what to do in each situation, players must put themselves "in the place of" anyone playing each of the other positions. They must, in short, learn to play roles in relation to role partners in social relationships.

Statuses and Roles   As children develop an awareness of themselves and others, they learn that their experience and behavior take place in the social context of statuses and roles that affect people's expectations, including their own. The adults who take care of them are mothers or fathers, wives or husbands, employees or bosses. As children begin to understand their positions in a family, they discover that siblings, mothers, and fathers have expectations and obligations that differ from those of casual playmates, aunts, uncles, grandparents, and total strangers. Although their parents have the legal right to hit them, other adults do not; and even parents do not have the right to physically injure them.

When children are told never to go anywhere with a stranger, they learn to make distinctions among people according to their social relationship with them. They learn that their alternatives depend on the situation, not merely on their impulses (such as to accept candy offered by a stranger). They are learning the basics of life in social structures, to choose among alternatives according to their positions in social relationships.

As early as the fourth year, children in the U.S. become aware of racial differences (Ambron, 1978); and they can identify their own gender by age 3. As children label themselves and others in terms of statuses such as gender, race, ethnicity, social class, age, and family position, they learn to categorize people just as they learn to distinguish rocks from plants and night from day. There is much more involved, however, for cultures attach ideas to each status and its occupant. By locating themselves in social structures, children learn "who they are" in the eyes of those who share their culture, how they are valued, how people feel about them, and what their rights and obligations are in relation to others. They are developing ideas about themselves that will become major parts of their *social* selves.

Self-Concepts and Self-Esteem

We experience the world largely through our senses until we learn to use language. With language we construct ideas, and just as we have ideas about objects outside us, so do we have ideas about ourselves. Taken together, they form a **self-concept**, the sum total of our beliefs and feelings about ourselves (Gecas, 1982; Rosenberg, 1979, 1981; Rosenberg and Kaplan, 1982).

Self-concepts are a curious phenomenon. When I describe myself, the object of my attention is "me"—myself. If I say, "I am a good dancer," I describe myself just as I might describe someone else. We use symbols to "split" ourselves into subject and object (Aboulafia, 1986; Mead, 1934), to feel love and hate, respect and contempt, tenderness and rage for our selves, and to hold beliefs about our selves that may or may not be true—that we are God or Wonder Woman, or that we cannot possibly understand calculus. Unlike ideas we have about objects outside ourselves, the self-concept is important to everyone because we bring it to almost every experience.

Self-concepts are rarely simple or objective, for they include evaluations of who we are, and emotions such as pride, contentment, and shame. Self-concepts are also difficult to confirm as true. We may believe that we are intelligent and place a great deal of importance on that image of ourselves, but we are continually vulnerable to evidence to the contrary. Self-concepts are fragile, and given their importance to us, they can produce considerable anxiety.

The Self in Social Mirrors   Where do self-concepts come from? Imagine Victor meeting Teresa

Which of these women from the Yanomami tribe of Brazil, Sweden, Taiwan, and Kenya is most beautiful to you? Which is least beautiful? How do you explain your preferences? What standards do you use to judge how you look? Where do they come from, and how do they affect how you feel about yourself?

on their first date. In such a situation, Cooley (1927) argued, we have:

1. The real Victor, known only to his maker.

2. Victor's idea of himself; such as, "I look terrific in this new shirt."

3. Victor's idea of Teresa's idea of him, such as "She thinks I look great."

4. Victor's idea of what Teresa thinks he thinks of himself, such as "Teresa thinks I think I look terrific."

5. Teresa's idea of what Victor thinks of himself, such as "Victor thinks he's something else."

6. What Teresa really thinks about how Victor looks, such as "That's the worst shirt I ever saw."
    And of course six analogous phrases that apply to Teresa.

In the simplest interaction, we use each other as mirrors, both casting another's reflection and looking for our own. Like the Queen in "Snow White," who chants "Mirror, mirror on the wall, who's the fairest one of all?" we look to others for confirmation of who we think we are. Social relationships are "an interweaving and interworking of mental selves" (Cooley, 1902): Victor imagines Teresa's mind, especially what she thinks about him. Unlike a mirror, however, we do not simply reflect each other; we evaluate and judge the selves we encounter, and those judgments are part of the reflection.

We all have ideas about how good looking we are, and they do not come simply from looking in a mirror on the wall. If we think others see us as plain, we think of ourselves as plain (until, perhaps, we meet someone who thinks we are beautiful). Whether or not others consider us beautiful depends in part on our culture, for each culture has its own standards for beauty. Like beauty, many aspects of our selves exist in the eye of the beholder, and each beholder is influenced by culture. Because we depend on other people's perceptions of us in order to see and evaluate ourselves, we tend to perceive ourselves as we believe others perceive and define us (Mead, 1934; Shrauger and Schoeneman, 1979).

When we imagine how others perceive and feel about us, we are constructing what Cooley (1927) called the **looking-glass self**. The looking-glass self is not who we actually are; nor is it how other peo-

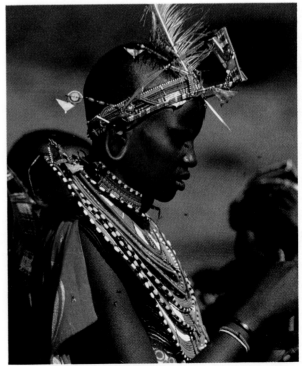

ple actually perceive us. Rather, it is our perception of how other people see us. A few studies show that we tend to see ourselves as others actually see us (Rosenberg, 1979), but most show relatively little correspondence between our self-concepts and how we are perceived by others (Gecas, 1982). The strongest relationship is between how we see ourselves and our *perception* of how others see us—our looking-glass self (Miyamoto and Dornbusch, 1956).

In many cases, we form a looking-glass self by using significant others as mirrors; but we also use perceptions of how the generalized other views us according to our statuses. Presidents are expected to be "presidential"—decisive, courageous, and "in charge" of the nation's affairs. Vice-presidents, on the other hand, are generally invisible—little if any real leadership is expected of them and they take a "back seat."

When vice-presidents suddenly become presidents—as Harry Truman and Lyndon Johnson did when Presidents Roosevelt and Kennedy died—they often surprise the public by "rising to the occasion" and displaying leadership abilities that no one thought they had. In many cases, rising to the occasion is a matter of looking at ourselves in a different mirror. When Harry Truman succeeded to the presidency, he was suddenly seen by other people as the president, and so he *became* the president.

Social Identities   From a sociological point of view, the most important parts of a self-concept are those that reflect our status sets. As we learn the cultural ideas associated with our statuses, we use them to describe ourselves not only to other people, but to ourselves as well. This social component of the self-concept is our **social identity** (Rosenberg, 1979; Stryker, 1981).

All cultures include categories that make distinctions such as "living" and "dead," "animal" and "mineral," "good" and "bad"; and at the moment of birth, children enter a variety of such categories. In Western societies, infants are described in terms of gender, race, age, nationality, and social class. Although such statuses have no meaning to infants, they do influence how others perceive them. A male Irish Catholic newborn living in Belfast, Northern Ireland, cannot know that members of society will tend to have differing expectations of him, his sister, and a male Irish Protestant newborn living across town, but as he matures and participates in the life of his society, he is likely to

use such external ideas about him as he forms his own ideas about himself.

Children expand their social identities by joining groups formed around shared interests or beliefs. Religious beliefs or interest in sports take on new meaning as children define themselves in terms of group membership. "I play baseball" becomes "I'm a Yankee in the Little League"; "I go to school" becomes "I'm a third-grader"; "I believe in Muhammad" becomes "I am a Muslim."

Social identities are also based on behavior. A child who steals may be labeled a "thief," a girl who is obedient and kind a "good girl," a boy who likes poetry a "sissy," a brilliant student a "genius," and a struggling one a "dummy." Thus, what we do may become an important part of who we think we are, and this, in turn, may influence our behavior and feelings. A child who accepts the label of "dummy" may give up in school, whereas a "genius" may feel the pressure to live up to extraordinary, if not impossible, expectations.

In forming identities we also draw upon an enormous number of psychological traits such as "generous," "aggressive," or "shy"—just a few examples of the more than 12,000 English words and phrases that describe such characteristics (Gordon, 1976). Although we tend to think of such traits as "personal," they often come from the roles attached to statuses. "Nurturant" mothers, "serious" bankers, and "scholarly" professors tend to be seen according to the expectations attached to their roles, often regardless of behavior and feelings to the contrary.

Although statuses, behavior, and psychological traits refer directly to individual characteristics, culture often extends the boundaries of social identities to include physical objects (Cooley, 1902). When people talk about the things they own, they often reveal that possessions form an important part of their sense of who they are (Csikszentmihalyi and Rochberg-Halton, 1981). Some people value expensive cars because they believe others will see them as rich and sophisticated. This principle also extends to people. When children taunt one another by saying, "Your mother has a mustache," it is clear to all involved that the attack is on the child, not the mother.

The most stable parts of our identities are those that other people will confirm, and for this reason when we describe ourselves, we tend to focus on our status sets. When Kuhn and McPartland (1954) asked people to answer the question, "Who am I?" with 20 words or phrases, their first answers most often referred to their social identities: "Mary Callahan, woman, graduate student, daughter, sister." Only after exhausting social categories did they describe themselves in terms of *personality*—the complex patterns of thought, feeling, and behavior that make each of us unique. Thus, in important ways, we know ourselves as we are known by others, and the vast majority of people know us only through our positions in relationships with them. If someone points to your sister and asks, "Who is she?" your first response will be, "She is my sister," indicating not what makes her a unique self, but her structural position in relation to you.

The last part of our social identity that distinguishes us as unique individuals is our name and, in complex societies, our numbers: social security, driver's license, credit cards. Although it may seem strange—if not offensive—to suggest that names and numbers are all that socially define us, it is important to remember that other people cannot possibly know the combination of characteristics (many of which are invisible) that presumably make each of our selves unique. I could describe a man's personality in the most minute detail, and yet you could not be certain that you knew him until I told you his name.

Social identities are powerful because we have little control over them. We can hide some statuses (if we lie about our education on a job application), but in many cases we cannot. Race, age, and gender are visible statuses, and we are severely limited in how much personal control we can exert over how other people perceive and respond to us as "white," "black," "woman," or "man."

By giving us a sense of who we are, social identities are like anchors that hold us in the world by connecting us to other people. This is never more apparent than when social identities are disturbed, especially when people do not confirm that we are who we think we are. When we lose important parts of our social identities—by being expelled from school, fired from a job, or losing a spouse—we often feel a sense of "nonexistence," as if we had been cut loose and were drifting aimlessly through the world, and in a social sense this is true. We still are "who we are" as individuals, but our ties to the social environment have been severely damaged, and until they are replaced or repaired, there is a feeling of loss, sadness, and disorientation.

Social identities, then, are the basis of our participation in social life, our feelings of belonging and being known by others. There is more to self-concepts, however, for social identities indicate not only who we are, but who we *ought* to be as well. (In light of what you have now learned about social identities, look back at Chapter 1, p. 11, and make a new self-survey of who you are.)

Ideals, Self-Esteem, and Reference Groups

When children are asked, "What do you want to be when you grow up?" their first answers tend to follow individual interests—to ride fire engines or dance in the ballet; but they soon learn that there is more involved than what appeals to them. In the U.S., we share the value that it is better to be a lawyer, doctor, engineer, or business executive than to be a firefighter, coal miner, or carpenter (Hodge, Siegel, and Rossi, 1964), and children draw upon such values to construct their **ideal self**.

In an important sense, culture is "the stuff that dreams are made of," dreams that become parts of self-concepts: "I am not only a little girl who writes stories; I am a girl who will someday be a great writer." Such images are important not only as descriptions of ourselves that we use as maps to guide our way into adulthood, but also as sources of **self-esteem**—the positive and negative feelings we have about ourselves (Rosenberg, 1979). Feelings such as pride and shame, or confidence and insecurity all reflect different levels of self-esteem (see Helen Lynd, 1958).

As children identify their places in social structures, they learn that cultural values rank some characteristics and statuses higher than others. In the U.S., they may learn that white is valued above black, yellow, red, and brown; male above female; intellectual labor above manual labor; and young above old. We rarely describe anything without passing judgment on it: "kind," "intelligent," and "beautiful" are not simply different from "cruel," "stupid," and "ugly"; they are culturally ranked as better.

When self-concepts correspond to culturally valued identities, we tend to feel good about ourselves, and if they do not, our self-esteem suffers, sometimes to the point of being stigmatized by negative labels such as "alcoholic," "mental patient," "thief," or "bum" (Goffman, 1963b; Snow and Anderson, 1987). Low self-esteem often has substantial consequences: a study of 5,000 high school students found that 80 percent of those with low self-esteem were highly depressed, compared with only 4 percent of those reporting high self-esteem (Rosenberg, 1965).

Through socialization, we use values to create an ideal self and to make judgments about ourselves. We also compare ourselves to **reference individuals** and **reference groups**, which we use as models of desirable or undesirable appearance or behavior (Hyman and Singer, 1968; Singer, 1981). Some research suggests that when political and entertainment celebrities commit suicide, extensive media coverage leads to higher suicide rates in the population at large. That celebrities who kill themselves may act as reference individuals can be seen in the fact that with extensive coverage of a *foreign* celebrity—with whom people are less likely to identify—suicide has no effect on domestic suicide rates (Stack, 1987).

We select reference individuals because we want to be like them or because we want to be *un*like them. Children often say they want to be like their mothers or fathers when they grow up, and evaluate themselves according to their parents' values. As adolescents, however, they often select new reference individuals— from professional athletes and rock musicians to teachers and famous writers—and this may involve a rejection of parental values. In this sense, a punk-rock musician replaces a parent as a positive reference individual, and parents become negative reference individuals.

We also compare ourselves with reference groups (Festinger, 1954). Students who are at the top of their high school senior class often find that they are no longer at the top in college, and may as a result feel they are not as capable as they thought they were. Their self-concept may change not because they have changed, but because they have adopted a new reference group.

We do not actually have to belong to a reference group in order to use it to evaluate ourselves. For many people the Ku Klux Klan is an example of racism at its worst, and, as a negative reference group, it gives them a point of comparison for favorably evaluating their own racial attitudes.

That we can use reference groups without being members is important for four reasons. First, it explains why we so often differ from the groups to which we do belong. The children of immigrant families may never learn their native language, because—as they aspire to become members of the surrounding society—they choose a reference group whose language differs from that of their parents.

Second, because we do not need to belong to reference groups, we can have more than one, and this contributes to conflicting self-evaluations. Lesbians may feel good about themselves when they use other lesbians as a reference group, but feel bad about themselves if they use co-workers who disapprove of homosexuality.

Third, the concept of reference groups helps explain why people begin to change their attitudes *in anticipation* of joining a group. This is called **anticipa-**

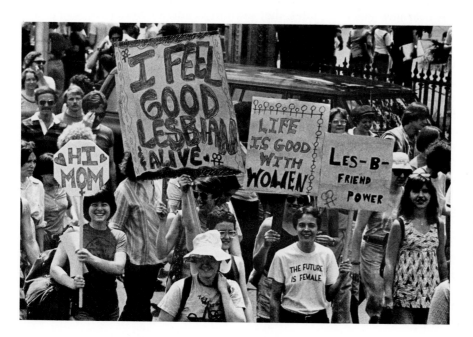

At rallies for gay rights, such as this one in Boston, marchers publicly assert a positive self-image for homosexuals. In what ways does your own sexual preference affect how others feel about you as well as how you feel about yourself?

tory socialization (Merton and Rossi, 1968), and it plays an important part in learning roles. When children try to act "grown up," they are using adults as a reference group long before they become adults themselves. Graduate students typically evaluate themselves in terms of the professional group they are preparing to join. A great deal of socialization, both among children and adults, is anticipatory, because we are learning about roles we do not yet perform.

Finally, our reference groups affect which parts of our identities we are most aware of and care the most about. Most characteristics have meaning only in comparison with other characteristics: the idea of "female" has no meaning without the idea of "male." To identify ourselves as "female," "black," or "heterosexual," we must have some point of comparison—such as those who are male, white, or homosexual. Without an awareness of people with contrasting characteristics, we have no reason to attach any special significance to our own.

In one study 500 high school students were asked to spend five minutes talking about themselves, saying anything that came to mind. Only 1 percent of the white students mentioned their race, whereas 17 percent of the blacks and 14 percent of the Hispanics mentioned theirs. Why the difference? The study was conducted in a school in which 83 percent of the students were English-speaking whites; only 9 percent were black and 8 percent were Hispanic. As far as racial identity was concerned, dominant whites compared themselves with students of their own race, whereas many of the visible minority of nonwhite students compared themselves with members of the dominant group and were thus more likely to be aware of their racial identity (McGuire et al., 1978).

If we are unhappy with how we compare with reference individuals or groups, we can change our identities by acquiring new statuses that have higher cultural value—getting a better job or going to college—or by concealing characteristics that lower our self-esteem. We can also choose (or create) new reference groups. When lesbians or blacks separate themselves from society, they are trying to create reference groups in which "lesbian" and "black" are highly valued characteristics.

Another way to narrow the gap between who we think we are and who we want to be is to lower our commitment to various parts of our ideal self. This changes not the content of our self-concept, but its structure, rearranging characteristics in terms of their importance to us. Like James Thurber's character Walter Mitty, we all have fantasies about who we might be, and so long as they are mere fantasies they do not threaten our self-esteem. Most of us spend our lives performing quite ordinary roles, and we protect ourselves when we say, "Sure, I'd like to be rich and famous, but I can live without it."

The most radical social solution to low self-esteem is not to change from one reference group to another, but to change the reference group itself. This is a major goal of many social movements such as the women's, civil rights, gay rights, and senior citizen movements. When blacks proclaim to a white-dominated society that "black is beautiful" or when feminist artists write song lyrics that celebrate being female, they are supporting their own self-esteem and sending a message to the surrounding society, exerting pressure for change in the prevailing value system. The goal is to create a culture in which people can participate fully and openly and have high self-esteem.

SOCIALIZATION AND THE LIFE COURSE

The fact that we adopt many different reference groups during our lives highlights an important fact about socialization. Childhood may be the most intense learning period of our lives, but socialization does not end when we reach adulthood.

Socialization takes place over the course of our entire lives, and is affected by major social institutions including the family, schools, the mass media, and the economy (see Part Five). We repeatedly discard old roles and learn new ones—a process called **resocialization**—and as our reference groups change, so do our perceptions and evaluations of who we are (Bush and Simmons, 1981; Gecas, 1981).

Rites of Passage

Because people's rights and responsibilities depend not on who they "really" are but on their social identities, control of the statuses people claim to occupy is important in all societies. In order to legitimately assume the status of "college graduate" or "married" we must participate in cultural ceremonies that mark our movement from one status to another. These **rites of passage** are a form of social control over our social identities (Van Gennep, 1909).

Puzzles: Are You a Child or an Adult?

How do you know that you are one and not the other? What about other people—do they always agree that you are what you think you are? If not, why?

As you will see in this chapter and again in Chapter 14, age is more than a matter of time. It is one of the most significant and universally recognized of all social statuses. That is why it is so important that we know which age group we are in and why being unsure can generate so much anxiety.

The passage from childhood to adulthood is perhaps the most universally important transition, for adulthood brings with it social power. In all societies people are children until they are culturally defined as adults, and this may take place long after they are physically mature.

In some societies the rite of passage from childhood to adulthood is well defined, involving, for example, a ceremony in which the child's genitals are mutilated (Van Gennep, 1909). In others, such as our own, the rites are more ambiguous: in most states young men and women are allowed to marry and have children before they are old enough to vote or purchase liquor. Although the law defines adulthood in terms of age, simply reaching the age of 18 or 21 does not necessarily lead others to treat us as adults. The important thing in the social world is not so much who we "really" are, but who other people think we are.

The following three sections take a brief look at the importance of social institutions in the socialization process.

Socialization in Families

One of the primary functions of the family as a social institution is to socialize children. How children are socialized as family members depends on the reference groups and individuals that parents orient themselves to (such as their own parents, their social class, or their ethnic subculture) and the structure of family relationships.

As they raise their children, lower-class parents generally value obedience to authority, neatness, cleanliness, and staying out of trouble more than middle-class parents do. Middle-class parents in a variety of societies are more likely to stress creativity, self-discipline, ambition, independence, curiosity, and self-direction (Ellis et al., 1978; Kohn, 1977; Slomczynski et al., 1981). Although lower-class parents evaluate their children's behavior primarily in terms of its positive or negative consequences, middle-class parents pay more attention to their children's intentions (Wright and Wright, 1976).

Class differences in family values produce differences in the methods parents use to socialize children. Lower-class parents who value obedience are more likely than middle-class parents to use physical punishment. Middle-class parents rely more on reasoning, guilt, and threatened loss of love to control their children (Maccoby and Martin, 1983; Wright and Wright, 1976).

Class differences in child-rearing values do not occur simply by accident. Lower-class children can eventually expect to depend on jobs that require them to follow orders rather than make independent judgments, and they are less likely to have advanced educations that lead to higher responsibilities within a given occupation. Middle-class children, on the other hand, are more likely to become professionals, managers, and administrators when they grow up. Parents tend to pass on to their children outlooks that are suited to their own experience in the world. A study of 122 cultures found that the more parents are supervised in their lives the more they tend to stress obedience and conformity in their children (Ellis et al., 1978).

Class differences in child-rearing values play an important part in the reproduction of classes. When working-class parents raise their children to be "good workers" who obey authorities, they unwittingly prepare them to participate in social relationships that will give them an unequal share of wealth, power, and prestige in the adult world. In similar ways, when upper-middle- and upper-class parents see to it that their children have the best educations, they, too, play a part in the reproduction of class relations (R. Robinson, 1984) (see One Step Further 6-1, p. 152–53).

Socialization in Schools

Like the family, the school is an institution whose major function is socialization. What most students learn in school consists primarily of formal studies—math, history, languages, and science—but perhaps the most important contribution of schools to socialization lies in their "hidden curricula," lessons imparted in the process of learning formal subjects.

Students in U.S. schools learn that they are expected to be punctual, neat, obedient, and polite. What they want to do is no longer important, and activities are rigidly scheduled. They learn that individual competition and success are more valued than working together in groups. For many middle-class students, the cultural messages in the hidden curriculum are an extension of socialization in their families; but for many others—including blacks, Hispanics, and poor people—the middle-class values of most schools differ sharply from those they experience at home. In fact, one of the major functions of early public schools in the U.S. was to weaken the ability of immigrant families to socialize their children according to their ethnic subcultures, so that their children would grow up sharing the dominant white, Anglo-Saxon culture (Lasch, 1977).

Because they help prepare children for adult life, schools play a major role in anticipatory socialization by shaping children's social identities, including their visions of which statuses they can occupy as adults. Lower-class students generally receive less encouragement to go on to college than middle- and upper-class students do; and they—along with blacks—are more likely to be placed in "slow" tracks in school, regardless of their test scores. Children from upper-middle and upper-class families, by contrast, are more likely to attend private prep schools where teachers assume their students will attend prestigious colleges and occupy high positions in business, government, or the professions (see Cookson and Persell, 1985).

In comparison with boys, girls receive relatively less encouragement to pursue careers, especially in science and the professions (Schaffer, 1981). As early as nursery school, boys generally receive more attention on academic work and more encouragement to work independently. Girls, on the other hand, are rewarded for showing dependency on the teacher and are more likely to have a teacher offer assistance whether or not they need it (Serbin and O'Leary, 1975; Sadker and Sadker, 1985).

The hidden curriculum of most American schools sends different messages to students of different genders, races, and social classes. In comparison with students who are nonwhite, female, or poor, those who are white, male, and middle- or upper-class generally receive more encouragement to perceive themselves as people who will one day occupy responsible positions that will bring them a disproportionately large share of wealth, power, and prestige. They are more likely to see themselves as people who will go to college and get good jobs, and in anticipation of this, they are more likely to do what they have to do in order to prepare themselves (Smith, 1981).

Peer Groups   The concept of **peer group** refers to people who have a similar level of social standing, especially in terms of age. Schools compete with families for influence in the socialization process, but adolescent peer groups compete with both families and schools. In his study of high schools, Coleman (1960, 1961) found that students worried about pleasing friends as often as they worried about pleasing parents. Whereas teachers generally place their highest values on academic performance, student peer groups do not; rather, they tend to value athletic ability and popularity, and rank academic performance a distant third.

Peer groups are particularly powerful in industrial societies because young people are excluded from adult statuses and their success as adults does not depend on their family ties. In small village societies, on the other hand, the entire village is regarded as a single family, and adult statuses are distributed according to people's positions in the village.

In industrial societies, the exclusion of young people from important adult statuses elevates the importance— and therefore the power—of peer groups.

Eisenstadt (1956) believes that adolescents in industrial societies turn to one another because they feel isolated from adult society. As they struggle toward adulthood, they are therefore likely to feel that other adolescents are the only ones who really understand what they are going through. The distinctive music, language, and dress of adolescent subcultures exist not in order to set them apart from adults, but as a reflection of the fact that society has already set them apart (Coleman, 1961). It is not surprising that pressure from peers is a frequent motivation for adolescents to engage in behavior—such as sex and the use of alcohol, cigarettes, and drugs—that violates the restrictions placed on them by adults.

The Importance of the Media

The mass media—television, radio, movies, books, newspapers, and magazines—produce a stream of cultural images. To sell products, advertisers tell us how we should look, smell, and behave as well as what we ought to own in order to be attractive to others. Cigarettes are associated with beautiful women who have "come a long way"; cars are described as "sexy" and offered as a way to show how "free-spirited," "independent," or "intelligent" their owners are. Expensive liquor is offered as a sign that those who drink it have succeeded in the world.

Like schools, the media often transmit hidden messages. Advertisements rarely portray women as the equals of men: women rarely instruct men and voice-overs are always male (Courtney and Whipple, 1983). Advertisements for products designed to make men and women sexually attractive never use men and women of different races in the same situation, implying that interracial attraction does not exist.

For many of us, the images portrayed in various media are like mirrors in which we look for reflections of ourselves as well as information about other people. "Is *my* breath bad? Is *this* what it's like to be in love? Is this what whites (or Hispanics or Chinese) are *really* like?" The media attempt to portray most aspects of life in our society, from the way police officers perform their jobs to family and work relationships, personal hygiene, and life in different social classes. In *All in the Family*, and, later, *Archie Bunker's Place*, Archie Bunker reinforced the stereotype that working-class people are ignorant racists (which draws attention away from racism among middle- and upper-class people) (Gans, 1980). The general absence of nonwhites in

leading roles in television and films (to which Bill Cosby is a notable exception) reinforces the stereotype that only whites have dramatic lives and are capable of heroic action (Withey and Abeles, 1980).

The power of the media lies primarily in the fact that they portray what is beyond the experience of many viewers; and, thus, images of social life can replace experience as our source of knowledge about

---

ONE STEP FURTHER 6-1:
Social Class, Race, and Who We Want Our Children to Be

The percentages in Table B-6-1 give a detailed picture of how child-rearing values vary among adults with different social statuses related to class and race. Each column represents a value measured by asking, "Which *three* qualities listed on this card would you say are the *most desirable* for a child to have?" The columns show the percentage of adults in each category—income, education, occupation, and race—who named each quality as one of the three most important.

There are a lot of numbers here, but if you follow them carefully it should all become clear. Column I shows percentages who mentioned "has good sense and sound judgment" as an important quality. If you look down the first column, you will see that the percentage increases as we go from lower to higher income, education, and occupational prestige, and from nonwhites to whites. The same is true for being "considerate" and "intellectually curious" (columns III and IV). Stop and find these patterns in the numbers. Take your time.

The opposite pattern, however, holds for obedience to parents (II) and being a good student (V). Whites and adults with more income, education, or occupational prestige are *less* likely to value these qualities most highly. Equally as important are the qualities of children for which there are *no* class or racial differences (not shown here): having good manners, being neat and clean, being honest, having self-control, trying hard to succeed, conforming to gender roles, getting along well with other children, and being responsible.

From what you have read in the text, how do you explain these findings?

Table B-6-1

Percentage of U.S. Adults Who Mention This Quality as One of Three Most Desirable for a Child to Have (1986)

| | QUALITY | | | | |
| | (I) | (II) | (III) | (IV) | (V) |
ADULT'S SOCIAL STATUS	Good Sense	Obeys Parents	Considerate	Intellectually Curious	Good Student
Income					
Less than $4,000	19%	49%	29%	19%	32%
$4,000–$13,999	32%	45%	35%	24%	22%
$14,000–$34,999	49%	35%	40%	22%	14%
$35,000 and over	49%	25%	37%	26%	15%
Education					
Less than high school	28%	54%	29%	15%	28%
High school graduate	43%	36%	38%	23%	18%
Some college	45%	28%	40%	23%	9%
College degree	46%	26%	45%	37%	11%
More than college	58%	21%	45%	42%	17%
Occupational Prestige					
Low	27%	49%	27%	14%	22%
Low-middle	41%	37%	39%	23%	18%
Upper-middle	43%	35%	36%	25%	16%
Upper	46%	23%	48%	35%	11%
Race					
Nonwhite	22%	56%	29%	21%	32%
White	44%	34%	39%	24%	16%

Source: Computed from raw 1986 General Social Survey data.

the social environment (van Dijk, 1987). Most people in the U.S. are strongly anti-communist and yet have never read Marx and have no experience of communism except through the images presented in the mass media. The media consistently emphasize the problems of countries such as the Soviet Union and China, which they usually attribute to failings of communism itself as a social system. Rarely do they raise critical questions about the fundamental problems of capitalism as a system (MacDonald, 1985). The mass media of communist countries present their citizens with biased views of capitalism, emphasizing problems such as poverty and racial inequality and paying less attention to such benefits as political freedom.

When images are oversimplified and distorted, they support stereotypes, but they also encourage us to experience life at such a distance that we do not feel the consequences of behavior. Most war movies focus on glory and heroics, not pain and suffering, and the thousands of fictional murders portrayed on television threaten to turn violence into a meaningless event for all but those who are directly involved.

The mass media also have the power to educate and to challenge stereotypes. Television shows such as *Roots*, *M*A*S*H*, *Holocaust*, and *The Day After*, and movies such as *Platoon* and *Full Metal Jacket* may have done much to make people more aware of racism, the human consequences of combat, the realities of persecution, and the horror of nuclear war.

Just how much influence the media have over us is still unknown (Withey and Abeles, 1980). Whether or not watching violent behavior on television stimulates aggressive behavior in children is still debated, and there are no consistent findings that point in one direction or the other (Milavsky et al., 1982; National Institute of Mental Health, 1982). Although some critics take the view that the media are a major socializing agent, it has yet to be demonstrated scientifically that they are any more than one piece of an intricate web of social factors.

It Never Ends: Adult Socialization

"I'm grown up now" is a statement that reflects an important and false belief that socialization is confined primarily to children, for we acquire new roles, drop old ones, and change current ones as we age (see Riley, 1987). Socialization continues throughout our lives, and often takes the form of *re*socialization as we adapt to changing circumstances (Gecas, 1981).

Paper Chases and Professional Training   In the television series based on *The Paper Chase*, John J. Osborn's 1979 book about life at Harvard Law School, Professor Kingsfield gives his first-year law students a crisp and clear statement about professional training: "You come in here with a head full of mush, and if you survive, you'll go out thinking like a lawyer." Notice that he does not say "knowing the law," but "*thinking* like a lawyer." "You will teach *yourselves* the law," he tells them, "but *I* will teach you how to *think*."

Like most people who undergo training for an occupation, many graduate students believe they are in school only to acquire skills or a degree; but they are often unaware that they are learning more than medicine, law, business management techniques, or sociology: they are also learning to *be* doctors, lawyers,

business executives, and sociologists. They are, in short, learning to perform roles that require far more than technical knowledge and skills.

Physicians are noted for paying less attention to patients as people than as "cases" that offer opportunities to diagnose and treat "conditions." A common explanation is that doctors practice role distance in order to protect themselves from repeated exposures to suffering and death. Becker and Geer (1958), however, offer another explanation based on participant observation in a medical school (see also Mizrahi, 1986).

First-year students, they found, enter medical school full of idealism based on sincerely held values and, in some cases, on a desire to disprove the common belief that doctors are greedy and self-serving. They are eager to help people, to heal the sick, and relieve suffering; but in their first two years, they rarely see—much less actually treat—patients. Instead, they study subjects such as chemistry and anatomy, taught by Ph.D.s who are not physicians. They soon learn that they cannot possibly learn everything there is to know about medicine, and quickly adjust to medical school as a place in which students learn to please their professors and pay as much attention to passing exams as to learning skills that will enable them to put their ideals into practice.

It is not until their third and fourth years that they see patients; but even then, they are constantly quizzed about technical knowledge:

> The student becomes preoccupied with the technical aspects of the cases with which he deals because the faculty requires him to do so. He is questioned about so many technical details that he must spend most of his time learning them. (p. 53)

There is good reason to believe that physicians who treat patients as "cases" rather than as people do so in part because they were socialized to think of patients in this way. As Becker and Geer note, however, many medical students become more concerned with human factors in medical practice as they near graduation, showing that in even the most intense socialization, individuals often hold on to their values until they are in a position to put them into action.

Starting Out: The Twenties   Between the ages of 20 and 30, a majority of Americans begin their first jobs, marry, and have children. In spite of the fact that most grow up with married parents, there are limits on how well anticipatory socialization can prepare anyone for marital roles. Emotional intimacy is one of the most difficult challenges adults face, and we tend to place heavy emotional demands on marriage.

Today, young married people must also struggle with change in the roles of women and men. It is no longer taken for granted that wives will stay at home while husbands devote themselves to paid work outside the home. For many couples, the families they grew up in do not serve as models, and husbands and wives must create their own roles to a considerable degree.

The birth of a first child brings with it readjustments. A new and demanding member is added to the family, and spouses acquire the new statuses of mother and father. In addition to learning how to parent, both must adjust to the loss of the continuous intimacy and free access they had to each other when they were first married (Glenn and McLanahan, 1983).

Those who remain single must also adjust to new roles as they make their way in a society dominated by married couples. In their early twenties, most of their friends are also single, but as they approach 30, many are married and interact primarily with other married couples. Single people nearing 30 must learn how to satisfy their emotional needs outside of marriage, and find themselves having to consider whether or not they will ever marry at all (Staples, 1981; Stein, 1981).

Married or not, most people in their twenties are employed, and because occupational roles occupy a large portion of people's time, they are important sources of socialization. Lawyers learn to focus more on legally relevant facts and winning arguments than their consequences for people; advertisers learn to value selling a product more than conveying accurate information about it. Teachers become disciplinarians and guides for their students, and office workers often adapt to bureaucratic settings by becoming rule-minded and rigid themselves (Merton, 1968).

Because we frequently change jobs during our lives, occupational resocialization is a common experience. We start our first jobs as the "new kid on the block," and after a period of probation and possible disappointment and confusion, earn our places as work-group members. When we change jobs, however, we must in some ways start all over again.

Decision Time: The Thirties
The twenties are generally an exciting and challenging period of trying new roles, and our youth makes us unaware

that our life spans are limited. By comparison, the thirties are often a time of serious reflection about our lives (Sheehy, 1974).

Parents must learn to give up control over their children who now approach adolescence. Many couples divorce during their thirties, and must adjust to the disruption of family life and the demands of living alone or raising children by themselves—often in poverty (Gordon, 1981; Rosenthal and Keshet, 1978).

Unmarried people must deal with the difficult question of whether or not to marry at all; and childless women in particular—whether married or not—must cope with the biological fact that their years of potential childbearing are limited. Whether or not to include motherhood as a part of their lives is a difficult and irrevocable decision, because unlike most other statuses, "mother" is limited by biological aging.

The thirties also are a time of intense reflection about occupations. The excitement over a "first job" in the twenties is often replaced by a disturbing question in the thirties: "Is this what I want to do for the rest of my life?" For many people—especially those in the working class—such questions are a luxury, for they have relatively little control over how to earn a living. For middle- and upper-class people, however, the choice is real—between the security of a job they do not like and the risks involved in cutting loose and looking for a better one.

The thirties appear to be a time for making important decisions about major roles. This period is, for many, like a pivot on which the rest of their lives will turn.

Mid-Life Crises: The Forties and Fifties
At midlife, we begin to adjust to the consequences of all the decisions we have made, and it is often a time of reconciling dreams with reality.

Marriage and parenthood are not the "bliss" that many thought they would be. Children leave home, and even parents who breathe a sigh of relief must adjust to their shrinking roles and loss of responsibilities. For childless women, time has run out, for childbearing is risky after 40 and by age 55, 96 percent of all women have experienced menopause (U.S. Department of Health, Education, and Welfare, 1961).

By this time, many have also discovered that dreams of success are unlikely to come true, and they must be content with what they have. With fresh generations of workers entering the labor force each year, older workers are less able to take occupational risks, because the chances of successfully competing for new jobs are relatively slim.

Perhaps the most difficult adjustment of midlife involves the realization that we are not immortal, especially in societies in which death before old age is rare. For younger people, death often seems only a remote idea; but in midlife, the "end of the tunnel" comes into view, and as we adjust to the failure of many dreams, we must also confront the reality of our eventual deaths.

Learning to Grow Old   Old age is a time of major readjustments in status and role sets (Riley et al., 1969). Retirement ends occupational roles, which —until old age—occupy most of people's daily lives. Aging can also mean the death of one's spouse and friends. Elderly men who become widowers and who do not remarry have death rates significantly above those for other men of their age (Helsing and Szklo, 1981); but Hyman (1983) found no massive short- or long-term negative effects on elderly women who become widows.

In industrial societies, people are forced to retire by specified ages (65 and 70 in the United States, depending on the job) and people who have worked their entire lives must adjust to the lower prestige of people who no longer earn a living. For many, old age causes sharp declines in income. In 1984, 80 percent of those over the age of 64 had incomes of less than $15,000, compared with only 50 percent of those between the ages of 35 and 44 (U.S. Census Bureau, 1986a).

Because women generally outlive men, a large proportion of older people are widows who live in poverty because Social Security is their only source of income. Elderly women are also more likely to live by themselves: in 1985, 38 percent lived alone compared with only 14 percent of elderly men (U.S. Census Bureau, 1986a).

Perhaps of most importance is the fact that the elderly must fully confront the reality of death, because for the first time in their lives many people of their own age are dying (Kübler-Ross, 1969, 1975). Time is literally running out at a rapid pace, and for many old age is a time of serious reflection about the meaning of their lives.

Stereotyped views of old age often portray it as a negative stage in life in which people are socialized to accept loss of loved ones and important roles and, ultimately, of life itself. It is important to emphasize, however, that for many elderly people old age is a very positive experience. The "loss" of roles is also an end to responsibilities—to children, spouses, and employers—and for many, old age is a time in which they have more freedom to run their own lives than ever before.

SOCIALIZATION AND FREEDOM

Socialization is a lifelong process that brings with it countless changes in the roles we play. It is a process that raises some important issues about the nature of social life.

Infants sometimes wake in the night and cry until someone picks them up and holds them for a while. They often have more difficulty falling asleep on a large bed than in a crib whose size is closer to their own. They seem to need *boundaries*, solid contact with people and things that give them a sense of where, if not who, they are. We are not unlike infants in this way. When we are left without limits we tend to feel lost, floating in a void, and we reach out for familiar things and people in order to reorient ourselves.

We are social animals who need one another, and yet our relationships are regulated by ideas we draw from a shared culture. As the studies of isolated children show, we cannot survive as autonomous, lone individuals, and so to satisfy our need for one another we must forgo a good portion of individual freedom.

Socialization is more than a process that prepares individuals for social life, however, for it is also a means by which societies are perpetuated. There is more at stake than what we become as individuals, how we adjust to social demands and succeed or fail. Also at stake is the kind of society we adjust to and the part we play in changing or perpetuating it. It is ironic that if we are socialized effectively, adjusting perfectly to our surroundings, we may at the same time perpetuate injustice and cruelty. For children who grew up in Nazi Germany during the 1930s, hating Jews and Poles was part of being a "good German," and their acceptance of this ultimately led to World War II, the Holocaust, and the destruction of Nazi Germany (see Peukert, 1987).

In similar ways, girls who learn to be "feminine women," and boys who learn to be "masculine men," are not merely acquiring roles and identities that allow them to operate in a sexist society. As we will see in Chapter 13, they are also learning to participate in the

In Nazi Germany, to be a good German was to be a good Nazi. What does it mean to be a good American?

dominance of women by men. Girls who adopt traditional roles learn to accept a subordinate position, whereas boys learn to use the power that comes with their gender. While we learn to be masculine or feminine in a sexist society, we also help to perpetuate sexism.

This raises a crucial point about socialization and the relationship between individuals and societies. All of us are socialized in the sense of becoming social beings. In every society, almost everyone forms a social identity and learns to interact with other people and to perform roles. This does *not* mean, however, that each of us is molded according to a uniform cultural model—that we all become no more than a mirror image of our social environment (Wrong, 1961).

Like individuals, societies constantly change, and how they change depends strongly on the choices individuals make. Without society the individual does not exist; it is also true, however, that without individuals there can be no society (see Giddeus, 1984). Because we are social beings, our dependence on others makes us vulnerable; and yet we have the power to resist the limitations of social environments, to define and redefine the terms by which we live.

SUMMARY

1. Socialization involves both what we learn and how we learn as we become social beings; these, in turn, depend heavily on culture and social structure. We learn to orient ourselves to cultural ideas according to our social statuses, and through this we acquire an awareness of ourselves and of others and develop self-concepts and self-esteem. Although our ability to be socialized is rooted in biological development, the process itself cannot unfold without interaction and language.

2. The behavioral, social learning, and cognitive perspectives are the three principal theories about how people learn. (1) According to the behavioral approach, our behavior results from the application of punishment and reward in classical and operant conditioning. (2) The social learning perspective pays attention to models whom we imitate. (3) Cognitive development theory focuses on developing the ability to make complex judgments. Although all three perspectives are useful, they do not take into account the crucial effects of social environments.

3. Socialization begins with our understanding of language, the basis for connecting our experience with the experience of others; through this, we develop mind, the ability to use symbols to put ourselves in the place of another person.

4. The "I" consists of our direct experience of ourselves and others, and the "me" is that part of us that looks upon the "I" as an object. Significant others are particular people we orient ourselves to, and the generalized other is our perception of what is expected in social situations. Through significant others we are able to discover ourselves as selves. Our self-concept is the total of our beliefs and feelings about ourselves; it is

strongly influenced by our looking-glass self, our perception of how other people perceive and evaluate us.

5. As we develop, we enlarge our status and role sets. The cultural ideas people share about the occupants of statuses are, in turn, used to form a social identity, an ideal self, and self-esteem. An important part of this process is the use of reference groups and individuals for comparison. This is particularly important for anticipatory socialization.

6. The family, schools, and the mass media are three major agents of socialization. Past childhood, we continue to adapt to new social circumstances throughout the life course. Rites of passage mark the transition from one status to another; and we adjust to change in work and family, modifying relationships as we grow into adulthood and old age. In many ways, we learn to play new roles and to reformulate our ideas and feelings about others and ourselves.

7. As we mature, the socialization process confers on us the power of selfhood, the ability to make our own choices, which at times may conflict with the same society that socialized us. We are not simply limited by our social environment; we are part of it, and so long as we participate in social life, we cannot help but punish and reward others and provide them with models. We are born into a world not of our own making, but as we are socialized and participate in social life, we become the makers who help fashion the social environment in which future generations will be born and become social beings.

KEY TERMS

Looking Elsewhere

Having studied Chapter 6, you might want to look at related discussions in *Human Arrangements*, which include

RECOMMENDED READINGS

ARIÈS, P. (1962). *Centuries of childhood: A social history of family life*. New York: Knopf. A fascinating look at how the definition of childhood has changed over the centuries, with a special emphasis on the ways in which this has affected the treatment of children.

BECKER, H. S., et al. (1976). *Boys in white: Student culture in medical school* (rev. ed.). New Brunswick, NJ: Transaction Books. The classic study of the socialization process that turns college graduates into doctors.

BRIM, O. G., JR., and WHEELER, S. (1966). *Socialization after childhood: Two essays*. New York: Wiley. Two classic essays that show that socialization only *begins* in childhood.

BROWN, R. (1965). *Social psychology*. New York: Free Press. In this classic text, chapters on the acquisition of language and morality are both extremely well written and full of ideas and information.

DAVIS, K. (1940). Final note on a case of extreme isolation. *American Journal of Sociology*, 45, 554–565. One of the few existing studies of a documented case of a child raised in isolation, Davis' 1940 article makes for fascinating reading.

FREUD, S. (1961). *Civilization and its discontents*. New York: Norton. Freud's classic theory about the tension between the demands of society and inborn human drives. (Original work published 1930)

GRACEY, H. L. (1972). Learning the student role: Kindergarten as academic boot camp. In D. H. Wrong (Ed.), *Readings in introductory sociology* (2nd ed.) (pp. 243–254). New York: Macmillan. This widely reprinted article shows how early training begins with amusing and sometimes disturbing insights into the world of kindergarten.

KÜBLER-ROSS, E. (1975). *Death, the final stage of growth*. Englewood Cliffs, NJ: Prentice-Hall. Kübler-Ross has been a pioneer in the study of death as a human experience. As the title of this book suggests, Kübler-Ross views death and dying as another stage of life that has its own lessons to be learned.

MCCARL, R. (1985). *The District of Columbia fire fighters' project: A case study in occupational folklife*. Washington, D.C.: Smithsonian Institution Press. An unusual and fascinating look at the process through which fire fighters are socialized into their occupational subculture.

MONTAGU, A. (1971). *Touching: The human significance of the skin*. New York: Columbia University Press. A fascinating look at the importance of touching in human development with a special emphasis on cross-cultural variation in how people touch each other.

ROSE, P. I. (Ed.). (1979). *Socialization and the life cycle*. New York: St. Martin's Press. A very good collection of readings on the socialization process throughout the life course.

ROSENBERG, M. (1979). *Conceiving the self*. New York: Basic Books. A thorough, thoughtful, and well-written look at key concepts in the sociological study of socialization, based on both a thorough review of existing research and the analysis of new data.

WRONG, D. H. (1961). The oversocialized concept of man in modern sociology. *The American Sociological Review*, 26 (April), 183–193. An important statement of the problems of viewing socialization as a process that is determined either by society or by forces within the individual. Wrong argues effectively for a more balanced view.

7 Social Interaction

In **social interaction**, we act in relation to one another. It is a complex process through which we organize and interpret our perceptions and expectations of people and situations; present ourselves to others; and try to understand who people are, what they are doing, and why. The behavior that results depends in part on the psychological characteristics of individuals; but culture, social structure, and population and ecology influence us in profound ways.

ACTION AND INTERACTION

Late one night in March 1964, a woman named Kitty Genovese was murdered outside her New York City apartment in a middle-class neighborhood of Queens. Thirty-nine people watched from their apartments as she screamed in agony and terror while her attacker stabbed her repeatedly in a struggle that lasted for more than 30 minues. He left her bleeding, but alive, only to return later and attack her again. Not one of the witnesses did anything to help her; no one even called the police until the final fatal wound had been inflicted.

The witnesses violated many important norms and values against which we might judge their behavior as outrageously immoral and unfeeling. In the public shock that followed, the question was raised repeatedly: How could people behave that way? For each one who raised that question, there was probably an underlying statement: "*I* would have done *something*."

If we think of the witnesses' behavior as simple actions carried out by individuals, our explanations will tend to be psychological: they were perhaps too insensitive, immoral, or frightened to pick up a telephone and call for help. Sociologists, however, are reluctant to settle for that kind of explanation, for it ignores the fact that when we act, we act in *relation* to one another and our environments.

Latané and Darley (1970) tried to answer the question "How could people behave that way?" and to test the common assumption that most people would have behaved differently (see also Dantin and Carver, 1982; Latané and Nida, 1981). As a participant in their experiment, you would have been invited to a small group discussion about personal problems. You are told that there are six of you, and to help you be more open about yourselves, each of you will sit in your own room from which you cannot see one another. Each person has two minutes to talk through an intercom system, and during that time, no one else can communicate with other members of the group. After everyone has spoken, each member may speak for an additional two minutes. You will go last.

The first person to talk mentions that he sometimes has violent seizures, especially when he is under strain. After you and other members talk about your lives and problems, the first person speaks again. Suddenly he says:

> I-er-if somebody could help me out it would—it would er-er s-s-sure be—sure be good . . . because er-the-er-er-a cause I-er-I-uh I've got a-a one of the-er-seiz . . . er-er-things coming on and-and-and I could really-er-use some help so uh-er-er-er-er c-could somebody er-er-help er-uh-uh-uh—(choking sounds) . . . I'm gonna die er-er-I'm . . . gonna die erer-seizure-er (choking sound again; then quiet).

What would you do? Immediately leave the room and look for help? Or sit and wonder if you should do anything? (At the end of the experiment, by the way, you learn that all the voices you heard were recorded.)

Latané and Darley wanted to explain why some subjects respond faster than others and why some fail to respond at all, and they focused not on personality differences but on how ecological characteristics of the situation affected the subjects' responses. In particular, they wanted to know how the number of people in a group affects behavior.

Their results were dramatic. Of those who believed they were in a six-person group, only 30 percent went for help, whereas 62 percent of those who believed they were in a three-person group responded to the plea. Of those who believed they and the victim were the only group members, fully 85 percent went for help. Although individual characteristics may explain why some people in six-person groups went for help and others did not, they cannot explain why those in larger groups were less likely to act than those in smaller groups.

A sociological explanation of why people may not help others combines social and ecological factors. First, the more bystanders there are, the more likely we are to assume that someone else will help; we spread responsibility over the entire group, and the larger the group is, the more thinly we can spread responsibility, leaving less for ourselves (Berkowitz, 1978).

Second, we are always in danger of misinterpreting situations and making fools of ourselves (being an "alarmist"), and the larger the number of people present, the more potential witnesses there are to ridicule us. Third, we are often unsure of our perceptions and interpretations, and we look to other people for confirmation: if no one else responds, it reinforces the interpretation that action is not called for. This is a classic "Catch-22" (Heller, 1955/1961). We wait for someone else to act first: hence, no one acts, because each potential "someone else" is also waiting for someone else to do something.

Such findings suggest that Kitty Genovese's neighbors were not cruel or callous, but that each felt their responsibility spread out over many others. Ironically, each may have refrained from helping because they could not imagine that *no* one would help. Had they seen someone go to her aid, they might well have called the police; or if each believed he or she was the only witness, they would have been far more likely to respond.

The sociology of interaction focuses on the way our awareness of ourselves, one another, and social environments influences our behavior. Basic to all social interaction are these two questions: Who are you? and Who am I?

Visibility: Seeing and Being Seen

Few things are more important to us than to be seen by other people. To be ignored for even a few minutes can make us feel shy and uninteresting, and to be shunned is one of the worst things that can happen.

In the prologue to Ralph Ellison's novel *The Invisible Man* (1952), a black man accidentally collides with a stranger on a dark street. The stranger insults the black man, and the black man violently attacks him:

The simple feeling that people can see us lies at the heart of our connection to social life. American artist Edward Hopper is known for his paintings that capture the sense of social isolation and loneliness—hallmarks of life in modern industrial societies.

And in my outrage I got out my knife and prepared to slit his throat . . . when it occurred to me that the man had not *seen* me, actually; that he, as far as he knew, was in the midst of a walking nightmare! . . . I ran away into the dark. . . . Poor blind fool, I thought with sincere compassion, mugged by an invisible man!

The black man feels that his low social standing makes him invisible to others, treated with so little regard by white society that he might as well not exist at all. The importance of this for social interaction is clear in his thoughts:

> Irresponsibility is part of my invisibility; any way you face it, it is a denial. But to whom can I be responsible, and why should I be, when you refuse to see me? Responsibility rests on recognition, and recognition is a form of agreement.

Our statuses affect whether or not people see us and how they see us; and these influence the terms by which we interact with one another, the often unspoken, unconscious "agreements" that structure social life.

Culture, Social Structure, and Perception

Since we cannot pay attention to everything at once, we necessarily select what we perceive. To remember and communicate, we must simplify and organize information. When we describe someone as "intelligent" we select a few observations from many, and simplify, organize, and interpret them in terms of an abstract category. Culture is a framework of ideas that we use in this process, and our statuses influence which parts of that framework we use and how we use them.

Perceptions of others depend on two kinds of information. The first consists of *impressions* of personal characteristics such as "kindness" or "cruelty," "beauty" or "ugliness." First impressions are particularly important because they foster expectations that influence our subsequent perceptions, feelings, and behavior.

In one experiment, college students read a description of a guest instructor just before he arrived (Kelley, 1950). The descriptions gave identical information about his academic background and experience, but differed in one detail: half read, "People who know him consider him to be a rather cold person, industrious, critical, practical, and determined," but in the other half, the words "very warm" were substituted for "cold."

The guest led the group discussion for twenty minutes—during which the researcher observed and recorded student participation—and after he left, students anonymously evaluated him. The single piece of information—"very warm" or "cold"—strikingly affected how students interacted with and evaluated him. Among students who were told he was very warm, 56 percent participated in the discussion, whereas only 32 percent of those who were told he was cold took part. When asked to evaluate his performance, students who were told he was cold thought that he seemed more self-centered, formal, unsociable, unpopular, irritable, humorless, and ruthless than did students who were told he was very warm.

Many social psychologists argue that perceptions of physical attractiveness are particularly important in forming first impressions (see Patzer, 1985). People we see as attractive, we also tend to see as having other positive features as well, such as being intelligent and likable. This can then become a **self-fulfilling prophecy**, a belief that comes true because people think and act as if it were, in fact, already true. Our beliefs about people lead us to treat them in particular ways; and our treatment, in turn, leads them to fulfill the prophecy contained in our beliefs (Merton, 1968). We treat those we see as unattractive as if they are also unlikable and this, in turn, makes it more likely that they will behave in ways that we will see as unlikable.

We use first impressions to form expectations around which we organize perceptions and judgments that strongly influence our behavior. From a sociological perspective, however, our expectations depend even more importantly on a second type of information: our perceptions of people's social identities, their status sets.

Stereotypes   Cultures contain thousands of beliefs: that the elderly are less capable than the young, that poor people are lazy (or victims of injustice), or that people from other societies value life less than we do. Although it is impossible to avoid using statuses as a source of information about people, they often lead to errors. When we select certain characteristics and make inferences from them, we not only lose the information we choose to ignore, but often add misinformation as well (McCall and Simmons, 1978).

These cultural "sketches" of people in different statuses are **stereotypes**—rigid, oversimplified beliefs that are applied to all members of a group or social category. We all depend on stereotypes to some degree when we interact with other people. In fact, without them we could not predict other people's behavior in role relationships.

When stereotypes are our only source of information, however, they cause several problems. First, they oversimplify. We forget that people we regard as heroes are human beings who dream, have fears, and make mistakes just like the rest of us. Second, stereotypes tend to be much more rigid than people. When

For many decades prior to the civil rights movement, the image of "Aunt Jemima" was a pervasive stereotype of black women as jolly cooks, maids, and caretakers of white children. In startling contrast, black artist Joe Overstreet's 1964 alternative depicts a proud, angry "New Jemima" wielding a machine gun.

we identify people as former mental patients, we tend to interpret their behavior as a reflection of mental instability, and expect them to continue to be "crazy" regardless of their actual behavior.

Third, although some characteristics are more common among those in one status than another, it is often a mistake to apply group characteristics to individuals. Men are far more likely than women to commit violent crimes; but this does not mean that every man you meet is likely to be a criminal.

Fourth, when we define people in terms of a social status, we often mistakenly assume that they represent all occupants of that status. A black college student may be called upon in class to give "the black point of view" on a particular issue, a request that ignores the enormous variation among black people.

Finally, stereotyping can have the effect of a self-fulfilling prophecy by encouraging people to conform to cultural beliefs about them. People often mistakenly assume that deaf people are mentally retarded because they express themselves with difficulty and in unusual ways. If, based on this stereotyped view, we deny deaf children regular schooling, they may in fact grow up with limited intellectual abilities.

Social interaction, then, is based on our perception of other people's social characteristics, from which we identify "who they are." We do not encounter them in a vacuum, however, for interaction occurs in social contexts whose characteristics affect both how we perceive others and how we and they define our expectations.

Defining the Situation

To interact we must define the situation by identifying the statuses and roles that define our expectations. How people define the situation is enormously important, for as W. I. Thomas once wrote, if we "define situations as real, they are real in their consequences" (Thomas and Thomas, 1928, p. 572).

In his movie *Take the Money and Run*, Woody Allen wants to rob a bank, and he hands a teller a note that reads, "I have a gun. Give me all your cash." The teller, however, is puzzled, because he reads, "I have a gu*b*."

"No, it's '*gun*,'" Allen says.

"Looks like 'gub' to me," the teller says, then asks another teller to help read the note, then another, and finally everyone is arguing over what the note means. Allen never robs the bank, because he is the only one who defines the situation as a robbery (see Watzlawick, 1976).

We continually activate and deactivate statuses in our daily lives, and as we do, we perform roles through which we express different aspects of our identities. One minute we are riders on a bus, then pedestrians, then restaurant customers, employees, or college students in class. When someone gives us a gift, it immediately activates the status of recipient and a role that includes gratitude and some obligation to return the favor (see Fisher, Nadler, and DePaulo, 1983).

The statement "I'm in love with you" is more than an expression of feeling; it is an attempt to define a relationship, and the response "I love you, too" invokes a complex set of expectations. In the same sense, the statement "I don't love you any more" is as much an attempt to redefine a situation as it is an expression of feeling.

When someone approaches us with a definition of a situation—such as "This is a holdup" or "We're lovers"—we must decide whether or not to adopt it, for once we do, we feel bound to perform the role implied. Doctors may lie to terminal patients about the seriousness of their conditions and justify their dishonesty in the name of protecting the patient from a horrible truth. From a sociological perspective, however, the deceivers also protect themselves, because once a patient is socially defined as "dying," other people must activate their own status of "attendant to a dying person" and face all of the sadness and frustration that go with it.

Our ability to define social relationships gives us considerable creative power. We can be taken care of as though we were children even when we reach adulthood, so long as there is someone willing to play the role of "adult" in relation to us as "child." Or we can be strong and domineering if someone is willing to be weak and submissive in relation to us. In many ways, we seek people who share our definitions of the situation, because they, in effect, allow us to be who we want to be.

The definition of the situation is important not only in the activation of statuses and roles, but also in the way people interpret one another. Studies in the sociology of sexuality have found that men who work with women tend to define business lunches as dates, while women do not. They also find that men are much more likely than women to interpret friendliness as sexual (see Gutek, 1985). Given that a smile or any other gesture can indicate many different emotions—from pleasure to embarrassment—how we define the situation in which it occurs has an enormous impact on what we think it means and, therefore, how we respond to it.

From a sociological perspective, interaction is based on a complex process of perception and interpretation of people and the situations in which we encounter one another, activate selected parts of our social selves, and, in responding to one another, interact. In some ways, interaction is like an elaborate dance in which we move in relation to one another, each creating variations on the "themes" contained in roles. If you observe department store clerks and customers, you will soon discover that although most of the interactions are between complete strangers, the patterns are astonishingly consistent throughout the day.

Interaction is a vital, functional activity in any society. It is literally the means through which social life takes place. It is in interaction that social structure and culture become more than ideas, for here they are reflected in what we actually do in relation to one another.

Social Attribution

When we interact with people, we often use the definition of the situation to explain their behavior. This process of interpretation is called **social attribution** (Heider, 1958; Kelley and Michela, 1980). Suppose a man picks your pocket and gets away with a week's pay, and the police catch him after he has spent your money. How severely would you want him punished? If you learned that he is a professional thief who drives a fancy car, you would feel quite differently than if you learned that he is desperately poor, was laid off from his job through no fault of his own, and used the money to buy fuel oil for his family during a bitterly cold winter. He is a thief in both cases, but your response to him depends on how you explain his behavior.

We cannot explain the thief's behavior simply by observing his actions—we need two basic types of additional information (Heider, 1958). First, we need to know the **internal causes** of the thief's behavior: personal motives, abilities, and emotional states. Was he desperate or just greedy? Or was he mentally ill and unaware of the seriousness of his behavior?

Second, we need to know the **external causes** to be able to explain behavior in any situation. If the thief is unemployed, poor, married, and the father of small children, his family roles require him to earn a living, but his statuses of "poor" and "unemployed" deprive him of socially legitimate ways to do so. We use people's statuses and roles to explain their behavior.

Several studies show that explanations of behavior vary according to the actor's gender. When asked to explain the success of a "Dr. Mark Greer" or a "Dr. Marcia Greer," people tend to attribute the man's success to his abilities and the woman's success to luck, hard work, or a less demanding job (Feldman-Summers and Kiesler, 1974). They also tend to explain a man's failure as a case of bad luck, while explaining similar failures of women as due to a lack of ability (Deaux, 1972).

We generally use internal causes to explain other people's behavior, but rely on external causes to explain our own (Davis and Stephan, 1980; Monson and Hesley, 1982; Reeder and Spores, 1983). When college students try to explain why their work is late, they are unlikely to offer "laziness," "lack of motivation," or "incompetence" as causes. They are more likely to refer to the demands of other roles ("I have four papers due this week") or circumstances beyond their personal control ("My dog ate my paper").

We add the demands of latent statuses (student in another course; dog owner) to our definition of the situation in order to explain our failure in a manifest status (notice also, in the "Dr. Greer" example above, how people used the latent statuses "male" and "female" to explain performance in the manifest status of "doctor"). Professors, on the other hand, are more likely to attribute student performance to internal causes and regard external factors as a poor excuse.

Why should this difference occur? Jones and Nisbett (1971) argued that as actors we "look outward" on the world and are therefore highly aware of the circumstances that affect our behavior. But, as Tetlock (1981) pointed out, we also want to appear in the best possible light and therefore tend to present ourselves to others as victims of circumstances we cannot control. As observers of other people, however, we tend to focus on individuals, not on their situations. All we see is them and what they do, and we therefore tend to believe that the causes of their behavior rest solely within themselves.

Social interaction is more than a dance between partners who share a rhythm and listen to the same music, for every act directed at someone else crosses a boundary that separates and protects that person from others. To interact is to act *upon* one another. It is important to examine the nature of those boundaries, how we cross them, and with what effects.

Social Boundaries

> Some thirty inches from my nose
> The frontier of my Person goes. . .
> Stranger, unless with bedroom eyes
> I beckon you to fraternize,
> Beware of rudely crossing it;
> I have no gun, but I can spit.
> —W. H. Auden

Physical contact is closely regulated in social life. While our skin separates and protects us from others, the cultural ideas that regulate human contact form an invisible boundary around us, and only those who occupy certain statuses in relation to us have the right to cross it, and even then only under certain circumstances. Clothes insulate us in public and shield us from other people's eyes, and only under special circumstances do we allow someone to reach the skin beneath. Strangers may shake our hands, but only those close to us may touch our faces. We allow dentists to work in our mouths and physicians to penetrate our skins, but they may do so only within the strict limits of their roles.

The right to forcibly move us from one place to another is limited to a narrow range of statuses, such as that of police officer (but only when arresting us) or parent (but only when we are still children). In general, people do not have the right to shoot, stab, or hit us; and yet, under culturally defined circumstances— "self-defense"—they may.

Our skin is a last line of defense, for the limits of our personal boundaries extend beyond it to include culturally prescribed limits to our selves. If you are sitting on a park bench and a stranger sits down right next to you, how do you feel? Chances are you feel less comfortable, as if there were no longer enough room for you, even though in a strict physical sense there is. Hall (1959, 1969) suggests that each culture contains ideas about appropriate physical distances between people for each situation.

In the U.S. the "zone of intimacy" extends to a distance of about 18 inches and is reserved for intimate acquaintances, whereas those who are close friends— but not intimate—must stay at a "personal distance"

As you study the people in this park, what can you infer about their social relationships solely from their physical position in relation to others?

of 18 inches to 4 feet. Impersonal interactions—those among workers—take place at a distance of from 4 to 12 feet; and the "public zone" of 12 feet or more is appropriate among strangers.

The use of physical space is an important ecological factor in social interaction. In the U.S., we use automobiles to insulate ourselves from others (although some interaction may result from aggression and competition) and prefer the stresses of rush hour traffic to the forced intimacy of buses and trains. Many Europeans (the French, in particular) and Latin-Americans, on the other hand, prefer being close to other passengers (Hall, 1969).

Each culture specifies the limits of physical zones. "Personal distance" in Latin cultures resembles the "zone of intimacy" in the U.S., and non-Latins often feel uncomfortable among Latins who seem to stand "too close." What we experience as natural boundaries are in fact social boundaries whose use depends on how we define the situation in a cultural context.

In an experiment about the use of physical zones, a researcher sat down six inches from people sitting alone on park benches (Sommer, 1969). He then re-corded how long the other person stayed, and compared this with observations of people who were left alone. Almost 50 percent of those whose social boundary was crossed left within five minutes, compared with only 10 percent of those who were left alone.

Norms do more than regulate physical contact, however, for they also specify expectations in role relationships. We may look at strangers, but folkways do not allow staring; even close friends may experience staring as an invasion of privacy, especially when directed at their eyes, which have been aptly described as "the windows of the soul." There are many ways to shield ourselves from other people. As children we tend to reveal ourselves openly and directly in social interactions, but as we are socialized, we learn subtlety and concealment (Cooley, 1902). Because we rely on gestures to express our feelings and thoughts to others, we can use them as screens that withhold or distort information about ourselves.

Many roles allow us to maintain contact with others without revealing ourselves. "Hello, how are you?" someone asks, to which we reply, "Fine, how are you?" On one level, such interactions are dishonest, for we rarely want to know how someone really feels when we pass them on the street, and "fine" is often an inaccurate description. Indeed, to describe our feelings in great detail violates the expectations attached to the role of "acquaintances meeting on the street."

As meaningless as such exchanges appear to be, they play an important part in social life, for without them we feel invisible and uncomfortable ("Why didn't you say 'hello'?"). Although the apparent question is "How are you?" the underlying question is often "How am I?" as we look for our reflection in other people's recognition of us. Without such roles, we would have to choose between extensive, revealing interactions or none at all. Few people are above the "small talk" that allows us to "keep in touch" with other people without revealing more of ourselves than we want to.

The importance of small talk illustrates a major tension in social life. We want to be known by others, to break down barriers that isolate us; and yet we are afraid of being known too well by people who may reject or abuse us. The psychotherapist Fritz Perls suggests that our cleverness with words encourages us to be superficial with one another, to conceal the feelings and thoughts that give meaning and depth to human relationships (Perls, Hefferline, and Goodman, 1965).

It is ironic that although social boundaries must be crossed if friendship is to occur, the likelihood of forming a friendship is diminished, not enhanced, when boundaries are unclear or too easily crossed. In one experiment, sailors volunteered to be isolated in pairs for ten days in a small chamber equipped with cots, tables, and toilet and eating facilities, as well as a video camera that recorded their interactions (Altman et al., 1971). Some became friends, but others did not get along.

The researchers noticed that friendship was more likely when the men established clear boundaries at the start of their stay: who would sleep where, what parts of the chamber were reserved for each man, how and when furniture was to be used. Those who failed to establish clear boundaries were far less likely to get along.

Interaction involves a complex balance among boundaries; and, as the definition of the situation changes, our boundaries swell and contract. Among intimate friends we draw boundaries close to ourselves and allow others to cross them with relative ease, but among strangers, boundaries expand and become increasingly difficult for people to cross.

Puzzles: When is Rape not a Crime?

When can a man force a woman to have sexual intercourse with him and not be charged with rape even if he confesses?

In most states of the United States, the answer is: when he is her husband and the couple is not legally separated. (A notable "exception that proves the rule" is a 1984 case in Florida in which a husband was tried and convicted of sexually assaulting his wife.) Power is often an important part of social interaction, and as explained in this chapter and in Chapter 13, the statuses of husband and wife have built-in power inequalities that allow husbands to behave toward their wives in ways that are prohibited in relation to other women.

Power and Social Interaction

We maintain some control over the extent and strength of our boundaries, but our ability to control contact and interaction with others is often limited by differences in power. As we saw in Chapter 4, power can take many forms, but most depend more on roles and the definition of the situation than on individual characteristics and will.

Most states define rape as sexual contact gained through the use of force or the threat of force. In rape, the woman's body as well as her right to control it are violated. As a member of society, she may call upon the legal system to support her right to be protected from assault (Brownmiller, 1975; Medea and Thompson, 1974). If her attacker happens to be her husband, however, the laws in many states define his behavior as "assault," not rape. In these states, "sexual contact gained through the use of force" simply cannot happen between spouses (see Russell, 1982). Why not?

Criminal laws exist to protect us from other people. Laws that forbid rape, murder, assault, robbery, and harassing telephone calls, or that limit a government's power to record our telephone calls, open our mail, or arrest us without good cause, all specify boundaries that people may not cross without risking punishment.

In many states, rape laws grant husbands the right to behave toward their wives in ways that would be criminal in relation to other women. Such laws are based on the seventeenth century writings of the English jurist Matthew Hale who argued that husbands cannot be held guilty of raping their wives, because upon marriage a wife is assumed to give unconditional consent to her husband's sexual desires, a consent which she "cannot retract" (Hale, 1847). This reflects the historical subjugation of women—in which they have been viewed as property, belonging first to their fathers, then "given" to their husbands in marriage. In every sexual interaction between spouses, the law grants a husband the right to cross his wife's personal boundaries at will, and although he may choose not to exercise that right, it is always nonetheless available (see Finkelhor and Yllo, 1985).

In the simplest sense, we all have personal power. Even small children have power in relation to adults: they can refuse to do what they are told, throw embarrassing tantrums in public places, or obey slowly and reluctantly. Sociologists, however, focus primarily on authority which differs from other forms of power in that it is socially supported, and rests on the belief that those who possess it have a right to it, and those who do not have a duty to obey. Our statuses determine who has the authority to invade our boundaries, to act upon us regardless of what we want. The statuses of child, mental patient, and "under arrest" have roles that include little authority, and people in those statuses must rely on personal power to control what happens with more powerful role partners.

Authority is not a form of personal power. It is attached to particular statuses under socially defined conditions. When military people salute each other, they pay respect to a person's rank, not to the individual who holds it; and when they remove their uniforms, they are no longer saluted.

Sociologically, authority is a particularly important source of power, because people in positions of authority can exercise power that is vastly beyond their resources and abilities. They act not in their own names, but in the name of an entire group if not society itself. Because society grants some status occupants power they would otherwise never have, authority is particularly subject to abuse (Sennett, 1981).

In a classic experiment (Haney, Banks, and Zimbardo, 1973), male college students volunteered to play the roles of prisoners and guards in a laboratory designed to resemble a prison. The students were paid to participate, and the "guards" were given complete control over the daily lives of their "prisoners." The experiment began with the handcuffing and arrest of the "prisoners" who were then transported to mock prison cells in a university building. The guards stripped and searched them, sprayed them with delousing fluid, took their pictures, and ordered them to remain silent in their cells. The researchers were testing the common belief that the brutality of guards in real prisons is caused by cruel personalities. Is it possible that the situation itself, in which some people have complete power over others, fosters abusive behavior?

As the days passed, the prisoners became increasingly depressed, sometimes crying or showing signs of rage and acute anxiety. Almost half had to be released before a week had passed, and the rest said they would gladly forfeit their pay in exchange for an early release.

The guards readily used their authority to abuse the prisoners. They rarely spoke to them except to deliver commands, frequently denied them privileges, and in one case locked a prisoner in the "solitary confinement" of a small closet all night. They concealed much of their abusive behavior from the experimenters, who they believed were "too soft" on the prisoners. Guards appeared to enjoy their work, volunteered to work overtime without pay, and were disappointed when the experiment ended prematurely. As one of the experimenters recalled:

> At the end of only six days we had to close down our mock prison because what we saw was frightening. It was no longer apparent to us or most of the subjects where they ended and their roles began. The majority had indeed become "prisoners" or "guards," no longer able to clearly differentiate between role-playing and self. There were dramatic changes in virtually every aspect of their behavior, thinking, and feeling. . . . We were horrified because we saw some boys ("guards") treat other boys as if they were despicable animals, taking pleasure in cruelty, while other boys ("prisoners") became servile, dehumanized robots who thought only of escape, of their own individual survival, and of their mounting hatred of the guards. (Zimbardo, 1971, p. 3)

These apparently decent young men gave support to Lord Acton's famous statement that "power tends to corrupt and absolute power corrupts absolutely." Why should power have this effect? Kipnis (1972) suggested that high levels of power lead to abuse for three reasons.

The Zimbardo experiment suggests that extreme power inequality is conducive to abuse. In few situations is this potential more dramatic than when we must remove our clothes in front of someone who has power over us—as do these Texas prison guards searching inmates. Can you imagine how you might feel in each of the social positions in this situation?

1. Status occupants will use as much power as is available to them. When we have only the power of persuasion, that is what we will use; if our roles allow us to punish and reward others, however, we will rely less on persuasion than on the more powerful means available to us.

2. Power allows people to control other people's behavior. In turn, those who have power may come to believe they are superior to those they control. Power may in fact lead to such a boost in self-esteem that the powerful believe they are exempt from usual standards of moral behavior, and they may feel contempt for those they are able to control.

3. Contempt for others and an exalted self-image cause people to distance themselves from those they control, to shield themselves from an awareness of how their actions affect others. Under such circumstances, abuse is more likely.

Although authority certainly provides the potential for abuse, there is no reason to expect that everyone will take advantage of it. Masculinity places a high value on the ability to control and dominate others, while femininity does not. Given this, it would be interesting to see if the Zimbardo experiment would yield similar results if repeated with female prisoners and guards.

The corrupting potential of power is great, but research suggests that powerlessness can have equally corrupting effects. When we believe that nothing we can do will affect what happens to us, we often become victims of "learned helplessness" and its resulting depression (Seligman, 1975). This occurs in extreme situations, such as prisons, and in everyday life, such as when students receive poor grades after hard work and better grades on papers they write hastily.

We all need to feel that we can affect other people. In one study, students visited elderly people living in homes for the aged. Half of the elderly people controlled the timing and length of visits, whereas the other half had no control and were visited at random (Schulz, 1976). At the end of two months, independent evaluators rated the health of the subjects, and the differences were dramatic. Those who controlled this small segment of their lives were judged to be healthier, more active, and more optimistic about life than those who did not (see also Rodin, 1986). In addition, other studies find that elderly people who *believe* they control their situations live longer than those who do not believe it, even when the actual levels of control are the same (Rodin and Langer, 1977; see also Deci, 1980; Schulz and Hanusa, 1980).

The importance of power is evident in what often seem to be the most insignificant behaviors and situations (see Molotch and Boden, 1985). When we interact with more powerful role partners, we tend to restrict our movements and sit erect with our legs uncrossed and our hands hanging at our sides or clasped in our laps; whereas more powerful people assume relaxed postures that indicate their relative invulnerability to how we judge them (Mehrabian, 1972). More powerful people are more likely to look at people they are speaking and listening to and hold eye contact longer when first meeting someone (Ridgeway et al., 1985).

The more powerful are also more likely to cross the boundaries of the less powerful by touching them, staring at them, initiating conversations, or interrupting during conversations (West, 1982). Observations of men and women show that men are more likely to touch women than women are to touch men (Henley, 1977). This tendency is especially evident in the workplace, where men usually occupy more powerful positions than women (Radecki and Walstedt, 1980).

Power, perception, definitions of the situation, and attribution are basic elements in all social interaction. Like all aspects of social life, however, interaction takes place in physical circumstances that affect what happens.

Microecology

As we saw in Chapter 5, ecology is primarily the study of the effects of physical environments on societies. The following sections describe **microecology**, which focuses on the ways in which the concepts of population and ecology help explain what goes on in social life on a smaller scale. How does the size of a group affect relationships among its members? How does the physical design of buildings affect interactions among those who live or work in them? How do individuals use physical distance to regulate the intimacy of their contact with other people?

Numbers Count   The old saying "Two's company, three's a crowd" is a statement about one of the simplest aspects of human population, the number of people involved in a social situation. How many people does it take to have a party? Two friends sitting around talking and laughing would hardly say, "What a wonderful party!" but 20 certainly might. Why do numbers matter?

Simmel (1908) pointed out that the key to a party is in the number of people. When two friends share dinner, a single mood dominates; but a party is dotted with small subgroups that display different moods and do different things, from dancing and joking to serious conversation. We enjoy parties precisely because they allow us to move freely and find a subgroup in which

we feel comfortable regardless of our mood. A party requires enough people to allow subgroups to form.

The smallest group (a dyad) has two members, and we can see some of the effects of size by comparing dyads with three-person groups (**triads**). As Simmel (1908) noted, dyads have the unique property that both members control the relationship's survival, for if either leaves it no longer exists. So long as each partner is free to leave, a dyad depends on consensus, giving each person considerable control over the other and motivating both to resolve conflicts through compromise. In addition, each member of a dyad is highly visible, and any violation of norms is easily noticed.

With three people, one person can lose control over relationships with the other two as their behavior becomes less visible and they form closer ties, or **coalitions** (Caplow, 1968; Gamson, 1968a; Simmel, 1908). Two roommates (or two siblings) may "gang up" on a third; or when a child is born, one parent may become jealous of the child's bond with the other parent. There is more involved in jealousy than human emotion, for such feelings come about when we perceive a threatening change in our relationships with other people.

As the number of people increases beyond 3, the patterns of interaction tend to change. We have all experienced the effect that class size has on classroom discussions. With 2 people, only 1 conversation is possible; with 3 people, 4 are possible; and with 4 people, 11 are possible (see Table 7-1, p. 172). As the numbers increase, however, the number of possible combinations of group members rises dramatically. With only 7 people there are 120 possible subgroups involving anywhere from 2 to 7 people at a time. With only 25 people (small by current classroom standards), there are 33,554,406!

In even relatively small groups—say ten—we find that those who are designated as leaders tend to take over more and more of the interaction (group discussions may be little more than conversations between the professor and one or two students). Other group members tend to feel stifled in their ability to express themselves (and guilty about taking up the group's time). Something as simple as "shyness," then, has its roots not only in personality, but in the ecology of groups.

As a characteristic of social interactions, the number of people who are involved is neither a cultural idea nor a set of shared expectations, and yet it clearly affects what goes on in social relationships. It is

Table 7-1

The number of possible combinations of members increases much faster than the size of a group. With two people, only one conversation is possible, but that number quadruples with the addition of a third member and almost triples with addition of a fourth.

GROUP MEMBERS	POSSIBLE COMBINATIONS OF MEMBERS
Anthony Barbara	Anthony-Barbara
Anthony Barbara Peter	Anthony-Barbara Anthony-Peter Barbara-Peter Anthony-Barbara-Peter
Anthony Barbara Peter Gloria	Anthony-Barbara Anthony-Peter Anthony-Gloria Barbara-Peter Barbara-Gloria Peter-Gloria Anthony-Barbara-Peter Anthony-Barbara-Gloria Anthony-Peter-Gloria Barbara-Peter-Gloria Anthony-Barbara-Peter-Gloria

a *physical* aspect of social situations within which individuals act and experience both themselves and other people.

Space and Social Interaction   Physical space is used to regulate social interaction. Intimate distances—6 to 18 inches—allow us to see facial details and detect body heat and odors, and make it difficult to be unaware of another's feelings. At moderate distances, we experience people more as objects; that is why we prefer such distances for conducting business or talking with casual acquaintances. Great distances allow us to act without an awareness of others; thus, long-range weapons such as guns and missiles enable us to kill one another with minimal awareness of the harm we do (Hall, 1969; Morris, 1967).

The arrangement of physical environments is often used to reinforce the structure of social relationships (Sommer, 1969). Waiting areas in airports are usually so large that people have little difficulty avoiding contact with one another. In Britain's House of Commons, members of opposition parties are seated across from one another and at close quarters, which encourages heated debate. By contrast, seating in the U.S. House of Representatives is comparatively spacious, resembling a large college lecture hall, and debate involving several members at once is rare.

Physical space is also used to reinforce differences in authority and is an important tool for social control. Judges in courtrooms and clergy in pulpits have physically elevated positions that reinforce their authority. The desks of senior executives are often placed far from office doorways, requiring visitors to cross a long expanse while their superiors can sit and examine them. The ability to limit people's access to our physical spaces also reinforces our power in relation to others. In many corporations the offices of lower-level personnel differ from those of their superiors by not having doors.

We often use space to insulate ourselves from others. Privacy and secrecy depend on people not being able to observe our behavior. When we vote, our behavior is concealed by booths; houses insulate their occupants from observation by others. Having "a room of one's own" is an important ecological aspect of family life, for it allows individuals a protected place.

When students write take-home exams, their role behavior is invisible to their professors, an ecological problem that is often dealt with through complex norms and values such as honor codes. With in-class exams, however, student behavior is visible both to the professor and other students, making cheating far less likely to occur. In both situations, the norms and values concerning cheating are the same, but the physical arrangements in which role performances take place are radically different.

One consequence of all this is that we often misperceive reality when we cannot observe what is happening. Congressional committees that meet "behind closed doors" force the public to depend on them to accurately report what they do (and on the media for information about what happens in the world). The president of the United States is unable to directly observe the actions of most people in the executive branch. This not only makes it impossible to control the everyday workings of government, but also makes the president almost completely dependent on others to act as "eyes and ears," a fact that greatly increases the opportunities for misinformation and poor decisions.

Notice how the seating in the U.S. House of Representatives is arranged similarly to a theater or large lecture hall. Attention is always focused on the front of the room. Compare this with the British House of Commons. Opponents sit directly across from each other and at close distance, an arrangement that is far more conducive to intense interaction.

Almost every president enters office with plans to bring the government under stricter control, but soon learns the ecological fact that it is almost impossible to control people whose behavior cannot be observed, as President Reagan discovered in the Iran-*contra* scandal of 1987.

A second consequence is that we often lack information that is important to us; and when this is the case, we sometimes make it up. In doing this, we may rely on our own beliefs about people: men may assume that they know what women talk about when there are no men around; whites may assume that they know what family life is like among blacks; the Internal Revenue Service may assume that most taxpayers cheat.

Microecology adds an important dimension to the many social factors that affect interaction, but interaction is more than the sum of such factors, for they are but pieces of a larger process. What does it look like? There are several models of interaction, and we will examine three of them.

THE DRAMATURGICAL APPROACH: INTERACTION AS THEATER

Interaction involves people who have ideas about who they are, who present themselves to one another in a variety of ways in order to achieve different effects or simply to act out their ideas of who they are (Tedeschi and Riess, 1981). Officials who act "official" and students who act "studious" are creating and maintaining impressions of themselves in the minds of others, just as actors perform before an audience; and, in this sense, all interaction is *dramaturgical*—in other words, it includes an element of theater (Goffman, 1959, 1981).

Teachers often present themselves to students as knowledgeable and capable, thoroughly in command of their subject and able to answer any question. Students support this image by blaming themselves when they do not understand what a teacher says, by assuming they have nothing to teach the teacher, or by refraining from asking challenging questions.

With their colleagues, however, teachers may reveal a very different side of themselves: one that includes feelings of inadequacy, doubts about knowing what they are doing in class, fear of being unable to answer a question, or hostility toward students. Are professors capable, confident, and knowledgeable? Or are they insecure, doubting, and afraid? The most likely answer is that teachers (and everyone else) feel all of these emotions at one time or another, but control how they reveal themselves to others depending on the social situation.

In *The Presentation of Self in Everyday Life* (1959), Erving Goffman described the **dramaturgical approach** to the analysis of social interaction as a continuing performance of actors before audiences. As we saw earlier, we approach people with an awareness that their behavior is affected by their impressions of us and their definition of the situation. We thus have an interest in presenting ourselves to others in ways that produce the results we want (Sagatun and Knudsen, 1982). More important, we have an interest in working together to keep the "play" going, for it is only in this way that we can sustain the definition of the situation in which we perform our roles.

To Goffman, we are actors who interact with other actors who are our audience (Goffman's term for role partners). Our performances take place in physical settings, and are guided by the roles we play—the expected behaviors and feelings that we associate with

our status in each situation. Together, the roles we play make up a **social script**.

When we approach others, we present them with a **front**—our physical appearance, behavior, and definition of the situation—which audiences use to help define the situation for themselves. We rely on various cues to define situations, orient ourselves to the appropriate script, and align our behavior to fit the role we choose to perform.

Like theater, interaction has a **frontstage** on which roles are performed before an audience, and a **backstage** on which players are freed from the requirements of their role. Just as players are careful not to let the frontstage audience see what they do while backstage, so do social actors **segregate their audiences**.

We can see the sociological usefulness of the dramaturgical approach by seeing how it works in the classroom. Both students and professors are actors who use one another as audiences for their performances. Before the professor arrives, students sit among themselves and play a variety of frontstage roles appropriate to the "pre-class" situation: "casual acquaintance," "close friend," "stranger," "fellow athlete," and "self-absorbed and not wanting to be bothered." During this frontstage performance students often talk about the professor and the course, as if they are discussing the performance that is about to begin. In this sense, frontstage performances are often at the same time backstage performances in relation to another situation.

The professor's entrance is the first of several cues that redefine the situation. On the first day of class the professor's front is a particularly important set of cues for students, for if professors arrive dressed in dirty jeans and sweatshirts and sit in the back of the room, students lack signals to shift their attention from other students to the professor.

Students present fronts of their own that help professors define the situation for themselves. College professors expect to see a room full of young people dressed for the occasion, and if they found a group of people dressed in gym shorts and sporting tennis rackets, they would think they had walked into the wrong "theater."

When the professor stops shuffling papers and looks at the class, the redefinition of the situation is complete. Students then perform **aligning actions** (part of their front) to signal their acceptance of the new definition: they sit quietly, look at the professor, and perhaps take out pencils and open notebooks.

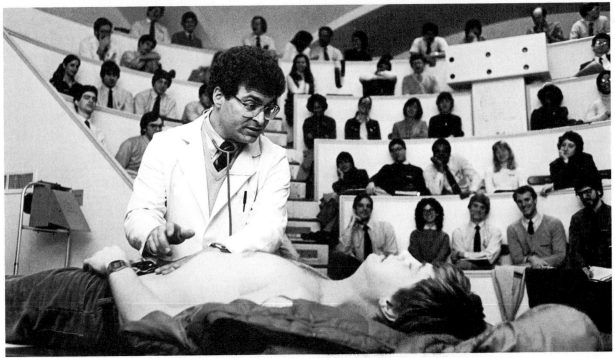

Interaction in this medical school classroom, among students before class and with the professor once the class begins, shows—according to the dramaturgical approach—how students and professors perform as actors and audiences for one another.

Frontstage is now the performance of students and professor in relation to one another, and the informal interactions among students that once took place frontstage now take place only backstage. Once actors and their audiences agree on the script, the performance begins.

Professors play their role, controlling who talks and when, and speaking with confidence. Students also play their role, taking notes, looking at the professor, and talking only after being recognized. Students are often reluctant to participate in class discussions because they risk making a bad impression on professors and other students. Yet, their role requires that they "be" there in mind as well as body, and they can indicate their involvement only through behavior.

To protect themselves, many students create an appearance of enough commitment to satisfy their role requirements without exposing themselves to unnecessary risks. They engage in "civil attention"—by nodding their heads or laughing at appropriate moments, taking notes, refraining from talking among themselves—and they participate when there are low-risk opportunities (Karp and Yoels, 1979). Civil attention allows us to play roles while minimizing the risks associated with them (Goffman, 1961b, 1963a).

Occasionally students go backstage for a moment to talk among themselves, but they must carefully conceal such behavior from their audience, the professor. Not only does such backstage behavior threaten their own performance, but it also threatens the professor's by redefining the situation and making the professor's script inappropriate. As the center of attention, however, professors have no immediately available backstage in which to escape the pressures of their role.

Throughout the performance, students and professors try to manage the impressions that others have of them, and this process lies at the heart of interaction as theater. In drama, it is not who we really are that matters; rather, it is who we *appear* to be that is central to our performance. Both students and professors try to appear confident and intelligent while concealing ignorance and feelings of insecurity from their respective audiences. They try to maintain the impression that they are seriously committed to the "play" (lest they appear to be cynical or insincere) and avoid behaviors that are "out of character."

Actors defend their performances in a variety of ways. They depend on the loyalty of those who share their status (students do not reveal to the professor that another student did not do the assigned reading); they try to choose their audiences carefully (professors may prefer young students, who are less likely to challenge them); and they control their faces, bodies, and voices, keeping them "in character." (We often prefer to use the telephone or letters to deliver bad news and lies to people, because it is easier to control the impression we make on them.)

If they fail in their role performance, they often feel embarrassment and are quick to align themselves once again to the situation and its script. Goffman (1956–1957) pointed out that embarrassment actually plays an important part in maintaining the integrity of the "play" and the actor's part in it. When we make foolish mistakes our embarrassed reaction is a way of signaling to everyone that we know what we were supposed to have done and an implication that we will do better from now on. Embarrassment thus expresses a commitment to the script that ties the actors together.

Audiences also feel obliged to help protect an actor's performance. If a professor makes a foolish mistake or stumbles and falls, students will also feel embarrassed and will support the professor's performance by acting as if they are unaware of what happened. Such "tactful inattention" protects both the performer and the audience by maintaining the integrity of the play in which all participate. In this sense, social interaction is unlike the theater, for participants are simultaneously audience and actors.

When professors give the appropriate cues, students know that the performance is over and all actors may retreat to backstage areas—faculty lounges, student dorms, coffee shops, or campus grounds—in which they are free to relax, drop their classroom fronts, and openly discuss what happened on the frontstage. Because the safety of backstage areas depends on controlling who enters them, both professors and students are careful to stay away from each other's respective backstages. (It is important to note that although college dorms and faculty lounges are backstage relative to the classroom, they are themselves frontstages, each with its own particular script.)

In many interactions the definition of a situation is unclear, and actors negotiate about the scripts they will follow. If a woman and man go out on a first date, their cues are often ambiguous, and they explore ways to arrive at a mutually agreeable definition of the situation. The cues each gives off are invitations—such as an invitation to perform the role of "friend."

Having agreed on a definition, one or both may later try to redefine the situation with a **realigning action**. Such actions constitute a new invitation (or demand), and require them to renegotiate the script.

The negotiation of scripts defines relationships by activating one or more statuses in a person's status set, and the struggle over definitions involves a conflict over which statuses will be defined as latent and which will be defined as manifest in a particular situation. In the workplace male employers often try to define a woman employee's manifest statuses as "female" and "sex object," while she struggles to define those statuses as latent, and defines "employee" as her manifest status.

Goffman's dramaturgical approach is useful because it focuses on the social mechanisms through which we create and maintain impressions of ourselves, choose and control audiences, and rely on one another for the successful performance of our roles and confirmation of our self-images. Only in the "theater" of social interaction can we perform before others and find out if they see us as we see ourselves.

When audiences accept our performance, they are in effect saying, "We believe in you." By accepting our presentation of ourselves, they also accept parts of us *as* selves. When audiences reject our performances, however, we are likely to feel embarrassment, if not shame, and may then defend ourselves by disowning our performances: "I'm not myself today."

FUNCTIONS AND CONFLICT: INTERACTION AS EXCHANGE

Exchange Theory

On one level, the Golden Rule—"Do unto others as you would have them do unto you"—is a norm that commands us to treat others well. We soon learn, however, that it is also a strategy for getting what we want: If I am kind to others, then they will tend to be kind to me. Because our behavior affects other people just as theirs affects us, interaction can be seen as a process of *exchange*.

Social **exchange theory** rests on four assumptions about human behavior:

1. We are motivated primarily to avoid pain and gain pleasure.

2. Other people's behavior is a source both of pleasure and pain for us.

3. Because human behavior is performed in relation to others, we can use our own behavior to influence what other people do in relation to us.

4. We try to maximize pleasure while minimizing our costs: we try to make the "best deal" we can in order to get what we want from others. (Blau, 1964; R. M. Emerson, 1981)

While we may believe that we love someone "just because," exchange theory suggests that loving is in part a strategy for gaining love for ourselves. In fact, Homans (1974) suggested that we behave according to an emotional "profit motive," by which we judge relationships according to how much we have to invest in them relative to what we gain from them (but see McClelland, 1986, for a different view). Caplow (1982) suggested from his study of families that the giving of Christmas gifts is often directed toward those whose relationships are both important to us and not secure enough to take for granted.

The importance of exchange in social life is made clear by the fact that all cultures have norms about what constitutes a "fair exchange" (Benedict, 1946; Malinowski, 1922). Norms about fairness and justice are vital to the well-being of any society (Gouldner, 1960), and apply across the entire spectrum of social behavior, from large questions of justice and equality to everyday interactions in which we expect others to do unto us as we have done unto them.

Competition, Cooperation, and Exploitation: The "Prisoner's Dilemma"

As a process of exchange, interaction gives rise to competition and exploitation as well as cooperation. Few studies illustrate the difficult choice between cooperation and exploitation more dramatically than the "prisoner's dilemma" (Luce and Raiffa, 1957).

Imagine a situation in which two criminals are arrested. The police are certain that these two committed the crime, but without a confession they have insufficient evidence to get a conviction. So the police put each in a separate room and present the following alternatives: "(1) If neither of you confesses, you'll be convicted on a minor, trumped-up charge and spend six months in jail; (2) If you both confess, the district attorney will recommend less than the maximum punishment, say four years; (3) If only one of you confesses, the one who does will go free while the other

Puzzles: Facing the Prisoner's Dilemma

Suppose that during an exam you and a friend help each other. Immediately afterward the professor asks your friend to wait in the classroom alone while she talks to you in her office. She tells you that she thinks the two of you cheated. "If neither of you confesses to me now," she tells you, "I'll find a way to give you both a D for the exam. If you both confess, you'll both flunk the course. If one of you confesses and the other doesn't, however, I'll let the one who confesses go unpunished while the one who doesn't will flunk the course and be reported to the dean's office, which could lead to expulsion from school." What would you do? Why?

This is a classic situation in the study of cooperation, exchange, and exploitation in social interaction.

Hence, there is a dilemma between cooperation and exploitation.

Luce and Raiffa presented volunteers with this dilemma and found that "prisoners" generally do not make cooperative choices: they usually confess, hoping that the other will not, and thus try to gain their own freedom at their partner's expense. Such dilemmas occur frequently in social interaction. When two people consider intimacy, each may feel reluctant to make a commitment, for those who fully commit themselves risk being abandoned or exploited by others. If neither makes a commitment, however, the relationship cannot be truly intimate (Table 7-2).

On a larger scale, the choice between cooperation and exploitation occurs frequently in economic behavior. Economic recessions sometimes confront workers with two alternatives: some lose their jobs so that others may keep theirs at their current rate of pay, or everyone's pay is cut so that no jobs are lost. The first choice is exploitative, for some workers gain only at the expense of others, while the second is cooperative. The prisoner's dilemma experiments suggest that people will exploit in such circumstances, but other evidence suggests that personal gain is not our only motive. In the 1982 negotiations between auto workers and manufacturers unions agreed to lower benefits in exchange for greater job security for all their members, a clear instance of cooperative behavior among group members.

Thus, although people rarely cooperate in prisoner's dilemmas in the laboratory, there are many situations whose structure compels us to run the risks

will receive the maximum sentence, ten years." As one of the prisoners, what would you do?

From one point of view, it is best to remain silent, for if neither confesses, both will suffer minimally. The problem with this cooperative strategy is that if you remain silent while your partner confesses, you suffer the maximum penalty while your partner goes free.

Table 7-2

The Prisoner's Dilemma Often Occurs in Social Relationships

Consider two people, Arthur and Valerie, who love each other but are unaware of each other's feelings. They can reveal themselves or not, and each option has its risks.

VALERIE'S OPTIONS	ARTHUR'S OPTIONS Reveal Himself	Not Reveal Himself
Reveal Herself	They might have a love affair.	Valerie may feel like a fool if Arthur doesn't love her too.
Not Reveal Herself	Arthur may feel like a fool if Valerie doesn't love him too.	They may miss out on the love of a lifetime.

One of the hallmarks of nonindustrial societies is the need for cooperation for survival. This 1854 picture of a quilting party in Virginia shows not only a common effort towards producing basic household goods, but also a sense of community. Both are more difficult to find in modern industrial societies where independence and competition have become more important than cooperation.

inherent in cooperation. In many cases we cannot get what we want without cooperation. When two people want intimacy or when nations want to reduce the risk of war, both parties must make a commitment.

The likelihood of cooperation or exploitation depends partly on the structural aspects of interactions—visibility, communication patterns, and the degree of interdependence (see Axelrod, 1984). In the prisoner's dilemma experiment, prisoners could not communicate with each other to share intentions, desires, and needs; nor was a long-term relationship involved. Similar structures can also be found outside the laboratory: when people hear rumors of a bank failure they may rush to withdraw their funds before others do, saving themselves at the expense of others. Or, when goods such as food seem to be in short supply, people may buy up more than they need, thereby depriving others of having any.

Social structures also specify how rewards and costs are distributed in interactions. In a race there is only one winner, and the prize can be had only at the expense of others. Such "zero-sum" games (Von Neumann and Morgenstern, 1964; Zagare, 1984) exist in many colleges: when grading is done on a curve that limits the number of students who can receive A's (and guarantees that a certain number at the bottom of the curve will fail), competition and exploitation are likely results, with students possibly refusing to help one another.

In other situations—such as among combat soldiers in the field or police officers on patrol—the team is no stronger than its weakest member. Each depends on the success of the others in order to survive. When relationships are structured in this way, competition and exploitation threaten the welfare of everyone involved.

promoted to management with two other groups of workers: those who had been promoted to union shop stewards and those who remained rank-and-file workers. Lieberman wanted to see how changes in social status affect people's beliefs, values, and attitudes.

He found that after a year, workers who became foremen adopted pro-management, anti-union ideas, whereas those who became union shop stewards became more pro-union and anti-management. Before changing statuses, almost none of the workers believed that management "really cared" about them. After a few years in their new statuses, however, 67 percent of the new foremen believed management really cared about workers, whereas none of those who became union shop stewards shared this positive view. By comparison, workers who had no change in status showed little change in their perceptions or feelings about unions and management. When Lieberman returned to the factory in 1954, he found that

the foremen who had been demoted to rank-and-file status tended to return to the attitudes they had held prior to their promotions. How do we explain such shifts?

Social exchange theory suggests that workers who become foremen adopt pro-management ideas because it is in their best interests. Balance theory, however, suggests that when we change statuses, we adopt new reference groups, and our positive feelings toward a new group produce a strain of imbalance if we continue to hold ideas associated with our former status and its reference group. In short, it is difficult to maintain positive feelings toward two reference groups that have a negative view of each other (Figure 7-3).

From a dramaturgical point of view, new foremen adopt roles whose scripts call for pro-management ideas and behaviors. Their foreman status becomes part of their social identity, and they can be true to their new self only by feeling, thinking, and acting accordingly. As Goffman (1961b) wrote, "A self vir-

In 1968, Eldridge Cleaver was a leader of the militant Black Panthers, who advocated the violent overthrow of the U.S. government; but, by 1982, he openly supported the U.S. political system, a change that illustrates the dramatic shift in social identity that exchange, interaction, and balance theory can help to explain.

Figure 7-3 Social Status, Attitudes, and Reference Groups

New foremen who identify with management, but who continue to share negative attitudes toward management find themselves in an unbalanced situation (a) which can be resolved by adopting positive attitudes. How else might the imbalance be resolved?

(a)
Unbalanced

(b)
Balanced

... It is in these roles that we know each other; it is in these roles that we know ourselves. (p. 249)

tually awaits the individual entering a position; he need only conform to the pressures on him and he will find a *me* ready-made for him." As we follow a new script, our behavior reinforces the new role. In Kenneth Burke's words, "doing is being."

Social life is full of such transformations: the radical political activist is elected to Congress and becomes "one of the boys," and although former friends may use exchange theory to explain the change ("She sold out"), the full explanation is undoubtedly more complicated than this, involving both problems of balance and changing identities (Gecas, 1981). Graduate students are among the severest critics of faculties, yet as professors they often become more pro-faculty and anti-student.

Because we play many roles, we may feel as though we have many different "selves" that we juggle as we shift from one situation to another (Alexander and Wiley, 1981; Goffman, 1961b). For many people, the dramaturgical perspective in particular paints a disturbing picture of people adopting one "mask" after another, "playing at" being different people in different situations. As Robert Park (1950) wrote,

It is probably no historical accident that the word "person," in its first meaning, is a "mask." It is a recognition of the fact that everyone is always and everywhere, more or less consciously, playing a role.

Goffman, however, was careful to point out that role playing does not necessarily imply insincerity or falseness. When we play a role, we reveal some aspects of ourselves while concealing others. We often put on a "mask" only to the extent that we select which parts of ourselves to reveal, and when we perform a role, we integrate one segment of who we are with selected segments of other people (Goffman, 1961b). In one situation, we display our "intelligent, competent, independent" self, in another, our "insecure, confused, dependent" self. We do not have to decide which is the "real me," for both are merely different parts of extraordinarily complex creatures.

Although we reveal different aspects of ourselves in different situations, our self-images are relatively stable, and we strive for consistency in our presentations of ourselves (Burke and Reitzes, 1981; Mortimer et al., 1981). The desire to maintain a self-image and the self-esteem that goes with it can be as powerful a motivation as the desire to gain through exchange, to balance relationships, or to act according to expectations inherent in social scripts (Rosenberg, 1979).

We are, of course, perfectly capable of faking performances, of donning masks that represent no segment of ourselves (except, perhaps, our desire for approval and other rewards). When capable, intelligent women act dumb and helpless in the presence of men, or when men who need emotional support act tough and self-sufficient, both misrepresent themselves by pretending to be what they are not. With time, others will expect such false performances (accepting and depending on them as real) and the contradictions between who we are and how we appear to others may cause an identity crisis.

In this sense, we struggle not only for balance in our relationships with others, but for an internal balance between what we do and who we think we are. If Goffman is correct that "we are who we present ourselves to be," then self-images will have powerful effects on how we present ourselves to others. This, then, is a central problem for individuals in social interaction: to satisfy our needs and respond to the demands of social life while maintaining a consistent, stable sense of who we are. Because our identities are heavily anchored in statuses whose roles often conflict, the problem of maintaining an "authentic self" can be formidable.

SUMMARY

1. Social interaction is the process through which people act in relation to one another. It depends on a complex process through which we organize and interpret our perceptions of people and situations.

2. How we perceive one another often rests on first impressions that rely heavily on stereotypes. When we act as though stereotypes were true, we may help bring about self-fulfilling prophecies.

3. The definition of the situation identifies which statuses and roles are relevant in a given situation. We often use such definitions in social attribution, which focuses on internal causes such as emotional states and external causes such as role requirements.

4. All cultures include norms about the physical distance between role partners, ranging from the zone of intimacy to personal, impersonal, and public zones. Social boundaries also regulate access to information about ourselves as well as behavior that may not involve physical contact.

5. Power is a factor in most social interaction. Sociologists are less interested in personal power than in authority, for authority is purely social in its origins. Extremes of both power and powerlessness can lead people to do things they would otherwise never consider themselves capable of.

6. Microecology focuses on the ways in which the number of people involved in a situation and physical arrangements affect social interaction. One difference between a dyad and a triad is that in a triad two people can gang up on the third by forming a coalition.

7. The dramaturgical approach to interaction focuses on individuals as actors who are also audiences for each other as they perform parts of a social script. Like the theater, there is a frontstage and a backstage, and audiences and actors use various techniques to protect performances and ensure the continuation of the "play." Realigning actions introduce new definitions of the situation, and aligning actions signal acceptance of them.

8. Exchange theory looks on interaction as a process in which we give to others in exchange for what we want. It assumes that we want to avoid pain and gain pleasure and that these are accomplished primarily in relation to other people. It also assumes that we try to maximize our gains while minimizing our costs. This can be accomplished in ways that, depending on the situation, may involve cooperation, competition, or exploitation.

9. Balance theory suggests that we organize our perceptions of people and objects into units, and that we strive for some consistency in the positive and negative feelings among them. Balance theory helps predict not only how we will feel toward others, but also how we may feel toward ourselves in a particular set of relationships.

10. A major problem for us is to satisfy our needs and respond to social demands while maintaining a consistent, stable sense of who we are.

KEY TERMS

balance theory   180
dramaturgical approach   174
    aligning action   174
    audience segregation   174
    backstage   174
    front   174
    frontstage   174
    realigning action   177
    social script   174
exchange theory   177
microecology   171
    coalition   171
    triad   171
self-fulfilling prophecy   163
social attribution   165
    external causes   165
    internal causes   165
social interaction   161
stereotype   163

Looking Elsewhere

Having studied Chapter 7, you might want to look at related discussions in *Human Arrangements*, which include

- interaction in college classrooms (Chapter 1, p. 8; Chapter 16, pp. 441–43)
- interaction in families (Chapter 14, p. 384; Chapter 15, pp. 412–14)
- group size and social interaction (Chapter 8, p. 200)
- spatial relationships and interaction in groups (Chapter 8, pp. 200, 202)
- coalitions in groups (Chapter 8, pp. 203–204) and in politics (Chapter 19, pp. 532–33)
- racial stereotyping (Chapter 12, pp. 313–14)
- racial differences in explanations of racial inequality (Chapter 12, p. 334)
- interaction between men and women (Chapter 13, pp. 350–52)
- sexual harassment and violence (Chapter 13, pp. 351–52)
- when doctors lie to their patients (Chapter 14, p. 386)

RECOMMENDED READINGS

BAILEY, F. G. (1983). *The tactical uses of passion: An essay on power, reason, and reality*. Ithaca, NY: Cornell University Press. Evoking feelings of recognition often evoked by reading Erving Goffman's work, a social anthropologist looks at the ways in which we use emotion and reason in "conflict talk."

GOFFMAN, E. (1959). *The presentation of self in everyday life*. New York: Doubleday. Goffman's classic introduction to his dramaturgical perspective. See also *Forms of talk* (1981). Philadelphia: University of Pennsylvania Press. A collection of essays that focus on the importance of how we talk to each other.

HALL, E. T. (1969). *The hidden dimension*. New York: Doubleday. An anthropological look at how the human uses of physical space affect social interaction.

SOMMER, R. (1969). *Personal space: The behavioral analysis of design*. Englewood Cliffs, NJ: Prentice-Hall. An important book that explores the effects of architecture and interior design on social interaction.

Group Culture

Group Norms

Pressures to Conform

The Structure of Groups

Boundaries: Members and Nonmembers

Role and Sociometric Structures

Power and Leadership

Who Talks to Whom: Structures of Communication

Ties That Bind: Primary and Secondary Groups

Formal and Informal Groups

Bureaucracies

Population, Ecology, and Groups

Group Size

Space and Social Structure

What Goes On: Group Process

Group Process and Changing Power Structures

Powerful Combinations: Coalitions

Getting the Job Done: Explaining Group Effectiveness

Staying Together, Falling Apart:
Cohesion and Conflict in Groups

Individuals, Freedom, and Life in Groups

Culture, Groups, and Individuals

Social Structure, Groups, and Individuals

8 Groups and Formal Organizations

The group is a basic unit of sociological analysis for several reasons. We orient most of our lives to groups, from the intimacy of romantic couples to the overwhelming complexity of bureaucracies. We experience our most intense desires to "belong" in relation to groups, our greatest fears of rejection, and our deepest conflicts as we perform roles in exchange for the privileges of membership. Some groups are like tiny islands—havens in which we are known and accepted, or prisons from which there is no escape—whereas others are so large and complex that we feel lost and insignificant in them.

Groups meet many of our needs, including those for approval, acceptance, protection, safety, and support for our values. We use reference groups to define important parts of who we are and to establish and maintain our self-esteem. We grow up in groups, learn, earn livings, and practice religion in them. It is through them that societies govern and defend themselves, distribute justice, heal the sick, distribute rewards, and inflict punishments. Groups are also a source of social conflict and problems. Persecution, discrimination, oppression, and warfare are often based on relationships between groups.

The social characteristics of groups affect the way they achieve their goals as well as their success in doing so. Social life centers on groups, and by understanding how they work, we can better understand ourselves as participants. We can also understand how groups affect the welfare of society itself: the ability of families to raise children, of governments to govern, of criminal justice systems to control crime, of hospitals to provide health care—all are vitally important.

The sociological study of groups centers on several kinds of questions, which this chapter examines in some detail. How can we describe groups in ways

> ## Puzzles: What Kept the Wehrmacht Going?
>
> During World War II, units of the German Army often kept fighting even when things looked hopeless, and long after most U.S. units in similar circumstances would have stopped fighting. Why did the German soldiers hang on so long?
>
> Many observers at the time thought (as you might) that perseverance among the German soldiers came from their dedication to their country and the Nazi cause, but as explained in this chapter, the social organization of military units in an army has more to do with the behavior of individual soldiers than any amount of ideology.

that allow us to see the cultural, structural, and ecological differences among them? How do they distribute power and assign roles to their members? How do group structures and cultures affect what goes on in them? How do groups survive, manage conflict, and maintain the loyalty and obedience of their members? How are individuals affected by groups? How do groups affect our freedom and the quality of our lives?

GROUP CULTURE

All groups are based on shared cultural ideas. Stein and his colleagues argue that whites often exclude nonwhites from groups not only because of race, but because they assume that nonwhites do not share their values and beliefs (Stein et al., 1965).

Researchers asked white high school students to answer questions about their values—the desirability of having school spirit, being intelligent, neat, and attractive, or being concerned about other people. They then used these responses to create for each student descriptions of two pairs of fictitious teenagers. One pair of teenagers shared the respondent's values, whereas the second did not. In each pair, one of the teenagers was black, and the other was white.

Respondents were then asked how interested they would be in different kinds of contact with the teenagers, such as inviting them home to dinner, going to a party together, attending the same school, belonging to the same group, living in the same building, or working together on the same committee. Although the willingness for close contact was negatively affected by race, a wide range of contact was not. What did make a difference in these cases was the respondents' perception of shared values.

Group Norms

The power of group norms is illustrated by a study of workers who built telephone switchboards at the Hawthorne plant of Western Electric (Roethlisberger and Dickson, 1939). In trying to find how to increase productivity, researchers were surprised to discover

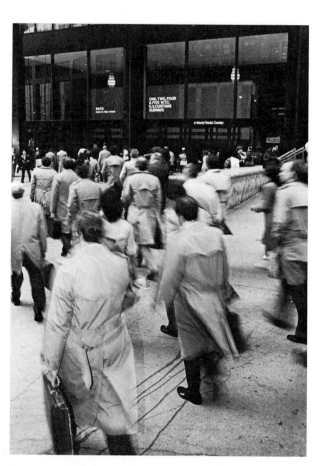

In each of these scenes—artists in eighteenth-century America, late-nineteenth-century Chinese immigrants in San Francisco's Chinatown, and New York City's Wall Street today—certain aspects of dress make people identifiable as members of the same culture. When people dress "outrageously," they usually conform to what are defined by their culture as "appropriately" outrageous ways.

that workers often violated company norms (trading jobs) and seemed unaffected by company rewards for increased production. They worked quickly in the mornings, but slowly in the afternoons, and never reported fellow workers who failed on the job. Men who worked too hard were labeled "rate busters," whereas those who worked too slowly were "slackers."

By working together, these men formed a subgroup with its own subculture that affected their behavior more strongly than the company's norms and values. That this subculture supported violations of company rules stems in part from sharing a common position in relation to the company and society as a whole. As members of the working class, they shared a long-standing tradition of resistance against the attempts of management to extract as much work from them as possible.

The common circumstances of these workers help explain the formation of their subgroup and the conformity of members to its norms; but in many groups, individuals conform even when they do not want to. What conditions allow groups to exert such power over their members?

Pressures to Conform

Pressures to conform in groups have three sources. First, by defining reality and expectations, group culture specifies requirements for membership. Whether we value a group for itself or as a means for achieving personal goals, conformity is the surest way to remain members: we conform to keep our jobs, to stay in school, or to keep the love and respect of family members.

Second, we conform to the cultural ideas of reference groups whether or not we are members. Our admiration and affection for the members of a close-knit work group will lead us to use them as models, and when such models are part of our social identity, conformity to the ideas that make up their culture is important if we are to maintain a stable sense of who we are. When we have "heroes and heroines" we often adopt their standards of behavior as our own.

Third, we depend on one another to support our perceptions of reality. If you sit with friends and suddenly smell gas, you are most likely to turn to other people for confirmation: "Do you smell gas?" If they do not support us, we are likely to conclude that our perceptions are faulty; but if they *do* support us, we are far more likely to act on our perceptions as if they were accurate.

The pressures to conform are illustrated by an experiment in which eight-member groups were shown a series of sets of four lines for which they were asked to judge which of three lines was the same length as a fourth "standard" line (Asch, 1952; see also Perrin and Spencer, 1980). Look at Figure 8-1 and imagine that you participated. Each member makes a judgment out loud, and you go last. With the first two sets of lines everyone agrees on which line is the same length as the "standard," but, with the third set, you hear the first person match the standard line with line 1, which is obviously not the same length. As you think about what a big mistake that was, you hear the second member make the same error, then the third, the fourth, and all the rest. Now it is your turn. Do you agree with the group's unanimous judgment or insist on your own?

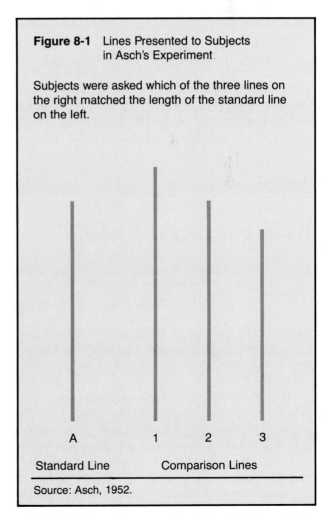

Figure 8-1   Lines Presented to Subjects in Asch's Experiment.

Subjects were asked which of the three lines on the right matched the length of the standard line on the left.

A   1   2   3

Standard Line   Comparison Lines

Source: Asch, 1952.

Asch found that chances are quite good that you would agree with the majority even though their judgments are clearly wrong. Faced with overwhelming opposition, only 20 percent of Asch's subjects openly disagreed with the group. Those who conformed reported afterward that they feared ridicule ("Every time I disagreed I was beginning to wonder if I looked funny") and doubted their own perceptions ("Maybe where I'm sitting is making me see the lines wrong").

Fear of ridicule and social isolation are especially important, as Asch (1952) discovered in a later experiment (see also Noelle-Neumann, 1984). This time, only one of the eight people was employed by Asch and instructed to make errors. As the lone confederate made wrong judgments, the volunteer subjects laughed and expressed disbelief and sarcasm. As one subject said later, "I felt the person was attempting a stupid joke. . . . Then I felt sorry for a person with such poor eyesight." Other studies found similar effects of group pressure on individuals (Deutsch and Gerard, 1955; Sherif, 1936; but see also Perrin and Spencer, 1980).

Groups exert strong pressures to conform, especially on people who are attracted to them (Kelley, 1952). Such pressures are particularly important for moral questions that rest less on fact than on values and abstract principles of right and wrong. These studies help us appreciate how extraordinary it is for individuals to defy majority judgments, and how difficult it is to maintain a sense of who we are and what we "know" in group contexts.

THE STRUCTURE OF GROUPS

As we saw in Chapter 4, social relationships have many structural characteristics that affect what goes on in them. Groups differ in the boundaries that define membership, and in the number and content of the roles their members are expected to perform. They have patterns of affection that may bind some members more closely to one another than to the group as a whole.

Groups differ in the amount of power they have in relation to other groups and the ways in which power and prestige are distributed among their members. Patterns of communication describe which members interact, with whom, how often and for what length of time.

Groups such as families and friendship groups are primary, existing for their own sake, enduring through time, and involving members in many aspects of one another's lives. Others—such as work groups—are secondary, limited to specific goals that, once reached, usually end a member's involvement in the group. Groups may be informal, relying on folkways to control behavior; or they may be formal, with specific rules that rigidly define and control role relationships.

Boundaries: Members and Nonmembers

All groups have boundaries that distinguish nonmembers from members. Norms define not only who is eligible for membership, but how long the group is expected to exist and individuals are expected to belong.

Membership takes different forms that depend on participation. Students who rarely talk during class are **peripheral**, for although they are subject to group norms, their interaction with others is minimal. Those who regularly skip classes are **nominal** members, for although their names are on the class list, the norms that guide classroom interaction do not affect them.

There are also different kinds of nonmembers (Merton, 1968). Some are eligible to belong whereas others are not; and some want to belong more than others. A large pool of eligible members who refuse to join a group can harm it by raising questions about its attractiveness. In this sense, groups have relationships not only among their members, but with nonmembers as well.

Time, Space, and Boundaries   Time is used to define group boundaries. Whereas some groups exist only briefly, others survive across many generations of members. Individual membership also varies in duration from a few hours to a lifetime. Some groups literally use time to define themselves, such as "the college class of 1993."

If you listed the members of your family, you would probably include only living relatives. A family tree, however, spans hundreds of years and includes both living and deceased members. We expect membership in a family to endure for a lifetime, and the family itself to endure long after we die. Such expansive time boundaries give us a sense of permanence, continuity, and stability, and make the family the most important group in our lives (Back, 1981).

In contrast, work groups are defined primarily by time and place (Homans, 1950); and, although the groups may survive indefinitely, their members generally do not stay very long, which makes it difficult to maintain a strong commitment of members to the group.

During the Vietnam War, U.S. troops were trained in one group, then transferred to others for one-year tours of duty. Because membership was clearly limited in time, soldiers cared less about the goals of their unit or the army than they did about the safety of themselves and their friends (George, 1971; Moskos, 1969). Their attitude toward replacements tended to be, "I've done my time; let the others do theirs."

> The end of the war is marked by the date a man leaves Vietnam, and not by its eventual outcome—whether victory, defeat, or stalemate. Even discussion of broader military strategy and the progress of the war . . . appears irrelevant to the combat soldier: "*My war is over when I go home.*" (Moskos, p. 16)

Clarity and Openness

All groups and organizations need to have clear boundaries in order to tell who is a member and who is not, and all vary in the degree to which their boundaries are open or closed. Intelligence services such as the CIA go to great lengths to ensure that their members are not actually enemy spies, and when a spy (often called a "mole") is discovered, it triggers a period during which members cannot be sure of who is a "real" member and who is not.

Groups draw boundaries in ways that restrict membership (Simmel, 1950). College fraternities and sororities discriminate on the basis of gender, and on many campuses, they have come under pressure to drop this restriction. In some cases, they have given in to this pressure but insisted on maintaining a semblance of their old boundaries. In one college, a fraternity agreed to admit women, but male members reinforced their gender boundary by insisting that female members be referred to as "brothers."

In her study of corporations, Kanter (1977b) found that since women almost always constitute a tiny minority at middle and upper job levels, men try to "heighten" group boundaries in order to exclude women as outsiders. The men were more likely to make sexual remarks in front of women than in front of other men. At meetings, they sometimes apologized for an off-color expression they were about to use and then went ahead and used it anyway. This simple act singles women out as outsiders who interfere with what is defined as the normal functioning of the group. By making the presence of "token" women more visible, men increased their solidarity with one another by heightening their own visibility as the dominant members.

Voluntary and Involuntary Membership

People often join groups because they value the group as an end in itself. Many people are church members because they enjoy the ritual of the services and the contact with other people who share their faith. Similarly, many people attend college because they enjoy learning, or work because they find it satisfying.

In other cases, individuals join groups as a means to an end. Some people attend church to avoid damnation, to make business contacts, or to impress their neighbors. Almost a fifth of all people employed in the U.S. work only to earn money and say they would quit if they won the lottery (Davis and Smith, 1987). Students often attend college not to satisfy a desire to learn, but to earn the degrees required for good jobs.

Whereas membership in some groups is voluntary, in others—mental hospitals, prisons, and elementary schools—it is not. In such cases, membership is a means to someone *else's* end. Involuntary membership not only ensures a group's survival, but also gives it more control over its members who are deprived of the right to make many decisions and are vulnerable to abuse and exploitation by those whose ends their membership serves.

The draft illustrates the importance of involuntary membership for the survival of groups, for many argue that without it the military cannot get the number of members it needs to achieve its goals. While ensuring a sufficiently large membership, however, the draft is dysfunctional for social cohesion. People who are forced to join have a low commitment to the organization, which can have disastrous consequences in combat. The draft also raises important questions about individual rights, as it forces young men to kill and risk their lives for goals they do not choose.

In voluntary groups, members sometimes develop a strong sense of loyalty that may lead them to adopt hostile, superior attitudes toward nonmembers, and these can be an important part of group boundaries.

In-Groups and Out-Groups

William Graham Sumner (1906) believed that groups become **in-groups** by developing a strong sense of "we-ness" and hostile attitudes toward **out-groups**. "Loyalty to the group, sacrifice for it, hatred and contempt for outsiders . . . all grow together, products of the same situation" (p. 13). There are many examples of this: the hostility of students toward "arch rival" schools, intense hatreds between nations, and the hostility that underlies the use of hundreds of slurs and epithets that different racial and ethnic groups apply to one another (Allen, 1983).

This photograph shows a portion of the tragedy of Jonestown. As evidence of their commitment to the group, hundreds of people killed themselves, their children, and the relatively few members who were reluctant to commit suicide.

In the late 1970s a religious cult called the People's Temple formed around a single man, the Reverend Jim Jones, and settled in the South American country of Guyana. While the cult gave many downtrodden people a sense of purpose, it maintained its boundaries by requiring such intense in-group loyalty that members had to cut their ties with all outsiders, fearing out-groups as "the enemy," and labeling criticism from the outside as lies.

When a congressman, several journalists, and concerned relatives visited the colony, Jones convinced his followers that the visitors wanted to destroy the cult. Not only were several of the visitors murdered, but over 900 members obeyed Jones' command to commit suicide, accepting his belief that the only alternative was the destruction of their colony.

Although there is ample evidence that groups develop a strong sense of in-group loyalty and a hostile, superior attitude toward nonmembers, such attitudes are by no means inevitable (Merton, 1968). Many groups are subgroups of larger groups. Members of college athletic teams may have a strong sense of group loyalty, but they are also members of other groups—dorms, fraternities, sororities, and classes—on whom they depend for support.

Role and Sociometric Structures

As groups develop, members take on different roles that form a *role structure*, which includes task and expressive roles (Bales, 1950). Members of families perform many roles in addition to those of parent, adult, child, and sibling. Parents often divide task and expressive roles, as when wives take responsibility for "kinkeeping," or, keeping family members in touch with one another (Rosenthal, 1985). Children may perform several different roles—caring for a lonely or alcoholic parent or younger children, or soothing conflicts between parents.

Role structures differ in content and complexity. A married couple has two statuses (wife and husband), whereas a group of workers may include hundreds. Large groups are usually more complex than smaller ones, but this is not always true, for a family consisting of two parents, a daughter, and a son has eight statuses (husband, wife, mother, father, son, daughter, brother, and sister), but a college freshman English course has only two: teacher and student (see Table 8-1).

The complexity of groups is reflected not only in the diversity of roles their members play, but also in

Table 8-1

As these examples show, groups come in all combinations of size and complexity.

	SMALL GROUP	LARGE GROUP
SIMPLE STRUCTURE	Discussion group Dance class Tennis team Jazz trio	Members of a group tour Veterans group Church congregation
COMPLEX STRUCTURE	Operating room staff Family Basketball team Army squad Movie-making crew (small budget)	Internal Revenue Service Army division U.S. House of Representatives Movie-making crew (blockbuster)

the emergence of subgroups based on ties of affection. Even in groups with as few as five or six people, members often form "friendship cliques." The patterns of affection that define a group's sociometric structure reveal that members frequently value subgroups more than the group as a whole. Office workers may become good friends and value being with one another at least as much as they value the achievement of organizational goals. Subgroups often develop their own cultures and share a sense of common destiny.

Power and Leadership

Who controls groups, and why are some groups more powerful than others? Groups distribute power in distinct ways, and sociologists are interested in the effects of this distribution on groups and their members. Power differences between groups are also important, for groups are often a source of social conflict.

Members who are able to define a group's culture have considerable control over group life. In Jonestown, Jones had the power to define all nonmembers as "enemies," and his control over group beliefs and values resulted in mass obedience to his command to commit suicide. Individuals derive power from their ability to control resources: when children play baseball, it is not unusual for the one who supplies the bat and ball to have a disproportionate share of power to decide which rules to play by. Control over patterns of communication is an additional source of power: committee chairpersons decide who talks during meetings, and can use their power to stifle dissenting points

of view. Those who perform roles that are important to a group or organization—and who perform them well—also tend to have a relatively large share of power (Pfeffer, 1981).

In democratic groups, power is distributed evenly among members, but in authoritarian groups, power is concentrated in the hands of a relative few. Most groups are neither purely democratic nor purely authoritarian, but fall somewhere in between.

A group has a leadership structure when power is assigned according to norms, and, therefore, takes the form of authority. Leaders perform a variety of roles: coping with external and internal threats, maintaining unity and order, managing anxiety and conflict among members, and motivating them to participate. As Whyte (1981) observed in his study of urban gangs, some groups depend on leaders for their very identity as a group:

> The leader is the focal point for the organization of his group. In his absence, members of the gang are divided into a number of small groups. There is no common activity or general conversation. When the leader appears . . . the small units form into one large group. . . . The leader becomes the focal point in the discussion. A follower starts to say something, pauses when he notices that the leader is not listening, and begins again when he has the leader's attention. When the leader leaves the group, unity gives way to the divisions that existed before his appearance. (p. 258)

There are three basic types of group leaders, and they have different effects on how groups function (Lippitt and White, 1947). **Authoritarian leaders** dominate group interactions and generally do not participate in group activities. **Democratic leaders** act as guides who give advice and suggest alternatives, but leave decisions to the group. **Laissez-faire** (a French phrase meaning "allow to act") **leaders** rarely participate unless asked to by the group, and withhold positive or negative evaluations of the group and its members.

Many groups do not have leaders, but even in those that do, authority is not necessarily concentrated in a few hands. This is particularly true in complex organizations. The presidents of corporations are clearly the most powerful leaders; and yet their effectiveness depends on hundreds if not thousands of employees organized into small work groups. Leaders depend on their followers to perform their roles and keep them informed of what is happening in the organization. The ability of followers to withhold or distort information gives them considerable power in spite of their low position in leadership structures (Weber, 1925).

Different leaders strongly affect how groups function. A study of adult leaders in children's groups found that members are more dependent on authoritarian leaders, demand more attention, and take less initiative (Lippitt and White, 1947). They also are more critical of the leader and less friendly and confiding.

With democratic leaders, members work more independently, are less critical of and more friendly toward the leader, and are more likely to work together as a group. Laissez-faire groups, however, generate anxiety from members who are far more likely to ask for guidance and suggestions.

Some groups (such as friends) have no leadership structure, whereas others have a pluralistic structure, in which authority in specific areas is assigned to specialists. In colleges and universities the administration is responsible for financial decisions, admissions, and financial aid, and the faculty controls what goes on in classrooms. Power in the U.S. House and Senate is divided among a number of committees, each of which exerts considerable control over different areas such as defense, budgets, health, and the behavior of group members.

Some groups have no leaders, while others do. Why?

When Are Leaders Necessary? Although people are generally reluctant to surrender individual freedom by giving power to a leader, several social conditions prompt the emergence of leaders (Brehm, 1966). First, members often give power to leaders in order to achieve highly valued goals (Marak, 1964). A group of friends usually lacks specific goals, and, therefore, has no leader; but people adrift in a lifeboat share a deep commitment to survival and are far more likely to appoint one.

Second, the more complex a group's role structure is, the more it needs a leader to coordinate the different roles its members perform. Students working on a project may not need a leader until they divide tasks.

Third, regardless of complexity, large groups are more likely to have leaders than small ones are. Studies of groups of varying sizes reveal that regardless of members' personalities, as size increases, a few members tend to dominate group interaction (Reynolds, 1971).

Finally, leaders tend to emerge when a crisis threatens the group (Hamblin, 1958). Many nations and organizations have given enormous power to leaders during crises: Robespierre during the French Revolution, Adolph Hitler in Germany, Stalin after the Russian Revolution, Franklin Roosevelt during the Great Depression, and Lech Walesa during the labor crises in Poland in the 1980s. For this reason, times of crisis are particularly dangerous for groups, because leaders are in a position to abuse the power given to them by their members.

Where Do Leaders Come From? Crises, group size and complexity, and a commitment to common goals help explain why groups have leaders, but how do members decide who will lead them? Professors are not hired by the students they teach; nor do workers appoint managers. In such cases, the selection of leaders depends on norms, and from a sociological point of view, such processes are straightforward and of relatively little interest. A more interesting case is the emergence of leaders in groups that initially lack a leadership structure. How are such leaders selected?

During the 1930s and 1940s, researchers identified personality characteristics shared by leaders, including self-confidence, intelligence, dominance, empathy, and an outgoing personality. Their research methods were so varied and ambiguous, however, that later research found many contradictions: traits that were related to leadership in one study were unrelated in others. Although personality certainly makes a difference (shy, retiring people are unlikely to become leaders), the personality approach was abandoned in the 1950s as researchers focused on behavior in groups (Bass, 1960).

One factor that affects the rise of individuals to leadership is their *rate of participation in group interactions*: the more members talk, the more influence they tend to have. Even shy people can become leaders if they are encouraged to participate. In an experiment, Hastorf (1965) asked small groups to discuss case studies; during the first session, he identified individuals whose participation was next to the lowest. In the second phase, members were separated by panels equipped with green and red lights. Participants were told that experts on group interaction controlled the lights, that "green" encouraged talk, while "red" advised silence.

During this phase, the lights were used to encourage the previously silent members to talk, and their contributions jumped by 50 percent. In the third phase, discussion continued without the lights, yet these members continued to talk the most; and in members' final ratings of one another's contributions, the initially silent member moved from third to second place.

Apparently, under the right circumstances, anyone has the potential to play a leadership role. People who cannot imagine themselves as leaders may find that merely by speaking up, they acquire surprising levels of power. This underscores the fact that leadership is a social status, that leaders are those whom group members *identify* as leaders (see Zelditch and Walker, 1984).

From this perspective, it is easier to see how "unlikely people"—Presidents Harry Truman and Lyndon Johnson—who are thrust into leadership positions during crises can perform very well. It is also easier to understand how people who are unfit for leadership nonetheless attain positions of authority through frequent, highly visible participation in group activities.

A second factor in leader selection is *latent statuses* that have no recognized role in group activities (Markovsky, Smith, and Berger, 1984; Ridgeway, 1981; Ridgeway and Berger, 1986). In newly formed groups, members lack specific information about one another and therefore tend to rely on their general expectations and judgments of other, nongroup statuses such as race, gender, occupation, and age. On juries men

and those with high-prestige occupations will tend to be given greater credibility and have more influence than women and those with lower-prestige occupations (see One Step Further 8-1, p. 196).

Conformity to norms is a third factor in the selection of leaders, especially in a group's early stages. Hollander (1960) planted confederates in problem-solving groups and supplied them with the correct answers to the problem. The groups established norms, which the confederates violated (by speaking out of turn) at different stages of the meeting.

Although the confederates always offered the correct solution to the problem, when they spoke out of turn at the beginning of the session they were generally ignored; when they obeyed the rules until midways in the meeting, the confederates' influence was greater; and when they conformed until the meeting was nearly over, their influence reached a maximum. Members initially identified as nonconformists are unlikely to become leaders regardless of their contributions.

Ridgeway (1981) used a similar experiment and found that the effect of conformity may not be as simple as Hollander suggests. She found that nonconformity can increase influence by attracting the attention of other members, but that this can be tricky since nonconformists may be seen as caring more about themselves than the group. Nonconformity was particularly dangerous for members who occupy latent statuses that are relatively low in prestige. Ridgeway concluded that the most important factors in determining influence are other people's perceptions of a member's motivation and competence in performing group tasks and, as we saw above, latent statuses such as gender and occupation.

The Power of Groups   Group power depends on culture and social structure. Like individual members, groups may exercise authority that rests on norms in the surrounding society. Police departments, the Internal Revenue Service, and employers all hold power over others by virtue of socially defined authority.

Groups also draw power from their structural position in relation to other groups and valued resources. Undergraduate college students conform to professors' demands not only to maintain their membership in undergraduate classes, but also because professors occupy a key position between undergraduate colleges and graduate schools.

ONE STEP FURTHER 8-1:
Gender, Occupation, and Power on Juries

In their study, Strodtbeck et al. (1957) selected people from community jury pools in Chicago and St. Louis and formed mock juries to study how decisions are made. The process through which the juries deliberated and formed a verdict was recorded, transcribed, and analyzed.

In most cases, the selection of a foreman was done quickly and with little debate, and men and those with high-prestige occupations were far more likely than others to be selected. The figures in Table B-8-1 show that men and those with high-prestige occupations tended to participate more and were more likely to be named as the juror who contributed most to the group. Section (C) shows that, even among those who have similar occupations, men consistently participated more and received higher ratings from the group than women.

Table B-8-1

SOCIAL CHARACTERISTICS	PARTICIPATION RATE	MOST HELPFUL JUROR (AVERAGE VOTES)
(A) *Gender*		
Women	6.6	2.3
Men	9.6	4.3
(B) *Occupation*		
Professional, Managerial	11.8	6.0
Clerical	9.2	3.4
Skilled Worker	7.1	3.5
Semi- and unskilled worker	6.4	2.3
(C) *Gender and Occupation*		
Professional, Managerial		
Women	9.1	3.2
Men	12.9	6.8
Clerical		
Women	7.8	2.7
Men	10.8	4.2
Skilled Worker		
Women	4.8	2.0
Men	7.9	3.9
Semi- and unskilled worker		
Women	4.6	1.5
Men	7.5	2.7

Source: Strodtbeck et al., 1957, Tables 2 and 3.

The control of valued resources is also a major source of power. Employment, professions, governments, and universities are controlled by people who are white, middle-aged, male, and wealthy, and this gives them power over nonwhites, women, the poor, and the elderly, whom they can exclude from socially legitimate avenues to money, power, and prestige.

Groups draw power from culturally based authority as well as structural positions in the surrounding society. This power is then distributed among group members, whose roles and power affect their position in prestige structures that rank members in terms of the respect they receive from others.

Communication Structures

Groups differ not only in how they distribute roles, affection, power, and prestige, but also in their *communication structures*. Figure 8-2 shows several family communication structures. In *(a)*, family members interact with one another a great deal, whereas in *(b)*, the father interacts heavily with the mother, but little with his children. In *(c)*, which represents many families with divorced parents, the father is "absent," interacting minimally with other family members, and in *(d)*, the heaviest interaction takes place between the children, as might occur when both parents are employed.

Such differences are important in several ways. First, observations of small groups show that frequent interaction strengthens attachments to the group and tends to make them happier. Thus, group cohesion and member satisfaction will tend to decrease as we go from *(a)* to *(c)*.

Second, members must communicate in order to know about each other and get feedback about their behavior. In *(b)*, the father and children depend largely on the mother for information about each other, while in *(c)*, they are isolated from each other. In comparison with *(a)*, then, the structures in *(b)* and

(c) are likely to result in considerably more misunderstanding and conflict between the father and his children.

Third, because interaction strengthens ties between group members, communication structures affect the formation of subgroups. The tendency to form subgroups will be least in *(a)*, while in *(b)* three distinct subgroups are likely: mother-father, mother-son-daughter, and son-daughter. In *(c)*, the father is a peripheral or nominal member and may be excluded by the mother-son-daughter subgroup, and in *(d)* the children may develop a bond that strongly influences family decisions.

Ties That Bind: Primary and Secondary Groups

The distinction between **primary groups** such as families and small groups of close friends and **secondary groups** such as those found in school classrooms and most work settings, is important to individuals and groups. Primary groups are at the heart of social life, for it is within them that we are valued and protected simply because we are members of the group. They give our lives a sense of continuity and stability and provide the only opportunities for affection and being known by others as complex individuals.

Secondary groups cannot give us a sense of stability and continuity, of belonging and worth, for they value group goals more than the welfare of individual

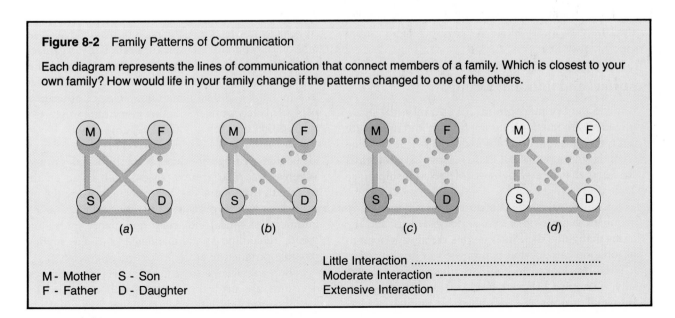

Figure 8-2 Family Patterns of Communication

Each diagram represents the lines of communication that connect members of a family. Which is closest to your own family? How would life in your family change if the patterns changed to one of the others.

(a)   (b)   (c)   (d)

M - Mother   S - Son
F - Father   D - Daughter

Little Interaction ....
Moderate Interaction -
Extensive Interaction ─────────────

members. We can lose our places in them quite easily, and the groups themselves can quickly dissolve. When individuals heavily invest themselves in secondary groups—such as at work—they often find that their world "falls apart" if they suddenly lose their jobs. Secondary groups, however, offer us greater control over our participation, including the aspects of ourselves we reveal to others (for this reason many people use workplaces as a refuge from the revealing intimacy of family life).

It is generally more difficult for a secondary group to control its members, since their loyalty is usually limited to specific goals and activities. It is difficult for employers to have much control over what workers do outside of working hours. Secondary groups, on the other hand, are more likely to survive across generations, because they can replace their members more easily. They can also coordinate large numbers of people in order to accomplish complex goals. It would be impossible to organize a university or a large army solely around primary relationships.

Primary groups are often regarded as superior to secondary groups because they help meet human needs such as those for intimacy and emotional support. They also can be sources of considerable problems for their members. We lose a great deal if we "quit" a family and such ties are difficult to replace. By exposing many aspects of our personal lives in them, we make ourselves vulnerable to exploitation, humiliation, and abuse. Many emotional problems that plague us as adults have their roots in our experiences in the family, and studies of family violence identify the family as one of the most dangerous of all groups (see Chapter 15).

Formal and Informal Groups

By definition, primary groups have an informal structure in which relationships are flexible and norms are rarely stated explicitly. Although this is true of some secondary groups (social clubs), most have a formal structure that clearly defines role relationships (see Table 8-2).

In informal groups, relationships among group members change with varying circumstances, and the terms that guide their interactions are always open to negotiation. An act that is punished in one situation may be overlooked in another: friends may tolerate silly, disruptive behavior one day, but not the next. **Informal groups** are identified by implicit under-

Table 8-2

Primary groups are always informal, but as these examples show, secondary groups can be either formal or informal.

	INFORMAL	FORMAL
PRIMARY	Family	None
	Close friends	'
	Small commune	
SECONDARY	Trial jury	Bureaucracy
	Tupperware party	Surgery team
	College class	Airline crew

standings of norms rather than by explicit statements, and by flexible relationships among group members.

In groups with specific goals, however, it is difficult to coordinate people's behavior in predictable ways. Especially when groups have many members who specialize in a variety of tasks, they cannot depend on members to negotiate the terms of their relationships as they go along (Simmel, 1950). A response to this problem is the **formal organization**, in which relationships are regulated by clearly stated, rigid norms oriented to the achievement of specific goals.

Bureaucracies

As we saw in Chapter 4, the ideal bureaucracy is a set of formal secondary relationships rationally organized to achieve specific goals. People specialize in roles that are narrowly and rigidly defined. Power is distributed in a hierarchy, and administrators oversee other people's role behavior to ensure that everything works as it is supposed to (Weber, 1922a, 1922b).

Bureaucracies are organized around cultural ideas that distinguish them from informal groups. Whereas informal groups place a high value on the welfare of their members, bureaucracies value the organization and its goals most highly, and place a premium on technical efficiency, rationality, precision, speed, reliability, strict obedience, and the highest possible production at the lowest possible cost.

Bureaucracies also rest on beliefs that the best decisions are made by experts (without regard for feelings) and that efficiency is highest when leaders are authoritarian and members are motivated by the desire to maximize their own rewards, rather than by ties of love and affection. A bureaucracy is a particularly passionless organization that tries to rely exclusively on rationality, impersonal relationships, inequality, specialization, and loyalty based on calculations of individual self-interest.

Tumin (1964) argued that bureaucracies also rest on beliefs that protect them from external threats. Because the organization is valued more highly than its individual members, for example, bureaucracies share what Tumin called "the myth of infallibility." Businesses, Tumin noted, rarely admit violations of the law, no matter how compelling the evidence; and prosecutions of large organizations usually end not in criminal convictions, but in settlements by which the company agrees to "stop doing what it never admitted to doing in the first place." When bureaucracies cannot defend themselves in this way, they usually use individuals (or "the computer") as scapegoats, preserving the integrity of the organization itself.

Bureaucracies are unique in the norms that structure relationships among their members. The ideal bureaucracy rests solely on norms that clearly specify how roles are assigned, how power and rewards are distributed, and how decisions are made. Such norms specify what members should do in every situation and forbid the use of personal feelings and individual discretion: decisions are made "by the book," not on a case-by-case basis. Expectations are loose in informal groups, and each member has some power over group interactions ("You can't do that." "Who says?"). In a bureaucracy, however, even the most powerful member is limited by clear norms that anyone can refer to ("According to the bylaws, you can't do that").

In a bureaucracy, individual members are easily replaced, for unlike informal groups, bureaucracies do not depend on particular individuals for their survival. Whereas a family is a group of specific *individuals*, a bureaucracy is a collection of social *statuses* whose relationships are structured not to benefit individuals, but to achieve goals within a rigid, stable set of mutual expectations among members. The bureaucratic ideal represents a complete submersion of individuals in a social organization and the resulting irrelevance of individual feelings and needs.

The Birth of a Bureaucracy
Whyte's (1950) study of restaurants shows how bureaucracies emerge as groups grow larger and more complex. Suppose two people decide to open a small restaurant. In its early stages, the structure is informal and may have some of the characteristics of a primary group. Everyone is identified as an individual; shares specific tasks such as cooking and serving food, paying bills, and ordering supplies; and handles crises as they arise. Because they interact continually with each other, they can negotiate responsibilities as they go along.

Business booms and they add several employees to cook and serve the food. The owners now face the problem of coordinating the activities of several different people. This requires them to create formal expectations about work hours, dress, and conduct on the job. If their business is highly successful, they might open several restaurants, or perhaps expand into a chain extending across many states. Now they must hire managers to direct each restaurant, accountants to keep the books, and, if they sell stock in their company, a board of directors to oversee the entire operation.

What began as a small informal group grows into a large bureaucracy in which relationships are formally defined. The company becomes more important than its members, any of whom can be replaced with relative ease. Although the original members had equal levels of power, the more complex, formal organization has a clearly defined hierarchy of power and prestige, with directors at the top and dishwashers at the bottom.

The structural complexity represented by modern bureaucracies is rooted in the development of more complex societies over the last 1,000 years. Murdock's data on preindustrial societies (1967) show that only 29 percent of villages in advanced horticultural societies were autonomous, free of dominating governments above them, whereas in simple horticultural societies, fully 79 percent were governed solely at the local level. The establishment of central governments spawned increasingly complex societies with formal legal codes, standing armies, and thousands of administrators (Lenski and Lenski, 1987).

The Industrial Revolution gave the growth of bureaucracy an enormous boost by bringing together large numbers of people with specialized roles. The increased scale and the complexity of production changed the organization of society itself as governments, schools, hospitals, and other organizations adopted the bureaucratic model (Zucker, 1983). The bureaucratic ideal has influenced criminals, for although organized crime once revolved around primary family ties, it now operates much like large corporations (see Figure 8-3).

POPULATION, ECOLOGY, AND GROUPS

The number of people involved is an important part of the rise of bureaucracy, and the ecological perspective draws attention to both group size and the spatial arrangement of its members, two important ecological characteristics that affect the cultures and structures of groups.

Group Size

Although the smallest group has only two members, it is difficult to establish the upper limit on possible group size. At some point, however, a group ceases to be a group and becomes a **collectivity**, in which people identify themselves as members but do not interact with one another. The American Civil Liberties Union began with only a few members who, together, made up a group; but it now has tens of thousands of members and hundreds of chapters across the country. Since many of its members never interact with other members (they join simply by making a donation), the ACLU is no longer a group.

As group size increases beyond three, members tend to specialize in different tasks, and the group may become more formal in order to control a more complex role structure. In addition, members of large groups are less visible than those in smaller ones and can violate group norms with less chance of being detected.

A large group allows its members to "hide," which lowers their sense of responsibility to the group. As a result, large groups generally have less cohesion than smaller ones, and individuals tend to feel less valued. Some students prefer small group discussions for this reason—they feel more involved, important, and visible—whereas others avoid such classes for the same reason (see Sale, 1980).

A large group is also more likely to include members with unusual characteristics. If only 10 percent of a student body are political radicals, a four-member student judiciary board is unlikely to have a radical member. A 100-member Student Senate, on the other hand, can expect to have at least ten radicals (10% of 100) simply by chance. Larger groups are more likely

to be heterogeneous, which increases the chances for internal conflict.

The power of groups in relation to other groups is also affected by size. Although small groups are generally weaker than large ones, the relationship between size and power depends both on a group's *absolute* size and its *relative* size (Merton, 1968; Simmel, 1950). Three hundred blacks fighting for their civil rights have far less power in a city of a million whites than in a small town with 500 residents.

Group power also depends on the *completeness* of membership—the proportion of eligible members who are actual members (Simmel, 1950). Seventeen million U.S. workers belong to labor unions; but 78 million workers do *not* belong to unions, even though many of them could if they wanted to (U.S. Census Bureau, 1986a). While the absolute and relative size of the labor movement gives it considerable power, it is undermined by the visible pool of eligible workers who refuse to join.

Space and Social Structure

Spatial relationships affect the structure of groups in many ways. Family members interact frequently simply because they share the same dwelling; and while children are young, frequent interaction supports family unity and allows members to exert considerable control over one another. When children mature and leave home, interaction declines, often causing severe shocks to parental power and the family's sense of itself as a group. Members may lose touch with one another, and no longer share important events such as holidays. At best, they may feel they no longer know one another; at worst, they may feel they no longer have a family at all.

The spatial arrangement of people within groups also affects patterns of interaction. When discussion groups are arranged in a circle people tend to talk with those across from them more than the ones next to them (Steinzor, 1950). At rectangular tables, the people sitting at each end tend to interact more frequently (Strodtback and Hook, 1961)—and, as we saw earlier, those who interact the most in groups are the most likely to emerge as leaders.

The military often uses spatial relationships to build cohesion in small units such as platoons. In the U.S., recruits enter the military with a variety of backgrounds and personal characteristics that distinguish them from one another. During training, they are

Figure 8-3   Organizational Chart for the Benguerra Crime "Family"

As you can see, bureaucracy has extended into areas of life where you would not expect to find it. The lines show directions of authority (who is answerable to whom). An underboss sees to it that the orders of the boss are carried out and is like a vice-president who takes over in the absence of the president. The counselor and treasurer are answerable only to the boss and have no authority of their own. There are ten "capos"—leaders of subgroups that control particular areas (such as neighborhoods) or operations (such as numbers, drugs, bookmaking, loansharking, or prostitution)— and below each capo are the lowest-ranking group members who carry out the work of a subgroup (such as collecting bets, enforcing loans, bribing public officials, and murder).

Source: Anderson, *The Business of Organized Crime,* 1979.

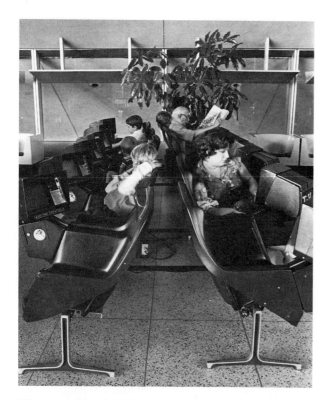

The seating arrangement shown here at New York's Kennedy airport seems designed to insure that no one talks to anyone else.

housed in open barracks that give them no privacy and force them to live in the same conditions. No personal articles—such as pictures—may be displayed.

The physical environment of basic training is designed to submerge the recruits' sense of themselves as unique individuals in order to foster a new, common identity as platoon members. As we will see later, such ties are vitally important for the performance of groups and individuals. When prisoners of war are isolated from one another, the resulting lack of interaction seriously damages group cohesion and the support that each member receives (Schein, 1957).

Spatial relationships are also used to reinforce distributions of power and prestige in groups. In his study of restaurants, Whyte (1950) observed that cooks often avoid face-to-face interaction with waitresses, because they dislike "taking orders" from workers who are ranked below them in prestige. In most restaurants, cooks and waitresses are separated by physical barriers; and in larger ones, orders are written and then passed to the cooks without any direct contact between cooks and waitresses.

The preceding descriptions and analyses of how groups vary in culture, structure, size, and spatial arrangements may give the false impression that groups consist of rigid relationships that lead their members to behave in predictable ways all of the time. What members *do*, however, often changes group structures and cultures.

WHAT GOES ON: GROUP PROCESS

Group process—what members actually do in groups—is a vital aspect of group life. It causes groups to change in response to new circumstances and to the behavior of their members.

After participating in a small group discussion, you would have many impressions of what happened, such as "So-and-so talked a lot," "We got nowhere," "I felt good," or "I couldn't wait to get out of there." Although such impressions help us make sense of what happens in groups, they are not a scientific description of what is going on. You might describe one member's contributions as "stupid," but someone else might describe that same person as "daring and constructive." In short, you most likely do not use an objective point of view that would yield the same results no matter who did the observing. Your impressions also tend to be highly selective. You may pay little attention to the remarks of people you do not like or miss large chunks of the meeting while you are thinking about what you are going to do afterwards.

The problem of inaccuracy in observing group process is especially great when it blinds us to systematic patterns that underlie important social differences. In their study of sexism in schools, Sadker and Sadker (1985) showed a film of a classroom discussion to teachers and administrators and then asked them who talked more, the boys or the girls. The educators reported overwhelmingly that the girls talked more; but trained observers who counted each act of talking found that boys talked more than three times as much as girls. The dominance of boys in the classroom was apparently masked by the expectation that girls are more talkative than boys.

In response to such problems, Bales (1950) and his colleagues developed a method for observing and recording interaction in small groups. They developed a set of categories (Table 8-3) to measure who does what in relation to whom, how and when they do it, under what conditions, and with what effects on other

Table 8-3

Bales' Group Process Categories

TYPE OF ACT	EXAMPLE
Shows Solidarity	"I think we've done well."
Shows Anger	"You stink."
Agrees	"I'll vote for that."
Disagrees	"That's not how it happened."
Shows Tension	Taps a pencil on the table.
Releases Tension	"I'll drink to that!" (laughs)
Makes a Suggestion	"Let's take a vote."
Asks for Suggestion	"Any ideas?"
Gives an Opinion	"I don't think it'll work."
Asks for Opinion	"Will it work?"
Gives Orientation	"We're running out of time."
Asks for Orientation	"What was the assignment?"

members and the group as a whole. To use this method, observers must record everything members say and do in the appropriate category.

The result is a record of (1) the total number of each type of act; (2) each member's total participation, overall and for each category; and (3) the patterns of interaction—who did what in relation to whom. Such records create a "map" of group interactions. In solving problems, all groups tend to pass through a series of stages that can be charted using Bales' categories (Bales and Strodtbeck, 1951).

Groups begin with pleasantries—saying hello, making jokes—that heighten feelings of group solidarity and lower tension. When the group gets down to work, behavior shifts to asking for and giving orientation as members try to see clearly what they are to accomplish. Then opinions and suggestions increase, followed by disagreement and, sometimes tension and anger.

Tension marks a critical phase, for groups can bog down if they cannot release tensions and regain a sense of solidarity. Acts that increase solidarity ("I think we can work this out if we stop fighting"), release tension (jokes), or orient the group ("I think we've lost sight of the problem") are very important, for, as groups thrash their way toward a solution, they can tear themselves apart with anger, disagreement,

and frustration. If the group passes through this difficult phase, interaction shifts to releasing tension and repairing any damage to group solidarity.

Group Process and Changing Power Structures

Clearly, groups need members who specialize in task roles (offering suggestions, opinions, and orientation) and expressive roles (providing solidarity and releasing tension). Bales' system allows us to identify how and when group process breaks down, and helps show why some groups succeed and others fail. It also reveals how members change their position in group structures.

Unlike less powerful members, leaders tend to speak to the group as a whole more than to individuals. When a member begins to speak to the group as a whole ("This is what *we* should do" instead of "This is what *I* want to do"), it may indicate an attempt to raise his or her position in the power structure.

If members support such bids for power by not arguing, the power seeker is free to continue addressing the group as a whole and is likely to compile a high rate of overall participation. As Bales (1968) noted, "For most individuals there is no better indicator of relative power or . . . position in the evaluation of the group than his total participation compared to that of others." Especially in formal groups, this can create tension by challenging group leadership structures and even altering the distributions of power and prestige.

Powerful Combinations: Coalitions

A second avenue to power is to form **coalitions**, subgroups of two or more members who join forces in order to increase their control over a group. Since Simmel's (1950) observations about the tendencies of two people to combine forces against a third member of a triad, two theories have emerged to explain why coalitions occur in groups. Caplow (1956, 1968) suggested that members form coalitions to maximize their control over others and minimize the control others have over them.

Gamson (1961, 1964), however, argued that power is not the only motivation—that members also try to maximize their rewards. They realize that if they form a coalition with other members, their share of any rewards may depend on the size of their contribution. From this perspective, coalitions form when (1) there is a decision to be made and individuals want to maximize their own gains from it; (2) no alternative will maximize every member's gain; (3) no member has the power to make decisions alone; and (4) no member has veto power.

The two theories lead to similar predictions except in the case of a weak member who contemplates joining with a strong member when there are substantial rewards at stake. To see how these theories predict coalition formation, let us apply them to three different situations (see Figure 8-4).

In the first there are three roommates—Sam, Bill, and Mark—who have equal amounts of power. Three coalitions are possible: Sam-Bill, Sam-Mark, and Bill-Mark. Both theories predict that all three coalitions are equally likely: Sam's power increases no more by joining with Bill than with Mark; nor does his share of rewards depend on whom he chooses for a partner.

The second case is a family consisting of Ann and her parents, both of whom have equal power. Ann increases her power regardless of which parent she joins with, and in both coalitions her partner has more power than Ann does. The parents will tend not to form a coalition between them, because each already has more power than Ann. On the other hand, a parent who forms a coalition with Ann gains increased control over the other parent. The most likely coalition is between Ann and one of her parents.

The third case is a group of nations, one of which is more powerful than any of the others and yet is *less* powerful than all of the others combined. Which coalitions would you predict? In this third situation, Caplow and Gamson make different predictions.

Caplow's theory predicts that weak nations will join with the strong in order to increase their power in relation to other weak countries. The strong country would welcome such a coalition because it increases its power while still controlling its partners. Gamson's theory, however, predicts that the most likely coalition combines the weaker nations against the strongest. Why?

Weak countries increase their power by combining with the stronger one, but when it comes time to divide up any rewards, they cannot prevent their more powerful partner from taking the lion's share. By combining only with each other, weak countries can both control a stronger one *and* share equally in the rewards, since their partners are equally powerful.

The study of coalitions is important because it shows how members of groups combine to change distributions of power even when there is no formal leadership structure. Weak members of groups and societies can use coalitions to end domination and exploitation by other groups. As individuals, black members of Congress have no more power than white representatives, but as a coalition, they have considerable power over legislation.

It is through social interaction that groups and organizations achieve their goals. Although the failure of groups to cope with disagreement and tension is an important factor in their performance, group cultures and structures also influence their effectiveness.

Getting the Job Done: Explaining Group Effectiveness

Groups confront a variety of tasks. Factory workers produce goods, and universities produce graduates and research. Groups of scientists solve problems involved in sending a rocket to a distant planet, and families figure out how to balance their budgets and keep everyone happy. Research teams judge the effectiveness of new drugs and juries judge the guilt or innocence of defendants in criminal trials.

Most group work involves one or more of these areas: balancing a family budget requires judgment (estimates of future needs and income) and problem solving (how to raise income or cut spending). Regardless of the mix of tasks involved, all groups must cope with the problems of keeping their members satisfied and maintaining the commitment of their members to the group.

The sociological study of group performance grew out of the Industrial Revolution and the concentration of production in larger and more complex groups. Although early research focused on finding ways to increase productivity (and profits), the study of group performance now includes many groups, such as schools, government bureaucracies, the military, and scientific research laboratories. The settings vary, but the sociological question remains the same: How do the cultural, structural, and ecological characteristics of groups influence their performance? Before describing the importance of such characteristics, we should first examine a fundamental question: Do groups perform better than individuals?

Individual versus Group Effectiveness   "Two heads are better than one," the poet John Heywood wrote, and most research comparing the performance of individuals and groups bears the poet out. Individ-

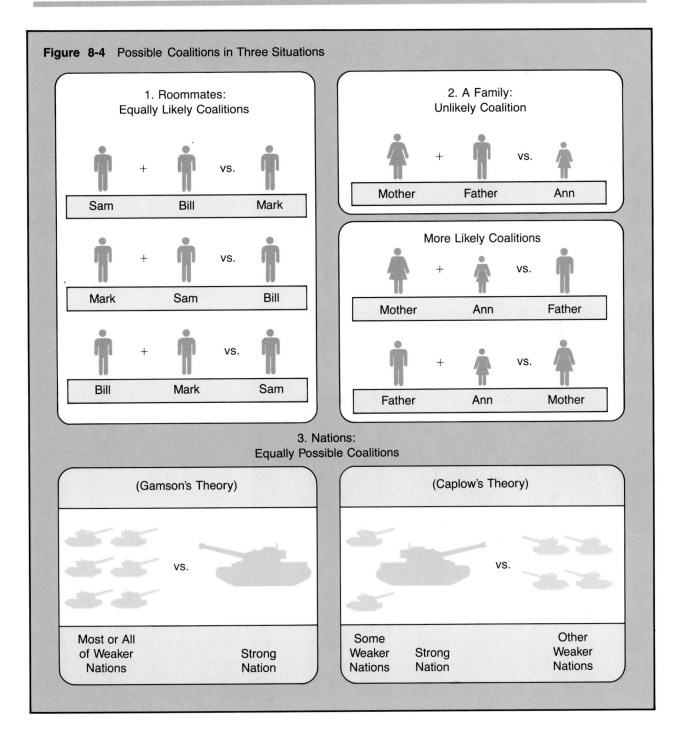

Figure 8-4 Possible Coalitions in Three Situations

1. Roommates:
Equally Likely Coalitions

Sam + Bill vs. Mark

Mark + Sam vs. Bill

Bill + Mark vs. Sam

2. A Family:
Unlikely Coalition

Mother + Father vs. Ann

More Likely Coalitions

Mother + Ann vs. Father

Father + Ann vs. Mother

3. Nations:
Equally Possible Coalitions

(Gamson's Theory)

vs.

| Most or All of Weaker Nations | Strong Nation |

(Caplow's Theory)

vs.

| Some Weaker Nations | Strong Nation | Other Weaker Nations |

uals usually learn better and faster in the presence of others (Perlmutter and Montmollin, 1952), and groups solve puzzles more quickly than individuals do (Hill, 1982; Laughlin, 1980). When Warnick and Sanders (1980) asked groups and individuals to recall details of a videotape portraying a crime, the groups produced more accurate and more detailed accounts.

Although two heads are often better than one, are they *twice* as good? Research suggests they are not, because individuals tend to reduce their effort as a

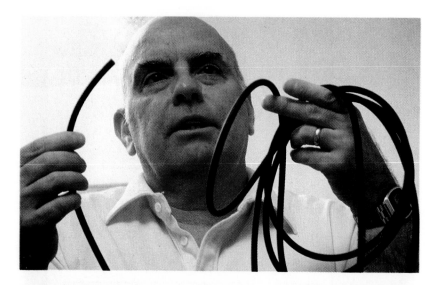

Roger Boisjoly was the engineer who first warned of the flaws in the Challenger's O-rings. After the disaster, he was treated so badly by co-workers that he resigned. He has been awarded the Prize for Scientific Freedom and Responsibility from the American Association for the Advancement of Science.

group grows in size (Harkins, 1981; Harkins, Latané and Williams, 1980). In one experiment, Moede (1927) asked men to pull as hard as they could on a rope attached to a machine that, unknown to them, measured their pull. By themselves, men pulled twice as hard as they did in groups of eight.

Although groups are generally more effective than individuals, they do have their disadvantages, especially when they are small and members want to maintain group harmony at all costs. When the desire for unity is strong, individuals are less likely to object to poor decisions and suggest alternatives. Groups, in other words, are vulnerable to what Irving Janis (1968, 1982) called **groupthink**, in which the desire for consensus overpowers group members' better judgment.

The events leading up to the destruction of the U.S. space shuttle Challenger and its crew illustrate how disastrous groupthink can be. Years before, many engineers who worked for NASA and the company responsible for building the Challenger (Morton Thiokol) were convinced that the shuttle was unsafe, but pressure both within NASA and Thiokol to keep the project on schedule silenced many of those who would have objected. As one member of the presidential investigative commission put it, "No one wanted to be the one who raised a show-stopping problem. No one had the guts to stand up and say, 'This thing is falling apart'" (New York Times, June 29, 1986, sec. 3, p. 1).

Hall and Watson (1970) asked groups of management trainees to decide what equipment would be needed in order to live on the moon. "Consensus groups" were instructed to reach a collective solution, whereas "conflict groups" were told to avoid changing views simply for the sake of harmony, to view differences of opinion as healthy and constructive, and to *not* use majority votes to reduce conflict.

Both individuals and groups submitted solutions, which were compared to those prepared by experts. Not only did conflict groups produce better solutions, but 75 percent of the conflict groups produced better solutions than their most capable individual member. By comparison, only 25 percent of the consensus groups performed better than their most capable member.

Groups and individuals differ not only in effectiveness, but in willingness to take risks as well. When stakes are high, groups tend to be more cautious than individuals (Knox and Safford, 1976). When the Soviet Union placed nuclear missiles in Cuba in 1964 most of President Kennedy's advisers initially urged an extreme response: the invasion of Cuba. Kennedy, however, insisted that his advisers reach a consensus. As a result, they made a "conservative shift" to a more moderate solution: a naval blockade around Cuba.

In less dangerous cases, groups make riskier decisions than individuals do. In one study, groups were asked to consider the following situation (Stoner, 1961):

> A man with a severe heart ailment must seriously curtail his customary way of life if he does not undergo a delicate medical operation that might cure him completely or might prove fatal. What would you advise? (p. 58)

Members were asked to consider the problem alone first and then as a group, and the results showed that group decisions were consistently more risky than those reached by individuals. In a group, individuals made a "risky shift."

Such findings raise disturbing questions: Do governments make group decisions that are riskier than those individuals would reach? Is group decision making more conducive to recklessness? Were decisions such as those to drop the atomic bomb on Japan or to seize the U.S. Embassy in Iran caused by risky shifts in groups? Why do such shifts occur?

In some cases, groups value risk taking as a sign that the group is "tough" and unafraid, and members increase their prestige by suggesting and supporting risky alternatives. Also, people tend to feel less individual responsibility when they are in groups and may feel less responsible for any failure that results from a risky decision. Finally, as Simmel (1950) noted, groups tend to release the inhibitions of their mem-

bers: we often feel freer to act out wild impulses at a large party than we do in a small group.

Groups tend to be more effective than individuals in achieving goals, but the results depend on the task and the size of the risks involved. Groups differ not only from individuals, however, but from one another, and such differences strongly influence their effectiveness.

Effectiveness and Group Culture   Although norms are supposed to help groups achieve their goals, they sometimes have just the opposite effect. Bureaucratic norms cannot anticipate all possible situations, and yet members are expected to obey the rules no matter what. Soldiers are required by law to obey the orders of their commanders, no matter how foolish those orders may appear to be.

Bureaucratic norms often become ends in themselves, obeyed not because they help accomplish group goals, but because "a rule is a rule." Procedures that work in one situation, however, may be totally inappropriate in another. In such cases, highly disciplined training becomes what Veblen called a "trained incapacity." During the Japanese attack on Pearl Harbor in 1941, some U.S. officers refused to issue weapons to soldiers without "proper written authorization" from the commander, even though they were being shot at by enemy planes.

In some cases, the content of norms affects group performance. In bureaucracies members are supposed to ignore feelings as they make decisions, to deal with each person as a "case," not as an individual. This often causes the arrogance, abruptness, and coldness so often associated with "bureaucrats," and creates hostile attitudes between bureaucracies and those they serve.

Effectiveness and Group Size   Larger groups tend to perform better than smaller ones when problems require a large number of skills or have a single solution (Watson, 1928). Small groups, however, tend to be more stable (James, 1951), and their members can communicate more easily. Small groups perform better when tasks require a limited range of skills and more creative solutions.

Small groups also appear to be better at satisfying their members, but this can be deceiving. Slater (1958) gave problems to 24 groups ranging in size from two to seven members and afterward asked members if they thought their group was too small or too large. The proportion responding "too small" decreased steadily with greater size, whereas the proportion of "too large" responses increased (Table 8-4).

Table 8-4

Percentage of Occasions on Which Subjects Felt Group Was Too Small or Too Large to Carry Out Assigned Task, by Size of Group

SIZE	PERCENT TOO SMALL	PERCENT TOO LARGE
2	34	0
3	17	0
4	11	0
5	0	0
6	0	14
7	0	13

Source: Slater, 1958.

Table 8-5

Issues on Which Large-Group Members Agreed More Often Than Small-Group Members[1]

1. The time available to solve the problem is insufficient.
2. This group doesn't make the best use of its time.
3. This group needs somebody to keep it on track.
4. Some people in this group talk too much.
5. Some people in this group are crowded out of the discussion.
6. Some people in this group should participate more.
7. There are considerable differences of ability and competence between members of this group.
8. There is too much competition among members in this group.
9. This group is not accomplishing as much as it could.

[1]Small groups have 2, 3, or 4 members, large groups 5, 6, or 7.

Source: Slater, 1958.

Only in groups of five members did no one feel the group was either too large or too small. In addition, members of large groups were more likely to complain about the group and its members (Table 8-5), whereas those in the smallest groups expressed no complaints at all. Why should size have this effect?

One might argue that in small groups we feel more important and freer to speak our minds. Yet, when Bales and Borgatta (1955) examined Slater's data, they found that in smaller groups members rarely showed tension or anger, whereas in larger groups anger and disagreement were common.

Bales and Borgatta explained these findings by suggesting that as groups increase in size, some problems are diminished while new ones emerge. The smallest groups depend on agreement and harmony for their survival (Simmel, 1950), and although they may lack the resources they need to accomplish a task, members are likely to conceal disagreement and anger and give a rosy picture of group life.

Large groups, however, have more resources and do not need the agreement of all their members in order to survive or reach a decision. Members feel freer to disagree and show anger because this poses a less serious threat to the group and their standing in it. This suggests that whereas *physical* freedom (to talk) is greater in small groups, *psychological* freedom (to express unpopular opinions) is greater in large groups (Mullen, 1983).

This contradicts the common belief that small groups are the only places where we can truly be ourselves. Large groups limit our participation, but small ones limit expression of feelings and outrageous impulses (Simmel, 1950). Whereas large groups tend to make us feel insignificant and lost, small groups tend to inhibit us by making us feel highly visible.

Effectiveness, Roles, and Leadership   As we saw earlier, the more complex a group is, the better it accomplishes complicated tasks that require a wide range of skills. Complex groups, however, also find it more difficult to coordinate and control their members' behavior.

Group complexity creates problems when it *becomes an end in itself*. The essence of a bureaucracy is the management of some members by others. In order to demonstrate their importance, bureaucrats often create work that requires assistants, which results in more paperwork as assistants report to their bosses. More assistants are then added, and the organization continues to grow, using more and more resources to manage its mushrooming staff (Parkinson, 1957).

Other problems arise from the ways in which groups decide who plays which roles. Bureaucracies try to secure the loyal, devoted service of their members by offering them job security and clear lines of promotion so long as they obey the rules. This causes three problems.

First, members may use their security to do no more than what the norms require of them. College professors are often criticized for working less after achieving the security of tenure. Second, because advancement in bureaucracies requires obedience to norms, people may become timid and overly conservative, afraid to show initiative for fear of risking their promotion to higher positions (Merton, 1968). Third, in bureaucracies people tend to be promoted to higher positions on the basis of performance in *lower* positions. Inevitably, members reach positions that are beyond their abilities and there they stay, unable to perform well enough to reach the next rung on the ladder.

Peter and Hull (1969) called this phenomenon the Peter Principle: "In a hierarchy each employee tends to rise to his level of *incompetence*; every post tends to be occupied by an employee incompetent to execute its duties." They suggested that the only reason top positions are sometimes occupied by competent people is that "there are not enough ranks for them to have reached their level of incompetence: in other words, *in that hierarchy* there is no task beyond their abilities." Although complex role structures increase group effectiveness in many ways, they also produce unanticipated negative consequences that affect their members and interfere with group performance.

Social situations affect not only the emergence and selection of leaders in groups, but their effectiveness as well. Task leaders are most effective in extreme situations—when groups verge on falling apart during disasters or when they are cohesive and strong. Expressive leaders, however, are more effective than task leaders in less extreme circumstances, when members have less need of a task leader and are in a stronger position to question a leader's authority (Fiedler et al., 1976). A leader who improves group performance in one situation may damage it in another.

Effectiveness and Communication We saw in Chapter 4 that communication patterns affect both success at different tasks and member satisfaction. When members can interact freely with one another (a "circle"), groups have more difficulty solving puzzles with single solutions than they do with tasks having many workable solutions (Shaw, 1954). In ad-

dition, although groups that channel communication through a single member (a "wheel") are efficient problem solvers, their members are less satisfied.

From this point of view, it is easier to see why large numbers of people with free and open communication structures (such as street mobs) are inefficient at solving problems. It is also easier to see why bureaucracies have so much trouble satisfying their members and performing efficiently. Their communication structures often leave members feeling insignificant and powerless. They also make it difficult for one part of the organization to know what other parts are doing, for each piece of information must pass through many hands before reaching its ultimate destination.

We have seen, then, that the ability of groups to achieve goals depends on their cultural and structural characteristics. No group, however, can perform well or even survive if it cannot maintain its members' loyalty. All groups must continually cope with the problem of social cohesion.

Staying Together, Falling Apart: Cohesion and Conflict in Groups

What makes groups stay together? When membership is involuntary as in junior high schools, **social cohesion** is maintained by the power of authority; but in voluntary groups, the attraction of members is more difficult to maintain. In the simplest sense, a group cannot exist unless people are motivated to interact with one another, and a group survives only if the forces keeping it together are stronger than those that would tear it apart.

In many groups, members are joined by a shared culture. Family members value family life itself and members of rural communities or urban neighborhoods may feel bound together by shared values about what constitutes "a good life," norms that regulate relationships among neighbors, suspicious attitudes toward "outsiders," and religious beliefs. Group cohesion that is based on common experience and culture is called **Gemeinschaft** ("community") (Tönnies, 1887) or **mechanical solidarity** (Durkheim, 1893). Because of the closeness of social relationships in Gemeinschaft groups, they are almost always primary.

The primary ties of Gemeinschaft are often the source of cohesion in the subgroups of larger organizations. In the last days of World War II, the German army maintained its effectiveness even though it was badly outnumbered, undersupplied, and had to rely

Gemeinschaft ties, such as those in the Little Italy neighborhood in New York City in the early 1900s, are based primarily on common culture and similar life experiences. They enabled millions of immigrants to come to the U.S. and immediately establish a sense of familiarity and belonging.

on damaged and inferior equipment. Some analysts believed that the German army continued to function as a cohesive unit because its soldiers strongly believed in their cause; but in a postwar study, Shils and Janowitz (1948) found that German soldiers were generally indifferent to Nazi ideology.

What held them together? Shils and Janowitz concluded that it was the loyalty that each soldier felt toward the members of his small combat squad or platoon (see also Van Creveld, 1982). The German soldier, they wrote,

> was likely to go on fighting, provided he had the necessary weapons, so long as the group possessed leadership with which he could identify himself, and so long as he gave affection to and received affection from the other members of his squad or platoon. . . . As long as he felt himself to be a member of his primary group and therefore bound by the expectations and demands of its other members, his soldierly achievement was likely to be good. (p. 284)

Studies of U.S. soldiers during World War II also showed that primary ties were vital sources of group cohesion in small combat units (Stouffer et al., 1949). A study of soldiers in Vietnam, however, suggests that although primary ties were important, they arose in part from the fact that soldiers could not survive on their own.

> The fact is that if the individual soldier is realistically to improve his survival chances, he must *necessarily* develop and take part in primary relationships. Under the grim conditions of ground warfare, an individual's survival is directly dependent upon the support . . . he can expect from his fellows. He gets such support to the degree that he reciprocates to the others in his unit. In other words, primary relations are at their core mutually pragmatic efforts to minimize personal risk. (Moskos, 1969, p. 18)

In contrast, the communist Vietcong, against whom the U.S. fought, were organized in small "cells" of 3–5 soldiers each, an arrangement that promoted strong

The caring shown by these two U.S. soldiers during the Korean War illustrates the importance of primary relations in holding small combat units together. In other respects, the units are merely specialized task groups in an enormously complex organization.

primary ties of loyalty more than ideological fervor (Karnow, 1983).

The primary ties in Gemeinschaft groups are based on common experience and a shared culture; but the example of the war in Vietnam introduces a second major source of cohesion: the degree to which members must depend on one another. The concepts of **Gesellschaft** (Tönnies, 1887) and **organic solidarity** (Durkheim, 1893) describe groups that stay together because their structures make it difficult to achieve important goals unless their members cooperate with and depend on one another even in spite of cultural differences. Whereas *culture* is the major source of cohesion in Gemeinschaft, cohesion within the secondary relations of Gesellschaft is largely a matter of *social structure.*

The most recognizable example of Gesellschaft is the bureaucracy. While small combat units are often held together by primary ties, the larger organizations of which they are a part—battalions, divisions, and armies—cannot function unless each of their units does its specialized job. A small unit that delivers food,

ammunition, and other supplies, or one that specializes in communications can stay together as a unit based on the primary ties among its members. An army, however, stays together only insofar as its various units function effectively as parts of the whole.

Social structure affects group cohesion by defining not only relationships within groups, but among them as well. As Thomas Jefferson and Winston Churchill noted, groups that conflict during peacetime suddenly pull together during wartime in the face of a common enemy, burying their differences and sacrificing individual interests for the common good. When the external threat is removed, old differences resurface, unity breaks down, and group conflicts resume (Coser, 1956).

During World War II, German leaders believed that continuous bombing of Britain's cities would beat its population into submission; but the bombings had the opposite effect, for they aroused a sense of solidarity and defiance in the British people. Later in the war, Allied commanders failed to learn from the German mistake, and researchers discovered after the war

The German bombing of British cities during World War II only strengthened the refusal of Britain to give up. Here, Prime Minister Winston Churchill tours London streets after a German raid, inspects damage and, as is plain to see, bolsters morale.

that saturation bombing of German cities only increased German resistance and prolonged the war (Janis, 1951). Nor did the U.S. heed this lesson thirty years later during the Vietnam War when it tried unsuccessfully to break communist resistance through massive bombing of North Vietnam (Karnow, 1983; Neustadt and May, 1986).

When group cohesion is low, leaders may increase solidarity by convincing members that other groups threaten their survival (Markides and Cohen, 1982). During its revolution, Iran was torn by power struggles and disagreements about how the country should be run, and its leaders frequently unified their followers by directing attention to "foreign devils"—the U.S.—who, the leaders claimed, wanted to destroy them. Libya's leader, Mohamar Khadafi, has used similar tactics to calm discontent at home.

In groups, we interact, work toward goals, and try to maintain a sense of cohesion. These are the basic elements of group life, but what are the implications for group members? How do the characteristics of groups affect the quality of our lives?

INDIVIDUALS, FREEDOM, AND LIFE IN GROUPS

The social characteristics of groups affect societies and their people. Groups are capable both of supporting and protecting their members and of corrupting and harming them. Through groups, human beings have accomplished stunning and wonderful things, but groups are also the source of our most astonishing cruelty and destruction. How do groups and organizations affect us?

Culture, Groups, and Individuals

Perhaps one of the most significant cultural changes during the last 2,000 years has been the enormous increase in the social value of individuals and their freedom in relation to groups. Durkheim (1893) went so far as to suggest that in the simplest societies with their uncomplicated divisions of labor, the idea of an "individual" simply did not exist. The group, he argued, was everything, and it never occurred to people to stand apart from it as unique individuals.

From Durkheim's point of view, "individuality" cannot exist without supporting cultural beliefs (such a thing is possible), values (the individual is important), and norms (individuals have rights in relation to groups); and these ideas are relatively new in history. In this sense, if sociology had existed thousands of years ago, it would not even have identified the effects of groups on individuals as a problem.

The social value of individuals has reached its highest point in complex industrial societies. As societies raise the value of individuals, people are less vulnerable to being "buried" in the group, to having no right to stand apart and celebrate their uniqueness. This, however, creates the danger of being *isolated* from groups.

In industrial societies, we spend increasingly large portions of our lives in groups and organizations that value efficiency, precision, speed, control, production, and obedience more than they value the happiness and satisfaction of their members. In addition, Slater (1971) argued that an extreme emphasis on individuals and their uniqueness creates a cultural environment that frustrates basic human needs to trust and cooperate with others, to deal directly with interpersonal problems, and to share responsibility for the conduct of our lives.

In short, Slater argued that modern cultures not only raise the social value of individuals to new heights, but also create unprecedented levels of isolation and loneliness. "Who am I?" is perhaps the most common and disturbing question individuals face in modern cultures, because simple group membership is no longer a complete basis for our existence. Whereas ties between individuals and groups may have been too strong in the simplest societies, in complex societies they are in danger of being too weak (Durkheim, 1897).

Such cultural changes, however, do not simply "happen" by accident; they are often responses to changing social structures that define relationships. Weber (1946) and Durkheim (1893) saw in the Industrial Revolution a threat to human welfare. What changes in the structure of group life did they see and why were they so concerned?

Social Structure, Groups, and Individuals

Gemeinschaft societies are held together by a common culture, and groups tend to be small, informal, and primary. Work, family, and religion form a unified whole. Those who share in the culture and obey its norms have a secure place in the social world.

The Industrial Revolution, however, accelerated a long-term change in which social relationships became increasingly rational, secondary, and formal in Gesellschaft societies based less on shared culture than on rational calculations of individual self-interest (Weber, 1922a). This change resulted from the rise of the bureaucracy as a model of social organization.

In complex industrial societies, we are known as individuals, and as individuals, we are known primarily by the social statuses we occupy. Children no longer grow up confident of their place in society, knowing exactly what is expected of them, what roles they will play as adults. To survive in modern societies, each of us must achieve a place for ourselves somewhere in the complex division of labor.

Nowhere are the consequences of these structures clearer than in bureaucracies with their formal rules, rigidly defined relationships, and inattention to individual feelings and needs. Argyris (1957) suggested that bureaucracies actually interfere with the needs of healthy people. Maturity includes the ability to act and make judgments independently, to think abstractly and in terms of long-term consequences of behavior. Bureaucracies encourage dependency and timidity, short-term thinking, and ignorance of long-term consequences.

Argyris concluded, "Formal organizations are willing to pay high wages and provide adequate seniority if mature adults will, for eight hours a day, behave in a less mature manner." As a result, we often feel frustrated and helpless because we have little control over our environment, goals, or behavior, and the lack of control creates anxiety and uncertainty. Karl Marx described the resulting feelings of being lost and insignificant as *alienation*—a feeling of helplessness and detachment in relation to work and its results.

Unlike primary groups, bureaucracies do not derive their security from the welfare of their members. We may be fired when it is no longer in an employer's "best interests" to keep us, regardless of our abilities. Middle-aged executives often lose jobs because they are *too* experienced and *too* capable and therefore command higher salaries than younger employees.

Some people defend themselves by leaving the organization (a risky choice), or by achieving more powerful positions within the organization. Others, however, who can neither advance nor afford to leave, retreat into apathy and daydreams, or create informal groups that support their feelings of alienation.

The rational basis of bureaucracy leads many to participate in order to achieve personal—not organizational—goals, the most important of which is earning a living (Moore, 1962). We can work in a bureaucracy without valuing its goals or liking our jobs or other workers. This often minimizes feelings of loyalty to large organizations and encourages members to exploit every opportunity for personal gain—whether on the large scale of criminal embezzlement or the small scale of stealing office supplies and equipment, padding expense accounts, or using company cars for personal trips—a clear example of social factors that foster criminal behavior (Gracey, 1972a).

As bureaucracy spreads, we find ourselves with fewer and fewer groups in which we are known and valued as individuals. We spend increasing portions of our lives in secondary groups that involve limited parts of ourselves, and our lives are divided into separate spheres of family, work, friendships, and religion that have little if any connection to one another. In such environments, it is difficult to maintain a sense of "wholeness" about our lives; rather, we tend to feel torn in many directions at once as we divide our time, energy, and loyalty between family, friends, and the formal demands of work (Moore, 1962).

The structures of complex societies create feelings of insignificance and rootlessness in their members, yet how do they differ from Durkheim's vision of simple societies in which individuals are indistinguishable from their groups? Is it not true that individuals have little significance in both simple Gemeinschaft societies and the bureaucracies of modern Gesellschaft societies?

Although individuals tend to be "lost" in both types of societies, there is an enormously important difference between the two. In the simple societies Durkheim referred to, individuals had no need to stand apart from their groups, because groups and their members depended on each other for their survival. There was a close connection between the welfare of groups and the welfare of their members.

A bureaucracy, however, uses people as a means for achieving goals that they neither determine nor control, and may not even share. In a bureaucratic society, individuals cannot afford to place their welfare in the hands of organizations that can and often do quickly dispense with them. It is no accident of history that as social structures become increasingly bureaucratic, concern for the rights and welfare of individuals grows stronger. As groups become more exploitative, members must establish new sources of protection and security, and aside from the family, the individual is the last line of defense.

The increased size, complexity, and formality of groups and organizations also affect the welfare of entire societies, for although bureaucracies support efficiency, control, and complex divisions of labor, they also oppose the strong emotional ties that are the basis of human morality, compassion, and empathy. In bureaucracies we are supposed to simply do our jobs and leave the establishment of group goals to our leaders. This gives bureaucracies what Sabini and Silver (1982) have called "a genius for organizing evil."

Nazi Germany was a model of bureaucratic efficiency, and prided itself on the strict formal organization of its society. When Adolph Eichmann managed the railway systems that transported millions of people to their deaths in concentration camps, he behaved as a model bureaucrat, carrying out his orders quickly, efficiently, and without question. In the final chaotic months of World War II, when Germany was defending itself on three fronts, Eichmann's proudest achievement was his astonishing ability to keep the trains running on time.

Marx believed that bureaucracy turns individuals into cogs in machines and that as we are more alienated from our work and its results, we are also more alienated from one another. In bureaucratic societies, in which organizations and their rules assume primary importance, it is not surprising that we are often motivated by rational self-interest ("What's in it for *me*?") and insensitive to the fate of others.

Groups will always be a part of human life, and it is for this reason that decisions about their structures and cultures are so important. We cannot survive alone, and the characteristics of groups set the terms on which we live our lives in relation to other people.

The same bureaucratic structures that enable railroads to perform the complex task of transporting large numbers of people and great quantities of goods were also used by the Nazis to send millions of victims to their deaths in concentration camps.

SUMMARY

1. The group is an important sociological concept because individuals perform their most important roles in them; groups meet many human needs and are an important source of social conflict; and the performance of groups strongly affects the achievement of important social goals such as socialization.

2. All groups rest on a shared culture to which members are expected to conform. In most cases, it is very difficult for us to defy the majority opinion in a group to which we belong.

3. Group structures differ in many ways, defining their existence in terms of time and space, and drawing boundaries that differ in their clarity and openness. Membership in some groups is voluntary, whereas in others it is compulsory. Group members may think of themselves as members of superior in-groups and express hostile attitudes toward out-groups.

4. The division of labor in groups is reflected in their role structures, and the distributions of affection, power, respect, and communication are revealed in sociometric, power, leadership, prestige, and communication structures.

5. Primary groups such as the family are valued for their own sake, endure through time, and involve many aspects of members' lives. Secondary groups such as many work groups are valued for limited goals, are relatively short-lived, and involve limited aspects of members' lives. Secondary groups range from informal organizations (in which norms are often vaguely stated and loosely applied) to formal organizations (in which norms are clearly stated and rigidly applied).

6. Democratic, authoritarian, and laissez-faire leaders emerge under a variety of conditions as groups struggle to stay together and achieve goals. Some groups have no leadership structure, whereas others have more than one.

7. The growth of bureaucracy as a form of social organization is one of the most significant transformations of the past two centuries and was given an enormous boost by the Industrial Revolution.

8. Groups can be as small as a dyad or as large as an army of tens of thousands. Absolute and relative size are important factors in the power of groups and the complexity of their structures.

9. Spatial relationships affect the frequency and duration of interaction in groups, which in turn affects the level of cohesion. Spatial relationships also serve to reinforce power structures.

10. Group process refers to what members actually do, regardless of the expectations attached to roles. Bales' techniques for recording group process are useful in identifying critical stages in the life of a group.

11. Members may try to form coalitions to increase their power or rewards. Coalition theorists try to predict the conditions under which coalitions will occur.

12. Many factors affect group effectiveness, depending on the goals involved. Factors include group size, the formality of norms, the complexity of role and communication structures, and the presence of leaders.

13. Group cohesion depends on the degree to which members share a common base of culture and experience (Gemeinschaft) and the degree to which members depend on one another in order to accomplish goals (Gesellschaft). Cohesion based on Gemeinschaft is called mechanical solidarity and is most often found in primary groups such as the family and preindustrial communities. Cohesion based on Gesellschaft is called organic solidarity and is most often found in bureaucratic organizations and complex industrial societies.

14. The characteristics of groups profoundly affect the experience and behavior of their members, their levels of self-esteem, their feelings of belonging and security, their ability to determine and pursue their own goals, and their power to control others and protect themselves.

KEY TERMS

authoritarian leader   193
coalition   203
collectivity   200

Looking Elsewhere

Having studied Chapter 8, you might want to look at related discussions in *Human Arrangements*, which include

• power structures in small army units (Chapter 4, pp. 91–92)
• coalitions in social relationships (Chapter 7, p. 171)
• coalitions in politics (Chapter 19, pp. 532–33)
• the political power of interest groups (Chapter 19, p. 532)
• more on bureaucracy (Chapter 4, pp. 94–97)
• the school as bureaucracy (Chapter 16, pp. 443–44)
• the effects of physical space on social interaction (Chapter 7, pp. 172–73)
• Gemeinschaft and Gesellschaft communities (Chapter 9, pp. 230–32)
• conformity in groups as a cause of deviance (Chapter 10, pp. 264–67)
• organizations as a source of crime (Chapter 10, p. 259)
• alienation in the workplace (Chapter 18, pp. 503–504)

RECOMMENDED READINGS

CHACKERIAN, R., and ABCARIAN, G. (1984). *Bureaucratic power in society*. Chicago: Nelson-Hall. A compelling critique of bureaucracy with a special emphasis on the connection between schools and the economy. An excellent source for students who want to deepen their understanding of bureaucracy.

JANIS, I. (1982). *Victims of groupthink*. Boston: Houghton Mifflin. A look at the sometimes disastrous effects of groupthink on decision making, focusing on U.S. foreign policy.

KANTER, R., and STEIN, B. A. (Eds.). (1979). *Life in organizations*. New York: Basic Books. A collection of essays about work experiences in formal organizations.

OLMSTEAD, M. S., and HARE, A. P. (1978). *The small group* (2nd ed.). New York: Random House. A well-written summary of important research on small groups. See also Paulus, P. B. (1983). *Basic group processes*. New York: Springer-Verlag.

SLATER, P. E. (1971). *The pursuit of loneliness*. Boston: Beacon Press. Slater's compelling analysis of a central tension in group life between independence, freedom, and a sense of belonging and commitment is one of those books that many people read more than once.

WEBER, M. *From Max Weber: Essays in sociology*. (1946). Edited and translated by H. H. Gerth and C. Wright Mills. New York: Oxford University Press. One of the best and most accessible sources of Weber's ideas on bureaucracy.

WHYTE, W. F. (1981). *Street corner society* (3rd ed.). Chicago: University of Chicago Press. Whyte's classic participation observation study of groups in an Italian slum in Boston.

Some Basic Types of Communities

The Rural-Urban Continuum

Traditional and Modern Communities

Communities and Culture

The Myth of Suburban Culture

Norms and Community Life

The Social Structures of Community Life

Community Boundaries and Xenophobia

The Importance of Time

Who Lives Here? The Social Composition of Communities

The Scale of Community Life: Groups and Formal Organizations

Community Power Structures

Relationships: Gemeinschaft and Gesellschaft

Community Ecology

Community Populations

Niches and Ecosystems

Land Use: Where People Do What They Do

How Communities Change

World Patterns of Change

Trends in the United States

Community Change in Developing Nations

Communities in Trouble: Possibilities for Change

9 Communities

What does the word "community" make you think of? Friends, family, home town, neighborhood, politics, school, church, work, "a place where I belong," busy streets, quiet country lanes, burglar alarms, doors locked only at night? Whatever the association, "community" refers to one of the most important aspects of our lives—where we live; and where we live affects *how* we live, for it is in communities that we are born, attend school, make and lose friends, find jobs, lose jobs, raise families, grow old, and die. Communities may be sources of attachment that make us feel rooted in the world; they may be like prisons from which we see little chance of escape; or they may be no more than stopovers on the way to someplace else.

A **community** is a collection of people who share a physical environment and meet their needs through daily interaction with other members (Schnore, 1973). (Groups, by contrast, often are not defined in relation to a physical territory.) The study of community life occupies an important place in the development of sociology in the U.S. At the University of Chicago, a number of sociologists, Robert Park (1864–1944), Ernest Burgess (1886–1966), W. I. Thomas (1863–1947), and Florian Znaniecki (1882–1938), combined a commitment to social reform with an intense curiosity about urban life. They were particularly interested in ecological studies of social problems created by rapid industrialization and urbanization, and massive immigration. Chicago abounded with a variety of human adaptations to the dizzying pace of urban life, and these members of what came to be known as the "Chicago School" used the city as a natural laboratory for the study of everything from urban gangs, slums, dance halls, and racism to life among the wealthy (Blumer, 1984; Coser, 1977).

We begin by describing basic types of communities, and then use sociological analysis to examine how their characteristics affect the lives of the people who live in them and cause communities to change.

SOME BASIC TYPES OF COMMUNITIES

There are many ways to describe differences among communities, but perhaps the two most important sociological distinctions are *rural* or *urban* and *traditional* or *modern*.

The Rural-Urban Continuum

Rural communities consist of small, homogeneous, sparsely settled populations, whereas **urban communities** are large, heterogeneous, and densely settled (Wirth, 1938).

How large and densely settled must a population be in order to be "urban"? Any limit is somewhat arbitrary, but most sociologists use the 1982 U.S. Census Bureau definition of 2,500 or more people. Although this figure has the practical advantage of being clear and precise, the concepts of urban and rural are most useful if we think of them as two extremes of a continuum.

At one end are tiny, isolated villages such as early North American settlements. The larger and more densely settled a population is, the more urban it is. An **urbanized area** is a city and the densely settled territory around it (its **suburbs**) that together contain 50,000 or more people.

On a larger scale, a **metropolitan area** is either a city with 50,000 or more inhabitants or an urbanized area that is socially and economically linked with surrounding counties that bring its total population to 100,000 or more (U.S. Census Bureau, 1986a). The specific definitions of urbanized and metropolitan areas are less important, however, than the basic concept behind them: they are large, densely settled population centers whose economic and social activities are closely linked with those of surrounding communities.

New York City contains over 7 million people, and activities in the city are tied to the populations

The obvious difference of sheer size that distinguishes tiny Topsham, Vermont (above) and New York City (below) is only a starting point for a sociological understanding of the variety and complexity of communities. In what ways would you expect life in these communities to differ, and why?

of surrounding counties in New York, New Jersey, and Connecticut. Many residents of these neighboring counties work and shop in New York City, making the city and its adjacent counties an integrated unit containing more than 9 million people (U.S. Census Bureau, 1986a).

Urban communities are divided into **neighborhoods**—collections of people who live close to one another—which often serve as communities for their residents (Gans, 1982; Greer, 1968; Hallman, 1984). Neighborhoods are where people carry out most of the small details of everyday life: they are where children play and where adults shop for groceries, have shoes repaired and clothing cleaned. Neighborhoods are communities in which we are most aware of and affected by other people's behavior and where, therefore, conformity is most highly valued.

Traditional and Modern Communities

Communities differ in the degree to which they are *traditional* or *modern* (Inkeles and Smith, 1974). The Amish in the U.S. live in **traditional communities** that are culturally isolated from the rest of society (Kephart, 1987). Their religious beliefs preclude the use of scientific technology, and they reject most aspects of the modern society that surrounds them—including electricity, indoor toilets, jewelry, machinery, politics, watches, life insurance, loans, and social security. Their style and color of dress—simple and black—is the same as it was 250 years ago.

In comparison with traditional communities, **modern communities** tend to have more complex divisions of labor, more sophisticated technology, more highly developed mass media, and higher levels of education and literacy. Residents of modern communities are more likely to accept new ideas, and social relationships tend to be more secondary and formal than primary and informal.

Urban communities are not necessarily modern, nor are rural communities necessarily traditional. Many cities in less developed countries—particularly in Africa and Asia—are traditional communities, while many rural communities in Europe and North America are, in relative terms, quite modern.

The concepts of urban, rural, traditional, and modern describe communities only in very general terms. In the rest of this chapter, we will focus on the detailed cultural, structural, and ecological characteristics of communities, and how they affect the lives of those who live in them.

COMMUNITIES AND CULTURE

Like groups, communities are characterized by a culture which, in some cases, lies at the core of a community's existence: the early Puritan settlements in New England came into being because their members wanted religious freedom. Throughout history, groups such as communes have been based on decisions to live according to cultural ideas considered deviant in the surrounding society (Kanter, 1972; Zablocki, 1980). The Twin Oaks commune in Louisa, Virginia, was inspired by the community described in B. F. Skinner's novel *Walden Two*. At Twin Oaks, cooperation is valued more than competition for individual advantage, and decisions based on consensus are valued more than leadership by a few. With the exception of private belongings, which members must keep in their rooms, all property is held in common and all that is earned or produced is contributed to the group (Cordes, 1984; Kanter, 1972).

A major focus in sociological analysis has been on cultural differences between rural and urban communities. As politicians need to remember, most rural communities rest on traditional values, and their members tend to be less open to change and less tolerant of strange life-styles than their urban counterparts. In the United States, rural dwellers are more likely to be religious fundamentalists and political conservatives: major opposition to the Equal Rights Amendment has come mostly from sparsely settled rural states.

In comparison with urban dwellers, people in rural communities generally place less value on literacy, formal education, the arts and mass media, the use of sophisticated technology, and individual advancement through competition (Inkeles and Smith, 1974; Larson, 1968). They tend to share a common set of cultural ideas and to place higher values on large families, traditional roles for men and women, conformity, cooperation, and loyalty to the community.

City populations represent great cultural diversity (diversity was, in fact, a major part of Wirth's 1938 definition of cities as communities). Cities contain a vast array of people in different occupations, social classes, and racial and ethnic groups. Cities are more likely to have substantial numbers of artists and musicians, judges and college professors, political radicals, the very wealthy and the very poor, as well as criminals and their victims. The mix of people from different cultural backgrounds is also far greater in cities: there

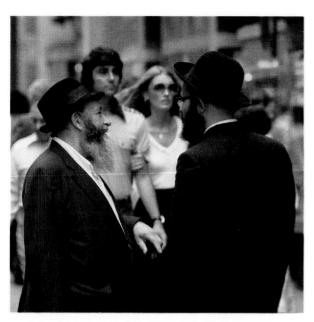

Hasidic Jews, like the Amish, maintain their traditional beliefs, customs, and manner of dress, even while living within modern communities such as New York.

are more Poles in Chicago than in Warsaw, the capital of Poland, and the Detroit area has the largest concentration of Arabic-speaking people outside of the Middle East.

One result is a generally higher level of tolerance for nonconformity in urban areas although this level has fallen somewhat in recent years (Abrahamson and Carter, 1986). Stephan and McMullin (1982) found that people who live in the largest cities report far more tolerance for homosexuality, pornography, and extramarital and premarital sex than do people living in smaller cities and towns. They found even greater differences in attitudes toward sexual nonconformity when they compared people in terms of the size of the communities they lived in as adolescents (see also Wilson, 1985).

Why should such cultural differences occur between small, sparsely settled communities and large, densely populated ones? Early sociologists such as Simmel (1908) and Wirth (1938) attributed urban-rural differences to the physical characteristics of the communities themselves—the number of people who occupy a given area. Large populations are bound to be more heterogeneous than small ones, and conformity will be valued more highly in small communities where people cannot escape awareness of one an-

other's behavior. When we are surrounded by large numbers of people, we protect our privacy, Simmel believed, by being aloof and superficial toward others.

Simmel's approach is purely ecological, because it suggests that physical differences between urban and rural communities (population size and density) cause cultural differences among their inhabitants. The ecological approach, however, ignores the effects of culture on the formation of communities. In other words, as more recent urban sociologists argue, it is culture that created the city—not the other way around (Castells, 1977; Gans, 1962; Jaret, 1983).

Since the beginnings of the Industrial Revolution in the eighteenth century, the most important characteristic of urban areas has not been their size and density; rather, it is their *industrial and commercial activity* that has affected community culture and structure. Industrial and commercial communities require large pools of workers in a complex occupational structure; to advance, individuals must compete for jobs and be willing to move to different neighborhoods or communities in search of better opportunities. These two facts help explain why industrial communities attract large numbers of people with a variety of cultural backgrounds.

People also choose to live in cities because cities foster a variety of subcultures, communities-within-communities in which shared interests draw people together. People with unusual interests or beliefs often feel isolated in small towns, but city populations are so large that people have a variety of supportive subcultures to choose from (Fischer, 1975, 1982, 1984; Wilson, 1986).

The cultural differences between urban and rural communities are not caused simply by the population characteristics that define communities as urban or rural, and nowhere has this misinterpretation been more evident than in early sociological studies of "suburbia."

The Myth of Suburban Culture

Although suburbs existed in the U.S. as early as 1815 (Binford, 1985), they did not emerge as a major community form until the turn of this century. Suburbs were inhabited by people who could afford country homes from which they commuted by train and streetcar to work in cities (see Jackson, 1986). In the 1920s, suburbs grew rapidly with the mass production of cars and paved roads, and after World War II they were built on a massive scale for returning veterans and their families (Long, 1981; Muller, 1981).

Suburbia received considerable attention from sociologists because it appeared to represent a new kind of community with a distinctive culture that emphasized family life, home ownership, security and safety, active community involvement, and close, friendly relations among residents—all the things that made for "the good life." It was also seen as a social environment in which conformity and "keeping up with the Joneses" were valued more than anything else. Wives were prisoners in their homes, and husbands could not escape the deadening daily commute to the city. With the help of movies (such as *Rebel Without a Cause*) and literature (such as John Cheever's short stories), suburbia was identified as a culturally unique form of community life.

In the last 20 years, however, sociologists have challenged the idea that a suburban culture exists at all. Rather, they argue that the cultures found in suburban communities depend on the social statuses of their residents: their social class, occupation, age, marital status, and race. Berger's 1960 study of a working-class suburb in California reveals a social life that contradicts the suburban ideal, with little participation in local affairs, limited social involvement with neighbors, and an almost exclusive concentration on the family, home, and television.

Other studies report a variety of cultures in different suburban communities (see Bell, 1969; Gans, 1962, 1982). Knowing that a woman lives in a suburb or city tells us far less about her than do statuses such as occupation, ethnicity, race, income, education, age, and marital status.

Outside the U.S., the variety of suburban lifestyles is even more apparent. In suburbs of Rome, residents focus almost completely on their families and have little to do with neighbors or community decisions (Ferrarotti, 1970). In the suburbs surrounding Kampala, Uganda, however, close ties with neighbors and active participation in community life are highly valued (Gutkind, 1966). For the most part there is little about the physical characteristics of suburbs that dictates a particular kind of culture.

Norms and Community Life

Like all norms, those that regulate life in communities differ in their formality, the strictness with which they are applied, and their content.

The small populations and relatively simple division of labor in traditional communities, such as the Amish, allow them to control their members with informal sanctions that are strictly applied. Individual behavior and appearance are highly visible in such communities: any member of an Amish community who violated prohibitions on smoking cigarettes or who dressed inappropriately would be quickly noticed. Because most residents know one another and interact on a regular basis, there is little need for formal mechanisms—police departments, courts, and correctional systems—for enforcing norms.

In cities it is impossible to regulate people's behavior through informal mechanisms. Populations are large and culturally heterogeneous, which makes it relatively easy for people to conceal their behavior. In cities, therefore, norms tend to be formal, enforced through a complex division of labor designed to discover, prosecute, and punish those who violate laws. Urban neighborhoods, however, are often small communities themselves and often rely on the informal mechanisms used by traditional communities (Jacobs, 1961).

Because cities offer residents a variety of neighborhood environments and a relatively high degree of anonymity, norms cannot be strictly applied, especially if they apply to personal choices such as sexual preferences and clothing. Urban communities tend to be far more tolerant of individual differences than rural communities (Fischer, 1982, 1984).

Urban and rural communities differ not only in the formality of norms and how strictly they are enforced, but in their content as well. This fact, too, results from the cultural and structural complexity of industrial and commercial communities. In his classic book *The Division of Labor in Society* (1933), Durkheim identified differences in the *content* of norms that hold communities together by regulating the behavior of their members (see also Lukes and Scull, 1983). He described two types of social solidarity that correspond to the content of community norms: mechanical and organic solidarity.

As we saw in Chapter 8, the concept of mechanical solidarity refers to social cohesion based on a relatively simple division of labor and a common culture—conditions found most often in small, traditional communities. In communities that are held together in this way, most norms take the form of criminal laws that prohibit specific behaviors because they are considered "wrong."

Organic solidarity, on the other hand, is based not on how alike people are, but on how different they are. City residents are connected to one another not so much by a shared culture as by their dependency on one another. Each resident performs a specialized task—food store manager, doctor, police officer, trash collector, department store clerk, electrician—in a complex division of labor. Because each person specializes in a narrow portion of the activities required to meet people's needs, city dwellers depend on people with whom they often have very little in common.

In communities that depend on organic solidarity—most of which are urban—only a relatively small proportion·of the norms focus on forbidden behaviors. Instead, most norms that govern community life are civil laws that regulate relationships involving groups and individuals who may never be more than strangers to one another. Commercial law, procedural law, constitutional law, contract law, and tort law regulate social relationships rather than prohibit specific behaviors.

To Durkheim, such differences in norms reflect differences in how communities stay together. The Industrial Revolution brought with it communities of such complexity and diversity that a vast body of civil law was needed to regulate a web of social relationships involving enormous numbers of people.

The concepts of organic and mechanical solidarity represent theoretical ideal types, and social cohesion in communities is rarely based purely on one or the other. Mexican villages and small African tribes are examples of communities held together primarily by mechanical solidarity, but many small, rural communities combine the two. Farming communities in most industrial societies have close relationships with urban and international markets.

To sum up, it is impossible to fully understand cultural differences between communities without paying attention to the way relationships among individuals and groups are structured: how boundaries are drawn and maintained, how roles, power, and prestige are distributed, and how interaction is patterned in predictable ways.

THE SOCIAL STRUCTURES OF COMMUNITY LIFE

On the level of role relationships, social structure refers to patterns of expectation among individuals. At the community level, however, social structure also refers to relationships among groups as well as to the mix of social statuses found in community populations.

The following sections describe the structural characteristics of communities: boundaries, the uses of time, role structures, the distribution of power and prestige among individuals and groups, and the kinds of relationships through which residents know and interact with one another.

Community Boundaries and Xenophobia

Like groups, communities have culturally defined boundaries; but community boundaries also have a physical dimension, for a shared physical space is part of the definition of a community. In both their social and physical aspects, community boundaries vary in clarity and openness.

Physical boundaries may be actual barriers such as the walls that protected ancient cities (see Braudel, 1981). They may also be geographic boundaries that are drawn politically (the "city limits"). Political boundaries are important because they define the area within which officials have jurisdiction and, thereby limit their authority. One of the most important aspects of communities, however, is that they provide us with a sense of belonging. Crossing physical boundaries does not necessarily mean that newcomers will be accepted as members of the community; it is here that the clarity and openness of a community's social boundaries are important.

In small communities, the clarity of boundaries depends on the simple fact that residents know one another. In some cases—resort communities and university towns—the massive influx of outsiders blurs community boundaries and leads permanent residents to adopt new ways of maintaining their sense of community, including hostile attitudes toward the "invaders." Each summer in Nantucket, a small island community just off the Massachusetts coast, tourists outnumber the permanent residents. Some residents spend most of their time at home in order to avoid feeling that they have lost their community to strangers; others display bumper stickers that read "Native."

Particularly in urban neighborhoods, people often draw symbolic boundaries that define the area with which they identify (Suttles, 1972). These may not correspond to physical or political boundaries and may include a variety of ethnicities, races, and social

Most community boundaries lack the clarity of this medieval walled French city.

classes. Harlem and Greenwich Village in New York, the Back Bay and Beacon Hill sections of Boston, and the Nob Hill and Haight-Ashbury sections of San Francisco are all well known neighborhoods whose residents think of them as their "real" home.

Boundaries are sometimes drawn in ways that select residents on the basis of statuses; the exclusion of blacks, Jews, and various ethnic minorities is a longstanding practice in U.S. communities. Until recently, the only true national urban policy centered on the value of "culturally homogeneous neighborhoods"—a thinly disguised way of saying that nonwhite and poor families should be excluded from white, middle-class neighborhoods. During the housing construction boom that followed World War II, the National Association of Real Estate Boards' code of ethics discouraged realtors from selling housing to members of "incompatible"—that is, black—groups. This deliberate policy of segregated housing was supported by the Federal Housing Administration, whose official guidelines for realtors and banks (which provided mortgages) forbade integration (Berry and Kasarda, 1977; Muller, 1981; Stahura, 1986).

In many cases, attempts to maintain closed community boundaries are based on **xenophobia**—the fear of strangers. The United States is a nation of immigrants (with the exception of American Indians), but this has not prevented people from claiming their communities as their own. The Protestant English who inhabited the early colonies attempted to exclude Jews and Catholics, and in the seventeenth century, Mary Dyer was hanged in the Massachusetts Bay Colony for preaching Quaker religious doctrine. The Pennsylvania Quakers, on the other hand, opposed the influx of German Protestants in the 1750s, and Benjamin Franklin (1751) was among those who believed that America should be reserved for Anglo-Saxon whites.

Throughout the nineteenth century, cities such as New York, Boston, and Philadelphia experienced widespread fear over the influx of Catholic immigrants, most of whom were Irish and German. The late 1800s was a period of bewildering social change in the rapidly industrializing Northeast, and residents found a convenient explanation for crime and corruption in the expanding population of "foreigners." Numerous groups—such as the Oriental Exclusion League, the Native American Party, and the Immigration Restriction League—tried to limit immigration into the U.S. (Curran, 1974). In California the excluded became the excluders as Irish workers formed the Workingmen's Party in 1877 and urged exclusion of Chinese immigrants who competed with them for jobs (see Boswell, 1986). In 1915 the Ku Klux Klan expanded its list of enemies to include Jews and Catholics.

Xenophobia and exclusion have not ended in the U.S.; all that has changed are the statuses used to define community membership. Now Mexican-Americans, Puerto Ricans, and Asian refugees are perceived by many as a threat to jobs held by "natives," a burden on public welfare systems, and a source of crime. Whites continue to exclude blacks from their neighborhoods and, if unsuccessful, are likely to move because they now consider their neighborhoods to be "less desirable" (Farley et al., 1978).

To some degree, it is inevitable that communities will accept some newcomers more readily than others, for a boundary that anyone can cross is no longer a boundary. When cities become "wide open," residents often lose their sense of community and then create smaller communities within the city (Gans, 1982). The ethnic neighborhoods of large cities attest to the human desire to maintain physical spaces within which life goes on according to predictable social arrangements.

A continuing problem with closed boundaries is that some communities and neighborhoods offer better schools, housing, health care, and jobs than others do. In this sense, boundaries not only maintain cultural homogeneity, but also perpetuate social inequality.

The Importance of Time

Time is an important aspect of community structure because communities and neighborhoods differ in age, and residents stay for varying lengths of time. In the simplest sense, the age of communities and neighborhoods is important because as communities age, their buildings, roads, sewer and water systems deteriorate. It takes a considerable amount of time to transform a neighborhood of large, stately homes into an urban slum that is falling apart.

Because communities differ widely in age, it is often difficult to compare them. The first U.S. suburbs were primarily "bedroom" communities in which people lived but did not work, and were, therefore, strikingly different from cities. In more recent years, however, businesses—including factories—have begun to move from central cities to the suburbs. As a result, suburbs may in time resemble cities with all their problems of overcrowding, pollution, and physical decay.

Time is also important because the longer we live in a community, the more likely we are to make the status of "resident" a part of our social identity ("I'm a Chicagoan"), and this motivates us to conform to the community culture. We are also more likely to care about a community if we believe we will live there a long time. If we are "short-timers," we have less stake in a community, because however bad it may be, we expect its effect on us to be temporary.

In highly mobile societies—in which job changes usually involve a change of residence—it is difficult for communities to foster loyalty and involvement among residents. The populations of college towns, vacation resorts, and communities near military bases are heavily populated with temporary residents whose home towns are far away. In such cases the problems of community loyalty and unity are particularly acute.

Who Lives Here?
The Social Composition of Communities

Our status sets tell a great deal about our probable beliefs, values, attitudes, and expectations. Similarly, the mix of statuses in a community tells a great deal about its social life. Retirement communities face different problems than do small suburbs with large numbers of young children; and wealthy suburbs offer a social environment very different from that of a working-class suburb or an inner-city neighborhood in which most residents live in poverty.

Many of the differences between communities are caused by the mix of statuses found in their populations. In comparison with suburban populations, central-city residents in the U.S. tend to be nonwhite, elderly, female, single, unemployed, and poor. Nonmetropolitan communities (most are rural) have a racial composition similar to that of suburbs, but tend to be poorer than central cities (Table 9-1).

Central cities and suburbs, however, are equally likely to include well-off families. In other words, central cities have a wider *mix* of incomes, with relatively high proportions of both the very poor and the well-to-do. Bloomfield, Michigan (the home of many auto executives), is homogeneously prosperous, whereas Manhattan contains both the wealthy residents of Park Avenue and the poorest ghetto dwellers.

Central cities tend to be poor and nonwhite because for centuries they have been a receiving area for

Table 9-1

Type of Community by Various Characteristics, United States

| | TYPE OF COMMUNITY | | |
| | Metropolitan Areas | | |
CHARACTERISTICS	Central Cities	Suburbs	Nonmetropolitan Areas
Race (1981)			
% White	68	90	88
% Black	22	6	9
% Hispanic	11	5	3
Median Family Income (1986)			
Whites	$28,800	$33,000	$22,800
Blacks	$15,900	$21,400	$12,400
Spanish origin	$16,600	$23,000	$15,800
% Below poverty level	15	6	15
% Above $50,000 (households)	15	28	8

Source: U.S. Census Bureau, 1982, 1987g.

impoverished migrants seeking industrial jobs (Goldstein and Mayer, 1965). The heaviest concentrations of blacks in the U.S. are in industrial cities such as Atlanta, Detroit, Newark, and Gary, Indiana.

Until the 1970s, blue-collar workers were heavily represented in urban labor forces, but as many manufacturers have moved to suburbs, the mix of occupations in cities has become more concentrated in white-collar jobs: professionals, administrators, clerks, and secretaries. Blue-collar jobs, however, have long been the major source of employment for poor migrants; and because they cannot afford to follow manufacturing jobs to the suburbs, many of them are trapped in central cities. This helps explain why unemployment rates in central cities are twice as high as those in suburban communities (Berry and Kasarda, 1977).

White-collar workers are increasingly likely to live in suburbs and work in central cities. Those who *work* in cities, then, tend to be in white-collar occupations, but those who *live* in cities are more likely to have blue-collar job skills. Unlike rural and suburban communities, then, the urban population during the day differs substantially from the nighttime population (Melbin, 1978).

In cities, women outnumber men, whereas rural communities have more men than women. The reason is the relative scarcity of opportunities for women in rural areas compared with the relative abundance of jobs elsewhere (Hunt, 1965). Cities are also more likely to include single people and childless couples because people tend to prefer the physical and social conditions in suburbs for raising children (Frey, 1983).

Such differences are not found in all societies or in all U.S. cities. In many developing countries, poverty is worse in rural areas than in cities, and men are more likely to migrate to cities than women are. Mexico City's poorest neighborhoods are on its fringe, not at its center, primarily because the city lies in a "bowl" of mountains and the most desirable land is in the middle. There are, in other words, few "green suburbs" to which the wealthy can flee. One of the wealthiest sections of Boston is Beacon Hill, located in the middle of the city. Although wealthy families left Beacon Hill for the nearby Back Bay neighborhood at the turn of the century, the poor people who moved in were eventually displaced by affluent Bostonians whose sentimental attachment to Beacon Hill prompted them

Differences in social composition— a relatively affluent elderly population in a Florida retirement community contrasted with the high concentration of poverty and children found in New York City's Lower East Side—create different problems and needs from health care and education to recreation and crime control.

to buy and restore its stately homes (Abrahamson, 1980; Firey, 1945).

In spite of such exceptions, the social composition of U.S. central cities differs sharply from suburban and rural areas. Such differences are important because the mix of statuses found in communities affects the beliefs, values, attitudes, and expectations of their inhabitants. The values people place on personal advancement, music and the arts, material possessions, conformity, and family life are determined more by their social class than whether their community is urban, suburban, or rural.

Communities with young populations have different values than do those with larger proportions of the middle-aged and elderly. Ann Arbor, Michigan, and Berkeley, California, are sites of major universities, and have been the birthplaces of radical social movements. Ann Arbor was the first U.S. community to pass a local ordinance classifying the possession of marijuana as only a minor offense.

The Scale of Community Life: Groups and Formal Organizations

In addition to the mix of statuses, communities also differ substantially in the degree to which social life is organized around various groups. Life in small, rural villages is often organized on a small scale in that relationships among individuals are more important than those among groups. In the cities of industrial societies, however, groups are more important and tend to hold a large share of wealth and power. In a few small New England towns, decisions are still made at town meetings in which residents have an opportunity to present their views and cast their votes. In larger communities, power is primarily concentrated in groups and formal organizations such as labor unions, government agencies, businesses, political parties, and neighborhood associations.

The large scale of city life makes it difficult for individuals to participate directly in community decisions. At best, city residents are heard only through groups that represent them; and those who do not belong to influential groups are virtually powerless.

Community Power Structures

In communities the occupancy of important statuses and control of resources such as land, wealth, and jobs are two main sources of power (Spinrad, 1965).

Some statuses are recognized by residents as legitimate authorities whose roles require them to make decisions about the community. Mayors, city managers, and councils pass laws and ordinances and decide how to spend tax revenues; police officers decide when to enforce particular laws; school boards decide which books students will read and how many teachers to hire.

Such statuses also include that of "voter"; and, when organized, voters can exert considerable power. In many small towns voters have the power to approve (or reject) local budgets and to override the decisions of elected officials. In cities, neighbors often form associations that, because they represent relatively large numbers of voters, vastly multiply the power of individual residents.

A more subtle source of power lies in the functional importance of a particular status. Trash collectors are not thought of as powerful by most people, but if they go on strike their power is revealed as residents watch garbage pile up on the sidewalks. Statuses also

give power to their occupants by allowing easy access to local officials. Business leaders and local politicians often belong to the same clubs, and in locker rooms and private dining rooms they have far greater access to one another than do other citizens.

In addition to social statuses, power also comes to those who control valued resources. Landowners can tear down low-rent tenements in order to build office buildings or luxury condominiums. Affluent residents can affect local government decisions by giving or withholding contributions to political campaigns. Bankers decide how to invest the money that residents put into savings, and their decisions can have important effects on community life. Recently, communities have become aware of the practice of "redlining," in which bankers decide that some neighborhoods are poor investment risks and refuse to give home improvement loans in those neighborhoods. In some cases, residents have expressed outrage at the fact that their money is being used to improve other neighborhoods at the expense of their own.

Control over jobs can give businesses considerable power. Companies may threaten to move and take hundreds if not thousands of jobs with them unless they receive special treatment (such as tax breaks or exemption from antipollution laws) from local governments. This affects not only workers and their families, but the financial health of the entire community: businesses are major sources of tax revenues, both directly through the taxes they pay and indirectly through the taxable income of their employees; and local businesses cannot survive if residents have little money to spend (Bluestone and Harrison, 1982; Raines, Berson, and Gracie, 1982). This is especially true in communities whose economies are dominated by a single company that shuts down (Buss and Redburn, 1983).

Given these basic sources of power, a major focus of sociological research has been to understand how they fit together to produce power structures. How is power distributed, and who influences which kinds of decisions?

Structures of Power: Who Rules?   Since sociologists began to study community power structures some 50 years ago, two major views have emerged. The first argues that power in communities is concentrated in the hands of a **power elite** whose members dominate all important areas of community life. A second and more recent view is **pluralism**, which holds that power is distributed among a wide variety of groups and individuals who influence decisions in different areas of community life.

The power-elite view first appeared in Robert and Helen Lynd's monumental "Middletown" studies (1929, 1937), in which they tried to identify a community's most influential individuals. They did this by living in the community for many months, interviewing residents, examining newspaper articles and official records, and acquainting themselves with the community's historical background. From this emerged the conclusion that an elite group of upper-class residents dominated community life in their own interests.

Floyd Hunter (1953, 1980) studied Atlanta, Georgia, and reached similar conclusions with the more efficient "reputational" method. Hunter located people he believed to be knowledgeable about various aspects of community life and asked them to compile a list of influential people. A panel of judges then used these lists to compile a final list of people whose names were mentioned most often, and these people were then interviewed and asked such questions as: "Which ten people on this list would you choose to make a decision about the community?" and "Who is the biggest man in town?"

The problem with these studies and their findings is that they focus not on who actually *makes* decisions about school expenditures, taxes, zoning, housing, or attracting businesses, but on who people *believe* make decisions or have the greatest potential to make decisions. More recent studies try to solve this problem by focusing on events rather than individuals: Who makes actual decisions, and what does this reveal about a community's power structure?

Dahl (1961) studied decisions made in New Haven, Connecticut, and Banfield (1965) conducted similar research in Chicago. Both studies (as well as many others) suggest that decisions in urban communities are influenced by a broad range of groups and individuals; that is, power is pluralistic, rather than concentrated among a single elite. Although specific decisions—how to zone a particular area or whether to build a new school—are usually controlled by small segments of a community, elite groups are not unified into a single, integrated whole that dominates community life, and they often have competing interests (Weissberg, 1981). Insurance companies, police departments, and groups of citizens may favor raising the legal drinking age in a community, but liquor companies and bar owners may oppose it.

Dahl found that few business leaders influenced community decisions, and then only in the area of urban redevelopment. None participated in decisions affecting education, and only a few were involved in political parties. The mayor and school officials made most decisions about education, and political party regulars were most influential in nominating candidates. As Mintz and Schwartz (1985) argue, however, the close connections that tie most business communities together can often overwhelm conflicts of interest to produce a powerful united front on important community issues (see also Domhoff, 1983).

In general, the larger and more diverse a community's population is, the more pluralistic its power structure. No single group can hold absolute power in cities such as Dallas, Chicago, or Los Angeles, for the structure of city life depends on too many different groups, any one of which has the power to cause conflict simply by refusing to perform its role. As societies become more urban, therefore, communities are increasingly vulnerable to disruption as groups struggle to improve their positions by increasing their power.

Whichever view of community power structures we adopt, the fact remains that in most communities power is unequally distributed among individuals and groups. Immigrants and the poor generally have little if any influence over community decisions, and in cities, residents are governed by representatives who clearly have more power than those they represent. The distribution of power in communities is an enduring source of conflict in community life and an important area of sociological analysis.

Relationships: Gemeinschaft and Gesellschaft

To sociologists such as Simmel, Weber, and Tönnies, industrialization and urbanization caused a disturbing shift in social relationships. Small, intimate communities gave way to large cities and the complex divisions of labor characteristic of mass production and bureaucracy. Weber (1922a) was disturbed by the increasing importance of rationality in social life, the rise of the "specialist," and impersonal bureaucratic models. To Simmel, city populations were so large and diverse that individuals protected themselves from overstimulation by becoming distant and aloof from other people.

Tönnies used a pair of concepts—*Gemeinschaft* and *Gesellschaft*—to describe this shift in social relationships (see Chapter 8). Gemeinschaft refers to a "'community of feeling' . . . that results from likeness and from shared life-experience" (Miner, 1968). Gemeinschaft relationships are what Cooley later referred to as primary.

A Gesellschaft relationship is held together less by a common culture than by rational considerations of self-interest and role structures that make people depend on one another. The city dweller who manufactures farm equipment and the farmer who uses it live sharply different lives, but each depends on the other in order to survive. Whereas Gemeinschaft rests on shared values and interpersonal liking, the secondary relations of Gesellschaft do not. Lawyers in small towns might refuse to defend an innocent man for fear of alienating a community certain the defendant is guilty, and city lawyers may represent clients they personally dislike and believe to be guilty.

The concepts of Gemeinschaft and Gesellschaft are ideal types; that is to say, there is no such thing as a community with relationships that are purely one or the other. The concepts are useful, however, for comparing the general character of relationships in different communities or in the same community over time. Since the colonial period, social relationships in the U.S. have dramatically shifted from Gemeinschaft toward Gesellschaft.

In colonial America, people who grew food and exchanged it for products such as candles knew those they were dealing with. Today, however, the structures through which goods are produced and exchanged are far more complex and impersonal. The lettuce eaten by someone in Kansas City was probably grown in California, picked by migrant farm workers from Mexico, sold to a wholesaler and then to a retailer, transported by truckers, and ultimately sold to an individual in a supermarket for money earned, perhaps, by working in a candle factory. Our relationship with lettuce growers is now based less on a shared culture than on a complex structure through which we exchange goods and services and thereby satisfy our needs and desires.

The first urban sociologists were as pessimistic about cities as they were optimistic and romantic about life in Gemeinschaft communities. To Wirth (1938), rural communities were cozy and intimate: people knew one another well, actively participated in community life, and could turn to others for comfort and support in times of trouble.

Cities, on the other hand, were seen as cold and impersonal places in which people disappeared in

anonymous and superficial relationships and rarely participated in community affairs, because they were "just passing through." As Tönnies (1887) wrote, in Gesellschaft communities,

> Everybody is by himself and isolated, and there exists a condition of tension against all others . . . intrusions are regarded as hostile acts . . . nobody wants to grant and produce anything for another individual . . . (p. 65)

Sociological research, however, suggests that neither the Chicago School's pessimism about urban life nor its romanticism about what anthropologist Robert Redfield (1947) called the "folk society" represents reality. When Kasarda and Janowitz (1974) interviewed residents of urban and rural communities in Britain, they found little difference in the satisfaction people reported about their social lives. In fact, urban residents tended to report more friendships than their rural counterparts. In two U.S. studies, Fischer (1982, 1984) found that urban dwellers reported no more isolation than rural residents, no less involvement with their families, and, in some cases, higher levels of social support. Fischer found no evidence that urban and rural dwellers differ in the amount or the quality of their social relationships.

People who live in cities are no more likely than others to report feeling always rushed in their daily lives. Nor are they more likely to report dissatisfaction with community conditions such as schools and police protection. Indeed, they are *less* likely to report dissatisfaction with health care, transportation, and annoyances such as street noise or poor street lighting or repair (U.S. Census Bureau, 1985; Farmers Home Administration, 1987). The larger the community, however, the more likely people are to feel afraid to walk alone in their neighborhoods at night (see One Step Further 9-1, p. 232–33).

How do people maintain social ties in cities? One explanation is that when confronted with astounding numbers of people and a dizzying cultural diversity, people tend to form communities within cities. Whereas Simmel believed that urban dwellers orient themselves to the entirety of a city and its population, Gans (1982) argued that the neighborhood is their primary focus. The size and diversity of city populations foster and sustain the strong subcultures found in many urban neighborhoods, and it is within them that people meet their needs for a sense of belonging and involvement in what Robert Park (1925/1967) called "little worlds that touch, but do not interpenetrate" (p. 40) (see also Popenoe, 1985).

Even those who appear to be isolated—such as elderly people living alone—often form "telephone communities" through which they maintain contact with one another (National Center for Health Statistics, 1986). Whereas Simmel and Wirth believed that the size of cities caused isolation and weak social ties, Fischer's analysis suggests just the opposite: although city dwellers may avoid interaction with *most* people, they have such a wide range of subcultures to choose from that their ties to other people are often stronger than they might be in small communities.

Although cities certainly have their share of serious problems—higher crime rates and higher percentages of poor people—they are free from the stifling pressures to conform found in small communities where "everyone knows your business." Life in Gesellschaft communities can be as overstimulating as Simmel suggests, but it is no less true that the homogeneity and closeness of a Gemeinschaft community can be very boring.

For over 1,000 years, people have migrated from rural communities to the attractive diversity of cities. Although during the late 1970s and early 1980s there was a shift of population away from cities and towards suburbs and rural areas, since 1982 the flow has reverted to its familiar historical pattern with cities drawing people to "the wonder and the terrors of human life" (Aronson, 1971, p. 300; U.S. Census Bureau, 1986c).

COMMUNITY ECOLOGY

Whereas the concepts of culture and social structure draw our attention to the social environments that distinguish one community from another, ecology focuses on characteristics of populations and their physical environments. Communities differ in the size and density of their populations as well as in how rapidly they grow or shrink. In addition, they find themselves in a variety of physical settings to which they adapt by organizing activity and using technology.

Community Populations

The size and density of a community's population are sociologically important in several ways. In comparison with small, sparsely settled communities, those that are large and densely settled can support a more complex division of labor—a greater variety of people

ONE STEP FURTHER 9-1:
Feeling Safe: The Social Distribution of Fear

Feeling secure in our neighborhoods is a product of social life and, not surprisingly, how much of a secure feeling we have depends on our communities and our positions in them. The numbers in Table B-9-1 are the percentages of U.S. adults who say that they are afraid to walk alone at night within a mile of their homes. There is a column for each of three community sizes ranging from less than 100,000 to a million or more inhabitants.

There is a lot to see in this table. The top row shows that fear rises dramatically with community size, from 30% to 53%. The rows below it show how fear is affected by community size for a variety of social categories. The second and third rows, for example, show how fear rises among women (from 46% to 69%) and men (from only 9% to 28%). Look at each row and you can see that community size increases fear regardless of age, race, education, or income. Stop for a moment and check for yourself.

Notice also that *regardless of community size* feeling afraid in our communities depends strongly on social statuses. Look down the first column and you will see that in communities of less than 100,000 people, women are more afraid than men, nonwhites are more afraid than whites, older people are more afraid than younger people, and those with less education and income are more afraid than those with more. The more powerful and privileged the statuses we occupy, the less frightened—and more secure—we tend to feel in our communities. This pattern holds in larger communities as well (second and third columns).

Why should fear be distributed in this way? What do you think?

performing specialized tasks. They tend to be culturally more heterogeneous, including people with a greater diversity of backgrounds. Because they cannot grow their own food, they are more dependent on technology—both in agriculture (so that farmers can grow enough to feed themselves as well as the urban population) and in industry (to provide employment for city residents).

Table B-9-1

	SIZE OF COMMUNITY		
	Less than 100,000	100,000 to 1 Million	A Million or More
Percent who report being afraid to walk alone at night.	30%	44%	53%
SOCIAL CHARACTERISTICS			
Sex			
Female	46%	60%	69%
Male	9%	20%	28%
Race			
Nonwhite	37%	63%	60%
White	29%	41%	50%
Age			
Less than 30	25%	37%	50%
30–39	24%	42%	46%
40–49	27%	40%	46%
50–64	30%	52%	65%
65 and older	48%	51%	61%
Education			
Less than high school graduate	36%	47%	61%
High school graduate	28%	47%	46%
Some college or more	26%	39%	52%
Income			
Less than $7,000	26%	40%	51%
$7,000–$14,999	31%	48%	51%
$15,000–$24,999	24%	39%	44%
$25,000 or more	7%	24%	38%

Source: Computed from raw 1984 General Social Survey data.

By current standards, the earliest cities hardly qualified as cities at all, for their populations rarely exceeded 20,000. In comparison, New York City had 7 million inhabitants in 1980 and Mexico City had over 11 million. Such large populations allow a division of labor whose complexity dwarfs that of previous cities. Tax records for fourteenth-century Paris list 157 occupations (Russell, 1972), but the number of different jobs found in New York City is in the tens of thousands.

In comparison with small rural communities, cities are more vulnerable to social disruption for three reasons: their division of labor is complex, they are highly dependent on energy such as electricity, and they are far less self-sufficient. An electrical black-out in a city brings economic activity to a halt, and if

What is experienced as overcrowding in one society may be just right in another. In this picture, 15,000 people enjoy the beginning of the summer holidays at Korakuen pool, the largest in Tokyo, Japan.

transportation from rural areas is disrupted by a strike, no food can reach the city.

Although much has been written about the supposed negative effects of crowded living conditions on human health and behavior, the evidence is far from conclusive (Baldassare, 1983; Simmel, 1950; Wirth, 1938). Simmel and Wirth argued that crowded living conditions in cities cause social relationships to be superficial and transitory; and others argue that crowding causes deviant behavior, mental illness, and poor physical health.

Most arguments linking high population density to deviant behavior and poor health are based on animal studies (such as Calhoun, 1962) and have yet to be demonstrated conclusively among humans (Hawley, 1981). International comparisons also raise questions about the effects of population density on human behavior. The density of Japan's 1983 population was almost 13 times greater than that of the U.S. and individual housing units were twice as crowded. Yet, in comparison with Japan, infant mortality rates in the United States were 57 percent higher, homicide rates were 9 times higher, and suicide rates were only slightly lower (U.S. Census Bureau, 1982, 1983c).

It cannot be denied, however, that social life is affected by the size and density of community populations in the diversity of cultures found among residents and the ways in which communities organize activity in relation to physical environments.

Niches and Ecosystems

Each community participates in an ecosystem—a physical environment that includes both natural resources and other species of life—and survives through its relationships with it. The ways in which a population participates in an ecosystem comprise its ecological niche, and communities differ both in the kinds of ecosystems they inhabit and how they interact within them.

Communities that survive by hunting game and gathering wild food can support only small, sparsely settled populations with minimal divisions of labor. The earliest cities were made possible by revolutionary advances in technology—such as the plow—that enabled people to produce more food than they needed for their own survival; this surplus, in turn, supported cities, whose residents did not grow their own food.

The greatest leap in world urbanization resulted from the Industrial Revolution, which rested on innovative technology and changing values. When machines were introduced on farms, the resulting increase in efficiency created a labor surplus in rural communities. At the same time new machinery, sources of energy, and ways of organizing factories allowed factory owners to vastly increase production and profits.

These changes affected urban communities. Masses of people who could no longer find work in rural communities—here and in Europe—migrated to urban areas in search of factory jobs (the enormous influx of Irish immigrants to U.S. cities in the middle of the nineteenth century was caused in large part by the Irish Potato Famine of 1846). Figure 9-1 shows how profound this change was in the U.S. Between 1820 and 1980 the percentage of people employed in nonagricultural occupations increased from a low of 21 percent to a current high of 98 percent. At the same time the percentage of people living in urban areas increased from around 10 percent to 76 percent. Work became increasingly specialized and this fostered diversity by attracting migrants with a vast range of backgrounds.

The phenomenal growth of cities during the last two centuries did not just "happen" and then create cultural differences between rural and urban communities. The size and density of city populations were caused by changes in both culture and social structure: in technology, the values of profit and mass production, and the increasingly complex divisions of labor that resulted.

The Industrial Revolution transformed community life by creating cities whose survival depended on increasingly complex technology, vast amounts of energy, and expanding markets in which to sell manufactured products. This change in the ecological niche of communities altered societies and relations among them. The colonial expansion of urbanizing European nations during the eighteenth and nineteenth centuries was the direct result of industrial needs for raw materials and markets in which to sell finished goods. In the late twentieth century, the phenomenal growth of cities across the world created an enormous demand for energy that dominates international politics. Industrial nations such as the United States, Japan, and most of Europe depend heavily on the stability of oil-producing countries in the Middle East, because without a steady supply of oil, the industries and cities that dominate these countries cannot survive.

The ecological shift from communities based on agriculture to industrial cities dependent on technology, huge supplies of energy, and vast markets brought with it increased interdependency among communities and nations and, therefore, increased vulnerability to economic disruption and international conflict. A drop in the demand for oil in 1982 brought the economy of Mexico to the edge of bankruptcy, and a major war in the Middle East could seriously damage the economies of countries located thousands of miles away.

The shift to industrial communities also increases damage to the physical environment by producing enormous amounts of waste. Until quite recently, death rates in cities were higher than in rural areas, largely because human waste was thrown into the streets or into rivers that were also used as water supplies. As recently as the nineteenth century the

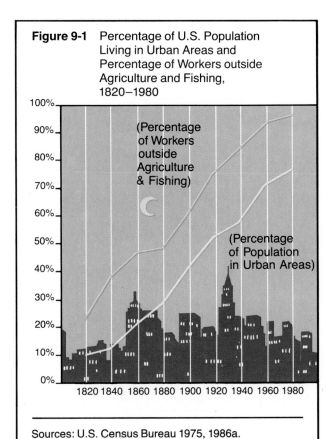

Figure 9-1   Percentage of U.S. Population Living in Urban Areas and Percentage of Workers outside Agriculture and Fishing, 1820–1980

(Percentage of Workers outside Agriculture & Fishing)

(Percentage of Population in Urban Areas)

100% 90% 80% 70% 60% 50% 40% 30% 20% 10% 0%

1820 1840 1860 1880 1900 1920 1940 1960 1980

Sources: U.S. Census Bureau 1975, 1986a.

Thames River in London was an open sewer, and London streets were littered with horse manure (see Wohl, 1983). In the 1980s Mexico City is in serious danger of depleting its supplies of drinkable water, New York City produces more waste than it can dispose of without seriously threatening the natural environment, and raw sewage from Tijuana, Mexico, is polluting the beaches of San Diego. The population of Houston, Texas, has grown so rapidly that its water supply is decreasing, and because most of its water is in the ground beneath the city, the city is steadily sinking as the water is consumed (Reinhold, 1982).

Land Use: Where People Do What They Do

Within any community, people and their activities are distributed spatially; the larger a community is, the more complex these arrangements are. With the boom in urban growth during the last century, ecologists and urban sociologists have tried to describe how the uses of space give communities their physical shape (Figure 9-2).

Early in this century Park, Burgess, and McKenzie (1925) theorized that cities develop in *concentric zones* or "rings" of activity around a core devoted to business and entertainment. As commercial activity "spills" into the next ring, residents flee outward, leaving behind a mixture of commercial activity and relatively impoverished residential neighborhoods, including ethnic neighborhoods such as "Chinatown" and "Little Italy." The next ring consists mostly of the homes of blue-collar workers, and as we move farther from the core, neighborhoods rise in social class, with the upper-middle and upper classes living in the outermost rings (Guest, 1976).

The **concentric-zone** view of city growth assumes that business activities are concentrated in a single core, and that rings develop as people compete for land away from industrial activity and poor neighborhoods. Although this model fit Chicago early in this century, city development is generally more irregular than a smooth set of concentric rings. Paris has no single business district (Caplow, 1952).

Hoyt's (1939) variation on the concentric zone model takes into account the effects of transportation

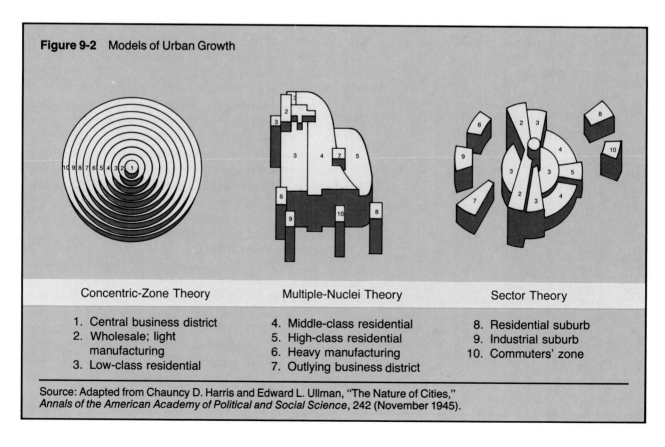

Figure 9-2   Models of Urban Growth

Concentric-Zone Theory   Multiple-Nuclei Theory   Sector Theory

1. Central business district
2. Wholesale; light manufacturing
3. Low-class residential
4. Middle-class residential
5. High-class residential
6. Heavy manufacturing
7. Outlying business district
8. Residential suburb
9. Industrial suburb
10. Commuters' zone

Source: Adapted from Chauncy D. Harris and Edward L. Ullman, "The Nature of Cities," *Annals of the American Academy of Political and Social Science*, 242 (November 1945).

on patterns of land use. Like the zone model, Hoyt's **sector model** suggests that cities develop outward from a core. Instead of a ring pattern, however, cities grow along transportation lines that go out from the center like pieces of a pie. According to Hoyt, upper-class neighborhoods are not necessarily clustered in an outer ring, but can be found at varying distances from the center of the city along transportation lines.

Harris and Ullman (1945) suggested the **multiple-nuclei theory**, which de-emphasizes central business districts and suggests that cities have centers for different kinds of activities—finance, theater, restaurants, clothing, and industry.

What do we make of these theories, none of which accounts for the variety of spatial arrangements? Perhaps their greatest usefulness lies in what they have in common: they acknowledge that the intensity of land use for different purposes varies from one part of a community to another, which affects not only what people do, but how communities change.

HOW COMMUNITIES CHANGE

The process of community change involves a combination of cultural, structural, and ecological factors. Although large cities have existed for many centuries, the rapid urbanization of the world was created by the Industrial Revolution, which represented a shift in values and technology and a change in structure toward increasingly complex divisions of labor.

These social changes, however, produced cities only in combination with ecological factors such as massive immigration of workers. The poverty of U.S. cities results not simply from inequality in the distribution of wealth, but also from the migration of businesses and middle- and upper-class families away from central cities. Community change is a complicated process, and finding solutions to community problems continues to be a particularly difficult task.

World Patterns of Change

Across the world there are some clear patterns of change in the social and ecological arrangements of communities. There is a general trend toward modernism—seen in the acceptance of change, the increased use of technology, and the spread of mass media such as newspapers and television (Inkeles and Smith, 1974).

The most dramatic trends, however, are ecological and structural, for the world's population is increasingly concentrated in urban areas. Only about 3 percent of the world's population lived in urban communities in 1800, but by the year 2000, cities will contain an estimated 55 percent (Table 9-2). As industrialization attracts migrants, city populations mushroom and include an astounding diversity of races, ethnic groups, occupations, and social classes.

Increasingly complex divisions of labor cause community relationships to shift from Gemeinschaft to Gesellschaft. The organization of community life around family ties and local economies gives way to mass markets and rational, contractual relationships (Miner, 1968). As the scale of communities grows larger, power is increasingly concentrated in large, formal organizations such as governments and corporations, and as this happens, individuals are further and further removed from the decision-making process.

The rise of the city as the dominant form of community life also affects rural communities (Larson, 1968). The increased use of agricultural technology makes farm communities less autonomous and less isolated. Rural villages are increasingly oriented to distant urban markets on which they depend for cash income as well as for bank loans to finance investments in machinery, seed, pesticides, and irrigation.

The growing orientation to distant markets—rather than to local subsistence needs—encourages farmers to specialize in only a few crops, many of which (such as coffee) cannot be used as food. This specialization, in turn, makes them still more dependent on urban markets, for they can no longer survive

Table 9-2

Degree of World Urbanization, 1800–2000

YEAR	PERCENTAGE LIVING IN CITIES OF 5,000 OR MORE	PERCENTAGE LIVING IN CITIES OF 100,000 OR MORE
1800	3	3
1900	14	5
1950	28	16
1975	41	26
2000	55	40

Source: Population Reference Bureau, 1975.

by consuming what they produce themselves. Rural farm populations such as those in El Salvador—who spend their lives growing food—often find themselves in the ironic position of starving when the prices offered for their cash crops decline in urban markets.

Trends in the United States

Although the world trends described above also apply to the U.S., since 1970 urban areas have experienced significant changes that are not typical of the world as a whole. Between 1970 and 1980 the combined population of U.S. central cities remained unchanged while the suburban population grew by almost 16 million, a rate of increase almost double the national average (U.S. Census Bureau, 1982, 1983c). While the *size* of central-city populations remained generally unchanged, however, their social *composition* changed dramatically (Frey, 1983).

The number of blacks living in central cities grew by almost 2 million, whereas the number of whites declined by over 6 million. According to one estimate, nonwhites now constitute majorities of the residents of many large cities including New York, Baltimore, Chicago, Detroit, and Cleveland (Kasarda, 1986). Because those who left central cities generally had higher incomes than those who stayed behind and those who moved in, the percentage of people below the poverty level increased in central cities from 13 to 16 percent, but the incidence of poverty in suburban communities remained unchanged at 7 percent. In the central cities of large metropolitan areas, median family income actually dropped by almost $800 while family incomes in the suburbs of these cities increased by $700 (U.S. Census Bureau, 1980b, 1983c).

What caused these shifts in the composition of central-city populations? To some extent, the flight of middle- and upper-class whites from central cities is due to racism. The answer is not this simple, however, for affluent blacks have also been leaving central cities at an accelerated rate (Long and De Are, 1981).

An additional piece of the explanation lies in the relocation of many businesses to suburban communities, due in part to the attraction of less congested environments, but also to the fact that as central cities become poorer, governments must increase tax rates in order to maintain essential services such as sanitation, fire and police protection, and welfare programs.

It is here that cities find themselves in a vicious circle, for as businesses and their middle- and upper-

middle-class employees move to the suburbs, living conditions in cities (including tax levels) become worse, precipitating still more flight (Bradbury et al., 1982). Many cities find themselves in a downward spiral toward greater poverty and—as in New York City in the late 1970s—on the edge of virtual financial collapse.

The problems of central cities are bound up with changes taking place in the suburbs. Although most suburbs have been little more than "bedroom-community" appendages to nearby cities, in the late 1980s a new form of community—called **outer cities**—is emerging as suburbs become more densely settled and dominated by business and manufacturing that have moved from central cities (see Hartshorn and Muller, 1987). Industrial and office parks, shopping malls, major hotels and restaurants, and growing downtown centers of some suburban communities are, in some cases, competing successfully with major cities as centers of economic life.

Community change in the U.S. has not been confined to urban areas, for in the last half-century the use of sophisticated agricultural technology has caused the decline of small family farms, which have been replaced by huge corporations. Between 1930 and 1986 the number of farms dropped from 6.5 million to 2.2 million, and the average size of farms tripled. This, coupled with the migration to cities, has dramatically lowered the populations of rural communities: between 1930 and 1986 the number living on farms dropped from 30 million to just under 5.4 million (U.S. Census Bureau, 1986a).

Migration from rural areas, however, has been selective: those who leave tend to be young adults, leaving rural communities with relatively high percentages of children and the elderly—people who produce less than they consume—which helps explain why poverty is most common in rural communities (U.S. Census Bureau, 1987a).

Community Change in Developing Nations

Many early urban sociologists and ecologists shared the belief that urbanization took the same form in all societies (Wirth, 1938). The experience of the past 20 years, however, suggests that in developing countries it is quite different from the urban growth in Europe and the U.S. that accompanied the Industrial Revolution (see Bradshaw, 1987; Hawley, 1981; London, 1987). Whether or not these different lines of development will ultimately converge and produce cities like those of industrial societies is still an open question.

Urbanization in developing countries is unique in four ways. First, urbanization in Europe and the United States was a response to the needs of rapidly expanding industry. By comparison, the world's most rapid urbanization now takes place in poor, nonindustrial countries.

Second, the Industrial Revolution prompted a decline in birth and death rates in Europe and the U.S. Together, expanding industry and lowered birth rates allowed these countries to keep industrial production ahead of population growth. In developing countries, however, birth rates remain high while death rates have fallen sharply through the use of medical technology. In rapidly urbanizing poor countries, populations increase faster than production, and urban economies cannot absorb enormous numbers of migrants from rural areas (see Bradshaw, 1987).

A third unique aspect of urbanization in developing countries is the spatial distribution of residents (Peattie and Aldrete-Haas, 1981). In most U.S. cities the social class of residents increases with distance from the center of the city (although many city centers attract a small elite of wealthy residents). Urban growth in most developing countries, however, reverses this pattern, with poor immigrants settling at the outskirts of cities (Berry and Kasarda, 1977).

Fourth, special changes predicted by early sociologists have not occurred in many developing countries. Tönnies believed that the shift from Gemeinschaft to Gesellschaft relationships was inevitable—that all cities would be dominated by formal, secondary relationships in which the individuals' primary loyalties are to themselves, rational thought is most highly valued, and people are rewarded strictly according to their performance.

Kolb (1954) and Hauser (1959) argued, however, that early predictions were based on a U.S. model of city life that does not apply in the social context of many nonindustrial societies. The cultures of developing societies are more likely to value spiritual life, tradition, extended family ties, and religion—none of which match the "rational" model of Western bureaucracy. Although urbanization in Europe and the U.S. was synonymous with industrialization in a modern cultural context, this is often not the case in developing countries.

The most important consequence of this difference lies in the social relationships among urban dwellers. In Africa, urban and rural culture are similar because migrants to the cities bring their village culture with them. One writer describes the "gusto," "camaraderie," and "casual ease with which relations are established" in many African cities, and attributes this to the fact that "the African who comes to town rarely arrives as a complete stranger" (Epstein, 1967, p. 206). This pattern is repeated throughout the world in "squatter" settlements outside cities in countries such as India, Turkey, Mexico, Egypt, and Kenya, where traditions are grounded in family and tribal ties and do not give way to the rational, secondary relationships found in the cities of industrial nations.

Despite the variety of their forms and patterns of growth, however, the world's cities have one thing in common: as communities, they find it increasingly difficult to feed, house, and employ their residents, and still preserve their physical environments.

Communities in Trouble: Possibilities for Change

The most serious problems facing urban communities are overcrowding, poverty and unemployment, and a deteriorating physical environment. It is important to remember that all but the first of these are not unique to cities. Some of the worst poverty is found in rural areas, as are some of the most dangerous environmental conditions, such as land erosion and droughts. Revolutions in developing countries such as El Salvador often focus on rural communities where most of the land is owned by single families and farmed by poor peasants who may face starvation while their crops are exported abroad for sale in cash markets (Weller and Guggenheim, 1982).

Most of the world's population, however, will soon live in urban areas; and for this reason, poverty, overcrowding, and deteriorating physical conditions are most visible and serious in cities. What are some possible solutions? In the simplest sense, the answers are obvious: redistribute populations in order to alleviate overcrowding, provide jobs for community residents, rebuild cities. How to accomplish these goals, however, is another matter, and it is here that we find three major approaches to solving community problems: government planning, private enterprise, and social movements among community residents.

The most notable examples of government planning are found in Britain, the Soviet Union, Israel, and China. In the early years of this century, the British

In many communities, economic development conflicts with residential interests. This picture shows two of the 1,500 homes in Detroit, Michigan, that were condemned to make way for a new Chrysler plant. Needless to say, residents wanted to preserve their neighborhood.

government decided to build a series of "New Towns" near urban centers such as London. They were designed as self-contained communities—not suburbs—in which people would live and work; by 1971 their combined population had reached almost half a million. The planners seem to have achieved most of their goals: most residents work in their local areas, and physical conditions are better than those in crowded cities (Berry and Kasarda, 1977).

After the Russian Revolution in 1917, the Soviet government began long-term planning to organize cities according to the number of workers needed for local industries and to ensure socialist ideals of equality and eradication of social class differences. The result in many Soviet cities (and in those of some eastern European communist countries that used the Soviet Union as a model) has been massive construction of cheap, uniformly designed apartment houses forming neighborhoods whose residents represent a broad mix of occupations. Although physical conditions in the Soviet Union are harsh by Western standards, Soviet urban planners appear to have achieved some of their goals (Berry and Kasarda, 1977).

In Israel the construction of planned communities, or *kibbutzim*, continues to be a major part of

nation building. In a kibbutz, property ownership and decision-making are shared among residents, and the community as a whole provides care for children and the elderly (Bettelheim, 1969; Spiro, 1956). There is some dissatisfaction among members—primarily among younger people who strain under the pressures to conform to community norms and values—but in general, community planning has resulted in high production, emotional support for residents, and a high degree of social cohesion and loyalty.

China has tried to stem the flood of migrants from rural areas in order to combat enormous overcrowding in its cities. Migration is tightly controlled by the government, and it is illegal to change residence without permission. China has also made major investments in rural areas in an attempt to make rural life more attractive.

In developing countries such as Egypt, urban planners try to increase urban employment through industrialization and lure migrants back to rural communities. This planning, however, has been unsuccessful. Their populations grow so rapidly that industrial development cannot meet the demand for jobs; and rural poverty is so extreme that migrants are reluctant to leave the cities that, however unpleasant, provide better conditions than rural areas (see London, 1987).

Although many countries have developed planning strategies for community development, in the U.S. there has been strong resistance to government participation in community planning, leaving the fate of communities in private hands. The piecemeal planning that has taken place has often ignored the needs of residents and the social factors that brought cities to their current crises in the first place.

The current problems of U.S. cities result in part from uncoordinated decisions of business owners and families over the past 200 years. City populations grew rapidly in the nineteenth century because immigrants were attracted to factory jobs. Because cities have been like lightning rods—attracting the poor who seek a better life—they have for two centuries been the home of large populations of poor people crowded into substandard housing.

In many neighborhoods, low-income families have been forced to leave even substandard housing through a process called **gentrification**, in which real-estate developers buy up old, deteriorating housing largely inhabited by poor people who pay low rents. They then remodel the buildings and rerent or sell them at rates far beyond the means of their original tenants (Laska et al., 1982). Although gentrification restores old neighborhoods, increases property values (and city tax revenues), and makes large profits for developers, it also displaces low- and middle-income residents who have no choice but to move to less desirable neighborhoods (Besser, 1979).

For many who have no place to move, the result is homelessness (U.S. Department of Housing and Urban Development, 1981) (see Figure 9-3). Flophouses once provided more than 2 million single-occupancy rooms for many of the poorest people; but between 1970 and 1980 almost half were either destroyed

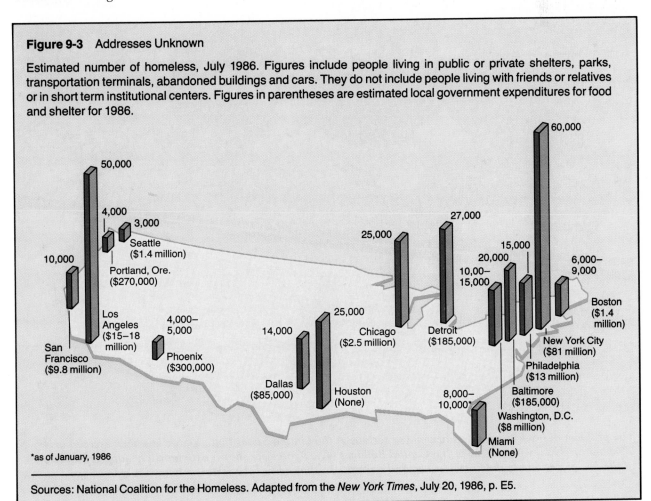

Figure 9-3   Addresses Unknown

Estimated number of homeless, July 1986. Figures include people living in public or private shelters, parks, transportation terminals, abandoned buildings and cars. They do not include people living with friends or relatives or in short term institutional centers. Figures in parentheses are estimated local government expenditures for food and shelter for 1986.

60,000

50,000

4,000

3,000

Seattle
($1.4 million)

10,000

Portland, Ore.
($270,000)

Los
Angeles
($15–18
million)

San
Francisco
($9.8 million)

4,000–
5,000

Phoenix
($300,000)

14,000

Dallas
($85,000)

25,000

Houston
(None)

25,000

Chicago
($2.5 million)

27,000

10,00–
15,000

Detroit
($185,000)

8,000–
10,000*

20,000

15,000

Washington, D.C.
($8 million)

Baltimore
($185,000)

Philadelphia
($13 million)

New York City
($81 million)

6,000–
9,000

Boston
($1.4
million)

Miami
(None)

*as of January, 1986

Sources: National Coalition for the Homeless. Adapted from the *New York Times*, July 20, 1986, p. E5.

or converted to higher-priced dwellings. New York City lost 87 percent of its single-occupancy rooms during this same period, and Denver, Seattle, and Rochester lost more than 50 percent (*Newsweek*, January 2, 1984).

The scattered efforts to improve life among poor populations in cities have failed because planners have assumed that the social aspects of community life depend primarily on ecology—the size and density of populations and the quality of buildings. They have largely ignored cultural and structural factors that affect life in communities—such as the inequalities produced by race and social class (Gans, 1982; Gottdiener, 1985).

In the last few decades, conditions in older U.S. cities have grown worse as businesses leave and take with them thousands of jobs. As cities become poorer, taxes increase, and to save money, landlords let their buildings deteriorate. This, in turn, makes cities increasingly unattractive places to live in, and middle-class families move to the suburbs (Gans, 1968).

The development of communities has thus depended primarily on what businesses and middle- and upper-class families consider to be in their own best interests, *not* on the overall needs of communities. What substitutes for a national urban policy

is a complex set of uncoordinated, often contradictory . . . random public policies and programs provided in

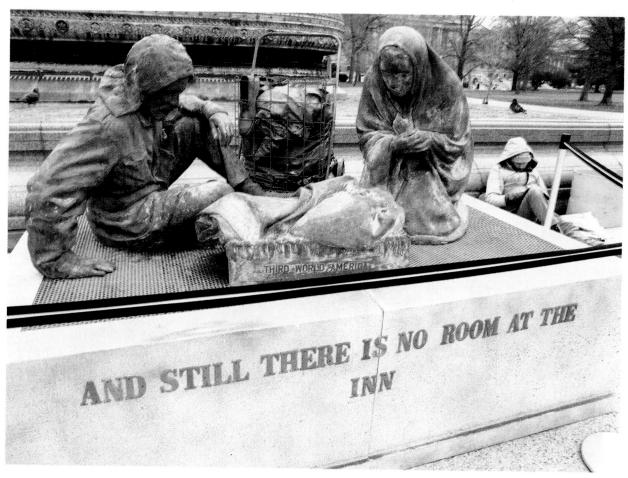

The problem of homelessness has become so serious in the United States that a statue has been erected in Washington, D.C. within sight of the Capitol Building. The figures are shown sitting on a heating grate, one of the few places where the homeless can find warmth. To the right of the statue, a homeless man sleeps.

the wake of strong economic forces which set the agenda for urban growth. Thus, if in the past urbanization has been governed by any conscious public objectives at all, these have been, on the one hand, to encourage growth, apparently for its own sake; and on the other hand, to provide public works and public-welfare programs to support piecemeal, spontaneous development impelled primarily by private initiative. (Berry and Kasarda, 1977, p. 371)

The populations of U.S. cities are increasingly poor, elderly, and nonwhite; and yet these groups have little power over the economic and political decisions that profoundly affect community development. So long as our culture values the right of organizations such as banks and corporations to act only in their self-interest—without regard for the fate of communities—how can conditions in our cities improve (see Gottdiener, 1985)?

One answer lies in the ability of community residents to organize and influence business and government (Fisher, 1984; Van Til, 1980). Neighborhood groups have successfully opposed the building of highways that threatened to split neighborhoods; tenants have successfully opposed the demolition of apartment houses or their conversion into luxury condominiums they cannot afford to buy. When companies that provide most of a community's jobs move out, residents sometimes pool their resources and become owners as well as workers, saving both themselves and their community.

Examples of residents organizing to fight for their communities are increasingly common, especially in less developed countries. In their extreme form, local efforts such as these are part of social movements that are sometimes revolutionary in scope. El Salvador and Mexico are vivid examples of citizen-initiated revolutions based in large part on the desire to improve economic and social conditions in communities.

SUMMARY

1. A community is a population that shares a territory and meets basic physical and social needs through daily interaction among residents. Rural communities are small, homogeneous, and sparsely settled; urban communities—or cities—are large, heterogeneous, and densely settled. Suburbs are communities around a city.

2. In comparison with modern communities, traditional communities tend to resist change, have relatively simple divisions of labor, use unsophisticated technology, have less highly developed mass media, and rely more on informal relationships than on secondary, formal relationships.

3. Community cultures differ in content and the homogeneity of community residents. There are no distinct urban, suburban, and rural cultures.

4. Community norms vary in their formality and strictness of application. They also differ in their content, and this corresponds to different sources of social cohesion. Mechanical solidarity refers to communities held together primarily by criminal laws; organic solidarity refers to communities held together by civil laws that regulate relationships in complex divisions of labor.

5. Communities differ in the clarity and openness of their physical and social boundaries. Closed boundaries are often based on xenophobia, the fear of strangers and outsiders.

6. Community structures also differ in age and how long residents stay; in social composition and the importance of groups and formal organizations; in distributions of power; and in the social relationships through which residents know and interact with one another.

7. Power in communities depends on authority and control of valued resources. Power-elite theory argues that an elite group dominates decision making; pluralist theory maintains that power is spread out among various interest groups.

8. Gemeinschaft communities are held together by primary relationships based on likeness and shared life experiences; Gesellschaft communities are held together by secondary relationships based on rationality and interdependence.

9. Communities differ in population size and density, and this affects the complexity of the division of labor. The Industrial Revolution caused a major change in the human niche by concentrating both production and people in relatively small areas (cities).

10. According to concentric-zone theory, cities develop in rings around a core of business activity. Outer rings are higher in social class than inner rings. The sector model states that cities grow in pie-shaped segments going out of a central business core. The multiple-nuclei theory maintains that cities have many different cores of activity. According to all three theories, the intensity of land use for different purposes varies from one part of a community to another, and residential neighborhoods tend to be segregated according to important social statuses.

11. Communities change through a complex process involving social and ecological factors. The world population is becoming increasingly urban and modern. In the United States, suburbs are growing faster than central cities, and some are becoming outer cities that rival the economic and political power of central cities. At the same time, city populations are becoming poorer and racially blacker, while suburbs are becoming wealthier and racially whiter. Urbanization is not the same in developing countries that lag behind in industrial growth.

12. The major approaches to solving community problems are government planning, private enterprise, and social movements among residents, and these can both solve and create problems.

KEY TERMS

Looking Elsewhere

Having studied Chapter 9, you might want to look at related discussions in *Human Arrangements*, which include
- population and the crisis of large cities (Chapter 5, pp. 103, 115–16)
- Gemeinschaft and Gesellschaft ties in groups (Chapter 8, pp. 209–12)
- mechanical and organic solidarity in groups (Chapter 8, pp. 209–12)
- urban-rural differences in crime (Chapter 10, p. 257)
- the distribution of national political power (Chapter 19, p. 526)
- racial segregation (Chapter 12, pp. 325–27)

RECOMMENDED READINGS

BOGGS, V., HANDEL, G., and FAVA, S. F. (Eds.). (1984). *The apple sliced: Sociological studies of New York City*. New York: Praeger. Drawing on the classical approach of the Chicago School, these 19 articles provide a richly entertaining and informative look at life in New York City.

BUSS, D. M., and REDBURN, F. S. (1983). *Shutdown at Youngstown: Public policy for mass unemployment*. Albany, NY: State University of New York Press. An examination of what happens when a "one-factory town" loses its factory.

FISCHER, C. S. (1984). *The urban experience* (2nd ed.). San Diego: Harcourt Brace Jovanovich. A critical appraisal of urban research with a particular emphasis on subcultures.

GANS, H. (1982). *The urban villagers* (2nd ed.). New York: Free Press. The second edition of an important study of tight-knit ethnic communities that struggle to maintain themselves in the midst of modern urban decay.

JACOBS, J. (1961). *The death and life of great American cities.* New York: Random House. Although more than 25 years old, Jacobs' observations about the problems of urban planning, urban renewal, and life in American cities are still of great value and make for interesting reading.

ROBERTS, B. (1979). *Cities of peasants.* Beverly Hills, CA: Sage. A look at the unique problems of cities in newly industrializing countries, with an emphasis on Latin America.

10 Deviance and Conformity

Deviance is any behavior or appearance that violates a norm, and **conformity** is behavior or appearance that is consistent with norms (Merton, 1968; Schur, 1971). We all violate norms—by overparking, telling "little white lies," failing to surrender a bus seat to an elderly passenger, or keeping a library book past its due date—but most of the time we do not risk serious punishment even, as with traffic violations, when we break a law.

Other deviance, however, has more serious consequences if it is detected. If we lie compulsively, commit murder or armed robbery, or cheat on college exams, we may be severely punished. Convicted criminals are sent to prison, and students who cheat may be expelled from school. Deviance and conformity are related to group boundaries; and, although everyone violates norms, we need to distinguish between the *kind* and the *intensity* of sanctions that result, sanctions that depend on cultural interpretations of behavior. To understand deviance, then, we must also pay attention to **social control**, "the organized ways in which society responds to behavior and people who are regarded as undesirable" (Cohen, 1985, p. 1).

This chapter focuses on three kinds of sociological questions about norms, deviance, and conformity. First, how do groups use norms to draw boundaries, and what are the resulting varieties of deviance? Second, how do culture, social structure, and ecology affect deviant behavior? (What kinds of people are the most likely to violate norms, and why? Why are some violators punished, but others are not? Why is deviance more common in some societies than others?) Third, how do conformity and deviance affect societies? What are their positive and negative consequences?

In short, what are deviance and conformity all about, and why are they important?

NORMS AND "THE NORM"

In any society, people behave in many different ways. Some behaviors are unusual—never eating meat—but their rarity in itself does not make them socially unacceptable. Most people in the U.S. eat meat, and such common behaviors are referred to as "**the norm**"; but the mere fact that individuals behave in ways that are statistically rare does not necessarily mean they are committing deviant acts. Performing heart transplant operations is an extraordinarily rare behavior in any society.

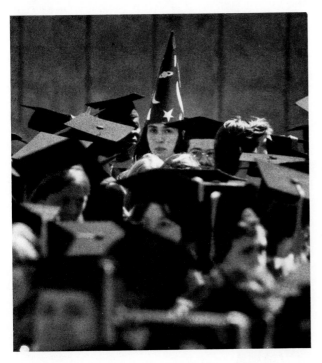

As much as we value our individuality, there are social risks associated with nonconformity. Which hat would you feel most comfortable wearing in this picture, and why?

What, however, of someone who eats people? Cannibalism is not simply unusual in the U.S., it also violates norms that define the moral acceptability of behaviors. In our culture there are thousands of different "acceptable" foods, but individuals who cross the cultural boundary and eat people are classified as *abnormal* and, to put it mildly, risk their standing as members of society (see Farb and Armelagos, 1980).

Norms are not merely ideas used to control individuals; they also establish social boundaries of acceptable and unacceptable behavior. This is clear in social responses to what is defined as immoral behav-

ior: "You are not one of us, and must either become one of us or leave." People who are identified as criminals or insane are either "rehabilitated" so they can once again fit within culturally defined limits of normality, or are excluded from society, through isolation in prisons and mental hospitals or—in more extreme cases—through death or exile.

Suicide clearly illustrates the connection between deviant behavior and social boundaries. By definition, suicide is an act in which the offender and the victim are one and the same (although other people certainly are affected). Even the most isolated individual, how-

During the final stages of World War II, a desperate Japan resorted to sending suicide pilots to crash explosive-laden planes into U.S. ships. These photographs show a hero's send-off for kamikaze pilots, and a kamikaze attack on the U.S. battleship Missouri.

ever, is legally forbidden to commit suicide. In England suicide was once viewed as so grave an act that the penalty for attempted suicide was a cruel death. How can we explain so extreme a response?

An obvious answer is that antisuicide laws support values about the importance of human life, but it is not this simple. Perhaps the clearest social boundary is the one that separates life from death. Life is difficult, and it is not uncommon for people to contemplate leaving society by ending their lives. In its simplest sense, the will to live is a basic prerequisite for the existence not only of individuals, but of groups and societies.

A society that allows suicide undermines its most fundamental hold on its members: "If you don't think life is worth living, why should anyone else?" Each time we prevent a suicide, we both save the potential victim's life and reaffirm the belief that even the most unhappy life is worth preserving.

What of societies in which suicide is sometimes permitted or expected? In feudal Japan, suicide was expected of those who had dishonored their families or their emperor (Douglas, 1968). The key to such exceptions is that suicide is not seen as rejection of life itself or of society; rather it affirms important values. When Japanese pilots committed suicide during World War II by crashing their planes into U.S. ships, they strengthened social boundaries by reaffirming the value that the emperor was more important than any citizen.

Although deviant behavior is by definition forbidden by norms, it is nonetheless common in many cases. In 1987, 81 percent of U.S. adults supported laws prohibiting marijuana use (Davis and Smith, 1987); yet more than half of all high school seniors had smoked marijuana at least once (Johnston et al., 1986). By their mid-20s, 80 percent of young adults have tried an illegal drug, and by age 27 roughly 40 percent have tried cocaine (Johnson, 1988).

The line between acceptable and deviant behavior varies both among cultures and within them. Ancient Greeks considered homosexuality a higher form of love than heterosexuality (Licht, 1932), and male homosexuality is an important part of rituals among Melanesian tribes (Herdt, 1984). Most societies, however, have persecuted homosexuals (including the murder of thousands in Nazi concentration camps). In 17th century colonial America, adultery carried the death penalty (D'Emilio and Freedman, 1988). Although 89 percent of adults in the U.S. profess the belief that adultery is wrong (Davis and Smith, 1987), adulterers today are far less likely to be shunned and are no longer punished under the law.

Prior to 1914 there were no legal controls on the use of addicting drugs such as opium and heroin in the United States. Cocaine, in fact, was an early ingredient in Coca Cola, and heroin and morphine were publicly advertised as over-the-counter drugs. In 1914 the federal government passed the Harrison Act, prohibiting the sale and use of opiates (Clausen, 1976). In 1937 marijuana was added to the list, as were LSD and other psychedelic drugs in the 1960s. More recently, tobacco smoking has been increasingly restricted by laws forbidding it in offices, airplanes, and public places, a

In 1885, cocaine was widely available in the U.S. as a pain remedy—much as aspirin or ibuprofen are today—advertised with pictures of children at play. Sigmund Freud believed that cocaine was a miracle drug that would cure a variety of physical and emotional ailments. In the century that followed, cocaine came to be regarded as a dangerous drug.

secretly and for personal gain. He is concerned not with challenging university norms, but with escaping their sanctions. If caught, he will defend himself not by appealing to higher values served by his behavior, but to circumstances that explain his actions ("I was desperate; I was overloaded with work this term").

The third student's behavior represents **retreatism** (Merton, 1968), a stance that rejects both norms and values without any interest in changing them. Like the rebel, he refuses to accept the university's norms and its values; but the retreatist offers nothing as a replacement. He has simply "dropped out" by refusing to participate. The retreatist's behavior is also aberrant, for it represents not an active concern with university culture, but a self-serving, apathetic rejection of the community itself.

Innovative behavior may be either aberrant (as in the case of the second student) or nonconformist. A student might share the cultural value of academic success and yet believe that exams are the wrong *means* for measuring accomplishment. Openly stealing the exam answers would then be an innovative, nonconforming act designed to protest norms while supporting cultural values.

These distinctions (shown in the box on this page) are important because social responses to deviant behavior depend on the type of deviance the act represents. Nonconforming rebels and innovators act in the name of important values and without consid-

---

Types of Deviant Behavior

NONCONFORMING BEHAVIOR   Done openly in the name of positive social change, not for personal gain; appeals to "higher values."

Rebellion   Openly rejects *both* norms and the values they support, and offers alternatives.

Example: Revolutionary.

Innovation   Openly rejects norms and offers alternatives; supports values that rejected norms enforce.

Example: Publicly burning a military draft card while calling for a volunteer army to meet defense needs.

ABERRANT BEHAVIOR   Done secretly for personal gain; concerned more with avoiding punishment than with positive change.

Retreatism   Rejects *both* norms and the values they support, but does not offer alternatives. Uses illegitimate means to achieve culturally illegitimate goals. "Dropping out."

Example: Skid row drug addict.

Innovation   Rejects norms, but accepts the values they support. Uses illegitimate means to achieve culturally legitimate goals.

Example: Robbing banks.

Source: Adapted from Merton, 1968, 1976a.

In 1963, police dogs were used against unarmed, nonviolent black demonstrators in Birmingham, Alabama. The willingness of blacks and whites to violate the law to call attention to racism and to endure the often violent efforts of police to stop them, appealed to deeply held American values about courage in the face of injustice.

eration of personal gain, so other people are more likely to support them. In addition, nonconformity often leads to positive social change. When blacks refused to sit in the back of buses or be turned away from "Whites Only" restaurants in the 1960s, they did so in order to promote social change. There can be little doubt that without such "civil disobedience," the black civil rights movement would never have achieved as much as it has (see Chapter 21).

Aberrant behavior, however, provokes harsher punishment because it is done for personal gain. Unlike nonconformists, people who commit aberrant acts such as theft cannot say to society, "I did this for our own good." The behavior of nonconformists reflects a concern for values that connects them with the society that considers punishing them, whereas aberrant and retreatist behavior identifies individuals as "outsiders."

The severity of punishment for aberrant behavior depends on the values involved. A starving woman who steals in order to feed herself violates a norm while conforming to important values about the preservation of human life. If she steals in order to feed starving children, she conforms to even more powerful values—helping others and caring for children. A man who steals simply because he wants to possess a luxury he cannot afford, however, acts only in his self-interest and conforms to a less-valued goal—accumulating possessions—and is therefore more likely to be punished harshly.

The social response to deviance also depends on the actors' orientations to values and norms as revealed by how they present themselves and their behavior to others. For this reason, people who describe themselves as "political terrorists" have something to gain by defending their behavior with appeals to "higher values" rather than personal gain (Rappoport and Alexander, 1982). In this way, they try to define killing as something other than murder, and abduction as something other than kidnapping, hoping to thereby escape punishment (Schafer, 1974).

Stigma: When Who We Are Is against the Rules

Stigmas, Goffman (1963b) wrote, are characteristics that render people "not quite human" in the eyes of others, who reduce them in their minds "from a whole and usual person to a tainted, discounted one." Bernard Pomerance's play (and, later, movie) *The Elephant Man* tells the true story of an Englishman who was horribly disfigured by a disease. Like many disfigured people, he was regarded as a freak and accepted only by a sympathetic physician and a rare few who were willing to seek out the witty, charming, and intelligent human being who lived within the deformed body. The 1985 movie *Mask* tells a similar story.

Most recently, people diagnosed as having AIDS have found themselves treated as outcasts. There are numerous cases of landlords who refuse to rent to

A hostage was taken by an Armenian at the Turkish consulate in Paris in 1981 to press demands related to long-standing Armenian grievances against Turkey. If caught, he would most likely defend his actions as nonconformist rather than as aberrant—as motivated by important cultural values rather than self-interest.

AIDS patients, of employers who refuse to hire them, and of health professionals—including physicians—who refuse to provide them with medical care. Children afflicted with AIDS have been excluded from schools, and in one Florida case the family's home was firebombed.

Stigmas are also attached to personality characteristics such as dishonesty or mental instability. Former convicts and mental patients may be treated as outcasts even when they "go straight" (or "go sane") (see Link et al., 1987). The mentally retarded are often subjected to humiliation even by those responsible for taking care of them (Dudley, 1983).

Stigmatized people are treated as deviants not for what they do, but because of who they *are* or are thought to be. It is perhaps the most damaging form of deviance, for while we can control our behavior, it is all but impossible to change our bodies or our pasts, no matter how much we may want to do so. Stigmas have the power to condemn people to lives of shame and isolation over which they have little if any control.

Formal and Informal Sanctions

In most cases, telling lies violates folkways that have informal sanctions such as expressions of anger. If we lie habitually, however, people may refuse to trust or associate with us, and as informal as such sanctions are, they can be powerful reasons to tell the truth.

Informal sanctions, however, are not strong enough to compel people to tell the truth in court. People often have powerful personal reasons for lying, and such behavior (perjury) can have serious consequences. In many cases, therefore, the norms take the form of *laws* with formal sanctions and specialists such as police officers, judges, and prison officials to enforce them. In general, *crime* is deviant behavior that violates the law, and the social causes of criminal behavior are a major focus of sociological research.

CRIME, CRIMINALS, AND VICTIMS

Although **crime** technically includes all acts that violate laws, it is important to note at the outset that many violations of law are not socially defined as crimes, and some crimes are not defined as deviant. Few people consider speeding on the highway a criminal act; and although restaurant waiters who fail to report all their tip income to the Internal Revenue Service are committing a crime, most people—includ-

ing restaurant owners—do not treat such people as deviants.

"There is no society that is not confronted with the problem of criminality," wrote Durkheim (1895), and the United States is a prime example. In 1986 a murder was reported to police every 25 minutes, a sexual assault every 6 minutes, an assault every 38 seconds, and a theft every 4 seconds (Table 10-1). In comparison with other modern industrial societies, the United States is the undisputed "murder capital of the world" (Table 10-2) in no small part because of the much greater availability and ownership of handguns and cultural support for the right of individuals to use them (see Wright et al., 1983).

The crime rate increased sharply during the last two decades. Between 1960 and 1983 the U.S. population grew by 31 percent, whereas the rate of reported crime grew by 460 percent—in spite of tripled public spending for law enforcement (U.S. Census Bureau, 1975a, 1986a). In 1973 about 16 percent of adults had had the experience of being shot at or threatened with a gun, but by 1987 the figure had risen to 20 percent (Davis and Smith, 1987).

We must remember that these statistics include only crimes reported to the police, and as people become more or less willing to report crimes, trends in *official* crime rates may not accurately reflect trends in *actual* rates. In the 1970s the U.S. Department of Justice began a series of national surveys to measure the incidence of crime (see Gottfredson and Hindelang, 1981). By comparing the results with police statistics, the researchers found that crime often goes unreported to the police (U.S. Department of Justice,

Table 10-1

Reported Incidence of Crimes (United States, 1960 and 1986)

	HOW FREQUENTLY EACH TYPE WAS REPORTED	
TYPE OF CRIME	1960	1986
Murder	60 minutes	25 minutes
Sexual assault	30 minutes	6 minutes
Assault	3 minutes	38 seconds
Theft	10 seconds	4 seconds

Source: U.S. Census Bureau, 1980b; FBI, 1987.

Table 10-2

Homicide Rates for Selected Countries, 1980–84 (Rates per 100,000 People)

COUNTRY	HOMICIDE RATE
United States	9.1
Canada	2.3
Australia	1.9
Israel	1.8
Denmark	1.4
France	1.4
Great Britain	1.2
Austria	1.2
Sweden	1.2
Norway	1.1
Japan	1.0
Switzerland	1.0
Netherlands	0.8
Greece	0.7
West Germany	0.7

Source: U.S. Census Bureau, 1983c; United Nations, 1985.

statistics on crime have been gathered. Prostitution is the only crime committed primarily (although not exclusively) by females (Cohen and Short, 1976).

In recent years the gender difference in crime has narrowed slightly in the U.S., particularly among non-whites and for relatively minor crimes. Smith and Visher (1980) suggest that as males and females increasingly come to occupy similar positions, such as occupation, their behavior—including deviance—should become more similar as well (see also Hagan et al., 1985, 1987). Gora's 1982 study of arrest rate trends, however, found no support for the common belief that increases in female criminal activity have been caused by the women's movement and a redefinition of women's roles.

Age Some crimes are defined literally by the age of the criminal. *Juvenile delinquency* refers to illegal acts committed by people under 18 years of age. Prior to the nineteenth century, "child criminals" were either shielded from the law or treated as adults, but during the last 100 years Western societies have created a separate legal category for youthful offenders, with its own set of procedures (Sutton, 1983).

Age is also important because it affects the likelihood of criminal behavior (see Hirschi and Gottfredson, 1983). A third of those arrested for theft in 1985 were under the age of 18, as were 41 percent of those arrested for arson (U.S. Census Bureau, 1986a). Adults are more likely to be arrested for violent crimes such as homicide and for crimes that require expertise (counterfeiting), money (drug smuggling), or special opportunities (embezzling bank funds) (Cohen and Short, 1976).

1980a). The victimization studies found that the incidence of violent crimes in 1984 was almost five times higher than that recorded by police (U.S. Census Bureau, 1986a).

Like most behavior, crime is influenced by social environments. Criminals are more likely to occupy some statuses than others, as are their victims, and criminals have relationships with one another. In addition, criminals, their victims, and those charged with law enforcement are related in ways that affect not only themselves, but the capacity of society to prevent crime as well.

Who Are the Criminals?

From a sociological point of view, criminal behavior is partly due to social structure, in that criminals as a social category differ from noncriminals in their likelihood of occupying important statuses such as gender, age, race, and social class.

Gender More than 10 million people were arrested in 1985, and 83 percent of them were male (U.S. Census Bureau, 1986a). The gender difference in known criminal behavior has existed in virtually all societies, communities, and age groups as long as

Puzzles: Who Constitutes the Criminal Class?

Who is most likely to break the law—someone from the lower class, the middle class, or the upper class?

If you answered, "the lower class," you might be right; and you might also be wrong. Popular stereotypes portray members of the lower class as particularly prone to criminal behavior, but, as this chapter shows, a long history of scientific research challenges this view amid a continuing debate among sociologists.

The high rate of arrests for teenage arsonists underscores the problem of estimates of crime based on arrests. Arrest information does not measure the *frequency* of crime, for it misses all unreported crimes as well as those reported crimes for which police do not make arrests. That teenagers are more likely to be arrested for arson may indicate not a greater likelihood of committing arson, but a lack of adult skills needed to get away with it.

Race and Social Class   The inadequacy of official statistics is particularly apparent when we try to estimate racial and class differences in criminal behavior. Nonwhites made up 15 percent of the U.S. population in 1985, but accounted for 28 percent of all arrests (U.S. Census Bureau, 1986a). The criminologists Wolfgang, Figlio, and Sellin (1972) kept track of almost 10,000 boys throughout adolescence and found that lower-class boys were twice as likely to be arrested as middle- and upper-class boys.

Do such findings indicate that nonwhites and the poor are more likely to commit crimes or that they are simply more likely to be singled out by police? Many studies that rely on private interviews suggest that official records are biased against nonwhites and people from the lower class. Hindelang (1978) reviewed studies based on reports from victims and concluded that whites and nonwhites have very similar overall rates of criminal behavior; and another review of 35 studies of crime and social class concluded that class has no effect on the likelihood of committing criminal

acts (Tittle, Villemez, and Smith, 1978). Although nonwhites living in inner cities are more likely to commit theft and violent crimes, the overall criminal tendencies of youths at all class levels are strikingly similar (Elliott and Ageton, 1980; R. Johnson, 1980).

The criminal acts of middle- and upper-class adults often go unrecorded because they tend to be **white-collar crimes**, crimes that people are able to commit because of the social statuses—usually occupations—that they occupy (Mars, 1983; Reiss and Biderman, 1980; Sutherland, 1983). Now that computers are used so heavily in business, for example, employees have new opportunities to steal. One computer operator with access to payroll records modified the computer program so that each employee's paycheck was rounded down to the nearest ten cents, with each small reduction transferred to the thief's own paycheck. With 3,500 employees this amounted to an additional $300 a week for the computer operator, whose real salary was only $120 (*New York Times*, January 29, 1984).

White-collar crimes may be committed by individuals or by groups. Factories that violate worker safety laws may cause the injury or death of employees. More people are killed each year because of unsafe working conditions than are murdered (see Hagan and Palloni, 1986; Hills, 1987). Companies that fix prices, violate patent and copyright laws, engage in fraud, or evade taxes cause three times more economic loss than do thieves and vandals (President's Commission on Law Enforcement, 1967). Although such acts

Table 10-3

Percentage of White Males Admitting Criminal Behavior during Last Five Years, by Social Class (United States)

CRIME	Upper	Upper-middle	Middle	Lower-middle	Lower
$5 theft	19	36	29	31	25
$50 theft	4	8	10	12	7
Gambling	38	54	50	48	36
Tax cheating	16	22	19	13	7
Assault	14	17	17	12	13
Marijuana use	16	25	19	13	24

Source: Tittle and Villemez, 1977.

Table 10-4

Violent Crimes and Property Crimes by Size of Place, United States, 1970 and 1985 (Rates per Year per 100,000 Population)

SIZE OF PLACE	VIOLENT CRIMES			PROPERTY CRIMES		
	1970	1985	% CHANGE	1970	1985	% CHANGE
Large metropolitan	458	658	+44	4389	5262	+20
Smaller cities	182	319	+75	2727	4262	+56
Rural	121	168	+39	1233	1635	+33

Source: U.S. Census Bureau, 1986a.

violate laws, they often go undetected; and, even when discovered, they are rarely considered true "crimes."

Even when companies are found guilty of crimes, the individuals involved are often not prosecuted; rather, the company itself is punished (usually a fine). Douglas and Waksler (1982) suggested that social ambivalence toward white-collar criminals reflects a deep underlying value conflict. On the one hand, we value honesty; but on the other hand, we also value "making the best deal" and "looking out for Number 1." W. C. Fields was not speaking only for himself when he said, "Never give a sucker an even break."

Because official statistics overlook most white-collar crime, some researchers suggest that middle- and upper-class people may actually be *more* prone to criminal activity than people from lower classes (Reckless, 1973). Tittle and Villemez (1977) interviewed a large sample of adults and found no evidence of greater criminality in lower classes (Table 10-3). Petty theft, gambling, and tax evasion were more commonly reported by upper- and upper-middle-class respondents.

There is, of course, reason to be suspicious of any study that relies on people to report their own criminal behavior. What is important to note here, however, is that these data do not support the common belief that lower-class people are more prone to criminal behavior than everyone else. The debate continues (see, for example, Braithwaite, 1981) and, so long as problems of measurement are as difficult to solve as they appear to be, it may be some time before the issue of social class and deviance can be resolved.

Urban, Rural, and In-between The likelihood that people will commit crimes depends not only on statuses such as gender, age, race, and class, but also on their ecological (or spatial) relation to one another. People who live in large cities are more likely to commit crimes than those who live in small cities or rural areas (Table 10-4). In some cities the rate of violent crime is extraordinarily high: The overall reported rate of violent crime in 1985 was 1,344 in large metropolitan areas, but the rate was over 2,000 in Baltimore and Detroit (U.S. Census Bureau, 1986a).

Historically, large cities have experienced more criminal behavior than smaller communities, but as Table 10-4 shows, small cities and rural communities are rapidly catching up. Between 1970 and 1985, violent crime rose by 44 percent in the largest cities, but by 75 percent in small cities. Small cities and rural areas both had higher rates of increase for property crimes.

As we found earlier with age and social class, the effect that the size of a community has on crime rates depends on the type of crime. Reported rates of violent crime are twice as high in large cities as in smaller ones, but rates of violent death among young people are highest not in cities, but in the sparsely settled "wide open spaces" of the Far West where population density is less than six people per square mile. According to Popper et al. (1987), the "frontier" still exists, complete with risk-taking and violent solutions to personal quarrels. Rates of death among whites in frontier areas are even higher than those for blacks in high crime rate cities. The answer to the question "Who are the criminals?" depends, then, on which crimes are involved.

The fact that crime involves both criminals and their victims brings us to a second question: What social characteristics distinguish victims from nonvictims?

Who Are the Victims?

Just as social statuses influence the likelihood of committing criminal acts, they also affect the likelihood of being victimized, and this too depends on the type of crime. Table 10-5 shows that for major crime categories, men are more likely than women to be victimized. In the case of sexual violence, however, almost all victims are women (U.S. Department of Justice, 1987). We can also see that nonwhites are more likely than whites to be victims. The murder of black men is astoundingly frequent, occurring at a rate almost six times greater than among white men.

The data in Table 10-6 show that victims of violent crime are heavily concentrated in younger age groups. In the case of sexual violence, most victims are young women between the ages of 16 and 24 (U.S. Department of Justice, 1987).

The effect of social class on victimization also depends on the type of crime. Lower-income people are more likely to be victims of violence (U.S. Department of Justice, 1987) and burglary (see Table 10-7). Higher-income people, however, are equally likely to suffer larceny (theft without breaking and entering or the use of force).

The most important thing these findings tell us about crime is that for *non-white-collar* crime, the statuses most likely to produce criminals are also those most likely to produce victims. For many types of crime, people who are young, nonwhite, poor, or city dwellers are more likely to be involved in crime either as offenders or as victims than are those who are older, white, with higher income, or living in smaller communities.

As we will see later in this chapter, the social characteristics of criminals and victims provide a basis for sociological explanations of criminal behavior. Be-

Table 10-6

Who Are the Victims? Violence and Theft by Victim's Age, United States, 1985 (Rates per Year per 1,000 Population)

	TYPE OF CRIME	
VICTIM'S AGE	All Violent Crimes	Theft
12–15	54	108
16–19	67	122
20–24	60	108
25–34	37	83
35–49	20	63
50–64	10	40
65 and older	4	19

Source: U.S. Department of Justice, 1987.

Table 10-7

Victims of Theft, by Income, United States, 1985 (Rates per Year per 1,000 Households)

	TYPE OF CRIME	
HOUSEHOLD INCOME	Burglary[1]	Larceny[2]
Less than $7,500	86	98
$7,500 to $9,999	60	101
$10,000 to $14,999	67	101
$15,000 to $24,999	59	104
$25,000 to $29,999	54	95
$30,000 to $49,999	58	98
$50,000 or more	56	104

[1] Burglary is unlawful entry in order to commit a crime.
[2] Larceny is stealing without illegal entry into a dwelling, force, violence, or fraud (e.g., shoplifting, pocket-picking, and auto theft).

Source: U.S. Department of Justice, 1987.

Table 10-5

Who Are the Victims? Violence and Theft by Victim's Gender and Race, United States, 1985 (Rates per Year per 100,000 Population)

	TYPE OF CRIME		
VICTIM'S RACE AND GENDER	Violence	Murder	Theft
White males	38	9	74
White females	21	3	66
Nonwhite males	47	51	76
Nonwhite females	31	11	53

Source: U.S. Department of Justice, 1987.

fore considering the causes of deviance, however, we must first examine criminal activity as a structured set of social relationships among criminals and between criminals and their victims.

Structures of Crime

The simplest element of crime's social structure is the number of people involved, ranging from individuals to large groups. Crimes may be committed by a small adolescent street gang, a large crime syndicate, or a major corporation. In the same way, victims may be either groups or individuals. Social relationships among criminals also vary in their complexity, from the simplicity of a pair of bank robbers to the bureaucratic complexity of organized crime. We need, then, to take a closer look at two kinds of relationships—those among criminals and those between criminals and their victims—in order to describe crime as social behavior.

Relationships among Criminals   Although violent crimes tend to have simple structures involving single offenders, crimes such as theft, prostitution, and drug smuggling involve more complex relationships (Miller, 1978). Thieves rely on "fences" to buy what they steal, and fences, in turn, rely on people who are willing to buy stolen property (which is itself a crime) (Steffensmeier, 1986). A fence may sell a truckload of stolen stereos to legitimate dealers who then sell them to an unsuspecting public. A simple act of theft often involves a variety of people playing different roles.

Just as industrialization made most institutions more bureaucratic, it also changed the organization of crime. **Syndicated crime** is highly bureaucratic, with rigid authority structures controlling complex divisions of labor (Abadinsky, 1983; Block and Chambliss, 1981). The smuggling and distribution of illegal drugs such as heroin and cocaine require large amounts of cash and precise coordination among overseas buyers, smugglers, and distributors, from the wholesaler to the lowliest pusher (see Adler, 1985).

Syndicated crime may be organized in a variety of ways, from a rigid military model of bureaucratic efficiency complete with salaried employees, to a tight-knit "family business." In some cases, syndicates operate as franchises (like fast-food chains), providing capital and expertise to local operators who then share their profits with the "parent company" (Anderson,

Table 10-8

Individuals and Groups as Criminals and Victims

	VICTIM	
CRIMINAL	*Individual*	*Group*
Individual	Assault Mugging Auto theft Sexual assault	Treason Tax evasion Bank robbery Embezzlement
Group	Gang burglarizes a home Mob collects "protection money" from merchant Ku Klux Klan lynches a black man	Job discrimination Mob bribes government officials Nazi group bombs Jewish synagogue

1979; Ianni, 1972), often making the structures of crime and legitimate business quite similar.

Criminals and Victims   Crime involves social interaction in which criminals victimize groups or individuals (Table 10-8). Most violent crimes involve people who are of the same race (O'Brien, 1987) and who know each other: a majority of murders, sexual and other assaults involve family members or acquaintances (U.S. Department of Justice, 1980a). White-collar crimes, however, tend to victimize groups, as do crimes that systematically victimize people on the basis of statuses such as race, ethnicity, age, or gender (illegal job discrimination).

In some cases, the distinction between individual and group victims is unclear. If a black man is lynched by the Ku Klux Klan as an example to blacks in general, the effects ripple beyond the immediate victim to all who share his racial status. Brownmiller (1975) made a similar point about sexual assault: the fact that some women are assaulted encourages all women to fear men.

Victimless Crime   Although most crimes involve an individual or group as victim, in **victimless crimes** there either is no victim or the criminal and the victim are one and the same. Most states define prostitution, some types of gambling, and the use of certain drugs as illegal, but who are the victims? If one argues that drug addiction victimizes the abuser, this means society punishes those who victimize themselves.

Schur (1965) argues that norms defining victimless crime exist not to protect people from victimization, but to prohibit behavior that is culturally defined as immoral. Because victimless crimes involve voluntary interactions, laws that prohibit them are difficult to enforce, for legal authorities are the only complainants.

The connection between victimless crime and morality helps explain why the response to such crimes is so severe even though individuals are not victimized. A society's mores reflect deeply held ideas about right and wrong and are an important part of the boundaries that define membership. In the case of prostitution, society itself is defined as the victim, and the punishment does more to maintain clear social boundaries than to protect individuals.

Structures of Justice and Injustice

Police, courts, and prisons constitute a **criminal justice system**, which carries out three basic social processes: identifying and arresting criminals, determining guilt and innocence, and deciding how to treat those who are convicted. How do culture and social structure affect who is arrested, prosecuted, and convicted? How effectively does the criminal justice system control crime?

Arrest   Arrest is a social process through which people enter the criminal justice system. Police face the impossible task of enforcing thousands of laws, and therefore have considerable discretion in deciding when to arrest someone. Police responses to criminal behavior depend on cultural definitions of the situation and the social statuses of those involved.

Until recently, our culture has defined wife beating as a "family matter," not a crime, so police have been reluctant to arrest men who abuse their wives, and usually persuaded the victim not to press criminal charges (Flynn, 1977). Enforcement agencies tend to ignore white-collar crime because our culture defines it as a less serious offense.

Participant observation studies of police reveal considerable racial prejudice, but also suggest that the high rate of black arrests is not due simply to race.

Rather, police are more likely to arrest those who are disrespectful or—as members of the lower class—objects of stereotypes that include shiftlessness, irresponsibility, and criminal tendencies (Piliavan and Briar, 1964). Donald Black (1971) suggested that racial prejudice among police officers leads blacks to assume they will be treated unfairly, and therefore approach police with defiance and hostility. Whatever the effect on their behavior toward police, blacks are far more likely than whites to perceive the police and courts as being unfair (Hagan and Abonnetti, 1982).

Although the evidence on racial discrimination is mixed, it is clear that poor people are frequently singled out for arrest. The better off a neighborhood, the fewer contacts there are between police and young people regardless of the amount of crime. Among young people who are arrested, the higher their socioeconomic status, the less likely they are to be prosecuted, regardless of their prior court records (Sampson, 1986). Smith (1987) found that the likelihood that a contact between police and criminal suspects will result in an arrest declines as the status of the neighborhood increases, and this occurs regardless of such factors as race, the type of crime, and how suspects behave towards police.

Chambliss (1973) studied the Saints and the Roughnecks—two gangs in the same town—and found that Saints committed more criminal acts than Roughnecks, caused more property damage, and often endangered other people's lives with their stunts and practical jokes. The Saints, however, were never arrested during Chambliss' two-year study, whereas the Roughnecks regularly found themselves in trouble with the law. Why? The Saints belonged to middle-class families, drove new cars, spoke politely to teachers, police, and others in positions of authority, and had parents whom the police knew might cause trouble if their children were arrested. Middle- and upper-class parents have resources to shield their children (and themselves) from arrest—resources that are unavailable to poor people. They are more aware of their legal rights, and their relatively high prestige gives them credibility when they guarantee their children's future good behavior. Most residents looked upon the Saints as no more than a group of "good boys" who were having a good time. The Roughnecks, however, were from the lower class and were assumed by residents to be "bad characters."

Police officers' perceptions influence their decisions to arrest individuals, and such perceptions are affected by cultural beliefs attached to social statuses.

Most evidence shows that the social statuses of defendants continue to influence the criminal justice system after arrests are made.

Prosecution   From the moment of arrest, legal procedures discriminate against the poor (Forer, 1984). Middle- and upper-class defendants can afford to hire their own lawyers rather than depend on overworked public defenders. This is especially true of white-collar criminals, who often can afford skilled lawyers who succeed in keeping damaging evidence from the prosecution (Mann, 1985). Poor people are also more likely to stay in jail while awaiting trial, for the bail system allows the wealthy to buy their freedom.

Trial verdicts may depend more on stereotypes about defendants and victims than on factual evidence. Under the law the only issues in a rape trial are the fact of sexual contact and whether or not the victim consented at the moment the act took place. People in the U.S., however, often blame the victim and treat her as if she were the actual defendant (Holmstrom and Burgess, 1983; Medea and Thompson, 1974).

Judges are obliged to decide cases on strict legal grounds, but juries are allowed to take extralegal factors into account, including stereotypes about women. Even when victims have been brutally beaten, their attackers may go free if the woman appears to be of "poor character" (typically, unmarried and sexually active). Juries often believe that such women "ask for it" and "deserve what they get." In so doing, they ignore the fact that a crime took place.

Defendants have the right to choose to be tried by a jury or by a judge alone, and Kalven and Zeisel's classic study, *The American Jury* (1966), shows why accused rapists prefer jury trials. Kalven and Zeisel examined 106 jury trials for aggravated rape (with physical evidence of brutality) and "simple" rape (when the victim was threatened with a weapon but not visibly beaten), and compared jury verdicts with those favored by the judge. In aggravated rape cases in which judges favored conviction on the basis of the evidence, juries acquitted defendants 14 percent of the time; but in "simple" rape cases in which judges favored conviction, *juries found defendants "not guilty" 95 percent of the time.*

In cases of "simple" rape, therefore, juries often ignore legal evidence, and judge the victim rather than the defendant. Judges favored conviction 52 percent of the time, whereas juries found defendants guilty in only 7 percent of such cases. By choosing a jury trial in which stereotypes about women can overshadow the facts of the crime, defendants are seven times more likely to go free.

Punishment   Once convicted, a defendant's statuses significantly affect the sentencing process. White-collar criminals usually receive lower sentences than other criminals (Seymour, 1973). In comparison

DOONESBURY

by Garry Trudeau

with whites, black juvenile delinquents are more likely to be prosecuted and to be committed to juvenile homes at younger ages, for less serious crimes, and with less damaging criminal records (Axelrad, 1952; Wilson, 1968). Nonwhite adults typically receive stiffer sentences than whites who commit the same crime (D. A. Bell, 1973), especially if the victim is white (LaFree, 1980). Black men are far more likely than whites to receive death sentences, especially when their victims are white. (See Nakell and Hardy, 1987.) In a study of 2,484 murders in Georgia, Baldus (1987) found that blacks who murdered whites were 22 times more likely to be sentenced to death than were blacks who murdered other blacks; and whites who murdered other whites were three times more likely to receive a death sentence than were whites who murdered blacks. Sociological documentation of such unequal treatment in fact formed the basis for the Supreme Court's 1968 decision to ban the death penalty (Zeisel, 1981).

Judges have great power to decide the severity of punishment, and an ingenious experiment illustrates the effects of a defendant's race on how judges use that power. Jackson (1974) gave descriptions of a typical case to 36 judges and asked them to decide on an appropriate sentence:

> "Joe Cut," 27, pleads guilty to battery. He slashed his wife on the arms with a switchblade. His record showed convictions for disturbing the peace, drunkenness, and hit-and-run driving. He told a probation officer that he acted in self-defense after his wife attacked him with a broom handle. The prosecutor recommended not more than five days in jail or a $100 fine.

Unknown to the judges, Jackson varied one detail in the descriptions: to half of the judges, the defendants were described as white; to the other half, they were described as black. White defendants received sentences ranging from three to ten days, compared with five to thirty days for blacks.

Criminologists have long maintained that the severity of punishment depends on the defendant's race and social class (Chambliss, 1969; Thornberry, 1973); but more recent evidence suggests that such discrimination may have declined substantially (Hagan and Bumiller, 1983). Sentences *do* depend on the culturally defined severity of the offense, however, and here there is a clear bias in favor of white-collar criminals (see Hagan and Parker, 1985).

In spite of the little evidence that criminal behavior is more likely among nonwhites and poor people

than among whites and the middle and upper classes, the U.S. prison population is overwhelmingly black and poor. Taken as a whole, the social processes of arrest, prosecution, and sentencing clearly discriminate against people in these social categories.

Does the System Work?   The criminal justice system is organized around a variety of goals (Cohen and Short, 1976), the most important of which are prevention, deterrence, and punishment. How effectively does the system achieve its goals, and how is this related to its social characteristics?

Criminal justice systems combat crime by increasing the size of police forces and, therefore, the ability to observe criminal acts; by imprisoning and thereby isolating criminals from potential victims; by imposing harsh penalties; and by attempting to alter the personalities of people who commit crimes. The evidence is clear that none of these methods has been very effective.

Between 1960 and 1983, per capita expenditures for police protection in the U.S. more than doubled (after adjusting for inflation); but in the same period, the rate of reported violent crime tripled and the rate of property crime almost tripled (U.S. Census Bureau, 1980b, 1986a). A doubled investment in crime prevention did not cut crime rates in half; instead, crime far outran efforts to prevent it. (It is of course possible that crime rates would have increased even more if expenditures had not increased.)

Most people who commit crimes are never caught, much less imprisoned. In 1985 the Justice Department's victim survey conservatively estimated a total of 22 million serious crimes. Of these, only half were reported to police and only 10 percent resulted in an arrest (U.S. Census Bureau, 1986a). More than 90 percent of serious criminal offenses never result in an arrest, much less in prosecution, conviction, and punishment.

Since the vast majority of criminals are never caught and convicted, the threat of punishment is too low to effectively discourage criminal behavior. In 1987, 79 percent of U.S. adults believed that courts do not treat criminals harshly enough (Davis and Smith, 1987), but dozens of studies show that long prison sentences are no more effective than short ones in preventing crime (Babst et al., 1976).

What does make a difference is the *certainty* of punishment (Chapman, 1976; Silverman, 1976; Tullock, 1974). In the United States over 90 percent of kidnappers are caught, convicted, and severely punished, and as a result, kidnapping is quite rare (*New York Times Magazine*, 1976). When public perception of the certainty of punishment for drunken driving increases, the incidence of drunken driving tends to decline (see Ross, 1984).

Finally, efforts to rehabilitate criminals by altering their personalities through therapy or by providing them with occupational skills have had, at best, mixed results (Lipton, Martinson, and Wilks, 1975; Martinson, 1974). A sociological point of view suggests several reasons for this failure.

Prison is what Goffman (1961a) called a **total institution**—in which inmates' lives are almost completely controlled. They are isolated from society, deprived of meaningful work and heterosexual contact, and can make few decisions for themselves. On entering prison, inmates experience **degradation ceremonies** (Garfinkel, 1956), in which they are stripped, searched, and labeled as inferior human beings. The physical and social organization of prisons is designed primarily to prevent escape, a goal that has little effect on crime rates since, as we have seen, few criminals are ever imprisoned. With prison inmates learning to adapt to and function in a social environment that bears little resemblance to the outside world (Sykes, 1958), it should come as no surprise that 74 percent are arrested for new crimes within four years of their release (Federal Bureau of Investigation, 1976).

A second reason for the failure of the U.S. criminal justice system lies in its assumptions about the *causes* of deviance. In particular, it assumes that fear of punishment is the most important factor in preventing deviance and that the causes of deviance have relatively little to do with the pressures and limitations imposed by social environments. We know, however, that fear of punishment has relatively little effect on behavior, including deviance (Piliavin et al., 1986), and there is no reason to believe that deviant behavior is any less affected by social life than any other form of behavior.

All of this points strongly to the importance of sociological explanations of deviant behavior. How do cultural ideas and the structures of human relationships increase the chances that people will commit crimes?

WHAT CAUSES DEVIANCE?

Researchers have long tried to identify biological and psychological causes of deviant behavior (see Kamin,

1986; Wilson and Herrnstein, 1985). Lombroso (1911) examined criminals and concluded that crime results from "animalistic body types"; but Goring (1913) later discovered that the physical appearance of criminals differs little from that of noncriminals. Sheldon (1949) found that delinquents tend to have sturdy, muscular bodies, and suggested that this increased the likelihood of aggressive behavior. The problem with such findings is that they ignore the ways in which people's social responses to physical appearances affect behavior (Glueck and Glueck, 1972). Muscular boys are more likely to be chosen as members of gangs that regularly engage in fighting, but this is a far cry from concluding that muscularity in itself causes deviance.

Personality certainly plays a part in deviant behavior, but psychologists have been unable to identify personality types that are consistently related to it (Schuessler and Cressey, 1950). Glueck and Glueck (1950) found that delinquents were only slightly more likely than nondelinquents to suffer from emotional disturbances, and mental illness appears to be no more common among prison inmates than among ordinary citizens (Hakeem, 1958).

Sociologically, choices between conformity and deviance depend a great deal on the social environments we find ourselves in. This does not mean that sociological explanations of deviance relieve individuals of personal responsibility; rather, they help identify social factors that encourage people to make deviant choices. To the extent that society itself fosters deviance, all the individual therapy in the world will only treat the symptoms of deviance, not its causes. Deviant behavior is an enormously complex puzzle, and researchers in all disciplines are far from identifying all its pieces, and even farther from putting them together. The following sections identify some of the pieces revealed by sociological analysis and research.

Deviance and Culture

In the simplest sense, culture contributes to deviance by defining some behaviors as deviant as part of the social boundaries. As Durkheim (1895) asserted, deviance is an inevitable consequence of social life, for societies use categories of deviant behavior to draw their boundaries and maintain social cohesion (Erikson, 1966).

The U.S. could reduce the annual number of arrests by more than 2 million if the law no longer defined public drunkenness, drug use, liquor sales to minors, prostitution, gambling, and vagrancy as crimes (U.S. Census Bureau, 1986a). When drugs such as heroin and cocaine are outlawed, their price skyrockets because they can be obtained only at great risk. For many addicts, crime is the only way to support an expensive habit. Schur (1965) argues that the criminal justice system would in fact be far more effective if certain behaviors, especially victimless crimes, were no longer defined as crimes.

Since deviance is inevitable in all societies, however, we are confronted with the problem of explaining why some people deviate from norms and others do not. Two sociological theories help explain the role of culture.

Deviance and Anomie   According to the first of these theories, we tend to conform to norms only insofar as we identify ourselves as members of society and feel an attachment to its values. Norms regulate social relationships, and if we feel cut off and isolated from groups, their norms will have little effect on us. In a related sense, if we live in a society in which there is wide disagreement and confusion about which behaviors are acceptable, we lack clear guidelines and are more likely to create new ones which may include innovative deviance.

Durkheim (1897) believed that human desire has no natural limits, and that if it were not for the pressure of norms and values, societies would be unable to control destructive behavior. When norms break down and people no longer feel a solid connection between themselves and society, the result is what Durkheim called **anomie**. During electrical blackouts, people often feel that "anything goes," and commit acts they would never consider in less chaotic conditions.

As Durkheim (1897) noted in his study of suicide, anomie is a dangerous social condition, for it "deceives us into believing that we depend on ourselves only." As Hirschi (1969) found in his comparisons of delinquents and nondelinquents, feelings of isolation are associated with deviant behavior. Typical delinquents are weakly attached to friends and family, and lack the close relationships and values that motivate most people to obey the law. Wiatrowski, Griswold, and Roberts (1981) supported Hirschi's findings and emphasize the particularly strong effects of adolescent attachments to parents and school as inhibitors of delinquent behavior (see also Liska and Reed, 1985).

The characteristics of individuals are often less important than the cultural *bonds* that tie individuals together. In her study of the elderly in the U.S., Blau (1973) found that when older people lose important roles either through retirement or the death of a spouse, they often protect themselves from the pain of the present by retreating into daydreams and nostalgia. This defense leads them to lose interest in social activities, isolating them from human contact and support.

In some cases, groups feel so weak a connection to society that they deviate by retreating, creating their own communities with deviant subcultures. In 1875, a religious group called the Hutterites rejected the capitalist, competitive way of life, and forbade marriage between their members and outsiders. Early in the same century, another religious group—called the Oneida Community—rejected ideas of marriage, the family, and private property. Sexual relations were unrestricted, and children were raised not by parents, but by the entire adult community. In more recent years, there have been numerous attempts in the U.S. to form "communes" that reject the values and norms that dominate our culture (Kephart, 1987; Zablocki, 1980).

Deviance as Conformity   A second cultural perspective raises the paradoxical idea that deviance may represent conformity. Even when there is general agreement about which behaviors are deviant and how serious each is, the larger and more complex a group or society is, the more likely subgroups are to form, and their subcultures may include norms, values, attitudes, and beliefs that conflict with those of the rest of society (Newman, 1976).

In the U.S., drug use, vandalism, theft, and teenage drinking and sex are defined as deviant behaviors; but adolescent friendship groups are powerful reference groups that may support such behavior. Not yet recognized as adults with important roles to play, adolescents must find other ways to feel rooted in society, and when they turn to peer groups to satisfy their desire to "belong," they encounter strong pressures to conform to adolescent subcultures.

In defiance of an adult society that refuses to grant them full membership, adolescent subcultures often include norms that require *non*conformity to norms and values in the surrounding culture (Coleman, 1961; Douvan and Adelson, 1966). Adolescents who refuse sex, drugs, and alcohol may be treated as deviants by their peers, excluded and ridiculed. Society defines car theft as criminal, but a street gang's subculture may define it as conformity. Reporting crime to the police conforms to legal norms, but criminal subcultures define it as deviant ("ratting," "snitching," and "finking"). For this reason, gang members who act as police informants occupy an insecure position between two cultures, neither of which may be willing to support or protect them.

The pressures to conform in small groups are often rooted in larger subcultures. Miller (1958) spent three years observing lower-class gangs, and concluded that the high value they place on toughness (being brave, daring, and strong), autonomy ("No one tells me what to do"), smartness (ability to "con" others), excitement (risk and danger), and fate (luck), reflected not the subculture of the gang itself, but elements of lower-class culture as a whole.

Miller did not suggest that lower-class subculture values criminal behavior; rather he suggested that values prevalent in that subculture increase the likelihood of behaviors defined as deviant by middle- and

upper-class authorities. We should also note that the lower class has no monopoly on values such as "toughness" and "machismo." In comparison with men in Northern European countries, U.S. men in general place a high value on such characteristics (Block, 1973). Many U.S. presidents have been motivated by the desire to maintain a "tough" and "manly" image (Halberstam, 1972) (see One Step Further 10-1, p. 266).

From this perspective, deviant behaviors are often *learned* through socialization. Toughness and defiance are learned through the same process as politeness and respect for the law. Prostitutes learn their craft just as plumbers, lawyers, and accountants learn theirs (Heyl, 1977). Why, however, are some people socialized into deviance, but others are not?

According to Sutherland's theory of **differential association**, complex societies offer many beliefs, values, and attitudes, including both respect and disrespect for the law (Matsueda, 1982; Sutherland and

The value placed on masculine toughness is not restricted to the lower class.

ONE STEP FURTHER 10-1:
Violence and Social Class

It is a commonly held belief that physical violence is largely a phenomenon of the lower and working classes, but a variety of evidence suggests otherwise in terms of experience and values. In Table B-10-1 the first column of percentages shows that the more income or education people have, the *more* likely they are to ever have been punched or beaten. This is true, also, for whites in comparison with non-whites. The second column shows no clear differences in the likelihood of having been shot at or threatened with a gun.

The third column focuses on values about violence rather than actual experience, and here the differences are even more striking. When people were asked if they could think of situations in which they would approve of a man hitting an adult male stranger, the percentage who could is considerably higher among those with more income or education and among whites. Such findings raise questions not only about the kind of public violence most often associated with crime, but also with more hidden violence such as child and spouse abuse (see Chapters 13 and 15).

Table B-10-1

| | PERCENT WHO HAVE EVER BEEN | | |
SOCIAL CHARACTERISTICS	Punched or Beaten	Shot At or Threatened with a Gun	Approve of Hitting?[1]
Income			
Less than $4,000	37%	24%	59%
$4,000–$12,999	33%	18%	58%
$13,000–$33,999	36%	21%	68%
$34,000 or more	43%	19%	75%
Education			
Less than high school graduate	34%	23%	50%
High school graduate	35%	19%	66%
Some college	36%	17%	75%
College degree	39%	18%	80%
More than college	45%	24%	83%
Race			
Nonwhite	32%	23%	50%
White	37%	20%	69%

[1]"Can you imagine a situation in which you would approve of a man punching an adult male stranger?" Percent answering "yes."

Source: Computed from raw 1986 General Social Survey data.

Cressey, 1978). Which ideas we adopt depends on the intensity of our exposure to competing alternatives. If we grow up associating primarily with professional thieves who define burglary as acceptable, we are more likely to accept it as legitimate. In the same way, if our parents regard income tax evasion as acceptable, we are likely to evade taxes ourselves, *unless we experience more intense exposure to alternatives.* Complex societies contribute to deviance by fostering the formation of subcultures whose ideas may conflict with the surrounding culture. Complex cultures also contain a variety of conflicting standards; and differences in exposure to competing alternatives during socialization produce different definitions of acceptable behavior.

Although cultural explanations reveal that deviant behaviors are often learned and transmitted from one generation to the next, they do not explain where such patterns come from in the first place. Why would anyone choose crime as an occupation? Why do some groups require members to conform to norms and values that society defines as deviant? A sociological response to such questions depends on a second major concept in the sociological perspective—social structure.

Deviance and Social Structure

If we focus on how statuses and roles limit people's choices, three structural theories help explain deviant behavior. First, people may violate norms from a sense of *duty*—because they believe that the legitimate demands of their roles require it. Second, societies can create deviant roles by *labeling* people as deviants and expecting them to violate norms. Third, people may find themselves in situations in which they can achieve legitimate goals only by violating norms—in other words, situations in which legitimate means will not work. The following section discusses each of these theories in turn.

Deviance as Duty According to the Uniform Code of Military Justice, U.S. soldiers are required to obey the orders of their superiors; during wartime, the penalty for disobedience is death. This raises a serious dilemma: What happens when a commander orders troops to commit illegal acts?

In Vietnam a platoon of U.S. soldiers, demoralized and frustrated by ambushes, booby traps, and an elusive enemy, wandered into the village of My Lai (Hersch, 1970). Most of the residents were women, children, and old men, and there was no reason to believe they threatened the soldiers in any way. Yet, within minutes, the GI's had killed several Vietnamese, and shortly thereafter both the platoon leader and the company commander ordered the soldiers to kill everyone in the village.

By day's end, between 450 and 500 civilians had been murdered in spite of their cries and pleas for

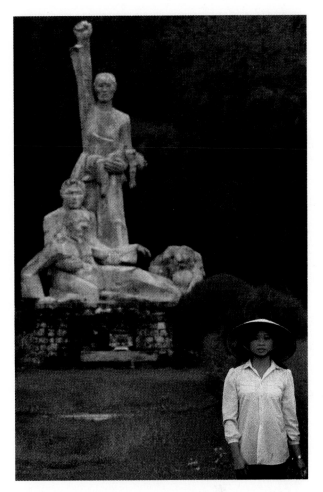

Pham Thic Trinh was nine years old when her entire family and the population of My Lai was massacred. She played dead by crawling beneath the bodies of her parents. Here she stands in 1988 in front of a memorial in My Lai. William Calley, the lieutenant who was held primarily responsible for the killings, was placed under house arrest for three years. More than twenty years later, Trinh tends the monument and lives with her nightmares.

mercy. They were stabbed, thrown down wells, pushed into ditches and shot, or forced into huts and then blown up with grenades.

> One further incident stood out in many GIs' minds: seconds after the shooting stopped, a bloodied but unhurt two-year-old boy miraculously crawled out of the ditch, crying. He began running toward the hamlet. Someone hollered, "There's a kid." There was a long pause. Then Calley ran back, grabbed the child, threw him back in the ditch and shot him. (Hersch, 1970, p. 74)

Puzzles: At What Point Would You Stop Obeying Legitimate Orders?

If the president of the United States ordered you to push a button that would execute a stranger for no good reason that you could see, would you do it?

If your answer is "no," pay particular attention to the following discussion of the Milgram experiment, for it suggests that you may not know yourself as well as you think you do.

How could people do this? Although their state of mind helps explain their behavior, one thing is clear: had their leaders not ordered them to fire, or had they ordered them *not* to fire, the massacre never would have happened.

From a sociological point of view, the soldiers did their duty by obeying orders. As Hersch noted, those who did not like what was happening "kept their thoughts to themselves," for disobeying orders during wartime is a serious crime. It seems incredible to most people that anyone would obey such orders, and yet, as Milgram discovered in his classic experiments, we tend to violate norms when an authority we define as legitimate tells us to.

Milgram (1965) conducted an experiment in which people volunteered to assist in a "learning experiment" at a prestigious university. Each subject (who was paid to participate) was told by a man dressed in an official-looking white lab coat that researchers were interested in the effects of punishment on learning.

The subjects stood in a small room equipped with a large electronic panel with a series of 30 buttons, each of which, they were told, delivered increasingly severe shocks to a man strapped to a chair in the next room. The lowest shock level (15 volts) was labeled "SLIGHT SHOCK," the third highest (420 volts) was labeled "DANGER: SEVERE SHOCK," and the last two switches (435 and 450 volts) had the ominous label "XXX." Subjects were told to read a list of words to the "learner" in the next room, and to punish him with shocks when he failed to recite the list correctly. (In fact, the "learner" worked for Milgram and there were no actual shocks.) A window allowed each "teacher" to see the "learner."

The learner consistently failed, and each time the experimenter told the teacher to increase the shock by 15 volts. At 75 volts, the learner grunted, and by 150 volts, he banged on the walls and begged to be released. When subjects protested to the experimenter, they were told, "The experiment requires you to continue" or "You have no other choice; you must go on." The learner said he had a weak heart, and after 330 volts was reached, he no longer responded at all. How do you think these ordinary people behaved? Did they refuse to endanger a person's life in the name of scientific research?

Milgram expected few subjects to deliver what they believed to be dangerous shocks, and a sample of 40 psychiatrists predicted that most would stop at the 150-volt level and that only a rare neurotic individual would deliver the maximum shock (Milgram, 1974). In fact, however, almost *two-thirds* of the subjects were fully obedient and went all the way to the most dangerous level. In doing so, they showed a great deal of anxiety—verbally attacking the experimenter, twitching or laughing nervously—but, nonetheless, most did as they were told.

Some argue that Milgram's experiment was unethical, that he did not have the right to manipulate people's beliefs and coerce them into committing what they believed were harmful acts (Baumrind, 1964; Mixon, 1972). In fact, only 2 percent of the subjects expressed regret that they had participated; the rest said they were glad.

Milgram's experiment dramatically illustrates the ability of authorities to force people to violate norms. When presidents order illegal wiretaps or the assassination of foreign leaders, or when business executives order subordinates to fire an employee without good reason, they are likely to be obeyed by people who define obedience to legitimate authority as part of their role obligations.

In the simplest sense, then, social structure often encourages deviance by giving some people the authority to demand deviant behavior from subordinates as a requirement for successful role performance (see Clinard, 1983). Deviant behavior is also encouraged, however, when societies label deviance as a social status whose role includes the violation of norms.

The Power of Labels   When people steal, they are usually punished if discovered; but the social response to deviance often goes beyond mere punishment. In some cases, both the actor *and* the behavior are labeled as deviant: the person who steals is labeled a "thief," or the student who cheats is labeled a "cheater." According to the **social labeling perspective**, societies often reinforce their boundaries by labeling *people* as deviants as well as their behavior. In this sense, behaviors such as theft, cheating, or drug use are transformed into statuses that people may make part of their social identities (Becker, 1964, 1973).

Deviant acts that are performed before any labels are applied (such as trying cocaine while out with your friends) are called **primary deviance**. People— including those who perform the act—do not consider primary deviance to be deviant, either because they are unaware of the behavior or because they think it is trivial. If you were caught and arrested, however, and referred to and treated as a "junkie" and a criminal, you might find that the label itself fosters further deviance—called **secondary deviance** (Lemert, 1951). If people who shun drug use also shun you once the label of junkie is applied, then you are more likely to seek the company of others who are also labeled as junkies; and at this point you might be on your way to a career of deviance and repeated arrests. Secondary deviance, then, may have nothing to do with the original cause of the primary deviance—giving in to peer pressure to use drugs. Secondary deviance represents a way of responding to or defending against the labeling and punishment that occur when primary deviance is discovered.

As the case of the Saints and the Roughnecks showed, high school students are often labeled as "troublemakers" or "good students." When a student is labeled a troublemaker, it alters people's expectations and interpretations of behavior: if teachers catch a "troublemaker" outside of class without a pass, they are likely to assume the student is doing something wrong. Finding a "good student" under the same circumstances, however, teachers are more likely to assume the student is there for a good reason (Balch and Kelly, 1974).

Although students who get into trouble may not initially define themselves as deviant people, cultural labels are sticky, and make it difficult for people to resist seeing themselves as others see them—the looking-glass self (see Link, 1987). As Hawthorne wrote in *The Scarlet Letter*, his novel about a colonial woman labeled an "adulteress" by her community,

No man, for any considerable period, can wear one face to himself, and another to the multitude, without finally getting bewildered as to which may be the true.

In some cases, a deviant status becomes a master status. Others use stereotypes attached to the deviant master status to form expectations, interpret the deviant's behavior, and decide how to respond. When former convicts apply for jobs they often find that their status as "ex-cons" overshadows all others in the eyes of potential employers (Schwartz and Skolnick, 1962).

Thus, latent statuses may become the most important part of a person's current status set, a fact that can lead to secondary deviance whether or not stigmatized people actually accept the label as part of their social identities. If the "thief" or "drug addict" label excludes them from jobs they may then have to steal in order to survive. Whether or not individuals accept the deviant label, secondary deviance is an example of a self-fulfilling prophecy: people are treated in ways that increase the chances that they will violate norms, and they do.

In a dramatic illustration of the power of cultural labels, Rosenhan (1973) planted volunteer "patients" in 12 different mental hospitals. Each reported a simple symptom—hearing a voice that said "empty," "hollow," and "thud." All were admitted with diagnoses of schizophrenia, and all *stopped reporting symptoms immediately after being admitted as patients*. They openly made written observations of ward activity, and when asked how they felt, replied that they felt fine and no longer heard voices.

"Despite their public show of 'sanity,' the pseudopatients were never detected" by the hospital staff. They were hospitalized for an average of 19 days (some as long as 52 days) and all were discharged with diagnoses of "schizophrenia in remission." Once the "mentally ill" label was applied, the staff used it to interpret patients' behavior. Note taking was described as "behavior indicative of psychological disturbance." When a "patient" paced up and down a corridor, a nurse asked, "Are you nervous?" "No. Bored," he replied. When a psychiatrist saw a group of patients sitting outside the lunchroom half an hour before mealtime, he remarked to other staff members that this was a compulsive behavior typical of schizophrenics, ignoring the fact that meals are one of the few events that interrupt the boredom of hospital life.

Rosenhan's study clearly shows the power of labels such as "crazy" and "schizophrenic":

Once the impression has been formed that the patient is schizophrenic, the expectation is that he will continue to be schizophrenic. When a sufficient amount

Jack Nicholson, in the movie version of One Flew Over the Cuckoo's Nest, *portrayed an inmate of a mental institution who heroically resisted the labeling and the consequent dehumanization imposed upon him and the other patients by the staff.*

of time has passed, during which the patient has done nothing bizarre, he is considered to be in remission and available for discharge. But the label endures beyond discharge. . . . Such labels, conferred by mental health professionals, are as influential on the patient as they are on his relatives and friends, and it should not surprise anyone that the diagnosis acts on all of them as a self-fulfilling prophecy. Eventually, the patient himself accepts the diagnosis, with all of its surplus meanings and expectations, and behaves accordingly. (pp. 253–254)

Some authors use the labeling perspective to argue that "mental illness" is as much a social role that is forced upon people as it is an illness (Scheff, 1975, 1984; Szasz, 1987). Others note, however, that although such labels have devastating effects on people, they cannot account for the years of serious emotional disturbance that precede most mental hospital admissions. As Clausen (1976) wrote:

It is probably true that in the past we launched many acutely disturbed persons on careers of chronic mental illness by keeping them in mental hospitals until every spark of motivation and zest for life had been snuffed out. But mental illness existed long before psychiatry and mental hospitals, and it simply will not do to blame psychosis on labeling. (p. 127)

When It Pays to Break the Rules Although labeling limits people's access to legitimate ways of achieving goals, such limitations also exist on a broader level. A major characteristic of social structures is the distribution of opportunities to attain rewards such as wealth. Roles include values that define goals, but they also include norms that define appropriate *means* for achieving goals. From a structural perspective, the likelihood of deviance depends on our access to legitimate means for achieving goals, the *adequacy* of legitimate means, and our access to illegitimate means. In other words, we are more likely to commit deviant acts if we cannot achieve goals in legitimate ways and if we can achieve them in illegitimate ways.

Earlier, we saw how social responses to deviance depend in part on the relationship between deviant acts and cultural values. "Innovators" support values, but reject norms by using deviant methods to achieve them. This approach helps explain the *causes* of deviance as well as social responses to it.

Merton (1938) expanded Durkheim's concept of anomie to pose a fundamental question about structural causes of deviance: What happens when we share important values but, because of our statuses, are cut off from socially legitimate ways of achieving them? Many poor people share the value of financial success and yet find themselves hopelessly cut off from well-paying jobs. They tend to have few marketable skills, are chronically unemployed, and have poor schooling opportunities. How then are they to share in the "American dream" of prosperity and security?

Merton argued that we often conform to norms when we do not *need* to break laws in order to get what we want, and we may violate norms when our social statuses leave us no alternative but to change our values and abandon our goals. People who are limited in this way are more likely to find new ways to achieve goals, and these are often defined as deviant by elites who *do* have access to legitimate means. Cultures that emphasize that everyone can and should succeed ("*Any* citizen can become president") exert strong pressures on disadvantaged people to resort to crime.

Given the American stigmatization of manual labor, *which has been found to hold rather uniformly in all social classes*, and the absence of realistic opportunities for advancement beyond this level, the result is a marked tendency toward deviant behavior. (Merton, 1968, p. 199)

In his study of crime rates in large U.S. metropolitan areas, Jacobs (1981) found that levels of property crime—burglary and larceny—tended to be higher in areas in which income inequality was the greatest. Property crime rates were *not* related, however, to the absolute levels of poverty—only to the size of the gap between the rich, the poor, and those in the middle.

Merton's theory is important because it shows how an aspect of social structures—the **opportunity structure**—distributes legitimate opportunities among the occupants of different statuses and predicts that deviance is more common when legitimate means for achieving important values are unequally distributed.

Conflict theory also explains deviance as a response to political and economic conditions. Industrial societies—capitalist societies in particular—depend on consumers to buy the products produced by the system, most of them luxuries not necessary for survival. Capitalism also depends on workers who are willing to spend their lives at dull, tedious, unrewarding jobs; and in order to motivate them, capitalists depend on large pools of impoverished people who stand ready to take the jobs of dissatisfied workers ("If you don't like this job, there are plenty of people who will take your place") (Bottomore and Rubel, 1965; Marx, 1867; Marx and Engels, 1846).

Industrial societies create "both the desire to consume *and*—for a large mass of people—an inability to earn the money necessary to purchase items they have been taught to want" (Chambliss, 1978, p. 192). Many crimes are committed because the opportunity structure limits people's opportunities *without* limiting their goals. Crime is not caused simply by "deviant subcultures" that create and support "criminal personalities" and disrespect for the law. It also depends on values and the structural distribution of opportunities for achieving them.

It is important to point out that Merton relies on a functional approach by identifying how the "normal" operation of societies creates deviance. That some conflict theorists explain deviance from the same perspective underscores the fact that the two points of view are complementary, not contradictory, because societies often produce social conflict as part of their normal functioning.

Societies distribute not only legitimate opportunities but illegitimate ones as well (Cloward and Ohlin, 1960). Government officials occupy statuses that allow them to do favors for others in exchange for bribes; computer programmers in banks are in an ideal position to embezzle funds by altering records; police officers who use their discretion in making arrests or responding to calls for help can demand various kinds of "payoffs" ranging from bribes from criminals to free services from local merchants who want to ensure adequate protection. Regardless of individual motives and personalities, social structures create opportunities and temptations that increase the likelihood of certain types of deviance.

Social structure also contributes to deviance when culturally defined ways of achieving goals are *available*, but *inadequate*. The most important goals of police officers are to prevent crime and apprehend criminals; and, on every level, they are rewarded only when they produce results. An officer's role also includes norms that define legitimate *means* for controlling crime. In the U.S., they are not allowed to torture prisoners, to wiretap telephones without a court order, to arrest people without informing them of their rights, or to search people's homes without due cause.

The best efforts of police to control crime, however, are largely unsuccessful. If you were a police officer, what would you do in the face of repeated failures to achieve the goals that define your job? Many officers believe that their roles limit them so severely that it is impossible for them to control crime. Public pressures on police provide incentives for them to *break laws in the name of enforcing the law* (Reiss, 1971; Skolnick, 1975). (As recent news stories make clear, police officers in many societies are not as restrained as they are in the U.S. Torture has been widely used by authorities in many countries, including Chile, Argentina, Uruguay, Iran, and the Philippines.)

Maximizing business profits is a value in our culture, in pursuit of which executives may bribe public officials, misrepresent income to tax collectors, falsely advertise products, or dispose of hazardous wastes in economical but dangerous ways. Many corporations contend that if they obeyed all antipollution laws, they could not survive and many jobs would be lost. Faced with bankruptcy, some business owners hire arsonists to burn their buildings so that they can collect insurance payments. Similarly, government agencies have been known to illegally wiretap telephones or break into homes or offices in search of information—all in the name of "national security."

Another response to the inadequacy of legitimate means is **ritualism**—which results when people, convinced they cannot achieve their goals, "go through the motions" by conforming to norms without fully supporting the values those norms support (Merton, 1938, 1968). Office workers who see no hope for promotion may simply show up each day and do no more than their roles require of them. College students who believe their grades will be mediocre no matter how hard they work may also "give up" by lowering their aspirations and working only enough to get passing grades. Although ritualism is often not viewed as true deviance (since norms are obeyed), it clearly poses a problem for societies.

A sociological approach helps us understand why some people conform to norms and others deviate from them, but additional questions remain: Why do *rates* of deviant behavior change over time and why is deviance more likely in some societies than in others? Such questions require us to think of culture and social structure in larger terms: How do the characteristics of populations and their ecological relationship to physical environments affect rates of deviant behavior in societies?

Population, Ecology, and Deviance

Rates of crime vary according to population characteristics such as age, urbanization, complexity, diversity, and equality. Between 1960 and 1985, crime rates in the U.S. tripled. During this same period, the population became younger (as the percentage of people 14 to 24 years old increased by a fifth) and 5 percent more urban (U.S. Census Bureau, 1986a). Some of the increase in crime may be the result of an increasingly young, urban population (Blumstein and Nagin, 1974; Cohen and Land, 1987).

Population characteristics also help explain variations in crime rates among social categories. Because birth rates are higher among blacks than among whites, the black population has a higher percentage of young people (U.S. Census Bureau, 1987a). Blacks are also more likely to live in cities. The distribution of blacks by age and residence contributes to higher rates of deviance. (Remember, however, that these statements do *not* include white-collar crime, most of which is committed by adults and rarely included in official crime statistics.)

Differences in age structures and urbanization also suggest a partial explanation for cross-cultural differences in crime. Crime rates in European countries, for example, are generally lower than in the U.S. Only one-fifth of the people of Europe live in large cities, compared with more than a third of all Americans (Goldstein and Sly, 1977; U.S. Census Bureau, 1986). Decades of low birth rates have also made European populations considerably older than the U.S. population.

Durkheim's theory of anomie suggests that deviance is more likely when social cohesion is low, and this implies that large, complex societies with many subcultures will have higher rates of deviance. It also suggests that highly *mobile* societies, in which people frequently move, will have more deviance because people will have weaker ties to communities and their norms. The U.S. has one of the most heterogeneous and mobile populations in the world, as well as one of the highest crime rates. More than one-third of the population changes residence every three years, producing an average of 13 moves in each person's lifetime (Long and Boertlein, 1976).

Iceland provides a particularly interesting comparison, for its population is homogeneous and stationary (the vast majority of its 230,000 inhabitants are native born and share a common heritage). There is only one jail in the entire country, and it is rarely used (Markham, 1982).

Iceland's low crime rate is not due simply to a small, homogeneous population, however, for Iceland's opportunity structure is far more egalitarian than that of the U.S. The Icelandic standard of living is considerably higher, and prosperity is distributed far more evenly among Icelandic citizens. Literacy is universal and unemployment is virtually nonexistent. These cultural and structural differences offer a partial explanation for Iceland's relatively low rate of crime.

It is important to emphasize the *tentative* nature of such explanations: evidence from so few comparisons is not conclusive, and the effects of population and ecology are complex. Japan is more urban than the U.S. but its crime rates are lower, not higher. Why? One explanation is that the Japanese population is more culturally homogeneous, resulting in greater social cohesion. No single factor operates alone: the high rate of crime in the U.S. is produced, in part, by a *combination* of social and ecological factors.

SOCIAL CONSEQUENCES OF DEVIANCE

Most of this chapter has focused on descriptions and explanations of deviance (for a summary, see the box on p. 273). We come now to a final question: What are the social consequences of deviance?

Much deviant behavior exacts enormous costs from individuals, groups, and societies. In the U.S. in 1985, 19,000 people were murdered and 5 million assaulted—including 180,000 sexual assaults (U.S. Census Bureau, 1986a). In 1987, 38 percent of adults said they were afraid to walk alone at night within a mile of their homes (Davis and Smith, 1987).

Crime not only causes suffering and fear, it results in enormous economic losses. Seventeen million people are robbed each year; automobile thefts in New York City alone amount to annual losses exceeding $400 million (Basler, 1982); and, nationally, the profits of syndicated crime amount to tens of billions of dollars a year. Conservative estimates put annual losses from white-collar crimes such as embezzlement and tax evasion at more than $250 million a *day*

Causes of Deviance: A Summary

Cultural Explanations

Anomie (Durkheim)
    Confusion, disagreement, ambiguity
    Weak social ties of individuals or groups to society

Deviance as Conformity
    Socialization in subcultures (Miller)
    Differential association in complex cultures (Sutherland)

Social Structural Explanations

Deviance and role behavior
    When legitimate roles require deviant behavior
    Social creation of "deviant roles"—labeling (Becker)
        "Primary" and "secondary" deviance

Deviance and oportunity structures
    Unequal access to legitimate means (Merton)
    Unequal access to illegitimate means (Cloward and Ohlin)
    Inadequacy of legitimate means

Population and Ecological Explanations

Age of population
Urbanization
Diversity of population
Size, complexity, and formation of subcultures
Mobility and cohesion

(Meier and Short, 1982). Even "victimless" crimes such as alcoholism cause annual losses in the billions of dollars.

The costs of deviance are not this simple, however, for the line between "victim" and "offender" is often unclear. Criminal behavior results in the labeling and punishing of thousands of lower-class, nonwhite people; and thousands of people labeled as "mentally ill" are forcibly committed to mental institutions. Homosexuals are regularly discriminated against in housing and jobs—40 percent of U.S. adults believe homosexuals should be denied teaching jobs in colleges and universities. Almost half would also bar communists and atheists from college faculties (Davis and Smith, 1987). Deviants themselves are often victims not only of social inequality, but of cultural stereotypes and stigmas as well.

Many people benefit from deviance. Tens of thousands of jobs depend on crime, for without it there would be no need for police officers, criminal lawyers, judges, prison guards, probation officers, locksmiths, and the thousands of people who record and report criminal activity. Although it is in the interests of some of these people to diminish crime (if only to justify keeping their jobs), it is not in their interests to eradicate it completely (Chambliss, 1978).

Furthermore, behaviors that some regard as problems are regarded by others as *solutions* to problems (Merton, 1976a). Homosexuality, adultery, divorce, drug use, alcoholism, prostitution, and tax evasion are culturally defined as deviant behaviors that constitute social problems. Yet, divorce is a common solution to the problem of unsatisfying and destructive marriages, homosexuality allows millions of people to express themselves sexually, and families and businesses often rely on tax evasion in order to survive.

Conformity is important because it gives social life a sense of predictability, continuity, and stability. As important as these manifest functions of conformity are, however, there are also latent dysfunctions that no group or society can afford to ignore. Too much conformity tends to stifle creativity and constructive criticism. Conformity can also be disastrous when values and norms are destructive as in the case of racism. Deviance also has unanticipated consequences, some of which are functional. Nonconformity stimulates social change by challenging the status quo (Janeway, 1987). The well-being of society and its members, then, depends on a delicate balance between deviance and conformity.

SUMMARY

1. Deviance is any appearance or behavior that violates a norm; conformity is obedience to norms. What most people actually do is "the norm," but the rarity of a behavior does not make it deviant. Because deviance is a cultural creation, the classification of behaviors as deviant varies historically and between cultures.

2. The functional perspective views deviant acts as violations of a moral consensus, and outraged responses of citizens as beneficial for social cohesion. The conflict perspective argues that deviance reflects social inequality, and that the law protects the interests of the powerful rather than a moral consensus.

3. Nonconformists openly violate norms in order to bring about positive change. Nonconformists may be either rebels who challenge both norms and values, or innovators who accept values but reject the norms that define legitimate means for achieving them. Aberrance is the secret violation of norms for personal gain. It may be either retreatist, in which a person withdraws from social life by rejecting values and norms without offering alternatives, or innovative, in which a person secretly uses illegitimate means to attain goals.

4. A stigma is a personal characteristic that others treat as deviant.

5. Some violations of law (overparking) are not defined as crimes or as deviance; many forms of deviance (lying to a friend) are not defined as crimes; and an act defined as criminal may be regarded as normal in a subculture.

6. Males are more likely than females to commit crimes. Young people are more likely to commit many traditional crimes such as burglary, but older people are more likely to commit white-collar crimes. Nonwhites and the poor are more likely than whites and the nonpoor to be arrested; but most evidence shows that class and race differences in crime influence the kinds of crime committed, not the amount. Crime is more common in urban areas than in suburban or rural areas, but the difference is greater for violent crimes than for those against property, and has been shrinking.

7. Men are more likely than women to be victimized by crime, except in the case of sexual assault. Nonwhites are more likely to be victimized than whites, and young people are more vulnerable than older people.

8. Relationships among criminals vary in complexity. Both criminals and victims may be either individuals or groups, and most victims of violence know their assailant. Some crimes—such as prostitution—are victimless, representing an offense against society.

9. Social class and race affect the likelihood of being arrested, prosecuted, and convicted of a crime, as well as the length of sentence. At all stages, the criminal justice system discriminates against blacks and lower-class people.

10. The criminal justice system responds to crime with punishment, rehabilitation, and isolation of criminals from society. Most evidence indicates that these do not control crime.

11. Culture contributes to deviance in several ways, the most basic of which is the definition of deviant acts. When norms are unclear or disputed, or when individuals are weakly attached to their society, anomie results, and deviance is more likely to occur. Deviance may also be conformity to subcultural values and norms that support behavior regarded as deviant in the surrounding society. In complex cultures, people are exposed to competing standards, and differential association helps explain why some adopt cultural ideas that are defined as deviant in society at large.

12. Social structure also contributes to deviance. Deviance is sometimes required in the performance of legitimate roles.

13. Primary deviance is behavior that people do not treat as deviant—either because they are unaware of it or they regard it as trivial. Secondary deviance occurs when people are labeled and treated as deviant, and "deviant" becomes an important part of their identity. This encourages secondary deviance, which conforms to people's expectations of those labeled deviant.

14. Structure also causes deviance by unequally distributing legitimate opportunities for achieving goals; by creating illegitimate opportunities for some status occupants; and by providing inadequate means for achieving goals.

15. In general, deviance is more likely in populations that are large, diverse, young, and urban.

16. Deviance results in negative consequences, including injury, fear, and economic loss. Widespread deviance weakens group boundaries and lowers social cohesion. Deviance also damages groups and individuals identified as deviant. Despite the costs of deviance, some benefit by holding jobs designed to record and control it.

KEY TERMS

anomie   264
collective conscience   250
conformity   247
crime   254

    syndicated crime   259
    victimless crime   259
    white-collar crime   256

criminal justice system   260

    degradation ceremony   263
    total institution   263

deviance   247

    aberrance   251
    innovation   251
    nonconformity   251
    rebellion   251
    retreatism   252
    ritualism   271
    stigma   251, 253

differential association   265
"the norm"   247
social control   247
opportunity structure   271
social labeling perspective   269

    primary deviance   269
    secondary deviance   269

Looking Elsewhere

Having studied Chapter 10, you might want to look at related discussions in *Human Arrangements*, which include
- the scientific validity of crime statistics as measures of criminal activity (Ch. 2, pp. 33–34)
- pressures to conform in groups (Chapter 8, pp. 189–90)
- conformity as a source of power in groups (Chapter 8, p. 195)
- rites of passage and deviance among the young (Chapter 14, pp. 383–84, 391)
- peer pressure and deviance (Chapter 6, pp. 151–52)
- family violence (Chapter 15, pp. 423–25)
- deviance among scientists (Chapter 17, pp. 466–67)
- civil disobedience and democracy (Chapter 19, p. 523)
- deviance as a source of religious change (Chapter 20, pp. 552–53)

RECOMMENDED READINGS

BOWERS, W. J. (1984). *Legal homicide: Death as punishment in America, 1964–1982.* Boston: Northeastern University Press. A passionate and unusually thorough discussion of the uses and effects of the death penalty.

GOFFMAN, E. (1963). *Stigma: Notes on the management of a spoiled identity.* Englewood Cliffs, NJ: Prentice-Hall.

KADISH, S. H. (1983). *Encyclopedia of crime and justice* (3 Vols.). New York: Free Press. An extraordinarily comprehensive, interdisciplinary summary of what is known about criminal behavior and social responses to it.

REASONS, C. E., and RICH, R. M. (Eds.). (1978). *The sociology of law: A conflict perspective.* Toronto: Butterworths. A provocative set of articles that examine the ways in which the law and definitions of deviance help maintain social inequality and oppression.

RUTTER, M. and GILLER, H. (1984). *Juvenile delinquency: Trends and perspectives.* New York: Guilford Press. An excellent survey of the causes and consequences of juvenile delinquency.

FOUR

Social Stratification

FEW AREAS OF SOCIAL life provoke as much strong feeling and conflict as social inequality. The gulf that separates rich and poor, the damage to individuals, families, communities, and societies caused by racial, ethnic, and gender prejudice and discrimination—all touch some of our most deeply held values about justice and fairness. The problem is far from simple, however, for in many societies, including the United States, the issue of how rewards such as wealth, power, and prestige are distributed also touches deeply held values about individualism, hard work, self-reliance, and the importance of merit. In short, while there is widespread support for justice and fairness in our society, there is also strong support for cultural and structural arrangements that produce inequality, in spite of the damage it inflicts on millions of people's lives.

We begin with Chapter 11, a detailed examination of the general problem of social stratification—the process through which wealth, power, and prestige are distributed. We will look at the nature and extent of inequality both within societies and between them and consider some major theories that try to explain why inequality exists at all. We will also look at the social processes through which some people gain a greater share of wealth, power, and prestige than others. In the remaining three chapters of Part Four we look at prejudice, discrimination, and social inequality based on the ascribed statuses of race, ethnicity, gender, and age.

Stratification, Inequality, and Social Class

Marx: Class, Production, and Social Relationships

Weber: Class, Prestige, and Power

Comparing Marx and Weber:
The Case of Carol, Susan, and George

Explaining Inequality

The Functional View:
Social Structure and Cultural Values

The Conflict Perspective:
To Each According to the Ability to Take

Culture, Ideology, and Inequality

Social Stratification in the United States

From Marx's Perspective

Through Weber's Eyes: Dimensions of Inequality

Social Mobility: Going Up and Going Down

How Much Mobility?

Who Goes Up and Who Goes Down?

Is Mobility an Illusion?

Marx: Mobility as an Uninteresting Problem

International Stratification

Varieties of Inequality within Societies

Inequality between Societies

Prospects for Change

Mobility and Equal Opportunity

Equality and Classlessness

11 Social Stratification: Who Gets What, and Why?

All societies produce rewards that are valued in their culture. Some are possessions such as land, automobiles, or buildings; money represents the power to buy possessions and services. Other rewards, such as respect, are nonmaterial, but are very important to us.

The central question is this: How do societies distribute rewards among their members? In other words, who gets what, and why? In this chapter, we use the functional and conflict perspectives to describe and explain inequality in societies, and apply both to the U.S. and other societies. We also look at the causes and consequences of inequality *among* societies.

STRATIFICATION, INEQUALITY, AND SOCIAL CLASS

"Justice," "fairness," "respect," "equality," "discrimination," "exploitation," and "oppression"—these are words that evoke strong feelings because they refer to fundamental aspects of social life: how we are treated by other people, how we treat them, and how we share in wealth, power, and prestige. The concept of **social stratification** refers to the social structures through which rewards are distributed unequally among the occupants of different statuses.

The definition of stratification has three aspects that you should understand before going on. First, stratification is a social *process*, even though the word calls up images of layers of rock. Societies continually sort people into different statuses and distribute rewards among them.

Second, a society is stratified only if wealth, power, and prestige are distributed unequally according to people's social statuses—age, gender, education, occupation, and ethnicity. If we took all the income produced in the U.S. during each year and distributed it through a lottery that gave more to some than others, the distribution of income would be unequal but *not* stratified. The difference is that in a stratified society rewards are distributed *systematically* according to social status, not randomly.

Third, *what* is distributed in a society varies according to cultural values. In a poor village society, food and clothing may be the major rewards, while in wealthier, more complex societies, political power, leisure time, health care, and luxuries are also distributed.

Stratification has long been a major area of sociological analysis because few aspects of social environments affect the quality of people's lives so profoundly. Our positions in stratified societies make the difference between respect and contempt, full stomachs and starvation, keeping warm and freezing during harsh winters, working and being unemployed, living long and dying young, living in hope and in despair, controlling our own lives and being controlled by others.

The most important concept in the study of stratification is *social class*, an idea developed most notably by Karl Marx and Max Weber. Their perspectives differ in important ways, however, and lead to different views of stratification.

Marx: Class, Production, and Social Relationships

To Marx, the most basic human activity is the production of necessities such as food, clothing, and shelter, and he focused on two key questions about that process: How do societies produce goods and services and how does the relationship between people and the ways in which goods are produced affect their lives?

Because Marx (1867) was primarily interested in how societies produce goods, he defined **social class** as an aggregate of people who occupy similar positions in relation to the production process. Although he identified several social classes, the most important are the **capitalists** (the **bourgeoisie**), who own the means of production (capital) such as factories, and the **workers** (the **proletariat**), who survive by selling their *labor power* to capitalists.

The distinction between labor and labor power is important in Marx's theories. **Labor** refers to the production of products and services that can either be *used* (shoes to wear, food to eat) or *exchanged* for something else (one farmer trades surplus wheat for another's surplus milk, or farmers sell crops or milk in the marketplace).

Farm workers, however, who spend their days picking lettuce that grows in someone else's fields are not selling their labor. It is not as if they pick the lettuce and "sell" it to the farmers, who then sell it on the market. The workers do not own the lettuce, the fields, or the machinery. What, then, *do* they sell? They sell their *time* in exchange for *wages*. They control neither what they do with that time nor what becomes of the products. Workers sell their **labor power**—so many dollars for each day's work—and not their labor. Unlike labor, labor power represents only the *potential* to produce something, not production itself.

In any society, Marx argued, the production process determines social relationships, and to understand social life we must pay attention to people's positions

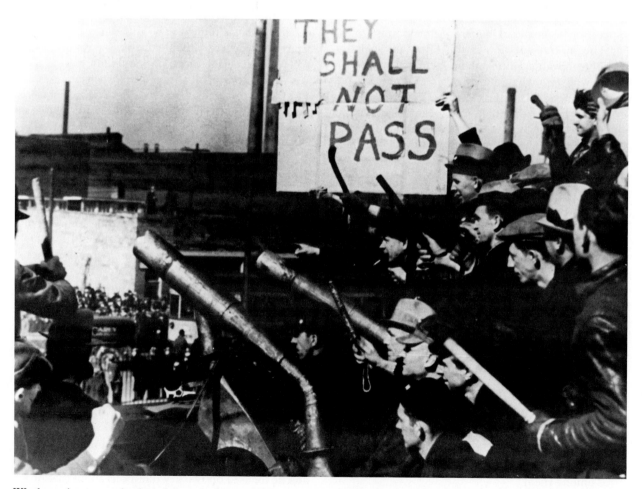

Workers, having only their labor power to sell, can control production by going on strike to prevent the use of capital to produce goods. Strikes occasionally involve armed confrontations. During this 1935 strike at Chrysler, workers armed themselves with billy clubs and auto parts to keep away "scabs"—replacement workers hired by management to break strikes.

in those relationships. Those who control the means of production also control jobs, while workers must sell their labor power for whatever wages they can get—or not work at all. When the means of production are privately owned, the capitalist class is in a position to exploit workers and accumulate wealth and power.

The complexity of modern societies makes it difficult to categorize everyone as either owners or workers. Professionals, such as physicians and lawyers, cannot easily be categorized as capitalists or workers, nor can managers and administrators in government and business (Gagliani, 1981). For this reason, it makes more sense to define classes according to *control* over production, which may or may not take the form of ownership. Wright et al. (1982) use this perspective to divide the labor force into six class categories based on the amount of control workers have over the means of production, other workers, and their own work (Figure 11-1) (see also Wright, 1985). Using data from a national survey, they estimated that roughly 45 percent of all workers are in Marx's working class, 2 percent are capitalists (the bourgeoisie), and 7 percent are "small" capitalists, or what Marx called the "petit bourgeoisie." The remainder are in the "gray areas" of social class: 30 percent are managers or supervisors, 6 percent are small employers, and 10 percent are semiautonomous wage earners such as college professors.

Weber: Class, Prestige, and Power

Whereas Marx focused on how the production process causes inequality, Weber (1946) paid more attention to the levels of wealth, power, and prestige people actually have than to how they come to have it. From Weber's perspective, stratification has three major dimensions—wealth, power, and prestige—and to identify social classes, we must first decide which one we are referring to.

Weber used "**class**" to describe the ability of people to get what they want in the market—their "life chances." A highly paid lawyer, or someone who inherits income-producing property such as land or stocks, is in a higher class than a secretary or factory worker because the lawyer has greater access to the goods and services that are bought and sold in the marketplace (see One Step Further 11-1, p. 282).

Weber referred to power as **party**. The term is important because it reflects the fact that most social power in modern societies is held by large organiza-

Figure 11-1   The American Class Structure from a Marxist Perspective

2% 6% 7% 30% 10% 45%

Percentage of All Workers

Social Class

Bourgeoisie (capitalists): Own means of production; ten or more employees (the owners of a factory; the controlling stock holders of a major corporation)—2%.

Small employers: Own means of production; two to nine employees (an electrical contractor with three employees)—6%.

Petite bourgeoisie (small capitalists): Own means of production; no more than one employee (people who knit sweaters at home and sell them through stores)—7%.

Managers and supervisors: Do not own means of production; moderate to high levels of autonomy and authority (office supervisor; personnel manager; military officer)—30%.

Semiautonomous wage earners: Do not own means of production; low to moderate levels of autonomy and authority (journalist; teacher)—10%.

Proletariat (workers): Do not own means of production; little autonomy; no authority (assembly-line worker; secretary; telephone operator)—45%.

Source: Adapted from Wright et al., 1982.

tions and bureaucracies, and the power of individuals depends very much on their position in such organizations. For prestige, Weber used the term **status** (unlike our earlier usage of this term to stand for a social position).

Unlike Marx's approach to stratification, Weber's leads us to rank people from "upper" to "lower" in terms of these three different dimensions, and people

ONE STEP FURTHER 11-1:
Social Class and the Distribution of Happiness and Unhappiness

Weber described class differences in terms of our "life chances" to get what we want and need in the marketplace. This has obvious effects on well-being when it involves the necessities of life such as food and shelter; but in a society that places as much importance as ours does on the ability to consume luxuries from VCRs and cars to a home, class position can strike at the heart of happiness itself.

The figures in Table B-11-1 show the percentage of people with different class characteristics who describe themselves as generally "very happy" (first column) or "not too happy" (second column). At the top of the first column, 30 percent of those with less than high school diplomas describe themselves as very happy. At the top of the second, 16 percent of this same group report being not too happy.

If you look down the first column, you can see that the more highly placed people are, the more likely they are to say they are very happy. People who say they belong to the working class are only half as likely to say they are very happy as are those who put themselves in the upper class (28 percent as opposed to 55 percent).

The second column shows that class differences in being not too happy are even more striking. People in the lowest class categories are three and five times more likely to say they are not too happy than those in the highest class categories.

Notice that education makes less of a difference than the other three variables. Why do you think this is so?

Table B-11-1

SOCIAL CHARACTERISTICS	PERCENT WHO SAY THEY ARE	
	Very Happy	Not too Happy
Education		
Less than high school graduate	30%	16%
High school graduate	31%	12%
Some college	32%	9%
College graduate	40%	8%
More than college	34%	5%
Income		
Less than $4,000	22%	23%
$4,000–$13,999	26%	17%
$14,000–$34,999	36%	8%
$35,000 or more	38%	5%
Social Class[1]		
Lower	16%	38%
Working	28%	12%
Middle	38%	8%
Upper	55%	8%
Occupational Prestige		
Lower	24%	17%
Lower-middle	28%	13%
Upper-middle	33%	11%
Upper	42%	5%

[1] The class people place themselves in.

Source: Computed from raw 1986 General Social Survey data.

who rank high on one dimension usually rank high on the other two. It takes a great deal of money to be elected to powerful, prestigious political offices in the United States, and the winners tend to be those who spend the most money in their campaigns (U.S. Census Bureau, 1986a).

The tendency of wealth, power, and prestige to go together leads many sociologists to classify people according to **socioeconomic status**, a concept that combines wealth, occupational prestige, and educational attainment into an average rank, usually expressed in terms of "upper class," "middle class," and "lower class" (see Powers, 1982). There are many exceptions, however, that make it difficult to assign people an overall rank. Successful criminals may rank high on wealth and power, but low on prestige; college professors and religious leaders rank high on prestige, but relatively low on wealth and power. Which of these has the highest overall rank in the stratification system and which has the lowest?

Many sociologists (such as Parsons, 1964) believe that prestige is valued more highly than wealth and power. Even if we confine ourselves to this single reward, however, ranking individuals is difficult because each of us occupies a variety of statuses whose levels of prestige may be *inconsistent* with each other (a phenomenon called **status inconsistency**). Physicians rank higher on prestige than do factory workers, and heterosexuals rank higher than homosexuals. Who, then, will be treated with greater respect in a heterosexual society—homosexual physicians or heterosexual factory workers?

One way to identify who is in which social class is simply to *ask* people which class they think they belong to. In 1987, 5 percent of U.S. adults placed themselves in the lower class, 44 percent in the working class, 47 percent in the middle class, and 4 percent in the upper class (Davis and Smith, 1987). This is a useful measure insofar as self-perceptions of class position affect our expectations and behavior, but it is misleading insofar as *actual* positions in a stratification system are more important than *perceived* positions. For example, 6 percent placed themselves in the lower class in 1986, while 13 percent had incomes below the poverty level (Davis and Smith, 1987; U.S. Census Bureau, 1987d). It is doubtful that *thinking* we are not poor is enough to undo the effects of poverty.

In spite of these complications, most sociologists use Weber's framework when they refer to social class—from the upper class, whose members generally rank high in prestige, wealth, and power, to the lower class, whose members rank at the bottom in all three areas. In addition, sociologists commonly make a class distinction based on occupation. The term **blue-collar workers** refers to people—factory workers, carpenters, and plumbers—whose jobs involve manual labor. **White-collar workers**—professionals, business executives, and secretaries—have jobs that are more mental than manual. Blue-collar occupations are also divided according to the skills involved. Carpenters depend on their mental abilities far more than do assembly-line workers. In fact, highly skilled blue-collar workers rely on mental abilities more than do many white-collar workers such as file clerks.

Neither Marx's nor Weber's approach allows us to unambiguously assign everyone to clearly defined categories, but we do not need to do this in order to understand how societies distribute resources and re-

wards. Marx draws attention to how the means by which goods and services are produced affect social relationships; Weber focuses on the *results* of the distribution process in a stratified society: sets of people with similar levels of wealth, power, or prestige. Marx and Weber concentrate on different aspects of a complex social process. The difference between their approaches is important because each leads us to pay attention to fundamentally different aspects of stratification and its effects on people's lives.

Comparing Marx and Weber: The Case of Carol, Susan, and George

Carol is a self-employed plumber in a small city. She owns her own tools, employs an apprentice, and, after paying all her expenses, earns $22,000 a year. She rents a modest apartment, drives an old Ford pickup truck, rarely takes vacations, and usually dresses in jeans and sneakers. She never attended college, is divorced, and her daughter attends a community college.

Susan works on an assembly line in an automobile plant. She earns $25,000 a year, drives a three-year-old car, takes a week off every year, rents a large apartment, and wears jeans and work boots to work. She earned a college degree by taking night courses at a community college. She is married and has three teenage children.

George is a design engineer at Susan's plant. He earns $60,000 a year (plus a bonus in good years), supervises ten employees, owns his own home, drives a new car, takes a three-week vacation each summer, and wears tailored suits. He has a graduate degree in engineering, and his only child attends an Ivy League college.

How would we compare these three people in terms of their relative standing in the U.S. stratification system? From Weber's perspective, George ranks highest because he has more wealth, a graduate degree, a more powerful and prestigious job, enjoys long vacations, and can point with pride to his child's Ivy League education. Susan is a distant second and Carol a close third, because although Susan has a higher income and a college degree, most would rank Carol's occupation higher in prestige (Hodge, Siegel, and Rossi, 1964).

Marx would look at these people very differently, however, for while Carol sells her labor and owns some capital—her plumbing equipment—George and Susan neither own nor control any means of production and must sell their labor power to whoever will pay them for it. From Marx's perspective, Carol is a small capitalist (a "petit bourgeois") and George and Susan are workers; and there may be reasons to prefer Carol's class position to George's and Susan's.

Susan and George have little control over their jobs and, therefore, little control over the rewards they receive by performing them. In the early 1980s, the U.S. automobile industry experienced a deep slump in sales, and unemployment in Detroit was the highest in the nation. While George's position as an engineer is better protected than Susan's, if a company closes an entire plant, virtually everyone except top managers is likely to be laid off. Carol's position has an important advantage, for, as she might put it, "People always say, 'you can never find a plumber when you need one'—and that's me. I can always get work."

Marx and Weber pay attention to fundamentally different aspects of people's positions in stratification systems. Weber focuses on how much wealth, power, and prestige people have, while Marx concentrates on how the production process fosters social relationships through which rewards are distributed. Because our positions in social relationships determine our rights and obligations, Marx's perspective focuses on an important fact that Weber's does not: whatever our class position may be now, our security depends on our control over the social relationships that keep us there.

EXPLAINING INEQUALITY

Sociologists use both the functional and conflict perspectives to explain stratification. There are many ways in which these perspectives generate different explanations of inequality, but they are most useful if we think of them as revealing different aspects of a complex puzzle. If we adopt either of them as "the one true perspective," we inevitably produce an oversimplified and, therefore, distorted explanation.

The Functional View: Social Structure and Cultural Values

Kingsley Davis and Wilbert Moore's (1945) functional theory of stratification focuses on two functions of inequality: first, differences in the level of rewards are necessary to motivate people to perform important roles; second, a complex division of labor requires

unequal distributions of power, because some must coordinate the activities of everyone else.

Davis and Moore pointed out that each culture values some activities more than others, in part because not all activities contribute equally to the well-being of society. They then argued that the most important tasks require abilities that few people possess, and that to prepare themselves, they must undergo rigorous training that requires considerable self-sacrifice. Given these requirements, societies inevitably confront the major problem of motivating people to play important, demanding roles. How do we motivate young people to endure the long years of study required to become physicians? How do we motivate people to run businesses, command armies, or govern societies?

Davis and Moore answer that in order to ensure that the most important roles are adequately performed, we must offer high levels of prestige and wealth to those who are able and willing to perform them. Conversely, jobs which rank lower on cultural scales of values—washing dishes, driving trucks, or assembling cars—will carry lower levels of reward, because it is relatively easy to find people who can and will adequately perform them and there is, therefore, no need to offer special rewards in order to make sure such jobs are performed.

If the Davis-Moore theory is correct, we should find that the most highly trained people receive the highest levels of reward. This is generally true for formal education (Table 2-6, p. 48): for both men and women, more years of schooling mean higher average incomes.

Studies of occupational prestige in the U.S. and elsewhere are also consistent with the Davis-Moore argument. Hodge, Siegel, and Rossi (1964) analyzed national survey data in which adults rated 91 occupations from "excellent" to "poor" in terms of how much respondents "look up to them." The most important finding is that the relative prestige of these occupations has remained essentially unchanged since the first study was done in 1925. The stability of occupational prestige rankings may be interpreted as a reflection of stable cultural evaluations of jobs and their importance to society.

In an international study, Hodge, Treiman, and Rossi (1966) compared prestige ratings of occupations in 31 countries that varied considerably in culture and level of industrialization. In general, there was strong agreement across societies about which occupations are most prestigious, which, the authors suggest, supports the idea that some occupations are more important than others regardless of the society.

> Specialized institutions to carry out political, religious, and economic functions, and to provide for the health, education, and welfare of the population, exist in one form or another in all national societies. Considering the importance of these functions to the maintenance of complex social systems, it is not surprising that occupations at the top of these institutional structures should be highly regarded. (p. 310)

The functional explanation also emphasizes that complex divisions of labor require that some individuals have authority to make decisions about what people do and how resources are distributed and used. To Parsons (1964, 1971), equality of power is simply impossible in any society with a complex division of labor.

While Davis and Moore's theory identifies some important functions of inequality, it has been criticized on six major grounds (Tumin, 1953). First, motivation to perform roles competently is a problem for *all* jobs—if garbage collectors fail to perform, life rapidly becomes intolerable for everyone. That our culture values engineers or business managers more than garbage collectors has less to do with maintaining

society than with maintaining the privileged position of managers and engineers.

Second, Tumin challenged the belief that those who occupy highly rewarded positions have made sacrifices for which they must be compensated with a lifetime of privilege. The costs of professional education are often borne by families and government, not the trainees themselves. Even when they bear a considerable portion of the cost, they quickly earn it back with higher-than-average incomes and then go on to 20 or 30 years of relatively high prestige and income. In addition, while trainees are in professional schools, they enjoy a higher level of prestige than many who work in low-level jobs and have greater opportunities for leisure.

Third, Tumin questioned the belief that wealth and prestige are necessary to motivate people to perform important roles. Davis and Moore minimized the importance of the satisfactions that come with important roles: the challenges, creative opportunities, high levels of control over work conditions, and the chance to make an important contribution to one's community and society.

Fourth, the Davis-Moore theory cannot explain why some people in some statuses—women and blacks—receive fewer rewards regardless of their

Given how difficult life becomes when garbage collectors go on strike, it is not clear that those who work in advertising agencies receive higher income and prestige simply because they contribute to society more.

training. Table 2-6 (p. 48) shows that the average income of women with graduate training is less than that of men who never finished college, and women college graduates average $2,500 less than men who never went beyond high school. Nor can their explanation account for wide variations in income among people who work at the same or similar jobs and have the same levels of education, skill, and experience (Thurow, 1975).

Fifth, Tumin criticized Davis and Moore for not making full use of the functional perspective, which focuses on *dys*functions as well as functions. The talent of those at the "bottom of the heap" is less likely to be discovered, encouraged, and developed; and, as a result, society is denied the full range of its population's abilities. Inequality encourages hostility, suspicion, and distrust between those at the top and those at the bottom; and those who must go through life with little prestige and little hope of a better life are less likely to be loyal to a society that deprives them.

Finally, while Davis and Moore argued that people receive high incomes because their jobs are perceived as being more important, some sociologists argue just the opposite—that we tend to perceive those who make a lot of money as being more important than the rest of us *because* of their high incomes and not because their jobs make a more important contribution to society (Jenkins, 1981a).

If the best interests of society do not explain the existence of stratification, why is systematic inequality so pervasive? Marx and other conflict theorists propose an answer.

The Conflict Perspective: To Each According to the Ability to Take

If societies cannot produce an abundance of food, clothing, and shelter to satisfy everyone's needs fully, it is inevitable that some will be in a position to take

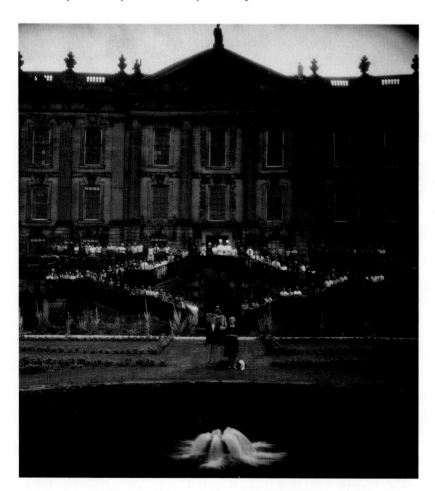

The Duke and Duchess of Devonshire, England, have a 175-room house and 170 personal servants. An enormous amount of surplus production and the labor of many people is needed to support two people in such lavish style as well as a social system that permits large concentration of wealth.

more than their share; and, as they accumulate wealth and power, they will use their dominant position to create and sustain a social environment that perpetuates their privileged position (Marx and Engels, 1846). Marx explained stratification as the result of conflict over scarce resources and of the ability of those who dominate society to maintain their privileged position by exploiting those below them.

Lenski (1966) supported Marx's view by tracing the development of societies and showing that stratification exists only in those that produce a surplus. (He does not say that there is no inequality in societies that barely survive; only that inequality is not determined by social statuses.) Hunter-gatherer societies such as the Kung Bushmen of Africa do not produce their own food, and they move from place to place in order to find it. This way of life discourages the production of surpluses and the accumulation of private property. As technology created greater surpluses, settlements became more permanent, elite groups accumulated wealth and power, and eventually stratification became an enduring characteristic of societies.

Conflict theorists argue that stratification benefits the dominant class, not society as a whole (Gans, 1973). The existence of poverty ensures that "dirty work" will get done: cleaning streets, collecting garbage, picking lettuce, scrubbing floors, and emptying bedpans in hospitals. Such jobs would go undone if no one was driven by the threat of poverty to perform them. Poverty also creates jobs for welfare and social workers, pawnbrokers, and government bureaucrats who administer antipoverty programs.

In addition, the lower class usually bears a disproportionately large share of the costs of social change: they are the first to lose their jobs when factories are automated; when homes are torn down to make way for highways, it is the poor, not the wealthy who lose. Even unemployment benefits those who own or control the means of production. When there are many people without jobs, competition leads them to accept lower wages, for if they refuse to work for low pay, there is always someone else desperate to take their place. Low wages, in turn, mean higher profits for the owners.

John Steinbeck portrayed this in his novel, *The Grapes of Wrath*, in which Oklahoma farmers who were wiped out by the Great Depression go to California in search of jobs in fruit orchards. Each day, the owners spread rumors that large numbers of jobs are available; an enormous crowd gathers at the gate, and the owners announce a pitifully low rate of pay. The people looking for work can see that only a few of them will get jobs, that they are hungry and homeless, and that even a low wage is better than none.

This scene is not unique to the Great Depression. In 1983, 10,000 people stood in freezing rain for four hours in Cleveland, Ohio, to apply for 1,000 public-service jobs that paid $4.50 an hour, were to last only 12 weeks, and involved cleaning up public parks and vacant lots. Some of the applicants were unemployed auto and steel workers with 25 years of experience in the steel industry (*New York Times*, March 22, 1983).

If inequality is imposed by the powerful on the weak, why does the lower class stand for it? The first response is, "They often don't." Throughout the last thousand years, people have been drawn to the idea of equality. During the Middle Ages, European peasants often joined bands of robbers and revolted against landowners. The story of Robin Hood, who "stole from the rich to give to the poor," has found a place in the folk histories of many societies (Hobsbawm, 1971). Peasant revolts were common in England, France,

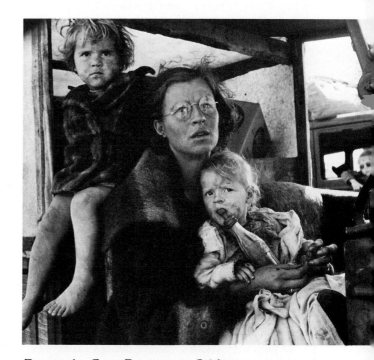

During the Great Depression, California represented the "Land of Milk and Honey". But, for migrants such as these, the dreams were quickly replaced by a harsh reality of exploitation and continued deprivation.

and other European countries (Froissart, 1961; Genicut, 1966).

Why, then, does stratification persist? Part of the answer lies in the ability of elite classes to use force to take what they want and keep what they have—by controlling police, armies, and governments. Moreover, stratification is an enduring characteristic of most societies, few of which resemble a police state. The rest of the answer lies deeper, in the *acceptance* of inequality by members of *all* social classes.

Culture, Ideology, and Inequality

In the *Manifesto of the Communist Party*, Marx and Engels (1848) argued that members of dominant classes use their privileged positions to influence the cultural ideas that affect people's perceptions of reality, aspirations, feelings, and expectations. Upper-class people tend to be among the best-educated members of society and occupy positions of authority—in government, university boards of trustees, the mass media, and legal systems (see Freire, 1985; Parenti, 1986; Peschek, 1987). They provide financial support for political candidates and universities. They are in a position to foster beliefs, values, attitudes, and norms that keep those in lower classes "in their place."

Norms   Norms are an important tool through which the upper class perpetuates its privilege. Norms that protect private property favor the wealthy more than the poor, and most inheritance laws allow families to accumulate wealth over many generations. By extreme contrast, in some American Indian tribes, no one is allowed to own land. An individual may lease land for a lifetime, but when he or she dies, the land becomes community property once again, to be leased to someone else (Matthiessen, 1984).

U.S. income tax laws were once designed to tax the wealthy at substantially higher rates than everyone else. This policy was based on several principles: the wealthy are more able to pay and therefore should pay more; they have more to gain from a healthy society and therefore should contribute more; and they receive a disproportionately large share of income, and therefore the burden of supporting society should fall more heavily on them.

In practice, however, income tax laws always allowed many of the wealthy to avoid paying taxes on much of their income (Devine, 1983).

Deductions sometimes enable millionaires to pay no tax at all, and few wealthy individuals pay the full

rate. Because upper-class people have considerable influence over the passage of laws, they are often able to bring about laws that serve their best interests (such as lowering the 70 percent rate to 50 percent in 1982 and then to only 33 percent in 1988). The effects of this are clear in Table 11-1, which shows the effect of income taxes on the distribution of income in 1985. In terms of before-tax income, the poorest 20 percent of the population received less than 4 percent of all income, while the richest 20 percent received almost 46 percent. The second column shows the distribution of after-tax income, and you can see that it differs very little from the distribution of before-tax income.

The tax structure has little effect on the distribution of income (see also Pechman, 1984). In addition, however, the Congressional Budget Office (1987) estimates that the drastic tax law changes enacted during the Reagan administration have shifted some of the tax burden from the highest to the lowest income families. In 1988, the poorest tenth of people in the U.S. will be paying 20 percent *more* in total federal taxes than they did in 1977, while the richest one percent will pay 20 percent *less*.

Culture and the Uses of Ideology   When Marx (1843) described organized religion as "the opiate of the masses," he was not attacking religion itself; rather, he was arguing that religion can function as a distraction for workers. The more attention they

Table 11-1

Distribution of Before-Tax and After-Tax Household Income (United States, 1985)

INCOME GROUP	SHARE OF BEFORE-TAX INCOME (Percentage)	SHARE OF AFTER-TAX INCOME (Percentage)
Lowest Fifth	3.9	4.6
2nd Fifth	9.7	11.0
3rd Fifth	16.3	17.2
4th Fifth	24.4	24.7
Top Fifth	45.7	42.6
	100.0	100.0

Source: U.S. Census Bureau, 1987b.

pay to heaven, hell, and the "hereafter," he argued, the less attention they pay to social relations on earth through which they are exploited.

Religious beliefs often cloud awareness of classes and their relationships with one another, especially in societies whose workers are poorly educated. Religion focuses attention on individuals, and this, too, draws attention away from social factors that affect living conditions, experience, and behavior. Marx called this lack of awareness of the true extent and causes of social inequality **false consciousness**, an important concept that shows how social conditions persist when we misperceive important aspects of reality.

Religion is not the only potential source of false consciousness. We commonly believe that the U.S. is a "land of equal opportunity," and value the right of individuals to own property. In 1987, 66 percent of adults in the U.S. reported the belief that hard work is the most important factor in "getting ahead" (Davis and Smith, 1987), and most believe that success and failure are due primarily to individual, not social, causes (Kluegel and Smith, 1982, 1986). A major part of the "American Dream" is to "make it big" and share in the affluence of the upper class.

Such aspects of culture support stratification by legitimating the social arrangements that produce it and by explaining our success or failure in purely individual terms. The belief in the importance of hard work is functional for maintaining the privilege of dominant classes. It keeps the lower classes hard at work and in a state of false consciousness. It does so without threatening members of the upper class, most of whom depend on inheritance (rather than hard work) for most of their wealth (Projector and Weiss, 1966). Instead, it legitimizes their privilege (if they are wealthy, they must have worked hard). When lower-class people fail to get ahead, they tend to blame themselves rather than a stratification system that severely limits their opportunities no matter how hard they work. After all, the U.S. was founded on the idea that "All men are created equal" (a constitutional ideal that still excludes women). By blaming themselves, members of lower classes tend to ignore the fact that while higher-class people may work no harder than they, they still receive far greater rewards.

When cultural ideas are used to justify a social arrangement, they constitute an **ideology** (see Swidler, 1986; Turner, 1986). In the late eighteenth and early nineteenth centuries, England enjoyed an unprecedented period of prosperity which included virtual economic dominance of most of the Western world. In that social environment, it is not surprising that the English philosopher and sociologist Herbert Spencer developed a theory that Britain's dominance and prosperity were justified by the superiority of the British society and culture.

Spencer's theory tried to apply Charles Darwin's theory of evolution to social inequality by arguing that the wealth, privilege, and power of some, and the deprivation and misery of others, was a "natural" and inevitable result of some people being more "fit" than others (see Jones, 1980). According to Spencer's theory, which became known as **social Darwinism**, the most capable people will and should gain more in the "struggle" for survival than the less capable.

Spencer's ideas found an enthusiastic audience in the U.S. which was then experiencing an orgy of economic speculation, the building of vast personal fortunes, and increasingly dismal living and working conditions (Hofstader, 1955). In his book, *What Social Classes Owe to Each Other* (1883), sociologist William Graham Sumner applauded Spencer's ideas and argued that the upper classes deserve their privilege because the mere fact of *having* it demonstrated their greater "fitness." The main problem with this argument is that it is circular and thereby true by definition. If we accept the idea that wealth is a valid measure of "fitness," then by definition the wealthy must be more fit than everyone else.

In general, those who benefit most from an ideology tend to be its strongest supporters (see Rytina, Form, and Pease, 1970; Kluegel and Smith, 1986). As Marx argues, however, dominant classes tend to use their influence to shape culture in their own interests, including promoting widespread acceptance and support for the status quo. Rarely do the mass media in the U.S. criticize capitalism as an economic system. Problems such as high unemployment, poverty and homelessness, or the 1987 crash of the stock market tend to be attributed to factors such as poor worker training, unfair foreign competition, or investor panic—not to inherent flaws in capitalism. When it comes to problems in socialist societies such as the Soviet Union, however, the media are far more likely to explain them as the result of inherent flaws in socialism as a system.

As a result, there is a high level of consensus in the United States that the stratification system functions fairly, that inequality is based primarily on personal attributes and talent, and that educational opportunity is available to all (last column of Table

Table 11-2

Perceptions of Class Inequality, by Family Income, United States, 1984

PERCENT WHO AGREE	FAMILY INCOME						
	$0–$4,999	$5,000–$14,999	$15,000–$24,999	$25,000–$34,999	$35,000–$49,999	$50,000 or more	ALL
The U.S. has an open society and that what one achieves in life no longer depends on family background, but on the abilities one has and the education one acquires.	78%	84%	88%	86%	89%	85%	86%
Everyone in this country has an opportunity to obtain an education corresponding to their abilities and talents.	72%	72%	71%	69%	74%	62%	71%
Differences in social standing between people are acceptable because they basically reflect what people made out of the opportunities they had.	72%	76%	75%	75%	71%	75%	74%
All in all, social differences in this country are justified.	54%	51%	54%	55%	52%	66%	54%

Source: Computed from raw 1984 General Social Survey data.

11-2). This holds regardless of family income: looking across each row in Table 11-2, you see that the percentages are quite similar from one income category to another. Such findings tend to support Marx's view that culture is used to support the privileged position of the dominant class.

The preceding sections introduce the major perspectives we use to describe and explain stratification, and those that follow apply these perspectives to the U.S. and less developed societies.

SOCIAL STRATIFICATION IN THE UNITED STATES

Because the United States was founded, in part, as a reaction against the aristocracies of Europe with their rigid divisions between nobility and commoners, we like to think of our society as classless. We may locate ourselves in the "lower class," "middle class," or "upper class," but we tend to believe that people who work hard can go as far as they want. Is this a classless society?

From Marx's Perspective

To Marx, there are two basic classes in industrial societies, those who own or control the means of production and those who do not. A classless society is one in which the means of production are collectively owned and controlled by everyone, and in which no one has the power to deny someone the right to earn a living. No industrial society has achieved Marx's ideal; but we can use his perspective to describe our class structure by answering two questions: (1) How likely are we to work for ourselves rather than for someone else? and (2) How concentrated is the ownership of the means of production?

In the early 1800s around 80 percent of working people were self-employed, mostly as farmers. By the 1870s, when the Industrial Revolution was in full swing, roughly 33 percent worked for themselves; but by 1985 the figure was under 9 percent (Mills, 1951; U.S. Census Bureau, 1986a). While we began as a country in which most people owned and controlled some means of production, the vast majority of contemporary workers work for someone else.

While this suggests the existence of capitalist and worker classes in the U.S., we have to remember that ownership and control of the means of production is not as simple now as it was in the 1800s when most businesses were family-owned. Most businesses are now owned by stockholders, and anyone who has money to spare can own a "piece of the action" by purchasing stocks and bonds.

This brings us to the second question: How *concentrated* is ownership of business? In 1983 the wealthiest 10 percent of the population owned 90 percent of all bonds and corporate stock; the wealthiest *one* percent owned 51 percent of all bonds and 60 percent of all stocks; and 80 percent owned *no* stocks or bonds at all (Joint Economic Committee, 1986a; U.S. Census Bureau, 1986a).

The above, when added to the findings shown in Figure 11-1, shows that from Marx's perspective, the U.S. is divided into classes defined by their relationship to the means of production. The dominant class is a small minority who are either self-employed professionals, own means of production, or occupy top management positions. Most of us are in the working class; for whether we are professors, engineers, fire fighters, or clerks, we cannot work unless those who control jobs are willing to buy our labor power.

The importance of Marx's concept of class was painfully evident to millions of workers in 1982, when almost 20 percent of those who wanted to work were either out of work and still looking for jobs or had given up the effort. Many of the newly unemployed had occupied well-paid positions, lived in mortgaged houses, and had children in college; they were shocked to suddenly find themselves without a way to earn a living. By drawing our attention to the importance of owning and controlling the means of production, Marx reveals that whatever our level of rewards may be today, in a class society, what workers earn today may be gone tomorrow no matter how hard they work or how competent they may be.

It is no accident that in the 1980s labor unions are shifting their focus from the rewards of work—pay, benefits, and vacation time—to control over working conditions. Auto unions now demand membership on corporate boards of directors, so that workers can have some control over the organizations on which they depend for a living. While pay was the issue of the 1960s and 1970s, job security is the issue of the 1980s, and this inevitably involves a struggle over control of the means of production (*New York Times*, July 7, 1987).

Through Weber's Eyes: Dimensions of Inequality

Unlike Marx, Weber divided societies according to the distribution of wealth, power, and prestige. How evenly are wealth, power, and prestige distributed?

Wealth and Income   It is important at the outset to distinguish between wealth and income. **Wealth** refers to valued possessions, including cash, property, stocks and bonds, buildings, jewels, and cars. **Income** refers to money that we receive each year. Wealth is what we *have*, while income is what we take in. The distinction is important because wealth is often a source of income: interest on investments, rent payments from tenants, or profits from a business or the sale of property that has increased in market value.

A small minority owns most of the wealth in the U.S. In 1983, the richest 10 percent of the population held 67 percent of all the wealth, including 87 percent of all cash assets, 49 percent of all real estate, 94 percent of all business assets, and 90 percent of all stocks and bonds (Joint Economic Committee, 1986a).

Like wealth, the distribution of income is also unequal. In 1985 the wealthiest 5 percent of families received 17 percent of all income—more than three times what they would have received if everyone got equal shares; and, the wealthiest 20 percent received 44 percent of all income. Meanwhile, the lower 60 percent received only 32 percent; the poorest 20 percent received 4.6 percent—less than a quarter of what they would have received if income were distributed equally; and the income of one out of every nine families fell below the poverty level (U.S. Census Bureau, 1986a).

Puzzles: Does Education Increase Mobility?

In the last twenty years, the educational attainment and level of training in the population in the U.S. has grown dramatically. As a result, has the distribution of income become less unequal, more unequal, or stayed just about the same?

The answer is that the distribution of income has become *more* unequal in the last ten years. This chapter explains why.

It is important to note that income figures based on tax returns understate the true extent of inequality, for much of the income of wealthy families and individuals is never reported to the Internal Revenue Service. Top executives enjoy large expense accounts that pay for travel and entertainment, and are often given the opportunity to buy stocks at a cost far below their actual value. The most lucrative tax-free investments are typically beyond the reach of all but the wealthy.

Power   C. Wright Mills (1956) argued that power is concentrated in the hands of an elite, that business, political, and military leaders share common backgrounds, values, and attitudes, and cooperate with each other in order to maintain their dominance. Business leaders are often appointed to top positions in government agencies designed to regulate business; or, those in charge of government agencies that regulate business may later work for corporations, using their special knowledge to help businesses avoid government regulations.

Alexander Haig was an army general until the 1970s, when he became a close aide to President Nixon. He then served as president of United Technologies, a large corporation that makes jet engines for the military. In 1980 he became Ronald Reagan's secretary of state, and after resigning that position, returned to United Technologies. In 1987, he decided to run for president of the United States. From Mills' point of view, Haig is an example of elite individuals who move from one powerful position to another—whether economic, political, or military—and because these people know each other well and share values and experiences, they are in a position to exercise considerable control over important decisions.

Domhoff (1967, 1971) compiled a list of the upper class—those at the highest levels of wealth and education—and found that while its members may belong to different political parties, they are closely related through intermarriage, attendance at the same elite schools, and club memberships (see also Cookson and Persell, 1985). Most important, they strongly value free enterprise and the rights to accumulate private property and make profits, and are far more likely to occupy powerful positions in business and government than are those in the classes below them. A majority of U.S. presidents have had upper-middle or upper-class origins (Pessen, 1984), and the highest reaches of the corporate world are generally reserved for members of the upper class (Useem and Karabel, 1986; see also Domhoff, 1983; Useem, 1983).

Riesman (1961), on the other hand, argued that Mills overstated the power of elites. To Riesman, power is *pluralistic*, concentrated in a wide variety of interest groups: labor unions, professional organizations such as the American Medical Association, consumer action groups, political parties, the National Association for the Advancement of Colored People (NAACP), the Civil Liberties Union, the Urban League, and the National Organization for Women.

Both views are correct to a degree. The upper class clearly has more control over economic and political decisions than do people in any other class. The power of the upper class is by no means absolute, however. While no group controls the U.S., it is also true that most citizens have good reason to feel powerless unless they are represented by an interest group.

Prestige   Unlike power and wealth, the distribution of prestige depends heavily on cultural values. Parsons (1964) argued that the respect we receive from others depends on how our culture values *possessions, qualities* (such as "natural talent" or ascribed statuses such as race, gender, and the social class of our parents), and *performance* (including achieved statuses such as education, marital status, and occupation).

If a culture values possessions, such as cars and stereos, respect tends to go to those who own them regardless of their power. For this reason, people often buy things (such as designer clothes) not simply to use or enjoy them, but to indicate to others that they have achieved an important cultural value and deserve respect. This is what Thorstein Veblen (1934) called **conspicuous consumption**—owning objects in order to enhance or affirm prestige.

Conspicuous consumption has not always brought with it higher levels of prestige. Harris (1974) argued that historical shifts in the *basis* for distributing prestige have helped perpetuate stratification in industrial societies. In the early stages of capitalism, prestige went to those who were frugal. When the privileged position of the rich became more secure, they engaged in conspicuous consumption—building enormous estates and spending their wealth openly and freely as a symbolic expression of their power and privilege.

As production increased and capitalists needed people to buy their goods, conspicuous consumption became associated with prestige among the middle and lower classes. Most recently, as the gap between rich and poor has become a source of social conflict, the "old rich" protect their high prestige by regarding conspicuous consumption as "vulgar." This shift

In the late 1800s, the upper class attempted to enhance its prestige by flaunting its wealth—conspicuous consumption. The marble "summer cottages," such as this mansion built for William K. Vanderbilt, were used for only two months of each year; otherwise, they were occupied only by the servants.

lowers their visibility and changes the "rules of the game," once again reserving the highest levels of prestige for themselves.

Prestige is also distributed according to ascribed statuses such as race, gender, and ethnicity—characteristics that we are born with and powerless to change. When people are asked to rank the prestige of occupations, they tend to rank them lower if they are presented with a hypothetical person holding the job who is a woman, or if they perceive the job as being held more often by women than by men (Bose, 1985). The prestige of occupations, in short, depends in part on the gender of those who hold them.

Prestige is also affected by cultural values attached to achieved statuses. Since 1947, several studies have measured the amount of prestige attached to different occupations by asking respondents to rate occupations as "excellent," "good," "average," "somewhat below average," or "poor" (see Table 11-3). Each occupation is given an average rank (Hodge, Treiman, and Rossi, 1966; North and Hatt, 1947; Treiman, 1977). The most prestigious occupations either require extensive formal education or involve high levels of responsibility and power—professionals and technical workers, business owners and managers, and high public officials. At the bottom are jobs that depend mainly on manual work, require relatively little training, and involve little or no power.

In 1985 only 27 percent of U.S. workers held jobs whose prestige was rated "good" or "excellent"—professionals and technical workers, managers, and administrators. Like wealth, income, and power, the distribution of prestige is highly unequal; and, as Studs Terkel (1974) found when he interviewed people in many different occupations, the high prestige of those at the top is paid for by those at the bottom. As a washroom attendant in a large Chicago hotel put it:

> I'm not particularly proud of what I'm doing. . . . I don't go around saying I'm a washroom attendant. . . . Outside of my immediate family, very few people know what I do. . . . This man shining shoes, he's had several offers . . . where he could make more money. But he wouldn't take 'em because the jobs were too open. He didn't want to be *seen* shining shoes. . . . No, I'm not proud of this work. (p. 108)

Whether we view stratification from Weber's point of view or Marx's, the United States is, like every complex society, clearly divided into social classes. The degree of inequality is only one aspect of strati-

Table 11-3

Prestige Ratings[1] of Occupations in the United States

OCCUPATION	RATING	OCCUPATION	RATING	OCCUPATION	RATING	OCCUPATION	RATING
Physician	82	Social worker	52	Postal clerk	43	Shoe repair	33
College teacher	78	Athlete	51	Mail carrier	42	Stone cutter	33
Judge	76	Computer		Tool and die maker	42	Bus/truck driver	32
Lawyer	76	programmer	51	Practical nurse	42	Cashier	31
Dentist	74	Editor or reporter	51	Farmer	41	File clerk	30
Bank officer	72	Optician	51	Plumber	41	Painter	30
Architect	71	Radio or TV		Railroad conductor	41	Precision machine	
Airplane pilot	70	announcer	51	Tailor	41	operator	29
Chemist	69	Bank teller	50	Carpenter	40	Sales clerk	29
Minister	69	Buyer, Wholesale	50	Telephone operator	40	Shipping clerk	29
Biologist	68	Office manager	50	Receptionist	39	Assembly line	
Civil engineer	68	Sales manager	50	Restaurant/bar		worker	27
Sociologist	66	Electrician	49	manager	39	Mine worker	26
High school teacher	63	Aircraft mechanic	48	Telephone installer/		Childcare worker	25
Registered nurse	62	Bookkeeper	48	repair	39	Garage worker	22
Dental hygienist	61	Dental assistant	48	Barber	38	Guard	22
Pharmacist	61	Machinist	48	Dancer	38	Taxi driver	22
Public official/		Police officer	48	Building		Bartender	20
administrator	61	Insurance agent	47	superintendent	38	Waiter	20
School administrator	60	Science technician	47	Auto mechanic	37	Household maid	18
Author	60	Musician or		Jeweler/Watchmaker	37	Peddler	18
Elementary school		composer	46	Airline stewardess	36	Garbage collector	17
teacher	60	Secretary	46	Brickmason	36	Laborer	17
Accountant	57	Office machine		Radio/TV repair	35	Fast food worker	15
Actor	55	operator	45	Baker	34	Janitor/cleaner	15
Librarian	55	Firefighter	44	Hairdresser	33	Shoe shiner	9
Funeral director	52	Real estate agent	44	Plasterer	33		

[1] Rated on a scale of 1 to 100.

Source: Davis and Smith, 1987, Appendix F.

fication systems, however, for societies also differ in how *rigidly* they are stratified. In other words, societies differ in how easily individuals can change their social class or their standing within a class. Such changes can be positive or negative, for people can move down as well as up. Together, the movement of individuals within and between classes is called **social mobility**.

The following sections look at mobility in terms of Weber's and Marx's concepts of social class. As you might guess, the resulting picture of mobility depends on which concept we use.

> ## Puzzles: What Are the Most Important Factors that Determine Who Gets Ahead?
>
> If your answer includes "education" and "hard work," you agree with most people in the U.S. But as this chapter explains, if your answer includes "luck," "race," "sex," and "who your parents are," you might be closer to the truth.

SOCIAL MOBILITY: GOING UP AND GOING DOWN

There are two types of mobility. We can think of *lifetime* mobility—a woman begins as a researcher in a publishing company and retires as a senior editor; or, she becomes an editor at age 36, loses her job when the company goes bankrupt, and ends her work life as a waitress. Or, we can compare people's class position with that of their parents in order to detect *intergenerational* mobility.

In a **closed stratification system**, classes are called **castes**. Caste membership is based on ascribed statuses such as ethnicity and race, and because it is assigned at birth, it cannot be changed. While individuals can improve their position within a caste, it is impossible to change their caste. Before the abolition of slavery in the U.S., caste was an important aspect of race relations, and in some respects it still is (Frederickson, 1981). Housing is highly segregated by race, and most whites disapprove of racial intermarriage.

In an **open stratification system**, individuals may freely compete for wealth, power, and prestige regardless of their ascribed statuses. In the U.S., as in most of the world's societies, the system allows some mobility from positions of lower power, wealth, or prestige to higher ones. Most people believe that whatever our class position is today, with hard work, education, and a little luck, there are few limits on what we can achieve. Sociological research suggests that our perceptions are accurate in the sense that we often do improve our positions; but it also shows that how *far* we can move is, for most of us, very limited.

The next three sections try to answer three basic questions about social mobility. First, what characteristics of societies determine how much mobility there is in their populations? Second, which social

As one of India's "untouchables," the lowest among the caste of laborers, the woman holding a broom she uses to clean toilets was assigned her status (and even her occupational specialization) at birth. The teacher is a member of a higher caste, but her status, too, was ascribed, based on her parents' caste. This traditional closed stratification system has been undergoing changes since India achieved its independence.

characteristics allow some individuals to be more mobile than others? Third, does mobility lead to greater equality in society as a whole?

How Much Mobility?

The extent of upward mobility in a society depends on two basic aspects of its structure. People cannot move up to better positions if there are none available; and in order to occupy higher positions, we must have the characteristics and abilities required for entry into those statuses.

Feudal societies were divided into two classes—the land-owning nobility and the peasants—and mobility was severely limited. There were very few positions available, and since only the eldest son could inherit his father's estate, the younger sons had few options other than a religious career. The daughters of nobility could marry a nobleman, spend their life in their father's house, or enter a convent. It was impossible for peasants to move upward, since the only higher status in the system was the ascribed status of "noble."

Industrialization accounts for the relatively high rates of mobility found in the U.S. and other modern societies (Blau and Duncan, 1967; Lipset and Bendix, 1959). Industrialization caused a vast expansion of educational opportunities: of people 18 to 24 years old, the percentage in college increased from 1 percent in 1870 to 26 percent in 1985, and since 1918 the number of people in vocational training programs has increased from under 100,000 to more than 16 million (U.S. Census Bureau, 1980b, 1986a).

By creating thousands of different jobs, industrialization created mobility by dividing the distance between the highest and lowest class into a series of very small steps. Whereas in feudal societies the "ladder" of success had only two rungs—with the top rung hopelessly beyond the reach of those on the bottom—the "ladder" in industrial societies has thousands of "rungs." While the poor still have almost no chance of reaching the upper rungs, they can experience some progress and may eventually make it to the middle class.

Kahl (1961) found that between 1920 and 1950, 67 percent of sons were in higher-ranked occupations

In feudal societies, the nobility was at the top and the peasants were at the bottom; there were few social positions in between.

Puzzles: Mobility and Affluence—Real and Apparent

Average family income in the United States has risen in the last decade, as has the number of possessions such as washers, dryers, televisions, and home computers that people have in their homes. Given this progress, why do most people report that the "lot of the average man" is growing worse?

The answer, as this chapter explains, has less to do with what people have than with how they come to have it.

than their fathers. Blau and Duncan (1967) compared the educations and occupations of fathers and sons and found that 37 percent of men with white-collar jobs had fathers who worked in blue-collar jobs. Both studies, however, find that the *degree* of movement from one generation to the next is quite small. The vast majority of those who occupy high statuses in

government and business come from upper-class families, and a study of professionals in the 1960s found that 40 percent had fathers who were professionals as well (Jackson and Crockett, 1964; Lipset and Bendix, 1959).

As the structure of the job market—the kinds of jobs available—changes, it causes both upward and downward mobility. In the 1980s the job market is expanding in industries that require technical training—computer programming—and service occupations such as veterinarians, legal assistants, tax preparers, and employment interviewers. There are not enough children of upper- and middle-class parents to fill these jobs—fertility is lower in the middle and upper classes than in the lower class. Structural changes in the economy and relatively low birth rates in the middle and upper classes have created opportunities for the children of lower-class parents to move into the middle class.

Technological advances that create thousands of jobs for those with technical training can spell disaster for millions of manual workers. The automobile industry will increasingly replace workers with robots on assembly lines, and while this creates jobs for

Although the use of robots in factories has increased efficiency, it has cost thousands of people their jobs. The widespread use of computers has had a similar effect in offices; here, word processors enable typists to do work that earlier required the labor of several people.

engineers and technicians, it causes severe downward mobility for many skilled and unskilled blue-collar workers. Some can go back to school, but this is a long-term solution that ignores short-term effects of downward mobility. Bills—including medical bills and those for college tuition and home mortgages—must be paid now, not later. In many cases, the shock of downward mobility is so severe that families never recover.

Who Goes Up and Who Goes Down?

Sociologists identify several social statuses that affect who moves up and who moves down in the stratification system, the most important of which are education, social class of parents, race, gender, occupation, and age.

People in the U.S. generally agree that education is the most important factor in upward mobility. In 1976 almost half of all parents hoped their young children would eventually receive a college or graduate degree; and in 1978, 35 percent of adults believed that a college education is "very important." The perceived importance of higher education is strongest among those with the most to gain: 45 percent of those with incomes below $7,000 consider college "very important," compared with only 32 percent of those with annual incomes above $15,000 (U.S. Census Bureau, 1980b).

Research generally supports our faith in education as a route to higher income (see Table 11-4). The beneficial effects of education are not guaranteed,

however. In 1985, 38 percent of college-educated workers had lower incomes than the average worker with only a high school diploma; and 18 percent of workers with high school diplomas had *higher* incomes than the average college-educated worker (U.S. Census Bureau, 1987a). As Thurow (1975), Jencks et al. (1972), and Bane and Jencks (1972) concluded, training and skill cannot explain why some people have more income than others. Bane and Jencks went so far as to suggest that "luck" is the single most important factor.

If we compare the incomes of brothers who have similar IQ scores and similar educations, they differ by an average of $5,300. If we choose pairs of men at *random*, however, the average difference between their incomes is only slightly higher—$6,200. As explained by Bane and Jencks:

> These estimates mean that people who start off equal end up almost as unequal as everyone else. Inequality is not mostly inherited: It is re-created anew in each generation. . . . Adult success must depend on a lot of things besides family background, schooling, and the cognitive skills measured by standardized tests. (p. 39)

The positive effects of education also depend on ascribed statuses such as race and gender. In Table 2-6, we saw that while education increases women's incomes, they still lag far behind men with far less formal education.

Although education has long been viewed as a great "equalizer," this depends on the belief that everyone has an equal chance to go to college; but this is far from true. In 1985, 54 percent of children with family incomes of $50,000 or more attended college; but in families making less than $20,000, only 25 percent were enrolled (U.S. Census Bureau, 1986a). While education promotes mobility regardless of parents' class, and lower-class parents are the most likely to value higher education, *access* to education strongly depends on parents' resources.

Even when children begin schooling with equal IQ and grow up to have equal education, class background strongly affects adult income. Bowles and Nelson (1974) found that among white males 35 to 44 years old, children from families in the top tenth of the population were three times as likely to wind up in the top fifth as children from families in the poorest tenth (Table 11-5).

Table 11-4

Income by Educational Attainment, 1984

EDUCATIONAL ATTAINMENT	AVERAGE INCOME
Professional degree	$46,500
Doctorate	$39,200
Master's degree	$27,500
Bachelor's degree	$22,100
Associate's degree	$16,200
High school diploma	$12,300
Less than high school diploma	$ 8,300

Source: U.S. Census Bureau, 1987f.

Table 11-5

The Effect of Class Background on the Chance of Winding Up in the Top Fifth of the Income Distribution as Adults, for Those with Equal Childhood IQ and Educational Attainment

INCOME OF FAMILY OF ORIGIN (10th)	CHANCE OF BEING IN THE TOP 5th OF INCOME AS AN ADULT (Percentage)
Bottom 10th	10
2nd 10th	14
3rd 10th	16
4th 10th	17
5th 10th	19
6th 10th	20
7th 10th	22
8th 10th	24
9th 10th	27
Top 10th	32

Source: Bowles and Nelson, 1974.

Studies of mobility in the U.S., then, give us a mixed picture. People often enjoy higher incomes and more prestigious occupations than their parents, but in general the differences are small. Achieved statuses, such as education, are important, but they offer no guarantee of success and their effects are often limited by ascribed statuses such as race and gender. The number and variety of jobs available are a structural characteristic of society itself and are beyond the control of workers. As that structure changes, it inevitably produces opportunities for some and hardship for others.

We come now to our third question about social mobility: What effect does it have on stratification? Does mobility lead to a less stratified society?

Is Mobility an Illusion?

While upward mobility appears to be a common occurrence, in several respects our faith in the equalizing effects of mobility is not justified. First, in spite of the findings of mobility studies, we increasingly believe that our financial conditions are growing worse, not better. Second, so long as the stratification system remains intact, mobility has little effect on the relative

standing of social classes and our ability to control our society and our own lives.

Between 1960 and 1984, the percentage living in poverty dropped from 22 percent to 14 percent, and, after taking inflation into account, the median income of husband-wife families increased by 44 percent. In addition, luxuries such as cars, washers, dryers, and stereos became increasingly common: between 1965 and 1984 the worth of all such goods in U.S. households more than doubled (U.S. Census Bureau, 1986a).

During much of this period, however, we continued to believe that our financial positions were growing worse. Between 1972 and 1987 the percentage who reported that their financial condition had grown worse recently held steady at around 20 percent, and those who agreed that "the lot of the average man is getting worse, not better" never dropped below 50 percent. In addition, people's perceptions of which class they belong to shifted downward: in 1964, 61 percent of adults placed themselves in the middle class, and 35 percent in the working class (Hodge and Treiman, 1968). By 1987 only 46 percent placed themselves in the middle class and the working class swelled to 43 percent (Davis and Smith, 1987; see also Blackburn and Bloom, 1985; Kuttner, 1984). How can things be getting better and worse at the same time?

Part of the answer is that while incomes rose between 1960 and 1984, the relative position of the middle class grew worse (see Levy, 1988). The richest 40 percent of families in the U.S. enjoyed a slight increase in their share of national income, while of the rest, the share of all but the poorest fell, even though actual incomes rose (U.S. Census Bureau, 1986a). At the same time, the distribution of wealth became far more lopsided in favor of the wealthiest families. The share of all wealth owned by the richest .5 percent of all families rose from 25 percent to 35 percent, while the share owned by the "bottom" 90 percent of all families fell from 35 percent to only 28 percent (Congressional Budget Office, 1988; Joint Economic Committee, 1986).

Under these conditions, we tend to feel **relative deprivation** (Williams, 1975). Whether or not we feel deprived depends only in part on *absolute* levels of income and wealth; it also depends on how much other people in our community and society have. If everyone lives at the same standard of living, no one is likely to feel deprived; but, if some live at a moderate level while others are wealthy, even a moderately good standard of living no longer feels adequate in comparison with others.

A second part of the answer lies in the *source* of increased income. Between 1960 and 1984, the percentage of husband-wife families that depended on the earnings of both spouses rose from 43 percent to 63 percent. Although family income rose by 39 percent, this was caused in part by a 47 percent increase in the percentage of families depending on the earnings of both spouses. Making a living also became more difficult for single, widowed, and divorced people: the percentage of people working at two or more jobs increased by 42 percent among single people and by 26 percent among those widowed or divorced (U.S. Census Bureau, 1981, 1986a).

What of our increased stock of luxury goods? This represents upward mobility only if we ignore the fact that between 1970 and 1982, the amount of consumer debt almost doubled after adjusting for inflation. This means that a substantial portion of these new possessions is owned by banks and loan companies that allow people to buy on credit. We increased our stock of luxuries in large part by going into debt. In fact, if spread evenly over the population, unpaid consumer debt in 1985 amounted to about $2,800 for every man, woman, and child (U.S. Census Bureau, 1986a).

While it appears on the surface that we are better off than ever before, most of us are working harder just to keep up, while those in the upper class maintain their privileged position with relative ease. This brings us to a deeper level, on which mobility is an illusion: in spite of all the moving around within classes, the class structure itself remains intact, and except for those in the poorest class, movement of people to a higher one is not common. Why is this true, and how is the illusion of mobility perpetuated?

Stone (1974) examined the steel industry in the early part of this century and argued that employers created mobility within the working class in order to encourage them to work harder and to control their dissatisfaction with working conditions and pay. Before the Industrial Revolution, goods were produced by skilled workers who were familiar with all aspects of production. From roughly the 1870s on, however, the factory assembly line, by splitting the production process into a series of small steps, few of which require great skill, led to a decline of skilled workers. As the range of skills in the steel industry narrowed, workers could be replaced with relative ease, and most found themselves stuck in "dead-end" jobs (Gordon, Edwards, and Reich, 1982).

Employers responded by creating "job ladders." Put simply, they took a narrow range of jobs and made fine distinctions among them, attaching slightly higher levels of pay to each. While the jobs were as "dead-end" as before, the job ladder gave workers the *feeling* of moving upward. Job ladders also encouraged workers to compete with one another for promotion, rather than unite against their employers.

"If debt is a measure of consumer confidence, we have become very confident indeed."
Drawing by Lorenz © 1983, The New Yorker Magazine, Inc.

The illusion of mobility is also supported by the greater value placed on white-collar jobs than on blue-collar jobs. Blau and Duncan (1967) interpreted the white-collar jobs of the children of blue-collar workers as a sign of upward mobility, but "white-collar" includes many low-level occupations; and many blue-collar jobs require more mental ability than many white-collar jobs. Is a typist's work any less "manual" or any more "mental" than a skilled tool and die maker's?

Stone argued that the distinction between mental and physical labor is both unnecessary and artificial, and "only serves to maintain the power of employers over their workers" (p. 28). It does this by fostering the illusion that becoming a white-collar worker—no matter how lowly the position—is a step upward.

Many people improve their levels of income, wealth, and prestige, both during their own lifetimes and in comparison with their parents; but the gap between those who control the means of production and those who do not is virtually unaffected by such individual progress. For the vast majority, upward mobility is strictly limited by the stratification system. Most of us spend our work lives inching up a short ladder with many rungs, and even when we reach the top of it, we are not very high and do not have much of a view (see Duncan et al., 1984).

Marx: Mobility as an Uninteresting Problem

Our tendency to focus on social mobility and competition for rewards *within* a stratified society leads us to ignore the stratification system itself (see Mach and Wesolowski, 1986). From Marx's perspective, so long as the upper class controls the means of production and the working class must sell its labor power, mobility from one income or occupational level to the next is largely a case of those at the lower levels fighting to keep from being on the bottom. After all, if everyone made it to the middle class, the middle class would no longer be "middle"—it would be the lower class in comparison with everyone else.

To Marx, the key to understanding how rewards are distributed lies in how goods are produced and whether or not the means of production are privately owned. The self-employed, who by definition control their own means of production, are twice as likely to be in the top income brackets as are those who work for someone else (U.S. Census Bureau, 1981).

To Marx, social mobility as we often view it is largely irrelevant and only contributes to false consciousness. More important, Marx's concept of social class focuses on the considerable *downward* mobility that most studies ignore. As we saw earlier, the percentage of people who are self-employed dropped from around 80 percent in the early 1800s to 9 percent in 1985. In addition, the *control* of the means of production remains concentrated in a relatively small portion of the population. Between 1900 and 1985, the percentage of employed people who were managers, administrators, or officials only increased from 6 percent to 11 percent (U.S. Census Bureau, 1980b, 1986a).

If we define "upward mobility" as movement from less control over the means of production to more control, then Americans have been *downwardly* mobile for almost two centuries, and only a small percentage have risen to positions that afford any real control over the means of production.

What of societies other than our own? How does stratification differ among societies, and why are some societies wealthier than others?

INTERNATIONAL STRATIFICATION

Countries differ in the degree of inequality and the amount of mobility they allow. In addition, there is enormous inequality between countries. International stratification is particularly important, for the amount of wealth that is available for distribution *within* a society often depends on relationships among societies.

Varieties of Inequality within Societies

In general, inequality is less severe in industrial countries than in poor countries that are just beginning to industrialize (Kerbo, 1983; Weede, 1980). Mexico is typical of industrializing countries: when the economy grows, the rich get richer and the poor get poorer. Increased production is used not to better the living and working conditions of the entire population but to satisfy the elite's desire for luxuries (Herman, 1975). As a former president of Brazil put it, "Brazil is doing well but the people are not" (in Barnet and Muller, p. 149).

Increased production in less developed countries is also used to protect the privileged position of the upper class. Countries such as Argentina, Chile, Indonesia, the Dominican Republic, and South Korea

The disparity between rich and poor is nowhere more apparent than in the large cities of countries in the early stages of industrialization. In this picture of Bombay, India, the shacks of the poor are built adjacent to luxury high-rise apartments.

invest heavily in military and police units whose primary function is to control the local population and prevent revolutions that would threaten the privileged upper class.

In socialist countries such as the Soviet Union and China, wealth, power, and prestige are unequally distributed, just as they are throughout most of the world (see Szelenyi, 1983). Party leaders are wealthier, live in better housing, and have access to a variety of luxury goods beyond the reach of most people. While the means of production are not owned by the elite, they are tightly controlled by a relative few (Connor, 1979; Hollander, 1982).

While the vast family fortunes of the Rockefellers and Hunts have no parallel in socialist countries, socialist and capitalist societies are similar in an important way. In socialist societies surpluses are appropriated by the state and controlled by the party elite. In capitalist societies surpluses are appropriated by capitalists who can then use them for their own benefit. In neither type of society do the workers have the power to control and dispose of what they produce.

Social Mobility   Nineteenth-century India was divided into four **castes**: priests and scholars at the top, then nobles and warriors, merchants and skilled workers, and common laborers. Below all of these were the outcasts, or "untouchables," with whom physical contact was avoided at all costs by members of castes. In 1949 the caste system was officially abolished. Its importance has declined in urban areas, but caste remains an important force in traditional rural areas (Berreman, 1973).

South Africa is one of the few remaining caste societies. Although whites make up only 17 percent of the population, they dominate all aspects of social life through a rigid policy of racial segregation called **apartheid**. Blacks are not allowed to vote in national elections, are forced to live in impoverished areas, and are allowed to enter "white" areas only to work for whites. All skilled and the better unskilled jobs are reserved for whites, blacks are forbidden by law from striking, and the average black worker's income is only one-seventh that of the average white (Frederickson, 1981; Lever, 1981).

In comparison with caste societies, class systems are relatively open, allowing varying degrees of mobility from lower to higher positions and using a variety of criteria to determine who is most likely to move. Does the U.S. offer more or less opportunity for mobility than other industrial societies?

If we measure mobility in terms of moving from blue-collar to white-collar jobs, the rates in West Germany, Sweden, Japan, France, and Britain are similar to those in the U.S. (Lipset and Bendix, 1959). If we define mobility more narrowly—focusing on movement from the working class to professional or highly technical occupations—the U.S. seems to offer better opportunities. In the 1960s roughly 10 percent of the U.S. working class advanced to professional and technical jobs, compared with 2 percent in West Germany, 7 percent in Japan, and 4 percent in France (Blau and Duncan, 1967; Fox and Miller, 1965). Note, however, how small the percentages are, even in the U.S.

Inequality is a pervasive feature of the world's societies. Perhaps the most striking levels of inequality in the world, however, are found *between* societies, not within them.

Inequality between Societies

In 1985, *per capita income* (what each person would receive if income were distributed evenly) in industrialized societies ranged from highs of $16,400 in Switzerland and the United States to a low of $6,500 in Italy. In socialist countries (excluding China), per capita income ranged from a high of $7,400 in the Soviet Union to a low of $2,100 in Poland and Yugoslavia. In the remaining countries, per capita income was startlingly low: $310 in China, $700 in Egypt, $250 in India, and $110 in Kenya (Population Reference Bureau, 1987).

These differences are even more striking if we remember that per capita income is the amount of money each person would receive *if* income were distributed equally *within* countries. While under conditions of equality each person in India would receive $250 a year, the vast majority of Indians must actually live on far less. Even if income were distributed equally within countries, the people of the wealthiest countries would receive more income each *week* than most of the world's inhabitants would receive each *year*.

The effects of world stratification extend to every aspect of living conditions. Almost half of the people in Africa and Asia can neither read nor write. The U.S. contains less than 5 percent of the world's people, and yet we use 25 percent of the energy consumed each year. China, however, contains roughly 21 percent of all the people in the world, and yet its annual share of energy is only 7 percent. In industrial societies, less than 2 percent of all infants die during their first year of life; but in many nonindustrial societies, between 15 and 25 percent die. The average person in Japan can expect to live 76 years, but in Nigeria life expectancy is only 39 years (Population Reference Bureau, 1987; U.S. Census Bureau, 1986a). In industrial societies, death by starvation is rare; but in Ethiopia, hundreds of thousands died of starvation when prolonged drought and crop failure wiped out the country's food supply in 1984 and 1985.

Part of the explanation of such inequality is ecological. The U.S. is rich in natural resources, and industrialization both here and in Europe took place when populations were relatively small. In most of today's poor countries, on the other hand, populations already outstrip food supplies and are growing faster than the ability to provide jobs and basic necessities.

The answer, however, is not this simple, for the poverty of most of the world is linked with the prosperity of the rest. The Industrial Revolution in Europe depended on **colonialism**, an arrangement through which a "parent" country controls and dominates another. England's colonies provided raw materials for its industry, and England then sold the finished goods to colonies. Because England controlled its colonies, it would not allow them to trade with any other country or develop industries of their own. Colonialism guaranteed colonial powers a source of raw materials and a "captive" market in which to sell their manufactured goods (Emerson, 1968; Fieldhouse, 1968).

This arrangement enriched colonial powers; but for the colonies themselves it was an exploitative relationship that left them poorer. Although the colonialism of the seventeenth, eighteenth, and nineteenth centuries no longer exists today, the relationships between rich and poor countries still contain elements of it. Many of the industries in less developed countries are owned and operated by U.S., European, or Japanese corporations. Many people believe that poor countries should be grateful to wealthy foreigners who build businesses and provide jobs, but this belief ignores some important facts (Barnet and Muller, 1974).

When a U.S. corporation builds a factory abroad, if often uses little of its own money. Instead, it borrows from banks in the host country that prefer to risk their money on established U.S. corporations. Many new industries in less developed countries do not represent a flow of resources (capital) from the wealthy countries to the poor. In addition, although less developed countries provide most of the financing for new industry, they receive a small share of the profits.

Such relationships resemble colonialism. Poor countries are less likely to develop industries owned and controlled by local inhabitants, and become dependent on the dominant country. Most important, they stay relatively poor, partly because profits are not reinvested in their own economies. In many respects international stratification is functional for wealthy nations whose power enables them to dominate and exploit other countries (Evans, 1981; Evans and Timberlake, 1980).

Why do the people in less developed countries tolerate such exploitation? In many cases, the exploitation of poor nations by rich ones is supported by the poor countries' elites, who grow richer while the majority of the population stays poor. They often maintain stability (and their privileged position) with large numbers of soldiers and police, often financed with generous contributions from the U.S. and other wealthy nations (Herman, 1975).

Mobility among Nations   For the world, estimated per capita income increased by 13 percent between 1970 and 1980, over and above the increase caused by inflation. While all but a handful of small countries shared in this, some took a much larger share than others. Between 1970 and 1980, per capita income increased by 17 percent in the wealthiest 15 countries (from $7,100 to $8,300) and by only 2 percent in the remainder (from $632 to $645) (U.S. Census Bureau, 1983c).

In the poorest 15 countries, per capita income rose to about $360; but in the wealthiest countries, the *increase* in per capita income ($1,200) was more than three times larger than *total* per capita income in the poorest countries. What makes these figures even more disturbing is the fact that the 15 poorest countries contain 48 percent of the world's population and income is distributed very unequally within them. This means that most of the world's people receive a very small share of what is *already* a very small share of all income (U.S. Census Bureau, 1983c).

While virtually all countries improved their incomes during the 1970s, the gap between the wealth-iest and the poorest was unchanged. In 1970 and 1980, the wealthiest fifth of the world's population received around 75 percent of all income (U.S. Census Bureau, 1983c). In many Third World countries, per capita income has actually been falling since 1980, and in parts of Africa "there is now the real possibility that it will be lower by the end of the 1980s than it was in 1960" (World Bank, 1983, p. 2).

There is little question that stratification among societies is similar to stratification within them. Like upper-class elites, the wealthy maintain the gap between themselves and those who have less. Although individual countries make progress, the international "pecking order" remains largely intact, just as the relative positions of social classes remain unchanged. It is a dismal picture and raises important questions: What are the prospects for change? Is such extreme inequality inevitable? Under what social and ecological conditions is equality most likely to come about, both within societies and between them?

PROSPECTS FOR CHANGE

Aristotle once defined justice as "a virtue of the soul distributing that which each person deserves." How can wealth, power, and prestige be distributed in ways that satisfy both the functional requirements of a society and our beliefs and values about justice and fairness? Debate over stratification centers on two kinds of change: equality of *opportunity* in the form of increased mobility, and equality of *outcomes*—an end to stratification itself.

Mobility and Equal Opportunity

In the early 1830s Alexis de Tocqueville visited America and recorded his impressions of the new country. In *Democracy in America* he wrote:

> I know of no country . . . where the love of money has taken stronger hold on the affections of men and where a profounder contempt is expressed for the theory of the permanent equality of property.

Tocqueville's observation remains largely true today. In their study of Boston and Kansas City, Coleman and Rainwater (1978) found that most people did not favor an end to stratification. In explaining their positions, people mentioned beliefs that this is a land of opportunity, that inequality is an important source of motivation for hard work, and that the possibility of mobility gives people a feeling that their lives are going somewhere. One of the major suggestions for change was to increase mobility by making higher education available to all and ending discrimination based on ascribed statuses such as race, ethnicity, and gender.

Coleman and Rainwater's study also revealed several important misperceptions of the U.S. stratification system. First, people commonly reported the belief that the gap between the upper class and those below is closing, although most evidence shows that it is widening. Second, they used a definition of social class that narrowly defines a class society as one organized around rigid castes.

Third, they reported a great deal of faith in education as a route to upward mobility. Recent evidence suggests, however, that while higher education aids upward mobility more than any other factor, it is no guarantee of success, and its impact is growing weaker as college degrees become more common (Freeman, 1976; Jencks et al., 1979; Thurow, 1975). If a relative few have college degrees, its value is high, but when college education is a common characteristic of job applicants, it represents less of an advantage.

Fourth, and perhaps most important, people generally thought of stratification in individualistic terms. The responses of many are summarized by one answer: "We're still a competitive society; *people are still trying to get ahead of the next person*, and if that ever changes, it won't be America anymore" (p. 294). This kind of response suggests that we tend to accept stratification because we believe that mobility will allow us to escape being at the bottom of the distribution system. In effect, they are saying, "Inequality is acceptable so long as I can feel that I'm doing better than someone else."

This ignores the *structure* of stratified societies. So long as an elite controls most of wealth and income, a stratification system can become open only to a very limited degree, whether the society is capitalist or socialist. However freely we may move from the lower to the middle class, 80 percent will still be competing with one another for the relatively small portion of wealth and income that remains after the wealthiest 20 percent takes its "share."

Herman (1975) argued that a significant shift toward equality will occur only when the lower 80 percent focus not on competition among themselves, but on the share of wealth and income left to them by the top 20 percent.

> Change, if it comes, will likely arise out of a continued series of shocks and a failure of the system to "deliver," not only to the bottom 20 percent, but to the lower 80 percent. Only substantial material blows are apparently capable of breaking through false consciousness. (p. 117)

Equality and Classlessness

To Weber, a classless society is one in which everyone receives an equal share of wealth, power, and prestige. Marx went further by defining a classless society as one in which the distinction between owners and workers is removed and no one has the power to control opportunities to earn an equal share of what a society produces. Weber's view tells us little about how to achieve a classless society, because it pays little attention to the ways in which classes are created and perpetuated. Marx, however, was primarily interested in change, and suggested how it might come about.

Davis and Moore (1945) held that inequality is functional, but they were uncertain about its inevitability (Davis, 1953). Marx believed that inequality will persist until societies are able to produce an abundance of goods without depending heavily on physical labor. He saw capitalism as a necessary step in a long historical process toward the utopian goal of equality, because capitalism dramatically increases production. Marx believed that *all* forms of inequality will disappear in advanced societies—for which he reserved the term "communist"—and capitalism will no longer be necessary. Indeed, Marx (in Marx and Engels, 1846) contended that the division of labor itself will disappear:

> In a communist society, where nobody has one exclusive sphere of activity, but each can become accomplished in any branch he wishes, society . . . makes it possible for me to do one thing today and another tomorrow, to hunt in the morning, fish in the afternoon, rear cattle in the evening, and criticize after dinner. (p. 22)

This vision is clearly utopian, and even Marx's colleague, Engels, believed that the most advanced societies will depend on complex divisions of labor that require some people to occupy positions of authority (see also Dahrendorf, 1959). Many functional theorists also see inequalities of prestige as inevitable, for high prestige is, by definition, always in short supply: There is no such thing as "high prestige" except in relation to those who have lower prestige. What is unclear, however, is whether inequality of prestige requires that some receive levels of respect so low that it damages their self-esteem.

The United States appears to have the ability to produce the abundance that Marx believed is necessary for equality. If all income for 1985 were distributed evenly among families, each would receive $32,900. In fact, however, 52 percent of all families had incomes more than $5,000 below this amount, and 40 percent had incomes more than $10,000 below. In order for family income to be equally distributed (20 percent going to each fifth of the population), 28 percent of all income would have to be redistributed from the top 40 percent of the population to the lower 60 percent (U.S. Census Bureau, 1987a).

While the United States clearly produces enough to provide for all its people, the actual distribution is far from this goal. Efforts to redistribute income—by taxing the rich at higher rates and supplementing poor people's incomes with welfare payments, food stamps, and free medical care—have only slightly increased the share of income going to the poorest class. At the same time, they have lowered the share received by the middle class (Beeghley, 1983; U.S. Census Bureau, 1987a) and done nothing to weaken the dominance of the upper class (Devine, 1983; Page, 1983).

In addition, by defining the problem of inequality primarily in terms of poverty, we ignore the fact that even if poverty were eradicated entirely, the enormous gulf separating the wealthiest 20 percent from everyone else would remain. In many ways, a single-minded concentration on poverty as *the* problem maintains inequality by distracting both lower- and middle-class people from the fact that they have far more in common with each other than either has with the upper class.

Why does stratification persist, even though we produce a huge surplus?

Class Consciousness and Social Change

Marx believed that even in societies that produce an abundance of goods, classes will disappear only when members of the working class achieve **class consciousness**—when they become aware of the true extent of inequality as well as its social causes. Without this, classes are little more than social aggregates—collections of people who have a status in common. With class consciousness, however, common interests become a basis for organizing social movements.

Why have the middle and lower classes not achieved class consciousness and demanded change? As we saw earlier in this chapter, we have a strong cultural ideology that supports stratification; but, there is more involved than simple ideology. Life for many *has* improved within the existing class system, and each small step upward reinforces the belief that it is possible to reach the top. This belief, in turn, supports competition as a way of life, and when people are competing with each other, they are unlikely to come together and recognize their common interests.

An additional piece of the answer lies in the concept of **alienation**—a psychological condition in which people feel disconnected from other people or their own behavior (Marx, 1884). When we work for someone else rather than for ourselves, we lose control over the conditions under which we live and work. The resulting lack of autonomy and self-control causes us to be something less than fully human, for as we lose control over work, we feel separated from it—alienated—and because work is such an important part of our lives, alienation from it produces feelings of alienation from each other. The alienation produced by a class society, then, makes it less likely that members of the working class will critically examine the true nature of their condition.

C. Wright Mills (1951) suggested that an important part of alienation is fear. Because those who control the means of production control our ability to make a living, we tend to live in a constant state of anxiety over our future. If we fear what employers may decide to do with us, we are less likely to threaten them and more likely to turn our anxieties on those who have less power over us—on other workers. In socialist countries fear is directed at the state, which, like employers in capitalist societies, controls people's ability to earn a living.

This explains why to many white male workers in the U.S. the "enemy" is not the upper class, but nonwhites and women who compete with them for jobs; and to many nonwhites and women the "enemy" is the white male worker who stands in the way of their upward mobility by trying to maintain a monopoly over skilled jobs. As a result, members of different racial, gender, and ethnic categories fail to see what they have in common—membership in the working class. Instead, they tend to explain their circumstances in terms of *one another*, rather than as the inevitable consequence of the stratification system itself.

While inequality within societies is likely to cause severe strains in the coming years, inequality between nations is an increasingly serious source of international tension and conflict. Countries that once supplied industrial nations with raw materials—rare metals and oil—are becoming more militant and demanding an end to relationships through which wealthy nations prosper at the expense of poorer ones. Less developed countries, realizing that industrial nations depend on them for raw materials, are using this awareness to exact higher prices for their goods.

While it may seem unlikely that Aristotle's notion of justice will ever come to pass in industrial societies, one thing is certain: change toward a more equitable and just system for distributing wealth, power, and prestige requires a full understanding of the structures and cultural ideas that produce and sustain stratification. The lot of individuals will improve little until we appreciate that each of us participates in social systems that affect our lives.

SUMMARY

1. Social stratification refers to the structures through which the products of social life—including wealth, power, and prestige—are distributed unequally. Stratification is a process in which statuses strongly affect rewards.

2. One of the most important concepts in the study of stratification is social class. To Marx, class position depends on a person's relationship to the means of production. Capitalists own or control the means of production, while workers sell their labor power to capitalists.

3. To Weber, class position depends on the *outcomes* of stratification; in other words, on how much power, prestige, or wealth a person has.

4. Davis and Moore's functional theory of stratification argues that inequality exists because some tasks are more important than others and it is necessary to offer higher rewards in order to motivate individuals to acquire the training to perform them. Complex divisions of labor also require that some people have authority over others.

5. Conflict theorists argue that inequality benefits only those who are in dominant positions and that culture often serves the interests of the elite and constitutes an ideology that supports the status quo. False consciousness exists when people misperceive the true nature and causes of the inequalities in their lives.

6. From the perspectives of both Marx and Weber, almost all societies are stratified. In the United States, the control of the means of production is concentrated in the hands of a small minority and the distributions of wealth, power, and prestige are very unequal.

7. Social mobility is the movement of people within or between social classes. In closed systems class position is based on ascribed statuses (or castes) and no movement between them is allowed. There is a moderate amount of mobility in the United States and other industrial societies, but most upward moves are quite small.

8. The most important factors in mobility are education, social class of parents, race, gender, occupation, and age. Mobility has little effect on the relative positions of social classes. Family mobility often requires that both spouses work and that the family go into considerable debt. Job ladders often foster the illusion of mobility by dividing a short distance into many small steps.

9. Societies differ in the degree of inequality and there is great inequality between societies. Inequality is more severe in poor and newly industrializing societies than in industrial countries. While socialist countries do not base inequality on ownership of the means of production, they still have considerable inequality.

10. The gap between rich and poor nations is stable, in part because wealthy nations are in a position to exploit poorer ones.

11. Debate about change in stratification focuses on two issues: an end to the inequality and social classes of stratification and equality of opportunity within a stratified society.

12. Marx's communist utopia, in which social classes would disappear, is unlikely to ever come to pass. Both conflict and functional theorists

believe that inequality of authority will always be necessary, and some functional theorists also believe that inequality of prestige is inevitable.

13. Efforts to redistribute income in the U.S. have slightly improved conditions among the poor but have had no effect on the upper class.

KEY TERMS

Looking Elsewhere

Having studied Chapter 11, you might want to look at related discussions in *Human Arrangements*, which include

RECOMMENDED READINGS

BEEGHLEY, L. (1983). *Living poor in America.* New York: Praeger. An important book that challenges many common beliefs about welfare and the causes of poverty.

BENDIX, R., and LIPSET, S. M. (Eds.). (1966). *Class, status, and power* (2nd ed.). New York: Free Press. A comprehensive collection of articles about social stratification.

BOWLES, S., and GINTIS, H. (1976). *Schooling in capitalist America: Educational reform and the contradictions of economic life.* New York: Basic Books. An important book about the ways in which schooling reproduces social classes and inequality in the United States.

KERBO, H. R. (1983). *Social stratification and inequality.* New York: McGraw-Hill. A clear, interesting, and thorough introductory text.

LENSKI, G. (1966). *Power and privilege.* New York: McGraw-Hill. A fascinating look at the relationship between historical changes in the mode of production and the emergence of social inequality. The early chapters are particularly useful as overviews of the general problem of social stratification.

MARX, K. (1964). *Selected writings in sociology and social philosophy.* Edited by T. Bottomore and M. Rubel. Baltimore, MD: Penguin. A highly accessible introduction to Marx's major ideas on social stratification.

SENNETT, R., and COBB, J. (1972). *The hidden injuries of class.* New York: Vintage. A thought-provoking look at the ways in which social class differences affect how people feel about themselves and one another.

12 Race and Ethnicity

Chapter 11 described basic aspects of all social stratification systems through which rewards are distributed unequally within and among societies. Whereas Chapter 11 focused primarily on the importance of achieved statuses such as occupation, in this and the next two chapters we look at the importance of ascribed statuses such as race and ethnicity, gender, and age in the distribution of wealth, power, and prestige.

We begin with some basic concepts—race, ethnicity, minority group, and social oppression—and then examine cultural, structural, and ecological aspects of social inequality based on race and ethnicity. Then we use conflict and functional perspectives to explain why societies have for centuries used ascribed statuses as bases for inequality, and, finally, we explore what it might take to end social oppression.

RACE AND ETHNICITY

Imagine that you apply for a copy of your birth certificate one day, and when you receive it, you discover that it lists your "race" as something other than what you and everyone else always considered it to be. You are black, and the certificate says you are white; or you are Asian, and it says you are black. How would you feel?

This is exactly what happened in 1977 to Susie Guillory Phipps—a New Orleans resident who had always been white, to herself and to everyone who encountered her. She had twice married white men, and her family album was filled with pictures of blue-eyed, white ancestors. The state of Louisiana, however, defined her as "colored."

When she protested to state authorities, they carefully traced her ancestry back 222 years and found that although her great-great-great-great grandfather was white, her great-great-great-great grandmother was black. Under Louisiana law, anyone whose ances-try was at least 3 percent black was considered black. Even with an ancestry 97 percent white, the state defined her as black (Jaynes, 1982).

Susie Phipps spent $20,000 to force Louisiana to change her birth certificate, and in 1983 Louisiana repealed the law. Why would a state have a formula for officially deciding what each person's race is? Why would a tiny percentage of black ancestry cause her to be considered black, while an overwhelmingly white ancestry would not mean she is white?

The key lies in the word "mean" in the previous sentence, for as we have seen, what things objectively *are* is often less significant to people than what things *mean* culturally. As a biological concept, **race** refers to people who share a genetic heritage that results in distinct physical features, such as the color of skin, eyes, and hair, or the shape of the eyes.

The biological concept, however, is useful only if different races remain separate from one another and do not combine their genes in reproduction. Most scientists agree that the genes that determine biological race have become so mixed that the vast majority of people have a mixed racial heritage. From a biological point of view, the concept of race has lost most of its usefulness (Dobzhansky, 1973; Richardson and Spears, 1972).

Most cultures, however, define race as an ascribed status which has important consequences for the occupants of different racial statuses. A biologist would have to say that Susie Phipps is certainly more white than black, but her dilemma has little to do with biology and everything to do with a culture in which, once she is defined as black, she is perceived, evaluated, and treated as black.

The cultural meaning of race is far more important than biological distinctions. Although Adolph Hitler's claim that there exists a distinct Aryan "race" of tall, blond, blue-eyed people is scientifically incorrect, his error (as well as the fact that he was short and dark-haired) did not prevent him and his followers from identifying Jews, Gypsies, Poles, and others as members of inferior "races." Nor did it prevent them from exterminating millions of people who fell into the wrong "racial" category.

Whereas the sociological concept of race refers to statuses based on a shared biological heritage, **ethnicity** refers to a shared cultural heritage. An **ethnic group** is a collection of people who identify with a common culture, share a common heritage of food and styles of dress, music and literature, and look back upon a history that reflects the collective experience of "their people." Jews, Italians, Egyptians, white Anglo-Saxon Protestants (WASPs), Irish, Ugandans, and Mexicans all constitute distinct ethnic groups whose members identify with a particular cultural and historical heritage.

The U.S. contains an extraordinary variety of ethnic backgrounds. In 1980, 10 percent of all those 5 to 17 years old spoke a language other than English at home, and 14 percent spoke English only with difficulty. Fifty-four percent of adults trace their origins to single ethnicities—the largest of which are German, English, Italian, Spanish, Polish, and Irish—and 46 percent report multiple origins (U.S. Census Bureau, 1982).

Race and ethnicity are often a major basis for feelings of pride and solidarity among people, but they also have been used for centuries as a basis for distributing wealth, power, and prestige, as well as for systematic violence, exploitation, and oppression.

Puzzles: When Is 80 Percent of a Population Not a Majority?

When they are blacks living in South Africa. It is also true that women do not rule any known societies even though they are a numerical majority in virtually all of them.

Minorities and Social Oppression

All of us trace our origins to ethnic groups that constitute relatively small percentages of the U.S. population. The largest set of people who cite only one ethnic origin are German, but they make up only 10 percent of the population. In terms of *numbers*, we all belong to ethnic minorities.

Sociologists, however, are less concerned with relative numbers than with the social consequences of ethnic and racial differences. From this point of view, a **minority** is a category of people

who, because of their physical or cultural characteristics, are singled out from the others in the society in which they live for differential and unequal treatment. (Wirth, 1945, p. 351)

A minority is defined not by relative numbers of people with certain characteristics, but by how they are treated as a result of such characteristics. In South

In South Africa, blacks are treated as a social minority even though they are an overwhelming numerical majority comprising more than 80 percent of the population. The extreme poverty they are forced to endure vividly underscores the fact that relative numbers have nothing to do with minority standing.

Africa, blacks are a minority because they are singled out for unequal treatment in spite of the fact that they make up the vast *majority* of the population. Regardless of their relative numbers, South African blacks would not be a minority in a society that treated whites and blacks in the same way. What all minorities have in common is that they are the objects of socially supported mistreatment, injustice, and exploitation that are the essence of **social oppression**.

It is important to understand that individuals may be abused or exploited without being oppressed. The concept of oppression describes relationships in which minorities are defined as inferior by dominant groups. Individuals are mistreated simply because they are members, regardless of their behavior or personal characteristics. When a man is beaten and robbed because his attacker wants his money, he is not being oppressed; but, if he is beaten and robbed because his attacker hates him as a member of a minority group, then he is a victim of oppression.

Moreover, a group may be defined as a minority even though some members are not oppressed; and a group may be socially dominant even though some members do not personally oppress minority people. Oppression is a social phenomenon that is based on the relative standing of different groups. Because some are culturally defined as superior to others, they are in a social position that allows them to benefit from the exploitation and mistreatment of those defined as inferior.

Whether or not we behave as victims or victimizers, the oppressive relationships between groups nonetheless exist. I, as a white man, may not personally oppress blacks; but this does not wipe away the fact that blacks as a group occupy an oppressed position in the United States, and I, as a white man, may benefit from their oppression whether I want to or not.

What are the social bases of oppression? What forms does it take and what are the consequences? As with other social phenomena, the sociological perspective focuses on three basic aspects of oppression—culture, structure, and ecology.

CULTURE, RACE, AND ETHNICITY

Culture plays an important part in the mistreatment of minorities. How people perceive and evaluate others, as well as how they feel and behave toward them, is strongly affected by beliefs that describe them, values

that rank them, attitudes that direct positive and negative feelings toward them, and norms that restrict people as participants in social relationships.

Prejudice: Racism and Ethnicism

Prejudice is an attitude based on stereotypes about members of a group (Allport, 1958; see also Seeman, 1981). Like all attitudes, prejudice includes beliefs that describe different kinds of people as well as values that rank their relative worth. Prejudice based on race is **racism**; and prejudice based on ethnicity is **ethnicism**. Prejudice may be either positive or negative: the belief that Hindus are superior to Muslims is just as prejudiced in favor of Hindus as it is against Muslims.

Whether positive or negative, prejudice has four characteristics that make it an important part of social oppression (Memmi, 1964). First, prejudice is based on real or imagined differences between groups. Prejudice against blacks includes the belief that they are lazy, stupid, happy-go-lucky, dirty, musical, and oversexed—descriptions that have also been applied to European Gypsies and poor people in southern Italy (Pettigrew, 1968). With the notable exception of Bill Cosby, family life among nonwhites is rarely portrayed, and nonwhites rarely have lead roles in television shows. When they do, they are usually cast in comic, servile roles (Unger, 1983; Withey and Abeles, 1980). Say the words "organized crime" and many people immediately think of Italians. Many people think of Jews as ambitious, sly, and dishonest, and of white Anglo-Saxon Protestants (WASPs) as snobs who only attend Ivy League schools.

People often form beliefs about personal characteristics of people in ethnic groups even when they have no personal experience of them (Karlins, Coffman, and Walters, 1969; van Dijk, 1987). In one study, college students even had beliefs about ethnic groups that do not exist—"Wallonians" and "Pirenians"—and their beliefs were usually negative (Hartley, 1946).

Second, prejudice attaches values to differences in ways that benefit dominant groups at the expense of minorities. To many Irish Protestants—who dominate Northern Ireland—"Protestant" is good and "Catholic" is bad. The drive to feel superior then leads people in the dominant group to *maximize* the perceived difference between themselves and minorities, for "the smaller he makes his victim, the bigger he becomes"

Historically, blacks in the U.S. have been confined to the most menial occupations, such as washing and ironing clothes. This status has been based on prejudiced beliefs that blacks are capable of little else.

(Memmi, 1964, p. 189). Many Irish Catholics respond with prejudice of their own against Protestants.

Third, prejudice is generalized to all members of a target group—in other words, each individual's self is summarized by stereotypes (Lieberson, 1982). Stereotypes often have a "grain of truth"—the average black score on school achievement tests is lower than the white average; the Italian word "Mafia" does describe *some* criminal organizations; and WASPs are more likely than others to occupy top positions in large corporations. Stereotypes, however, ignore enormous differences between individuals who share social characteristics: many blacks are more intelligent than most whites; most Italians are not criminals; and the vast majority of white Anglo-Saxons are neither executives nor professionals and do not attend Ivy League colleges.

Fourth, in order to ensure their superior position, members of dominant groups support the belief that the inferior position of those in a minority is absolute and inevitable because it results merely from membership in the group. This is often extended back in time and into the future: "Jews have always been greedy and blacks have always been inferior; therefore, they always *will* be." In the case of racism, biology is often used to explain the disadvantaged position of minorities, and biological racism is enormously powerful because, once accepted, it defines differences as absolute and, therefore, unchangeable. As Memmi (1964) put it:

biological racism . . . penetrates the flesh, the blood and the genes of the victim. It is transformed into fate, destiny, heredity. From then on, the victim's very *being* is contaminated, and likewise *every manifestation of that being:* behavior, body, and soul. (p. 190)

For centuries, scientists and others have tried to prove that members of minorities are biologically inferior. Jensen (1969) has asserted that most of the difference between the average IQ scores of blacks and whites is due to genetic factors. The crux of his position is that racial differences in IQ persist even among people who have similar social class backgrounds. From this he argued that since racial differences persist even when social environments are similar, then genetics must be the cause. He concluded that blacks as a group will always be intellectually inferior to whites, regardless of educational efforts.

There are several problems with Jensen's argument (Tumin, 1973). First, IQ tests measure a set of mental skills that are developed in and reflect a particular cultural context—that is, the world of the white middle class. Many black children do relatively poorly on IQ tests, not because they are less intelligent, but because the examples and language used in test questions reflect white middle-class culture and experience. The tests used to measure IQ are to some degree *culturally biased* in favor of whites.

Second, a genetic explanation of racial differences rests on the false assumption that blacks and whites represent pure racial types. Hunt and Walker

(1974) estimated that 70 percent of all U.S. blacks have some white ancestors and that 20 percent of all whites have some black ancestors.

The most serious criticism of Jensen, however, is that he misinterpreted his own evidence (Lewontin, 1970). Specifically, Jensen assumed that when he compared the IQs of blacks and whites who came from the same social classes, he was comparing people whose social environments were the same. As we have seen in earlier chapters, however, the measurement of social class is, at best, quite crude. To conclude that people whose parents had similar educations and occupations are alike on all the known and unknown social factors that affect the development of intelligence is simply unjustified. In other words, we do not *know* how social environments affect intelligence, and controlling for social class does not eliminate the social causes of IQ differences.

Racism and ethnicism therefore rest on negative stereotypes about minorities and positive stereotypes about dominant groups. They are more than simple sets of ideas, however, for they play a vital part in justifying and perpetuating the interests of dominant groups. Racism and ethnicism, in other words, are used as *ideologies*.

Undoubtedly, racism contributed to the actions of U.S. soldiers when they massacred close to 500 women, men, and children in the Vietnamese village of My Lai. Despite pleas for mercy, the victims were stabbed, thrown down wells, pushed into ditches and shot, or forced into dwellings, which were then blown up with grenades.

Ideology and Oppression

Racism and ethnicism support oppression by denying the existence of oppression itself. This is accomplished primarily by blaming the negative consequences of oppression on its victims.

Many people in the U.S. believe that theirs is a land of opportunity in which ability and motivation largely determine success and failure. Such a belief can be used to "mask" the oppression of minorities, however: "America is a land of equal opportunity; if you have failed, you must be at fault." Not surprisingly, whites are far more likely than blacks to believe that blacks have equal opportunity, for such a belief effectively blames blacks for their disadvantaged position (L. Harris, 1977).

Blaming victims often takes a more direct form. In 1986, 21 percent of white adults believed that blacks have worse jobs, income, and housing than whites because blacks have "less in-born ability to learn"; and 64 percent answered that blacks "don't have the motivation or will power to pull themselves out of poverty" (GSS, 1986). In 1981, 43 percent of whites believed that laziness was the major cause of black unemployment (Clymer, 1981).

Within the framework of prejudiced ideologies, members of minorities are not perceived as varied and complex individuals who have many of the same feelings, goals, and needs as other people. This view makes it easier to perceive them as faceless objects, and, therefore, easier to treat them in ways that members of dominant groups would never accept for themselves.

During the Vietnam War, Asians were labeled "gooks" and were stereotyped as people to whom "life is cheap." This made it easier to kill large numbers of Vietnamese civilians since, after all, the U.S. military was not taking away something of much importance to *them*. Members of minorities often have ideologies of their own that justify violence toward members of dominant groups. During the 1960s some black militants labeled all police officers "pigs," and some used this stereotyped label to justify killing them.

The Destruction of Culture

How is a society affected by the coming together of people from different ethnic backgrounds? Mexico is a good example of **amalgamation**, which occurs when diverse cultures merge into a single new culture. Modern Mexico is a mixture of Indian and Spanish culture. This is what Zangwill (1909/1933) meant when he mistakenly described the U.S. as a "melting pot."

Assimilation occurs when people from different backgrounds conform to the dominant culture; and **pluralism** occurs when people of different ethnicity live side-by-side and maintain their cultural diversity.

Assimilation best describes cultures in most heterogeneous societies, including the U.S. In spite of our immigrants' varied backgrounds, the most important elements of our culture are Anglo-Saxon. English is our language, our legal system is based on English Common Law, and basic cultural ideas about liberty and the rights of individuals are based on the English Magna Carta.

Assimilation often requires ethnic minorities to abandon their cultures as the price of escaping minority status and participating fully in the life of a society. The first U.S. public schools were designed to enforce "Anglo-conformity" among immigrants (Cole and Cole, 1954), and immigrant children still find that their native language and customs are unacceptable in white schools that regard non-Anglo-Saxon cultures as inferior. The children of immigrants typically do not learn the language of their parents, and it is not uncommon for children to have difficulty understanding their own grandparents. As a result, entire cultural traditions may eventually be lost (see Conklin and Lourie, 1983; Stevens, 1985).

The decline of non-English languages in the U.S. is not uniform, however. While native speakers of European languages such as French have declined, Spanish and Portuguese language groups have grown, fostering a strong "Latino" ethnic identity (see Stevens and Swicegood, 1987). In some states, especially those with large Spanish-speaking populations such as California, Texas, and New York, this has prompted controversial proposals to make English the "official" language by no longer printing voting ballots in both Spanish and English. Supporters of such bills argue that widespread use of languages other than English undercut a sense of national cultural unity, while opponents see them as an attempt to destroy ethnic subcultures in the interest of enforcing uniformity and the dominant position of the Anglo culture.

By devaluing ethnic and racial differences, racism and ethnicism destroy cultural diversity (Blauner, 1972). When blacks were brought to America as slaves, their African cultures were systematically destroyed by their white owners. They were forced to take new names, and family members were separated from one another. They were not allowed to govern themselves, to administer justice, or practice their religions. Blacks found themselves in the midst of a white culture that excluded them in every way except as slaves (Frederickson, 1981).

American Indians also experienced systematic efforts by whites to destroy their cultures. For centuries, they had been free peoples who effectively governed themselves and administered justice. Since their conquest by whites, however, they have been forced to adopt a uniform type of government modeled after Anglo-Saxon institutions: constitutionally elected tribal officers, tribal courts, and legislatures (Josephy, 1973). Most power, however, is vested in a federal agency—the Bureau of Indian Affairs—not in the tribes (Barsh and Henderson, 1980).

With autonomy and self-government went many beliefs and values. Some tribes valued cooperation more than competition, group success more than personal ambition, the careful management of nature more than its conquest and exploitation. People were seen as an integral part of the natural world, not separate from it, and had neither the need nor the right to dominate it.

Such values were unacceptable in the Judeo-Christian tradition of whites, a tradition that included centuries of individualism, political domination, economic development, and exploitation of the natural environment. Indians and their culture stood in the way of white "progress," and so the dominant whites forced the Indians to choose between adopting white culture and being annihilated (Josephy, 1973).

The destruction of cultural diversity often takes more subtle forms. It is common, for example, to use a single term, "Hispanic," to refer to people with enormously varied backgrounds—Mexicans, Puerto Ricans, Cubans, Brazilians, Colombians, Chileans, Argentinians, Salvadorans, and Nicaraguans. In each of these countries, people certainly distinguish themselves from other Latin American peoples; but in the U.S., Hispanic is used by the white majority to conveniently label nonwhites who are not black. In the same way, Africans are referred to as if they were culturally homogeneous, when in fact there are hundreds of different languages and cultures on the African continent.

Racist and ethnicist ideologies support social relationships in which minorities are oppressed, partic-

The devastation of American Indian societies by white conquest is reflected in many ways, including lowering Indian culture to the point of selling it as a commodity to tourists, most of whom are white.

ularly through the destruction of culture. What do the social structures that result from racism and ethnicism look like?

SOCIAL STRUCTURE, RACE, AND ETHNICITY

On the microlevel of role relationships, oppression occurs as exploitation, abuse, and injustice in social interactions between members of different groups. On the macrolevel of social structure, race and ethnicity are statuses that powerfully affect the distribution of wealth, power, and prestige.

Patterns of Interaction: Discrimination

Whereas prejudice is an attitude, **discrimination** refers to unequal *treatment* of people based on stereotypes. Expectations and feelings during interactions depend on how people define social situations, and this, in turn, depends on how they perceive other people. When we see people dressed in police uniforms, we immediately act and feel as though we have significant information about them. In the same way, when we identify people's race or ethnicity, we draw upon cultural ideas that identify how we should behave, what we should expect of them, and how we feel toward them.

In 1970 college students conducted an experiment in which pairs of black, Mexican, and white students tried to rent apartments in Los Angeles. All 12 students dressed similarly, spoke English equally well, and had equal educations. They applied for a total of 25 apartments, and in virtually every case the white couples were the most likely to be accepted. Black and Mexican couples were more often told there were no apartments available, or were quoted higher rents. Only 5 of the 25 apartment managers did not discriminate in any way (Johnson et al., 1971).

Prejudice differs from discrimination in the same way that our beliefs about people differ from what we *do* in relation to them. In this sense, our behavior and attitudes may often contradict each other (Merton, 1948). Some members of dominant groups are not prejudiced and do not discriminate against minorities, while other unprejudiced people may nonetheless discriminate against minorities when it is expedient or profitable to do so.

Prejudice does not necessarily result in discriminatory behavior. Our culture strongly values equality for all, and both prejudice and discrimination are against the "American creed." Prejudiced people are under pressure to conceal their prejudice, and for this reason some people are what Merton (1948) called "timid bigots."

In the 1930s, a Chinese couple stopped at 250 restaurants and hotels as they traveled across the U.S. and were refused service only once. Later, they sent letters to the establishments and asked if they served "members of the Chinese race." About half replied, and of these, 90 percent said they did not (Lapiere, 1934).

A later study in a northeastern suburb had similar results: both white and black couples were treated well in restaurants, but attempts to make telephone reservations for black groups were strongly resisted (Kutner et al., 1952).

Regardless of our attitudes, whether or not we *act* on them depends strongly on the social situation. It is far easier for people to discriminate over a telephone or through the mail than it is when they are face-to-face with the person who will be hurt by discriminatory behavior. It is also easier to discriminate in secondary relationships ("It's nothing personal"), because people can then claim that they are simply following rules formulated and enforced by others. In this way, they are able to conceal their own motives, which may or may not rest on prejudiced attitudes.

Social interaction is an important arena in which the attitudes of racism and ethnicism are played out to the benefit of dominant groups and at the expense of minorities. It is here, on the smallest level, that cultural ideas about race and ethnicity become visible in social relationships. On a larger structural level, however, race and ethnicity affect the material conditions of people's lives, for it is here that these statuses play an important part in social stratification.

Wealth, Income, and Life Chances

Race exerts a powerful effect on the distribution of income and wealth in the U.S. As of 1984, white households had accumulated an average of eleven times the net wealth of black households, and almost a third of all black households had no net wealth at all (see Table 12-1).

The 1985 median income of white households was $24,900, but it was only $17,500 for Hispanics and $14,800 for blacks. Black households constituted 11 percent of the population and yet received only 7 percent of all income, 64 percent of what they would receive if income were distributed equally. Only 5.8 percent of black households had incomes of $50,000 or more, compared with 7.3 percent of Hispanics and 15.8 percent of whites. Blacks and Hispanics were almost three times more likely than whites to have incomes below the poverty level (U.S. Census Bureau, 1986a, 1987a).

Why do whites make so much more money than nonwhites? Education appears to explain some of the difference, for whites are 15 percent more likely than blacks to have high school diplomas and almost twice as likely to have college degrees. There are three problems with education as an explanation, however.

First, average education is slightly higher among blacks than among Hispanics, but average income is lower. Second, when we compare families whose adults have similar educational levels, the racial difference remains: in families with a college-educated householder, mean income in 1985 was $50,000 for whites, $42,000 for Hispanics, and $38,000 for blacks. Third, unemployment is more likely among nonwhites regardless of education: in 1986, blacks and Hispanics with four or more years of college were 39 and 57 percent more likely to be unemployed than similarly educated whites (U.S. Census Bureau, 1986a).

What about occupation? Do whites have higher incomes because they have better jobs? Here the evidence is more convincing: whites have a 60 percent greater chance of holding upper-level white-collar

Table 12-1

Distribution of Wealth, by Race, United States, 1984

WEALTH	WHITES	BLACKS	HISPANIC
Median net worth[1] of households	$39,100	$3,400	$4,900
Percent with			
zero or negative net worth	8%	30%	24%
$100,000 or more	26%	4%	8%
Percent who own homes	68%	44%	40%

[1]Net worth is the sum of assets minus debts and other liabilities.

Source: U.S. Census Bureau, 1986d.

Although the civil rights movement has enabled a small minority of blacks to make it to the middle and upper-middle classes, the vast majority of blacks are no closer to equality with whites than they were 30 years ago. Nowhere are these effects more widespread or compelling than among black children, almost half of whom live in poverty.

jobs, a 25 percent greater chance for lower-level white-collar jobs, and a 40 percent greater chance for upper-level blue-collar jobs. Nonwhites, on the other hand, are 55 percent more likely than whites to have low-paying, unskilled jobs (Table 12-2, p. 320). Take a moment to study Table 12-2. Check the jobs you would like to have, and then see which columns they are in.

Racial differences in income are affected not only by the kinds of jobs people have but also by whether or not they have jobs at all. In 1985 the unemployment rate among blacks was 15 percent—more than twice as high as the rates for whites and 50 percent higher than the rate for Hispanics (U.S. Census Bureau, 1986a). It is generally true that unemployment levels whites experience as a recession—6 or 7 percent—represent relative prosperity for nonwhites. If whites experienced the unemployment risks that are usual for blacks, they would consider themselves in the midst of a deep depression.

Whites are not only more likely than nonwhites to have *a* job, but are also more likely to be working at two or more jobs. What is most interesting, however, is that the reasons for working at more than one job vary by race. Blacks are more likely than whites to have extra jobs in order to pay regular bills, pay off debts, or save for future needs. Whites, on the other hand, are more likely to work at extra jobs in order to gain new work experiences or to make "special" pur-

chases (U.S. Census Bureau, 1982). Even though whites are more likely to have two or more jobs, they are less likely to have them because they *must*.

While blacks generally have poorer jobs and less education than whites, these differences do not fully explain why the income of black families is so much lower. Nor do education and occupation fully explain the income gap between blacks and other nonwhites and their greater likelihood of being unemployed. What, then, is left?

What is left is racial discrimination. The cost of being black includes being systematically paid less than whites for jobs that require comparable levels of skill and training (National Committee on Pay Equity, 1987). As Duncan (1969) demonstrated with his sophisticated analysis of data describing U.S. men 25 to 64 years old,

> At least one-third of the income gap arises because black and white men in the same line of work, with the same amount of schooling, with equal ability, from families of the same size and same socio-economic level, simply do not draw the same wages and salaries. (p. 108)

Although discrimination plays a major part in perpetuating the minority standing of blacks, William J. Wilson (1978) and Hout (1984) argued that race, itself, is slowly losing its importance. Until recently,

Table 12-2

Representation of Nonwhites in Various Occupations (United States, 1985)

OCCUPATIONS IN WHICH NONWHITES ARE UNDERREPRESENTED, BY DEGREE

Severe[1]	*Substantial*[2]	*Slight*[3]	*Overrepresented*
Engineer	Accountant	Public official	Social worker
Lawyer	Social scientist	Elementary teacher	Military, enlisted grade
Judge	Computer programmer	Electronic technician	Vocational counselor
Librarian	Personnel worker	Mail carrier	Police officer
Dentist	Nurse	High school teacher	File clerk
College teacher	Military officer	Shipping clerk	Clerical supervisor
Scientist	Pharmacist	Science technician	Recreation worker
Physician	Health technician	Stock clerk	Computer operator
Journalist	Bank teller	Storekeeper	Mail clerk
Writer	Drafter	Billing clerk	Stenographer
Artist	Restaurant or bar manager	Health administrator	Telephone operator
Entertainer	Secretary	Public administrator	Crane operator
Editor	Counter clerk	Painter	Typist
Financial manager	Cashier	Hairdresser	Factory assembler
Sales representative	Insurance adjustor	Punch and stamp	Seamstress
Bookkeeper	Receptionist	Press operator	Laundry worker
Carpenter	Plumber	Child care worker	Food service worker
Electrician	Machinist	Welder	Machine operator
Sheet metal worker	Auto mechanic	Stock handler	Barber
Tool and die maker	Butcher	Telephone installer	Meat or produce packer
Radio and TV repair	Blue-collar supervisor	Electric line worker	Textile factory worker
Type compositor	Aircraft mechanic	Printing press operator	Chauffeur
Typesetter	Baker		Truck, bus, taxi driver
Mine worker	Psychologist		Freight handler
Farmer or farm manager			Construction laborer
Waiter			Cook
			Practical nurse
			Gardener
			Cleaning worker
			Guard
			Hospital orderly
			House servant

[1]Percentage less than half the percentage of nonwhites in the labor force.
[2]Percentage between half and three-fourths of nonwhite percentage in the labor force.
[3]Percentage just under nonwhite percentage in the labor force.

Source: U.S. Census Bureau, 1983c.

blacks were discriminated against universally simply because they were black; but, during the last few decades, some blacks have entered the middle and upper-middle classes. While the historical legacy of racism still affects *all* blacks, Wilson argued that the disadvantaged position of most blacks is now caused more by social *class* than by race. Many blacks are poor not because of *current* racial discrimination, but because a history of systematic racism and discrimination has concentrated them in the lower class, thereby confining them to unemployment and jobs that offer little hope of advancing into the middle class.

Wilson was sharply criticized by Willie (1978, 1979) who maintained that race was becoming *more* significant, not less, and was having an increasingly damaging effect on the quality of life among blacks. Thomas and Hughes (1986) took Willie's position a step further by focusing on measures of psychological harm taken between 1972 and 1985 and found that "blacks have lower life satisfaction, less trust in people, less general happiness, less marital happiness, more anomie, and lower self-rated physical health than whites regardless of social class, marital status, age, or year" (p. 839).

Blacks are the largest racial minority in the U.S., but American Indians are in the worst position. Most of the roughly 1 million Indians are confined to impoverished reservations. Unemployment averages roughly 45 percent, and average family income is under $2,000 (Burnette, 1971; Rose, 1981).

Clearly, race is an ascribed status that affects class membership. Nonwhites are heavily overrepresented in the lower class and virtually absent from the upper class. Ethnicity also affects class membership, although to a lesser degree than race. White Anglo-Saxon Protestants and Jews have higher average incomes, better jobs, and more education than do most other ethnic groups (see Farley and Neidert, 1984).

Ethnicity played its strongest role in social stratification during the nineteenth and early twentieth centuries. Successive waves of immigrants were confined to the worst jobs and living conditions in urban ghettos. Mexicans were perceived as "aborigines" who were inferior to white Anglo-Saxons (Pratt, 1935). Each new wave of immigrants, however, brought a fresh supply of poor people to occupy the bottom rung of the stratification ladder, and those who had come before were able to move upward, although only with considerable effort (Hutchinson, 1965). Those whose culture was most similar to that of the dominant Anglo-Saxons—Germans and Scandinavians—were able to move upward with greater ease than those who were culturally more different: Catholic Irish, Poles, and other East Europeans.

Ethnicity has become a relatively minor determinant of social class among whites (see Neidert and Farley, 1985). Nonwhite ethnics, however, continue to lag behind whites in average income. Among college graduates, average income among American Indians, Chinese, and Filipinos amounted to only two-thirds of the average income for all college graduates; and Hispanic and Japanese earnings amounted to roughly 85 percent of the national college-graduate average (Jencks, 1983a; see also Farley and Neidert, 1984).

The legacy of racial prejudice and oppression persists largely because race is more visible than ethnicity, but also because nonwhites have a unique history in the U.S. Whites killed Indians in vast numbers as they seized their land. Blacks were property to be bought and sold and used in any way their owners saw fit. As oppressed as minorities such as the Irish once were, they were never slaves, were never systematically slaughtered, and were never forced to abandon their cultural heritage.

Prejudice against most European minorities was largely sporadic—there were many places where the Irish were not treated as a minority—but prejudice against blacks and Indians was universal and has lasted for generations.

> Discrimination only poses a serious barrier to economic success if it is almost universal, or if its existence transforms the victims' behavior in self-defeating ways. Discrimination against European minorities was common but never anything like universal. The descendants of European immigrants have almost all had the option of shedding their ethnic identity and "passing" as just plain "Americans." Physical differences, combined with extreme social sensitivity to the significance of these differences, made this much more difficult for most blacks and somewhat more difficult for Asians, American Indians, and even Latin Americans. (Jencks, 1983a, p. 34)

As an ethnic group, Jews are an exception to these generalizations (see Johnson, 1987). For centuries, Jews were not allowed to own land, were regarded by Christians as the embodiment of evil, and were periodically murdered in large numbers, culminating in the World War II Holocaust during which an estimated 6 million were murdered. A few, however, were allowed such financial pursuits as banking and tax collecting, for when banking first came into being, it was regarded as immoral, and tax collectors were far from popular. Some Jews were "middlemen" between the upper and lower classes. This allowed the upper class to profit while avoiding the resentment of people in the lower class.

Through this, many Jews developed important skills, and when banking and business became more culturally respectable, they flourished. Because they made the best of what was left to them, Jews have, for

Jews in Nazi Germany and countries under Nazi control were regularly subjected to humiliation. In this rare 1933 photograph (top), a Jewish boy is forced to cut off his father's beard while German soldiers look on with contempt. As the Holocaust proceeded, Jews were forcibly segregated and deported by the millions, usually to their deaths by disease, starvation, torture, and mass execution by machine gun or in gas chambers.

centuries, been despised and envied. Their somewhat unique position is duplicated by some racial and ethnic minorities in other societies: Chinese merchants in Indonesia and Malaysia, and Muslim merchants in eastern and southern Africa (Pettigrew, 1968).

It is important to remember, however, that while Jews have relatively high *average* education and income, most are in the middle and working classes. The popular image of Jews as bankers is nothing more than a stereotype. Jews are rarely found on the boards of large corporations, including those of commercial banks (Domhoff and Zweigenhaft, 1983).

Power

In caste societies such as South Africa and, until recently, India, power is sharply divided according to race. The Indian constitution specifies which castes are eligible for benefits such as college scholarships, welfare, and government jobs. South African blacks are denied the vote in national elections and representation in the national parliament. They cannot travel freely, conduct strikes against employers, or choose where they will eat, work, live, or educate their children. Almost every aspect of life in South Africa is segregated by race—including public transportation, restaurants, beaches, residential neighborhoods, and schools (Price and Rosberg, 1980). In 1985 Desmund Tutu—1984 winner of the Nobel Peace Prize—became the first black bishop of the Anglican Church in Johannesburg; but he had to obtain special permission to enter the white neighborhood where the ceremony appointing him to his office took place.

Until quite recently, the situation of blacks in the U.S. was as bad as or worse than that of today's South African blacks (Elkins, 1963; Frederickson, 1981). Slavery flourished for 200 years before the Civil War, and even "free Negroes" were denied the rights to vote, testify in court, own land, or make contracts. In spite of federal efforts after the Civil War, the late 1800s and early 1900s were a period in which blacks had little power to participate in their society or to live in safety. In southern states, "Jim Crow" laws restricted blacks in every conceivable aspect of their lives. Literacy tests and poll taxes prevented many from using newly won voting rights, and they were "kept in their place" by the terror of lynchings and church burnings.

In the last 20 years blacks have greatly increased their collective power, largely by using the federal courts to fight discrimination, registering as voters, running for public office, and staging mass demonstrations. After the passage of the 1965 Voting Rights Act, the registration of black voters in the South more than doubled, and the percentages of whites and blacks registered are now nearly equal. Between 1970 and 1986 the number of political offices held by blacks increased from 1,479 to 6,384. Blacks have become mayors of large cities: Chicago, Philadelphia, Los Angeles, Atlanta, Washington, D.C., Detroit, Cleveland,

In the 1988 U.S. presidential race, Jesse Jackson stunned political experts with his ability to win not only the overwhelming support of black voters, but an unprecedented number of white voters as well. He is the first black in U.S. history to emerge as a serious contender for the nomination of a major party.

and Newark. In 1966 Edward Brooke became the first black senator in this century, and between 1962 and 1981 the number of black representatives quadrupled (U.S. Census Bureau, 1982, 1986a). In 1988, Jesse Jackson became the first black to come within striking distance of being the Democratic nominee for president or vice-president.

While such gains are important, power is still disproportionately concentrated in the hands of whites. In 1980 blacks comprised 12 percent of the U.S. population but held only 1 percent of all public offices. As of 1988, there were no blacks in the U.S. Senate, and blacks made up only 5 percent of the House of Representatives.

Nowhere is inequality of power between whites and blacks more evident than in the criminal justice system. Because blacks are more likely than whites to be poor, they are more often unable to use bail in order to stay out of jail during their trials; and numerous studies show that accused criminals are more likely to be convicted if they are imprisoned during their trials (Wice, 1973). Once convicted, blacks receive harsher sentences than whites—more than 10 times greater for murder or kidnapping, and twice as great for rape, robbery, or the sale or possession of illegal drugs (U.S. Census Bureau, 1975c). Those who murder whites receive far more severe sentences than do those who murder blacks.

As with ethnic differences in income, ethnicity plays a less important part than race in the distribution of power. Major corporations and government bodies

such as the U.S. Congress are still dominated by whites of Anglo-Saxon descent, but the ethnic lines that once clearly defined elite groups are becoming increasingly blurred (see Alba and Moore, 1982).

Prestige and Self-Esteem

When we find ourselves in an achieved status, such as occupation, that brings little respect from others, we may suffer; but we may be able to increase our standing by achieving a higher-level status. With ascribed statuses such as race and ethnicity, however, it is, by definition, impossible to change our status, unless we misrepresent ourselves.

Racism and ethnicism involve strong cultural values, attributing superior qualities to members of dominant groups and inferior qualities to those subordinate to them. Just as the relative ranking of occupations has remained quite constant, so, too, has the ranking of different ethnicities and races (Bogardus, 1928, 1959). Generations of whites have defined nonwhites as undesirable and inferior: light skin is better than black, yellow, brown, or red skin; wavy and straight hair is better than "wooly" hair. Generations of white Anglo-Saxon Protestants have defined those who do not speak English or who are non-Protestant as inferior and undesirable. The world, they believed, was reserved for those of "superior" ethnicity and race—for those like them (Hofstadter, 1955).

Inevitably, the low value placed on minority groups is attached to individuals who must confront a fundamental problem: How do I perceive and value *myself* in a culture that thinks so little of me? If my life is bad, does that mean *I* am bad?

As we grow up in a society, we acquire social identities that define who we are in relation to other people, and an important part of our identities is self-esteem. We cannot define and evaluate ourselves without taking into account how we think others see and evaluate us—what Cooley (1927) called our looking-glass self. Culture provides "mirrors" in which we see images of ourselves that are difficult to reject. Minority status is a stigma that carries with it the danger of leaving individuals with "spoiled identities" (Goffman, 1963b). As Kenneth Clark (1965) wrote:

> Human beings . . . whose daily experience tells them that almost nowhere in society are they respected and granted the ordinary dignity and courtesy accorded to others, will, as a matter of course, begin to doubt their self-worth. . . . These doubts become the seeds of pernicious self- and group-hatred. (p. 64)

When Robert Coles (1968) observed the first black children to attend integrated schools in the South, he found that the hatred directed toward them and their families strongly affected how they saw themselves. When one black girl—Ruby—drew pictures,

> she drew white people large and more lifelike. Negroes were smaller, their bodies less intact. A white girl we both knew to be her own size appeared several times taller. While Ruby's own face lacked an eye in one drawing, an ear in another, the white girl never lacked any features. (p. 47)

More recent studies suggest that the negative effects of racial stereotypes on self-esteem have grown weaker since the civil rights movement of the 1960s, during which many blacks participated in a collective reevaluation of blackness. For centuries, blacks had been named by others—niggers, coloreds, and then Negroes; but in the 1960s, blacks aggressively insisted on naming themselves and establishing their own value as people. When they adopted the label "black," they intended to create a cultural category free of associations with slavery and oppression.

In the early 1970s Rosenberg and Simmons (1971) found that many children in Baltimore schools were relatively unconscious of racist stereotypes about them and many others discounted stereotypes, saying that they did not apply to them, personally, and were based on the irrationality of whites. Nonetheless, black gains in self-esteem have been won in *spite* of a culture that still often places a relatively low value on them. Unlike whites, blacks and other minorities must continually maintain levels of pride and self-esteem that are contrary to the evaluation of those who dominate their society. What whites can take for granted—the relatively high standing of their race—is, for blacks, a daily struggle against a waning, but still formidable, tide of prejudice.

Minorities and Social Mobility

As we saw in Chapter 11, social mobility in the U.S. is, for most people, very limited. Many ethnic groups have shared in this limited progress (Farley and Neidert, 1984; Neidert and Farley, 1985); but until quite recently, nonwhite minorities have not.

Between 1959 and 1985 the percentage of blacks living below the poverty level dropped from 55 to 31 percent, and the average income of black families (taking inflation into account) increased by 56 percent. The percentage of blacks working in professional and technical jobs tripled, and the percentage in managerial positions doubled (U.S. Census Bureau, 1980b, 1986a, 1987a).

What these numbers miss is the fact that the position of blacks *relative* to whites has not improved greatly, primarily because while black standards of living have risen, so have those for whites. In 1959 blacks were three times more likely than whites to live in poverty. By 1985—26 years later—blacks were 2.75 times as likely to live in poverty (U.S. Census Bureau, 1980b, 1986a).

By many measures, the relative position of blacks has scarcely improved. In 1947 blacks living in families received a share of national income equal to 56 percent of what they would receive if income were distributed equally; by 1985 they received 65 percent. The average black family's income in 1950 was 54 percent of the white average, and by 1985 it had only risen to 62 percent (U.S. Census Bureau, 1980b, 1986a). While the distribution of blacks in occupations indicates some progress, it has been extraordinarily slow and has had little effect on the distribution of income. Why is mobility so much more difficult for blacks, and why does it have so little effect on the distribution of income?

Harrington (1963) maintained that blacks stay poor because

> they made the mistake of being born to the wrong parents. . . . Poverty breeds poverty. . . . Poor parents cannot give their children the opportunities for better health and education needed to improve their lot. Lack of motivation, hope, and incentive is a more subtle but not less powerful barrier than lack of financial means. Thus the cruel legacy of poverty is passed from parents to children. (p. 21)

In other words, blacks inherit the disadvantages of *poverty* from their parents.

Duncan (1969) and others (Blau and Duncan, 1967; Jencks et al., 1972) have argued, however, that the inheritance of *race* is the crucial factor that distinguishes blacks from others (see also Pomer, 1986). Even when we compare blacks and whites whose fathers had similar occupations, educations, and who came from the families of the same size, blacks have jobs considerably below those of whites. Even blacks who enter the same occupations as whites, with equal education levels, have incomes that average only 63 percent of white incomes (Jencks et al., 1972; see also National Committee on Pay Equity, 1987).

Undoubtedly, some blacks have made impressive gains; but, after more than 20 years of mass protest and federal programs to remove the disadvantages of race, the vast majority of blacks have barely improved their relative standing.

Prejudice can be a self-fulfilling prophecy, for the position of minorities is often exactly what cultural stereotypes predict. For centuries, the dominant white culture has defined blacks as childlike, inferior beings with no use for education. The prophecies inherent in racism came true for many blacks because, as a result of racism, they were denied access to education and decent jobs. They were not allowed to vote and were excluded from juries. Perhaps most important, generations of blacks were taught by experience that, regardless of ability, ambition, or effort, they were unlikely to escape poverty and the stigma of their race.

The social oppression of minorities rests on cultural beliefs, values, norms, and attitudes that, in turn, are reflected in relationships among groups and individuals. Oppression, however, depends not only on the characteristics of social environments, but also on *ecology*—the relationship between populations and their physical environments.

THE SOCIAL ECOLOGY OF OPPRESSION

The ecological perspective focuses on the ways in which societies use natural resources and technology, on population size and growth, and on the spatial distribution of people and their activities. Each of these plays a part in social oppression.

Technology and Production

Oppression often plays an integral part in the production process. Slaves were first brought to America in response to a labor shortage, but the sharply increased black population made white slaveowners fear a rebellion. They protected themselves with harsh, rigid codes that severely restricted black freedom (Pettigrew, 1976).

Slavery was most profitable in colonies that had warm climates and fertile land—Maryland, Virginia, and South Carolina—and was, therefore, uncommon in New England. In the early 1800s, aided by Eli Whitney's cotton gin, cotton production jumped enormously, as did the demand for slaves, whose numbers rose from fewer than 1 million in 1800 to almost 4 million by 1860 (U.S. Census Bureau, 1918). The Industrial Revolution mechanized agriculture and created masses of unemployed farmers and farm workers, while at the same time creating an enormous demand for cheap industrial labor. This led to exploitation of European immigrants from Ireland, Germany, and Poland.

While technology often facilitates social oppression, it can also have the opposite effect. When agriculture in the South was mechanized early in this century, the demand for black farm labor dropped sharply and blacks migrated to cities in great numbers (Baron, 1976). What progress blacks have made since then is due largely to their migration from rural to urban areas, for it was in cities that they found new opportunities for employment in industry and a less-racist social environment (Pettigrew, 1971, 1975).

Segregation: The Social Uses of Physical Space

Most U.S. cities are **segregated**: people who differ in occupation, education, race, religion, ethnicity, and income tend to live in different neighborhoods. Studies of Chicago, Cleveland, and Hartford show that the farther apart people are in racial and ethnic status or social class, the greater is the physical separation of their homes (Duncan and Duncan, 1955; Feldman and Tilly, 1960; Uyeki, 1964).

This simple ecological observation has profound social implications for racial and ethnic groups. Physical segregation heightens awareness of status differences by associating social characteristics with specific communities or neighborhoods. This, in turn, reinforces stereotypes by making it unlikely that members of different groups will experience each other directly.

The physical segregation of minorities also reinforces their disadvantaged social position (Massey and Denton, 1985). The more highly segregated immigrants are, the less likely they are to learn English, become naturalized citizens, or be occupationally mobile in comparison with their parents (Duncan and Lieberson, 1959; Lieberson, 1961).

Next to American Indians, blacks are the most highly segregated minority in the U.S., particularly in the large urban areas in which most blacks now live. In 1980, the most segregated cities were Chicago, Cleveland, and St. Louis, in which *90 percent* or more of all residents would have to move in order for each neighborhood to reflect the racial composition of the cities as a whole. In most other major cities, at least 75 percent would have to move in order to achieve integration (Taeuber, in Farley, 1984, p. 35; see also Massey and Denton, 1987). In general, Asian and Hispanic Americans are far less segregated—with the exception of Puerto Ricans, whose rates of segregation are similar to those of blacks (Massey, 1981b).

What Causes Neighborhood Segregation?

As Farley and his colleagues (1978) suggest, many cities are well on their way to becoming what a popular song described as "chocolate cities with vanilla suburbs" (Malbix/Ricks Music, BMI, 1976). How do we explain this trend?

The most common explanations are that blacks cannot afford to live in white neighborhoods and prefer all-black neighborhoods, and that whites resist the entry of blacks into their neighborhoods, move out when blacks move in, and will not move to integrated neighborhoods. Numerous studies (summarized in Farley et al., 1978) show, however, that residential segregation increased in Detroit in spite of black economic gains; and in national studies, blacks increasingly express a preference for integrated neigh-

borhoods. In Farley's Detroit study, 83 percent of blacks preferred integrated neighborhoods.

What of white resistance to integration? Most studies ask whites if they would be upset if blacks of similar economic status moved into their neighborhoods, and in 1972 fully 84 percent of whites in national samples said they would not be upset (National Opinion Research Center, 1972). What, then, is going on?

Farley and his co-researchers tested two additional explanations of segregation in Detroit. First, they tested the hypothesis that blacks overestimate the cost of housing in white neighborhoods or differ from whites in their evaluation of the relative attractiveness of different neighborhoods. Second, they used a new measure of attitudes toward integration, for they suspected that the "black on your block" question was too general because it failed to confront whites with specific residential possibilities.

Their findings show clearly that whites and blacks accurately perceive the cost of housing in different areas and share views of which areas are the most attractive to live in. In addition, while blacks report a strong preference for integrated neighborhoods, whites generally believe that blacks want to "stick to their own kind." In other words, whites seriously underestimate blacks' preference for integration.

Apparently, this misperception reinforces the reluctance of whites to share neighborhoods with blacks, for Farley's most important finding is that whites do not want to live in integrated neighborhoods. Rather than ask whites if they would mind living near a black family of similar economic status, Farley presented them with diagrams that showed different neighborhood mixes of black and white families. The diagrams showed 15 houses colored white or black with the center house labeled "your house." Hypothetical neighborhoods ranged from all white to just over half black (8 out of 15 houses).

Whereas in most surveys a majority of whites say they would not mind living near blacks, Farley's results tell a very different story (Table 12-3). As the hypothetical neighborhoods become increasingly black, the reported discomfort of whites, their desire to move out, and their reluctance to move in all rise sharply.

If Detroit is typical of U.S. cities, Farley's results offer little hope that segregation in housing will ease in the near future. While better-educated whites tend to be more tolerant of integration, the differences be-

Table 12-3

White Responses to Racial Integration Possibilities (Detroit, 1976)

PROPORTION OF WHITE RESPONDENTS WHO WOULD:	HYPOTHETICAL NEIGHBORHOODS: PERCENTAGE OF FAMILIES THAT ARE BLACK			
	14	20	33	53
Feel uncomfortable in the neighborhood	24	42	57	72
Try to move out of the neighborhood	7	24	41	64
Would not move into such a neighborhood	27	50	73	84

Source: Farley et al., 1978, Figure 7.

tween the least and most educated are small. Higher-*income* whites, however, are *less* tolerant of racial integration than are lower-income whites, while higher-income blacks are *more* likely to accept integrated neighborhoods than are lower-income blacks (Farley et al., 1978). Racially segregated housing, complete with its negative effects on black people, is likely to remain for some time to come.

Segregated Schools and Living with Contradictions

There are two basic causes of school segregation. **De jure** segregation is required by law, a type of segregation found in southern states until the 1954 Supreme Court decision outlawed segregated schools. **De facto** segregation is caused by residential segregation: children live in segregated neighborhoods and, since they attend neighborhood schools, their schools are segregated, as well.

As of 1978, roughly half of all public school students would have to change schools in order to make the racial composition of schools match that of the entire population. In Chicago, 90 percent would have to move, and in most other major cities the percentages amount to two-thirds or more (Farley, 1984). School segregation denies white and black children the opportunity to know one another and negatively affects the educational careers of black children.

Blacks who attend segregated schools are less likely to finish high school, attend college, and secure white-collar jobs than are blacks who attend integrated schools (Crain, 1975).

Racial segregation also affects whites, for those who attend integrated schools are least likely to prefer all-white classes and all-white friends (Coleman et al., 1966). White adults who attended integrated schools are also more willing to live in integrated neighborhoods, have their children attend integrated schools, and have black friends (U.S. Commission on Civil Rights, 1967).

Residential and school segregation illustrate a basic contradiction in our culture, for while most whites say they do not object to living in integrated neighborhoods, most reverse their position when they are presented with specific integration possibilities. A similar reversal occurs with school segregation. Data for 1984 to 1986 show that 92 percent of whites believe white and black students should attend school together, and 79 percent say they would not object to their children attending a school whose student body was half black; and yet, 75 percent opposed the busing of black and white students from one school district to another and 49 percent supported the right of whites to deliberately exclude blacks from their neighborhoods by refusing to sell their houses to them (GSS, 1984, 1986).

These contradictions illustrate that individuals may support general cultural values and yet violate them when they believe their interests are threatened. Many people are what Merton (1948) called "Fair-Weather Liberals," who support the "American Creed" until it threatens them personally. We value equality and fairness, but we also live with a centuries-old legacy of racism and value the right of individuals to control basic aspects of their lives, including who will live near them and where their children will go to school. These are deep contradictions that will not be resolved easily or quickly.

Population and Minorities

In the simplest sense, superior numbers make it easier for one group to oppress another. In the late 1800s and early 1900s, many prominent people in the U.S. worried that relatively high rates of population growth among nonwhite peoples of the world (including the U.S.) would soon make it difficult for whites to maintain their dominant position (Hofstadter, 1955).

In some cases, those who dominate a society try to control the size and growth of minority populations. The most extreme form of this is **genocide**, the deliberate attempt to annihilate an entire racial or ethnic group (see Kuper, 1977, 1982, 1985). The most brutal was the Nazi Holocaust during World War II (see Dawidowicz, 1975; Gilbert, 1986), but there are other examples. The early Hebrews tried unsuccessfully to exterminate the Canaanites; entire tribes of American Indians were all but annihilated during the nineteenth century; between 1917 and 1919, Turks massacred over a million Armenians (Dadrian, 1971); and massacres have plagued many newly independent African states (Kuper, 1977). In a single attack in 1983, 600 Moslems were slain by Hindus in the rural area of Assam, India (Hazarika, 1983).

A less extreme form of population control is **expulsion**—forcing an entire race or ethnicity to move. In 1830, the Indian Removal Act forced thousands of American Indians of many different tribes in the Southeast to move west of the Mississippi, primarily to allow whites to seize their tribal lands. During their long forced marches—often covering thousands of miles—some tribes lost as many as 40 percent of their people to disease and starvation.

This girl and her family were among the thousands of U.S. citizens of Japanese descent who were forced to live in concentration camps for the duration of World War II. They lost most of what they owned, including homes, businesses, and some of the richest agricultural land in California.

After the Japanese attacked Pearl Harbor in 1941, 77 thousand U.S. citizens of Japanese descent were confined to "relocation camps" for the duration of the war. They were loyal citizens, many of whose sons fought in Europe as members of an all-Japanese unit that earned more battle decorations than any other in the U.S. Army. Nonetheless, they were removed from their homes and effectively imprisoned simply because of their ancestry, while Americans of German and Italian descent—culturally and racially more similar to the dominant Anglo-Saxons—retained their full rights as citizens. It was not until 1983 that U.S. courts awarded financial compensation to those who were interned (Irons, 1983).

We come now to the central problem in understanding oppression and prejudice—why do they exist at all?

EXPLAINING SOCIAL OPPRESSION

Sociologists use the conflict and functional perspectives to explain the mistreatment of minorities. A conflict perspective focuses on competition and the ability of some groups to exploit others. A functional view tries to identify the functional and dysfunctional consequences of oppression.

The Conflict Perspective

There is historical evidence that prejudice and discrimination are most likely to occur when there is intense competition over scarce resources and rewards (Noel, 1968; Vander Zanden, 1972). In Hawaii and on the U.S. West Coast there was little open prejudice against Japanese until whites and Japanese competed for the same jobs; and the economic success of Chinese in Southeast Asia preceded sharp rises in prejudice against them. In the 1980s, many countries in Western Europe depend heavily on foreign workers and have larger foreign-born populations than the U.S. In France, West Germany, Britain, and the Netherlands there have been increasing pressures to expel foreign workers in order to decrease competition for jobs (*New York Times*, August 5, 1986, p. A6).

In the U.S., lower-class whites are more likely to express racist attitudes than are higher-class whites, which is consistent with a competition explanation of discrimination. Until recently, many white-dominated labor unions resisted increases in black membership,

In 1987, hundreds of KKK members gathered in Forsyth County, Georgia, to harass protestors objecting to the exclusion of blacks in a white community. Membership in the KKK is overwhelmingly lower and working class.

means of production and those who do not. From this perspective, racial and ethnic prejudice benefit the capitalist class (Reich, 1981). The existence of minorities provides a continuing source of cheap labor, for "inferior" people cannot demand high wages. Prejudice against minorities also divides the working class by setting workers of different ethnicity and race against one another. This perpetuates inequality by contributing to false consciousness and interfering with solidarity within the working class: rather than blame the upper class or the class system itself, lower-class groups blame each other. As Lipset and Bendix (1959) put it:

> A real social and economic cleavage is created by widespread discrimination against minority groups, and this diminishes the chances for the development of solidarity along class lines. . . . This continued splintering of the working class is a major element in the preservation and the stability of the class structure. (pp. 105–106)

During the first third of this century, few blacks belonged to unions, and white employers actively recruited blacks as strikebreakers to take the place of striking union workers (Griffin et al., 1986). This intensified racism among working-class whites and, until blacks were actively recruited as union members, divided the working class along racial lines.

To Marx, prejudice and exploitation are inevitable in class societies—whether the targets are defined by race, ethnicity, or gender. Oppression maintains upper-class privilege and the class system. It also encourages members of lower classes to vent their anger and frustration on relatively safe—and undeserving—targets by using minorities as **scapegoats**.

Scapegoats In the ancient Roman Empire, Christians were "thrown to the lions" whenever disaster struck. When Christians became a majority, Jews replaced them as scapegoats, and when plagues ravaged Europe during the fourteenth century, Jews were blamed and hundreds of their communities were wiped out. The ruling class often used Jews as tax collectors, making them convenient targets for the dissatisfaction of those whose taxes supported the wealthy. During the Great Depression of the 1930s, Hitler used Jews and Communists as scapegoats on which Germans could blame all their political and economic troubles (Dawidowicz, 1975; Johnson, 1987).

In nineteenth-century America, Irish immigrants were blamed for crime, poverty, and political corrup-

in part because unemployment was already a problem for white members (Gould, 1968). Large unions—the AFL-CIO—however, are now among the most integrated of all organizations.

The openness of large labor unions to minorities suggests that prejudice is not simply a result of competition, for we need to remember that competition among the lower classes is caused in large part by the fact that the upper classes take a disproportionately large share of wealth and income. The scarcity of rewards in the lower classes is, itself, a product of a class system.

To Marx, the most important aspect of capitalist societies is the division between those who own the

For almost a thousand years, Jews have been used as convenient targets. It was a common practice to blame Jews whenever a child was killed in suspicious circumstances. An artist's rendition depicts the eve of the Third Crusade led by England's Richard the Lionheart in 1189, when Jews throughout London were attacked, in part to stir up Christian solidarity.

tion. When they became established, prejudice was turned against other ethnic and racial groups—Germans, Polish Catholics, Chinese, and Japanese. During the Depression, anti-Semitism grew sharply (Strong, 1941). After World War II, veterans who felt they had received bad breaks in the army were more likely than others to report anti-Semitic attitudes (Bettelheim and Janowitz, 1950). Campbell (1947) found

that people who report themselves as being dissatisfied with economic and political conditions are almost three times more likely than satisfied people to express dislike for Jews, avoid them, or show hostility toward them. Whites who are dissatisfied with community services and local government are more likely than others to express hostile attitudes toward blacks (Campbell, 1971). Hispanics, blacks, and Asian refugees are the current scapegoats on which many blame urban decay, the "welfare mess," unemployment, disorder in schools, and crime.

Social oppression is connected to both competition for scarce rewards and the exploitation of classes, and from this perspective it is easier to understand why prejudice is more often expressed by lower-class people (Adorno et al., 1950; Selznick and Steinberg, 1969). The upper class can *afford* to appear liberal and unprejudiced because minority gains pose no threat to them (Kerbo, 1983). In the lower class, however, people are more vulnerable to unemployment and a loss of prestige and income; and, because they depend on the upper class for their jobs, they are more likely to vent their anger and frustration on people who are less powerful than they.

From a conflict perspective the existence of minorities benefits only members of dominant groups, particularly those in the upper class. Does this mean that oppression never has latent functional consequences for society as a whole?

A Functionalist Perspective on Prejudice and Discrimination

The oppression of minorities is often part of the basic fabric of social life. On the simplest level, racial and ethnic stereotypes help maintain social boundaries. In homogeneous societies, negative stereotypes about outsiders (and positive ones about insiders) allow insiders to draw clear boundaries between themselves and the rest of the world, boundaries that often reinforce superior self-images.

In eighteenth- and nineteenth-century America, stereotypes about immigrants contributed to social solidarity among Anglo-Saxons by heightening awareness of racial and ethnic differences and by devaluing all non-Anglo-Saxons. Racism was functional for the economy of southern states prior to the mechanization of agriculture; many whites of that period believed they were doing blacks a *favor* by enslaving them, for this was a way of introducing Christianity to the "African heathen" (Pettigrew, 1976).

In spite of their negative effects on minorities, prejudice and discrimination have some latent functional consequences in the U.S. Oppression ensures that "dirty work" will be done: cleaning streets and collecting trash, maintaining and cleaning buildings, washing dishes in restaurants, and performing the countless tasks required in low-paid, unskilled factory jobs. The oppression of migrant farmworkers—most of whom are nonwhite—keeps the price of fruits and vegetables relatively low.

The functional perspective also identifies *dysfunctions* of oppression. In addition to the obvious negative consequences of prejudice and injustice, it keeps substantial portions of the population in poor health and contributes to hostility, suspicion, and fear. It denies millions of people the opportunity to develop fully and use their abilities, not only depriving society of the full range of talents found in its population, but also contributing to crime, growing welfare and unemployment rolls, and community decay.

Ethnic and racial groups themselves are not the problem. The problem is their mistreatment which has become an enduring structural, cultural, and ecological aspect of our environment. The elimination of prejudice and discrimination involves more than changes in attitudes, for oppression is deeply embedded in the arrangements that make up social life.

SOCIAL CHANGE: ENDING PREJUDICE AND OPPRESSION

As we have seen, oppression has three major sociological aspects: prejudice (culture), discrimination and inequality (social structure), and population control and segregation (ecology). What are the prospects for change in each of these areas?

Cultural Change: Reducing Prejudice

One way to reduce prejudice is by attacking its legitimacy. Racial and ethnic prejudice runs deep in our culture; and yet, at the same time, we value equality, fairness, equal opportunity, and freedom from oppression. Our culture pulls us in opposite directions; and as Myrdal (1945) wrote in his classic analysis, *An American Dilemma*, the resulting strain makes social change inevitable.

One of the major accomplishments of the U.S. civil rights movement of the 1960s was that it forced many people to confront serious cultural contradictions. As Myrdal predicted, Martin Luther King, Jr., and other civil rights activists used one part of our culture—beliefs and values about equality—to attack another—racial prejudice. This is a particularly effective method of bringing about social change, for it makes people confront uncomfortable contradictions

Much of the progress made by blacks has been due to the willingness of civil rights supporters to risk their lives in order to confront the white power structure. In 1965, when 600 marchers left Selma, Alabama as part of a drive to increase black voter registration, they were attacked by police using dogs and tear gas. When the march resumed, it was joined by volunteers from around the country; and by the time it reached Montgomery, the state capitol, its ranks had swelled to an estimated 25,000 people.

between what they envision as their *ideal* culture and the cultural ideas they actually live by.

As prejudice is exposed and becomes unacceptable in a culture, however, people often respond merely by withholding expressions of prejudice or by expressing it in less visible ways (see Wilson, 1987). Although surveys show a steady decline in outward expressions of racial and ethnic prejudice in the U.S., this does not prove that prejudice itself is declining (Dovidio and Gaertner, 1986). Recent evidence suggests that while most people favor equality in principle, they do not support concrete changes and programs that might actually do something to bring it about (Schuman et al., 1985). This is an important distinction, because if prejudice remains strong while its outward expression declines under social pressure, it can quickly reemerge under less restrained conditions.

A second approach to reducing prejudice is to change people's perceptions of minorities, which involves the destruction of stereotypes as bases for our knowledge about one another.

Changing Perceptions of Minority Groups

Because prejudice focuses on differences between groups, one solution is for minorities to assimilate—to change their culture so they conform to the dominant culture. When Hispanics or Asians adopt English as their primary language, or when Jews change their names, they may become more acceptable and less visible as members of a minority (my great grandfather emigrated from Norway to the U.S. and changed his name from Mokestaad to Johnson in order to fit in). Many immigrants avoid prejudice by replacing ethnic customs, styles of dress, and modes of speech with those favored by dominant ethnic groups.

The problem with this solution is that it requires minorities to surrender unique cultural identities, which can be yet another form of social oppression. In addition, while assimilation can reduce ethnic prejudice, it is largely ineffective for reducing racism, since race is much more difficult to conceal. Black Americans are oppressed, in part, simply because of their race. How, then, can minorities keep their unique cultural identities and free themselves from negative stereotypes and prejudice?

We use **stereotypes** as substitutes for direct experience and knowledge of people. They lead us to overestimate differences between groups, to underestimate the amount of variation within them, and to apply general descriptions of entire groups or social categories to all individuals within them. They distort reality in many different ways.

It is easiest to maintain stereotypes if we avoid evidence that contradicts them, and one way to avoid such evidence is to avoid interacting with people of different races or ethnicities, so there is no opportunity to compare stereotypes with the actual people those stereotypes describe. So long as we are isolated from one another, we can make up our own private explanations for people's behavior without ever taking their point of view into account (Newcomb, 1947).

This suggests that we can reduce prejudice if we change the structure of social relationships by increasing interaction among members of different groups. Contact with people of other races or ethnicities makes us more likely to see them as unique. Many studies support the idea that increased interaction reduces prejudice (see Miller and Brewer, 1984). Deutsch and Collins (1951) compared two housing projects. In one, residents were randomly assigned to dwellings; in the other, blacks and whites were segregated. Blacks and whites in integrated housing were more likely to interact informally and to report interracial friendships. Other studies show that integrated housing reduces the tendency to stereotype members of minorities (Wilner et al., 1955); and the desegregation of elementary schools increases interaction among children of different races and desire for friendships with one another (Koslin et al., 1969).

A simple increase in interaction is not a guaranteed cure for prejudice, however. Blacks and whites interacted with each other for several hundred years in the American South without decreasing the level of racism. Interaction is most likely to reduce prejudice when people: (1) occupy the same status (such as co-workers); (2) share common goals (as in problem-solving groups); (3) can achieve their goals only by working together (as in athletic teams and military units); and (4) have the support of authorities (Allport, 1954). After President Truman ordered an end to discrimination and segregation on U.S. merchant ships, racial prejudice among white seamen decreased with each integrated voyage.

The reduction of prejudice through interaction illustrates how cultural, structural, and ecological factors affect one another. New ecological arrangements (integration of schools, workplaces, or neighborhoods) produce structural change (the frequency of interaction) that, in turn, often reduces prejudice (a cultural attitude). The 1954 Supreme Court decision to integrate public schools attacked racism by creating ecological arrangements and patterns of interaction in which stereotypes are more difficult to maintain. Other structural changes—putting people of different races or ethnicities in similar statuses in which they must depend on one another for the achievement of common goals—also affect how we value, feel and think about, and behave toward others.

Structural Change: Reducing Inequality

Expressions of racial and ethnic prejudice seem to be declining in the U.S., and many whites infer from this that blacks are no longer oppressed. In 1977, roughly 60 percent of whites reported the belief that blacks receive equal treatment when applying for housing and white-collar jobs, or when dealing with police; and 68 percent reported the belief that blacks are treated equally when they apply for skilled-labor jobs. Blacks, on the other hand, reported very different perceptions. Less than a quarter said they receive equal treatment in the economy, housing, and by police (Harris, 1977). In more recent studies, blacks were far more likely than whites to perceive the police and courts as unfair (Hagan and Abonnetti, 1982). In short, whites are far more likely than blacks to believe that race is no longer an important factor in social stratification (see One Step Further 12-1, p. 334).

There is little question that some segments of the black population have made considerable gains over the last 20 years, especially those who are young, married, and well educated; but, in general, the relative standing of blacks has improved very little (Farley, 1980), and there is considerable evidence that a large black underclass is being left behind in conditions of desperate poverty, especially in large cities (Wilson, 1987). During the 1970s, the earnings gap between white and black *workers* decreased slightly. The gap between white and black *families*, however, did not change at all, and actually increased between 1980 and 1985 (Commission on Minority Participation, 1988). How could this happen?

Part of the answer is that for blacks and whites single-parent families headed by women became increasingly common during the 1970s, and such families have lower average incomes than two-parent families. Because this trend was stronger among blacks than among whites, black gains in the labor market were offset by changes in family structure (Farley, 1980, 1984). Wilson (1987) argues that the strong trend toward single-parent families among blacks is itself due in part to the terrible job prospects for young black males.

In spite of black gains in occupational status, an enormous racial gap remains, and Kluegel and Smith (1982) estimated from a national study of white adults that almost three-quarters of whites overestimate recent economic progress by blacks and the level of their opportunities. In 1980 white workers had a 67 percent greater chance than blacks to have upper-level white-collar jobs and a 39 percent greater chance to have skilled blue-collar jobs (U.S. Census Bureau, 1981). In fact, the percentage of blacks with upper-level white-collar jobs was lower than the comparable percentage for whites in 1950 (Farley, 1980).

While employed blacks have made some progress, even they are vulnerable, for when unemployment increases, blacks are among the first to be laid off. Each year since 1947, unemployment rates have been twice as great among nonwhites as among whites. Compared with whites in 1986, unemployment rates were twice as high among blacks and 60 percent higher among Hispanics (U.S. Census Bureau, 1980b, 1986a). In the late 1980s, corporate mergers and acquisitions resulted in the loss of many managerial positions. Blacks were far more likely than whites to be affected, therefore undoing many of the gains of the 1970s and early 1980s (*New York Times*, January 4, 1987, Section 3).

It is important to point out that the progress made by blacks came about only with the assistance of the federal government and a decade of mass protests and riots in cities such as Los Angeles, Detroit, and Washington, D.C. R. B. Freeman (1975) showed the close relationship between black progress and antidiscrimination activities of federal agencies such as the Equal Employment Opportunity Commission. The likelihood that companies would hire blacks was directly related to the amount of pressure applied by the federal government, as were changes in discriminatory hiring, firing, and promotion practices.

The most controversial attempt to eliminate economic inequality is **affirmative action**, the practice of giving minorities preferential treatment when they apply for jobs or college. Opponents argue that it is "reverse discrimination"—progress for minorities at the expense of others. Our culture, they argue, values ability as the main consideration in distributing resources and rewards, and affirmative action violates this important value.

ONE STEP FURTHER 12-1:
Race and Perceptions of Inequality

Blacks and whites disagree not only about the extent of inequality, but about its causes. There are also interesting differences by gender. The figures in Table B-12-1 show the percentage of different race and gender categories who attribute inequality in jobs, income, and housing to various causes. There are six columns, three for each racial category. The first two columns describe black women and men, and the third describes all blacks regardless of gender. The last three columns show comparable figures for whites. Stop for a moment and be sure you see this.

There are several interesting patterns here. First, Row (A) shows that both blacks and whites express relatively little support for the belief that blacks have less in-born ability to learn.

Second, blacks are far more likely than whites to attribute inequality to discrimination (B), somewhat more likely to attribute it to lack of educational opportunity (C), and far *less* likely to attribute it to a lack of will power or motivation (D).

A third interesting pattern is that gender makes a difference among blacks but not among whites. In all four rows the percentages for white women and men are virtually the same, but black men are more likely than black women to attribute inequality to discrimination and education. Significantly, however, there is no difference between black women and men in their views of in-born differences and lack of will power. How would you explain this?

Table B-12-1

On the average, blacks have worse jobs, income, and housing than white people. Do you think these differences exist mainly because of:

EXPLANATION	BLACKS			WHITES		
	Women	Men	All	Women	Men	All
(A) Blacks have less in-born ability to learn	18%	20%	18%	20%	22%	21%
(B) Discrimination	70%	82%	74%	41%	40%	40%
(C) Blacks lack educational opportunities	60%	73%	65%	51%	52%	51%
(D) Blacks lack motivation or will power to pull themselves out of poverty	38%	39%	38%	64%	64%	64%

Source: Computed from raw 1986 General Social Survey data.

Supporters of affirmative action point out that individual ability has relatively little to do with inequality (see Chapter 11). In addition, the ability argument ignores the cumulative effect of centuries of oppression, because it assumes that blacks and whites are now in equally strong positions to compete. It is not enough to say, "From now on, everyone has an equal chance," when history has left minorities with relatively low levels of education, training, and job experience.

While affirmative action programs have helped blacks who are highly skilled, well educated, or who have long, steady work histories, in some ways it has hurt blacks by reinforcing racial prejudice. The mere existence of a double standard reinforces the belief that blacks are inferior to whites. As Jencks (1983b) points out, when colleges recruit blacks whose average preparation for college is weaker than the average white's, it reinforces perceptions that "blacks just aren't very bright":

The logic is precisely the same as the logic that convinces students and faculty that athletes, who are also admitted even if they are academically unpromising, aren't very bright. The difference is that encouraging the nation's future professional and managerial elite to think athletes are nitwits does no serious social harm, whereas encouraging the belief that blacks are nitwits does incalculable harm. (Jencks, 1983b, p. 14)

Racial oppression is strongly linked with class systems, with both upper- and middle-class whites benefiting from the exploitation of nonwhites. Many whites have relatively little to lose by giving up racist ideas; but unequal distributions of wealth, income, and power will be with us for a long time to come, for they have been deeply embedded in our economic, social, and political fabric for centuries. As Farley (1980) wrote:

> We are a long way from the segregated society of 1950, but we are still far from the dream of Martin Luther King. If the next generation of blacks is not to remain a generation behind whites, society has a long road ahead. (p. 16)

Violence and Social Change   Just as dominant groups often use violence to oppress minorities, so, too, do minorities sometimes resort to violence as the only way to end prejudice and discrimination.

Gandhi and his followers freed India from Britain's colonial rule largely without the use of violence, and Martin Luther King, Jr., used Gandhi as a model. There can be little doubt, however, that the U.S. did not pay serious attention to civil rights until blacks asserted their willingness to engage in violence. The riots in Detroit, Los Angeles, and other cities during the 1960s prompted the appointment of a national commission whose conclusions focused on the frustrations of blacks in a racist society.

More recently, many South African blacks have concluded that peaceful, legal action will not bring about an end to their oppressed minority status. Denied any effective voice in government and forbidden to protest by breaking even the most minor laws, many blacks believe that their government will only allow opposition that it knows will be ineffective; this leads them to the conclusion that "the only language the government understands is force" (Slambrouck, 1983, p. 13).

Gamson (1974, 1975) studied 53 social movements in U.S. history and found that the more "unruly" social movements were, the more likely they

The unwillingness of a militarily powerful white minority to grant equality to blacks, and the determination of blacks to settle for nothing less, has made violence inevitable in South Africa. At a rally in the township of Soweto outside Johannesburg, students protest the death of a 16-year-old after being jailed for participating in a protest march.

were to achieve their goals. As Gamson concluded, "the meek don't make it."

Ecological Change

One of the most important ecological aspects of social oppression is physical segregation. Paradoxically, both more and less segregation have been proposed as responses to the oppression of minorities in the United States and elsewhere.

For years many French Canadians in the province of Quebec have urged a separation of Quebec from the rest of Canada and the establishment of an independent state in which "French Canadian" is no longer treated as a minority status (Hughes, 1963). Israel is the only country in the world in which "Jew" is not a minority status. During the 1920s Marcus Garvey proposed seizing European colonies in Africa and transforming them into a free United Black Africa populated by U.S. blacks and sympathetic Africans. More recently, the Republic of New Africa movement suggested taking over several southern states for an independent black nation (Weisbord, 1975).

ONE STEP FURTHER 12-2:
What Racial Isolation Looks Like

The map of Connecticut, Figure B-12-2, provides a vivid example of how isolated black and white students are from one another in the United States. Although nonwhite children make up 22 percent of the student population, notice that in the vast majority of school districts the nonwhite share falls below 5 percent (white areas). Most nonwhites are concentrated in larger cities such as Hartford, New Haven, Bridgeport, Waterbury, and Stamford where they make up as much as 90 percent of the student population. Even if Connecticut schools were perfectly integrated *within* school districts, racial isolation would guarantee that most students would still have relatively little contact with students of other races.

Figure B-12-2   Percentage of Minority Students by School District, 1986

Source: Adapted From the *New York Times,* January 31, 1988, p. C1.

All of these efforts to preserve cultural diversity and escape exploitation and mistreatment involve **separatism**, which calls for greater segregation, not less, and rests on the belief that separation is the only way people can control the social and ecological conditions in which they live. In most cases, they have not been successful, primarily because those who control necessary resources benefit from the oppression of minorities.

In contrast to separatists are those who advocate greater integration, and their efforts have focused on two major areas—housing and schools.

Desegregation and Resegregation In 1954 the Supreme Court decided that separate schools for whites and blacks are "inherently unequal," and ordered an end to segregated schools. As we saw earlier, however, segregation persists.

When measuring change in the distribution of blacks and whites, it is important to distinguish between racial **integration** and racial *isolation*. Within school districts, schools are integrated if whites and blacks are evenly distributed among schools. In other words, if the population is 10 percent black and 90 percent white, full integration exists only if every school has that racial composition.

Racial **isolation**, on the other hand, refers to comparisons *between* school districts. Suppose one district's population is entirely white and another's is entirely black; *within* each district, schools are integrated, because the racial composition of the schools matches the racial composition of the communities they serve. Black and white students, however, are isolated from each other, because they live in different school districts (see One Step Further 12-2).

Although segregation has decreased, it remains high in many large cities such as Chicago, Cleveland, and Newark. In fact, segregation in these and other cities actually increased in the 1970s (Wurdock, 1979; Wurdock and Farley, 1979; Farley, 1984). This occurred primarily because *residential* segregation *within* school districts increased: whites moved from integrated neighborhoods to all white neighborhoods in the same school district. Thus, de facto *re*-segregation is slowly undoing much of the desegregation achieved between 1954 and 1967.

Racial isolation fell between 1967 and 1976, but as whites leave central cities in increasing numbers, the separation of white and black students is likely to increase once again. Only two of the nation's 20 largest cities—Phoenix and San Jose—have school districts in which whites outnumber nonwhites; and whites make up only 4 percent of enrolled students in Washington, D.C., 18 percent in Detroit, and 25 percent in Chicago (Wurdock and Farley, 1979). Increased interaction between blacks and whites made possible by desegregation is likely to be undone by increased racial isolation caused by changing racial compositions of communities (see also Farley, 1984).

Coleman, Kelly, and Moore (1975) argued that desegregation in many communities has actually caused increased racial isolation, because white parents leave rather than send their children to integrated schools. Farley, Richards, and Wurdock (1980) showed, however, that the migration of whites away from cities has been going on continuously for several decades, and when such communities desegregate their schools, white migration increases only for the following year and then settles back to its former rate. In other words, school desegregation has a relatively small and temporary effect on the "flight" of white families from communities.

Migration is only one factor in segregated schools, however, for in the last decade the number of private schools has grown rapidly while the number of public schools has decreased (U.S. Census Bureau, 1987a). Many of these schools exclude blacks—some of them on supposedly religious grounds—and this introduces a major new way for whites to separate their children from blacks.

If the goal of integration is to reduce prejudice and discrimination by improving educational opportunities for blacks and by increasing contact between students of different races, we clearly have a long way to go. In fact, there is reason to believe that we are retreating from the goal of a society in which people from different ethnic and racial backgrounds can share the same neighborhoods and schools.

SUMMARY

1. Biological races are collections of people whose distinct physical characteristics are passed on through reproduction. Social race is a status defined in physical terms. An ethnic group is a collection of people with a common cultural heritage.

2. A minority is a group of people who are singled out for unequal treatment. Social oppression is

the systematic, socially supported abuse or exploitation of one group by another.

3. Prejudice is a positive or negative attitude directed toward members of a group. Prejudice is based on real or imagined differences between groups, attaches values to group differences, is generalized to all members of a target group, and usually includes the belief that group differences are absolute and inevitable.

4. Prejudice functions as an ideology by denying the existence of oppression and by blaming minorities for the effects of oppression.

5. Cultural differences within societies are dealt with in several ways. Amalgamation occurs when several cultures mix to become a new culture; assimilation occurs when ethnic groups conform to the culture of a single group; and pluralism occurs when diverse ethnic groups maintain their differences within a society.

6. Discrimination is unequal treatment of people because they belong to certain groups. Whether or not our treatment of each other is consistent with our attitudes depends on the situation.

7. Race strongly affects the distribution of wealth, occupation, education, income, prestige, employment, power, health, and living conditions. Ethnicity has weaker effects because it is less visible and has weaker prejudices attached to it.

8. Upward mobility among blacks has been slow and has barely affected the distribution of wealth, income, power, and prestige. Blacks are handicapped not only by poorer education and occupation, but by the stigma of race itself. Prejudice often creates self-fulfilling prophecies.

9. Ecology often affects the creation and perpetuation of minorities. Discrimination and prejudice often are encouraged by economic arrangements.

10. Segregation reinforces the disadvantaged position of minorities. Residential segregation is the norm in the U.S. and results mostly from the refusal of whites to live near blacks. *De jure* segregation is required by law; *de facto* segregation is a latent consequence of other social or ecological arrangements. Most children attend segregated schools because they live in segregated neighborhoods.

11. Genocide is the systematic killing of members of a group. Expulsion is a form of oppression in which minorities are forced to leave their community or society.

12. Conflict theorists believe that prejudice and discrimination arise out of competition for scarce resources in which some groups exploit others. Prejudice serves the interests of dominant groups and contributes to false consciousness among subordinate groups that often use minorities as scapegoats.

13. The functional perspective shows that, in spite of their negative consequences both for minorities and societies, prejudice and discrimination also have functional consequences.

14. Prejudice may be reduced by attacking its social legitimacy or by reducing perceived differences between minorities and dominant groups. Increased interaction often lowers prejudice when people occupy the same statuses and share common goals that can be achieved only through cooperation. Affirmative action programs—preferential treatment given to minorities—have generally had little effect on the disadvantaged position of minorities in the U.S.

15. Separatism is a belief in increased segregation as a way of preserving minority culture and ending discrimination.

16. Racial integration of schools exists when the racial composition of schools matches the composition of their communities. Racial isolation refers to comparisons between school districts and communities and the degree of contact between people of different races. U.S. schools have become more racially integrated and less isolated since 1954, but in many large cities the trend toward less isolation is reversing as whites move out of integrated neighborhoods.

KEY TERMS

affirmative action   333
amalgamation   315
assimilation   316
discrimination   317
ethnicity   312
ethnic group   312

Looking Elsewhere

Having studied Chapter 12, you might want to look at related discussions in *Human Arrangements*, which include

- racism, ethnicism, and xenophobia (the fear of outsiders) in communities (Chapter 9, pp. 224–26)
- race, crime, and punishment (Chapter 10, pp. 256–57, 258, 260–62)
- South Africa as a caste system (Chapter 11, p. 302)
- learning and school segregation (Chapter 16, p. 447)
- race and I.Q. (Chapter 16, pp. 435–36)
- how minorities are treated in schools (Chapter 16, pp. 440, 453, 454, 457)
- women as a unique minority (Chapter 13, pp. 372–73)
- origins of the civil rights movement (Chapter 21, pp. 582, 586–91)
- race and health (Chapter 5, p. 108)

RECOMMENDED READINGS

ALLPORT, G. (1958). *The nature of prejudice*. Cambridge, MA: Addison-Wesley. A classic exploration of the nature of prejudice, including a look at the ways in which minorities often respond.

CONKLIN, N. F., and LOURIE, M. A. (1983). *A host of tongues: Language communities in the United States*. New York: Free Press. A study of linguistic assimilation through which the diverse cultural origins of the American people are dominated by a single language.

DUNBAR, L. W. (Ed.). (1984). *Minority report: What has happened to blacks, Hispanics, American Indians, and other American minorities in the eighties*. New York: Pantheon. Seven civil rights activists argue that while many cultural aspects of racial and ethnic inequality have changed, economic discrimination continues and will continue without government intervention.

FERNANDEZ, J. P. (1981). *Racism and sexism in corporate life*. Lexington, MA: D. C. Heath. A study of attitudes among managers toward existing company-sponsored affirmative action programs. One major finding is that the more highly placed executives are, the more racist and sexist their personal attitudes tend to be.

SIMPSON, G. E., and YINGER, J. M. (1985). *Racial and cultural minorities: An analysis of prejudice and discrimination* (5th ed.). New York: Plenum. The latest edition of an important source book on discrimination and prejudice, which pays attention to both theory and research.

WILSON, W. J. (1978). *The declining significance of race*. Chicago: University of Chicago Press. A provocative book that argues that class, not race, is the most important impediment to progress for American blacks. See, also, his new book—(1987). *The truly disadvantaged*. Chicago: University of Chicago Press—about public policy and the black underclass.

Biology, Culture, and Social Structure

Gender, Culture, and the Ideology of Sexism

Language and Gender

Beliefs: Masculine and Feminine

Values: Vive la Différence?

Attitudes

Norms

Gender and Social Structure

Gender Roles, Status Sets, and Social Identity

Divisions of Labor: Ecology and Social Structure

Wealth and Income

Power, Patriarchy, and Matriarchy

Prestige

Socialization: Learning to Be Male and Female

Gender Roles and the Family

Schools and Gender Roles

Gender Roles and the Media

Gender and Adult Socialization

Explaining Inequality

The Functional View: Are Gender Roles Necessary?

The Conflict Perspective: Perpetuating Patriarchy

Gender Roles and Social Change

New Ideologies and Cultural Change

Social Change and Social Structure

Why Is Change So Difficult and Slow?

13 Gender

A man and his son go for a walk. The boy falls and injures himself seriously. The father rushes his son to a hospital, and while the father waits, his son is taken into a treatment room. A doctor enters the room, looks at the boy and exclaims, "My God! It's my son!"

Who is the doctor?

I have heard many complex answers to this riddle (such as the doctor is the boy's real father and the other man is his stepfather), but it also has a very simple one: the doctor is the boy's mother. When most of us hear it for the first time, the "obvious" answer is not obvious at all; Russians, however, would probably figure it out quickly since most physicians in the Soviet Union are women.

The riddle reveals a fragment of a much larger phenomenon found in most societies: we make social distinctions among other people based upon their biological sex, and this affects our perceptions, evaluations, feelings, and behavior. Most important, however, is the fact that in most societies sex plays a part in social stratification, the unequal distribution of wealth, power, and prestige. In many cases, it is also the basis for prejudice and discrimination; that is, the treatment of females as members of a social minority.

Unlike most minorities, females are a numerical majority in all societies, which makes their minority standing all the more compelling (Hacker, 1951). How have culture, social structure, and ecological arrangements been used to transform a numerical majority into a social minority?

We begin by looking at the difference between sex as a biological characteristic and gender as a social status. From there we go into a detailed analysis of cultural, structural, and ecological aspects of inequality based on gender and the socialization process through which we learn to take our place as males and females and play the roles associated with them. The rest of the chapter uses the ecological, functional, and conflict perspectives to explain why gender is used as a basis for inequality, and closely examines the myths and realities of change in contemporary society.

BIOLOGY, CULTURE, AND SOCIAL STRUCTURE

Biological sex is a crucial and relatively simple characteristic, for it takes two types of people to create new people. All fetuses initially look the same, but after the first few months, males develop testicles and penises and females develop vaginas, clitorises, ovaries, wombs, and fallopian tubes. These differences occur because males have an "X" and "Y" pair of chromosomes and females have two "X" chromosomes.

Males and females also differ in body chemistry, for while both have the same hormones, they differ in how much of each they have. Females generally have more estrogen and males more testosterone, and this difference plays an important part in physical development (determining, among other things, the size of our bodies, amounts of body hair, potential for muscle development, and the size of breasts and hips).

Sociologically, however, there is more to being male or female than chemistry, physiology, and the parts we play in reproduction, for these *physical* differences have been culturally transformed into two **genders**, which are distinguished by different social characteristics. Cultural beliefs define the basic nature of males and females in different ways; values rank males higher than females; norms support male privilege; and females are the object of both positive and negative attitudes—from the adoration of the Virgin Mary to the contempt for women expressed in pornography.

Most societies also assign males and females to different statuses and, on this basis, distribute wealth, power, and prestige unequally. Women are frequently the ones who care for the children, whereas most men spend their time producing goods. Even among people who work outside the home, there are sharp differences in what men and women do: all but a few women follow instructions given by men; men are far more likely to make decisions and supervise other people. Women are also more likely than men to live in poverty, and to have no paid work at all.

People differ by gender not only in what they do, but in how they do it, for in most societies, male and female patterns of response to other people differ in many ways. Men tend to display more aggressiveness and self-confidence, whereas women display more tenderness, vulnerability, and emotion.

Because all societies make important social distinctions between females and males, it is tempting to conclude that such distinctions are biologically determined and are, therefore, "inevitable" and "natural." Edward O. Wilson (1975) revived this point of view in his study of **sociobiology** and the genetic basis of

social behavior among humans and other species. Females, he asserted, are nurturant toward children because the species needs such behavior in order to successfully reproduce itself. There is, he contended, a nurturant gene, and biological differences between males and females explain important differences we observe in what men and women do and how they do it.

This conclusion, however, fails to pay enough attention to the crucial fact that cultures distinguish between males and females in different ways, and the distinctions made within cultures often change over time. As Wilson (1977) later acknowledged, "The evidence is strong that almost but probably not quite all differences among cultures are based on learning and socialization rather than on genes" (p. 133) (see also Boyd and Richerson, 1985).

Biological determinism also ignores the fact that aside from the roles males and females play in reproduction, there is little scientific evidence that other differences are biologically caused; and those differ-

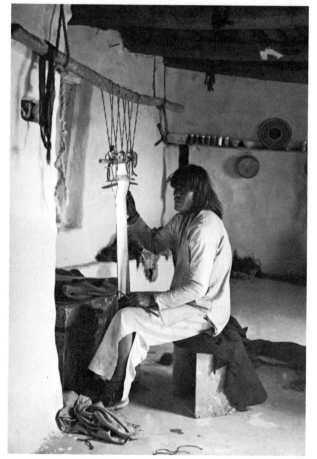

Although Hopi and Navajos share the same territory, their gender divisions of labor are quite different. Among the Navajo, women are the weavers; but among the Hopi, it is the men who weave. Only social factors can account for such differences.

ences that are biological are relatively few in number (Maccoby and Jacklin, 1974). Males are more vulnerable than females to hemophilia and color blindness. They tend to have better visual-spatial and mathematical abilities but poorer verbal abilities, and they tend to be more active physically (Petersen, 1980).

Females display more sensitivity to sound, odor, and touch, are more dexterous in the use of their fingers, and are more likely to sing in tune. Males are generally more sensitive to light and are more adept at manipulating objects in space and "seeing" spatial relations in their minds—as in reading a map or getting through a maze. Female infants pay more attention to facial expressions than to moving objects, whereas the pattern in infant males is just the opposite (Durden-Smith and DeSimone, 1983; Gove and Carpenter, 1982). In each of these cases, however, the differences are between *averages* for males and females, and there is considerable overlap: many girls have better spatial ability than many boys do.

There is little evidence that hormones cause gender differences in behavior (Maccoby and Jacklin, 1974). Studies of testosterone levels and hostility and aggressiveness in men find no consistent relationship.

The lack of scientific support for biological determinism does not mean there is no connection between "male" and "female" as biological and as social characteristics, however (Rossi, 1984). The confinement of women to child care is no mere accident of history. The important point is that biological differences do not *determine* social differences, although they are often used as the basis for them. Sex does not determine gender (see Bleier, 1984; Fausto-Sterling, 1985).

This chapter focuses on two major sociological questions about gender: How do societies use biological characteristics to distinguish among their members, and under what social circumstances do these distinctions lead to the definition of women as a minority? From a sociological perspective, the position of women as a minority depends on the cultural, structural, and ecological aspects of our environments, and each of these factors is connected to the other two in often complex ways.

GENDER, CULTURE, AND THE IDEOLOGY OF SEXISM

Male and female are ascribed statuses, attached to which are *gender roles*—sets of expectations about how males and females should appear and behave. As you read the following sections, keep in mind that although females are treated as a minority in most societies today, this has not always been the case. In most hunter-gatherer and some horticultural societies, the division of labor was based on gender, but women were not treated as inferior. In fact, in many societies they were highly revered (Etienne and Leacock, 1980; Lerner, 1986).

In social interaction, we first define the situation. We decide who other people are in relation to us. Culture is the source of such definitions, providing us with the categories through which we "know" and evaluate people, decide what to expect of them as well as what they will expect of us. At the heart of definitions is language, which makes important distinctions between females and males.

Language and Gender

Language is more than a tool for communication, for our use of a particular language focuses our attention on some aspects of reality more than others. We are less likely to focus on women's adult strengths if we think of them as "girls" rather than "women."

Language reinforces the minority status of females in four ways (Richardson, 1981). First, in many languages, females do not exist independently of males. In English, "man" and masculine pronouns such as "he" are commonly used to refer to both males and females (as in "Peace on earth and good will toward men"). When women marry, they usually replace their own last name with their husband's, surrendering a unique part of their social identity. In general, men are referred to as "Mr."—a title that reveals nothing about their marital status—while women are known either as "Miss" or "Mrs."—in other words, according to their relationship with men. In French, the word "femme" means both "woman" and

Puzzles: What Word Means "Hatred of Males"?

There is no such word. This chapter explains why this is so, even though we have the word misogyny, which means "hatred of females."

"wife," but "husband" and "man" are distinct words—"mari" and "homme." A French man can be referred to independently of his relationships with women, whereas a French woman's identity as "woman" is synonymous with a relationship with a man.

Some argue that "it's only semantics" and "everyone knows that 'man' and 'he' refer to both males and females"; but both common experience and research suggest otherwise. When the word "man" is used, it is more likely to evoke male images than female ones, so the idea that women can be "congressmen" often puzzles children. Scheider and Hacker (1973) asked college students to submit photographs for a new textbook. Half the students were given chapter titles such as "Urban Life" and "Political Behavior," and the other half received titles such as "Urban Man" and "Political Man." The second group produced far more pictures of men than of women, reflecting the subtle but powerful influence of cultural imagery.

Second, we tend to associate masculine and feminine pronouns with specific statuses. We refer to telephone operators and elementary school teachers as "she," but use "he" to refer to college professors, engineers, and physicians. When men or women hold jobs dominated by the other gender, we draw attention to the exception by using titles such as "male nurse" and "policewoman" (Lakoff, 1975). In both cases, language reflects beliefs about who occupies each status, rather than the objective fact that both men and women do.

We also use masculine and feminine pronouns to label nonhuman objects in ways that reflect the subordinate social position of females. Things that men build and control (or try to)—airplanes, ships, and nature—are "she's," while forces that are too powerful for men to control—the Devil and God—are "he's" (see Griffin, 1978).

Third, we use language in ways that portray women as weak, incompetent, and undesirable, and men as strong, competent, and socially valued. Women are often called "girls," but men are rarely called "boys" unless they occupy inferior statuses such as "busboy," or, in some cases, "black." Unmarried older men are called "bachelors," a far more flattering label than comparable words for women—"old maid" and "spinster."

Most sexual slang that is applied to women describes their desirability to men ("fox," "chick," and "broad"), whereas slang that applies to men refers to power over women ("stud"). Many people are familiar with the word for "excessive sexual desire in a female"

Puzzles: Is Your Language Sexist?

Read the following sentences, filling in the masculine or feminine pronoun (his/her, he/she) you think is most appropriate. Do not take a lot of time thinking about your choice.

Professor Blandon of Oxford won the Nobel Prize for _____ discoveries in biochemistry.

_____ sang softly to the baby cradled in _____ arms.

The memo from the boss said _____ would award bonuses next Friday.

As the senator accepted the presidential nomination, _____ eyes filled with tears of joy.

My secretary has increased _____ average typing speed to 80 words per minute.

The smartest student in the class often waited until the last minute to finish writing _____ term papers.

If you can honestly say that both male and female pronouns seem equally right for most or even all these sentences, you may have learned to go beyond the gender orientation of language and to concentrate on what people, as individuals, can do and be.

(nymphomania), but few have ever heard the word for comparable males (satyriasis). In addition, although English includes words for the hatred of females (**misogyny**) and the hatred of all people (**misanthropy**), few dictionaries list a word for the hatred of males.

Japanese contains two vocabularies and grammars—one of which expresses ideas more directly and assertively than the other—and females are expected to use the less assertive form (Shibamoto, 1985; see also Cherry, 1988). American speech produces parallel examples: women are more likely than men to use words such as "lovely," "cute," and "precious," and less likely to use strong profanity or make direct, powerful statements (Lakoff, 1975). Not only do males and females tend to use different vocabularies, but in some cases people assign different meanings to words depending on the speaker's gender. Many people support the belief that when a woman says "no," she really means "yes."

Language reinforces the minority status of women in a fourth way: there is a clear historical trend through which words used to describe women acquire negative meanings. "Madam" and "mistress" went from respectful forms of address to "keeper of a whorehouse" and "lover kept by a man." "Hussy" once meant "housewife"; "tart" and "biddy" were affectionate names; "whore" once meant "lover of either sex"; "nymph" meant "beautiful young woman"; and "broad" meant "young woman," with no negative connotations. Words that describe men, however, have not been degraded in this way. In fact, favorite insults directed toward men are often derived from words that describe women—as in "sissy" (from "sister"), "pussy," and "son of a bitch" (which attacks men by insulting their mothers). Interestingly, "bitch" was originally a term of great reverence for the pre-Christian Goddess, Artemis-Diana, and "son of a bitch" referred to a spiritual son of the pagan Goddess (Walker, 1983).

Language does not cause women to occupy inferior positions, but it plays an important part because we use it to think about ourselves and other people. The fact that there is no English word for "the hatred of males" does not mean that no one hates males; it does mean, however, that systematic, socially supported negative attitudes toward males are unlikely to be a part of a society whose culture includes no such word. In the same way, the existence of the word "misogyny" does not mean that everyone will hate females, but it reflects a cultural idea that lends legitimacy to prejudice and discrimination against them.

Beliefs: Masculine and Feminine

At the heart of cultures are beliefs that we use to define reality, and these include gender stereotypes: men are smarter than women; women cannot take pressure like men can; men are less emotional than women and are only interested in sex; women make better parents and housekeepers than men; aggressive men are "go-getters" and aggressive women are "pushy"; women's talk is all chatter and women only think about clothes; women want to be raped; menstruation makes women unreliable; there is something wrong with women who enjoy sex; there is something wrong with men or women who do *not* enjoy sex.

These are only a few examples of the beliefs that have been used to distinguish between males and females. Together, they portray a vision of the "true nature" of females and males, and in our culture these "natures" are summarized by the concepts of "masculine" and "feminine."

Regardless of gender, race, age, or social class, we generally agree that **masculinity** describes people who are aggressive, rational, strong, independent, competitive, self-confident, dominant, active, tough, emotionally insensitive, and reluctant to show their feelings. **Femininity** describes people who are intuitive, emotionally excitable, weak, vulnerable, dependent, insecure, submissive, noncompetitive, passive, tender, sensitive, and quick to show their emotions (Broverman et al., 1972).

Like all stereotypes, the concepts of masculinity and femininity describe people in oversimplified terms that bear little relation to what individual men and women are really like (Lott, 1981). No one is aggressive or passive all the time; we all have moments of intelligence and moments of stupidity. Gender stereotypes also ignore the enormous variation *among* women and *among* men: there are many men who come closer to the feminine ideal than many women do. Perhaps most important, stereotypes about gender are strongly linked to cultural values.

Values: Vive la Différence?

To many people, beliefs that distinguish females and males do no more than just that: the two genders differ from each other, and what is the harm in that? The harm lies in the fact that most cultures also generally value males more than females, and different criteria are used to evaluate men and women.

Schur (1984) goes so far as to suggest that the status of "female" is treated in many ways as a deviant, stigmatizing characteristic. Several studies reveal a preference for male children among parents in most societies (Coombs, 1977; Williamson, 1976). In parts of rural India, infanticide—the killing of infants—is relatively common and is more likely to be inflicted on female children (Korbin, 1983). Not only is maleness a preferred characteristic, but traits associated with masculinity are valued more highly than those associated with femininity. Broverman et al. (1970) asked male and female mental health professionals to use lists of personality traits to describe the "mature, healthy, competent" male, female, and human being. Although they described the ideal male and ideal human being in similar terms, they described the ideal female in sharply different terms. Females who fulfill their cultural ideals are valued less than men who conform to theirs (see also Showalter, 1985).

The higher value placed on maleness leads to different perceptions and evaluations of men's and women's behavior. In a study of 600 male and female undergraduates (Lao et al., 1975), students watched videotapes of men and women playing roles that differed in assertiveness. Role players were matched for age, physical attractiveness, and intelligence; but, in every case, male role players were judged to be more intelligent and likable than their female counterparts. Highly assertive men were evaluated as more intelligent than less assertive men; but the results for women were in the opposite direction: higher assertiveness resulted in *lower* evaluations of intelligence.

It is significant that cultures commonly value maleness and masculinity more highly than femaleness and femininity; but we also tend to evaluate men and women according to different criteria. An important basis for evaluating women is their physical attractiveness to men, and women often go to great lengths to force their bodies to conform to male values about how they should look (see Lakoff and Scherr, 1984). As Chernin (1981) describes in her powerful

analysis of values about female slenderness, dieting and being thin are a national obsession among U.S. females as young as 7 years old (Feldman et al., 1988; see also Simmons and Blyth, 1986).

Slenderness is far from a natural or universal criterion for beauty in women. In Western Samoa most women gain weight with each pregnancy and are, by U.S. standards, "fat" by the time they reach middle age. Rather than suffering shame, they are widely admired and perform "humorous, almost lascivious" dances on public occasions (MacKenzie, 1980). In the U.S., however, as married couples age, changes in the wife's physical appearance have a much greater negative effect on how attractive they are to their husbands than physical changes in husbands have on how attractive they are to their wives (Margolin, 1987).

To make their legs appear attractive, many women wear shoes whose high heels make it difficult to walk or run and cause back pain. In 1984, 95,000 U.S. women submitted themselves to surgery in order to increase the size of their breasts (American Society of Plastic and Reconstructive Surgeons, 1985). The Chinese practiced footbinding, the gross distortion of women's feet that made it painful and almost impossible for them to walk (Dworkin, 1974). Tiny feet were

 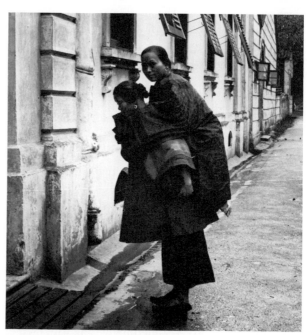

The practice of footbinding shows how class and gender can have bizarre effects. The peasant woman oaring her boat has healthy feet that were considered crude and ugly. The maidservant must carry her aristocratic employer everywhere because footbinding has tortured her feet into "perfect" but useless stumps.

culturally valued as delicate, beautiful, and feminine, and feet of normal size were considered ugly.

Footbinding was accomplished by bending all toes except the big one under a girl's foot and into the soles of her feet. The result—in addition to excruciating pain, chronic bleeding, and infection—was a woman who could barely do more than shuffle. Although footbinding is a far cry from chronic dieting and wearing high-heeled shoes, it is hard to escape the parallel, for in each case women's bodies are subjected to distortion and pain in order to conform to cultural values.

The major criteria for evaluating men, however, are power, wealth, and prestige, not physical attractiveness. The values applied to women do not increase their power, except through relationships with men who find them attractive. Such power, however, is very insecure, for it depends on men's evaluations of women. The cultural values that apply to women encourage them to depend on men, and provide them with no independent basis of power; values that apply to men have just the opposite effect.

Attitudes

Several authors argue that beneath beliefs and values that define females as inferior are negative attitudes. Pornography usually portrays women as objects that exist to please men, and women are often the victims of verbal abuse and physical violence (Lederer, 1980; Malamuth and Donnerstein, 1984).

Chernin's (1981) analysis of values about female beauty shows their relationship with negative attitudes toward females. American women, she observes, are often dissatisfied with their bodies and regard them as enemies that refuse to conform to cultural ideals of slenderness. The desire to live in a different body reflects

> a bitter contempt for the feminine nature of my own body. The sense of fullness and swelling, of curves and softness, the awareness of plentitude and abundance, which filled me with disgust and alarm, were actually the qualities of a woman's body. (p. 18)

The dislike that many women feel for their bodies reflects negative cultural attitudes toward the natural physical characteristics of female bodies (Chernin, p. 22), just as the Chinese belief that normal female feet were crude and unattractive reflected attitudes of that culture.

Negative attitudes toward females are common throughout the histories of many societies (see Dijkstra, 1987). Ancient Greeks believed women were evil, and misogyny was a recurring theme in literature that portrayed women as the cause of all human problems (Pomeroy, 1975). The Greek philosopher and mathematician Pythagoras wrote, "There is a good principle which created order, light, and man, and an evil principle which created chaos, darkness, and woman" (in Morgan, 1970, p. 34). In the 15 centuries after the death of Christ, women and sexuality were increasingly associated with evil in many cultures, and negative attitudes peaked in Europe during the Middle Ages when millions were persecuted as witches (Ben-Yehuda, 1980; Dworkin, 1974).

As this etching shows, in classical mythology, Pandora was credited with opening a box that loosed on the world all the evils that trouble humanity, claiming men as the first victims.

Norms

Laws have limited the rights of females in many societies. Until quite recently, women could not vote in the U.S., own property, dispose of their earnings, or enter into contracts. A majority of states still do not include a husband's use of force to have sex with his wife in their legal definition of rape (Finkelhor and Yllo, 1985). In 1982 the Equal Rights Amendment to the Constitution was defeated, and women do not yet enjoy equal standing and protection under the law.

The effects of the folkways and mores on the everyday lives of men and women are no less important than the effects of law. Women are expected to marry and, once married, to have and raise children, leaving the job of breadwinning to men. In 1987, 47 percent of U.S. adults agreed that, "It is much better for everyone involved if the man is the achiever outside the home and the woman takes care of home and family" (Davis and Smith, 1987). Even when women do work outside the home, they are expected to put family obligations before their jobs (Pleck, 1977).

In their interactions with men, women are expected to conceal their intelligence and strength. When a man is sexually aroused, many women feel an obligation to do something to satisfy him. Many men feel they should open doors for women, defend them if another man offends them, and pay the check when they go out with them.

On a superficial level, these may appear to be no more than harmless courtesies that make life more pleasant. On a deeper level, however, they reinforce the minority status of women by expecting them to pretend they are inferior when they are not, to subjugate their own feelings to men's desires, and to pretend that they are incapable of providing for, taking care of, and defending themselves.

Because we use culture to make sense of the world, we are often unaware that it is a human creation until we look at cultures other than our own. In her classic study of New Guinea tribes, Margaret Mead (1935) found startling departures from Western ideas about gender. Among the Arapesh, both men and women conformed to our ideas about femininity: both took care of children, aggressive behavior was discouraged for both genders, and gentleness and warmth were valued.

Among Mundugamoors, however, the opposite prevailed: both men and women were aggressive and violent, and men and women attacked each other with equal ferocity. The third tribe—the Tchambuli—distinguished between men and women, but the behavior of women corresponded to our ideas of masculinity, whereas the men conformed to our ideas of femininity.

In a study of college students in various Western societies—Norway, Sweden, Denmark, Finland, and the United States—Block (1973) found that men in the U.S. place more importance on "manliness" than do men from the other countries, and women in the U.S. describe the ideal woman in more masculine terms than other women do. Students also place more importance on competitive achievement and less emphasis on the control of aggressive behavior in males.

Culture is a framework that we use to make sense of ourselves and others. Ideas that apply to males and females, however, go beyond the task of "making sense" of the world, for they also help justify and perpetuate social structures in which females are treated as a minority. Most cultures are **sexist** because they support prejudice against females; and because sexism is used to justify inequality, it is an *ideology*. What do these structures of inequality look like, and how do they affect our lives?

GENDER AND SOCIAL STRUCTURE

The social structures of most of today's societies clearly place women in the position of a minority; but, as we saw earlier, gender-based inequality is by no means universal. In most hunter-gatherer and in some horticultural societies, women and men have shared equally in wealth, power, and prestige, in spite of their different positions in divisions of labor (Etienne and Leacock, 1980; Sanday, 1981).

Gender Roles, Status Sets, and Social Identity

Gender roles define expectations for males and females. When we interact with people of different genders, we use beliefs to identify and describe them as male or female, values to determine their rank in relation to us, attitudes to direct positive and negative feelings and behavior toward them, and norms to form expectations of them and ourselves in relation to them.

We do not have to think, evaluate, feel, and behave according to roles, but we have strong reasons to do so. Roles have coercive power over us because reward and punishment depend on them and because we use roles to orient ourselves to other people. If we deviate from a gender role, we risk punishment or lost rewards. At the very least, we may lose our sense that we know who we are and who other people are in relation to us.

In our culture, gender roles correspond to masculinity and femininity. Females who conform to their gender role define physical beauty as "slenderness"; value the ability to be attractive to and supportive of men more than they value independence; admire and look up to men; and behave in ways that perpetuate their subordinate position (letting men interrupt them, asking men to do things for them that they could easily do themselves, or allowing men to dominate them sexually).

Men who conform to their gender role believe they are more intelligent than women; value wealth, power, and prestige more than intimate relationships; feel hostility toward women (often expressed as humor); and behave in ways that reinforce their dominance (controlling conversations, "defending" women without asking them if they want to be defended, or being sexually aggressive regardless of women's feelings).

As important as gender roles are, however, they are only the "tip of the iceberg," *because gender is a status that affects which other statuses are included in our status sets.* Men dominate society not simply because they are masculine, but because they have greater access to powerful achieved statuses. They control legislatures, governments, courts, labor unions, corporations, religious organizations, schools, universities, and important professions such as law and medicine.

Women's inferior position rests on more than the demands of femininity, for women are confined to relatively powerless statuses. As wives or mothers, they have little power outside the home, and those who do not work for pay must depend on men for their security. In families, they enjoy few legal protections from abuse by their husbands. In the workplace, most hold the lowest paying, least powerful jobs.

Gender roles have an enormous impact on our status sets and, with them, our identities. In our culture a successful woman is not simply feminine: she is also a supportive wife and devoted mother who values her children's happiness and her husband's occupational success more than her own. She is content with poorly paid or part-time jobs. In the same way, a

---

Puzzles: Why Are the Husbands of Some Working Wives So Troubled?

White husbands whose wives work often report more symptoms of psychological distress (such as difficulty sleeping and nervousness) than those whose wives do not work. Why?

If your answer is that husbands whose wives work have harder lives because they have to do more housework, you are wrong. As this chapter explains, working wives still do most of the housework and husbands tend to feel threatened by a wife's earning power.

---

successful man is not simply masculine. He has a beautiful wife, a highly paid, prestigious job, his own home, and a new car.

Gender roles are not single, unified roles. There are several that make up much of men's and women's social identities (Janeway, 1971).

Role and Status Conflict: Binds and Double-Binds   The variety of statuses we occupy and the complexity of their role sets often produce conflicting expectations that cause status and role strain. Working mothers experience status strain because they are expected to stay home to care for a sick child and go to work (see Barnett and Baruch, 1983). Added to this is the widespread belief that children's development suffers if women work (Davis and Smith, 1986)—a belief that consistently finds no support in scientific research (Hayes and Kamerman, 1983). Men experience role strain when other men (and many women) expect them to be strong and domineering, and yet many women expect them to behave with tenderness and treat them as equals.

Although everyone experiences conflict because of gender, a society that treats women as a minority generally produces more strain for them than for men (see Michelson, 1985). Unless women can hire someone to care for their children, they have a difficult time combining marriage, motherhood, and full-time work. Men are in less of a bind, for our culture makes relatively few demands on husbands and fathers, enabling men to have families and commit themselves to their occupations. Men are able to separate their different roles from one another in time and space. One

Women who want to work outside the home and have children face status strain that men have been able to avoid. What are the different ways in which such strain might be resolved What changes would they require?

result of this is that early marriage disrupts the educational progress of women but not that of men (Alexander and Reilly, 1981).

Women who marry and have children, however, cannot separate family and nonfamily roles so easily (Janeway, 1971). The result is considerable strain for many women who want to work or who must work (because their husbands cannot support their families or because they are divorced and are the sole source of support).

The conflicts and dilemmas that confront males and females in social relationships are most apparent in the interactions of everyday life.

Patterns of Interaction We saw earlier that men and women tend to use language differently in ways that contribute to the inferior social position of women. Observations of interactions between men and women reveal inequality of power in other ways as well, most notably in the control men tend to exercise over conversations (see Kollock, Blumstein, and Schwartz, 1985).

Women tend to say less than men and more often abandon topics they introduce in favor of what men want to talk about (Fishman, 1975). In mixed-gender couples, men are usually the ones who interrupt; but, when men and women talk with people of their own gender, interruptions are more evenly distributed (Zimmerman and West, 1975). When women interact with men, they often appear to be "a class of speakers . . . whose rights to speak are casually infringed

upon by males" (p. 117). As a female student wrote in her journal, "he assumes that *whatever* I'm doing is interruptible; that I will be ready to do what he wants to do when he wants to do it" (in Richardson, 1977, p. 29).

Men and women differ not only in control over conversations, but in the content of what they say. It is generally true that people of higher status are not required to reveal as much of themselves as are people of lower status (Goffman, 1967), and this appears to be true for women and men. Masculine men are expected to hide emotion and weaknesses, while feminine women are expected to be open and vulnerable (Henley, 1973; see Friedman, Riggio, and Segall, 1980).

Language is only one of the tools we use in social interaction, and in many cases our bodies send non-verbal messages that are more important than what we say. Women tend to smile more often than men regardless of how they are feeling (Deaux, 1976). Females tend to remember people's faces more accurately than males, a difference that has been detected in children as young as 4 years old; females also are more willing to make eye contact with others and to hold it for longer durations (see Haviland and Malatesta, 1981). A substantial body of research shows that women are more sensitive than men to nonverbal expressions of how people are feeling (see Hall, 1978).

Men are more likely to touch women than to be touched by them (Henley, 1973, 1977; Mayo and Henley, 1981); and, as Goffman (1967) reminds us, if we are more powerful than others, we feel greater freedom to touch them when we want to (teachers touch students more than students touch teachers). In public we are more likely to see a man's arm around a woman's shoulders than the other way around, and even when holding hands, men tend to hold the back of their hand facing forward, as if leading a child.

Men and women also tend to touch in different ways. When a man "cuddles" a woman in his arms, his position is a controlling one, for her arms are confined by his. Men, however, rarely allow themselves to be cuddled, especially in public, because this threatens to reduce them to a childlike status (Henley, 1973).

Women encounter a variety of difficulties in their interactions at work. Both men and women generally prefer to have male supervisors and resent women who are placed above them (Greene, 1976; Kanter, 1976). When competent women have jobs that match their abilities, male co-workers tend to dislike them and exclude them from informal activities such as meeting for lunch or coffee—all of which are important in being accepted as co-workers (Hagen and Kahn, 1975).

In corporations, highly placed women are often the only women in their workplace. Such "tokens" are pressured to conform to stereotypes that have nothing to do with their jobs. Executive women may be expected to "mother" male executives—by preparing coffee or providing emotional support. They are often looked upon as sexual objects that men compete for, or as "office pets" who play the role of a "younger sister" who adds humor and does not threaten men (Kanter, 1977b). In 1983, one of Atlanta's leading law firms sponsored a swimsuit contest for female law interns (Morello, 1986).

Among all the pressures and conflicting expectations women face in their interactions with men, one of the most serious is sexual harassment—repeated and unwanted sexual comments, looks, propositions, and physical contact (Gutek, 1985). Whether at work, on the street, or on campus, women often experience a violation of their social boundaries:

> "Hey honey, where you going? Can I go too? Where's your bra, honey? Don't they get cold that way? I'll keep 'em warm. . . . What a nice piece. . . . You got real nice legs. . . . Got anything between 'em? What's the matter with you? You stuck up or something?" (in Medea and Thompson, 1974, p. 47)

Most women can tell stories of similar experiences, including "those mysterious hands that sud-denly appear from under attaché cases, coats, or simply out of nowhere"—what Medea and Thompson call "little rapes." One study estimates that 75 percent of working women have experienced sexual harassment at work (Kolson, 1979). That men so often assume that women enjoy such experiences reflects a culturally supported lack of regard for women's right to choose the circumstances under which they will interact with others (see Beauvais, 1986; Gutek, 1985).

Minorities are commonly the victims of violations of social boundaries, which often extend to physical violence. Using data from the National Victimization Studies, Johnson (1980) estimates that as many as one-third of U.S. females will experience an attempted or completed criminal sexual assault in their lifetime (see also Russell and Howell, 1983). A nationwide study of college women conservatively

AT&T

It is company policy that all employees have a right to work in an environment free of discrimination, which encompasses freedom from sexual harassment. A.T.&T. prohibits sexual harassment of its employees in any form.

Such conduct may result in disciplinary action up to and including dismissal. Specifically, no supervisor shall threaten or insinuate either explicitly or implicitly that any employee's submission to or rejection of sexual advances will in any way influence any personnel decision regarding that employee's employment, evaluation, wages, advancement, assigned duties, shifts or any other condition of employment or career development.

Other sexually harassing conduct in the workplace, whether physical or verbal, committed by supervisors or non-supervisory personnel is also prohibited. This includes repeated offensive sexual flirtation, advances, propositions, continual or repeated abuse of a sexual nature, graphic verbal commentary about an individual's body, sexually degrading words to describe an individual and the display in the workplace of sexually suggestive objects or pictures.

Employees who have complaints of sexual harassment should in appropriate circumstances report such conduct to their supervisors. If this is not appropriate, they should seek the assistance of their equal opportunity complaint investigator. Where investigations confirm the allegations, appropriate corrective action will be taken.

Only in the last few years have corporations taken the issue of sexual harassment seriously enough to issue formal statements that both define and prohibit it. AT&T's policy was issued in 1986.

estimated that 15 percent had been raped since the age of 14 and an additional 12 percent had been victims of attempted rape (Koss et al., 1987). Virtually all rape is committed by males against females and damages the victim's life in serious and often irreparable ways (Brownmiller, 1975; Holmstrom and Burgess, 1983; Russell, 1984).

Gender roles affect interactions among women and among men, as well as between them. Except for handshaking and contact during sports, men rarely touch each other, for to do so may threaten the power of the man who is touched (Deaux, 1976). Women, however, have less power to lose through touching, and are more likely than men to touch people of their own gender (Rands and Levinger, 1979). In one experiment, experimenters stood very close to men and women on a street and found that men moved away from men but not from women. Women, however, were more tolerant of such "invasions" of space, regardless of the "invader's" gender (Dobbs, 1972).

Gender roles affect not only inequalities of power, but also the kinds of relationships people have. Friendships among women tend to be more intense than among men (Rubin, 1973), tend to last longer (Wheeler and Nezlek, 1977), and involve more emotional support (Weiss and Lowenthal, 1975). The evidence suggests that men pay a price for dominance—fewer enduring, self-revealing, personal ties that provide emotional support (Fox et al., 1985).

Divisions of Labor: Ecology and Social Structure

Divisions of labor in most societies use gender as a basis for sorting people into adult statuses (Nielson, 1978), but only a few statuses such as mother and father are directly tied to biological sex. Historically, however, mother and father have been statuses of enormous importance in creating and perpetuating gender inequality (Huber, 1976).

In early hunter-gatherer societies, the dependence of children on their mothers confined women to tasks that allowed them to remain in one place for long periods. Although women participated in hunting, men were in the best position to be hunters who left their villages for days at a time. Some anthropologists argue that hunting provided the most important source of food for these societies, and biological roles allowed men to monopolize the most culturally valued social roles (Friedl, 1975).

Harris (1977) argued that different reproductive roles also created inequality by allowing men to dominate warfare:

> Warfare required the organization of communities around a resident core of fathers, brothers, and their sons. This led to the control over resources by paternal-fraternal interest groups and the exchange of sisters and daughters between such groups . . . to the allotment of women as a reward for male aggressiveness. . . . The assignment of drudge work to women and their ritual subordination and devaluation follows automatically from the need to reward males at the expense of females. (p. 86)

Early ecological arrangements enabled men to monopolize the most important tasks and laid the groundwork for cultural values that rank males higher than females.

Others maintain that the gender division of labor did not result in inequality in hunter-gatherer societies or in most horticultural societies. In all societies, adult standing depends on performing socially productive labor (Huber and Spitze, 1983). In the earliest societies, all labor contributed to the community. The "domestic" work of women was no less socially productive than the hunting and warfare conducted by males, and even when women were less powerful than men, they were treated as full adults. There is considerable evidence that the importance of hunting in many of these societies is much less than previously believed and that, in fact, women provided most of the food in a diet that was largely vegetarian. In addition, women's control over childbearing, before the male role in reproduction became known, gave them a highly revered place, long before the development of patriarchal ideas about male deities who created life (see Fisher, 1980; Lerner, 1986).

Among the Hopi Indians, families are headed by women, not men; Hopi women do not depend on marriage for their security; and privilege based on gender does not exist. Although men are primarily responsible for hunting, herding, and farming, these tasks are not more highly valued than women's work—making pottery, baskets, and clothing. It is revealing to note that Hopi society differs sharply from our own in another crucial way: child care is the responsibility of the entire community, not of women alone (Leavitt, 1971).

Engels (1891), Sacks (1974), Goody (1976), and others argue that it was when technology enabled societies to produce surpluses that the position of women dropped dramatically. The ability to produce surpluses created two distinct types of production: goods that were consumed and goods that were traded. Here the concept of "private property" emerged, and while men monopolized the production of surplus goods, women were confined to producing goods for immediate consumption.

The distinction is crucial because surplus goods are wealth that is a basis for exchange and social power. The family emerged as a social unit separate from the community; production was for the family, not the community; and because domestic work no longer contributed to the community, women lost adult standing and were viewed as little more than the wives and daughters of men (Etienne and Leacock, 1980).

As divisions of labor became more complex, gender distinctions went beyond childbearing, child care, hunting, and warfare to include a wide range of occupations. In colonial America, families produced most of what they consumed, and although men and women usually did different things, women performed important productive roles—weaving cloth, making products such as soap and candles, and trading in the marketplace. Some women worked as blacksmiths, tailors, printers, and shopkeepers, and when husbands died, wives often assumed full control of family businesses (Baxandall et al., 1976; Demos, 1970).

In colonial times, family life and production of goods were usually carried on in the same place, but this ecological arrangement changed with the Industrial Revolution (Cherlin, 1983; Tilly and Scott, 1978). With the introduction of factories, home became a "private sphere," separated and isolated from the "public sphere" of paid work. Ecological changes made it increasingly difficult for women to occupy the statuses of wife and mother and perform more highly valued and powerful roles outside the family (Sachs, 1983). This, in turn, affected the division of labor within families.

Divisions of Labor in Families   In most families in the U.S., husbands are considered to be the "heads" of their households and dominate decision making. However, women who work outside the home, and who have more education than their husbands, tend to have more power within their families than women who do not (Gillespie, 1971; Hood, 1983).

In most families, women still do most of the housework (Miller and Garrison, 1982), and a recent study of high school seniors reveals little interest in changing this division of labor (Herzog, Bachman, and Johnston, 1983). In families with two working parents, husbands generally do a small fraction of the domestic work their wives do, mostly shopping or doing dishes (Huber and Spitze, 1983). Fathers, as a whole, spend an average of only 12 minutes a day alone with their children (Tavris and Wade, 1984), time more likely spent in play than in caretaking (Berk and Berk, 1979). Among women who work full time, roughly 90 percent do most or all of the family cooking and shopping (*New York Times*, February 24, 1988, p. 1).

Women are not only expected to devote themselves to family life, but must live with a cultural contradiction: they are expected to value family roles above all, yet those roles have a relatively low cultural value. We tend to value people who work more than we value those who do not, and family roles are not defined as "productive work." The U.S. Census Bureau does not count homemakers in the labor force, and if you ask a full-time homemaker, "Do you work?" she will most likely say, "No, I'm a housewife."

The relatively low value placed on family roles puts women in an insecure position in which they receive little outside support. Few businesses provide day-care facilities for employees; the demands of child care make it difficult for women to establish themselves in secure, well-paying jobs; and the status of "homemaker" has little financial security, lasting only as long as the marriage.

The division of labor within families affects the position of women in society. The domestic responsibilities of women are not only the historical root of gender inequality, but a major aspect of social structure that continues to deny women equality.

Gender and the "Public" World   Most women in all societies are part of the labor force. In 1986, 65 percent of single women in the U.S. were in the labor force, as were 55 percent of married women, including 54 percent of those with preschool children and 68 percent of those with children of school age. Among divorced women, 76 percent were in the labor force, including 74 percent of those with young children and fully 85 percent of those with school-age children (U.S. Census Bureau, 1986a).

The persisting ideal that a "woman's place is in the home" clearly does not describe our society and is, in fact, a curious idea, both in comparison with other societies and historically. Yet, while most women work, they are still less likely than men to be in the labor force. In 1985, 76 percent of males over the age of 15 were in the labor force, compared with 54 percent of females. Women are also more likely than men to work at part-time jobs: in 1985 only 10 percent of men over the age of 16 worked part-time, compared with 27 percent of women (U.S. Census Bureau, 1986a).

Even among those who work full-time, however, women are in jobs at the lowest levels of income, power, and prestige (Rytina, 1981). There is also increasing evidence that when men and women perform different jobs that require comparable skills, women are consistently paid less simply because the job is defined as a woman's job (Bureau of National Affairs, 1984; Treiman and Hartmann, 1981; Women's Research and Education Institute, 1984).

The contents of Table 13-1 are important enough to study carefully. Each column shows occupations according to how well women are represented in them, *relative to their representation in the entire em-*

ployed labor force. In 1985, women made up 44 percent of the employed labor force. If women had an equal share of all jobs, they would comprise 44 percent of every occupation, but they make up only 7 percent of engineers and 15 percent of lawyers (top of first two columns), whereas 87 percent of all librarians (top of last column) were women.

The table reveals three patterns that describe the position of women in the labor force. First, they are overrepresented in jobs that involve taking care of other people's needs (nurses, secretaries, elementary school teachers, and child-care workers), few of which include authority over other adults, and all of which carry low pay and prestige. Second, women are severely or substantially underrepresented in the best white-collar jobs (engineer, lawyer, physician) as well as blue-collar jobs that are highly skilled or represented by unions (plumbers and electricians, machinists, truck drivers, and police officers). In 1985, only 13 percent of employed women belonged to unions, compared with 22 percent of working men (U.S. Census Bureau, 1986a). Third, in virtually all jobs in

Table 13-1

Representation of Women in Selected Occupations, United States, 1985

UNDERREPRESENTED			OVERREPRESENTED	
Severely[1]	*Substantially*[2]	*Slightly*[3]	*Moderately*[4]	*Heavily*[5]
Engineer	Lawyer	Accountant	High school teacher	Librarian
Dentist	Judge	Psychologist	Personnel worker	Nurse
Senator or	Natural scientist	Social scientist	Vocational	Therapist
representative	Chemist	Computer	counselor	Health technician
Carpenter	Physician	programmer	Editor	Social worker
Plumber	Pharmacist	College teacher	Buyer	Elementary/
Electrician	Science technician	Writer	Health	kindergarten
Firefighter	Sales manager	Artist	administrator	teacher
Construction	Insurance agent	Entertainer	Building manager	Bank teller
worker	Stockbroker	Bank officer	Real estate agent	Office manager
Metalcraft worker	Mail carrier	School	Insurance adjustor	Computer operator
Machinist	Telephone installer	administrator	Assembly-line	Clerk
Mechanic	Storekeeper	Restaurant manager	worker	Cashier
Police officer	Farm supervisor	Typesetter	Bus driver	Bookkeeper
Heavy equipment	Security guard	Postal clerk	Commercial cook	Secretary
operator	Salesworker (except	Cleaning worker		Telephone operator
Meat cutter and	clerks)	Sales representative		Clerk supervisor
butcher	Blue-collar	Baker		Stenographer
Mine operative	supervisor	Public official		Typist
Welder	Precision machine	Machine operator		Receptionist
Taxi and truck	operator	Religious worker		Textile worker
driver	Farmer or farm			Laundry worker
	manager			Dressmaker
				Waiter
				Child-care worker
				Household servant

[1]Equal to less than ¼ of women's share of the employed labor force.
[2]Equal to between ¼ and ¾ of women's share of the employed labor force.
[3]Equal to between ¾ and all of women's share of the employed labor force.
[4]Less than ⅓ more than women's share of the employed labor force.
[5]More than ⅓ more than women's share of the employed labor force.

Source: U.S. Census Bureau, 1986a.

which women are heavily overrepresented, they are supervised by men.

Women not only occupy inferior positions *among* occupations, but within them (Brown, Moon, and Zoloth, 1980). In medicine, women are rarely surgeons (the highest paid specialty) and are more likely than men to be psychiatrists, pediatricians, or internists, all of which are at the bottom of the medical hierarchy (AAMC, 1987). Women with Ph.D.'s in science and engineering are more likely than comparable men to be unemployed, earn lower salaries, and work for less prestigious institutions regardless of the quality of their graduate department or their professional experience (Haas and Perrucci, 1984). In writing for movies and television, males get more jobs than women, with better pay and higher prestige (Writers Guild of America, 1987), and few women make it to top posts in the media (Wilson, 1988). In college faculties, women are less likely than men to have tenure or have full professorships, and women in the military rarely reach the rank of general. Among lawyers, women are more likely than men to work in government agencies, whereas men more often work in higher-paying private law firms (Epstein, 1983). Women who manage to make it into large private firms are overrepresented among associates but severely underrepresented among partners (Table 13-2).

Over the course of their lives, women as a whole tend to be somewhat downwardly mobile, whereas men tend to move upward (Marini, 1980; Sewell et al.,

---

Table 13-2

Representation of Women Lawyers among Associates and Partners in Selected Large U.S. Law Firms

LAW FIRM (City)	PERCENT-AGE OF ASSOCIATES WHO ARE WOMEN	PERCENT-AGE OF PARTNERS WHO ARE WOMEN
Sidley & Austin (Chicago)	31	6
Shearman & Sterling (New York)	34	2
Morgan, Lewis, & Bockius (Philadelphia)	28	1
Gibson, Dunn, & Crutcher (Los Angeles)	35	4
Skadden, Arps, Slate, Meagher, & Flom (New York)	29	3
Vinson & Elkins (Houston)	28	3
Jones, Day, Reavis, & Pogue (Cleveland)	30	4
Finley, Kumble, Wagner, Heine, Underberg, Manley, & Casey (New York)	22	2
Squire, Sanders, & Dempsey (Cleveland)	31	4
Fulbright & Jaworski (Houston)	26	2

Source: *National Law Review*, May 21, 1984.

1980). Spenner, Otto, and Call (1982) found that the greater opportunities for men mean that over the course of their working lives, the educational "payoff" in terms of occupation prestige, complexity, and skill is nearly three times as great as it is for women.

Divisions of labor that place women in inferior positions are found throughout the world. In socialist countries such as the Soviet Union, women are far less likely than men to occupy positions of high income, prestige, or power (see Holland, 1985). The Chinese family is still heavily dominated by men (Johnson, 1983; Stacey, 1983); and although roughly three-quarters of all Soviet physicians are female, they have less prestige than U.S. physicians and earn only two-thirds the income of skilled Soviet workers (Lapidus, 1978).

Wealth and Income

Men are far more likely than women to be among the top wealthholders under 50 years of age in the U.S. Among older top wealthholders, women fare better, but this is largely because women outlive men and therefore outnumber them at the older ages (U.S. Census Bureau, 1986d).

Among full-time workers in 1985, women earned only 63¢ for every dollar earned by men; and families headed by unmarried women were more than twice as likely to live in poverty than were those headed by unmarried men (U.S. Census Bureau, 1986a). Divorce is perhaps the leading cause of the impoverishment of women. In California, divorce causes an average drop of 73 percent in the standard of living of divorced women and their children, but brings a 42 percent *increase* in the average standard of living of divorced men (Weitzman, 1985).

As we saw in Chapter 2, women earn less in part because they have relatively low-paying jobs regardless of their qualifications, and even when they work at the same jobs or jobs requiring comparable skills, they tend to be paid less (Hartmann, 1985; Remick, 1984) (see Figure 13-1). Duncan et al. (1984) conclude that at least two-thirds of the gender gap in wages is "undeserved" in that it cannot be accounted for by differences in education, work experience, work continuity, and differences in socialization and on-the-job training.

Income inequality between men and women exists regardless of race, but it is more severe among whites than among nonwhites. This is largely because nonwhites are crowded into a narrow range of low

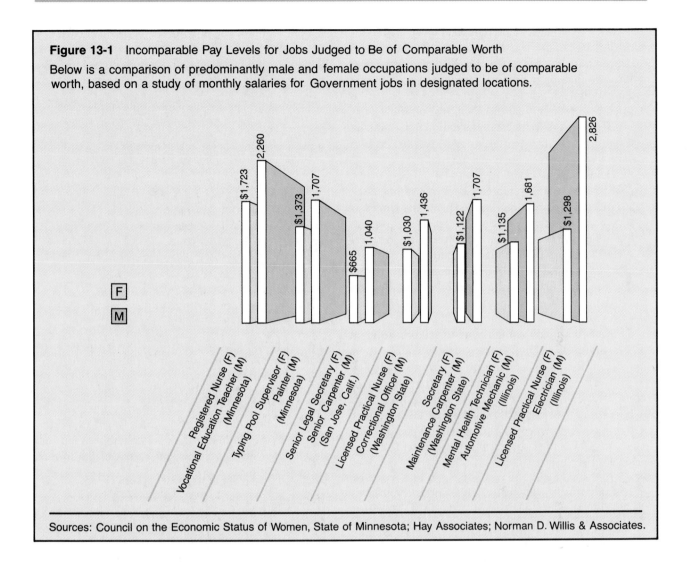

Figure 13-1 Incomparable Pay Levels for Jobs Judged to Be of Comparable Worth

Below is a comparison of predominantly male and female occupations judged to be of comparable worth, based on a study of monthly salaries for Government jobs in designated locations.

F

M

Registered Nurse (F)
Vocational Education Teacher (M)
(Minnesota)

Typing Pool Supervisor (F)
Painter (M)
(Minnesota)

Senior Legal Secretary (F)
Senior Carpenter (M)
(San Jose, Calif.)

Licensed Practical Nurse (F)
Correctional Officer (M)
(Washington State)

Secretary (F)
Maintenance Carpenter (M)
(Washington State)

Mental Health Technician (F)
Automotive Mechanic (M)
(Illinois)

Licensed Practical Nurse (F)
Electrician (M)
(Illinois)

$1,723 2,260 $1,373 1,707 $665 1,040 $1,030 1,436 $1,122 1,707 $1,135 1,681 $1,298 2,826

Sources: Council on the Economic Status of Women, State of Minnesota; Hay Associates; Norman D. Willis & Associates.

incomes, and so the potential for large gender differences in income *among* nonwhites is small. Black women made up 55 percent of the black population in 1985 and received 44 percent of all income received by blacks—80 percent of what they would receive under conditions of equality *among* blacks. White women, however, made up 52 percent of the white population, and yet received only 33 percent of all income received by whites—only 63 percent of their proportional share (U.S. Census Bureau, 1987a).

Power, Patriarchy, and Matriarchy

Patriarchy and matriarchy describe the distribution of power by gender in a society. A **patriarchy** is a society in which men dominate women, children, and major social institutions, and a **matriarchy** is a society dominated by women. So far as we know, there has never been a truly matriarchal society, although there have been numerous societies in which women were highly regarded and held some major institutional power (Bamberger, 1974; Lerner, 1986).

Men control business and banking, government, religious organizations, the mass media (including most magazines written for women), schools and universities, legal and correctional systems, prestigious professions such as law, medicine, and science, the military, and most of the nation's wealth (Epstein and Coser, 1981). As of 1988, women made up only 2 percent of the U.S. Senate, 5 percent of the House of Representatives, and 15 percent of state legislatures (Mandel, 1987). In Scandinavian countries, such as

Norway, women have more political power than in the U.S., but, as in the U.S., women's power is more likely to be focused on traditionally female concerns such as child care than on male-dominated areas such as economic policy (Haavio-Mannila et al., 1985). Iceland is a notable exception. In 1987 a feminist political party won 10 percent of the seats in the national parliament, enough to make it a pivotal force in national politics (*Los Angeles Times*, August 19, 1987, p. 1).

On a smaller scale Goldberg (1973) argued that women have great power, because their feminine qualities and child-rearing role make them "the directors of societies' emotional resources" (p. 140). Most of women's power is over children, however. Such power is short-lived and ironic in its consequences, for insofar as women raise their children to conform to gender roles, they are, like the Chinese mothers who bound their daughters' feet, perpetuating a society in which females are treated as a minority (Rich, 1976).

Women *do* have some power in relation to men; but as Hacker (1951), Janeway (1971), and others point out, it is the peculiar kind of power wielded by subordinate groups. Few would argue that small children are powerful in our society, and yet they often control their parents with astonishing effectiveness. Like children, women are often stereotyped as "manipulative," *but their social status gives them few other sources of power.*

> As part of her traditional role, it is only in intimate situations that she can use power and feel its rewards. The more she is precluded from acting for herself in man's world and limited to managing emotions . . . the likelier it becomes that her need for autonomy, her search for identity . . . and the unused energies she possesses will come to expression in private because they can't be put to work in public. The negative role of bitches is almost built into a woman's role and it surfaces at the heart of the duality of marriage *if this is to be the only place where she has a chance to exercise power* [italics mine]. (Janeway, 1971, p. 205)

Women also derive power from their unique position as a minority, for while virtually all other minorities are segregated from those who dominate them, intimate relationships between men and women lie at the heart of the most universal of all social institutions, marriage and the family. Although women are a minority, most women also live in relationships in which they depend on men and men depend on them.

Women, Virginia Woolf (1929) noted, serve as "looking-glasses possessing the magic and delicious

power of reflecting the figure of man at twice its natural size" (p. 35). She then described how men depend on women to play this role in order for men to feel powerful:

> Without that power, the earth would still be swamp and jungle. The glories of all our wars would be unknown. . . . mirrors are essential to all violent and heroic action. That is why Napoleon and Mussolini both insist so emphatically upon the inferiority of women, *for if they were not inferior, they would cease to enlarge. That serves to explain the necessity that women so often are to men. And it serves to explain how restless they are under her criticism; how impossible it is for her to say to them that this book is bad, this picture is feeble, or whatever it may be. . . . For if she begins to tell the truth, the figure in the looking-glass shrinks; his fitness for life is diminished. How is he to go on giving judgement, civilizing natives, making laws, writing books . . . unless he can see himself at breakfast and at dinner at least twice the size he really is?* (italics mine) (pp. 35–36)

As Janeway (1971) put it, "Here is the paradox: women are weak because they can be strong only through giving. They are strong because what they give is needed" (p. 57).

Social structures distribute power unequally between women and men in complex ways. Men dominate, but the unique interdependency between men and women gives women power unavailable to most other minorities.

Prestige

In most societies, males generally have more prestige than women, because they are male and because the roles they perform are valued more highly (see Bose, 1985). When men conform to their role by committing themselves more heavily to work than to family, they increase their prestige. Women who fulfill their role through femininity, marriage, motherhood, and working at low-level jobs, however, automatically place themselves in low-prestige positions.

The generally low prestige of women is powerfully reflected in everyday experience. Women office workers are often treated as servants who are incapable of making independent decisions. Many domestic tasks that women are regularly expected to perform involve chores—washing floors, changing soiled diapers, and cleaning bathrooms—that, as occupations, rank at the bottom of the prestige scale (Oakley, 1974). Women's work, therefore, is work that men avoid because it detracts from their prestige (Polatnick, 1973).

The preceding sections give a detailed look at cultural and structural factors that perpetuate gender inequality. Male and female are social positions, and just as we must learn to play the roles associated with statuses such as "teacher" or "lawyer," so, too, must we learn to play gender roles as our culture defines them.

SOCIALIZATION: LEARNING TO BE MALE AND FEMALE

Most socialization centers on roles we are currently trying to play, as when children learn to play a game or adults learn to perform in a job. Anticipatory socialization, however, involves preparation for roles we hope to perform later. Gender roles involve both types of socialization, for as we learn to be feminine or masculine, we also prepare ourselves for adult statuses that are defined as appropriate for us. In this process, we locate ourselves in relation to our families, and then in a continually widening scope of relations in the larger social world. The most important agents of socialization are the family, schools, the media, and occupations.

Gender Roles and the Family

Most studies show few gender differences in the behavior of infants, but many show that parents tend to treat infant girls and boys differently and to have different expectations of them. Parents generally give boys and girls different toys, and discourage aggressive behavior in girls, but not in boys. They also tend to give sons less help than they give to daughters. When parents are asked if they treat sons and daughters differently, however, they generally report no awareness of the differences observed by researchers (Fischer and Lazerson, 1984).

The expectations adults have of male and female children also tend to lead them to perceive the behavior of children differently. In one study, parents watched videotapes of infants at play, and when they were told the infant was a boy, men tended to describe "his" behavior in terms of independence, aggressiveness, activity level, and alertness. When the infant was identified as a girl, on the other hand, men described "her" behavior in terms of passivity, delicacy, and dependency. Although women made distinctions,

In almost all societies—from nonindustrial to high-tech laundromats—it is women who take care of the personal needs of other people, including washing dirty clothes.

men paid more attention to gender-appropriate behavior than women did (Meyer and Sobieszek, 1972).

Both social learning and developmental theory have been proposed as explanations of gender-role socialization in childhood. Social learning theorists argue that children learn gender roles through a combination of conditioning—reward and punishment—and imitation of adults of their own gender. Most studies, however, show that conditioning and imitation explain only part of the process. Both boys and girls imitate adults who display warmth, dominance, and power, regardless of the adult's gender (Bandura et al., 1963b); and most studies find no consistent evidence that children imitate adults of one gender more than the other (Maccoby and Jacklin, 1974).

Developmental theorists focus on the way children think about gender. In the first stage of development, children discover that there are two sexes and learn to identify people as male or female. At first they use physical characteristics such as hair length to distinguish males and females, but by age seven their idea of gender is more stable and they begin to identify which behaviors are appropriate for each. Most studies, however, reveal few gender differences in behavior among young children (Maccoby and Jacklin, 1974).

In the second stage, children develop a sense of value about their gender and begin to imitate people of their own gender as they strive for acceptance as males or females. In the third stage, children develop deep emotional bonds with their same-sex parent, bonds that generally assure gender-role socialization.

Developmental theory is more comprehensive than social learning theory, but does not explain how children select behaviors from the many that are defined as appropriate for their gender. In addition, both perspectives ignore the fact that the particular abilities children develop depend on the activities they are encouraged or allowed to perform. In families, sons and daughters tend to be assigned domestic tasks that conform to gender roles—cooking and cleaning for girls and lawn mowing for boys (White and Brinkerhoff, 1981). Less self-confidence among women reflects more than conformity to roles or imitation of models. It also rests on the fact that girls tend to be excluded from activities such as sports, through which children develop self-confidence.

In addition to being models of masculine and feminine behavior, adults offer children a preview of the statuses they can expect to occupy. Most research on occupational mobility uses only the father's occupation to predict mobility among sons and daughters. More recent research, however, shows that whether or not a mother works, as well as the kind of job she holds, affects career plans and mobility among both daughters and sons (Hoffman, 1977; Stephan and Corder, 1985). Working mothers provide role models of mothers who work outside the home; and fathers in such families can provide role models of men who work outside the home and share domestic responsibilities.

Schools and Gender Roles

Children begin school with a clear idea of their own gender, but know relatively little about adult gender roles. In schools, children learn about gender roles from what they are taught and from the structure of the school itself, which serves as a mirror of the adult world.

Textbooks reinforce gender roles. Most characters are male, as are almost all important people. Men are shown in a wider variety of jobs than women; in rare instances where working mothers are portrayed, they are in support roles as nurses, secretaries, and elementary school teachers. Girls are portrayed as passive—jumping rope and playing with dolls, or performing traditionally female chores such as cooking—while boys are portrayed as active—climbing mountains or saving girls who are in danger (St. Peter, 1979; Women on Words and Images, 1975a).

The structure of schools also reinforces gender roles. In elementary grades, when school work has little prestige in the outside world, most teachers are female. Their role is similar to a mother's, and much of the day is spent in play, nurturing, and discipline. Most principals, however, are male. In high school and college, work is more demanding and more prestigious, and most teachers are male. The structure of schools reinforces cultural expectations that women take care of others and men are authorities with serious roles in the world outside the home (Mickish, 1971).

There is evidence that teachers treat girls and boys differently as early as nursery school. One study found that teachers gave twice as much instruction to boys as they gave to girls. Boys got more attention on academic subjects and were encouraged to work independently. Girls were rewarded for being dependent and staying close to their teachers; and teachers were more likely to intervene in a girl's work and complete it for her (Serbin and O'Leary, 1975). In their study of more than a hundred fourth-, sixth-, and eighth-grade classes in the U.S., Sadker and Sadker (1985) found that boys received more attention, dominated classroom discussions, and were allowed to be more academically assertive (by calling out answers rather than waiting to be called upon).

In higher grades, girls are often discouraged from participating in serious athletic competition and advanced courses in math and science, whereas boys are encouraged to study science and math but are discouraged from developing their skills in less marketable areas such as language, home economics, and literature (Schaffer, 1981). As children strive for stable identities as males or females, schools play an important role—by presenting cultural images of men and women, by mirroring adult gender roles, and by selectively encouraging boys and girls to engage in activities that develop different skills.

Gender Roles and the Media

Television, radio, films, literature, and journalism provide us with streams of images in words, pictures, and sound. Such images do more than represent the world as it is; they also reflect ideas about how the world ought to be. On television shows most leading characters are male (McArthur, 1982; Women on Words and Images, 1975b). In his analysis of the uses of gender in advertising, Goffman (1976) identified ways in which men and women are presented that contribute to gender inequality (see also Courtney and Whipple, 1983, for a review of research findings). In most ads, there are clear patterns:

1. Women are taller than men only when they are their social inferiors.

2. Women's hands are rarely portrayed as holding anything firmly—only touching it lightly.

3. Women never instruct men; even among children, the boy is the one who instructs the girl.

4. Men are rarely shown lying down; it is usually a woman or child who is in this vulnerable pose.

5. The eyes of men focus only on important people; the eyes of women focus on men.

6. Women are often portrayed as "dreamlike" and physically close to a man, as if they did not need to be aware of their surroundings so long as there was a man present to look out for them.

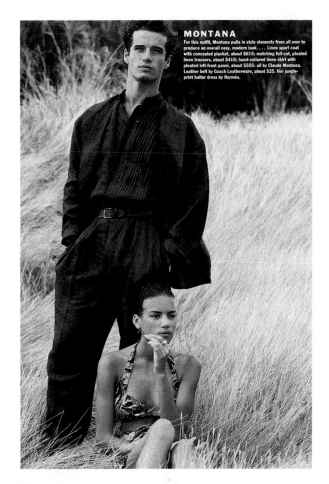

This advertisement is typical in portraying men in a physically dominant position over women. How would the impression change if their positions were reversed?

7. Women are more likely than men to be shown in a state of shock or surprise.

Particularly in commercial advertising, images of women and men do more than sell products. As Gornick (1979) wrote, they also

serve the social purpose of convincing us that this is how men and women are, or want to be, or should be, not only in relation to themselves, but in relation to each other. . . . That orientation accomplishes the task a society has of maintaining . . . order, an undisturbed on-goingness, *regardless of the actual experience of the participants* [italics mine]. (p. vii)

The media often seem to be an independent force in society, but it is important to remember that the images they present are designed to fit the expectations of their audience (when did you last see an ad for laundry detergent in which a man was trying to remove a stubborn stain?). As such, the media often function as mirrors in which we look for familiar reflections, both of ourselves and the world we live in.

Gender and Adult Socialization

Learning gender roles involves more than masculinity and femininity, for the place of men and women in society depends on their entire status sets. For this reason, socialization extends throughout our lives as we learn to perform roles associated with adult statuses considered appropriate for our gender.

It is often not until after women marry that they learn how their new status limits their rights in relation to husbands, and for many women, childbearing confronts them with the fact that they no longer control their own bodies. As Rich (1976, p. 28) wrote, "The new life of my third child was a kind of turning point for me. I had learned that my body was not under my control; I had not intended to bear a third child."

At work, men learn that most women are there to serve them, and that their success as men is measured by the size of their paycheck and their ability to compete (Gould, 1973; Silverstein, 1972). Women learn that they are expected to occupy subordinate, inferior positions (Epstein, 1970). Even in the professions, they are excluded from informal interactions through which vital professional knowledge is passed. They are less likely to be made assistants to those in powerful positions, and are thus more likely to find their upward mobility blocked (Speizer, 1981).

When their children reach adulthood, most mothers must adjust to the fact that their major activity in life is now a low-level job that offers few rewards. Although men escape this, they face their own crisis when retirement forces them to surrender their most important status and live at a diminished standard of living (Bock, 1972). Among the elderly, women must learn to live as widows (Lopata, 1979): among people 65 years old and older who lived alone in 1985, there were more than four times as many women as there were men (U.S. Census Bureau, 1986a). This is due in part to the fact that women generally live longer than men do. It is also due, however, to the tendency of men to marry women who are younger than they, giving elderly women relatively few potential husbands who are their age or older.

Socialization is a lifelong process through which we learn to participate in a society that treats men as a privileged class and women as a minority. All of this, however, begs the most important question of all: Why are women a minority in the first place?

EXPLAINING INEQUALITY

Both the functional and conflict perspectives contribute important pieces to the puzzle of stratification based on gender.

The Functional View: Are Gender Roles Necessary?

The functional perspective raises a basic question: In what ways are gender inequality and the division of labor between men and women functional, and in what ways are they dysfunctional?

Ecological conditions in early societies encouraged women to take primary responsibility for child care and allowed men to monopolize hunting and warfare. These gender divisions of labor were clearly functional for the survival of populations; but even here, women were not a minority.

Ecological conditions in modern countries, however, are quite different. Bottled formulas free women from having to remain close to children in order to feed them; contraceptives allow women to limit childbearing to relatively small periods of their lives; women live much longer now and have many years to live after their children have grown; and people no longer range far from home in search of food (Rossi, 1984). What functional consequences, then, do inequality and the gender division of labor have now?

Parsons and Bales (1953) argued that because people now live and work in different places, the most efficient division of labor is one in which parents split paid and domestic work. If we accept the belief that women are better suited for child care than men are, then the gender division of labor is functional for reproduction and socialization and making sure that economic, political, and other public roles are performed properly.

We certainly *believe* that "child care" and "mother" are two terms that mean the same thing. Most interpret the verb "to mother" as meaning "to care for," but attach very different meaning to the verb "to father" (to impregnate a woman). Although our association between women and child care is strong, there is considerable evidence that it is based more in myth than fact. As Albert (1971, p. 29) put it, "Having babies is one thing, raising them another."

In his famous experiments, Harlow (1958; see also Harlow and Harlow, 1969) raised monkeys with nonliving "mother substitutes" (wire cages shaped like adults) and found that providing food is not the most important part of "mothering"; rather, warmth, cuddling, and physical comfort make the most difference in the healthy development of infant monkeys. "The American male," he concluded, "is physically endowed with all the really essential equipment to compete with the American female on equal terms in . . . the rearing of infants" (Harlow, 1958, p. 685).

People, of course, are not monkeys, but Harlow's evidence challenges the notion that only women can give infants what they need. To this we must add the fact that some women dislike children and show little inclination to take care of them, and many men care for children very well. An experiment in Washington, DC (Herzig and Mali, 1980), found that ten-year-old boys welcomed the opportunity to take care of babies

There is every reason to believe that men have the potential to provide infants with the physical and emotional comfort, contact, and care that are necessary for healthy development. What is less clear is what it will take for men to feel responsible for such care.

and eagerly learned how to take care of them (their first response on entering the nursery was characterized by the title of Herzig and Mali's book—*Oh, Boy! Babies!*). In their exhaustive review of the research literature, Maccoby and Jacklin (1974) concluded that whether or not people are "positively nurturant or indifferent" toward children "depends in large measure on how much contact they have with children and how much responsibility they have for child care" (p. 372).

Even if we believe that females are better suited than males for child care, a functional analysis shows that discrimination against women is unjustified. A large number of women never marry or have children. In 1985, of all U.S. women over the age of 44 (beyond childbearing age), almost 2 million—or 12 percent—had either never married or were childless (computed from U.S. Census Bureau, 1986a,g); and an estimated 29 percent of white women born after 1950 may not have children (Bloom, 1982). Even women who do marry and have children have, on the average, around two children, and children begin to spend their days in school by the age of six.

Davis and Moore (1945) argued that social inequality is functional for ensuring that the most qualified people perform the most important roles, but evidence strongly suggests that discrimination against women does not serve this end. As Table 13-3 (p. 364) shows, women college graduates have lower average incomes than men who never finished high school. Discrimination against women appears to have little to do with ensuring that the most capable, highly trained people perform the most important roles (Treiman and Roos, 1983).

A functional analysis also reveals ways in which the exclusion of women from important nonfamily statuses is *dys*functional, for it excludes more than half of our population from contributing their talents and abilities to important roles in business, government, education, and other vital institutions. There is also evidence that gender roles are dysfunctional for women's mental health (see Franks and Rothblum, 1983). For every category of mental illness, married women have higher rates than single women, whereas married men have lower rates than single men (Gove and Tudor, 1973). Weiss (1981) found that female graduate students who were divorced or separated were more productive and self-confident than those who were married, but that the effect was just the opposite among men.

Table 13-3

Median Income by Years of Education and Gender for Year-Round, Full-Time Workers (United States, 1985)

YEARS OF SCHOOL COMPLETED	MEDIAN INCOME		FOR EACH DOLLAR MEN EARN, WOMEN EARN:
	WOMEN	MEN	
Elementary			
0 to 7 Years	$ 9,700	$14,800	66¢
8 Years	$11,400	$18,600	61¢
High School			
1 to 3 Years	$11,800	$18,900	62¢
4 Years	$15,500	$23,900	65¢
College			
1 to 3 Years	$18,000	$27,000	67¢
4 Years	$21,400	$32,800	65¢
5 Years or More	$25,900	$39,300	66¢

Source: U.S. Census Bureau, 1987a.

Bernard (1972) argued that the role of "housewife" is so boring and frustrating, and brings so few rewards or support, that it contributes to disillusionment and depression among women; and depression is the most prevalent mental illness among middle-aged women (Bart, 1971). Kessler and McRae (1981), however, reported that in the last decade the great influx of women into the U.S. labor force has narrowed the gender difference in symptoms of psychological distress.

The pressures men experience appear to be dysfunctional for their health, as well. Their heavy investment in work makes them particularly prone to depression when they lose their jobs or retire (Schaffer, 1981), and weak family ties often leave them without emotional support during personal crises. The strains of the male role may be reflected in suicide rates, for men are almost three times more likely than women to kill themselves, and among older men— who face retirement and the end of their work lives— suicide rates are four to ten times higher than for women of the same age (see Table 13-4). The masculine ideal of "toughness" may also be dysfunctional for men's health, for men are four times more likely than women to be murdered (U.S. Census Bureau, 1983c). Men are also more likely than women to be

treated for psychotic disorders involving drug and alcohol abuse and violence toward others (Dohrenwend and Dohrenwend, 1976).

A functional analysis makes it clear that a division of labor based on the demands of child care, and

Table 13-4

Suicide Rates by Age, Race, and Gender (United States, 1983)

Age	WHITES		BLACKS	
	Males	Females	Males	Females
15–24	21	5	12	3
25–34	26	7	19	3
35–44	23	8	14	4
45–54	26	10	12	3
55–64	27	9	12	2
65–74	33	8	14	1
75–84	52	7	16	1
85 and older	57	5	13	2

Source: National Center for Health Statistics, 1987.

the inequalities between men and women that result, are not socially necessary. Many women never become wives or mothers, and those who do spend a small portion of their lives with small children; and men, with proper socialization, can perform most child-care tasks. The gender-based division of labor and its resulting inequalities also appear to be dysfunctional for both society and the health of men and women. How, then, do we explain the persistent and pervasive position of women as a minority? One approach to this question is to rephrase it from a conflict perspective: Whose interests does gender inequality serve?

The Conflict Perspective: Perpetuating Patriarchy

The conflict perspective focuses on the struggle over the distribution of wealth, power, and prestige. From this perspective the gender division of labor benefits males at the expense of females. Child care is the key to women's inferior position, for so long as women are responsible for child rearing and men are not, women will be unable to securely establish themselves outside the family, and it is such work that primarily determines shares of wealth, power, and prestige (see Bergmann, 1986). Why do women accept child-care responsibility and why do men avoid it?

Polatnick (1973) and others argue that women accept child-rearing responsibilities because existing societies are dominated by men and offer women few socially supported alternatives. Most men, on the other hand, avoid child-rearing responsibilities because their gender role does not require them to take care of children, and because taking care of children does nothing to improve or maintain their dominant position in society.

Women's labor has been exploited for well over a century in the United States, from providing cheap labor in nineteenth-century factories to performing vital industrial jobs during World War I and World War II, only to be replaced by returning veterans at war's end.

Although women have long been treated as a minority, Marxian analysis argues that industrialization—and capitalism in particular—sharply lowered the social standing of women. Engels (1891) argued that when the family became the "private sphere" in industrializing nations, women were denied full and equal participation in production, and their resulting dependency on men rendered them little more than domestic slaves.

Capitalists have been quick to exploit women, using them as cheap labor and quickly dispensing with them when they are no longer needed (Smith, 1981). Married women contribute domestic labor each year that, by market standards, amounts to billions of dollars; and yet, they do so in return for only a share of their husbands' earnings over which they have only partial control. Domestic labor, however, includes socializing future workers, and thus the domestic exploitation of women also serves the interests of capitalism (Sacks, 1974).

Gender, like ethnicity and race, is also part of a larger system of classes that share unequally in the control over the means of production and the distribution of rewards. The treatment of women as a minority does not result simply from a "war between men and women," but is also tied to larger structures that maintain general inequality in societies. It is here that the functional and conflict perspectives come together.

Unlike other minorities, the subordinate position of women results from more than their relationship to the means of production, for in a patriarchy, *that* relationship is directly tied to women's roles in reproduction and child care (Mitchell, 1966). *Within* each social class, women have unequal standing, just as do the members of other minorities. From this perspective it is easier to understand why lower-class men are more likely to oppose equality for women, for gender divides the working class in the same way that race and ethnicity do. Working-class men are already at the bottom of the stratification system and are likely to experience women's equality as a threat to their already deprived conditions (explaining, in part, why some labor unions exclude women). Black women in particular find themselves doubly discriminated against because they occupy two minority statuses that they cannot change.

Just as the most highly placed black is, in some ways, culturally defined as inferior to lower-class whites, so, too, is the most wealthy woman culturally defined as inferior in some ways to lower-class men.

The parts of our culture that degrade women and define masculinity and femininity apply to males and females of all social classes.

Both the functional and conflict perspectives make it clear that gender inequality is deeply rooted in cultural, structural, and ecological characteristics of societies. How, then, do we move from a patriarchal society to one in which females and males have equal standing?

GENDER ROLES AND SOCIAL CHANGE

To understand how gender roles and inequality might change, we need to appreciate how we got to where we are now. Most families in frontier America lived in isolated farm communities. Families were large, and women were valued primarily as domestic laborers. Children were valued as economic assets, for the cost of raising them was relatively low and they began to share the load of farm work at an early age (Riley and Waring, 1976).

Urbanization and the Industrial Revolution caused major shifts in the social positions of men and women (Harris, 1979). Children became less valuable as producers—and, therefore, more costly to raise—and the only way that women could participate in paid labor was to limit child-care responsibilities by limiting their fertility. From 1800 on, the average number of children born by each woman in the U.S. and Europe steadily declined.

As nineteenth-century women became increasingly aware that wealth, power, and prestige were distributed according to statuses outside the family, dissatisfaction over their confinement to family roles formed the basis for the early stages of the women's movement, which sought, among other goals, the right to vote, own property, and enter into contracts, as well as equal access to higher education and the professions. The first Equal Rights Amendment was proposed in the 1920s but received little support.

Women made slow progress in education and employment until World War II created a massive demand for industrial workers. At the war's end, however, women workers were displaced by returning veterans (Milkman, 1987), and as the postwar economy boomed, women retreated to traditional domestic labor in the newly emerging suburbs (J. Freeman,

1975), and the long downward trend in fertility reversed itself in the "Baby Boom" that followed.

After 1950 women's participation in the labor force increased dramatically (Bergmann, 1986), in part because as the economy expanded, so, too, did the demand for low-level service workers such as secretaries and waitresses. In the 1960s the Baby Boom ended and the costs of raising children increased as more and more young people attended college. As women devoted less time to child care, they once again looked outside the family for roles that would redefine their social identity and increase their share of social rewards. In 1963 Betty Friedan published *The Feminine Mystique* in which she urged women to reevaluate their traditional roles and demand the opportunity to fully develop their abilities; and in 1966 Friedan and others formed the National Organization for Women and rejuvenated the women's movement.

Pressures for social change, therefore, did not occur simply because people began to change their ideas about men and women. Rather, changes in economic production coupled with a decline in the birth rate provided new opportunities for women. As they took advantage of them by dramatically increasing their participation in the labor force, their social position as a minority became increasingly obvious as they were systematically excluded from all but the most low-level occupations.

Changes in population and the economy created ideal social conditions for a new and pervasive "consciousness-raising" among women, and many began a concentrated attack on the inferiority of their social statuses *and* on the cultural ideas that underlie them.

New Ideologies and Cultural Change

Just as cultural ideas about gender have been used as an ideology supporting patriarchy, the women's movement is based on **feminism**—an ideology that directly opposes sexism by supporting gender equality and portraying women and men as equals (see Tavris and Wade, 1984).

The women's movement is too diverse to be guided by a single ideology, and, in fact, there are at least three approaches (see Ferree and Hess, 1985; Kahn-Hut et al., 1982). **Liberal feminism** defines gender inequality as the result of arbitrary arrangements such as child care, and argue that women and men can have the same opportunities for work and child care to the benefit of both. Their focus is primarily on achieving equal rights and economic opportunities for women without challenging the basic masculine values on which our society is based and by which rewards are distributed.

Marxist feminism argues that the causes and cures of gender inequality run much deeper, that women cannot achieve equality without challenging the capitalist system that profits from their exploitation (see Chapter 18). The economic system has made the subjugation of women an integral part of its functioning, and the fact that equality may enrich the lives of both men and women is not enough to bring it about.

Radical feminism goes even further than Marxists by arguing that in a patriarchal society, women and men have fundamentally different interests, and equality will require sacrifices of power, wealth, and prestige that men will be unwilling to make (see MacKinnon, 1987). Even if the exploitative arrangements of capitalism were overthrown, men would still benefit from the oppression of women, just as they do in most socialist societies, although to a somewhat lesser degree.

Culturally, the women's movement has focused on masculinity and femininity by publicly challenging the definition of females as inferior, and by promoting **androgyny**, a concept that combines masculinity and femininity.

Androgynous people are neither masculine nor feminine. Rather, they choose their behaviors without regard to gender. Androgynous men would not avoid child care simply because they feared others might consider them "feminine." In the same way, androgynous women base their decisions about bearing and caring for children on their personal preferences, not to protect an image as "feminine" women.

Lott (1981) criticized the concept of androgyny on the grounds that it depends on and therefore supports the practice of thinking of people in terms of the masculine and feminine stereotypes. Masculinity and femininity, she argues, are artificial concepts that arbitrarily divide the wide range of human traits into sets associated with each gender. To talk of combining these two sets of traits still treats them as if they are real. A different approach would be to end *all* references to gender when discussing behavior and personality, a position that argues against the use of androgyny as much as it does against the concepts of masculinity and femininity.

The women's movement also focuses on norms that perpetuate their oppression. Working through legislatures and courts, women have struck down many discriminatory laws (such as those excluding women from military service academies) and have lobbied successfully for new laws that equalize opportunity (such as those forbidding discrimination against women in pay, hiring, and promotion).

The more subtle norms found in folkways are also the target of the women's movement. Women's insistence that they pay their own way on social occasions, that they be referred to as "Ms.," that men stop rushing to open doors for them, that women be re-spected when they say "no" in sexual situations, or that they no longer be expected to clean up after men—all reflect a growing awareness that an end to patriarchy depends on more than what happens in courts, legislatures, and boardrooms of large corporations. It also depends on what happens in the interactions of everyday life—on the street, in offices, classrooms, kitchens, and bedrooms.

We often feel surrounded by rapid social change, and there are many who believe that most aspects of sexism have been eliminated in our society. As Figure

Figure 13-2   Change in Beliefs and Values about Gender in the U.S., 1977 and 1986

Percent Who

0% 10% 20% 30% 40% 50% 60% 70% 80% 90% 100%

1. *Disagree* that women should take care of running their homes and leave running the country to men.

2. *Approve* of a married woman earning money if she has a husband capable of supporting her.

3. *Would* vote for a qualified woman nominated for president.

4. *Disagree* that most men are better suited emotionally for politics than are most women.

5. *Disagree* that a preschool child is likely to suffer if his or her mother works.

6. *Agree* that a working mother can establish just as warm and secure a relationship with her children as a mother who does not work.

7. *Disagree* that it is much better for everyone involved if the man is the achiever outside the home and the woman takes care of the home and family.

8. *Disagree* that it is more important for a wife to help her husband's career than to have one herself.

1977 ☐
1986 ☐

Source: Davis and Smith, 1982, 1987.

13-2 shows, it is certainly true that there have been significant changes in values and beliefs about gender. In the nearly ten years between 1977 and 1986, increasing percentages of adults support the political and economic rights of women in general and wives and mothers in particular. It is also true that the Equal Rights Amendment was defeated in 1982. Even now fewer than half of all adults disagree with the erroneous belief that preschool children suffer when their mothers work, and less than a majority disagree with the traditional idea that women should stay home and care for the family (5 and 7 in Figure 13-2).

Perhaps most serious is the enduring appeal of the masculine ideal. As Roszak and Roszak (1969, p. viii) wrote, "the world belongs to what . . . masculinity has become"—we value rationality more highly than intuition, control of emotions more highly than their open and free expression, toughness more than vulnerability, the conquest of nature more than respect for it, independence more than dependence, being perceived as right more than admitting we are wrong. For many, then, the liberation of women merely allows them to participate in a male-dominated society according to the cultural ideas associated with masculinity. In this sense, the liberation of women implies the *negation* of women and the cultural ideas associated with them.

On a deeper level, some segments of the women's movement seek to change our culture from one based on masculinity to one based on the full range of human potential. This is a radical goal that would affect not only the positions of men and women, but our basic cultural assumptions about how people in general ought to think, feel, and behave.

Social Change and Social Structure

A second major focus of the women's movement is on the confinement of women to statuses that offer relatively low levels of wealth, power, and prestige. This includes access to higher education and occupations previously monopolized by men; but on a deeper level it extends to the family, for a division of labor that leaves child care to women lies at the heart of their minority status.

It is true that women "have come a long way" since the earliest women's movement. They are more likely now to be in the labor force than at any time since the Industrial Revolution, and they occupy many positions previously reserved for men. They work in

coal mines and in police and fire departments; they drive trucks, work on construction crews, manage businesses, and teach in universities. In art, music, and literature, there has been a virtual explosion in new works created by women. In 1981 the first woman was appointed to the Supreme Court, and women are found in increasing numbers among lawyers, judges, and physicians. In 1983 the first American woman astronaut was included in the crew of a space shuttle. Between 1977 and 1987 female representation in the U.S. armed forces doubled from five to ten percent (*New York Times*, March 13, 1988, p. E5). In 1984 the top-ranked graduate of the United States Naval Academy was a woman, and Geraldine Ferraro became the first woman nominated by a major political party as a candidate for vice-president of the United States. In 1987, major civic organizations such as the Lions and Kiwanis Clubs voted to admit women for the first time. The Rotary Club was ordered to do so by the Supreme Court. In 1988, the Boy Scouts allowed women to serve as scout masters for the first time.

In families, there is evidence that some men are making greater commitments to child care, most notably in seeking custody of their children during divorce proceedings (Greif, 1985). During the last few years, there has been a dramatic increase in research examining the importance of fathers for child development (Cath, Gurwitt, and Ross, 1982; Furstenberg et al., 1987) and the ways in which married couples can adjust to the demands of work and family. There is also evidence that wives who seek careers are increasingly likely to have the support of their husbands (Huber and Spitze, 1981; Wallston et al., 1978), although most research shows that working women are still held primarily responsible for domestic work even when they work full time (Michelson, 1985; Pleck, 1985).

Such gains sound impressive—especially when highly publicized—but the vast majority of women are still heavily concentrated in low-level, poorly paid occupations (see One Step Further 13-1, p. 371). Relative to men, working women were less well off financially in 1985 than they were in 1955, in spite of the fact that women have outnumbered men among college students since 1979 (U.S. Census Bureau, 1986a). Men still rarely involve themselves in the care of infants (Entwistle and Doering, 1981; Lamb and Goldberg, 1982), and the high divorce rate means that the overall child-care burden still falls overwhelmingly on women (Rossi, 1984).

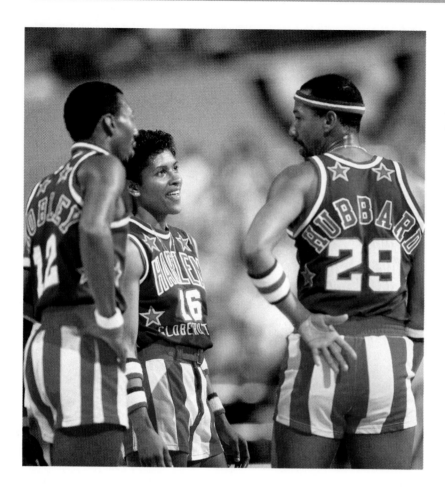

Women have managed to break into many occupations once reserved exclusively for men. In 1985, Lynette Woodward made sports history by becoming the first woman to play for the Harlem Globetrotters.

Why Is Change So Difficult and Slow?

It will be difficult for women to free themselves of their minority standing because their position in the public world is strongly tied to their roles in the family; they are a minority in all classes, including within other minorities; and gender is one of the most important bases for the identities of both men and women.

Social Structure   Even if women were not discriminated against, so long as men avoid the responsibilities of child care they will have a huge advantage in the marketplace. Coverman (1983) found that among married, white, employed men and women, the more time people spend on domestic tasks, the lower their income tends to be, especially if they are working-class men or middle- to upper-class women. Coltrane (1988) studied 90 societies and found that the less involved fathers are in child care, the less likely women are to be involved in community politics and to occupy positions of authority. This leads many feminists to look upon the right to choose abortion as critical for women's liberation, for without it they cannot control their commitment to child care (Luker, 1984). Even in socialist countries that proclaim equality for women as a major goal, gender equality does not include bringing large numbers of men into child care (Huber and Spitze, 1983).

Industrial societies are structured in ways that make it convenient to hold women responsible for child care—"If women are allowed to have careers, who will take care of children?" It is vital to remember, however, that such a question is relevant only in societies that isolate the family from other social institutions by separating production from reproduction; and if the family is isolated, women are isolated with it (Sacks, 1974).

Most societies are controlled by men, and it serves men's interests if society is structured so that it

ONE STEP FURTHER 13-1:
Who Supports the Women's Movement?

As we saw in Chapter 11, those who stand to benefit most from an ideology tend to be among its strongest supporters. Thus far, progress for women has occurred primarily among those with relatively high education and class background—especially those who aspire to careers in business and the professions. Are these social categories also the most likely to take feminist positions on issues related to women's equality?

As a partial answer, Table B-13-1 shows responses to the traditional idea that a woman's place is in the home. If you look down each column, you can see that, for both women and men, higher income, education, or occupational prestige goes along with greater opposition to the idea that a woman's place is in the home (a pattern that holds for several other similar questions as well). Notice also that the answers of blacks and whites are almost identical, and that with few exceptions, so are the responses of men and women.

How would you explain the similarity of women's and men's responses? Of blacks and whites? What are the implications of the other patterns for the women's movement?

Table B-13-1

It is much better for everyone involved if the man is the achiever outside the home and the woman takes care of home and family.

SOCIAL CHARACTERISTICS	PERCENT WHO DISAGREE AMONG		
	Women	Men	All
Education			
Less than high school graduate	30	35	32
High school graduate	54	47	52
Some college	66	63	65
College graduate	74	58	66
Some graduate training	76	77	77
Income			
Less than $4,000	40	49	42
$4,000–$13,999	43	45	44
$14,000–$34,999	60	50	55
$35,000 or more	62	60	61
Occupational Prestige			
Very Low	47	30	40
Low	52	46	50
Middle	59	57	58
Upper	58	60	59
Race			
Black	52	49	52
White	53	53	52

Source: Computed from raw 1986 General Social Survey data.

is difficult for women to gain equal standing. It is true that the liberation of women would destabilize society to some degree, requiring massive change in social institutions such as the family, government, and the economy. The other side of this, however, is that in order to perpetuate patriarchy, domestic labor must continue to be defined as nonwork; and, therefore, females must continue to be treated as a minority.

Faced with the choice between child care and careers, women are increasingly choosing to remain single, at least during their twenties (see Goldscheider and Waite, 1986). Between 1970 and 1985 the number of unmarried couples in the U.S. almost quadrupled, and the number of young adults living alone more than doubled. Between 1960 and 1986 the percentage of women who had never married rose from 28 to 58 percent among women from 20 to 24 years old, and from 10 to 28 percent among women from 25 to 29 years old (U.S. Census Bureau, 1986a, 1986f) (see Figure 13-3).

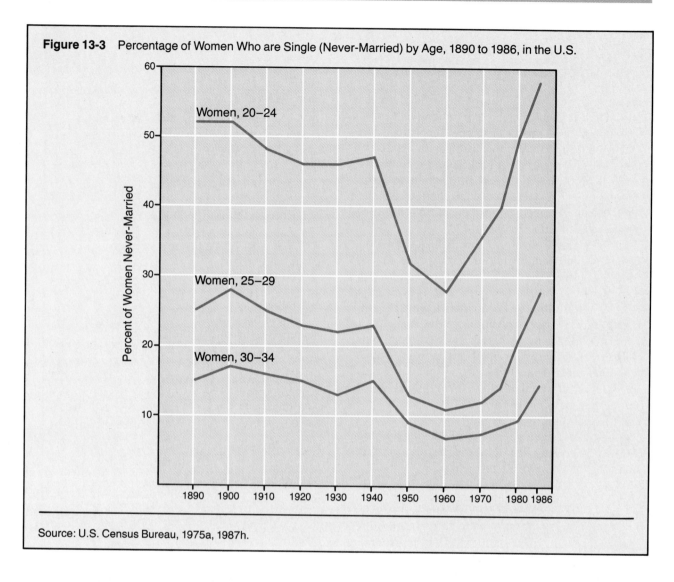

Figure 13-3   Percentage of Women Who are Single (Never-Married) by Age, 1890 to 1986, in the U.S.

Source: U.S. Census Bureau, 1975a, 1987h.

Changing the division of labor in families may be the last and most difficult goal of the women's movement, for as long as rewards are distributed according to performance in the public world rather than in the family, most men will resist substantial commitments to domestic labor (Coverman, 1983; Polatnick, 1973).

There is also recent evidence that married men do not like their wives to work full time, especially when wives earn more than their husbands, as they do in one out of five two-earner marriages (U.S. Census Bureau, 1986e). In a national study of white married couples, Kessler and McRae (1982) found that although employment lowered the incidence of depression, poor self-esteem, and psychological distress symptoms (such as insomnia) among wives, it increased such problems among husbands. Nothing indicated that the increased problems of husbands resulted from demands such as a greater contribution to domestic work. The problem, concluded the authors, seemed to be largely a matter of men having a difficult time accepting new definitions of the roles of husbands and wives (see also Michelson, 1985).

Women as a Unique Minority   The fact that the formation of families requires women to join with members of the social category that dominates them means that they are at the bottom of whatever other minority they belong to. This means that men will dominate social movements that promote an end to inequality based on social class, race, and ethnicity. Historically, women have made enormous contributions to movements for social justice (including the movement to abolish slavery in the early nineteenth century and the labor union movement in the late nineteenth and early twentieth centuries); but their own cause has been, for the most part, ignored (Kessler-Harris, 1982; Stimpson, 1971).

This is due, in part, to the fact that women's liberation threatens the social standing of all men regardless of their minority status. During the 1960s the United States experienced violent social movements protesting injustice against blacks and the poor; and yet women were often treated as a minority *within* these movements. In extreme cases, some leaders looked upon women as no more than envelope stuffers, bed partners, and domestic workers (Morgan, 1970).

Identity and the Power of Social Mythology

Janeway (1971) observed that many cultural ideas about men and women are myths—beliefs rooted more in emotion than in factual evidence. Such mythology is "illogical—or, at least, pre-logical" and rarely describes real men or women accurately; but *this has nothing to do with its importance to us*, for "from this very fact, it gains a certain strength: logic may disprove it, but it will not kill it" (p. 27).

Myths are important because regardless of their accuracy, they are beliefs that give us a feeling that the world makes sense and always will. We also value them because as social beings, we locate ourselves within them and depend on them for a stable sense of who we are. From this point of view, it is easier to understand why many women resist their own liberation, for they can free themselves only by shattering myths that define important parts of their social identities. It is often easier to hang on to social arrangements that are familiar and yet oppressive than it is to give them up in favor of new ones that are both alien and only potentially better.

As Langer (1962, p. 147) wrote, "We live in a web of ideas, a fabric of our own making." However necessary it may be to tear the web that holds us tightly in a world of meaning and social relationships, once we do, we experience the chaos of not knowing who we are, until we create a new social environment in which to live.

SUMMARY

1. Women are a minority in most societies in spite of the fact that they are a numerical majority. Sex refers to the physical characteristics that distinguish males and females; gender refers to social distinctions between them.

2. There is little scientific evidence that biological factors cause more than a very few gender differences in behavior or ability.

3. As part of culture, language reinforces gender inequality by always connecting the status of women with men, by associating male and female pronouns with social statuses, by portraying men and women in different terms, and by degrading the words used to describe women.

4. Masculinity and femininity are sets of beliefs about men and women that make up gender roles.

5. Cultural values both rank maleness above femaleness and evaluate men and women according to different criteria.

6. Historically, cultural attitudes have long reflected hostility toward females.

7. Both laws and folkways are used to reinforce the subordinate position of females.

8. Gender roles define expectations for people according to sex. Gender roles cause considerable status and role strain for both men and women and result in many different patterns of interaction that reflect the subordinate status of females.

9. In most societies, adult standing depends on productive labor, and as production has become separated from the home, the standing of women has steadily declined.

10. In families, women still perform the majority of domestic work. Outside the home, women are concentrated in the poorest paying, least prestigious jobs with the lowest chance of advancement.

11. The concept of patriarchy refers to dominance by men, and the concept of matriarchy refers to formal dominance by women. There is some debate over whether there has ever been a matriarchal society.

12. Gender role socialization takes place primarily through the family, schools, and the media. It depends on portrayals of what males and females are supposed to be like and on how we are treated depending on our gender. Socialization continues throughout adulthood as we occupy marital, parental, and occupational statuses.

13. Functional analysis shows that gender inequality has few functional consequences in an industrial society and that it has many dysfunctional consequences.

14. Conflict analysis shows that women are a minority in all classes and that the gender division of labor serves the interests of men as a group and rests primarily on the ability of men to avoid domestic work.

15. Pressures for change have grown in recent decades as women have entered the labor force in greater numbers and birth rates have declined.

16. The passage of the Equal Rights Amendment and the elimination of sexism are major cultural goals of the women's movement. Major structural goals include access to better occupations and a full sharing of domestic responsibilities with men.

17. Change toward gender equality is slow because women are a unique minority, because many ideas about gender are deeply rooted in cultural mythology, and because gender inequality is rooted in the structure of important institutions such as the family and the economy.

KEY TERMS

androgyny   367
femininity   345
feminism   367
   liberal   367
   marxist   367
   radical   367
gender   341
gender role   348
masculinity   345
matriarchy   357
misanthropy   344
misogyny   344
patriarchy   357
sexism   348
sociobiology   342

Looking Elsewhere

Having studied Chapter 13, you might want to look at related discussions in *Human Arrangements*, which include gender and

- suicide (Chapter 1, pp. 10, 12–13)
- income inequality (Chapter 2, pp. 44–47)
- poverty among the elderly (Chapter 14, pp. 388–89)
- role strain (Chapter 4, pp. 83–84)
- power on juries (Chapter 8, pp. 195, 196)
- preference for male children (Chapter 5, p. 105)
- choosing role models (Chapter 6, p. 137)
- social identity (Chapter 6, pp. 140, 144–45, 146)
- rites of passage to adulthood (Chapter 6, p. 150; Chapter 14, pp. 382–84)
- attributions of success and failure (Chapter 7, p. 166)
- sexual violence as social interaction (Chapter 7, pp. 168–69)
- group boundaries that exclude women (Chapter 8, p. 191)
- crime (Chapter 10, pp. 255, 258)
- kinship systems (Chapter 15, pp. 405–406)
- sexual values (Chapter 15, pp. 407–408)
- marriage rules (Chapter 15, pp. 409–10)
- family divisions of labor (Chapter 15, p. 412)
- distributions of power in families (Chapter 15, p. 414)
- family violence (Chapter 15, pp. 423–25)
- the defeat of the ERA (Chapter 19, pp. 533–34)
- religion (Chapter 20, p. 550)
- abortion (Chapter 22, pp. 599–600)
- problems with functional explanations of gender inequality (Chapter 22, pp. 600–601)

RECOMMENDED READINGS

BERK, S. F. (1985). *The gender factory: The apportionment of work in American households*. New York: Plenum. A recent study of the gender division of labor in families and the ways in which this affects both family life and gender stratification.

COOK, A. G., LORWIN, V. R., and DANIELS, A. K. (1984). *Women and trade unions in eleven industrial countries*. Philadelphia: Temple University Press. A collection of articles that compare the status of women in unions and segmented labor markets in Denmark, West Germany, Finland, France, Great Britain, Ireland, Italy, Japan, Norway, the United States, and Sweden.

EPSTEIN, C. F. (1983). *Women in law*. New York: Anchor Press/Doubleday. An insightful study of what women encounter as they try to enter, survive, and succeed in the male-dominated legal profession.

ETIENNE, M., and LEACOCK, E. (Eds.). (1980). *Women and colonization: Anthropological perspectives*. New York: Praeger. A collection of articles on non-Western societies that focus on the sources of gender inequality.

HAYES, C. D., and KAMERMAN, S. B. (1983). *Children of working parents: Experiences and outcomes*. Washington, DC: National Academy Press. A thorough examination of the ways in which the participation of both parents in the labor force affects the education and everyday experience of children. A major finding is the absence of any direct negative effect of mothers' working on child development.

PETRAS, J. W. (1975). *Sex:Male/Gender:Masculine*. Port Washington, NY: Alfred. A stimulating collection of articles about men.

ROLLINS, J. (1985). *Between women: Domestics and their employers*. Philadelphia: Temple University Press. An important book that, by focusing on black female domestics and their white female employers, explores the complex relationship between gender, race, and social class.

SAYWELL, S. (1985). *Women in war*. New York: Viking. Fascinating portraits of twenty-five women that illustrate the many roles played by women in combat, from World War II to El Salvador.

14 Age Stratification

How old are you? Are you a child, adolescent, adult, middle-aged, elderly? If your answer is "adult," how would you feel if people thought of you as an adolescent or a child? Or, if your answer is "adolescent," how would you feel if people thought of you as an adult?

As your feelings about these questions may tell you, the importance of age goes far beyond the passage of time, and the physical process of development, gradual deterioration, and death. Age and aging are socially important because cultures divide the human life span into **age groups** and apply different beliefs, values, attitudes, and norms to each. Age is a social status that affects our relationships with people who are younger, older, or the same age as we are; and aging is a continuous transition from one status to another.

We begin by comparing biological and sociological approaches to age and aging, and then see how age inequality is reflected in cultural, structural, and ecological arrangements. We then use the functional, conflict, and ecological perspectives to help explain the existence of age stratification; and we close by considering the possibility of change towards equality among age groups.

SOME DIFFERENT VIEWS OF AGE AND AGING

As a status, age is unique in three ways. First, age is always a temporary, transitional status, for we inevitably move from one age status toward another. Second, unlike other statuses (except, perhaps, gender), age provides a cultural "map" of our entire lives. All cultures include ideas that describe the **life course**—the "normal" set of passages from one age to another (Eisenstadt, 1956; Hogan, 1980). Our "map" tells us where we are expected to be and what we are expected to be doing: in school as children, at work in our early twenties, married and raising families by our thirties,

Drawing by Chas. Addams © 1983, The New Yorker Magazine, Inc.

and at our peak of wealth, prestige, and power by our fifties. When we are defined as elderly, we are expected to stop working, lose interest in sex, and become less active, less intelligent, and more rigid and conservative in our thinking.

As individuals we can deviate from cultural expectations tied to stages in the life course; but like all deviants, we risk being treated as outsiders and losing our sense of who and where we are. Age is more than a set of statuses whose roles influence our thoughts, feelings, and behavior in a given time and place, for it also defines our futures. It describes where we are going as much as where we are and where we have been.

Third, more than any other social characteristic, age affects which statuses we achieve. It determines

Does this reflect the continuing effort of young males to prove their manhood in the absence of clear rites of passage? Do high rates of sexual behavior and pregnancy among adolescent girls reflect a desire to be regarded and treated as adults, even though such behavior violates norms? Is the "identity crisis" that seems to be so common among adolescents caused by cultural ambiguity about the passage from adolescence to adulthood?

Margaret Mead's (1928/1953) study of life in Samoa during the 1930s suggests that the answer to these questions is "yes." Samoan adolescents, she observed, were fully integrated into adult life: they participated in production, observed sexual behavior among adults, and freely experimented with sexuality. They were not confined to a vaguely defined area between childhood and adulthood, and they showed little of the awkwardness and anxiety so common among adolescents in the U.S.

By telling us who we are in relation to other people, social identities are like anchors that hold us firmly in our social environment. We may know how many years we have lived, but it is our social age that really matters. The clarity of the boundaries that distinguish one age group from another is enormously important, for without it we may find ourselves feeling lost, as if we do not know where we are in social space. This, in turn, makes it difficult for us to clearly define social situations, including our expectations of ourselves and others.

Age, Role Sets, and Social Interaction

Like all statuses, age affects our choice of role partners, and the roles attached to age affect our perceptions, evaluations, feelings, and expectations of ourselves and other people. This, in turn, produces patterns of interaction that vary according to the ages of those involved.

Cohorts, Peer Groups, and Subcultures
One of the most important concepts in the sociological study of age is the birth cohort. Strictly speaking, a birth cohort is an aggregate of people born in the same year, but sociologists often use a wider range of time—usually 5 years—to define birth cohorts. We could define those born between 1930 and 1935·and those born between 1960 and 1965 as two different cohorts.

The birth cohort is an important concept because it defines peer groups on the basis of age and because it shows how different groups of people experience the

stages of the life course during different historical periods. Each cohort tends to identify with its own unique history. My cohort reached adulthood during the 1960s, and many of us identify with the trauma of Vietnam, the civil rights movement, and the protest music created by people such as Bob Dylan. Today's elderly are drawn together by the shared experience of the Great Depression and World War II. Cohorts born in the late 1960s and early 1970s have had to grow up in a society in which global nuclear annihilation is an everyday possibility. Because of AIDS, they are perhaps the first cohorts for whom sexual coming of age involves risks not only of unwanted pregnancy and venereal disease, but of death.

Such shared experiences can create subcultures that isolate cohorts from each other; but many aspects of social environments—such as primary family ties—encourage interaction among members of different cohorts. Almost 75 percent of people in the U.S. over age 65 have living children, and 25 percent live with them. The percentage of adults who think it is a good idea for elderly parents to live with their children increased from 31 percent in 1973 to 50 percent in 1987; and those who thought it was a bad idea dropped from 58 percent to 35 (Davis and Smith, 1987).

Parents and adult children interact quite frequently in the United States. In 1986, 31 percent of adults with living parents reported spending social evenings with them at least once a week, and 42 percent did so at least several times a month (Davis and Smith, 1987). In addition, most people—regardless of age—say they *prefer* to spend their time with people of different ages rather than with peers (National Council on Aging, 1975).

Our society encourages and discourages interaction between age groups. We benefit by interacting with people who are younger and older than we are, for it gives us a continuing sense of where we are in the life course by reminding us of where we have been and where we are going. Yet, the unique experience of each cohort as it moves along the life course encourages us to limit ourselves to our peers, and the more isolated we are from other age groups, the less aware we are of the effects of ageism, age discrimination, and age inequality on our relationships with other people.

Age and Patterns of Interaction   Each age status has a role set. Young adults orient themselves to different sets of expectations when they interact with

children, adolescents, peers, middle-aged adults, and the elderly. We readily call a boy by his first name, but would wait for permission to call a 70-year-old woman by hers.

Role sets change as people move from one age group to another. In the U.S., children have few responsibilities or rights, and their roles consist more of what they should *not* do than what they should do. They are surrounded by an adult world whose statuses are forbidden to them, and aside from attending school and doing what they are told, they live with relatively few important expectations from their society.

Rights and responsibilities increase in adolescence and adulthood, especially in relation to people in younger age groups. As adolescents, for example, we feel obliged to help a lost child or an ailing elderly person in ways that rarely occurred to us as children. The older we become, the more responsible we tend to feel for other people and the groups and communities we belong to.

In the United States, however, old age reverses the upward trend of rights and responsibilities. The social position of the elderly reverts in many ways to that of children, which consists more of what they should not do than what they should.

Like members of other minorities, children and the elderly are often treated by young and middle-aged adults as if they were socially invisible, and this reflects and perpetuates their subordinate position in society. Adults frequently discuss children's problems with other adults even when the children are present and often refer to them in the third person, as if they were not there. The elderly also find themselves treated in this way, often because younger people assume they are senile and either unable to hear what is said or to understand what they hear.

There is a deeper reason for treating the elderly as if they were invisible, however. Especially in industrial societies, the death of young people is rare, so most of our awareness of death is associated with the elderly, who remind us that death is inevitable. In the U.S., people over the age of 75 constituted less than 5 percent of the population in 1983 but accounted for 46 percent of all deaths (National Center for Health Statistics, 1987).

Although the old have always died, the dying have not always been old. It is only in very recent decades that death has become primarily the province of the elderly, rather than an event scattered erratically across

Unlike most elderly people in the U.S., the grandfather in this family died at home under the care of his wife, his grandson, and his grandson's family. This arrangement brings out many of the roles involved in dying as a social event, including saying goodbye.

enrolled in school climbed from 47 to 97 percent (U.S. Census Bureau, 1975a, 1986a). During the same period, the percentage of those 10 to 15 years old who were employed dropped from 18 percent (25 among boys) to virtually zero. Even though a substantial percentage of older adolescents are now in the labor force, they are more than four times as likely as older workers to be unemployed (Riley and Waring, 1976; U.S. Census Bureau, 1986a).

The elderly have experienced a similar transition. Between 1890 and 1986, the percentage of men over the age of 65 who were in the labor force dropped from 68 to 16 (U.S. Census Bureau, 1975a, 1986a). Mandatory retirement laws created "room at the top" for upwardly mobile younger workers. In 1967, however, the Age Discrimination Act protected workers between the ages of 40 and 65, and by 1987 the act had been amended to eventually forbid forced retirement even at age 70 (Graebner, 1980; *New York Times*, February 16, 1987, p. D1).

It is important to note that the exclusion of children and the elderly from productive work does not occur in many societies, especially those that are nonindustrial. The elderly in Soviet Georgia, as well as those in many other less developed societies, continue to work as long as they are able, in part because they own their own land (Nash, 1965; Weg, 1975). In industrial societies, however, both the youngest and the oldest age groups have been virtually excluded from the productive work through which wealth, power, and prestige are distributed.

Wealth and Income

The elderly are among the poorest age groups in the U.S. with incomes generally being highest among people 35 to 54 years old (Table 14-1). In 1985, 10.4 percent of those 22 to 64 years old lived below the poverty level, but the figure was 12.6 percent for those over 65. Individuals had an average income of $15,800, but for those 65 and over, the average was only $11,400. Of all the money earned in 1985, 12 percent went to the elderly, although they made up 16 percent of the adult population (U.S. Census Bureau, 1986a, 1987a). Their share of the national income was 75 percent of what they would have received if income were distributed equally.

Among the elderly who are female or nonwhite, incomes are even lower (Table 14-1). Only 11 percent of elderly whites lived in poverty in 1985, compared with 32 percent of blacks and 24 percent of Hispanics (U.S. Census Bureau, 1986a).

Households headed by elderly women were twice as likely to live in poverty in 1985 than were those headed by elderly men. Elderly men's share of national income equaled their share of the population (6.5 percent); but, whereas women over the age of 65 made up 9.2 percent of the population, they received only 5.5 percent of all income (U.S. Census Bureau, 1987a).

The poor position of elderly women illustrates how cultural, structural, and ecological factors combine to produce minorities. Cultural values rank elderly women relatively low, but this alone does not explain their high rates of poverty. Their position as women excludes them from good jobs for most of their adult lives, which, in turn, makes them dependent on their husbands. In addition, women live longer than men, which means that widowhood is far more common among women. In 1985, 51 percent of women over the age of 64 were widows, while only 14 percent of men over 64 were widowers (U.S. Census Bureau, 1986a).

Widows are also more common than widowers because elderly widowers are more likely than widows to remarry. Cultural values encourage men to marry younger women, while elderly women are expected to

---

Puzzles: Financially, Being Elderly Makes One Better Off and Worse Off at the Same Time. How Is This Possible?

As you will see later in this chapter, the answer lies in the difference between the effects of aging and the differences between cohorts. On the one hand, it is true that today's elderly are much better off than previous generations. It is also true, however, that if we compare the financial condition of today's elderly cohorts with their own financial condition when *they* were younger, they are considerably *worse* off.

If we compare different *cohorts* of elderly, those today are better off; but if we look at changes in financial conditions *within* cohorts, we find that growing older means substantial downward mobility.

Table 14-1

Average (Median) Money Income by Age, Gender, and Race (United States, 1985)

	TOTAL	GENDER		RACE	
AGE GROUP	POPULATION	MEN	WOMEN	WHITES	BLACKS
15–19	$1,800	$1,900	$1,800	$1,900	*
20–24	$7,300	$8,600	$6,200	$7,800	$4,400
25–34	$14,300	$18,700	$9,900	$15,000	$12,200
35–44	$17,100	$25,400	$10,300	$17,700	$12,500
45–54	$16,400	$25,900	$9,600	$16,900	$12,200
55–64	$12,400	$20,300	$7,200	$13,000	$7,900
65–69	$8,900	$12,600	$6,500	$9,400	*
70 and older	$7,500	$10,000	$6,200	$7,800	*

*Too few cases to estimate.

Source: U.S. Census Bureau, 1987a.

look for husbands among men who are *older* than they. Widowed elderly men have a larger pool of prospective mates than do elderly women. Among people 65 years or older in 1985, there were only 26 unmarried men for every 100 unmarried women (U.S. Census Bureau, 1986a).

Unlike income, the distribution of wealth favors the elderly because the longer we live, the more wealth we can accumulate. In 1976, 55 percent of the wealthiest individuals were more than 49 years old, even though this age group made up only 24 percent of the population. Among the wealthy, at least, age generally favors women, because they tend to outlive their husbands and become wealthy through inheritance. The majority of wealthy women are over the age of 50; the majority of wealthy men are less than 50 years of age (U.S. Census Bureau, 1983c).

Much has been made in recent years of the economic progress made by the elderly, especially through increased Social Security benefits (Pear, 1982). In general, the "poverty gap" between the elderly and the rest of the population has closed substantially since the 1950s, and the elderly are only slightly more likely to be poor than the population as a whole. The incidence of poverty, however, is only one way of comparing the incomes of people in different social categories and ignores the fact that age generally acts as an income "leveler" because most people are

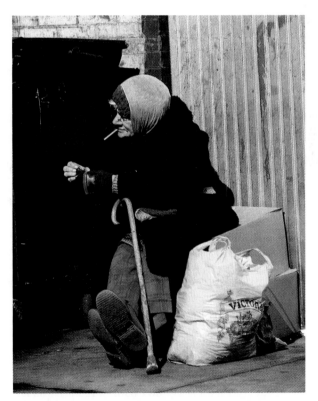

The elderly—and elderly women in particular— constitute one of the poorest age groups in the United States. They are often found—as this woman—among the homeless.

Figure 14-1 Cohort Effects

Social change makes it almost inevitable that different cohorts will experience each stage of the life course under different social circumstances. Males born in 1920 (top row) were far more likely to serve in the military as young adults (World War II) than were males born in 1960 (bottom row).

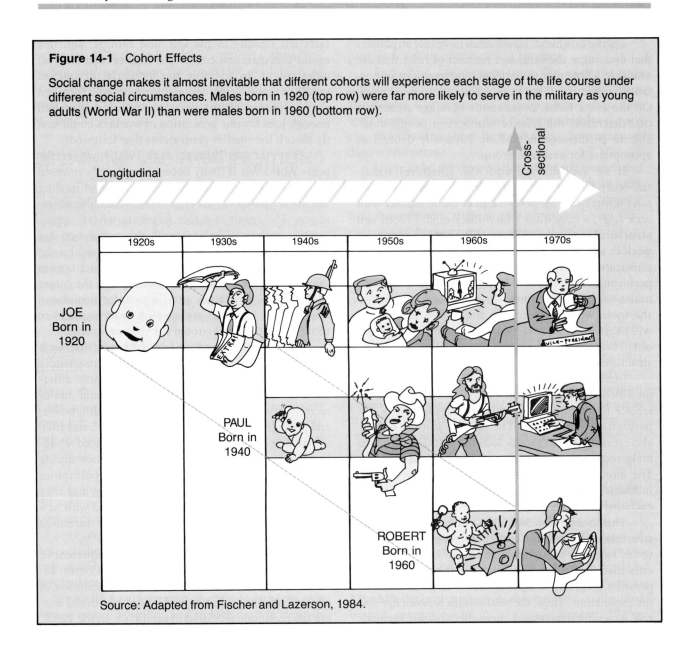

Source: Adapted from Fischer and Lazerson, 1984.

labor market, and the relatively low education of older workers poorly equips them to compete for these jobs.

As each new cohort benefits from expanded educational opportunities, it enlarges its advantage in relation to older cohorts, but eventually *loses* ground in relation to *younger* cohorts. While older workers are less likely than younger workers to *lose* their jobs, if they do, it is much harder for them to find new ones (Riley and Foner, 1968).

The preceding sections indicate some of the functional and ecological aspects of age stratification. While these perspectives contribute important pieces

of the puzzle of age stratification, other pieces are missing, which brings us to the conflict perspective.

Age and Social Conflict

The conflict perspective identifies relationships between age stratification and the conditions that create and maintain social classes. Beliefs that portray adolescents as incapable of performing adult roles and that define the elderly as senile arose in part from class conflict. Nineteenth-century laws that prohibited child labor were strongly supported by labor unions that wanted to reduce competition for jobs. Mandatory retirement for older workers increased in popularity during the 1930s—the years of the Great Depression—when jobs were scarce and labor unions were becoming more powerful (Atchley, 1982).

The low standing of the elderly in the U.S. is also related to class conflict, because competition between age groups is produced by the concentration of wealth and income in the upper class. Forced retirement benefits the capitalist class by lowering costs and increasing business profits. Employers can replace experienced—and more expensive—older workers with younger workers who, although they are generally better educated, are willing to work for lower wages because they are inexperienced (Haber, 1983).

As the age structure of the population becomes older, the potential for conflict increases. When Social Security was enacted in 1935, it was designed as a self-supporting fund that would provide supplementary benefits for all elderly people who contributed to the fund during their working years. Workers and employers would contribute, and when workers retired they would draw from the fund. By design, then, each cohort contributed to a "safety net" that would protect those who survived to old age from living in poverty.

In practice, however, the system has worked quite differently. In 1956, disabled workers under age 65 became eligible for benefits; in 1961, workers retiring before age 65 also became eligible; and in 1965, hospital insurance under the Medicare plan was added to the list of benefits. Because the elderly population was still relatively small in the early 1970s, the fund had a huge surplus, and Congress decided to adjust social security payments according to the level of inflation.

In the 1970s, however, the cost of living—as measured by inflation—was rising *faster* than the income of workers. Between 1970 and 1981 average real family income actually *dropped* by almost one percent, but social security benefits increased by 40 percent. At the same time, the age structure of the population was becoming older at a rapid rate. Together, these two factors meant that for the first time money was flowing *out* of the fund faster than it was coming *in*, and by 1983 the social security system was losing money at the rate of $20,000 each *minute*.

As benefits rose rapidly, retired workers were drawing far more from the social security fund than they and their employers had contributed. The average person who retired in 1980 had, together with his or her employer, contributed $24,000 to the system; but those retirees could expect to draw $125,000 in benefits.

The result is a growing burden on the young and middle-aged working population, whose contribution to social security is now used immediately to pay *current* benefits to those who are already retired. In 1945 there were 42 workers to provide benefits for each retired person. The elderly population is now much larger relative to the working population that pays social security taxes, and there are only 3 workers to support each retired person (*Newsweek*, January 24, 1983; U.S. Census Bureau, 1986a).

It is important to point out that conflict over the social security issue is *within* the lower and middle classes. Eighty percent of those over the age of 65 have incomes below $10,000 and depend on social security for more than half their annual income (*Newsweek*, January 24, 1983; U.S. Census Bureau, 1986a). As we saw in Chapter 11, the lower and middle classes are hardly in a position to support the elderly, but the burden, nonetheless, falls largely on them.

Consequently, the social security problem is not simply a matter of changing age structures and rising retirement benefits, for it also reflects the economic structure of our society. The large population of retired people is produced in part by an economy that cannot provide jobs for everyone who wants to work, and from this perspective, retirement programs benefit upper-class capitalists as well as (if not more than) middle- and lower-class workers. Without such programs, workers would either insist on remaining in the labor force well into old age or would demand wages high enough to provide for retirement (Smith, 1981). In this way, retirement programs operate as "a kind of insurance for capitalists and corporations" (O'Connor, 1973, p. 138).

The position of the elderly rests on both functional requirements of societies and conflict over wealth, power, and prestige. It is also closely tied to changing age and role structures and to biological aspects of age and aging. The uniqueness of age as a social status produces barriers to social change and pressures for change.

AGE STRATIFICATION AND SOCIAL CHANGE

Pressures toward equality between age groups come from organized social movements, the unique characteristics of age as a social status, changing age structures of populations, and the changing characteristics of age cohorts.

In the U.S., the elderly have greatly increased their political power in the last decade. They are not only more numerous than ever before but are more likely to vote than almost any other age group (U.S. Census Bureau, 1986a). The American Association of Retired Persons has 24 million members, and the Gray Panther organization has over 70,000 who actively challenge stereotypes while promoting equal rights for the elderly. Says Maggie Kuhn, the 78-year-old founder of the Gray Panthers:

> We have used street theater, we have marched, we have demonstrated, we have picketed. . . . But more than that, we have brought together a group of people

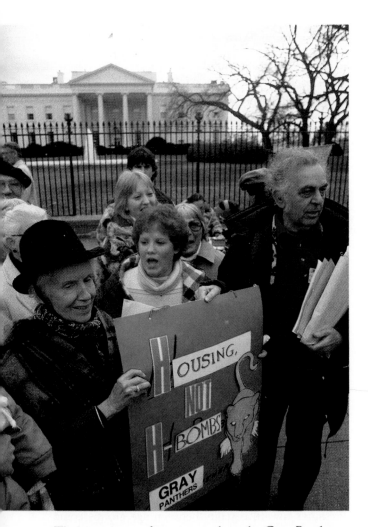

The emergence of groups, such as the Gray Panthers, signaled a major growth in the organized political influence of the elderly in the United States.

who have first-class minds and who read a lot, who have the ability to think and who have a creative social analysis. (*Hartford Advocate*, July 28, 1982, p. 6)

The Gray Panthers is an intergenerational organization that attracts people of all ages. In part, its attractiveness rests on the uniqueness of age as a social status, for we all face the time when we will be culturally defined as "old." Whites can ignore the oppression of blacks; men can ignore the oppression of women; and adults can ignore the disadvantaged position of children. Few can ignore the fate of the elderly, however, without also ignoring the inevitability of old age itself.

Perhaps the most important pressure for change results from long-term shifts in the age structure of populations and the flow of generations through the life course. For almost two hundred years, birth rates have declined steadily in Europe and North America, and this has caused major shifts in population age structures. By the year 2025, an estimated 20 percent of our population will be over the age of 64, compared with 12 percent in 1985 and only 4 percent in 1890 (U.S. Census Bureau, 1975a, 1986a). From 1980 to the year 2000, the number of centenarians—people 100 or more years old—is expected to jump by seven times, from 15,000 to more than 100,000 (U.S. Census Bureau, 1987i). Throughout Europe, populations are expected to be even older than in the U.S., with more than 25 percent over the age of 64 in West Germany (O.E.C.D., 1987).

The resulting "graying" of the U.S. will increase the political power of the elderly and pressure decision makers to devote larger portions of national resources to elderly people's needs, such as health care and retirement income and housing. Opposition to mandatory retirement laws will grow along with the size of the elderly population, and this will put pressure on a job market that excludes the elderly in order to provide jobs for young and middle-aged adults.

Such changes are particularly important in southern parts of the U.S. whose populations have swelled with elderly migrants attracted by warm climates and low costs of living. People over the age of 64 made up 12 percent of the U.S. population in 1985, but 18 percent of Florida's (U.S. Census Bureau, 1986a). Many communities in Florida and other Sun Belt states are being designed and built specifically to meet the needs of older residents, and the elderly increasingly dominate local and state politics.

Increased power among the elderly also results from the different social characteristics of cohorts. In 1985, 37 percent of those over the age of 64 had never gone beyond elementary school; only 12 percent had college degrees; and 20 percent were foreign-born and relatively unfamiliar with U.S. laws and the political process. By comparison, less than 10 percent of the elderly in 2010 will have never gone beyond elementary school; roughly 20 percent will have college degrees; and almost all will be native-born (U.S. Census Bureau, 1981, 1986a). This, combined with an increasing consciousness of the importance of age as a social status, will probably result in considerable increases in the social power of the elderly.

Greater tension between age groups appears to be an inevitable consequence of changing age structures and the increased political power of each succeeding generation of elderly people. How might these tensions be resolved? Is equality a possible answer?

Is Equality Possible?

Age stratification results primarily from the use of age to determine which statuses people may occupy and, therefore, which roles they may perform in the division of labor. Equality among age groups implies that age would no longer limit people's access to statuses, especially jobs. This kind of arrangement, however, would inevitably result in renewed age stratification, because societies still have to allocate roles among their members, and the most likely criteria are strongly related to age (Riley and Waring, 1976).

Suppose that work roles were allocated on the basis of skill and ability. Adolescents would be at a disadvantage, and the middle-aged and elderly would have to compete with healthy and vigorous younger cohorts fresh out of college where they have learned the latest technological skills. If work experience were the most important factor, young and middle-aged workers would lose their competitive edge over the elderly. If jobs went to those who needed them most—such as those with families—the middle-aged would benefit, because they are the most likely to have families with college age children (Oppenheimer, 1974).

This analysis suggests that age stratification among adolescents, adults, and the elderly is unavoidable, but it rests on an assumption that may not be. All of these hypothetical consequences of age equality would occur only in a society that cannot provide jobs for everyone, making it necessary to exclude some people from the labor market in order to employ everyone else. Competition between groups tends to breed prejudice, and prejudice is the cultural bulwark of discrimination (Noel, 1968; Vander Zanden, 1972).

To Marx, such conditions are main features of capitalist, industrial societies in which the means of production are privately owned, and competition among workers keeps wages low and profits high. Marx argued that these conditions would disappear in a technologically advanced communist society, and, with them, all forms of social inequality. From Marx's perspective, age inequality is directly related to the same social conditions that produce social classes.

Marx's view is utopian, and we cannot know if the ideal society he envisions is possible. His perspective is powerful, however, because it underscores the fact that social change is severely limited by the basic ways in which societies organize production and distribute wealth, power, and prestige. It is impossible to eliminate age stratification in industrial societies—including capitalist and socialist countries—without changing fundamental economic and political structures that perpetuate social inequality. To see why this is true, consider the recommendations of two panels of scientists who studied the disadvantaged positions of the young and the elderly in the U.S. (Coleman et al., 1974; Riley, 1974).

In industrial societies, education is confined primarily to children and adolescents who, in turn, spend most of their time in school. Similarly, young and middle-aged adults are confined to work, and the elderly are largely excluded from paid work. In spite of the fact that they focused on dramatically different age groups, the panels made similar recommendations: education, work, and leisure should not be rigidly distributed among age groups; rather, they should be distributed evenly throughout the life course (see Vaupel and Gowan, 1986).

Under this arrangement, adolescents would split their time between school and on-the-job training. Young and middle-aged adults would work less in order to make room for continuing education and increased leisure. The elderly would continue to work—although perhaps at reduced levels—while enjoying increased amounts of leisure and education. These proposals rest on the idea that the total amount of time devoted to education, work, and leisure would remain the same in the population as a whole. What would change would be the distribution of these activities over the life course.

There is some evidence that this kind of shift has already begun. Adults are increasingly likely to change careers at least once and such changes often require a return to school for additional training. Between 1960 and 1985 the percentage of adults over the age of 29 who were enrolled in school more than doubled (U.S. Census Bureau, 1986a).

Unless total production and income increase, however, redistribution of education, work, and leisure across age groups will reduce inequality of income only if people in higher-income age groups are willing to lower their incomes. Raising the average income of elderly people to the 1985 national average of $15,800 would cost more than $119 billion, or $800 for every adult under the age of 65.

Where would this money come from? From the 64 percent of younger adults who *already* earn less than the national average? Or from the upper classes that not only control most of the nation's wealth and income but also heavily influence those who make our laws? Will the upper class weaken itself in order to bring about equality for the elderly, especially given that old age does not threaten *them* with financial insecurity? Certainly this seems unlikely.

Inequality, whether based on gender, race, ethnicity, or age, is ultimately created by social conditions that produce and perpetuate social stratification itself. In capitalist societies, an end to age stratification would require the redistribution of the enormous wealth, power, and prestige now concentrated in the upper class. In socialist societies, the state and those who control it would have to surrender their power over the economy and the distribution of what is produced. So long as control over the means of production is unequally distributed, there will be scarcities and competition; and so long as people must compete for scarce rewards, privileged groups will use their advantages to maintain their position (see Lenski, 1966).

In order for some groups to be privileged, others must pay the cost. In capitalist and socialist societies, the most important question is not, Will minorities continue to exist? but, Who will the minorities be?

SUMMARY

1. Societies divide the life span into age groups, each of which is a social status with its own role set.

2. As a social status, age affects the distribution of wealth, power, and prestige. Age is unique in that it is always temporary, provides a map of the life course, and affects the content of status sets more than any other status. Because we all belong to subordinate and dominant age groups at one time or another, subordinate age groups are only quasi-minorities.

3. Relationships between age groups are supported by a variety of beliefs, values, attitudes, and norms; and in many societies, the prejudice of ageism perpetuates age stratification and creates self-fulfilling prophecies.

4. Like other statuses, age groups have boundaries, and in some societies rites of passage clearly indicate when people move from one age group to another.

5. In social interaction, the role sets attached to age statuses affect our perceptions, evaluations, feelings, and expectations. In many relationships age acts as a latent status that affects how we play other roles.

6. The birth cohort is an important concept because it defines peer groups on the basis of age and because it reveals how different groups of people experience the stages of the life course during different historical periods.

7. Divisions of labor use age as a basis for assigning roles, and this, in turn, creates and supports

Ziggy by Tom Wilson. © Universal Press Syndicate.

social inequality. In the U.S., children and the elderly generally occupy lower positions than young and middle-aged adults, and while most elderly people are not poor, they are worse off than they were as younger adults, especially if they are women.

8. Age stratification is functional for the socialization and motivation of children to perform adult roles, and is also closely connected to ecological arrangements, population growth, and changing age distributions. Work and family roles are assigned according to age, and when structural lag causes the role structure in a society to be out of balance with the population age structure, opportunities increase for some age groups at the expense of others.

9. Age stratification also has dysfunctional consequences. It creates large numbers of dependent people who consume more than they produce, and fosters feelings of alienation and frustration among young and old alike.

10. While age stratification has many functional consequences, it is also perpetuated by conflict among social classes. The exclusion of children and the elderly from employment lessens competition for jobs made scarce by a class society. It also contributes to false consciousness among young and middle-aged adult workers by focusing attention on competition between age groups rather than on the upper class whose privileged position creates the scarcities over which people compete.

11. While social movements for age equality have benefited the elderly, the strongest pressures for change center on changing population age structures and characteristics of new generations. Each new cohort of elderly people is more numerous, educated, and politically aware than the last, which increases their political power.

KEY TERMS

age group   377
ageism   378
cohort effect   393
gerontocracy   390
hospice   386
life course   377
structural lag   393

Looking Elsewhere

Having studied Chapter 14, you might want to look at related discussions in *Human Arrangements*, which include

- birth cohorts and age structures (Chapter 5, pp. 119-20)
- age structure and unemployment (Chapter 18, p. 505)
- age and crime (Chapter 10, pp. 255–56)
- socialization throughout the life course (Chapter 6, pp. 149–56)
- changing patterns of education and the life course (Chapter 16, p. 456)

RECOMMENDED READINGS

FONER, N. (1984). *Ages in conflict: A cross-cultural perspective on inequalities between old and young.* New York: Columbia University Press. A richly detailed look at the varieties of age stratification and their effects on relations between age groups in traditional societies.

MCPHERSON, B. D. (1983). *Aging as a social process: An introduction to individual and population aging.* Toronto: Butterworths. An excellent introduction to aging as a social process, including the ways in which that process is affected by historical, gender, racial, social class, and cross-cultural factors.

RILEY, M. W., HESS, B. B., and BOND, K. (Eds.). (1983). *Aging in society: Selected reviews of recent research.* Hillsdale, NJ: Lawrence Erlbaum Associates. An excellent collection of papers originally written for the 1981 White House Conference on Aging, and touching on topics such as aging and economics, the family, work, retirement, mortality, stress, learning and memory, health and mortality, nutrition, and geographic mobility.

ZELIZER, V. A. (1985). *Pricing the priceless child: The changing social value of children.* New York: Basic Books. A fascinating analysis of how children in the U.S. became economically useless and emotionally "priceless" at the turn of the 20th century, and the relationship between these two transformations.

FIVE

Social Institutions

IN PARTS ONE AND TWO we laid out a basic conceptual framework of sociological analysis—the organization of human life through cultural, structural, and ecological arrangements. In Part Three we applied this to basic aspects of social life: the socialization process, interaction, groups, formal organizations, communities, and the ways in which groups and societies try to control the behavior of their members. In Part Four we focused on the ways culture, social structure, and ecology produce and perpetuate inequality based on characteristics such as social class, race, ethnicity, gender, and age.

Part Five focuses on social *institutions*, the most important arrangements in any society. As we saw in Chapter 4, institutions are enduring sets of cultural ideas and social relationships organized to accomplish important social goals. All societies rely on some variation of the *family* to produce, socialize, protect, and care for new members. In many societies, *schools* provide additional education and skills; *economic institutions* produce and distribute goods and services; *political institutions* distribute and apply collective power; and *religious institutions* help members of society grapple with enduring questions about the meaning of life itself.

Marriage and the Family as Institutions

Your Family, My Family, and The Family

Cultural Variations

Beliefs and the Concept of Kinship

Values

Attitudes

Norms

Varieties of Social Structure

Basic Elements of Family Structures

Divisions of Labor and Role Structures

Patterns of Interaction

Power, Matriarchy, and Patriarchy

Family Wealth and Power in Stratified Societies

The Social Ecology of Family Life

Reproduction: Marriage, Family, and Society

Birth Rates, Death Rates, and the Structure of Family Life

Technology, Production, and Families

Marriage, Family, and Society

Functions and Dysfunctions

The Conflict Perspective on Marriage and the Family

Family Disorganization

Understanding Divorce

Family Violence

Families and Social Change

Cultural Change and the Family

Shifting Structures

Families Come and Families Go, but The Family Is Here to Stay

15 Marriage and the Family

Look through a Sunday newspaper and you will find announcements of engagements, weddings, births, and divorces. In the obituary columns you will find the names of people who "survive" those who die. On a residential street you will see houses and apartments, each with its own assortment of people living together. Think about your childhood, and more than anything else you will probably think of your family—a group that may include anyone from you and one parent to scores of people—parents, stepparents, sisters and brothers, grandparents, distant cousins, aunts, and uncles, some of whom are no longer alive.

On the surface, such aspects of marriages and families seem to involve no more than people's personal decisions about their lives, and we may think that each relationship is unique for the people who define themselves as a married couple or a family. Sociologically, however, marriages and families exist in environments that affect how they are formed, how they fall apart, and what goes on among their members; just as what goes on in families affects the nature of those environments. In spite of variations from one family to another, families tend to conform to predictable social and ecological patterns within societies. These patterns, and their importance to both society and to us as individuals, are what this chapter is all about.

We begin by looking at how culture and social structure characterize the family in different societies and how these are affected by ecology and population. We then use the functional and conflict perspectives to better understand the place of families in societies. The closing sections include a systematic sociological analysis of family disorganization—divorce and violence in particular—and the causes of change in the family as a social institution.

"We are gathered here to join together this man and this woman in matrimony—a very serious step, with far-reaching and unpredictable consequences."
Drawing by Booth © 1985, The New Yorker Magazine, Inc.

MARRIAGE AND THE FAMILY AS INSTITUTIONS

The definition of marriage is relatively simple, regardless of the society. **Marriage** is a socially supported union between individuals in what is intended to be a stable, enduring relationship that involves sexual interaction as one of its key elements. As such, the institution of marriage is the basis for the institution of the family.

If asked to define a "family," you would probably describe it as a group consisting of parents and their children. In an Israeli kibbutz, however, the entire community serves as a family, and all women take collective responsibility for child care (Rabin, 1965); among India's Nayar, fathers have no role relationship with their children (Gough, 1952); and Indonesia's Dani have no word for "family" at all (Heider, 1972). Although these examples reveal cultural differences in the definition of the family, all three have one thing in common. In each case the family is a social institution—an enduring set of cultural ideas and social relationships that contribute to the achievement of social goals.

In virtually all societies the **family** performs six basic social functions, and these define the family as an institution. First, it regulates sexual behavior by specifying who may have sexual contact with whom. Second, the family is responsible for *reproduction*. As we saw in Chapter 5, the norms, values, and beliefs that regulate family life often affect the number of children born.

Third, families nurture and protect children and provide emotional support for adults. Fourth, the fam-

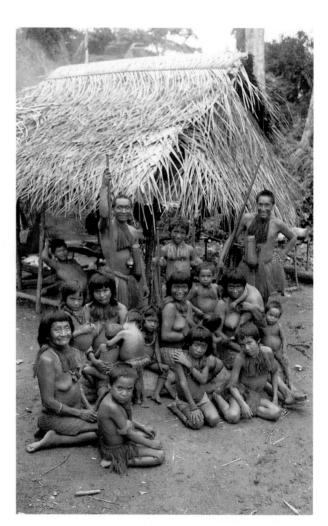

All societies have families, but they vary greatly in cultural and structural forms—the relatively simple parent–child families found in most industrial societies; families that include several generations, such as those in Turkey; and families that include entire communities, such as the Yagua Indians of Brazil.

ily is the main socializing institution charged with teaching new members of society what they need to know in order to participate in their social environment.

Fifth, the family plays a part in the production and consumption of goods. In many societies the family is a center of economic production, and its members produce most of what they consume. In others, such as our own, families produce little of what they consume.

Finally, families are a source of ascribed social statuses—race, ethnicity, and social class—that affect people's life chances. Caste membership in India and South Africa depends solely on the characteristics of families into which people are born.

Even among the Dani—who have no word for the family—the institution nonetheless exists in social relationships that perpetuate the culture and social structures of Dani society. Since the essence of the family lies in *why* it is organized rather than *how*, we should not be surprised by the astounding variety found in the world, for the same goals can be achieved in many ways.

Your Family, My Family, and The Family

If we compared your family and mine, we would find many differences—in values, beliefs, and attitudes that we share; in norms that define our rights and responsibilities; and in the number of children, patterns of interaction and affection, and divisions of labor and power. Just as no two individuals are exactly alike, individual families also have some unique characteristics.

As an *institution*, however, the family is more than a collection of families, just as a group is more than the sum of its members. An institution is a social "blueprint" that defines how family relationships ought to be structured and what goals families and their members should pursue in order to make sure that important social goals are achieved.

Each of us participates in family life in relation to cultural models that produce patterns of family relationships, and these patterns are at the heart of the family as an institution. In the United States fathers generally have more power than mothers; children have few legal rights until they reach 18 years of age; and most families have three or fewer children and do not have aunts, uncles, and grandparents living in the same dwelling.

Although some societies have a single model for the family, others—such as ours—include several, each of which reflects a different subculture. In some ways all families in the U.S. are alike, but ethnic and racial subcultures often produce unique patterns of family relationships. It is misleading to refer to the institution of "the American family" as if it has only one meaning.

This chapter focuses on six of the many aspects of marriage and the family that interest sociologists: How does culture define marital and family relationships and regulate behavior within them? How are these relationships structured? How do ecological arrangements affect family life? What are the relationships between families and the rest of society? How do we explain the problems that threaten the well-being of marriages and families? How and why do the institutions of marriage and the family change?

CULTURAL VARIATIONS

Marriages and families are affected by a variety of cultural ideas. Beliefs define who is related to whom; values motivate us to form families and guide our choices within them; attitudes affect our feelings toward family members and outsiders; and norms define family roles and govern how family relationships are established, maintained, and broken.

Beliefs and the Concept of Kinship

At the heart of all family institutions is the concept of **kinship**, which refers to social relationships based on common ancestry, adoption, or marriage. In all societies children and their mothers are defined as relatives (or *kin*); but beyond this there are great differences among the world's cultures.

In the U.S., there are special terms for hundreds of relatives: such as spouses, parents, children, aunts, uncles, nieces, nephews, in-laws, and grandparents. To these we can add fictive kin, such as godparents and "honorary aunts and uncles," who are not formal members of a family but nonetheless may play important roles. The number of possible kin relationships is enormous, and for this reason virtually all societies simplify kinship by considering only some to be "true" relatives.

Trobriand Islanders are unaware of the biological tie between fathers and children, and although fathers are affectionate with their children, they are regarded

Kinship provides what is perhaps our most important social connection, one that can extend backward in time across many generations. In this picture, more than 200 descendants of a Cape Cod pioneer celebrate their heritage as one of the oldest families in the U.S.

as outsiders (Malinowski, 1929). Southern India's Nayar acknowledge the biological role of fathers; but, as in several other societies, the mother's eldest brother is responsible for her children (Gough, 1974).

Kinship, therefore, depends more on cultural definitions than on biology, and if "fate makes our relatives," then part of that fate is the culture we happen to be born into (Sahlins, 1976). For societies, kinship provides continuity from one generation to the next by establishing ties between the generations who carry a society's culture and those who must learn to live by it. For individuals, kinship is important because it links each of us to the past, present, and future.

Unlike all other social relationships, those among kin have the power to transcend death itself. In most horticultural societies, people worship their ancestors, believing that if they do not appease them, their spirits might return to harm them (Shiels, 1975). Even in societies such as our own that do not worship ancestors, we often refer to deceased relatives as living parts of our social identities.

Kinship is defined in one of three ways. In societies with **matrilineal descent**, ancestry is traced through mothers and their blood relatives, and children are not defined as relatives of their father's family. Matrilineal descent is relatively rare among known societies, and is found most often in horticultural societies in which women produce most of the food (Aberle, 1961; Murdock, 1967).

The situation is reversed in societies with **patrilineal descent**, in which children are related only to

their father's blood relatives. In most societies, descent is either matrilineal or patrilineal (Murdock, 1949); there are only a few with **bilateral descent**, tracing ancestry through both the mother's and father's families. Murdock (1949) found that of the 86 societies on which information on descent is available, fully 71 percent are patrilineal, compared with 27 percent that are matrilineal, and only 2 percent that are bilateral.

While kinship defines basic family ties, other beliefs affect relationships within families. Until recently, Americans believed that when men and women marry, they become "one," and the "one" is the husband. This belief affects family relationships by undermining a wife's standing as a separate individual with her own rights in relation to her husband and the rest of society. It is still evident in the tendency of most married women to adopt their husband's last name as their own. In contrast, the Swedish Parliament ruled in 1982 that husbands and wives are free to choose their own last names, and that if they choose no last name for a newborn child, after three months it automatically takes its *mother's* name (*Ms.* magazine, 1982).

Many people in the U.S. believe that marriage is better for women than it is for men, a belief reflected in jokes about women "trapping" men into marriage and about husbands continually trying to escape married life. Most research, however, shows just the opposite: single women report greater happiness and less psychological stress than married women of the same age, while married men report less psychological distress than single men.

The worship of ancestors among the Chinese includes annual meetings at burial grounds and offerings of food and incense to reinforce their sense of attachment with kin both living and dead.

Values

Cultural values strongly affect both the formation and dissolution of marriages and families and social interactions within them.

There are many reasons for marrying, and in the U.S., romantic love is generally considered to be the most important. Rural Greeks, however, still arrange marriages as economic exchanges between the bride's family and the groom's, and spouses rarely know each other before they marry (Friedl, 1962). Similar arrangements are found among North America's Blackfeet Indians and the Swazi of southeast Africa (Kuper, 1963; Wissler, 1911). In northern Australia, the marriages of Tiwi girls are arranged before they are even born, and they grow up as members of their future husband's family (Hart and Pilling, 1960).

Many of us flinch at the idea of basing marriage on economic and political values; but these values have their advantages. Romantic love thrives on rushes of excitement that come with exploring the mysteries of another person (as well as the mystery of why they find *us* so exciting). Married life, however, makes heavy, practical demands on spouses, from earning a living to cleaning house, caring for children, and managing relationships with in-laws.

We also value virginity in brides and sexual fidelity in marriage, particularly on the part of women. In 1987, 89 percent of U.S. adults considered extramarital affairs to be wrong, and in spite of rapidly changing values, 36 percent held similar values about premarital sex (Davis and Smith, 1987).

Strong values supporting virginity at marriage are relatively rare among societies—Murdock (1949) estimated that premarital sex is prohibited in less than 5 percent of them. Virginity has no value among Samoans or Trobriand Islanders, and the Mentawei of Indonesia go so far as to require women to give birth before marriage in order to prove they are fertile (Malinowski, 1929; Mead, 1928; Murdock, 1949). Women in Scandinavian countries increasingly choose to have children without marrying the father (Westoff, 1978b), and Blake (1982) believes that similar trends are occurring in the U.S. as disapproval of premarital sexual behavior declines and acceptance of children born out of wedlock increases.

Values about adultery also differ among societies. Eskimos and Australian aborigines consider it to be good manners to share wives with visitors (Montagu, 1971), and a Nayar wife is free to have sex with any man, so long as he belongs to her husband's caste (Gough, 1974).

Although many societies place a lower value on virginity and fidelity than we do, others value them much more highly. In Muslim societies, a family's honor depends on the virginity of its daughters (Pastner, 1974), and although Trobriand Islanders do not value virginity, they strongly value fidelity between spouses. Virginity was a required condition for marriage among ancient Hebrews, and a bride who failed to show signs of virginity on her wedding night (such as spots of blood) was killed and her family was shamed (Brownmiller, 1975). More recently, when thousands of single women in Bangladesh were raped by invading Pakistani soldiers, they lost all chance of marrying, even though they had no control over the loss of their virginity.

It is important to note that in no society are virginity at marriage and marital fidelity valued more highly in men than in women, and this clearly reflects the subordinate position of women, especially in societies that regard them as actual property of their fathers or husbands.

Other values also play a part in family relationships. We tend to value the success of individuals more than loyalty to kin, and value marital ties more highly than those to the families in which we grow up. In contrast with children of traditional Japanese families, adult offspring in the U.S. are expected to control their own lives, even when they conflict with their parents' desires, and the independence of husbands, wives, and their children from the influence of parents-in-law is closely guarded.

Values also affect how many children parents have. The cultural value of small families tends to increase with industrialization. In the U.S. lower-class families generally have more children than those in the middle and upper classes, but this is due more to ineffective birth control than to differences in values. Income makes little difference in the number of children people say they want to have, only in the number they actually do have (Ryder and Westoff, 1971).

Attitudes

Our attitudes toward marriage and the family are a curious blend of opposites. Regardless of social class, we attach intense emotional needs to families and look upon the idea of the family with a great deal of reverence. We worry about whether or not the family is being destroyed by a rapidly changing industrial society; over 90 percent marry at some time in our lives and although roughly half will experience a divorce, around 65 percent of those who divorce remarry within five years (Grady, 1980; Thornton and Rodgers, 1983; U.S. Census Bureau, 1982). We celebrate Mother's Day and Father's Day and regard holidays such as Thanksgiving, Christmas, and Hanukkah as important family events.

Such positive attitudes, however, exist side by side with negative ones. Hostile jokes about mothers-in-law, "hen-pecked husbands," and "Jewish mothers" are a staple ingredient of our humor, and comedians typically include hostile remarks about spouses in their routines.

We often avoid revealing our negative attitudes toward families—even to ourselves—in part because the cultural ideal of the happy family is so strong that we tend to bury feelings of disappointment, frustra-

The requirement that women wear veils in Tunisia and other Moslem countries underscores their status as closely guarded sexual property in patriarchal societies.

tion, and bitterness that inevitably arise in intense primary relationships. Perhaps this is why hostile jokes about marriage and families are so popular, for they express negative feelings that we, ourselves, would rather not see or let others see in our own lives.

The importance of marriage and the family—as institutions and as basic aspects of our lives—causes us to make heavy emotional investments in them. Individuals' needs and the perpetuation and stability of societies require their continued existence in one form or another. We cannot live without them, and we often find it difficult to live with them. From this point of view, the existence of ambivalent cultural attitudes about marriage and the family should not surprise us.

Norms

Cultural norms affect almost every aspect of social relationships in marriages and families, and generally fall into one of two categories: norms that regulate the formation and dissolution of marriages, and those that regulate role behavior among kin.

Marriage Rules   In all cultures, **marriage rules** put limits on whom people may marry, when, and under what conditions. Incest rules prohibit marriage between people who are defined as close relatives. With the exception of a few ancient societies in Hawaii, Egypt, and Mexico, all societies include parents and their children, as well as brothers and sisters, in that category. Even in Hawaii and Egypt incest was regarded as a privilege reserved for royal families (see Rubin and Byerly, 1983), although Lewis (1983) argues that in ancient Egypt brother-sister marriage was fairly common in the urban middle class as well.

U.S. law prohibits marriages involving parents and their children, siblings, grandparents and grandchildren, aunts and nephews, and uncles and nieces, and 30 states prohibit marriages between first cousins. Shoshone Indians, however, do not distinguish between siblings and cousins, and therefore prohibit marriages that involve even the most distant cousins.

That incest taboos are universal suggests a biological basis for them, but cross-cultural differences in the definition of incest and illogical definitions within cultures show that incest rules are as much a matter of culture as biology (see Arens, 1986). In some societies people commit incest if they marry a child of their mother's sister or father's brother; but they are often *expected* to marry a child of their mother's *brother* or father's *sister*. Biologically, the son of a mother's sister is no closer a relative than the son of a mother's brother, but the incest rule clearly defines marriage to the first as revolting and marriage to the second as socially desirable.

Incest taboos are not the only norms that regulate who marries whom. Norms of **endogamy** require people to marry those belonging to their own group. Nazi Germany forbade marriage between Jews and gentiles. Orthodox Jews may not marry gentiles, and a Balinese woman may not marry a man from a caste lower than her own (Mead, 1968). Norms of **exogamy**, however, require marriage to someone who is culturally defined as an *outsider*.

In the U.S., marriage rules are generally endogamous in relation to race and religion. In 1985, less than 2 percent of married couples were interracial, and in 1987 almost a quarter favored laws prohibiting interracial marriage (Davis and Smith, 1987; U.S. Census Bureau, 1986a). Our marriage rules are exogamous, however, in relation to gender, for the law does not yet provide for marriage between people of the same gender. In contrast, East Africa's Nuer and Nandi tribes allow childless women to marry younger women and claim their children as heirs (Lévi-Strauss, 1956; Obaler, 1985).

Norms also specify how many people can be married to each other at one time. In his survey of 238 societies, Murdock (1949) found that 18 percent insist on **monogamy**—marriage to only one spouse at a time—while the remainder permit some form of multiple marriage, or **polygamy**. Men are allowed to have more than one wife (**polygyny**) in 80 percent of all societies, including the Swazi of Africa, the Tiwi of Australia, and, until 1896, U.S. Mormons. Murdock found that women may marry more than one husband (**polyandry**) in only three societies: the Toda of India, the South Pacific Marquesian Islanders, and the Sherpa of Nepal.

Most of these 238 societies are small, preindustrial, and contain a small fraction of the world population. Although most societies permit multiple marriage, most people live in societies that expect monogamy.

Once couples marry, norms also affect where they can live. In **matrilocal societies**—the American Hopi Indians—married couples live in or near the wife's mother's household, whereas in **patrilocal societies**—Greek villages and Africa's Swazi—they live in or near the husband's father's household. In **bilocal**

A Bakhtiari man stands with his three wives and many children. Although polygyny is allowed in many societies, most men are monogamous since they cannot afford to pay the bride price often associated with marriage in such societies.

societies—the Blackfeet Indians—couples may choose between the husband's and the wife's families (but they cannot choose neither). In contrast, couples may live wherever they want in most **neolocal** industrial societies, with couples starting new households. Murdock's (1949) survey of 238 societies shows that 73 percent are patrilocal, 18 percent are matrilocal, and 9 percent allow a free choice of residence.

These patterns describe residence rules in most but not all societies. Among western Africa's Ashanti, husbands and wives do not live together at all—each lives with his or her own mother's relatives. Children may eat meals at their father's house and then return to their mother's house for the night (Fortes et al., 1947). In India, once a Nayar husband has spent three nights with his wife, he leaves her, and the wife lives as a member of her mother's household (Gough, 1974).

Together, values and norms affect who marries whom in other ways as well. In most societies, spouses tend to have similar social statuses. In the U.S., we generally marry people of similar ages (Leslie, 1982) and rarely marry people of different races, although the rate of interracial marriage is highest in communities in which there is the least amount of racial inequality (South and Messner, 1986). We also tend to marry people who are similar to us in educational attainment, social class, and religion. In the late 1970s, 93 percent of Protestants, 89 percent of Jews, and 81 percent of Catholics married people of their own religious faith (Smelser, 1981). As factors such as religion and ethnicity become less important in the choice of marriage partners, however, the rate of intermarriage has increased and the level of endogamy has declined (Stevens and Swicegood, 1987).

Although marriage patterns—those of age, race, and religion—are largely due to culture, they are also affected by social relationships that limit our interactions to people who have statuses in common with us. We live in neighborhoods that tend to be homogeneous with respect to social class, race, and ethnicity; college students are more likely to meet and fall in love with each other than with high school graduates who are already in the labor force. The relative frequency of intermarriage across ethnic, class, and religious boundaries is strongly affected by how homogeneous the population is, with intermarriage far more common in large heterogeneous cities than in small rural communities (Blau, Blum, and Schwartz, 1982).

Just as norms regulate the conditions of marriage, so, too, do they regulate their dissolution. Until quite recently, most U.S. states permitted divorce only under a limited set of circumstances—adultery and desertion—and the Catholic Church does not recognize divorce as legitimate although the practice of annulment is often used to accomplish the same end. Only in recent years have states adopted no-fault divorce laws under which spouses can divorce each other by nothing more than mutual consent.

Norms and Family Relationships   In addition to regulating the formation and dissolution of marriages, norms define roles within marriages and families. While most norms about sex set limits on it, marital norms define sexual access to spouses as a right, and refusal to have sex is grounds for divorce in most U.S. states.

Although all societies define sex as a basic part of marriage, norms regulate sexual behavior in sharply different ways. In India and most Muslim countries, husbands may not sexually approach wives who are menstruating or who have recently given birth. In the U.S., many states still have laws that specifically prohibit certain sexual behaviors—such as oral and anal sex—even between spouses.

Family norms differ sharply from those found in other groups in their informality and the way in which they are applied. In comparison with other groups, family norms are often applied in different ways to each member depending on his or her personal characteristics and needs. Because families are intimate primary groups, members are more likely to be treated as unique individuals, each with his or her own special needs, abilities, and limitations.

Much of the world outside the family, however, operates under formal norms that apply to everyone who occupies a particular social status. Relationships in school are secondary, and when children first attend school they are often jarred by the fact that they no longer receive the individual attention and special considerations that they enjoy as family members.

Major aspects of family relationships include the distribution of labor, wealth, power, and prestige among family members, and the patterns of interaction that are the social fabric of life in families.

VARIETIES OF SOCIAL STRUCTURE

Sociologists study the institutions of marriage and the family on both the micro- and macrolevels of social structure, for what goes on in families is affected by the relationships between families and other institutions. It is no less true, however, that societies are affected by what goes on in their families. The following sections describe some basic family structures and then look at variations in their major characteristics: role structures, patterns of interaction, and distributions of wealth and power.

Basic Elements of Family Structures

Although kinship includes people who are related to us whether they live with us or not, family boundaries generally include only people who live together. From this point of view, the family composition usually takes one of four forms (see Figure 15-1).

A **nuclear** family consists of parents and their natural or adopted children, and this structure describes most families in industrial societies. **Extended**

Figure 15-1   Some Types of Families

Nuclear	Compound	Extended
Mother, father, children (daughter and son)	Mother, father, their daughter and son, and father's daughter by a previous marriage ended by divorce	Mother, father, daughter, son, mother's widowed sister and her son, mother's widowed father, father's unmarried brother and parents

families include additional relatives such as grand-parents, aunts, uncles, or cousins.

The remaining two structures are variations on the nuclear family. **Single-parent** families are nuclear families with one parent absent. In **compound** families children are related to only one of the parents. When a divorced parent with children remarries, the resulting family—parent, children, and stepparent—constitutes a compound family.

Even when they are relatively small, compound families can have very complicated structures. Both wife and husband may bring to their new family children from prior marriages and then have children together. Compound families have the potential to include a variety of complicated relationships in which children have closer family ties to one parent than the other and, in the most complicated cases, other children have equally strong family ties to both parents.

Although these four structures describe families in most societies, there are other variations as well. In the Israeli kibbutz child care is the responsibility of adult females as a group; and yet, nuclear family ties exist within the larger structure and parents spend time with their children at the end of each day. Among Indonesia's Dani the family as an isolated social group barely exists at all; the community as a whole is the major focus of social life. Spouses, parents, and children spend relatively little time together, and children live with other relatives by the time they are ten years old (Heider, 1972).

Divisions of Labor and Role Structures

Biological reproduction, socialization, consumption, and the regulation of sexual behavior are the most important functions of families in all societies; and in nonindustrial societies, production is still a major family function. It is around such functions that family divisions of labor are organized.

In virtually all societies responsibility for child care falls almost exclusively on women; but women are also economically active in production. The "ideal" division of labor in the U.S.—women are confined to housework and child care and men are solely responsible for breadwinning—has not been achieved in any society, including our own.

In the U.S., 55 percent of married women were in the labor force in 1986, as were 54 percent of those with preschool children and 68 percent of those with

school-age children. Divorced mothers had the highest rate—fully 85 percent of those with school-age children (U.S. Census Bureau, 1986a).

In all societies, then, women contribute heavily to important family functions—reproduction, socialization, and production—while in almost all societies fathers focus most of their attention on production. This is true even in the Israeli kibbutz, for while child-rearing tasks are not the responsibility of each individual mother, child care and other domestic work are still defined as "women's work" (Lesser-Blumberg, 1983). Within this basic structure, however, there is much variation between and within societies.

Women in industrial societies are not only less likely to be economically active than are women in nonindustrial societies, but the higher their family's class position, the more likely it is that outsiders will be hired to perform housekeeping and child-rearing roles.

Child rearing, however, is a complex role, and families often assign different aspects of child rearing to mothers and fathers. In working-class families, mothers have primary responsibility for meeting children's emotional needs, while fathers generally play the role of punisher (LeMasters, 1975). Regardless of social class, fathers rarely participate in child care before their children are 18 months old (Entwistle and Doering, 1981); and while fathers are more likely to play with children than care for them, the pattern is the opposite for mothers (Lamb and Goldberg, 1982).

Divisions of labor are different in middle-class families, for both parents are expected to support their children emotionally. These variations reflect different child-rearing values. Middle-class families tend to stress children's emotional development, while working-class families are more concerned with obedience to authority.

Children are also part of family role structures. In nonindustrial societies, they play economic roles from an early age, whereas in industrial societies, they are usually confined to school and nonproductive household chores. Children in lower- and working-class families are far more likely than their middle- and upper-class counterparts to work in order to help support their families.

Patterns of Interaction

Like all groups, individual married couples and families develop their own patterns of interaction, but because each is part of a social institution, interactions in families often have similar structures. In the U.S., for example, nighttime is identified as the "appropriate" time for sex, in part because the structure of work in industrial society requires absence from the home during the day. This pattern may give rise to rigid expectations ("It's night; we're in bed; therefore we should make love") that can convert a natural pleasure into a burden.

In monogamous societies, frequent interaction between spouses affects their perceptions, values, and attitudes. As Berger and Kellner (1964) suggested, when marriage involves intense and relatively exclusive relationships between wives and husbands, spouses tend to adopt similar beliefs, values, and attitudes, even when they initially disagree. They may enter their marriage disagreeing about everything from politics to the likability of friends; but the longer they live together, the more similar their views become (see also Mirowsky and Ross, 1987).

This occurs for two reasons. First, we all depend on other people to confirm our perceptions of reality and support our values and attitudes, and we tend to depend on the people with whom we interact the most. In the U.S. in particular, when people marry they tend to focus their attention more on each other than on friends they had before marrying. Friends often perceive a husband and wife as a couple—not as two individuals—and no longer feel free to spend time with one without including the other. It is difficult to invite a married woman to a dinner party without including her husband. Cultural ideas about married couples help produce exclusive and intense interactions between husbands and wives.

Second, the stability of intense and exclusive marital relationships depends in large part on the *perception* of a strong common bond between husbands and wives. Constant disagreement produces a strain in relationships, and this encourages the creation of a "common ground" on which spouses can live together in relative peace.

Marital interactions are also affected by major structural characteristics of families. In matrilocal societies—where married couples join the wife's mother's household—the husband occupies the status of "outsider." This undermines his position in the family, contributes to his being left out of important interactions, and makes him vulnerable to coalitions formed against him by family "insiders." All these observations apply equally to wives in patrilocal societies.

Patterns of interaction in families are even more complex than between spouses. The presence of children makes married life far more complex and, in most cases, more difficult. Introducing children into a marriage tends to reduce interaction between spouses, increase the amount of conflict, tension, and nervousness, especially in relation to the division of labor within the family, and to decrease marital satisfaction (Glenn and McLanahan, 1983).

In nuclear families, where child care is the responsibility of the wife alone, children tend to interact far more with mothers than with fathers. In many cases mothers are children's only source of adult contact and, as a result, mothers frequently feel "overloaded" and children become heavily dependent on a single adult. This problem is especially acute in single-parent families—which made up 23 percent of all families with children under 18 in 1985—and affects both single mothers and single fathers (U.S. Census Bureau, 1986a).

Such patterns help explain why children often feel jealous of newborn babies with whom they must compete for the parent's attention. If the family structure includes more than one adult who is available to children, they are less likely to feel that the attention paid to newborns causes a loss of attention for them. In extended families the availability of several adults means that no one adult must bear the entire burden alone. This is also true of societies—the Dani of Indonesia and the Israeli kibbutz—in which entire communities share the responsibility of child care.

The structure of compound families can create very complex patterns of interaction (Cherlin and Furstenberg, 1983; Matilda Riley, 1983) and considerable stress and strain (White and Booth, 1985). Because children have a closer tie with a natural parent, they may form coalitions against the stepparent and defy a stepparent's authority ("You aren't my *real* mother"). Stepparents may feel left out of family jokes, secrets, and memories that were created before they joined the family, and often feel in competition with the natural parent who no longer lives with the children. One result of such complexity is greater strain in compound families, especially when both spouses are remarried and there are stepchildren. In these families, divorce is more likely, children tend to leave home at an earlier age, and spouses express less satisfaction with married life (White and Booth, 1985).

A large body of research (summarized in Hess, 1970) shows that family interactions vary a good deal among social classes. In general, the higher a family's social class position, the more likely parents are to talk with their children, reason with them, use complex language in talking to them, express warmth and affection, and avoid physical punishment. These social class differences in family interactions have been found in a variety of societies, and in the U.S. (Hess and Shipman, 1965; Kamii and Radin, 1967).

Power, Matriarchy, and Patriarchy

Who rules the family? In a **patriarchy** husbands are culturally defined as the heads of major institutions, including the family; in a **matriarchy** women dominate; and in **egalitarian marriages** power is shared equally between husbands and wives. In spite of variations among families, almost all existing societies are patriarchies. Even in matrilineal societies—the Trobriand Islanders—which trace kinship through the mother's family, family power structures are patriarchal. There is, in fact, some debate over whether or not there has ever been a society in which women held most of the power (Bamberger, 1974).

There is considerable doubt that any society has ever been truly matriarchal (Bamberger, 1974), but most archeological evidence suggests that for most of human history gender equality has been the rule. Patriarchy is barely five thousand years old, which is not as old as it may seem when we put in the context of upwards of two *million* years of human history (see Fisher, 1980; Lerner, 1986).

Although patriarchy describes family institutions in most societies, the distribution of power varies considerably among both societies and families. This depends on a variety of cultural and structural factors. The cultural valuing of egalitarian marriage tends to be stronger in the middle and upper classes than in the working and lower classes. This may be due in part to the fact the husbands in higher classes have more power outside the home than lower-class husbands do, and therefore have less need to use the family as a situation in which they can feel powerful. Although middle- and upper-class families tend to be more egalitarian, they are still patriarchal, and husbands generally control most important decisions, such as what kind of car to buy or where the family will live.

In all societies individuals' authority depends in part on their contribution to production, and this holds between husbands and wives. In the U.S., wives who work tend to have more power than wives who do

not; and the higher a wife's education or income is, the more power she tends to have in family decision making (Gillespie, 1971; Hood, 1983; see also Mirowsky, 1985).

Residence rules also affect authority relations in families (Warner et al., 1986). In a matrilocal society a husband's authority is undermined by the fact that his wife's kin can "gang up" on him. In patrilocal societies, however, the dominance of men is increased enormously by the wife's isolation from her family, and her greatest source of power is to leave the marriage and return to her parents' house. From this point of view, matrilocal residence supports egalitarian marriage by giving the wife more authority. Societies that allow married couples to freely choose where they will live also support equality by separating husbands and wives from their families.

Keep in mind that the concepts of matriarchy, patriarchy, and egalitarianism refer to cultural models of the family and prevailing patterns of authority, and although some women in patriarchal societies may be in charge of families, this does not mean that matriarchy prevails. If we describe single-parent families headed by divorced women as "matriarchal," we distort the basic meaning of matriarchy, for these women dominate by default, not because society defines women as the legitimate heads of families. Single-parent families headed by women deviate from the patriarchal ideal.

This distinction is important because single-parent families are increasingly common in the U.S., particularly among blacks. Without this distinction, we might conclude that black families are more matriarchal than white families simply because they are more likely to be headed by women. Among intact families, however, patriarchy prevails among both blacks and whites.

The preceding sections describe basic structural characteristics of families and how they affect relationships and interaction within families. As groups, however, families occupy positions in relation to their surrounding societies, and one of the most important of these is their position in systems of social stratification.

Family Wealth and Power in Stratified Societies

In hunter-gatherer and horticultural societies community life is organized around kinship ties, and the family is the most powerful institution. Even in agrarian societies political authority rests largely in family units. Industrial societies, however, are too large and complex to be dominated by even the largest kin group, and authority lies in institutions outside the family—in schools, government, courts, corporations, churches, and the professions. Legal norms prohibit preferential treatment for relatives in occupations and the legal system. Families, in short, are not powerful groups in industrial societies.

This does not mean that all families have equal amounts of power. Inequality of wealth and income among families is common, and wealth is a source of power. Engels (1891) went so far as to argue that the existence of family units in communities and societies is a basic cause of social stratification itself. It is only when families can accumulate wealth and have an interest in passing it on to their heirs that intense competition within societies comes into being.

The chapters in Part Four describe a variety of social statuses—race, ethnicity, gender, age, education, and occupation—that affect the distribution of income in stratified societies, and these characteristics affect inequality among families as much as they affect inequality among individuals. The structure of families, however, in addition to the statuses of their members, also affects the distribution of income.

In the U.S., family income is greatest in intact families (especially if both parents work) and single-parent families headed by men. Families with the lowest income are headed by unmarried women, a pattern that holds regardless of race (take a moment to study Table 15-1 carefully).

Clearly, families headed by unmarried women—whether divorced, single, or widowed—are in a poor economic position, especially if they are nonwhite. In comparison with intact families, families headed by white females are over four times as likely to live in poverty and over seven times as likely to depend on food stamps. These differences are less severe among blacks, primarily because they are crowded into a much narrower income range (U.S. Census Bureau, 1986a).

THE SOCIAL ECOLOGY OF FAMILY LIFE

The ecological perspective is basic to any study of marriage and family institutions since reproduction, production, and consumption are among their most important social functions.

Reproduction: Marriage, Family, and Society

In all societies, cultural and structural aspects of marriage and the family affect birth rates and population growth in several ways.

The more common marriage is and the younger the age at marriage, the higher birth rates tend to be. An estimated 44 percent of all African females 15 to 19 years old are married, and in countries of Western Africa the estimate is 70 percent. By comparison, less than 10 percent of U.S. and European females 15 to 19 years old are married (Population Reference Bureau, 1980; U.S. Census Bureau, 1986a).

Table 15-1

Median Family Income, by Race and Family Structure (United States, 1985)

FAMILY STRUCTURE	FAMILY INCOME			
	All Families	*Whites*	*Blacks*	*Hispanics*
Intact married couple	$31,100	$31,600	$24,600	$22,300
Wife works	$36,400	$36,900	$30,500	$28,100
Wife does not work	$24,600	$25,300	$15,100	$17,100
Male head—wife absent	$22,600	$24,200	$16,400	$19,800
Female head—husband absent	$13,600	$15,800	$ 9,300	$ 8,800

Source: U.S. Census Bureau, 1986a.

Birth rates also depend on the degree to which married couples limit childbearing. Contraception is used by 64 percent of married women in the U.S., and this results in longer periods between births and fewer births over the life cycle. Between 1955 and 1985, the birth rate among married women 20 to 24 years old dropped by 50 percent. The result has been a steady decline in the average size of families. Between 1967 and 1985 the percentage of women 30 to 34 years old who expect to have two or fewer children increased from 31 to 68 percent, and the percentage who expect to bear four or more children dropped from 55 percent to 10 (U.S. Census Bureau, 1986a).

While delayed marriage and childbearing are more common, men and women are more likely than before to live together without marrying and to have children without marrying. Between 1960 and 1985 the number of unmarried couples increased from just over 100,000 to almost 2 million (Glick and Norton, 1979; U.S. Census Bureau, 1986a). In the same period birth rates increased by 44 percent among unmarried women and doubled among unmarried teenagers, the latter increase being due largely to increased sexual activity and a failure to use effective contraception (U.S. Census Bureau, 1981; Zelnick and Kantner, 1976 and 1978). Although overall teenage pregnancy and birth rates began to drop in 1983, the rates for the U.S. are still higher than in many industrial societies (see Table 15-2). This results in part from a loss of control

by the institutions of marriage and the family over sexual behavior and reproduction, but it is also due to a failure to recognize how widespread teenage sexuality and the need for contraception and effective sex education are in the U.S. (see Guttmacher Institute, 1987; Maciak, 1987).

Changing values and norms about family life also affect birth rates (see Mason, 1982). Hindus in India's West Bengal prohibit sexual intercourse between husbands and wives for almost 100 days out of every year, and in some societies intercourse is forbidden for two or three years after childbirth (Nag, 1962, 1967). Before 1975, birth rates among American Catholics were higher than among non-Catholics primarily because Catholicism forbids the use of contraceptives and encourages childbearing. Since 1975, however, Catholics have increasingly ignored the ban on contraceptive use and abortion, and their birth rates are virtually equal to those of other major religious groups (GSS, 1987; Westoff and Jones, 1979).

Finally, family size is strongly related to the nonfamily statuses that wives and mothers occupy. In nonindustrial and industrial societies women who work outside the home tend to have fewer children than women who do not, especially if their work is highly paid (Weller, 1977; Weller and Bouvier, 1981). In addition, the more highly educated women are, the fewer children they tend to have. Education lowers fertility not only by increasing the chances that women will work outside the home, but also by delaying the entry of women into marriage and increasing the chances that they will never marry (Kammeyer and Ginn, 1986).

While the institutions of marriage and the family affect birth rates and population growth, changing birth rates, death rates, and age structures also have important effects on individual families and the institution of the family.

Birth Rates, Death Rates, and the Structure of Family Life

As birth and death rates fall and families grow smaller and people live longer, the structure of the family tends to change. In colonial America the average married woman bore an estimated eight children during a lifetime that, by current standards, was short (Grabill, Kiser, and Whelpton, 1959). Each woman could expect to have few years during which she was not pregnant or responsible for young children.

Table 15-2

Teenage Pregnancy and Birth Rates[1] in Industrial Societies, 1981

COUNTRY	PREGNANCY RATE	BIRTH RATE
United States	96	53
England/Wales	45	29
Canada	44	26
France	43	23
Sweden	35	14
Netherlands	14	9

[1] Number of pregnancies and number of births per 1,000 females 15–19 years old.

Source: Alan Guttmacher Institute, 1987.

By comparison, average lifetime fertility among married women is now just over two children, and life expectancy is far higher than it was in colonial times. This means that married women spend a relatively small portion of their lives bearing and caring for children. By the time most married women reach their early thirties, their children are in school, and these mothers have an average of 43 more years of life ahead of them (U.S. Census Bureau, 1986a).

These population changes encourage women to work outside the home, especially in career occupations that require years of training and involve steady advancement. This, in turn, breaks the monopoly that husbands have had over the breadwinner role ever since the Industrial Revolution separated the family—and mothers—from production. As women increase their share of earning power, they also tend to increase their prestige and power in marriages and families.

Falling birth rates have had the additional effect of decreasing the number of relatives people have. As children, today's elderly had an average of 5 siblings, 20 uncles and aunts, and perhaps as many as 40 cousins. Children born in the last decade, however, have on the average less than half that number of relatives with whom they can form close ties (Bane, 1976). As the number of kinship ties falls, so does the importance of extended kinship networks in everyday life.

The potential effects of declining birth rates on kinship systems is particularly startling in the case of China whose government, as we saw in Chapter 5, is trying to limit each family to just one child. If this plan succeeded for many generations, the result would be a family system in which there literally would be no siblings, aunts, or uncles (Kertzer, in Riley, 1987). Given the importance of family ties in traditional Chinese society, it is difficult to imagine how deeply such a change might affect the richness of family life.

Technology, Production, and Families

Social institutions change in response to changes in population and ecological arrangements. The family is certainly no exception, for it has changed dramatically over the last few centuries in response to industrialization, population growth, and urbanization.

With small populations and a relatively simple division of labor, hunter-gatherer and horticultural societies organize social life almost exclusively around kinship ties (Coon, 1971; Service, 1966). Production, education, religion, law, and government all revolve around kinship groups. The extended family is the source of individual rights, responsibilities, and social identities, and marriage is based more on economic and political considerations than on individual preferences.

The larger and more complex agricultural societies, however, include a variety of kinship groups, none of which can dominate all aspects of social life. Even here, though, family membership is closely related to wealth and political power, for some families monopolize political offices that are inherited.

As recently as the turn of the century, there were many areas of the U.S. in which women spent much of their lives bearing children, as did this mother of nine in rural Tifton, Georgia in 1909.

The Industrial Revolution rapidly accelerated a process that began centuries before: kinship ties were losing their importance as families lost control over societies. This ecological change affected families in important ways and continues to affect them in societies that are beginning to industrialize today.

As production shifts to factories and relies on more sophisticated technology, child labor loses its value and large families become a liability. Birth rates began a steady decline in Europe in the early 1800s and somewhat later in the U.S.—well over a century before the invention of effective contraceptives. Thompson and Whelpton (1933) estimated that the U.S. birth rate was 55 births per 1,000 people at the end of the eighteenth century, but by 1900 it had fallen to 30 per 1,000 (Weller and Bouvier, 1981).

Unlike hunter-gatherer and horticultural societies, industrial societies are dominated by secondary relationships and formal bureaucracies, and many of the functions once performed by the family have been transferred to other social institutions. Responsibility for education shifts to schools; wealth and power depend more on individual performance and characteristics than on family ties. While discrimination in favor of relatives in politics and employment is expected in preindustrial societies, it is commonly outlawed (although not unknown) in industrial societies.

As vital social functions are transferred from the family to other institutions, the importance of economics and politics in the formation of marriages declines. This is one reason why romantic love is far more important in industrial than in preindustrial societies (Goode, 1959). As a basis for marriage, romantic love allows people to separate from the families they grew up in. Young people no longer have to wait to inherit the positions held by their elders, and can escape parental authority at a relatively early age (Cherlin, 1981). Romantic love also promises to provide the emotional support once provided by extended families, and encourages people to marry in societies in which marriage is no longer required to preserve the power of kinship groups.

The extended family's loss of control over marriage increases the power of women. In agrarian societies, women were property to be exchanged by families for economic and political gain. In industrial societies, however, women are freer to choose their own husbands and have more bargaining power in the "marriage market."

Industrialization also creates social conditions in which the importance of nuclear families increases at the expense of extended families (Goode, 1963). Industrial societies need workers who can move from one place to another as new industries are built, and the loose ties of nuclear families to relatives increases geographic mobility. Industries also need people who are willing to be *socially* mobile—who will break away from the lower-class occupations of their parents and strive for middle-class jobs.

Finally, industrialization and the rise of the nuclear family affect the division of labor within families. Among Alaskan Eskimos and the Gusii of Kenya women work in or near their homes and strap their infants to their backs while they work (Montagu, 1971; Whiting, 1963). In industrial societies, however, the separation of production and the home makes it diffi-

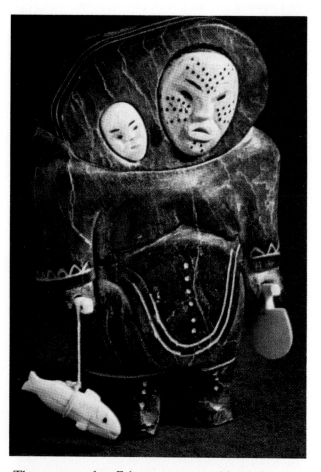

This carving of an Eskimo woman and her baby portrays what was a universal aspect of family life for almost all of human history prior to industrialization. She carries a knife in one hand and a fish in another, showing that production and reproduction were not mutually exclusive activities.

cult for both parents to work (Cherlin, 1983). As a result, child care and production are more specialized in industrial than in preindustrial societies: child care is almost the exclusive province of women, and men tend to be the primary breadwinners.

Over a period of many centuries, then, the family has been dramatically transformed from an extended kinship network that dominated social life to a relatively small primary group whose most important functions are to meet the emotional needs of its members, care for young children, and regulate sexual behavior. The powerful extended family of preindustrial societies has been largely replaced by a variety of social institutions. Families, however, are not isolated groups insulated from the outside world. They are a vital part of the social environment, charged with the responsibility for reproducing that environment in new generations. As such, they affect and are affected by surrounding social institutions.

MARRIAGE, FAMILY, AND SOCIETY

As institutions, marriage and the family are defined by the social functions they perform. This does not mean, however, that the characteristics of families always have functional consequences. Nor does it mean that conflict does not exist, both within families and between them and other institutions.

Functions and Dysfunctions

While marriage and the family are defined in terms of major functions discussed earlier in this chapter, particular cultural and structural aspects of family life—incest taboos and marriage rules—can also be looked at from this perspective (Mead, 1968).

Incest taboos draw boundaries that distinguish close kin from everyone else and promote family stability by preventing hostility and jealousy among family members. They help keep family structures unambiguous and clear, and this minimizes status strain. If a mother and son had a daughter, the son would be the newborn's father and her brother. By forcing people to look outside the family for sexual partners, incest taboos also encourage social ties between families and the growth and solidarity of larger kinship networks and communities.

Incest taboos are related to rules of exogamy that require people to marry outside their group, and exogamy performs an important function for communities.

Among hunter-gatherers marriage between people of different communities helps establish cooperative political and economic ties (Service, 1962).

Endogamous marriage can also be functional because by restricting marriage to group members outside the immediate family, it keeps group boundaries clear and helps maintain group solidarity. Endogamy among Orthodox Jews helps ensure the perpetuation of their religious and cultural traditions and strengthens the in-group loyalties that support them against anti-Semitism. Ironically, Nazi Germany also imposed endogamous marriage to isolate Jews from the rest of German society.

The dysfunctions of some family characteristics illustrate again that all social arrangements have costs as well as benefits. The nuclear family is by definition isolated from extended kinship networks, and this means that its members depend on relatively few people for emotional and material support. If a spouse dies in an extended family, other adults are available to assume important roles, but in nuclear families the absence of a spouse through death or divorce can cause a major crisis that threatens the survival of the family itself.

Extreme interdependency among nuclear family members may create severe emotional strain. We spend most of our lives in secondary relationships and often rely on the family as our main source of emotional support. This makes nuclear families particularly vulnerable to emotional overload, and the intensity of family relationships may breed hostility and bitterness as well as love (A. Skolnick, 1975).

The structure of the nuclear family—unlike that of the extended family—excludes the elderly from meaningful roles, and this is dysfunctional for the well-being of the elderly and for society. Thousands of widowed, elderly parents spend their last years alone or in institutions, and even those who join their children's nuclear families often have no meaningful part to play in family life. In Japan, however, the extended family is more common, and not only provides meaningful roles for the elderly, but also supports women working outside the home by providing child care (Morgan and Hirosima, 1983).

Although the nuclear family has many functional consequences in industrial societies, it brings with it social costs. Its structure contributes to family vulnerability, instability, and strain, and leaves elderly people in a "roleless" position. Like all social structures, its form produces both positive and negative consequences.

The Conflict Perspective on Marriage and the Family

From a conflict perspective, social institutions like the family are arenas in which struggles for wealth, power, and prestige take place. Conflict takes place both within marriages and families and between them and society, and is related to the social characteristics of institutions in different societies and historical periods.

In lower- and middle-class families relationships among family members are strongly affected by the family's position in relation to economic institutions. In industrial societies workers have little control over work conditions that often have negative effects on family life. Many industries operate 24 hours a day. Although this increases industrial efficiency and profits, it creates severe strains on the families of both blue- and white-collar workers (Lipset, Trow, and Coleman, 1956; Rowbotham, 1973). Working spouses often must be away from their families during the night, and repeated changes in work shift assignments subject individuals to a variety of negative effects, such as insomnia and chronic fatigue.

Work conditions also affect families in the middle and upper-middle classes. Managers are under intense pressure to care more about their jobs than their families, and because their jobs often take them away from home, they must choose between family life and the rewards of their occupations (Pleck, 1977). Given the emotional needs that nuclear families are expected to satisfy, it is easy to see how industrial economies create strains within families by calling upon workers to neglect their families in the name of supporting them.

A more important effect of economic institutions on marriages and families comes from the structure of the economy itself. In industrial societies, families do not produce what they consume and must sell their labor power for money they can exchange for goods and services. Families, however, do not receive a substantial portion of what is produced by their members' labor power—a large percentage is kept as profit in capitalist societies or is appropriated by the state in socialist societies. The resulting strain on families is inevitable, for workers are paid less to make a product than it costs to buy it. One result of this is that most families have a hard time making ends meet and must depend on the earnings of both spouses. In 1890, only 14 percent of all women in the labor force were married. In 1986, 55 percent of women in the labor force were married, and 55 percent of these were mothers (U.S. Census Bureau, 1975a, 1986a).

Most of what is produced in industrial societies—food, clothing, appliances, housing, and medical care—is consumed by families. This means that the stress and strain that workers experience is inevitably reflected in the families that depend on their occupational success (Rubin, 1976). In a study of urban husbands and wives, Blood and Wolfe (1960) found that disagreements about money made up 42 percent of marital disputes, while sex, in-laws, religion, politics, and family roles together accounted for only 22 percent.

It should not surprise us to find that marital and financial instability go together. Goode (1976) estimated that marriages involving service workers and laborers are twice as likely to be unstable as are those involving professional and technical workers, differences which are found in many industrial societies (Goode, 1962).

It is ironic that the family's most important function as an institution is to reproduce the very society that often has negative effects on families (Landes, 1977–1978). Families are not simply isolated groups that are affected by social conditions. Whether they live in Manhattan or Moscow, parents who raise children to obey authorities and be "good workers" reproduce not only people, but the social relationships that create and sustain social inequality. In turn, they also help reproduce and perpetuate the stressful conditions under which their children will, themselves, marry and raise families. In this way, the victims of social inequality are expected by their society to perpetuate the social conditions that victimize them and their children.

FAMILY DISORGANIZATION

A group is organized if all its statuses are occupied by people who adequately perform their roles. A nuclear family is organized if it includes a mother and father and children, all of whom perform their roles. **Family disorganization** occurs when a status is unoccupied or when one or more members fail to perform their roles. It is of interest to sociologists because it affects a family's ability to perform important social functions and because it affects the lives of family members.

Structural incompleteness takes a variety of forms, the most common of which is separation of spouses through divorce. It also occurs, however, when women have children without marrying at all or when a spouse dies. Inadequate role performance also takes many forms—from mental or physical breakdowns or unemployment to an "empty shell" family in which members go through the motions of task roles while ignoring the emotional roles that make up the core of primary relationships (Goode, 1976).

Divorce was outlawed in Catholic Europe during the Middle Ages and in Puritan New England, and most family disorganization was caused by the death of a spouse (Stephens, 1963). In mid-eighteenth-century Sweden, roughly half of all marriages ended because a spouse died, as did approximately 60 percent of marriages in France and 70 percent in India (Lenski and Lenski, 1982).

As death rates fell over the past century, divorce became the major form of family disorganization. Between 1860 and 1984 the divorce rate in the U.S. increased from 1.2 per 1,000 married couples to 23.1 per 1,000—a nineteen-fold increase (Thornton and Freedman, 1983; U.S. Census Bureau, 1975a, 1986a). In 1987, 34 percent of those who had ever been married had also experienced a divorce or legal separation (Davis and Smith, 1987), and an estimated 50 percent of recent marriages will end in divorce if current rates continue (Weed, 1982).

Understanding Divorce

Sociological reseach has much to say about trends in divorce rates. Once again, the explanation rests on the key sociological concepts of culture, social structure, and ecology.

Divorce and Culture   Just as cultural beliefs, values, norms, and attitudes affect the organization of marriages and families, so, too, do they affect their disorganization. As one would expect, divorce rates tend to be highest where norms restrict it the least and where values and attitudes place little stigma on divorced people.

Socially legitimate grounds for divorce vary enormously among cultures (Stephens, 1963). Stinginess and laziness are grounds among the Hopi Indians, and the Iban of Borneo may divorce if they see a bad omen or have an ominous dream. In patrilocal societies the husband's parents can initiate divorce by sending his wife home if they do not like her. Divorce rates in nineteenth-century Japan were very high for this reason (Goode, 1976).

In some societies—such as the Navaho Indians—divorce involves no elaborate ceremonies (Stephens, 1963). In pre-Civil War New England, however, married couples could not divorce without a special act of the state legislature (Goode, 1976). Divorce rates in the U.S. have risen as the legal grounds for divorce have expanded and become less specific. In the nineteenth century the only grounds were desertion, adultery, and physical abuse, but since then "abuse" has been expanded to include mental cruelty, and the new grounds of incompatibility include virtually any behavior that one spouse dislikes in the other (Bane, 1976). Almost half of all the states now have "no-fault" laws that allow couples to divorce without proving that either spouse was guilty of misbehavior.

Divorce has also been made easier by changing values about marriage, the family, and happiness. In societies that base marriage and the family primarily on economics and alliances between kinship groups, the fact that spouses are unhappy with each other is relatively unimportant. In the U.S., however, marriage is valued primarily as a relationship that satisfies emotional needs, and when these are not met divorce is defined as a legitimate solution (see Thornton and Freedman, 1982).

As values and norms about divorce have changed, so, too, have attitudes. It was not that long ago that no divorced person could run for the office of president and win; but that changed with the election of Ronald Reagan. Until the 1960s most looked on divorce as a shameful admission of failure, and divorced women were assumed to be "loose," "wild," and promiscuous. These stigmas have lost most of their importance.

Divorce and Social Structure   The structural causes of rising divorce rates take three forms: the changing relationship of married couples to kinship networks, the changing structure of families, and increased visibility of divorced people.

First, the more people a marriage involves, the higher the pressures are against divorce. Among the Subanum in the Philippines, marriage is an economic exchange between two families, including a "bride-price" paid by the groom's family to the bride's. If couples divorce and the wife is found to be at fault, her family must repay up to twice the bride-price to the husband's family and turn over the children and most of the couple's property to them. Among the Navaho, marriage joins two kinship networks and divorce threatens to disrupt important social ties (Stephens, 1963). In such cases extended families often oppose divorce because they stand to lose a great deal. In industrial societies, however, extended families lose relatively little when couples divorce and so offer less opposition.

The isolation of nuclear families from extended kin also makes divorce more likely by increasing the emotional and financial insecurity of married couples. In prerevolutionary China, the relationship between spouses was less important than the contribution of each to the extended family, and spouses depended on a large set of family relationships to satisfy their needs (Goode, 1976). Married couples in industrial societies, however, are both more independent and more isolated: spouses depend on each other to satisfy their needs, and in times of stress they can count on relatively little support from kinship networks.

Paradoxically, the increased importance of the nuclear family has contributed to higher divorce rates in some societies and lower divorce rates in others. In Japan divorce rates fell as parents-in-law lost the power to send their daughters-in-law home. In the U.S., where in-laws never had that power, the isolation of nuclear families has had just the opposite effect on divorce rates.

A second structural cause of rising divorce rates is the changing structure of the nuclear family and its relationship with the economy. In extended families production is shared among many adults, and divorce has little effect on either spouse's ability to survive. Each can simply return to the extended family from which they came. Divorce in nuclear families, however, threatens the financial security of both spouses (but particularly of wives). Divorce rates normally drop during economic depressions, because most couples cannot afford to separate (Jacobson, 1959).

Divorce rates increase as wives work outside the home more and become financially independent of their husbands (South, 1985). When both spouses are heavily committed to demanding jobs, conflicts inevitably occur around the performance of domestic work, and although many couples succeed in creating marriages that are more egalitarian, it is, at best, difficult (see Kingston and Nock, 1987).

Husbands who earn less than their wives often feel threatened. If one spouse wants to take a job in a distant city, the other must choose whether to move at the expense of an existing job. In some cases, husbands and wives decide to live in different places—maintaining a "commuter marriage"—in order to keep their relationship intact while pursuing their occupational goals (Gerstel, 1976; Gross, 1980). How the stability of such marriages compares with that of other marriages is yet to be seen.

Family finances and economic relationships between husbands and wives help explain historical changes in social class differences in divorce rates. In the nineteenth century, when divorce was expensive and difficult to obtain, it was more common in the upper class than in the middle and lower classes (Bane, 1976). Since that time, however, legal costs have dropped sharply and are within the reach of many more lower- and middle-class couples, and divorce is now more common among lower-class couples than among those in the upper class.

As divorce has become more accessible, other legal changes encourage upper-middle and upper-class couples to stay together. In particular, community property laws force divorcing couples to split their property evenly, and wealthier couples often own valuable assets such as stock and real estate. This means that both spouses—but husbands in particular—have a great deal to lose in a divorce and may stay with an otherwise unattractive marriage.

The third structural change that helps explain rising divorce rates is the sheer increase in the number—and therefore the visibility—of divorced people. When divorce was rare, people who contemplated it correctly believed that divorce would place them in a small, deviant minority. Their only reference group consisted of married couples, and they got little support for the decision to end a marriage.

As more and more people occupy the status of "divorced person," however, divorced people are increasingly visible to married people who contemplate divorce, and this provides unhappy spouses with a new reference group on which they can model their behavior and from which they can draw emotional support and social approval (see Thornton, 1985).

Divorce, Population, and Ecology   Changes in population and ecology have contributed to rising divorce rates by making divorce easier and by making lifelong marriage harder.

When nuclear families produced most of what they needed, each spouse needed the other to perform important productive work. Prior to the late 1800s most U.S. families lived on farms, and it took at least two adults working together to produce enough to support them. A man who divorced his wife lost far more than a companion, for he also lost a producer of a variety of essential goods.

By shifting production out of the home, industrialization creates economies in which people work for money that they use to buy what other people produce. This means, in turn, that wives and husbands can survive by their own labor, and this weakens the economic dependency of spouses on each other. As their dependency on each other lessens, so does the material cost of divorce.

Population trends also affect divorce rates by making lifelong marriage more difficult. In the eighteenth century, adult death rates were relatively high—especially among women of childbearing age—and people rarely spent their entire lives with a single spouse. High death rates contributed to relatively low divorce rates by ending marriages before the need for divorce ever arose. Death rates have fallen sharply over the last century, however, and this means that people who married in their early twenties could look forward to roughly 50 years of married life (U.S.

Census Bureau, 1986a). This inevitably increases the chance that divorce will occur, because it is simply much harder to spend 50 years with one person than it is to live together for 10 or 20 years.

Population changes, therefore, have made "'Til death do us part" an increasingly difficult ideal to achieve.

Family Violence

One of the most important functions of families is to provide a safe haven for its members. The U.S. Constitution protects our homes from unlawful intrusions. Families, we believe, should be safe, and for this reason family violence is particularly disturbing—and difficult to control.

Straus, Gelles, and Steinmetz (1980) conservatively estimated that 8 million Americans are assaulted by family members each year. Violence occurs in one out of four marriages. Rape occurs in at least one out of ten. At least half of all adolescents and as many as 1.5 million younger children are the victims of parental violence. As many as 2.5 million elderly family members are abused each year (Gelles and Cornell, 1985; see also Straus and Gelles, 1986; Pagelow, 1984). Sixteen percent of all murder victims are killed by members of their own family (FBI, 1987).

These data paint a picture of family life that is a far cry from our cultural ideal of harmony and love. From a sociological perspective, however, the level of violence in families comes as no great surprise. Why?

In industrial societies, in which long lives are becoming the rule rather than the exception, "'Til death do us part" is an increasingly difficult commitment to honor, although not, apparently, for this Swedish couple.

Ecology and Family Violence   Interpersonal violence depends on people being physically close, and the nuclear family brings a small group of people into close and frequent interaction. Physical proximity is just as necessary for hitting another person as it is for hugging.

The chance of violence is also increased by the isolation of the nuclear family, since outsiders cannot see what goes on inside the home. The less publicly visible our behavior is, the more likely we are to commit deviant acts.

Violence and Social Structure   Ironically, the very fact that the ideal nuclear family functions as a "haven in a heartless world" (Lasch, 1977) increases the chances for violence. Most families have difficulty satisfying all their members' needs. The extreme emotional and material dependency of nuclear family members on one another inevitably creates some tension, anger, and bitterness because many family decisions—such as how to spend money—cannot satisfy everyone (Gelles, 1972; Shupe et al., 1987) (see One Step Further 15-1).

Defining the family as a haven also supports violence because the family becomes the only place in which we feel free to "let off steam." You pay a much higher price if you punch your boss than you do if you punch your spouse, because your boss has far fewer reasons to tolerate such behavior. As Coser (1956) put it, the nuclear family is a "safety-valve institution," and this makes it conducive to violence. In general, the more stress a family undergoes—financial worry, trouble at work, legal problems, prolonged illness, or death of someone close—the more violence there is, especially towards children (Straus et al., 1980).

Because the family and its home are valued as private places, public officials are reluctant to intervene in what is culturally defined as a "family affair" (Berk and Loseke, 1981; Pagelow, 1984). This insulates family members from standards of behavior that prevail in the outside world and makes violence more likely to occur (Sherman and Berk, 1984; Berk and Newton, 1985).

Structural distributions of power in patriarchal families also contribute to violence by making women and children highly vulnerable (Dobash and Dobash, 1979; Klein, 1982). Children are generally powerless to leave abusive families, and wives often find themselves in the same position because they cannot support their children and themselves with their own earnings.

ONE STEP FURTHER 15-1:
Patriarchy, Power, and Family Violence

The tensions that inevitably arise in family life are most conducive to violence when power is unequally distributed between husbands and wives, especially in patriarchal homes in which the husband dominates. If we look at violence against wives in Figure B-15-1, the most violent homes are those in which husbands dominate (the right side of the graph), followed by those dominated by wives (the left side of the graph). The least violent homes are those in which husbands and wives share equally in power and neither dominates (the center of the graph). Child abuse is also more frequent in families with unequal distributions of power (Straus et al., 1980). Why do you suppose this would be true?

Figure B-15-1

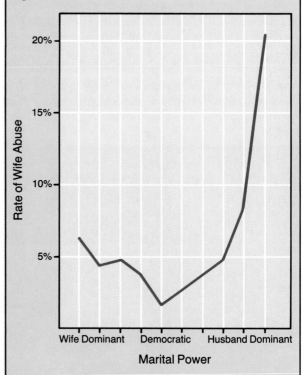

Source: Adapted from Straus, Gelles, and Steinmetz, 1980.

Culture and Family Violence   Although our culture includes a disapproval of family violence, it also contains ideas that support it. Most parents regard the physical punishment of children as both legitimate and necessary and rarely define it as violence (Gelles, 1972).

Our norms often allow behavior within families that would not be tolerated among nonfamily members. Parents may slap children who refuse to eat their vegetables and the police will not intervene; but they risk punishment for criminal assault if they slap restaurant customers who do not eat their vegetables. The social sanctions are quite different in these two situations, even though in both cases the violent behavior might be defended as "for the victim's own good."

In a majority of states, a husband may force his wife to have sex with him by threatening violence if she refuses; but the same behavior toward any other woman is legally punishable as rape. How do we live with such contradictory norms? One way is to use cultural beliefs to define many physically violent acts as "nonviolent." In general, we do not define an injurious act as violent if the act is permitted or required by a social role. A national study of men in the U.S. found that most do not define the killing of a criminal by police as violence (Blumenthal et al., 1972), and most parents do not define spanking a child as a violent act, because they regard it as a necessary part of their role (Gelles, 1972). From this perspective, family violence is often neither defined nor treated by outsiders as such because family roles condone violence within limits that are always subject to interpretation.

Culture, social structure, and ecology help explain many aspects of family disorganization. As disorganization becomes more visible in families, however, we must confront issues about the future of the family that have disturbed many people for a number of years: Is the family as an institution in danger? Can it be destroyed?

FAMILIES AND SOCIAL CHANGE

Like all groups, families change in response to changes in their social and physical environments; but unlike most other groups, change is an inevitable part of family life. Membership in families spans the entire life course, and as individuals inevitably age, their families must also change (Boss, 1980).

In families with young children, socialization, protection of the young, and children's obedience to their parents are highly valued, and family norms support those values. Interaction is frequent because they live in the same household, and power is unequally divided between parents and children and between husbands and wives.

When children reach adulthood, however, family culture and structure change dramatically. Children are expected to make their own decisions, and parents lose much of their authority along with their socializing roles. Interaction drops sharply as children move away from home; and as parents enter old age, inequality between them lessens, particularly when the husband was once the primary breadwinner. In many societies family changes over the life course are not as dramatic as they are in the U.S. In patrilocal and matrilocal societies newlyweds live with their in-laws, and adult children have far less autonomy.

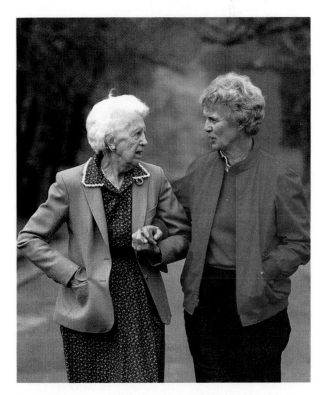

As parents age, parent–child roles are often reversed as children assume the responsibility of caretaker. As this picture of mother and daughter suggests, daughters are more likely than sons to take this role, in part because tending to the personal needs of others is culturally associated with the female gender role.

Our concern in the following sections, however, is less with such internal changes than with changes in the family as an institution. What kinds of changes are taking place in the cultural ideas and social structures that define and regulate marriage, divorce, and family relationships? What is the future of the family as an institution?

Cultural Change and the Family

Some of the most profound cultural changes during the last few decades focus on marriage and divorce. One of the most important social functions of marriage is the regulation of sexual behavior, and in the U.S. we increasingly support values that promote sexual unions between unmarried people. Between 1960 and 1986, the percentage of adults who believed that premarital sex is always or almost always wrong dropped from 80 to 29 percent (Davis and Smith, 1977, 1987).

We are also increasingly tolerant of interracial marriage. Between 1972 and 1987 the percentage of adults who favor laws prohibiting interracial marriage dropped from 38 to 23 percent. Disapproval of homosexual unions, however, has remained virtually unchanged over the last ten years. In 1987, 78 percent of U.S. adults believed that homosexual relationships between adults are always or almost always wrong (Davis and Smith, 1987).

Values and norms about relationships within marriages and families are also changing. Marriage has always been a contract relationship—the moment we say "I do," we enter into a culturally defined set of rights, obligations, and expectations that are not explicitly stated in marriage ceremonies. Increasingly, however, couples are basing marriage on written contracts that specify the spouses' expectations of each other—sometimes including details about who does which domestic tasks (Weitzman, 1981).

Both the surge of women into the labor force and the women's movement have contributed to a shift toward egalitarian values in some middle- and upper-class marriages. As wives become financially independent, the tendency toward equality is inevitable, and husbands have less and less choice about whether or not they will share in household tasks.

Values about adultery have remained unchanged since 1973; and in 1987, 89 percent of all adults disapproved of it. Perhaps in reaction to the fact that divorce has become easier to obtain and no longer carries the stigma it did 20 or 30 years ago, a slim majority believe that it should become *harder* to obtain (Davis and Smith, 1987).

Changing values also affect the composition of families. Although the value of large families has declined sharply, other values have changed in ways that may increase the size of households. Between 1973 and 1987, for example, the percentage of adults who believe that it is a good idea for elderly people to share a home with their grown children increased from 31 to 50 percent (Davis and Smith, 1987).

What do all these statistics tell us about the U.S. family? As a set, they seem to describe changes that go in more than one direction. We are more tolerant of premarital sex, but oppose adultery; divorce is easier to obtain, but a majority would make it harder. In an important sense, such patterns of change in our most important social institutions are just what we should expect.

In a changing society, marriage and the family inevitably reflect those changes since they are the focal point of most people's lives. Nevertheless, because marriage and the family are so important to us as individuals, we tend to resist change in the interests of stability and continuity. When it comes to changing major institutions, in other words, we tend to be cautious. A liberal attitude toward change in some areas is often balanced by conservative attitudes toward change in others.

Shifting Structures

In the U.S., the composition of families is the most visible change in family structure. Adults are less likely to live in nuclear families and families are becoming smaller, less likely to be headed by a married couple, and more likely to include nonrelatives.

Between 1960 and 1985 the percentage living in families dropped from 93 to 88 percent. At the same time, the number of people living alone almost tripled to 21 million and more than quadrupled to 8 million among those under 45 years old. In the last ten years, the number of households whose members are unrelated to one another—including unmarried couples—tripled to 24 million, while the number of families rose by only 39 percent (U.S. Census Bureau, 1986a).

These numbers suggest that we are experimenting with alternatives to the nuclear family. For many unmarried couples, living together is a new form of courtship that may lead to formal marriage (Tanfer,

1987)—a pattern that exists in a number of societies, including Poland and, especially, Sweden (Popenoe, 1987). It is possible, however, that a growing minority in the U.S. is reluctant to take on the burdens and restrictions of marriage and parenting, and although more than 90 percent of young people say they intend to marry, that figure may come down in the future (Thornton and Freedman, 1982) (see Table 15-3).

What about the structure of families themselves? How are they changing? (Before you read on, take a moment to study Table 15-4, p. 428, carefully.)

Between 1960 and 1985 average family size dropped by 11 percent among whites and 18 percent among blacks. Although the nuclear family headed by a married couple is still the most common family structure, it is losing ground. Between 1960 and 1985 the percentage of families headed by a divorced, separated, or single mother increased by 44 percent among whites and 100 percent among blacks.

As a result, a growing percentage of children are living in single-parent families, and, as a result, in poverty (McLanahan, 1985). Between 1960 and 1985 the percentage of all children living with both parents dropped from 89 to 74 percent, and to less than half among black children. Since 1970, single-parent families headed by women who have never married have also become more common. The percentage of all children living in such families was seven times greater in 1985 than in 1970, and among whites, ten times greater. Hofferth (1985) projects that 70 percent of white children and 94 percent of black children born in 1980 will spend at least part of their childhood with one parent.

The compound family is another structure that is becoming increasingly common in the U.S. In 1981, roughly half of all marriages were a remarriage for at least one of the spouses (U.S. NCHS., 1985). A sixth of all children were living in compound families and there were 2.3 million households with stepchildren (Cherlin and McCarthy, 1985).

The nuclear family is also changing by becoming more extended in some ways and less extended in others. A **subfamily** is a family that lives in the household of another family, and subfamilies can be either related or unrelated to the host family. Between 1960 and 1980 the number of related subfamilies dropped by 26 percent, indicating a decline in extended family networks. By 1986, however, the number of related subfamilies had climbed by 96 percent to its highest level since 1950. At the same time, the number of

Table 15-3

Nonmarital Cohabitation among Never-Married Women, 20–29 Years Old (United States, 1983)

As you can see, although there are no substantial racial differences among the percentage of women who are currently or have ever lived with a man, there are sharp differences by education and religion. Cohabitation is strongly related to lower levels of education and to expressing no religious preference (but note there is no difference between Catholics and nonCatholics).

SOCIAL CHARACTERISTICS	CURRENTLY COHABITING OR EVER COHABITED	
	Current	Ever
Race		
Black	10%	29%
White	13%	30%
Education		
Less than high school graduate	23%	46%
High school diploma	15%	36%
More than high school	9%	22%
Religion		
Catholic	11%	29%
NonCatholic	12%	28%
None	15%	48%

Source: Tanfer, 1987, Table 1.

unrelated subfamilies more than doubled. In addition, the number of unrelated individuals in family households almost tripled (U.S. Census Bureau, 1986a). In addition to subfamilies, there has also been a recent trend towards single young adult children returning to live with their parents, often because of difficult times brought on by unemployment or divorce (see Glick and Lin, 1986).

The United States has never been a society in which most households included extended families (Demos, 1986; Thornton and Freedman, 1983), and although the importance of kinship seems to be declining as increasing numbers of adults live by them-

Table 15-4

The Changing Composition of American Families, by Race, 1960 to 1985

FAMILY STRUCTURE	ALL FAMILIES		WHITES		BLACKS		HISPANICS
	1960	1985	1960	1985	1960	1985	1985
Average family size	3.7	3.2	3.6	3.2	4.4	3.6	3.9
Percentage of Families with:							
Married couple	87	80	89	84	74	51	72
Female head	10	16	9	13	22	44	23
Percentage of All Children Who Live with:							
Both parents	89	74	92	80	69	40	72
Mother only	8	21	6	16	21	51	25
Percentage of All Children Who Live with:							
Single mothers[1]	0.8	5.6	0.2	2.1	4.4	24.8	6.5

[1]Single means never married, children are those under 18 years old, and figures are for 1970 and 1985.

Source: U.S. Census Bureau, 1986a.

selves, families also seem to be expanding their households by including nonrelatives. This trend is paralleled by the increased number of nonfamily households in which unrelated adults live together and share expenses and housework. We seem, in short, to be trying out a number of ways of meeting our needs for companionship and financial and emotional security. The fact that we are less likely to live with extended kin does not mean that we have become a nation of "loners" and isolated nuclear families.

Families Come and Families Go, but The Family Is Here to Stay

Fear that the family is "falling apart" is nothing new in our history (see Demos, 1986). The historical durability of the family as an institution suggests that in spite of high divorce rates and a growing minority of young people who postpone marriage or forgo it altogether, the family will always be a part of society. We end marriages in record numbers, but we also remarry in record numbers (see Glick and Lin, 1986; Norton and Moorman, 1987). Although many grow disillusioned with particular marriages, or delay marrying,

there is little evidence that marriage itself is losing its appeal.

Both historical and cross-cultural variations in marriage and family highlight the fact that social institutions are defined by the functions they perform, not by particular cultural and structural arrangements. From this perspective, institutions may change structurally or culturally; but they "die" only if other institutions take over their functions or the functions themselves lose their social importance.

Many functions of the family have been taken over in part by other institutions such as schools, but there is no society in which the family does not exist in some form. Even the Soviet Union—which tried to replace the family with schools and day-care centers in the years following the Russian Revolution—returned to the family as the primary group in which children are cared for and socialized.

The family as we know it is changing and will most certainly continue to change; but primary groups in which people are born and grow up, and which meet their needs for emotional support and a sense of continuity in their lives are, as Bane (1976) put it, "here to stay."

SUMMARY

1. An institution is a social "blueprint" for groups. The family as an institution is not the same as your family or mine.

2. Marriage is a socially supported union between individuals in what is intended to be a stable, enduring relationship that involves sexual interaction. It is the basis for the family, an institution defined by six social functions: regulation of sexual behavior, reproduction, nurturance and protection of children, socialization, production and consumption, and the passing on of ascribed statuses such as race.

3. Marriage and the family rest on many beliefs, the most important of which is kinship. Matrilineal societies trace descent through the mother's blood relatives, whereas patrilineal societies trace descent through the father's. In bilateral societies descent is traced through the relatives of both parents.

4. Among the most important values and attitudes in marriage and the family are those focusing on the basis for marriage (such as love or economic exchange), sexual experience before and during marriage, and the relative importance of family ties and those with outsiders.

5. Marriage rules limit whom people may marry, when, and under what conditions. Incest rules prohibit marriage between kin; rules of exogamy require marriage outside the group; and rules of endogamy require marriage within it. Marriage rules define the acceptability of multiple spouses (polygamy), whether it be multiple wives (polygyny) or husbands (polyandry). In matrilocal societies married couples must live with the wife's family, whereas in patrilocal societies they live with the husband's. In bilocal societies couples must choose between the two. In neolocal societies, couples live wherever they want.

6. Families have a variety of structures, from the nuclear family consisting of parents and children, to extended families that include additional relatives, single-parent families, and compound families that include children from other marriages.

7. In all societies women are the primary caretakers of children, but they also participate in production. The more industrial a society is, the less likely women are to be economically active.

8. Patterns of interaction in families depend on the structure of family institutions. The intensity of monogamy encourages couples to reach agreement on important views.

9. Most societies are patriarchies, and no known societies have been matriarchies. Egalitarian marriages are increasingly common in industrial societies.

10. The characteristics of families strongly affect birth rates. The younger the age at which people marry the higher birth rates tend to be. Changes in birth rates, in turn, affect family structure. Compared with colonial women, women in the 1980s bear far fewer children and are more likely to work outside the home.

11. The way in which goods are produced in a society affects the power of family groups and the ways in which families are organized. In industrial societies, many of the functions once performed by the family have been transferred to other institutions.

12. The functional perspective identifies functional and dysfunctional consequences associated with different aspects of family organization. A conflict perspective shows how the interests of individual families and economic and political institutions clash.

13. Family disorganization occurs when statuses are not occupied or roles are not performed. Divorce, death, and violence—themselves caused by social and ecological factors—are major causes of family disorganization.

14. As an institution, the U.S. family has undergone a variety of cultural and structural changes, particularly as families adjust to changes in the economy and the roles of men and women.

KEY TERMS

bilateral descent   406
egalitarian marriage   414
family   404

> extended   411
> nuclear   411

>> compound   412
>> single-parent   412

> subfamily   427

family disorganization   420
kinship   405
marriage   403
marriage rules   409

> bilocal   409
> endogamy   409
> exogamy   409
> matrilocal   409
> monogamy   409
> neolocal   410
> patrilocal   409
> polyandry   409
> polygamy   409
> polygyny   409

matriarchy   414
matrilineal descent   406
patriarchy   414
patrilineal descent   406

Looking Elsewhere

Having studied Chapter 15, you might want to look at related discussions in *Human Arrangements*, which include

- sexual values and norms (Chapter 3, pp. 66–67, 72–73)
- socialization in families (Chapter 6, p. 150)
- marital rape (Chapter 7, pp. 168–69)
- family divisions of labor and gender inequality (Chapter 13, pp. 353, 362–65, 367, 369, 370–71)
- patriarchy, matriarchy, and gender inequality (Chapter 13, pp. 357–58)
- socialization, families, and gender roles (Chapter 13, pp. 359–60)
- learning to be spouses and parents (Chapter 6, pp. 154–55)
- age and changing patterns of family interaction (Chapter 14, pp. 384–85)
- social causes and consequences of fertility (Chapter 5, pp. 104–106)
- the effects of greater longevity on family life (Chapter 17, p. 481)
- conflict between families and schools (Chapter 16, p. 449)

RECOMMENDED READINGS

Demos, J. (1986). *Past, present, and personal: The family and the life course in American history*. New York: Basic Books. A fascinating history that shows not only the changes that have taken place in family life, but the remarkable durability of this vital institution.

Gelles, R. V., and Cornell, C. P. (1985). *Intimate violence in families*. Beverly Hills, CA: Sage. A recent summary of what is known about violence in U.S. families.

Goode, W. J. (1976). Family disorganization. In R. K. Merton and R. Nisbet (Eds.), *Contemporary social problems*. New York: Harcourt Brace Jovanovich. A useful sociological overview of family disorganization.

Hood, J. C. (1983). *Becoming a two-job family*. New York: Praeger. An in-depth study of 16 married couples in which both spouses work. Hood sheds light on a number of important issues, including the effects of a wife's work status and earnings on her power in the family and the ways in which spouses negotiate domestic responsibilities. See also Lein, L. (1984). *Families without villains: American families in an era of change*. Lexington, MA: D. C. Heath.

Journal of Marriage and the Family. Minneapolis, MN: National Council on Family Relations. The leading scholarly journal that focuses on marriage and the family.

KORBIN, J. E. (Ed.). (1983). *Child abuse and neglect: Cross-cultural perspectives*. Berkeley: University of California Press. A collection of papers that includes a disturbing study that finds that behaviors such as child abuse are more common in "developed" societies than in what many people think of as "primitive" societies.

SPIRO, M., and SPIRO, A. G. (1975). *Children of the kibbutz: A study in child training and personality*. Cambridge, MA: Harvard University Press. An analysis of the effects of a radically different approach to family life on the development of children.

STAINES, G. L., and PLECK, J. H. (1983). *The impact of work schedules on the family*. Ann Arbor: University of Michigan Press. A clearly written, interesting study that shows how work schedules for both men and women affect the feelings and behavior of family members.

School as a Social Institution
A Short Social History of Schools

Cultural Variations
Beliefs

Values

Norms

Attitudes

The Importance of Subcultures

Cultural Lessons in the Hidden Curriculum

Varieties of Social Structure
Boundaries

Patterns of Interaction

Complexity and Role Structures: The School as Bureaucracy

Distributions of Power

The Social Ecology of Schools
Population and the Business of Schooling

Segregation and Learning

Technology, Production, and Schools

Schools and Other Institutions
Schools and Families

The Social Economics of Schooling

Politics, Schools, and Nationalism

Schools and Social Conflict: Class and Classrooms
Inequality and the Hidden Curriculum

Opportunity and Outcome

Schools and Social Change
Changing Schools

Money and the Quality of Education

16 Education

Students often describe everything outside of schools as the "real world." "School," they say, "isn't part of the real world. It's just a place I have to go if I want to get a decent job. *Real* life doesn't begin until after graduation." They could not be more mistaken. Few social institutions mirror the social environment as faithfully as schools do, and that so many students are unaware of this fact gives schools enormous power and influence in their lives.

What are schools and how do their cultural, structural, and ecological characteristics define them as social institutions? How are they related to other institutions, such as the family, religion, the economy, and the state? In what ways are they functional and dysfunctional, and what part do they play in social inequality? These are the kinds of questions that this chapter will try to answer.

SCHOOL AS A SOCIAL INSTITUTION

All societies socialize their members to perform adult roles. In hunter-gatherer and horticultural societies, children learn informally from the adults who happen to be around them. They learn the same way in agricultural societies, but because skills are more specialized and the division of labor is more complex, some children are apprenticed to adults—such as carpenters and blacksmiths—and also learn through on-the-job training.

Training in industrial societies, however, is too complex to be left to informal relationships, and families do not have the resources to prepare their children for adult roles. As a result, children spend large portions of their childhood in **schools**—formal organizations whose main purpose is to educate people. From this perspective, **education** is a special form of socialization, which involves the systematic, formal trans-

In hunter-gatherer societies, such as that of the American Sioux Indians, it was possible for children to acquire all the adult skills they would need through informal instruction from adults. This boy learns to use a bow and arrow by shooting first at stationary targets and then at small game.

mission of skills, knowledge, and other aspects of a society's culture.

A Short Social History of Schools

Schools have existed for centuries, but until the late nineteenth century they were restricted largely to the children of elite families. The ancient Chinese used schools to train government officials, just as medieval Europeans used them to train priests. In Victorian

In many societies, scholarly learning has been a key to high prestige. This was especially true in China where, as recently as the turn of this century, scholars commanded far greater respect than millionaires. In this detail from an eleventh-century scroll, a scholar composes a poem.

As the Industrial Revolution took hold in the nineteenth century, the upper class monopoly over formal schooling began to loosen. Social life became more bureaucratic and rational, and the demand for training in specialized skills—from typing and filing documents to operating telegraphs, engineering, and managing complex business organizations—grew rapidly (Trow, 1961). Examinations and grades were used to certify competence. Education as a symbol of "cultured," elite status was gradually replaced by education as a means for producing a large number of workers with a wide range of skills (Weber, 1946).

In addition to a skilled work force, industrialists wanted "good" workers whose values and attitudes served the interests of employers and helped increase production (see Carnoy and Levin, 1985). Horace Mann—one of the strongest early supporters of public education—won the support of manufacturers by promising that educated workers would be "docile and quick to apply themselves to work," disciplined, punctual, and loyal (Mann, 1842).

By the 1850s every state supported public education. Between 1870 and 1900 the number of high schools grew from 160 to more than 6,000, and the percentage of young adults with high school diplomas more than tripled. By 1985, 86 percent of those 25 to 29 years old were high school graduates, and illiteracy had dropped from 11 percent of the population in 1900 to less than 1 percent (U.S. Census Bureau, 1975a, 1986a).

Colleges and graduate schools grew more slowly than public high schools, primarily because few families could afford to send their children to college, and higher education was widely perceived as a luxury until well into the twentieth century. In fact, around 1900, popular books giving advice on "success" generally told their readers that college was a waste of time for all but the wealthy, who did not have to worry about making a living (Huber, 1971).

Although the dramatic rise of schooling resulted largely from the Industrial Revolution, other factors also played a part. Nations used schools to instill patriotism and national solidarity ("I pledge allegiance to the flag . . ."). In the late 1800s and early 1900s the U.S. was flooded with immigrants, and schools were used to assimilate them into Anglo culture.

Over the last century education has also been perceived as the major source of upward mobility, an escape route leading out of poverty into the middle class. By the late 1970s—in sharp contrast to the early

England, elite private schools trained future high-level government officials and business leaders (Wilkinson, 1964), and this is still true today. In 1977, 86 percent of all senior officials in the Foreign Office (the British counterpart of the U.S. State Department) were graduates of just two elite colleges—Oxford and Cambridge (Sampson, 1983). Similar patterns are found in the U.S. in relation to elite prep schools and Ivy League colleges (see Cookson and Persell, 1985).

Education not only prepared the elite for prestigious and powerful occupations; it set them apart symbolically from the classes below them. The ability to read and write, or to speak Latin and Greek, was a cultural indicator of "high breeding" and superiority. Schooling was a major way for members of the upper class to prepare their children to be defined and treated as members of the upper class.

1900s—79 percent of parents said they would like their children to go beyond high school, and 36 percent of all adults rated college education as "very important." Most significant, the perceived importance of college is highest among people who are at the *bottom* of the stratification system—nonwhites and those with relatively low incomes and educations (U.S. Census Bureau, 1975a).

Whether or not such perceptions of education are accurate, one thing is certain: institutionalized learning affects not only societies, but the lives of millions of people. Given this, we need to understand how schools work—how cultural, structural, and ecological factors affect what goes on in them—as well as how schools affect and are affected by the social environments in which they exist. The next three sections analyze the characteristics of schools. Then, we take a broader perspective and examine the relationships between educational and other institutions and the effects of education on social inequality.

CULTURAL VARIATIONS

Like other institutions, schools rest on a foundation of cultural ideas. To understand what people do in schools, we first have to understand how people use culture to think about schools and about what goes on in them.

Beliefs

The most fundamental belief that underlies schooling in the U.S. is that in order to learn what we need to know as adults, someone must decide what it is that we need to know and then teach it to us. From the earliest grades, most students and teachers share the belief that teachers know what is true and students do not. It is not surprising that college students seldom challenge their teachers—even when they believe their teachers are wrong.

A second important belief is that knowledge is the key to individual happiness and the solution to social problems. Jefferson argued that a healthy democracy depends on a well-educated public capable of making critical, independent decisions about social issues and government. Half of U.S. adults believe that blacks and other minorities are relatively poor because they "don't have the chance for the education it takes to rise out of poverty" (Davis and Smith, 1987), a belief that, as we will see later in this chapter, is largely untrue.

A third belief underlying schooling is that tests and grades accurately measure mental abilities and how much students learn. Most research shows, however, that this is at best only partly true. Standardized tests—such as IQ tests and college SATs—have come under heavy criticism for being biased in favor of white middle- and upper-class students. Tests depend

DOONESBURY

by Garry Trudeau

sured by tests whose questions usually have only one correct answer. In addition to learning facts, such learning contains a hidden cultural lesson: all questions have a single correct answer, and that is what the teacher is looking for (Holt, 1964). Students are taught to *know* answers, not to search for them, and to value questions that have one correct answer.

When students enter college, they are often disturbed when professors ask questions that have more than one correct answer ("How can nuclear war be prevented? What is the poet trying to say in this poem?"). All of us know the uneasy silence that sometimes comes over a class when this kind of question is asked, the fear of being called on, the frantic search for the "right" answer somewhere in the readings, and the wondering, "Will this be on the exam?"

The hidden curriculum contains many such lessons (Gracey, 1972b; Holt, 1972). Even in kindergarten, children learn to value punctuality and being "good." They learn to value themselves according to their performance and their ability to compete, and to value an "expert's" judgments more than their own. Whether they personally want to do something is no longer important.

Minority students often learn to devalue their own subculture and replace it with the culture of the white, middle-class. At home Puerto Rican children learn that it is impolite to look directly into an adult's eyes; but their middle-class, white teachers often interpret—and punish—such behavior as "shifty" and untrustworthy. Until the late 1960s, the Spanish language was forbidden by law in Texas schools, and Mexican-American children were often punished—

sometimes by having to kneel and beg forgiveness—for saying a Spanish word (Silberman, 1971).

School norms emphasize order, obedience, and uniformity; and a student's reward is usually gained at the expense of others (Henry, 1963). In elementary classrooms, when one student cannot answer a question, the others often hold their hands high in the air, straining for the teacher's attention (Henry, 1963). Students are also encouraged to adopt attitudes of cheerful, willing acceptance of authority—to do what they are told to do until they are told to stop, without complaining or questioning.

As we will see later in this chapter, the importance of such hidden cultural lessons extends far beyond schools, for they play a major part in the perpetuation of social inequality.

VARIETIES OF SOCIAL STRUCTURE

Like all organizations, schools are held together by social relationships, and to understand schools from a sociological perspective, we need to take a detailed look at their structural characteristics.

Boundaries

Organizational boundaries vary in their clarity and in how open they are. Of these two characteristics, the degree of openness of school boundaries is far more important, for schools control the distribution of knowledge and skills as well as the credentials for jobs. Prior to the mid-nineteenth century, virtually all

In Japan, competition for acceptance to universities is so fierce that many students offer prayers to a Shinto guardian of studies. If they are successful, they write a note of thanks and place it at a religious shrine, as this student is doing in Tokyo.

schools were privately owned and reserved for the children—especially sons—of wealthy families. As recently as 1985, only a third of all U.S. high school graduates went on to college (U.S. Census Bureau, 1986a). In most other societies, higher education is even more restricted. In Britain, Japan, Switzerland, and France competition for college entrance is fierce, and only an elite few go beyond secondary school (Eurich, 1981).

Public education made elementary and secondary education available to most in the U.S., but "white" schools excluded blacks until the 1954 Supreme Court decision outlawed separate schools for whites and blacks (Ravitch, 1983). Until quite recently, women were largely excluded from professional education in law, medicine, business, engineering, and science.

Boundaries become more closed with each additional level beyond high school, owing primarily to competition for limited places and the high cost of college and professional education. This, in turn, affects the racial and class composition of college enrollments. As Table 16-1 shows, white male high school graduates are considerably more likely than comparable blacks to go to college, and enrollment increases steadily with each rise in family income (although the effect of income is less pronounced among blacks than among whites).

The exclusiveness of higher education has been lessened by the enormous growth of two-year junior colleges—especially the relatively inexpensive community colleges. Between 1960 and 1984, the number of junior colleges more than doubled; enrollments increased by ten times; and the number of part-time college students grew at a rate 55 percent higher than the number of full-time students (U.S. Census Bureau, 1986a).

Junior college students differ sharply from those in four-year colleges. They are more likely to be black, twice as likely to be married, are generally older, and most are employed. The rapid growth of alternatives to four-year colleges has opened up higher education for social categories that were generally excluded in the past, and almost half of all junior college graduates eventually transfer to four-year schools (AACJC, 1977).

Patterns of Interaction

Like other organizations, schools produce patterns of interaction among students, teachers, and administrators. In most classrooms the teacher is the focus of all

Table 16-1

College Enrollment among Those 18 to 24 Years Old, by Sex and Race and by Family Income (United States, 1985)

RACE AND SEX[1]	PERCENTAGE ENROLLED
White males	37
White females	34
Black males	28
Black females	25

RACE AND FAMILY INCOME[2]	
Whites	
Under $10,000	16
$10,000–$19,999	24
$20,000–$29,999	35
$30,000–$39,999	44
$40,000–$49,999	50
$50,000 or more	54
Blacks	
Under $10,000	12
$10,000–$19,999	24
$20,000–$29,999	23
$30,000–$39,999	38
$40,000–$49,999	39
$50,000 or more	*

[1]For sex and race, figures are percentages of high school graduates who are enrolled in college.
[2]Figures are percentages of all those 18 to 24 years old.
*Too few cases for accurate estimate.

Source: U.S. Census Bureau, 1986a.

interaction. Students speak only when asked and are generally forbidden to communicate with one another. This pattern is reinforced by physical arrangements in which students sit in fixed chairs facing the front of the room while teachers are free either to face the entire class or walk about and monitor student behavior.

Some schools have "open" classrooms in which students are allowed to move about the room and interact with one another more freely (Silberman, 1971). Open classrooms were introduced to encourage autonomy, initiative, and creativity, but they also tend the number of teachers more than tripled, the number of principals and administrators increased more than sevenfold (U.S. Census Bureau, 1975a, 1982, 1986a).

The transformation of schools closely paralleled a trend toward bureaucracy that was occurring throughout the U.S. Business leaders dominated school boards and evaluated schools with the same standards of efficiency and productivity they applied to business: How many math problems do students solve per hour? How many students graduate each year, and what does it cost per student? As Callahan (1962) put it:

> They saw schools not as centers of learning, but as enterprises which were functionally efficient if the students went through without failing and received their diplomas on schedule and if the operations were handled economically. (p. 247)

The signs of bureaucracy are found everywhere in schools. Public school teachers must be certified by state agencies. Formal records are kept not only on student behavior and performance but on teachers. Relationships between teachers, students, and administrators are clearly defined by school norms, as are those between administrators and outside authorities such as school boards, boards of trustees, and, in public institutions, state legislatures. Look at any college's "Student Handbook," and you will quickly see how many areas of student life are explicitly regulated by institutional norms.

College students are assigned identification numbers, and in many classes enrollments are so high that teachers do not know which student names go with which faces. Students are judged by their performance on tests that ignore individual needs and abilities, for attention to individuals is almost impossible under such circumstances. In many courses, students never meet their professors face-to-face, and when they need help, they turn to graduate students who run study sessions. Students have good reason to often feel lost in the crowd, because in today's bureaucratic schools, they often are.

In bureaucracies attention is on the organization as a whole rather than on individuals. The negative effect of this on educational goals is clear in the practice of **social promotion**, through which students who have not mastered the skills of the current grade are nevertheless sent to the next higher grade. Part of this is undoubtedly due to the desire of many teachers to spare students the humiliation of repeating a grade. We also have to remember, however, that one function

of schools is to produce graduates, and if large numbers of students are not promoted, the school's efficiency and productivity appear to decline.

How does this affect educational goals? In 1977, 40 percent of high school juniors in Florida failed a functional literacy test that included such questions as:

1. Joe gave a clerk a dollar for two dime candy bars and a nickel for a package of gum. If the tax was one penny, what change should he get back?

2. You want to call Mr. Jones on the telephone. You look in the telephone book for his number. You would find it between which names?
   A. Jackson and Jacobs
   B. James and Johnson
   C. Johnson and Judson
   D. Judson and Justus

In 1977 a 19-year-old sued a New York State school district for "educational malpractice," because although he was a high school graduate, he could not read above the fourth grade level (Hentoff, 1977). In 1979 the Carnegie Foundation's nationwide study found that 20 percent of high school graduates lacked basic skills in language and mathematics. In addition, the national average score on college entrance examinations has been declining steadily for over a decade, and in 1983 the National Commission on Excellence in Education concluded that a "tide of mediocrity" has seriously damaged education in America.

The negative effects of social promotion are most glaring among minority students. In 1975, one out of every five 17-year-old students in inner-city schools could not read a newspaper or the directions on a can of food (NAEP, 1977). While many may feel tempted to blame the students involved, such explanations ignore the fact that they were promoted in spite of the fact that they had not mastered basic skills.

It would be a gross oversimplification to suggest that bureaucratic structure is responsible for the decline of learning in U.S. schools. It is apparent, however, that the educational needs of many students have been ignored by an institution that serves several interests—including providing jobs for teachers and administrators—and that like all bureaucracies, schools may neglect individuals within them while perpetuating the organization itself (see Baldridge and Deal, 1983).

Distributions of Power

As institutions, schools are tied to the surrounding society. This means that power is distributed within schools and between them and other institutions. Whether or not they are structured as bureaucracies, most schools rely on highly unequal distributions of power, with students placed at the bottom. Distributions of power vary substantially, however, from one level of schooling to another.

In public elementary and secondary schools, administrators have power over teachers, teaching methods, and curriculum, and students have little power in relation to anyone but their peers. To some degree, however, the power of administrators over teachers is balanced by the fact that most public school teachers belong to labor unions that can use strikes to protect their interests.

In colleges and universities, the distribution of power is more complex. In many colleges, the administration controls the flow of money, which, in turn, allows it to affect the resources available to academic departments. Unlike public school teachers, college faculties generally control what goes on in classrooms—the kinds of courses that are taught and standards for grading—and play the most important role in deciding who will be hired, fired, or promoted.

In other ways, however, professors have less power than public school teachers. While most public school teachers belong to organized unions, professors often depend solely on the support of their own departments, which may consist of only a few members. Because faculty power generally lies in departments rather than the faculty as a whole, the administration can often overcome opposition because the faculty does not speak or act as an organized group.

The power of college faculties is also weakened by conflicting values and internal divisions of power. Senior, tenured members have a great deal of power over the careers of junior members, for promotions and tenure depend primarily on their recommendations. Heads of academic departments are almost always tenured professors, and the interests of senior members often conflict with those of junior members. Tenured professors do not have to worry about job security and may value the long-term survival of their departments more than anything else. Junior members, however, often have young families and must worry about their individual futures. When a college administration suggests saving money by cutting the size of the faculty, junior members are the ones most likely to lose their jobs. Tenured members, on the other hand, are less affected since the department can

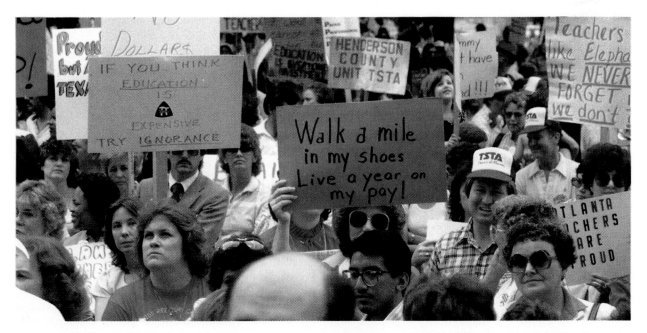

The complexity of today's schools is reflected in the many conflicting interests of the people involved—from parents, who argue about what should be taught, to teachers, who are among the lowest paid of all professionals.

still survive, and it is through departments that they exercise much of their power.

THE SOCIAL ECOLOGY OF SCHOOLS

Schools exist primarily for socialization, and this means that the demand for schooling depends on the number of young people in a population. In addition, the existence of schools depends on material resources, for schools are expensive, and if children are in school, they are not available for productive work.

Population and the Business of Schooling

In societies that use schools for education, when birth rates increase, so does the demand for schooling. Before reading on, take a moment to study Table 16-2, which shows how enrollment at the elementary, high school, and college levels has changed.

Enrollment in elementary school was stable until the effects of the post–World War II Baby Boom were felt in the 1950s and enrollment jumped by almost 50 percent. In the next decade it rose by only 14 percent, because the Baby Boom was winding down; and in the last decade, enrollment has actually declined as birth rates have fallen.

High school enrollment jumped by almost 50 percent in the 1950s and by another 50 percent in the

Table 16-2

School Enrollment (1,000s) by Level of Schooling (United States, 1930–85)

| | LEVEL OF SCHOOLING | | |
YEAR	ELEMENTARY	HIGH SCHOOL	COLLEGE
1985	30,936	13,741	12,247
1980	31,666	14,652	12,097
1970	34,190	14,418	7,136
1960	30,119	9,600	3,126
1950	21,033	6,453	2,281
1940	20,466	7,130	1,494
1930	22,954	4,811	1,101

Source: U.S. Bureau of the Census, 1975a, 1986a.

1960s; but it barely grew at all in the 1970s, and began to fall in the 1980s. Notice that enrollment began to fall earlier in elementary schools than in high schools. This occurs because high school students are older, and it takes longer for falling birth rates to affect the number of teenagers.

College enrollment rose sharply in the late 1940s because government benefits under the GI Bill allowed many returning World War II veterans to afford a college education. As the economy boomed and a college degree became an important factor in the job market, enrollment continued to climb in the 1950s and 1960s, and as the Baby Boom generations reached college age, enrollment rose sharply through the 1970s and continues to rise in the 1980s, although more slowly.

In spite of the importance attached to a college degree, falling birth rates may cause college enrollment to decline in the next 20 years. This is not inevitable, however, because there is already some evidence that although the number of people 18 to 23 years old is declining, the age structure of the college population is shifting upward. A large percentage of students in junior and community colleges, for example, are more than 21 years old (AACJC, 1977). Large numbers of married women are returning to school in order to improve their chances in the job market. Thus, while the age group traditionally served by colleges is shrinking, older students may make up the difference.

Why are these trends important? One answer is that education is the biggest business in the U.S. Over 5 million people earned a living by working in schools in 1985, and many more—from book publishers to construction workers—benefit from a large school population. The rapid increase in the student population over the last 30 years caused a dramatic increase in the number of teachers, and as the school population shrinks, thousands lose their jobs (U.S. Census Bureau, 1986a).

College faculties more than doubled in size between 1960 and 1975, and tenure was relatively easy to achieve. After 1975, however, college faculties barely grew at all, but the percentage having tenure did—to 66 percent in 1985 (U.S. Census Bureau, 1986a). If the number of college professors remains stable, the percentage with tenure will remain high, and the prospects for those without tenure will be grim regardless of their qualifications. There is "no room at the top," and many professors have been forced to change careers or wander from one part-time job to another (Abel, 1984).

Segregation and Learning

When public schools were first introduced in the U.S. on a massive scale at the end of the nineteenth century, blacks were largely excluded, either by law or because they had to work (Beale, 1975). In the early 1900s public education was available to most blacks, but the distribution of funds clearly favored whites. In one Southern county, expenditures per child in white schools were 33 times greater than in schools attended by blacks (Nasaw, 1979).

In 1954 the Supreme Court's landmark decision ruled that separate schools for blacks were inherently unequal, and the Court ordered an end to segregation "with all deliberate speed" (Ravitch, 1983). More than 30 years later, blacks and whites still attend schools that are predominantly of one race. As of 1976 full racial integration would have required the reassignment of 52 percent of all students (Wurdock and Farley, 1979).

In Chapter 12 we discussed the causes of racial segregation; but here we are concerned with its effects on students. It has long been noted that average scores on standardized tests are lower among blacks than among whites. Does segregation help explain this difference? Do blacks achieve higher scores in integrated schools?

At the request of the U.S. Civil Rights Commission, James Coleman and his colleagues conducted a survey of 570,000 students and 60,000 teachers in 4,000 public schools (Coleman et al., 1966). They expected to find lower quality in predominantly black schools than in predominantly white schools: older buildings, fewer library and science facilities, less qualified teachers, larger classes, fewer textbooks, and poorer funding. They were surprised, however, to find little difference between them. Average test scores for blacks were 15 points lower than for whites, and 84 percent of black students scored below the median score for whites; but Coleman also found that his measures of school quality explained little of the racial difference in achievement.

The factor that had the greatest impact on scores was social class. Regardless of race, students from middle-class families score higher than lower-class students. Most important, when students attend schools with students from a lower class than their own, their test scores suffer. When they attend schools with students primarily from higher social classes than their own, their scores tend to increase. Lower-class blacks who attend black schools whose students are mostly middle-class do better than lower-class blacks who go to school with other lower-class blacks. Coleman concluded that blacks generally score lower than whites because they are more likely to come from the lower class *and* attend school with other lower-class children.

Coleman's findings laid the groundwork for racial integration, and a number of later studies showed that, under the right circumstances, integration increases the average score of blacks by 2 to 3 points (Jencks, 1972). Notice, however, that most of the racial difference remains. It is apparent from these studies that changing the racial mix of student populations has only a limited effect on racial differences in educational achievement. As we will see later, this has important implications for ending racial inequality in our society as a whole.

Technology, Production, and Schools

In the U.S., more than 97 percent of those 5 to 17 years old were enrolled in school in 1985, and less than 1 percent over the age of 15 were illiterate. In many countries, however, illiteracy is common and only a small fraction of young people attend school. More than half of the populations of Africa and South Asia are illiterate, and in Ethiopia, Afghanistan, Saudi Arabia, and other countries, over 80 percent are illiterate (U.S. Census Bureau, 1986a).

A major reason for such wide variations in education and literacy is that formal schooling is expensive. It not only takes an enormous investment in buildings, teachers, and equipment, but also requires that young people spend their time away from productive labor. Most societies simply cannot afford to formally educate their young on the scale found in the United States.

If all the money spent on education in the U.S. in 1986 were equally distributed, it would amount to $1,080 for every woman, man, and child. For many countries, however, this level of spending would exhaust the entire national income: more than half of all the people in the world live in countries whose total per capita income is less than $400, a figure just under the U.S. per capita expenditure on higher education alone (U.S. Census Bureau, 1986a).

In countries such as India, the great expense of schooling means that the vast majority of the population is excluded from all but the most elementary form of training.

Take a moment to study Figure 16-1, which shows the relationship between per capita income and secondary school enrollment for a number of countries, each of which is represented by a dot. Note that most countries are clustered in the lower left-hand corner, with very low per capita income and secondary school enrollment. Most important is the fact that these countries contain almost three-quarters of the world's population, while the "educational elite" countries contain only 17 percent. The distribution of formal education among societies is just as unequal as the distribution of wealth and income.

While literacy and elementary education are nearly universal in industrial societies, secondary education is not. In the U.S. and Japan, over 72 percent of all those 15 to 19 years old are full-time students; but in France and West Germany, the figure is only 51 percent, and in Great Britain, only 44 percent (U.S. Census Bureau, 1980b).

The staggering expense of institutionalized learning raises serious questions about education and economic development in underdeveloped countries. Although universal literacy is relatively easy to achieve, it may be that our model of education with its heavy emphasis on advanced training beyond the elementary school level will be beyond the means of most of the world's population for a long time to come.

SCHOOLS AND OTHER INSTITUTIONS

As an institution, the school does not exist in a vacuum. It is connected to other institutions—the

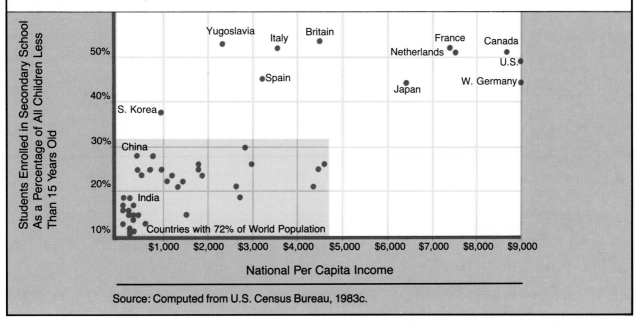

Figure 16-1   Secondary School Enrollment by Per Capita Income, Selected Countries

The wealthier a society is, the more likely it is to have a high proportion of young people enrolled in secondary school. There are no countries with low income and high enrollment (upper-left section) or with high income and low enrollment (lower-right section).

Source: Computed from U.S. Census Bureau, 1983c.

economy, the family, and the state—in ways that affect schools.

Schools and Families

Latent consequences of compulsory schooling affect families in a variety of ways. By acting as "baby-sitters," schools make it easier for both parents to work outside the home. In their role as socializers, schools relieve parents of much of the burden of preparing their children for adult work roles. In many schools, the food provided is cheaper and better than what is available at home.

While transfers of family functions to schools make life easier for parents in many ways, they also create problems. As responsibility for socialization shifts to schools, so does power over children. Before education became compulsory, families had greater control over socialization and could pass on subcultures to their children. Many advocates of public schooling, however, saw the family's influence as dysfunctional for social progress and wanted to use schools to break the family's hold on children, to replace "old-fashioned" ideas of many ethnic immi-

grants with the "modern" ideas of dominant groups (Lasch, 1977).

In many ways, parents feel threatened by schools, not because schools have so much power, but because they separate children from the family and give parents little control over what their children do all day long. In his study of high schools, Coleman (1961) found that students valued pleasing their friends almost as much as pleasing their parents. As we saw earlier, schools have played a major role in the creation of adolescent peer groups and subcultures, and it is in response to peer pressures that young people often have their first exposure to alcohol, drugs, cigarettes, and sex. As responsibility for children has shifted away from families, parents must compete with the formal and hidden curricula of schools and with the strong influence of student peer groups.

The Social Economics of Schooling

School and economy are related in several important ways. Because schools delay the entry of young people into the labor market, they help minimize competition for jobs. In 1985 there were 115 million people in the

U.S. labor force, of whom over 8 million were unemployed. Almost 27 million people were enrolled in high schools and colleges (U.S. Census Bureau, 1986a). If all those students suddenly entered the labor force, the number of unemployed could more than quadruple.

By evaluating and sorting students according to ability, schools also help determine which jobs students will qualify for as adults. As early as 1908, many educators shared the view of the president of Harvard who believed that schools "ought to sort the pupils and sort them by their evident or probable destinies" (in Nasaw, 1979, p. 138). Many U.S. and European schools assign students to "tracks." In Swiss schools, children are assigned to one of three tracks after four years of primary education. The lowest achievers finish primary school and then learn a manual trade; the middle group goes on to high school and trains for jobs in business and management. Only the highest track leads to college and graduate education and work in the professions, universities, and leadership in business and government.

Because schools do not produce a product that they sell in the market, they are not self-supporting; public schools must depend on tax revenues, local school boards, and state and federal governments for funding. When the economy is in a slump, schools are often among the first institutions to feel the effects as teachers are laid off and programs are cut.

The dependence of schools on outside support makes them vulnerable, for if they displease their supporters, they may lose the funds they need to operate. During the 1960s the University of California had a running battle with Governor Ronald Reagan, who disapproved of student demonstrations against the war and student demands for greater control over the university. One of his major weapons in that struggle was his influence over the state budget.

Finally, schools are connected to the economy because they are *part* of it. Most public school teachers belong to unions whose interests may conflict with educational goals. The National Commission on Excellence in Education (1983) recommended merit pay for teachers and regular evaluation of teacher performance. The American Federation of Teachers, however, opposed merit pay because it would weaken the union's bargaining position; it also believed teacher evaluation would undermine job security.

Even college professors have unionized on some campuses in order to protect job security and pay levels—even though professors traditionally look upon unions as being inappropriate for middle-class professionals. The unionization of professors shows clearly that in spite of the fact that many people like to think of colleges as "Ivory Towers" that stand aside from the mundane affairs of society, colleges and universities are organizations in which people earn a living, and the economic interests of different groups often conflict.

Politics, Schools, and Nationalism

If an unfriendly foreign power had attempted to impose on America the mediocre educational performance that exists today, we might well have viewed it as an act of war. . . . We have in effect been committing an act of unthinking, unilateral educational disarmament. (National Commission on Excellence in Education, 1983)

This startling conclusion about the current state of U.S. education reflects a strong belief in a connection between achievement in schools and the attainment of national goals. The Commission clearly defines education as a national armament that helps protect the U.S.

The use of schools to promote national goals is not a new practice (see Freire, 1985). The first public schools appeared in Germany at a time when Germans were trying to build a sense of national solidarity and patriotism, and in the 1930s the Nazis used children's literature to foster the image of Germans as a master race that would rule the world (Kamenetsky, 1984). Students in U.S. schools pledge allegiance to the flag every day and sing the national anthem at sporting events. Courses in U.S. history tend to neglect the more unattractive aspects of our past—racism, imperialism, and atrocities committed during wars—while emphasizing our accomplishments, praising the benefits of capitalism, and highlighting the shortcomings of socialism and communism.

Japanese textbooks were recently criticized for ignoring atrocities committed by Japanese troops during World War II; and German textbooks pay little attention to the Nazis and the Holocaust. Lessons in Russian schools glorify socialism and communism, condemn capitalism, and, depending on the political climate, either attack or glorify various leaders of the past. Until as recently as the 1960s, the study of sociology was not allowed in China or the Soviet Union; and current sociological work in the Soviet

Like schools in most societies, those in the United States tend to project a favorable image of national history by neglecting such subjects as the massacre of Sioux Indians at Wounded Knee in 1890 or, as shown here in Robert Lidneux's painting "Trail of Tears," the brutal 1838 forced migration of some 16,000 Cherokee Indians, during which more than 4,000 died.

Union rarely raises issues and problems that challenge basic characteristics of its society (*Footnotes*, 1980).

The tendency of the Soviet leadership to rewrite history is so pervasive that it has found its way into Russian jokes, one of which defines a Russian historian as "someone who can predict the past." More recently the new Soviet policy of *glasnost* (or "openness") has led them to adopt more accurate views of their history with a special emphasis on the problems of Soviet society. These revisions have been so extensive that in 1988 officials cancelled final secondary school exams in history while new texts were being written. There was, officials reasoned, no point in requiring students to continue learning a false history (*New York Times*, May 31, 1988, p. 1).

After World War II the U.S. and the Soviet Union engaged in a "Cold War" in which both sides struggled for economic and military superiority. In 1957 the Soviet Union launched the world's first space satellite—Sputnik I—and the U.S. reacted in fear to this startling technological advance. President Eisenhower argued that scientific education lay at the heart of self-defense and called for nationwide testing of high school students, incentives to pursue scientific careers, increased laboratory facilities, and better training for math and science teachers (Ravitch, 1983; Spring, 1976).

Within a year of the launch of Sputnik I, Congress passed the National Defense Education Act, which provided federal funding for counseling programs designed to identify the most gifted students, training programs for science teachers, graduate fellowships, and undergraduate student loans. Schools were clearly being regarded as an instrument of national political policy.

On many levels, then, schools perform a variety of functions—from socializing the young to advancing political goals. Because schools distribute skills and credentials, they have often been criticized as supporters of social inequality. Conflict theorists in particular focus on the ways in which cultural, structural, and ecological aspects of schools perpetuate inequality based on race, gender, and class.

SCHOOLS AND SOCIAL CONFLICT: CLASS AND CLASSROOMS

In the 1960s the civil rights movement targeted education as a major way of removing racial inequality (Bane and Jencks, 1972). A basic assumption was that lower-class children could not escape poverty without the basic cognitive skills—the ability to read, write, and do arithmetic—required in the job market.

As explained in the following sections, the assumptions underlying this strategy are false, because cognitive skills do not explain why some people are rich and others are poor, and because there is little evidence that schools can substantially reduce class or racial differences in basic skills. Social characteristics of schools, however, do help perpetuate social inequality in other ways, for

the real achievement of schools consists in their ability to train children to accept the prevailing class structure and their fate as workers within the industrial system. . . . What is learned in school . . . is rarely related to specific skills. . . . Rather students learn . . . to accommodate to the first requirement of industrial labor: respect for authority, the self-discipline needed to internalize the values of the labor process, and the place of the worker within the prevailing occupational hierarchies. (Aronowitz, 1973, p. 74)

Inequality and the Hidden Curriculum

There is a New England town in which most of the residents are connected in some way to a local private, elite college. The public schools are relatively new and well staffed, and a large percentage of the students are the children of college professors and administrators. The neighboring town is inhabited primarily by working-class people, some of whom work at the college (Smith, 1981).

In both towns high school students study the same subjects, but the hidden curriculums are very different. The working-class students cannot leave classrooms without a "hall pass"; their behavior is watched closely; they have little choice over the courses they will take; and the subject of college is rarely brought up. In the college town, however, students are not required to have hall passes; they are allowed to make many decisions for themselves, including selection from a wide variety of elective courses; and their teachers often express confidence that most if not all of them will go on to college.

If they learn their "lessons," students in these towns will graduate with quite different ideas about themselves and their place in society. Working-class students will learn that they are not to be trusted, that important decisions about their lives will rest in the hands of others. The middle- and upper-class students in the college town, however, will learn that they can be trusted to control their own lives and, most important, that they will become adults who will make decisions about *other* people's lives. The working-class students are being prepared to be workers under the authority of managers and professionals, while the middle- and upper-class students are learning to *be* managers and professionals (see Chackerian and Abcarian, 1984).

Through a detail as simple as how they are arranged in relation to their teachers, students in these two classes—one in a public school and the other in a private school—are receiving very different messages about who they are in the world and what is expected of them.

Nowhere are class differences in the hidden curriculum more apparent than when we compare public high schools and elite private academies. As Cookson and Persell (1985) point out, in many ways student life in elite private schools is more tightly regulated than life in public schools. The harsher discipline in elite schools serves a very different purpose, however, for it serves as a rite of passage that prepares upper-middle- and upper-class students for prestigious and powerful adult statuses. The discipline found in middle- and working-class schools, by comparison, prepares students to obey authority, a very different consequence that reinforces class differences in power.

Such differences between schools intensify class differences among adults by transmitting different expectations to students. When Leacock (1969) repeated the Rosenthal and Jacobson (1968) experiment in which teachers' expectations and behavior were affected by false reports of student potential, she found that the results were themselves affected by the school's social class. Teachers in schools whose students came primarily from the middle class treated students better if they were identified as bright and promising; but in lower-class schools, just the opposite occurred: "promising" students were often treated as "wise guys."

This raises a serious question about the study (Coleman et al., 1966), discussed earlier. Coleman found that measures of school quality did not explain the racial gap in academic achievement. Although these researchers did measure "teacher qualifications," they did *not* measure the beliefs, values, attitudes, and expectations that affect teachers' perceptions and behavior in relation to students. This suggests that the relatively poor performance of students in lower-class schools—many of whom are black—may be in part a self-fulfilling prophecy: they achieve less because their teachers *expect* them to, regardless of the "quality" of schools and their teachers.

Tracking and Inequality   **Tracking** is used to divide students according to tests of academic ability. The manifest function of tracking is to allow "slow" students to get extra attention and to allow "bright" students to move at their own speed, rather than having to wait for the "slow" students to catch up. It often has other consequences, however.

Nonwhite and lower-class students are more likely than others to be assigned to "slow" tracks, regardless of their test scores (Edelman et al., 1985).

Given what we know about the effects of expectations on student achievement, it is tempting to conclude that tracking helps explain racial and class differences in achievement (see Oakes, 1985). The evidence of past research tends to support this conclusion. In general, higher-ability students do better when placed in homogeneous classes; but lower-ability students do worse and fall even further behind. Many studies also show that the gain by higher-ability students is less than the lost ground of lower-ability students, which suggests that for society as a whole the costs of tracking may outweigh the benefits (see Dar and Resh, 1986; Oakes, 1985).

Tracking may also help perpetuate inequality in ways that have nothing to do with academic achievement. By affecting students' expectations, tracking may reinforce their acceptance of their position in society, whether it be high or low (see Hallinan and Sørensen, 1987). In this sense, tracking may contribute to false consciousness and, therefore, to the perpetuation of inequality.

Grades, Ideology, and False Consciousness

Grades have several functional consequences in schools. They reinforce the power of teachers, motivate students to work, and are fairly accurate predictors of future academic performance.

Grades also have dysfunctional consequences, however. Grades are poor predictors of performance outside the school environment (McClelland, 1973); they create tensions and anxieties that interfere with creativity and discourage close relationships between students and teachers; and they encourage students to manipulate teachers, to compete rather than cooperate with each other, and to avoid taking initiative and risks (Hoyt, 1965; Kirschenbaum et al., 1971; Sawyer, 1970).

The finding that grades are inaccurate predictors of adult performance is important, because schools are often viewed as sorters of talent for the job market. If grades are poor predictors of which students will make the best lawyers, business managers, scientists, or teachers, then why are they still used to "sort" students? Part of the answer comes from the conflict perspective.

As we saw in Chapter 11, the perpetuation of social classes depends in part on people's acceptance of their class position. Part of the basis for this acceptance is the belief that the system through which rewards are distributed is fair, that everyone has an equal opportunity to achieve desirable jobs and relatively high standards of living. If individuals support the belief that the system is basically fair, then they have no one but themselves to blame if they are in the lower class, and no one but themselves to credit if they live a life of privilege (Jencks and Riesman, 1968).

Students generally enter college with unrealistic job aspirations, for there are not enough good jobs to go around (Guzzardi, 1976). Grading dulls the aspirations of many students, but particularly those from the working and lower classes, for they are most likely to have below-average grades (Clark, 1960). Many students with low grades are advised to drop out of school altogether; but many others are encouraged to remain in school but to accept lower aspirations. This helps ensure that less desirable jobs will be performed; but, most important, it helps maintain the ideology of equal opportunity and, with it, the unequal distribution of rewards.

Trimberger (1971) and others claim that grading contributes to false consciousness among lower-class students by supporting the false belief that class position results more from individual abilities and performance than from the limitations imposed by a class society. Grading, however, also contributes to false consciousness among middle- and upper-class students, for it supports the equally false belief that their success is due entirely to their individual talent and effort.

You might be tempted to conclude from this analysis that if schools devised a grading system that did accurately predict adult performance, then actual ability would be the only basis for assigning people to adult roles, and the resulting distribution of rewards would be fairer. The problem with this solution, however, lies with the fact that the distribution of wealth, power, and prestige has relatively little to do with ability, however accurately it may be measured.

Opportunity and Outcome

From their earliest years, public schools were looked to as sources of economic prosperity, social equality, and upward mobility. A major part of the American dream is that individual ability and effort are the only limits on achievement, and equal opportunity for education is the key to equality of outcomes (Binder, 1974).

We saw earlier that lower class and minority members do not have equal access to higher educa-

tion; but as many sociologists point out, even if there *were* equal educational opportunity, this would not eliminate social classes, because inequality is created by economic arrangements, not educational ones (Bane and Jencks, 1972).

The educational attainment of the U.S. labor force rose sharply over the last two decades (see Table 16-3). Between 1960 and 1985 the percentage of adults completing high school increased by 55 percent, and among blacks the percentage almost tripled. Among blacks and whites, the percentage with college degrees more than doubled, with comparable gains for Hispanics. As we saw in Chapter 11, however, inequality between social classes *increased*, which suggests that while education is certainly not irrelevant to economic success, other factors play an equal, if not more important, part.

Like all major structural characteristics of societies, inequality is not the result of any one aspect of social life. No institution has the power to remove the inequalities of race, gender, or social class. That schools have been looked to so often as a remedy for inequality is due less to the actual power of schools than to the importance we attach to the cultural values of equal opportunity and reward based solely on ability and effort.

Table 16-3

Educational Attainment by Race and Sex (United States, 1960–85)

	HIGH SCHOOL GRADUATE		COLLEGE GRADUATE OR MORE	
RACE AND SEX	1960	1985	1960	1985
White males	22%	35%	10%	24%
White females	29%	42%	6%	16%
Black males	11%	32%	3%	11%
Black females	14%	36%	3%	11%
Hispanic males[1]	20%	27%	6%	10%
Hispanic females[1]	22%	30%	3%	7%

[1]Figures are for 1970 and 1985.

Source: U.S. Census Bureau, 1986a.

SCHOOLS AND SOCIAL CHANGE

If you wanted to change a major aspect of society, where would you begin? When I pose this question to college students, more often than not they reply, "You have to start with kids." It is an obvious solution: it is easier to teach children new ideas than to change old ideas that are already deeply embedded in adults.

For this reason, schools have often been a battleground in struggles for social change. Racial integration increases interaction between children of different races before they firmly adopt the fundamentals of racism. A major focus of the women's movement has been on the images of males and females in school textbooks. Sex education is offered as a way to increase young people's understanding of their sexuality and decrease the likelihood of teenage pregnancy and AIDS.

Opponents of change focus on schools as sources of social opportunity and stability. Religious fundamentalists oppose the teaching of the theory of evolution, and 16 percent of U.S. adults are against sex education. Just under half would bar atheists, communists, or advocates of military rule from teaching in colleges or universities, and 40 percent would also bar homosexuals (Davis and Smith, 1987).

Values also conflict in less specific areas. For many, schools exist in order to teach students to think for themselves, to solve problems, and to ask critical questions about their society—Thomas Jefferson's prescription for a healthy democracy. To others, however, the idea that any question can have more than one correct answer is unacceptable because it threatens the stability of predictable, orderly views of the world, especially those based on religion.

Schools embody a fundamental value conflict in social life: The freedom of people to think for themselves is highly valued in our culture and is the major source of innovation and creativity; and yet, at the same time, free inquiry inevitably leads to critical questions about social life. The late Brazilian educator Paulo Freire (1972) was expelled from his country because he taught peasants to read. The dominant groups—especially the landowners who exploited the peasants—felt threatened because literacy helped the peasants understand their oppressed position in Brazilian society.

Higher education, in particular, contributes to social change in ways that have nothing to do with

what students learn. Many college students are free of work and family responsibilities, and this gives them time and energy to participate in social movements. The civil rights and anti-Vietnam War movements of the 1960s drew heavily on the support of students. In the 1970s university students in France succeeded in leading what became a paralyzing national strike, and the 1987 demonstrations by students in South Korea were powerful enough to force a change in the country's leadership and constitution.

Education has also fostered the growth of intellectuals as a category—people who are separated from production and are therefore free to analyze and criticize their society (Flacks, 1970). The roots of sociology itself extend back to the turbulent 1800s in which scholars such as Durkheim, Weber, and particularly Marx, were motivated as much by a desire for

This French student, injured in a 1986 confrontation with riot police in Paris, is one of the hundreds of thousands who protested government proposals to allow public universities to employ more selective admissions policies. In a matter of weeks, strikes shut down 50 of France's public universities. The government eventually backed down.

positive social change as they were by intellectual curiosity. Most of the first U.S. sociologists saw themselves as social reformers, not detached intellectuals. Many of today's sociologists believe that it is their responsibility to use their research and analytic skills to bring about positive change.

Writers, artists, scholars, and professionals such as Lenin, Leon Trotsky, Fidel Castro, and Che Guevara have played major roles in revolutions. For this reason, intellectuals are often viewed with considerable suspicion, if not hostility. When the Nazis seized power in Germany in the 1930s, university professors and other intellectuals were among their first targets as the Nazis tried to stifle criticism and dissent. In the U.S., college professors and other intellectuals have often been punished for views that were perceived as threats to the status quo. Tenure was instituted for the purpose of defending academic freedom from those who would try to suppress unpopular views.

As institutions, schools contribute to social change and conflict *and* to continuity and stability; but schools, themselves, have also been the objects of movements for social change.

Changing Schools

As we have seen, schools may be understood in terms of how they operate and their relationships with the rest of society. In order to understand changes in schools, therefore, we have to pay attention to both of these levels of analysis.

Because the functions of schools are so highly valued, criticism of schools and efforts to change them are almost as old as schools themselves. The practice of grading has a long and checkered history in U.S. education. Over the last hundred years, schools have adopted grading, dropped it, re-adopted it, and modified it with innovations such as "pass-fail" (Kirschenbaum et al., 1971). In the 1980s there is a renewed call for higher standards and stricter grading of student work (National Commission on Excellence in Education, 1983).

Such changes reflect competition between opposing beliefs and values. Opponents argue that grading inhibits creativity and independent thought, that it encourages students to care more about grades than learning. Supporters stress different values—the importance of motivating students to learn what they need to know whether they like it or not, and sorting out students of different ability levels.

Underlying such positions are beliefs about the nature of childhood and values about how much power children should have, and such differences have produced some radical alternatives to traditional schooling. At a British school called Summerhill, teachers exercise virtually no authority over their students, who run the school through democratic meetings and decide what they will learn and when they will learn it. The school's founder, A. S. Neill, maintained that the most important thing for young people to learn is how to live with others and make decisions for themselves. Subjects such as history and science can be learned later, when children decide they need them (Neill, 1961).

Illich (1971) went so far as to advocate abolishing schools altogether and replacing them with "learning centers" in which people who want to learn get together with those who have something to teach. He objected to formal schooling not only because of his belief that it stifles the motivation to explore and learn about the world, but also because the hidden curriculum promotes control, obedience, and conformity more than enlightenment and independent thought. Illich and Neill were both embraced and ridiculed by experts in many fields, including education (see Gartner, Greer, and Riessman, 1973; Hart, 1970).

Beyond a few private experiments, it is unlikely that elementary and secondary schools will stray far from their current bureaucratic form in which power is sharply divided between adults and children (see Shor, 1986). In 1983 the National Commission on Excellence in Education strongly recommended that school days and years be lengthened, that student freedom to decide which subjects to study be severely limited, and that requirements for graduation be raised and strictly enforced.

There is evidence, however, that in higher education students are controlling their own education to an increasing degree. For the most part, this results from the fact that an increasing proportion of students are adults who are returning to school after spending several years in the labor force. It also results from the fact that many colleges are experiencing financial difficulties and shrinking enrollments, and they see the adult market as a new source of income.

This raises once again the economic reality that schools must have money in order to operate; and some of the most heated debates about schools focus on the issue of who will pay for them and how, and how this will affect the quality of education.

Money and the Quality of Education

Many reformers would improve schools by forcing them to improve—by raising graduation standards and by requiring teachers to pass competency tests at regular intervals. Others, however, suggest that the best way to improve schools is to set them in economic competition with each other. If parents can send children to the school of their choice, then schools will have to compete in order to survive.

One suggestion is to take a community's school budget and distribute it among parents in the form of "credits" or "vouchers" (La Noue, 1972). Parents could then redeem their vouchers in any way they wished, either by enrolling their children in a public school, or by seeking out private education. The best schools, of course, would get the most "business," and this would encourage inferior schools to improve their performance.

A second proposal would allow parents who send their children to private schools to pay less federal tax (Hegedus, 1976; Thomas and Levin, 1983). By subsidizing private schools, supporters argue, this plan would increase healthy competition between public and private schools and give parents greater freedom of choice and control over their children's educations.

Critics—the NAACP, the Civil Liberties Union, and professional educators—argue that both plans would make the distribution of education even more unequal than it is today. As additional family income, vouchers would enable middle-class parents to send their children to private schools, but would not be enough to give lower-class parents the same option. Tuition tax credits discriminate against lower-class families, who cannot afford private schools and already receive a relatively small share of educational resources. Critics fear that both proposals would further divide schooling into two separate and unequal systems: one well-financed, middle-class, and predominantly white, and the other poorly financed, lower-class, and predominantly nonwhite.

The characteristics of educational institutions seem forever tied to social conditions in society itself. Schools have been, are, and will continue to be important parts of the "real world."

SUMMARY

1. Education is a form of socialization that involves systematic, formal transmission of skills, knowledge, and other aspects of culture. In many societies this takes place primarily in schools—formal organizations whose primary purpose is education.

2. Education was once restricted to the upper classes, but with the Industrial Revolution public schooling gradually included increasingly large segments of the population.

3. Like all institutions, schools are organized around cultural ideas such as a belief in the accuracy of grades, values of punctuality and competition, and norms such as those embodied in honor codes. Within this environment, there are subcultures such as those among students. While the manifest function of schools is to teach subjects such as math, they also teach a hidden curriculum that consists of values such as obedience to authority and the relative desirability of different social classes or of different ethnic backgrounds.

4. In general, the higher the level of schooling, the more likely school boundaries are to exclude students from disadvantaged backgrounds.

5. Like all social behavior, patterns of interaction in schools are affected by definitions of the situation and people's perceptions of each other. Teachers and students often feel frustrated with each other when students define their role as giving correct answers and teachers expect students to think independently.

6. Schools, like many institutions, have become bureaucratic. Some argue that this interferes with education by creating competing interests such as those of teachers and administrators.

7. Distributions of power differ sharply among schools, according to the level of schooling. For example, students generally gain power as they advance to college, and power structures are more complex in college than in elementary school.

8. Population affects schools primarily through changes in the birth rate, increasing or decreasing the number of potential students. This affects communities and professionals who make a living from the business of schooling.

9. Ecological factors, such as the use of space, also affect schools. Racial segregation and different models of classroom interaction, such as open classrooms, affect what and how much students learn. The mode of production in a society is also important, because schooling is expensive. Industrial societies are in a far better position to school their children than are underdeveloped countries.

10. Schools are related to other institutions in many ways. They have taken over many functions once reserved for families; compulsory schooling keeps young people out of the job market; and schools are often used to promote national political goals such as allegiance to the state.

11. Schools play an important part in social conflict. The hidden curriculum, tracking, and grades support social class differences by sorting and preparing students to accept their class position. While schooling has long been perceived as a solution for social inequality, most research shows that the causes of inequality are to be found primarily outside of schools.

12. Because they socialize the young, schools have been viewed as vehicles for social change. This has made them an ongoing scene of conflict as various interest groups vie to determine school policy and curriculum.

KEY TERMS

education   433
extrinsic reward   438
hidden curriculum   439
intrinsic reward   438
school   433
social promotion   444
student subcultures

  academic   439
  collegiate   439
  nonconformist   439
  vocational   439

tracking   453
zero-sum game   438

Looking Elsewhere

Having studied Chapter 16, you might want to look at related discussions in *Human Arrangements*, which include

- schools and socialization (Chapter 6, pp. 150–52)
- socialization, schools, and gender roles (Chapter 13, pp. 360–61)
- interaction in college classrooms (Chapter 1, p. 8; Chapter 7, pp. 174, 175)
- student cheating as deviance (Chapter 10, pp. 251–52)
- education and social mobility (Chapter 11, pp. 298–99)
- the causes of neighborhood segregation (Chapter 12, pp. 326–27)

RECOMMENDED READINGS

BARR, R., and DREEBAN, R., with WIRATCHAI, N. (1983). *How schools work*. Chicago: University of Chicago Press. A study of how school systems work and their effects on education using a multi-level perspective ranging from political structures such as school boards to what goes on in classrooms.

BOOCOCK, S. (1980). *Sociology of education: An introduction* (2nd ed.). Boston: Houghton-Mifflin. An excellent introduction to the field. See also Parelius, A. P., and Parelius, R. J. (1978). *The sociology of education*. Englewood Cliffs, NJ: Prentice-Hall.

BOWLES, S., and GINTIS, H. (1976). *Schooling in capitalist America: Educational reform and the contradictions of economic life*. New York: Basic Books. An important analysis of the ways in which schools and formal education help to reproduce social classes in America.

ILLICH, I. (1971). *Deschooling society*. New York: Harper and Row. A revolutionary plan to do away with schools as we know them. For an equally provocative collection of critical articles written in response to Illich's ideas, see A. Gartner, C. Greer, and F. Riessman (Eds.). (1973). *After deschooling, what?* New York: Harper and Row.

JENCKS, C., ET AL. (1972). *Inequality*. An energetic challenge to the belief that education is the key to social mobility and reduction of social inequality.

RAVITCH, D. (1983). *The troubled crusade: American education 1945–1980*. New York: Basic Books. A thoughtful, well-written analysis of 35 years of attempts at educational reform in the United States.

ROHLEN, T. P. (1983). *Japan's high schools*. Berkeley: University of California Press. A highly recommended study that tries to explain how Japan's high schools produce levels of achievement unheard of in the United States. See also Cummings, W. K. (1980). *Education and equality in Japan*. Princeton, NJ: Princeton University Press.

17 Science, Technology, and Medicine

By definition, social institutions are conservative in that they try to preserve different aspects of social life. A major function of families and schools is to reproduce a culture by passing it from one generation to the next. It is in the nature of institutions to resist change, for they are designed to give social life a sense of continuity, regularity, and predictability.

As an institution, however, **science** is a unique case. Although it is an enduring set of arrangements that resist change as much as those of any institution, its major social function is to seek new knowledge, to test old assumptions, and approach what we think we know with a skeptical eye (see Barnes, 1985). It is perhaps the only social institution in human history dedicated to change, and, as such, it is a source of marvelous innovation and enormous conflict. From theories about the creation of the universe to an understanding of the social and biological aspects of race and gender differences, science continually tests a society's ability to make sense of itself and control its own affairs. While other institutions are designed to keep things as they are, the knowledge produced by science can change not only how we think about the world, but how we shape the physical and social world in which we live.

Unlike science, which consists solely of theories and knowledge, technology is the practical ability to manipulate and make use of the physical world. We are now able to splice genes and create forms of life, to transplant organs from one body to another, to enable one woman to bear a child for another; to use computers to store and retrieve detailed information on every citizen, and to destroy life on earth with nuclear weapons. However, we have barely begun to deal seriously with the profound moral, practical, and legal implications of such abilities.

In this chapter we take a detailed look at the social characteristics that make science a key institution in our society, and at the dramatic and complex effects of science and technology on social life. We then turn to medicine, an institution that exists in virtually all known societies but which in industrial societies is increasingly dominated by technology and science.

SCIENCE AS A SOCIAL INSTITUTION

Science is a set of social arrangements whose major function is the seeking of new, largely reliable knowledge (see Merton, 1973). As an institution, it provides a cultural "blueprint" that defines legitimate subjects for research, acceptable methods of seeking knowledge, and standards for evaluating and interpreting the results. The question of whether God exists falls beyond the realm of science because science concerns itself only with what can be observed and evaluated with objective evidence. Since the existence of God is a matter of faith rather than of observable evidence, it is not a legitimate question for scientific inquiry. The question, however, of whether a belief in the existence of God affects other aspects of our lives, such as happiness or tolerance for those who differ from us, can be answered scientifically, for it is possible to gather evidence about people's beliefs, their happiness, and their tolerance.

As an institution science is more than a set of ideas and symbols. It also involves social relationships through which knowledge is pursued by individuals and groups. Science, then, is a social process which itself can be understood in terms of how it operates and changes. It is not simply a source of change, for it is affected by its own findings and the social environment in which it operates (see Zuckerman, 1988). Science is a complex social process that affects social life with both wondrous and disastrous results. We begin with the cultural and structural characteristics that define science as an institution, and then take a broader look at the complex relationship between science and society.

THE CULTURE OF SCIENCE

Science is a cultural way of looking at the world, and, like all aspects of culture, it affects how we pay attention to it. Science, however, is unique in its dedication to understanding the world through the use of particular methods based on fundamental assumptions about the nature of reality.

Beliefs and Paradigms

At the heart of science as a cultural framework is the belief in science itself as a valid way of understanding the world. Most of us take this for granted, many going so far as to regard science as the ultimate authority determining what is true and what is not (Barnes, 1985). What we tend to overlook is how ethnocentric this view is, that as members of other cultures we might look at the problem of truth very differently. To a Zen Buddhist all aspects of the observable and unobservable world form an integrated whole, to be accepted as it is, not "understood" by picking it apart and figuring things out in terms of their parts and the relationships that bind them. From this perspective, scientific efforts to explain the world by identifying how things "work" is at best a silly distraction, and at worst a futile and dangerous effort to control a world that is inherently neither understandable nor controllable in that way.

Within science, the most important beliefs take the form of **paradigms**—sets of guiding assumptions, theories, and methods that define a particular approach to scientific problems (see Kuhn, 1970). A paradigm defines for scientists what they should pay attention to, how they should pay attention to it, and how they should interpret what they observe. As you might imagine, paradigms are enormously important in science because they have so much influence over what scientists do. Most scientists are socialized into the paradigms that dominate their fields and, as with

A Japanese Zen Buddhist sits and meditates on what he believes to be the undifferentiated wholeness of the natural world. Louis Pasteur, who discovered that germs cause disease, is typical of scientists who try to understand reality by taking it apart to see how it "works." These dramatically different approaches reflect not only different ways of understanding, but different ways of life.

any cultural belief system, they tend to hang on to them unless confronted with overwhelming evidence to the contrary.

The Ptolemaic view of the universe, which places the earth rather than the sun at the center, was the dominant paradigm in astronomy for many centuries until it was finally upset by the Copernican view. The new paradigm, however, was fiercely resisted for centuries after it was first introduced in 1543. The old paradigm not only dominated astronomy, but was also an important part of religious views that placed humanity at the center of existence as God's most important creation. Both Copernicus and, a century later, one of his strongest advocates, Galileo, were persecuted. Galileo was forced to recant his views under threat of torture and imprisonment. In more recent history, resistance to new paradigms is the rule rather than the exception in science. Charles Darwin's theory of evolution, Louis Pasteur's theories of germs, Gregor Mendel's theory of genetics, and Sigmund Freud's theory of the subconscious—all represented dramatic shifts in paradigms, and all were greeted with enormous resistance.

The Making of Scientific Revolutions

Because paradigms include basic assumptions that guide scientific work, they are the last element of any scientific field to change, and when they do, the result can be revolutionary.

As Kuhn (1970) describes this process in his classic book, *The Structure of Scientific Revolutions*, most scientists practice *normal* science, which means that they work within a particular paradigm without challenging its assumptions. A Ptolemaic astronomer would never try to measure the characteristics of the earth's orbit around the sun because according to the Ptolemaic paradigm the earth does not orbit around the sun. When a paradigm is wrong, however, its use will result in a growing number of findings that contradict the paradigm or make no sense. In the case of Ptolemy's view of the solar system, astronomers found that the planets were not where they expected them to be. Such findings that are inconsistent with a scientific paradigm are called **anomalies**, and as they accumulate, the position of the paradigm becomes increasingly insecure until a new paradigm is developed to account for the anomalies and replace the old one. It is this replacement of one paradigm with another that constitutes a **scientific revolution**.

One of the most intriguing new paradigms in science centers on the unpredictable side of nature found in the seeming chaos of everything from weather patterns to the irregular dripping of a leaky faucet. The principle of "chaos" is now being used to organize a revolutionary approach to understanding a wide range of natural and social phenomena that have, until now, had no place in existing scientific paradigms (see Gleick, 1987). In this paradigm, what we tend to think of as so disorderly and unpredictable as to be beyond our understanding is as normal as the regularities produced by gravity. In this emerging paradigm, such phenomena have a place in the natural order of things and can be understood in a systematic, scientific way.

Conflict between competing paradigms is probably the most vital issue confronting a scientific discipline, for it is nothing less than a struggle over the fundamental assumptions and views that determine the research that will be done. In sociology the functional and conflict perspectives have been seen as direct opposites of each other, and advocates of each have argued their positions for years, often with some bitterness. The functional paradigm promoted by Talcott Parsons was based on the idea of society as a set of integrated social institutions, such as the family, economy, and law, supported by a general consensus on cultural norms and values. Each part of a social system can be understood in terms of its dependency on other parts and the ways in which it contributes to or interferes with the operation of the system. Within societies, individuals choose among culturally defined alternatives and are motivated by norms and values to make choices that ultimately contribute to the maintenance of the system (Parsons, 1937, 1951).

Particularly in the 1940s and 1950s, many sociologists accepted the functional paradigm's assumptions about societies and how they work and used it to approach research problems as diverse as social stratification, gender inequality, and the organization of the family (see Chapters 11, 13, and 15). To many other sociologists, however, there were too many aspects of social life that seemed to contradict the assumptions of the functional paradigm. As the anomalies of injustice and social unrest revealed by the civil rights and anti-Vietnam War movements in the 1960s mounted, the conflict paradigm became increasingly popular, especially from a Marxist perspective. Parsons' critics charged that his functional paradigm assumed a false picture of society as a harmonious, stable collection of social relationships and cultural values and norms (see Dahrendorf, 1958; Gouldner, 1970; Mills, 1959). Societies, they argued, are not cohesive, unified

The Ptolemaic paradigm placed the earth at the center of the universe. Medieval thinkers also believed that the constant motion of the planets required some sort of "mover," which, in this fourteenth-century depiction, was provided by angels turning the wheels of the universe.

wholes in which all work for common goals. Most societies are dominated by groups that use their power and privilege to shape society to serve their own ends, and it is impossible to understand societies with an approach that fails to take this into account. All societies experience continuing conflict and change, not stability and equilibrium; and each part of society contributes to that conflict and change. The basis of social order is not consensus, but the coercive use of power (Dahrendorf, 1973).

Although the functional and conflict paradigms still have ardent advocates within sociology, as we have seen throughout this book, the result of this struggle has not been the replacement of one with the other. Instead, most sociologists have come to appreciate the paradigms as complementary parts of a larger sociological paradigm. The result here, then, has been one of integration, not revolution.

The Values of Science

As with any institution, scientific work is guided by values. Perhaps the highest scientific value is placed on verifiable knowledge itself, for this is the avowed goal of all scientific work. To a scientist, there is no "good knowledge" and "bad knowledge," although there are certainly good and bad *uses* of scientific knowledge.

The inability of scientists to control how knowledge is used raises a difficult value conflict: Should scientists seek knowledge that could be used for destructive purposes? If it were possible to demonstrate that women in general tend to have a genetic makeup that results in slightly lower *average* mathematical abilities, the high value placed by science on the pursuit of knowledge for its own sake might lead many scientists to go ahead. Other scientists, however, have a broader view of scientific values in the context of *other* cultural values such as the importance of social justice. These scientists would pay attention to how such findings might be used to reinforce negative cultural stereotypes about women and justify discrimination against individual women regardless of their mathematical abilities.

Such decisions cannot be made scientifically, for they force scientists to consider values that have nothing to do with science itself (see Fausto-Sterling, 1985). A scientist's decision to search for a cure for

AIDS or to develop a new plague that can be used against an enemy in war is not a scientific one. Nor is a biologist's decision to try to disprove the prejudiced belief that minorities are inferior to dominant groups. The mere act of choosing what questions to ask is, itself, profoundly influenced by a scientist's nonscientific values.

It is also important to remember that the individual scientist is not the only one whose values influence the choice of what knowledge to pursue. Scientific research today is so expensive that it requires the support of major social institutions such as universities, government, corporations, and private foundations, each of which has its own nonscientific reasons for preferring one line of research over another. Drug companies generally place a higher value on making a profit than on curing disease. They will often decide against pursuing cures for diseases that are devastating for their victims but which do not afflict enough people to result in a large profit for the company. Scientists often feel compelled to choose their research topics according to which kinds of problems are re-

"We want you to do some pure disinterested fundamental research into something immensely profitable."

Copyright *New Scientist,* London.

ceiving a high priority from government agencies, corporations, and foundations that control research funds. For these, the choice may appear to be between doing research on what others consider to be important or not doing research at all.

The heart of the scientific value system focuses less on the selection of research problems than on the conduct of scientific work itself and the social relationships that bind the scientific community together. Scientific values define the difference between "good science" and "bad science" and establish the goals to which all scientists are expected to aspire. It is here that the norms of the scientific community become most important in regulating the behavior of scientists.

The Norms of Science

Merton (1968) identified four norms that govern scientific work. The norm of **universalism** requires scientists to use the same objective criteria for evaluating scientific findings regardless of their source. The anti-Semitic ideology of Nazi Germany led to a complete rejection of the results of "Jewish science"—including the fundamental work of Albert Einstein—a clean violation of this norm.

Until quite recently, science in the Soviet Union was dominated by a rigid communist ideology which rejected many of the assumptions which underlay "Western" (which is to say, "capitalist") science, including many of the basic theories of genetic inheritance. The influence of political ideology on the interpretation of scientific evidence was so strong that it forced scientists to adopt the false view that acquired traits could be passed on genetically. According to Soviet genetic theory, if a crop of corn was particularly well-fertilized and watered and was therefore unusually productive, seed from that crop would also be highly productive. Since watering and fertilizing have no effect on the genetic makeup of corn or anything else, their effects cannot be passed on genetically. This fundamental error, dictated by the nonscientific standards of communist ideology, resulted in years of disastrous crops for Soviet farmers, and although the error was finally corrected in the 1960s, its long-term effects still keep the Soviet Union far behind the west in its ability to adequately feed its people.

The norm of **communism** (a term whose usage here has no connection with communism as a political system) requires scientists to share their findings freely with one another, based on the idea that knowledge is common, not private property that should be held in secret. This has produced conflict as scientific knowledge has become increasingly important in international power struggles between the United States and the Soviet Union. Scientists who do basic research for the U.S. Defense Department are often required not to share their findings with anyone outside the government for fear that it will be made available to the Soviets. This requirement has led many scientists to refuse to work for the government rather than violate the norm of communism.

Since the scientific community does not regard ideas and knowledge as private property to be used to advance the interests of the individual scientist, the norm of **disinterestedness** requires scientists to act more for the benefit of science than themselves. In spite of the fact that original discoveries are the key to a scientist's professional success, such concerns are not supposed to influence how science is conducted. Scientists who falsify results in order to make names for themselves violate this norm by placing their own interests above those of science.

The fourth norm ensures that all evidence will be subjected to **organized skepticism**. No finding, argument, or theory should be accepted without first carefully weighing the evidence and critically evaluating the methods used to generate it. This norm has been institutionalized in the practice of publishing articles in scientific journals only after they have been carefully reviewed by other scientists, and of accepting published findings only after enough time has passed to allow the broader scientific community to comment on them. Scientists feel a sense of obligation to hold no idea, theory, or paradigm sacred, except, of course, the beliefs, norms, and values that underlie science itself.

Conformity and Deviance in the Scientific Community

Because the focus of science is knowledge and truth, it depends on the ability of scientists to assume that other scientists are honest and forthcoming. Otherwise, scientists would be faced with the task of verifying independently every piece of research before accepting its results (see Zuckerman, 1988). This is impossible given that there are some 40,000 scientific journals in the world publishing upwards of a million articles each year (Broad, 1988). "The institution of science involves an implicit social contract between scientists so that each can depend on the trustworthiness of the rest . . . the entire cognitive system of science is rooted in the moral integrity of individual scientists" (Zuckerman, 1977, p. 113).

As with all values, however, those that underlie scientific norms are ideals that fallable humans will inevitably fail to achieve fully. As we have seen, it is impossible for scientists to ignore nonscientific values completely. In addition, scientific norms are difficult to enforce because violations of them are often invisible: no one may ever know of a finding that is kept secret, and scientists who reject the work of others because of their race, age, gender, or religion may do so without ever being discovered.

When norms are violated, the most severe sanction the scientific community can impose is to expel the scientist. Scientists found guilty of fraud may lose not only their jobs, but the respect of other scientists, their willingness to believe what they say and write. For a scientist, expulsion from the scientific community can amount to the virtual end of a scientific career.

Although known fraud is relatively rare in science in comparison with other spheres of social life, it does occur (see Broad and Wade, 1983; Merton, 1973). Jensen's (1969) argument in favor of a genetic explanation for racial differences in IQ drew heavily on the twin studies reported by British psychologist Cyril Burt. As it turned out, Burt's studies were marred by numerous contradictions, inconsistencies, missing documentation, and questions as to whether some of his co-authors ever existed (see Kamin, 1974; Wade, 1976). More recently there has been a rash of fraud cases, some of which have taken place in prestigious Ivy League universities such as Harvard and Yale.

Why do scientists sometimes cheat? As with other forms of deviance, a sociological answer focuses on the pressures and opportunities to violate norms that are inherent in the social situations in which people find themselves (Merton, 1957, 1973). University scientists—especially graduate students or younger professors—cannot make a name for themselves (or achieve the security that goes with academic tenure) without making original discoveries, and the intense competition among scientists means there is always the danger that someone else will "get there first." Scientists share the value of original discoveries, but they do not all have equal access to the opportunities to achieve them. Some have far greater access to research facilities, grant money, and support for time off to study and write. Ironically, it is those who are already established—and who, therefore, are least desperate in their need for recognition—who tend to have the greatest resources (see Merton, 1973). The system itself, then, by making rewards depend so heavily on producing quick, "new" findings, and by distributing unequally the opportunities to achieve those rewards, encourages scientists to break the rules by placing their own self-interest above the goals of science (see Broad and Wade, 1983; Merton, 1984).

THE STRUCTURE OF SCIENCE

As an institution, science has a structure in the form of social relationships through which scientists are trained and socialized, research is done, and knowledge is evaluated and shared within and beyond the scientific community. The structure of scientific work has changed dramatically over the last 300 years, especially in relation to social boundaries that define science as a profession and the complexity of social relationships through which science is conducted.

Boundaries: Science as a Profession

The forerunners of scientists worked primarily alone and identified themselves as "natural philosophers." By comparison, today's scientists share a sharply defined subculture of symbols, language, theoretical perspectives, and role expectations that distinguish them from nonscientists and establish their right to determine what is considered to be valid knowledge about the natural and social world. Science has been transformed from an individual pastime and hobby into a profession whose members go to great lengths to defend its boundaries.

From this perspective, the recent controversies over the teaching of evolution and "creation science" in public schools is far more than a disagreement over competing versions of the truth, for it also involves the power of scientists to control their professional boundaries and a monopoly over scientific knowledge (see Gieryn et al., 1985). Those who call themselves "creation scientists" claim that there is a scientific basis for a literal interpretation of the Biblical version of creation. In opposing them, scientists do not just argue that the Bible's version is a poor scientific theory that does not fit the facts; even more important, they argue that "creation science" is not science at all and its practitioners are not scientists because they violate the scientific norm of organized skepticism. Creationists, they argue, practice religion, not science. The core of the scientific approach to the world is the quest for

This seventeenth-century painting by an unknown Flemish artist shows that the gentleman of the day was expected to be well versed in the arts, literature, music, and science. Science was not organized as a profession and discoveries depended primarily on the work of isolated people who dabbled in science as a hobby.

new knowledge based on an ongoing willingness to examine evidence showing that what we believe to be true is, in fact, not true. Religion, however, is grounded in the belief that the truth has already been revealed and is simply there to be accepted and lived by. Unlike science, what holds religion together is an unquestioning faith that the truth is already known, which is a far cry from organized skepticism.

The distinction between scientists and nonscientists is important because it reflects an ongoing struggle over the authority to determine what is true in a society. As we will see later, this can have important implications for the distribution of power in societies and the way in which they are governed.

The Structural Complexity of Science

It was not until 1662 that the Royal Society was founded in London as the first organization dedicated to the idea that it is important for scientists to talk with one another, to support one another's work, and to discuss, evaluate, and share one another's theories and findings. Even here, however, science remained a relatively personal activity engaged in by amateurs who were wealthy enough to have the time to pursue it (Merton, 1938).

In the more than 300 years since the founding of the Royal Society, science has been transformed from an informal activity carried out by isolated individuals to a formal profession that takes place mostly within large organizations. Today most scientists work as employees, not as independent thinkers, and earn their living by their scientific work. This change mirrors the transformation of science itself from something that could be done with a minimum of equipment and financial resources to an activity that is so expensive that few individuals can afford to do it on their own. We left what Price (1986) calls "Little Science" behind with World War II and entered the age of "Big Science." The lone genius has been replaced by teams working in bureaucratic organizations that provide the necessary expensive equipment. The self-sufficiency of the upper-class philosopher/scientist has been replaced by a dependency on massive funding from foundations, corporations, and government agencies.

Royal academies of science in London and, as represented here, in Paris, were a dramatic leap forward in the organization of scientific activity. They brought scientists together and helped to establish science as a serious pursuit, not simply an amusement for those who could afford it. The excitement that the gathering generated is captured in this seventeenth-century engraving portraying different aspects of the dominant work of the time in mathematics, physics, and astronomy.

One consequence of this is that scientists have lost much of their independence and autonomy, for their dependence on institutional support is so great that their choice of research problems becomes more a matter of organizational priorities than their own interests. The distribution of power, in short, has shifted from the individual scientist to the organizations on which scientists depend, a trend that, as we have seen in other chapters, has been repeated in many other institutions. Ultimately, the decision to conduct research on the causes of AIDS is made not by research scientists but by leaders in business, government, and private foundations, many of whom are not scientists and do not feel bound by the norms or values of the scientific community. Shilts (1987) argues that research on AIDS was delayed not for scientific reasons, but because those who controlled research funds were slow to respond to the emerging crisis.

Against this, however, other social factors reinforce the autonomy of scientists. Perhaps the most important is the fact that the rewards that come from success in science depend more than anything on the recognition of other scientists (Barnes, 1985; Merton, 1973). For most people, successful job performance results in the payment of money which we use as currency to get what we want. In science, however, the currency is the recognition of other scientists, which is the basis for the major rewards scientists seek, from a better-paying job to landing a big research grant. Such recognition is controlled primarily by science as an institution, and this helps to insulate scientists from the potentially corrupting influences of organizations that offer money as a primary reward.

Another important consequence of the increased complexity of science is extreme specialization. As with most types of work, long gone is the scientific generalist who was familiar with a wide range of knowledge and theoretical perspectives. In part, this is due to the sheer magnitude of knowledge which is now so great that no one can master it all. The quantity of new findings generated each year is so vast that only a highly specialized network of specialists can sift through and evaluate it all in order to determine what should be accepted. Specialization also reflects, however, competition among scientists for scarce resources and the pressures on scientists to achieve the recognition of their peers. Zuckerman (1988) likens the process of specialization to mining for ore: As each area is exhausted, scientists try to identify and move on to new areas of ignorance in which to mine for new

knowledge (see also Merton, 1987). This kind of specialization is not unique to the physical sciences, for it has taken place in most areas of intellectual work, from philosophy to sociology (see Jacoby, 1987).

The Structure of Scientific Work

The major values of science—the production and sharing of verifiable knowledge about the world—is achieved through the structure of scientific work. Consider the process through which findings are shared with and evaluated by the scientific community (see Barnes, 1985). Most findings are reported in journals, which are typically edited by scientists. When authors prepare an article for possible publication, they must first orient themselves to a set of standards and conventions that govern such work. They know their work will be read and evaluated by other scientists who serve as referees, who will expect certain things, such as a review of previous research on the subject, a clear statement of how the research was conducted, and a discussion of how the new findings fit with what is already known. The specific people who serve as referees are anonymous to the author, which means that the author is guided by a general set of expectations associated with scientific work—the generalized other of the scientific community. This means that before a scientific report even reaches a journal it has already gone through a filtering process as authors make use of their knowledge of what other scientists expect of them.

The criticism provided by expert referees provides a second stage of filtering. Articles may be rejected or accepted outright or, more often, returned to the author for revision and resubmission. Once published, findings are then shared among scientists at large who then provide criticism or support of their own. Only after this has gone on for some time is a finding actually accepted as knowledge, and even then it is subject to continuing test in light of new evidence.

Although this complex process goes a long way toward ensuring the validity of scientific knowledge, in practice it is often less objective than it seems. How seriously a scientist's work is taken by other scientists depends in part on that scientist's reputation (just as, unfortunately, some professors feel they cannot assign a grade to a student's work without knowing who the student is). A paper written by a relative unknown might be judged by an editor to be nonsense; but that same paper might be seen in a far more positive light if the name of a famous scientist were attached to it. This means that a great deal of important scientific work may never come to light simply because of the unequal distribution of recognition and power within the scientific community.

All that this shows is that scientists are social beings like everyone else and that scientific knowledge, as with everything else we think we know about the world, is created through a social process that is inevitably affected by the characteristics of social environments (see Zuckerman, 1988). It is also true, however, that unlike other institutions, science is dedicated to identifying and minimizing the distorting effects of such social forces. That this value is, ultimately, unachievable is not surprising, since most major values that guide human life serve as ideals, not realistic goals.

TECHNOLOGY

Many scientists are dedicated simply to understanding the world in a clearer way regardless of what such understanding can be used for. It is usually through technology, however, that science affects social life. Technological innovation touches virtually every area of social life, from the machines and robots of industry and the tools of mass warfare to the ability to communicate with loved ones who are far away, to prevent unwanted pregnancies or cause wanted ones, to alter genetic structures or make ourselves feel better when we have a cold. It is the source of some of the greatest improvements in the quality of human life and some of its deepest, most troubling problems. It has enabled a mere five percent of the U.S. population to produce enough food for the entire country with plenty to spare; and it has, in varying degrees, poisoned much of the water we drink and the air we breathe.

Although people often think of science and technology as being essentially the same, they are in fact quite different and the development of one need not involve the other. It is certainly true that science, especially today, often depends on technology. Without the invention of the telescope Galileo could not have made his observations that led him to support the Copernican view of the solar system. Without the ability to cool objects to hundreds of degrees below zero, we might never have discovered superconductivity—the capacity of a substance to allow electricity to pass through it with virtually no resistance and, therefore, with no loss of power or build-up of heat. The development of the space shuttle has made possible experiments that require a weightless environment, something that was unavailable before space travel.

It is equally true, however, that many scientific and technological breakthroughs occur independently of each other. Einstein's theory of relativity was not based on any real-world experiments. In fact, it was some decades after he developed his theory that science had the technology necessary to begin to test his ideas. New technology is often simply an improvement over existing technology that depends more on the skill and imagination of inventors and engineers than on the theoretical breakthroughs of science

The technology that can keep people alive long after they would otherwise have died raises unprecedented ethical and moral issues. Who has the right to decide when to use such technology and when not to? Are we in danger of becoming so preoccupied with what we are able to do with sophisticated technology that we lose sight of the needs, rights, and interests of the people to whom the machines are attached?

(Barnes, 1985). This is especially true of technological growth before the rise of science as a social institution. Late in the horticultural period, when societies had developed the simple technology required to grow their own food, people discovered the beginnings of metallurgy, first with copper in the Middle East and then with bronze—a harder alloy of copper and tin—in Southeast Asia and China. This was a major discovery, for people could now make harder, more durable tools as well as deadlier weapons. As we saw in Chapter 5, the plow was one of the most revolutionary inventions of all time, and yet it came into being thousands of years before the advent of science around the seventeenth century.

The discovery of metallurgy illustrates how one development begets another: without the high temperatures of pottery ovens, it would not have been possible to extract metals from ores and melt, smelt, and mold them into different shapes. Next came the discovery of how to smelt iron and harden it into steel, and by the time of Jesus Christ the new technology had taken root throughout the Middle East, India, and China. In the next 1,000 years, it spread to Europe and Southeast Asia and then to the European colonies in the New World. Each technological advance produced still more inventions: gun powder, horseshoes and harnesses, screws, woodturning lathes, magnets, water- and wind-powered mills, the spinning wheel, printing, porcelain, wheelbarrows, and clocks. Still later, on the eve of the Industrial Revolution, the steam engine and power-driven tools were developed.

It is important to get some sense of the speed of technological innovation and its effects on industrial expansion during the early stages of the Industrial Revolution, for it shows how accumulated innovations and key inventions can bring about startling changes, even without scientific breakthroughs. The Industrial Revolution began in the mid-1700s, but by 1845, the production of textiles was five times greater than it was in 1760; iron production was 24 times greater; and coal mining was 9 times greater (Deane and Cole, 1962). By contrast, it took horticultural societies the better part of 4,000 years to advance from hoes and digging sticks to the plow.

In the mid-1800s the use of steam power in transportation boosted industrialization by linking distant markets, lowering the cost of moving goods, and stimulating demand and production. Goodyear discovered how to make rubber hold up in extreme hot and cold, and the emerging chemical and petroleum industries added to the momentum of technological change. Farmers traded in horse-drawn plows for threshers, mowers, reapers, steam plows, and chemical fertilizers. In 1860, electric power became a reality with the invention of dynamos and transformers. In the twentieth century the pace of technological innovation has increased dramatically. Long-distance communications, nuclear power and weapons, transistors and micro-chips, lasers, organ transplants, genetic engineering, superconductors, and the widespread use of computers in everything from toys to industrial robots are only a few of the major innovations.

Over the last two centuries, then, both the sophistication and the quantity of technology have increased dramatically; but technology has also become more complex, which brings its own problems. In his book, *Normal Accidents*, Perrow (1984) argues that such complex technologies as nuclear power plants are virtually certain to produce serious accidents regardless of how careful we are in running them or how many safety systems are involved. The key, Perrow shows, lies first in the complexity of such systems, for the more connections there are between different parts of a system, the more things there are that can go wrong *in unpredictable ways*. If one small part in a complex system fails, it will affect several others which, in turn, will affect still others. The number of possible combinations of causes and effects quickly becomes so huge that it is impossible to anticipate them all.

The second key lies in how "tightly coupled" a system is. In a tightly coupled system, there is little flexibility, which means that when one part fails it has immediate effects on other parts, which leaves little room for error. Perrow argues that a system that is *both* complex *and* tightly coupled is bound to fail sooner or later. The only way to prevent accidents in these cases, he believes, is to not build such systems in the first place.

The problem of tightly-coupled, complex systems seems to have also played an important role in the 1987 stock market crash. Although the workings of the stock market are too complex to go into here, the crux of the problem is this: Increasingly, computers have been used to decide whether to buy or sell stock depending on how market conditions change from one moment to the next. The decisions are made automatically, with lightning speed, and involve transactions that can amount to hundreds of millions of dollars. Huge transactions can change the market conditions to which other computers react, stimulating—

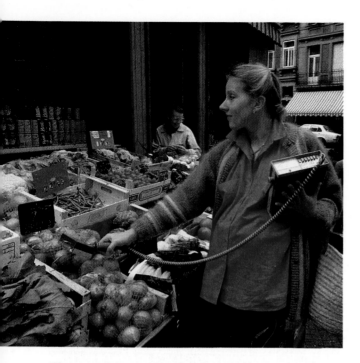

The complexity and tightly-coupled structure of nuclear power technology raise profound questions about its safety. In 1987, a reactor at Chernobyl in the Soviet Union melted down and sent radiation over most of Europe. In this picture taken in the Alsace region of France, a woman uses a Geiger counter to check produce in a local market. The extensive amount of radiation made it necessary to plow under many crops and to dump great quantities of milk and other foods.

within a matter of seconds—equally huge transactions. The result can be chaotic conditions in the market with stock prices fluctuating so much that investors begin to lose confidence in their understanding of what is happening, precipitating the kind of panic of which stock market crashes are made.

As the above suggests, and as we will see in the following section, as science and technology become increasingly complex, so do their effects on social life.

SCIENCE, TECHNOLOGY, AND SOCIETY

As the functional and conflict perspectives make clear, science can be understood both in terms of its consequences for society and social life and in terms of the unequal distribution of its benefits.

Functions and Dysfunctions

In looking at science from a functional perspective, it is important to pay attention to the ways in which its own structure and culture produce functional and dysfunctional consequences. Intense competition among scientists and pressures to succeed are certainly functional for promoting rapid innovation, but they also encourage secrecy, distortion of research results, fraud, sabotage of competing projects, and the publication of results that, although trivial, add to a scientist's list of publications. Shilts (1987) reports that some scientists, in their rush to be the first to achieve a breakthrough on AIDS research, withheld information from one another, a violation of the norm of communism that improved their competitive advantage at the expense of AIDS victims.

There is a similar mixture of functions and dysfunctions in the complex division of labor in modern science. On the one hand, narrow specialization makes science more efficient in generating and evaluating enormous amounts of new information. On the other hand, it discourages scientists in different disciplines—or even in different specialties of the same discipline—from talking with one another. This kind of isolation interferes with the crucial process through which discoveries and insights in one area have unanticipated benefits for work in others (see Barnes, 1985).

From a functional perspective, science and technology have a variety of functional consequences for society. Together, they have been responsible for unprecedented levels of agricultural and industrial production, revolutionary developments in communications, travel, energy, the storage and use of information (computers), and, as we will see shortly, enormous strides in health and longevity, from the virtual eradication of major infectious diseases to organ transplants and laser surgery.

As with most aspects of social life, however, science and technology also produce dysfunctional consequences. Control over infectious diseases saves millions of lives, especially those of small children; ironically, this has contributed to a population explosion, one of whose effects is to worsen already impoverished living conditions. Chemical pesticides have dramatically increased agricultural productivity around the world, and yet have also poisoned much of the natural environment. Although use of the lethal pesticide DDT has been banned in much of the world for some time, it was used so heavily that traces of it are now found everywhere, from the North Pole to mother's milk. At the same time that it enriches us, industry produces toxic wastes that poison water supplies and fall as acid rain on lakes and streams, defoliating trees and killing fish. In 1984, thousands of people were killed and hundreds of thousands injured by a leak of deadly gases from a U.S.-owned chemical plant in Bhopal, India. As we witnessed at Three Mile Island and, more recently, the Chernobyl accident in the Soviet Union, the benefits of nuclear power are offset by the continuing problem of disposing of nuclear wastes, and the danger of devastating accidents that affect people hundreds of miles away (see Perrow, 1984).

Technology has done much to make industrial production more efficient, but in the process it has also produced unemployment and hardship for millions of workers by making their skills obsolete. Although innovations such as assembly-line robots and word processors create some jobs for those with higher levels of skill, it leaves behind the millions of poor people who do not have access to such skills. Our ability to make production more efficient than ever threatens to create a permanent underclass.

As we have seen, the rise of science has been part of a general move towards the rationalization of social life, and science has become a dominant institutional approach to establishing truth in many societies. One problem with this is that as societies look to science as a source of truth, nonscientists—who include most citizens and politicians—are likely to lose confidence in themselves and implement decisions whose basis they do not fully understand. Habermas (1971) argues that the result can be a **technocracy** in which expertise is power and social problems are viewed in narrow and unrealistic terms as little more than technical issues of social management and maintaining and improving society as if it were only a machine (see also Barnes, 1985). Most of us find it difficult to form a clear opinion on highly technical issues such as the safety of nuclear power or the feasibility of the Star Wars Defense Initiative because they hinge on knowledge that most of us simply do not have. Given the enormous social importance of such questions, the social boundaries that separate scientists and nonscientists take on added significance as an important part of the distribution of power in society.

As you may have gathered from these many functional and dysfunctional consequences, most flow not from science itself, but from technology. Science consists of nothing but knowledge and theories about how the world works, and there is nothing inherent in

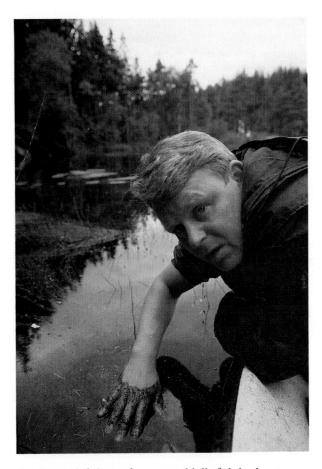

Acid rain defoliates forests and kills fish by leaving deposits such as these skimmed from a lake by a scientist in Sweden.

science that demands that it be used for anything. The knowledge of chemistry necessary to make plastics does not *have* to be used actually to make plastics, just as an understanding of atomic physics does not have to be used to make nuclear power plants or nuclear weapons. Such decisions usually rest with other institutions, which raises the critical issue of how different interests are served by science and technology.

Science, Technology, and Social Conflict

Although scientists are often seen as people who are insulated from the affairs of society, who carry out their work in the solitude of laboratories, the work of science is bound up with a wider social world. Nor does the high value science places on objectivity ensure that science will be simply a neutral vehicle for searching out truth regardless of whom it hurts or whose interests it serves. In increasingly complex ways, technology and scientific expertise are sources of power, and, as such, they play an important part in social conflict.

This is due, in part, to the dependence of "Big" science on the financial resources of large organizations, which often have goals that have little to do with objectivity or the pursuit of truth and much to do with social inequality. Many U.S. scientists do research that has military applications, which gives science a major role in political tensions, especially those involving the U.S. and the Soviet Union. This not only leads these scientists to engage in research projects that might otherwise have no appeal to them, but it can also lead them to make scientific judgments on political rather than scientific grounds. Such conflicts are even more apparent among engineers who design technology. The disastrous destruction of the space shuttle Challenger might never have happened were it not for the intense political and economic pressures being exerted on shuttle engineers to keep the launch program on schedule, pressures that led officials to ignore scientific judgments that the shuttle was unsafe.

Science and technology are also important in more general conflicts between wealthy and poor nations, for both military and economic power are more dependent than ever on scientific and technological abilities. A virtual monopoly over productive technology is one of the keys to the dominance of a relative few industrial nations over the world economy.

Within societies, science and technology play an important part in the perpetuation of social inequality.

Genetic technology may revolutionize agriculture by greatly increasing production, but as the Office of Technology Assessment (1986b) points out, this technology will be so expensive that only large farm corporations will be able to afford it. This, in turn, will make small and medium-size farms even less able to compete and will accelerate their demise and the increasing concentration of wealth and power in agriculture.

In industry, technology has been used increasingly to replace workers by making the production process more efficient. Strikes become less and less effective as employers are able to transfer work from one site to another (by sending computer files over telephone lines) or to get by with fewer workers through automation. Computers are being used extensively in many offices to closely monitor worker behavior—effectively the same as having someone looking over your shoulder every second of the work day. Such developments strengthen the position of capitalists and weaken that of workers by making workers easier to replace and by making it less likely that highly skilled and less skilled workers will organize around common interests. As production becomes increasingly dependent on sophisticated technology and less dependent on relatively unskilled labor, the position of the working class becomes still more insecure (see Zuboff, 1988).

Science also affects inequality when it is used to justify or explain inequality, or when it is used to refute prejudicial claims against minorities. On the one hand, scientific theory has often been looked upon as a source of support for prejudiced beliefs

Computer technology has greatly expanded the ability of employers to keep watch on and control workers. Many businesses regard such practices as reasonable steps to increase productivity. Many workers, however, view them as unwarranted invasions of privacy.

about nonwhites and women by giving prejudice the social legitimacy conferred by "scientific objectivity." This has been particularly true of the use of "nature" arguments to explain and justify the subordinate position of women on the grounds that the social arrangements around gender are dictated by biological differences. Science itself continues to be a largely male occupation dominated by strongly masculinist values, and it has only been recently that a feminist scholarship has emerged which systematically examines the impact of science on gender roles and inequality (see Bleier, 1984; Fausto-Sterling, 1985; Keller, 1985).

On the other hand, what progress there has been toward racial and gender equality in the last thirty years owes much to the research of social and physical scientists which has sustained a vigorous and effective attack on the cultural stereotypes and mythology that underlie prejudice and discrimination. From the sociologists whose findings were instrumental in the landmark 1954 Supreme Court school desegregation decision to the biologists and geneticists who have demonstrated that racial and gender differences have far more to do with social than biological factors, scientists have played a key role in the search for social justice.

Whether we use the conflict or the functional perspective, it is clear that the effects of science and technology on social life are increasingly pervasive and complex. Nowhere is this more visible than in the area of medical institutions and health care.

MEDICAL INSTITUTIONS

Human life is inherently frail—from the inevitability of dying to the ease with which new micro-organisms, such as the AIDS virus, can devastate us. Beyond their effect on individuals, death and disease have profound social effects on everything from families to entire societies. In the fourteenth century, the Black Death killed one-third of the entire population of Europe (Gottfried, 1983); in 1918 a worldwide influenza epidemic took some 20 million lives; and as we approach a new century, the true destructive potential of the AIDS pandemic looms as a frightening unknown. In the face of our fundamental vulnerability, it is no surprise that every known society has developed social arrangements around the issue of health.

Like other institutions, **medicine** is defined by basic social functions. The first two functions are to

maintain health by preventing illness and injury, and to restore health by healing injury and curing sickness. Third, medicine often performs a social control function, by defining the difference between "sanity" and "insanity," or by certifying births and deaths. Fourth, medicine is responsible for maintaining a society's store of knowledge about health and illness. In societies with highly developed scientific institutions, medicine also performs a research function by continually challenging existing understandings of health and illness and searching for better ones. In societies and subcultures in which science is not influential, medical knowledge is closer to religious belief than to scientific fact.

Medicine has changed enormously over the last two or three thousand years, and perhaps the clearest way to see this is by looking at the cultural and structural characteristics that make up medical institutions.

The Culture of Medicine

At the heart of any medical institution is a belief and value system—what amounts to a paradigm (although not necessarily a scientific one)—that both defines and makes sense of health and illness. Each society has ways of identifying and explaining what is going on in a human body, distinguishes between what is considered healthy and what is considered pathological, and defines appropriate ways to maintain health and cure illness. In nineteenth-century Europe, open enjoyment of sexuality by women was taken as a sign of ill health, and some physicians went so far as to surgically remove the clitoris as a way to "cure" this "condition." Today, by comparison, it is considered unhealthy for women *not* to enjoy their sexuality.

The earliest known medical paradigm is traced to the Greek physician Hippocrates, who, some 2,500 years ago, developed the view that health and illness depend on the balance between different sorts of bodily fluids. The human body, he believed, was like a furnace to which the lungs supply air and food supplies fuel. Hippocrates' approach was based on what amounted to the common sense of his culture, not on any scientifically verified knowledge of cause and effect.

This basic approach was influential throughout Europe for many centuries. As recently as the late eighteenth century in colonial America, typical treatments of disease included attempts to "purify" the body by drawing blood (a treatment that led to the death of George Washington, who had come down

Hospitals were once very dangerous places, in large part because the importance of germs was not understood and surgery was typically carried out in highly unsanitary conditions (note the absence of gloves and masks as surgeons bend over and work on the open wound).

with nothing more than a bad cold); blistering (burning the skin in the belief that the resulting pus was a healthy vehicle for removing toxic substances); inducing massive vomiting or giving powerful laxatives; and prescribing medicines, some of which themselves contained potent poisons such as mercury.

It was not until the mid-1800s that Louis Pasteur discovered the causal connection between germs and disease and revolutionized beliefs about health and illness. Germ theory was an entirely new paradigm that explained a wealth of health problems such as the high mortality rate of mothers after childbirth (doctors often went from performing autopsies on corpses to delivering babies without washing their hands in between). Germ theory did more than revolutionize medical knowledge, it also was instrumental in making medicine a scientifically based profession of enormous power.

Sociologists draw a sharp distinction between the social and medical models of illness. According to the medical model, illness is an objective state of being—something goes wrong in the body and needs to be fixed through medical intervention. The social model, however, also considers that what may be defined as illness in one social environment may be looked upon as quite normal in another, and that the pressures and limitations imposed by social environments can affect our health. The American Psychiatric Association defined homosexuality as a mental illness until the 1970s when, partly in response to pressure from gay rights groups, it redefined homosexuality as nothing more than a nonpathological sexual preference.

Going in the opposite direction, what is initially defined as a nonmedical problem may come to be identified as an illness. Alcoholism and drug abuse have increasingly been defined less as moral failings than as treatable diseases. Alcoholism is an interesting case, for even if biological factors predispose some people to it, this is unlikely to be an explanation for differences in the rate of alcoholism among societies or subgroups within societies. To understand the causes of alcoholism, either in a specific individual or in society as a whole, it is necessary to pay attention not only to individual characteristics, but to the ways in which they interact with the social environment. Our culture heavily promotes the use of alcohol, especially through advertising, and there are enormous pressures for people to drink at parties and other social occasions. A full understanding of something like alcoholism, then, depends on a combination of the medical and social models of illness.

Values and Social Conflict   Because medicine deals with issues of life and death, values play a crucial role in medical practice and are often the source of deeply divisive social conflict. The central value of traditional medicine is to at least "do no harm" to patients if it is not possible to achieve the higher values of healing and curing. In the U.S., prevention and health maintenance generally have lower value since physicians tend to be more interested in helping those who are already in ill health, but this is not true of many alternative approaches to medicine such as holistic medicine (which emphasizes the importance of proper diet).

The vital role played by physicians in life and death decisions often places them at the center of difficult moral dilemmas and bitter social conflicts. Is it preferable to live a long life plagued by chronic pain and dependence on machines or to live a shorter life with less pain and greater independence? Is it more important to save the life of an expectant mother or the life of her unborn child? Should badly deformed newborns or terminally ill patients be allowed to die? Should doctors and nurses have the right to refuse to treat patients who have dangerous infectious diseases such as AIDS? Should doctors have the right to force a pregnant woman to undergo surgery in order to ensure the safe delivery of her child even though she forbids it? Does the state have the right to participate in the relationship between doctors and their patients by forbidding abortion?

Given the close relationship between the growth of medicine and the growth of science and technology, it is not surprising that many of the moral dilemmas centering on health and illness are closely connected to innovations in technology. The ability to detect birth defects in unborn children through the use of sound waves confronts parents and doctors with the option of aborting a badly deformed fetus, a choice that simply did not exist before technology made such knowledge of the fetus available. Technology that enables doctors to keep patients alive long after they would otherwise have been left to die raises profound questions about the meaning of life and death (when is someone dead?) and equally profound dilemmas for doctors and family members who must decide whether to "pull the plug." Similarly, the technological ability to transplant organs from one body to another can create pressures to "give up" on one patient perhaps prematurely in the rush to secure organs for donation to another. All of these and scores of other moral dilemmas simply would not occur without the appropriate technology.

As we would expect with values, there are no simple answers to these moral dilemmas, and yet they occur every day. Physicians, patients, family members, judges, and hospital administrators must decide one way or another. To solve many of them, physicians rely on the guidelines established by their profession, which raise the question of how medical institutions are structured.

The Structure of Medicine

On the simplest level, the structure of medical institutions revolves around the role relationship between patients and healers. The sick role defines what is expected of people who are identified as ill, including the requirement to do whatever they can to get well and resume their usual role obligations (see Parsons, 1951). Physicians are bound by norms such as the expectation that they will keep confidential whatever their patients reveal to them.

The explosive growth and increasing complexity of science and technology over the past century have gone hand-in-hand with similar changes in the structure of medicine. Gone is the simple relationship between doctor and patient, for the role set of the typical physician now includes not only patients, but complex bureaucracies such as hospitals, insurance companies, state licensing boards, and professional organizations that set standards and discipline their members. In many states, physicians are moving away from private practice and becoming employees of health care corporations known as Health Maintenance Organizations (or HMOs, for short).

Like science, the role structure of medicine includes an expanding number of specialties in which doctors concentrate not only on particular parts of the body (such as eyes, ears, nose, and throat), but on particular treatments (such as surgery or anesthesiology) or diseases (such as cancer) (see Cockerham, 1986; Kurtz and Chalfant, 1984). The most profound structural changes in medicine, however, involve the distribution of power and authority, both within the practice of medicine and in the relation of medical institutions to society as a whole.

Power and Authority   From the perspective of the medical profession, one of the unanticipated effects of the development of germ theory and the emergence of scientific medicine is that physicians greatly increased their practical ability to cure and heal, to some degree by enabling them simply to avoid actually doing harm to their patients. Prior to the discovery of germs, hospitals were dangerous places that all but the poorest patients avoided (middle- and upper-class patients preferred to be treated at home). It was only when hospitals were perceived as doing more good than harm that they became popular, and this was due largely to an understanding of the role of germs in disease and death (see Rosenberg, 1987).

In an important sense, the perception that doctors really knew what they were doing had an enormous impact on their authority over health care. Medicine rapidly became a highly skilled profession requiring rigorous training and certification, and granting its members almost complete autonomy, the highest level of prestige accorded any occupation, and a monopoly over what was accepted as valid knowledge and practice about health and illness (see Starr, 1982). In 1846 physicians formed the American Medical Association (AMA) and soon persuaded state legislatures to grant them a legal monopoly over health care. Alternatives such as chiropractic medicine were denied legal standing, and midwives—who once delivered most babies—were gradually excluded from obstetrics (see Ehrenreich and English, 1979). So deliberate and persistent were the efforts of the AMA to discredit chiropractors, that in 1987 a federal court found the AMA guilty of "systematic, long-term wrongdoing with the intent to destroy a licensed profession" (*New York Times*, August 31, 1987).

Today, gender continues to affect the authority structure of medicine as nurse-practitioners (most of whom are women) take over many of the functions traditionally performed by physicians, such as routine physical exams. Although many doctors resist such changes on the grounds that it lowers the quality of patient care, there are clearly other issues involved including a desire by physicians to maintain professional boundaries and the rewards and privileges that come with them.

Although medicine is still the most powerful and prestigious profession, recently many physicians have felt threatened as they have found themselves working as employees of large health maintenance organizations. Many physicians who work for HMOs believe their independence and autonomy to make medical judgments are being interfered with by corporations whose primary interest is in making a profit from medical care. In some cases—such as in Minneapolis—physicians have begun to talk seriously of forming a union (*New York Times*, July 13, 1987, p. D1). This is a dilemma that is similar to that faced by many scientists, for science and medicine have become so dependent on expensive technology that it is difficult to practice either without accepting some measure of dependency on large organizations. The consequences of this include not only threats to the standing of individual doctors and the authority and autonomy of medicine as a profession, but also the people and society served by medical institutions (Hillman, 1987).

Medicine and Society: A Functional Approach

From a functional perspective, one of the most dramatic changes that has occurred over the last century

For most of history, child delivery has been exclusively in the hands of midwives. In this seventeenth-century engraving, midwives are shown with a special delivery table and obstetrical instruments. After more than a century of suppression by the medical profession, midwives are now making a comeback in many parts of the U.S.

has been in the **medicalization** of society, a process through which medicine and the medical model have come to play a role in areas of life not usually associated with health and illness.

This is seen most simply in the sheer growth of health care in industrialized societies. In 1940, total national expenditures for health care in the U.S. amounted to 4 percent of the gross national product (GNP—the value of all goods and services produced in that year). By 1985, however, the percentage of the GNP going to health care had almost tripled to 11 percent, or $1,721 for every woman, man, and child (U.S. Census Bureau, 1975a, 1986a). Even after taking inflation and the growth of the population into account, we spent almost eight times as much on health care in 1985 as in 1940 (Figure 17-1).

The medicalization of society also occurs through the growing influence of physicians and the medical perspective in many areas of life. The simple act of giving birth has been transformed from an event that

rarely involved doctors and took place in the home to a highly medicalized procedure taking place in hospitals under the control of physicians. In an increasing number of cases, doctors, with authority granted them by the courts, have claimed the right to force expectant mothers to undergo surgery when they believe it is in the best interests of the fetus, even when the mother is opposed to it.

Many other life events have come to be viewed in medical terms, including hyperactivity in children, child abuse, alcoholism, drug abuse, obesity, mental disorders such as schizophrenia, insomnia, depression, and even our physical appearance. In some cases the medical perspective plays a part in social control by redefining deviant behavior, such as by defining alcoholism and drug abuse not as moral failings but as diseases whose victims deserve help rather than blame. In criminal trials, the role played by psychiatrists in determining whether defendants are legally "insane" and therefore not legally responsible for their behavior has become increasingly controversial, especially since John Hinckley used the insanity defense to successfully avoid punishment for his attempted assassination of President Reagan in 1981.

As powerful as the medical profession is, public acceptance of its authority is far from absolute. Many argue against the use of psychiatry in courtrooms on the grounds that psychiatrists cannot accurately determine the state of mind of a defendant at the time a crime is committed and that the medicalization of crime is used inappropriately to relieve people of responsibility for their actions. In the health care system, patients have begun to organize and assert their rights in relation to physicians, from demanding access to their records and full disclosure of their medical conditions to resisting the authority of physicians to force unwanted surgery on them. Many doctors feel overwhelmed by the threat of malpractice suits and soaring malpractice insurance premiums, sometimes to the extent of refusing to treat patients with a history of suing their doctors, or of leaving medical specialties that involve risky treatments.

A Conflict Approach to Medicine

Health care is a product of social life, and as with most valued products, access to it is often distributed unevenly. As we saw in Chapter 5, although Great Britain, Canada, and most of Europe have national health insurance plans that guarantee equal access to health

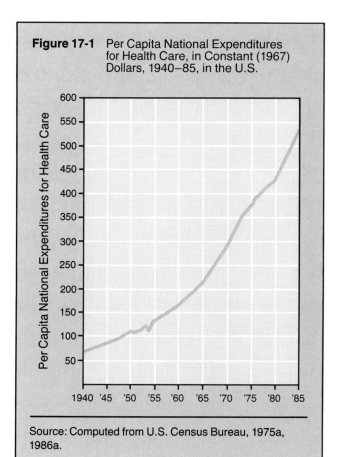

Figure 17-1   Per Capita National Expenditures for Health Care, in Constant (1967) Dollars, 1940–85, in the U.S.

Source: Computed from U.S. Census Bureau, 1975a, 1986a.

care, the United States is the only industrial country in which health care is marketed as a commodity whose availability depends on the ability to pay. A major consequence of this is that class position has a strong effect on health care, health, and, ultimately, mortality. Blacks and the poor have poorer health than whites and the middle and upper classes. Infant mortality is considerably higher among blacks, largely because of poor prenatal care (see One Step Further 17-1).

The conflict approach reveals not only unequal access to medical care, but unequal treatment by medical institutions for those who seek care and use of medical authority and expertise as a tool in social oppression. Involuntary surgery is far more likely to be forced on blacks and women—especially if they are poor—than on whites and others higher in the class system. One study found that elderly women are less likely than younger women to receive appropriate treatment for breast cancer even when they are otherwise in excellent health, a finding that may reflect discrimination based on both gender and age (Greenfield et al., 1987). In authoritarian societies, such as the Soviet Union and, until recently, Argentina, medicine is often used as a means for controlling political dissidents, who may be diagnosed as schizophrenics and committed to mental hospitals as a form of pun-

---

ONE STEP FURTHER 17-1:
Why Do So Many Babies Die in the U.S.?

In spite of the wealth and technological sophistication of the U.S., infants are more likely to die here than in almost any other industrial nation. Why? Part of the answer lies with our relatively large poor population, the inadequate prenatal health care they receive, and an unusually large rate of teenage pregnancy (also one of the highest among industrialized nations). Poor nutrition and the lack of good prenatal medical care are major causes of infant death. In addition, infants born to teenage mothers tend to be of low birth weight, which also makes infants vulnerable.

If you look at the percentages in the columns in Table B-17-1, you can see how the combination of these factors makes the health of expectant mothers and their babies especially vulnerable among blacks, who are far more likely than whites to be poor. In 1984, black babies were more than twice as likely as whites to be born to teenage mothers (24 percent vs. 11 percent) and 10 times more likely to be born to mothers under the age of 15 (1 percent vs. .1 percent). Black mothers were considerably less likely to begin prenatal care early (62 percent vs. 80 percent) and twice as likely to get little or no prenatal care at all (10 percent vs. 5 percent). As a result of these and other factors, black babies

are twice as likely to have a low weight at birth (12 percent vs. 6 percent) and, as the infant mortality rates at the bottom show, twice as likely to die before their first birthday.

Table B-17-1

	WHITES	BLACKS
PERCENT OF ALL		
Births, 1984	80	16
Births to teenage mothers	11	24
Births to mothers under age 15	0.1	1
Births of babies with low birth weight	6	12
Babies born to mothers who began prenatal care in first three months of pregnancy	80	62
Babies born to mothers who began prenatal care in the last three months of pregnancy or not at all	5	10
Infant mortality rate	9	18

Source: National Center for Health Statistics, in the *New York Times*, June 26, 1987, p. A20.

ishment. Physicians may also lend their medical knowledge to the torture and abuse of political prisoners (Stover and Nightingale, 1985).

Science, Technology, Medicine, and Social Change: The Social Effects of Longer Lives

As we have seen, science and technology are, by their very nature, sources of social change. This is particularly true of the ways in which they combine to produce dramatic changes in the structures of social life.

Consider the simple fact that scientific findings on everything from germ theory to the causes of heart disease, combined with medical technology—such as the ability to maintain clean drinking water supplies or perform open heart surgery or organ transplants—have greatly increased human longevity, especially in industrial societies. In the nineteenth century, only two-thirds of all children ever became adults compared with 98 percent today (U.S. Census Bureau, 1975a, 1986a). In the late 1980s centenarians—those 100 years or older—are our fastest growing age group (U.S. Census Bureau, 1987i). Since the first human heart transplant in 1967, the number of transplants has grown to almost 2,000 per year (*New York Times*, December 1, 1987).

The social consequences of the simple extension of the human life span are far-reaching and complex (see Riley, 1987). As the population ages, there is a strain to shift resources from the needs of the young to those of the elderly, and this can cause friction between generations. A longer life span allows us to prolong education. Retirement—once a rarity—becomes commonplace and occupies up to a quarter of our lives. Perhaps most dramatic are the effects on family relationships, for they are the only ties that last a lifetime. Instead of having one parent die early in a child's adulthood (as was common less than a century ago), most children today can expect to have living parents long into their own old age. This not only makes the goal of having marriages last "till death do us part" more difficult, but raises challenges for changing relationships between children and parents. Longer life for our parents means many years of working out relationships as relative equals or, if parents become disabled late in their lives, as their caretakers as the direction of the dependency is reversed.

Greater longevity also changes family structures by making them more complex. A century ago less than half of middle-aged married couples in the U.S. had any surviving parents; but today half have two or more parents living (Uhlenberg, 1980). One result is typical families whose living kin include at least four intact generations. When we combine this with high divorce and remarriage rates, the staggering complexity of kinship and step-kinship ties raises enormous challenges for family life. As Riley (1987) put it, "a new system of kinship is in the making" (p. 8).

Finally, as life is extended, often by technological means, the process of dying is itself being transformed (Riley, 1983). A century ago most people died outside of hospitals, many of them at home. By comparison, in the late twentieth century most elderly people die in institutions—hospitals, hospices, or nursing homes—that, by comparison, confine death to sterile, medical settings devoid of familiar surroundings and dominated by a view that death is primarily a medical event.

As with other changes associated with science and technology, none of these is inevitable, for they all depend on how we choose to use the knowledge and capabilities they make possible. The enormous potential benefits as well as the dangers that go along with such choices guarantee that science, technology, and medicine will continue to confront us with some of our deepest value conflicts and most disturbing moral dilemmas. What they cannot provide us, however, is a

This hospice patient knows that she is dying, and is allowed to do so with a level of emotional support and comfort generally unavailable in traditional hospitals.

resolution of our conflicts or a way out of our dilemmas. For these we must look elsewhere in the institutional structure of our society.

SUMMARY

1. In its dedication to seeking new knowledge and testing old assumptions, science is unique among social institutions.

2. By providing assumptions and beliefs about the world, paradigms form the cultural core of science and are the most resistant to change. When the practice of normal science generates enough anomalies that do not fit prevailing paradigms, the result is a scientific revolution in which new paradigms replace the old. The functional and conflict perspectives are examples of two major paradigms in sociology.

3. It is important to be aware of the ways in which nonscientific values affect scientific work, especially those that guide the choice of research problems that can have important social implications.

4. Scientific work is guided by the norms of universalism, communism, disinterestedness, and organized skepticism. Deviance from scientific norms, especially in the form of fraud, is often caused by the same factors that explain deviance in other areas of social life, such as pressures to succeed without access to the means to succeed.

5. Historically, science has been transformed from a pastime engaged in primarily by well-to-do individuals to a highly skilled profession that carefully maintains its boundaries and its control over the determination of truth. At the same time, the structure of science has become far more complex as it has been taken over by large institutions and scientists have increasingly specialized their interests.

6. The institutionalization of science has greatly diminished the autonomy of scientists; but this is to some degree balanced by the fact that the reward scientists want most is the recognition of other scientists.

7. The relationship between technology and science is complex and often, although not always, reciprocal. Breakthroughs in each area are often made independently. The impact of technology on social life has accelerated greatly as technology has become increasingly sophisticated, complex, and tightly coupled.

8. The functional and conflict perspectives reveal important aspects not only of the workings of science itself, but of the effects of science and technology on society and social inequality. Most of these effects are due not to science and technology per se, but to the ways in which they are used in other institutional settings.

9. As an institution, medicine is defined by its social functions, which include prevention and healing, social control, maintaining the store of knowledge about health and illness, and, in some societies, by conducting medical research.

10. The culture of medicine rests on a medical model of health and illness which defines human conditions in terms of bodily functions that can be improved through medical intervention. This contrasts with the social model that also pays attention to the use of culture to define the difference between health and illness.

11. As with science, the structure of medicine has grown increasingly professionalized and complex, and the authority for medical decisions has begun to shift from individuals to large bureaucratic organizations. From a functional perspective, medicine has assumed increasing social importance, most notably in the medicalization of many aspects of social life.

12. Medicine also plays a part in social inequality. This is seen in inequality within the medical profession, unequal access to medical care, and inequalities in the ways in which patients are treated depending on their social statuses.

13. The far-reaching and complex social effects of science, technology, and medicine are illustrated by advances in human longevity, which have affected everything from schooling and the structure of marriage and the family to retirement and the meaning of death.

KEY TERMS

anomalies   463
medicalization   479
medicine   475

Looking Elsewhere

Having studied Chapter 17, you might want to look at related discussions in *Human Arrangements*, which include

- the use of scientific methods in sociological research (Chapter 2, pp. 29–30)

- the socialization of physicians (Chapter 6, p. 154)

- professions as occupations (Chapter 18, pp. 500–501)

- doctor-patient role relationships (Chapter 4, pp. 79–80, 82, 85)

- when doctors lie to dying patients (Chapter 14, p. 386)

- the hospice as a place to die (Chapter 14, p. 386)

- epidemiology—the study of disease (Chapter 5, pp. 109–110)

- technology and human ecology (Chapter 5, pp. 123–25)

- technology and social change (Chapter 22, pp. 604–607)

- technology and family life (Chapter 15, pp. 417–19)

- technology, automation, and work (Chapter 18, pp. 494–95)

- religion, science, and sociology (Chapter 20, pp. 544–45, 547)

- technology and varieties of religious belief (Chapter 20, pp. 556–57)

RECOMMENDED READINGS

BARNES, B. (1985). *About science.* New York: Basil Blackwell. A brief, clearly written, and provocative look at the problems confronting science as a social institution.

FAUSTO-STERLING, A. (1985). *Myths of gender: Biological theories about women and men.* New York: Basic Books. A biologist critically examines the uses and misuses of biological science in trying to understand gender differences.

HARRISON, M. (1982). *A woman in residence: A doctor's personal and professional battles against an insensitive medical system.* New York: Penguin Books. A daily journal provides an inside look at the need for reform of the medical profession and what it will take to bring it about.

KUHN, T. S. (1970). *The structure of scientific revolutions.* One of the most influential books ever written about the process through which scientific thought develops and changes.

MERTON, R. K. (1973). *The sociology of science.* Chicago: University of Chicago Press. A classic collection of articles by the leading figure in the sociology of science.

PERROW, C. (1984). *Normal accidents.* New York: Basic Books. A fascinating sociological analysis of the unavoidable risks inherent in the structure of technological systems such as nuclear power and air travel.

STARR, P. (1982). *The social transformation of American medicine.* New York: Basic Books. A Pulitzer prize went to this sociological analysis of the history of medicine in the United States. It is essential reading for anyone interested in the sociology of medicine.

The Roots of Capitalism

Feudalism: A Shift in Power

Buying, Selling, and the Rise of the Merchant Class

Capitalism as an Economic Arrangement

The Transformation of Labor

Advanced Capitalism: Relations of Production

Distributions of Power

Occupational Structures and Segmented Labor Markets

Life in the Labor Force

Socialism and Communism

The Social Structure of Socialist Economies

The World Economy

Power and Multinational Corporations

The Social Consequences of Economic Arrangements

Functions and Dysfunctions

Conflict, Change, and the Contradictions of Capitalism

18 Economic Arrangements

Stop for a moment and look at the characteristics of this book as an object: the print, pictures, cover, binding, use of color, and strings of words that communicate ideas. Now think about two questions: What did it take to bring this book into being, and how did it wind up in your hands?

In the simplest sense, this book has physical origins: lumber and paper mills, photographic equipment, typewriters, word processors, artists' pens and brushes, typesetting machines, printing presses and ink, glue and binding machines. In order to get to you, it had to be packed, shipped to a store, and then given to you in exchange for money. This book is also the result of energy—from electricity to gasoline. Together, these constitute what Marx called the **means of production**. They are the physical means through which goods and services are produced in a society.

All this, however, is not the whole story of where this book came from, for the means of production were used by people who worked in relation to one another and to the means of production. The author, editors, administrators and managers, sociologists, clerks, secretaries, artists, designers, photographers, typesetters, bookbinders, market researchers, salespeople, bookstore owners—all these and many more participated in a set of social **relations of production** through which this book and thousands like it are produced and distributed. Together, the means of production and the relations of production constitute the **mode of production**.

Economic institutions are enduring sets of cultural ideas and social relationships through which goods and services are produced and distributed in societies. Cultural characteristics of economic institutions include values that define the goals of productive activity (to feed people, to make a profit, or both?). Structural characteristics of economic institutions refer to how people work in relation with one another and to the means of production: who owns and controls the means of production, who decides what will be produced and how, who controls what is done with the results, and the kinds of roles people play in the production process.

I, for example, work under contract with my publisher. I agree to produce a manuscript by a certain date, in return for which I am paid a share of the returns from selling the book. I work in my house and use a word processor that I own. No one checks to see if I am at work this morning. So long as I get the job done on time, *I* decide how and when I work.

Most of the others who helped produce this book, however (like most people in our society), work for employers who buy their time for wages and decide what they will do with that time. These employees do not get a percentage of the proceeds from selling what their labor power helps to produce; they do not decide how and when they will work; and, most important, they do not own any means of producing goods or services other than themselves.

The characteristics of economic institutions determine how societies produce goods and services and how individuals participate in the production process; and one way to see how economic institutions affect societies and their people is to look at how those institutions have changed over the course of history. Imagine that we can condense 35,000 years into a single life span, so that each of us can experience the changes that have occurred. Where do we begin, where do we end up, and how do we get from there to here?

THE ROOTS OF CAPITALISM

We begin with tiny societies whose members survive by hunting wild game and gathering plants. There are neighboring societies some distance away; but we rarely encounter them except on long hunting expeditions, and generally have little to do with them. Virtually everyone except the smallest child produces

In hunter-gatherer and other non-market societies, such as the Bushmen of southern Africa or this fishing society on Africa's Ivory Coast, virtually everyone contributes to production. Control over production is communal, and, since goods are neither sold nor traded, sharing is the rule.

something; we share what we produce with everyone else, for kinship is the most important tie that binds us together into a single society (Murdock, 1967). Our division of labor is simple and based entirely on age and gender. Although each of us contributes to production in different ways, no one's contribution is valued so highly that it gives him or her a great advantage of prestige or power.

We consume everything that we produce, which means that the value of everything from meat to clothing is based solely on its **use value**. Control of the means of production is *collective*, and our economy is *communal*, much like that of the Melanesian tribes that Malinowski (1922) studied in the 1920s. We help one another as friends and family members—not for personal gain, but because we feel a social obligation to cooperate with and help one another.

Thousands of years pass (until roughly 7000 B.C.), and we discover how to grow food. We invent simple tools, and as our technology grows—especially with the invention of the plow—we are able to produce more than we need to survive. Our population grows because we can feed more people; but, most important, our ability to produce a surplus affects both the structure of our society and its relation to others.

Everyone no longer must produce food. Some can make clay pots, mats to sleep on, or fancy clothes

to wear during celebrations. Whereas we once produced things only for their use value, we can now exchange some of what we produce for goods that we do not make ourselves. We can trade some of our fancy clothes for things produced in other societies: arrows or medicinal herbs. Even food—if we produce a surplus—takes on **exchange value** in addition to use value.

When goods have exchange value, they are **commodities**. For the first time, we trade with each other—commodity for commodity—and our economy is changing into a **market economy** in which the exchange value of goods determines what can be bartered for what. I make fancy clothes but I do not grow food; you grow food but do not make fancy clothes; so we trade one for the other. This means that we have to deal continually with the problem of deciding what amount of clothing is "worth" what amount of food. The basic mechanism in bartering is the balance between how much labor it takes to make clothing and food and how much each of us wants or needs what the other produces.

Although many aspects of our society—such as family life—do not operate like a market, a market economy significantly changes the culture and structure of our society. Getting a fair (if not the "best") deal replaces sharing as our most important economic value, and the means of production are no longer

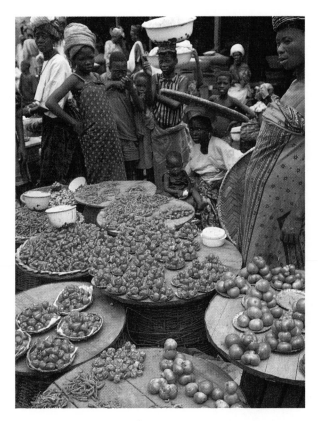

The seemingly simple shift from producing food, such as tomatoes and peppers, for the purpose of eating to producing in order to buy and sell in markets, such as this one in Nigeria, brings with it a profound shift in economic and other values.

collectively owned. Each of us owns and controls some means of production and uses it and what it produces to get what we need and want through market exchanges.

As the number of different goods and services grows, we discover that bartering is a very inefficient way of getting what we need and want. Once you have all the clothes you want, or if you think the clothes I make are ugly, how do I get food from you? How, in short, can I get something that you produce when you do not want what I produce? The answer that developed around 2000 B.C. was money, and it profoundly affected market relationships.

As a cultural yardstick for measuring wealth, money has taken many forms, including shells, furs, salt, cotton cloth, copper bracelets, bits of coral, dried fish, tobacco, sugar, cocoa, rice, and bitter almonds as well as precious metals such as gold and silver and,

more recently, paper (Braudel, 1981). Money is useful because it makes trading easier. Instead of trading commodities for commodities, we now use money. I trade my clothes for money and then trade my money for food. Exchanges now take the form of commodity-money-commodity, rather than the simpler form of commodity-commodity.

Feudalism: A Shift in Power

As the centuries pass (we are up to the early Middle Ages), populations grow more rapidly, divisions of labor are more complex, trade expands rapidly, and money is increasingly important as a medium of exchange. All of this supports an elite of nobles, kings, and queens, who maintain their positions by accumulating wealth in the form of money and land. The most significant aspect of this society, however, lies in the social relationships between producers and the elite.

Nobles use their power to protect people from other nobles; and many of these people are *serfs*, who give some of what they produce to the nobles in exchange for protection (Bloch, 1961). Although serfs are bound to the land and live generally miserable lives, both they and free workers control the means of production. They use land or tools and decide how much to produce. Unlike slaves, then, serfs control their own labor.

Serfs, however, are not allowed to dispose of what they produce as they choose. Even independent producers are regulated by craft guilds whose norms specify where and when they work, and what and how much they produce. Clearly, this new system—called **feudalism**—marks the beginning of a transformation that ultimately will affect almost every aspect of social life: *the control over the production process is shifting out of the hands of those who actually produce goods.*

Buying, Selling, and the Rise of the Merchant Class

Around the eleventh century, towns develop outside the walls of feudal estates, and after some struggle people free themselves from the dominance of the nobility (Dobb, 1947). Producers can now produce what they want, make the best trades they can, and accumulate a surplus.

At about this time some powerful residents of the towns make a discovery that will dramatically affect the development of societies: since economic

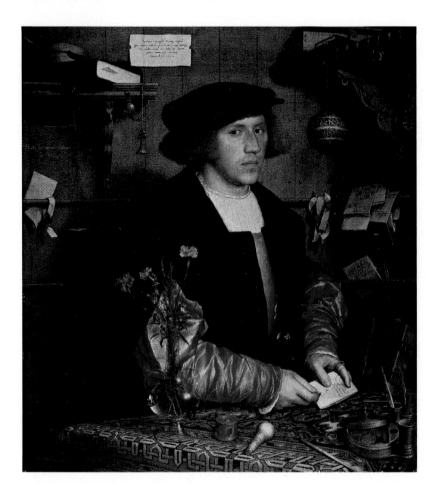

Merchants, such as this man in his London office in 1532, were the prime movers in the breakdown of feudalism and the elevation of profit and control over markets and labor to the highest levels of economic value.

exchange primarily involves money, why not use money to buy commodities and then sell them for still more money? These innovators—**merchants**—withdraw from the production process and make a radical transition from a commodity-money-commodity exchange to one that is money-commodity-money.

The new exchange is revolutionary because it changes the values that govern economic behavior. The purpose of exchange had been to get what we did not produce ourselves; and we were content to wind up with something whose value was comparable to what we gave up. Merchants, however, want to end up with more money than they start with. They make a profit by taking a share of what is produced through the labor of other people.

The appearance of merchants introduces a new social relationship—between producers and merchants; and the idea of profit is based on the terms of that relationship. In our earliest society goods had use value only; later they acquired exchange value determined by the value of the labor it took to produce them. Now, however, merchants want to sell goods at a higher price than they pay for them. One way to do this is to try to sell the goods for more than their value; but this makes it difficult to compete with other merchants.

A second alternative is to pay workers less than the value of their labor and keep what is left over. "What is left over" is called **surplus value**, and it is created by the relationships among workers, capital, and capitalists (Marx, 1867; see also Braverman, 1976). For the system to operate, workers must receive enough of the value of what they produce to maintain a standard of living that allows them to work (to buy enough food, shelter, clothing, and medical care to remain productive) and raise children who will become new workers. The "surplus" value consists of what is left over after taking out what is needed to maintain and reproduce workers.

It is important to understand that while surplus value is a form of profit, not all profit represents surplus value. When merchants buy goods in one place and sell them in another for more than their cost, they make a profit; but this is not surplus value, because the merchants do not own the capital used by workers to make the goods they buy and sell. Surplus value refers *only* to profit made by capitalists through their control over capital and, therefore, over workers.

Merchants increase profits by maximizing the difference between the value of goods and what it costs to produce that value—that is, by maximizing surplus value. Those who produce goods, however, can refuse to sell them to merchants if the offered price is too low, and consumers can refuse to buy if the price is too high. How, then, can merchants maximize their profits?

One answer is to increase control over those who produce goods and over the markets in which goods are sold—in other words, to change the structure of economic institutions. Before we see how this is accomplished, we have to understand the cultural and structural characteristics of *capitalism*—the economic arrangement toward which these changes are moving us.

Capitalism as an Economic Arrangement

As Adam Smith outlined in his enormously influential book, *The Wealth of Nations*, the values that underlie capitalism are those of private property, profit, rational self-interest, and free competition. The idea of private property does not refer to personal items such as clothing, but to **capital**, which is wealth—from hand tools to factories—that can be used to produce new wealth. **Capitalism** is an economic arrangement in which private individuals and groups have the authority to use and dispose of the means of production as they see fit. Capitalism values most highly the capitalist's self-interest—not loyalty to community, society, or kin. Capitalists compete with other capitalists, and the one who buys commodities at the cheapest cost and sells them at the highest price will be the most successful.

The growth of capitalism is facilitated in the sixteenth century when John Calvin founds the Calvinist religious sect. In his classic book, *The Protestant Ethic and the Spirit of Capitalism*, Max Weber argued that Calvinist religious doctrine and practices created conditions that contributed to the rise of capitalism as an economic arrangement. Calvinists believe that work is a "calling" done in the service of God, and that living in luxury is a sin. They also believe that whether people will go to heaven or to hell is decided at the moment of birth. Understandably, this creates a lot of anxiety since those who are to go to heaven do not know it and those who are condemned to hell can do nothing about it. In the face of this, it makes sense that people look for some sign of their eventual fate, something that indicates that they are among the select few who will go to heaven.

Given their beliefs about work and the importance of setting aside their wealth, it also makes sense that they interpret financial success as just such a sign. In the seventeenth century, Calvinism takes root in England and Scotland, and the accumulation of wealth becomes not only respectable, but almost a moral imperative. Members of the aristocracy, of course, were wealthy long before the seventeenth century, but Calvinism encourages them to accumulate wealth rather than use it to live luxuriously. Since capital is relatively expensive, a religious doctrine that encourages the accumulation of wealth was, Weber argued, an important cultural ingredient in the emergence of capitalism.

The rise of capitalism and the form it eventually acquires depends on far more than values and beliefs about work and wealth. In the 300 years after Calvin, technological revolutions and structural change will affect the relations of production and produce modern capitalism (see Kriedte, 1984). This brings us back to the basic problem of merchants and capitalists: how to control the cost of goods in order to maximize surplus value.

The Transformation of Labor

As goods increasingly are valued for exchange, landowners begin to use land in ways that radically alter social relationships. In feudal societies the ownership of land was the basis of power for the aristocracy: peasants grew food on land owned by the nobility and gave a share of what they produced to the lord in exchange for protection. Beginning in the sixteenth century, however, the demand for wool grows so large that landowners realize that they can do far better if they become capitalists and use their wealth to buy and use land to support sheep rather than to grow crops. Over a period of some 200 years, a great deal of agricultural land in England is "enclosed" and used entirely for sheepraising, and thousands of peasants become landless (Lazonick, 1974).

During the same period the cultural value placed on the right to own private property and do as one pleases with it reaches new heights (Dobb, 1947). The centuries-old relationship between serfs and the nobility begins to fall apart, producing thousands of landless peasants who, lacking a viable alternative, sell their labor power to capitalists. It is here that capitalists try to solve their problem of competing with one another by minimizing the cost of producing goods.

Landless peasants no longer control their own labor and are forced to sell their labor power to capitalists for whatever price capitalists are willing to pay. Labor power is transformed into a commodity: capitalists purchase it, put it to work in factories, and then sell what is produced. Unlike previous economic arrangements, this system allows people who sell their labor power to receive in return only a portion of the value of what they produce. When I sell chairs that I have made, I receive in return their full value, a value that is determined by the labor that went into them. If I sell my labor *power* to someone else, however, I receive less, because capitalists keep some of the value of what I produce—the surplus value—for themselves.

Capitalists increase their profits in four basic ways. First, they try to control the cost of production, which is facilitated by a growing class of landless peasants who have no choice but to work for someone since they no longer own or control any means of production. Capitalists are therefore in a position to exploit the landless peasants by paying them just enough to maintain and reproduce themselves (Dowd, 1974). Costs of production can also be minimized by introducing new ways of using labor power—assembly lines, for instance—or by replacing people with machines. In both cases, costs are reduced by increasing efficiency of production, which has become one of capitalism's most important values.

Second, capitalists can try to increase sales—through advertising, for example. Once they maximize the surplus value of each object they produce, they can then increase overall profits by selling as many of them as possible.

Third, capitalists can introduce new products and, possibly, new markets. Home video games and personal computers were unheard of just ten years ago, but opened up vast new markets for existing manufacturers and spawned a large number of new companies. To sell new products, however, capitalists must convince potential buyers to purchase them (something they failed at with home computers). As we will see later, advertising plays an important role in this by "manufacturing desire."

Fourth, they can increase profits by maximizing the price at which they sell finished goods, and one way to do this is to have a **monopoly**—in other words, to be the sole provider of a particular product. If everyone likes to drink tea, and I am the only one who imports tea from India and China, then you will either pay the price I ask or go without tea. This is, in fact, how some early English capitalists became rich—the king sold them monopolies over the tea trade (Hill, 1961).

Few sixteenth- and seventeenth-century English capitalists are able to buy monopolies from the king, and this means that the best way to increase profits is to exploit workers, and the control of labor power becomes one of the most important goals of capitalists. To compete with one another, capitalists must continually expand by making more and more profit and by acquiring still greater productive power. To expand, however, they must increase the surplus value of what their workers produce, and this means that they must give workers a shrinking share of what they make. Whereas expansion is the basic economic process through which capitalism develops, exploitation is the basic social process (Dowd, 1974).

We are now up to the nineteenth century, and the Industrial Revolution is in full swing. Before looking at modern capitalist societies as well as some alternative economic arrangements, go through Table 18-1 carefully, for it summarizes the major changes we have just described.

Notice how values and the social structures through which goods are produced and exchanged have changed. Values have shifted from use to exchange to surplus value. Social obligation, cooperation, and the importance of meeting social needs are giving way to rational self-interest, control over labor power, the ideal of free competition, and efficiency in the name of greater profit and capitalist expansion. Although the types of exchange are similar in feudal

Table 18-1

Summary of Economic Transformations: From Communalism to Capitalism

CHARACTERISTIC	COMMUNAL ECONOMIES	FEUDAL ECONOMIES	CAPITALIST ECONOMIES
Dominant Economic Values	Obligation to kin Use value of goods Cooperation Tradition Community control Social needs	Obligation to nobility and kin Exchange value of goods Regulated competition Tradition Control over labor Maintaining nobility	Rational self-interest Surplus value (profit) Free competition (capitalists) Innovation Control over labor power Efficiency
Types of Exchange	Sharing	Commodity-commodity (early) Commodity-money-commodity (early) Money-commodity-money (later)	Money-commodity-money (capitalists) Commodity-money-commodity (workers)
What Is Exchanged?	Labor	Labor, goods, and money	Labor, labor power, goods, and money
Who Owns the Means of Production?	Collective	Individual producers	Capitalists
Who Controls How Goods Are Disposed Of?	Collective	Individual producers Nobles	Capitalists
Division of Labor	Simple ⟶		Complex
Technology	Simple ⟶		Sophisticated
Social Organization	Gemeinschaft Primary group ⟶		Gesellschaft Bureacracy

and capitalist societies, *what* was exchanged changed dramatically when labor power became a commodity.

All of these changes were accompanied by rapid population growth, increasingly complex divisions of labor, and a shift in social organization from Gemeinschaft to Gesellschaft and from primary work groups to bureaucracies. Bureaucracy reinforces the separation of workers from the means of production, for it rests on such narrowly defined tasks and limited areas of responsibility that control over production is impossible for most workers; and in modern industrial societies, if people want to work, they must sooner or later find a place in bureaucratic organizations.

Before we examine twentieth-century capitalist societies in some detail, it is very important to raise some warning flags. The Industrial Revolution and the rise of capitalism were closely connected to each other.

Like all social arrangements, capitalism has both desirable and undesirable consequences, but it is difficult to know whether some of these are due to capitalism or to industrialization. Some of the negative aspects of capitalist societies—such as the alienation of workers—may occur in any industrial society whether it is capitalist or not.

As you read about capitalist societies you may also be tempted to conclude that their problems are not shared by noncapitalist societies such as the Soviet Union and China; but this is far from the truth. As ideal types capitalism and socialism differ sharply from each other. In practice, however, countries that are called "capitalist" and those that are called "socialist" have many of the same problems; and although socialist societies claim to have corrected many of the negative aspects of capitalism, in many areas of social life the conditions are far worse than they are under capitalism. Both kinds of societies, in short, have a long way to go before achieving their ideal economic arrangements.

Finally, the fact that socialist and capitalist countries share many common problems does not mean that the differences between them are merely theoretical. Workers in both types of societies have very little control over the economy; but the state has most of the power in socialist countries, whereas private individuals, groups, and organizations have most of the power in capitalist societies. The difference is a profound one, even though many of the consequences for workers are similar.

ADVANCED CAPITALISM: RELATIONS OF PRODUCTION

With the exception of the Soviet Union, the capitalist model guides the leading industrial societies of the world—Japan, the United States, West Germany, Great Britain, and France. What does capitalism look like in the twentieth century? How do capitalists pursue the goals of greater profit, efficiency, and control over labor power and markets? What does the division of labor look like, and how does it affect the perpetuation of capitalism and the positions of different social classes?

Distributions of Power

The ability of capitalists to compete with one another depends on two factors: control over labor power through which goods are produced and the control

---

Puzzles: Why No Revolution?

Karl Marx predicted revolutions in advanced industrial societies such as England and the United States, revolutions in which the working class would overthrow capitalism and install socialism. Obviously Marx's prediction has not yet come true. Why not?

The answer has to do with many social changes that Marx did not foresee, including the increasing power of the modern state and divisions within the working class, matters examined later in this chapter.

Puzzles: Why Do Workers Feel Powerless?

In spite of the fact that labor unions are supposed to benefit workers, more than 80 percent of workers in the U.S. do not belong to one. Why not?

While part of the answer certainly has to do with the bad reputations of many unions, most of the answer has to do with the structure of the U.S. economy and job market and the relatively powerless position of most workers within it, as this chapter explains.

---

over markets in which they are sold. To protect themselves, workers resist the attempts of capitalists to extract surplus value from them, and this, in turn, creates social conflict.

Controlling Labor   When wage labor was first introduced in the sixteenth century, peasants in England protested the exploited position they were being forced into, and the most radical among them believed that to be forced to work for wages was to lose their birthright as free Englishmen (Hill, 1967; Macpherson, 1973). It was a losing battle, however, for they eventually realized that they had few viable alternatives to selling their labor power. Unlike feudal serfs, workers in capitalist societies are not obliged to work for anyone, but they are obliged to sell their labor power to *some*one; and this basic structural fact about capitalism explains most of the power difference between capitalists and workers.

Although workers in the U.S. no longer protest the selling of labor power, they do make an issue of the terms on which it is sold. In the late nineteenth and early twentieth centuries, they began to organize unions because they knew that employers were powerful primarily because they could replace dissatisfied workers with others who also had no choice but to sell their labor power wherever they could find a buyer for it. If all workers refused to work under certain conditions, however, they would then have far greater power.

Capitalists—often with the active help of courts, legislatures, and government troops—retaliated against the rising power of organized labor in ways that sometimes resulted in confrontations of unprecedented violence (see Painter, 1987). Because they were willing to work for low wages, immigrants and blacks were often used to replace strikers. Unions were attacked directly through the use of spies, disruption of meetings, and bribery of public officials. Companies also used their considerable financial resources to mount massive propaganda campaigns in which union activists were portrayed as violent anarchists (see Boswell, 1986; Griffin et al., 1986).

Since the beginning of the twentieth century, relations between capitalists and workers have lost most of their violent character; but control of labor power continues to be a major means for increasing profits. How is it done? The most obvious source of control still lies in the structure of capitalist society, for so long as workers do not control the means of production, they do not control their own jobs. In his influential book, *White Collar*, C. Wright Mills wrote of the "new middle class," whose insecure position in the labor market contributes to increasing feelings of anxiety and powerlessness.

A second major source of control lies in the divisions within the working class that prevent unified action on the part of workers. In 1985, only 18 percent of workers belonged to unions (U.S. Census Bureau, 1986a). They represent an elite of the working class who often see themselves as having little in common with other workers (see Form, 1985). This was not always the case. When union organizing was at its height at the turn of this century, there was relatively little distance between the least and most skilled workers, and this provided a common base of experience from which to organize. By the 1930s, however, divisions within the working class were beginning to appear as the result of specialization, job ladders, pay scales, and a routinized work process that sharply distinguishes between skilled and unskilled labor (see Griffin et al., 1986).

The best evidence of a divided working class is the decline of union membership. Why is membership so low? Part of the answer is that most workers in industrial societies (nearly two-thirds in the U.S.) hold jobs that require relatively unsophisticated skills—clerks, assembly-line workers, farm laborers, and restaurant workers (U.S. Census Bureau, 1986a). Because there are always workers willing to take their place, most workers have a great deal to lose by making trouble, and employers generally define attempts to form unions as just that.

Union membership is also low because those who are most likely to hold low-level jobs—nonwhites, married women, college students, teenagers, and the elderly—tend to have little social power (Smith, 1981). Their position in society and the labor market gives them little ability or incentive to take the risks and make the investment of time and energy that it takes to form unions and improve working conditions and pay levels.

A third source of control lies in the segmented, bureaucratic nature of work in industrial societies. This not only makes it easier for employers to replace

During the late nineteenth and early twentieth centuries, the U.S. government openly acted against the rising tide of labor organizing. In 1912, for example, mill workers in Lawrence, Massachusetts, struck in protest over wage cuts, and the intervention of state militia troops resulted in both the end of the strike and the death of one of the strikers.

discontented workers, but puts most power over production in the hands of bureaucratic managers who specialize in controlling labor power. The proliferation of "management seminars" and courses in "labor relations" attests to the growing sophistication of capitalist methods for controlling workers.

One of the most important sources of control is the continuing drive for greater efficiency. In 1911 Frederick Winslow Taylor published *Principles of Scientific Management*, in which he espoused the use of scientific principles to determine the most efficient way to use workers. In time-and-motion studies, he tried to identify the single most efficient way for workers to accomplish narrowly defined physical tasks—such as screwing two pieces of wood together. The design and control of the human work process, he believed, should be no less rigorous and scientific than the design of machines (see Hounshell, 1984).

In the 1920s industrial sociologists focused on how to maximize the productivity of workers (and, therefore, the surplus value that could be extracted from them). The famous Hawthorne studies (discussed in Chapters 2 and 8) were attempts to identify working conditions—such as the amount of lighting and the frequency of rest periods—that would maximize the productivity of each worker. Studying productivity from another angle, Mayo and his colleagues discovered that small primary work groups establish norms about a "fair day's work" that often exert more control over worker productivity than do employers.

One of the most effective ways to increase efficiency and weaken the control of workers over productivity is to replace them with machines—a process known as **automation** (see Griffin et al., 1986; Shaiken, 1986). In the eighteenth century, British textile manufacturers developed power looms with which a single worker could replace hundreds; and as industrialization has expanded over the last two centuries, increasingly sophisticated technology has rendered ever greater numbers of skills—and, in some cases, workers themselves—obsolete. Automakers in Japan and the U.S. use robots to perform many assembly-line tasks that once provided thousands of jobs. To cut costs and maintain profits, the printing industry now uses so much high technology that skills among printers have declined and the printing craft has lost its once envied position as the epitome of skilled craftwork (Wallace and Kalleberg, 1982).

The capitalist valuing of efficiency increases productivity, but workers often bear the costs. Productivity—as measured by the average value of goods produced by each worker in a day—is lower in Japan than it is in the U.S. The reason for this lies not with the characteristics of workers, the use of technology, or the organization of work; rather, it lies with the structural relationship between employers and workers.

In capitalist Japan workers generally are not laid off when sales decline; thus, during economic "slumps," production is cut back while the number of workers remains the same, and productivity per worker falls. In the U.S., however, efficiency is often increased by laying workers off when sales decline; and this keeps the statistical measure of worker productivity at a higher level. Increased efficiency often benefits capitalists more than workers. Understandably, some labor unions have opposed automation and have been accused by many as being opposed to progress and efficiency. This is one of the major contradictions of capitalism, for greater efficiency often worsens the relative position of workers (Smith, 1981).

In industries whose unions are strongest, workers have increased their power, in some cases by placing a representative on corporate boards of directors. It is important to note, however, that this kind of shift in the distribution of power is achieved only under intense pressure, for it works against one of capital-

Printers were once among the proudest and most satisfied of all workers, due in large part to their highly developed skills, autonomy, and close connection to the production of printed knowledge and ideas. High technology, however, has made their skills obsolescent and deprived them of much of what made their work meaningful.

ism's primary values: the maximization of surplus value by controlling labor power.

Controlling Markets: Monopoly and Oligopoly

Adam Smith believed that the ideal capitalist economy is controlled not by individuals, groups, or organizations (including governments), but by the "invisible hand" of economic forces that underlie market activities. Detroit automakers lost ground to foreign competition in the 1970s because they continued to manufacture large, expensive, gas-guzzling cars long after a preference for small, inexpensive, efficient cars appeared. From Smith's point of view, they suffered losses because they did not match consumer demand with a supply of desired goods at a price people were willing to pay.

Smith believed that in order to make a profit and compete successfully with one another, capitalists must give consumers what they want at prices they are willing to pay. Competition forces them to introduce both new products at attractive prices and more efficient ways of producing them, and in the end everyone benefits. In the ideal capitalist society, the market is controlled by competition among producers and by the balance of supply and demand—the market forces that make up the "invisible hand."

In practice, capitalist economies do not come close to Adam Smith's ideal. Increased profits depend on control over both production and markets. Not only is free and open competition among capitalists anxiety-producing, but it also poses a constant threat to the ability of businesses to survive. Understandably, then, capitalists prefer an economy in which they are protected from competition (while at the same time perpetuating the belief that the market is free), and this has led to increasing control over production and marketing in the hands of a relatively few organizations—a condition known as **oligopoly** (Chamberlin, 1962).

Many believe that small businesses are the "bedrock" of the U.S. economy, but the truth is that businesses owned and operated by a few individuals have a tiny share of production and income. The fact is that a small minority of corporations controls the majority of economic activity. In 1985 there were almost 200,000 industrial corporations; but the largest 100 of these owned 70 percent of all business assets, and the largest 200 owned 85 percent. The 500 largest U.S. corporations had sales in excess of almost 1.8 *trillion* dollars, *an amount that exceeds the gross national product (GNP) of every other country in the world, with the exception of the Soviet Union* (U.S. Census Bureau, 1986a).

Oligopoly describes markets for many important products and services. More than 1,800 different makes of automobiles have been manufactured in the U.S. (Table 18-2 lists some of them). In 1988 there were only 3 major U.S. automakers. A handful of companies controls our entire supply of oil and natural gas, a situation that is also true for cigarettes, beer, breakfast cereals, coffee, aluminum, and personal computers (Standard and Poor, 1978, 1979). Six huge airlines control 90 percent of U.S. domestic air traffic; just two companies—Coke and Pepsi—control almost three-quarters of the entire soft drink industry. Ten corporations control NBC, ABC, and CBS (both

---

Table 18-2

Some of the Makes of Automobiles Once Manufactured in the United States

PRODUCTION DATES	NAMES	PRODUCTION DATES	NAMES
1914–1922	Allen	1909–1958	Hudson
1916–1926	Anderson	1888–1941	Hupmobile
1901–1926	Apperson	1905–1912	Johnson
1904–1913	Atlas	1908–1928	Lexington
1900–1936	Auburn	1904–1925	Maxwell
1899–1911	Autocar	1910–1925	Mercer
1915–1922	Bell	1918–1958	Nash
1915–1937	Brewster	1907–1932	Oakland
1871–1873	Cahart Steamer	1906–1930	Overland
1909–1927	Case	1899–1958	Packard
1908–1923	Chalmers	1900–1932	Peerless
1913–1922	Commonwealth	1901–1938	Pierce-Arrow
1929–1937	Cord	1904–1936	Reo
1910–1936	Cunningham	1896–1925	Stanley
1950–1955	Cunningham	1912–1930	Stearns Knight
1915–1924	Dixie Flyer	1906–1966	Studebaker
1921–1934	Dusenberg	1913–1935	Stutz
1915–1933	Dupont	1908–1928	Velie
1910–1932	Essex	1908–1923	Washington
1902–1934	Franklin	1908–1925	Westcott
1946	Frazer	1914–1932	Willys-Knight
1919–1931	Gardner	1896–1924	Winton

Source: Ash, *Automobile Almanac*, 1967.

television and radio); 34 affiliated television stations; 201 cable television franchises; 59 magazines including *Newsweek* and *Time*; 20 record companies; 41 book publishers; and 58 newspapers including the *Wall Street Journal*, the *Washington Post*, the *Los Angeles Times*, and the *New York Times* (Parenti, 1985).

The importance of oligopoly lies in the ability of an organization to control prices while maintaining the appearance of a competitive marketplace. For example, we spend more than $200 billion on food each year, but less than 40 cents out of every dollar goes to farmers. Most of what we spend on food goes to "middlemen"—food processors—and only 50 companies control 90 percent of the food market (Hightower, 1980). Beatrice Foods owns more than a hundred companies whose products include ice cream, yogurt, bread, milk, pickles, bottled water, cheese, Chinese food, cat food, whiskey, orange juice, hot dogs, taco sauce, peanut butter, nuts, ketchup, sausage, tomato sauce, cocoa mix, turkeys, popcorn, smoked meats, cooking oil, pudding, refried beans, "sloppy Joe," and soup mix.

Judging from commercials on Saturday morning television, you might think that there is intense competition among the enormous number of different breakfast cereals—Wheaties, Cheerios, Total, and so on; but most of these brands are made by a few companies that, to a degree, compete against themselves. The extensiveness of oligopoly results in considerably less competition than there appears to be.

When production of goods or services is controlled by a single corporation, it is said to have a monopoly. Most people buy utilities such as natural gas and electricity from companies that control the entire market in a given geographical area, and until recently, telephone service in the U.S. was controlled entirely by AT&T.

A **conglomerate** is a collection of companies in different industries that are owned by a single corporation. Conglomerates form when one company uses its profits to buy others, or when two or more companies merge to form a single organization. Beatrice is a conglomerate, as is the International Telephone and Telegraph company which owns more than 150 different corporations that provide products and services that have nothing to do with telephones—including Wonder Bread and Hostess Twinkies.

Conglomerates have enormous power in the marketplace because their vast and diversified resources allow them to compete in the marketplace in ways that

are beyond the resources of independent companies. As conglomerates increase their control over markets and drive smaller, independent firms out of business, oligopoly tends toward monopoly.

The Manufacture of Desire   All economies shape people's needs to fit what is produced to some degree; but the capitalist imperatives of expansion, profit, and competition make it important to control what consumers think they want and need (see Schudson, 1984). In order to expand, capitalists must increase people's perceived needs and then try to meet them in a profitable way.

The manufacture of desire is an important part of capitalist economies and is often accomplished by introducing "new" products. In many cases, the products are not new at all: new dishwashing detergents often differ from old ones only in their packaging and smell. Production goes on as usual, but advertising campaigns foster the illusion of change (Baran and Sweezy, 1966).

Desire is also manufactured by introducing products that substitute new ways of doing things for old

"Lester, shouldn't we be upgrading something?"
Drawing by Saxon © 1984, The New Yorker Magazine, Inc.

ways that were quite sufficient. People have always managed to entertain themselves—with singing, parties, games, dancing, storytelling; but now "entertainment" generally involves products or services that are sold in markets—television, records, radios, cassettes, CDs, VCRs, and movies.

In many cases the production process creates real needs that create new sources of profit. As Best and Connolly (1976) wrote:

> When industrial production pollutes the air, urban dwellers come to equate the need for air with a vacation, air conditioning, or a more expensive home in the suburbs. . . . When food packaging, processing, and distribution create tasteless food fortified with potentially dangerous preservatives, consumers identify the need for nutrition with expensive organic foods and natural vitamins. (pp. 57–59)

The effort to manufacture the desire to consume products that generate profits for capitalists often leads to contradictions. Full-page advertisements for cigarettes often picture people smoking after they have obviously engaged in healthy exercise—a handsome man sitting in a locker room or a beautiful young dancer sitting next to a dance studio mirror.

Who's in Charge?   That the economies of most advanced capitalist societies are dominated by large organizations raises the important question of who, in turn, dominates these powerful corporations? In the early stages of industrial capitalism there were no corporations, and businesses were owned and operated by no more than a few individuals who often belonged to the same family. Family control of business organizations continued well into the twentieth century and formed the basis for the fortunes of families such as the Rockefellers, Vanderbilts, Kennedys, and Hunts.

In the twentieth century, however, ownership of large businesses appeared to slip from the control of families and individuals as stock ownership spread. As business became more bureaucratic, large numbers of managers and administrators took over control of day-to-day decision making. These two developments led some to believe that ownership and control of the means of production were no longer in the same hands, and that economic power was, therefore, becoming less concentrated (Berle and Means, 1968).

This view is sharply countered by a number of social scientists. Burch (1972) gathered data on the largest U.S. corporations and divided them into two groups. Corporations that were controlled by single families or groups of families who owned a controlling interest and placed some of its members in key management positions (such as chairman of the board or a top executive) were classified as "owner-dominated." If controlling interest was owned by a family or group of families who did *not* also have family members in key management positions, then the corporation was classified as "management-dominated."

Burch concluded that "owner-dominance" characterized almost 60 percent of the top 300 industrial corporations, 72 percent of the top 50 merchandising corporations, and just over half of all corporations that deal in banking and transportation. In addition, the wealthiest 1 percent of U.S. families own 60 percent of all corporate stock, whereas 80 percent own no stock at all (Joint Economic Committee, 1986). Although bureaucracy and its managers play increasingly important roles in production, business is still primarily controlled by a small elite.

Herman (1981) studied the 200 largest U.S. corporations and disagreed with Burch by concluding that there is no small economic elite. He agreed with Burch, however, when he noted that many high-level managers own substantial amounts of stock in their companies; and even those who do not, have the same goals and interests as those who do. In short, Herman concluded that managers and owners have essentially the same interests (see also James and Soref, 1981; Domhoff, 1983).

The Role of Government   To Adam Smith, government never interferes with the economy in the ideal capitalist society: "laissez faire" (or, "leave it alone") was his motto. Early in this century, however, U.S. officials came to believe that unrestrained capitalist expansion threatened to damage and deplete natural resources, and that corporations were amassing so much power that monopoly and oligopoly threatened free competition and the welfare of consumers. Railroads typically charged "what the market would bear," and their monopoly over hauling freight allowed them to charge exorbitant prices.

The government played an expanding role in the regulation of business, primarily in order to ensure a stable social environment in which capitalists could pursue their interests (Weinstein, 1969). U.S. immigration policy played an important part in the development of capitalism by allowing millions to enter the U.S. for most of the nineteenth century when the need

Franklin Roosevelt, shown here with a West Virginia coal miner in 1932, dramatically increased the involvement of the federal government in attempts to control the causes and consequences of the recurring crises that are characteristic of capitalism.

for cheap industrial labor was great, but then virtually excluding immigrants in the 1920s when industrial capitalism had become firmly established (see Calavita, 1984). Antitrust laws forbade monopolies; and in 1983 the government won a long legal battle to end AT&T's monopoly over telephone service. During the Depression of the 1930s, Franklin Roosevelt's administration set a precedent for government action—unemployment compensation, farm subsidies, the minimum wage, social security, regulation of banking and the stock exchange, and vast government spending in the marketplace—all signaled a growing economic role of government (Heilbroner, 1977).

The areas in which government plays a regulatory role include work safety regulations; control of natural resources; antipollution laws; fair trade practices (such as rules that govern our rights and obligations when we sign a lease or credit agreement); regulation of nuclear power plants; product safety (such as drugs, food, and cars); and labor-management relations (such as laws that forbid employers from firing employees who promote unions).

The Federal Reserve Board controls the nation's money supply and determines, among other things, how much money is available for business investment and personal loans. When the government charges tariffs on goods imported from abroad, it helps protect U.S. industries from competition. The government subsidizes the production of various agricultural

products—such as tobacco—by guaranteeing a certain level of prices, and regulates the price of vital commodities such as oil, gasoline, and natural gas.

The state seems to have a great deal of power, but how and in whose interests particular administrations use that power, and how effectively they control what goes on in the marketplace, are other matters. The trend toward oligopoly strongly suggests that the government's ability (or willingness) to limit the power of corporations is itself quite limited (see Bowles and Gintis, 1986; Clawson et al., 1986).

Occupational Structures and Segmented Labor Markets

As we have seen, labor power is a commodity that is bought and sold in capitalist societies. Although complexity is the most obvious characteristic of labor markets in industrial societies (the Labor Department lists over 35,000 different occupations), of more interest to sociologists is the fact that modern labor markets are divided into separate parts: they are *segmented*, and this affects the opportunities available to workers (Gordon, Edwards, and Reich, 1982).

The U.S. labor market is divided into two basic segments (study the characteristics of different jobs in Table 18-3 and see which labor market you would prefer to be in). The **primary** market includes jobs that encourage stable work habits, involve skills that

Table 18-3

Segmented Labor Markets

LABOR MARKET SEGMENT	CHARACTERISTICS
Primary	Encourages stable work habits. Skills often acquired on the job. Relatively high-paying. Job ladders. Strong unions.
Subordinate primary	Routine jobs that encourage dependability, discipline, obedience to authority. EXAMPLES: Police officer, skilled blue-collar worker, bank teller, office supervisor, computer programmer, public school teacher, military officer.
Independent primary	Creative jobs that require problem solving, initiative, and decision making. EXAMPLES: Scientist, executive, college professor, public official, school principal, lawyer, newspaper editor, police chief.
Secondary	Does not require stable work habits. Relatively low-paying. High turnover. Few job ladders ("dead end jobs"). Weak unions or none at all. EXAMPLES: Laborer, clerk, day-care worker, factory assembly-line worker, restaurant worker, taxi or bus driver.

are often learned on the job, are relatively high-paying, and have job ladders. The primary segment is, itself, divided into two smaller segments. **Subordi-nate** primary jobs involve routine tasks that encourage workers to be dependable and obedient to authority. **Independent** primary jobs, on the other hand, involve more creativity, autonomy, and power. Roughly two-thirds of workers were in the primary market in 1985, but only around 16 percent of all workers had "independent" jobs (compiled from U.S. Census Bureau, 1986a).

The **secondary** market does not require stable work habits, is relatively low-paying, has few chances for advancement, and, as a result, has a high rate of turnover (people leave jobs after relatively short periods of time). Roughly a third of all workers were in this segment of the labor market in 1985.

The structure of labor markets in capitalist societies reflects the importance attached to controlling labor power, for only a small minority of all workers have jobs that bring them some measure of power, autonomy, and creativity. In their theory of **labor market segmentation**, Reich, Gordon, and Edwards (1973) argued that the goal of controlling labor power actually caused the development of labor markets. During the late nineteenth century industrialization had the effect of homogenizing labor—factory work fragmented the production process and no longer required highly skilled workers who were familiar with all phases of production. This, combined with having to sell their labor power for wages, gave workers a common basis for organizing unions and opposing the power of capitalists.

Reich, Gordon, and Edwards believed that twentieth-century capitalists responded to the threat of organized labor in part by creating different jobs, making the division of labor more complex than it needed to be for efficiency. The steel industry created job ladders that made trivial distinctions between job levels and assigned slightly higher pay levels to each (Stone, 1974). This fostered an illusion of upward mobility and weakened the bond of common experience that held the labor movement together. Unlike workers in the nineteenth century, in other words, twentieth-century workers had less in common with one another because some were better off. The "division of labor" literally "divided" the labor movement.

The structure of the economy also changed in ways that reinforced a segmented labor market. In the nineteenth century the economy was competitive, with large numbers of small businesses competing against one another. In the twentieth century, however, some areas of business—the steel, auto, and chemical industries—were slowly dominated by monopolies and oligopolies, largely because there was a steady demand for their products. Others—such as restaurants, stores, construction companies, and auto dealers—remained competitive because the demand for their goods fluctuated and they had to compete in order to stay in business.

As a result, a **dual economy** emerged—part monopolistic and part competitive—and the position of workers in them strongly affects their position in the labor market. Primary and secondary jobs exist in both sectors of the economy; but primary workers are far more likely to be found in the monopoly sector, whereas most secondary workers are in the competitive sector.

Unions are weak in the competitive sector because most of the workers are in the secondary labor market and can be replaced with relative ease. Low pay and job insecurity are, in fact, major ways in which such businesses remain competitive and control workers: when business is slow, employers simply "lay them off" (see Juravich, 1985). In late 1983 the Greyhound bus company insisted that workers agree to a cut in pay so that the company could remain competitive. Workers went on strike, and the company threatened to replace them. After almost nine weeks the workers accepted the pay cut and returned to work.

Monopolistic business, however, depends on a stable demand for products and employs a larger number of highly skilled workers who cannot be replaced easily. If employees leave because they dislike working

conditions, monopoly businesses stand to lose far more than competitive businesses; and, for this reason, workers have more leverage in monopoly industries, and unions are more common and more powerful.

When people think of "labor," many think of highly publicized unions such as the Teamsters or the United Auto Workers, who often use their power to exact relatively high wages from their employers. It is important to remember, however, that the vast majority of workers—roughly 80 percent—do not belong to unions, and only a portion of the 20 percent who are members belong to powerful unions. When the United Auto Workers gains major concessions from employers, it results in relatively few benefits for the vast majority of workers. For most, low pay and job insecurity are permanent features of their positions in a segmented job market.

Professions and Professionalization   Some occupations—both within and outside the primary labor market—are **professions**, and these have unique cultural and structural characteristics (Greenwood, 1962). Professional jobs are based on systematic, formal knowledge about a particular field, such as law, medicine, or engineering. Compared with other occupations, professionals are relatively autonomous and can determine the conditions under which they work.

Professionals, however, are generally bound by codes of conduct and standards that are determined by professional organizations. Physicians and lawyers are answerable primarily to other physicians and lawyers

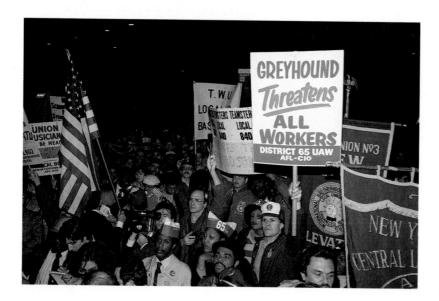

The vulnerability of unions in the competitive economy played a large part in the failure of the Greyhound bus strike in 1983. As in many other industries, workers often have to choose between agreeing with the terms offered by their employers or losing their jobs.

who decide what constitutes malpractice. In 1987, the American Medical Association declared that it was unethical for any physician to refuse to treat an AIDS patient. In similar ways, scientists establish norms for competent research and ethical conduct.

The boundaries of professions are tightly controlled. Scientists and professors must have advanced degrees in order to practice their profession; doctors, lawyers, nurses, and engineers must pass licensing examinations and be certified by state boards; public school teachers must be certified by the state in order to teach; and only lawyers with special training are allowed to argue cases before the Supreme Court.

Because professions provide valued services, are relatively free of outside interference, require extended training, control the size of their membership, and enjoy relatively high levels of prestige, they generally have high levels of income. The average income of U.S. physicians in 1984 was $102,000; and the average starting salary for graduates with Ph.D.s in engineering, chemistry, mathematics, and physics was more than $35,000. By comparison, the average earnings of all full-time workers amounted to $17,000 (U.S. Census Bureau, 1986a).

Roughly 12 percent of U.S. workers are professionals, and most of these work for someone else—in other words, they are part of the labor market. Engineers, accountants, librarians, religious workers, scientists, nurses, reporters, and teachers sell their labor power as members of what Marx considered to be the working class. Most of them are better off than other workers, and many have authority over other workers (such as secretaries). Nonetheless, as members of the working class, these professionals must live with the uncertainties of a job market they do not control.

An even smaller minority—just over 2 percent—are professionals who work outside the labor market—physicians, dentists, and lawyers in private practice. It is among these professionals that autonomy, financial well-being, and job security reach their highest level in a capitalist economy.

Some occupations are "semi-professions" that have only some of the characteristics of professions (Etzioni, 1969). A growing number of business executives have graduate degrees, and often like to refer to business as a profession with its own code of ethics. In addition, professions that exist primarily as part of the labor market—such as public school teaching—have less autonomy and control over their members than do those that are largely outside the labor market.

The attractiveness of professional standing encourages many people to try to *professionalize* their occupation (Caplow, 1964). The first step in **professionalization** is to form a professional group or organization whose boundaries restrict membership and create a sense of occupational identity for its members. Often, a new name for the occupation (such as "educator" for "teacher") is a part of establishing boundaries, for it helps to break the cultural association of an occupation with its previous nonprofessional standing.

The second step is to create a code of ethics to indicate to the outside world that the group intends to regulate its own members. It is an early assertion of one of the most important characteristics of a profession—autonomy from outside control. The third and final step is to gain formal public recognition—usually from political authorities—that establishes the autonomy of the organization and, in some cases, creates legal criteria for membership (such as state licensing).

Once an occupation is professionalized, its members may gain a substantial increase in collective power. The American Psychological Association (APA) limits competition by opposing the professionalization of psychotherapists who are not psychiatrists (with M.D. degrees) or clinical psychologists (with Ph.D.s). This is accomplished by having the services of competing therapists legally ineligible for health insurance policy benefits. Since people are less likely to use uninsured medical services, this limits competition. Only recently have some states included some other mental health care providers—such as psychiatric social workers—in health insurance benefits.

Postindustrial Society and Changing Occupational Structures

In preindustrial societies, most people earn a living by working directly with raw materials—by growing or gathering food—what Daniel Bell (1973) called a "game against nature" (p. 126). In industrial societies, however, most economic activity involves manufactured goods. The early 1950s the U.S. began a third stage in which most economic activity involved neither raw materials nor manufacturing, but *service* occupations such as sales clerk, telephone operator, travel agent, secretary, banker, real estate agent, office manager, public official, teacher, police officer, and soldier.

Bell believed that this signaled the beginning of **postindustrial society**—in which the production of goods is overshadowed by the provision of services,

BLOOM COUNTY   by Berke Breathed

and relations between people and machines are gradually replaced by relationships among people. In this kind of society, he argued, social interaction becomes the most important aspect of work; disputes between workers and employers are handled through negotiation rather than angry confrontation; and most people work for small organizations rather than large corporations.

Braverman (1974) and others, however, have pointed out that although the job market is changing from factory work to office work, the relations of production—between workers and employers and between workers and their work—have not changed. The central values of capitalist societies—expansion, profit, and the exploitation of labor power—are as strong as ever. The most rapidly expanding occupations—sales and service—are in the secondary, competitive labor market, where unions are weak or nonexistent and where wages are low and profits relatively high.

Life in the Labor Force

How do different economic arrangements affect the lives of workers? Do relations of production in a postindustrial society differ substantially from those in an industrial society? Are the gaps between social classes narrower? Do people have more control over what they do?

Sophisticated technology—computers, word processors, and telecommunications equipment—is used increasingly in offices, but it is unclear whether this improves the lives of workers as much as it in-

creases profits. Textile workers once stood for hours tending machines that turned thread into cloth; but secretaries and clerks now sit for hours in front of computer terminals. They "process" information—taking it from one place and putting it in another—without affecting it in any way (see Zuboff, 1982, 1988).

One study of clerical workers in two New England companies found that computer operators were instructed to enter information just as they received it even when they spotted obvious errors. "They were not expected to be able to decide if the information was correct." The work of customer representatives (who work primarily over the phone) was closely monitored by computers that allotted them a specific number of minutes to handle each customer; and if workers paid extra attention to a difficult case, they were often penalized for falling short of their work quota for the day (*Hartford Courant*, January 5, 1983). One recent study estimated that as many as seven million workers in the U.S. are already being monitored and evaluated by computers (Office of Technology Assessment, 1987).

High technology in a postindustrial society certainly has the potential to make work more interesting; but the drive for greater efficiency and profit creates enormous numbers of "dumb," rigidly controlled jobs that involve "intelligent" technology. Just as early machines degraded skilled work by taking over complex manual tasks, so too does computer technology further this process by taking over increasing numbers of mental tasks (Braverman, 1974). As one skilled worker put it, "You don't have to think anymore. You lose touch with what you're actually doing. . . . and . . . you yourself become a robot, because you don't get to use your mind" (in Gill, 1985, p. 84; see also Zuboff, 1988).

Computer technology and automation are functional for productivity and profits, but how do they and other characteristics of capitalist societies affect the lives of workers?

Going Through the Motions: Alienation in the Workplace   To Marx (1845), **alienation** is the feeling that the world we live in is, itself, alien to us. In the workplace alienation represents a lack of connection between people and what they produce and between themselves and other people. It is the feeling that they do not know why they are doing what they are doing, and yet must go on doing it anyway.

Imagine that you are a bootmaker in seventeenth-century Paris. You own a little shop, and on a typical day a man comes in and tells you he wants a pair of boots. If he is insulting, you might tell him to go to another shop and leave you alone. If not, you discuss different styles and kinds of leather, measure his feet, fix a price, and tell him when they will be ready.

Your life is far from ideal. You are relatively poor, and there are months when it seems that no one needs boots. You do, however, decide when you will work, whose boots you will make, how you will make them, and for what price. Most important, you produce and sell boots by interacting both with materials that you transform into finished boots and with other people—from the purchase of leather to the final sale.

Now imagine that you work in a twentieth-century boot factory. You do not make boots; you cut out soles on a stamping machine—thousands of them every day—and you are paid a wage for each hour of work. While you work, you stand alone and tend the machine, feeding the leather in and taking the soles out. You do not control which kinds of boots are made in the factory, the leathers that are used, the style, the quality, the price for which they are sold, or to whom they are sold. Your wages are determined by your employer. You punch the time clock at 8:00 A.M., work until noon with a ten-minute break at 10:00, and then punch out at 4:00 and go home. The next day, you return to the factory and cut out thousands of soles again; and this is what you do year after year.

Stop for a moment and imagine yourself in each of these situations. Which would you prefer and why?

In comparison with the seventeenth-century worker, the twentieth-century factory worker lacks control over the process of work and the results. The process of making boots is now fragmented into many separate tasks, and what workers do has little connection to their thoughts or feelings about what they do. The shopowner could sit back occasionally and think about what he was about to do with the leather, and the unity of thought and action is what produced the boots. In the factory, however, the boots are disconnected from what the workers think or feel about them.

When we have no control over our work or what is done with the result, we lose our sense that work has

This engraving shows a seventeenth-century shoemaker's shop. Under the guild system, all members of the shop lived in the same house, and the design, making, and selling of shoes all occurred in the same place. Industrialization drove most such shops out of business because they could not compete with the low prices (and inferior quality) that came with mass production.

meaning and value; and work is one of the most important of all human activities. If what we do lacks meaning and value, and if our social identities are bound up in what we do, then we are in danger of feeling that *we* are meaningless.

Alienation is one of the most important concepts in the sociological analysis of work (see, for example, Seeman, 1959). In his classic study of alienation in four U.S. industries—car, textile, chemical, and printing—Blauner (1964) tried to identify structural characteristics of work that affected what he believed were four key aspects of alienation: powerlessness, meaninglessness, social isolation, and a lack of personal attachment and commitment to work.

Alienation was highest among auto workers, most of whom performed dull, repetitive jobs on assembly lines that isolated them from other workers and gave them no control over the work process. Alienation was lowest among printers who performed a craft with deep historical roots and controlled many aspects of production, including the pace at which they worked. Printers were able to interact with one another, and rather than perform a tiny portion of a work process, they did the "whole job" and had the satisfaction of seeing the final product, much like our seventeenth-century bootmaker (see Lipset, Trow, and Coleman, 1956, for a classic study of printers).

Chemical workers were only slightly more alienated than printers. Although they had relatively little control over production, they worked in teams of skilled workers who closely monitored production and made many decisions. In comparison with auto workers, chemical workers enjoyed far more interaction with one another and their decision-making powers gave them a stronger feeling of attachment to their work.

Other studies show similar patterns. A 1973 national study asked workers if they would choose their present occupation again, and the results showed that as the level of skill, prestige, and control over work increases, so does satisfaction with work (U.S. Department of Health, Education, and Welfare, 1973). More recent data show that those who are self-employed or who have higher prestige occupations are considerably more likely to say they are very satisfied with their jobs and considerably less likely to report being dissatisfied (see Table 18-4).

Alienation seems to be closely tied to powerlessness, meaninglessness, social isolation, and fragmentation of work tasks (see also Kalleberg and Griffin,

Table 18-4

Percent Very Satisfied or Dissatisfied with Their Jobs, by Occupational Prestige and Self-Employment, U.S., 1986

OCCUPATIONAL PRESTIGE[1]	VERY SATISFIED	DISSATISFIED
Very low	36%	24%
Low	45%	12%
Moderate	51%	9%
Upper	63%	8%
SELF-EMPLOYMENT		
Self-employed	65%	8%
Work for someone else	46%	12%

[1]Occupations rated on a scale from 1 to 100: very low = 10–19; low = 20–39; moderate = 40–59; upper = 60–89.

Source: Computed from raw 1986 General Social Survey data.

1980; Kohn and Schooler, 1983; and Mottaz, 1981). In 1987, a sample of U.S. workers was asked which aspects of occupations were most important to them; whereas half ranked "a feeling of accomplishment and importance" at the top, only 22 percent placed "high income" in that position (Davis and Smith, 1987).

The structure of occupational life in industrial societies makes it difficult for people to care about and feel attached to their work. What, however, of those who want to work, but are unemployed? What are the social causes of unemployment, and how does it affect our lives?

Causes and Consequences of Unemployment

Wanting a job but not having one is often a personal problem that individuals must deal with on their own. Unemployment has obvious financial consequences for families and individuals; when workers are the only earners in their families, the loss of a job is like firing the entire family. One study of workers who lost their jobs when a plant closed found a sharp increase in symptoms of poor physical and mental health. Reported levels of anxiety, tension, pessimism, depression, and insomnia increased, as did the incidence of high blood pressure and ulcers (Institute for Social Research, 1980; see also Buss and Redburn, 1983).

From a sociological perspective, unemployment is also a social problem with cultural, structural, and ecological causes. When unemployment rates are high, the personal desperation and despair of individuals is multiplied by thousands:

> In Detroit last month, several thousand desperate people, ranging from a 19-year-old unmarried mother to a 55-year-old unemployed automobile worker, lined up for a handful of job openings as unskilled laborers. In New York, 60 people spent the weekend in line, sleeping on the sidewalk to assure acceptance of their applications as carpenters' apprentices. Some of the out-of-work families who left the industrial mid-west for the supposedly greener pastures of Texas are being forced to live in their cars. In Austin, 2,817 applicants lined up for 187 jobs.

The above is not a description of the Great Depression of the 1930s; it was written in 1982 (*New York Times*, November 3, p. C1). Between 1980 and 1982 the number of unemployed people increased by 37 percent, as did the average number of weeks that people were out of work; and in many countries—including France, Great Britain, and most of Latin America—the picture is far bleaker than it is in the U.S. (U.S. Census Bureau, 1982). In addition to those who are looking for work without success, more than six million workers have become so discouraged that they have given up looking altogether. Of those who have jobs, as much as a third are "underemployed"—which means that although they are employed, their jobs are either part-time or so poorly paid that they cannot earn enough to live on (Bureau of Labor Statistics, 1986, 1987; Lichter, 1988) (see One Step Further 18-1, p. 506).

Most of us look upon unemployment as a fact of life. We are so accustomed to the monthly unemployment statistics that it is hard to imagine a society in which everyone who wants to work has a job. The fact that we tend to accept it as an inevitable part of economic life strongly suggests that its causes lie in the nature of the social environment that we also tend to take for granted.

As Smith (1981) pointed out, once labor power becomes a commodity, then the demand for labor (and the opportunity for work) is no longer controlled by the willingness of individuals to work and the demand for the goods they produce. New factors come into play, such as the desire of capitalists to expand, to increase their profits, or to compete more successfully with one another. Most important is the fact that the historical transformation of labor into a commodity has created an ongoing conflict between employers and workers.

One of the most important types of unemployment is **structural unemployment**—so called because it is caused by changes in the structure of occupations (see Ashton, 1986). The mechanization of agriculture throws unskilled farm laborers out of work, just as automation creates unemployment by replacing workers with machines (Rasmussen, 1982). Automated bank tellers replace human tellers; word processors enable secretaries to do work that once required several people; robots on auto assembly lines not only take over dull "dumb" jobs, but leave many assembly-line workers with no jobs at all. Since the cost of labor power is the largest single expense in many industries, automation increases profits by lowering costs; but it does so at the expense of people.

In some cases structural unemployment has demographic causes, for as populations grow and age structures change, so does the size of the labor force in relation to the number of jobs. In the 1950s, the labor force grew slowly because the low birth rates of the 1930s resulted in a relatively small number of young adults. The Baby Boom of the late 1940s and 1950s, however, created a huge influx of young people looking for jobs in the 1970s and 1980s. Combined with a surge of women into the job market, the labor force expanded more rapidly than the job market.

As age structures change, so does the demand for certain goods and services. The large numbers of children produced by the Baby Boom fostered a sharp rise in the demand for teachers; in the 1980s, however, the size of the school-age population is considerably smaller, and thousands of teachers must choose between unemployment and training for new occupations.

Sweezy (1942) also argued that the antagonistic relations between workers and employers in capitalist societies create recurring crises that inevitably raise unemployment levels. A basic tension in capitalist societies is between the desire of capitalists to expand by giving workers the smallest possible share of what they produce and the desire of workers to increase their share. When profits are high (a "boom"), workers are in a better position to demand a bigger share—in other words, an increase in wages. If their wages go up, then business profits go down, and economic growth slows (a "slump" or, in the worst cases, a "bust"). If employers are able to keep wages from rising, then

ONE STEP FURTHER 18-1:
Who's Who in the Underside of the Labor Market

Both unemployment and underemployment are distributed quite unevenly in the United States. As you can see from the figures in Table B-18-1, although women are only slightly more likely than men to be unemployed (out of work but actively looking for a job), they are almost twice as likely as men to have given up the search for a job even though they want to work, or to be working for the minimum wage. The differences between blacks and whites are even more dramatic, with blacks more than twice as likely to be unemployed and to have given up, but only slightly more likely to be working for the minimum wage. Age differences show that all three types of experience decline sharply with age as workers get a more stable place in the job market.

Table B-18-1

SOCIAL CHARACTERISTICS	PERCENT WHO WANT WORK, BUT HAVE GIVEN UP LOOKING	PERCENT UNEMPLOYED	PERCENT WORKING FOR MINIMUM WAGE
Gender			
Women	5.1	7.4	10.5
Men	2.6	7.0	5.4
Race			
Black	8.3	15.1	8.7
White	3.2	6.2	7.8
Age			
16–19	10.3	18.6	28.7
20–24	4.6	11.1	10.1
25–59	2.8	5.2	4.6
60 and older	1.2	3.2	*

*not available

Source: Bureau of Labor Statistics, 1987, 1988; U.S. Census Bureau, 1986a.

workers do not have enough money to buy all of the goods being produced in a "boom" period, and this in turn causes business profits to fall and, with them, the expansion of the economy.

When the economy goes into a slump, wages fall (as they did during the Great Depression and as they have during the last decade) and workers are in a weak bargaining position. This sets the stage for higher profits and renewed economic expansion, and the cycle begins again.

SOCIALISM AND COMMUNISM

In the 1800s the Industrial Revolution and the growth of capitalism went hand in hand; and, as we saw in earlier chapters, Marx wrote in response to the economic and social conditions spawned by these developments. He believed that capitalism was a stage in history that was necessary because it would bring about an enormous increase in production and technology. Because capitalism generated intense class conflict, however, Marx also believed that eventually it would be replaced by *socialism* and then by *communism*.

As an ideal type, socialism differs from capitalism in that under **socialism** the means of production are owned by the state, not by private individuals and groups. Marx believed that socialism would end class conflict by doing away with classes and by creating a workers' state. Private ownership of capital would not exist; satisfying social needs such as adequate housing, food, and defense would be valued more than surplus value and profit; full employment would be valued above efficiency; and cooperation would be valued more than competition.

As is true of capitalist societies, however, socialist societies have yet to get close to their ideal. Although capitalism and socialism differ dramatically from each other, many socialist and capitalist societies have some problems in common that stem from industrialization and the complexity of their societies.

The Social Structure of Socialist Economies

The distribution of power is the most important structural difference between socialist and capitalist societies. Under socialism the party and its government officials decide what wages are paid for each kind of work, which goods and services are produced and in what amount, and how goods and services are distributed (Hollander, 1982; Lane, 1982). Whereas capitalist societies are dominated by privately owned monopolies and oligopolies, socialist societies are dominated by state-owned monopolies and oligopolies.

Ideally, there should be no economically based social conflict in socialist societies because the state supposedly acts in the best interests of everyone. In existing socialist societies, however, there is a conflict between the workers and the state that tries to control them. Bureaucracy is more pervasive in China and the Soviet Union than in most capitalist societies, for socialist countries are trying to control the entire social life of large, complex societies from single, centralized sources of authority. The result is astounding inefficiency (although, see Burawoy and Lukacs, 1985). Goods are produced long after the demand for them has been satisfied, while goods in short supply go unmade. In late 1983 a large new opticians' center was opened in Moscow and lacked only one thing—eyeglass frames and lenses, waiting times for which ranged from several months to a few years.

Inefficiency is the least of the problems of most socialist countries, for most are also authoritarian states in which governments rule by force and are not elected by the people. In practice, the socialist ideal of

In the Soviet Union, almost everyone has a job with a decent income, but there are chronic shortages of quality goods, as is evident from the long line that formed quickly outside a Moscow shoe store when news spread of a new shipment (top). Capitalist countries have solved the problem by producing huge quantities of quality goods, but also create far higher levels of poverty and unemployment, as shown in this 1983 picture of more than 1,000 people who lined up in Chester, Pennsylvania to apply for 30 job openings.

Political Power and the State

The Emergence of the State

Culture, Politics, and the State

Structures of Power: Basic Types of Political Institutions

Distributions of Power: Democracy, Oligarchy, and Autocracy

How Much Power? Authoritarianism and Totalitarianism

Who Rules? Power in U.S. Politics

Political Ecology

The Geography of Political Power

The Uses of Political Power

Functions and Dysfunctions

The State and Social Conflict

Politics and Social Change: Rebellions, Coups, and Revolutions

19 Political Institutions

In 1983 the government of Rumania, a socialist country in southeastern Europe, banned the ownership of typewriters by former convicts or anyone who posed "a danger to public order or state security" (*New York Times*, April 24, 1983). People could not buy a typewriter without permission from the government, and those who already owned one had to register it with the police, including a sample of the typewriter's print for identification of anything written on it. It is easier to own a gun in most of the U.S. than it is to own a typewriter in Rumania.

Politics refers to the social process through which power is distributed and used at all levels from groups to societies, and the preceding example illustrates important aspects of political structures. The Rumanian government's decision is an exercise of power that affects all members of its society, and this by itself is enough to make it political.

It is also political in that it was designed to make it more difficult for opponents to publish antigovernment leaflets. The government's attempt to control the use of something as simple as a typewriter is an attempt to maintain its power and perpetuate the form of government that rules Rumania.

Previous chapters explored the importance of power in social interaction (Chapter 7), groups and organizations (Chapter 8), and communities (Chapter 9). In this chapter, we are interested primarily in the distribution of power in societies. In particular, we focus on **political institutions**—the relatively permanent social arrangements through which power is distributed and exercised. Who has the power to make what kinds of decisions? How evenly distributed is decision-making power? How are decisions actually made and how are they put into effect? How do political institutions affect the people who occupy different statuses in a society? What are the functional and dysfunctional consequences of different political arrangements, and what is the relationship between political power and social change?

Since the sociological study of politics centers on the concept of power, we begin by taking a closer look at this by-now-familiar concept.

POLITICAL POWER AND THE STATE

We have defined power as the potential to have an effect on ourselves or our environment even when there is resistance. This includes not only direct control over people—such as the conditions under which they can own typewriters or guns—but also the ability to decide how the resources of a society will be used. Deciding how tax money will be spent is as much a use of political power as the ability to force people to pay taxes in the first place.

As we now know, the most important form of social power is authority, a unique form of socially supported power that rests on the beliefs that those who possess it have a right to it and those who do not have a duty to obey. Weber identified three types of authority, the first of which is **legal-rational authority**, which is power based on clearly stated norms. The norms that define legal-rational authority specify who holds power in relation to whom and under what circumstances. The power of professors to grade students, of people to control who enters their houses, and of bosses to hire and fire workers are all examples of legal-rational authority. In the U.S. the police may not enter your home without a proper warrant; but in many countries such as Chile and Argentina, it has not been uncommon for the police literally to kidnap "suspects" who are never heard from again.

Unlike legal-rational authority, **charismatic authority** is based on the belief that someone possesses

Sociologists are interested not simply in the amount of authority someone has, but its social basis. Gandhi had enormous charismatic authority as leader of India's successful struggle for independence from Britain, but he never held political office. Japan's Emperor Hirohito, in contrast, wielded absolute traditional and legal-rational authority before Japan's defeat in World War II. Later, however, Japan's new constitution stripped him of virtually all of his authority.

special abilities or characteristics. Prophets, heroes, demagogues, and mass murderers—from Jesus Christ to Gandhi, from Napoleon Bonaparte to Adolph Hitler—all have this type of authority (Willner, 1984). When the more than 900 disciples of the religious cult leader, Jim Jones, obeyed his instructions to commit suicide by swallowing poison (and poisoned their children, as well), they dramatically illustrated the power of charismatic authority (although it should be noted that some members were forced to take the poison). In this case, Jones' power came not from the social status of "religious leader," but from his followers' close identification with him as an individual.

The third form is **traditional authority**, which rests on the belief that the occupants of certain statuses are legitimately powerful because "that's the way it's always been." The authority of kings, queens, and

emperors and, on a smaller scale, of elderly Japanese over their adult children—does not depend solely on legal-rational rules; rather, it also flows from a commitment to traditional arrangements that confer power on the occupant of particular statuses.

It is important to emphasize that legal-rational and traditional authority are not forms of personal power, for they are attached to particular social statuses under socially defined conditions. When soldiers salute each other, they pay respect to a person's rank, not to the individual who holds it. When police officers go "off duty," they lose much of their authority, just as former U.S. presidents no longer control the use of nuclear weapons.

A number of sociologists (see Haskell, 1984) point out that in technologically sophisticated societies *expertise* in a specialized area is becoming an increasingly important source of authority in addition to Weber's three classic types. Experts in fields such as medicine, computer science, economics, business management and accounting, and nuclear weapons technology often exercise considerable authority because they command information necessary for important decisions.

In sharp contrast with authority, **coercive power** lacks social legitimacy. When one country invades another and imposes its will on the inhabitants, its control over that society is not socially supported. Rather, it is based on fear and, for this reason, tends to be relatively unstable. In the aftermath of revolutions (such as that in Nicaragua) and invasions (such as the Soviet Union's invasion of Afghanistan), guerilla warfare often becomes a fact of everyday life, and the new leaders live with continuing awareness that they might be overthrown at any time. In countries such as Japan and the U.S., however, leaders know that while they may lose office with the next election, their opponents do not question their basic right to use the authority of their office.

Weber's three forms of authority are ideal types that rarely exist by themselves. A president may combine legal-rational, charismatic, and traditional authority, and the power of parents in relation to their children combines both traditional and legal-rational authority. If one source of power declines, status occupants rely more heavily on others. Former national leaders have no legal-rational authority over their government but may try to use charismatic or traditional authority to influence decisions long after they leave office.

How is authority organized in societies? This question brings us to perhaps the most important concept in the study of political institutions—the *state*.

The Emergence of the State

Weber (1921) defined the **state** as the institution that "claims the monopoly of the use of force within a given territory" (p. 78). Like other institutions, the state is defined in part by the social functions it performs. It is responsible for establishing and enforcing legal norms; it sets goals; it acts as an "umpire" in disputes among individuals, groups, and communities; and it establishes and maintains relationships with other societies, including trade agreements and military alliances. One function underlies all of these: the state is responsible for maintaining order and stability.

States vary in how they perform these functions, and it is these differences that are the focus for most of this chapter. In this sense, the state is not a static "thing"; rather, it is a set of cultural ideas and dynamic social relationships through which power is used by some individuals and groups over others.

The U.S. judicial system—going all the way to the Supreme Court—is, above all, a social mechanism for resolving disputes and using the authority to determine guilt and innocence and inflict punishment. The rules that regulate what happens in courts are part of the normative structure of the state and affect many aspects of social life.

The state is not the same as the *government*, just as "The American Family" is not the same thing as your family or mine. A **government** is the collection of people who occupy positions of authority within the framework of relationships that define the state. There are two answers to questions such as "What is the Soviet Politburo?" As a part of the Soviet government, it is a collection of leaders who come and go, different people at different times. As part of the Soviet state, it is a group whose members—*whoever they may be*—have particular powers in relation to the citizens of the Soviet Union and particular relationships with the leaders of other societies.

The U.S. government may change considerably with each presidential election, but the state remains unchanged. The Bill of Rights (the first 10 amendments to the Constitution) is a set of norms that defines relationships between the state and its citizens, and it applies no matter which government is in power. The distinction between the state and government may be clearer if we remember that although many governments during our history have violated the Bill of Rights by abusing the power of the state, such violations have had a relatively small effect on the nature of the state itself.

Historically, the state is a relatively recent social institution. Hunter-gatherer societies had no state; decisions generally rested on community consensus, and the kinship group was the only focus of power. Horticultural societies often had a few leaders who depended on traditional authority, but it was not until the agricultural era produced surpluses of wealth that social classes and the state emerged.

Kings and emperors were at the center of the first states. Their authority was strictly traditional, and they were involved in continuous power struggles with nobles and with religious and military leaders. It

Like most hunter-gatherer societies, Eskimo bands have no formal leaders. Important decisions are based on a consensus or, where specialized knowledge is needed, by those considered best qualified to decide.

was not until the last few centuries—particularly in Europe and then the United States—that the state began to acquire a monopoly over political power and the many social functions that characterize its modern form. With the emergence of the state came new cultural concepts—"nation" and "patriotism"—that have become basic organizing concepts in relations between societies. As the Industrial Revolution spawned a growing middle class of well-educated citizens who demanded a voice in the exercise of power in their societies, and as divisions of labor made social life increasingly complex, the functions of the state—and its power—expanded enormously.

Some authors believe that the emergence of powerful states was inevitable as societies industrialized and became more complex (Davis, 1949; Service, 1975); but as explained later in this chapter, the development of the state and its power has served some social classes more than others. Since the prime function of the state is to maintain order and stability in a social environment, and since a given social order usually favors some groups over others, the state inevitably plays an important part in the perpetuation of

social inequality. This also means that the social characteristics of the state inevitably mirror to some degree the social environment it is designed to protect and perpetuate.

CULTURE, POLITICS, AND THE STATE

The power exercised by the state represents the collective ability of a society to "mobilize its resources in the interest of goals" (Parsons, 1969, p. 204). In other words, the state uses laws and policies to support selected values. How do such values and norms differ from one society to another, and how are they reflected in the state as an institution?

Does the state value personal freedom more than social order and conformity, a strong military more than a healthy population free of poverty, equality more than the freedom to pursue individual gain, the rights of accused criminals more than the rights of their victims? The answers to such questions define a basic aspect of any state—the goals it pursues in the name of society—and affect how particular governments use political power.

In capitalist societies, the right to own and use the means of production for private gain is an important value in economic life. The state, in turn, is responsible for protecting private property rights and fostering social conditions in which capitalists can maximize profits (see Smith, 1981). From Marx's perspective, economic arrangements form the most important institutions in any society, and a key function of a capitalist state is to support the values of the capitalist class.

Consider antitrust laws that forbid monopolies in which one organization completely dominates a product or service. Whose interests do such laws best serve? Do they protect consumers from the ability of monopolies to dictate any price they want? Apparently not, for a few large companies in an industry can maintain high prices even though no one of them has a monopoly. There are three major U.S. automobile manufacturers, for example, and yet there is little price competition. Each waits for one of the others to raise prices at the beginning of the new model year and then one by one the others raise their prices by a comparable amount. The only serious price competition in the automobile market has come from foreign manufacturers, which has nothing to do with U.S. antitrust laws.

From Marx's perspective, antitrust laws primarily serve those who own and control capital. This appears to be a contradiction, for why would the state serve the interests of capitalists by restricting them? One answer is that antitrust laws protect capitalists from being driven out of business by other capitalists who monopolize a market. The breakup of AT&T in 1983 was urged less by consumer groups than by companies that wanted a larger slice of the long distance telephone market. The long and unsuccessful antitrust suit against IBM was inspired primarily by IBM's competitors—such as Xerox—not by consumers. In both cases, the millions of dollars spent by the government to sue the companies involved were supplied by taxpayers.

The protection of private property rights is not the only function of the state in capitalist countries. Values such as privacy and the freedoms to vote, express opinions, move from one place to another, and follow religious beliefs are also legally protected. The state takes major responsibility for providing for the poor, for protecting consumers against fraud or the hazards of dangerous products, for supporting public education, and for protecting the environment.

Some of the values supported by the state in socialist countries such as the Soviet Union and Rumania are very different from those emphasized in capitalist countries. Personal freedom is far more restricted, and people live in continuing fear that they will be reported to the authorities for doing something that might offend officials. Rock music was recently banned in the Soviet Union because of its supposed "subversive" effects; and artists, musicians, and writers are regularly persecuted for "undermining" the state.

The announced aim of such societies is to promote equality by refusing to support what is, in capitalist societies, one of the most important personal freedoms—the right to own capital. The welfare of the community, socialists argue, is of more value than the freedom of individuals to exploit the community for personal gain. Consequently, full employment is more highly valued than efficient production.

The contrast between capitalist and socialist states might lead one to conclude that personal freedom and equality are inherently incompatible values, that it is impossible for a society to vigorously support both at the same time. It is important to remember, however, that the right to own property is only one of many personal freedoms, and human history is full of examples—including most hunter-gatherer and horticultural societies—of societies in which people owned little private property and inequality was minimal and in which personal freedom in other areas of life was *not* tightly restricted as it is in so many socialist societies today. Whether or not freedom and equality can be achieved simultaneously in industrial societies remains to be seen.

It is also important to remember that most socialist societies were created through violent revolutions or foreign invasions that transformed societies in which private property rights and severe inequality had existed for hundreds of years. To Lenin (1917), the most powerful leader of the Russian Revolution, the state had to assume great powers over individual freedom in order to crush opposition to the revolution and break the control of the ruling class over the society.

Regardless of their differences, all societies where the state has developed as an institution have one value in common: the preservation of the state itself. The state is the institution that monopolizes the use of force, and when the perpetuation of the state is threatened, the governments of the U.S. or Britain are

When the state is used as an instrument of social oppression of minorities, its monopoly over the use of force becomes all the more important and dangerous. This picture was taken near Cape Town, South Africa, where blacks, whose shantytown was being demolished by the government, demonstrated in protest because they had no other place to live. The response from the police was a volley of tear gas. Like most minorities, South African blacks cannot begin to match the enormous military power of their government.

no less likely to respond with force than are those of China, Rumania, or the Soviet Union. It is a federal crime to advocate—even by merely writing a letter or making a speech—the violent overthrow of the U.S. government; but it is legal for the state to use police and soldiers to disperse a crowd of demonstrators.

The state, then, is an institution that, at best, walks a fine line between the protection of citizens and their oppression. In the name of safeguarding society, it seeks to increase its powers; but those same powers—the monopoly of violence—can then be used against those same citizens.

STRUCTURES OF POWER: BASIC TYPES OF POLITICAL INSTITUTIONS

It is in the structures of power—how it is distributed and used—that the greatest differences between societies are found. As we have seen before, power struc-

tures have two basic characteristics: the equality of distribution, and the amount of power a group, organization, community, or society has.

Distributions of Power: Democracy, Oligarchy, and Autocracy

The word **democracy** joins the Greek words "cracy" ("rule") and "demo" ("of the people"), and in pure democracies power is shared equally by all members of a society. In ancient Greece, decisions were made at meetings in which every citizen had a vote. Virtually all hunter-gatherer societies operated as democracies, and some New England towns still have town meetings in which residents voice their opinions and vote on the issues. Democracies always place some restrictions on who is defined as a "citizen" eligible to participate in decision making. Children cannot vote, just as slaves and women could not in ancient Greece.

Few states take the form of pure democracy, in large part because it is impractical in large complex

In Vermont, the first Tuesday in March is a holiday which allows citizens to attend town meetings held across the state. People of all ages fill halls such as this one shown. It is a time to renew social ties and to make decisions on matters ranging from school budgets and bridge repairs to resolutions calling for a freeze on nuclear weapons.

societies. How would millions of citizens meet to thrash out national issues? If every decision required a vote by the entire population, we would spend most of our time at the polls. One common response to this problem is the **representative democracy**, in which citizens delegate authority to elected representatives—such as those who serve in legislatures. Theoretically, the elected representatives speak for the voters, who are too numerous to speak for themselves.

Democracy depends on several key cultural and structural characteristics. Countries with advanced economies and urban, literate, middle-class populations tend to be more democratic than societies that are underdeveloped and have largely illiterate, rural, peasant populations (Lipset, 1959). Although Bollen (1983) found that economic development and democratic institutions tend to go hand in hand, he also found that democracy depends on the position of a country in the world economy (see Chapter 18). Democracy is most common in wealthy core countries such as the U.S., West Germany, and Japan and least common in peripheral countries such as Nigeria.

Cultural characteristics of a society also play a part. Democracy depends on norms that restrict the power of the state in relation to the people—such as the U.S. Constitution and its Bill of Rights. Values and attitudes are also important, especially those that tolerate and support dissent (see McClosky and Brill, 1983). In the U.S. **civil disobedience**—the deliberate and open violation of a norm for the purpose of changing it because it is perceived as being unjust—is cul-

turally defined as legitimate behavior, even though those who engage in it are punished. Our culture reserves a special respect for those who openly defy unjust laws and willingly accept the consequences in the name of improving society. Many observers have noted that Russians, by contrast, tend to hold just the opposite view and value conformity and obedience to authority far more highly than do those in the U.S. (Shipler, 1983).

Two important aspects of social structure also support democracies. Since citizens must be in a position to elect representatives who act in their best interests, it is important for citizens to know what their representatives are doing with their authority. This produces a continuing tension between the desire of those in authority to keep their activities secret and the need of the people to know about government decisions and activities.

In some cases, secrets do protect "national security." If the public had access to the military's plans for national defense, so would its enemies. In other cases, however, secrecy serves the interests of leaders who want to conceal activities that the public would oppose. Many instances of official misconduct—such as the sale of arms to Iran in return for hostages—are concealed by government officials on the grounds of "national security," when in fact the only security involved is that of the government officials themselves.

Democracy also depends on diffusion of power among many different individuals, groups, and organizations, for when power is concentrated in the hands of a relative few, democracies are in danger of becoming *oligarchies* and, in the most extreme cases, *autocracies*.

Oligarchy and Autocracy Michels (1911) argued that the mere existence of leaders in a society guarantees that democracy cannot last, because power is corrupting no matter how noble a leader's intentions may be. Michels believed that an "Iron Rule of Oligarchy" dictates that complex societies always become **oligarchies**, in which the power of the state is monopolized by an elite.

Michels based his rule on three arguments, the first of which is that most people, either because of apathy or incompetence, would rather let others make decisions for them. It is difficult for most of us to actively involve ourselves in debates over nuclear weapons and the economy without a thorough understanding of the complex issues involved.

Second, Michels argued that in complex societies it is impossible to pay attention to every point of view. Although we may have opinion polls, elections, and referenda on important issues, it is impossible to conduct a "national debate" that includes the active participation of more than 240 million people. Decisions are left to a small number of leaders.

Third, leaders enjoy the privileges that come with power and, therefore, want to keep their positions of power. In order to keep their power, leaders seek more power, trying to control their rivals or silence their opposition by limiting criticism in the media.

From Michels' point of view, the increasing complexity of societies and their reliance on leaders results in a loss of individual power and freedom and growing opportunities for abuses that result in social oppression. As Tannenbaum (1968) pointed out, however, things are not so simple. Industrial societies are organized around complex bureaucracies that control complex divisions of labor. No small group can control national governments in countries such as the U.S. Every four years, new presidents vow to control the vast federal bureaucracy and, inevitably, realize that they cannot possibly do it. As Etzioni-Halévy (1983) argued, bureaucracy is necessary for managing the affairs of a complex representative democracy, and yet its size and power coupled with its inherent rigidity constitute a threat to democratic institutions.

Socialist countries such as the Soviet Union and China are, in comparison with North American and most European countries, far more oligarchic and bureaucratic. When Soviet jet fighters shot down a Korean airliner that strayed into Soviet airspace in 1983, one fact that became clear in the aftermath was that the Soviet oligarchy—the Politburo—had great difficulty monitoring and controlling military units far on the other side of the country. As tightly controlled as many aspects of social life are in socialist countries, gross inefficiency is one of their hallmarks, and this is due in no small part to the vastness and complexity of the bureaucracies through which a relatively small number of leaders try to govern entire societies.

The most extreme concentration of political power is found in an **autocracy** in which the power of the state is wielded by a single leader. Hitler in Germany, Stalin in Russia, Idi Amin in Uganda, and the Shah of Iran were all autocrats, as were most kings and

A true autocrat—such as Libya's Qaddafi shown here in 1987 celebrating the anniversary of the revolution that brought him to power—is a relative rarity today.

queens prior to the twentieth century. Autocracy describes only a few national leaders in recent years, including the head of the royal family in Saudi Arabia, Muammar al-Qaddafi in Libya, the Ayatollah Khomeini in Iran, and Augusto Pinochet in Chile.

The scale running from democracy to autocracy describes the range within which states distribute political power. A second important dimension of the state, however, is the amount of power it has.

How Much Power?
Authoritarianism and Totalitarianism

The concept of **authoritarianism** describes the degree to which the state controls the lives of its citizens. Since all states, by definition, monopolize the use of force, they are all authoritarian to some degree; but sociologists generally reserve the term "authoritarian" for states that exercise high levels of control over people's lives.

Most of the population of the world lives in authoritarian states, from China, the Soviet Union, and the countries of Eastern Europe to military dictatorships in Latin American countries such as Chile, Paraguay, and Guatemala (see Rubin, 1987). Under authoritarianism, the state has the power to control the mass media, schools, and the economy. It often uses terror—inflicted by military and secret police organizations—to control its citizens. The ability of people to migrate often is restricted, and there are few restraints on the government's ability to enact and enforce laws, however unjust they may be (Friedrich and Brzezinski, 1965).

The most extreme form of authoritarianism is **totalitarianism**, under which the state attempts to control not only people's behavior, but virtually all aspects of their private lives. Best described in George Orwell's 1949 classic novel, *Nineteen Eighty-four*, the totalitarian state tries to control what people think and feel as well as what they do through complete control over all social institutions, from the family and mass communications to religion. In Orwell's nightmarish vision, a society is ruled by "Big Brother"; television sets are two-way, allowing authorities to monitor people's homes; history is rewritten in order to conform to the state's version of the truth; and those who refuse to conform are tortured until they think and behave "correctly."

Of all the forms that the state can take, totalitarianism is probably the least stable and is as uncommon as pure democracy (Walzer, in Howe, 1983). In the twentieth century, Nazi Germany and Russia under Stalin came closest to Orwell's vision of totalitarianism, but even these extreme cases were far from monolithic states that effectively ruled the private lives of their citizens. In both cases dissent was not uncommon and there were frequent power struggles (Peukert, 1987). History seems to show that the totalitarian state is unattainable (see Nee and Mozingo, 1983; Schlesinger, 1983).

In general, the likelihood of authoritarianism increases as a society becomes more unstable, especially during crises such as wars or internal upheaval. In 1986, as anti-apartheid protests increased in South Africa, the government made it illegal for anyone to criticize the government in public. The most authoritarian states in the world today—China, the Soviet Union, and military dictatorships in a number of countries—all came into existence in the aftermath of violent revolutions.

In 1798, shortly after the American Revolution, Congress passed the Sedition Act, which allowed the government to prosecute anyone who wrote or published anything that was "false, scandalous, or malicious" against any branch of the federal government (Beard and Beard, 1944). In short, open criticism of the government was banned by law. In the early 1950s the fear of communism allowed Senator Joseph McCarthy to conduct his infamous Senate hearings to identify communists. Hundreds of people were subpoenaed to testify before his committee, and anyone who had ever belonged to a communist organization, or who had associated with those who had, was labeled a communist (or a communist sympathizer). McCarthy never identified a single communist in the government, but by the time he was stopped, hundreds of innocent people—from government employees to teachers, writers, artists, and actors—had lost their jobs and suffered permanent damage to their reputation.

There is no such thing as a state that cannot become more authoritarian under the control of a particular government, and the state's monopoly over the use of force creates a continuing tension between the functional importance of state institutions and the potential for abuse of authority by groups and individuals. Nor is "majority rule"—a hallmark of democracy—a guarantee that the power of the state will not be used to oppress citizens. More than a century ago, Alexis de Tocqueville (1835/1954) visited the U.S. and warned of the possibility of a "tyranny of the major-ity," in which the rights of minorities would not be protected. In a racist, sexist, anti-Semitic society conformity to prevailing norms results in the oppres-sion of nonwhites, women, and Jews for whom the law—which is controlled by the state—is "a sword, not a shield" (Burns, 1973). Without the acceptance of Nazi ideology by millions of Germans, the Nazi state never would have been able to perpetrate the Holocaust in which more than 6 million people were murdered.

It is important to note that while many of today's authoritarian states are also socialist countries, there is no necessary connection between economic and polit-ical arrangements. Nazi Germany was both capitalist and anti-socialist; some of the world's most oppressive military dictatorships are allies of the U.S.; and in semi-socialist countries such as Sweden and Norway, the state is not authoritarian.

Who Rules? Power in U.S. Politics

Sociologists have developed several views of the distri-bution of political power in societies, two of which we encountered in Chapter 9. Mills (1956) and Hunter (1953) argued that power is monopolized by an elite of business, government, and the military leaders who have similar backgrounds and move easily from one sphere of power to another (see also Useem, 1983). Below the power elite a variety of interest groups have some power, and at the bottom lies the mass of un-organized people who have little power to affect na-tional decisions.

The power elite, Mills argued, is bound together by common interests. Military leaders want to expand the number and sophistication of weapons, and corpo-rations want to build such weapons for huge profits. As a result, decisions about the nuclear arms race are based not only on national defense, but on the eco-nomic interests of corporations as well. The concept of a power elite identifies several consequences of con-centrated political power, the most important of which are the growth of corporate power and the decline of public participation in decision making (Domhoff and Ballard, 1968).

Riesman (1961) offered a very different view, ar-guing that power is divided pluralistically among a variety of interest groups over which the mass of unorganized citizens has some power. Different inter-est groups dominate decision making in different

areas, and recognize that they have limited power and depend on others in order to accomplish their goals.

Riesman (1961) believed, however, that when pluralism is taken to extremes it interferes with leader-ship because each interest group exercises "veto" power over the issues that define its goals. Governing bodies such as the Congress have difficulty making decisions because they are besieged by well-organized interest groups at every turn. The result is often legis-lation that offends a minimal number of groups but also fails to establish clear and decisive directions for national programs and policy.

Lieberson (1971) also contended that when inter-est groups become so numerous and powerful that they dominate political decision making, it is difficult for a national consensus to emerge on any given issue. Each group tends to fight for its special interest and for nothing else, and this tends to fragment society and break down social cohesion.

There is little doubt that political power is con-centrated in the U.S., although certainly not to the degree found in authoritarian societies. Domhoff's 1967 study and Freitag's study in 1975 both support Mills' belief in the existence of a power elite (see also Domhoff, 1983). Freitag found that almost 90 percent of federal cabinet officers between 1897 and 1973 had also served as high-level officers in corporations (see One Step Further 19-1).

This does not mean the power elite is a unified group whose members meet to agree on how political decisions are to be made. It does imply that a relatively small number of people have far greater access to political power than do most citizens, and their inter-ests tend to coincide. Middle- and lower-class people have some voice in selecting presidents and congres-sional representatives, but they have virtually no power in choosing cabinet members and the heads of powerful federal agencies such as the departments of State and Defense. Nor does the average citizen have any access to these officials once they are appointed (when was the last time you or your parents attended a dinner party whose guests included high-level govern-ment officials?).

Members of the power elite certainly differ on various issues and may oppose one another; but when they choose to work toward common goals, they wield enormous political power. As one study of corporate campaign contributions in the 1980 elections showed, businesses as a group tend to support the same candi-dates (Clawsen et al., 1986); and when businesses go

ONE STEP FURTHER 19-1:
The Political Power of the Upper Class

Although Domhoff estimates that the U.S. upper class makes up only 0.5 percent of the population, its share of politically powerful positions is considerably larger. The data in Table B-19-1 are from two historical studies of U.S. cabinet members from 1897 to 1973 and from 1932 to 1964. In both periods, roughly two-thirds of cabinet members had upper-class family origins (percentages that, although omitted below, are only slightly higher for Republican cabinets than for Democratic). The first set of percentages shows how presidential cabinets compared with the entire U.S. adult population on a variety of class indicators. Notice how strong the elite Anglo-Saxon background of cabinet members is in comparison with a miniscule percentage of the general population.

If we add to this Mintz's finding that 90 percent of cabinet members were either from the upper class or were associated with major corporations, it becomes clear that the upper class and those who share its interests have a virtual monopoly over high level positions in the administrative branch of the federal government. Freitag (1975) finds that this pattern is not only quite stable over time, but varies little from one cabinet position to another, including secretary of labor.

Table B-19-1

1897–1973

PERCENT	CABINETS	GENERAL U.S. POPULATION
in the business elite	78%	less than 0.5%
in the social elite	66%	less than 1.0%
listed in the *Social Register*	25%	less than 0.1%
who belong to elite clubs	48%	less than 1.0%
who attended elite schools	29%	less than 0.5%
with British background	82%	19%

1932–1964

PERCENT IN THE UPPER CLASS		
Secretaries of state	63%	
Secretaries of defense	62%	
Secretaries of treasury	63%	

Source: For 1897–1973, Mintz (1975); for 1932–1964, Domhoff (1967).

against the tide and support candidates or issues that are generally unpopular in the business community, there are powerful sanctions that can be used to enforce conformity (see Mintz and Schwartz, 1985; Useem, 1984). If the U.S. political system is pluralistic, it is what Kornhauser (1966) called an "elite pluralism," in which a select few vie with one another over control of the state (see also Knoke, 1981).

The U.S. Voter The right to vote is the most direct form of political power available. Although we rarely use it to decide specific issues, we can use it to elect nominated candidates for public office. This represents a very indirect form of power in an important respect, for once candidates are elected, their need to worry about pleasing their constituents lessens until the next election. In the 1964 presidential election, Lyndon Johnson overwhelmed his opponent, Barry Goldwater, in large part because voters feared that Goldwater would be too quick to involve the U.S. in war. Within a few years after his election, however, Johnson had led us deep into the disastrous war in Vietnam. Ronald Reagan won landslide victories as a presidential candidate in part by promising to control the federal budget deficit. Under his leadership, however, it has grown to record high levels.

We are considerably less likely to vote in national elections than are the citizens of other industrial societies (Table 19-1). This may be due in part to the fact that responsibility for registering as voters rests entirely with the individual, whereas in Canada, Finland, Great Britain, and West Germany registration is either required or actively facilitated by the government by allowing registration by mail or automatically registering all citizens. Among U.S. registered voters, fully 88 percent voted in the 1984 election, which suggests that if registration were more widespread, voting might be as well (U.S. Census Bureau, 1986a).

There is also evidence, however, that we generally pay little attention to political issues. In 1987 only 23 percent reported that they were "very interested in politics and national affairs," and more than a third said they were "only somewhat interested" or "not at all" (Davis and Smith, 1987). National surveys suggest that these relatively low levels of political involvement may reflect a lack of faith in government and the belief that government is not responsive to the people. In 1987, more than two-thirds reported the belief that

most public officials have little interest in the average citizen's problems, and less than 20 percent expressed a great deal of confidence in either the Congress or the executive branch. Voter nonparticipation is also related to the statuses people occupy. In general, those who occupy the highest positions are the most likely to vote (Table 19-2). An exception to this is that women and men are equally likely to vote, even though women as a category occupy an inferior social position.

Table 19-2

Who Votes in Presidential Elections? (United States, 1984)

CHARACTERISTIC	PERCENTAGE VOTING[1]
Gender	
Male	59
Female	61
Race	
White	61
Black	56
Hispanic	33
Age	
18–20	37
21–24	44
25–34	54
35–44	64
45–64	70
65 and older	68
Education	
8 years or less	43
1–3 years high school	44
High school graduate	59
1–3 years college	68
College graduate or more	79
Employment Status	
Employed	62
Unemployed	44

[1]Percentage of adult citizen population that actually voted in the 1984 presidential election.

Sources: U.S. Census Bureau, 1982, 1986a.

Table 19-1

Voter Participation in Selected Countries

COUNTRY	PERCENTAGE VOTING[1]
Switzerland	52
United States	59
India	60
Canada	71
Finland	74
Ireland	76
Israel	79
Great Britain	79
Norway	83
Denmark	89
West Germany	91

[1]Percentage of population of voting age that actually voted in national elections.

Source: U.S. Census Bureau, 1980b.

Is our general lack of political interest and participation some kind of national "personality trait"? While this is a possible explanation, sociologists are more likely to consider how the structure of political institutions affects the ability and motivation of individuals to participate in them. For more insight into this, we turn to political parties, the first level of political organization above the "unorganized mass of people" (see Teixeira, 1987).

Political Parties   A **political party** is an organization whose main goal is to acquire power by placing members in positions of authority. In authoritarian countries, such as the socialist countries of Eastern Europe, a single party dominates the state and voters must choose between voting for the official party candidates or not voting at all. In a few countries, such as Mexico, the state is not authoritarian, but the ruling party is so firmly entrenched that opposition parties rarely win elections. Most countries have a handful of parties, and a few, such as Italy, have a dozen or so.

Since parties are the main source of candidates for public office, they are an important link between citizens and government. Through their candidates, parties define positions on issues, map solutions to problems, and transmit public opinion to those who make decisions. If voters, then, feel unmotivated to participate in political activities, part of the explanation may lie in the characteristics of political parties through which most of our power as individual voters is felt.

The sociological importance of parties lies in two areas that distinguish parties in the U.S. from those in most other representative democracies. The first concerns the legal norms that control elections, which, in turn, define the relationship between parties and the state. The second focuses on the structural and cultural characteristics of parties themselves, both of which are closely tied to the first.

Unlike elections in most democracies, U.S. norms dictate a "winner-take-all" system in which a candidate must receive more votes than any other candidate. The composition of Congress is determined by the outcome in each of 50 state elections. Under this system, even if 49 percent of the voters favor candidates from party "A," it is possible that *none* of those who are elected will be from that party. In this extreme hypothetical case the interests of almost half of the adult population would have no representation in Congress.

In most other representative democracies, the composition of legislatures is proportional, which is to say it is determined by the percentage of the vote received by each party, not whether individual candidates get more votes than do their opponents. If only 10 percent of the voters favor party "A," then 10 percent of the seats in the legislature will be filled by members of that party. Such legislatures reflect the diversity of their populations in a way that is almost impossible in the U.S.

The norms that govern elections affect the composition—the structure—of governing bodies such as the Congress and state legislatures or European parliaments. If U.S. voters want to use their votes to elect candidates, their only hope is to vote for a candidate who can beat all other opponents. If the candidate who seems most likely to win does not represent their views, then from a practical standpoint, their votes have no effect on the ultimate composition of the government.

The effects of the winner-take-all system extend to the social characteristics of parties themselves, and U.S. parties differ from those in other representative democracies in several ways (Lipset, 1959). Suppose that you belong to the "Freedom Party," whose members favor, among other things, legalization of marijuana, a position shared by only 16 percent of adults in 1987 (Davis and Smith, 1987). How does your party win seats in Congress?

In most democracies, you could gain as many as 16 percent of the legislative seats—in other words, representation in direct proportion to the percentage of your supporters in the population. In the U.S., however, you would win no seats unless you ran candidates in congressional districts where most voters favor legalization of marijuana—an extremely unlikely possibility. If you are serious about winning—rather than merely expressing your views—one response to this problem is to do whatever you can to avoid offending potential supporters, and one obvious way to do this is not to take a clear and open stand in favor of legalizing marijuana.

In most representative democracies, when parties take a clear stand on the issues, it does not destroy their chances of gaining some political power; but in the U.S., it can be disastrous, as Barry Goldwater and George McGovern discovered in the presidential elections of 1964 and 1972. Both took clear positions in their campaigns and both were defeated overwhelmingly by their opponents—Lyndon Johnson in

1964 and Richard Nixon in 1972. In 1984 many analysts agreed that Ronald Reagan's landslide victory over Walter Mondale was helped considerably by Reagan's avoidance of controversial issues and his refusal to reveal his plans for a second term. Mondale announced that he would raise taxes in order to lower the federal deficit, while Reagan said he would not raise taxes but did not reveal any alternative.

To avoid such defeats, parties try to attract a majority of voters by offending as few people as possible. As a consequence, **party platforms**—statements of positions on important issues—tend to be vague and wishy-washy, and members of the same party may hold sharply different views. Southern Democrats are often more conservative than northern Republicans.

This, in turn, makes it difficult for parties to be tightly organized on a national level. More important, it forces voters to choose between candidates whose political differences are often hard to detect and who do not represent what voters want. (The disaffection of voters was perhaps best expressed by a candidate who tried unsuccessfully to change his name to "None of the Above," figuring that he would attract a large number of voters.) As a result, we tend to base our votes more on our perceptions of candidates' personalities than on their positions on issues. Early in the 1988 presidential campaign, front-runner Gary Hart dropped out after reports of extramarital affairs, and Joseph Biden withdrew after it was revealed that he quoted the words of others in his speeches without giving credit and had been convicted of plagiarism in law school. By comparison, most other democracies do not share our intense focus on the personal behavior and characteristics of candidates and instead vote for the political party, not individual candidates.

The relative importance of parties and individual candidates affects the characteristics of parties. In France individuals can gain public office only through the success of their parties. There are no primary elections; party officials decide who will occupy the seats won in an election. This gives parties enormous power over officeholders, for those who fail to support party positions on important issues may be expelled from the party and, therefore, denied access to office. Under this system, representatives must either reflect the views of those who elected them or leave office.

In the U.S., by contrast, the focus is on the candidate, not the party, and this means that parties have

The emphasis on the personalities and private behavior of politicians as a major factor in U.S. political life was dramatically apparent in the rapid rise and fall of presidential candidate Gary Hart in the 1988 campaign. Considered by most to be a front-runner for the democratic nomination, he withdrew from the race after reports that he was involved in an adulterous affair.

little control over those they help elect. Individuals can defy their parties and maintain their power on the basis of their own resources. Since most voters do not follow politics closely, they often have no idea of what their representatives are actually doing, and when election time rolls around, personality often plays a far more important part than ability or political ideology.

It should come as no surprise that we are less and less likely to vote in elections and increasingly identify ourselves as "independents" rather than as members of a political party. Between 1972 and 1987 the proportion of adults who identified themselves as independents rose from 26 to 32 percent, and in 1987 only 29 percent classified themselves as strong members of a major political party (Davis and Smith, 1987).

Political parties, then, are not very powerful in the U.S. Given the fact that voters are, for the most part, disorganized and not very committed to actively following political affairs, where else can we look for concentrations of political power? One answer is the interest group.

Interest Groups   Whereas the avowed goal of political parties is to place their members in positions of authority, an **interest group** attempts to affect political decisions by supporting candidates who are sympathetic to their goals and by influencing those who are already in positions of authority.

Parties generally have broad platforms that cover many issues, but interest groups usually focus on single issues such as abortion, gun control, consumer affairs, the arms race, prayer in public schools, the environment, benefit levels for retired people, the Fqual Rights Amendment, or legislation that affects a

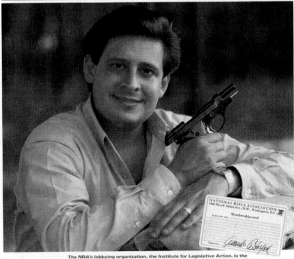

The issue of gun control in the U.S. has spawned numerous interest groups, the most powerful of which is the National Rifle Association (NRA). Pro-gun-control groups, such as Handgun Control, reflect the views of the majority of U.S. adults, but the NRA has nonetheless been able to block most efforts to control the sale of handguns.

particular business, industry, or category of workers. As you can see, the list could go on and on, and this gives you some sense of how many different interest groups focus their attention on officials.

Interest groups influence officials primarily by providing them with expert information on complex issues and by contributing money to election campaigns. When legislators consider bills that would affect nuclear power plants, they must take into account a vast array of scientific information that describes, among other things, the risks of nuclear disasters. Few legislators in the U.S. Congress are scientists (most, in fact, are lawyers), and they therefore depend on outsiders for the technical information needed to make informed decisions.

This is where interest groups often exert influence by employing **lobbyists**—representatives who meet with officials and provide expert information, which tends to support the interest group's goals. Lobbyists for pronuclear power groups, then, might provide studies that indicate that nuclear power is both safe and economical, while lobbyists for antinuclear interest groups might provide information that underscores the dangers and high cost of nuclear power. Since legislators usually lack independent sources of expertise on complex issues, their own positions often result from the relative persuasiveness of different lobbyists.

Because some interest groups are well organized and can hire full-time lobbyists, they can exert far more influence over government decisions than citizens who have neither the time nor the money to lobby. This is particularly true of corporations whose financial resources are greater than those of any other organization with the exception of the state. In 1986, lobbyists spent a total of $61 million to influence congressional legislation, an average of more than $113,000 per legislator (Associated Press, 1987).

The importance of money in politics goes beyond lobbying, for elected officials depend on contributions in order to finance their campaigns for reelection. As the late humorist Will Rogers put it in 1931, "Politics has got so expensive that it takes a lot of money even to get beat with." When politicians take positions that affect interest groups, they cannot ignore the fact that they might offend those whose contributions could make the difference in a campaign for reelection.

Some political writers, such as Drew (1983), argue that the connection between money and politics is unnecessary. The greatest campaign expense is television advertising, and in Great Britain television time is given to candidates free of charge, substantially reducing candidates' dependence on private contributions from interest groups. Others urge public campaign financing through which candidates receive equal amounts of money from tax revenues and are forced to rely exclusively on these funds.

Efforts to limit the dependency of officeholders on private supporters have generally been unsuccessful. The Federal Election Campaign Act severely limited the amount that each individual could contribute to a campaign, but interest groups soon found a way around the law. There is no limit on the amount that groups and organizations can contribute, and interest groups—from corporations to social movements—have formed political action committees (called "PACs") through which great amounts of money from individuals are funneled into campaigns.

Organized interest groups are a major focus of political power in many countries; but groups can multiply their power by temporarily forming coalitions with other interest groups.

Political Coalitions   Interest groups often combine in order to accomplish goals that temporarily overlap, and this can produce strange combinations. The American Civil Liberties Union generally fights against the activities of the Ku Klux Klan; but when the Klan tries to conduct demonstrations in public, the Civil Liberties Union has often defended the right of Klan members to assemble publicly and express their views. As Charles D. Warner (1870) put it a century ago, "politics makes strange bedfellows."

Coalitions abound in the political life of any complex society, in part because as the number of interest groups grows, the relative power of any group declines in relation to all the rest. In the debate over abortion, organizations that favor free choice for women include the Planned Parenthood Federation, the American Civil Liberties Union, the National Organization for Women, and a variety of religious and feminist groups. While these groups form a coalition around the issue of abortion, however, they sometimes oppose one another on other issues. Some feminist groups oppose the free availability of hard-core pornography; the Civil Liberties Union, however, opposes this position on the grounds that it would interfere with constitutionally guaranteed freedoms.

Coalitions are also a part of everyday life within governments. In Congress, senators and representatives regularly form coalitions in order to muster enough votes to pass their favorite bills ("I'll vote for your bill if you'll vote for mine"). In some countries—such as Italy and Israel—there are so many political parties that it is rare for any one party to win a majority of the vote in elections; so they are forced to form a coalition government in which several parties share ruling power.

The stability of such governments depends on the ability of diverse groups to maintain a consensus, and if that consensus breaks down, the government falls and new elections are called. This is in sharp contrast to our winner-take-all system in which one candidate controls the entire administration after being elected president.

While most coalitions are temporary and focus on specific issues, some appear to be permanent. In the U.S., one of the most powerful coalitions is what President Dwight D. Eisenhower (a former army general) called the **military-industrial complex**—a coalition consisting of the military and industrialists who make huge profits by manufacturing military hardware. Both share the goal of developing expensive new armaments, but for different reasons. The military justifies its budget and its importance as an institution only by justifying the need for more and better weapons which, in turn, provide profits for industry. Both use their expertise and financial resources to lobby Congress to authorize increased military spending.

As we have seen in the preceding sections, the cultural and structural characteristics of political arrangements define them as social institutions through which decisions about life in a society are made. Political power is also affected by ecological arrangements, for the definition of the state itself includes the physical territory within which governments exercise authority.

POLITICAL ECOLOGY

Geography and population are two of the most important factors that affect the ability of a government to exercise the power of the state. The territory of the Soviet Union is more than twice as large as the U.S., four times as large as Europe, and slightly larger than all of Latin America. Obviously, for a central government to control a vast territory is at best an enormously difficult task, and that helps explain why the state in societies such as the Soviet Union, China, and the U.S. depends so heavily on a huge bureaucracy, military, and police force. It also helps explain why

such governments are so inefficient, for it is very difficult for central planners in Moscow (or Washington) to monitor what is happening 4,000 miles away in Vladivostok (or 3,000 miles away in Los Angeles).

The government of China faces additional obstacles to controlling its population, for not only is China large (roughly the area of the U.S.) but it has a population of more than 1 billion people—four times larger than the U.S. population and amounting to a fifth of all the people in the world (Population Reference Bureau, 1987). It is one thing for the government to institute a policy—such as limiting families to one child in order to lower birth rates—and quite another to enforce it.

In any society, regardless of its size, the state cannot effectively control its citizens without their cooperation; but this is particularly true in societies with large populations or territories. If just 20 percent of U.S. taxpayers refused to file income tax returns, the Internal Revenue Service would be faced with tracking down and prosecuting 18 *million* lawbreakers distributed over almost 4 million square miles.

The Geography of Political Power

Geography is an important aspect of the distribution of political power. In the simplest sense, geographical boundaries define legal jurisdictions—the territories that are under the authority of the governments of towns, cities, counties, states, and nations. Geography, however, often plays a more complex part in political life.

Consider the problem of adding the Equal Rights Amendment to the U.S. Constitution. The amendment was passed by both houses of Congress and sent to state legislatures, 38 of which had to ratify the amendment in order for it to become part of the Constitution. In the spring of 1982, 91 percent of adults reported that they had heard of and understood the ERA, and of these, 75 percent favored its passage (Davis and Smith, 1987); yet when the deadline for passage came, the amendment had fallen 3 states short of ratification.

There are many explanations for the ERA's defeat (see McGlen and O'Connor, 1983), but one aspect simply involves the social geography of political power. Regardless of the relative size of its population, each state has an equal vote in deciding the fate of constitutional amendments. A significant portion of ERA opponents are religious fundamentalists, most of whom live in rural southern and western states with small populations. The combined populations of the states whose legislatures opposed the ERA made up only 28 percent of the U.S. population, and yet because each of these sparsely settled states had an equal vote, they were able to block the amendment. The ERA failed in part because most of its supporters were concentrated in a relatively small number of states, each of which could cast only one vote for the amendment (an arrangement designed by the framers of the Constitution to ensure that large urban states could not dominate and exploit small, rural states).

Political geography has perhaps its greatest effects on relationships between societies. The vastness and harsh climate of Russia condemned to failure Napoleon's and Hitler's dreams of conquest. The flat, level terrain of Western and Central Europe makes the passage of armies so easy that this region has been a recurring battleground for centuries. Before the invention of nuclear weapons, the Atlantic and Pacific oceans virtually ensured that no invader from beyond the Americas could easily attack the U.S., just as the stormy English Channel has protected the British Isles for almost 1,000 years.

In many cases, the distribution of natural resources plays an important part in determining the power of societies in relation to one another. Were it not for their great supplies of oil, most of the countries of the Middle East would have far less influence over industrial societies than they now enjoy; nor would the U.S. be as hesitant as it has been to take action against apartheid in South Africa were it not for the important minerals that South Africa supplies to the U.S.

Many societies are influenced by the belief that a nation is powerful in direct proportion to the size of its population, and that efforts by industrial countries to encourage birth control in Third World countries is an attempt to limit their power. Although the world is now dominated by countries that contain only a small fraction of total world population, it is understandable that many poor societies see the sheer size of their populations as their only hope for influence in a world dominated by economic and technological superpowers.

THE USES OF POLITICAL POWER

Like all institutions, political arrangements have cultural, structural, and ecological characteristics. In what ways are they functional and dysfunctional, what part do they play in social conflict, and how are they related to social change?

Functions and Dysfunctions

Like all social institutions, political arrangements produce both functional and dysfunctional consequences. Representative democracy allows a great deal of public debate and criticism of government. Many officials—from presidents to city council members—are elected and can, therefore, be held accountable for their decisions.

These characteristics of democracies are functional for restraining the power of government and encouraging authorities to weigh their decisions carefully. Compared with authoritarian states, democratic governments have much less authority to arrest, detain, and punish people without due cause, to invade privacy or use torture to extract information.

Widespread opportunities for participation in the political process strengthen the social legitimacy of the state and, therefore, help to perpetuate it. We may oppose a particular government, but since representative democracy is the source of our ability to protest in the first place, it is less likely to be challenged.

These same characteristics also produce dysfunctional consequences, however. Public debate often requires a great deal of time, and it can take years for new policies to emerge and take effect. While the accountability of authorities to the public limits their power, it also tends to make officials wary of making decisions that will offend voters, especially voters of interest groups. In 1984, the federal budget deficit was projected to be in the neighborhood of 200 billion dollars, and although most officials agreed that programs such as Social Security would have to be cut in order to bring the budget under control, neither the president nor Congress was willing to "do what was necessary" and risk alienating elderly voters so close to an election.

The relative openness of democratic societies also encourages conflict as interest groups clash over the goals a government pursues and the means it uses to accomplish them. The turbulent decade of the 1960s is a perfect example of the great instability that can occur when the public takes full advantage of the right to protest government policies.

Unlike democracies, authoritarian states do not have to first consider public opinion. They enjoy much greater freedom to make decisions and act on them as they see fit, which can lead to greater efficiency. There was no public debate in the Soviet Union over the invasion of Afghanistan; the violent and nonviolent protests that took place in the U.S. over the

Vietnam War never would have been tolerated in the Soviet Union. Nor is there public debate in Russia over the Soviet position at international arms control negotiations.

The price that is commonly paid for such efficiency, however, is rigidity, stagnation, and oppression (Stojanovic, 1981). Without criticism and public debate, governments can easily fall into a set of inflexible policies that discourage the introduction of new and better ideas. The Soviet state's control over the economy is a perfect example of inefficiency and backwardness that is so extreme that it is a favorite source of sarcastic humor among Russian citizens themselves. It is too soon to tell how the new Soviet policy of openness will effect it.

The primary goal of authoritarian states is to control as many aspects of social life as possible, and this produces a number of dysfunctional consequences. Beyond the obvious problem of abused authority through which people are arrested, tortured, and imprisoned without legal representation or due process of law (Stojanovic, 1981), there are less obvious effects. Authoritarian societies often appear to be very stable, for example, as if the government is in complete control and can do as it pleases. Authoritarian governments, however, stay in power by taking maximum advantage of the state's monopoly over the use of force, and this means that their stability depends heavily on coercive power. "The one means," wrote Adolph Hitler (1924, p. 53) "that wins the easiest victory over reason: terror and force."

Leaders in all societies face the problem of knowing what people are thinking, but the problem is even more acute in authoritarian states because they forbid dissent. This necessitates enormous and complex institutions—such as secret police—whose sole function is to find out if people are thinking and doing anything that might threaten the government (Hollander, 1982).

Authoritarian leaders sometimes try to increase their security by identifying themselves with the state—in other words, by removing the distinction between the state and a government. "I am the state," declared Napoleon Bonaparte to the French Senate in 1814. This statement, in effect, implied that since Napoleon was the state, the state as an institution could not be used to limit his authority. The dangers inherent in this view make clear why the separation of government from the state is an important principle in representative democracies. The principle—"no one is above the law, not even the president"—was the

In the 1970s, between 6,000 and 15,000 people in Argentina were kidnapped, tortured, and murdered by government security forces in an attempt to silence opposition to strict military rule. After a new civilian government was elected, protests spread throughout Argentina as the families of those who had disappeared demanded justice. This picture shows mothers with posters of their missing children.

basis for Richard Nixon's forced resignation in 1974. His removal from office underscored the supremacy of the state over any particular government.

The State and Social Conflict

As the institution responsible for maintaining order and stability, the state inevitably plays a part in social conflict. The state, however, is rarely a neutral "umpire," for by preserving the cultural and structural arrangements of a society, it also preserves arrangements that create social inequality.

This is most apparent in authoritarian states. In socialist authoritarian societies, such as East Germany and the Soviet Union, the power of the state is used to maintain the wealth, power, and prestige of government and military leaders, and there is a basic conflict between the government and the people. In capitalist authoritarian societies, the state also supports the interests of capitalists, whether or not they occupy formal positions in the government. In El Salvador, leaders of labor unions are regularly harassed by the police and military, and many have been kidnapped and murdered by "death squads" who support the government.

State support for those who dominate society is less visible in representative democracies, but it is important and widespread nonetheless. The U.S. is a capitalist democracy where government rarely uses the power of the state to hurt the interests of capitalism as an economic system. This means that most government programs support the interests of capitalists.

The French philosopher Jean-Jacques Rousseau (1762/1950) believed that the state came into being because the right to own property caused such chaotic competition over ownership that an institution was needed to restore order. Rousseau also believed, however, that the state did more than maintain order: It also defended the wealthy—the largest and most influential class of property owners.

Marx expanded Rousseau's analysis and concluded that democracy is an illusion, that because the masses of people do not control *economic* institutions the belief that we can still control political institutions is false. It is of course true that we can elect anyone we want to public office, but Marx believed that the basic structure of the state supports the interests of capitalism and capitalists, not the vast majority of people who must sell their labor power in order to survive.

In the simplest sense, the state in capitalist democracies supports capitalism by refraining from doing anything that hurts the interests of capitalists as a class. Although many laws defend the interests of working people—minimum wage laws, occupational health and safety laws, and laws protecting labor unions, for example—none threatens capitalism as a system. Nor have they significantly altered the unequal distribution of wealth, power, and prestige between classes (see Chapter 11).

In a more complex sense, the state actively supports capitalism by creating and maintaining social conditions that enable capitalists to expand and more efficiently profit from the labor power of workers. In the world economy, the State Department conducts relations with other countries in ways that foster a stable social order in the world, within which capitalists can invest money in other countries and be assured that their investments are safe. This often puts the U.S. in the position of supporting authoritarian states such as South Korea and Chile because U.S. corporations have huge investments in those countries.

In the U.S. many domestic government programs that are officially defined as for the benefit of workers also support capitalism (O'Connor, 1973), particularly those that increase the productivity of labor and help to train and educate new workers. Each year the government spends billions of dollars on research that benefits industry and also maintains railroads, highways, airports, and other utilities that directly benefit businesses. The military provides huge sources of income and profit to business, and policies of the Treasury Department and the Federal Reserve affect interest rates and the money supply—both of which are vital to the investment needs of capitalists.

Businesses depend on a steady supply of trained, educated workers. Public education, subsidized housing, federally guaranteed mortgages, school lunch programs, and publicly funded daycare centers not only benefit families but also capitalists, by helping to prepare each generation of workers at public expense. Without such programs, individuals would have to shoulder the expense and would, therefore, be far more likely to demand much higher wages from their employers.

A variety of other programs benefit capitalists in ways that are not readily apparent. Welfare and unemployment insurance obviously benefit workers and families; but they also soften the negative effects of job shortages, and this makes it easier for employers to lay off workers when it is profitable to do so. Social Security lessens the need for workers to set aside money during their working years, and this lessens the pressure for higher wages.

Perhaps the most important way in which all states—whether authoritarian or democratic, capitalist or socialist—maintain economic arrangements and the resulting inequalities is by legitimating them by identifying with them. We tend to think of the U.S. as both capitalist and democratic, and most of us have a hard time imagining one without the other. We tend to believe that democracy *implies* capitalism and that capitalism implies democracy; that socialism implies authoritarianism (and, erroneously, that authoritarianism implies socialism). Because economic institutions affect so many aspects of life in a society, and because the state's prime function is to maintain order and stability, when people affirm their loyalty and affection for their country, they also tend to affirm their support for its economic system. When children learn the pledge of allegiance to the flag and develop a love for their country, they also are socialized to accept prevailing economic institutions as the "right" way to produce and distribute wealth.

In this sense, political and economic institutions are so intertwined that we need to think in terms of **political economy**—the social arrangements through which political and economic institutions support and maintain each other (see Froman,

1984). We may think of them as separate, but as is true of so many social arrangements described in earlier chapters, these two institutions are integral parts of the same whole and do not operate independently of each other (Domhoff, 1983).

The state cannot single-mindedly pursue the interests of one class or interest group, however, without alienating the vast majority of its citizens and threatening the legitimacy of state authority. As O'Connor (1973) put it, this produces a serious tension:

> The state must try to maintain or create conditions in which profitable capital accumulation is possible. However, the state also must try to maintain or create conditions for social harmony. A capitalist state that openly uses its coercive forces to help one class accumulate capital at the expense of other classes loses its legitimacy and hence undermines the basis of its loyalty and support. But a state that ignores the necessity of assisting the process of capital accumulation risks drying up the source of its power, the economy's surplus production capacity and the taxes drawn from this surplus. (p. 6)

This source of conflict is even more apparent in authoritarian states such as the Soviet Union. On the one hand, civilian leaders must support the interests of powerful groups such as the military, who demand a huge share of national resources. On the other hand, high levels of defense spending leave a relatively small share for consumer goods—from meat to decent housing. One of the most persistent social problems of Soviet society is the demoralization of its people, who are frustrated in their desire to improve their standard of living; and their frustration often supports a crisis of faith in society itself (Shipler, 1983; Silk, 1983).

In most societies, then, governments use the power of the state to maintain what is often a delicate balance between the demands of interest groups, the needs of the population, and the pressures of maintaining the legitimacy of the state itself. When a government can no longer maintain that balance, political change may be unavoidable.

Politics and Social Change: Rebellions, Coups, and Revolutions

Political change generally takes one of three basic forms. A **rebellion** challenges the policies of a government without trying to change the cultural or structural characteristics of the state. In 1786, poverty was widespread in the American colonies in the aftermath of the Revolutionary War; and poor farmers, unable to pay their debts, were stripped of their possessions—their land, animals, and equipment—by the courts. Led by Daniel Shays, mobs of farmers prevented Massachusetts courts from meeting to prosecute indebted farmers, and eventually there was an armed confrontation between Shays' followers and the Massachusetts militia (Morison, 1965). "Shays' Rebellion" was not an attempt to change the form of political institutions. Its goal was to change the policies of government—in other words, to change the ways in which the government used the power of the state.

In 1982 and 1988 Polish shipyard workers went on strike, not to call for an end to socialism in Poland, but rather to demand better living and working conditions for workers (see Ash, 1984).

Like rebellion, a **coup d'état** (pronounced "coo day ta"—whose meaning in French is "a blow concerning the state") does not try to change the character of the state; but unlike rebellion, a coup is an illegal attempt to replace one government with another, often with the use of force. In many countries—especially in Latin America and Africa—coups are so frequent

In Haiti, General Henri Namphy appears on television in the summer of 1988 shortly after a successful coup. Namphy ousted Haiti's president who, a week before, had fired the general on a charge of insubordination. The president fled to safety in a neighboring country.

that they have become the primary way in which leadership passes from one group to another. Because the military has a virtual monopoly on the instruments of force, it is often the source of coups. In the simplest case, military leaders decide that they can do a better job of governing a country than civilian leaders can. One morning the president wakes up to find that the presidential residence is surrounded by tanks and that key resources—television and radio stations, telephone exchanges, airports, and power plants—are under military control. In other cases, coups occur while the leader is out of the country. It was through a coup that General Noriega seized power in Panama in 1987 after the president tried to fire him from his post as leader of the military.

Of all the forms of political change, **revolution** is by far the most serious, both in its goals and its methods. Unlike rebellions and coups d'état, revolutions seek to install a new government *and* to change the fundamental character of the state and society (Skocpol, 1979). Because revolutions seek to change the most fundamental cultural and structural characteristics of a society and its institutions, they almost always include considerable violence. In 1789 French revolutionaries toppled the autocracy of Louis XVI in what was to be the first stage of a prolonged period of violence and chaos as France searched for new political and economic institutions. In March 1917 the Russian Revolution forced Czar Nicholas II to give up his throne (he and his family were killed) and installed a new provisional government; but in October, a second revolution brought Lenin and his communist followers to power, and Russia became the Soviet Union. In the decades that followed—particularly under the rule of Stalin—millions of Russians who were suspected of opposing the new state were imprisoned, exiled, or executed.

Revolutions have been common occurrences in the twentieth century. In 1949 the Communist forces of Mao Tse-tung defeated the armies of Chiang Kai-shek and established a socialist state in mainland China. In 1954 Vietnamese revolutionaries under the leadership of Ho Chi Minh defeated a French army and ended French colonial rule in Indochina. North Vietnam became an authoritarian socialist state and South Vietnam became an authoritarian capitalist state. In 1959 revolutionaries under the leadership of Fidel Castro overthrew Batista's authoritarian capitalist state and replaced it with an authoritarian socialist state. In 1973 the socialist government of Chile's Salvador Allende was overthrown by a military coup and

---

Puzzles: When Are Revolutions Most Likely to Occur?

Are revolutions more likely when injustice and miserable living conditions persist for long periods of time or when there are rapid improvements in social justice and standards of living?

As surprising as it may seem, revolutions are more likely when conditions are getting better than they are when they remain steadily poor. This apparent paradox is explained here and in Chapter 22.

---

replaced by an authoritarian capitalist state. In 1979 Marxist revolutionaries overthrew the government of Nicaragua, and Islamic revolutionaries replaced the Shah of Iran with an authoritarian state based on Islamic religious law.

The American Revolution actually began as a rebellion in which colonists demanded the same rights as those enjoyed by British citizens living in Britain. It became a revolution when colonists declared their independence from Great Britain and precipitated a war that resulted in a new country with political institutions that differed sharply from those of the past. Although the new state borrowed heavily from British political institutions, the Constitution, the office of the president, and the two houses of Congress were all major departures from the British form of government.

Why do revolutions occur? Sociologists have identified several cultural and structural characteristics of political institutions and societies that are conducive to revolution (Goldstone, 1982). From a cultural perspective, revolutions are based on a profound shift in beliefs and values and a sharp drop in the acceptance of norms. Belief in the legitimacy of the state tends to crumble and this is often due to a chronic inability of the state to solve routine problems of government and meet the needs of the people, coupled with a rising expectation among the people that those needs should be met. The Russian Revolution occurred in a society in which a huge peasant class had, for centuries, lived in poverty under the oppressive rule of the czars. In 1914 Germany declared war on Russia and in the three years that followed, millions of Russians died and shortages of food and other necessities became critical. Russia's continued participation in the war greatly aggravated long-standing social problems (Skocpol, 1979).

Revolution is also more likely to occur when people begin to share the beliefs that inequality and injustice are widespread and that more effective political institutions are possible. Perhaps most important is the shared belief that radical change cannot be achieved peacefully, that the state can be changed only through violence because the government will not respond positively to the needs and desires of the people.

Shifts in beliefs are closely related to changing values, particularly those that affect what people expect for themselves. When expectations are rising—when people think that living conditions, freedoms, and other aspects of social life should improve—they are far more likely to question the legitimacy of a state that offers little hope of making those expectations a reality.

As values change, so too does allegiance to norms that define legitimate means for achieving goals. If the legal norms of the state support values that the people oppose, then the norms begin to lose their power over people's behavior.

Cultural shifts are closely tied to important aspects of social structure. The belief that peaceful change is impossible is often based on the refusal of government authorities to communicate with the people. In January 1905, 12 years before the 1917 Russian Revolution, thousands of Russian workers peacefully marched to the czar's winter palace to protest poverty and hunger. They were met by troops who attacked the crowd, wounding and killing hundreds of unarmed people. The response to "Bloody Sunday" was a series of strikes and protests. Since even these did not bring about change, the eventual response was revolution.

As allegiance to the state erodes, and as lines of communication are blocked (or shown to be nonexistent in the first place) the state loses its authority and the government increasingly relies on coercion in order to stay in power. This further erodes the population's belief that the state and its government are legitimate, and only increases the chances for a revolution.

In the aftermath of revolution, the state is often authoritarian—sometimes more authoritarian than the state it replaced (Goldstone, 1982). This occurs primarily because the new government sets as its first goal the crushing of all opposition. There were even hints of this in the years following the American Revo-

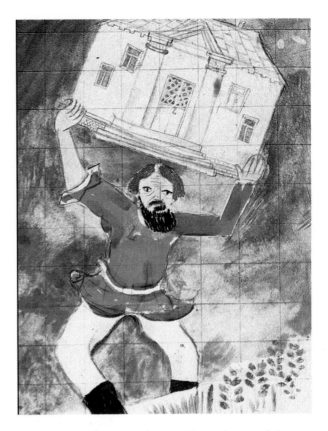

Revolution often pits the wealthy and powerful against the impoverished and weak; but when the state is vulnerable, as it was in Russia before the 1917 revolution, the weak can band together to bring down the powerful. This is suggested in Marc Chagall's 1919 painting, War on the Palaces.

lution, when the Sedition Act made it a crime to publish criticism of the government.

It should come as no surprise that revolutions are as violent or rare as they are, for no social institution regularly serves the function of deliberately turning itself into something else. What Miliband (1969) observed in capitalist societies is true in virtually all societies in which the state exists as a social institution:

> The politics of advanced capitalism have been about different conceptions of how to run the same economic and social system and not about radically different social systems. (p. 72)

In most societies, governments come and go and the balance of power between interest groups shifts one way or another; but the cultural and structural form of the state remains largely intact. As with economic arrangements, real change in political institutions is rare.

SUMMARY

1. Political institutions are enduring sets of cultural ideas and social structures through which power is distributed and used in societies.

2. Authority is the most important form of political power; it may be based on legal-rational, charismatic, or traditional grounds, or on expertise in an important field. Coercion, on the other hand, is the use of power not considered legitimate by those who are subject to it.

3. The state is the institution that has a monopoly over the use of force. A government is a collection of people who happen to occupy the positions of authority that make up the state.

4. As an institution, the state may support a variety of cultural values, such as those promoting equality or individual freedoms.

5. States differ in how power is distributed. In a democracy, power is shared equally by all citizens. In a representative democracy, citizens elect people to exercise authority in their name. Democracy is fostered by a number of social factors, including economic development, cultural homogeneity, norms that restrict the power of the state, tolerance of dissent, and access to information about government activities.

6. Unlike democracy, an oligarchy is ruled by an elite, and an autocracy is ruled by one person. According to Michels' "Iron Rule of Oligarchy," oligarchy is inevitable because of citizen apathy, the complexity of societies, and the desire of leaders to keep their power.

7. States also vary in how authoritarian—or powerful—they are in relation to their citizens. Totalitarianism is an extreme in which the state tries to control virtually all aspects of life.

8. The power structure in the U.S. is neither dominated by a unified power elite nor spread pluralistically among many different interest groups. Rather, it is an elite pluralism in which a relatively small number of interest groups struggle over control of the state.

9. U.S. citizens are less likely to vote and be involved in politics than citizens of most democracies. Generally those in the most advantaged social positions are the most likely to vote and be involved in politics.

10. Political parties are organizations whose main goal is to place members in positions of authority, and parties in the U.S. differ sharply from those in European democracies. U.S. elections are based on a winner-take-all system that encourages candidates to take ambiguous positions on issues and weakens the ability of parties to control their candidates once elected. Unlike parties, interest groups do not try to place members in positions of authority but rather try to influence elected officials.

11. A political coalition is a set of interest groups who temporarily combine in order to increase their power. This often means that groups that oppose each other on one issue work together on another.

12. Geography often plays an important part in political life. The larger a society is the more difficult it is for the state to control its citizens.

13. Like all social institutions, a given political arrangement will have both functional and dysfunctional consequences. Democracy is functional for protecting individual freedoms but is dysfunctional for reaching rapid decisions in times of crisis.

14. Its monopoly over the use of force inevitably means that the state will play a role in social conflict. While it sometimes acts as an umpire between conflicting groups, it more often promotes the interests of dominant groups. This is particularly true of those who dominate economic institutions. Through political economy, political and economic institutions support each other and promote the interests of those who dominate them.

15. Political institutions change through rebellion, in which policies are changed without affecting the state, through coups d'état, in which only the government is changed by forcibly replacing old leaders with new, and through revolution, in which the state itself is changed. Revolution is most likely to occur in societies in which the state is no longer able to perform basic governmental tasks, citizens no longer view the state as a legitimate wielder of authority, and beliefs in the existence of injustice and inequality become widespread.

KEY TERMS

Looking Elsewhere

Having studied Chapter 19, you might want to look at related discussions in *Human Arrangements*, which include

- communication structures in authoritarian and democratic governments (Chapter 4, p. 93)
- gerontocracy: age and political power (Chapter 14, p. 390)
- schools, propaganda, and nationalism (Chapter 16, pp. 450–51)
- the role of government in the economy (Chapter 18, pp. 497–98)
- socialism as a political system (Chapter 18, pp. 506–509)
- religious support for the state (Chapter 20, pp. 550–53, 558–59, 561–64)
- the state as a substitute for religion (Chapter 20, pp. 561–64)
- the origins and effects of social movements (Chapter 21, pp. 580–91)

RECOMMENDED READINGS

ELDER, C. D., and COBB, R. W. (1983). *The political use of symbols.* New York: Longman. A valuable introduction to the use of symbols in the political processes through which power is distributed, held, and used.

FROMAN, C. (1984). *The two American political systems: Society, economics, and politics.* Englewood Cliffs, NJ: Prentice-Hall. How does the U.S. political system *really* operate? The author provides one answer in a clear, straightforward look at political economy—the important relationship between political and economic institutions—in the United States.

MILLS, C. W. (1956). *The power elite.* New York: Oxford. A sociological classic in which Mills provides a provocative answer to the question, "Who rules America?"

ORUM, A. M. (1983). *Introduction to political sociology* (2nd ed.). Englewood Cliffs, NJ: Prentice-Hall. A comprehensive text on the many sociological aspects of politics, from socialization to the structures of power.

REJAI, M., and PHILLIPS, K. (1983). *World revolutionary leaders.* New Brunswick, NJ: Rutgers University Press. A short, readable book that explores the relationship between leaders and revolutions. Do revolutions create leaders or do leaders make revolutions?

SKOCPOL, T. (1979). *States and social revolutions.* New York: Cambridge University Press. An important study of the causes of revolution in China, Russia, and France.

TUFTE, E. R. (1978). *Political control of the economy.* Princeton, NJ: Princeton University Press. An important and highly interesting exploration of the connection between politics and economics.

20 Religious Institutions

Have you ever taken the time to sit down and seriously ask yourself, "What will happen to me after I die?" I vividly remember the first time I thought about that question and the other questions it inevitably raised: What do I mean by "me"; what is there about me that might exist after my body does not; and what might that existence be like? In struggling over the meaning of death, I inevitably had to think about the meaning of life.

As I thought about it that first time, I imagined my life as a slender slice out of an infinity of time before my birth and an infinity of time after my death. Suddenly, I felt frightened, as if my life would be replaced by nothingness and meaninglessness. The most frightening thing was to realize that I did not know what would happen.

People have wrestled with the meaning of death and life for thousands of years. Sociologically, the most important thing about these concepts is that they deal with the known, the unknown, and meaning. Although people place great emphasis on the truth of particular beliefs, our interest centers on the fact that people in all cultures wrestle with these basic themes.

At the core of culture are symbols and ideas that we use to attach meaning to objects, events, and experiences, those that we can see and touch and smell, and those which we cannot perceive. An important latent consequence of our ability to give meaning to

As with much of art, the universal, enduring mysteries of life and death, as portrayed in Gustav Klimt's famous painting, Death and Life, *are at the core of all religious institutions.*

life is that it creates the possibility of meaninglessness. I doubt very much that my dog contemplates the meaning of life after death, just as he never contemplates the meaning of life before death. Meaning and meaninglessness, the known and the unknown are not problems for him; but they are for us.

As social animals, we tend to join together to solve such problems, and these collective solutions lie at the heart of religion and religious institutions. We begin our examination of these subjects by defining some basic concepts and then look at the variety of religious ideas and ways of structuring religious institutions. From there we explore the effects of population and ecology on religious institutions, and use the functional and conflict perspectives to better understand the relationship between religion, society, and social change.

WHAT IS RELIGION?

The substance of **religion** is a set of cultural symbols and ideas that focus on the meaning of human life and the nature of the unknown. The symbols are important because they describe visions of the ultimate nature of both the world and human experience in it, and they establish in people "powerful, pervasive, and long-lasting moods and motivations" that affect their feelings and behavior (Geertz, 1973, p. 90).

Just as words do not constitute a language unless they are shared by members of a speech community, ideas about human existence and the unknown constitute a religion only when they are shared among members of a community of believers. I may believe that there is a heaven and that no one who flies in an airplane or talks on a telephone can go there after they die; but, from a sociological perspective, my beliefs are not part of a religion unless a group of people shares them.

Religion is not the only source of ideas about the unknown. Scientists spend their lives trying to understand the unknown. How, then, do science and religion differ? In the simplest sense, science looks upon the unknown as something that is ultimately knowable through observation, experiment, and verifiable fact.

Religion, however, is not a method for pursuing truth; it is the embodiment of what is already believed to be true. Christians regard their beliefs about the

origins of the universe as truths to be learned and shared in the community of believers. The only confirmation of such beliefs lies within the community itself: individuals must look to the faith of others in order to confirm their own. To cosmologists, on the other hand, beliefs about the universe are scientific hypotheses waiting to be tested.

There is a more important difference between religion and science, a difference that focuses both on the aspects of the unknown to which people pay attention and on how they pay attention to them. In his classic sociological study of religion, Durkheim (1912/1965) noted that all religions distinguish between the *sacred* and the *profane*. To consider an object, experience, or unknown force as **sacred** is to give it meaning and value that inspire feelings of awe and place it outside of the natural human world. To Christians, the cross, the idea of God, and the life of Jesus Christ are all sacred, just as the city of Jerusalem is sacred both to Jews and Muslims, and the cow is sacred to Hindus.

The concept of the **profane** refers to what we can experience directly as ordinary aspects of the natural world. As a profane experience, death involves the cessation of biological functioning and of a dying person's physical and mental experience. The concept of the sacred focuses on the *meaning* of death, on its place in a cosmic order of things. In sacred terms, we are concerned not with what death consists of or how it happens, but why people die and what it means to die—and, therefore, what it means to live—in an ultimate sense.

Science and religion pay attention to fundamentally different aspects of the unknown. What causes a dying person to suffer is something that scientists can determine; but why suffering seems to be an inherent part of human experience is a question that scientists consider to be unanswerable in scientific terms and therefore irrelevant to scientific inquiry. In most religions, however, the meaning and reason for earthly suffering are major concerns.

The sacred and the profane are not two separate and disconnected cultural realms; on the contrary, the sacred is used to give a sense of ultimate understanding and meaning to the profane, and by doing so it affects it (Geertz, 1973). In a religion that includes the belief that death is always a matter of divine will that is not to be interfered with, believers will refuse medical intervention and will be much more likely to die. By providing an account of what the world is like in an ultimate sense, religion can affect what the world in fact becomes.

In some cases, science and religion focus on similar problems, but from different perspectives. In the debate over the origins of human life some religions frame explanations in sacred terms, as Christianity does with the belief that a male God created man in "His" own image and then created woman from Adam's rib. As far as we know, the existence of God cannot be proved or disproved with objective evidence and, hence, the Christian explanation of the origin of human life holds little interest for scientists. By definition, science cannot draw upon supernatural explanations, for the province of science is the natural world.

Religion, then, is defined by its concentration on the sacred and supernatural. The sociology of religion is principally concerned with the place of religions and religious institutions in societies.

Religion and Society

The distinction between the sacred and the profane lies at the heart of religion, but religious institutions are sociologically significant primarily because of their social functions and dysfunctions. From a cultural point of view, religion attaches meaning and value to human life and supports major cultural ideas. All religions offer believers some form of salvation—whether it be the heaven of Christianity, the earthly peace offered by Buddhism and Taoism, Hindu reincarnation into a higher social caste, or the simple curing of an illness (Wilson, 1982).

Most important, religion helps believers explain and accept the suffering that plagues human life, by offering a coherent world view in which suffering makes sense and is, therefore, sufferable.

> The dumb senselessness of intense or inexorable pain, and the enigmatic unaccountability of gross iniquity all raise the uncomfortable suspicion that perhaps the world, and hence man's life in the world, has no genuine order at all—no empirical regularity, no emotional form, no moral coherence. And the religious response to this suspicion is in each case the same: the formulation, by means of symbols, of an image of such a genuine order of the world which will account for, and even celebrate, the perceived ambiguities, puzzles, and paradoxes in human experience. The effort is not to deny the undeniable—that there are unexplained events, that life hurts, or that rain

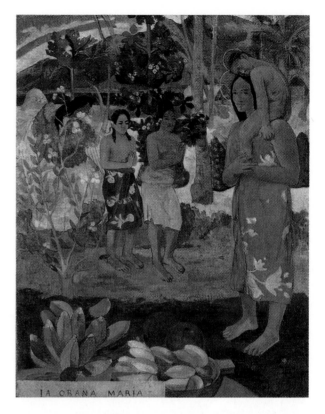

French artist Paul Gauguin's We Greet Thee Mary *is more than an idealization of the Tahitian society in which he lived for much of his life. Its vision of paradise and bliss reflects a desire for salvation that is a part of most religious faiths.*

falls upon the just—but to deny that there are inexplicable events, that life is unendurable, and that justice is a mirage. (Geertz, 1973, p. 108)

Religion locates a community of believers in relation to spiritual and supernatural forces as well as the profane world (the meaning of life, the nature of the universe) and this is an important ingredient in collective definitions of who we are in the ultimate scheme of things (Mol, 1976). In most religions, people are not lost bodies floating aimlessly through time and space. Life has meaning and an ultimate purpose, and people are part of something larger than themselves and their societies. Religion, then, can reduce anxiety and uncertainty in its believers by connecting the profane world with the mysteries of life, which are given sacred meaning and value. In the same way, religion can increase anxiety—by leading people to believe that they will suffer endless torture in another world after they die.

Religion can also perform important structural functions, for it is a major source of social cohesion. The roots of the word "religion" lie in the Latin words "re" and "lig" which together mean to tie or bind again. A community of believers shares basic ideas about the known and the unknown. They can therefore give one another comfort and support when suffering and misfortune strike their members or share in joy or ecstasy when something happens that suggests that their lives are in harmony with the sacred order of things. When people come together for a funeral or other ceremony, they reinforce their bonds with one another. When two people marry, religious ceremonies bind them to their cultural community as well as to each other, for it

is their society and its religious institutions that legitimate and assign meaning, value, and expectations to their relationship.

Religious institutions also legitimate other social institutions. In medieval Europe, the Church supported the "divine right of kings" to rule: the coronations of kings and queens were, more than anything else, religious ceremonies in which rulers of the profane world identified with the sacred and therefore drew power from those who represented sacred powers (Kendall, 1962). In return, religious institutions often received large amounts of property and other wealth from kings and emperors (Lenski, 1966).

Most modern states no longer depend on the blessing of religious institutions and their leaders to justify their power; but they often identify with religious symbols in order to reinforce their authority

For these Jewish mourners in Jerusalem, a funeral is a ceremony that brings people together and reinforces bonds by sharing in a common faith that makes sense of both their lives and the fact that they, too, will die.

(Warner, 1961). U.S. coins bear the words "In God We Trust"; political leaders often refer to God as being "on our side"; the Pledge of Allegiance to the Flag includes the words "one nation, under God"; the song "America the Beautiful" includes the words "God shed His grace on thee"; both houses of Congress begin their sessions with prayer.

Hunter-gatherer and horticultural societies had no state (see Chapter 19); and in his studies of such societies Durkheim (1912/1965) first formulated his theory of the relationship between religion and society. In the aboriginal tribes of Australia, each clan worshiped a **totem**—an animal or plant considered sacred in that society. Each totem represented not a god, but the clan itself, and from this simple observation, Durkheim argued that religion is in fact a way in which people worship their own societies. A totem gives supernatural significance and power to the social bonds that hold people together and through which they survive.

Durkheim was one of the first in a long line of sociologists who accepted the belief that religion and religious institutions are part of culture and are, therefore, of human and not divine origin. Is it therefore necessary to accept this belief in order to study religion from a sociological point of view?

Can a Sociologist Believe in God?

The first sociologists who studied religion—Comte, Marx, Durkheim, and Weber—were part of a social revolution in which science challenged religion as the dominant cultural framework for interpreting and explaining the world and human experience. These early sociologists were in the thick of an intense conflict between the supporters of religion and of science as points of view. In that social environment, they found themselves trying to explain the existence of religion—why people hold beliefs even though they may appear to be untrue—and to explain religion *away* (Wilson, 1982).

Modern sociology is not antireligious, but the definition of religion as a humanly created part of culture is generally accepted in the sociological study of religion. This raises a disturbing question for those who use sociology as a perspective and who belong to a community of religious believers: Can sociologists be religious? Can a Christian, Muslim, or Jewish sociologist study religion as a set of cultural ideas and believe in the existence of a Supreme Being?

The answer to all these questions is yes, and the reason is quite straightforward: It is not the goal of sociologists to test the truth or falsity of religious beliefs. "Does God exist?" is not a sociological question; but "Do people believe that God exists?" is. Sociologists want to understand how religious ideas and practices affect the lives of those who belong to a community of believers and influence the societies in which those people live. They want to understand how religious institutions are organized and how they affect other institutions. They want to understand the functions and dysfunctions of religion and the part religion plays in social conflict and change.

None of these sociological problems requires that we assume that particular religious beliefs are either true or false. Wherever specific religions may have come from, they affect social life in a variety of ways in different societies, and it is the job of sociology to understand those effects in cultural, structural, and ecological terms.

CULTURE: LINKING THE KNOWN AND THE UNKNOWN

The core of any religion is a set of cultural ideas and practices that constitute a framework for interpreting the known and unknown in relation to the sacred world of the supernatural. While all four components of culture are important parts of religion, beliefs are what distinguish different religions most clearly from one another.

Religious Belief: Some Major Types of Religion

Religious belief systems focus on describing the ultimate nature of reality and the place of human beings in it. Most religions can be categorized as one of only a few major types, each of which corresponds to a different view of the sacred, the profane, and the relationship between the two.

Theistic Religion   A theistic religion includes the belief in one or more supreme beings. Christianity, Judaism, and Islam are **monotheistic** religions because each generally recognizes the existence of only one Supreme Being. To Christians it is God; to Jews it is Yahweh; and to Muslims it is Allah; but what all have in common is a single Supreme Being who allows allegiance only to Himself (note that all also envision the Supreme Being as male).

Hinduism is a **polytheistic** religion; it allows for the existence of five gods. The concept of god is not central in the Hindu religion, for the power of the supernatural is vested in a spiritual concept of "Oneness" through which people are born into social castes and are **reincarnated** in succeeding lives as members of higher or lower castes, depending on how well they satisfy the duties associated with their current caste. The Hindus of India, Pakistan, and Bangladesh do not believe in a single supreme being that decides their fate but in a vision of life as a succession of lives in which the ultimate goal is a state of unity with supernatural forces.

Animistic and Totemic Religion Many religions ignore the idea of a Supreme Being. Some African and American Indian tribes practice **animistic** religions in which spirits and ghosts are believed to inhabit sacred objects such as trees, rocks, or animals. To the Mbuti of Africa, the forest is the sacred giver of life and death (Turnbull, 1965). The Shinto religion of Japan vests supernatural power—Kami—both in objects such as stones and trees and in ancestors (and, for this reason, Shintoism is also a religion involving **ancestor worship**). As we saw earlier, **totemic** religions believe that certain objects—or **totems**—have supernatural powers. The totemic approach to unknown forces is similar to the way people think of "good luck charms."

Abstract Ideals A large portion of the world's population—living mostly in India and East Asia—have religions that focus more on sets of abstract ideals than on supernatural powers vested in gods, objects, or animals. The largest of these religions are Buddhism, Confucianism, and Taoism, and they are concerned with how we can achieve a better life on earth. Buddha was a sixth-century B.C. Indian Hindu who believed that we can escape suffering by freeing ourselves of all desire, an ideal state called Nirvana.

Confucius was a Chinese contemporary of Buddha who believed that salvation depended on behaving according to correct manners and respecting those of higher social rank. Taoism is still more abstract and focuses on harmonious living and personal ethics that conform to concepts of a universe held together by ethical principles. In both Confucianism and Taoism, supernatural power lies in the universe itself and the harmonious relationships among the things and creatures in it. The task of believers in these **ethical religions** is to behave in ways that enable them to fit into the scheme of things in a harmonious way.

Ritual Religions use a variety of practices—called **rituals**—to maintain relationships among believers and between believers and the supernatural. Ritual may be as simple as uttering a sacred word or as complex as an elaborate ceremony involving sacred objects and specialized roles. Religions that include one or more gods use ritual to reaffirm loyalty to supernatural powers and to satisfy their gods. The ancient Aztecs of Mexico performed gory rituals in

This ceremonial Eskimo mask represented a shaman's vision of spirits believed to be found in animals and the forces of nature. The mask shows the spirit of the shaman riding the spirit of a beaver.

which a priest cut the heart from a living person, in the belief that this would appease their gods (Diaz, 1974). Christians, Jews, and Muslims use prayer to maintain their connection with the supernatural. Christianity is one of the few religions that emphasizes the concept of sin and uses ritual to reestablish a state of "grace" that will enable sinners to enter heaven when they die (Wilson, 1982).

The Trobriand Islanders use magic in their efforts to control the powers of the unknown (Malinowski, 1948), and the followers of the Shinto religion worship both nature and their ancestors in order to maintain a relationship with the supernatural power of the Kami. Buddhists, Taoists, and Confucians meditate in order to establish an inner sense of harmony between themselves and the ethical principles they believe tie all the parts of the universe into a single, integrated whole.

These are only major differences between the belief systems of the major religions, to which must be added thousands of specific beliefs about the universe and our place in it. Most religions, for example, pay little attention to life after death.

It is important to be aware that there is a great variety of beliefs not only between religions, but within them as well. Some Orthodox Jews differ sharply from other Jews in their strict adherence to the belief that the Jews may not have their own homeland until God sends a Messiah. This means that these Jews oppose the existence of the state of Israel.

There are also different beliefs among Christians, even on such central issues as the existence of God, Jesus as the Son of God, life after death, and the importance of religion (see Glock and Stark, 1968).

Sharp differences exist not only between denominations (Table 20-1) but also between societies that are predominantly Christian (Table 20-2, p. 550). In societies whose people are predominantly white, Christians believe that Jesus was white; but many African Christians believe he was black.

Religious Values, Norms, and Attitudes

One of the most important goals in any religion is salvation, although each religion defines it in its own way (Wilson, 1982). To the Melanesian tribes of Southern Indonesia, salvation is safety on the sea when they go fishing. For many Christians, it includes going to heaven rather than hell when they die. In Judaism, salvation is the coming of the Messiah, signaling that Jews once again enjoy the favor of God.

In Hinduism, salvation is reincarnation into a higher social caste in the next life, which, after an appropriate number of lives results in a complete identification with the Divine. In Buddhism, salvation is the achievement of a mystical state of "Oneness" with the Divine. In Taoism and Confucianism, salvation is oriented to the present life. In Taoism, it takes the form of withdrawing from all earthly pleasures and ending all desire and, therefore, all feelings of deprivation and suffering; in Confucianism, it is harmonious living by the principles of a unified universe. In animistic and totemic religion, salvation often takes the form of deliverance from the misfortunes of everyday life such as disease and accidents.

Religious norms define socially approved means for achieving salvation. Orthodox Judaism requires obedience both to the Ten Commandments and to the

Table 20-1

Varieties of Religious Beliefs among U.S. Christians, 1986

PERCENT WHO BELIEVE	BAPTIST	METHODIST	LUTHERAN	PRESBYTERIAN	EPISCOPALIAN	CATHOLIC
The Bible is literally true	65	38	38	33	11	26
There is life after death	84	86	92	89	83	80
Life after death is very much like life on earth	50	36	43	17	50	40
God is a judge	63	64	54	42	68	63
Women should be ordained	50	80	75	77	71	55

Source: Computed from raw 1984 and 1986 General Social Survey data.

Table 20-2

Percentage of People Reporting Belief in God or Universal Spirit and in Life after Death (Selected Countries)

COUNTRY	PERCENTAGE WHO REPORT BELIEF IN "GOD" OR A "UNIVERSAL SPIRIT"	PERCENTAGE WHO REPORT BELIEF IN LIFE AFTER DEATH	PERCENTAGE WHO VALUE RELIGIOUS BELIEFS AS "VERY IMPORTANT"
United States	94	69	56
Canada	89	54	36
Italy	88	46	36
Australia	80	48	25
Belgium	78	48	26
United Kingdom	76	43	23
France	72	39	22
West Germany	72	33	17
Sweden, Norway, Denmark, and Finland	65	35	17

Source: Gallup Report, September 9, 1976.

complex set of laws contained in the Talmud, including dietary laws forbidding the eating of pork. Among Hindus, reincarnation into a higher social caste depends on performing the duties associated with their current caste, including obedience to sacred laws such as those forbidding the killing of cows.

In Buddhism, meditation is the chief means for achieving the end of desire, which is believed to lead to the salvation of a nonexistence free from earthly suffering. As in animistic religions, the Shinto of Japan appease the spirits in objects and ancestors by worshipping them and by taking care not to harm them. Followers of totemic religions carry totems to appease supernatural forces.

Ethical religions such as Taoism and Confucianism stress respect for others and goodness and love as the means for achieving harmony with the universe. Confucianism in particular stresses respect for the family and those in higher classes. Confucianism demands support for the existing social system as the means for achieving religious values.

To sociologists, the most important religious attitudes focus on relationships among people, not between believers and the sacred and supernatural. Among Hindus, religious beliefs and values underlie a caste system that includes attitudes of respect for those in higher castes and contempt for the "untouch-

ables." Confucianism stresses attitudes of respect and subservience toward family elders and those in higher classes. Christianity and Judaism tend to regard females as inferior, and Catholicism in particular—in spite of its adoration for the Virgin Mary—carries a deep tradition of negative attitudes toward women, beginning with the belief that Eve was responsible for Adam's fall from grace in the Garden of Eden (Daly, 1973).

Together, beliefs, values, attitudes, and norms form the cultural core of religion, but a full sociological understanding of the importance of religion in society must also pay attention to how religious ideas are expressed through socially structured relationships.

SOCIAL STRUCTURE: THE SOCIAL ORGANIZATION OF RELIGION

As institutions, religions are more than collections of cultural ideas, for they also include relationships within a community of believers and between it and society. These relationships affect how religious ideas are expressed and in many cases how social life in general is carried out in a society.

Religious institutions have boundaries that define both active and potential membership, role structures that divide labor and power, and patterns of interaction through which religious ideas are expressed and perpetuated. In relatively simple societies, religious institutions are not separate from family, economic, and political institutions; but in complex industrial societies, religious institutions stand apart and are related to other social institutions in complex ways.

These structural differences can be described in terms of several major types of religious institutions: the *ecclesia*, the *church*, the *denomination*, the *sect*, and the *cult*.

The Ecclesia

The ecclesia is the most powerful of all religious institutions. Islam in Iran and Catholicism in Italy are examples of an **ecclesia**, in which all or most of the people in the society belong to the community of believers from the moment they are born.

The role structure of an ecclesia is formal and bureaucratic. It has a highly trained corps of religious leaders and workers, and one leader usually dominates the entire structure. Authority is primarily traditional and legal-rational, although in some cases charismatic leaders, such as Iran's Ayatollah, emerge. In no ecclesia, however, is charismatic authority the main source of power.

The time structure of an ecclesia is indefinite (Islam's followers expect it to last forever), and religious practices consist primarily of rituals that include relatively little expression of emotion.

Perhaps the most important structural characteristic of the ecclesia is that unlike all other religious institutions, it is closely identified and allied with political, economic, and family institutions. In ancient Egypt, the Pharaohs were, themselves, regarded as gods and thus the rulers of both the profane and sacred worlds (Woolley, 1963).

The ecclesia is less common today than it once was, but it still exists. In Iran, the Islamic ecclesia is virtually amalgamated with the government. Criminals are tried in religious courts under religious law, and no major governmental decision can be made without the approval of the country's highest religious leader. In Italy, the position of the Catholic ecclesia is not so powerful, but the pattern is similar nonetheless. The pope is a powerful figure in Italy, and while the government often makes decisions that the pope condemns—such as allowing divorce or abortion—the

The Muslim religion in Iran is a powerful example of an ecclesia in which the highest religious leader—the Ayatollah Khomeini—is also the leader of the government.

government cannot afford to ignore completely the views of the Catholic ecclesia.

The Church

A **church**—the Church of England, the Catholic Church outside of Italy, the Methodist, Episcopalian, and Lutheran churches in the United States, and the Greek Orthodox Church—is similar to an ecclesia in several ways. Membership is usually ascribed at birth and includes people from all social classes. There is a formal bureaucracy with a highly trained priesthood, authority is based more on tradition and legal-rational rules than on charisma, the institution is expected to last indefinitely, and religious practice is highly ritualized with relatively little display of emotion (Troeltsch, 1912).

Two important structural characteristics distinguish churches from ecclesia, however. Membership does not include all members of a society, and the relationship between churches and other social institutions is far looser. Churches such as the Church of England generally ally themselves with the ruling class and support the status quo; but they do not have the power of an ecclesia to influence political and economic institutions. In many authoritarian societies, churches oppose the power of the state, in some cases because the state at best only tolerates religion.

The Denomination

Denominations—such as Congregational and Unitarian Universalists—are the smallest religious institutions that still have a formal role structure with trained religious leaders. Like churches and ecclesiae, denominations generally draw new members from families that already belong to the community of believers, and religious rituals usually involve little expression of emotion.

Unlike churches and ecclesiae, denominations draw members from a limited range of class backgrounds. Congregationalists and Unitarians are most likely to come from the upper-middle and upper classes, while almost 70 percent of Baptists are in the working and lower classes (Chalfant, Beckley, and Palmer, 1981). Mintz's (1975) study of U.S. presidential cabinet members from 1897 to 1972 found that almost half were either Presbyterians or Episcopalians, even though these denominations account for only 7 percent of the entire U.S. population.

Denominations also lack the bureaucratic structure that is the hallmark of ecclesiae and churches, and they have a much looser power structure based on traditional authority. The relationship between denominations and other social institutions is also far more remote. Rather than allying themselves with governments, denominations are more likely to coexist with them and avoid active involvement in political or economic issues.

The U.S. is one of the few religiously pluralist societies, in which no single church dominates. As we will see later, this results in a high degree of religious tolerance and freedom, but also tends to lessen the influence of religion on social life.

The Sect

Sects are religious groups that have broken off from churches and denominations, and their structures are radically different (Troeltsch, 1912; Wilson, 1982). Membership is usually through conversion rather than ascribed at birth, and new members are converted through persuasion. Their role structure is informal and leaders have little if any formal training.

There are minimal divisions of power and leaders are usually chosen by the community. Religious ceremonies encourage spontaneous shows of emotion and have little of the rigid, abstract form found in the ecclesia, church, or denomination.

Sects also differ from other religious institutions in their opposition to other institutions. Members of the lower classes are more likely than others to belong to religious sects, perhaps because they have less to gain by supporting existing political and economic institutions that place them at the bottom of the social stratification system. Engels (in Feuer, 1959) draws striking parallels between revolutionary movements and the early history of Christianity as a religious sect:

> Christianity was originally a movement of oppressed people; it first appeared as the religion of slaves and emancipated slaves, or poor people deprived of their rights, of peoples subjugated or dispersed by Rome. (p. 168)

Niebuhr (1929) argued that sects form when churches develop to a point where they no longer serve the interests of lower- and working-class members, and this helps explain why Christianity is divided into many different sects. As churches become more established, they also come to be dominated by the more prosperous middle and upper classes and reflect their needs and interests more than those of members lower in the class system. Those who are deprived often look to religion to provide comfort and reassurance that their deprivation during life will be compensated for after death. Their orientation tends to be away from the material conditions of life and towards a direct relationship with God and the supernatural.

Those who are prosperous, however, have less reason to escape or reject the material conditions of life, and will tend to shape their religion in ways that accept, if not actively support, their material well-being. The result is a more abstract, detached orientation to God and the supernatural, which does not meet the needs of those who must reconcile themselves with deprivation. Consequently, as churches become increasingly dominated by the upper classes, lower-class members are more likely to break away and establish sects that more effectively meet their religious needs. Over time, sects may succeed to the point where the cycle begins again. The Mormons began as a sect but today more closely resemble a denomination.

In the 1970s roughly 55 percent of sect members in the U.S. belonged to the working and lower classes, compared with just over 40 percent of Presbyterians and Jews and just over 30 percent of Episcopalians. Only around 14 percent of those who belong to sects are from the upper class, compared with 30 percent of Presbyterians and Jews and 40 percent of Episcopalians (Chalfant, Beckley, and Palmer, 1981).

The deviant status of many sects often causes tense and hostile relationships both with the parent church and the surrounding society. In the fifth century B.C., the first Buddhists were persecuted as a sect of Hinduism. Early Christians were a sect of Jews who believed that Jesus was the Son of God, and they were persecuted by the Romans. In the seventeenth century, English Quakers were persecuted by Christians, as were Mormons in the eighteenth century; in this century, members of the Baha'i sect are persecuted in countries such as Iran; and in India, members of the Sikh sect of Hinduism have frequent violent confrontations with other Hindus.

The Cult

Cults are the least organized religious institutions (see Merton and Moore, 1982). Most members join through conversion—usually in response to a personal crisis—and tend to come from the poorest social classes. Ceremonies tend to be highly emotional and spontaneous. The role structure of cults is informal, but power is concentrated in a charismatic leader.

The cult is the only religious institution in which charisma is the main form of authority. For this reason, the time structure of a cult tends to be no longer than the life of its leader, for once he or she is gone (or loses charismatic appeal), the central organizing force in the cult disappears. The importance of charismatic authority in cults also creates conditions in which leaders may easily abuse their power. For example, in 1978 the Reverend Jim Jones led 900 of his followers in a mass suicide (Hall, 1979).

Cults also differ from other religious institutions in their rejection of and withdrawal from the rest of society (see Flowers, 1984). While sects are critical of other social institutions, cults tend to reject them entirely. This perhaps explains why cults attract so many people from the poorest social classes, people who see little to be gained by trying to participate in the existing institutions of their society.

The followers of Jim Jones were almost all poor people who saw the Jones cult as their last hope for a decent life, and who willingly left the U.S. to create

Defeated and forced to live on desolate reservations, the Sioux Indians were deep in despair and starvation in 1881 when they heard of a prophecy of a return to the prosperity and peace they had once known. This developed into the Ghost Dance cult, named for the dance they believed would drive whites away and realize the prophecy. The Ghost Dance included religious frenzy, and semiconscious trances and visions. The shirt they wore was believed to protect its wearer from the bullets of white soldiers.

their own colony in the small South American country of Guyana. Their mass suicide (in which a few unwilling participants were murdered) was based on the same kind of fear of outsiders that prompted them to move to Guyana: they believed that outsiders were coming to destroy their cult.

It is important to be aware that all major religions began as cults. Islam, Buddhism, and Christianity have enormous influence in the world today, and yet all were once regarded by the societies in which they first appeared as deviant. In this sense, the cult represents true religious innovation in a society, for although sects often form in rebellion against churches, they remain within the same religious tradition. As different as the many Christian sects are, they are all, nonetheless, Christian.

We have seen, then, that religions differ both in their ideas and the ways in which institutional arrangements are structured (see Table 20-3, p. 554). Not all religious institutions can be classified in terms of the major types described in the preceding sections, for the social structures of religious institutions are connected with the cultural ideas contained in reli-

Table 20-3

Summary of Major Types of Religious Institutions

STRUCTURAL CHARACTERISTIC	ECCLESIAE	CHURCHES	DENOMINATIONS	SECTS	CULTS
Boundaries and Membership	Ascribed; most people belong	Mostly ascribed; broad membership	Mostly ascribed; limited in social class	Mostly achieved, through persuasion; lower class	Mostly achieved, through emotional crisis; poor people
Time Structure	Indefinite	Indefinite	Indefinite	Moderately long	Usually temporary
Role Structure	Formal and bureaucratic with trained clergy	Formal and bureaucratic with trained clergy	Formal but not bureaucratic; relatively untrained clergy	Informal with relatively untrained leadership chosen by community	Informal, loosely organized; charismatic leadership
Authority Structure	Legal-rational and traditional	Legal-rational and traditional	Traditional	Minimal authority structure	Charismatic
Patterns of Interaction	Highly abstract ritual; relatively little emotion	Highly abstract ritual; relatively little emotion	Abstract ritual; relatively little emotion	Few formal rituals; spontaneous show of emotion	No formal rituals; highly emotional
Relation to Other Institutions	Closely identified with political and economic institutions	Often allied with ruling class and status quo	Coexist with political and economic institutions	Oppose institutions; nonconformist	Reject institutions; retreatist

gions. Ecclesiae and churches are more common among monotheistic religions such as Christianity, Judaism, and Islam than they are among polytheistic religions such as Hinduism and ethical religions such as Taoism and Confucianism. Religions based on belief in a single all-powerful god are more likely to develop complex social structures—including bureaucracies—through which religious leaders represent and administer what is believed to be the will of the Supreme Being. Monotheism also creates a need for institutions that have power to force followers to be religiously faithful, for monotheistic gods are generally viewed as jealous and intolerant of allegiance to any other sacred force (Wilson, 1982).

Ethical religions, on the other hand, do not view sacred power as flowing from a single source such as a god; rather, the sacred consists of all things—of which each believer is a part. This cultural aspect of ethical religions gives them less need for formally structured religious institutions. It is one thing to have a church leadership that "represents God on earth"; but it makes little sense to have church leaders who represent the entire universe.

THE SOCIAL ECOLOGY OF RELIGIOUS INSTITUTIONS

Like all cultural and structural aspects of social life, religions and religious institutions are affected by how populations grow and distribute themselves and the ways in which societies use physical environments to meet their material needs.

The Importance of Size

The number of people who belong to a community of believers directly affects the power of religious institutions (see Tables 20-4 and 20-5); but as we saw in Chapter 8, the effect of numbers on group power depends as much on relative size as it does on absolute size (Merton, 1968; Simmel, 1950).

As an ecclesia, the Iranian Islamic religion is powerful because its membership is large and because it includes almost all of Iran's population. Under such conditions, it is difficult for other religious institutions to survive, much less compete successfully. In a religiously pluralistic society such as the U.S., however, no single religion dominates religious life, in part because there are so many different communities of believers. Absolute size alone, then, does not determine social power.

Size helps account for several social characteristics of smaller religious groups such as sects and cults. Small numbers not only lessen their power but also

Table 20-5

Membership in Major Religions (United States, 1984)

RELIGION	NUMBER OF MEMBERS	PERCENTAGE OF U.S. POPULATION
Protestant	78,700,000	33.2
Roman Catholic	52,300,000	22.1
Other Catholic	1,000,000	0.4
Eastern Orthodox	4,000,000	1.7
Jewish	5,800,000	2.4
Other	290,000	0.1
Nonmembers	95,000,000	40.1

Source: U.S. Census Bureau, 1986a.

Table 20-4

Estimated Membership in Major Religions of the World, by Region, Late 1980s

RELIGION	NORTH AMERICA	SOUTH AMERICA	EUROPE[1]	ASIA	AFRICA	OCEANIA	WORLD
Total Christian	87.1%	93.6%	66.8%	7.0%	45.4%	83.9%	32.9%
Roman Catholic	(33.2)	(88.1)	(33.4)	(2.8)	(17.2)	(29.0)	(18.3)
Protestant	(17.7)	(3.2)	(11.4)	(1.8)	(12.1)	(29.6)	(6.6)
Other Christian	(36.2)	(2.3)	(22.1)	(2.4)	(16.1)	(25.3)	(8.0)
Jewish	3.0	0.2	0.6	0.2	*	0.3	0.4
Muslim	1.0	0.1	5.2	19.5	41.4	0.4	17.1
Hindu	0.3	0.2	*	22.4	0.2	1.1	13.2
Buddhist	0.1	0.1	*	10.7	*	*	6.2
Other Religions[2]	0.3	2.1	0.4	13.2	12.7	0.9	9.3
Nonreligious	7.3	3.1	17.0	22.2	0.3	11.4	16.4
Atheists	0.4	0.6	10.0	4.8	*	2.0	4.5
TOTAL	100.0%	100.0%	100.0%	100.0%	100.0%	100.0%	100.0%
(N in millions)	(265.8)	(415.6)	(774.5)	(2,870.7)	(571.6)	(26.2)	(4,924.4)

*less than 0.1%.
[1]Europe includes the Soviet Union where official lack of recognition of organized religion makes it difficult to estimate religious membership.
[2]Other religions include Chinese folk religionists, new religionists, tribal religionists, sikhs, shamanists, confucians, bahai's, shintoists, and jains.

Source: The World Almanac and Book of Facts: 1988. New York: Newspaper Enterprise Association, Inc., 1987.

make it more difficult to perpetuate themselves across generations. This problem is particularly acute in the predominantly black Father Divine cult in the United States, whose norms forbid marriage and sexual relations among its members. Since reproduction is a major way to increase community size, this policy removes what is obviously a very important source of new members (Kephart, 1976).

The instability of cults reinforces members' fears of the surrounding society and their urge to isolate and protect themselves from it; but this is not restricted to sects and cults. The state of Israel is attractive to many Jews in part because while Jews are a tiny minority around the world, in Israel they constitute an overwhelming numerical majority. Vulnerability to persecution and discrimination is substantially lessened by the ecological arrangement that exists in Israel.

Technology, Production, and Religion

Sociologists and anthropologists have long noted aspects of religion that vary between societies according to differences in ecological arrangements (Table 20-6). The religions of most hunter-gatherer societies do not include belief in a Supreme Being who created the earth, while this belief is found in the religions of almost all herding societies. Among hunter-gatherers,

animism is the most common form of religion (Turnbull, 1961).

Notice in Table 20-6 that as we move toward societies that use more advanced technology, belief in a Supreme Creator who is active in human affairs and supports moral behavior becomes more common— with the interesting exception of herding societies, 80 percent of whose religions do include this belief. Although we do not know just why the belief in an active and caring creator is so common among herders, it is possible that they draw upon their own experience as herders to envision a Supreme Being that cares for them in the same way that they care for their animals (Lenski and Lenski, 1982).

The mode of production in a society is also related to whether or not its religion includes the worship of ancestors. Ancestor worship is found in only 17 percent of hunter-gatherer societies, but in more than two-thirds of simple and advanced horticultural societies. This difference may be due to the simple fact that unlike hunter-gatherers, peoples who live by tending small gardens tend to live in one place and this keeps them near the graves of their ancestors (Shiels, 1975).

Before the explosive growth of scientific thinking and knowledge in seventeenth- and eighteenth-century Europe, **fatalism**—the belief that we can do nothing to control events—was a common religious belief, and magic was often viewed as the only way to

Table 20-6

Percentage of Societies Whose Religion Includes Selected Beliefs, by Type of Society

	TYPE OF SOCIETY				
RELIGIOUS BELIEF	Hunting and Gathering	Herding	Simple Horticultural	Advanced Horticultural	Agrarian
No concept of a Supreme Creator	61	4	61	21	23
Belief in a passive Supreme Creator who is unconcerned with human affairs	29	10	35	51	6
Belief in an active Supreme Creator who does not support human morality	8	6	2	12	5
Belief in an active Supreme Creator who supports human morality	2	80	2	16	66
PERCENTAGE TOTAL	100	100	100	100	100
(Number of Societies)	(85)	(50)	(43)	(131)	(66)

Source: *Human Societies*, Lenski and Lenski, 1978.

escape helplessness (Banfield, 1967; Levi, 1947). Scientific thought, however, offered the possibility of control over the physical world, and with the rising influence of science, fatalism and belief in magic declined.

Technology and modes of production are also related to the size, power, and complexity of religious institutions. As is true of political institutions, a full-time, highly trained, and powerful class of religious leaders can only be supported in a society that is able to produce a surplus of goods, and it was not until the agrarian age that ecclesiae and churches came into being.

Religious institutions in industrial societies, however, are far less powerful than they were in agrarian Europe of the Middle Ages. As we saw in Chapter 19, church and state in medieval Europe were the two dominant and competing sources of power, but religious change, science, and the Industrial Revolution weakened the economic and political power of religious institutions. The Protestant Reformation inspired by Martin Luther in the sixteenth century challenged the absolute authority of the Catholic Church and undermined its claim to obedience and wealth. In the eighteenth and nineteenth centuries, science weakened the monopoly of religion over cultural explanations of the world; and with the Industrial Revolution the state and the emerging capitalist class claimed an increasing share of wealth. The result was a dramatic decline in the economic and political power of religious institutions.

Here it is especially important to remember that religions and religious institutions are not the same thing. Nowhere in the world, perhaps, has the power of the state caused so dramatic a decline in the power of a church as it did in Russia after the 1917 revolution that began the transformation of feudal Russia into the socialist Soviet Union. In today's Soviet Union, the Russian Orthodox Church has no authority as a social institution; but the religious ideas and practices of Christianity still have considerable power in a large segment of the Russian population (Shipler, 1983).

FUNCTION, DYSFUNCTION, AND SOCIAL CONFLICT

All religious institutions are defined in part by the functions they perform in a community of believers. As we have seen in other chapters, however, this does not mean that institutional characteristics cannot also have dysfunctional consequences, or that they never play a part in social conflict.

Some Dysfunctions of Religion and Religious Institutions

Religious ideas often have dysfunctional consequences for societies. Because religious communities often view their beliefs and values as absolutely correct, it is only a short step to the ethnocentric view that their religion is superior to all others. The absoluteness with which many religious ideas are held also increases the chance that religion will serve as an ideology.

No war is so fierce as a "holy war" fought in the name of religion, and as the seventeenth-century French philosopher and mathematician Pascal wrote, "Men never do evil so completely and cheerfully as when they do it from religious conviction." As long as the religion of ancient Rome was polytheistic, Christians were favorite objects of persecution; but when Christianity became the official religion of Rome in the fourth century, Jews became the new target and have remained an object of persecution based on the mistaken belief that Jews were responsible for the death of Christ. The crusades of the eleventh, twelfth, and thirteenth centuries pitted Christians against Muslims. The Spanish Inquisition at the turn of the sixteenth century sent thousands of suspected heretics to their death, focusing particularly on Jews and Christians with Moorish backgrounds. In the sixteenth century, French Catholics and Protestants fought for more than 30 years during which massacres and other atrocities were commonplace.

Religion still plays a part in aggression and war. Catholics and Protestants in Northern Ireland have been fighting for most of this century. Muslims and Christians in Lebanon have fought with each other in religious wars that continue into the 1980s. Violence against Jews in France, the Soviet Union, the U.S., and many other countries still occurs. In India, violence between Muslims and Hindus is common, and in 1984 members of the Sikh religious sect assassinated Prime Minister Indira Gandhi in retaliation for alleged mistreatment by the government. The 1979 revolution in Iran replaced the oppressive authoritarian state of the shah with an equally or more oppressive authoritarian state based on Islamic religious law. Arrest, torture, and execution of those who oppose Islamic rule has become common in Iran, and the ensuing war with Iraq has been characterized by Iranian leaders as a "holy war" whose ultimate goal is to bring about the supremacy of Islam as the basis for all political institutions in the Middle East.

Religion is not the sole cause of such violence; as in the case of Northern Ireland, conflict often has more to do with economic and political issues than with differences of faith. Religion, however, fuels conflict by giving each side the belief that their cause is "just" in an ultimate and absolute sense.

Social conflict is more likely to involve monotheistic religions such as Islam, Christianity, and Judaism than polytheistic religions such as Hinduism or ethical religions such as Buddhism, Confucianism, and Taoism. By definition, monotheism includes the belief that there is not only a god, but one god only. Any other religion that does not focus on that god is likely to be seen as a threat to believers in a monotheistic religion.

Violence is not the only dysfunction of religion. The Buddhist emphasis on people removing themselves from earthly concerns and putting an end to all feelings of desire tends to remove them from the ongoing conflict through which positive social change often occurs (Wilson, 1982). The Islamic religion carries a strong sense of fatalism in the belief that everything that happens on earth is a matter of Allah's will. This interferes with economic progress that usually involves long-range planning and a belief that the future can be affected by what people do in the present (Hall, 1959).

In the simplest sense, religion can be dysfunctional when it includes false beliefs. In Europe of the Middle Ages and into the eighteenth century, the advance of science and technology was slowed by religious doctrines that argued a very different view of how things work. Scientists such as Galileo and Copernicus were persecuted by the Catholic Church for their theories about the solar system, and early medical researchers were forbidden from cutting open corpses and had to steal them from graveyards.

In general, sociologists are not very interested in the truth or falsity of particular religious beliefs, because the social power and importance of religion does not lie in the content of religious ideas; rather, it lies in the commitment of a community of believers to a set of ideas that form a sacred framework within which people interpret and explain the world and their experience in it. In general, the ideas that make up a religion are far less significant than the fact that people believe in them.

Religion, Class, and Social Conflict

The relationship between religious institutions and class systems in stratified societies is both long-standing and widespread. The rise of religious institutions was spurred by the same ecological and social changes that supported the emergence of stratification systems and the state. Since religious and political institutions depend on wealth that they do not produce, it is not surprising that they have often found themselves either supporting each other or competing for a greater share of power. Religious leaders constituted one of the first elites to emerge when societies began to produce a surplus of goods that allowed the accumulation and concentration of wealth and power.

Religious beliefs and values have supported social inequality in many different cultures. The Hindu caste system is supported by the religious belief in reincarnation and the importance attached to caste boundaries. Respect for elders and others in positions of authority is an important part of Confucianism that supports inequality of wealth and power. Buddhist values and beliefs support the status quo by denying the importance of anything that occurs in the profane world and striving for a cessation of all desire for wealth, power, and prestige (Wilson, 1982).

For centuries the Catholic Church was one of the most powerful social institutions in Europe, rivaled only by the nobility; and even when the state emerged as the dominant social institution, the church contin-

Iranian Revolutionary Guards kiss the holy book of Islam, the Koran, before going to the front to fight in Iran's long "Holy War" against Iraq.

ued to have great wealth and influence. In Mexico, the Catholic Church was so closely allied with the upper class that during the violent revolutions of the nineteenth century the church and its priesthood were targets of the anger and frustration of the peasant class. Not only did the church lose most of its wealth, but for several years priests were forbidden to wear religious clothing in public, and they are still constitutionally prohibited from voting or holding public office.

Religion does not always serve the interests of dominant classes and the status quo, however. While the Mexican revolutionaries identified the church as an enemy, the Mexican people were at the same time deeply religious. Here the distinction between religion and religious institutions is once again impor-

tant, for it was the church and not religion that Mexicans rejected.

In some societies, religious institutions openly oppose the state, especially when it is oppressive and authoritarian. This is true of most religious sects and cults that draw their members largely from the lowest social classes; but it is also true of the Catholic Church in Latin American countries that are ruled by dictatorships. The church in such societies becomes a place for people to meet, to discuss political and social issues that affect their lives, and to make plans for change. In a few Latin American countries, such as El Salvador and Nicaragua, the priesthood serves as an active source of criticism of government policy and of awareness of the true conditions of life in the profane world. Most important, religion in these societies—and others such as socialist Poland—is a source of emotional attachment and power whose mere existence threatens the dominance of the state. In 1984, the Polish government ordered the enforcement of a previously passed law banning the display of crucifixes in public schools and universities, a move that prompted violent demonstrations against the government.

Religious faith has played an important part in the struggle of Polish workers against their government. During the 1980 general strike which included formation of the union, Solidarity, striking workers and their families knelt to pray in front of a portrait of Pope John Paul, himself a Pole.

Religion and False Consciousness   When Karl Marx described religion as the "opium of the people," he was saying that the focus of religion on the sacred and unknown world distracts our attention from the realities of life in the profane world of inequality and injustice. As Max Weber (1923) wrote, "It was possible for the working class to accept its lot as long as the promise of eternal happiness could be held out to it" (p. 369).

Marx's use of "opium" as an image is powerful because opium is a depressant drug that dulls sensation, including pain. To Marx, religion is often used to explain and justify the suffering that we experience during our lives. The key, however, is that religion explains earthly conditions not as the result of social relationships but as part of a natural, sacred order.

In this way, religion contributes to false consciousness by substituting a sacred explanation of earthly conditions for a social one. The problem, argued Marx, lies not with the conditions created by sacred or supernatural forces, but with those created by societies, and when we focus attention on the sacred as the source of all things—including poverty, oppression, and suffering—we are less likely to identify the social sources of inequality and the suffering and deprivation that result.

Slaves in the American South were told that their condition was a matter of God's will (Stampp, 1956); and mill owners in North Carolina near the turn of the twentieth century supported local churches primarily in order to distract workers from the social causes of their deprivation (Pope, 1942). Many Christians believe that inequality between men and women is based on the word of God as revealed in the Bible, a belief that prompted pioneer feminist Elizabeth Cady Stanton to argue that "The first step in the elevation of women under all systems of religion is to convince them that the great Spirit of the Universe is in no way responsible for any of these absurdities" (in Daly, 1973, p. 13).

Harris (1974) argued that false consciousness lay at the heart of the persecution of witches throughout Europe during the Middle Ages. In those times of severe economic hardship, women accused of being witches served as scapegoats, which encouraged the poor to believe that "they were being victimized by witches and devils instead of princes and popes" (p. 237).

Christianity is not the only religion that contributes to false consciousness in this way. The Hindu religion is a perfect example, for people who are born into lower castes cannot hope to return in a higher caste unless they accept their current lot in life and meet their prescribed obligations to the castes above them.

In a deeper sense, all religion contributes to false consciousness by alienating people from the simple fact that the social world and its institutions are the products of human activity. When family roles, the roles of men and women, or the roles of kings are shrouded in religious symbolism, we tend to treat them as inevitable parts of the ultimate reality that religious ideas purport to describe.

> Just as religion mystifies and thus fortifies the illusionary autonomy of the humanly produced world, so it mystifies and fortifies its introjection in individual consciousness. The internalized roles carry with them the mysterious power ascribed to them by their religious legitimations. Socialized identity as a whole can be apprehended by the individual as something sacred, grounded in the "nature of things" as created or willed by the gods. As such, it loses its character as a product of human activity. (Berger, 1967, p. 95)

There is nothing about religion that necessarily means that it supports false consciousness and, therefore, existing social conditions. Some argue that Jesus

Christ was one of many Jews who led the Jewish rebellion against the Roman Empire (Harris, 1974). The Mexican revolution that overthrew Spanish rule early in the nineteenth century was led by a soldier and a priest, and a Catholic bishop played a key role in the ousting of Philippine President Ferdinand Marcos in 1986.

In the U.S., priests and ministers played active roles in the civil rights movement, and Martin Luther King, Jr.—one of the most powerful of all civil rights leaders—was himself a minister. In the 1980s many U.S. religious leaders are playing an active part in the nuclear freeze movement that opposes the spread of nuclear weapons (Castelli, 1983), and the Reverend Jesse Jackson almost captured the Democratic presidential nomination.

Religion and religious institutions, therefore, have both opposed and inspired social conflict aimed

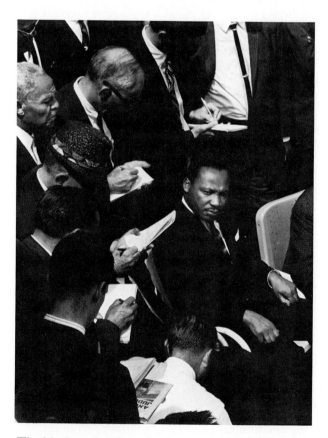

The black civil rights movement depended heavily on the leadership of ministers such as Martin Luther King, Jr. Throughout the South, churches served as a focus not only of religious faith, but of political organization and action.

at changing the social conditions in which people live. Religions and religious institutions themselves, however, are also subject to the pressures that lead to change.

RELIGION AND SOCIAL CHANGE

Like all aspects of social environments, religions and religious institutions change, for they do not exist in a vacuum and thus are affected by change in the surrounding society.

Cultural Change

In general, the ideas that constitute a religion change less easily than the structures through which a community of believers practices its religion, for these ideas form the most basic visions of what life is about, both in this world and in the unknown.

Nevertheless, they do change. Norms once forbade the participation of women in religious services among Catholics, Jews, and several Protestant denominations; but under the pressure of the women's movement, those norms are breaking down. There is continuing pressure on the Catholic Church to relax norms that forbid abortion, divorce, and the use of contraceptives, as well as those that forbid priests from marrying.

In 1983 the National Council of Churches released a new translation of key passages in the Bible, designed to remove the male-oriented, sexist bias of earlier translations. The new version replaces "mankind" with "humankind," refers to God as "my Mother and Father" and to Jesus as the Child of God rather than as the Son of God. For all of the protest and praise the new version has inspired, it is important as an institutional acknowledgement of the impact of religious ideas on the most basic aspects of social life and of the pressures exerted on religion by change in the surrounding society.

Specific changes such as these are not isolated social phenomena, for they are part of a much broader and more powerful trend in industrial societies called *secularization*.

Secularization Secularization is a social process through which "beliefs concerning the supernatural and practices associated with them are discredited and the institution of religion loses social influence" (J. Wilson, 1978, p. 397). Secularization involves cultural and structural change within reli-

gions as well as changes in the relationship between religious and other institutions.

In 1984, only 26 percent of U.S. Catholics said they believed that the Bible is the literal word of God as did only roughly a third or less of most major Protestant denominations (see Table 20-1). In 1987 only 29 percent of U.S. adults had "a great deal of confidence" in the leaders of organized religion (Davis and Smith, 1987). For many, religious holidays are no longer occasions of worship but opportunities to escape the demands of work and spend time with families.

The declining influence of religion is common in industrial societies, and sociologists have identified several likely causes. The most obvious is the steady rise of scientific thinking that began in the seventeenth century and undermined religion as a framework for explaining the natural world (Berger, 1967). Physical science challenged the Christian view of the origins of the universe and human life, and in no industrial society is the Biblical version of creation widely used as an explanation (Wilson, 1982). As we saw earlier, Weber, Marx, and Durkheim challenged religion by focusing on social rather than divine causes of social conditions. They even went so far as to argue that religion, itself, was a human creation.

The Industrial Revolution added to this an explosion of material goods and, with it, an increased social value placed on material prosperity at the expense of religion's orientation to the sacred and spiritual worlds (J. Wilson, 1978). Industrialization also brought with it the need for increased mobility and migration, and with this the ties between church and community became increasingly difficult to maintain. Perhaps most important, the Industrial Revolution rationalized both thought and social relationships, and this undermined the social importance of sacred forces.

As a cultural system, religion has not simply changed in response to cultural changes in society, however, for as the structures of industrial societies have become more complex, religious institutions have been challenged by other institutions.

Changing Structures

Secularization affects not only the cultural ideas that constitute religions but also the structures of religious institutions and their relationships with the rest of society. The most dramatic structural change in religious institutions has been a drastic decline in power and authority. In preindustrial societies religion is directly involved in virtually all aspects of social life, from the rituals that mark the passage from one stage of the life course to another—birth, adulthood, marriage, and death—to healing the sick, caring for the poor, administering justice, explaining the world, and educating the young.

In industrial societies, however, many of these social functions are performed by other institutions. It is now possible to marry and have children with no involvement with religious institutions; physicians heal the sick, schools educate the young, scientists in universities and business provide socially acceptable explanations of the world, and the state determines what the law will be, administers justice, and provides for the poor.

In comparison with preindustrial societies in which religion and religious institutions are deeply embedded in all aspects of social life, religious institutions in industrial societies tend to be separate, private, and isolated (see Bellah et al., 1985). They must compete with a variety of other institutions that perform many of the former functions of religion and place demands on the attention of believers (Luckmann, 1967). Religious institutions are no longer the major source of cultural ideas that they once were, a fact that is particularly apparent in the high degree of religious tolerance found in most industrial societies. As Wilson (1982) wrote:

> The very fact that religion becomes an optional matter, the fact that there is freedom of religion, tolerance, and choice, is an indication that religion is apparently of little direct consequence to the functioning of the social order, at least as that order is understood by those who have helped to build it, modify it, and maintain it. (p. 46)

There are some indicators that suggest that while the power of religious institutions has certainly diminished in relation to society as a whole, they have held a steady appeal to their members. Among Protestants, the percent who attend church on a weekly basis was roughly the same in 1984 as it was in 1939; and although weekly attendance among Catholics is lower now than it was (due primarily to disagreements with the pope on issues of sexual morality) the drop is not very great (Hout and Greeley, 1987; see Table 20-7). Since 1950, religious membership has remained relatively constant at around 60 percent, and those who say they "believe in God or a universal spirit" have stayed very close to 95 percent (Caplow et al., 1983; see also Bilheimer, 1983; National Council of Churches, 1987).

Table 20-7

Percent Who Attended Church in the Preceding Week, by Religion, U.S., 1939–84

YEAR	PROTESTANTS	CATHOLICS	JEWS	OTHERS
1939	40%	64%	12%	**
1950	36%	63%	32%	56%
1959	39%	72%	20%	49%
1960	39%	70%	11%	57%
1969	39%	64%	8%	18%
1979	40%	53%	19%	40%
1980	43%	47%	5%	16%
1984	42%	52%	13%	46%

Source: Hout and Greeley, 1987, Table 1.

Although religious institutions in general have declined in importance in most other ways in industrial societies, this has been confined largely to ecclesiae, churches, and denominations. Cults such as the Unification Church of Sun Myung Moon and the Hare Krishna movement and the various fundamentalist Christian sects involved in the new evangelicalism still constitute a very small portion of the U.S. population, but have nonetheless enjoyed large increases in membership over the last decade (Hadden and Swann, 1981; Lofland, 1977). In comparison with larger religious institutions, cults and sects offer a mystical and absolute view of the world that may be a backlash against the secularization process that helps make the world increasingly rational, bureaucratic, impersonal, and unemotional.

Civil Religion and Other Alternatives

If involvement in religion is declining, what becomes of its most important social functions—increasing social cohesion and providing a sense of individual and group identity that rests on a set of shared ideas about the meaning of life and our relation to the unknown?

Durkheim argued that religious institutions in preindustrial societies allowed people to worship their societies. The sociologist Robert Bellah (1973) contended that in industrial societies, the state itself has become a religious institution. Through **civil religion**, we worship society directly rather than indirectly through religious institutions. Civil religion cuts across all lines drawn by churches, denominations, sects, and cults and helps to unite a pluralistic society (Bellah and Hammond, 1980).

The evidence of civil religion is everywhere. God is mentioned at most important public occasions: at the opening of Congress, in courts, in the Pledge of Allegiance to the Flag, at presidential inaugurations. The words "In God We Trust" appear on money; the bald eagle and the U.S. flag are sacred symbols of national unity, purpose, and strength; the Fourth of July and Memorial Day are ritual celebrations of a common heritage and the belief that God is somehow on our side. National monuments such as the Lincoln Memorial in Washington, DC, resemble religious shrines.

Perhaps the most striking example of civil religion is the Soviet Union, which, paradoxically, officially opposes religious institutions. From its revolutionary beginnings in 1917, the Soviet state identified religious institutions as a negative force that did little more than contribute to false consciousness and the dominance of the ruling class. The Soviet state has tried to replace religion with the state itself and with a Marxist theory of the world based entirely on the production process (Duverger, 1959). Yet in this society that officially opposes the very idea of the "sacred," Russians stand in line for hours to visit the tomb of Lenin in which the Soviet Union's first Marxist leader lies in his casket, perfectly preserved for all to view with quiet religious reverence.

In some ways, the concept and the reality of civil religion represent a contradiction in terms. Religion focuses on sacred and unknown forces that are believed to affect human life, whereas the word "civil" refers to the profane world of our ordinary lives as members of a society. Marxism is grounded in the material conditions of human existence, not in unknown forces beyond the understanding of everyday experience. This is also true of civil religion in the U.S.: we may love our country, we may feel awe in the presence of monuments, and we may feel full of emotion when we hear "America the Beautiful"; but it remains to be seen if our attachment to our country can substitute for answers to the ultimate questions that religions try to answer.

Civil religion cannot explain why we were put on this earth; nor can it tell us what will become of us when we die. It cannot, by definition, provide a meaning of life grounded in beliefs that have a sacred source beyond everyday human experience. While it can, in short, bind us to our society, it cannot secure a place for us in the universe and the endless stretches of time that include our short earthly existence.

While civil religion performs some of the functions once performed by religious institutions, it is not a true religion. Bellah (1973), in fact, believed that civil religion is little more than a "broken and empty shell" (p. 142) and that our increased reliance on science, technology, and the state to provide ultimate solutions to human dilemmas will cause a crisis of major proportions.

The rise of the state and civil religion and the declining influence of religious institutions do not necessarily mean that people are no longer concerned with understanding the unknown and attaching a cosmic meaning to life. While sociologists can measure how often people attend church, it is very difficult to measure aspects of religious faith and concern scientifically. In 1987, 72 percent of adults in the U.S. reported a belief in life after death, and although only a minority of adults attend church on a regular basis, 61 percent oppose the Supreme Court's ban on religious observances in public schools (Davis and Smith, 1987). One out of every three adults opposes allowing atheists to give speeches in their communities and half do not think atheists should be allowed to teach in colleges and universities (Davis and Smith, 1987).

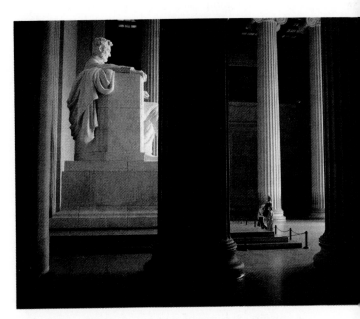

The immensity and majesty of the Lincoln Memorial in Washington, D.C., inspires in many a sense of awe that has sacred overtones typical of those associated with the idea of civil religion.

Again we can see the importance of the distinction between religion and religious institutions. Although attendance at church services in many industrial societies is declining, there is some evidence that people are turning to more private settings for religious behavior. Televised services have a growing—although still relatively small—audience in the United States (Hadden and Swann, 1981). In 1983 the coach of a professional football team, a U.S. senator, professional athletes, and prominent businessmen all appeared on television to promote a book that, they promised, would give its readers "a personal relationship with God."

Major religious institutions appear to be losing much of their former authority as sources of the ultimate meanings and truths that make up a religion, and, at the same time, religion has become a more private matter. Rather than adopting the organized beliefs of a particular religion, individuals are now more likely to construct their own view of ultimate truth from a variety of available beliefs and values. With the decline of primary religious institutions, other institutions have taken over some of the role of spreading ideas that ultimately become part of people's religious framework. The family, schools, and the media all offer and support an assortment of ultimate truths from which individuals construct what amount to private religious systems (Luckmann, 1967).

It appears that religion is becoming less visible as people turn away from major institutions as the main setting for religious expression; but a lack of visibility does not mean such feelings and beliefs no longer exist. It does suggest, however, that religion is on the decline as a social force that binds people together and forms a basis for group identity. Whether or not other institutions can perform this important social function remains to be seen.

SUMMARY

1. Religion consists of symbols and ideas that focus on the meaning of life and the nature of the unknown. The profane is what we can experience directly as ordinary aspects of the natural world, but the sacred is outside the natural world and inspires feelings of awe.

2. Like all institutions, religion is defined in part by the functions it performs. It helps believers cope with pain and suffering and contributes to social cohesion.

3. It is not the task of sociology to prove the truth or falsity of religious beliefs; rather, sociologists try to understand how religion affects the lives of individuals, groups, and societies.

4. Religions differ primarily in their beliefs. Theistic religion includes the belief in one (monotheism) or more (polytheism) supreme beings. Animists believe that spirits inhabit objects such as trees, and totemists believe objects (totems) have supernatural power. Ancestor worshippers believe the dead can influence life among the living. Religions such as Buddhism and Confucianism focus more on abstract ideas as guides for ethical living than on supernatural forces. Religions employ practices called rituals through which religious beliefs are acted out.

5. Salvation is one of the most important values in any religion, and many religious norms define appropriate means for achieving it. Religions also include a variety of attitudes, from adoration of sacred figures to hatred of nonbelievers.

6. Ecclesiae, churches, denominations, sects, and cults are five basic structural types of religious institutions. They differ from each other in how powerful they are and how universal their membership is in a society; in how bureaucratic they are; in the closeness of their ties to other institutions, especially the state; in the selectivity of their membership, especially in terms of social class; and in the ways in which people become members.

7. As with all institutions, religions are affected by population and ecology. The relative and absolute number of followers helps account for both the power of ecclesiae and the weakness of cults. Religious ideas are also affected by technology and the mode of production in a society. The more technologically advanced a society is, the more likely are its religions to include belief in a supreme being who takes an active interest in human affairs.

8. Like all institutions, religion has both functional and dysfunctional consequences. Belief in the absolute truth of religious ideas fosters ethnocentrism and conflict with followers of other religions.

9. Frequently religious institutions are either allied with or actively opposed to the state and dominant social classes. Marx believed that religion often contributes to false consciousness by distracting members of oppressed groups from the true nature and causes of their oppression.

10. A major trend in religious change has been secularization, the process by which religious institutions lose influence to nonreligious institutions such as the state and schools. Compared with religious institutions in preindustrial societies, those in industrial societies have far less authority and influence over people's lives.

11. Some have pointed to the emergence of civil religion as a substitute for the declining influence of religious institutions. In civil religion, society is the focus of worship. In some ways, however, civil religion is a contradiction in terms.

KEY TERMS

ancestor worship   548
animism   548
church   551
civil religion   562
cult   553
denomination   552
ecclesia   551
ethical religion   548
fatalism   556
monotheism   547
polytheism   548
profane   544
reincarnation   548
religion   544
ritual   548
sacred   544
sect   552
secularization   561
totemism   548
   totem   547, 548

Looking Elsewhere

Having studied Chapter 20, you might want to look at related discussions in *Human Arrangements*, which include

- the Jim Jones cult as an in-group (Chapter 8, p. 192)
- anti-Semitism (Chapter 12, pp. 314, 321–22, 328, 329–30)
- religion and science (Chapter 17, pp. 461–62, 467–68)
- the caste system and social inequality (Chapter 12, p. 295)

RECOMMENDED READINGS

BERGER, P. L. (1969). *A rumor of angels: Modern society and the rediscovery of the supernatural.* New York: Doubleday. A thoughtful exploration of the place of religion in modern industrial societies.

FOWLER, J. W. (1981). *Stages of faith.* New York: Harper and Row. A study of religious socialization that focuses on the ways in which people acquire religious faith.

HUNTER, J. D. (1983). *American evangelicalism: Conservative religion and the quandry of modernity.* New Brunswick, NJ: Rutgers University Press. A historical study that shows how the traditional basis of evangelicalism has adapted and survived alongside modernization in most major regions of the world.

ROBBINS, T., and ANTHONY, D. (Eds.). (1980). *In gods we trust: New patterns of religious pluralism in America.* New Brunswick, NJ: Transaction Books. An important set of articles that focus on religious change in the United States, from social conflict to the rise of civil religion and new religious institutions.

WILSON, J. (1978). *Religion in American society: The effective presence.* Englewood Cliffs, NJ: Prentice-Hall. An excellent introduction to the sociology of religion in the United States. See also Wilson, B. (1982). *Religion in sociological perspective.* New York: Oxford.

SIX

Social Change

MOST OF THIS BOOK has focused on trying to describe the cultural, structural, and ecological aspects of social life and to explain how they operate as human arrangements that affect our lives. We have covered a considerable distance—from the process through which children learn language and discover themselves and other people to the ways in which political and economic systems work.

Most of the chapters end with a section on change, and this in itself indicates an important sociological problem that extends across all of the areas we study: it is not enough to describe and explain human social arrangements, for the arrangements change, and each change presents us with new problems to solve. It is one thing to see clearly how things are and to describe how they work; but it is quite another to understand how things got to be the way they are, and still another to have some idea of how things will be in the next year or the next decade. And given the rapid pace of change in today's societies, it is more important than ever that we wrestle successfully with these kinds of issues.

These last two chapters look at two areas of sociology that focus on social change. Chapter 21 focuses on collective behavior, an area that includes social movements, which are organized efforts to either bring about or interfere with social change. Why do social movements emerge when they do, and how do we account for the success of some and the failure of others? What causes revolutions to occur? In the final chapter we examine specific theories that try to explain the patterns, speed, and causes of change.

Crowds, Masses, and Collective Behavior

Mobs

Riots

Panics

Hysteria

Some Theories of Behavior in Crowds

Le Bon and "Mob Psychology"

Collective Behavior as Social Interaction

Social Movements

Classical Social Movement Theory

Resource Mobilization Theory

Political Process Theory

21 Collective Behavior and Social Movements

In the spring of 1982, 700,000 people marched peacefully in New York City to protest the nuclear arms race. There was little violence associated with the demonstration, and no clashes with police. In the months just before Christmas in 1983, however, the "Cabbage Patch" brand of dolls became wildly popular in the United States. In Charleston, West Virginia, 5,000 shoppers started a near riot in a department store. "They knocked over tables, fighting with each other—there were people in mid-air," reported the store manager. "It got ugly." Huge crowds waited for hours—often in biting cold winds—for a chance to snatch up the dolls, and the rush often resulted in injuries, including broken bones (Associated Press, 1983).

In that same fall hundreds of thousands of people gathered in cities across Western Europe to protest the deployment of nuclear missiles. In England protesters chained themselves to fences surrounding military bases; many people were arrested and police used water cannons to disperse some of the crowds. In late 1984, two members of the Sikh religious sect in India murdered Prime Minister Indira Gandhi, and in the days of enraged rioting that followed, more than 1,000 people were killed, most of them Sikhs. In 1987, a panic seized the New York Stock Exchange, and as the average value of stocks crashed as dramatically as they did in the crash of 1929, the panic spread around the world to stock exchanges from London to Tokyo.

Where in the sociological framework do we find a place for people pushing and shoving over a doll, battling with police in the streets, calmly marching in huge numbers without violence, killing strangers only because they belong to the same religious group as two

In 1982, more than 700,000 people gathered peacefully in New York City's Central Park in support of a freeze on the production and deployment of nuclear weapons.

murderers? A clue lies in the concept of collective behavior, and in this chapter we examine the forms it takes and some major attempts to understand it sociologically. We begin with some basic concepts.

CROWDS, MASSES, AND COLLECTIVE BEHAVIOR

Collective behavior refers to how people think, feel, and behave as members of crowds and masses (Lofland, 1981; see also McPhail and Wohlstein, 1986). A **crowd** is a temporary collection of people who happen to be in the same place at the same time and close enough so that they can interact with and affect one another. A collection of people on a sidewalk, the audience at a rock concert, passengers on a bus—all are examples of crowds, in which membership is a temporary, situational social status. Standing in a telephone booth, we are not part of a crowd; but when we open the door and step out on the sidewalk, we suddenly are.

Unlike a crowd, a **mass** is a collection of people who pay attention to and react to the same thing without being in one another's presence. The 1963 assassination of President John F. Kennedy set off a wave of shock and sadness that went around the world and was shared by tens of millions of people who were thousands of miles apart. The collective shock and mourning were examples of mass shock and grief, within which people also expressed their feelings as members of crowds such as those that lined the route of the funeral procession. One of the most telling indicators of the mass experience of Kennedy's assassination is that virtually everyone who was old enough to be aware of the event knows exactly what they were doing when they first heard about it.

Since collective behavior refers to what we think, feel, and do in crowds or masses, what distinguishes it from other behavior is not so much what we do, but the structure of the situations in which we do it.

There are four basic types of collective behavior (Blumer, 1939) that can occur either in crowds or in masses (see Table 21-1). **Casual** collective behavior—such as people walking on a sidewalk—involves no common purpose or goal around which people interact or focus attention. **Conventional** behavior involves a specific purpose such as watching a parade. **Expressive** collective behavior—as you might suppose—centers on feelings. Protest marches, riots, reli-

Table 21-1

Examples of Collective Behavior in Crowds and Masses

TYPE OF BEHAVIOR	IN A CROWD	IN A MASS
Casual	Waiting for bus	Watching the Superbowl
Conventional	Church service	4th of July celebrations
Expressive	Protest march	Nationwide fear over AIDS
Acting	Lynch mob Social movement	Voting Social movement

Sources: Based on Blumer, 1939, and Lofland, 1981.

gious revival meetings, funerals, and the congregation of tens of thousands of people in New York City's Times Square each New Year's Eve are all examples of expressive collective behavior. Finally, **acting** behavior is oriented to specific goals—whether it be to lynch someone, block traffic, prevent workers from crossing a picket line, elect a new government, or topple an existing one.

These four general categories include most types of crowd behavior, but miss several kinds of collective behavior that take place in masses. **Fashion** refers to relatively temporary standards of appearance and behavior that are considered to be socially acceptable or desirable. Men's hairstyles in this country were generally short in the 1950s, longer in the 1960s and 1970s, and shorter again in the 1980s.

Fads have a shorter life span than fashions and rarely become general standards for behavior or appearance; but what they lack in staying power and social acceptability they make up for in the enthusiasm of their followers. In the 1930s trying to swallow goldfish was popular among college students, just as trying to fit as many people as possible into a telephone booth (or a Volkswagen Beetle) was in the 1950s.

Collective behavior has long been an important problem for sociologists because it so often has an impact on societies. Crowd behavior is highly visible, and when it is focused on grievances over social condi-

Nowhere has fashion played a more powerful role than in ideas about women's clothing. In the early 1900s, middle- and upper-class women were expected to wear corsets—such as those sold in this Paris shop—which caused a variety of ailments in pursuit of the "hour-glass" shape. Although fashions for women have changed, our cultural preoccupation with how women's bodies appear has not.

tions, it openly threatens the status quo and stability of social institutions and those who occupy positions of authority in them. People in crowds also have the collective capacity to seriously threaten both life and property, from killing people and destroying property to overthrowing a government. Such violence may provoke equal or greater violence from authorities, resulting in a polarization of society as people take sides. It is also not uncommon, however, for authorities such as the police to violently attack a peaceful but disruptive crowd. This, in turn, often provokes a violent response from the crowd.

Most important, the behavior of people in crowds seems to be highly unpredictable, and the combination of danger and unpredictability provides a compelling reason to understand it. In addition—as we will see later in this chapter and in Chapter 22—social movements are, as the definition implies, a form of collective behavior aimed directly at changing or maintaining the cultural, structural, or ecological conditions of social life.

Mobs

A **mob** is an emotionally aroused, acting crowd that typically has a leader and focuses on a specific goal, the achievement of which usually involves violence. In the late 1800s and early 1900s, lynch mobs were common in the U.S. and resulted in the murder of more than 5,000 people, most of them blacks living in the South (Cantril, 1963; Raper, 1933).

Mobs often play an important part in causing or preventing social change. In the 1930s mobs of Nazis roamed German cities and established a pattern of intimidation of opponents and persecution of Jews that solidified Adolph Hitler's authority and laid the groundwork for the Holocaust. In the 1970s mobs of Japanese tried to prevent the opening of a new airport

In 1970, students at Kent State University in Ohio gathered to protest the war in Vietnam and the presence of ROTC on campus. When National Guard troops mistook the crowd for a dangerous mob, they panicked and opened fire, killing four undergraduates.

near Tokyo. In 1980 a mob of Iranians seized the U.S. embassy in Tehran, made hostages of the embassy employees, and precipitated an international crisis that—among other things—played a major part in ending President Carter's hopes for a second term.

Its potential for violence has always made the mob an object of fear. Authoritarian governments rarely allow crowds to gather unless they are tightly controlled, in part to prevent a crowd from turning into a mob. In some cases, however, authorities allow mob violence when this supports their goals. In the U.S. South early in this century, attacks on blacks served to keep blacks "in their place," and were often inflicted as punishment for "offenses" such as trying to vote or daring to use facilities reserved for whites (Raper, 1933). The mobs in Nazi Germany served Hitler's purposes in a similar way.

Riots

Unlike mob action, a **riot** lacks leadership, organization, and clear goals. Riots often allow people to express frustration and anger that have been contained for years. Riots may involve the destruction or theft of property or attacks on people. In 1984, thousands of people in the Tunisian capital of Tunis rioted for three days after the government doubled the price of bread and other staples. Shops that sold luxury goods were attacked, as were drivers of expensive cars, and some 50 people were killed. The government then restored the lower prices, and within a few hours the streets were filled with people in a festive mood.

As a form of violent collective behavior, the riot has played an important part in the life of most societies. India is struck periodically by riots over the unavailability of food. In the 1960s French students rioted over unpopular government educational policies and the riots eventually resulted in a national strike that brought down the government. In late 1986, hundreds of thousands of French college students staged violent protests against the government's plan to allow universities to be more selective in admitting students and granting degrees, reforms that students believed threatened the principle of free higher education for all. The government eventually reversed its decision. In 1987, riots by South Korean students forced their government to make reforms in that country's election laws.

In 1863 residents of New York City rioted in protest against military draft laws instituted to recruit

soldiers for the Civil War. In Chicago in 1919 and in Detroit in 1943 rioting whites attacked blacks in two of the U.S.'s worst race riots. In the 1930s conflict between striking workers and management resulted in frequent riots. In the 1960s blacks rioted in U.S. ghettos to protest poverty and racial discrimination. In 1968 at the Democratic National Convention in Chicago, hundreds of anti-Vietnam War demonstrators clashed with police in the streets outside the convention hall, and although many observers defined the demonstrators as the rioters, an Illinois Commission later decided that it was the police who had rioted by attacking nonviolent demonstrators indiscriminately and without justification.

Riots often pose a more serious danger to social order than mobs do precisely because they have neither leadership nor clear goals. A mob can often be stopped through its leader or by meeting its goals without violence. Once a riot has started, however, it is difficult to stop without the use of equal or greater violence, and each use of official violence often has the effect of only deepening the anger and motivation of rioters.

Panics

As a form of collective behavior, a **panic** is an attempt by people in a crowd or mass to escape a perceived danger or respond to acute uncertainty. By definition a panic is an irrational response in that cooperation breaks down completely and this usually results in greater danger, not greater safety. When someone yells "Fire!" in a crowded theater, a panic reaction would be for everyone to try to run to the exits at once. The result would most likely be injury or death for most of the people and escape for a relative few.

Panics can also occur at the level of masses. When people hear that a bank is about to fail, they may panic and rush to withdraw their money, an action that ensures the bank's failure. In 1984 false rumors that the Continental Illinois bank was about to fail began to spread, and large-scale depositors withdrew billions of dollars in a matter of weeks. The bank—the eighth largest in the U.S.—was not in good financial shape when the rumors began to circulate, but it was not in immediate danger of failing. By mid-summer, however, more than $20 billion had been withdrawn and neither the government nor the bank management was able to restore public confidence. Finally, the Federal Depositor's Insurance Corporation stepped in and made an arrangement to ensure the bank's survival. Panic withdrawals were prevented in Ohio in 1985 because the governor ordered the temporary closing of the state's savings and loan institutions after one of the largest failed.

Hysteria

Panic in crowds and masses is often preceded by mass **hysteria**, which is a state of rapidly spreading anxiety based on a danger or opportunity that is usually misperceived.

In 1982, people in the U.S. became aware of a new disease called Acquired Immune Deficiency Syndrome (AIDS) that appeared to be confined to a small subgroup of the population—most notably male homosexuals (Fettner and Check, 1984; Shilts, 1987). Anxiety over AIDS spread quickly. Although discrimination against homosexuals was certainly nothing new, it now took on an added dimension of open fear of any physical contact with homosexuals, a fear based on the mistaken belief that the disease could be transmitted merely by being near or touching an AIDS victim. Suddenly, homosexuals were losing jobs and being denied housing that was formerly open to them. Many health workers and ambulance personnel refused to handle possible AIDS victims; some police officers wore rubber gloves and protective masks while arresting homosexuals.

As telephone hot lines were flooded with thousands of anxious calls from around the country, it became clear that mass hysteria had set in and that a medical emergency was compounded by widespread fear based on false beliefs. For homosexuals, the result was a double-victimization—once by the disease and again by the mass hysteria that followed.

Mobs, riots, panics, and mass hysteria are forms of collective behavior that have attracted much attention from sociologists, and for more than a century they have tried to explain why and how they occur.

SOME THEORIES OF BEHAVIOR IN CROWDS

Perspectives on crowd behavior can be divided into two types. The earliest theories—and some later ones—saw behavior in crowds in largely psychological terms. Crowds were viewed as having personalities and tendencies that explained the behavior of people

In the hysteria that accompanied the AIDS epidemic, police and other public workers responded with extreme measures to protect themselves from what they erroneously believed to be a highly contagious disease.

in them. In fact, the earliest theories treated crowds as if they were some kind of distinct organism with a mind and life of their own. Later theories have placed much more importance on the social conditions that cause collective behavior and the social processes through which it occurs. In short, over the last century thinking about collective behavior has become less psychological and more sociological.

Like sociology itself, theories of crowd behavior first emerged in the nineteenth century, a period full of rapid social change that often involved violence and revolution. While this led thinkers to pay a lot of attention to social conditions and the characteristics of social environments, it provided particular reasons to focus on crowds and masses, for in many cases—the most notable being the French Revolution—

they played a direct and important role in bringing about dramatic change.

Those opposed to change tended to see crowds and masses as menacing forces that threatened the very fabric of civilized society, whereas those in favor of change often saw them as evidence of an aroused lower class whose awareness of social conditions was, to paraphrase Marx, the engine of progress. Clearly, many early theorists were particularly affected by the times they lived in; they used unscientific data and often had a personal ax to grind. Nowhere was this more apparent than in the nevertheless pioneering work of Gustave Le Bon.

Le Bon and "Mob Psychology"

Writing at the end of the nineteenth century, Le Bon made one of the earliest serious attempts to analyze collective behavior with a psychology of crowds— **mob psychology**. Like all thinkers, his ideas reflected the social conditions and the dominant ideas of his time. France had endured a violent revolution a century before and the pace of change had, if anything, quickened since. The working class struggled for better working conditions and a greater share of political power, and the emerging capitalist middle class threatened the dominance of the upper class. The old feudal order was gone, but capitalism was too new to provide a sense of order and continuity in social life.

In short, change was rapid and often accompanied by violence, and Le Bon (1895/1960) feared that his society was going out of control. Without the social bonds and obligations of feudalism, Le Bon feared that society would be ruled by mobs of ignorant and irresponsible members of the lower class. As he put it,

> Today the claims of the masses are becoming more and more sharply defined, and amount to nothing less than a determination to utterly destroy society as it now exists, with a view to making it hark back to . . . before the dawn of civilization. (p. 16)

Le Bon believed that collective violence occurs because people who are prone to violence are drawn together by an event, what Turner (1964) called Le Bon's **convergence theory**. Crowds consist of like-minded people who assemble in one place. Collective violence depends on individuals who are already prone to violent behavior.

Perhaps most important in Le Bon's theory is his reliance on leaders who control crowds through a kind of hypnotism. "A crowd," he wrote, "is a servile flock that is incapable of ever doing without a master" (p. 118). Le Bon believed that leaders exert power by flattery, strong rhetoric, the presentation of only one side of an issue, repetition, and the clever use of symbols. In short, they succeed by appealing to the nonrational, emotional, and unconscious motivations of people in crowds. People can be controlled through such techniques, he believed, because in crowds they are "leveled"—which is to say, everyone comes to think, feel, and behave in the same way. Le Bon believed that in a crowd people no longer exist as individuals: only the crowd exists.

According to Le Bon, once a crowd forms, several consequences follow. People lose their ability to think rationally, and they lose touch with abstract ideas (especially those about right and wrong). Crowd members are very suggestible in this state and will readily do what they are told. They become shortsighted and misperceive what is going on around them. To Le Bon, then, crowds are suggestible, blind, and fickle.

As a process, crowd behavior in Le Bon's view is quite simple and depends on what he called **contagion**. People copy one another's behavior, and this sets off a chain reaction. Le Bon deserves credit for making an early connection between social conditions and collective behavior and for drawing attention to the importance of unconscious psychological motivations (such as those that play a role in lynch mobs). Most important, he focused serious attention on crowds as a subject of study. His ideas, however, have little credibility among sociologists. There is no compelling evidence that contagion either describes or explains what goes on in crowds, or that social influence in crowds differs substantially from social influence in general. Nor is there any evidence that hypnotism operates in crowds.

Le Bon's most serious shortcomings are his view of the nature of crowds and his reliance on the power of leaders as an explanation of collective behavior. As we will see shortly, many studies find that people in crowds are far more rational than Le Bon thought they were; and there is a division of labor in most crowds that is ignored by Le Bon's view of crowds as a group in which all members are alike. During anti-Vietnam War demonstrations in the 1960s, some demonstrators specialized in acting as "medics" who took care of the injured, while others looked out for police movements and possible avenues of escape.

People do not all think, feel, and act alike in crowds (see McPhail and Wohlstein, 1983). Watch a crowd at a sporting event and you will see a lot of variation in what people do and appear to feel. Some watch the game enthusiastically; some talk with friends and seem to ignore the game; some play games that compete with what is happening on the field. Le Bon barely scratched the surface of the complexity of collective behavior in even the most common social situations.

Blumer and Stampeding Cattle   In the 1930s the U.S. sociologist Herbert Blumer (1939) used many of the same assumptions that underlay Le Bon's work. Unlike Le Bon, however, Blumer focused on interaction among crowd members rather than between leaders and followers, and this was an important shift in emphasis.

Like Le Bon, Blumer assumed that crowds are homogeneous and that individuals in crowds are irrational. Blumer also relied on a concept he called **circular reaction**, which was like the concept of contagion in viewing crowd behavior as a chain reaction, but differed in an important way: people in crowds do not simply set each other off; rather, when one person affects a second, the act of witnessing the result acts back on the first person and *amplifies* the affect. So, my excitement stimulates you, and when I see your excitement I become still more excited, and so on. In this way, Blumer believed, feelings and tendencies in crowds spread and increase rapidly. To describe this, Blumer used the image of a herd of cattle in which cows progressively become more and more excited until they stampede.

Blumer believed that crowds form around some precipitating incident. Then people "mill around," talking with one another, being stimulated by and amplifying one another's moods. Someone does something, and instead of interpreting the behavior as they would normally do, people react without thinking. As collective excitement builds, it focuses on a common object, and in the final stage of excitement, people act impulsively and irrationally toward it.

Blumer's ideas have many problems in common with those of Le Bon—most notably his reliance on the idea of circular reaction and his assumptions about the homogeneity and irrationality of people in crowds. Also like Le Bon's theory, Blumer's theory of circular reaction describes more than it explains and cannot explain why not everyone in a crowd is aroused or why the mood in a crowd can change quickly.

Le Bon's and Blumer's theories have a deeper problem, however, for both viewed crowds as irrational, uncivilized collections of people. This meant that neither fully appreciated the fact that many crowds contain people who can protest social conditions in no other way. Unlike theorists discussed later in this chapter, Le Bon and Blumer de-emphasize the importance of collective behavior as both a reflection of social problems and an important vehicle for positive social change.

Collective Behavior as Social Interaction

From a social interaction perspective, collective behavior poses no theoretical problems that are any more challenging than those posed by any other social behavior. How are collective situations defined? How do people make choices within them? What do the patterns of interaction in crowds look like?

Emergent Norms   One of the paradoxes of collective behavior is that individuals in crowds behave in a variety of ways, but at the same time often feel a sense of shared purpose with people they have never met. Often there is no prior planning in crowd behavior, and yet clearly discernible patterns of expectation and interaction emerge from crowd situations, and participants feel constrained by a set of informal norms. How does this happen? Where do these norms come from?

Turner and Killian (1972) offered **emergent norm theory** to explain how patterns of interaction and expectation evolve in crowds. In most situations, we rely on the definition of the situation in order to know what is expected of us and others. When shopping in a store we are bound by certain legal norms (paying for what we buy) and informal folkways (waiting our turn). In a crowd, however, the definition of the situation may be unclear. Suppose that we have been waiting for eight hours outside a department store in Buffalo, New York, in order to buy Cabbage Patch dolls as Christmas presents. People are cold, a little irritable, and anxious that there will not be enough dolls to go around or that the announcement

These shoppers, waiting for a bell to signal the opening of a department store sale, may well be wondering what norms will apply to them. The unpredictability of such situations and the fact that norms do eventually emerge is the focus of emergent norm theory.

of a new shipment was false. What norms apply here as the store-opening time nears? How do you know "what goes" and what does not?

Chances are that you would look around at what other people are doing. Are they staying in line? Are people slowly inching their way toward the door so that they will be in a better position when the store opens? In usual circumstances the norms about waiting in line would be clear; but the tension in this situation creates unusual circumstances in which no one is sure if other people will abide by the usual norms. There is, in short, a sense of anomie—or normlessness—in this situation, and people look at what others are doing in order to establish the norms. This is just the opposite of what usually happens: rather than having the patterns of interaction emerge out of an established set of norms, the norms emerge out of a pattern of interaction.

According to emergent norm theory, in crowds we look for signs of what norms will apply in that situation. This is due, in part, to earlier experiences in groups in which behavior is rewarded or punished depending on whether or not it conforms to group norms. Since we are actively looking for norms to emerge, we are unusually susceptible to suggestion and are likely to accept emerging norms with little criticism. We tend, in short, to approach all collective situations with a certain amount of anxiety and, therefore, a desire to define the situation quickly so that we know what is going on. This, in turn, means that we

tend to accept definitions of crowd situations without exercising very much independent critical judgment.

The desire of crowd members to identify quickly a set of norms to guide their behavior means that some visible members can have considerable power to define the situation through the example set by their behavior. In a tense, yet ambiguous crowd situation, the difference between violence and peaceful protest may hinge on whether someone yells "Get them!" or "Everybody stay calm!"

Emergent norm theory is useful because it focuses on the ways in which social interaction in crowds establishes norms. Crowds generally contain a collection of people who have diverse motives, feelings, and beliefs about what is going on, and yet somehow through social interaction a common purpose and set of shared expectations often emerge.

Emergent norm theory contains traces of a problem found with its predecessors: a tendency to view behavior in crowds as less rational than that in other social situations. More recent theories have directly challenged that longstanding view, arguing that interaction is no less rational or intelligent in a crowd than in any other situation.

Decision Theory   As a view of human nature and behavior, decision theory is about as far as one could get from Le Bon's view of uncivilized mobs. Decision theory has been applied to many aspects of human behavior, and essentially rests on the idea that people usually act rationally in order to solve problems. From this perspective, collective behavior represents the efforts of people in crowds to act together in order to solve problems.

Problem-solving—whether by an individual on a desert island or by members of a crowd at a football game—is a process that may be thought of as consisting of a series of steps (Luce and Raiffa, 1957; Raiffa, 1970). We gather and interpret information about what is happening and about what might happen; we may list our options and rank them according to the desirability of their probable consequences; and we make choices in order to gain the best possible outcome.

Suppose that you are eating lunch in a college dining room and suddenly some people start throwing food at each other. It is the last day of the term and there is a lot of laughing as food flies through the air. What do you do? According to decision theory, the behavior of most people will depend on some weighing of the probable consequences: What happens if I join in? What happens if I just sit here? If I try to stop it? If I leave?

If you join in, you might have some fun or release some tension; you might also get covered with food, be punished by college authorities, and offend other students. If you just sit there, you run the risk of having some students think you do not like to have a "good time"—and you will probably end up with food on you anyway. If you try to stop it, even those students who do not participate might think you are being a "wet blanket"; and if you leave, you leave your lunch behind along with everything else.

Somewhere among those options you will decide which consequences are the most important to you, and this will be the basis of your decision. Notice that in this and many other crowd situations, people are not all behaving in the same way, even though you might later describe the incident as a "food riot." There is at least circumstantial evidence that people are making decisions about their behavior, rather than blindly copying the behavior of others.

Notice also that your decision depends on how other people react, both to your behavior and the behavior of others. This kind of situation—in which consequences for an individual depend on what other people do—is called a *game*.

Game Theory   According to **game theory**, we try to achieve what is called a "minimax" solution, one

that minimizes our costs and maximizes our rewards (Luce and Raiffa, 1957; Zagare, 1984). In order to discover such a solution in a crowd situation, each member has to consider what other people are likely to do, a process that is central to the game theory approach to collective behavior (Berk, 1974a, 1974b).

In game theory, the decision facing crowd members boils down to two problems: Will others support what I do, and what difference will it make? Of the two, predicting whether or not other people in the crowd will support what we do is the most difficult problem, and the ability to predict depends on a number of structural and ecological characteristics of crowds (Berk, 1974b). The more people there are who appear to act in a particular way and the more visible their behavior is, the more likely we are to perceive support for ourselves if we join in.

From a gaming perspective, collective behavior is a case of collective problem solving in which individuals compromise and cooperate with one another in order to maximize their rewards through mutual support. "Each crowd member tries to make the most of the situation while constrained by the need for support from others" (Berk, 1974b, p. 73). This approach is most useful in explaining why people participate in crowds that require cooperation.

It is also useful, however, for understanding crowds that involve competition among members (Berk, 1974b). Suppose that you hear on the radio that a nuclear power plant is about to "melt down" and cause a nuclear disaster in your city. A rational response would be for everyone to leave the city in a rapid but orderly manner, for if everyone makes a mad dash for the highways and public transportation systems, the confusion and inevitable accidents might make it virtually impossible for all but a few to escape.

Suppose, however, that you notice a few people driving wildly toward the highway entrance ramp, screaming out their car windows for everyone else to get out of the way and waving pistols in the air just to make sure everyone gets the point. You might conclude that those few people have panicked unnecessarily and that the best thing for everyone to do is to proceed in a quick and orderly manner and ignore the panicked few.

It is also possible, however, that the mad dashers know something that you do not—that, perhaps, the reactor has already melted down and fatal radiation is only minutes behind you. In that case, it may be impossible for everyone to get out alive, and only those who force their way through will escape un-harmed. This is a very different kind of game from a peace demonstration in which people cooperate with one another in pursuit of common goals, for in this game the rational choice is to maximize the chance of survival by struggling against everyone else.

The line between cooperation and competition, then, is a thin one, and which side of it you wind up on depends on your perceptions of what is going on; and, as we have seen before, our perceptions of the world are strongly affected by the social environment. The environment provides us with *information*, a key in-gredient in collective behavior; and *rumor* is an impor-tant social mechanism through which information is communicated.

Rumor A **rumor** is an unverified belief that arises from informal interaction. Most rumors arise in situations in which we need to have information that is otherwise unavailable to us (Rosnow and Fine,

1976): when daily routines are disrupted (the buses are all running late); when the environment changes drastically (there is an earthquake); when we must make choices but are uncertain of the outcomes (which courses to sign up for); when there is sustained tension (families of prisoners of war must wait for news); or when there is prolonged boredom with-out knowing the cause (people wait in a theater line that stretches halfway around the block and does not move).

That rumor spreads informally does not mean that it is a random process in which everyone is equally likely to be included. Instead, most rumors are nurtured by established social networks of people who share statuses that make the content of the rumor relevant to them (Milgram, 1977). In Lillian Hellman's powerful play, *The Children's Hour*, a girl in a boarding school mentions to her grandmother that she saw the two women who run the school hugging each other in their room. This simple observation soon becomes

Rumor often plays a part in panic situations in which vital information is missing. This has been the case in stock market crashes such as the one that occurred first in the U.S. and then in major world markets in 1987. Like everyone else, these traders on the London exchange are trying to find out what is happening in time to protect themselves from financial loss. Often the rumors themselves spur further panic and still greater losses than would otherwise have occurred.

embellished into a supposed lesbian relationship, and the rumor spreads quickly among the parents of girls who attend the school—but not in the community as a whole. In similar ways, rumors about the 1987 stock market crash spread more quickly among executives than among building custodians.

As a social process, rumor has been viewed as an example of human failing and as a normal part of social life. In early studies of rumor, Bartlett (1932) and later Allport and Postman (1947) treated rumors as accounts passed in series from one person to another, and they used experiments to explore how this occurs. They asked one person to repeat a simple statement to the next person in a chain and recorded each transmission until the last person was reached.

In these and many subsequent experiments the findings were the same: as the account is transmitted down the line, it tends to become shorter, more concise, and easier to understand (an effect called *leveling*); limited to a relatively few details (*sharpening*); and more coherent and consistent with the interests and beliefs of the participants (*assimilation*). The general conclusion from these experiments was that distortion is inevitable in rumor because of faulty perception and memory, and the inability to repeat a message verbatim.

In spite of the fact that many replications of the Allport and Postman experiments generated similar results, many researchers have challenged the results because they were obtained in an artificial laboratory setting. Caplow (1947) argued that in many situations—such as combat—the accuracy of information is so important that people are critical about what they accept and what they subsequently pass on to others. The fact that rumor usually travels through established social networks means that unreliable people tend to be discounted and eliminated from the network. The result, he believed, is that rumors may become more—not less—accurate as they go along.

Others, such as Festinger (1948) and Peterson and Gist (1951), have also pointed out that in many situations rumors become longer and more elaborate—not shorter and simpler—as they are spread through a network. This may be due in part to the fact that since rumors are social beliefs they must be plausible for us to believe in them; and this encourages the development of details related to the main piece of information.

Several researchers have argued that rumor is part of a collective effort to define social situations (Shibutani, 1966, 1968; Turner, 1964). So long as

something important is unexplained, there is "a distracting sense of incompleteness" and a desire "to understand the new circumstances by completing the incomplete" (Shibutani, 1968, p. 579). The more important it is to us to understand a situation and the more ambiguous the available information is, the more likely it is that rumors will develop as a way for increasing our understanding and defining the situation with greater clarity (Jaeger, Anthony, and Rosnow, 1979). As rumors develop, they tend to become more plausible and complete. Details that do not fit are eliminated, whereas those that are consistent with the rumor are added, thereby making it more convincing.

According to Shibutani, the ways in which rumor develops depend on the social situation. When the situation is relatively unimportant to the participants, information is handled through established social networks. In situations of high excitement, however, such as during natural disasters, established networks tend to break down and new lines of communication spring up spontaneously. Under such conditions, it is harder to verify new information before it is spread further.

When people are bored, rumor can serve quite different functions: it can be a source of entertainment or a vehicle for expressing attitudes. Students may spread bad rumors about a disliked teacher because it lets them express negative feelings; and by passing it through the student network, they strengthen the bonds among them. The ultimate truth or falsity of the rumor is, in this case, irrelevant to its social functions.

Like all social behavior, the process of spreading rumors has a structure that can involve a variety of different roles (Shibutani, 1966, 1968). Transmitters simply pass on messages ("I heard that today's final exam is going to include the whole book."), while interpreters place them in context, evaluate their truth or falsity, and speculate about details that are left out ("That doesn't make any sense; I was in class when the announcement was made. Then again, worse things have happened in that course."). Skeptics play the important role of challenging new information ("That can't be true."), and agitators urge action based on the rumor ("That's totally outrageous; let's go see the dean.").

This model of the rumor process clearly reflects more recent views of collective behavior, in that it looks upon such behavior as a rational process through which we try to achieve goals, define situations, and take action that we perceive to be in our best interests. From this perspective, collective behavior is a normal consequence of the social and ecological conditions in which we live. Nowhere is this more apparent than in social movements—collective behavior that focuses on social change.

SOCIAL MOVEMENTS

Social movements are organized attempts to cause or prevent social change. In addition to being organized, they are social in that they attempt to change cultural or structural aspects of society; but they are social in another perhaps more important respect as well. So long as members of minorities do not identify themselves as members of a minority, they have no other explanation for their disadvantages and mistreatment than luck or their personal characteristics. Once they identify prejudice and discrimination as causes of their condition, however, they can see the social problems of which their personal troubles are a part. It is only when people go beyond psychological and biological frameworks and focus on their relationships to their environments that social movements become possible.

The anti-nuclear power movement is a powerful example of a resistance movement that has had considerable success. In 1983, these marchers protested the Shoreham nuclear power plant on Long Island, New York, on the grounds that it would be impossible to evacuate residents in the event of an accident. After years of protest, the power company was ordered in 1988 to dismantle the completed plant before it was put into operation.

Social movements usually focus on reform, revolution, or resistance to change. **Reform movements** try to improve existing arrangements by altering specific aspects of them. Various civil rights movements—of blacks, women, or gays—do not seek to dismantle and change the entire society; rather, they demand that members of those social categories have the right to participate fully in political and economic life and receive a fair share of wealth, power, and prestige. In similar ways, movements to save the physical environment often focus on specific arrangements (such as the choice between solar or nuclear technology to provide energy) rather than society as a whole.

Unlike reform movements, **revolutions** attempt to replace an existing social or ecological arrangement (Goldstone, 1982; Skocpol, 1979). The French Revolution attempted to replace a monarchy with a more democratic government; and the American Revolution—which began as a reform movement to guarantee colonists the same rights as other British subjects—rapidly turned into a revolution that completely separated the colonies from the British Empire. In early 1917 the Czar of Russia was overthrown and replaced by a government that began to introduce a kind of Western democracy. Later in that same year, the Bolsheviks under the leadership of Lenin carried out yet a second revolution that led to the socialist state that rules the Soviet Union today.

More recently, religious fundamentalists in Iran joined with other dissatisfied groups to overthrow the shah's monarchy and replace it with a government strictly guided by religious principles. In Nicaragua a revolutionary movement in the early 1980s installed a socialist government; as of 1987, a *counter*revolutionary movement was still trying to depose that government; and in neighboring El Salvador a socialist revolutionary movement was trying to depose a capitalist government with strong ties to the U.S.

Although social movements often cause change, their purpose is sometimes just the opposite—to oppose or undo change (Lo, 1982)—in which case they are called **resistance movements**. In 1982, organized opposition defeated the Equal Rights Amendment in spite of the fact that a clear majority of adults supported it. In 1983, a nuclear weapons freeze movement grew rapidly, and opposed the introduction of newer, more deadly weapons. Other movements support a return to prayer in public schools, the dismantling of school busing programs, and the reversal of Supreme Court decisions that support women's rights to have abortions.

Social movements have attracted increasing attention from sociologists during the past 40 years and have been a topic of intense debate since the mid-1970s. Why do social movements emerge when they do? What determines their success or failure? In the following sections, we look at some attempts to answer such questions.

Classical Social Movement Theory

Like early theories of behavior in crowds, early social movement theories often relied heavily on psychological explanations for what is essentially a social phenomenon. What McAdam (1982) called **classical social movement theory** actually includes several specific approaches, all based on the same general model: some kind of strain or disturbance (such as an economic depression) creates disruptive psychological states in individuals (such as anxiety) and individuals then channel their energy into social movements in order to relieve their emotional difficulties (Figure 21-1).

Frustration, Deprivation, and Aggression Dollard and colleagues (1939) were the first to outline the **frustration-aggression theory** of social movements, according to which social strain in the form of frustration is an underlying motive for aggressive behavior, including that which leads to the formation of social movements. A frustration-aggression explanation of lynch mobs in the South during the late nineteenth and early twentieth centuries would go like this: Cotton is the main crop in southern states and most poor whites make a living from it. When the cotton market is good and prices are high, everyone does reasonably well. When the market is bad, poor whites suffer and in their frustration seek a relatively safe target on which to vent their feelings. The obvious choice was blacks. (Blacks suffered too from poor economic conditions, but lacked a safe target.) (Dollard et al., 1939).

In trying to explain violent social movements, Gurr (1970) argued that frustration most often arises from people's anger at not getting what they think they deserve—in other words, from what is known as *relative deprivation*. **Absolute deprivation** is a state in which we feel we do not have what we need—our stomachs growl from hunger and we feel weak much of the time. **Relative deprivation**, however, is the perception that we do not have enough in comparison with others who we think should not be any better off than we are. If I have enough food to guarantee good nutrition, I may feel physically fit and therefore not

---

Figure 21-1 Classical Theories of Social Movements

"Classical" theories of social movements are psychological in that they argue that social movements are a way for people to relieve uncomfortable and disruptive feelings that are caused by social conditions. They tend to ignore the social factors that determine whether a social movement will emerge or succeed.

The Classical Model:	Structural Strain	Disruptive Psychological State in Individuals	Social Movement
Frustration-Aggression Theory (Dollard):	Deprivation	Frustration	Social Movement
Mass Society Theory (Kornhauser):	Social Isolation	Anxiety and Anomie	Social Movement
Structural Strain Theory (Smelser):	Structural Strain	Normative Ambiguity	Social Movement

Source: McAdam, 1982.

suffer any absolute deprivation. If my reference groups (such as friends and co-workers) can afford fancy wines and lots of meals in restaurants, however, I will experience relative deprivation.

The distinction between absolute and relative deprivation is important, for the use of one concept rather than the other generates quite different predictions. If we think in terms of absolute deprivation, we would predict that societies with the highest incidence of poverty will be the ones to experience the highest levels of violent behavior, and that the most violent society will be one in which everyone is poor. If, however, we use the concept of relative deprivation, we would predict that the highest levels of collective violence will occur in societies in which the *gap* between the richest and the poorest is perceived to be the widest and the most out of line with people's expectations, even though no one might be poor in an absolute sense. This can result in a paradoxical situation, for an improvement in absolute conditions may stimulate people's expectations to rise even faster, and as this widens the gap between what people have and what they think they should have, the chances for violence should increase.

This is how some sociologists explained the increase in urban riots and other collective violence in the U.S. during the 1960s (Graham and Gurr, 1979; Gurr, 1970). In 1954 the Supreme Court banned racial segregation in schools, and segregation in other public facilities—such as restaurants, buses, and restrooms—was outlawed shortly thereafter. The economy boomed during the 1960s, President Johnson declared a war on poverty, and civil rights legislation outlawed racial discrimination and strengthened blacks' voting rights.

In an absolute sense, then, conditions were improving for many blacks, but for many others conditions remained largely the same. What were changing dramatically, however, were black people's perceptions of what they ought to have relative to everyone else. Severe inequality continued while the social acceptability of poverty and inequality declined and the promise of an end to poverty was offered by the federal government. It is likely that one result of this was a widespread feeling among poor urban blacks that the promise was an empty one, that economic prosperity was passing them by, and that in a relative sense, they were worse off than ever before.

In addition to relative deprivation, frustration-aggression theorists focus on two other sources of frustration. In the above account, for example, federal antipoverty programs may have created the hope and the expectation among blacks that things would improve rapidly for them. Such **rising expectations**, argue some sociologists, form the basis for frustration and then social movements when they fail to materialize. Davies (1962) argued that social movements are more likely if a period of rapid improvement is followed by a sharp downturn. According to his "**J-curve**" theory of black rebellion in the 1960s, a period of rising expectations and actual improvements in living conditions was followed by a rapid worsening of the relative position of blacks, a sudden reversal that was intolerable.

Theories that rely on frustration, relative deprivation, rising expectations, and sudden reversals to explain social movements have been criticized on a number of grounds (see McAdam, 1982; Morris, 1984). First, most studies that use this framework have not measured the existence of these key psychological states over time. Since the theories argue that it is an *increase* in such disruptive feelings that prompts social movements, the failure to link movements with changes in levels of frustration is a crucial one.

Second, studies do not compare the levels of frustration in those who participate in social movements with those who do not. When Orum (1972) did this in his study of black student participation in civil rights protests, he found that those who participated were no more likely to have experienced rising expectations than those who did not.

Third, the indicators that are typically used to measure the presence of strain do not correlate with the level of social movement activity. McAdam (1982) compared economic indicators—such as the ratio of black incomes to white incomes—with the annual number of black civil rights movement events for the period between 1948 and 1976. He found no significant relationship between them.

Fourth, as Shorter and Tilly (1974) and Tilly (1978a) argued, emotional arousal—however intense—is not enough to create a social movement. As they wrote in their study of strikes in France, "individuals are not magically mobilized for participation in some group enterprise, regardless of how angry, sullen, hostile, or frustrated they may feel. Their aggression may be channeled to collective ends only through the coordinating, directing functions of an organization, be it formal or informal" (p. 38). In short, a

In 1983, hundreds of thousands of people gathered in Washington, D.C. to mark the 20th anniversary of Martin Luther King's "I have a dream" speech. The level of organization and resources needed for this kind of collective action raises serious questions about the theory that social movements can result simply from psychological states such as frustration.

collection of angry people is not a social movement. To be a social movement, the anger and energy must be organized, and frustration-aggression, relative deprivation, rising expectations, and J-curve theories ignore this vital *social* aspect of social movements.

Kornhauser, Mass Society, and Social Isolation   In the aftermath of World War II Kornhauser (1959) focused on social conditions in societies as a whole and how these promoted or inhibited collective violence that seemed—to many living in the cold-war atmosphere of the 1950s—to lead to authoritarian governments. Kornhauser believed that collective action is most likely when people feel a lack of connection between themselves and their communities. This happens when there are no groups through which people can affect political decisions or feel like they belong in their communities. Kornhauser called this condition of widespread social isolation **mass society**, and the social isolation it reflects is similar to Durkheim's concept of anomie that we discussed in Chapter 10 as a cause of deviant behavior.

To Kornhauser, large numbers of unattached and alienated people are the raw material of collective behavior and social movements. When people feel submerged in a mass, they feel disconnected from meaningful involvements and relationships, and this leads them to experience strong feelings of anxiety. In order to escape these feelings, people engage in extreme behavior, including social movements (see Figure 21-1).

Kornhauser argued that social movements are ultimately caused by social conditions; but it is important to see that he did not see social movements as attempts to *change* those conditions. Rather, he explained them as mechanisms through which individuals try to reduce unpleasant psychological conditions such as strain and anxiety. Violent behavior may discharge tension, and participation in a social movement may provide feelings of belonging and connection with other human beings. "Mass movements," he wrote, "appeal to the unemployed on psychological . . . grounds, as ways of overcoming feelings of anxiety and futility, of finding new solidarity and forms of activity" (p. 167).

Smelser and Structural Strain   Like Kornhauser, Smelser (1962) focused on social conditions that give rise to psychological states that in turn motivate people to participate in social movements; but Smelser's theory is more complex and tries to encompass a wider range of various social factors—from the characteristics of societies to the dynamics of crowds—in order to explain social movements. To Smelser, collective behavior and the emergence of social movements depend on a series of factors.

To illustrate and describe Smelser's theory, consider the wave of antinuclear protests that swept over Europe in the late fall of 1983 when the United States and its European allies began to install cruise and Pershing II nuclear missiles in Europe. In many countries mass demonstrations were held to protest the introduction of new weapons, and these demonstrations often ended in violent confrontations with police. In one incident in Frankfurt, West Germany, an estimated 4,000 people gathered in the center of the city for an antinuclear rally. They then marched to a nearby U.S. Army arms depot to continue their protest. As they marched past the U.S. consulate, many shook their fists and threw tin cans and firecrackers. In the hours that followed, roughly half of these drifted away, and when police blocked the road between the remaining demonstrators and the Army depot, demonstrators threw rocks and firecrackers at the police, used garbage cans to build barricades in the street, and set fire to the barricades. Police responded by firing water cannons into the crowd and then waded in to arrest about 100 people.

How does Smelser's theory help explain why this happened? To Smelser, the ultimate cause of social movements is some form of **structural strain** that leads to a state of uncertainty among people. People then participate in collective behavior—and social movements in particular—as a way of reducing uncertainty and relieving anxiety. As we have seen in many earlier chapters, contradiction, tension, and conflict exist to some extent in virtually all societies, especially if they are complex. In a general sense, Smelser's concept of strain refers to differences between social conditions as they are and conditions as people want or expect them to be. As we saw in Chapter 12, the U.S. faces what Gunnar Myrdal called "an American dilemma" because we discriminate on the basis of race and deeply value equality and fairness. The contradiction between the social reality of racism and discrimination on the one hand and deeply held values on the other creates structural strain.

Strain certainly abounds in the area of nuclear weapons. It is fair to say that most people are afraid of nuclear war; governments are expected to represent the best interests of the people, especially in representative democracies; and many people share the expectation that life should get better, not worse. Confounding these expectations, however, is the fact that the destructive capacity of the world's militaries in general and nuclear arsenals in particular are growing at a rapid rate, and the superpowers show continued willingness to use armed force in order to further what they define as their own interests.

One result is a considerable amount of anxiety as millions of people live in the shadow of nuclear destruction and look to their governments to make the world a safer place. When the Western allies decided to introduce new nuclear weapons, it was inevitable that strain would develop as many people perceived this move as making things worse, not better.

Strain also exists within societies. Ever since the defeat of Germany in World War II, U.S. troops have been on the soil of what became West Germany; and although West Germany rules itself, for many Germans sovereignty and independence can never be complete so long as thousands of foreign troops and their weapons are in Germany. Add to this the fact that the weapons being introduced are U.S.-made and will be under the control of U.S. commanders, and the potential for strain is clear. (Try to imagine, for a moment, how you might feel if a large German army base was located near your neighborhood, even if they were there as allies of the U.S.)

Smelser believed that we respond to ambiguity, uncertainty, and strain by trying to make sense of things as a way of relieving the strain. This results in what Smelser referred to as **generalized beliefs**, which we seize upon in order to justify our actions and reduce feelings of uncertainty. Smelser believed that generalized beliefs are often if not usually irrational because they exist not to provide a rational framework for bringing about social change, but to provide a common motivation and justification for us to take part in movements in order to reduce strain.

> These beliefs differ . . . from those that guide many other types of behavior. They involve a belief in the existence of extraordinary forces—threats, conspiracies, etc.—which are at work in the universe. They also involve an assessment of the extraordinary consequences which will follow if the collective attempt to reconstitute social action is successful. The beliefs on which collective behavior is based . . . are thus akin to magical beliefs. (p. 8)

In the case of nuclear weapons in Europe, there are many beliefs that antinuclear forces use to explain and define the social situation and to justify collective responses to it. The most important of these are the beliefs that new weapons increase the danger of war and that protests have the potential to halt their spread. Antinuclear forces also blame military establishments, claiming that they want to increase their power and importance by acquiring expensive and powerful weapons. They blame industrialists, claiming that they profit from the sale of arms and want the arms race to continue. They blame the U.S. government, claiming that it cares more about competition with the Soviet Union than about the security of Europe, and that it is trying to use Europe as a battlefield in order to avoid a war that would involve U.S. territory.

These West Germans protesting the arms race in 1983 carry a banner portraying the U.S. and the Soviet Union as vultures perched on "eggs" (bombs) in a "weapons nest." In Germany the vulture is often a symbol of old, worn out ideas, and the people shown between the two world powers are obviously taking things into their own hands.

Smelser went on to argue that in a society in which there is a sufficient level of strain and generalized beliefs about the sources of strain, social movements then depend on a **precipitating incident** that, as interpreted by generalized beliefs, triggers a collective response. In the case of the nuclear missiles, the most important precipitating incident was the actual introduction of cruise and Pershing II missiles in late 1983.

Mobilization is the next step—in which people gather into a crowd that is capable of producing collective behavior. Mobilization depends on a number of social factors. Communication must be good enough for people to know about what is happening and to be aware of opportunities for collective action. People must be available to participate and able to get together (McPhail and Miller, 1973). This last factor helps explain why young people—students in particular—are so well represented at demonstrations. Since they are less likely to have job or family responsibilities, they are more available.

Once mobilization occurs, the forces of **social control** are all that stand in the way of collective action, and these represent Smelser's final condition affecting the likelihood that collective behavior will take place. In South Korea, all of the first five of Smelser's social conditions for collective behavior are present, but, until recently, demonstrations have been rare. Why? One major reason appears to be the strict social control exercised by the South Korean government. Public assembly without official permission was illegal, and leaders of demonstrations were usually arrested and often jailed or beaten by police. Only when discontent with the government was severe enough to overcome such obstacles was collective action successful.

Some Problems with Mass Society and Structural Strain Theories Kornhauser's and Smelser's theories are sociologically important because they explicitly include social conditions in their explanations of social movements. They have been criticized, however, on several grounds, the most important being their heavy reliance on psychological explanations.

Structural strain and social isolation are always present in complex societies, but social movements are relatively rare occurrences. When a movement occurs, one can always note the existence of structural strain or social isolation. What this ignores is the fact that there are often *no* social movements in *spite* of the existence of strain or mass society conditions. It may be that social movements will not occur without strain in a society, critics argue, but strain by itself is not enough to bring it about.

In addition, as Tilly (1978a) and others argued in relation to theories of frustration and aggression, any attempt to explain social movements as an expression of individual psychological need ignores the importance of social organization. Classical theories underestimate the importance of social movements as organized political attempts to bring about change. As McAdam (1982) put it,

> If movement participants are motivated only by the desire to . . . manage "feelings of anxiety and futility," then we would hardly expect social movements to be effective. . . . In fact, however, movements are, and always have been, an important impetus to sociopolitical change. The American colonists defeated the British on the strength of an organized insurgent movement. Mao, Lenin, Khomeini, and Castro all came to power as a result of similar movements. An incumbent American president, Lyndon Johnson, was forced from office and this country's policy on Vietnam altered as a result of the antiwar movement. And through the collective protest efforts of blacks, the South's elaborate system of Jim Crow racism was dismantled in a matter of a decade. Are we to conclude that such significant historical processes were simply the unintended byproducts of a collective attempt at tension management? The argument is neither theoretically nor empirically convincing. (p. 18)

Oberschall (1973), McAdam (1982), and others argue that classical social movement theory falls short because it rests on a false view of the societies in which movements occur. Specifically, classical theories assume a pluralistic distribution of power in which no group dominates decision making and everyone has some access to major institutions. In such a world, it makes sense to view social movements and other forms of collective behavior as aberrations resulting from the personal troubles of individuals. Why else, after all, why would great numbers of people take to the streets and protest when legitimate avenues were available to them to make grievances known and to effect change?

One answer is that the distribution of power is not pluralistic. From a conflict point of view, legitimate means for changing a society are controlled by an elite, and the only way to bring about change is through some organized action. To go against dominant groups, however, requires *resources* as well as

motivation, and this brings us to more recent—and more sociological—theories of social movements.

Resource Mobilization Theory

Inequality, discontent, frustration, anxiety, and social isolation are nothing new to complex societies, and the relative rarity of social movements underscores the fact that such conditions, even when shared by many people, are not in themselves sufficient to bring about collective action (Jenkins and Perrow, 1977; Oberschall, 1973). In response to this inadequacy of classical social movement theories, **resource mobilization theory** argues that people with common interests form social movements only when they have access to resources—time, people, skills, money, and organization—that give them some hope of achieving their goals in spite of opposition from the powerful groups that dominate society (Jenkins, 1983; Lofland, 1985).

It takes time, energy, and money to change the world, and most people can spare little of either, especially if they are poor. This simple fact helps explain why so many social movements—even those that act in the interests of poor people—tend to draw heavily on the time and energy of middle- and upper-class, relatively well-educated people. The Cuban Revolution that brought Fidel Castro to power was founded by young professionals and well-educated intellectuals (Draper, 1962). Over two-thirds of the founders of the Chinese Communist Party came from upperclass—not peasant—backgrounds (Lee, 1968). A large percentage of the activists in the civil rights, anti-Vietnam War, women's, and nuclear freeze movements have been young college students, middle-class, nonworking women, professionals such as physicians and lawyers, and the elderly—all of whom have relatively high levels of free time and autonomy (Snow, Zurcher, and Eckland-Olson, 1980).

The fact that disadvantaged groups are the least likely to command the resources necessary to sustain a social movement has led several theorists to argue that such movements succeed only with support from the outside. In the civil rights movement, blacks had to attract the support of elite outsiders—in this case the federal government, upper-middle- and upper-class Northern whites, and young college students (McCarthy and Zald, 1973; Oberschall, 1973). Similarly, the farm workers movement relied on strong support from liberal churches and powerful labor unions (Jenkins,

1981b, 1983). As Jenkins and Perrow (1977) wrote, "collective action is rarely a viable option because of a lack of resources and the threat of repression. . . . When deprived groups do mobilize, it is due to the interjection of external resources" (p. 251).

As McAdam (1982) pointed out, this view suggests that most groups are powerless and that initiation of social movements lies with groups that control crucial resources. It is they, and not deprived groups, who are ultimately responsible for social movements and, therefore, for social change.

Resource mobilization theory is a substantial improvement over classical theories in several respects (see McAdam, 1982). First, it explicitly defines social movements as organized social behavior rather than characterizing them as little more than manifestations of shared feelings of tension, anxiety, and discontent. It has, in short, put the "social" back into social movements. Second, by taking social movements out of the realm of the psychological problems of individuals, mobilization theory makes movements more understandable as political actions that are as rationally motivated as any other political behavior including that of those who control social institutions.

Third, mobilization theory includes the influence of groups outside social movements in order to explain the emergence and development of social movements. Classical theories focused primarily on the characteristics of movements and their participants. Finally, mobilization theory underscores the importance of organization to the success of social movements. Movements do not depend only on the motivation of their participants; rather, like all organizations, they require a steady supply of resources that include everything from money to administrative skills.

Although mobilization theory has stimulated a great deal of interest in what was considered by many to be a dying field in sociology, it has several weaknesses. In general, it is more effective at explaining the success or failure of movements initiated by those who already have some power in society, as was the case with environmental and consumer groups (McCarthy and Zald, 1973). It is less successful at explaining movements among minorities who are generally excluded from legitimate means for bringing about change (Piven and Cloward, 1979).

It is important to note that the involvement of elites in social movements by powerless groups can have negative as well as positive effects (Jenkins, 1981b; Jenkins and Eckert, 1986). If a movement becomes dependent on outside support, it may take fewer risks for fear of alienating its sponsors. Since members of the elite have an interest in preserving the social arrangements that support their elite status, they may support some social movements in order to ultimately gain control over them and limit their effectiveness.

A more serious problem with resource mobilization theory is that by focusing on the importance of outside support, it underestimates the resources of minorities and their ability to bring about change on

In societies with substantial college populations, social movements find a valuable resource in students. In fact, student protests such as this one in the U.S. to protest South African apartheid often use boycotts of classes and other responsibilities as a form of protest, an action that is more likely to be tolerated by deans and professors than by employers.

Although leaders such as Martin Luther King, Jr., were more prominent and provided a national focus, it was from local black churches that the civil rights movement drew much of the strength and organization necessary for a prolonged struggle against enormous odds.

their own. McAdam's (1982) analysis of the black civil rights movement during the late 1950s suggests that it was not a sudden infusion of outside support that led to an increase of black civil rights activity; it was just the other way around. Increased militancy led to increased levels of outside support. In their analysis of strikes in France, Shorter and Tilly (1974) emphasized the importance of preexisting organization among workers and "the availability of a structure which identifies, accumulates, and communicates grievances on the one hand, and facilitates collective action on the other" (p. 284). As Morris (1984) shows, this was particularly important in the U.S. civil rights movement which was planned, organized, and led primarily on the local level using community resources and networks of urban churches and their ministers (see also Jenkins, 1985; Jenkins and Eckert, 1986; Morrison, 1987).

An additional problem with mobilization theory is that it has yet to include a clear definition of "resources." Since the concept can include anything from organizational skills to money, it is usually possible to find an increase of some kind of resource that precedes the emergence, rise, or decline of a social movement. It is also possible, therefore, to find many instances in which resources increased without leading to a social movement. As theorists define resources more narrowly, it will be possible to test the theory more conclusively.

Political Process Theory

As we have seen, whereas classical movement theory focuses on the intensity of feeling among participants, resource mobilization theory focuses on the importance of support from outside the movement. Skocpol (1979), Tilly (1978a), and McAdam (1982), and others concentrate on an important additional aspect of the problem: what goes on inside and outside social movements. At the heart of **political process theory** is the idea that social movements "develop in response to an ongoing process of interaction between movement groups and the larger sociopolitical environment they seek to change" (McAdam, 1982, p. 40).

The emergence of a political protest movement depends on a combination of factors. First, there must be an opportunity to bring about change, which means that the more vulnerable dominant groups and institutions are, the more likely open opposition to them will be. When the general political situation in a country is unstable, protest movements are more likely to occur, because the forces that might oppose them are weaker and less well organized. In their analysis of strikes in France, Shorter and Tilly (1974) found that strike activity in France was most common during times of intense struggle over who would rule the country.

As Skocpol (1979) argued in her analysis of the French, Chinese, and Russian revolutions, this is particularly true in the case of revolutions through which entire social systems may undergo radical change. In each of these cases the state was in crisis, and its inability to perform the basic tasks that defined its role as a social institution prompted opposition from deprived groups such as the peasantry and aggravated old conflicts among dominant groups as well. The 1917 Russian Revolution took place while the Russian state was in turmoil over repeated defeats in World War I. More recently, the Solidarity labor movement in Poland began amid general social unrest over poor economic conditions (Ash, 1984).

Second, the emergence and success of movements depends on the level of organization that exists among opposing groups. The black civil rights movement owed much of its success to the existing organizational network of black churches (Morris, 1984). Widespread church membership among southern blacks provided a source of social movement members, facilitated communication, gave members a sense of belonging that encouraged them to stay with the movement, and generated leaders such as Martin Luther King. Tilly's (1978a) studies of social movements in Europe show a steady change over the past 400 years from temporary disorganized movements to more organized efforts with lasting influence (see also Shorter and Tilly, 1974; Tilly and Tilly, 1981; and Tilly, Tilly, and Tilly, 1975).

Third, even when dominant groups and institutions are vulnerable to pressure and subordinate groups have the potential to organize a social movement, collective action depends on how potential participants *think* about their situation. Movements tend to emerge only when people begin to (1) question the legitimacy of authorities, (2) assert what they want as rights, and (3) believe that they are not helpless and that they have the potential to bring about change (Piven and Cloward, 1979).

As McAdam (1982) summarized this part of political process theory, the emergence of social movements depends on expanding political opportunities, the organizational strength of subordinate groups, and "cognitive liberation," or new ways of thinking about their situation and prospects for change (see Figure 21-2). Both the availability of political opportunities and organizational potential are the result of long-term social changes, and "cognitive liberation" results both from the perceived vulnerability of dominant

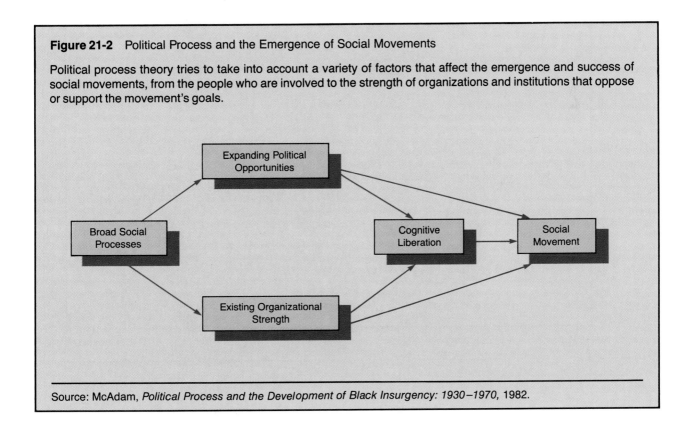

Figure 21-2 Political Process and the Emergence of Social Movements

Political process theory tries to take into account a variety of factors that affect the emergence and success of social movements, from the people who are involved to the strength of organizations and institutions that oppose or support the movement's goals.

Source: McAdam, *Political Process and the Development of Black Insurgency: 1930–1970*, 1982.

ONE STEP FURTHER 21-1:
The Civil Rights Movement, White Opposition, and the Government: Political Process Theory in Action

The civil rights movement provides a vivid illustration of political process theory, for as McAdam (1982) shows, blacks used political protest to provoke responses from their white supremacist opponents which were so extreme that the federal government intervened on behalf of blacks.

Figure B-21-1 covers the period from 1961 into 1965 and shows the timing of actions by civil rights groups, white supremacists, and the government. What is most striking is that the peaks in civil rights activity (blue line) almost always occur *before* peaks in white supremacist activity (red line) which, in turn, are often followed by peaks in government action (gold line). In other words, the data show how civil rights activities provoked white supremacist reactions which in turn forced the government to act. As a result, the movement skillfully elicited federal involvement in the defense of their rights and the promotion of their cause.

Figure B-21-1

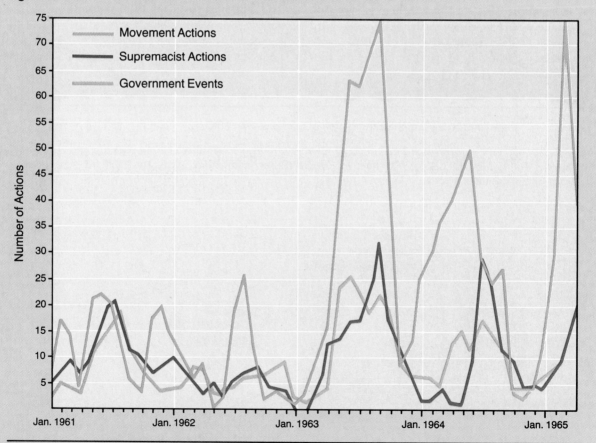

Source: McAdam, 1982, Figure 7.5.

groups and institutions and from the organizational strength of the subordinate group.

Once a movement emerges, its success depends on a variety of factors that involve dynamics within the movement, its opposition, and the relationship between the two (see One Step Further 21-1). Protest movements may encounter violent opposition from governing institutions. This, in turn, may provoke outraged responses that strengthen the movement's organization by increasing membership and outside support. It may also produce a response that is so violent and repressive—as was the case with the Solidarity movement in Poland—that even the most well organized movement cannot sustain itself. To a lesser degree, this also has been true of the U.S. labor union movement which, especially in the early part of this century, had to struggle against the powerful and often overwhelming opposition of the capitalist class whose resources included not only great wealth and control over capital, but influence over government officials, legislatures, and the courts (see Griffin et al., 1986).

A political process approach offers some advantages over its predecessors. Its most important feature may be its inclusiveness, for it tries to cover the entire range between the characteristics of participants and groups and the society in which they and the forces they oppose exist. It fills an enormous gap between classical and resource mobilization theory and goes significantly beyond them. Sociological understanding of collective behavior in general and social movements in particular has come a long way from Le Bon's crowd psychology.

As we have seen, social movements often play an important part in changing the cultural, structural, and ecological conditions in which people live, but they are only one of many sources of social change. A fuller discussion of these appears in the next chapter.

SUMMARY

1. Collective behavior refers to how we think, feel, and behave as members of crowds and masses. In crowds, collective behavior includes casual, conventional, expressive, and collective action. In addition to these kinds of collective behavior, fads and fashion also occur in masses.

2. Some of the most volatile forms of collective behavior are mobs, riots, panics, and hysteria.

3. Le Bon's theory of mob psychology was one of the earliest attempts to understand collective behavior. His theory emphasizes the importance of leaders, the like-mindedness and irrationality of crowd members, and people copying one another's behavior. Blumer also viewed crowds as irrational, uncivilized collections of people.

4. From a social interaction perspective, collective behavior involves interpretations of behavior and defining the situation. Emergent norm theory argues that people observe one another's behavior in crowds in order to establish the norms that will apply in that situation. Decision theory and game theory emphasize the rational calculations that we make in deciding how to behave in crowd and mass situations.

5. Rumor is an important ingredient in the social interaction that makes up collective behavior because it is often a major source of information. As in all social situations, people perform different roles in the rumor process, and the patterns through which rumor develops and spreads depend on the situation.

6. Social movements are organized, collective attempts to change or preserve some aspects of a social environment.

7. Classical theories have in common a reliance on the view that movements develop in order to relieve psychological strain brought about by strain in the social environment. Frustration-aggression theory argues that relative deprivation leads to frustration, which in turn leads to social movements. Rising expectations as well as rapid improvement followed by sharp declines (the J-curve) have also been suggested as causes of frustration and social action.

8. According to Kornhauser, the existence of mass society in which people feel socially isolated produces feelings of anxiety, and people engage in collective behavior and social movements in order to relieve such feelings and restore a feeling of connection with others.

9. Smelser's structural strain theory is more complex than most preceding theories, but shares with them a view of collective behavior and social movements as based in psychological needs that arise from social conditions. Strain in social conditions, he argues, leads to uncertainty and

tension among people who then seize upon generalized beliefs to explain their condition in much the same way that people appeal to magic. Such beliefs are then used to justify collective action around a precipitating incident. The success of collective behavior depends both on the ability of the movement to mobilize participants and on the ability of authorities to exercise social control.

10. Classical theories have been criticized on many grounds, including their reliance on psychology to explain social phenomena; their failure to link changes in psychological states such as frustration and relative deprivation with the occurrence of collective behavior; and their failure to see the importance of social change as a major goal of social movements.

11. Resource mobilization theory focuses on social organization by explaining the development of social movements in terms of available resources.

12. Political process theory goes beyond resource mobilization and classical theory by looking at what goes on both within social movements and in their relationship to major social institutions. In this model, movements depend on opportunities, existing organizational resources, and a shared perception that collective behavior is legitimate and has some chance of success.

KEY TERMS

Looking Elsewhere

Having studied Chapter 21, you might want to look at related discussions in *Human Arrangements*, which include

- the women's movement (Chapter 13, pp. 366–73)
- the civil rights movement (Chapter 12, pp. 331–35, 337)
- the labor movement (Chapter 18, pp. 492–94, 497–500)
- revolution and political change (Chapter 19, pp. 537–39)

RECOMMENDED READINGS

FREEMAN, J. (Ed.). (1983). *Social movements of the sixties and seventies*. New York: Longman. A penetrating look at the factors that affected the emergence and progress of 18 social movements of the 1960s and 1970s.

GAMSON, W. A., FIREMAN, B., and RYTINA, S. (1982). *Encounters with unjust authority*. Homewood, IL: Dorsey Press. An intriguing experimental study of what it takes for small groups to rebel against the unjust demands of those in authority.

GENEVIE, L. (Ed.). (1978). *Collective behavior and social movements*. Ithaca, IL: Peacock. A useful collection that surveys the broad range of collective behavior.

LIEBMAN, R. C., and WUTHNOW, R. (1983). *The new Christian right*. New York: Aldine. A collection of essays that tries to explain why many conservative evangelicals have joined social movements to bring about political change in the U.S., and the significance of this political activism for both religion and politics.

NYDEN, P. W. (1984). *Steelworkers rank-and-file: The political economy of a union reform movement*. New York: Praeger. Based on interviews with dozens of union workers in a midwest steel plant, this excellent study shows how rank-and-file union members rebelled against authorities in an attempt to gain a voice in the affairs of their own union.

WELLER, R. P., and GUGGENHEIM, S. E. (Eds.). (1982). *Power and protest in the countryside: Studies of rural unrest in Asia, Europe, and Latin America*. Durham, NC: Duke University Press Policy Studies. A collection of articles that explores protest and rebellion in the rural areas of a variety of societies.

22 Social Change

Questions about social change are relatively easy to ask, but they are among the most difficult of those that sociologists try to answer. Why did the women's movement emerge with such strength in the 1960s? Where did capitalism and socialism come from? Will the widespread use of computers make it easier for government to invade the privacy of individuals? How will AIDS affect homosexual and heterosexual relationships?

Much of the relevant information about social change is historical, and it is, therefore, especially difficult to scientifically measure the factors that might account for the change. Added to this is the difficulty with most research problems that sociologists deal with: social change involves simultaneously many factors that affect one another in complex ways. New social ideas and relationships do not come about through "events" that can be precisely located in time or simply explained. We cannot say that the modern women's movement began on January 4, 1963, in New York City. History is not a simple sequence of events, each of which is neatly caused by previous events. It is, rather, like a river into which flow many streams that mingle and affect both one another and the river itself in countless different ways.

CULTURE, STRUCTURE, AND SOCIAL CHANGE

As we have seen in many previous chapters, the functional and conflict perspectives provide two major sociological frameworks for explaining what goes on in societies. These perspectives have also been applied to the problem of social change. Before discussing and evaluating their usefulness, we turn first to a look at some of the ways in which culture and social structure contribute to change.

Cultural Sources of Change

As we saw in Chapter 18, Weber's classic book *The Protestant Ethic and the Spirit of Capitalism* analyzed the impact of beliefs and values on the structure of economic activity. According to the Calvinist religion, the assignment of people to heaven or hell is determined at birth, and nothing a person can do will alter that fate. Calvinism also placed a high value on frugal living and hard work, and only through success in a "calling" could people lower their anxiety over what their fate would be. Prior to Calvin, the idea of a "calling" in Christianity applied only to religious occupations. Calvin, however, defined all occupations as callings and this injected into everyday work a new religious fervor.

Weber argued that Calvinist beliefs and values contributed to a social environment that fostered the emergence of capitalism, for as an economic system capitalism depends on the accumulation of wealth, which is then available for investment in capital. Weber did not argue that Calvinism alone *caused* capitalism to appear, but he did believe that in this case religious belief played an important part in fostering the development of a new economic system.

There are countless examples of the effect of ideas on social environments. Albert Einstein's theories about the laws that govern the universe were basic to the discovery of atomic fission and the invention of nuclear weapons that have changed the nature of warfare and the structure of political power in the world. The writings of Karl Marx and Friedrich Engels became the cultural basis for revolutions that have radically affected social life in a wide range of societies from the Soviet Union to China to Cuba and Nicaragua. In similar ways the U.S. Declaration of Independence and Constitution embody ideas that have been used as inspirations and blueprints in the transformation of many societies.

As the last two examples show, the effect of culture on social change is particularly evident when ideas take the form of ideology, for an ideology is a set of ideas that serves the function of explaining or justifying particular social arrangements. In his role as leader in the civil rights movement, Martin Luther King, Jr., increased his support among whites by appealing to strongly held values placed on equality, fairness, and justice. He was able to enlist the support of whites who otherwise did not share the high value he placed on racial equality in its own right.

Culture also causes change in more direct ways, especially through norms that explicitly require change. The 1954 Supreme Court decision that outlawed racially segregated schools and the 1983 decision that banned the use of gender by insurance companies in setting rates for life insurance and annuities changed the social environment, as did federal regulations requiring affirmative action in hiring and federal legislation requiring equal treatment of male and female students in schools that receive federal aid.

Structural Sources of Change

Just as new ideas often bring about change in social structure, so too does structural change affect culture. One way to break down stereotypes is to increase social interaction between those who hold stereotypes and those who are the object of them (see Miller and Brewer, 1984). This is particularly true when the people involved must cooperate with one another in order to achieve shared goals (Allport, 1954).

Laws that forbid racial segregation are aspects of culture that affect the structure of social relationships. Increasing the frequency of interaction between people of different races is a structural change that can, in turn, have the effect of weakening cultural stereotypes. It has long been noted that it is almost impossible to change people's beliefs about and perceptions of others by requiring them to do so; but this example shows how changes in the structure of social relationships—how often people of different races interact with one another—can affect how they perceive and think about other people.

Such effects of structure on culture are common in social life. Over the last several decades people in the U.S. have become increasingly tolerant and supportive of women working outside the home and having careers. Some of this cultural shift is probably due to the entry of massive numbers of women into the labor force as the economy shifted from industry to services and the demand for secretaries and other service workers mushroomed. As women had fewer children and growing opportunities outside the home, they had new reason to question the terms on which they were living their lives and to seek alternatives. It

Even the strongest stereotypes and prejudices may not survive situations whose structure requires people to depend on one another. In this 1971 picture, a black marine in Vietnam refuses to leave his wounded white friend.

was only a matter of time before cultural ideas about men and women began to adjust to this structural change.

It is important to keep in mind that behind the relatively small scale structural changes that we identify around us often lie major macro-structural changes that take place over many generations. As Tilly (1984) argues, in order to understand social change it is necessary to include what he calls "big structures" and "large processes" such as the development of capitalism or the emergence of powerful nation states. The macro-structures that make up economic, political, and religious systems form the basic limitations of social life from which many aspects of everyday life take shape. Changes in the roles of men and women, the organization of family life, or the importance of religion in people's lives can only be understood in the context of major institutional arrangements which, barring revolutions, change only over long periods of time.

We turn now to the ways in which the functional and conflict approaches explain social change in terms of the effects of culture and social structure on societies.

The Functional Perspective

Durkheim developed the idea that a society is a complex network of interdependent parts—such as the family, government, religion, and economy—each of which either contributes to or interferes with the maintenance of the whole. Parsons (1937, 1951, 1966b, 1971) built on Durkheim's work by exploring what he regarded as the most important sociological problem: What causes groups and societies to stay together or to fall apart? How do culture and social structure affect the adaptability and maintenance of society?

Parsons believed that societies have built-in mechanisms that help them adapt and remain stable. Shared cultural ideas and the relationships between their various parts help a society maintain equilibrium—or "balance"—among its different parts. When strain develops within the system or is introduced from the outside, it stimulates change that helps to reduce it. Social change, then, is a process through which societies "regain their balance" as they adjust to strain that arises through their normal functioning as systems.

Consider what happened in 1986 when police and federal agents began a major effort to stem the flow of the potent form of cocaine known as "crack" in New York City. Their efforts were so successful that the criminal justice system was soon faced with overcrowded jails and prisons, long court backlogs, and overburdened prosecutors, public defenders, and probation officers (*New York Times*, November 24, 1986, p. A1). The policing system was working just as it was supposed to, and yet enormous strains in the criminal justice system resulted from it.

Several changes are possible in this kind of situation. Crimes such as drug use might be reclassified as

Overcrowding in jails and prisons has become one of the most pressing problems in the U.S. criminal justice system. It is a problem that is, ironically, aggravated by vigorous law enforcement.

legal acts (as some officials recently urged), reducing the number of arrests and prosecutions. More prisons might be built, diverting resources from other uses, such as the relief of poverty. Or, courts might dispense with some civil rights that "slow down" trials—such as the right of appeal. Each of these changes is a possible response to strain that develops through the normal operation of the institutional "parts" that make up a society.

Although Parsons' ideas had considerable influence in the 1940s and 1950s, they came under attack during the 1960s. Because he was interested primarily in the problem of how societies maintain themselves as systems of social relationships and cultural ideas, he paid relatively little attention to social conflict and social change. Like all investigators, he was selective in his choice of research problems; but his focus on social order during a period of intense unrest and awareness of injustice in existing social conditions led many sociologists to misperceive Parsons and the entire functional perspective as inherently supportive of the status quo, including social inequality. As civil rights and antiwar protests challenged the status quo in the United States, any focus on the maintenance of social order as a theoretical problem became increasingly unpopular among sociologists.

In fact, however, leading functional theorists had recognized since the late 1940s that "strain, tension, contradiction, and discrepancy between the component parts of social structure" are inevitable in any society and that these often produce positive social change (Merton, 1948). Merton and others, such as Lewis Coser (1956, 1967), incorporated important elements of social conflict into the functional perspective and highlighted the fact that cultural ideas and social structures can have dysfunctional as well as functional consequences.

The Conflict Perspective

While Parsons' functional theory views change as an adaptive response to disturbances in an otherwise balanced society, the conflict perspective focuses on different aspects of society and social change. Both perspectives view change as a normal social process, but they differ in their view of what holds societies together. To Parsons, society is held together primarily by a consensus over values. The conflict perspective, however, views society as held together by the ability of the powerful to coerce the weak, and the resulting

conflict among different groups is a continuing source of change.

Marx and Engels (1848/1932) believed that "All history is the history of class conflict"—which in capitalist societies means a struggle between those who own the means of production and those who do not. Class divisions inevitably lead to struggles to alter social conditions that produce and support exploitation and inequality. As Schaff (1970) summarized some of Marx's early ideas,

> To liberate the individual . . . it is necessary to effect a change in social relations and institutions, to overthrow them by overthrowing the prevalent pattern of class relations. (p. 31)

From a conflict perspective, oppressed groups cannot depend on their society to reach an equilibrium that includes social justice, for without conflict, social arrangements change slowly and tend to remain stable. Consequently, Marx believed that societies inevitably change, but not necessarily for the better; rather, they often perpetuate inequality and injustice in the name of stability and in the interests of powerful elites.

The conflict perspective identifies important aspects of social change, but, like Parsons' functional views, in its extreme form it oversimplifies societies and the process of change. As Dahrendorf (1958) pointed out, the functional and conflict perspectives focus on different but complementary aspects of social life. All societies represent an ongoing tension between social forces that would pull them apart and those that keep them together. Social structure is a source of cohesion and conflict (Merton, 1968).

It is important to note as Simmel did in 1904 that conflict is often functional in societies, and supports cultural values. In the simplest sense, in order to fight with one another we must *interact*, both with our allies and with our enemies. Increased interaction, in turn, can increase solidarity in groups and reveal important differences in points of view that must then be dealt with. In this way, conflict can improve relations within and between groups.

Conflict is often functional in a larger sense as well (Coser, 1956, 1967). Our legal system is based on "adversarial" relationships in which both sides in a dispute are represented by lawyers who openly conflict as they fight for their clients. Our government is based on conflict among various political parties, an arrangement that we consider more desirable than

Puzzles: What Made Abortion a Public Issue?

Prior to the 1970s abortion was never a seriously debated moral issue in the United States. Why did it suddenly emerge as a hotly contested passionate debate that involved primarily women?

The answer has much to do with the women's movement and the Supreme Court, as you will discover in this chapter.

rule by a single group. In many ways, conflict is deliberately used to ensure that our society functions in certain ways.

Social conflict arises because internal contradictions are inevitable in any complex society. We generally value equality and fairness and yet our society includes cultural ideas and social structures that discriminate against minorities such as nonwhites and women. We value both economic progress and a physical environment free of pollution; and we value the efficiency of rationally structured bureaucracies, and yet we also value the attention to individuals and their feelings that bureaucracies ignore.

The division of industrial societies into social classes based on unequal distributions of wealth, power, and prestige produces an inherent structural contradiction: each class often prospers at the expense of another. The structure of industrial society produces conflict between classes, and conflict, in turn, produces pressures for new arrangements and accommodations.

Social Movements   As we saw in Chapter 21, social movements are one of the most noticeable manifestations of social conflict and are a major source of change. Social movements are structural in that they are organized and focus on changing some aspect of social relationships, particularly those that affect inequality.

It is important to remember that the appearance of social movements itself depends on both culture and social structure; that is, that social movements are as much an effect of social change as they are a cause. The importance of social conditions in the emergence of social movements is startlingly clear in the case of

the abortion controversy in the U.S. Luker (1984) found that before the 1850s there were no legal restrictions on abortion. Abortion was widespread and practiced primarily by nonphysicians such as midwives and herbalists, and the first attempts to restrict abortion were mounted by physicians as part of their attempt to build a professional monopoly over medical care. To do this they attacked both the competence of nonphysicians and the relatively open availability of abortion to women. They were so successful in both areas that between 1850 and 1890 every state of the Union passed laws that allowed only physicians to perform abortions and then only when the pregnancy threatened the mother's life.

The effect of these laws was not to outlaw abortion, but to grant physicians a monopoly over the medical procedure and therefore to limit its availability. For the next half-century, abortion was not a public issue. It was regarded as a medical issue, not a moral one. In the early 1960s, some physicians became concerned over the fact that the law was ambiguous about the growing practice of performing abortions not only to save a mother's life, but to safeguard her mental health as well by terminating a pregnancy when the emotional strain of bearing a deformed child threatened to overwhelm the mother. This concern led 16 states to amend their statutes to include mental health as a valid consideration in abortion decisions. Once again the decision was prompted by the medical community without a public moral debate.

In 1973, however, the Supreme Court's decision in *Roe* v. *Wade* overturned all laws designed to regulate abortion and returned to women control over the decision to have an abortion. The Court focused on the Fourteenth Amendment which states that no State "shall deprive any person of life, liberty, or property without due process of law." A fetus, the Court ruled, is not a person subject to the protection of the Constitution.

Since that decision, abortion has been available on demand, and it was here, Luker argued, that the current struggle began. The pro-choice movement is led primarily by highly educated professional career women for whom the right to abortion is crucial to their ability to maintain their position in highly demanding, competitive careers. The anti-abortion movement, however, consists largely of less educated housewives whose husbands are either skilled workers or small businessmen. For them, Luker argued, abortion on demand is an attack on motherhood itself, and,

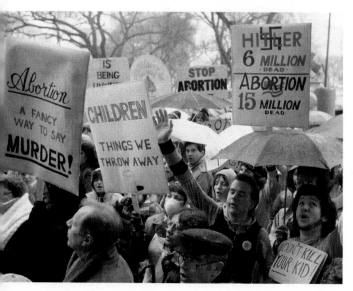

These pro-choice marchers in San Francisco and their opponents typify the forces that oppose each other in the continuing controversy over the rights of women and the rights of unborn children.

therefore, on the role that provides their lives with much of their worth and meaning.

Both these social movements depended on a particular set of cultural and structural conditions in order to emerge as opposing forces. It is unlikely that the Supreme Court decision would have occurred without the activism of professional women in a decade of intense feminist activity. It is also unlikely that the response of the pro-life movement would have been so extreme were it not for the threat to the roles of housewife and mother that many women experienced in the face of the women's movement and the continuing surge of mothers into the labor force.

Some Problems with Functional and Conflict Theories

Functional theories explain cultural and structural change as adaptations to social and physical conditions. From this point of view, it is tempting to think of particular social arrangements as necessary. Some argue that divisions of labor based on gender allow societies to accomplish the essential tasks of production and reproduction more efficiently (Parsons and Bales, 1953). In some ways, such arguments are based on the commonsense notion that if something exists, there must be a good reason for it. After all, the complex relationships between men and women did not come about by accident, and so we may search for the cause that explains their origins as well as their continuing existence.

Goody (1976) argued that in early hunter-gatherer societies, it was more efficient for men to hunt and women to care for children, since hunting requires days of extended travel and children require almost continuous attention. It would be difficult for mothers to both tend to the breast-feeding of their children and go on long, arduous hunting expeditions. Physical conditions provide an explanation for a gender-based division of labor in such societies. As revealing as such perspectives are, however, they can mislead us if we use them to explain or justify existing social arrangements by searching single-mindedly for their adaptive value to society. They must be used carefully for several reasons.

First, if we think long and hard enough, we can always think of a reason for the existence of a cultural idea or social structure, and this may lead to the conclusion that all social arrangements are necessary simply because they exist. It is like the old story of a peasant who first shoots holes in the fence and then paints bull's-eyes around them (Geertz, 1973). As Merton (1948) pointed out some time ago, "whatever is, is right" is both a fallacy and a misapplication of the functional perspective.

Second, social structures are closely related to one another. Industrial societies are structured in such a way that most workers do not live and work at home. In families with children it is difficult for both parents to work and still care for their children. Many argue from this that society suffers when mothers work and leave the care of their children to others, often relying on the justification that the identification of women with child care goes back thousands of years. This ignores the fact that the economy and the family are related to each other, and that if the economy were organized as it was before the Industrial Revolution, women would not experience this conflict. That is why some segments of the women's movement argue not for an end to the family, but for a restructuring of economic life and its relation to the family.

Third, it is easy to argue that a social arrangement is necessary for the perpetuation of the status quo, but this does not mean that it is desirable to do so (Friedman, 1974; Harris, 1979). As functional analysis has long indicated, social arrangements frequently benefit some groups at the expense of others. The division of labor between men and women may have some adaptive value for society; but a male monopoly on the most culturally valued tasks—such as production, politics, and warfare—allows them to maintain a privileged position at the expense of women.

Even when a social arrangement has functional consequences, it often not only harms those in some social categories, but also produces latent dysfunctions for society as a whole (Merton, 1968). Discrimination against women, for example, deprives society of the skills and talents of more than half the population and has negative effects on the happiness and mental health of millions of women (Bernard, 1972). It is not enough to say, "we must confine men and women to different roles in order to preserve our way of life," for we must ask if our way of life is worth preserving intact.

Finally, even if a social arrangement once had adaptive value, as conditions change, its usefulness to society may change as well. It is like the story of the man who watches his wife cut two inches from the end of a ham before she puts it in a large roasting pan. "Why do you do that?" he asks. "The pan is big enough for the whole ham."

"Because my mother always did," she replies.

He asks her mother, who answers, "I guess because that's the way *my* mother always did it." The grandmother's response is simple: "We were poor, and my roasting pan was too short."

We do not feed ourselves by ranging far from home in search of wild game—economic production and military defense in industrial societies depend far more on brains than on physical strength. Some scholars estimate that some 29 percent of white women born during the 1950s may remain childless (Bloom, 1982). In comparison with earlier generations, those women who do become mothers have fewer children and spend a far smaller portion of their lives caring for them. Infants no longer must depend on a mother's breast for nourishment, and children spend most of their waking hours in schools, with friends, and in front of television sets. Under such conditions, it is unclear that *any* role except the actual bearing of children must necessarily be performed exclusively by women or by men.

Just as single-minded attention to functional aspects of change can lead us astray, so can the attempt to explain all change in terms of social conflict. New technologies and their impact on social life often do not result from social conflict. Nor does conflict theory fully explain the complex ways in which changes in one area, such as economic arrangements, affect others, such as the family.

A sensible approach to theories of change recognizes that each illuminates selected aspects of an enormously complex process. From a conflict perspective, the women's movement represents the organized dissatisfaction of millions of women with their social circumstances. From a functional point of view, equality for women would have many functional consequences, including a healthier economy, improved health for both men and women, and the realization of important values about social justice.

POPULATION, ECOLOGY, AND SOCIAL CHANGE

Theories that focus on population and ecology as sources of change try to predict patterns of change and the speed with which it occurs. Many early theories tended to be descriptive—focusing primarily on patterns of change; but some recent theories pay attention to explanations as well. Before discussing and evaluating these theories, we begin by applying the ecological framework: How do population, the environment, and technology stimulate change?

Ecology and the Physical Environment

Because they represent interdependencies among living things in relation to physical environments, ecosystems constantly change through a process called **succession** (see Hawley, 1986). As one species thrives by consuming others, its food source declines as its population grows, and resulting starvation sends its population on a downward slide. Or, a change in the physical environment may benefit some forms of life at the expense of others: water pollution kills fish but supports bacteria and algae. Humans benefit from covering land with buildings, but most other forms of life do not (except, perhaps, for rats and cockroaches).

Human populations initiate succession by changing patterns of consumption (what and how much we consume); by altering the physical environment; and by changing population size or distribution. These sources of change depend heavily, in turn, on technology. Our preference for eating beef leads us to use land inefficiently. Land that could be used to cultivate crops is, instead, used to grow food for cattle, and the nutritional value of their meat is less than that of the food they consume. It is more efficient to eat corn than it is to feed it to cattle that transform it into beef.

Succession also takes place as we alter the physical environment. Much of the early work of sociologists such as Robert Park and Ernest Burgess focused on how urban areas develop as physical environments (Park, Burgess, and McKenzie, 1925). Over the last century, for example, New York City's Harlem changed from an area of pastures to an upper-class neighborhood, then a lower-middle-class neighborhood, and finally, today, a largely black ghetto (Osofsky, 1966). Succession is still commonplace in urban environments. "Urban renewal," for example, typically transforms run-down neighborhoods by restoring buildings. This, however, displaces residents who can no longer afford to live there, and what was, perhaps, a working-class neighborhood becomes a middle-class neighborhood.

Such changes also result from the migration of groups whose subculture differs from that of those already living there. One ethnic group moves in, and another moves out in search of a culturally homogeneous environment (Bressler, 1960).

Population

Perhaps the most important source of ecological succession is the size and distribution of population, for these directly affect how much people consume and how they use land. A growing population creates pressure that may lead to technological innovation—such as the invention of the plow—and this, in turn, both supports larger populations and alters their relationship with physical environments by making it possible to overcultivate the land, exhaust the fertility of the soil, and promote soil erosion (Harris, 1974).

The rapid growth of the world's population during the last two centuries has resulted primarily from increased production supported by new technology and increasingly complex divisions of labor, and from the dramatic lowering of death rates, particularly among infants and children. In many societies, however, control over many causes of death has made populations grow faster than the production of goods needed to support them.

The technology for controlling disease was first discovered in rapidly developing industrial societies in North America and Europe at a time when birth rates were falling. As death rates declined, so did birth rates; and, while populations grew because death rates fell faster than birth rates, expanding industry allowed them to support more people. Once these medical technologies were discovered, however, they were easily and cheaply applied in societies whose birth rates remained high and whose economies could barely support rapidly growing populations. This ecological change has reached crisis proportions in much of the world in which population now grows much faster than production. While world population grew slowly prior to 1800—perhaps no more than 0.1 percent per year—it now grows by more than 1.7 percent. While it once took nearly 700 years for the world population to double, at current rates it will double in only 40 years (Population Reference Bureau, 1987; Thompson and Lewis, 1965).

The resulting imbalance between population and production contributes to extreme poverty in rural areas that make up most of developing countries, whose people migrate in droves to already crowded cities, seeking opportunities that simply do not exist. Such "overurbanization" plagues many developing countries, such as India, Egypt, and Mexico. In New Delhi, India, thousands of urban "squatters" sleep in vacant lots, school playgrounds, and city streets. As we saw in Chapter 5, Mexico City is rapidly becoming the largest city in the world—inhabited primarily by unemployed peasants—and demands for water will soon outrun the supply. It is ironic that what threatens to become a major ecological and social disaster was precipitated by an undeniably positive innovation—the elimination of many diseases as causes of death.

Population processes also prompt social change by altering the age structure. As we saw in Chapter 14, the job opportunities available in a society may not match the age structure, creating an imbalance that is difficult both for individuals and societies as a whole. As the U.S. population ages, the number of teenagers declines and the number of elderly increases. One result is that there are more opportunities for young people than there are young people to fill them; and there are more elderly people who would like to continue working than there are jobs for them. This is a case of structural lag in which the occupational struc-

ture has not yet "caught up" to changes in the age structure (Riley et al., 1988).

When we realize that humans affect ecosystems in countless ways by initiating thousands of ecological changes, we can see how difficult it is to understand where the process of ecological succession will lead. The danger of this is that our ecosystems may change in ways that no longer support human life. In ecosystems, one form of life is no more "valuable" than another: to us, a polluted lake may be awful, but to bacteria and algae, it is an ideal environment. Although most cultures may value humanity as the most important form of life, in ecosystems, we enjoy no such privileged standing.

Cohorts   The birth cohort is an important concept in the study of social change, for as each new generation is socialized, its members continue existing traditions and modify them through their own fresh

The shift in the portrayal of "Uncle Sam" between World War II enlistment posters and a 1972 anti-Vietnam War protest illustrates the changes that can occur between cohorts who grow up under different social conditions. How do you feel about each of these? What does that say about your cohort?

experience (Ryder, 1965; Riley, 1987). Each generation has a comparatively low level of commitment to a past it has not experienced, and so it brings with it an openness to new ideas and social relationships (Mannheim, 1952). The inevitable movement of new cohorts through the stages of the life course under historical circumstances that differ for each generation makes social change inevitable.

During the 1960s, older generations had a hard time understanding or accepting the antiwar activities of many young people. Many older people identified the Vietnam War with their experience of World War II and the Korean War—it was simply another occasion for patriotism, self-sacrifice, and obedience to the government. Young people who were not even born when World War II ended were less likely to identify Vietnam with previous wars and were able to be far more critical of the government's policies. In turn, many of those who now read this book have no memory of the Vietnam War and the protest movements of the 1960s, and so might have difficulty understanding why young men would refuse to fight.

Each generation is both a source of new ideas and a continuing threat to the perpetuation of social environments. In the Israeli Kibbutz, younger members often feel a strong pull toward the comforts of city life, for they did not share in the early years of excitement and challenge when the Kibbutz was first tried as a new form of community and family life (Bettelheim, 1969). Many Jews also worry because the number of people who actually experienced the Holocaust grows smaller each year. There are fewer "witnesses" who can speak of the horror, who can perpetuate the memory of it in order to ensure that it will never happen again.

Technology

Technological change occurs in three basic ways. A **discovery** is an instance of finding out about something that already exists (such as gravity or the effects of cocaine on the brain), whereas an **invention** is something new created from things that already exist (such as the plow or the computer chip). Although discovery and invention obviously have been crucial sources of innovation in the world as a whole, the introduction of new technology in most societies has occurred through the process of **diffusion**, which is the borrowing of knowledge from other societies (see Rogers, 1983). As far as we know, printing was invented in the sixth century by Chinese who used

engraved wooden blocks. During the next 1,000 years printing technology spread from China through the Middle East and Europe, and a German printer named Johann Gutenberg is credited with inventing movable reusable type in the fifteenth century. Printing technology is now used around the world, and yet it was not invented anew in each society.

A major part of the ecological perspective focuses on the ways in which societies apply discoveries and inventions to physical environments. As we have seen, technology affects the niches human societies occupy in ecosystems; but it also affects the cultural and structural characteristics of social environments. Money transformed economic activity by making it possible to engage in trade for profit, and without money, capitalism could never have developed. The invention of printing and movable type made books available to a wide population for the first time. This greatly increased literacy, and the rapid spread of ideas stimulated the development of scientific, political, religious, and philosophical thought (see Eisenstein, 1980). In similar ways, the computer is now revolutionizing our ability to store, retrieve, and communicate information with phenomenal speed and accuracy.

The invention of the cotton gin in the late 1700s made the production of cotton in the American South far more profitable, and this led to a dramatic increase in the slave population (Rasmussen, 1982). The Industrial Revolution rested on an astonishingly rapid series of innovations in the design of machinery and the development of nonhuman sources of energy. Industrialization, in turn, virtually transformed work and affected institutions such as the family and schools.

The mechanization of agriculture in the 1930s and 1940s helped to transform the U.S. from a nation of farmers into a nation of urban workers whose entire food supply is provided by less than 3 percent of the population (Rasmussen, 1982). The decline in the demand for manual farm labor also stimulated a mass migration of southern blacks from rural areas, first to southern cities, and then to the cities of the North. The urbanization of blacks led to better education and job opportunities, and these, in turn, helped to lay the groundwork for the civil rights movement of the 1960s.

Technological innovation often has social effects that are not readily apparent. The automobile is more than a means of transportation: in the early 1900s it

In no area of technology has the power of diffusion been more frightening than with nuclear weapons. Even the poorest countries —such as Pakistan and India—have managed to borrow the technology needed to manufacture them. If carried far enough, diffusion could make the use of such weapons all but inevitable.

provided young people with a way to escape the watchful eyes of their parents. The mass migration of people from northern to southern states such as Texas in recent decades has been due in no small part to the development of air conditioning, which has made life in the southern climate far more bearable.

Technology often creates dilemmas around deeply held values, in part because technological change moves at a faster pace than changes in cultural ideas, creating what W. F. Ogburn called **culture lag**. We develop new technologies faster than we develop new cultural ideas that regulate how we use them (Ogburn, 1922, 1964). Medical technology enables doctors to artificially inseminate a woman with any man's sperm, making it possible for wives to bear children even if their husbands are sterile. It also makes it possible for married couples to have the husband's sperm used to impregnate another woman

when the wife is infertile. In the late 1980s, several couples tried this approach. They signed legal contracts with what were called "surrogate mothers" who, for a fee, agreed to turn over the child after it was born. What happens, however, when the mother, who is carrying the child, decides to keep it? Who is the actual mother under the law, the woman who bore the child or the woman who paid the surrogate mother? How are the biological father's rights balanced against those of the biological mother (who is not his wife)? Where in all of this do the child's best interests lie?

Although in a major case involving "Baby M" a New Jersey court awarded custody of the child to the natural father and his wife, the issue is far from settled. Many states are considering laws that would outlaw such agreements altogether. Without the reproductive technology that allows artificial insemination the legal and moral questions raised by such cases would never

Puzzles: Who Owns the Eggs?

In 1981 an Australian married couple discovered that the only way they could have children was through test tube fertilization. Several eggs were removed from the wife and fertilized with the husband's sperm. Two of the resulting embryos were frozen while the third was implanted in the wife. She miscarried 10 days later. In 1983 the couple was killed in a plane crash and left an estate valued at several million dollars.

Are the frozen embryos heirs to the estate? Does anyone own them? Can they be destroyed? If they are implanted in a woman who becomes their mother, can she claim part of the estate on their behalf?

These and other difficult questions that faced Australian legal authorities are examples of the kinds of problems that arise when technology allows us to do things faster than we create norms, beliefs, and values to deal with the consequences.

arise in the first place. In this case, as with so many others like it, our cultural grasp of the ethical and legal issues lags far behind our technological capabilities.

Culture lag also involves norms, for the introduction of new technology often alters human behavior and interaction patterns faster than groups and societies are able to construct new norms to regulate them. Prior to the widespread use of computers, most records in business, government, and other organizations were kept in written form, and this made it relatively easy to control who had access to them. As computers have taken over the job of filing and keeping track of vast quantities of information, however, entirely new security problems are introduced (Parker, 1983). In 1983, operators of home computers—called "hackers"—began to figure out how to "break into" large computers by guessing passwords. When hospitals, banks, the military, and government agencies became alarmed at the prospect of unauthorized entry into and alteration of highly important information, they discovered that no laws existed which dealt with "breaking and entering" a computer through the use of a telephone.

The rapid growth of computer technology introduces other problems as well (see Sherman, 1985). Because most information held by governments in the past was in written form, it was relatively difficult to keep track of detailed information from diverse sources about millions of citizens. Computers, however, make it possible for government agencies to compile and access detailed records about citizens quickly and efficiently, and Marx and Reichman (1984) and others have argued that this gives the state an unprecedented ability to invade the privacy of individuals (see Office of Technology Assessment, 1986a).

The rate at which new ideas and technologies are introduced depends on a variety of social and ecological factors (see Rogers, 1983). In the simplest sense, scientific and technological knowledge is largely cumulative: the more we know, the more we are able to know. Since inventions are new combinations of existing ideas and inventions, the more we start with, the more combinations we can invent. Large populations can be conducive to innovation because the more people there are, the more likely it is that someone will come up with something new (Ogburn, 1922). Population size, however, like any other factor, is not sufficient to guarantee innovation, as the examples of India and China during the last few centuries illustrate. A quarter of the world's population lives in China, and yet in terms of industrial technology China is an underdeveloped country.

A third factor affecting the rate of innovation is the stability of environments. A society that must adapt to rapidly changing physical or social conditions will tend to produce more innovations than a society that exists in stable conditions. In the 1970s, oil-producing nations in the Middle East refused to sell oil to the U.S., and the ensuing shortages stimulated the development of solar energy technology. The nuclear arms race is another example of rapidly shifting environmental conditions that stimulate an equally rapid pace of technological development as each country struggles to "keep up" with the other.

Since most innovation occurs through diffusion, a fourth factor affecting the rate of innovation is the amount of contact between societies. Isolated societies have less opportunity to borrow from others than societies that are actively engaged in trade or other forms of exchange.

In some cases, societies try to isolate themselves in order to avoid new ideas. This was true of Japan prior to the nineteenth century and in important ways is still true of the Soviet Union, whose government fears the diffusion of Western culture into their society. The importation of magazines, films, and books from the West is tightly controlled by the government, and Soviet citizens are discouraged from interacting with tourists from Western countries. Only recently has the Soviet policy of *glasnost* (or "openness") begun to loosen this control.

Having examined the effects of population and ecology on societies, we look now at some specific theories that draw heavily on these factors in their attempts to predict and explain social change.

Evolutionary and Unilinear Theory

In trying to identify laws of social change, early thinkers often used biological evolution as a model. Herbert Spencer drew on Darwin's ideas about natural evolution to develop a theory of **social evolution** through which societies naturally change toward superior forms (Spencer, 1891, 1896). From this point of view, social change is **unilinear**, which means that all societies pass through predictable stages: from primitive to civilized, simple to complex, "inferior" to "superior," from militant to peaceful, and from agricultural to industrial.

Like all ideas, Spencer's reflected his social environment, for England was rapidly colonizing much of the world and encountering a vast array of peoples living in relatively simple societies at comparatively low levels of economic development. The theory of social evolution supported the Europeans' belief in their own superiority by focusing on economic development as the most important indicator of a superior society.

The U.S. sociologist Thorstein Veblen also used evolutionary theory as a framework, but focused more on the effect of technology on social change (see Lerner, 1948). Like later theorists, however, Veblen did not believe that social change is unilinear, for he was aware of how easily technology can be transplanted from one society to another. China is still a largely agricultural society, and yet trade agreements signed with the U.S. in 1984 will bring computer and nuclear power technology to what is otherwise a technology-poor society. Despite their poverty, both India and Pakistan now have the ability to manufacture nuclear weapons.

Cyclical Theory

Early in this century, the German philosopher Spengler (1926) produced a variation on evolutionary theory by suggesting that societies change in predictable cycles, in the same way that people progress from birth toward maturity, old age, and death. Like Spencer, Spengler's ideas about **cyclical change** reflected his environment, for the chaos and mass destruction of World War I shook Europeans' belief that societies naturally progress toward better forms. Obviously, change did not necessarily imply an improvement in social life, for in the midst of the greatest economic progress ever known, millions of people were systematically slaughtering one another.

The U.S. sociologist Pitirim Sorokin also believed in cyclical change. According to his principle of **immanent change**, cultures have material and nonmaterial characteristics that cause societies to develop in certain directions. Eventually they are taken to their logical extreme, after which they go too far and "become less and less capable of serving as an instrument of adaptation, as an experience for real satisfaction of the needs of its bearers, and as foundation for their social and cultural life" (Sorokin, 1937–41).

Sorokin argued that as a society develops the ability to produce goods, it will tend to go too far, and as people focus on owning more and more possessions, life begins to lose its sense of meaning and they will turn away from the material aspects of their culture to nonmaterial aspects such as religious belief. During the two decades that followed World War II, the U.S. enjoyed a period of great economic prosperity. In the 1960s there was a strong movement away from "materialism" and toward various forms of spiritualism, especially in the form of Eastern religions such as Zen Buddhism. This movement was strongest among college students, many of whom came from prosperous families. In the 1970s and 1980s there also has been a strong growth in fundamentalist religion and religious cults.

In spite of the insights that the early evolutionary and cyclical theories of change provide, they have a number of drawbacks that make them of relatively little interest to today's sociologists (Zeitlin, 1981). Their most obvious shortcoming is that they often do not fit the facts: as Veblen noted, societies often "skip" stages of development, especially when technology is introduced from the outside. It took the Industrial

The unprecedented carnage of World War I shattered the illusion that civilization inevitably progresses towards higher and better forms. So fierce was the slaughter in some battles that within periods of only a few days hundreds of thousands of soldiers were killed or wounded by rifle and artillery fire. This picture was taken after the battle of the Somme in 1916.

Revolution to ultimately produce the telephone, television, computer, nuclear reactor, and such deadly weapons as hydrogen bombs. These technologies, however, have spread rapidly to societies that have yet to industrialize. These theories also do not appreciate the enormous complexity of social change and the phenomenal variation found among societies.

Multilinear Theories

More recent evolutionary theories show greater appreciation for the complexity of social change. **Multilinear** theories in particular identify certain changes that appear to be universal—from small, simple, rural, and low technology to large, complex, urban, and high technology—and yet acknowledge that such changes take place in a variety of ways and do not necessarily result in "progress" (Smelser, 1973; Steward, 1955).

Perhaps the best developed of the recent multilinear theories is Lenski's theory of social evolution (Lenski and Lenski, 1987). There are important similarities between the biological evolution of living species and the social evolution of human societies. Both depend on the transmission of information—via DNA molecules in genes in the case of biological evolution and via cultural symbol systems in social evolution. Both forms of evolution arise from the interaction of populations with their environments, and in each case the evolutionary trend involves an increase in amount and complexity of information. In comparison with the simplest virus, human genes hold a million times more information (Curtis and Barnes, 1981). In similar ways, industrial societies are far more complex than hunting and gather societies.

Biological and social evolution differ in important ways, however. The genetic information that

ARRIVALS

PESTILENCE	4:02
FAMINE	4:15
MARTIAL LAW	4:21
TRIPLE LOCKS	5:00
UNEMPLOYMENT	5:20
INFLATION	5:32
SHORTER SUMMERS	5:43
LONGER ZIP CODES	5:46
PLASTIC SILVERWARE	6:01

DEPARTURES

GOOD TASTE	3:32
SLEIGH RIDES	3:49
ALL-BEEF BURGERS	4:25
HAPPINESS	5:11
SECURITY	5:15
FRIENDLY LOAN COMPANIES	5:58
WARM BLANKETS	6:10
HARDWOOD FLOORS	6:15
HOMEMADE ICE CREAM	6:31

Drawing by Ziegler © 1979, The New Yorker Magazine, Inc.

controls biological evolution can be transmitted only through reproduction, and two different species cannot mate—that is, they cannot exchange genetic information. Since different species of life cannot share the same genetic information, biological evolution tends to produce greater diversity as each species develops in its own way.

Human societies, on the other hand, can share information quite easily, and in this way they tend to become more similar. Less than a century ago, basic technologies such as electricity and telecommunications were found in only a few countries, but now exist in almost every society. Other aspects of culture, from fast food restaurants and computers to jeans and rock music, have spread rapidly throughout the world.

Like some earlier theorists, Lenski regards information as the key to social change. It was new technology that enabled populations and societies to grow. The expanding resources of larger societies spawned new cultural and structural developments: systems of written language, new vocabularies, more complex divisions of labor, and greater production of goods. According to modern evolutionary theory, in short, information is the engine of social change. Social change, in turn, creates pressures for new information and further change. One consequence of industrial technology has been damage to the physical environment (pollution) and, therefore, to the well-being of populations. This, in turn, has created pressures for new technology (such as pollution control devices) and for change in political arrangements (such as greater government regulation of industry).

Modernization Theory

The concept of **modernization** refers to a process through which the social and ecological characteristics of societies change in predictable ways (Parsons, 1951; Rostow, 1960). In its earliest form, which was most popular during the 1950s and 1960s, modernization theory was actually a form of evolutionary theory that tried to describe the process of industrialization. For two decades the idea of modernization dominated thinking about economic and social change in underdeveloped countries, and it held out the expectation that the economic prosperity and democratic political institutions found in the countries of North America and Western Europe would spread throughout the world.

According to modernization theory, development depends on more than complex technology, for it also involves a variety of structural, cultural, and ecological changes. Cultures become more heterogeneous and subcultures flourish. People become more oriented to the future and open to change, and the rights of the individual increase in value. Social relationships shift from informal and primary to formal, bureaucratic, and secondary, and populations become more urban.

Social inequality increases during the early stages of modernization as an elite profits from exploiting an unsophisticated, unskilled labor force; but as a society industrializes, social mobility increases and rigid stratification systems based on ascribed statuses such as race and gender tend to break down. Traditional sources of authority—such as respect for the elderly—also tend to weaken as social institutions such as schools and the state take on increasing responsibility and power.

At the heart of modernization is technological innovation that makes industrialization possible, and scientific research and technological innovation are highly valued in modern societies. With industrialization comes a specialized division of labor, a more skilled and educated work force, and greater alienation in the workplace. Contact with modern working conditions, in turn, tends to make workers more modern in their values and beliefs, more supportive of democratic institutions, and more committed to the rights of individuals (Inkeles and Smith, 1974). As we saw in Chapter 18, some theorists believe that the most advanced stage of modernization is *postindustrial* society, in which sophisticated technology replaces much of human labor and most people work as service providers (such as nurses and computer programmers) rather than as producers of goods (Daniel Bell, 1973).

There is little doubt that most societies are committed to economic development, for the lure of higher standards of living is a strong one. What is not clear, however, is how useful the theory of modernization is for predicting the patterns of change in underdeveloped societies. As we saw in Chapter 11, the gap between rich and poor nations has been growing, not shrinking. Is economic prosperity an attainable goal for all countries of the world as modernization theory seems to suggest? Supporters of world-system theory believe the answer is no.

World-System Theory

World-system (or **dependency**) **theory** was developed in the 1970s as a direct challenge to modernization theory, most notably by Immanuel Wallerstein (1976, 1979, 1980). As we saw in Chapter 18, Wallerstein divides societies into three categories. Core societies such as Britain, the U.S., and Japan occupy dominant positions in the world economy by controlling the development and flow of new technology as well as the wealth necessary for the creation of new capital. Countries in the periphery—such as most of Africa and much of Asia—are poor and underdeveloped and supply core societies with raw materials, food, and other products that can be produced without sophisticated technology or an educated work force. Semiperiphery countries such as Brazil and Taiwan stand between the core and the periphery and often provide cheap but well-trained industrial labor when labor costs in core countries go up. Many automobile spare parts are manufactured in Mexico, just as many U.S. companies have their products made in South Korea.

A world-system perspective has important implications for social change, for it is based on the view that economic development depends not simply on a society's internal structure, culture, population, and ecology, but also on its position in the world system. It argues that even the leading socialist country in the world—the Soviet Union—cannot be completely socialist so long as it must deal with a largely capitalist world economy (Wallerstein, 1979). It also argues that "backward" conditions found in many peripheral societies arise not only from their internal conditions, but also from their relationship with societies at the core or in the semiperiphery of the world system. We cannot understand the phenomenal economic growth in Taiwan over the past 30 years without taking into account Taiwan's close relationship with the U.S.

An important aspect of world-system theory focuses on the ways in which core and peripheral societies change due to their positions in the system. When Great Britain was an empire, it systematically destroyed the textile industry in India—one of its colonies—and forced Indians to purchase cloth made in Britain by not allowing them to produce any themselves. This eliminated competition and provided a captive market for British goods. One result of this policy was increased revenues for Britain, which contributed to the industrial revolution that was the basis for modern core societies (Baran, 1957).

The economic problems of many countries are also tied to dependency relationships in the world system. Mexico is an urban, industrial, rich country compared to most underdeveloped nations, and yet in spite of its wealth of natural resources it has widespread poverty and an enormous gap between rich and poor. Gonzalez Casanova (1980) argued that this is due in part to the relationship between Mexico and corporations in core countries, the U.S. in particular. So much of Mexico's industry is owned by foreigners, and so much of its foreign sales depend on a few customers, that Mexican leaders lack the flexibility they need to make the domestic investments that lead to improved living conditions.

Like all theories, world-system theory has its shortcomings. Few social scientists would deny that a world system exists or that there are dependent relations between societies. What is unclear, however, are the reasons that some societies are at the core and others are in the periphery or semiperiphery. Brenner (1976) showed that economic "backwardness" in eastern Europe arose less from economic dependence than on a lack of technology that preceded the development of its dependent position in the world system (see also Chirot, 1980, 1985; Chirot and Hall, 1982; and Lenski, 1976b).

For all their shortcomings, theories of social change have come a long way from the relatively simplistic notions of unilinear evolution. Multilinear evolutionary theory and world-system and dependency theory show a development toward more comprehensive theories that appreciate the complexity of social change.

SUMMARY

1. Social change refers to the ways in which social and ecological arrangements change.

2. Cultural ideas often promote change. New beliefs alter ways of perceiving the world; shifting values affect our goals; and changing norms alter expectations in social relationships.

3. The structure of social relationships also causes change. Prejudice may be reduced by changing patterns of interaction between members of different groups. Social movements focus explicitly on change.

4. A functional perspective views social change as an adaptive response to the strains that arise through normal activity in a society. When mothers enter the labor force in increasing numbers, for example, subsequent changes in beliefs,

values, attitudes, and norms that apply to working mothers affect social cohesion and order.

5. The conflict perspective focuses on social change as the result of struggles between groups. This perspective would focus on protest as a source of changing beliefs, values, attitudes, and norms that apply to working mothers.

6. Succession is the process through which ecosystems change, and it often causes social change. The shift from hunter-gatherer to horticultural and then agricultural societies laid a foundation for the emergence of social stratification and complex divisions of labor.

7. Rapid population growth and the changing characteristics of populations promote social change in a variety of ways. The pressure of an expanding population stimulates the development of new technology; overpopulation contributes to poverty, urban congestion, and pollution; the movement of cohorts through the life course under social conditions that differ for each generation makes change inevitable.

8. New technology acquired through discovery, invention, or diffusion is one of the most important sources of change. Culture lag occurs when technology changes faster than other aspects of culture, as when medical technology raises moral questions that have yet to be resolved.

9. The rate of innovation in a society depends on existing knowledge, population size, the stability of social and physical environments, and the extent of contact with other societies.

10. Early evolutionary theory drew on Darwin's theory of evolution and argued that societies progress toward superior forms. Some theorists believed that change is unilinear, always taking place in the same stages.

11. According to Spengler's cyclical theory, societies have periods that correspond to youth, middle- and old-age in humans. Sorokin believed that societies tend to overdevelop dominant cultural characteristics and then go into a period of decline.

12. More recent multilinear evolutionary theories show greater appreciation for the complexity of change. Lenski's theory suggests that social and

biological evolution have much in common, especially their reliance on the accumulation and transmission of information.

13. Modernization theory attempts to describe the process through which societies change from traditional to modern, rural to urban, nonindustrial to industrial, simple to complex, and from primary, informal relationships to those that are predominantly secondary, formal and bureaucratic.

14. World-system theory argues that modernization is not a universal phenomenon but rather depends on the position a society occupies—core, semiperiphery, or periphery—in the world economic system. Dependent relationships between periphery and core societies, for example, often make it difficult if not impossible for periphery societies to modernize.

KEY TERMS

culture lag   605
cyclical change   607

    immanent change   607

diffusion   604
discovery   604
ecological succession   602
invention   604
modernization   609
multilinear change   608
social evolution   607
unilinear change   607
world-system (dependency) theory   610

Looking Elsewhere

Having studied Chapter 22, you might want to look at related discussions in *Human Arrangements*, which include change and

- the importance of groups (Chapter 8, pp. 213–14)
- communities (Chapter 9, pp. 237–43)
- the class system (Chapter 11, pp. 304–307)
- race relations (Chapter 12, pp. 331–37)
- gender inequality (Chapter 13, pp. 366–73)
- age inequality (Chapter 14, pp. 395–98)
- the family (Chapter 15, pp. 425–28)
- schools (Chapter 16, pp. 455–57)
- science and technology (Chapter 5, pp. 123–25; Chapter 17, pp. 461, 463–64, 470–72)
- scientific revolutions (Chapter 17, pp. 463–64)
- capitalism (Chapter 18, pp. 512–13)
- political revolution (Chapter 19, pp. 537–39)
- religion (Chapter 20, pp. 563–66)
- social movements (Chapter 21, pp. 580–91)
- world-system theory and international inequality (Chapter 18, pp. 509–11)

RECOMMENDED READINGS

BERGESEN, A. (Ed.). (1983). *Crises in the world system*. Beverly Hills, CA: Sage. A collection of articles, all of which try to understand the cycles of recurring crisis believed by world-system theorists to characterize the world economy.

CHIROT, D. (1977). *Social change in the twentieth century*. New York: Harcourt Brace Jovanovich. An interesting look at social change from a world-system perspective. See also his recent book (1986). *Social change in the modern era* which changes many of his earlier views.

JENKINS, J. C. (1983). "Resource mobilization theory and the study of social movements." *Annual Review of Sociology 9*, 527–553. A comprehensive, up-to-date review of an important theoretical approach to social change.

LAUER, R. H. (Ed.). (1981). *Perspectives on social change* (3rd ed.). Boston: Allyn and Bacon. An introduction to social change that focuses on both theory and research.

MARSH, J. C., GEIST, A., and CAPLAN, N. (1982). *Rape and the limits of law reform*. Boston: Auburn House. A case study that examines the effect of a radical rewriting of Michigan's sexual assault laws on the ways in which subsequent cases were handled. Illustrates the difficulty of bringing about change through legal reform in an area of entrenched beliefs and values such as those that surround gender and violence.

PRICE, J. (1982). *The antinuclear movement.* Boston: Twayne. A richly drawn portrait of the antinuclear movement, starting with its beginnings in the 1950s.

ROBERTSON, C. C. (1984). *Sharing the same bowl: A socioeconomic history of women and class in Accra.* Bloomington: Indiana University Press. A book that adds an important piece to dependency and world-system theory by looking at the ways in which colonialism, capitalism, and peripheral status in the world system have changed the status of women in urban Africa.

Appendix A
A Student Research Guide

At some point during your study of sociology, you may have to write a research paper, and this appendix will help you (see Figure A-1). You have probably never done original research; and even if you are an old hand at using libraries, sociology has its own resources, of which you should be aware before you start.

DECIDING WHAT YOU WANT TO KNOW

Whether you do your own research or use the results of someone else's in order to write a paper, you cannot get very far without a clear idea of what it is you want to know. Without a doubt, this is the most difficult part of research for most people, amateurs and professionals alike. Notice that saying, "I want to write a paper on the family" is not a statement of what you want to know; rather, it defines a general area within which lie hundreds of different topics.

One of the best ways to define a topic is to put it in the form of questions to which you can imagine clear answers. For example: How common is family violence in the U.S.? What kinds of families are the most prone to violence? How is the likelihood of violence affected by such things as the age of spouses and children, the employment status and relative earnings of wives and husbands, whether or not both parents are living at home, whether or not parents were victims of abuse as children? Is family violence more common in some societies than in others? Why? With each of these questions, you can have a clear idea of what you are looking for—an idea you cannot have with something like "I want to write a paper on the family."

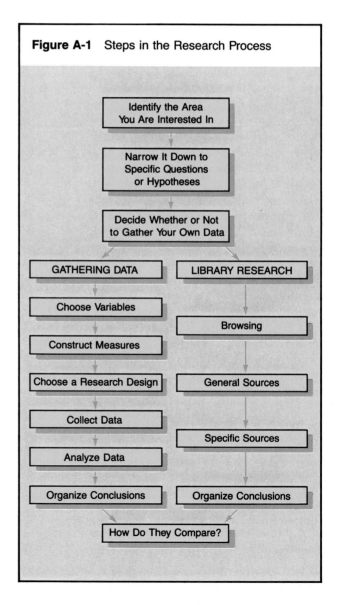

Figure A-1 Steps in the Research Process

Identify the Area You Are Interested In

Narrow It Down to Specific Questions or Hypotheses

Decide Whether or Not to Gather Your Own Data

GATHERING DATA

Choose Variables

Construct Measures

Choose a Research Design

Collect Data

Analyze Data

Organize Conclusions

LIBRARY RESEARCH

Browsing

General Sources

Specific Sources

Organize Conclusions

How Do They Compare?

Once you have made up clear, specific questions, you will probably still have to narrow your topic even further since you are working at a disadvantage that you do not share with most other researchers: College terms rarely last more than 12 or 13 weeks, and you may have less than a month to complete your work. Any one of the questions in the preceding paragraph could lead to a substantial term paper.

DESIGNING YOUR RESEARCH

Once you have decided what you want to know, the next thing to do is to plan how you are going to go after it. You may decide to use only published sources or you may supplement this by gathering new information. You might be interested in finding out just how prevalent family violence is in the U.S. As part of your research, you would use the library to review what is known about family violence. You might want to supplement this, however, by doing a survey of students in your college in order to find out how many of them come from families in which violence has taken place during the past year.

If you decide to supplement library research with your own fieldwork, I suggest that you assume that it will take you at least twice as long to do your fieldwork as you think it will. This is not meant to discourage you from gathering your own data—far from it. There are few things as exciting in academic work as doing your own research. It is meant to help you to be realistic about the time constraints you are probably working under. Writing questionnaires and having them duplicated, distributed, returned, tabulated, and analyzed takes a lot of time. One excellent way to deal with this problem—if your professor allows it—is to work in teams of two or three students so that you can divide the labor.

HOW TO USE A LIBRARY

Many people go through their entire educational career without realizing what extraordinary resources libraries and their staffs are. To use a library well, however, you will first have to get to know your way around it.

The first thing you have to know is how a library is laid out. In writing this book, I have spent a great deal of time just wandering through the stacks of my library, getting a sense of what is located where. You will find that most sociology books are shelved in the same general area, and you can get an excellent feel for any discipline by spending an hour or so just browsing. You can benefit from this both in getting to know the field as a whole and in becoming familiar with specific areas within it, such as demography, the sociology of gender, stratification, urban studies, or the family. How do you find out what is where? Ask a librarian. Most librarians are justifiably proud of their libraries and are more than happy to show people how to use them.

Some subjects will be catalogued in several locations. You will find sources that discuss family violence under sociology as well as anthropology, psychology, and government studies that treat family violence as a problem in law enforcement.

Whether or not you decide to gather data of your own, at some point you should make yourself aware of what others have found and had to say about the topic you are investigating. Out of the millions of books and articles contained in many libraries, you need ways of locating just the ones that are most likely to help you understand the relatively narrow subject you have selected.

General Sources

The most obvious place for you to begin is with the references in *Human Arrangements*, provided that this book discusses the topic you are interested in. The section in Chapter 15 on family violence indicates several recent sources. Rather than spend hours finding them on your own, take advantage of the fact that I have already done some of your work for you—just as other authors did some of my work for me.

Another place to look is a general source such as an encyclopedia. In addition to widely known ones such as *Britannica*, there is the *International Encyclopedia of the Social Sciences*, which contains hundreds of articles written by specialists. Although it is a bit dated for some purposes (it was published in 1968), for general background discussions of major concepts and areas of the social sciences it is an excellent resource.

You might also look at recent issues of *Annual Review of Sociolgy*, a hardbound book containing reviews of entire areas of sociological inquiry. If you are lucky enough to find a recent review of your area of interest, it can save you a great deal of time.

Specific Sources in Sociology

Sociological articles appear in a number of journals (see Table A-1), and you should familiarize yourself with them. An hour or so spent browsing through the tables of contents for the previous year can give you a good idea of the kinds of subjects found in each.

Tracking Down Sources

There are several ways to find scholarly writings. Card catalogues usually consist of two sections. One lists books by author and title and the other lists them by subject. If you are doing a project on family violence, for example, you might look under "family," "violence," "domestic violence," or "child abuse." In general, it is best to go after the most recent titles, since they are likely to include summaries of previously published research.

Table A-1

Useful Journals in Sociological Research

MAJOR SOCIOLOGICAL JOURNALS

American Sociological Review
American Journal of Sociology
British Journal of Sociology
Social Forces

MORE SPECIALIZED JOURNALS IN SOCIOLOGY

Contemporary Sociology (Book reviews)
Journal of Marriage and the Family
Journal of Health and Social Behavior
Public Opinion Quarterly
Social Problems
Sociology of Education
Demography
Population Studies

JOURNALS IN SOCIAL PSYCHOLOGY

Social Psychology Quarterly
Journal of Experimental Social Psychology
Journal of Applied Social Psychology
Journal of Abnormal and Social Psychology
Personality and Social Psychology

In addition to the card catalogue, there are books in the reference department that you can use to locate books and articles about a particular subject. The multivolume annual *Books in Print* lists all currently published books by subject, author, and title, and it can be a useful guide to books that your library does not own but which may be obtained through interlibrary loan systems. The *Social Science Index* and *Sociological Abstracts* are published each year and contain brief descriptions of every article and book of interest to sociologists. There are similar volumes for other areas, such as education, psychology, and crime. As before, begin with the most recent year and work backward. Most reference departments also have a variety of annotated bibliographies: books that describe articles and books that focus on a particular subject, such as blacks or women. These can be enormously useful.

For some topics, none of these sources will provide you with information, and this often happens when you are interested in a subject that focuses on recent events. If you cannot find what you need in scholarly sources, turn to the *Reader's Guide to Periodical Literature*, which is published each year and gives listings by subject of articles that appear in magazines such as *Newsweek*. In addition, newspapers of record, such as the *New York Times* and the London *Times*, publish annual indexes that list every person, event, or subject that has appeared in their newspapers. Be careful when using popular sources such as those found in the *Reader's Guide*, however, for they are not generally bound by the same rigorous scientific standards that sociologists try to follow.

Finding Statistical Information

Perhaps the best source of statistical information about the U.S. is the federal government. Some libraries are Government Document Depositories which contain most major documents published by the federal government (and usually have a documents librarian to help you find them). The Census Bureau publishes not only the results of the census but also the periodic *Current Population Reports*, whose surveys cover such important areas as race, income and poverty, marital status and living arrangements, divorce and marriage, and migration.

The National Center for Health Statistics publishes detailed information on births, deaths, marriages, and divorces each year, often broken down by race, gender, and age. The Department of Labor publishes highly detailed reports on work and earnings, and the Justice Department reports on crime and law enforcement.

If you do not have access to a depository library, the best source is the annual *Statistical Abstract of the United States*, which presents highlights of all federal statistics, with supplements from other sources as well. In addition, the federal government publishes other excellent statistical source books, including *Historical Statistics of the United States from Colonial Times to 1970* and *Social Indicators*, the latter being a series of volumes that periodically report on selected social conditions and trends with some comparative data from other countries.

Many libraries also own annual volumes of the Gallup Opinion Poll Index (usually found in the reference section), which lists each question asked along with the responses, which are often broken down by characteristics such as age, gender, race, religion, education, or income.

For statistical information about countries in addition to the U.S., the best source is the United Nations, especially its *Demographic Yearbook*, which contains the most complete and accurate information available on the social, political, and economic conditions of all states belonging to the United Nations. For more recent information on issues related to population, a good source is the Population Reference Bureau, whose current, inexpensive publications are available at Box 35012, Washington, DC 20013.

Appendix B
Using Samples: A Primer on Statistical Inference

Researchers often try to describe very large populations, such as the adult population of the United States, with the results of surveys that involve only a relatively small sample, such as 1,300 to 1,500 people. If you have ever followed a national election, you know that such polls can predict results with astonishing accuracy. How is this possible? The procedure is called **statistical inference**. It involves some sophisticated mathematics that we will not go into here; but you can get some idea of the reasoning behind it by considering the following example.

Suppose you shoot dice with Fred (using his dice) and he rolls a total of "7" three times in a row. "Lucky throws," you think. Then he rolls three more 7s, for a total of six straight. "*Very* lucky," you think. "Maybe *too* lucky." As Fred keeps rolling 7s, you begin to doubt the "fairness" of the dice, and at some point you will conclude that something is fishy with the dice, and perhaps with Fred.

Without knowing it, you are performing some sophisticated statistical reasoning. You start with a **null hypothesis**, a testable assumption that both dice are "fair," which means that on each throw, all numbers have an equal chance to come up. You then watch the dice, and after a sample of three rolls, you note the result: "all 7s." At this point, there are two possibilities: (1) the dice are fair (the null hypothesis is correct) and Fred is lucky, or (2) a fair pair of dice would hardly ever give a total of "7" three times in a row, and the null hypothesis is wrong. After only three rolls, you would most likely choose the first possibility.

With a sample of ten rolls of all 7s, however, the second possibility looks more likely: A fair pair of dice would almost never give you ten 7s in a row. Therefore, the dice are *almost certainly* loaded.

"But," protests Fred, "ten 7s in a row isn't *impossible* with fair dice."

"True," you reply, "but if I call the dice loaded, *the chances are mighty slim that I'm wrong*."

This last statement is an example of statistical inference, and it is the key to the use of samples to draw conclusions about populations. Theoretically the population of all possible throws of a pair of dice is not just very large, it is *infinitely* large (we could keep throwing dice forever); but instead we use a sample of only ten throws to draw a conclusion about the population that consists of "all possible throws of a pair of dice."

Scientists in many disciplines use samples to test ideas. Physicians testing a new drug begin with the assumption that the drug is useless. They administer it to a sample of people and find, perhaps, that it is effective half the time. They then must choose between two possibilities: (1) the drug is in fact useless and its effectiveness in half the cases was a "fluke" or (2) a useless drug is very unlikely to be effective half the time; therefore, it must be a useful drug. The key here is the phrase "very unlikely" (and this is where the sophisticated mathematics comes in): *if the sample is properly selected, it is possible to mathematically calculate the chances that a useless drug would be effective half the time simply by chance.*

This is essentially how pollsters predict election winners long before all the votes are in. If they draw a sample that shows candidate Mary Jones the winner, they start with the assumption that, at best, the election will end in a tie when all votes are counted. They then ask, "How likely is it that Jones would win in a sample we drew from a population in which she actually has no more votes than her opponent? (the same reasoning as "How likely are ten 7s with a pair of fair dice?"). If this possibility is very *unlikely*, they reject the assumption that at best Jones will tie, and predict her victory.

There are four important points to be made here. First, when scientists draw conclusions from samples, there is always a possibility that they are wrong (just as ten 7s in a row is possible, however improbable it is). The mathematics of statistical inference, however, allows researchers to know just how likely such a mistake is. When election predictors say, "It's too close to call," they are in effect saying that if they predict a winner, the chances of being wrong are unacceptably high.

Second, they can make such statements only if they can *calculate* the chance of making an error, and this can only be done with samples selected so that every member of the population has an equal chance of being included. With "haphazard" samples there is no way to draw a conclusion and calculate the chances of making a mistake. They might be right; they might be wrong. More than that, they cannot say.

In the 1936 U.S. presidential election, the *Literary Digest* selected a sample of adults from telephone directories and found overwhelming support for Republican Alfred Landon among its two million replies. The magazine predicted an easy victory over his Democratic opponent, Franklin Roosevelt. George Gallup, however, used a far smaller sample and correctly predicted Roosevelt's victory. What happened?

The *Literary Digest* violated the most important principle of scientific sampling when it used telephone directories to select its sample. During the Depression, only middle- and upper-class people could afford telephones, and such people tended to vote Republican. Less affluent people, on the other hand, heavily favored Roosevelt and were never considered for the *Digest* sample. By using scientific techniques to draw his sample, Gallup accurately predicted the outcome with a far smaller sample (Hennessy, 1971).

Third, note that the conclusion, "Jones will win the election" rests on the *rejection of other possible outcomes*. This illustrates a basic aspect of scientific research. We cannot explain something merely by finding an explanation that "fits the facts," because there may be many competing explanations that also might "fit the facts." The only way to prove a theory, then, is to systematically eliminate every alternative theory. To test the theory that employers discriminate against women by paying them less than men for doing the same work, we must first eliminate alternative explanations—men are more competent, have more experience or higher educations. Only if we eliminate all possible alternative causes of pay differences, can we attribute any differences in earnings to discrimination.

Fourth, statistical inferences must be carefully interpreted. When a drug company tests its toothpaste against competing brands, it selects samples of children. One group uses "Brand A" and the other uses "Brand B," and after several years, the two groups are compared. The null hypothesis in this case is: "There is no difference between the two Brands." Suppose the Brand A group has fewer cavities than the Brand B group. Does this mean Brand A is better?

The problem is that it is possible to have two equally effective products produce differences *by chance* in a sample of users (just as it is possible to get six 7s in a row with a fair pair of dice). Researchers then use the mathematics of statistical inference to answer the question: "Could the difference between the two groups have occurred simply by chance?" Suppose they conclude the following: "It's *very* unlikely that two samples using equally effective toothpastes would differ this much simply by chance. Therefore, the two brands must *not* be equally effective: Brand A is better."

Such conclusions are frequently presented as "Children using Brand A had *significantly* fewer cavities." This is where caution is needed, for to most people, "significant" means "important" or "substantial"; but scientific "significance" has a much narrower meaning. To say that two groups are "significantly different" means *only* that we are very certain they are not exactly the same. By itself, it does *not* mean that the difference is either large or important.

Many studies show that when punishment is swift and certain, crime rates tend to fall. The swiftness and certainty of punishment have "significant effects" on crime rates. While this is an important finding, it is also important to ask, "How much of an effect?" The answer, disappointingly, is, "Not very much" (Andenaes, 1975; Tittle, 1975). Whenever you read a scientific report that refers to "significant differ-ences," be sure to search for statements that indicate the actual magnitude of the difference.

Used correctly, samples and statistical inference are very efficient research tools, for they enable us to study populations that would otherwise be too large to study at all.

Glossary

Aberrant behavior (aberrance) Behavior that violates norms in secret and for personal gain. **251**

Absolute deprivation A lack of basic necessities relative to a fixed standard such as the amount of food necessary for survival. **581**

Abstract ideal (See **Ethical religion**.)

Academic subculture The type of student subculture that encourages hard work and learning for its own sake. **439**

Achieved status A status entered after birth and usually due at least in part to individual behavior. **81**

Acquired status (See **Achieved status**.)

Acting collective behavior Crowd or mass behavior oriented to specific goals. **570**

Affirmative action A social policy of preferential treatment for minorities, the purpose of which is to erase disadvantages caused by a history of prejudice and discrimination. **333**

Age group One of the categories into which the life span is divided in a particular culture. **377**

Ageism Prejudice based on age. **378**

Age structure The relative number of people of each age in a population. **118**

Aggregate A collection of people who happen to be in the same place at the same time. **86** (See also **Situational status**.)

Agrarian society A society in which agriculture is the primary means of subsistence. **124**

Alienation The psychological condition in which individuals feel detached from work, social relationships, and the results of their own behavior. **306, 503**

Aligning action An action that signals an actor's acceptance of a new definition of the situation. **174**

Amalgamation The combination of several cultures in a society to produce a new culture. **315**

Ancestor worship The religious worship of ancestors based on the belief that they possess supernatural power. **548**

Androgyny The combining of masculine and feminine personality traits in a single individual. **367**

Animism A religion based on the belief that spirits and ghosts inhabit sacred objects such as trees and rocks. **548**

Anomalies Scientific findings that either contradict or cannot be explained by a paradigm. **463**

Anomie A social condition in which members of groups, communities, or societies no longer feel allegiance to norms. **264**

Anthropology The study of culture in small, preindustrial societies. **18**

Anticipatory socialization The process of learning how to perform a role attached to a status we do not yet occupy. **148–49**

Apartheid South Africa's rigid policy of racial discrimination and segregation. **302**

Ascribed status A status assigned at birth. **81**

Assimilation The conformity of members of ethnic groups to the culture of the dominant group. **316**

Attitudes Positive or negative evaluations of people, objects, or situations that often predispose people to feel and behave positively or negatively toward them. **15, 74**

Audience segregation In the dramaturgical approach to interaction, the effort by social actors to keep their "frontstage" and "backstage" selves separate. **174**

Authoritarian leadership structure A leadership structure in which power is concentrated in the hands of a relative few. **91**

Authoritarianism The degree to which the state controls the lives of its citizens. **525**

Authoritarian leader A leader who dominates social interaction in a group. **193**

Authority Power assigned according to norms and generally accepted as legitimate by those over whom it is exercised. **91**

Autocracy A state that is ruled by a single person. **524**

Automation The replacement of human labor with machines. **494**

Backstage In the dramaturgical approach, the place where players are freed from the requirements of their role. **174**

Balance theory A theoretical perspective on social interaction that suggests that people organize their perceptions of people and objects into units and strive for some consistency in the positive and negative feelings among them. **180**

Behavioral approach (to learning) A theoretical approach to learning and behavior that focuses on the importance of reward and punishment and classical and operant conditioning. **135**

Beliefs Statements about what is real. **15, 63**

Bias The tendency of research results to be in error in one respect more than in any other. **36**

Bilateral descent Kinship arrangements in which descent is traced through both the mother's and father's blood relatives. **406**

Bilocal A society in which married couples must live near or in the household of the wife's mother or the husband's father. **409**

Biological determinism The belief that individual differences are biologically caused and, therefore, unchangeable. **343**

Birth cohort   People who share the same year of birth. **119**

Birth rate   The number of children born each year for every thousand members of a population. **111**

Blue-collar   Referring to occupations that primarily involve manual work. **283**

Boundary   The specification of who may occupy a particular status. **86** The **clarity** of boundaries describes how easily people can tell who occupies a status. **86** The **openness** of boundaries refers to how easy it is for individuals to occupy a particular status. **86**

Bourgeoisie   (See **Capitalist**.)

Bureaucracy   A complex set of formal, secondary relationships in which (1) entry into statuses is controlled by rigid norms; (2) people specialize in narrowly-defined tasks; (3) roles are rigidly defined by rules; (4) power is distributed in a clear hierarchy; (5) managers specialize in making sure everything works according to the rules; and (6) decisions are based on rational considerations of the organization's best interests rather than on personal feelings of individuals. **94**

Capital   Wealth such as machinery that can be used to produce more wealth. **489**

Capitalism   An economic system in which the means of production are privately owned and controlled. **489**

Capitalist   A person who owns means of production. **280, 489**

Case study   A research design that focuses on a single example rather than a representative sample. **37**

Caste   A social class in which membership depends on ascribed statuses and cannot be changed after birth. **302**

Casual collective behavior   Crowd or mass behavior that involves no common goal or purpose around which people interact. **570**

Census   A gathering of information on all members of a population. **35**

Charismatic authority   Authority based on belief that a particular individual possesses special abilities or characteristics. **517**

Church   The second most powerful religious institution, with a broad membership that includes a majority of the members of a society, a formally trained and bureaucratic clergy, governed by legal-rational and traditional authority, focusing on highly abstract unemotional ritual, and often although not always allied with the ruling class. **551**

Circular reaction   In Blumer's theory of collective behavior, the belief that people copy one another and amplify their emotional state in the process. **575**

Civil disobedience   The deliberate and open violation of a norm for the purpose of changing it. **523**

Civil law   A norm that regulates social relationships in order to prevent or undo the negative effects of particular acts. **73**

Civil religion   A set of cultural ideas, symbols, and practices oriented to the direct worship of a society by its members. **562**

Clarity   (See **Boundary**.)

Class consciousness   An awareness among members of a social class of the true extent and social causes of inequality in a society. **306**

Classical conditioning   A form of learning in which a biological reflex is conditioned to respond to a new stimulus. **136**

Classical social movement theory   A theory (including several specific approaches) that is based on the following general model: some kind of strain or disturbance in the social environment (such as an economic depression) creates disruptive psychological states in individuals (such as anxiety) and individuals then channel their energy into social movements in order to relieve their emotional difficulties. **581**

Closed (stratification) system   A stratification system in which class membership is based on ascribed statuses and movement from one class to another is difficult if not impossible. **295** (See **Caste**.)

Coalition   A subgroup whose members join forces in order to increase their control over group process. **171**

Coercive power   Power that lacks the social legitimacy of authority and is based on fear and the use of force. **519**

Cognitive development perspective (theory)   A theoretical perspective of socialization that focuses on the growth of mental abilities to make increasingly complex judgments about ourselves as well as our physical and social environments. **137**

Cohort   (See **Birth cohort**.)

Cohort effect   Effects on people's lives that arise from the characteristics of the historical periods during which they experienced stages of life such as childhood or middle age. **393**

Collective behavior   The relatively unstructured behavior of people in crowds and masses. **570**

Collective conscience   The term—used by proponents of the functional perspective—for the moral consensus that is violated by deviant acts. **250**

Collectivity   A set of people who share a culture and think of themselves as a unit, but do not interact with one another. **200**

Collegiate subculture   The type of student subculture that values social activities above others. **439**

Colonialism   The relationship between countries in which one dominates the other and exploits its natural and human resources. **303**

Commodity   A good or service produced primarily for its exchange value, not for direct consumption by the producer. **486**

Communal economy   An economy based on collective ownership of means of production, primary ties, and sharing. **486**

Communication structure   The frequency and duration of interaction among members of a group. **92**

Communism   A utopian economic system in which the means of production are communally owned and there is no state. **508**

Communism, norm of   A norm that requires scientists to share their findings with one another. **465**

Community   A collection of people who share a common territory and meet their basic physical and social needs through daily interaction with one another. **219**

Compound family   A nuclear family in which children are directly related to only one of the parents. **412**

Compound status   A status that consists of one or more statuses joined together as one—as "policewoman" joins occupation with gender.

Concentric-zone theory   A theory of urban land use according to which cities develop in rings around a core of business activity; outer rings are higher in class than inner rings. **236**

Conflict perspective   A theoretical perspective that focuses on the struggle among different social groups over scarce rewards. **22**

Conformity   Behavior or appearance consistent with norms. **247**

Conglomerate   A collection of companies in different industries that are owned by a single corporation. **496**

Conspicuous consumption   Consumption intended to affirm or enhance an individual's prestige. **292**

Constant   A behavior or characteristic that does not vary from one individual, group, or society to another. **32**

Contagion   In Le Bon's theory of collective behavior, the belief that people uncritically copy one another's behavior, setting off a chain reaction. **574**

Content analysis   Analysis of words and images contained in written, spoken, and visual media. **42**

Control group   A group of people in an experiment who are not exposed to the experimental stimulus under study. **40**

Control variable   A variable introduced into a statistical analysis to see if a statistical relationship holds among people who are alike on a particular characteristic. **46**

Conventional collective behavior   Crowd or mass behavior that involves a specific purpose such as watching a parade. **570**

Convergence theory   Le Bon's belief that crowds consist of like-minded people who assemble in one place. **574**

Core society   In world-system theory, a society that is in an economically dominant position. **510**

Correlation   A measure of association used in regression analysis. **49**

Coup d'état   An attempt to illegally replace one government with another, often through the use of force. **537**

Crime   The term for acts that violate laws. **254**

Crime rate   The number of crimes per year per thousand people in a population. **254**

Criminal justice system   A set of institutions including police, courts, and prisons. **260**

Criminal law   A norm that links specific acts with punishments. **73**

Cross-cultural study   Research that tries to identify the origins of cultural ideas, social structures, or ecological arrangements by comparing different societies. **44**

Crowd   A relatively temporary collection of people who happen to be in the same place at the same time in close enough proximity to one another so that they can interact with and be affected by one another. **570**

Crude birth rate   (See **Birth rate.**)

Crude death rate   (See **Death rate.**)

Cult   A relatively temporary religious group whose members are generally recruited among poor people in a state of emotional crisis, which has an informal, loosely organized structure governed by charismatic leadership, involves no formal rituals, relies on emotional displays during ceremonies, and actively rejects the major institutions of society. **553**

Cultural determinism   The belief that individual differences are caused by socialization and are, therefore, changeable.

Cultural relativism   A concept that refers to the fact that the importance of a particular cultural idea varies from one society or subgroup to another. **65**

Cultural universal   A cultural product found in all societies. **65**

Culture   The material products of social life, and the entire set of beliefs, norms, values, and attitudes that govern social relationships in groups, communities, or societies. **14, 57**

Culture lag   An instance in which technological change occurs before cultural norms can be introduced to govern its use. **605**

Cyclical theory of social change   The theory that the development of societies occurs in cycles (rather than a straight line) that parallel the lives of individuals. Societies are born, mature, age, and die. **607**

Death rate   The number of people who die in a given year for every thousand people in a population. **107**

Decision theory   A theoretical perspective that views collective behavior—and human behavior in general—as the result of rational attempts to solve problems. **576**

De facto segregation   Segregation that is an unintended consequence of social or ecological arrangements. **327**

Definition of the situation   The determination of which statuses and roles are relevant in a social situation. **82**

Degradation ceremony   An important part of the socialization process in total institutions, in which inmates are subjected to humiliation and labeled inferior human beings. **263**

De jure segregation   Segregation that is required by law. **327**

Democracy   A social structure in which power is evenly distributed. **522**

Democratic leader   A leader who exercises little authority and acts primarily as a moderator in group interactions. **91, 194**

Democratic socialism   An economic system in which the state owns and controls only selected important means of production such as utilities and airlines. **508**

Demographic transition theory   A theory describing the pattern of falling death and birth rates that has characterized the recent history of industrialized countries. **112**

Demography   The study of the size, composition, growth, and distribution of human populations. **104**

Denomination   The third most powerful type of religious institution, with a membership generally dominated by a single social class, a formal but not bureaucratic role structure, a trained clergy, traditional authority, abstract relatively unemotional ritual, and a condition of coexistence between it and dominant political and economic institutions. **552**

Dependency theory   (See **World-system theory.**)

Dependent variable   A variable affected by another variable. **45**

Deviance   Any behavior or appearance that violates a norm. **247**

Differential association (theory)   A theory of deviance that argues that in the socialization process people vary in the norms and values they feel allegiance to because they are not equally exposed to the same norms and values. **265**

Diffusion   The process through which knowledge spreads from one society to another. **604**

Discovery   An instance of finding out about something that already exists. **604**

Discrimination   Positive or negative behavior based on stereotyped beliefs about the occupants of a status. **317**

Disinterestedness, norm of   A norm that requires scientists to not allow personal or other nonscientific interests to influence their work. **466**

Division of labor   The allocation of different roles among the members of a group, organization, community, or society. **123**

Dramaturgy (dramaturgical approach)   The study of social interaction as theater in which actors play roles before audiences. **24, 174**

Dual economy   An economy that is part monopolistic and part competitive. **500**

Dyad   A group with two members. **85**

Dysfunction   The interference of a cultural idea or social structure with the maintenance or adaptation of a society. **21**

Ecclesia   The most powerful of religious institutions, including most members of a society, dominated by a formal and bureaucratic clergy, governed by legal-rational and traditional authority, focusing on highly abstract ritual, and closely identified with dominant political and economic institutions. **551**

Ecological succession   The process through which ecosystems change. **602**

Ecology   The study of the relationship between populations and their physical environments, including the ability to use natural resources and technology. **16, 104**

Economic institutions   Enduring arrangements of cultural ideas and social relationships through which goods and services are produced and distributed in societies. **485**

Ecosystem   All forms of life that live in relation to one another and a shared physical environment. **121**

Education   The systematic formal transmission of skills, knowledge, beliefs, values, attitudes, and norms. **433**

Egalitarian family (marriage)   A family in which authority is evenly divided between husbands and wives. **414**

Ego   In Freudian theory, the rational part of the self that "manages" the desires of the id and the demands of the superego. **141**

Emergent norm theory   A theory of collective behavior that tries to explain how patterns of expectation and interaction emerge in crowds that involve no prior planning. **575**

Emigrant   Someone who moves out of a territory. **113**

Endemic disease   A disease that is normally found in a population. **109**

Endogamy   A marriage rule that requires people to marry someone belonging to their own social group or community. **409**

Epidemic disease   A disease not normally found in a population which spreads rapidly. **109**

Epidemiology   The study of where diseases come from, how they are distributed geographically and socially, and how they are transmitted from one place or person to another. **109**

Ethical religion   A religion that focuses more on sets of abstract ideals than on supernatural powers vested in gods, objects, or animals. **548**

Ethnic group   A set of people who identify with a common cultural heritage. **312**

Ethnicism   Prejudice based on ethnicity. **313**

Ethnicity   A concept that refers to statuses based on a shared cultural heritage. **312**

Ethnocentrism   The tendency of people to regard the ideas and practices of other cultures as incorrect, if not inferior. **65**

Ethnomethodology   The study of the unspoken rules and meanings through which people interpret one another's behavior and form expectations of one another. **23**

Evolutionary theories of social change   Theories that argue that all societies develop along predetermined paths that take them from inferior to superior forms, from simple to complex, and from "primitive" to "civilized." **607**

Exchange theory   An approach to social interaction that focuses on how people exchange one thing for another in social relationships. **177**

Exchange value   The attribution of value to goods or services based upon how much can be gotten for them in exchange for other goods and services. **486**

Exogamy   A marriage rule that requires people to marry someone outside their own social group or community. **409**

Experiment   A research design in which similar groups of subjects are exposed to conditions that differ in only one respect (the independent variable) in order to establish cause-and-effect relationships. **39**

Expressive collective behavior   Crowd or mass behavior that focuses on the expression of feelings toward some common object or event. **570**

Expressive role   A role that focuses on maintaining harmony among members. **89**

Expulsion   A form of social oppression in which minorities are forced to leave their communities or societies. **328**

Extended family   A family that includes a nuclear family plus additional relatives such as grandparents, aunts, or cousins. **411**

External causes   In social attribution, aspects of people's social situations that are used to explain their behavior. **165**

Extrapolation   An estimate of future conditions based on the assumption that "current trends will continue."

Extrinsic reward   A reward given to someone by someone else. **438**

Fad   A short-lived standard of appearance or behavior marked by great enthusiasm among its followers. **570**

False consciousness   A state of unawareness of, or misperception of, social conditions and their causes, especially when applied to social stratification. **289**

Family   A primary group organized around kinship ties and designed to regulate sexual behavior and reproduce, nurture, protect, and socialize the young. **404**

Family disorganization   The result of unoccupied statuses or inadequately performed roles within a family. **420**

Fashion   A relatively temporary standard of appearance or behavior that is considered to be socially acceptable or desirable. **570**

Fatalism   The belief that we can do nothing to control events. **556**

Femininity   A set of beliefs describing the ideal female. **345**

Feminism   An ideology that directly opposes sexism by supporting gender equality. **367** (See **Liberal feminism**; **Marxist feminism**; **Radical feminism**.)

Feudalism   The social structure that characterized medieval Europe and other preindustrial societies, based upon a system of mutual obligation between the nobility and serfs. **487**

Field experiment   A non-laboratory experiment. **40**

Folkways   The set of manners and customary acts that characterize everyday life in a society. **69**

Formal organization (group)   A group that exists for a specific purpose and is dominated by social relationships governed by clearly stated, rigidly enforced norms. **198**

Formal relationship   A relationship governed by norms that rigidly control interactions among status occupants. **93**

Formal sanction   A clearly defined reward or punishment with specific people empowered to deliver it. **73**

Front   In the dramaturgical approach, a person's physical appearance, behavior, and definition of the situation. **174**

Frontstage   In the dramaturgical approach, the place where roles are performed before an audience. **174**

Frustration-aggression theory   A theory that argues that collective behavior is a way of relieving feelings of frustration. **581**

Function   A contribution of a cultural idea or social structure to the maintenance and adaptation of a group or society. **21**

Functional perspective   A theoretical perspective that focuses on the ways in which cultural ideas and social structures contribute to or interfere with the maintenance or adaptation of a group or society. **21**

Game theory   A theoretical perspective that views collective behavior—and human behavior in general—as an attempt by people to maximize their rewards while minimizing costs. **577**

Gemeinschaft   A concept that describes communities in which social cohesion is based on primary relationships, shared culture, and similarity of life experience. **209** (Referred to by Durkheim as **Mechanical solidarity**.)

Gender   Social statuses to which males and females are assigned in a society. **341**

Gender role   A role that applies to people of different genders. **348**

Generalized belief   In Smelser's theory of social movements, an irrational belief seized upon as a way of justifying collective behavior and reducing uncertainty and feelings of anxiety. **584**

Generalized other   Our perception of the expectations that generally apply to people in a particular social situation. **143**

Genocide   The systematic attempt to kill all occupants of a particular status. **328**

Gentrification   A process of community change through which housing in old neighborhoods is restored, resulting in higher rents and the displacement of previous tenants who can no longer afford to live there. **241**

Gerontocracy   A society that is ruled by an elderly elite. **390**

Gesellschaft   A concept that describes communities in which social cohesion is based on secondary relationships and interdependencies created by complex divisions of labor. **211** (Referred to by Durkheim as **Organic solidarity**.)

Gesture   An action that has symbolic meaning. **57**

Government   The collection of people who happen to occupy positions of authority within the framework of social relationships that define the state. **519**

Group   Two or more people who interact with each other in patterned ways and are identified as members. **85**

Group effectiveness   The extent to which a group accomplishes the goals it sets for itself. **204**

Group process   What group members actually do, regardless of role expectations. **202**

Groupthink   An example of group process in which a shared desire for consensus outweighs members' better judgment. **206**

Hawthorne effect   A distortion of research results caused by the response of subjects to the special attention they receive from researchers. **39–40**

Hidden curriculum   In schools, knowledge, values, attitudes, norms, and beliefs that people acquire because of the process that is used to learn something else. **439**

Historical (analysis) research   The use of historical documents to analyze the development and change of culture, social structure, and ecology. **42**

Horticultural society   A society in which subsistence needs are met primarily through cultivation of small gardens, but without the use of the plow. **123**

Hospice   An organization designed to care for the terminally ill. **386**

Hunter-gatherer society   A society in which subsistence needs are met primarily by hunting wild game and gathering existing vegetation. **123**

Hypothesis   A statement that predicts a relationship between variables. **45**

Hysteria   A state of rapidly spreading anxiety that affects people in crowds and masses. **573**

I   Mead's concept that refers to that part of us that directly experiences ourselves and others. **142**

Id   In Freudian theory, that part of the self that is the source of unregulated desires and impulses. **141**

Ideal self   Our image of ourselves as we believe we ought to be. **147**

Ideal type   A concept that describes a "pure" type that does not actually exist. **93**

Ideology   A set of interrelated beliefs, values, attitudes, and norms that are used to explain and/or justify existing social relationships. **289**

Immanent change   Sorokin's principle that cultures have material and nonmaterial characteristics that cause societies to develop in certain directions. **607**

Immigrant   Someone who moves into a territory. **113**

Incest taboo   A norm that forbids sexual intercourse between people who are culturally defined as kin. **419**

Income   Money that people receive each year. **291**

Independence   The condition in which one variable has no effect on another. **49–50**

Independent primary (labor market) jobs   In the primary labor market, jobs that involve relatively high levels of creativity, autonomy, and power. **499**

Independent variable   A variable considered to cause variation in a second variable. **45**

In-depth interview   An interview or series of interviews designed to collect extensive information. **37**

Infant mortality rate   The number of infants under the age of one who die in a given year for every 1,000 births that occur during that year. **105**

Informal organization (group)   A group in which social relationships are governed by flexible, implicit norms. **198**

Informal relationship   A relationship governed by flexible, implicit norms. **93**

Informal sanction   A loosely defined reward or punishment with no specific people authorized to impose it. **73**

In-group   A group to which we belong and in which we share a sense of "we-ness" that often excludes and devalues members of other groups. **191**

Innovation   A form of deviance in which a person accepts values but rejects the norms that define legitimate means for achieving them. **251**

Institution   An enduring set of cultural ideas and social relationships that are designed to accomplish one or more goals. **98**

Insulation   The practice of managing our role performances so that role partners cannot observe our behavior in two or more conflicting roles. **85**

Integration   The degree to which members of groups in a community are distributed according to their relative numbers. **337**

Interaction   (See **Social interaction**.)

Interactionist perspective   A major theoretical perspective that focuses on the causes and consequences of social behavior, based on the importance of assigning meaning to appearance, behavior, and experience. **23**

Interest group   An organization that attempts to affect political decisions by supporting candidates who are sympathetic to their interests and by influencing those who are already in positions of authority. **531**

Intergenerational mobility   When the class position of children differs from that of their parents. **295**

Internal causes   In social attribution, personal motives, abilities, and emotional states that are used to explain behavior. **165**

Internal migration   Migration within a society.

International migration   Migration between societies.

International stratification   Stratification among societies. **301**

Interview   A method of gathering data through which people are asked a series of questions. **36**

Intrinsic reward   A reward that people give to themselves. **438**

Invention   Something created from things that already exist. **604**

Iron rule of oligarchy   Michels' theory that all states inevitably become oligarchies. **524**

Isolation   The degree to which groups do not share the same communities. **337**

J-curve theory   A theory of social movements that argues that movements are most likely to occur when a period of rising expectations is followed by sharp and rapidly worsening conditions for members of deprived groups. **582**

Juvenile delinquency   Criminal acts committed by minors. **255**

Kin   People who are bound together by ties of ancestry, adoption, or marriage. **405**

Kinship   Social relationships that are based on common ancestry, adoption, or marriage. **405**

Labor   The production of goods or services that can either be used directly or exchanged. **280**

Labor market segmentation   The division of job markets into distinct parts to which access is unequally distributed among workers. **499**

Labor power   The potential to produce goods—usually measured in terms of time—which workers sell to employers in return for wages. **280**

Laissez-faire leader   A leader who does not participate in group interaction unless asked to do so. **194**

Language   A collection of symbols (words) and rules for their usage (syntax and grammar). **60**

Latent dysfunction   A negative unintended effect of a cultural idea or social structure on the maintenance or adaptation of a group or society. **21**

Latent function   A positive unintended effect of a cultural idea or social structure on the maintenance or adaptation of a group or society. **21**

Latent status   A status that is not included in the definition of a situation, but nonetheless affects the expectations of the participants. **83**

Law   A norm whose sanctions are formal. **73**

Leadership   The exercise of authority that is supported by group norms and accepted by members. **91**

Leadership structure   A structure that exhibits the distribution of authority in a group or organization. **91**

Legal-rational authority   Power that is based on culturally defined rules that regulate social interaction. **517**

Liberal feminism   A branch of feminism that argues that gender equality can be achieved without challenging men as a group or changing basic economic and political arrangements such as capitalism. Equality is primarily a matter of gaining equal legal rights and equal access to higher level statuses. **367** (See **Marxist feminism**; **Radical feminism**.)

Life course   The culturally defined "normal" set of passages from one age group to another. **377**

Life expectancy   The average number of remaining years people can expect to live if current death rates remain unchanged throughout their lifetime. **107**

Lifetime mobility   The degree to which individuals change class position within their own lifetimes. **295**

Lobbyist   A representative of an interest group who meets with government officials and tries to influence decisions by providing information that tends to support the goals of the group. **532**

Longitudinal (study) survey   A research design in which information is gathered from the same sample of people at specified intervals of time. **38**

Looking-glass self   Our perception of how other people perceive and evaluate us. **145**

Macrosociology (macrolevel)   A branch (level) of sociology that focuses on the cultural and structural characteristics of groups and societies. **98, 597**

Manifest dysfunction   A negative intended effect of a cultural idea or social structure on the maintenance or adaptation of a group or society. **21**

Manifest function   An intended positive effect that a cultural idea or social structure has on the maintenance or adaptation of a group or society. **21**

Manifest status   A status that is explicitly included in the definition of a situation. **83**

Market economy   An economy based primarily upon exchange of goods and services rather than sharing. **486**

Marriage   A socially supported union between individuals in what is intended to be a stable, enduring relationship that involves sexual interaction as a key element. **403**

Marriage rules   Norms that regulate whom people may marry, when, and under what circumstances. **409**

Marxist feminism   A branch of feminism that argues that patriarchy is closely connected with capitalism, and that equality for women cannot be achieved without also making major political/economic changes in capitalism as a system. **367**

Masculinity   A set of beliefs describing the ideal male. **345**

Mass   A collection of people who pay attention to and react to the same thing without being in one another's presence. **570**

Mass society theory   Kornhauser's theory that collective behavior is caused by a social condition in which people feel isolated from one another and from their communities. **583**

Master status   A status that is treated as more important than any other status in a status set. **81**

Material culture   Objects made by people as they interact with one another and the physical world. **15, 74**

Matriarchy   A society or family system dominated by females. **357, 414**

Matrilineal descent   A kinship arrangement in which descent is traced through mothers and their blood relatives. **406**

Matrilocal family (society)   A kinship arrangement in which married couples live in or near the household of the wife's mother. **409**

Me   Mead's concept that refers to the part of the self that looks upon the self as an object. **142**

Mean   A statistical measure used to describe the average score in a sample or population. It is computed by adding all the scores together and dividing by the number of scores. **44**

Means of production   The physical means through which goods and services are produced in a society. **485**

Measurement instrument   A procedure that classifies individuals, groups, or societies according to a behavior or characteristic. **32**

Measure of association   A number varying between + 1.0 and − 1.0 that indicates how accurately an independent variable can be used to predict a dependent variable. **50**

Mechanical solidarity   **209** (See **Gemeinschaft**.)

Median   A statistical measure used to describe the typical score in a sample or population. It is equal to the score that divides a sample or population so that half the members are above the median and half are below. **45**

Medicalization   The process through which medical perspectives and treatment become increasingly influential and common in a society. **479**

Medicine   The social institution responsible for maintaining health, healing injury, and curing disease. **475**

Merchants   In a market economy, those who do not produce, but make a living by buying and selling what others produce. **488**

Metropolitan area   A city with at least 50,000 inhabitants, or an urbanized area that is socially and economically integrated with surrounding communities that bring the total population to 100,000 or more. **219**

Microecology   The study of how the number of people involved in a social situation and their physical arrangement in relation to one another affect social interaction. **171**

Microsociology (microlevel)   A branch (level) of sociology that focuses on social relationships among individuals. **16**

Migration   The movement of people from one place to another, either between societies or within them. **113**

Military-industrial complex   A coalition consisting of the military and industrialists who profit by manufacturing arms and selling them to the government. **533**

Mind   The ability to use symbols in order to understand other people's thoughts, feelings, and expectations. **141**

Minority (group)   A collection of people who, because of physical or cultural characteristics, are singled out from others for differential and unequal treatment. **312**

Misanthropy   Hatred of all people. **344**

Misogyny   Hatred of females. **344**

Mob   An emotionally aroused, acting crowd that typically has a leader and focuses on a specific goal, the achievement of which usually involves some form of violence. **571**

Mobilization   In Smelser's theory of collective behavior, the phase in which people gather into a crowd. **585**

Mob psychology   A theoretical approach that tries to explain collective behavior solely on the basis of the psychological states of its members. **574**

Mode   A statistical measure used to describe groups, equal to the most frequent score in a sample or population. **44**

Model   A person whose behavior or appearance we use as an example of what to imitate or what to avoid. **136**

Mode of production   The way in which a society goes about producing goods and services, consisting of the means and relations of production. **485**

Modern community   A community with a relatively complex division of labor, whose inhabitants tend to welcome change, use sophisticated technology, have well-developed mass media, and rely more on formal, secondary relationships than on primary or informal relationships. **221**

Modernization   A concept describing a process through which societies are believed to change from less to more developed forms through the introduction of new technology and other social change. **609**

Monogamy   Marriage to only one spouse at a time. **409**

Monopoly   An arrangement in a market economy in which a particular good or service has only one provider who, therefore, controls the market. **490**

Monotheism   Religious belief in a single supreme being. **547**

Morbidity   Any condition that causes illness. **107**

Mores   The set of deeply held ideas about how people ought to behave. **70**

Multilinear (change) theory   Theories of change that identify some change as universal, but also acknowledge that change takes place in ways that do not necessarily result in "progress." **608**

Multinational corporation   A large business organization whose operations extend across international boundaries. **510**

Multiple-nuclei theory (model)   A theory of urban land use according to which cities have many different "cores" of activity. **237**

Multistage sample   A sample selected in stages, beginning with the most unspecific level (such as regions) and ending with the most specific (such as houses on selected city blocks). **36**

"Nature versus nurture" debate   A debate arising from the question of whether nature (genetics) or nurture (environment) plays a greater role in human development. **134**

Negative relationship   A relationship in which high scores on one variable are related to low scores on another. **49–50**

Neighborhood   Collections of people who live close to one another within a community. **221**

Neolocal society (family)   A kinship arrangement in which married couples start new households. **410**

Niche   The position a species of life occupies in an ecosystem. **121**

Nominal member   Someone who is considered to be a member of a group but who rarely if ever participates in group activities. **190**

Nonconformist behavior (nonconformity)   Behavior that openly violates norms in order to bring about social change. **251**

Nonconformist subculture   The type of student subculture that values rebellion against authority and open deviation from the academic, collegiate, and vocational subcultures. **439**

Nonmaterial culture   The products of collective human activity that have no physical reality, including symbols, language, music, art, beliefs, values, norms, and attitudes. **15**

Norm   A rule that attaches sanctions to the behavior or appearance of status occupants. **15, 69**

"The norm"   The common behaviors of a society. **247**

Nuclear family   A family consisting of parents and their natural or adopted children. **411**

Null hypothesis   A testable assumption about a population. (See Appendix B.)

Oligarchy   A state that is ruled by a privileged elite. **524**

Oligopoly   An economic arrangement in a market economy in which production of a good or service is controlled by a few organizations. **495**

Openness   (See **Boundary**.)

Open (stratification) system   A stratification system in which people are allowed to move from one class to another regardless of their ascribed statuses. **295**

Operant conditioning   A form of learning in which punishment and reward are used to reinforce or discourage a behavior. **136**

Opportunity structure   The distribution of opportunities to achieve goals. **271**

Organic solidarity   **211** (See **Gesellschaft**.)

Organization   A situation in which two or more groups are related to each other through shared expectations and goals.

Organized skepticism, norm of   A norm that requires scientists to scrutinize all findings carefully before accepting them as true. **466**

Outer city   A new form of community emerging as suburbs become more densely settled and dominated by business and manufacturing that have moved from central cities, and which in some cases compete successfully with major cities as centers of economic life. **238**

Out-group   A group toward which hostile attitudes are directed by members of another group. **191**

Overpopulation   An ecological condition in which a society is unable to support all its members with available technology and natural resources. **125**

Pandemic disease   An epidemic that spreads across several different populations, even to include the entire world. **109**

Panic   A form of collective behavior in which people try to escape from a perceived danger in an uncooperative, often irrational way. **572**

Paradigm   A framework of guiding assumptions, theories, and methods that define a particular approach to scientific problems. **462**

Participant observation   A research method in which researchers observe behavior in real-life settings in which they are participants. **40**

Party   Weber's term for people who share similar levels of social power. **281**

Party platform   A statement of a political party's position on important issues. **530**

Patriarchy   A society or family system dominated by males. **357, 414**

Patrilineal descent   A kinship arrangement in which descent is traced through fathers and their blood relatives. **406**

Patrilocal family (society)   A kinship arrangement in which married couples live near or in the household of the husband's father. **409**

Pattern of communication   (See **Communication structure**.)

Peer group   People who share a level of social standing, especially in terms of age. **151**

Percentage   The number of people in a sample or population who have a particular characteristic, divided by the size of the population or group, and multiplied by 100.

Performative language   A meaningful utterance that alters people's positions in social relationships. **62**

Peripheral member   A group member who meets with other members but rarely interacts with them. **190**

Peripheral society   In world-system theory, a society that is in an economically subordinate position. **510**

Personality   The complex patterns of thought, feeling, and behavior that make each individual unique.

Personal power   Power that is based not on status occupancy, but on personal attributes such as physical strength or persuasiveness. **169**

Pluralism (ethnic)   The coexistence of diverse ethnic groups in the same society. **316**

Pluralism (political)   The distribution of power among a variety of interest groups. **229**

Pluralistic leadership structure   A structure in which the right to make decisions is divided among different specialists. **91**

Pluralist theory   The theory that holds that power is distributed among a wide variety of groups and individuals. **229**

Political economy   The social arrangements through which political and economic institutions support each other. **536**

Political institution   The relatively permanent cultural ideas and social structures through which power is distributed and exercised in societies. **517**

Political party   An organization whose main goal is to acquire political power by placing members in positions of authority in political institutions. **529**

Political process theory   An approach to social movements that concentrates both on what goes on within movements and on the relationship between movements and the institutions in the surrounding society. **588**

Politics   The social process through which power is distributed among and used by groups, communities, and societies. **517**

Polyandry   Marriage between a woman and more than one man. **409**

Polygamy   Marriage to more than one spouse at a time. **409**

Polygyny   Marriage between a man and more than one woman at a time. **409**

Polytheism   In religion, the belief in more than one god. **548**

Population   A collection of people who share a geographic territory. **35** In research, any precisely defined set of objects, people, groups, or societies. **16, 104**

Population density   The number of people per unit of area (e.g., per square mile). **120**

Population distribution   A concept that refers to (1) the density of populations, (2) how people of different social statuses are distributed spatially, and (3) the physical arrangement of individuals as they interact with each other. **120**

Population growth rate   The net result of births, deaths, in-migration, and out-migration in a population. **110**

Positive relationship   A statistical relationship in which high scores on one variable are related to high scores on another variable. **49–50**

Postindustrial society   A society in which the production of goods is overshadowed by the provision of services, and in which relations between people and machines are gradually replaced by relationships between people. **501**

Power   The potential to have an effect on ourselves, others, or our environment in spite of opposition. **90**

Power elite   A group of people who dominate decision making in all important areas of life in a community or society. **229**

Power-elite theory   The theory that argues that power in communities is concentrated in the hands of a relatively small group. **229**

Power structure   The distribution of power among members of groups, organizations, communities, or societies. **91**

Precipitating incident   In Smelser's theory of collective behavior, an event that triggers a collective response. **585**

Prejudice   A positive or negative attitude directed toward people simply because they occupy a status. **313**

Prestige   Respect accorded to people because of the social statuses they occupy. **92**

Primary deviance   Behavior that is not identified as deviant by the actor or by significant others. **269**

Primary group   A group valued for its own sake rather than for the achievement of specific goals, which endures through time and involves many aspects of its members' lives. **197**

Primary labor market   The portion of the segmented labor market that includes jobs that require stable work habits, involve skills that are often learned on the job, are relatively high-paying, and have job ladders. **498**

Primary relationship   A social relationship that exists for its own sake, endures through time, and involves people in many aspects of each other's lives. **93**

Prisoner's dilemma   An experimental situation in which actors must choose between the risks of cooperation and competition. **177**

Profane   In religion, the designation of an object, experience, or person as being part of the natural world. **544**

Profession   An occupation that is based on systematic, formal knowledge about a particular field (such as law) and involves high levels of autonomy and codes of conduct formulated and administered by other members of the occupation. **500**

Professionalization   The social process through which an occupation acquires the cultural and structural characteristics of a profession. **501**

Proletariat   In Marx's framework, the working class, which neither owns nor controls any means of production. **280**

Pull factor   In migration, a positive social or ecological condition in one area that motivates people living in another area to move there. **113**

Push factor   In migration, a negative social or ecological condition in people's home areas that motivate them to leave. **113**

Questionnaire   A method of gathering information in which respondents complete a written form. **36**

Race (biological)   A collection of people with distinct physical characteristics that are passed on through reproduction. **311**

Race (social)   A social status defined in terms of beliefs about biological race. **311**

Racism   Prejudice that is based on perceived racial differences. **313**

Radical feminism   A branch of feminism that argues that patriarchy centers on a fundamental difference in interests between men and women, and that equality for women cannot be achieved unless men as a group give up the power, wealth, and privilege that patriarchy grants them. **367**

Random sample   A sample drawn so that all members of the population have an equal chance of being included. **36**

Rate of natural increase   The difference between birth and death rates in a population. **110**

Realigning action   An action through which an actor tries to introduce a new definition of the situation. **177**

Rebellion   A form of deviance in which a person challenges values and norms that define legitimate means for achieving them. **251** In politics, a **rebellion** challenges the policies of a government without trying to change the cultural or structural characteristics of the state. **537**

Reference group   A group that someone uses as a standard of desirable or undesirable appearance or behavior. **148**

Reference individual   An individual that someone uses as a standard of desirable or undesirable appearance or behavior. **148**

Reform movement   A social movement that seeks to improve existing social environments. **580**

Reincarnation   Rebirth in new bodies. **548**

Relations of production   The social relationships through which goods or services are produced. **485**

Relative deprivation   The perception that one's position in a stratification system is worse than the position of others with whom one compares oneself. **299, 581**

Reliability   The degree to which a measurement instrument gives the same results with repeated measurements (assuming that whatever is being measured does not change). **33**

Religion   A set of cultural ideas, symbols, and practices that focus on the meaning of life and the nature of the unknown. **544**

Replication   The scientific practice of repeating research studies in order to confirm the original findings. **40**

Representative democracy   A state in which citizens delegate authority to elected representatives. **523**

Research design   The set of procedures that guide the gathering of research data. (See Appendix A.)

Resistance movement   A social movement intended to stop social change. **580**

Resocialization   The process of learning new roles that replace ones we once performed. **149**

Resource mobilization theory   An approach to social movements that tries to explain their emergence, success, or failure in terms of access to resources such as time, money, people, and leadership and organizational skills. **586**

Retreatism   A form of deviance in which a person withdraws from social life by rejecting values and norms without offering alternatives. **252**

Revolution   A social movement seeking to change the fundamental character of one or more social institutions in a society. **538, 580**

Riot   A leaderless, unorganized crowd whose members often focus on destruction and the expression of frustration and anger. **572**

Rising expectations   The hope or expectation of a deprived group that social conditions will improve in the near future—thought by some sociologists to be a cause of social movements. **582**

Rite of passage   A ceremony marking the transition of individuals from one social status to another. **149**

Ritual   A religious practice intended to maintain the relationship between believers and the supernatural and among one another. **548**

Ritualism   Conformity to norms without a commitment to values. **271**

Role   A set of beliefs, values, norms, and attitudes shared by status occupants in their relationships with the occupants of other statuses. **81**

Role distance   The disassociation or "distancing" of people from a role they are performing in order to distract themselves and others from negative aspects of the role performance. **85**

Role partner   The occupant of a particular status in relation to whom we perform roles as status occupants. **82**

Role performance   The actual behavior of people who occupy a status. **82**

Role segregation   The practice of avoiding occupying statuses for which specific individuals are role partners for more than one of our roles. **85**

Role set   A set of roles attached to a single status. **82**

Role strain   The tension that results when we have difficulty performing a role or satisfying the conflicting demands of two or more roles in a role set. **83**

Role structure   The set of roles performed by members of a group. **89**

Rumor   An unverified belief that arises from informal social interaction. **578**

Rural community   A small, homogeneous, and sparsely settled community. **219**

Sacred   In religion, the designation of an object, person, or experience as having meaning and value that inspire feelings of awe and place it outside of the natural human world. **544**

Sample   A subgroup of a population. **35**

Sanction   A social punishment or reward associated with obeying or violating a norm. **69**

Scapegoat   A person blamed for the troubles of others. **329**

School   A formal organization whose primary function is education. **433**

Science   A social institution responsible for seeking verifiable knowledge about the natural world. **461**

Scientific method   A method of posing and answering questions that relies on clear, objective guidelines for gathering and interpreting observable evidence. **29**

Scientific revolution   The replacement of one scientific paradigm with another. **463**

Secondary analysis   The use of information already gathered by others, such as government agencies and universities. **41**

Secondary deviance   Deviant acts performed in order to conform to people's expectations of those labeled "deviant." **269**

Secondary group   A group valued by its members only insofar as it enables them to achieve specific and limited goals. **197**

Secondary labor market   That segment of the labor market that includes jobs that do not require stable work habits, are relatively low-paying, have few chances for advancement, and have a high turnover. **499**

Secondary relationship   A relationship that is limited to goals that, once achieved, usually end a person's involvement. **93**

Sect   A religious group that draws most members by persuasion from the lower class, that has an informal structure and an untrained clergy, is governed with minimal authority, has few formal rituals, involves spontaneous displays of emotion, and generally opposes the dominant institutions of its society. **552**

Sector theory (model)   A theory of urban land use according to which cities grow in "pie-shaped" segments going out of a central business core. **237**

Secularization   The social change process through which religious beliefs and practices lose influence in a society. **561**

Segregation   The practice of physically separating the occupants of some social statuses from the occupants of others. **325**

Self-concept   The sum total of our thoughts and feelings about ourselves. **144**

Self-esteem   The positive and negative feelings people feel toward themselves. **147**

Self-fulfilling prophecy   A false belief that becomes true because we think and act as if it were. **163**

Semiperipheral society   In world-system theory, a society that is in the process of industrializing. **510**

Separatism   An ideology that holds that increased segregation is the only way to preserve minority cultures and end social oppression. **337**

Serfs   In a feudal economy, those who give a share of what they produce to the nobility in exchange for protection and use of the noble's land. **487**

Sex   Biological differences that define male and female. **341**

Sexism   Prejudice based on gender. **348**

Sex role   (See **Gender role**.)

Significant other   A particular individual whose beliefs, evaluations, attitudes, and expectations affect our appearance or behavior. **142**

Single-parent family   A nuclear family with one parent. **412**

Situational status   A status occupied only in a particular social situation. **81**

Social attribution   The process through which we interpret and explain other people's appearance and behavior. **165**

Social boundary   The protection from various kinds of social contact, offered by the roles attached to social statuses. **166**

Social category   Two or more people who have a social status in common, but who do not interact in patterned ways. **86**

Social change   The ways in which cultural and structural characteristics of social environments change.

Social class (Marx)   A set of people who occupy a similar position in relation to the means through which goods and services are produced in a society. **280**

Social class (Weber)   A set of people who have similar levels of wealth. **281**

Social cohesion   The degree to which members of groups, organizations, communities, or societies feel committed to group beliefs, values, attitudes, and norms, as well as to the well-being of other members. **209**

Social control   The organized ways in which society responds to behavior and people who are regarded as undesirable. **247, 585**

Social Darwinism   A late nineteenth-century theory (used to explain and justify social inequality) that held that the most capable people will and should gain more in the struggle for survival than the less capable. **289**

Social environment   Culture and social structure.

Social evolution   Spencer's theory (adapted from Darwin's ideas about natural evolution) that all societies naturally change toward superior forms. **607**

Social identity   The sum total of who we think we are in relation to other people. **146**

Social institution   (See **Institution**.)

Social interaction   The process through which individuals act in relation to one another. **161**

Socialism   An economic arrangement in which the means of production are owned and controlled by the state, not by private individuals or groups. **507**

Socialization   The process through which people learn to think, feel, evaluate, and behave as individuals in relation to social and physical environments. **133**

Social labeling perspective   A perspective that holds that societies often reinforce their boundaries by labeling people as well as their acts as deviant. **269**

Social learning theory (perspective)   A theory of socialization that focuses on learning through the imitation of models. **136**

Social mobility   The process through which people move from one position in a stratification system to another. **294**

Social movement   A collective effort aimed at either changing or preserving some aspect of social environments or ecological arrangements. **580**

Social oppression   The systematic, socially supported mistreatment and exploitation of one group or social category by another. **313**

Social promotion   A practice in which students who have not mastered the skills of a particular grade or level are nevertheless sent on to the next higher grade. **444**

Social psychology   The study of the effects of social environments on the psychological functioning and behavior of individuals.

Social script   In the dramaturgical approach to social interaction, the role we perform in relation to a particular audience. **174**

Social status   A position in a social relationship, a characteristic that locates individuals in relation to other people and sets of role expectations. **80**

Social stratification   The systematic, uneven distribution of valued products of social life such as wealth, power, and prestige among the occupants of different social statuses. **279**

Social structure   The arrangement of people in relation to one another and the patterns of expectation attached to positions in social relationships. Also patterns of expectation between groups, the distribution of people among various social positions, and the distribution of social rewards. **16, 80**

Social system   Any arrangement of social relationships that functions as a whole and can be thought of as a unit. **20**

Society   A population whose members share a cultural identity and way of life, interact in patterned ways, and occupy common geographic territory. **17, 90**

Sociobiology   A perspective that views social patterns among humans and other species as the result of genetics. **342**

Socioeconomic status   A single, overall rank many sociologists use to describe people's positions in stratification systems. **282**

Sociogram   A method of "mapping" patterns of loyalty and affection among group members. **90**

Sociology   The systematic study of social environments and their effects on human experience and behavior. **7**

Sociometry   The study of patterns of affection and loyalty that bind some group members more closely than others. **90**

Special language   A language developed by a subgroup in order to set themselves apart from others. **62**

Speech community   A set of people who share a language. **61**

Spurious relationship When two variables that have no causal connection are, nonetheless, statistically related to each other. **48**

State The social institution that claims the monopoly of the use of force within a given territory. **519**

Statistical independence A condition in which scores on one variable do *not* differ according to scores on another. **49–50**

Statistical inference A mathematical procedure used to test null hypotheses by comparing sample information with an assumption about a population. (See Appendix B.)

Statistical relationship A condition in which scores on one variable differ according to scores on another. **49–50**

Statistics A collection of numerical data; also, the branch of mathematics dealing with the collection and analysis of numerical data. **44** (See also Appendix B.)

Status Weber's term for the amount of prestige people receive. **281** (See also **Social status** for additional meaning.)

Status inconsistency The occupancy of statuses whose levels of prestige are inconsistent with one another. **283**

Status segregation (See **Role segregation**.)

Status set The entire collection of social statuses occupied by an individual. **81**

Status strain The tension that results from the inability to satisfy the requirements of roles attached to different statuses. **83**

Stereotype A rigid, oversimplified belief that is applied to all members of a group or social category. **163, 332**

Stigma Personal characteristics that others treat as deviant. **251, 253**

Structural lag A condition that occurs when a structural aspect of a society changes more slowly than other related aspects of society and is therefore out of balance with them. **393**

Structural strain In Smelser's theory of collective behavior, the result when people perceive a contradiction between the reality of social life and what their values say it ought to be. **581, 584**

Structural unemployment Unemployment caused by changes in the structure of occupational opportunities, such as when a steel factory closes and the number of steelworker jobs declines. **505**

Subculture A distinctive set of cultural ideas that sets a group of people apart from the culture of a surrounding community or society. **65**

Subfamily A family that shares a household with another family. **427**

Subgroup A group that is part of a larger group. **85**

Subordinate primary (labor market) jobs In the primary labor market, jobs that involve routine tasks and encourage workers to be obedient to authority. **499**

Suburb A community lying close to a city. **219**

Succession (See **Ecological succession**.)

Superego In Freudian theory, the conscience—the part of the self that is concerned with morality and living up to the expectations of adult society. **141**

Surplus value The value of goods and services that is kept by employers as profit after paying workers whatever is needed to sustain their labor power and reproduce themselves. **488**

Survey A method of gathering data through which people are asked a series of questions either by an interviewer or in questionnaire form. **36**

Symbols Objects, characteristics of objects, gestures, or words that represent more than themselves. **57**

Symbolic interaction The use of symbols by people to present themselves to others and interpret each other's behavior. **24**

Syndicated crime Highly bureaucratic crime, with rigid authority structures and complex divisions of labor. **259**

Systematic sample A sample drawn by selecting a random starting point in a list of a population and skipping through the list at regular intervals. **36**

Task role A role that focuses on achieving goals. **89**

Technocracy A society dominated by experts, especially those in the sciences. **473**

Technology A society's accumulated knowledge of how to use the natural environment. **16, 123, 470**

Temporary status A status occupied for a limited time. **81**

Theoretical perspective A non-explanatory, general framework that defines a point of view within a discipline, including basic assumptions that draw attention to particular aspects of a phenomenon and, therefore, generate particular kinds of questions about it. **20**

Theory A set of interrelated propositions designed to explain a phenomenon. **19**

Time structure The ways in which social relationships are defined, conditioned, and regulated by time. **88**

Token People who have a social characteristic that is unusual in a particular social situation. **41**

Total institution An organization such as a prison in which all aspects of people's daily lives are controlled by authorities. **263**

Totalitarianism The political condition in which the state attempts to control not only people's behavior, but virtually all aspects of their private lives as well. **525**

Totem In totemist religions, a sacred object believed to possess supernatural power. **547, 548**

Totemism A religion based on the belief that sacred objects (totems) possess supernatural power. **548**

Tracking An educational practice in which students are divided into groups on the basis of such factors as ability as measured by test scores. **453**

Traditional authority Authority that rests on the belief that the occupants of certain statuses are legitimately powerful because "that's the way it's always been." **518**

Traditional community A community with a relatively simple division of labor, whose inhabitants tend to resist change, use unsophisticated technology, have less developed mass media, and rely more on informal relationships than on secondary, formal relationships. **221**

Transitional status A status occupied for a limited time as a "stepping stone" toward the occupancy of other statuses. **81**

Triad A group with three members. **171**

Unilinear (change) theory A theory of social change according to which all societies follow the same path of development. **607**

Universalism, norm of A norm that requires scientists to evaluate scientific findings using the same criteria regardless of the source of the findings. **465**

Urban community A large, heterogeneous, and densely settled community. **219**

Urbanized area A city and the densely settled territory around it that, together, contain 50,000 or more people. **219**

Use value The attribution of value to goods and services based upon their usefulness to those who consume them. **486**

Validity The degree to which a measurement instrument measures what it is intended to measure. **32**

Value An idea about what is socially desirable. **15, 66**

Variable In sociology, a behavior or characteristic that varies from one individual, group, or society to another. **32**

Victimless crime   Criminal acts that violate legal norms but do not involve individuals as victims. **259**

Vocational subculture   A student subculture that values hard work for its "pay off" in terms of a good job after graduation. **439**

Wealth   Valued possessions not needed for immediate consumption. **291**

White-collar   Referring to occupations that primarily involve mental work. **283**

White-collar crime   Crimes that people are able to commit because of the power and opportunities afforded by social statuses—usually occupations—they occupy. **256**

Worker   (See **Proletariat**.)

World economy (system)   The economic arrangement among all nations, in which there is a division of labor and no nation is self-sufficient. **509**

World-system (dependency) theory   A theory that divides nations into three groups (based on the worldwide distribution of wealth and power) and argues that the economic development of societies depends on their position in the world system. **510, 610**

Xenophobia   The fear of strangers and outsiders. **225**

Zero-sum game   A game in which the success of one player requires the failure of another. **438**

References

Boldface numerals indicate pages on which references have been cited. References without page numbers, although not cited in the text, have been included because they may be of interest to the reader.

AACJC (American Association of Community and Junior Colleges). (1977, May). *Students in two-year colleges.* **441, 446**

AAMC (American Association of Medical Colleges). (1987, June 29). Reported in the *New York Times.* **355**

Abadinsky, H. (1983) *The criminal elite: Professional and organized crime.* Westport, CT: Greenwood Press. **259**

Abbey, A. (1987). Misperceptions of friendly behavior as sexual interest. *Psychology of Women Quarterly, 11(2),* 173–194. **24**

Abel, E. K. (1984).*Terminal degrees: The job crisis in higher education.* New York: Praeger.

Aberle, D. (1961). Matrilineal descent in cross-cultural perspective. In D. Schneider & K. Gough (Eds.), *Matrilineal kinship* (p. 677). Berkeley, CA: University of California Press. **406**

Aboulafia, M. (1986). *The mediating self: Mead, Sartre, and self-determination.* New Haven, CT: Yale University Press. **144**

Abrahamson, M. (1980). *Urban sociology* (2nd ed.). Englewood Cliffs, NJ: Prentice-Hall. **228**

Abrahamson, M. & Carter, V. J. (1986). Tolerance, urbanism, and region. *American Sociological Review, 51(2),* 287–294. **222**

Adler, P. A. (1985). *Wheeling and dealing: An ethnography of an upper-level drug dealing and smuggling community.* New York: Columbia University Press. **65, 259**

Adorno, T. W., et al. (1950). *The authoritarian personality.* New York: Harper & Row. **330**

Ageton, S. S. (1983). *Sexual assault among adolescents.* Lexington, MA: Lexington Books.

Alba, R. D., & Chamlin, M. B. (1983). A preliminary examination of ethnic identification among whites. *American Sociological Review, 48*(April), 240–247.

Alba, R. D., & Golden, R. (1986). Patterns of ethnic marriage in the United States. *Social Forces, 1,* 202–223.

Alba, R. D., & Moore, G. (1982). Ethnicity in the American elite. *American Sociological Review, 47*(June), 373–383. **323**

Albert, E. (1971). The unmothered woman. In H. Garskof (Ed.), *Roles women play.* Belmont, CA. **363**

Alexander, K. L., & Reilly, T. W. (1981). Estimating the effects of marriage timing on educational attainment. *American Journal of Sociology, 87,* 143–156. **350**

Alexander, N. C., & Wiley, M. G. (1981). Situated activity and identity formation. In M. Rosenberg & R. Turner (Eds.), *Sociological perspectives on social psychology.* New York: Basic Books. **183**

Allan, L. J. (1978). Child abuse: A critical review of the research and the theory. In J. P. Martin (Ed.), *Violence and the family.* New York: Wiley. **391**

Allen, I. L. (1983). *The language of ethnic conflict.* New York: Columbia University Press. **62, 191**

Allport, F. H. (1920). The influence of the group upon association and thought. *Journal of Experimental Psychology, 3,* 159–182.

Allport, G. W. (1935). Attitudes. In C. Murchison (Ed.), *A handbook of social psychology.* Worcester, MA: Clark University Press. **15, 74**

Allport, G. W. (1954). *The nature of prejudice.* Garden City, NY: Doubleday/Anchor Books. (1958 refers to the paperback edition.) **313, 332, 596**

Allport, G. W., & Postman, L. (1947). *The psychology of rumor.* New York: Holt. **579**

Alreck, P. L., & Settle, R. B. (1985). *The survey research handbook.* Homewood, IL: Richard D. Irwin. **36**

Altman, D. (1986). *AIDS in the mind of America: The social, political, and psychological impact of a new epidemic.* Garden City, NY: Anchor. **109**

Altman, I., Taylor, D. A., & Wheeler, L. (1971). Ecological aspects of group behavior in social isolation. *Journal of Applied Social Psychology, 1,* 76–100. **168**

Ambron, S. R. (1978). *Child development* (2nd ed.). New York: Holt, Rinehart & Winston. **143**

American Society of Plastic and Reconstructive Surgeons. (1985). In *Newsweek,* May 27, 1985, pp. 66–67. **346**

Amin, S. (1975). Toward a structural crisis of world capitalism. *Socialist Review, 5*(April), 9–44. **511, 512**

Anderson, A. G. (1979). *The business of organized crime.* Stanford, CA: Hoover Institution Press. **201, 259**

Anderson, B. A., Silver, B. D., & Abramson, P. R. (1987). The effects of race of the interviewer on race-related attitudes of black respondents in SRC/CPS national election studies. Population Studies Center Research Report 86-113. Ann Arbor, Michigan: Population Studies Center, University of Michigan. **34**

Archer, D., & Gartner, R. (1984). *A comparative perspective on the legitimation of homicide.* New Haven, CT: Yale University Press.

Arens, W. (1986). *The original sin: Incest and its meaning.* New York: Oxford University Press. **409**

Argyris, C. (1957). The individual and organization: Some problems of mutual adjustment. *Administrative Science Quarterly, 1,* 1–24. **213**

Ariès, P. (1962). *Centuries of childhood: A social history of family life.* New York: Knopf. **380, 386**

Aronowtiz, S. (1973). *False promises.* New York: McGraw-Hill. **452**

Aronson, S. H. (1971) The city: Illusion, nostalgia, and reality. In D. H. Wrong & H. L. Gracey (Eds.), *Readings in introductory sociology* (2nd ed.) (pp. 288–300). New York: Macmillan. **232**

Asch, S. E. (1952). *Social psychology.* Englewood Cliffs, NJ: Prentice-Hall. **189, 190**

Ash, D. (1967). *Automobile Almanac.* New York: Essandess/Simon & Schuster. **495**

Ash, T. G. (1984). *The Polish revolution: Solidarity.* New York: Charles Scribner's Sons. **537, 589**

Ashton, D. N. (1986). *Unemployment under capitalism: The sociology of British and American labor.* Westport, CT: Greenwood Press. **505**

Association of American Medical Colleges. (1987, June 29). Reported in Women as surgeons: Fighting for success. *New York Times.* **36**

Atchley, R. C. (1982). Retirement as a social institution *Annual Review of Sociology, 8,* 263–287. **395**

Auden, W. H. (1965). Prologue: The birth of architecture. In *About the house,* New York: Random House.

Axelrad, S. (1952). Negro and white male institutionalized delinquents. *American Journal of Sociology,* (May), 569–574. **262**

Axelrod, R. (1984). *The evolution of cooperation.* New York: Basic Books. **179**

Babst, D. V., et al. (1976). Assessing length of institutionalization in relation to parole outcome. *Criminology, 14*(May). 41–54. **262**

Back, K. W. (1981). Small groups. In M. Rosenberg & R. H. Turner (Eds.), *Social Psychology: Sociological perspectives* (pp. 320–343). New York: Basic Books. **190**

Balch, R. W., & Kelly, D. H. (1974). Reactions to deviance in a junior high school: Student views of the labeling process. *Journal of Instructional Psychology, 1*(1). **269**

Baldassare, M. (1983). Residential crowding and social behavior. In J. S. Pipkin, M. LaGory, and J. R. Blau (Eds.), *Remaking the city* (pp. 148–162). Albany, NY: State University of New York Press. **234**

Baldridge, J. V., & Deal, T. (1983). *The dynamics of organizational change in education.* Berkeley, CA: McCutchan. **444**

Baldus, D. (1987, April 23). Research on the death penalty reported in the *New York Times,* March 23. See also *New York Times,* p. A1. **262**

Bales, R. F. (1950). *Interaction process analysis: A method for the study of small groups.* Cambridge, MA: Addison-Wesley. **89, 192, 202**

Bales, R. F. (1954). Task roles and social roles in problem-solving groups. In E. E. Maccoby, T. M. Newcomb, & E. L. Hartley (Eds.), *Readings in social psychology* (3rd ed.). New York: Holt, Rinehart & Winston. **91**

Bales, R. F. (1968). Interaction process analysis. In D. L. Sills (Ed.), *The international encyclopedia of the social sciences* (Vol. 7). New York: The MacMillan Company/The Free Press. **203**

Bales, R. F., & Borgatta, E. F. (1955). A study of group size: Size of group as a factor in the interaction profile. In A. P. Hare, E. F. Borgatta, & R. F. Bales, *Small Groups.* New York: Knopf. **208**

Bales, R. F., and Slater, P. E. (1955). Role differentiation in small decision-making groups. In T. Parsons, R. F. Bales, and P. E. Slater, *The family, socialization, and interaction process.* New York: The Free Press. **91**

Bales, R. F., and Strodtbeck, F. L. (1951). Phases in group problem-solving. *Journal of Abnormal and Social Psychology, 46,* 485–495. **203**

Bamberger, J. (1974). The myth of matriarchy: Why men rule in primitive society. In M. Z. Rosaldo & L. Lamphere (Eds.), *Women, culture, and society* (pp. 263–280). Stanford, CA: Stanford University Press. **357, 414**

Bandura, A. (1977). *Social learning theory.* Englewood Cliffs, NJ: Prentice-Hall. **136**

Bandura, A., Ross, D., & Ross, S. (1963b). Vicarious reinforcement and imitative learning. *Journal of Abnormal and Social Psychology, 67,* 601–607. **360**

Bane, M. J. (1976). *Here to stay: American families in the twentieth century.* New York: Basic Books. **417, 421, 422, 428**

Bane, M. J., & Jencks, C. (1972, September 16). The schools and equal opportunity. *Saturday Review of Education,* pp. 37–42. **298, 451, 454**

Banfield, E. C. (1965). *Political influence.* New York: The Free Press. **230**

Banfield, E. C. (1967). *The moral basis of a backward society.* New York: The Free Press. **557**

Baran, P. A. (1957). *The political economy of growth.* New York: Monthly Review Press. **610**

Baran, P. A., & Sweezy, P. M. (1966). *Monopoly capital.* New York: Modern Reader Paperbacks. **496**

Barnes, B. (1985). *About science.* New York: Basil Blackwell. **90, 461, 462, 469, 471, 474, 475**

Barnet, R. J., & Muller, R. J. (1974). *Global reach.* New York: Simon & Schuster. **301, 303**

Barnett, R. C., & Baruch, G. K. (1983). *Women's involvement in multiple roles, role strain, and psychological distress.* (Working Paper 107). Wellesley, MA: Wellesley College Center for Research on Women. **349**

Baron, H. M. (1976). The demand for black labor. In J. H. Skolnick & E. Currie (Eds.), *Crisis in American institutions* (3rd ed.). Boston: Little, Brown. **325**

Barsh, R. L., & Henderson, J. Y. (1980). *The road: Indian tribes and political liberty.* Berkeley and Los Angeles, CA: University of California Press. **316**

Bart, P. B. (1971). Depression in middle-aged women. In V. Gornick & B. K. Moran (Eds.), *Woman in sexist society* (pp. 163–186). New York: Signet. **364, 383**

Barth, H. (1976). *Truth and ideology.* Berkeley, CA: University of California Press.

Bartlett, F. C. (1932). *Remembering.* Cambridge, England: Cambridge University Press. **579**

Barton, A. (1985). Determinants of economic attitudes in the American business elite. *American Journal of Sociology, 91,* 54–87.

Barton, E. M., Baltes, M. M., & Orzech, M. J. (1980). Etiology of dependence in older nursing home residents during morning care. *Journal of Personality and Social Psychology, 38,* 423–431. **391**

Basler, B. (1982, April 18). Auto thefts in city. *New York Times.* **273**

Bass, B. M. (1960). *Leadership, psychology, and organizational behavior.* New York: Harper & Row. **195**

Baumrind, D. (1964). Some thoughts on the ethics of research: After reading Milgram's 'Behavior study of obedience.' *American Psychologist, 19,* 421–423. **268**

Bavelas, A. (1950). Communication patterns in task-oriented groups. *Journal of Acoustical Society of America, 22,* 725–730. **92**

Baxandall, R., Gordon, L., & Reverby, S. (1976). *America's working women.* New York: Vintage. **42, 353**

Beale, H. K. (1975). The education of Negroes before the Civil War. In J. Barnard & D. Burner (Eds.), *American experience in education* (pp. 88–90). New York: Watts. **447**

Beard, C. A., & Beard, M. R. (1944). *A basic history of the United States.* New York: The New Home Library. **525**

Beauvais, K. (1986). Workshops to combat sexual harassment: A case study of changing attitudes. *Signs: Journal of Women in Culture and Society, 12*(1), 130–145. **351**

Beauvoir, S. de. (1952). An androgynous world. In B. Roszak and T. Roszak (Eds.), *Masculine/feminine* (pp. 148–157). New York: Harper & Row.

Becker, G. (1981). *A treatise on the family.* Cambridge, MA: Harvard University Press. **112**

Becker, H. S. (1953). Becoming a marijuana user. *American Journal of Sociology, 59*(November), 235–242.

Becker, H.S. (Ed.). (1964). *The other side.* New York: The Free Press. **269**

Becker, H. S. (1973). *Outsiders: Studies in the sociology of deviance* (rev. ed.). New York: The Free Press. **269**

Becker, H. S., & Geer, B. (1958). The fate of idealism in medical school. *American Sociological Review, 23,* 50–56. **158**

Beeghley, L. (1983). *Living poorly in America.* New York: Praeger. **306**

Bell, D. (1973). *The coming of postindustrial society.* New York: Basic Books. **362, 501, 610**

Bell, D. (1987). *And we are not saved: The elusive quest for racial justice.* New York: Basic Books.

Bell, W. (1969). Urban neighborhoods and individual behavior. In P. Meadows & E. H. Mizburchi (Eds.), *Urbanism, urbanization, and change.* Reading, MA: Addison-Wesley. **223**

Bellah, R. N. (1970). *Beyond belief.* New York: Harper & Row.

Bellah, R. N. (1973). *The broken covenant.* New York: Seabury Press. **562, 563**

Bellah, R. N., & Hammond, P. E. (1980). *Varieties of civil religion.* New York: Harper & Row. **563**

Bellah, R. N., Madsen, R., Sullivan, W. M., Swidler, A., & Tipton, S. M. (1985). *Habits of the heart: Individualism and commitment in American life.* Berkeley, CA: University of California Press. **562**

Bem, S., & Bem, D. (1976). Training the woman to know her place: The power of nonconscious ideology. In S. Cox (Ed.), *Female psychology: The emerging self.* Chicago: St. Martin's Press. **140**

Bendix, R., & Lipset, S. M. (Eds.), (1966). *Class, status, and power.* New York: The Free Press.

Benedict, R. (1934). *Patterns of culture.* New York: New American Library. **68, 79, 135**

Benedict, R. (1946). *The chrysanthemum and the sword.* Boston: Houghton Mifflin. **177**

Benoliel, J. Q. (1973). *The nurse and the dying patient.* New York: Macmillan. **386**

Bensman, J., & Rosenberg, B. (1979). The peer group. In P. I. Rose (Ed.), *Socialization and the life cycle.* New York: St. Martin's Press.

Ben-Yehuda, N. (1980). The European witch craze of the 14th and 17th centuries: A sociologist's perspective. *American Journal of Sociology, 86*(1), 1–31. **347**

Berger, B. M. (1960). *Working class suburb: A study of autoworkers in suburbia.* Berkeley, CA: University of California Press. **223**

Berger, P. L. (1963). *Invitation to sociology: A humanistic perspective.* Garden City, NY: Anchor Books. **19**

Berger, P. L. (1967). *The sacred canopy.* New York: Doubleday. **560, 561**

Berger, P. L. (1970). *A rumor of angels.* Garden City, NY: Doubleday.

Berger, P. L., & Kellner, H. (1964). Marriage and the Construction of reality. *Diogenes, 45,* 1–25. (Reprinted in H. Robboy, S. L. Greenblatt, and D. Clark (Eds.). *Social interaction* (pp. 308–322). New York: St. Martin's Press.) **181, 413**

Berger, P. L., & Luckman, T. (1967). *The social construction of reality.* Garden City, NY: Anchor Books. **61**

Bergesen, A. (Ed.). (1980). *Studies of the modern world system.* New York: Academic Press. **509**

Bergmann, B. R. (1986). *The economic emergence of women.* New York: Basic. **47, 365**

Berk, R. A. (1974a). A gaming approach to crowd behavior. *American Journal of Sociology, 79*(June), 355–373. **577**

Berk, R. A. (1974b). *Collective behavior.* Dubuque, IA: William C. Brown. **577**

Berk, R. A., & Berk, S. F. (1979). *Labor and leisure at home: Content and organization of the household day.* Beverly Hills, CA: Sage. **353**

Berk, R. A., & Berk, S. F. (1983). Supply-side sociology of the family. *Annual Review of Sociology, 9,* 375–395.

Berk, S. F., & Loseke, D. R. (1981). Handling family violence: Situational determinants of police arrest in domestic disturbances. *Law and Society Review, 15,* 315–346. **424**

Berk, R. A., & Newton, P. J. (1985). Arrest and wife battery. *American Sociological Review, 50*(2), 253–262. **424**

Berkowitz, L. (1978). Decreased helpfulness with increased group size through lessening the effects of the needy individual's dependency. *Journal of Personality, 46,* 299–310. **162**

Berle, A. A., Jr., & Means, G. C. (1968). *The modern corporation and private property* (rev. ed.). New York: Harcourt Brace and World. (Original work published 1932). **497**

Bernard, J. (1972). *The future of marriage.* New York: Bantam. **364, 601**

Berreman, G. D. (1973). *Caste in the modern world.* Morristown, NJ: General Learning Press. **302**

Berry, B. J. L., & Kasarda, J. D. (1977). The congruence of social and spatial structure: Neighborhood status and white resistance to residential integration as an example. In *Contemporary urban ecology* (Chapter 2). New York: Macmillan. **225, 227, 239, 240, 243**

Besser, J. D. (1979, January). Gentrifying the ghetto. *The Progressive,* pp. 30–32. **241**

Best, M. H., & Connolly, W. E. (1976). *The politicized economy.* Lexington, MA: D. C. Heath. **497**

Bettelheim, B. (1969). *Children of the dream.* New York: Macmillan. **240, 604**

Bettelheim, B., & Janowitz, M. (1950). *Dynamics of prejudice: A psychological and sociological study of veterans.* New York: Harper & Row. **330**

Bilheimer, R. S. (Ed.). (1983). *Faith and ferment: an interdisciplinary study of Christian beliefs and practices.* Minneapolis: Augsburg. **562**

Binder, F. M. (1974). *The age of the common school: 1830–1865.* New York: Wiley. **454**

Binford, H. C. (1985). *The first suburbs: Residential communities on the Boston periphery, 1815–1860.* Chicago: University of Chicago Press. **222**

Birren, J. E. (1968). Psychological aspects of aging and intellectual functioning. *The Gerontologist, 8*(1, Part II), 19. **378, 379**

Black, D. J. (1971). The social organization of arrest. *Stanford Law Review, 23*(6). 1104–1110. **260**

Blackburn, M. L., & Bloom, D. E. (1985). What is happening to the middle class? *American Demographics, 7,* 18–25. **299**

Blake, J. (1972). Coercive pronatalism and American population policy. In R. Parke, Jr., & C. F. Westoff (Eds.), *Aspects of population growth policy* (Vol. 6 of U.S. Commission on Population and the American Future Research Reports). Washington, DC: U.S. Government Printing Office. **106**

Blake, J. (1982). Demographic revolution and family evolution: Some implications for American women. In P. W. Berman and E. R. Ramey (Eds.), *Women: A developmental perspective* (pp. 299–

312) (NIH Publication No. 82-2298). Washington, DC: U.S. Department of Health and Human Services. **407**

Blake, J. (1985). Number of siblings and educational mobility. *American Sociological Review, 50*(1), 84–93.

Blalock, H. M. (1964). *Causal inferences in nonexperimental research.* Chapel Hill: University of North Carolina. **39**

Blalock, H. M. (Ed.). (1985). *Causal models in experimental and panel designs.* Chicago: Aldine. **39**

Blau, P. M. (1964). *Exchange and power in social life.* New York: Wiley. **177**

Blau, P. M. (1973). *The dynamics of bureaucracy* (2nd rev. ed.). Chicago: University of Chicago Press. **264**

Blau, P. M. (Ed.). (1975).*Approaches to the study of social structure.* New York: The Free Press.

Blau, P. M., Blum, T. C., & Schwartz, J. E. (1982). Heterogeneity and intermarriage. *American Sociological Review, 47*(1), 45–62. **410**

Blau, P. M., & Duncan, O. D. (1967). *The American occupational structure.* New York: Wiley. **296, 297, 301, 303, 325**

Blau, Z. S. (1982). *Old age in a changing society* (2nd ed.). New York: Watts.

Blauner, R. (1964). *Alienation and freedom.* Chicago: University of Chicago Press. **504**

Blauner, R. (1972). Racism as the negation of culture. In *Racial oppression in America.* New York: Harper & Row. **316**

Bleier, R. (1984). *Science and gender: A critique of biology and its theories on women.* New York: Pergamon Press. **134, 343, 473**

Bloch, M. (1961). *Feudal society.* Chicago: University of Chicago Press. **487**

Block, A. A., & Chambliss, W. J. (1981). *Organizing crime.* New York: Elsevier North Holland. **259**

Block, J. (1973). Conceptions of sex role: Some cross-cultural and longitudinal perspectives. *American Psychologist, 28,* 512–526. **265, 348**

Block, N. J., & Dworkin, G. (Eds.). (1976). *The IQ controversy.* New York: Pantheon.

Blood, R. O., Jr., & Wolfe, D. M. (1960). *Husbands and wives.* New York: The Free Press. **420**

Bloom, D. E. (1982). What's happening to the age at first birth in the United States? A study of recent cohorts. *Demography, 19*(3), (August), 351–370. **363, 601**

Bluestone, B., & Harrison, B. (1982). *The deindustrialization of America: Plant closings, community abandonment, and the dismantling of basic industry.* New York: Basic Books. **229**

Blumenthal, M. D., et al. (1972). *Justifying violence: Attitudes of American men.* Ann Arbor, MI: Institute for Social Research. **425**

Blumer, H. (1951). Collective Behavior. In A. M. Lee (Ed.), *New outline of the principles of sociology.* New York: Barnes and Noble. (Original work published 1939). **570, 575**

Blumer, M. (1984). *The Chicago school of sociology: Institutionalization, diversity, and the rise of sociological research.* Chicago: University of Chicago Press. **219**

Blumstein, A., & Nagin, D. S. (1974). *Analysis of arrest rates for trends in criminality.* Pittsburgh: Carnegie Mellon University School of Urban and Public Affairs. **272**

Bock, E. W. (1972, January). The significance of marital kinship and alternative relations. *The Family Co-ordinator,* pp. 71–78. **362**

Bogardus, E. S. (1928). *Immigration and race attitudes.* Boston: D. C. Heath. **323**

Bogardus, E. S. (1959). Race reactions by sexes. *Sociology and Social Research, 43,* 439–441. **323**

Bok, S. (1979). *Lying: Moral choice in public and private life.* New York: Vintage. **71**

Bollen, K. (1983). World system position, dependency, and democracy. *American Sociological Review, 48*(August), 468–479. **523**

Bollen, K., & Jackman, R. W. (1985). Political democracy. *American Sociological Review, 50*(4), 438–457.

Booth, A., & Edwards, J. N. (1985). Age at marriage and marital instability. *Journal of Marriage and the Family, 47,* 67–75.

Bose, C. E. (1985). *Jobs and gender: A study of occupational prestige.* New York: Praeger. **293, 358**

Bosrup, E. (1981). *Population and technological change.* Chicago: University of Chicago Press. **120, 127**

Boss, P. G. (1980). Normative family stress: Family boundary changes across the life span. *Family Relations, 29,* 445–450. **425**

Boswell, T. E. (1986). Discrimination and Chinese immigration. *American Sociological Review, 51*(3), 352–371. **226, 493**

Bottomore, T. (Ed.). (1963). *Karl Marx: Early writings.* London: Watts.

Bottomore, T. Structure and history. (1975). In P. M. Blau (Ed.), *Approaches to the study of social structure.* New York: The Free Press.

Bottomore, T., & Nisbet, R. (Eds.). (1978). *A history of sociological analysis.* New York: Basic Books.

Bottomore, T., & Rubel, M. (Eds.). (1965). *Karl Marx: Selected writings in sociology and social philosophy.* New York: McGraw-Hill. **271**

Bouvier, L. F., & Gardner, R. W. (1986). Immigration to the U.S.: The unfinished story. *Population Bulletin, 41*(1, November). Washington, DC: Population Reference Bureau. **113, 115, 116, 117**

Bouvier, L. F., Shyrock, H. S., & Henderson, H. W. (1977). International migration: Yesterday, today, and tomorrow. *Population Bulletin, 30,* 3–24. **114**

Bowles, S., & Gintis, H. (1976). *Schooling in capitalist America: Educational reform and the contradictions of economic life.* New York: Basic Books.

Bowles, S., & Gintis, H. (1986). *Democracy and capitalism.* New York: Basic Books. **498, 511**

Bowles, S., & Nelson, V. (1974). The 'inheritance of IQ' and the intergenerational reproduction of economic inequality. *Review of Economics and Statistics, 56* (1, February). **298, 299**

Boyd, R., & Richersen, P. J. (1985). *Culture and the evolutionary process.* Chicago: University of Chicago Press. **342**

Bradbury, K., Downs, A., & Small, K. A. (1982). *Urban decline and the future of American cities.* Washington, DC: The Brookings Institution. **238**

Bradshaw, Y. W. (1985). Dependent development in black Africa. *American Sociological Review, 50*(2), 195–206.

Bradshaw, Y. W. (1987). Urbanization and underdevelopment: A global study of modernization, urban bias, and economic dependency. *American Sociological Review, 52*(2), 224–239. **116, 238, 239**

Braithwaite, J. (1981). The myth of social class and criminology reconsidered. *American Sociological Review, 46*(February), 36–57. **257**

Braudel, F. (1977). *Afterthoughts on material civilization and capitalism.* Baltimore: Johns Hopkins University Press.

Braudel, F. (1981). *The structures of everyday life: Civilization and capitalism, 15th–18th century, volume one.* New York: Harper & Row. **66, 224, 487**

Braudel, F. (1983). *The wheels of commerce: Civilization and capitalism, 15th–18th century, volume two.* (S. Reynolds, Trans.). New York: Harper & Row. **509**

Braudel, F. (1984). *The perspective of the world: Civilization and Capitalism, 15th–18th century, volume three.* New York: Harper & Row.

Braverman, H. (1974). *Labor and monopoly capital.* New York: Monthly Review Press. (1976 refers to the paperback edition.) **488, 502**

Breault, K. D. (1986). Suicide in America: A test of Durkheim's theory of religious and family integration. *American Journal of Sociology, 92*(3), 628–656. **30**

Brehm, J. W. (1966). *A theory of psychological reactance.* New York: Academic Press. **194**

Brenner, R. (1976). Agrarian class structure and economic development in pre-industrial Europe. *Past and Present, 70,* 30–75. **611**

Bressler, M. (1960). The Myers' case: An instance of successful racial invasion. *Social Problems, 8,* 133. **602**

Brim, O. G., Jr. (1966). Socialization after childhood. In O. G. Brim, Jr., & S. Wheeler, *Socialization after childhood: Two essays.* New York: Wiley.

Broad, W. J. (1988, February 14). Science can't keep up with flood of new journals. *New York Times,* p. C1. **466**

Broad, W., & Wade, N. (1983). *Betrayers of the truth: Fraud and deceit in the halls of science.* New York: Simon and Schuster/Touchstone. **467**

Brody, J. A. (1983). Life expectancy and the health of older people. *American Journal of Geriatric Sociology.*

Bronfenbrenner, U. (1970). *Two worlds of childhood.* New York: Russell Sage Foundation.

Broverman, I. K., Broverman, D., Clarkson, F., Rosenkrantz, P., & Vogel, S. (1970). Sex-role stereotypes and clinical judgements of mental health. *Journal of Consulting and Clinical Psychology, 34,* 1–7. **345**

Broverman, I. K., Vogel, S., Broverman, D., Clarkson, F., & Rosenkrantz, P. (1972). Sex-role stereotypes: A current appraisal. *Journal of Social Issues, 28,* 59–79.

Brown, D. L., & Wardwell, J. M. (Eds.). (1980). *New directions in urban-rural migration: The population turnaround in rural America.* New York: Academic Press.

Brown, R. (1965). *Social psychology.* New York: The Free Press. **69, 141**

Brown, R. S., Moon, M., & Zoloth, B. S. (1980). Incorporating occupational attainment in studies of male-female earnings differentials. *Journal of Human Resources, 15,* 3–28. **355**

Brownmiller, S. (1975). *Against our will: Men, women, and rape.* New York: Simon & Schuster. **168, 259, 352, 408**

Burawoy, M., & Lukacs, J. (1985). Capitalist and socialist work. *American Sociological Review, 50*(6), 723–737. **507**

Burch, P. H., Jr. (1972). *The managerial revolution reassessed.* Lexington, MA: D. C. Heath. **497**

Bureau of Justice Statistics. (1987a). Recidivism of young parolees. Washington, DC: U.S. Government Printing Office.

Bureau of Justice Statistics. (1987b). Violent crime by strangers and nonstrangers. Washington, DC: U.S. Government Printing Office.

Bureau of Labor Statistics. (1986, November 30). Findings reported in the *New York Times,* Business Section, p. 1. **505**

Bureau of Labor Statistics. (1987, September 27). Findings reported in the *New York Times,* Business Section, p.1. **505, 506**

Bureau of Labor Statistics. (1988, January 24). Findings reported in the *New York Times.* **506**

Bureau of National Affairs. (1984). *Pay equity and comparable worth* (Report 45 LDSR 28). Washington, DC: Bureau of National Affairs. **354**

Burke, K. (1935). *Permanence and change.* New York: Republic.

Burke, K. (1945). *A grammar of motives.* Englewood Cliffs, NJ: Prentice-Hall. **139**

Burke, P. J., and Reitzes, D. C. (1981). The link between identity and role performance. *Social Psychology Quarterly, 44,* 83–92. **183**

Burnette, R. (1971). *The tortured Americans.* Englewood Cliffs, NJ: Prentice-Hall. **321**

Burns, H. (1973). Black people and the tyranny of American law. *The Annals, 407*(May), 156–166. **250, 526**

Burnside, I. M. (1975). Sexuality and the older adult: Implications for nursing. In I. M. Burnside (Ed.), *Sexuality and aging.* Los Angeles: Ethel Percy Andrus Gerontology Center. **379**

Bush, D. M., & Simmons, R. G. (1981). Socialization processes over the life course. In M. Rosenberg & R. H. Turner (Eds.), *Social psychology: Sociological perspectives* (pp. 133–164). New York: Basic Books. **133, 149**

Buss, T. F., & Redburn, F. S. (1983). *Shutdown at Youngstown: Public policy for mass unemployment.* Albany, NY: State University of New York Press. **229, 504**

Calavita, K. (1984). *U.S. immigration law and the control of labor: 1820–1924.* Orlando, FL: Academic Press. **498**

Calhoun, J. B. (1962). Population density and social pathology. *The Scientific American, CCVI,* pp. 139–148. **234**

Callahan, R. E. (1962). *Education and the cult of efficiency.* Chicago: University of Chicago Press. **444**

Campbell, A. A. (1947). Factors associated with attitudes towards Jews. In T. Newcomb & E. Hartley (Eds.), *Readings in social psychology.* New York: Holt, Rinehart & Winston. **330**

Campbell, A. A. (1971). *White attitudes toward black people.* Ann Arbor, MI: Institute for Social Research, University of Michigan. **330**

Campbell, A. A., and Schuman, H. (1968). Racial attitudes in fifteen American cities. In *Supplementary studies for the National Advisory Commission on Civil Disorders* (see Kerner Commission). Washington, DC: U.S. Government Printing Office.

Cantor, M. G., and Pingree, S. (1983). *The soap opera.* Beverly Hills, CA: Sage. **42**

Cantril, H. (1963). *The psychology of social movements.* New York: Wiley. **571**

Caplow, T. (1947). Rumors in war. *Social Forces, 25,* 298–302. **579**

Caplow, T. (1952). Urban structure in France. *American Sociological Review, XVII,* 544–549. **203, 236**

Caplow, T. (1956). A theory of coalitions in the triad. *American Sociological Review, 21,* 489–493. **203**

Caplow, T. (1964). *The sociology of work.* New York: McGraw-Hill. **501**

Caplow, T. (1968). *Two against one: Coalitions in triads.* Englewood Cliffs, NJ: Prentice-Hall. **171, 203**

Caplow, T. (1982). Christmas gifts and kin networks. *American Sociological Review, 47*(June), 383–392. **177**

Caplow, T., et al. (1983). *All faithful people.* Minneapolis: University of Minnesota Press. **562**

Caplow, T., & McGee, R. J. (1958). *The academic marketplace.* New York: Arno Press. **439**

Carnegie Council on Policy Studies in Higher Education. (1979, December 3). Giving youth a better chance: Options for education, work, and service. *The Chronicle of Higher Education,* pp. 11–13. **439**

Carnegie Foundation for the Advancement of Teaching. (1988). *An imperiled generation: Saving urban schools.* New York: Carnegie Foundation. **439**

Carnoy, M., & Levin, H. (1985). *Schooling and work in the democratic state.* Stanford, CA: Stanford University Press. **434**

Castelli, J. (1983). *The bishops and the bomb: Waging peace in a nuclear age.* New York: Image. **560**

Castells, M. (1977). *The urban question: A Marxist approach.* (A. Sheridan, Trans.) Cambridge, MA: The MIT Press. **222**

Castells, M. (1980). *The economic crisis of American society.* Princeton, NJ: Princeton University Press. **512**

Cath, S. H., Gurwitt, A. R., & Ross, J. M. (Eds.). (1982). *Father and child: Developmental and clinical perspectives.* Boston: Little, Brown. **369**

Chackerian, R., & Abcarian, G. (1984). *Bureaucratic power in society.* Chicago: Nelson-Hall. **452**

Chafetz, J. S. (1984). *Sex and advantage: A comparative, macrostructural theory of sex stratification.* Totowa, NJ: Rowman & Allanheld.

Chafetz, J. S., & Dworkin, A. G. (1986). *Female revolt: Women's movements in world and historical perspective.* Totowa, NJ: Rowman & Allanheld.

Chalfant, H. P., Beckley, R. E., & Palmer, L. E. (1981). *Religion in contemporary society.* Palo Alto, CA: Mayfield. **552, 553**

Chamberlin, E. H. (1962). *Theory of monopolistic competition.* Cambridge, MA: Harvard University Press. **495**

Chambliss, W. J. (1969). *Crime and legal process.* New York: McGraw-Hill. **262**

Chambliss, W. J. (1973). The Saints and the Roughnecks. *Society, 11,* 24–31. **250, 251, 260**

Chambliss, W. J. (1978). Toward a political economy of crime. In C. E. Reasons & R. M. Rich (Eds.), *The sociology of law: A conflict perspective.* Toronto: Butterworths. **271, 273**

Chapman, J. I. (1976). An economic model of crime and police: Some empirical results. *Journal of Research in Crime and Delinquency, 13*(January), 48–63. **262**

Chen, X. (1985). The one-child population policy, modernization, and the extended Chinese family. *Journal of Marriage and the Family, 47*(1), 193–202. **106**

Cheng, L., & Bonacich, E. (1984). *Labor immigration under capitalism: Asian workers in the United States before World War II.* Berkeley: University of California Press.

Cherlin, A. (1981). *Marriage, divorce, remarriage.* Cambridge, MA: Harvard University Press. **418**

Cherlin, A. (1983). Changing family and household: Contemporary lessons from historical research. *Annual Review of Sociology, 9,* 51–66. **353, 419**

Cherlin, A., & Furstenberg, F. F. (1983, June). The American family in the year 2000. *The Futurist,* pp. 7–14. **413**

Cherlin, A., & McCarthy, J. (1985). Remarried households: Data from the June 1980 Current Population Survey. *Journal of Marriage and the Family, 47*(1), 23–30. **427**

Chernin, K. (1981). *The Obsession: Reflections on the tyranny of slenderness.* New York: Harper & Row. **346, 347, 380**

Cherry, K. (1988). *Womansword: What Japanese words say about women.* New York: Kodansha International. **344**

Childe, V. G. (1953). *Man makes himself.* New York: Mentor. **123**

Childe, V. G. (1964). *What happened in history.* Baltimore: Penguin. **123, 124**

Chirot, D. (1977). *Social change in the twentieth century.* New York: Harcourt Brace Jovanovich.

Chirot, D. (1980). Changing fashions in the study of the social causes of economic and social change. In J. F. Short (Ed.), *The state of sociology* (pp. 259–282). Beverly Hills, CA: Sage. **611**

Chirot, D. (1985). The rise of the west. *American Sociological Review, 50*(2), 181–194. **611**

Chirot, D. (1986). *Social change in the modern era.* San Diego: Harcourt Brace Jovanovich.

Chirot, D., & Hall, T. D. (1982). World-system theory. *Annual Review of Sociology, 8,* 81–106. **611**

Chomsky, N. (1957). *Syntactic structures.* The Hague: Mouton.

Chomsky, N. (1966). *Cartesian linguistics.* New York: Harper & Row. **134**

Clark, B. R. (1960). The cooling-out function in higher education. *American Journal of Sociology, 65*(May). **454**

Clark, B. R., & Trow, M. (1966). The organizational context. In B. R. Clark & M. Trow (Eds.), *College peer groups.* Chicago: Aldine. **439**

Clark, C. (1987). Sympathy biography and sympathy margin. *American Journal of Sociology, 93*(2), 290–300. **74**

Clark, G. K. (1962). *The making of Victorian England.* Cambridge, MA: Harvard University Press.

Clark, G. K., & Piggott, S. (1965). *Prehistoric societies.* New York: Knopf. **123**

Clark, K. B. (1965). *Dark ghetto.* New York: Harper & Row. **324**

Clausen, J. A. (1976). Drug use. In R. K. Merton & R. Nisbet (Eds.), *Contemporary social problems.* New York: Harcourt Brace Jovanovich. **249, 270**

Clawson, D., Neustadtl, A., & Bearden, J. (1986). The logic of business unity. *American Sociological Review, 51*(6), 797–811. **498, 526**

Clinard, M. B. (1983). *Corporate ethics and crime: The role of middle management.* Beverly Hills, CA: Sage. **268**

Clinard, M. B., & Yeager, P. C. (1980). *Corporate crime.* New York: The Free Press. **250**

Cloward, R. A., & Ohlin, L. E. (1960). *Delinquency and opportunity: A theory of delinquent gangs.* New York: The Free Press. **271**

Clymer, A. (1981, August 28). Polls find black-white gaps on variety of issues. *New York Times.* **315**

Coale, A. J. (1964). How a population ages or grows younger. In R. Freedman (Ed.). *Population: The vital revolution.* New York: Anchor Books. **119**

Cockerham, W. C. (1986). *Medical sociology* (3rd ed.). Englewood Cliffs, NJ: Prentice-Hall. **477**

Cohen, A. K. (1955). *Delinquent boys: The culture of the gang.* New York: The Free Press.

Cohen, A. K., & Short, J. F., Jr. (1976). Crime and juvenile delinquency. In R. F. Merton & R. Nisbet (Eds.), *Contemporary social problems* (4th ed.). New York: Harcourt Brace Jovanovich. **255, 262**

Cohen, L. E., & Land, K. C. (1987). Age structure and crime: Symmetry versus asymmetry and the projection of crime rates. *American Sociological Review, 52*(2), 170–183. **272**

Cohen, S. (1985). *Visions of social control.* Cambridge: Polity Press. **247**

Cole, S. G., & Cole, M. W. (1954). *Minorities and the American promise.* New York: Harper & Row. **316**

Coleman, J. S. (1960). The adolescent subculture and academic achievement. *American Journal of Sociology, 65,* 337–347. **151, 439**

Coleman, J. S. (1961). *The adolescent society.* New York: The Free Press. **151, 152, 264, 439, 449**

Coleman, J. S., et al. (1966). *Equality of educational opportunity.* Washington, DC: U.S. Government Printing Office. **327, 447, 453**

Coleman, J. S., et al (1974). *Youth: Transition to adult.* Chicago: University of Chicago Press. **397**

Coleman, J. S., Kelly, S. D., & Moore, J. A. (1975). *Trends in school segregation: 1968–1973.* Washington, DC: The Urban Institute. **337**

Coleman, R. P., & Rainwater, L. (with McClelland, K. A.). (1978). *Social standing in America.* New York: Basic Books. **304**

Coles, R. (1968). *Children in crisis.* New York: Dell. **324**

Collins, R. (1975). *Conflict sociology: Toward an explanatory science.* New York: Academic Press. **23**

Collins, R. (1982). *Sociological insight: An introduction to nonobvious sociology.* New York: Oxford University Press.

Coltrane, S. (1988). Father-child relationships and the status of women: A cross-cultural study. *American Journal of Sociology, 93*(5), 1060–1095. **370**

Commission on Minority Participation. (1988). *One-third of a nation.* Washington, D.C.: American Council on Education. **333**

Congressional Budget Office. (1987, November 12). Findings reported in the *New York Times*, p. A26. **288**

Congressional Budget Office. (1988, February 2). Reported in the *New York Times*, p. 1. **299**

Conklin, N. F., & Lourier, M. A. (1983). *A host of tongues: Language communities in the United States.* New York: Free Press. **316.**

Connor, W. P. (1979). *Socialism, politics, and equality.* New York: Columbia University Press. **302**

Cook, R. C. (1957). World migration: 1945–1955. *Population Bulletin, 13,* 77–94. **114**

Cookson, P. W., & Persell, C. H. (1985). *Preparing for power: America's elite boarding schools.* New York: Basic Books. **151, 292, 434, 453**

Cooley, C. H. (1927). *Life and the student.* New York: Knopf. **145, 324**

Cooley, C. H. (1962). *Social organization.* New York: Schocken Books. (Original work published 1909). **93**

Cooley, C. H. (1964). *Human nature and the social order.* New York: Schocken. (Original work published 1902). **139, 145, 146, 167**

Coombs, L. C. (1977). Preferences for sex of children among U.S. couples. *Family Planning Perspectives, 9*(6), 259–265. **345**

Coon, C. S. (1971). *The hunting peoples.* Boston: Little, Brown. **417.**

Cooper, H. M., & Good, T. L. (1983). *Pygmalion grows up.* New York: Longman. **443**

Cordes, C. (1984, November). Easing toward perfection at Twin Oaks: Walden Two model now 17. *APA Monitor,* p. 1. Washington, DC: American Psychological Association. **221**

Coser, L. A. (1956). *The functions of social conflict.* Glencoe, IL: The Free Press. **211, 424, 598**

Coser, L. A. (1967). *Continuities in the study of social conflict.* New York: The Free Press. **598**

Coser, L. A. (Ed.). (1975a). *The idea of social structure.* New York: Harcourt Brace Jovanovich.

Coser, L. A. (1975b). Structure and conflict. In P. M. Blau (Ed.), *Approaches to the study of social structure.* New York: The Free Press.

Coser, L. A. (1977). *Masters of sociological thought* (2nd ed.). New York: Harcourt Brace Jovanovich. **219**

Coser, R. L. (1966). Role distance, sociological ambivalence, and transitional status systems. *American Journal of Sociology, 77*(2), 173–187. **81**

Coulton, G. G. (1926). *The medieval village.* London: Cambridge University Press. **386**

Courtney, A. E., & Whipple, T. W. (1983). *Sex stereotyping in advertising.* Lexington, MA: Lexington Books. **152, 361**

Coverman, S. (1983). Gender, domestic labor time, and wage inequality, *American Sociological Review, 48,* 623–637. **370, 372**

Crain, R. L. (1975). School integration and occupational achievement of Negroes. In Pettigrew (1975), pp. 206–224. **327**

Croll, E., Davin, D., & Kane, P. (Eds.). (1985). *China's one-child family policy.* New York: St. Martin's. **106**

Crowne, D. P., & Marlowe, D. (1980). *The approval motive.* Westport, CT: Greenwood. **34**

Csikszentmihalyi, M., & Rochberg-Halton, E. (1981). *The meaning of things: Symbols in the development of the self.* Cambridge: Cambridge University Press. **146**

Curran, T. J. (1974). Xenophobia in America. In F. J. Coppa & P. C. Dolce (Eds.), *Cities in transition: From the ancient world to urban America.* Chicago: Nelson Hall. **225**

Curtin, P. D. (1969). *The Atlantic slave trade.* Madison, WI: University of Wisconsin Press. **115**

Curtis, H. (1968). *Biology.* New York: Worth. **60**

Curtis, H., & Barnes, N. S. (1981). *Invitation to biology* (3rd ed.). New York: Worth. **608**

Dadrian, W. N. (1971). Factors of anger and aggression in genocide. *Journal of Human Relations, 19,* 394–417. **328**

Dahl, R. A. (1961). *Who governs? Democracy and power in an American city.* New Haven: Yale University Press. **230**

Dahrendorf, R. (1958). Out of utopia: Toward a reorientation of sociological analysis. *American Journal of Sociology, 64,* 115–127. **463, 598**

Dahrendorf, R. (1959). *Class and class conflict in industrial society.* Stanford, CA: Stanford University Press. **23, 303**

Dahrendorf, R. (1973). Toward a theory of social conflict. In A. Etzioni & E. Etzioni-Halevy (Eds.), *Social change: Sources, patterns, and consequences.* New York: Basic Books. **464**

Daly, M. (1973). *Beyond God the Father.* Boston: Beacon Press. **550, 560**

Dantin, H. M., & Carver, C. S. (1982). Induced competences and the bystander effect. *Journal of Applied Social Psychology, 12*(2), 100–111. **16**

Dar, Y., & Resh, N. (1986). *Classroom composition and pupil achievement: A study of the effect of ability-based classes.* New York: Gordon and Breach. **453**

Darwin, C. (1962). *On the origin of species.* New York: Macmillan. (Original work published 1859).

Davies, J. C. (1962). Toward a theory of revolution. *American Sociological Review, 27,* 5–18. **582**

Davis, J. A., & Smith, T. W. (1977). *General Social Surveys, 1972–1977: Cumulative Codebook.* Chicago: National Opinion Research Center. **426**

Davis, J. A., & Smith, T. W. (1984). *General social surveys, 1972–1984: Cumulative codebook.* Chicago: National Opinion Research Center. **32**

Davis, J. A., & Smith, T. W. (1986). *General Social Surveys, 1972–1983: Cumulative codebook.* Chicago: National Opinion Research Center. **349**

Davis, J. A., & Smith, T. W. (1987). *General social surveys, 1972–1987: Cumulative codebook.* Chicago: National Opinion Research Center. **66, 191, 249, 254, 262, 273, 282, 289, 294, 299, 348, 407, 409, 421, 426, 435, 455, 504, 528, 529, 531, 533, 561, 563**

Davis, K. (1940). Extreme social isolation of a child. *American Journal of Sociology, 45,* 554–564. **135**

Davis, K. (1947). Final note on a case of extreme isolation. *American Journal of Sociology, 50,* 432–437. **135**

Davis, K. (1949). *Human society.* New York: Macmillan. **520**

Davis, K. (1953). Reply to Tumin. *American Sociological Review, 18*(August), 394–397. **305**

Davis, K. (1955). The origin and growth of urbanization in the world. *American Journal of Sociology, 60,* 429–437. **125**

Davis, K. (1963). The theory of change and response in modern demographic history. *Population Index, 29*(4), 345–366. **113**

Davis, K. (1974). The migrations of human populations. *Scientific American, 231,* 92–105. **115**

Davis, K., & Blake, J. (1956). Social structure and fertility: An analytic framework. *Economic Development and Cultural Change, 4,* 211–235. **105**

Davis, K., & Moore, W. E. (1945). Some principles of stratification. *American Sociological Review, 10,* 242–249. **284, 305, 363**

Davis, M. H., & Stephan, W. G. (1980). Attributions for exam performance. *Journal of Applied Social Psychology, 10*(3), 235–248. **166**

Davis-Friedmann, D. (1983). *Long lives: Elderly and the Communist Revolution.* Cambridge: Harvard University Press. **381**

Dawidowicz, L. S. (1975). *The war against the Jews: 1933–1945.* New York: Holt, Rinehart & Winston. **73, 328, 329**

Deane, P., & Cole, W. A. (1962). *British economic growth 1688–1959: Trends and structure.* London: Cambridge University Press. **471**

Deaux, K. (1972). To err is humanizing. But sex makes a difference. *Representative Research in Social Psychology, 3,* 20–28. **166**

Deaux, K. (1976, December). Ahhh, she was just lucky. *Psychology Today 10*(7), p. 70ff. **350, 352**

Deci, E. L. (1975). *Intrinsic motivation.* New York: Plenum Press. **438**

Deci, E. L. (1980). *The psychology of self-determination.* Lexington, MA: Lexington Books. **170**

D'Emilio, J., and Freedman, E. B. (1988). *Intimate matters: A history of sexuality in America.* New York: Harper & Row.

Demos, J. (1970). *A little commonwealth: Family life in Plymouth Colony.* New York: Oxford University Press.

Demos, J. (1986). *Past, present, and personal: The family and the life course in American history.* New York: Basic Books. **427, 428**

Deutsch, M., & Collins, M. (1951). *Interracial housing: A psychological evaluation of a social experiment.* Minneapolis: University of Minnesota Press. **332**

Deutsch, M., & Gerard, H. B. (1955). A study of normative and informational social influences upon individual judgement. *Journal of Abnormal and Social Psychology, 51,* 629–636. **190**

Devine, J. A. (1983). Class inequality and state policy. *American Sociological Review, 48*(October), 606–622. **288, 306**

Diaz, B. (1974). *The conquest of New Spain* (J. M. Cohen, Trans.). London: The Folio Society. **549**

Dijkstra, B. (1987). *Idols of perversity: Fantasies of feminine evil.* New York: Oxford University Press. **347**

Dobash, R. E., & Dobash, R. (1979). *Violence againt wives.* New York: The Free Press. **424**

Dobb, M. (1947). *Studies in the development of capitalism.* New York: International Publishers. **487, 490**

Dobbs, J. (1972). *Sex, setting, and reactions to crowding on sidewalks.* Paper presented at the American Psychological Association meeting, Honolulu. **352**

Dobzhansky, T. (1973). *Genetic diversity and human equality.* New York: Basic Books. **311**

Dohrenwend, B. P., & Dohrenwend, B. S. (1976). Sex differences in psychiatric disorders. *American Journal of Sociology, 81,* 1447–1454. **364**

Dollard, J., et al. (1939). *Frustration and aggression.* New Haven: Yale University Press. **581**

Domhoff, G. W. (1967). *Who rules America?* Englewood Cliffs, NJ: Prentice-Hall. **292, 527**

Domhoff, G. W. (1971). *The higher circles.* New York: Random House. **292**

Domhoff, G. W. (1983). *Who rules America now?* Englewood Cliffs, NJ: Prentice-Hall. **230, 292, 497, 526, 537**

Domhoff, G. W., & Ballard, H. T. (Eds.). (1968). *C. Wright Mills and the power elite.* Boston: Beacon Press. **526**

Domhoff, G. W., & Zweigenhaft, R. L. (1983, April 24). Jews in the corporate establishment. *New York Times.* **322**

Douglas, J. D., & Waksler, F. C. (1982). *The sociology of deviance: An introduction.* Boston: Little, Brown. **257**

Douvan, E., & Adelson, J. (1966). *The adolescent experience.* New York: Wiley. **264**

Dovidio, J., & Gaertner, S. (Eds.). (1987). *Prejudice, discrimination, and racism.* Orlando: Academic Press.

Dowd, D. F. (1974). *The twisted dream: Capitalist development in the United States since 1776.* Cambridge, MA: Winthrop. **490**

Draper, T. (1962). *Castro's revolution: Myths and realities.* New York: Praeger. **586**

Drew, E. (1983). *Politics and money.* New York: Macmillan. **523**

Dudley, J. R. (1983). *Living with stigma: The plight of people we label mentally retarded.* Springfield: IL: Charles C. Thomas. **254**

Duncan, G. J., Coe, R. D., Corcoran, M. E., Hill, M. S., Hoffman, S. D., & Morgan, J. N. (1984). *Years of poverty, years of plenty: The changing economic fortunes of American workers and families.* Ann Arbor, MI: Institute for Social Research, University of Michigan. **47, 301, 356**

Duncan, O. D. (1961). From social system to ecosystem. *Sociological Inquiry, 31,* 140–149. **104**

Duncan, O. D. (1969). Inheritance of poverty or inheritance of race? In D. P. Moynihan (Ed.), *On understanding poverty* (pp. 85–110). New York: Basic Books. **319, 325**

Duncan, O. D., & Duncan, B. (1955). Residential distribution and occupational stratification. *American Journal of Sociology, 60*(5), 493–503. **326**

Duncan, O. D., & Lieberson, S. (1959). Ethnic segregation and assimilation. *American Journal of Sociology, 64*(January), 364–374. **326**

Duncan, O. D., & Schnore, L. F. (1959). Cultural, behavioral, and ecological perspectives in the study of social organization. *American Journal of Sociology, 65.* **104**

Dunn, J., & Kendrick, C. (1982). *Siblings: Love, envy, and understanding.* Cambridge, MA: Harvard University Press.

Durden-Smith, J., & DeSimone, D. (1983). *Sex and the brain.* New York: Arbor House. **343**

Durkheim, E. (1933). *The divison of labor in society.* New York: The Free Press. (Original work published 1893) **74, 209, 211, 213, 223**

Durkheim, E. (1938). *The rules of the sociological method.* New York: The Free Press. (Original work published 1895) **14, 19, 20, 250, 254, 263**

Durkheim, E. (1951). *Suicide.* New York: The Free Press. (Original work published 1897) **29, 213, 264**

Durkheim, E. (1965). *The elementary forms of religious life.* New York: The Free Press. (Original work published 1912) **544, 547**

Durkheim, E. (1974). *Sociology and philosophy.* New York: The Free Press. (Original work published 1924) **69, 250**

Duverger, M. (1959). *Political parties* (B. North & R. North, Trans.). London: Methuen. **529, 563**

Dworkin, A. (1974). *Woman hating.* New York: E. P. Dutton. **347**

Easterlin, R. A. (1967). Effects of population growth on the economic development of developing countries. *Annals of the American Academy of Political and Social Science, 371,* 98–108. **119**

Easterlin, R. A. (1978). What will 1984 be like? Socioeconomic implications of recent twists in age structure. *Demography, 15,* 397–432. **111**

Edelman, M. W., & Howe, H., et al. (1985). *Barriers to excellence: Our children at risk.* Boston: National Coalition of Advocates for Students. **453**

Edgerton, R. B. (1985). *Rules, exceptions, and social order.* Berkeley: University of California Press. **70**

Edwards, J. (1984). Language, diversity, and identity. In Edwards, J. (Ed.), *Linguistic minorities: Policies and pluralism* (pp. 277–310). New York: Academic Press. **62**

Ehrenreich, B., & English, D. (1979). *For her own good: 150 years of the experts' advice to women.* Garden City, NY: Anchor. **478**

Eisenstadt, S. N. (1956). *From generation to generation.* New York: The Free Press. **152, 378, 392**

Eisenstein, E. (1980). *The printing press as an agent of change.* Cambridge, England: Cambridge University Press.

Elder, G. H. (1974). *Children of the Great Depression.* Chicago: University of Chicago Press. **391**

Eldridge, H. T. (1968). Population policies. In D. L. Sills (Ed.), *The international encyclopedia of the social sciences* (Vol. 12). New York: The Macmillan Company/The Free Press. **105**

Elkins, S. M. (1963). *Slavery: A problem in American institutional and intellectual life.* New York: Grosset and Dunlap. **322**

Elliott, D. S., & Ageton, S. S. (1980). Reconciling race and class differences in self-reported and official estimates of delinquency. *American Sociological Review, 45*(February), 95–110. **256**

Ellis, G. J., Lee, G. R., & Peterson, L. R. (1978). Supervision and conformity. *American Journal of Sociology, 84*, 386–403. **150**

Ellison, R. (1952). *The invisible man.* New York: Random House. **162**

Emerson, R. (1968). Colonialism: Political aspects. In D. L. Sills (Ed.), *The international encyclopedia of the social sciences (Vol. 3).* New York: The Macmillan Company. **303**

Emerson, R. M. (1981). Social exchange theory. In M. Rosenberg and R. H. Turner (Eds.), *Social psychology: Sociological perspectives* (pp. 30–65). New York: Basic Books. **177**

Emerson, R. M. (1981). Observational field work. *Annual Review of Sociology, 7*, 315–378. **40**

Empey, L. (1982). *American delinquency: Its meaning and construction.* Homewood, IL: Dorsey.

Engels, F. (1962). *Conditions of the working class in England in 1844.* Moscow: Foreign Languages Publishing House. (Original work published 1845) **387**

Engels, F. (1972). *The origin of the family, private property, and the state.* New York: Pathfinder Press. (Original work published 1891) **352, 366, 415**

Entwistle, D. R. & Doering, S. G. (1981). *The first birth: A family turning point.* Baltimore: Johns Hopkins University Press. **369**

Epstein, A. L. (1967). Urbanization and social change in Africa. *Current Anthropology, 8*, 275–295. **239**

Epstein, C. F. (1970). Encountering the male establishment. *American Journal of Sociology, 75*, 965–982. **36, 362**

Epstein, C. F. (1983). *Women in law.* New York: Doubleday/Anchor. **356**

Epstein, C. F., & Coser, R. L.(Eds.). (1981). *Access to power: Cross-national studies of women and elites.* London: Allen Unwin. **357**

Erikson, E. H. (1963). *Childhood and society* (2nd ed.). New York: Norton.

Erikson, E. H. (1968). *Identity, youth, and crisis.* New York: Norton.

Erikson, K. (1986). Work and alienation. *American Sociological Review, 51*(1), 1–8.

Erikson, K. T. (1966). *Wayward Puritans: A study in the sociology of deviance.* New York: Wiley. **250, 262**

Espenshade, T. (1980). Raising a child can now cost $85,000. *Intercom, 8*, 1–2. **111**

Espenshade, T. J. (1984). *Investing in children: New estimates of parental expenditures.* Washington, DC: Urban Institute Press. **111**

Etaugh, C., & Kasley, H. C. (1981). Evaluating competence: Effects of sex, marital status, and parental status. *Psychology of Women Quarterly, 6*(2, Winter), 196–203. **39**

Etienne, M., & Leacock, E. (Eds.). (1980) *Women and colonization: Anthropological perspectives.* New York: Praeger. **343, 348, 353**

Etzioni, A. (1969). *The semi-professions and their organization.* New York: The Free Press. **501**

Etzioni-Halévy, E. (1983). *Bureaucracy and democracy: A political dilemma.* Boston: Routledge and Kegan Paul. **524**

Eurich, N. P. (1981). *Systems of higher education in twelve countries.* New York: Praeger. **441**

Evans, P. B. (1979). *Dependent development: The alliance of multinational, state, and local capital in Brazil.* Princeton, NJ: Princeton University Press.

Evans, P. B. (1981). Recent research on multinational corporations. *Annual Review of Sociology, 7*, 199–223. **304, 510, 511**

Evans, P. B., and Timberlake, M. (1980). Dependence, inequality, and the growth of the tertiary: A comparative analysis of less developed countries. *American Sociological Review, 45*(4), 531–552. **304**

Farb, P. (1973). *Word play: What happens when people talk.* New York: Knopf. (1975 refers to the Bantam paperback edition.) **61**

Farb, P., & Armelagos, G. (1980). *Consuming passions: The anthropology of eating.* Boston: Houghton Mifflin. **248**

Farley, R. (1980). The long road: Blacks and whites in America. *American Demographics, 2*(2), 11–17. **333, 335**

Farley, R. (1984). *Blacks and whites.* Cambridge, MA: Harvard University Press. **326, 327, 333, 337**

Farley, R., Bianchi, S., & Colasanto, D. (1979). Barriers to the racial integration of neighborhoods: The Detroit case. *Annals of the American Academy of Political and Social Science, 441* (January), 97–113.

Farley, R., & Neidert, L. J. (1984). *How effective was the melting pot? An analysis of current ethnic differences in the United States* (Population Studies Center Research Report 84-68). Ann Arbor: University of Michigan. **321, 324**

Farley, R., Richards, T., & Wurdock, C. (1980). School desegregation and white flight: An investigation of competing models and their discrepant findings. *Sociology of Education, 53*(3), 123–139. **337**

Farley, R., Schuman, H., Bianchi, S., Colasanto, D., & Hatchett, S. (1978). 'Chocolate city, vanilla suburbs:' Will the trend toward racially separate communities continue? *Social Science Research, 7*(4), 319–344. **226, 326, 327**

Farmers Home Administration. (1987, February 20). Report discussed in the Hartford *Courant.* See also *American Demographics,* January–February, 1987. **231**

Fatemi, N. S., Williams, G. W., & de Saint-Phalle, T. L. T. (1982). *Multinational corporations* (rev. 2nd ed.). New Jersey: A. S. Barnes. **511.**

Fausto-Sterling, A. (1985). *Myths of gender: Biological theories about women and men.* New York: Basic Books. **343, 464, 473**

Featherman, D. L. (1983). Life-span perspectives in social science research. In P. B. Baltes & O. G. Brim (Eds.), *Life-span development and behavior* (Vol. 5, pp. 1–59). New York: Academic Press.

Featherman, D. L., & Lerner, R. M. (1985). Ontogenesis and sociogenesis. *American Sociological Review, 50*(5), 659–676. **133.**

Federal Bureau of Investigation. (1976). *Uniform crime reports for the United States: Crime in the United States: 1976.* Washington, DC: U.S. Government Printing Office. **263**

Federal Bureau of Investigation. (1987). *Uniform Crime Reports: Crime In the United States, 1986.* Washington, DC: U.S. Government Printing Office. **254, 423**

Feldman, A. S., & Tilly, C. (1960). The interaction of social and physical space. *American Sociological Review, 25*, 877–884. **326**

Feldman, D. A., & Johnson, T. M. (1986). *The social dimensions of AIDS: Method and theory.* New York: Praeger.

Feldman, W., Feldman, E., & Goodman, J. T. (1988). Children's attitudes towards thinness and fatness. *Pediatrics, 81*(2, February), 190–194. **346**

Feldman-Summers, S., & Kiesler, J. (1974). Those who are number two try harder: The effects of sex on attributions of causality. *Journal of Personality and Social Psychology, 30*, 846–855. **166**

Ferrarotti, F. (1970). *Roma da capitale a pereferia.* Rome: Laterza. **223**

Ferree, M. M., & Hess, B. B. (1985). *Controversy and coalition: The new feminist movement.* Boston: Twayne. **367**

Festinger, L. (1948). A study of rumor: Its origin and spread. *Human Relations, 1*, 464–485. **579**

Festinger, L. (1954). A theory of social comparison processes. *Human Relations, 7*, 117–140. **148**

Festinger, L., Riecken, H. W., & Schacter, S. (1956). *When prophecy fails.* New York: Harper & Row. **40**

Fettner, A. G., & Check, W. A. (1984). *The truth about AIDS*. New York: Holt, Rinehart & Winston. **573**

Feuer, L. (Ed.). (1959). *Marx and Engels: Basic writings on politics and philosophy*. Garden City, NY: Doubleday. **552**

Fidell, L. (1970). Empirical verification of sex discrimination in hiring practices in psychology. *American Psychologist, 25,* 1094–1097. **40**

Fiedler, F. E., Chemers, M. M., & Mahan, L. (1976). *Improving leadership effectiveness*. New York: Wiley. **209**

Fieldhouse, D. K. (1968). Colonialism: Economic aspects. In D. L. Sills (Ed.), *The international encyclopedia of the social sciences* (Vol. 3). New York: The Macmillan Company/The Free Press. **303**

Finkelhor, D., Gelles, R. J., Hotaling, G. T., & Straus, M. A. (Eds.). (1983). *The dark side of families: Current family violence research*. Beverly Hills, CA: Sage.

Finkelhor, D., & Yllo, K. (1985). *License to rape: Sexual abuse of wives*. New York: Holt, Rinehart, & Winston. **169, 348**

Firey, W. (1945). Sentiment and symbolism as ecological variables. *American Sociological Review, 10*(April), 140–148. **228**

Firestone, S. (1970). *The dialectic of sex: The case for feminist revolution*. New York: William Morrow.

Fischer, C. S. (1975). Toward a subcultural theory of urbanism. *American Journal of Sociology, 80* (May), 1319–1941. **222**

Fischer, C. S. (1982). *To dwell among friends: Personal networks in town and city*. Chicago: University of Chicago Press. **222, 223, 231**

Fischer, C. S. (1984). *The urban experience* (2nd ed.). San Diego: Harcourt Brace Jovanovich. **222, 223, 231**

Fischer, H. W., & Lazerson, A. (1984). *Human development*. New York: W. H. Freeman. **133, 243, 359, 394**

Fisher, E. (1980). *Woman's creation: Sexual evolution and the shaping of society*. New York: McGraw-Hill. **352**

Fisher, H. T., & Fisher, M. H. (Eds.). (1966). *Life in Mexico: The letters of Fanny Calderon de la Barca*. Garden City, NY: Doubleday. **103**

Fisher, J. D., Nadler, A., & DePaulo, B. M.(Eds.). (1983). *New directions in helping: Recipient reactions to aid,* (Vol. 1). New York: Academic Press. **70, 165**

Fisher, R. (1984). *Let the people decide: Neighborhood organizing in America*. Boston: Twayne. **243**

Fishman, P. (1975). *Study of male-female conversations*. Paper presented at the American Sociological Association Annual Meeting, San Francisco. **350**

Flacks, R. (1970, June). Young intelligentsia in revolt. *Transaction*. **455**

Flowers, R. B. (1984). *Religion in strange times: The 1960s and 1970s*. Macon, GA: Mercer University Press. **553**

Flynn, J. (1977). Recent findings related to wife abuse. *Social Casework, 58,* 13–20. **260**

Foner, N. (1984). *Ages in conflict: A cross-cultural perspective on inequalities between old and young*. New York: Columbia University Press. **378**

Footnotes. (1980). Sociology in China: Its restoration and future role. Volume 8, No. 4 (October). **451**

Forer, L. G. (1984). *Money and justice*. New York: Norton. **261, 378**

Form, W. (1985). *Divided we stand: Working class stratification in America*. Champaign, IL: University of Illinois Press. **493**

Fortes, M., Steel, R. W., & Ady, P. (1947). Ashanti survey, 1945–46: An experiment in social research. *Geographical Journal, 110,* 149–179. **410**

Fox, M., Gibbs, M., & Auerbach, D. (1985). Age and gender dimensions of friendship. *Psychology of Women Quarterly, 9,* 489–502. **352**

Fox, R. W. (1981). Mexico City shows global 2000 stresses. *Intercom, 9*(7), 1. Washington, DC: Population Reference Bureau. **116**

Fox, T., & Miller, S. M. (1965). Intra-country variations: Occupational stratification and mobility. *Studies in Comparative International Development, 1,* 3–10. **303**

Franklin, B. (1974). *Observations concerning the increase of mankind*. (Original work published 1751) **225**

Franks, V., & Rothblum, E. D. (Eds.). (1983). *The stereotyping of women: Its effects on mental health*. New York: Springer. **363**

Frederickson, G. M. (1981). *White supremacy: A comparative study in American and South African history*. New York: Oxford University Press. **295, 302, 316, 322**

Freedman, D. S., Freedman, R., & Whelpton, P. K. (1960). Size of family and preference for children of each sex. *American Journal of Sociology, 66,* 141–146. **105**

Freeman, D. (1983). *Margaret Mead and Samoa: The making and unmaking of an anthropological myth*. Cambridge, MA: Harvard University Press. **41**

Freeman, J. (1975). The women's liberation movement: Its origins, structures, impact, and ideas. In J. Freeman (Ed.), *Women: A feminist perspective* (pp. 448–460). Palo Alto, CA: Mayfield. **366**

Freeman, R. B. (1976). *The overeducated American*. New York: Academic Press. **305**

Freire, P. (1972). *Pedagogy of the oppressed*. New York: Herder and Herder. **442, 455**

Freire, P. (1985). *The politics of education: Culture, power, and liberation*. South Hadley, MA: Bergin & Garvey. **288, 450**

Freitag, P. (1975). The Cabinet and big business: A study of interlocks. *Social Problems, 2* (December), 137–152. **527**

Freud, S. (1952). *Totem and taboo*. New York: Norton. (Original work published 1913) **141**

Freud, S. (1960). *The Ego and the Id*. New York: Norton. (Original work published 1923) **141**

Freud, S. (1961). *Civilization and its discontents*. New York: Norton. (Original work published 1930) **141**

Freud, S., & Dann, S. (1951). An experiment in group upbringing. *Psychoanalytic study of the child*. New York: International Universities Press. **135**

Freudenburg, W. R. (1986). The density of acquaintanceship: An overlooked variable in community research? *American Journal of Sociology, 92*(1), 27–63.

Frey, W. H. (1983). *Lifecourse migration of metropolitan whites and blacks and the structure of demographic change in large central cities* (Research Report No. 83-47). Ann Arbor, Michigan: University of Michigan Population Studies Center. **227, 238**

Frey, W. H., & Kobrin, F. (1982). Changing families and changing mobility: Their impact on the central city. *Demography, 19,* 261–277. **392**

Frey, W. H., & Speare, A. (1988). *Regional and metropolitan growth and decline in the United States*. New York: Russell Sage.

Friedan, B. (1963). *The feminine mystique*. New York: Dell. **367**

Friedl, E. (1962). *Vasilika: A village in modern Greece*. New York: Holt, Rinehart & Winton. **407**

Friedl, E. (1975). *Men and women: An anthropologist's view*. New York: Holt, Rinehart & Winston. **352**

Friedman, H. S., Riggio, R. E., & Segall, D. O. (1980). Personality and the enactment of emotion. *Journal of Nonverbal Behavior, 5,* 35–48. **350**

Friedman, J. (1974). Marxism, structuralism, and vulgar materialism, *Man, 9,* 444–469. **601**

Friedrich, C. J., & Brzezinksi, Z. (1965). *Totalitarian dictatorship and autocracy* (Vol. 2). Cambridge, MA: Harvard University Press. **525**

Froebel, F., Heinrichs, J., & Kreye, O. (1980). *The new international division of labor.* New York: Cambridge University Press. **509**

Froissart, Sir J. (1961). *The chronicles of England, France, and Spain.* New York: Dutton. **228**

Froman, C. (1984). *The two American political systems: Society, economics, and politics.* Englewood Clifss, NJ: Prentice-Hall. **536.**

Furstenberg, F. F., Jr., & Spanier, G. B. (1984). *Recycling the family: Remarriage after divorce.* Beverly Hills, CA: Sage.

Furstenberg, F. F., Jr., Morgan, S. P., & Allison, P. D. (1987). Paternal participation and children's well-being after marital dissolution. *American Sociological Review, 52*(5), 695–701. **369**

GSS (General Social Survey). For whatever year is given, the source is raw unpublished (to the best of my knowledge) General Social Survey data for that year analyzed by the author. **32, 33, 67, 73, 315, 327, 334, 371, 416, 504, 549**

Gagliani, G. (1981). How many working classes? *American Journal of Sociology, 87*(2), 259–285. **281**

Gamson, W. A. (1961). An experimental test of a theory of coalition formation. *American Sociological Review, 26,* 565–573. **203**

Gamson, W. A. (1964). Experimental studies in coalition formation. In L. Berkowitz (Ed.), *Advances in experimental social psychology* (Vol. 1). New York: Academic Press. **203**

Gamson, W. A. (1968a). A theory of coalition formation. *American Sociological Review, 22,* 373–379. **171**

Gamson, W. A. (1968b). *Power and discontent.* Homewood, IL: Dorsey Press.

Gamson, W. A. (1974, July). Violence and political power: The meek don't make it. *Psychology Today, 8*(2), pp. 35–41. **335**

Gamson, W. A. (1975). *The strategy of social protest.* Homewood, IL: Dorsey Press. **335**

Gans, H. J. (1962). Urbanism and suburbanism as ways of life: A re-evaluation of definitions. In A. Rose (Ed.), *Human behavior and social processes.* Boston: Houghton Mifflin and Routledge & Kegan Paul. **222, 223**

Gans, H. J. (1968). *People and plans.* New York: Basic Books. **242**

Gans, H. J. (1973). *More equality.* New York: Pantheon. **285**

Gans, H. J. (1980). *Deciding what's news.* New York: Vintage. **152**

Gans, H. J. (1982). *The urban villagers* (2nd ed.). New York: The Free Press. **221, 223, 226, 231, 242**

Garfinkel, H. (1956). Conditions of successful degradation ceremonies. *American Journal of Sociology, 61,* 420–424. **263**

Garfinkel, H. (1967). *Studies in ethnomethodology.* Englewood Cliffs, NJ: Prentice-Hall. **23**

Gartner, A., Greer, C., & Riessman, F. (Eds.). (1973). *After deschooling, what?* New York: Harper & Row. **456**

Gecas, V. (1981). Contexts of socialization. In M. Rosenberg and R. Turner (Eds.), *Social psychology: Sociological perspectives.* New York: Basic Books. **149, 154, 183**

Gecas, V. (1982). The self-concept. *Annual Review of Sociology, 8,* 1–33. **144, 146**

Geertz, C. (1973). *The interpretation of cultures.* New York: Basic Books. **57, 544, 545, 601**

Geller, D. M., Goodstein, L. S. M., & Sternberg, W. C. (1974). On being ignored: The effects of violation of implicit rules of social interaction. *Sociometry, 37,* 541–556. **162**

Gelles, R. J. (1972). *The violent home: A study of physical aggression between husbands and wives.* Beverly Hills, CA: Sage. **198, 424, 425**

Gelles, R. J., & Cornell, C. P. (1985). *Intimate violence in families.* Beverly Hills, CA: Sage. **423**

Genicut, L. (1966). Crisis from the Middle Ages to modern times. In M. M. Postan (Ed.), *The agrarian life of the Middle Ages* (Vol. 1 of *The Cambridge economic history of Europe*). Cambridge: The University Press. **288**

George, A. L. (1971). Primary groups, organization, and military performance. In R. W. Little (Ed.), *Handbook of military institutions* (pp. 293–318). New York: Russel Sage Foundation. **191**

Gergen, M. M. (1980). The effects of age and type of residence on forms of social explanation. Unpublished doctoral dissertation, Temple University, Philadelphia. Cited in Gergen, K. J., and Gergen, M. M. (1981). *Social psychology,* p. 331. New York: Harcourt Brace Jovanovich, 1981. **391**

Gerstel, N. R. (1976). The feasibility of commuter marriage. In P. J. Stein, J. Richman, & N. Harmon (Eds.), *The family.* Reading, MA: Addison-Wesley. **422**

Giddens, A. (1973). *The class structures of advanced societies.* New York: Harper & Row.

Giddens, A. (1975).*The class structure of advanced societies.* New York: Harper & Row.

Giddens, A. (1983). *A contemporary critique of historical materialism.* Berkeley and Los Angeles: University of California Press.

Giddens, A. (1984). *The constitution of society: Outline of a theory of structuration.* Berkeley and Los Angeles: University of California Press.

Gieryn, T. F., Bevins, G. M., & Zehr, S. C. (1985). The professionalization of American scientists. *American Sociological Review, 50*(3), 392–408. **467**

Gilbert, M. (1986). *The holocaust: A history of the Jews in Europe during the second world war.* New York: Holt, Rinehart, & Winston. **328**

Gill, C. (1985). *Work, unemployment, and the new technology.* Cambridge, England: Polity Press (Basil Blackwell). **503**

Gillespie, D. (1971). Who has the power? The marital struggle. *Journal of Marriage and the Family, 33,* 445–458. **353, 414**

Giniger, H. (1981, October 5). Quebec meets defiance in enforcing language law. *New York Times,* p. 2. **62**

Glaser, B. G. (1966). Disclosure of terminal illness. *Journal of Health and Human Behavior, 7,* 83–91. **386**

Glaser, B. G., & Strauss, A. (1965). *Awareness of dying.* Chicago: Aldine. **386**

Glass, J., Bengston, V. L., & Dunham, C. C. (1986). Attitude similarity in three-generation families: Socialization, status inheritance, or reciprocal influence? *American Sociological Review, 51*(5), 685–698.

Gleick, J. (1987). *Chaos: Making a new science.* New York: Viking. **463**

Glenn, N., & McLanahan, S. (1983). Children and marital happiness: A further specification of the relationship. *Journal of Marriage and the Family, 44,* 63–72. **155, 413**

Glick, P. C., & Lin, S. (1986a). More young adults are living with their parents: Who are they? *Journal of Marriage and the Family, 48*(1), 107–112. **427**

Glick, P. C., & Lin, S. (1986b). Recent changes in divorce and remarriage. *Journal of Marriage and the Family, 48*(1), 737–747. **428**

Glick, P. C., & Norton, A. J. (1979). Marrying, divorcing, and living together in the U. S. today. *Population Bulletin, 32*(5). Washington, DC: Population Reference Bureau. **416**

Glock, C. Y., & Stark, R. (1968). *American piety: The nature of religious commitment.* Berkeley: University of California Press. **549.**

Glueck, S., & Glueck, E. (1950). *Unraveling juvenile delinquency.* New York: The Commonwealth Fund. **263**

Glueck, S., & Glueck, E. (1972). *Physique and crime: A biopsychosocial approach.* New York: Seminar Press. **263**

Goffman, E. (1956–1957). Embarrassment and social organization. *American Journal of Sociology, 62,* 264–271. **176**

Goffman, E. (1959). *The presentation of self in everyday life.* New York: Doubleday & Company. **8, 24, 174**

Goffman, E. (1961a). *Asylums*. New York: Anchor Books. **37, 40, 263**

Goffman, E. (1961b). *Encounters*. Indianapolis, IN: Bobbs-Merrill. **85, 176, 182, 183**

Goffman. E. (1963a). *Behavior in public places*. New York: The Free Press. **176, 442**

Goffman, E. (1963b). *Stigma: Notes on the management of a spoiled identity*. New York: Prentice-Hall. **147, 251, 253, 324**

Goffman, E. (1967). *Interaction ritual*. New York: Anchor Books. **350**

Goffman, E. (1976). *Gender advertisements*. New York: Harper Colophon. **361**

Goffman, E. (1981). *Forms of talk*. Philadelphia: University of Pennsylvania Press. **24, 174**

Goldberg, S. (1973). *The inevitability of patriarchy*. New York: William Morrow. Excerpted in J. Bensman & B. Rosenberg (Eds.), *Sociology* (pp. 136–140). New York: Praeger. **358**

Goldscheider, F., & Lebourdais, C. (1986). The falling age at leaving home, 1920–1979. *Sociology and Social Research, 70,* 99–102.

Goldscheider, F. K., & Waite, L. J. (1986). Sex differences in the entry into marriage. *American Journal of Sociology, 92*(1), 91–109. **371**

Goldstein, S., & Mayer, K. B. (1965). The impact of migration on the socio-economic structure of cities and suburbs. *Sociology and Social Research, 50*(1), 5–23. **227**

Goldstein, S., & Sly, D. F. (1977). Recent and projected trends in world urbanization. In S. Goldstein & D. F. Sly (Eds.), *Patterns of urbanization: Comparative country studies*. Bolhain: Ordina Editions. **272**

Goldstone, J. A. (1982). The comparative and historical study of revolutions. *Annual Review of Sociology, 8,* 187–207. **538, 539, 580**

Gonzalez Casanova, P. (1980). The economic development of Mexico. *Scientific American, 243,* 192–204. **127, 610**

Goode, W. J. (1959). The theoretical importance of love. *American Sociological Review, 24,* 38–47. **418**

Goode, W. J. (1962). Marital satisfaction and instability: A cross-cultural class analysis of divorce rates. *International Social Science Journal, 14,* 507–526. **420**

Goode, W. J. (1963). *World revolution and family patterns*. New York: The Free Press. **418**

Goode, W. J. (1976). Family disorganization. In R. K. Merton & R. Nisbet (Eds.), *Contemporary social problems* (4th ed., pp. 513–554). New York: Harcourt Brace Jovanovich. **420, 421, 422**

Goodman, L. W. (1980). Horizons for research on international business in developing nations. *Latin American Research Review, 15,* 225–240. **511**

Goodsell, C. T. (1983). *The case for bureaucracy: A public administration polemic*. Chatham, NJ: Chatham House.

Goody, J. (1976). *Production and reproduction*. New York: Cambridge University Press. **352, 600**

Goolrich, W., & Tanner, O. (1980). *The battle of the bulge*. New York: Time-Life Books. **86**

Gora, J. G. (1982). *The new female criminal: Empirical reality or social myth?* New York: Praeger. **255**

Gordon, C. (1976). Development of evaluated role identities. *Annual Review of Sociology, 2,* 405–433. **46**

Gordon, D. M., Edwards., R., & Reich, M. (1982). *Segmented work, divided labor*. Cambridge: Cambridge University Press. **300, 498**

Gordon, M. (1978). *Final payments*. New York: Ballantine. **381**

Gordon, S. L. (1981). The sociology of sentiments and emotion. In M. Rosenberg & R. H. Turner (Eds.), *Social psychology: Sociological perspectives*. New York: Basic Books. **74, 155**

Goring, C. (1913). *The English convict*. London: His Majesty's Stationery Office. **263**

Gornick, V. (1979). Introduction. In E. Goffman, *Gender advertisements*. New York: Harper Colophon. **361**

Gottdiener, M. (1985). *The social production of urban space*. Austin: University of Texas Press. **242, 243**

Gottfredson, M. R., & Hindelang, M. J. (1981). Sociological aspects of criminal victimization. *Annual Review of Sociology, 7,* 107–128. **254**

Gough, E. K. (1952). Changing kinship usages in the setting of political and economic change among the Nayars of Malabor. *The Journal of Royal Anthropological Institute of Great Britain and Ireland, 82,* 71–87. **404**

Gough, E. K. (1974). Nayar: Central Kerala. In D. Schneider & E. K. Gough (Eds.), *Matrilineal kinship*. Berkeley, CA: University of California Press. **406, 407, 410**

Gould, R. E. (1973, June). Measuring masculinity by the size of a paycheck. *Ms.* **362**

Gould, W. B. (1968). Discrimination and the unions. In J. Larner & I. Howe (Eds.), *Poverty: Views from the left* (pp. 168–183). New York: William Morrow. **329**

Gouldner, A. W. (1960). A norm of reciprocity: A preliminary statement. *American Sociological Review, 25,* 161–178. **70, 177**

Gouldner, A. W. (1970). *The coming crisis of western sociology*. New York: Avon. **463**

Gove, E., & Tudor, J. (1973). Adult sex roles and mental illness. *American Journal of Sociology, 78,* 812–835. **363**

Gove, W. R. (1980). Labeling and mental illness: A critique. In Gove, W. (Ed.), *Labeling deviant behavior* (pp. 53–109). Beverly Hills, CA: Sage.

Gove, W. R. (1982). The current status of the labeling theory of mental illness. In Gove, W. R. (Ed.), *Deviance and mental illness* (pp. 273–300). Beverly Hills, CA: Sage.

Gove, W. R., & Carpenter, G. R. (1982). *The fundamental connection between nature and nurture*. Lexington, MA: Lexington Books. **343**

Grabill, W. H., Kiser, C. V., & Whelpton, P. K. (1959). *The fertility of American women*. New York: Wiley. **416**

Gracey, H. L. (1972a). Morality in the organized society. In D. H. Wrong and H. L. Gracey (Eds.), *Readings in introductory sociology* (2nd ed). New York: Macmillan. **214**

Gracey, H. L. (1972b). *The civil structure and ideology of an elementary school*. Chicago: University of Chicago Press. **440**

Grady, W. R. (1980). Remarriages of women 15–44 years of age whose first marriage ended in divorce: United States, 1976. *Advancedata, 58*(February), 1–12. **408**

Graebner, I., & Britt, S. H. (Eds.). (1942). *Jews in a gentile world*. New York: Macmillan. **329**

Graebner, W. (1980). *A history of retirement: The meaning and function of an American institution, 1885–1978*. New Haven: Yale University Press. **388**

Graham, H. D., & Gurr, T. R. (Eds.). (1979). *The history of violence in America*. National Commission on the Causes and Prevention of Violence. New York: Bantam. **582**

Graham, L. (1981). *Between science and values*. New York: Columbia University Press.

Greene, S. (1976). Attitudes toward working women have a long way to go. *The Gallup Opinion Index* (Report No. 128, March). **351**

Greenfield, S., Blanco, D. M., Elashoff, R. M., & Ganz, P. A. (1987). Patterns of care related to age of breast cancer patients. *Journal of the American Medical Association, 257*(20), 2766–2770. **480**

Greenwood, E. (1962). Attributes of a profession. In S. Nosow and W. H. Form (Eds.), *Man, work, and society*. New York: Basic Books. **500**

Greer, S. (1968). Neighborhood. In D. L. Sills (Ed.), *The International Encyclopedia of the Social Sciences, Vol. 11,* (pp. 121–125). New York: The MacMillan Company/The Free Press. **221**

Greif, G. L. (1985). Single fathers rearing children. *Journal of Marriage and the Family, 47*(1), 185–191. **369**

Griffin, L. J., Wallace, M. E., & Rubin, B. A. (1986). Capitalism and labor organization. *American Sociological Review, 51*(2), 147–167. **329, 493, 494, 591**

Griffin, S. (1978). *Woman and nature.* New York: Harper & Row. **344**

Griffith, J. (1973). Social pressure on family size intentions. *Family Planning Perspectives, 5*(4), 237–242. **106**

Gross, H. E. (1980). Dual-career couples who live apart: Two types. *Journal of Marriage and the Family, 42*(August), 567–576. **422**

Grossholtz, J. (1984). *Forging capitalist patriarchy: The economic and social transformation of feudal Sri Lanka and its impact on women.* Durham, NC: Duke University Press.

Guest, A. M. (1976). Occupation and the journey to work. *Social Forces, 55,* 161–181. **236**

Gulliver, P. H. (1968). Age differentiation. In D. L. Sills (Ed.), *The international encyclopedia of the social sciences* (Vol. 1, pp. 157–162). New York: Macmillan. **383**

Gurr, T. R. (1970). *Why men rebel.* Princeton, NJ: Princeton University Press. **581, 582**

Gutek, B. A. (1985). *Sex and the workplace: The impact of sexual behavior and harassment on women, men, and organizations.* San Francisco: Jossey-Bass. **24, 165, 351**

Gutkind, P. C. W. (1966). African urban family life and the urban system. *Journal of Asian and African Studies, 1,* 35–42. **223**

Guttmacher Institute. (1987). Teenage pregnancy in industrialized countries. New York: Alan Guttmacher Institute. **416**

Guzzardi, W. (1976, January). The uncertain passage from college to job. *Fortune Magazine.* **454**

Haas, V. B., & Perucci, C. C. (Eds.). (1984). *Women in scientific and engineering professions.* Ann Arbor: University of Michigan Press. **355**

Haavio-Mannila, E. (1985). *Unfinished democracy: Women in Nordic politics.* Oxford: Pergamon Press. **358**

Haber, C. (1983). *Beyond sixty-five.* Cambridge: Cambridge University Press. **395**

Habermas, J. (1971). *Toward a rational society.* London: Heinemann. **475**

Hacker, H. (1951). Women as a minority group. *Social Forces, 30,* 60–69. **341, 358**

Hadden, J. K., & Swann, C. E. (1981). *Prime time preachers: The rising power of Televangelism.* Reading, MA: Addison-Wesley. **562, 564**

Hagan, J., & Abonnetti, C. (1982). Race, class, and the perception of criminal injustice in America. *American Journal of Sociology, 88*(2), 329–355. **260, 333**

Hagan, J., & Bumiller, K. (1983). Making sense of sentencing: A review and critique of sentencing research. In A. Blumstein, J. Cohen, S. Martin, & M. Tonry (Eds.), *Research on sentencing: The search for reform* (Vol. 2, pp. 1–54). Washington, DC: National Academy Press. **262**

Hagan, J., Gillis, A. R., & Simpson, J. (1985). The class structure of gender and delinquency: Toward a power-control theory of common delinquent behavior. *American Journal of Sociology, 90*(6), 1151–1178. **255**

Hagan, J., & Palloni, A. (1986). Structural criminology. *Annual Review of Sociology, 12,* 431–449. **256**

Hagan, J., & Parker, P. (1985). White-collar crime and punishment. *American Sociological Review, 50*(3), 302–316. **262**

Hagan, J., Simpson, J., & Gillis, A. R. (1987). Class in the household: A power-control theory of gender and delinquency. *American Journal of Sociology, 92*(4), 788–816. **255**

Hagen, R., & Kahn, A. (1975). Discrimination against competent women. *Applied Social Psychology, 5,* 362–376. **351**

Hagestad, G. O. (1984). The continuous bond: A dynamic multigenerational perspective on parent-child relations between adults. In M. Perlmutter (Ed.), *Minnesota symposium on child psychology* (pp. 129–158).

Hakeem, M. (1958). A critique of the psychiatric approach to the prevention of juvenile delinquency. *Social Problems, 5,* 194–205. **263**

Halberstam, D. (1972). *The best and the brightest.* New York: Random House. **265**

Hale, M. (1847). A husband cannot be guilty. In *History of the pleas of the crown* (Vol. I, p. 628). Philadelphia: R. H. Small. **169**

Hall, B. (1981). The cost of raising a child—Update. *Consumer Close-Ups #8.* Ithaca, NY: Cornell University Cooperative Extension. **111**

Hall, E. T. (1959). *The silent language.* Greenwich, CT: Fawcett. **89, 166, 558**

Hall, E. T. (1969). *The hidden dimension.* Garden City, NY: Anchor. **70, 89, 166, 167, 172**

Hall, J., & Watson, W. H. (1970). The effects of normative intervention on group decision-making performance. *Human Relations, 23,* 299–317. **206**

Hall, J. A. (1978). Gender effects in decoding nonverbal cues. *Psychological Bulletin, 85,* 845–857. **350**

Hall, J. R. (1979, September/October). Apocalypse at Jonestown. *Society,* pp. 52–61. **553**

Hallinan, M. T., & Sørensen, A. B. (1987). Ability grouping and sex differences in mathematics achievement. *Sociology of Education, 60*(2), 63–72. **453**

Hallman, H. W. (1984). *Neighborhoods: Their place in urban life.* Beverly Hills, CA: Sage. **221**

Hamblin, R. L. (1958). Leadership and crisis. *Sociometry, 21,* 322–335. **194**

Hammel, L. (1974, July 2). Why do few women hold apprenticeships? *New York Times,* p. 26. **36**

Hammer, H., & Gartrell, J. W. (1986). Canada and mature dependency. *American Sociological Review, 51*(2) 201–213.

Haney, C., Banks, C., & Zimbardo, P. G. (1973). Interpersonal dynamics in a simulated prison. *International Journal of Criminology and Penology, 1,* 69–97. **169**

Hansberry, L. (1950). *A raisin in the sun.* New York: Random House. **5, 6**

Hare, A. P. (1962). *Handbook of small group research.* New York: The Free Press. **89**

Hare, A. P. (1968). Group role structure. In D. L. Sills (Ed.), *The international encyclopedia of the social sciences* (Vol. 6). New York: The MacMillan Company/The Free Press. **89**

Harkins, S. G. (1981). *Effects of task difficulty and task responsibility on social loafing.* Presentation to the First International Conference on Social Processes in Small Groups, Kill Devil Hills, NC. **206**

Harkins, S. G., Latané, B., & Williams, K. (1980). Social loafing: Allocating effort or taking it easy? *Journal of Experimental Social Psychology, 16,* 457–465. **206**

Harlow, H. F. (1958). The nature of love. *The American Psychologist, 69* (December), 685. **363**

Harlow, H. F., & Harlow, M. K. (1969). Effects of various mother-infant relationships on rhesus monkey behaviors. In B. M. Foss (Ed.), *Determinants of infant behavior* (Vol. 4). London: Methuen. **363**

Harriman, A. (1985). *Women/men management.* New York: Praeger.

Harrington, M. (1963). *The other America: Poverty in the United States.* Baltimore: Penguin Books. **325**

Harris, C. D., & Ullman, E. L. (1945). The nature of cities. *The Annals of the American Academy of Political and Social Science, 242,* 7–17. **236, 237**

Harris, M. (1974). *Cows, pigs, wars, and witches.* New York: Random House. **71, 292, 560, 602**

Harris, M. (1977). *Cannibals and kings: The origins of cultures.* New York: Random House. **122, 315, 333, 352**

Harris, M. (1979). *Cultural materialism.* New York: Random House. **68, 122, 125, 366, 601**

Harris, M. (1985). *Good things to eat: Riddles of food and culture.* New York: Simon and Schuster.

Harris, M., & Ross, E. B. (1987). *Death, sex, and fertility: Population regulation in preindustrial and developing societies.* New York: Columbia University Press.

Hart, C. W. M., & Pilling, A. R. (1960). *The Tiwi of North Australia.* New York: Holt, Rinehart & Winston. **407**

Hart, H. H. (1970). *Summerhill: For and against.* New York: Hart. **456**

Harter, C. L. (1977). *The 'good times' cohort of the 1930s* (PRB Report 3, April). Washington, DC: Population Reference Bureau. **119, 120**

Hartley, E. L. (1946). *Problems in prejudice.* New York: Columbia University Press/King's Crown Press. **313**

Hartmann, H. I. (Ed.). (1985). *Comparable worth: New directions for research.* Washington, DC: National Academy Press. **356**

Hartshorn, T. A., & Muller, P. O. (1987). *Suburban business centers: Employment implications.* U. S. Department of Commerce. Washington, DC: U.S. Government Printing Office. **238**

Haskell, T. L. (Ed.). (1984). *The authority of experts.* Bloomington, IN: Indiana University Press. **518**

Hastorf, A. H. (1965). The 'reinforcement' of individual actions in a group situation. In L. Krasner and L. P. Ullmann (Eds.), *Research in behavior modification: New developments and implications.* New York: Holt, Rinehart & Winston. **195**

Haug, M., & Lavin, B. (1983). *Consumerism in medicine: Challenging physician authority.* Beverly Hills, Ca: Sage.

Hauser, P. (1959). Cultural and personal obstacles to economic development in the less developed areas. *Human Organization, 18,* 82. **239**

Haviland, J. J., & Malatesta, C. Z. (1981). The development of sex differences in nonverbal signals: Fallacies, facts, and fantasies. In C. Mayo & N. M. Henley (Eds.), *Gender and nonverbal behavior* (pp. 184–208). New York: Springer-Verlag. **350**

Hawley, A. H. (1968). Human ecology. In D. L. Sills (Ed.), *The international encyclopedia of the social sciences* (vol. 4, pp. 328–337). **120**

Hawley, A. H. (1981). *Urban society: An ecological approach* (2nd Ed.). New York: Wiley. **234, 238**

Hawley, A. H. (1984). Human ecological and Marxian theories. *American Journal of Sociology, 89,* 904–917.

Hawley, A. H. (1986). *Human ecology: A theoretical essay.* Chicago: University of Chicago Press. **104**

Hawthorne, N. (1979). *The Scarlet Letter.* New York: Dodd. **269**

Hayes, C. D., & Kamerman, S. B. (1983). *Children of working parents: Experiences and outcomes.* Washington, DC: National Academy Press. **349**

Hazarika, S. (1983, February 21). 600 reported dead after Hindu raids on Indian villages. *New York Times,* p. 1. **328**

Heer, D. M. (1966). Economic development and fertility. *Demography, 3,* 423–444. **119**

Hegedus, R. (1976). Voucher plans. In S. E. Goodman (Ed.), *Handbook on contemporary education* (pp. 128–131). New York: Bowker. **457**

Heider, F. (1946). Attitudes and cognitive organization. *Journal of Personality, 21,* 107–112. **180**

Heider, F. (1958). *The psychology of interpersonal relations.* New York: Wiley. **165**

Heider, K. G. (1972). *The Dani of West Irian.* Andover, MD: Warner Modular. **404, 412**

Heilbroner, R. L. (1977). *The economic transformation of America.* New York: Harcourt Brace Jovanovich. **498**

Heiss, J. (1981). Social roles. In M. Rosenberg & R. H. Turner (Eds.), *Social psychology: Sociological perspectives* (pp. 94–129). New York: Basic Books. **81**

Heller, J. (1961). *Catch-22.* New York: Dell. (Original work published 1955) **162**

Hellman, L. (1979). *The children's hour.* In *Six plays by Lillian Hellman.* New York: Vintage. (Original work published 1934) **578**

Helsing, K. J., & Szklo, M. (1981). Mortality after bereavement. *American Journal of Epidemiology, 114,* 41–52. **156**

Henley, N. M. (1973). Status and sex: Some touching observations. *Bulletin of the Psychonomic Society, 2,* 91–93. **350, 351**

Henley, N. M. (1977). *Body politics: Power, sex, and nonverbal communication.* Englewood Cliffs, NJ: Prentice-Hall. **171, 350**

Henry, J. (1963). *Culture against man.* New York: Random House. **440**

Hentoff, N. (1977). Who's to blame? The politics of educational malpractice. *Learning, 6*(October), 40–49. **444**

Herdt, G. H. (Ed.). (1984). *Ritualized homosexuality in Melanesia.* Berkeley and Los Angeles: University of California Press. **249**

Heritage, J. (1984). *Garfinkel and ethnomethodology.* New York: Basil Blackwell. **23**

Herman, E. S. (1975, January 3). The income 'counter-revolution.' *Commonweal.* Reprinted in J. H. Skolnick & E. Currie (Eds.). (1976). *Crisis in American institutions* (3rd ed.). Boston, MA: Little, Brown. **301, 304, 305**

Herman, E. S. (1981). *Corporate control, Corporate power.* New York: Cambridge University Press. **497**

Hernandez, D. J. (1985). Fertility reduction policies and poverty in third world countries: Ethical issues. *Studies in Family Planning, 16*(2), 76–87. **127**

Hersch, S. M. (1970). *My Lai 4: A report on the massacre and its aftermath.* New York: Vintage. **267**

Herzig, A. C., & Mali, J. L. (1980). *Oh boy! Babies!* Boston: Little, Brown. **363**

Herzog, A. R., Bachman, J. G., & Johnston, L. D. (1983). Paid work, child care, and housework: A national survey of high school seniors' preferences for sharing responsibility between husband and wife. *Sex Roles, 9*(1). **353**

Hess, R. D. (1970). Social class and ethnic influences upon socialization. In P. H. Mussen (Ed.), *Carmichael's manual of child psychology* (Vol 2). New York: Wiley. **413**

Hess, R. D., & Shipman, V. C. (1965). Early experience and the socialization of cognitive modes in children. *Child Development, 34,* 869–886. **414**

Hetherington, E. M. (1967). The effects of familial variables on sex-typing on parent-child similarity, and on imitation in children. In J. P. Hill (Ed.) *Minnesota Symposium on Child Psychology* (Vol. 1). Minneapolis: University of Minnesota Press. **137**

Heyl, B. S. (1977). The madam as teacher: The training of house prostitutes. *Social Problems, 24*(5). **265**

Hightower, J. (1980). Food monopoly. In M. Green & R. Massie (Eds.), *The big business reader* (pp. 9–18). New York: Pilgrim. **496**

Hill, C. (1961). *The century of revolution.* Edinburgh: Thomas Nelson and Sons. **490**

Hill, G. W. (1982). Group versus individual performance: Are n + 1 heads better than one? *Psychological Bulletin, 91,* 517–539. **205**

Hill, R. J. (1967). *Reformation to Industrial Revolution.* London: Weidenfeld and Nicolson. **492**

Hill, R. J. (1981). Attitudes and behavior. In M. Rosenberg & R. H. Turner (Eds.), *Social psychology: Sociological perspectives* (pp. 347–377). New York: Basic Books. **15, 74**

Hillman, A. L. (1987). Financial incentives for physicians in HMOs: Is there a conflict of interest? *New England Journal of Medicine, 317,* 27, 1743–1748. **478**

Hills, S. L. (1987). *Corporate violence: Injury and death for profit.* Totowa, NJ: Rowman & Littlefield. **256**

Hindelang, M. J. (1978). Race and involvement in common law personal crimes. *American Sociological Review, 43,* 93–109. **256**

Hirschi, T. (1969). *Causes of delinquency.* Berkeley, CA: University of California Press. **264**

Hirschi, T., & Gottfredson, M. (1983). Age and the explanation of crime. *American Journal of Sociology, 89*(3, November), 552–584. **255**

Hirschi, T., & Gottfredson, M. (1985). Age and crime: Logic and scholarship. *American Journal of Sociology, 90*(5), 1330–1333.

Hitler, A. (1948). *Mein Kampf* (R. Mannheim, Trans.). Boston: Houghton Mifflin. (Original work published 1924) **535**

Hobsbawm, E. (1971). Bandits. New York: Dell. **287**

Hochschild, A. (1979). Emotion work, feeling rules, and social structure. *American Journal of Sociology, 85,* 551–575.

Hodge, R. W., Siegel, P. M., & Rossi, P. H. (1964). Occupational prestige in the United States, 1925–1963. *American Journal of Sociology, 70,* 286–302. **147, 282, 284**

Hodge, R. W. & Treiman, D. J. (1968). Class identification in the United States. *American Journal of Sociology, 73,* 535–547. **299**

Hodge, R. W., Treiman, D. J., & Rossi, P. H. (1966). A comparative study of occupational prestige. In R. Bendix & S. M. Lipset (Eds.), *Class, status, and power: Social stratification in comparative perspective* (2nd ed.). New York: The Free Press. **284, 293**

Hoebel, A. (1972). *Anthropology: The study of man* (4th ed.). New York: McGraw-Hill. (1966 refers to the third edition.) **60**

Hofferth, S. L. (1985). Updating children's life course. *Journal of Marriage and the Family, 47*(1), 93–115. **427**

Hoffman, L. (1977). Changes in family roles, socialization, and sex differences. *American Psychologist, 32,* 644–657. **360**

Hofstadter, R. (1955). *Social Darwinism in American thought.* Boston: Beacon. **289, 323, 327**

Hogan, D. P. (1980). The transition to adulthood as a career contingency. *American Sociological Review, 45*(April), 261–276.

Holland, B. (Ed.). (1985). *Soviet Sisterhood.* Bloomington: University of Indiana Press. **356**

Hollander, E. P. (1960). Competence and conformity in the acceptance of influence. *Journal of Abnormal and Social Psychology, 51,* 365–369. **195**

Hollander, P. (1982). Research on Marxist societies: The relationship between theory and practice. *Annual Review of Sociology, 8,* 319–351. **302, 507, 508, 535**

Holmes, L. D. (1986). *Quest for the real Samoa: The Mead/Freeman controversy and beyond.* South Hadley, MA: Bergin and Garvey. **41**

Holmstrom, L. L., & Burgess, A. W. (1983). *The victim of rape.* New Brunswick, NJ: Transaction Books. **261, 352**

Holt, J. (1964). *How children fail.* New York: Dell. **440**

Holt, J. (1972, June). The little red prison. *Harper's, 244,* pp. 80–82. **440**

Homans, G. C. (1950). *The human group.* New York: Harcourt Brace Jovanovich. **85, 190**

Homans, G. C. (1974). *Social behavior: Its elementary forms* (rev. ed.). New York: Harcourt Brace Jovanovich. **177**

Hood, J. C. (1983). *Becoming a two-job family.* New York: Praeger. **353, 414**

Horowitz, I. L. (1965). *The rise and fall of Project Camelot.* Cambridge, MA: MIT Press. **51**

Hounshell, D. A. (1984). *From the American system to mass production 1900–1932: The development of manufacturing technology in the United States.* Baltimore: Johns Hopkins University Press. **319, 494**

Hout, M. (1984). Occupational mobility of black men: 1962–1973. *American Sociological Review, 49*(June), 308–322. **319**

Hout, M. (1986). Opportunity and the middle class. *American Sociological Review, 51*(2), 214–223.

Hout, M., & Greeley, A. M. (1987). The center doesn't hold: Church attendance in the United States, 1940–1984. *American Sociological Review, 52*(3), 325–345. **562**

Howe, I. (Ed.). (1983). *1984 revisited: Totalitarianism in our century.* New York: Harper & Row. **525**

Hoyt, D. (1965). The relationship between college grades and adult achievement. *American Council on Testing Research Reports.* **453**

Hoyt, H. (1939). *The structure and growth of residential neighborhoods in American cities.* Washington, DC: Federal Housing Authority. **236**

Hoyt, M. F., & Raven, B. H. (1973). Birth order and the 1971 Los Angeles earthquake. *Journal of Personality and Social Psychology, 28,* 123–130.

Huber, J. (1976). Sociology: Review essay. *Signs: Journal of Women in Culture and Society, 1*(3, Part 1), 605–697. **352**

Huber, J., & Spitze, G. (1981). Wife's employment, household behaviors, and sex-role attitudes. *Social Forces, 60,* 150–169. **369**

Huber, J., & Spitze, G. (1983). *Sex stratification: Children, housework, and jobs.* New York: Academic Press. **106, 112, 352, 353, 370**

Huber, R. M., (1971). *The American idea of success.* New York: McGraw-Hill. **434**

Hughes, E. C. (1963). Race relations and the sociological imagination. *American Sociological Review, 28*(December), 879–887. **335**

Humphreys, L. (1970). *Tearoom trade: Impersonal sex in public places.* Chicago: Aldine. **50**

Humphreys, L. (1975). *Tearoom trade: Impersonal sex in public places* (2nd ed.). Chicago: Aldine. **51**

Hunt, C. (1965). Female occupational roles and urban sex ratios in the United States, Japan, and the Philippines. *Social Forces, 43* (March), 407–417. **227**

Hunt, C., & Walker, L. (1974). *Ethnic diversity.* Homewood, IL: Dorsey Press. **314**

Hunter, F. (1953). *Community power structure: A study of decision makers.* Chapel Hill, NC: University of North Carolina Press. **230, 526**

Hunter, F. (1980). *Community power succession.* Chapel Hill, NC: University of North Carolina Press. **230**

Hutchinson, E. P. (1965). *Immigrants and their children.* New York: Wiley. **321**

Hyde, J. S. (1979). *Understanding human sexuality.* New York: McGraw-Hill. **65**

Hyman, H. H. (1972). *Secondary analysis of sample surveys.* New York: Wiley. **41**

Hyman, H. H. (1983). *Of time and widowhood.* Durham, NC: Duke University Press. **156**

Hyman, H. H., & Singer, E. (Eds.). (1968). *Readings in reference group theory and research.* New York: The Free Press. **148**

Ianni, F. A. J. (1972). *A family business: Kinship and social control in organized crime.* New York: Russell Sage Foundation. **259**

Illich, I. (1971). *Deschooling society.* New York: Harper & Row. **456**

Immigration and Naturalization Service. (1986, February 21). Reported in the Hartford *Courant.* **115**

Inkeles, A., & Smith D. H. (1974). The fate of personal adjustment in the process of modernization. *International Journal of Comparative Sociology, 11*(June), 101–103. **221, 237, 610**

Institute for Social Research. (1980, August). Faltering economy takes its toll on Americans' mental health. *Institute for Social Research Newsletter,* p. 3. **504, 511**

Irons, P. (1983). *Justice at war.* New York: Oxford University Press. **328**

Ishii-Kuntz, M., & Lee, G. R. (1987). Status of the elderly: An extension of the theory. *Journal of Marriage and the Family, 49*(3), 413–420. **381**

Itard, J.-M.-G. (1962). *The wild boy of Aveyron* (G. & M. Humphrey, Trans.). Englewood Cliffs, NJ: Prentice-Hall. (Original work published 1801) **135**

Jackson, D. (1974, January 11). Justice for none. *New Times*, pp. 48–57. **262**

Jackson, E. F., & Crockett, H. J., Jr. (1964). Occupational mobility in the United States. *American Sociological Review, 24*, 5–15. **297**

Jackson, K. T. (1986). *The suburbanization of the United States.* New York: Oxford University Press. **222**

Jackson, P. (1968). *Life in classrooms.* New York: Holt, Rinehart & Winston. **439**

Jacobs, D. (1981). Inequality and economic crime. *Sociology and Social Research, 66*(1), 12–28. **270**

Jacobs, J. (1961). *The death and life of great American cities.* New York: Vintage. **223**

Jacobson, P. H. (1959). *American marriage and divorce.* New York: Rinehart. **422**

Jacoby, R. (1987). *The last intellectuals.* New York: Basic Books. **469**

Jaeger, M. L., Anthony, S., & Rosnow, R. L. (1979). Some determining factors in the transmission of a rumor. Unpublished study, London School of Economics, London, and Temple University, Philadelphia. Cited and discussed in K. J. Gergen & M. M. Gergen. (1981). *Social psychology* (p. 366). New York: Harcourt Brace Jovanovich. **579**

James, D., & Soref, M. (1981). Profit constraints on managerial autonomy: Managerial theory and the unmaking of the corporation president. *American Sociological Review, 46*, 1–18. **497**

James, J. (1951). A preliminary study of the size determinant in small group interaction. *American Sociological Review, 16*, 474–477. **207**

Janeway, E. (1971). *Man's world, woman's place.* New York: Dell. **349, 350, 358, 373**

Janeway, E. (1987). *Improper behavior: When and how misconduct can be healthy for society.* New York: William Morrow. **273**

Janis, I. L. (1951). *Air war and emotional stress: Psychological studies of bombing and civilian defense.* New York: McGraw-Hill. **212**

Janis, I. L. (1968). Group identification under conditions of extreme danger. In D. Cartwright & A. Zander (Eds.), *Group dynamics: Research and theory.* New York: Harper & Row. **206**

Janis, I. L. (1982). *Victims of groupthink.* Boston: Houghton Mifflin. **206**

Jaret, C. (1983). Recent neo-Marxist urban analysis. *Annual Review of Sociology, 9*, 499–525. **222**

Jaynes, G. (1982, September 30). Suit on race recalls lines drawn under slavery. *New York Times*, p. B16. **311**

Jencks, C. (1983a, March 3). Discrimination and Thomas Sowell. *New York Review of Books*, p. 33ff. **321**

Jencks, C. (1983b, March 17). Special treatment for blacks? *New York Review of Books*, p. 12ff. **334, 335**

Jencks, C., & Reisman, D. (1968). *The academic revolution.* New York: Doubleday. **454**

Jencks, C., et al. (1972). *Inequality: A reassessment of the effect of family and schooling in America.* New York: Basic Books. **298, 325, 447**

Jencks, C., et al. (1979). *Who gets ahead? The determinants of economic success in America.* New York: Basic Books. **305**

Jenkins, J. C. (1981a). On the neofunctionalist theory of inequality. *American Journal of Sociology, 87*(1), 177–179. **286**

Jenkins, J. C. (1981b). Sociopolitical movements. In S. Long (Ed.), *Handbook of political science* (pp. 81–153). New York: Plenum Press. **586, 587**

Jenkins, J. C. (1983). Resource mobilization theory and the study of social movements. *Annual Review of Sociology, 9*, 527–553. **586**

Jenkins, J. C. (1985). *The politics of insurgency: The farm worker movement in the 1960s.* New York: Columbia University Press. **588**

Jenkins, J. C., & Eckert, C. M. (1986). Channeling black insurgency: Elite patronage and professional social movement organizations in the development of the black movement. *American Sociological Review, 51*(6), 812–829. **587, 588**

Jenkins, J. C., & Perrow, C. (1977). Insurgency of the powerless: Farm workers movements (1946–72). *American Sociological Review, 42*(April), 249–268. **586, 587**

Jensen, A. R. (1969). How much can we boost IQ and scholastic achievement? *Harvard Educational Review, 39*(Winter), 1–123. **314, 466**

Johnson, A. G. (1980). On the prevalence of rape in the United States. *Signs: Journal of women in culture and society, 6*(1), 136–146. **351**

Johnson, A. G. (1988). *Statistics.* San Diego: Harcourt Brace Jovanovich.

Johnson, D. A., et al. (1971). Racial discrimination in apartment rentals. *Journals of Applied Social Psychology, 1*, 364–377. **317**

Johnson, D. G., & Lee, R. D. (1986). *Population growth and economic development.* Washington, DC: National Academy of Sciences. **125, 249**

Johnson, D. L. (1988, April 12). Cited in the *New York Times*, p. A1.

Johnson, K. A. (1983). *Women, the family, and peasant revolution in China.* Chicago: University of Chicago Press.

Johnson, P. (1987). *A history of the Jews.* New York: Harper and Row. **321**

Johnson, R. E. (1980). Social class and delinquent behavior: A new test. *Criminology, 18*, 86–93. **256**

Johnston, L. D., O'Malley, P. M., & Bachman, J. G. (1986). *Use of licit and illicit drugs by American high school seniors, college students, and other young adults.* Ann Arbor, MI: Institute for Social Research. **249**

Joint Economic Committee. (1986a). *The concentration of wealth in the United States.* Washington, DC: Joint Economic Committee of the U.S. Congress. **291, 299, 497**

Joint Economic Committee. (1986b). *The great American job machine: The proliferation of low wage employment in the U.S. economy.* Washington, DC: Joint Economic Committee of the U.S. Congress.

Jones, E. E., & Nisbett, R. E. (1971). *The actor and the observer: Divergent perceptions of the cause of behavior.* Morristown, NJ: Silver Burdett/General Learning Press. **166**

Jones, G. (1980). *Social Darwinism and English thought: The interaction of biological and social theory.* Atlantic Highlands, NJ: Humanities Press. **289**

Jones, R. (1977). *The other generation: The new power of older Americans.* Englewood Cliffs, NJ: Prentice-Hall. **379**

Josephy, A. M., Jr. (1973). Freedom for the American Indian. *The Critic.* Chicago: Thomas More Associates. Reprinted in J. Skolnick & E. Currie (Eds.). (1976). *Crisis in American institutions* (3rd ed.). Boston: Little, Brown. **316**

Juravich, T. (1985). *Chaos on the shop floor: A worker's view of quality, productivity, and management.* Philadelphia: Temple University Press. **500**

Kagan, J., & Havemann, E. (1980). *Psychology: An introduction* (4th Ed.). New York: Harcourt Brace Jovanovich. **136**

Kahl, J. A. (1961). *The American class structure* (2nd ed.). New York: Holt, Rinehart & Winston. **296**

Kahn-Hut, R., Daniels, A. K., & Clovard, R. (Eds.). (1982). Unresolved questions: Three feminist perspectives. In *Women and work: Problems and perspectives.* New York: Oxford. **367**

Kalish, R. A. (1976). Death and dying in a social context. In R. H. Binstock & E. Shanas (Eds.), *Handbook of aging and the social sciences.* New York: Van Nostrand Reinhold. **386**

Kalish, R. A. (1981). *Death, grief, and caring relationships.* Monterey, CA: Brooks/Cole. **386**

Kalleberg, A., & Griffin, L. (1980). Class, occupation, and inequality in job rewards. *American Journal of Sociology, 85,* 731–768. **504**

Kalton, G. (1984). *Introduction to survey sampling.* Beverly Hills, CA: Sage. **36**

Kalven, H., Jr., & Zeisel, H. (1966). *The American jury.* Boston: Little, Brown. **261**

Kamenetsky, C. (1984). *Children's literature in Hitler's Germany.* Athens, OH: Ohio University Press. **450**

Kamii, C. K., & Radin, N. L. (1967). Class differences in the socialization practices of Negro mothers. *Journal of Marriage and the Family, 29,* 302–310. **414**

Kamin, L. J. (1974). *Science and the politics of IQ.* Hillsdale, NJ: Erlbaum. **466**

Kamin, L. J. (1986). Is crime in the genes? The answer may depend on who chooses what evidence. *Scientific American,* (February), 22–27. **263**

Kammeyer, K. C. W., & Ginn, H. (1986). *An introduction to population.* Chicago: The Dorsey Press. **107, 108, 416**

Kanter, R. M. (1972). *Commitment and community: Communes and utopias in sociological perspective.* Cambridge, MA: Harvard University Press. **221**

Kanter, R. M. (1976). Why bosses turn bitchy. *Psychology Today* 9(May), pp. 56–59. **351**

Kanter, R. M. (1977a). *Men and women of the corporation.* New York: Basic Books. **40, 42**

Kanter, R. M. (1977b). Some effects of proportions on group life: Skewed sex ratios and responses to token women. *American Journal of Sociology, 82,* 965–990. **40, 191, 351**

Kaplan, N. (1955). *Reference group theory and voting behavior.* Unpublished doctoral dissertation, Columbia University. Quoted in R. K. Merton, (1957/1968). **87**

Karlins, M., Coffman, T., & Walters, G. (1969). On the fading of social stereotypes: Studies in three generations of college students. *Journal of Personality and Social Psychology, 13,* 1–16. **313**

Karnow, S. (1983). *Vietnam: A history.* New York: Viking Press. **211, 212**

Karp, D. A., & Yoels, W. C. (1979). The college classroom: Some observations on the meanings of student participation. In H. Robboy, S. L. Greenblatt, & C. Clark (Eds.), *Social interaction.* New York: St. Martin's Press. **176, 442**

Kart, C. S., & Manard, B. B. (Eds.). (1976). *Aging in America: Readings in social gerontology, Part III.* Sherman Oaks, CA: Alfred. **379**

Kasarda, J. D. (1986, October 22). Reported in the *New York Times,* p. A1. **238**

Kasarda, J. D., & Janowitz, M. (1974). Community attachment in mass society. *American Sociological Review, 39,* 328–339. **231**

Katz, D., & Braly, K. W. (1933). Racial stereotypes of 100 college students. *Journal of Abnormal and Social Psychology, 28,* 280–290. **313**

Keller, E. F. (1985). *Reflections on gender and science.* New Haven: Yale University Press. **473**

Kelley, A., & Williamson, J. (1984). *What drives third world city growth? A dynamic general equilibrium approach.* Princeton: Princeton University Press.

Kelley, H. H. (1950). The warm-cold variable in first impressions of people, *Journal of Personality, 18,* 431–439. **163**

Kelley, H. H. (1952). Two functions of reference groups. In G. E. Swanson, T. M. Newcomb, & E. L. Hartley (Eds.), *Readings in social psychology* (rev. ed.). New York: Holt. **190**

Kelley, H. H., & Michela, J. L. (1980). Attribution theory and research. *Annual Review of Psychology, 31,* 457–501. **165**

Kemper, T. D. (1987). How many emotions are there? *American Journal of Sociology, 93*(2), 263–289. **74**

Kendall, P. M. (1962). *The Yorkist age.* Garden City, NY: Doubleday. **546**

Kephart, W. M. (1987). *Extraordinary groups: An examination of unconventional life-styles* (3rd ed.). New York: St. Martin's Press. (1976 refers to the first edition.) **221, 556**

Kerbo, H. R. (1983). *Social stratification and inequality: Class conflict in the United States.* New York: McGraw-Hill. **301, 330**

Kerner Commission (National Advisory Commission on Civil Disorders). (1968). *Report of the National Advisory Commission on Civil Disorders.* New York: Bantam.

Kessler, R. C., & McRae, J. A., Jr. (1981). Trends in the relationship between sex and psychological distress: 1957–1976. *American Sociological Review, 46*(August), 443–452. **364**

Kessler, R. C., & McRae, J. A., Jr. (1982). The effects of wives' employment on the mental health of married men and women. *American Sociological Review, 47*(April), 216–227. **372**

Kessler, S. (1975). Psychiatric genetics. In D. A. Hamburg & K. Brodie (Eds.), *American handbook of psychiatry* (Vol. 6). New York: Basic Books. **134**

Kessler-Harris, A. (1982). *Out to work: A History of wage-earning women in the United States.* London: Oxford University Press. **373**

Kingston, P. W., & Nock, S. L. (1987). Time together among dual-earner couples. *American Sociological Review, 52*(3), 391–400. **422**

Kipnis, D. (1972). Does power corrupt? *Journal of Personality and Social Psychology, 24,* 33–41. **169**

Kirschenbaum, H., et al. (1971). *Wad-ja-get?* New York: A & W. **436, 453, 456**

Klein, D. (1982). The dark side of marriage: Battered wives and the domination of women. In N. H. Rafter & E. A. Stanko (Eds.), *Judge, lawyer, victim, thief: Women, gender roles, and criminal justice.* Boston, MA: Northeastern University Press. **424**

Kluegel, J. R., & Smith, E. R. (1982). Whites' beliefs about blacks' opportunity. *American Sociological Review, 47*(August), 518–532. **289, 333**

Kluegel, J. R., & Smith, E. R. (1986). *Beliefs about inequality: Americans' views of what is and what ought to be.* New York: Aldine. **289**

Knoke, D. (1981). Power structures. In S. Long (Ed.), *Handbook of political behavior.* New York: Plenum. **527**

Knottnerus, J. D. (1987). Status attainment research and its image of society. *American Sociological Review, 52*(1), 113–121.

Knox, R. E., & Safford, R. K. (1976). Group caution at the racetrack. *Journal of Experimental Social Psychology, 12,* 317–324. **207**

Kohlberg, L. (1963). The development of chidren's orientations toward a moral order: I. Sequence in the development of moral thought. Vita hum., Basel. **68**

Kohn, M. L. (1977). *Class and conformity.* Chicago: University of Chicago Press. **151**

Kohn, M. L., & Schooler, C. (1983). *Work and personality: An inquiry into the impact of social stratification.* Norwood, NJ: Ablex. **504**

Kolb, W. (1954). The social structure and function of cities. *Economic Development and Cultural Change, 3,* 30–46. **239**

Kollock, P., Blumstein, P., & Schwartz, P. (1985). Sex and power in interaction. *American Sociological Review, 50*(1), 34–46. **350**

Kolson, A. (1979, February 4). Sexual harassment on the job. *Detroit Free Press,* p. 1C. **351**

Korbin, J. E. (Ed.). (1983). *Child abuse and neglect: Cross-cultural perspectives.* Berkeley, CA: University of California Press. **345**

Kornhauser, W. (1959). *The politics of mass society.* New York: The Free Press. **583**

Kornhauser, W. (1966). 'Power elite' or 'veto groups'? In R. Bendix & S. M. Lipset (Eds.), *Class, status, and power.* New York: The Free Press. **527**

Koslin, S., Amarel, M., & Ames, N. (1969). A distance measure of racial attitudes in primary grade children. *Psychology in the Schools, 6,* 382–385. **332**

Koss, M. P., Gidycz, C. A., & Wisniewski, N. (1987). The scope of rape. *Journal of Consulting and Clinical Psychology, 52*(2), 162–170.

Kriedte, P. (1984). *Peasants, landlords, and the merchant capitalists: Europe and the world economy, 1500–1800.* Cambridge: Cambridge University Press. **489**

Kübler-Ross, E. (1969). *On death and dying.* New York: Macmillan. **156, 386**

Kübler-Ross, E. (1975). *Death, the final stage of growth.* Englewood Cliffs, NJ: Prentice-Hall. **156, 386**

Kuhn, M. H., & McPartland, T. (1954). An empirical investigation of self-attitudes. *American Sociological Review, 19,* 68–76. **146**

Kuhn, T. S. (1970). *The structure of scientific revolutions* (2nd enlarged ed.). Chicago: University of Chicago Press. **462, 463**

Kuper, H. (1963). *The Swazi: A South African kingdom.* New York: Holt, Rinehart & Winston. **407**

Kuper, L. (1977). *The pity of it all: Polarization of racial and ethnic relations.* Minneapolis: University of Minnesota Press. **328**

Kuper, L. (1982). *Genocide: Its political use in the twentieth century.* New Haven: Yale University Press. **328**

Kuper, L. (1985). *The prevention of genocide.* New Haven: Yale University Press. **328**

Kurtz, R. A., & Chalfant, H. P. (1984). *Sociology of medicine and illness.* Boston: Allyn & Bacon. **477**

Kutner, B., et al. (1952). Verbal attitudes and overt behavior involving racial prejudice. *Journal of Abnormal and Social Psychology, 47*(July), 649–652. **318**

Kuttner, R. (1984). *The economic illusion.* Boston: Houghton Mifflin. **299**

LaFree, G. D. (1980). The effect of sexual stratification by race on official reactions to rape. *American Sociological Review, 45*(October), 842–854. **262**

Lakoff, R. (1975). *Language and woman's place.* New York: Harper & Row. **344**

Lakoff, R. T., & Scherr, R. L. (1984). *Face value: The politics of beauty.* Boston: Routledge & Kegan Paul. **346**

Lamb, M. E., & Goldberg, W. A. (1982). The father-child relationship: A synthesis of biological, evolutionary, and social perspectives. In L. W. Hoffman, R. Gandelman, & H. R. Schiffman (Eds.), *Parenting: Its causes and consequences* (pp. 55–73). Hillsdale, NJ: Lawrence Erlbaum. **369, 412**

Landes, J. B. (1977–1978). Women, labor, and family life. *Science and Society, 41*(Winter), 386–409. **420**

Lane, D. (1982). *The end of social inequality? Class, status, and power under state socialism.* London: Allen Unwin. **507, 508**

Langer, S. K. (1962). The growing center of knowledge. In *Philosophical sketches.* Baltimore: Johns Hopkins Press. **373**

La Noue, G. R. (Ed.). (1972). *Educational vouchers: Concepts and controversies.* New York: Teachers College Press, Columbia University. **457**

Lao, R., Upchurch, W., Corwin, B., & Grossnickle, W. (1975). Biased attitudes toward females as indicated by ratings of intelligence and likeability. *Psychological Reports, 37,* 1315–1320. **346**

Lapidus, G. (1978). *Women in Soviet society.* Berkeley, CA: University of California Press. **356**

Lapiere, R. T. (1934). Attitudes versus actions. *Social Forces, 13*(December), 230–237. **317**

Larson, O. F. (1968). Rural society. In D. L. Sills (Ed.), *The international encyclopedia of the social sciences* (Vol. 13 pp. 580–588). New York: The Macmillan Company/The Free Press. **221, 237**

Lasch, C. (1977). *Haven in a heartless world: The family besieged.* New York: Basic Books. **424**

Laska, S. B., Seaman, J. M., & McSeveney, D. R. (1982). Inner-city reinvestment: Neighborhood characteristics and spatial patterns over time. *Urban Studies, 19,* 155–165. **241**

Latané, B., & Darley, J. M. (1970). *The unresponsive bystander: Why doesn't he help?* New York: Appleton-Century-Crofts. **161, 442**

Latané, B., & Nida, S. (1981). Ten years of research on group size and helping. *Psychological Bulletin, 89,* 308–324. **161**

Lauer, R. H. (1981). *Temporal man: the meaning and uses of social time.* New York: Praeger. **89**

Laughlin, P. R. (1980). Social combination processes of cooperative problem-solving groups on verbal intellective tasks. In M. Fishbein (Ed.), *Progress in social psychology.* Hillsdale, NJ: Lawrence Erlbaum.

Lazonick, W. (1974). Karl Marx and enclosures in England. *The Review of Radical Economics, 6*(2, Summer), 1–32. **490**

Leacock, E. (1969). *Teaching and learning in city schools.* New York: Basic Books. **453**

Leavitt, H. J. (1951). Some effects of certain communication patterns on group performance. *Journal of Abnormal and Social Psychology, 46,* 38–50. **92**

Leavitt, R. (1971). Women in other cultures. In V. Gornick & B. K. Moran (Eds.), *Woman in sexist society* (pp. 393–427). New York: Basic Books. **44, 352**

Le Bon, G. (1960). *The crowd: A study of the popular mind.* New York: Viking. (Original work published 1895) **574**

Lederer, L. (Ed.). (1980). *Take back the night: Women on pornography.* New York: William Morrow. **347**

Lee, M. T. (1968). The founders of the Chinese Communist party. *Civilizations, 18.* **586**

Leibert, R. M., Sprafkin, J. N., & Davidson, E. S. (1982). *The early window: Effects of television on children and youth* (2nd ed.). New York: Pergamon.

LeMasters, E. E. (1975). *Blue-collar aristocrats.* Madison, WI: University of Wisconsin Press. **412**

Lemert, E. M. (1951). *Human deviance, social problems, and social control.* New York: McGraw-Hill. **269**

Lenin, V. I. (1949). *The state and revolution.* Moscow: Progress Publishers. (Original work published 1917) **521**

Lenski, G. E. (1966). *Power and privilege.* New York: McGraw-Hill. **287, 398, 546**

Lenski, G. E. (1975). Social structure in evolutionary perspective. In P. M. Blau (Ed.), *Approaches to the study of social structure.* New York: The Free Press. **89**

Lenski, G. E. (1976a). History and social change. *American Journal of Sociology, 82*(3, November), 548–564.

Lenski, G. E. (1976b). Immanuel Wallerstein. The modern world system. *Social Forces, 54,* 701–702. **611**

Lenski, G. E., & Lenski, J. (1987). *Human societies* (5th ed.). New York: McGraw-Hill. **199, 608**

Lepper, M. R., Greene, D., & Nisbett, R. E. (1973). Undermining children's intrinsic interest with extrinsic reward: A test of the 'overjustification' hypothesis. *Journal of Personality and Social Psychology, 28,* 129–137. **438**

Lerner, G. (1986). *The creation of patriarchy.* New York: Oxford. **343, 357**

Lerner, M. (Ed.). (1948). *The portable Veblen.* New York: Viking Press. **607**

Leslie, G. R. (1982). *The family in social context* (5th ed.). New York: Oxford University Press. **410**

Lesser-Blumberg, R. (1983). Kibbutz women: From the fields of revolution to the laundries of discontent. In M. Palgi, J. R. Blasi, M. Rosner, & M. Safir (Eds.), *Sexual equality: The Israeli kibbutz tests the theories* (pp. 130–150). Norwood, PA: Norwood Editions. **412**

Lester, D. (1983). *Why people kill themselves.* Springfield, IL: Charles C. Thomas.

Lever, H. (1981). Sociology of South Africa: Supplementary comments. *Annual Review of Sociology, 7,* 249–262. **302**

Levi, C. (1947). *Christ stopped at Eboli.* New York: Farrar, Straus. **557**.

Lévi-Strauss, C. (1956). The family. In H. L. Shapiro (Ed.), *Man, culture, and society.* New York: Oxford University Press. **409**

Levy, F. (1988). *The changing American income distribution.* New York: Russell Sage Foundation/Basic Books. **299**

Lewis, N. (1983). *Life in Egypt under Roman rule.* Oxford: Clarendon Press. **409**

Lewontin, R. (1970, March). Race and intelligence. *Bulletin of the Atomic Scientists,* pp. 23–25. **315**

Lewontin, R., Rose, S., & Kamin, L. J. (1984). *Not in our genes: Biology, ideology, and human nature.* New York: Pantheon.

Licht, H. (1932). *Sexual life in ancient Greece.* London: Routledge. **249**

Lichter, D. T. (1988). Racial differences in underemployment in American cities. *American Journal of Sociology, 93*(4), 771–797. **505**

Lieberman, S. (1956). The effects of changes in roles on the attitudes of role occupants. *Human Relations, 9,* 385–402. **181**

Lieberson, S. (1961). The impact of residential segregation on ethnic assimilation. *Social Forces, 40,* 52–57. **326**

Lieberson, S. (1971). An empirical study of military-industrial linkages. *American Journal of Sociology, 76*(January), 562–583. **526**

Lieberson, S. (1980). *A piece of the pie.* Berkeley: University of California Press.

Lieberson, S. (1982). Stereotypes: Their consequences for race and ethnic interaction. In R. M. Hauser, D. Mechanic, A. O. Haller, & T. S. Hauser (Eds.), *Social structure and behavior* (pp. 47–68). New York: Academic Press. **314**

Lieberson, S. (1985). *Making it count: The improvement of social research and theory.* Berkeley: University of California Press.

Liebert, R. M., et al. (1982). *The early window: The effects of television on children and youth.* Elmsford, NY: Pergamon. **133**

Limerick, P. N. (1987). *The legacy of conquest: The Unbroken past of the American west.* New York: W. W. Norton & Company. **113**

Link, B. G. (1987). Understanding labeling effects in the area of mental disorders: An assessment of expectations of rejection. *American Sociological Review, 52*(1), 96–112. **269**

Link, B. G., Cullen, F. T., Frank, J., & Wozniak, J. F. (1987). The social rejection of former mental patients: Understanding why labels matter. *American Journal of Sociology, 92*(6), 1461–1500. **254, 269**

Linton, R. (1936). *The study of man.* New York: Appleton-Century Crofts. **80, 81**

Lippitt, R., & White, R. K. (1947). An experimental study of leadership and group life. In T. M. Newcomb & E. L. Hartley (Eds.), *Readings in social psychology.* New York: Holt, Rinehart & Winston. **193, 194**

Lipset, S. M. (1959). Democracy and working-class authoritarianism. *American Sociological Review, 24,* 482–501. **303, 523, 529**

Lipset, S. M. (1963). *Political man.* New York: Anchor Books.

Lipset, S. M., & Bendix, R. (1959). *Social mobility in industrial society.* Berkeley, CA: University of California Press. **269, 297, 329**

Lipset, S. M., Trow, M., & Coleman, J. S. (1956). *Union democracy.* Glencoe, IL: The Free Press. **420, 504**

Lipton, D., Martinson, R., & Wilks, J. (1975). *The effectiveness of correctional treatment.* New York: Praeger. **263**

Lipton, M. (1984). Urban bias revisited. *Journal of Development Studies, 20*(3) 139–166.

Liska, A. E., & Reed, M. D. (1985). Institutions and delinquency. *American Sociological Review, 50*(4), 547–560. **264**

Lo, C. Y. H. (1982). Countermovements and conservative movements in the contemporary U.S. *Annual Review of Sociology, 8,* 107–134. **580**

Lofland, J. (1977). *Doomsday cult* (enlarged ed.). New York: Irvington. **562**

Lofland, J. (1981). Collective behavior: Elementary forms and processes. In M. Rosenberg & R. Turner (Eds.), *Social psychology: Sociological perspectives.* New York: Basic Books. **570**

Lofland, J. (1985). *Protest: Studies in collective behavior and social movements.* Brunswick, NJ: Transaction Books. **586**

Lombroso, C. (1911). *Crime: Its causes and remedies.* Boston: Little, Brown. **263**

London, B. (1987). Structural determinants of third world urban change: An ecological and political economic analysis. *American Sociological Review, 52*(1), 28–43. **116, 241**

Long, J. E. (1981). *Population deconcentration in the United States.* (Special Demographic Analysis COS-81-5). Washington, DC: U.S. Government Printing Office. **223**

Long, L. H., & Boertlein, C. (1976). *The geographic mobility of Americans* (Current Population Reports, Series P-23, No. 64). Washington, DC: U.S. Government Printing Office. **272**

Long, L. H., & De Are, D. (1981, September). The suburbanization of blacks. *American Demographics.* **238**

Lopata, H. Z. (1979). *Women as widows.* New York: Elsevier. **362**

Lopata, H. Z., Miller, C. A., & Barnewolt, D. (1984). *City women: Work, jobs, occupations, careers: Vol. 1. America.* New York: Praeger.

Lopata, H. Z., Barnewolt, D., & Miller, C. A. (1985). *City women: Work, jobs, occupations, careers: Vol. 2. Chicago.* New York: Praeger.

Lott, B. (1981). A feminist critique of androgyny: Toward the elimination of gender attributions for learned behavior. In C. Mayo & N. M. Henley (Eds.), *Gender and nonverbal behavior* (pp. 171–180). New York: Springer-Verlag. **345, 367**

Luce, R. D., & Raiffa, H. (1957). *Games and decisions.* New York: Wiley. **177, 577**

Luckmann, T. (1967). *The invisible religion.* New York: Macmillan. **562, 564**

Luker, K. (1984). *Abortion and the politics of motherhood.* Berkeley, CA: University of California Press. **370, 599**

Lukes, S., & Scull, A. (Eds.). (1983). *Durkheim and the law.* New York: St. Martin's Press. **223**

Lynd, H. (1958). *On shame and the search for identity.* New York: Harcourt Brace. **147**

Lynd, R. S. (1939). *Knowledge for what?* Princeton, NJ: Princeton University Press.

Lynd, R. S., & Lynd, H. M. (1929). *Middletown: A study in American culture.* New York: Harcourt Brace. **37, 230**

Lynd, R. S., & Lynd, H. M. (1937). *Middletown in transition: A study in cultural conflicts.* New York: Harcourt Brace. **230**

Maccoby, E. E., & Jacklin, C. N. (1974). *The psychology of sex differences.* Stanford, CA: Stanford University Press. **343, 360, 363**

Maccoby, E. E., & Martin, J. A. (1983). Socialization in the context of the family: Parent-child interaction. In P. H. Mussen (Ed.), *Handbook of child psychology* (4th ed.): Vol. 4. E. M. Hetherington (Ed.), *Socialization, personality, and social behavior.* New York: Wiley. **150**

MacDonald, J. F. (1985). *Television and the red menace: The video road to Vietnam.* New York: Praeger. **153**

Mach, B., & Wesolowski, W. (1986). *Social mobility and social structure.* London and New York: Routledge & Kegan Paul.

Maciak, B. J. (1987, October 20). Reported in the *New York Times.* **416**

MacKenzie, M. (1980). *The politics of body size: Fear of fat.* Los Angeles, CA: Pacifica Tape Library. **346**

MacKinnon, C. A. (1987). *Feminism unmodified*. Cambridge, MA: Harvard University Press. **367**

Malamuth, N. M., & Donnerstein, E. (Eds.). (1984). *Pornography and sexual aggression*. Orlando, FL: Academic Press. **347**

Malandro, L. A., & Barker, L. L. (1983). *Nonverbal communication*. Reading, MA: Addison-Wesley. **57**

Malbix/Ricks Music, BMI. (1976). *Chocolate city*. (Available on Casablanca Records, NBLP 7014). **326**

Malinowski, B. (1922). *Argonauts of the western Pacific*. New York: Dutton. **177, 486**

Malinowski, B. (1929). *The sexual life of savages*. New York: Harcourt Brace and World. **406, 407**

Malinowski, B. (1948). *Magic, science, and religion*. New York: The Free Press. **549**

Malthus, T. (1960). *Essay on the principle of population*. New York: Modern Library. (Original work published 1798) **127**

Mamdani, M. (1981). The ideology of population control. In K. L. Michaelson (Ed.), *And the poor get children*. (pp. 39–49). New York: Monthly Review Press. **127**

Mandel, E. (1968). *Marxist economic theory*. New York: Monthly Review Press.

Mandel, R. B. (1987, May 26). Findings reported in the *New York Times*. **357**

Mann, H. (1842). *Fifth annual report to the secretary of the board*. Boston: Dutton and Wentworth, State Printers. **434**

Mann, K. (1985). *Defending white-collar crime: A portrait of attorneys at work*. New Haven: Yale University Press. **261**

Mann, T. (1956). *The magic mountain*. New York: Knopf. (Original work published 1924) **88**

Mannheim, K. (1952). *Essays on the sociology of knowledge*. London: Routledge and Kegan Paul. **604**

Marak, G. E., Jr. (1964). The evolution of leadership structure. *Sociometry, 27*, 174–182. **194**

Marcus, G. E. (1983, March 27). One man's Mead. *New York Times Book Review*, p. 3. **41**

Margolin, L., & White, L. (1987). The continuing role of physical attractiveness in marriage. *Journal of Marriage and the Family, 49*(1), 21–27. **346, 380**

Marini, M. M. (1980). Sex differences in the process of occupational attainment. *Social Science Research, 9*, 307–361. **356**

Markham, J. M. (1982, April 4). In barren Iceland, culture blossoms. *New York Times*. **272**

Markides, K. C., & Cohen, S. F. (1982). External conflict/internal cohesion: A reevaluation of an old theory. *American Sociological Review, 47*(February) 88–98. **212**

Markovsky, B., Smith, L. R. F., & Berger, J. (1984). Do status interventions persist? *American Sociological Review, 49*(June), 373–382. **92, 195**

Mars, G. (1983). *Cheats at work: An anthropology of workplace crime*. Winchester, MA: Allen Unwin. **256**

Marshall, L. (1965). The !Kung Bushmen of the Kalahari Desert. In J. Gibbs (Ed.), *Peoples of Africa*. New York: Holt, Rinehart & Winston. **120**

Martinson, R. (1974). What works? Questions and answers about prison reform. *The Public Interest, 35*(Spring), 22–54. **263**

Marx, G. T., & Reichman, N. (1984). Routinizing the discovery of secrets: Computers as informants. *American Behavioral Scientist, 27*(4, March/April), 423–452. **606**

Marx, K. (1935). Theses on Feuerbach. In F. Engels, *Ludwig Feuerbach and the outcome of classical German philosophy* (pp. 73–75). New York: International Publishers. (Original work published 1845) **503**

Marx, K. (1961). *Economic and philosophical manuscripts of 1884*. (T. B. Bottomore, Trans.) in E. Fromm, *Marx's Concept of Man*. New York: Ungar. **306, 312**

Marx, K. (1967). Critiques of Hegel's Philosophy of Rights. In L. D. Easton & K. Guddat (Trans. and Eds.), *Writings of the young Marx on philosophy and society*. New York: Doubleday. (Original work published 1843) **288**

Marx, K. (1970). *A contribution of the critique of political economy*. New York: International Publishers. (Original work published 1859)

Marx, K. (1975). *Capital: A critique of political economy*. New York: International Publishers. (Original work published 1867) **127, 271, 280, 488**

Marx, K., & Engels, F. (1932). *Manifesto of the Communist party*. New York: International Publishers. (Original work published 1848) **23, 288, 598**

Marx, K., & Engels, F. (1976). The German ideology. In *Collected works of Marx and Engels: Vol. 5*. New York: International. (Original work published 1846) **23, 271, 287, 305**

Mason, K. O. (1982). Norms relating to the desire for children. In R. A. Bulatao & R. D. Lee (Eds.), *Determinants of Fertility in developing countries: A summary of knowledge* (Panel on Fertility Determinants, Report No. 3). Washington, DC: National Academy Press. **416**

Massey, D. S. (1981a). Dimensions of the new immigration to the United States and prospects for assimilation. *Annual Review of Sociology, 7*, 57–85. **115**

Massey, D. S. (1981b). Hispanic residential segregation: A comparison of Mexicans, Cubans, and Puerto Ricans. *Sociology and Social Research, 65*. **326**

Massey, D. S., Alarcon, R., Durand, J., & Gonzalez, H. (1987). *Return to Aztlan: The social process of international migration from Western Mexico*. Berkeley: University of California Press. **115**

Massey, D. S., & Denton, N. A. (1985). Spatial assimilation as a socioeconomic outcome. *American Sociological Review, 50*(1), 94–105. **326**

Massey, D. S., & Denton, N. A. (1987). Trends in the residential segregation of blacks, hispanics, and asians: 1970–1980. *American Sociological Review, 52*(6), 802–825. **326**

Mathais, P. (1983). *The first industrial revolution: An economic history of Britain 1700–1914* (2nd ed.). London and New York: Methuen. **125**

Matsueda, R. L. (1982). Testing control theory and differential association. *American Sociological Review, 47*(August), 489–504. **265**

Matthiessen, P. (1984). *Indian country*. New York: Viking Press. **288**

Mayo, C., & Henley, N. M. (Eds.). (1981). *Gender and nonverbal behavior*. New York: Springer-Verlag. **350**

McAdam, D. (1982). *Political process and the development of black insurgency 1930–1970*. Chicago: University of Chicago Press. **581, 582, 586, 587, 588, 589, 590**

McArthur, L. Z. (1982). Television and sex role stereotyping. *The Brandeis Quarterly, 2*(January), 12–13. **361**

McCall, G., & Simmons, J. (1978). *Identities and interactions* (rev. ed.). New York: The Free Press. **163**

McCarthy, J. D., & Zald, M. N. (1973). *The trend of social movements in America: Professionalization and resource mobilization*. Morristown, NJ: General Learning Press. **586, 587**

McClelland, D C. (1973). Testing for competence rather than for 'intelligence.' *American Psychologist, 29*(January). **453**

McClelland, D. C. (1986). Some reflections on the two psychologies of love. *Journal of Personality*, (July), 334–353. **177**

McClosky, H., & Brill, A. (1983). *Dimensions of tolerance: What Americans believe about civil liberties*. New York: Russell Sage Foundation. **523**

McDougall, W. (1950). *An introduction to social psychology* (30th ed.). London: Methuen. (Original work published 1908) **134**

McGlen, N., & O'Connor, K. (1983). *Women's rights: The struggle for equality in the 19th and 20th centuries.* New York: Praeger. **533**

McGuire, W. J., McGuire, C. V., Child, P., & Fujioka, T. (1978). Salience of ethnicity in the spontaneous self-concept as a function of one's ethnic distinctiveness in the social environment. *Journal of Personality and Social Psychology, 36,* 511–520. **149**

McLanahan, S. (1985). Family structure and the reproduction of poverty. *American Journal of Sociology, 90*(4), 873–901. **427**

McPhail, C., & Miller, D. (1973). The assembling process: A theoretical and empirical examination. *American Sociological Review,* (December). **585**

McPhail, C., & Wohlstein, R. T. (1983). Individual and collective behaviors within gatherings, demonstrations, and riots. *Annual Review of Sociology, 9,* 579–600. **575**

McPhail, C., & Wohlstein, R. T. (1986). Collective locomotion as collective behavior. *American Sociological Review, 51*(4), 447–463. **570**

Macpherson, C. B. (1973). *Democratic theory: Essays in retrieval.* Oxford: Clarendon Press. **492**

McRae, K. D. (1984). *Conflict and compromise in mutilingual societies: Vol. 1. Switzerland.* Waterloo, Ontario: Wilfrid Laurier University Press. **62**

McRae, K. D. (1986). *Conflict and compromise in multilingual societies: Vol. 2. Belgium.* Waterloo, Ontario: Wilfrid Laurier University Press. **62**

Mead, G. H. (1934). *Mind, self, and society.* Chicago: University of Chicago Press. **24, 141, 143, 144, 145**

Mead, M. (1953). *Coming of age in Samoa.* New York: Modern Library. (Original work published 1928) **41, 44, 384, 407**

Mead, M. (1963). *Sex and temperament in three primitive societies.* New York: Morrow. (Original work published 1935) **348**

Mead, M. (1968). Incest. In D. L. Sills (Ed.), *The international encyclopedia of the social sciences* (Vol. 7, pp. 115–122). New York: MacMillan. **409, 419**

Medea, A., & Thompson, K. (1974). *Against rape.* New York: Farrar, Straus, and Giroux. **168, 261, 351**

Mehrabian, A. (1972). *Nonverbal communication.* Chicago: Aldine-Atherton. **171**

Meier, R. F., & Short, J. F., Jr. (1982). The consequences of white-collar crime. In H. Edelhertz & T. D. Overcast (Eds.), *White-collar crime: An agenda for research* (pp. 23–50). Lexington, MA: Lexington Books. **273**

Melbin, M. (1978). Night as frontier. *American Sociological Review, 43*(February), 3–22. **227**

Memmi, A. (1964) *Dominated man.* New York: Orion Press. **313, 314**

Merrick, T. W. (1986). World population in transition. *Population Bulletin, 41*(2, April). Washington, DC: Population Reference Bureau. **105, 115, 127**

Merton, J. G., & Moore, R. L. (1982). *The cult experience: Responding to the new religious pluralism.* New York: Pilgrim Press. **553**

Merton, R. K. (1936). The unanticipated consequences of purposive social action. *American Sociological Review, 1,* 894–904.

Merton, R. K. (1938). Social structure and anomie. *American Sociological Review, 3,* 672–682. **270, 271, 468**

Merton, R. K. (1940). Fact and factitiousness in ethnic opinion-naires. *American Sociological Review, 5,* 13–28. **38**

Merton, R. K. (1948). Discrimination and the American creed. In R. M. MacIver (Ed.), *Discrimination and national welfare* (pp. 99–126). New York: Harper and Brothers. **317, 327, 598, 601**

Merton, R. K. (1957a). *Social theory and social structure.* New York: The Free Press. **443, 466**

Merton, R. K. (1957b). Priorities in scientific discovery: A chapter in the sociology of science. *American Sociological Review, 22*(6), 635–659.

Merton, R. K. (1968). *Social theory and social structure* (enlarged ed.). New York: The Free Press. **21, 79, 81, 82, 83, 155, 164, 190, 192, 209, 247, 251, 252, 270, 271, 252, 270, 271, 443, 465, 555, 598, 601**

Merton, R. K. (1973). *The sociology of science: Theoretical and empirical investigations.* Chicago: University of Chicago Press. **461, 466, 469**

Merton, R. K. (1975). Structural analysis in sociology. In P. Blau (Ed.), *Approaches to the study of social structure* (pp. 21–52). New York: The Free Press.

Merton, R. K. (1976a). The sociology of social problems. In R. K. Merton & R. Nisbet (Eds.), *Contemporary social problems* (4th ed.). New York: Harcourt Brace Jovanovich. **251, 252, 273**

Merton, R. K. (1976b). *Sociological ambivalence and other essays.* New York: The Free Press.

Merton, R. K. (1978). *Science, technology, and society in seventeenth century England.* Atlantic Highlands, NJ: Humanities. (Original work published in 1938).

Merton, R. K. (1984, November 2). Scientific fraud and the first to be first. *Times Literary Supplement.* **467**

Merton, R. K. (1987). Three fragments from a sociologist's note-books: Establishing the phenomenon, specified ignorance, and strategic research materials. *Annual Review of Sociology, 1987,* 1–28. Palo Alto, CA: Annual Reviews. **469**

Merton, R. K., & Rossi, A. S. (1968). Contributions to the theory of reference group behavior. In Merton (1968), pp. 279–334. **149**

Meyer, J., & Sobieszek, B. (1972). Effect of a child's sex on adult interpretations of its behavior. *Developmental Psychology, 6,* 42–48. **360**

Michels, R. (1911). *Political parties.* (1967). New York: The Free Press. **524**

Michelson, W. (1985). *From sun to sun: Daily obligations and community structure in the lives of employed women and their families.* Totawa, NJ: Rowman & Allanheld. **349, 369, 372**

Mickish, G. (1971). Can women function as successfully as men in the role of elementary principal? *Research Reports on Educational Administration, 2*(4) (ERIC Documentation Reproduction Service, ED 062 679). **360**

Micklin, M., & Choldin, H. M. (Eds.). (1984). *Sociological human ecology: Contemporary issues and applications.* Boulder, CO: Westview Press. **104**

Milavsky, J. R., Kessler, R. C., Stipp, H. H., & Rubens, W. S. (1982). *Television and aggression: A panel study.* New York: Academic Press. **154**

Milgram, S. (1965). Some conditions of obedience and disobedience to authority. *Human Relations, 18,* 57–76. **268**

Milgram, S. (1974). *Obedience to authority.* New York: Harper & Row. **268**

Milgram, S. (1977). *The individual in a social world.* Reading, MA: Addison-Wesley. **578**

Miliband, R. (1969). *The state in capitalist society.* New York: Basic Books. **539**

Milkman, R. (1987). *Gender and work: The dynamics of job segregation by sex during World War II.* Chicago: University of Chicago Press. **366**

Miller, G. (1978). *Odd jobs: The world of deviant work.* Englewood Cliffs, NJ: Prentice-Hall. **259**

Miller, J., & Garrison, H. H. (1982). Sex roles: The division of labor at home and in the workplace. *Annual Review of Sociology, 8,* 237–262. **353**

Miller, N., & Brewer, M. B. (Eds.). (1984). *Groups in contact: The psychology of desegregation.* New York: Academic Press. **332, 596**

Miller, W. B. (1958). Lower-class culture as a generating milieu of gang delinquency. *Journal of Sociological Issues, 14* (Summer), 5–19. **265**

Millett, K. (1971). *Sexual politics.* Garden City, NY: Doubleday.

Mills, C. W. (1951). *White collar.* New York: Oxford University Press. **290, 306, 493**

Mills, C. W. (1956). *The power elite.* New York: Oxford University Press. **23, 292, 526**

Mills, C. W. (1959). *The sociological imagination.* New York: Oxford University Press. **19, 463**

Miner, H. M. (1968). Community-society continua. In D. L. Sills (Ed.), *The international encyclopedia of the social sciences* (vol. 3, pp. 174–180). New York: The Macmillan Company/The Free Press. **231, 237**

Mintz, B. (1975). The President's cabinet, 1897–1972: A contribution to the power structure debate. *Insurgent Sociologist, 5,* 131–148. **527, 552**

Mintz, B., & Schwartz, M. (1985). *The power structure of American business.* Chicago: University of Chicago Press. **230, 527**

Mirowsky, J. (1985). Depression and marital power: An equity model. *American Journal of Sociology, 91*(3), 557–592. **414**

Mirowsky, J., & Ross, C. E. (1987). Belief in innate sex roles: Sex stratification versus interpersonal influence in marriage. *Journal of Marriage and the Family, 49*(3), 527–540. **181, 413**

Mitchell, J. (1966, November/December). The longest revolution. *New Left Review,* pp. 11–37. **366**

Mitroff, I. I., Mason, R. O., & Barabba, V. P. (1983). *The 1980 census: Policymaking amid turbulence.* Lexington, MA: Lexington Books. **35**

Mixon, D. (1972). Instead of deception. *Journal of the Theory of Social Behavior, 2,* 145–177. **268**

Miyamato, S. F., & Dornbusch, S. (1956). A test of the symbolic interactional hypothesis of self-conception. *American Journal of Sociology, 61,* 399–403. **146**

Mizrahi, T. (1986). *Getting rid of patients: Contradictions in the socialization of physicians.* New Brunswick, NJ: Rutgers University Press. **154**

Moede, W. (1927). Die Richtlinien der Leitungspsychologie. *Industrielle Psychotechnik, 4,* 193–209. Cited and discussed in Raven (1968). **206**

Mol, H. (1976). *Identity and the sacred: A sketch for a new social-scientific theory of religion.* Oxford: Blackwell. **545**

Molotch, H. L., & Boden, D. (1985). Talking social structure. *American Sociological Review, 50*(3), 273–287. **170**

Money, J., & Ehrhardt, A. (1972). *Man and woman, boy and girl.* Baltimore, MD: Johns Hopkins University Press.

Monson, T. C., & Hesley, J. W. (1982). Causal attributions for behaviors consistent or inconsistent with an actor's personality traits: Differences between those offered by actors and observers. *Journal of Experimental Social Psychology, 18*(5), 416–432. **166**

Montagu, A. M. F. (1971). *Touching: The human significance of the skin.* New York: Columbia University Press. **134, 407, 418**

Moore, W. E. (1962). *The conduct of the corporation.* New York: Random House. **214**

Mor, V. (1987). *Hospice care systems: Structure, process, costs, and outcomes.* New York: Springer. **386**

Morello, K. B. (1986). *The invisible bar: The woman lawyer in America.* New York: Random House. **351**

Moreno, J. L. (1943). Sociometry and the cultural order. *Sociometry, 6,* 299–344. **90**

Morgan, R. (1970). *Sisterhood is powerful.* New York: Random House. **347, 373**

Morgan, S. P., & Hirosima, K. (1983). The persistence of extended family residence in Japan. *American Sociological Review, 48*(April), 269–281. **419**

Morgenstern, O. (1968). Game theory: Theoretical aspects. In D. L. Sills (Ed.), *The international encyclopedia of the social sciences* (Vol. 6). New York: The MacMillan Company/The Free Press. **438**

Morison, S. E. (1965). *The Oxford history of the American people.* New York: Oxford University Press. **328, 537**

Morris, A. (1984). *The origins of the civil rights movement: Black communities organizing for change.* New York: Free Press. **582, 588, 589**

Morris, D. (1967). *The naked ape.* New York: McGraw-Hill. **172**

Morrison, K. C. (1987). *Black political mobilization: Leadership, power, and mass behavior.* Albany, NY: SUNY Press. **588**

Mortimer, J. T., Finch, M. D., & Kumka, D. (1981). Persistence and change in human development: The multidimensional self-concept. In P. B. Bates & O. G. Brim, Jr. (Eds.), *Life-span development and behavior* (Vol. 4) New York: Academic Press. **183**

Moskos, C. C., Jr. (1969). Why men fight: American combat soldiers in Vietnam. *Transaction, 7*(1). **191, 210**

Mottaz, C. J. (1981). Some determinants of work alienation. *The Sociological Quarterly, 22*(Autumn), 515–529. **504**

Ms. (1982, October). Name styles of the future, p. 11. **406**

Mullen, B. (1983). Operationalizing the effect of the group on the individual: A self-attention perspective. *Journal of Experimental Social Psychology, 19*(4), 295–322. **208**

Muller, P. O. (1981). *Contemporary suburban America.* Englewood Cliffs, NJ: Prentice-Hall. **223, 225**

Mulligan, M. A. (1977). An investigation of factors associated with violent modes of conflict resolution in the family. Unpublished master's thesis, University of Rhode Island. Cited in Gelles (1978), p. 173.

Mumford, L. (1961). *The city in history.* New York: Harcourt Brace Jovanovich.

Munley, A. (1983). *The hospice alternative: A new context for death and dying.* New York: Basic Books. **386**

Munsinger, H. (1975). The adopted child's IQ: A critical review. *Psychological Bulletin, 82,* 623–659. **134**

Murdock, G. P. (1943). The common denominator of cultures. In R. Linton (Ed.), *The science of man in the world crisis.* New York: Columbia University Press. **64**

Murdock, G. P. (1949). *Social structure.* New York: MacMillan. **406, 407, 409, 410**

Murdock, G. P. (1967). *Ethnographic atlas.* Pittsburgh, PA: Pittsburgh University Press. **123, 124, 199, 406, 486**

Murray, C. (1984). *Losing ground: American social policy 1950–1980.* New York: Basic Books.

Myrdal, G. (1945). *An American dilemma.* New York: Harper & Row. **331**

NAEP (National Assessment of Educational Progress). (1977). Basic skills improve, but . . . *NAEP Newsletter, 10*(February), pp. 1–2. **444**

Nag, M. (1962). *Factors affecting human fertility in nonindustrial societies: A cross-cultural study.* New Haven, CT: Yale University Press. **416**

Nag, M. (1967). Family type and fertility. *Proceedings of the World Population Conference, Volume II,* pp. 160–163. New York: United Nations. **416**

Nakell, B., & Hardy, K. A. (1987). *The arbitrariness of the death penalty.* Philadelphia: Temple University Press. **262**

Nasaw, D. (1979). *Schooled to order.* New York: Oxford University Press. **447, 450**

Nash, M. (1965). *The golden road to modernity: Village life in contemporary Burma.* New York: Wiley. **388**

National Center for Health Statistics. (1986, May 25). Findings reported in the *New York Times,* p. 32. **232**

National Center for Health Statistics. (1987). *Vital statistics of the United States, 1983, Vol. II, Mortality, Part A.* Washington, DC: U.S. Government Printing Office. **364, 385**

National Center for Health Statistics. 1988). *Health United States 1987.* Washington, DC: U.S. Government Printing Office. **108**

National Commission on Excellence in Education. (1983). *A nation at risk: The imperative for educational reform.* Washington, DC: U.S. Government Printing Office. **95, 437, 444, 450, 456**

National Committee on Pay Equity. (1987, March 1). Ford Foundation study reported in the Hartford *Courant.* **319**

National Council of Churches. (1987). *Yearbook of American and Canadian Churches: 1987.* Nashville, TN: Abingdon Press. **562**

National Council on Aging. (1975). *The myth and reality of aging in America* (Mimeograph). Washington, DC. **379, 384**

National Institute of Mental Health. (1982). *Television and behavior: Ten years of scientific progress and implications for the eighties.* Washington, DC: U.S. Government Printing Office. **154**

National Law Review. (1984, May 21). **356**

National Office of Vital Statistics. (1956). *Death rates by age, race, and sex, United States, 1900–1953: Suicide* (Vital Statistics–Special Reports, 43, 30). Washington, DC: U.S. Government Printing Office. **10, 13**

National Opinion Research Center. (1972, Spring). *National Data Program for the Social Sciences (General Social Survey).* National Opinion Research Center, University of Chicago. **326**

Nee, V., & Mozingo, D. (1983). *State and society in contemporary China.* Ithaca: Cornell University Press. **525**

Neidert, L. J., & Farley, R. (1985). Assimilation in the United States. *American Sociological Review, 50*(6), 840–849. **321, 324**

Neill, A. S. (1961). *Summerhill.* New York: Hart. **456**

Nemeth, R. J., & Smith, D. A. (1985). The political economy of contrasting urban hierarchies in South Korea and the Philippines. In M. Timberlake (Ed.), *Urbanization in the world economy* (pp. 183–206). New York: Academic Press.

Neugarten, B. L., et al. (1965). Age norms, age constraints, and adult socialization. *American Journal of Sociology, 70,* 710–717. **386**

Neustadt, R. E., & May, E. R. (1986). *Thinking in time.* New York: Free Press. **212**

Newcomb, T. M. (1947). Autistic hostility and social reality. *Human Relations, 1,* 69–86. **332**

Newcomb, T. M. (1956). The prediction of interpersonal attraction. *American Psychologist* (Vol. 1, pp. 575–586). **181**

Newcomb, T. M. (1961). *The acquaintance process.* New York: Holt, Rinehart & Winston. **181**

Newman, G. (1976). *Comparative deviance: Perception in law in six cultures.* New York: Elsevier. **264**

Nichols, E. K. (1986). *Mobilizing against AIDS.* Cambridge, MA: Harvard University Press. **109**

Nielson, J. (1978). *Sex in society: Perspectives on stratification.* Belmont, CA: Wadsworth. **352**

Noel, D. (1968). A theory of the origin of ethnic stratification. *Social Problems, 16*(Fall), 156–172. **328, 397**

Noelle-Neumann, E. (1984). *The spiral of silence: Public opinion and our social skin.* Chicago: University of Chicago Press. **190**

Norton, A. J., & Moorman, J.E. (1987). Current trends in marriage and divorce among American women. *Journal of Marriage and the Family, 49*(1), 3–14. **428**

North, C. C., & Hatt, P. K. (1947). Jobs and occupations: A popular evaluation. *Opinion News, 9,* 3–13. **293**

Oakes, J. (1985). *Keeping track: How schools structure inequality.* New Haven: Yale University Press. **453**

Oakley, A. (1974). *Woman's work: The housewife, past and present.* New York: Pantheon. **358**

Oberschall, A. (1973). *Social conflict and social movements.* Englewood Cliffs, NJ: Prentice-Hall. **586**

Obaler, R. S. (1985). *Women, power, and economic change: The Nandi of Kenya.* Stanford: Stanford University Press. **409**

O'Brien, R. M. (1987). The interracial nature of violent crimes: A reexamination. *American Journal of Sociology, 92*(4), 817–835. **259**

O'Connor, J. (1973). *The fiscal crisis of the state.* New York: St. Martin's Press. **395, 536, 537**

OECD (Organization for Economic Cooperation and Development). (1987, November 15). Reported in the *New York Times,* p. E8. **396**

Office of Technology Assessment. (1986a). Electronic record systems and individual privacy. Washington, DC: U.S. Government Printing Office. **606**

Office of Technology Assessment. (1986b, March 18). Reported in the *New York Times.* **472**

Office of Technology Assessment. (1987, September 28). The electronic supervisor: New Technology, New Tensions. Washington, DC: Congressional Office of Technology Assessment. Reported in the *New York Times.* **502**

Ogburn, W. F. (1922). *Social change.* New York: Viking Press. **605, 606**

Ogburn, W. F (1964). Cultural lag as theory. In W. F. Ogburn (Ed.), *On culture and social change* (pp. 86–95). Chicago: University of Chicago Press. **605**

Oppenheimer, V. K. (1974). The life-cycle squeeze: The interaction of men's occupational and family life cycles. *Demography, 11*(2), 227–244. **397**

Orum, A. M. (1972). *Black students in protest.* Washington, DC: The American Sociological Association. **582**

Orwell, G. (1971). *Nineteen eighty-four.* New York: Signet. (Original work published 1949) **525**

Osborn, J. J., Jr. (1979). *The paper chase.* New York: Popular Library. **154**

Osofsky, G. (1966). *Harlem: The making of a ghetto.* Irvington. **602**

Page, B. I. (1983). *Who gets what from government.* Berkeley: University of California Press. **306**

Pagelow, M. D. (1984). *Family violence.* New York: Praeger. **423, 424**

Painter, N. I. (1987). *Standing at Armageddon: The United States, 1877–1919.* New York: W. W. Norton & Company. **493**

Parenti, M. (1985). *Inventing reality.* New York: St Martin's Press. **288**

Park, R. E. (1926). The urban community as a spatial pattern and moral order. In E. W. Burgess (Ed.), *The urban community.* Chicago: University of Chicago Press.

Park, R. E. (1950). The nature of race relations. In R. E. Park, *Race and culture* (pp. 81–116). Glencoe, IL: The Free Press. (Original work published 1939) **183**

Park, R. E. (1967). The city: Suggestions for the investigation of human behavior in the urban environment. In R. E. Park, & E. W. Burgess, (Eds.). *The City.* Chicago: University of Chicago Press. (Original work published in 1925) **231**

Park, R. E., & Burgess, E. (Eds.). (1921). *An introduction to the science of sociology.* Chicago: University of Chicago Press. **120**

Park, R. E., Burgess, E., & McKenzie, R. D. (Eds.). (1925). *The city.* Chicago: University of Chicago Press. **236, 602**

Parker, D. P. (1983). *Fighting computer crime.* New York: Charles Scribner & Sons. **606**

Parkinson, C. N. (1957). *Parkinson's law.* Boston: Houghton Mifflin. **208**

Parsons, H. M. (1982). More on the Hawthorne effect. *American Psychologist, 37*(7, July), 856–857. **40**

Parsons, T. (1937). *The structure of social action.* New York: McGraw-Hill. **463, 597**

Parsons, T. (1951). *The social system.* Glencoe, IL: The Free Press. **81, 463, 477, 597, 609**

Parsons, T. (1964). A revised approach to the theory of social stratification. In T. Parsons, *Essays in sociological theory* (pp. 386–439). New York: The Free Press. **282, 285, 292**

Parsons, T. (1966). *Societies: Evolutionary and comparative perspectives.* Englewood Cliffs, NJ: Prentice-Hall. **597**

Parsons, T. (1969). *Politics and social structure*. New York: The Free Press. **520**

Parsons, T. (1971). *The system of modern societies*. Englewood Cliffs, NJ: Prentice-Hall. **285, 597**

Parsons, T., & Bales, R. F. (1953). *Family, socialization, and interaction process*. Glencoe, IL: The Free Press. **362, 600**

Pascal, B. *Pensées*, Section XIV, No. 894. **557**

Pastner, C. (1974). Accommodations to Purdah: The female perspective. *Journal of Marriage and the Family, 36* (May), 408–414. **408**

Patterson, M. L. (1983). *Nonverbal behavior*. New York: Springer-Verlag. **57**

Patzer, G. L. (1985). *The physical attractiveness phenomena*. New York: Plenum Press. **163**

Paulus, P. B. (1983). *Basic group processes*. New York: Springer-Verlag.

Pavlov, I. P. (1960). *Conditioned reflexes*. New York: Dover. (Original work published 1927) **136**

Pear, R. (1982, December 19). How poor are the elderly? *New York Times*. **389**

Peattie, L., & Aldrete-Haas, J. A. (1981). 'Marginal' settlements in developing countries. *Annual Review of Sociology, 7,* 157–175. **239**

Pechman, J. A. (1984). *Who paid the taxes?* Washington, DC: Brookings Institution. **288**

Perlmutter, H. V., & Montmollin, G. (1952). Group learning of nonsense syllables. *Journal of Abnormal and Social Psychology, 47,* 762–769. **205**

Perls, F. S., Hefferline, R. F., & Goodman, P. (1965). *Gestalt therapy*. New York: Dell. **168**

Perrin, S., & Spencer, C. (1980). The Asch effect–A child of its time? *Bulletin of the British Psychology Society, 32,* 405–406. **189, 190**

Perrow, C. (1984). *Normal accidents: Living with high-risk technologies*. New York: Basic Books. **471, 475**

Perschek, J. (1987). *Policy-planning organizations: Elite agendas and America's rightward turn*. Philadelphia: Temple University Press.

Pessen, E. (1984). *The log cabin myth: The social backgrounds of the presidents*. New Haven: Yale University Press. **292**

Peter, L. J., & Hull, R. (1969). *The Peter Principle*. New York: William Morrow. **209**

Petersen, A. C. (1980). Biopsychosocial processes in the development of sex-related differences. In Parsons (1980), pp. 31–56. **343**

Peterson, W., & Gist, N. P. (1951). Rumor and public opinion. *American Journal of Sociology, 57,* 159–167. **579**

Pettigrew, T. F. (1968). Race relations: Social and psychological aspects. In D. L. Sills (Ed.), *The international encyclopedia of the social sciences* (Vol. 13, pp. 277–282). New York: The Macmillan Company. **313, 321, 329**

Pettigrew, T. F. (1971). *Racially separate or together?* New York: McGraw-Hill. **325**

Pettigrew, T. F. (1975). *Racial discrimination in the United States*. New York: Harper & Row. **325**

Pettigrew, T. F. (1976). Race and intergroup relations. In R. K. Merton & R. Nisbet (Eds.), *Contemporary social problems* (4th ed.). New York: Harcourt Brace Jovanovich. **325, 331**

Peukert, D. J. K. (1987). *Inside Nazi Germany: Conformity, opposition, and racism in everyday life* (R. Deveson, Trans.). New Haven: Yale University Press. **156, 525**

Pfeffer, J. (1981). *Power in organizations*. Marshfield, MA: Pitman. **193**

Pfeiffer, E., Verwoedt, A., & Davis, G. (1972). Sexual behavior in middle life. *American Journal of Psychiatry, 128*(10), 82. **379**

Piaget, J. (1965). *The moral judgement of the child*. Glencoe, IL: The Free Press.

Piaget, J., & Inhelder, B. (1969). *The psychology of the child*. New York: Basic Books. **138**

Piliavin, I., & Briar, S. (1964). Police encounters with juveniles. *American Journal of Sociology, 70,* 206–214. **260**

Piliavin, I., Gartner, R., Thornton, C., & Matsueda, R. L. (1986). Crime, deterrence, and choice. *American Sociological Review, 51*(1), 101–119. **263**

Piven, F. F., & Cloward, R. A. (1979). *Poor people's movements*. New York: Vintage. **587, 589**

Pleck, J. H. (1977). The work-family role system. *Social Problems, 24,* 417–427. **348, 420**

Pleck, J. H. (1985). *Working wives/Working husbands*. Beverly Hills, CA: Sage. **369**

Polatnick, M. (1973). Why men don't rear children: A power analysis. *Berkeley Journal of Sociology, 18,* 45–86. Reprinted in J. W. Petras (Ed.). (1975). *Sex: Male; Gender: Masculine* (pp. 199–235). Port Washington, NY: Alfred Publishing Company. **358, 365, 372**

Polit, D. F., & Falbo, T. (1987). Only children and personality development: A quantitative review. *Journal of Marriage and the Family, 49*(2), 309–325. **106**

Pollock, L. A. (1984). *Forgotten children: Parent-child relations from 1500 to 1900*. Cambridge: Cambridge University Press. **380**

Pomer, M. I. (1986). Labor market structure, intragenerational mobility, and discrimination: Black male advancement out of low-paying occupations. *American Sociological Review, 51*(5), 650–659. **325**

Pomerance, B. (1979). *The elephant man*. New York: Grove Press. **253**

Pomeroy, S. (1975). *Goddesses, whores, wives, and slaves*. New York: Schocken. **347**

Pope, L. (1942). *Millhands and preachers*. New Haven: Yale University Press. **560**

Popenoe, D. (1985). *Private pleasure, public plight: American metropolitan community life in comparative perspective*. New Brunswick, NJ: Transaction Books. **231**

Popenoe, D. (1987). Beyond the nuclear family: A statistical portrait of the changing family in Sweden. *Journal of Marriage and the Family, 49*(1), 173–183. **427**

Popper, F. J., et al. (1987, December 12). Reported in the *New York Times*, p. 13. **257**

Population Reference Bureau. (1975). *World urbanization: 1800–2000*. Washington, DC: Population Reference Bureau. **237**

Population Reference Bureau. (1980). *World's women data sheet.* Washington, DC: Population Reference Bureau. **415**

Population Reference Bureau. (1984). *World population data sheet: 1984*. Washington, DC: Population Reference Bureau.

Population Reference Bureau. (1987). *1987 world population data sheet*. Washington, DC: Population Reference Bureau. **104, 105, 107, 108, 110, 111, 112, 113, 120, 133, 303, 392, 533, 602**

Porter, J. N. (Ed.). (1982). *Genocide and human rights: A global anthology*. Lanham, MD: University Press of America.

Powers, M. G. (Ed.). (1982). *Measures of socioeconomic status*. Boulder, CO: Westview Press. **282**

Pratt, J. W. (1935). The ideology of American expansion. In *Essays in honor of William E. Dodd* (p. 344). Chicago. **321**

President's Commission on Law Enforcement. (1967). *Final Report*. Washington, DC: U.S. Government Printing Office. **256**

Price, D. J. (1986). *Little science, big science, and beyond* (2nd enlarged ed.). New York: Columbia University Press. **468**

Price, R. M., & Rosberg, C. G. (1980). *Apartheid regime: Political power and racial domination*. Berkeley, CA: University of California Institute of International Studies. **322**

Projector, D., & Weiss, G. (1966). *Survey of financial characteristics of consumers*. (Federal Reserve Technical Paper, p. 148.) Washington, DC: U.S. Government Printing Office. **289**

Przeworski, A. (1985). *Capitalism and social democracy.* Cambridge: Cambridge University Press.

Quadagno, J. S. (1976). Occupational sex-typing and internal labor market distributions: An assessment of medical specialties. *Social Problems, 23*(4), 442–453. **36**

Quinn, O. W. (1954). The transmission of racial attitudes among white Southerners. *Social Forces, 33*(1), 41–47. **136**

Quinney, R. (1972). The ideology of law: Notes for a radical alternative to legal oppression. *Issues in Criminology, 7*(1), 1–35. **250**

Rabin, A. I. (1965). *Growing up in the kibbutz.* New York: Springer. **404**

Radcliffe-Brown, A. R. (1948). *The Andaman Islanders.* Glencoe, IL: The Free Press. **381**

Radecki, C., & Walstedt, J. J. (1980). Sex as a status position in work settings: Female and male reports of dominance behavior. *Journal of Applied Social Psychology, 10*(1), 71–85. **171**

Raiffa, H. (1970). *Decision analysis.* Reading, MA: Addison-Wesley. **577**

Raines, J. C., Berson, L. E., & Gracie, D. (1982). *Community and capital in conflict.* Philadelphia: Temple University Press. **229**

Rands, M., & Levinger, G. (1979). Implicit theories of relationship: An intergenerational study. *Journal of Personality and Social Psychology, 37,* 645–661. **352**

Ransford, H. E., & Miller, J. (1983). Race, sex and feminist outlooks. *American Sociological Review, 48*(February), 46–59.

Raper, A. (1933). *The tragedy of lynching.* Chapel Hill: University of North Carolina Press. **571, 572**

Rappoport, D. C., & Alexander, Y. (Eds.). (1982). *The morality of terrorism: Religious and secular justifications.* New York: Pergamon Press. **253**

Rasmussen, W. D. (1982). The mechanization of agriculture. In *Scientific American. The mechanization of work* (pp. 15–30). San Francisco: W. H. Freeman. **505, 604**

Ravitch, D. (1983). *The troubled crusade: American education, 1945–1980.* New York: Basic Books. **327, 436, 437, 441, 447, 451**

Reckless, W. C. (1973). *The crime problem.* Englewood Cliffs, NJ: Prentice-Hall. **257**

Redfield, R. (1947). The folk society. *American Journal of Sociology, 52,* 293–308. **231**

Reed, J. (1960). *Ten days that shook the world.* New York: Random House.

Reeder, G. D., & Spores, J. M. (1983). The attribution of morality. *Journal of Personality and Social Psychology, 44*(4), 736–745. **166**

Reich, M. (1981). *Racial inequality: A political-economic analysis.* Princeton, NJ: Princeton University Press. **329**

Reich, M., Gordon, D. M., & Edwards, R. C. (1973). A theory of labor market segmentation. *American Economic Review, LXIII*(2, May). **499**

Reinhold, R. (1982, September 26). Houston's great thirst is sucking city down into the ground. *New York Times,* p. 28. **236**

Reiss, A. J. (1971). *The police and the public.* New Haven, CT: Yale University Press. **271**

Reiss, A. J., & Biderman, A. D. (1980). *Data sources on white-collar law-breaking.* Washington, DC: Bureau of Social Research. **256**

Remick, H. (Ed.). (1984). *Comparable worth and wage discrimination: Technical possibilities and political realities.* Philadelphia: Temple University Press. **356**

Reskin, B., & Hartmann, H. I. (1986). *Women's work, men's work: Sex segregation on the job.* Washington, D.C.: National Academy Press.

Reynolds, P. D. (1971). Comment on 'The distribution of participation in group discussions' as related to group size. *American Sociological Review, 36,* 704–706. **194**

Reynolds, P. D. (1979). *Ethical dilemmas and social science research.* San Francisco: Jossey-Bass. **50**

Reynolds, P. D. (1982). *Ethics and social science research.* Englewood Cliffs, NJ: Prentice-Hall. **50**

Reynolds, V. (1980). *The biology of human action.* San Francisco: W. H. Freeman. **134**

Rich, A. (1976). *Of woman born: Motherhood as experience and institution.* New York: Norton. **358, 362**

Richardson, K., & Spears, D. (Eds.). (1972). *Race and intelligence.* Baltimore: Penguin Books. **311**

Richardson, L. W. (1977). *The dynamics of sex and gender.* Boston: Houghton Mifflin. **350**

Richardson, L. W. (1981). *The dynamics of sex and gender* (2nd ed.). Boston: Houghton Mifflin. **343**

Ridgeway, C. L. (1981). Nonconformity, competence, and influence in groups. *American Sociological Review, 46*(June), 333–347. **195**

Ridgeway, C. L., & Berger, J. (1986). Expectations, legitimation, and dominance behavior in task groups. *American Sociological Review, 51*(5), 603–617. **91, 195**

Ridgeway, C. L., Berger, J., & Smith, L. (1985). Nonverbal cues and status: An expectation states approach. *American Journal of Sociology, 90*(5), 955–978.

Riding, A. (1983, May 15). Problems of Mexico City: Warning to the third world. *New York Times,* p. 1. **103**

Riesman, D. (1961). *The lonely crowd.* New Haven, CT: Yale University Press. **292, 526**

Rifkin, J. (1987). *Time wars.* New York: Holt & Company. **60**

Riley, J. W., Jr. (1983). Dying and the meanings of death: Sociological inquiries. *Annual Review of Sociology, 9,* 191–216. **481**

Riley, M. W. (1974). The perspective of age stratification. *School Review, 82*(1). **397**

Riley, M. W. (1976). Age strata in social systems. In J. E. Birren (Ed.), *Handbook of aging and the social sciences.* New York: Van Nostrand Reinhold. **366, 393**

Riley, M. W. (1983). The family in an aging society: A matrix of latent relationships. *Journal of Family Issues,* (September). **386, 413**

Riley, M. W. (1987). On the significance of age in sociology. *American Sociological Review, 52*(1), 1–14. **119, 154, 390, 393, 417, 481, 604**

Riley, M. W., et al. (1969). Socialization for the middle and later years. In D. A. Goslin (Ed.), *Handbook of socialization theory and research* (pp. 951–982). Chicago: Rand McNally. **156**

Riley, M. W., et al. (1970). *Aging and society* (Vol. 2). New York: Russell Sage Foundation. **379, 380**

Riley, M. W., & Foner, A. (1968). *Aging and society* (Vol. 1). New York: Russell Sage Foundation. **379, 380, 381, 383, 394**

Riley, M. W., & Foner, A. (1972). *Aging and Society* (Vol. 3). New York: Russell Sage Foundation. **393**

Riley, M. W., Foner, A., & Waring, J. (1988). A sociology of age. In N. J. Smelser, & R. Burt (Eds.), *Handbook of sociology.* New York: Russell Sage. **393, 603**

Riley, M. W., & Riley, J. W., Jr. (1986). Longevity and social structure: The added years. *Daedalus, 115,* 51–75.

Riley, M. W., & Stoll, C. S. Content analysis. (1968). In D. L. Sills (Ed.), *The international encyclopedia of the social sciences* (Vol. 3, pp. 371–377). New York: Macmillan. **42**

Riley, M. W., & Waring, J. (1976). Age and aging. In R. K. Merton & R. Nisbet (Eds.), *Contemporary social problems* (4th ed.). New York: Harcourt Brace Jovanovich. **379, 388, 397**

Rindfuss, R., Bumpass, L., & St. John, C. (1980). Education and fertility: Implications for the roles women occupy. *American Sociological Review, 45,* 431–447. **113**

Robinson, J. C. (1984). Racial inequality and the problem of occupation-related injury and illness. *Milbank Memorial Fund Quarterly, 62*(4), 567–590. **109**

Robinson, J. G. (1980). Estimating the approximate size of the illegal alien population in the United States by the comparative trend analysis of age-specific death rates. *Demography, 17,* 159–176. **115**

Robinson, R. V. (1984). Reproducing class relations in industrial capitalism. *American Sociological Review, 49*(June), 182–196. **150**

Robinson, W. P. (1972). *Language and social behavior.* Baltimore, MD: Penguin Books. **62**

Rodin, J. (1986, October 7). Reported in the *New York Times,* p. C1. **170**

Rodin, J., & Langer, E. (1977). Long-term effects of a control-relevant intervention with the institutionalized aged. *Journal of Personality and Social Psychology, 35,* 897–902. **170**

Roethlisberger, F. J., & Dickson, W. (1939). *Management and the worker.* Cambridge, MA: Harvard University Press. **40, 188**

Rogers, E. M. (1983). *Diffusion of innovations* (3rd ed.). New York: The Free Press. **604, 606**

Rogers, W. (1931, June 28). Syndicated newspaper column. In *Bartlett's quotations* (13th ed., p. 904) (1955). Boston: Little, Brown. **532**

Rose, P. I. (1981). *They and we: Racial and ethnic relations in the United States.* New York: Random House. **321**

Rosenberg, C. E. (1987). *The care of strangers: The rise of America's hospital system.* New York: Basic Books. **478**

Rosenberg, M. (1965). *Society and the adolescent self-image.* Princeton, NJ: Princeton University Press. **147**

Rosenberg, M. (1979). *Conceiving the self.* New York: Basic Books. **144, 146, 147, 183**

Rosenberg, M. (1981). The self-concept: Social product and social force. In M. Rosenberg & R. H. Turner (Eds.), *Social psychology: Sociological perspectives* (pp. 593–624). New York: Basic Books. **144**

Rosenberg, M., & Kaplan, H. B. (Eds.). (1982). *Social psychology of the self-concept.* Arlington Heights, IL: Harlan Davidson. **144**

Rosenberg, M., & Simmons, R. B. (1971). *Black and white self-esteem: The urban school child.* Washington, DC: The American Sociological Association. **324**

Rosenhan, D. L. (1973, January 19). On being sane in insane places. *Science, 179*(No. 4070), pp. 1–9. **269**

Rosenthal, C. J. (1985). Kinkeeping in the familial division of labor. *Journal of Marriage and the Family, 47*(4), 965–974. **192**

Rosenthal, K. M., & Keshet, H. F. (1978). Childcare responsibilities of part-time and single fathers. *Alternative Lifestyles, 1*(4, November). 465–491. **155**

Rosenthal, R., & Jacobson, L. (1968). *Pygmalion in the classroom: Teacher expectation and pupils' intellectual development.* New York: Holt, Rinehart & Winston. **443, 453**

Rosnow, R. L., & Fine, G. A. (1976). *Rumor and gossip.* New York: Elsevier. **578**

Ross, H. L. (1984). Social control through deterrence: Drinking-and-driving laws. *Annual Review of Sociology, 10,* 21–35. **263**

Rossi, A. S. (1969). Sex equality: The beginning of ideology. In B. Roszak and T. Roszak (Eds.), *Masculine/feminine* (pp. 173–186). New York: Harper & Row.

Rossi, A. S. (1984). Gender and parenthood. *American sociological review, 49*(February), 1–19. **343, 362, 369**

Rostow, W. W. (1960). *The stages of economic growth: A non-communist manifesto.* Cambridge: Cambridge University Press. **609**

Roszak, B., & Roszak, T. (Eds.). (1969). *Masculine/feminine.* New York: Harper & Row. **369**

Rousseau, J.-J. (1950). New York: E. P. Dutton. (Original work published 1762) **536**

Rowbotham, S. (1973). *Woman's consciousness, Man's world.* New York: Penguin Books. **420**

Rubin, B. (1987). *Third world coup makers, strongmen, and populist tyrants.* New York: McGraw-Hill. **525**

Rubin, L. B. (1976). *Worlds of pain.* New York: Basic Books. **38, 420**

Rubin, N. (1982, January 10). Learning how children learn from the first moments of life. *New York Times* (Education Supplement). **138**

Rubin, R., & Byerly, G. (1983). *Incest: The last taboo* (An annotated bibliography). New York: Garland. **409**

Rubin, Z. (1973). *Liking and loving.* New York: Holt, Rinehart & Winston. **352**

Ruffini, J. L. (Ed.). (1983). *Advances in medical social science.* New York: Gordon and Breach.

Russell, D. E. H. (1982). *Rape in marriage.* New York: Macmillan. **168**

Russell, D. E. H. (1984). *Sexual exploitation: Rape, child sexual abuse and workplace harassment.* Beverly Hills, CA: Sage. **352**

Russell, D. E. H., & Howell, N. (1983). The prevalence of rape in the United States revisited. *Signs, 8*(4), 688–695. **351**

Russell, J. C. (1972). *Medieval regions and the cities.* Bloomington, IN: Indiana University Press. **233**

Ryder, N. B. (1965). The cohort as a concept in the study of social change. *American Sociological Review, 30,* 843–861. **119, 393, 604**

Ryder, N. B., & Westoff, C. F. (1971). *Reproduction in the United States, 1965.* Princeton, NJ: Princeton University Press. **408**

Rytina, J. H., Form, W. H., & Pease, J. (1970). Income and stratification ideology: Beliefs about the American opportunity structure. *American Journal of Sociology, 75*(January), 703–716. **289**

Rytina, N. F. (1981). Occupational segregation and earnings differences by sex. *Monthly Labor Review, 104*(January), 49–53. **354**

Sabini, J., & Silver, M. (1982). *Moralities of everyday life.* New York: Oxford University Press. **214**

Sachs, C. E. (1983). *The invisible farmers: Women in agricultural production.* Totowa, NJ: Rowman & Allanheld. **353**

Sacks, K. (1974). Engels revisited: Women, the organization of production, and private property. In M. Z. Rosaldo & L. Lamphere (Eds.), *Woman, culture, and society* (pp. 207–222). Stanford, CA: Stanford University Press. **352, 366, 370**

Sadker, M., & Sadker, D. (1985). Sexism in the schoolroom of the '80s. *Psychology Today,* (March), 54–57. **151, 202, 361**

Sagatun, I. J., & Knudsen, J. H. (1982). Attributional self presentation for actors and observers in success and failure situations. *Scandinavian Journal of Psychology, 23,* 243–252. Cited in *Annual Review of Sociology, 9*(1983), p. 441. **174**

Sahlins, M. D. (1976). *The use and abuse of biology: An anthropological critique of sociobiology.* Ann Arbor, MI: University of Michigan Press. **58, 406**

Sahlins, M. D., & Service, E. R. (Eds.) (1960). *Evolution and culture.* Ann Arbor, MI: University of Michigan Press.

St. Peter, S. (1979). Jack went up the hill . . . but where was Jill? *Psychology of Women Quarterly, 4,*256–260. **42, 360**

Sale, K. (1980). *Human scale.* New York: Coward, McCann, and Geoghegan. **200**

Sampson, A. (1983). *The changing anatomy of Britain.* New York: Random House. **434**

Sampson, R. J. (1986). Effects of socioeconomic context on official reaction to juvenile delinquency. *American Sociological Review, 51*(6), 876–885. **260**

Sanday, P. R. (1981). *Female power and male dominance.* Cambridge: Cambridge University Press. **348**

Sawyer, J. (1970, February 25). The case against grades. *Emphasis, Daily Northwestern Magazine,* 44. **453**

Schafer, S. (1974). *The political criminal.* New York: The Free Press. **253**

Schaff, A. (1970). *Marxism and the human individual.* New York: McGraw-Hill. **75, 76, 598**

Schaffer, K. F. (1981). *Sex roles and human behavior.* Cambridge, MA: Winthrop. **151, 361, 364**

Scheff, T. J. (1975). *Labeling madness.* Englewood Cliffs, NJ: Prentice-Hall. **270**

Scheff, T. J. (1984). *Becoming mentally ill: A sociological theory* (2nd ed.). Chicago: Aldine. **270**

Scheider, J., & Hacker, S. (1973). Sex role imagery in the use of the generic 'man' in introductory texts: A case in the sociology of sociology. *American Sociologist, 8,* 12–18. **344**

Schein, E. J. (1957). Reaction patterns to severe chronic stress in American army prisoners of war of the Chinese. *Journal of Social Issues, 13,* 21–30. **202**

Schlesinger, A. (1983, September 25). Familiar barbarities [Review of Howe, 1983]. *New York Times Book Review,* p. 1. **525**

Schnore, L. F. (1973). Community: Theory and research on structure and change. In N. J. Smelser (Ed.), *Sociology: An introduction* (2nd ed.). New York: Wiley. **219**

Schroeder, R. C. (1974). Policies on population around the world. *Population Bulletin, 29.* Washington, DC: Population Reference Bureau. **105**

Schudson, M. (1984). *Advertising, the uneasy persuasion: Its dubious impact on American society.* New York: Basic Books. **496**

Schuessler, K. F., & Cressey, D. R. (1950). Personality characteristics of criminals. *American Journal of Sociology, 55,* 476–484. **263**

Schulz, R. (1976). Control, predictability, and the institutionalized aged. *Journal of Personality and Social Psychology, 33,* 563–573. **170, 391**

Schulz, R., & Hanusa, B. H. (1980). Experimental social gerontology: A social psychological perspective. *Journal of Social Issues, 36*(2), 30–46. **170**

Schuman, H., & Converse, J. M. (1971). The effects of black and white interviewers on black responses in 1968. *Public Opinion Quarterly, 35,* 44–68. **34**

Schuman, H., & Presser, S. (1981). *Questions and answers in attitude surveys.* New York: Academic Press. **34, 36**

Schuman H., Steeh, C., & Bob, L. (1985). *Racial attitudes in America: Trends and interpretations.* Cambridge, MA: Harvard University Press. **332**

Schur, E. M. (1965). *Crimes without victims.* Englewood Cliffs, NJ: Prentice-Hall. **260, 264**

Schur, E. M. (1971). *Labeling deviant behavior.* New York: Harper & Row. **247**

Schur, E. M. (1984). *Labeling women deviant: Gender, stigma, and social control.* New York: Random House. **345**

Schwartz, R. D., & Skolnick, J. H. (1962). Two studies of legal stigma. *Social Problems, 10*(2). **269**

Schwendinger, J. R., & Schwendinger, H. (1983). *Rape and inequality.* Beverly Hills, CA: Sage.

Seeman, M. (1959). On the meaning of alienation. *American Sociological Review, 24,* 783–789. **504**

Seeman, M. (1975). Alienation studies. In *Annual Review of Sociology, 1,* 91–123.

Seeman, M. (1983). Alienation motifs in contemporary theorizing: The hidden continuity of the classic themes. *Social Psychology Quarterly, 46,* 171–184.

Seeman, M. (1981). Intergroup relations. In M. Rosenberg & R. H. Turner (Eds.), *Social psychology: Sociological perspectives* (pp. 378–410). New York: Basic Books. **313**

Seligman, M. E. P. (1975). *Helplessness.* San Francisco: W. H. Freeman. **170**

Selznick, G. J., & Steinberg, S. (1969). *The tenacity of prejudice.* New York: Harper & Row. **330**

Sennett, R. (1981). *Authority.* New York: Vintage. **169**

Sennett, R., & Cobb, J. (1973). *The hidden injuries of class.* New York: Vintage.

Serbin, L., & O'Leary, K. (1975, December). How nursery schools teach girls to shut up. *Psychology Today, 9,* pp. 56–58. **151, 361**

Service, E. (1962). *Primitive social organization: An evolutionary perspective.* New York: Random House. **419**

Service, E. (1966). *The hunters.* Englewood Cliffs, NJ: Prentice-Hall. **417**

Service, E. (1975). *Origins of the state and civilization.* New York: Norton. **520**

Sewell, W. H., Hauser, R. M, & Wolf, W. C. (1980). Sex, schooling, and occupational status. *American Journal of Sociology, 8,* 551–583. **356**

Seymour, W. N. (1973). Social and ethical considerations in assessing white-collar crime. *American Criminal Law Review, 11,* 821–834. **261**

Shaiken, H. (1986). *Work transformed: Automation and labor in the computer age.* Lexington, MA: Lexington. **494**

Shaw, G. B. (1904). *Plays pleasant and unpleasant* (Vol. II, Preface). Chicago, IL: H. S. Stone. (Original work published 1898). **62**

Shaw, M. E. (1954). Some effects of problem complexity upon problem solution efficiency in various communication nets. *Journal of Experimental Psychology, 48,* 211–217. **93, 209**

Sheehy, G. (1974). *Passages: The predictable crises of adult life.* New York: E. P. Dutton. **155**

Sheldon, W. R. (1949). *Varieties of delinquent behavior.* New York: Harper. **263**

Sherif, M. (1936). Formation of social norms: The experimental paradigm. In M. Sherif, *The psychology of social norms.* New York: Harper & Row. Reprinted in H. Proshansky & B. Seidenberg (Eds.). (1966). *Basic studies in social psychology.* New York: Holt, Rinehart & Winston. **190**

Sherman, B. (1985). *The new revolution: The impact of computers on society.* New York: John Wiley & Sons. **606**

Sherman, L. W., & Berk, R. A. (1984). The specific deterrent effects of arrest for domestic assault. *American Sociological Review, 49*(June), 261–272. **424**

Shibamoto, J. S. (1985). *Japanese women's language.* New York: Academic Press. **344**

Shibutani, T. (1966). *Improvised news: A sociological study of rumor.* Indianapolis, IN: Bobbs Merrill. **579**

Shibutani, T. (1968). Rumor. In D. L. Sills (Ed.), *The international encyclopedia of the social sciences* (Vol. 13, pp 576–580). New York: The Macmillan Company/The Free Press. **579**

Shiels, D. (1975). Toward a unified theory of ancestor worship. *Social Forces, 54*(December), appendix, part B. **406, 556**

Shils, E. A., & Janowitz, M. (1948). Cohesion and disintegration in the Wehrmacht in World War II. *Public Opinion Quarterly, 12*(Summer), 280–315. **210**

Shilts, R. (1987). *While the band played on: Politics, people, and the AIDS epidemic.* New York: St. Martin's Press. **109, 110, 469, 474, 573**

Shipler, D. K. (1983, October 16). Russia: A people without heroes. *New York Times Magazine,* p. 29. **523, 537, 557**

Shor, I. (1986). *Culture wars: School and society in the conservative restoration 1969–1984.* Boston: Routledge & Kegan Paul. **456**

Shorter, E., & Tilly, C. (1974). *Strikes in France: 1830–1968.* London: Cambridge University Press. **582, 588, 589**

Showalter, E. (1985). *The female malady: Women, madness, and English culture, 1830–1980.* New York: Pantheon. **346**

Shrauger, J. S., & Schoeneman, T. J. (1979). Symbolic interactionist view of self-concept: Through the looking glass darkly. *Psychological Bulletin, 86,* 549–573. **145**

Shupe, A., Stacey, W. A., & Hazlewood, L. R. (1987). *Violent men, violent couples: The dynamics of domestic violence.* Lexington, MA: Lexington Books. **424**

Silberman, C. (1971). *Crisis in the classroom.* New York: Random House. **440, 441**

Silk, L. (1983, October 9). Andropov's economic dilemma. *New York Times Magazine.* **508, 537**

Silverman, M. (1976). Toward a theory of criminal deterrence. *American Sociological Review, 41,* 442–461. **262**

Silverstein, M. (1972). The history of a short, unsuccessful academic career. *Insurgent Sociologist*(Fall), 4–19. **362**

Simmel, G. (1950). *The sociology of Georg Simmel* (K. H. Wolff, Ed. and Trans.). New York: The Free Press. (Original work published between 1902 and 1917) **94, 191, 198, 200, 203, 207, 208, 234, 555**

Simmel, G. (1965). The poor (C. Jacobson, Trans.). *Social Problems, 13,* 118–140. (Original work published 1908) **171, 222**

Simmons, R. G., & Blyth, D. A. (1986). *Moving into adolescence: The impact of pubertal change and school context.* New York: Aldine de Gruyter. **346**

Singer, C., Holmyard, E. J., & Hall, A. R. (1954). *A history of technology* (4 volumes). New York: Oxford University Press.

Singer, E. (1981). Reference groups and social evaluations. In M. Rosenberg & R. H. Turner (Eds.), *Social psychology: Sociological perspectives* (pp. 66–93). New York: Basic Books. **148**

Skinner, B. F. (1938). *The behavior of organisms.* New York: Appleton-Century-Crofts. **136**

Skinner, B. F. (1948). *Walden Two.* New York: Macmillan. **221**

Skinner, B. F. (1971). *Beyond freedom and dignity.* New York: Knopf.

Skinner, B. F. (1981). Selection by consequences. *Science, 213,* pp. 501–504. **136**

Skocpol, T. (1979). *States and social revolutions.* New York: Cambridge University Press. **538, 539, 580, 588**

Skolnick, A. (1975). The family revisited. *Journal of Interdisciplinary History, 5*(4), 715. **271, 419**

Skolnick, J. H. (1975). *Justice without trial* (2nd ed.). New York: Wiley. **271**

Slambrouck, P. V. (1983, May 27). South Africa: The limits of dissent. *Christian Science Monitor,* p. 1. **335**

Slater, P. E. (1958). Contrasting correlates of group size. *Sociometry, 21,* 129–139. **207, 208**

Slater, P. E. (1970). *The pursuit of loneliness.* Boston: Beacon. (1971 refers to the paperback edition.) **68, 213**

Slomczynski, K. M., Miller, J., & Kohn, M. L. (1981). Stratification, work, and values. *American Sociological Review, 46,* 720–744. **150**

Smelser, N. J. (1959). *Social change in the Industrial Revolution.* Chicago: University of Chicago Press. **387**

Smelser, N. J. (1962). *Theory of collective behavior.* New York: The Free Press. **583**

Smelser, N. J. (1973). Toward a theory of modernization. In A. Etzioni & E. Etzioni-Halevy (Eds.), *Social change: Sources, patterns, and consequences.* New York: Basic Books. **608**

Smelser, N. J. (1981). *Sociology.* Englewood Cliffs, NJ: Prentice-Hall. **410**

Smith, A. (1982). *The wealth of nations.* New York: Penguin. **489**

Smith, D. (1987). The neighborhood context of police behavior. In A. J. Reiss & M. Tonry (Eds.), *Communities and cities.* Chicago: University of Chicago Press. **260**

Smith, D. A., & Visher, C. A. (1980). Sex and involvement in deviance/crime. *American Sociological Review, 45*(August), 691–701. **255**

Smith, J. (1981). *Social issues and the social order: The contradictions of capitalism.* Cambridge, MA: Winthrop. **151, 366, 395, 452, 493, 494, 505, 510, 511, 521**

Snow, D. A., & Anderson, L. (1987). Identity work among the homeless: The verbal construction and avowal of personal identities. *American Journal of Sociology, 92*(6), 1336–1371. **85, 147**

Snow, D. A., Zurcher, L. A., & Eckland-Olson, S. (1980). Social networks and social movements. *American Sociological Review, 45,* 787–801. **586**

Sommer, R. (1969). *Personal space: The behavioral analysis of design.* Englewood Cliffs, NJ: Prentice-Hall. **167, 172**

Sorokin, P. A. (1937–1941). *Social and cultural dynamics* (Vol. 4). New York: American Book Company. **607**

Sorokin, A., & Merton, R. K. (1937). Social time: A methodological and functional analysis. *American Journal of Sociology, 42,* 615–629. **89**

South, S. J. (1985). Economic conditions and the divorce rate: *Journal of Marriage and the Family, 47*(1), 31–41. **422**

South, S. J., & Messner, S. F. (1986). Structural determinants of intergroup association: Interracial marriage and crime. *American Journal of Sociology, 91*(6), 1409–1430. **410**

South, S. J., & Spitze, G. (1986). Determinants of divorce over the marital life course. *American Sociological Review, 51*(4), 583–590.

Spaeth, J. L. (1985). Job power and earnings. *American Sociological Review, 50*(5), 603–617.

Speizer, J. J. (1981). Role models, mentors, and sponsors: The elusive concepts. *Signs: Journal of Women in Culture and Society, 6,* 692–712. **362**

Spencer, H. (1891). *The study of sociology.* New York: Appleton. **607**

Spencer, H. (1896). *The principles of sociology.* New York: Appleton. **607**

Spengler, O. (1926). *The decline of West.* New York: Knopf. **607**

Spenner, K. I., Otto, L. B., & Call, V. R.A. (1982). *Career lines and careers.* Lexington, MA: Lexington Books. **47, 356**

Spinrad, W. (1965). Power in local communities. *Social Problems, V*(12, Winter), 335–356. **229**

Spiro, M. E. (1956). *Kibbutz: Venture in utopia.* Cambridge, MA: Harvard University Press. **240**

Spring, J. (1976). *The sorting machine.* New York: McKay. **451**

Stacey, J. (1983). *Patriarchy and socialist revolution in China.* Berkeley: University of California Press. **356**

Stack, S. (1987). Celebrities and suicide: A Taxonomy and analysis. *American Sociological Review, 52*(3), 401–412. **148**

Stahura, J. M. (1983). Determinants of change in the distribution of blacks across suburbs. *Sociological Quarterly, 24,* 423–433.

Stahura, J. M. (1986). Black suburbanization. *American Sociological Review, 51*(1), 131–144. **225**

Stampp, K. (1956). *The peculiar institution.* New York: Knopf. **560**

Standard and Poor. (1979). *Standard and Poor's industrial survey.* New York: Standard and Poor Corporation. **495**

Staples, R. (1976). *Introduction to black sociology.* New York: McGraw-Hill.

Staples, R. (1981). *The world of black singles.* Westport, CT: Greenwood Press. **155**

Starr, P. (1982). *The social transformation of American medicine.* New York: Basic Books. **478**

Steffensmeier, D. J. (1986). *The fence: In the shadow of two worlds.* Totowa, NJ: Rowman & Littlefield. **259**

Stein, D. D., Hardyck, J. A., & Smith, M. B. (1965). Race and belief: An open and shut case. *Journal of Personality and Social Psychology, 1*(4), 281–289. **187**

Stein, D. (1978). Women to burn. *Signs, 4,* 253–268.

Stein, P. J. (Ed.). (1981). *Single life.* New York: St. Martin's. **155**

Steinbeck, J. (1969). *The grapes of wrath.* New York: Bantam Books. (Original work published 1939) **114, 287**

Steinhart, P. (1981, October 25). The new green revolution. *New York Times Magazine.* **125**

Steinzor, B. (1950). The spatial factor in face-to-face discussion groups. *Journal of Abnormal and Social Psychology, 45.* Reprinted in Hare et al., (1961), pp. 348–353. **200**

Stephan, C. W., & Corder, J. (1985). The effects of dual-career families on adolescents' sex-role attitudes, work and family plans, and choices of important others. *Journal of Marriage and the Family, 47,*(4) 921–929. **360**

Stephan, G. E., & McMullin, D. R. (1982). Tolerance of sexual nonconformity: City size as a situational and early learning determinant. *American Sociological Review, 47*(June), 411–415. **222**

Stephens, W. N. (1963). *The family in cross-cultural perspective.* New York: Holt, Rinehart & Winston. **421, 422**

Sternglanz, S., & Serbin, L. (1974). Sex role stereotyping in children's television programs. *Developmental Psychology, 10,* 710–715. **42**

Stevens, G. (1985). Nativity, intermarriage, and mother-tongue shift. *American Sociological Review, 50*(1), 74–83. **313**

Stevens, G., & Swicegood, G. (1987). The linguistic context of ethnic endogamy. *American Sociological Review, 52*(1), 73–82. **63, 316, 410**

Steward, J. H. (1955). *Theory of culture change: The methodology of multilinear evolution.* Urbana, IL: University of Illinois Press. **608**

Steward, J. H. (1956). Cultural evolution. *Scientific American, 194,* 70–80.

Stimpson, C. (1971). 'Thy neighbor's wife, thy neighbor's servants': Women's liberation and black civil rights. In V. Gornick & B. Moran (Eds.), *Women in sexist society* (pp. 622–657). New York: New American Library. **373**

Stojanovic, S. (1981). *In search of democracy in socialism.* Buffalo, NY: Prometheus Books. **512, 535**

Stone, K. (1974). The origins of job structures in the steel industry. In R. C. Edwards, M. Reich, & D. M. Gordon (Eds.), *Labor market segmentation* (pp. 27–84). Lexington, MA: D. C. Heath Company. **300, 499**

Stoner, J. A. F. (1961). A comparison of individuals and group decisions involving risk. Unpublished master's thesis, Massachusetts Institute of Technology, Cambridge, MA. **207**

Stouffer, S. A., et al. (1949). *The American Soldier.* Princeton, NJ: Princeton University Press. **210**

Stover, E., & Nightingale, E. O. (1985). *The breaking of bodies and minds: Torture, psychiatric abuse, and the health professions.* New York: St. Martin's Press. **481**

Straus, M. A., & Gelles, R. J. (1986). Societal change and change in family violence from 1975 to 1985 as revealed by two national surveys. *Journal of Marriage and the Family, 48*(3), 465–479. **423**

Straus, M. A., Gelles, R. J., & Steinmetz, S. K. (1980). *Behind closed doors.* New York: Anchor. **196, 423, 424**

Strauss, A. L. (1959). *Mirrors and masks.* New York: The Free Press.

Strodtbeck, F. L., & Hook, L. H. (1961). The social dimensions of a twelve-man jury table. *Sociometry, 24*(December), 397–415. **200**

Strodtbeck, F. L., James, R. M., & Hawkins, C. (1957). Social status in jury deliberations. *American Sociological Review, 22,* 713–719. **92, 198**

Strong, D. S. (1941). *Organized anti-Semitism in the United States.* American Council on Public Affairs. **330**

Stryker, S. (1981). Symbolic interactionism: Themes and variations. In M. Rosenberg & R. H. Turner (Eds.), *Social psychology: Sociological perspectives* (pp. 3–29). New York: Basic Books. **24, 146**

Sudnow, D. (1967). *Passing on: The social organization of dying.* Englewood Cliffs, NJ: Prentice-Hall. **386**

Summers, G. F., & Hammonds, A. D. (1966). Effects of racial characteristics of investigator on self-enumerated responses to a negro prejudice scale. *Social Forces, 44,* 515–518. **34**

Sumner, W. G. (1883). *What social classes owe to each other.* New York: Harper. **289**

Sumner, W. G. (1906). *Folkways.* Boston: Ginn & Company. **65, 69, 70, 191**

Sutherland, E. H. (1983). *White collar crime: The uncut version.* New Haven, CT: Yale University Press. **256**

Sutherland, E. H., & Cressey, D. R. (1978). *Criminology* (10th ed.). Philadelphia: Lippincott. **265**

Suttles, G. D. (1972). *The social construction of communities.* Chicago: University of Chicago Press. **224**

Sutton, J. R. (1983). Social structures, institutions, and the legal status of children. *American Journal of Sociology, 88*(5), 915–947. **255**

Suzuki, D. T., Griffiths, A. J. F., & Lewontin, R. C. (1981). *An introduction to genetic analysis* (2nd ed.). San Francisco: W. H. Freeman. **134**

Swanson, G. E. (1960). *The birth of the gods: The origin of primitive beliefs.* Ann Arbor: University of Michigan Press.

Sweezy, P. M. (1942). *The theory of capitalist development: Principles of Marxian political economy.* New York: Modern Reader Paperbacks. **505**

Swidler, A. (1986). Culture in action. *American Sociological Review, 51*(2), 273–286. **289**

Sykes, G. (1958). *The society of captives: A study of a maximum security prison.* Princeton, NJ: Princeton University Press. **62, 89, 263**

Szasz, T. (1987). *Insanity: The idea and its consequences.* New York: Wiley. **270**

Szelenyi, I. (1983). *Urban inequalities under state socialism.* New York: Oxford University Press. **302**

Tanfer, K. (1987). Patterns of premarital cohabitation among never-married women in the United States. *Journal of Marriage and the Family, 49*(3). 483–497. **426, 427**

Tannenbaum, A. S. (1968). Leadership: Sociological aspects. In D. L. Sills (Ed.), *The international encyclopedia of the social sciences* (Vol. 9). New York: The MacMillan Company/The Free Press. **524**

Tavris, C., & Wade, C. (1984). *The longest war: Sex differences in perspective* (2nd ed.). New York: Harcourt Brace Jovanovich. **353, 367**

Taylor, F. W. (1911). *The principles of scientific maanagement.* New York: Harper & Row. **494**

Tedeschi, J. T., & Riess, M. (1981). Identities, the phenomenal self, and laboratory research. In J. Tedeschi (Ed.), *Impression management theory and social psychological research* (pp. 3–22). New York: Academic Press. **174**

Teitelbaum, M. S., & Winter, J. M. (1985). *The fear of population decline.* Orlando, FL: Academic Press.

Teixeira, R. A. (1987). *Why Americans don't vote.* Westport, CT: Greenwood Press.

Terkel, S. (1974). *Working.* New York: Pantheon. **293**

Tetlock, P. E. (1981). The influence of self-presentation goals on attributional reports. *Social Psychology Quarterly, 44,* 300–311. **166**

Thoits, P. A. (1985). Self-labeling processes in mental illness: The role of emotional deviance. *American Journal of Sociology, 91*(2), 221–249.

Thomas, J., & Levin, H. M. (1983). *Public dollars for private schools: The case of tuition tax credits.* Philadelphia, PA: Temple University Press. **457**

Thomas, M., & Hughes, M. (1986). The continuing significance of race: A study of race, class, and quality of life in America, 1972–1985. *American Sociological Review, 51*(6), 830–841. **321**

Thomas, R. K. (1966–1967). Powerless politics. *New University Thought, 4*(Winter).

Thomas, W. I. (1931). *The unadjusted girl.* Boston: Little, Brown. **59**

Thomas, W. I., & Thomas, D. S. (1928). *The child in America.* New York: Knopf. **164**

Thompson, W. (1942). *Population problems* (3rd ed.). New York: McGraw-Hill. **112**

Thompson, W., & Lewis, D. (1965). *Population problems* (5th ed.). New York: McGraw-Hill. **602**

Thompson, W., & Whelpton, P. K. (1933). *Population trends in the United States.* New York: McGraw-Hill. **418**

Thornberry, T. P. (1973). Race, socioeconomic status, and sentencing in the juvenile justice system. *Journal of Criminal Law and Criminology, 64,* 90–98. **262**

Thornton, A. (1985). Changing attitudes toward separation and divorce: Causes and consequences. *American Journal of Sociology, 90*(4), 856–872. **422**

Thornton, A., Alwin, D. F., & Camburn, D. (1983). Causes and consequences of sex-role attitudes and attitude change. *American Sociological Review, 48*(April), 211–227.

Thornton, A., & Freedman, D. (1982). Changing attitudes toward marriage and single life. *Family Planning Perspectives, 14*(6, November/December), 297–303. **421, 427**

Thornton, A., & Freedman, D. (1983). The changing American family. *Population Bulletin, 38*(4). Washington, DC: Population Reference Bureau. **421, 427**

Thornton, A., & Rodgers, W. L. (1983, February). *Changing patterns of marriage and divorce in the United States* (Final Report Prepared for the National Institute for Child Health and Human Development, Ann Arbor, MI). **408**

Thurow, L. (1975). *Generating inequality.* New York: Basic Books. **286, 298, 305**

Thurow, L. C. (1980). *The zero-sum society: Distributions and the possibilities for economic change.* New York: Basic Books.

Thurow, L. C. (1983). *Dangerous currents: The state of economics.* New York: Random House.

Tilly, C. (1978a). *From mobilization to revolution.* Reading, MA: Addison-Wesley. **582, 586, 588, 589**

Tilly, C. (Ed.). (1978b). *Historical studies of changing fertility.* Princeton, NJ: Princeton University Press. **105**

Tilly, C. (1984). *Big structures, large processes, huge comparisons.* New York: Russell Sage Foundation. **597**

Tilly, C. (1985). *Big structures, large prophecies, huge comparisons.* New York: Russell Sage. **99**

Tilly, C., Tilly, L., & Tilly, R. (1975). *The rebellious century.* Cambridge, MA: Harvard University Press. **589**

Tilly, L. A., & Scott, J. W. (1978). *Women work, and the family.* New York: Holt, Rinehart & Winston. **353**

Tilly, L. A., & Tilly, C. (Eds.). (1981). *Collective action and class conflict.* Beverly Hills, CA: Sage. **589**

Tissue, T. (1979). Downward mobility in old age. In P. I. Rose (Ed.), *Socialization and the life cycle* (pp. 355–367). New York: St. Martin's Press. **390**

Tittle, C. R. (1975). Deterrence of labeling? *Social Forces, 53*(March), 399–419.

Tittle, C. R., & Villemez, W. J. (1977). Social class and criminality. *Social Forces, 56*(2), 474–502. **256, 257**

Tittle, C. R., Villemez, W. J., & Smith, D. A. (1978). The myth of social class and criminality: An empirical assessment of empirical evidence. *American Sociological Review, 43,* 643–656. **256**

Tocqueville, A. de. (1954). *Democracy in America II.* New York: Random House. (Original work published 1835) **304, 525**

Tönnies, F. (1963). *Community and society.* New York: Harper. (Original work published 1887) **209, 211, 231**

Toynbee, A. (1956). *The Industrial Revolution.* Boston: Beacon Press.

Treiman, D. J. (1977). *Occupational prestige in comparative perspective.* New York: Academic Press. **293**

Treiman, D. J., & Hartmann, H. I. (Eds.). (1981). *Women, work and wages: equal pay for jobs of equal value.* Washington, DC: National Academy Press. **46, 354**

Treiman, D. J., & Roos, P. A. (1983). Sex and earnings in industrial society. *American Journal of Sociology, 89*(3, November), 612–650. **363**

Trimberger, E. K. (1971). The ideological function of grading in American education. Paper Read at the Annual Meeting of the American Sociological Association. **454**

Troeltsch, E. (1931). *The social teaching of the Christian churches.* New York: Macmillan. (Original work published 1912) **551, 552**

Trow, M. (1961). The second transformation of American secondary education. *International Journal of Comparative Sociology, 2,* 144–165. **434**

Tuchman, B. W. (1978). *A distant mirror.* New York: Knopf. **112**

Tuddenham, R. D., & McBride, P. (1959). The yielding experiment from the subject's point of view. *Journal of Personality, 27,* 259–271. **190**

Tullock, G. (1974). Does punishment deter? *The Public Interest,* (Summer), 103–111. **262**

Tumin, M. M. (1953). Some principles of stratification: A critical analysis. *American Sociological Review, 18,* 378–394. **285**

Tumin, M. M. (1964). Business as a social system. *Behavioral Science 9,* 2(April), 120–130. **199**

Tumin, M. M. (1973). *Patterns of society.* Boston: Little, Brown. **314**

Turk, A. (1969). *Criminalty and the legal order.* Chicago: Rand McNally. **250**

Turk, A. (1976). Law as a weapon in social conflict. *Social Problems, 23*(3), 276–291. **250**

Turnbull, C. (1961). *The forest people.* New York: Simon & Schuster. **556**

Turnbull, C. (1965). The Mbuti Pygmies of the Congo. In J. L. Gibbs, Jr. (Ed.), *People of Africa.* New York: Holt, Rinehart & Winston. **548**

Turner, B. S. (1986). *Equality.* New York: Tavistock.

Turner, J. H. (1987). Toward a sociological theory of motivation. *American Sociological Review, 52*(1), 15–27.

Turner, R. H. (1964). Collective behavior. In R. E. L. Faris (Ed.), *Handbook of modern sociology.* Chicago: Rand McNally. **574, 579**

Turner, R. H., & Killian, L. (1972). *Collective behavior* (2nd ed.). Englewood Cliffs, NJ: Prentice-Hall. **575**

Uhlenberg, P. (1980). Death and the family. *Journal of Family History, 5,* 313–320. **481**

Unger, A. (1983, May 10). TV is offering a fairer image, but mainly for certain groups. *Christian Science Monitor,* p. 12. **313**

United Nations. (1956). *The determinants and consequences of population trends* (Vol. 1). New York: Author. **378**

United Nations. (1973). The determinants and consequences of population trends: New summary of findings on interaction of demographic, economic, and social factors. I. *Population Studies, 50.* New York: United Nations Department of Economic and Social Affairs.

United Nations. (1985). *Demographic Yearbook: 1985.* New York: Author. **255**

United Nations. (1987). *The state of the world's population.* New York: Author. **126**

U.S. Census Bureau. (1918). *Negro population: 1790–1915.* Washington, DC: Government Printing Office. **325**

U.S. Census Bureau. (1975a). *Historical statistics of the United States: Colonial times to 1970.* Washington, DC: U.S. Government Printing Office. **84, 97, 235, 254, 372, 388, 392, 396, 420, 421, 434, 435, 444, 446, 479, 481**

U.S. Census Bureau. (1975c). *The social and economic status of the black population in the United States.* (Current Population Reports, Series P-23, No. 54). Washington, DC: U.S. Government Printing Office. **323**

U.S. Census Bureau. (1979). *Fertility of American women: June, 1978* (Current Population Reports, Series P-20, No. 341). Washington, DC: U.S. Government Printing Office. **105**

U.S. Census Bureau. (1980b). *Social indicators III.* Washington, DC: U.S. Government Printing Office. **108, 238, 254, 262, 298, 301, 324, 333, 448, 528**

U.S. Census Bureau. (1981). *Statistical abstract of the United States, 1981.* Washington, DC: U.S. Government Printing Office. **300, 301, 333, 397, 416**

U.S. Census Bureau. (1982). *Statistical abstract of the United States, 1982.* Washington, DC: U.S. Government Printing Office. **108, 219, 227, 234, 238, 312, 319, 323, 408, 444, 505, 528**

U.S. Census Bureau. (1983a). *Households, families, marital status, and living arrangements: March, 1983.* Washington, DC: U.S. Government Printing Office.

U.S. Census Bureau. (1983b). *Money income and poverty status of families and persons in the United States, 1982* (Current Population Report, Series P-60, No. 140). Washington, DC: U.S. Government Printing Office. **45**

U.S. Census Bureau. (1983c). *Statistical Abstract of the United States: 1984.* Washington, DC: U.S. Government Printing Office. **108, 234, 238, 255, 303, 320, 364, 389, 449**

U.S. Census Bureau. (1986a). *Statistical abstract of the United States: 1987.* Washington, D.C.: U.S. Government Printing Office. **45, 46, 47, 83, 84, 97, 105, 116, 156, 200, 219, 221, 235, 238, 254, 255, 256, 257, 262, 264, 272, 282, 290, 291, 296, 298, 299, 300, 301, 303, 318, 319, 323, 324, 333, 353, 354, 355, 356, 362, 363, 369, 371, 379, 388, 389, 391, 392, 393, 395, 396, 397, 398, 409, 412, 413, 415, 416, 417, 420, 421, 423, 426, 427, 428, 434, 441, 444, 446, 447, 450, 454, 479, 481, 493, 495, 499, 501, 506, 528, 555**

U.S. Census Bureau. (1986b, November 21). Reported in the Hartford *Courant.*

U.S. Census Bureau. (1986c, April 13). Advance report on geographical mobility reported in the *New York Times*, p. 1. **232**

U.S. Census Bureau. (1986d). Household wealth and asset ownership. Washington, DC: U.S. Government Printing Office. **318, 356**

U.S. Census Bureau. (1986e, May 7). Statistics reported in the Hartford *Courant*, p. A5. **372**

U.S. Census Bureau. (1986f, December 14). Findings reported in the *New York Times*. **371**

U.S. Census Bureau. (1986g). Fertility of American women: June 1985. *Current Population Reports* Series P-20, No. 406. Washington, DC: U.S. Government Printing Office. **363**

U.S. Census Bureau. (1987a). Money income of households, families, and persons in the United States: 1985. *Current Population Reports* Series P-60, No. 156. Washington, DC: U.S. Government Printing Office. **44, 45, 48, 238, 272, 298, 306, 313, 324, 337, 357, 364, 388, 389**

U.S. Census Bureau. (1987b). Household after-tax income: 1985. *Current population reports,* Series P-23, No. 151. Washington, DC: U.S. Government Printing Office. **288**

U.S. Census Bureau. (1987c). Male-female differences in work experience, occupation, and earnings: 1984. *Current Population Reports* Series P-70, No. 10. **46**

U.S. Census Bureau. (1987d, July 3). Poverty figure for 1986 reported in the *New York Times*, p. A12. **282**

U.S. Census Bureau. (1987e, October 1). Reported in the *New York Times*. **116**

U.S. Census Bureau. (1987f). What's it worth? Educational background and economic status: Spring 1984. Washington, DC: U.S. Government Printing Office. **298**

U.S. Census Bureau. (1987g). Money Income and Poverty Status of Families and Persons in the United States: 1986. *Current Population Reports* Series P-60, No. 157. Washington, DC: U.S. Government Printing Office. **227**

U.S. Census Bureau. (1987h). Households, Families, Marital Status, and Living Arrangements: March (Advance Report). *Current Population Reports* Series P-20, No. 417. Washington, DC: U.S. Government Printing Office. **372**

U.S. Census Bureau. (1987i). America's Centenarians. *Current Population Reports* Series P-23, No. 153. Washington, DC: U.S. Government Printing Office. **396, 481**

U.S. Commission on Civil Rights. (1967). *Racial isolation in the public schools (Vol. 1).* Washington, DC: U.S. Government Printing Office. **327**

U.S. Department of Health, Education, and Welfare. (1961). *U.S. health examination survey: 1959–1961.* Washington, DC: U.S. Government Printing Office. **48, 155**

U.S. Department of Health, Education, and Welfare. (1973). *Work in America.* Cambridge, MA: M.I.T. Press. **504**

U.S. Department of Housing and Urban Development. (1981). *Residential displacement: An update.* Washington, DC: U.S. Government Printing Office. **241**

U.S. Department of Justice. (1980a). *Criminal victimization in the United States: A comparison of 1977 and 1978 findings.* Washington, DC: U.S. Government Printing Office. **254, 259**

U.S. Department of Justice. (1987). Criminal victimization in the United States: 1985. Washington, DC: U.S. Government Printing Office. **258**

Useem, M. (1983). *The inner circle: Large corporations and the rise of business political activity in the U.S. and U.K.* New York: Oxford University Press. **292, 526**

Useem, M. (1984). *The inner circle.* New York: Oxford University Press. **527**

Useem, M. (1986). Paths to corporate management. *American Sociological Review, 51*(2), 184–200.

Useem, M., & Karabel, J. (1986). Pathways to top corporate management. *American Sociological Review, 51* (2), 184–200. **292**

U.S. NCHS. (1985). Advance report of final marriage statistics, 1981. *Monthly Vital Statistics Report, 32*(11, February 29). **427**

Uyeki, E. S. (1964). Residential distribution and stratification. *American Journal of Sociology, 69*(5), 491–498. **326**

Van Creveld, M. (1982). *Fighting power: German and U.S. Army Performance, 1939–1945.* Westport, CT: Greenwood Press. **210**

Van de Kaa, D. J. (1987). Europe's second demographic transition. *Population Bulletin, 42*(1, March). Washington, DC: Population Reference Bureau. **111, 112**

Vandenberg, S. G., Singer, S. M., & Pauls, D. L. (1986). *The heredity of behavior disorders in adults and children.* New York: Plenum. **134**

Vander Zanden, J.W. (1972). *American minority relations: The sociology of race and ethnic groups* (3rd ed.). New York: Ronald Press. **328, 397**

Van Dijk. (1987). *Communicating racism: Ethnic prejudice in thought and talk.* Newbury Park, CA: Sage. **313**

Van Gennep, A. (1960). *The rites of passage.* Chicago: University of Chicago Press. (Original work published 1909) **149, 150, 383**

Van Til, J. (1980). Citizen participation in neighborhood transformation: A social movements approach. *Urban Affairs Quarterly, 15,* 439–452. **243**

Vaupel, J. W., & Gowan, A. E. (1986). Passage to Methuselah. *Amerian Journal of Public Health,* (April). **397**

Veblen, T. (1934). *The theory of the leisure class.* New York: Modern Library. (Original work published 1928) **292**

Von Neumann, J., & Morgenstern, O. (1964). *Theory of games and economic behavior* (3rd ed.). New York: Wiley. **179, 438**

Vos, S. de. (1984). *The old-age economic security value of children in the Philippines and Taiwan.* Papers of the East-West Population Institute, No. 60-G. Honolulu: East-West Population Institute. **105**

Wade, N. (1976). IQ and heredity: Suspicion of fraud beclouds classic experiment. *Science, 194*(November 26), 916–919. **466**

Waite, L. J., Goldscheider, F. K., & Witsberger, C. (1986). Nonfamily living and the erosion of traditional family orientations among young adults. *American Sociological Review, 51*(4), 541–554.

Walker, B. G. (1983). *The women's encyclopedia of myths and secrets.* New York: Harper & Row. **345**

Wallace, M., & Kalleberg, A. L. (1982). Industrial transformation and the decline of craft: The decomposition of skill in the printing industry, 1931–1978. *American Sociological Review, 47*(June), 307–324. **494**

Wallerstein, I. (1974). Dependence in an interdependent world: The limited possibilities of transformation within the capitalist world-economy. *African Studies Review, 17,* 1–26.

Wallerstein, I. (1976a). *The modern world system.* New York: Academic Press. **509, 510, 610**

Wallerstein, I. (1976b). Semi-peripheral countries and the contemporary world crisis. *Theory and Society, 3,* 461–483.

Wallerstein, I. (1979). *The capitalist world-economy.* Cambridge: Cambridge University Press. **509, 610**

Wallerstein, I. (1980). *The modern world system II: Mercantilism and the consolidation of the European world economy, 1600–1750.* New York: Academic Press. **509, 510, 610**

Wallerstein, I. (1986). Marxisms as utopias: Evolving ideologies. *American Journal of Sociology, 91*(6), 1295–1308. **508**

Wallston, B., Foster, M., & Berger, M. (1978). I will follow him: Myth, reality, or forced choice. Job seeking experiences of dual-career couples. *Psychology of Women Quarterly, 3,* 9–21. **369**

Walum, L. R. (1974). The changing door ceremony: Notes on the operation of sex roles. *Urban Life and Culture, 2,* 506–515. **70**

Warner, C. D. b(1870). *My summer in a garden.* Quoted in Bartlett's, p. 645. **532**

Warner, R. L., Lee, G. R., & Lee, J. (1986). Social organization, spousal resources, and marital power: A cross-cultural study. *Journal of Marriage and the Family, 48*(1), 121–128. **414**

Warner, W. L. (1961). *The family of God.* New Haven: Yale University Press. **547**

Warnick, D. H., & Sanders, G. (1980). The effects of group discussion on eyewitness accuracy. *Journal of Applied Social Psychology, 10*(3), 249–259. **205**

Watson, G. B. (1928). Do groups think more efficiently than individuals? *Journal of Abnormal and Social Psychology, 23,* 328–336. **207**

Watson, J. B. (1928). *Psychological care of infant and child.* New York: Norton. **134, 207**

Watson, J. B., & Rayner, R. (1920). Conditioned emotional reactions. *Journal of Experimental Psychology, 3,* 1–14. **136**

Watzlawick, P. (1976). *How real is real? Confusion, disinformation, communication.* New York: Random House. **165**

Weber, M. (1946). *From Max Weber: Essays in sociology* (H. H. Gerth & C. W. Mills, Eds. and Trans.). New York: Oxford University Press. **213, 281, 434**

Weber, M. (1947). *The theory of social and economic organization.* New York: Oxford University Press. (Original work published 1925) **90, 194**

Weber, M. (1949). *The methodology of the social sciences.* New York: The Free Press. **34**

Weber, M. (1950). *General economic history.* New York: The Free Press. (Original work published 1923) **559**

Weber, M. (1922a/1954). In M. Rheinstein (Ed.), *Max Weber on law in economy and society.* Cambridge, MA: Harvard University Press. (Original work published 1922) **94, 198, 213, 230**

Weber, M. (1922b/1958). Bureaucracy. In H. H. Gerth & C. W. Mills (Eds. and Trans.), *From Max Weber: Essays in sociology.* New York: Oxford University Press (Original work published 1922) **94, 198**

Weber, M. (1958). Politics as a vocation. In H. H. Gerth & C. W. Mills (Eds. and Trans.), *From Max Weber.* New York: Oxford University Press. (Original work published 1921) **519**

Weber, M. (1958). *The Protestant ethic and the spirit of capitalism.* New York: Charles Scribner's and Sons. (Original work published 1904) **489, 595**

Weed, J. (1982). Divorce: Americans' style. *American Demographics, 4*(3, March), 13–17. **421**

Weede, E. (1980). Beyond misspecification in sociological analysis of income inequality. *American Sociological Review, 45,* 497–501. **301**

Weg, R. B. (1975). Changing physiology of aging: Normal and pathological. In D. S. Woodruff & J. E. Birren (Eds.), *Aging: Scientific perspectives and social issues.* New York: Van Nostrand. **388**

Weinstein, J. (1969). *The corporate ideal in the liberal state: 1900–1918.* Boston: Beacon Press. **497**

Weinstein, J. A. (1976). *Demographic transition and social change.* Morristown, NJ: General Learning Press. **112**

Weisbord, R. (1975). *Genocide? Birth control and the black American.* Westport, CT: Greenwood Press. **335**

Weiss, C. S. (1981). The development of professional role commitment among graduate students. *Human Relations, 34,* 13–31. **363**

Weiss, L., & Lowenthal, M. F. (1975). *Life course perspectives on friendship.* In M. F. Lowenthal, M. Thurner, & D. Chiriboga (Eds.), *Four stages of life.* San Francisco: Jossey-Bass. **352**

Weissberg, R. (1981). *Understanding American government* (alternate ed.). New York: Holt, Rinehart & Winston. **230**

Weitzman, L. (1981). *The marriage contract.* New York: The Free Press. **426**

Weitzman, L. J. (1985). *The divorce revolution: The unexpected social and economic consequences for women and children in America.* New York: The Free Press. **356**

Weller, R. H. (1977). Demographic correlates of women's participation in economic activities. *International Population Conference: Mexico 1977,* (pp. 497–516). Liege, Belgium: International Union for the Scientific Study of Population. **416**

Weller, R. H., & Bouvier, L. F. (1981). *Population: Demography and policy.* New York: St. Martin's Press. **116, 125, 416, 418**

Weller, R. P., & Guggenheim, S. E. (Eds.). (1982). *Power and protest in the countryside: Studies of rural unrest in Asia, Europe, and Latin America.* Durham, NC: Duke Univerity Press. **239**

Welsh, W. A. (Ed.). (1981). *Survey research and public attitudes in Eastern Europe and the Soviet Union.* New York: Pergamon Press. **512**

West, C. (1982). Why can't a woman be more like a man? *Sociology of Work and Occupations, 9,* 5–29. **171**

West, S. G., Gunn, S. P., & Chernicky, P. (1975). Ubiquitous Watergate: An attributional analysis. *Journal of Personality and Social Psychology, 32,* 55–65. **166**

Westing, A. (1981). Cited in the *New York Times,* October 6, 1981. **125**

Westoff, C. F. (1978a). Some speculations on the future of marriage and fertility. *Family Planning Perspectives, 10,* 79–83. **111**

Westoff, C. F. (1978b). Marriage and fertility in the developed countries. *Scientific American, 239*(6), 51–57. **407**

Westoff, C. F. (1983). Fertility decline in the West: Causes and prospects. *Population and Development Review, 9,* 99–105. **111**

Westoff, C. F., & Bumpass, L. (1973). The revolution in birth control practice of U.S. Roman Catholics. *Science, 179*(5), pp. 41–44. **105**

Westoff, C. F., / Jones, E. F. (1979). The end of "Catholic" fertility. *Demography, 16*(May), 290–317. **416**

Wheeler, L., & Nezlek, T. (1977). Sex differences in social participation. *Journal of Personality and Social Psychology, 35,* 742–754. **352**

White, K. L., & Brinkerhoff, D. B. (1981). The sexual division of labor: Evidence from childhood. *Social Forces, 60, 170–181.* **360**

White, L. K., & Booth, A. (1985). Stepchildren in remarriages. *American Sociological Review, 50*(5), 689–698. **413**

Whiting, B. (Ed.). (1963). *Six cultures–Studies in child rearing.* New York: Wiley. **418**

Whorf, B. L. (1956). *Language, thought and reality.* Cambridge, MA: MIT Press.

Whyte, W. F. (1950). The social structure of the restaurant. *American Journal of Sociology, 54,* 302–310. **199, 202**

Whyte, W. F. (1981). *Street corner society* (3rd ed.). Chicago: University of Chicago Press. **37, 40, 193**

Whyte, W. H. (1956). *The organization man.* New York: Simon & Schuster.

Wiatrowski, M. D., Griswold, D. B., & Roberts, M. K. (1981). Social control theory and delinquency. *American Sociological Review, 46*(October), 525–541. **264**

Wice, P. B. (1973). *Bail and its reform: A national survey.* Washington, DC: U.S. Government Printing Office. **323**

Wilentz, S. (1984). *Chants democratic: New York City and the rise of the American working class.* New York: Oxford.

Wilkinson, R. (1964). *Gentlemanly power: British leadership and the public school tradition.* London: Oxford University Press. **434**

Williams, B. B. (1987). *Black workers in an industrial suburb: The struggle against discrimination.* New Brunswick, NJ: Rutgers University Press.

Williams, R. M., Jr. (1975). Relative deprivation. In L. A. Coser (Ed.), *The idea of social structure* (pp. 355–378). New York: Harcourt Brace Jovanovich. **299**

Williamson, J. (1984). *The crucible of race.* New York: Oxford University Press.

Williamson, N. (1976). Sex preferences, sex control, and the status of women. *Signs: Journal of Women in Culture and Society, 1,* 847–862. **105, 345**

Willie, C. V. (1978). The inclining significance of race. *Society, 15*(10), 12–15. **321**

Willie, C. V. (1979). *The caste and class controversy.* Bayside, NY: General Hall. **321**

Willner, A. R. (1984). *The spellbinders: Charismatic political leadership.* New Haven, CT: Yale University Press. **518**

Wilner, D. M., et al. (1955). *Human relations in interracial housing: A study of the contact hypothesis.* Minneapolis: University of Minnesota Press. **332**

Wilson, B. (1982). *Religion in sociological perspective.* New York: Oxford University Press. **545, 547, 549, 552, 554, 558, 561, 562**

Wilson, E. O. (1975). *Sociobiology.* Cambridge, MA: Belknap. **342**

Wilson, E. O. (1977). Biology and the social sciences. *Daedalus, 106*(Fall), 127–140. **342**

Wilson, J. (1978). *Religion in American society: The effective presence.* Englewood Cliffs, NJ: Prentice-Hall. **319, 561**

Wilson, J. G. (1988, March 2). Reported in the *New York Times.*

Wilson, J. Q. (1968). The police and the delinquent in two cities. In S. Wheeler (Ed.), *Controlling delinquents.* New York: Wiley. **262**

Wilson, J. Q. (1983). *Thinking about crime* (revised ed.). New York: Basic Books.

Wilson, J. Q., & Herrnstein, R. J. (1985). *Crime and human nature.* New York: Simon & Schuster. **222, 263**

Wilson, R. S., & Harpring, E. B. (1972). Mental and motor development in infant twins. *Developmental psychology, 7,* 277–287. **134**

Wilson, T. C. (1985). Urbanism and tolerance. *American Sociological Review, 50*(1), 117–123. **222**

Wilson, T. C. (1986). Community population size and social heterogeneity: An empirical test. *American Journal of Sociology, 91*(5) 1154–1169.

Wilson, W. J. (1973). *Power, racism, and privilege.* New York: Macmillan.

Wilson, W. J. (1978). *The declining significance of race.* Chicago: University of Chicago Press. **319**

Wilson, W. J. (1987). *The truly disadvantaged: The inner city, the underclass, and public policy.* Chicago: University of Chicago Press. **333**

Wirth, L. (1938). Urbanism as a way of life. *American Journal of Sociology, 44,* 1–24. **219, 221, 222, 231, 234, 238**

Wirth, L. (1945). The problem of minority groups. In R. Linton (Ed.), *The science of man in the world crisis.* New York: Columbia University Press. **312**

Wissler, C. (1911). The social life of the Blackfoot Indians. *Anthropological Papers of the American Museum of Natural History, 7* (1). New York: American Museum of Natural History. **407**

Withey, S. B., & Abeles, R. P. (Eds.). (1980). *Television and social behavior.* Hillsdale, NJ: Erlbaum. **152, 154, 313**

Wohl, A. S. (1983). *Endangered lives: Public health in Victorian England.* Cambridge, MA: Harvard University Press. **236**

Wolfgang, M. E., Figlio, R. M., & Sellin, T. (1972). *Delinquency in a birth cohort.* Chicago: University of Chicago Press. **256**

Women on Words and Images. (1975a). *Dick and Jane as victims: Sex stereotyping in children's readers* (enlarged ed.). Princeton, NJ. **42, 360**

Women on Words and Images. (1975b). *Channeling children: Sex stereotyping on prime TV.* Princeton, NJ. **42, 361**

Women's Research and Education Institute. (1984). *Gender at work.* Washington, DC: Women's Research and Educational Institute. **354**

Woolf, V. (1929). *A room of one's own.* New York: Harcourt, Brace and World. **358**

Woolley, Sir L. (1963). *Prehistory* (Vol. 1, Pt. 2). New York: Harper & Row. **551**

World Bank. (1983). *World Development Report 1983.* New York: Oxford University Press. **304**

World Health Organization. (1978). *World Health Statistics Annual* (Vol. 1). Geneva, Switzerland: World Health Organization. **107**

World Health Organization. (1987, December 22). Reported in the Hartford *Courant,* p. A6. **110**

Worldwatch Institute. (1987). *State of the world in 1987.* Washington, DC: Worldwatch Institute. **127**

Wren, C. S. (1981, November 11). In China, millions use fuel produced from wastes. *New York Times,* p. C1. **125**

Wright, E. O. (1985). *Classes.* New York: Schocken Books. **281**

Wright, E. O., Hacken, D., Costello, C., & Sprague, J. (1982). The American class structure. *American Sociological Review, 47*(December), 709–726. **281**

Wright, E. O., & Martin, B. (1987). The transformation of the American class structure, 1960–1980. *American Journal of Sociology, 93*(1), 1–29.

Wright, J. D., Rossi, P. H., & Daly, K. (1983). *Under the gun: Weapons, crime, and violence in America.* Chicago: Aldine. **254**

Wright, J. D., & Wright, S. R. (1976). Social class and parental values for children: A partial replication and extension of the Kohn thesis. *American Sociological Review, 41*(June), 527–548. **150**

Writers Guild of America. (1987, June 24). Findings reported in the *New York Times.* **355**

Wrong, D. H. (1961). The oversocialized conception of man in modern sociology. *American Sociological Review, 26,* 183–193. **157**

Wrong, D. H. (1980). *Power: Its forms, bases, and uses.* New York: Harper & Row. **90**

Wurdock, C. (1979). Public school resegregation after desegregation: Some preliminary findings. *Sociological Focus, 12*(4), 263–274. **337**

Wurdock, C., & Farley, R. (1979). School integration and enrollments in the nation's largest cities: An analysis of recent trends. *Proceedings of the American Statistical Association (Social Statistics Section),* 359–363. **337, 447**

Wyman, D. S. (1984). *The abandonment of the Jews: America and the holocaust, 1941–1945.* New York: Pantheon.

Yarrow, L. J., Rubenstein, J. L., & Pedersen, F. A. (1975). *Infant and environment: Early cognitive and emotional development.* Washington, DC: Hemisphere Publishing Company (Distributed by Wiley). **135**

Zablocki, B. (1980). *The joyful community.* Chicago: University of Chicago Press. **221, 264**

Zagare, F. C. (1984). *Game theory: Concepts and applications.* Beverly Hills, CA: Sage. **179, 577**

Zald, M. N., & McCarthy, J. D. (Eds.). (1979). *The dynamics of social movements.* Cambridge, MA: Winthrop.

Zangwill, I. (1933). *The melting pot.* New York: Macmillan. (Original work published 1909) **316**

Zborowski, M. (1953). Cultural components in responses to pain. *Journal of Social Issues, 8,* 16–31.

Zeisel, H. (1981). Race bias in the administration of the death penalty. *Harvard Law Review, 95*(2), 456–468. **262**

Zeitlin, I. M. (1981). Karl Marx: Aspects of his social thought and their contemporary relevance. In B. Rhea (Ed.), *The future of the sociological classics* (pp. 1–15). London: Allen Unwin. **607**

Zeldich, M., & Walker, H. A. (1984). Legitimacy and the stability of authority. In E. Lawler (Ed.), *Advances in group process: Theory and research* (Vol. 1, pp. 1–27). Greenwich, CT: JAI Press. **91, 195**

Zelizer, V. A. (1985). *Pricing the priceless child: The changing social value of children.* New York: Basic Books. **391**

Zelnick, M., & Kanter, J. F. (1976). Sexual and contraceptive experience of young unmarried women in the United States, 1976 and 1971. *Family Planning Perspectives, 9*(March–April), 55–71. **416**

Zelnick, M., & Kanter, J. F. (1978). First pregnancies to women aged 15–19: 1976 and 1971. *Family Planning Perspectives, 10*(January–February), 11–20. **416**

Zerubavel, E. (1981). *The seven day circle: The history and meaning of the week.* New York: Free Press/Macmillan. **88**

Zerubavel, E. (1985). *The seven-day week: The history and meaning of the week.* New York: Free Press. **88**

Zimbardo, P. G. (1971). *The psychological power and pathology of imprisonment.* A statement prepared for the U.S. House of Representatives Committee on the Judiciary, Subcommittee No. 3; Hearings on Prison Reform, San Francisco, California, October 25. Cited and quoted in D. G. Myers. (1983). *Social psychology* (pp. 179–180). New York: McGraw-Hill. **169**

Zimmerman, D., & West, C. (1975). Sex roles, interruptions and silences in conversation. In B. Thorne & N. Henley (Eds.), *Language and sex: Difference and dominance.* Rowley, MA: Newbury House. **350**

Zorbaugh, H. W. (1929). *The Gold Coast and the slum: A sociological study of Chicago's Near North Side.* Chicago: University of Chicago Press.

Zuboff, S. (1982). New worlds of computer-mediated work. *Harvard Business Review,* (September/October). **502**

Zuboff, S. (1988). *In the age of the smart machine.* New York: Basic Books. **503**

Zucker, L. (1983). Organizations as institutions. In S. B. Bacharach (Ed.), *Research in the sociology of organizations* (Vol. 2). Greenwich, CT: JAI Press. **199**

Zuckerman, H. (1977). Deviant behavior and social control in science. In Sagarin, E. (Ed.), *Deviance and social change* (pp. 87–138). Beverly Hills, CA: Sage. **466**

Zuckerman, H. (1988). The sociology of science: A selective review. In Smelser, N. (Ed.). (1988). *Handbook of sociology.* Beverly Hills, CA: Sage. **462, 466, 469, 470**

Zuriff, G. E. (1985). *Behaviorism: A conceptual reconstruction.* New York: Columbia University Press. **136**

ILLUSTRATION CREDITS

Photos

PART OPENING PHOTOS: **One:** © Brian Brake/Photo Researchers; **Two:** © Dave Bartruff/FPG International; **Three:** © 1984 Ted Spiegel/Black Star; **Four:** © 1985 Stuart Cohen/Stock, Boston; **Five:** © Cary Wolinsky/Stock, Boston; **Six:** © Owen Franken/Stock, Boston

CHAPTER 1: **Page 6:** © Elliot Erwitt/Magnum; **7:** (left) © Jerry Schad; (right) © Susan Holtz; **9:** © Abigail Heyman/Archive; **14:** Hieronymus Bosch, *Hell*, 1505–1510. Right panel on triptych, oil on wood. Museo del Prado, Madrid. Photo MAS; **15:** Pulitzer Prize 1977 © Stanley Forman; **17:** Photographs by Joel Sackett, copyright © Michael O'Mara Books Ltd., London. All rights reserved; **22:** © Chip Hires/Gamma Liaison; **25:** (top) AP/Wide World; (bottom left) AP/Wide World; (bottom right) Terry Ashe/*Time* Magazine

CHAPTER 2: **Page 30:** Michelangelo, *The Temptation and Expulsion of Adam and Eve*, ceiling of the Sistine Chapel, 1508–1512. Fresco. The Vatican, Rome. Scala/Art Resource; **31:** Carmine Gallasco/*The Record*, Hackensack, N.J.; **34:** Anglo-Australian Telescope Board © 1987; **37:** © Nancy Moran 1975; **38:** © Jerry Cooke/Photo Researchers; **43:** (left) public domain; (right) Photograph by Joel Sackett, copyright © Michael O'Mara Books Ltd., London. All rights reserved; **49:** © Alice Kandell/Photo Researchers; **51:** © Robert Eckert/EKM-Nepenthe

CHAPTER 3: **Page 58:** (left) Katherine Young; (right) Elizabeth Crews; **59:** (left) © Malave/Stock, Boston; (right) Fabian/Sygma; **60:** Camerapix; **64:** © Lennart Nilsson, *A Child Is Born*, Dell Publishing Co.; **65:** (left) © Eric Roth/Picture Cube; (right) © Owen Franken/Stock, Boston; **69:** (top) Reuters/Bettmann Newsphotos; (center) Regis Bossu/Sygma; (bottom) © Eric Kroll/Taurus; **71:** AP/Wide World; **75:** Bill Romero/Union-Tribune, San Diego

CHAPTER 4: **Page 80:** The Museum of Modern Art/Film Stills Archive; **81:** © Stanley Tretick/*Newsweek;* **83:** © Terry Ashe/Sygma; **85:** HBJ Collection; **87:** Sara Krulwich/NYT Pictures; **88:** (left) © Ray Ellis/Photo Researchers; (right) © Melanie Carr/Zephyr; **91:** UPI/Bettmann Newsphotos; **94:** Western History Collections, Univ. of Oklahoma Libraries; **95:** © Sullivan/TexaStock; **96:** Ben Shahn, *Integration*. Tempera on kraft paper mounted on masonite, 36" x 48". Des Moines Art Center (James D. Edmundson Purchase Fund)

CHAPTER 5: **Page 103:** © Urraca/Sygma; **105:** (left) Reuters/Bettmann Newsphotos; (right) © Robin Laurance/Photo Researchers; **109:** Courtesy New York City Dept. of Health; **116:** Culver Pictures; **121:** Nogues/Sygma; **122:** Courtesy Australian News and Information Bureau; **124:** (top) Courtesy The City of Memphis; (bottom) © John Ross/Robert Harding Picture Library

CHAPTER 6: **Page 133:** © Douglas Faulkner/S. Faulkner Collection; **135:** Richard Lee/Anthro-Photo; **137:** © Donald Dietz/Stock, Boston; **140:** © Ruth Silverman/Stock, Boston; **142:** © Ellis Herwig/Picture Cube; **143:** (left) © Alan Carey/The Image Works; (right) © Carol Palmer/Picture Cube; **144:** (left) © 1983 V. Englebert/Black Star; (right) © Ted Speigel/Black Star; **145:** (left) © Nik Wheeler/Black Star; (right) © Y. Arthus-Bertrand/Peter Arnold; **148:** © Ellis Herwig/Picture Cube; **151:** © Catherine Ursillo/Photo Researchers; **157:** The Bettmann Archive

CHAPTER 7: **Page 162:** Edward Hopper, *Automat*, 1927. Oil on canvas, 28" x 36". Des Moines Art Center (Edmundson Collection); **164:** Joe Overstreet, *New Jemima*, 1964. Construction, 102½" x 61" x 17". Menil Foundation, Houston. Photo courtesy The Menil Collection, Houston; **167:** © Peter Menzel/Stock, Boston; **170:** © Danny Lyon/Magnum; **173:** (top) © Paul Conklin; (bottom) Rex Features; **179:** *The Quilting Party*, western Virginia, c. 1854. Oil on wood, 13¼" x 25¼". Based on an engraved illustration published in Gleason's *Pictorial* for October 21, 1854. Abby Aldrich Rockefeller Folk Art Collection, Wiliamsburg, VA. Photo courtesy Colonial Williamsburg Foundation; **182:** (left) AP/Wide World; (right) UPI/Bettmann Newsphotos

CHAPTER 8: **Page 188:** (top left) Matthew Pratt, *The American School*, 1765. Oil on canvas, 36' x 50¼". Metropolitan Museum of Art, New York (Gift of Samuel P. Avery, 1897); (bottom left) Library of Congress; (right) © Richard Laird/FPG International; **192:** UPI/Bettmann Newsphotos; **202:** © Eric Kroll 1978/Taurus; **206:** (top) © Philip Jones Griffiths/Magnum; (bottom) AP/Wide World; **210:** Library of Congress; **211:** U.S. Signal Corps; **212:** © The Keystone Collection; **215:** (top) © P. Vauthey/Sygma; (bottom) General Services Administration/Black Star

CHAPTER 9: **Page 220:** (top) © MacDonald Photography/EKM-Nepenthe; (bottom) © George Gardner; **222:** © 1978 Joel Gordon; **225:** SEF/Art Resource; **227:** (top) © Eric A. Roth/Picture Cube; (bottom) © Michael Weisbrot/Stock, Boston; **234:** © Matsumoto/Sygma; **240:** © Joanne M. Domka/Urban Center for Photogaphy; **242:** © Smiley/TexaStock

CHAPTER 10: **Page 247:** © Ellis Herwig/Stock, Boston; **248:** (top left) Mainichi Shimbun; (top right) U.S. Naval Institute; (bottom) U.S. Naval Institute; **249:** Al Freni/*Time* Magazine; **251:** © 1987 John D. Campbell/EKM-Nepenthe; **252:** AP/Wide World; **253:** Rancinan/Sygma; **265:** (left) Evans/The White House; (right) Laffont/Sygma; **267:** Geoffrey Clifford/Wheeler Pictures; **270:** The Museum of Modern Art/Film Stills Archive

CHAPTER 11: **Page 280:** The Archives of Labor and Urban Affairs, Wayne State University; **285:** (left) © George Gardner/Image Works; (right) Tom Tracy/Photophile; **286:** Courtesy Andre Deutsch, London; **287:** Library of Congress; **293:** The Preservation Society of Newport County; **295:** (left) © Marilyn Silverstone/Magnum; (right © J.P. Laffont/Sygma; **296:** Art Resource/Giraudon; **297:** © 1981 Arnold Zann/Black Star; **302:** Nik Wheeler/Sygma

CHAPTER 12: **Page 312:** Campbell/Sygma; **314:** Jacob Lawrence, *Ironers*, 1943. Gouache on paper, 21½" x 29½". Private collection. Photo courtesy Terry Dintenfass Gallery, New York; **315:** Ron Haeberle, *Life* Magazine © 1969 Time Inc.; **317:** © J.R. Holland/Stock, Boston; **319:** © George Gardner; **322:** (top) Bettmann Archive; (bottom) Roger-Viollet; **323:** © Jim Heenstra/Picture Group; **328:** National Archives; **329:** Randy Taylor; **330:** Culver Pictures; **331:** © James H. Karales/Peter Arnold, Inc.; **335:** AP/Wide World

CHAPTER 13: **Page 342:** (left) Courtesy of the Southwest Museum, Los Angeles, CA, Neg. No. 33,942; (right) Seaver Center for Western History Research, Natural History Museum of Los Angeles

County; **346:** Keystone-Mast Collection, California Museum of Photography; **347:** Bettmann Archive; **350:** © DEK/TexaStock; **351:** Courtesy AT&T; **359:** (top) © Paul Conklin; (bottom) © Charles Gupton/Stock, Boston; **361:** Courtesy *GQ.* Copyright © 1987 by The Condé Nast Publications Inc. Photo by Sacha Van Dorsen; **363:** © Paul Conklin; **365:** (top) Library of Congress; (bottom) Margaret Bourke-White, *Life* Magazine © 1943 Time Inc.; **370:** © All-Sport

CHAPTER 14: **Page 378:** © 1988 Erika Stone; **379:** © Barrera/TexaStock; **380:** Diego Velasquez, *Las Meninas,* 1656. Oil on canvas, approx. 10′5″ x 9′. Museo del Prado, Madrid. Photo MAS; **382:** Novosti; **383:** © Arthur Tress/Magnum; **386:** Mark Jury Communications; **387:** Photographs by Lewis Hine, International Museum of Photography, George Eastman House; **389:** © Christopher Morris/Black Star; **391:** © Michael Sullivan/TexaStock; **396:** © Dennis Brack/Black Star

CHAPTER 15: **Page 404:** (top left) © Ellis Herwig/Picture Cube; (bottom left) © Robert Fried/Stock, Boston; (right) © J.R. Holland/Stock, Boston; **406:** Manos/Magnum; **407:** Burton Pasternak; **408:** Rapho/Photo Researchers; **410:** Howarth/Woodfin Camp; **417:** Photograph by Lewis Hine, International Museum of Photography, George Eastman House; **418:** Reproduced by permission of La Federation des Cooperatives du Nouveau Quebec, Montreal; **423:** Larry Burrows, *Life* Magazine © 1957 Time Inc.; **425:** © 1985 Lynn Johnson/Black Star

CHAPTER 16: Page 433: National Anthropological Archives/ Smithsonian Institution; **434:** Anonymous, *A Scholar Composes a Poem while Sitting under the Shade of a Willow-tree,* Sung Dynasty (960–1279). Collection of the National Palace Museum, Taiwan, Republic of China; **440:** AP/Wide World; **443:** Culver Pictures; **445:** © Peter Silva/Picture Group; **448:** (top) Cary Wolinsky/Stock, Boston; (bottom) Diane Lowe/Stock, Boston; **451:** Robert Lidneux, *Trail of Tears,* 20th century. Oil on canvas. Woolaroc Museum, Bartlesville, Oklahoma; **452:** (left) © Michael Sullivan/TexaStock; (right) © J.D. Sloan/Picture Cube; **455:** Reuters/Bettmann Newsphotos

CHAPTER 17: **Page 462:** (top) © H.W. Silvester/Photo Researchers; (bottom) Reunion des Musées Nationaux, Paris; **464:** By permission of the British Library; **465:** Courtesy *New Scientist,* London; **467:** By unknown Flemish artist of the 17th century. National Gallery, London; **468:** Reproduced by permission of the Trustees of the British Museum; **470:** © Jan Halaska/Photo Researchers; **471:** Guterkunst/Gamma-Liaison; **473:** © 1982 Ted Spiegel/Black Star; **474:** © 1983 Catherine Ursillo/Photo Researchers; **476:** Thomas Eakins, *The Agnew Clinic,* 1898. Oil on canvas, 331.5 x 179.1 cm. University of Pennsylvania School of Medicine, Philadelphia; **478:** Bettmann Archive; **481:** © Melanie Kaestner/Zephyr Pictures

CHAPTER 18: **Page 486:** © Marc & Evelyne Bernheim/Woodfin Camp & Assoc.; **487:** © Owen Franken/Stock, Boston; **488:** Hans Holbein the Younger, *Georg Gisze,* 1532. Staatliche Museen, Berlin; **493:** Library of Congress; **494:** © James Skovmand/Union-Tribune Publishing Co.; **498:** UPI/Bettmann Newsphotos; **503:** Culver Pictures; **507:** (top) UPI/Bettmann Newsphotos; (bottom) © Brad Bower/Picture Group

CHAPTER 19: **Page 518:** (left) BBC Hulton/Bettmann Archive; (right) HBJ Collection; **520:** Courtesy American Museum of Natural History; **522:** Leslie Hammond/*The Argus*; **523:** AP/Wide World; **524:** AP/Wide World; **530:** Frank Micelotta/*Time* Magazine; **531:** (left) Handgun Control, Inc., Washington, D.C.; (right) © 1987

National Rifle Association of America; **535:** AP/Wide World; **537:** AP/Wide World; **539:** Courtesy *Soviet Life*

CHAPTER 20: **Page 543:** Gustav Klimt, *Death and Life,* 1908 and 1911. 5′10″ x 6′6″. Collection of Marietta Preleuthner, Salzburg. Photo Galerie Welz (reproduced from a collotype print); **545:** Paul Gauguin, *Ia Orana Maria,* 1891. Metropolitan Museum of Art, New York (Samuel A. Lewisohn Bequest); **546:** FPG International; **548:** Hamburgisches Museum für Völkerkunde 36.52:1; **551:** AP/Wide World; **553:** Museum of the American Indian, Heye Foundation; **558:** AP/Wide World; **559:** Jean-Louis Atlan/Sygma; **560:** © Danny Lyon/Magnum; **563:** © D.E. Cox/Click, Chicago

CHAPTER 21: **Page 569:** © Alan Carey/Image Works; **571:** (top) Eugène Atget, *Boulevard de Strasbourg, Corsets,* 1912. Gelatin-silver print by Berenice Abbott, 1940, 9⅜″ x 7″. Collection, The Museum of Modern Art, New York. Given anonymously; (bottom) © 1970 John Filo/*Valley Daily News,* Tarentum, PA; **573:** © Owen Franken/Sygma; **576:** © Richard Pasley 1985/Stock, Boston; **578:** P. Habans/Sygma; **580:** Tannenbaum/Sygma; **583:** © Bruce Hoertel/*Newsweek*; **585:** Regis Bossu/Sygma; **587:** © P.F. Bentley/*Time* Magazine; **588:** © Leonard Freed/Magnum

CHAPTER 22: **Page 596:** Larry Burrows, *Life* Magazine © 1971 Time Inc.; **597:** © Reed Kaestner/Zephyr Pictures; **600:** (top) © Cindy Charles/Gamma Liaison; (bottom) © David E. Kennedy/TexaStock; **603:** (left) Library of Congress; (right) © 1972 *Newsweek*; **605:** © E.C.P. Armees/*Newsweek*; **608:** Imperial War Museum, London

Figures

B-3-2: Copyright © 1986 by the New York Times Company. Reprinted with permission. **5-2:** Copyright © 1981 by the New York Times Company. Reprinted with permission. **5-3:** L.F. Bouvier and R.W. Gardner, "Immigration to the U.S.: The unfinished story," *Population Bulletin,* Vol. 41 No. 4 (November 1986). Adapted by permission of the Population Reference Bureau, Inc. **5-5:** Adapted from a computer graphic by Melvin L. Prueitt, Los Alamos National Laboratory. **B-5-1:** T.W. Merrick, "World population in transition," *Population Bulletin,* Vol. 41 No. 2 (April 1986). Adapted with permission of the Population Reference Bureau, Inc. **8-1:** Solomon E. Asch, *Social Psychology* (Englewood Cliffs, N.J.: Prentice-Hall, Inc., 1952). **8-3:** Adapted from *The Business of Organized Crime: A Cosa Nostra Family* by Annelise Graebner Anderson with permission of the publisher Hoover Institution Press. © 1979 by the Board of Trustees of the Leland Stanford Jr. University. **9-2:** Reprinted from "The Nature of Cities" by Chauncy D. Harris and Edward L. Ullman in volume no. 242 of *The Annals* of The American Academy of Political and Social Science. Chauncy D. Harris and Edward L. Ullman, "The Nature of Cities," *Annals of the American Academy of Political and Social Sciences* 242 (November 1945). **9-3:** Copyright © 1986 by the New York Times Company. Reprinted with permission. **11-1:** Wright, Hacken, Costello, and Sprague, "The American Class Structure," *American Sociological Review* 47 (December 1982): 709–726. **B-12-2:** Copyright © 1988 by the New York Times Company. Reprinted with permission. **14-1:** Kurt Fischer and Arlyne Lazerson, *Human Development* (New York: W.H. Freeman): 45. **B-15-1:** M. Straus, R. Gelles, and S. Steinmetz, *Behind Closed Doors* (Garden City, N.Y.: Anchor Press, 1980): 194. **B-16-1:** Copyright © 1988 by the New York Times Company. Reprinted with permission. **21-1, 21-2, B-21-1:** Doug McAdam, *Political Process and the Development of Black Insurgency: 1930–1970* (Chicago: The University of Chicago Press, 1982): 7, 9, 51.

COPYRIGHTS AND ACKNOWLEDGMENTS

Tables

Index

Page references in **boldface** indicate figures, tables, photographs, and other illustrative material.